BST

ACPL ITL ✓ Y0-CXH-446

DISCARDED

REFE

Not to leave the library

TITLES OF
UNITED STATES CODE
AND
UNITED STATES CODE ANNOTATED

**(See the note following Title 1, Section 204
for a list of the titles that have been
enacted into positive law.)**

---

1. General Provisions.
2. The Congress.
3. The President.
4. Flag and Seal, Seat of Government, and the States.
5. Government Organization and Employees.
6. Domestic Security.
7. Agriculture.
8. Aliens and Nationality.
9. Arbitration.
10. Armed Forces.
11. Bankruptcy.
12. Banks and Banking.
13. Census.
14. Coast Guard.
15. Commerce and Trade.
16. Conservation.
17. Copyrights.
18. Crimes and Criminal Procedure.
19. Customs Duties.
20. Education.
21. Food and Drugs.
22. Foreign Relations and Intercourse.
23. Highways.
24. Hospitals and Asylums.
25. Indians.
26. Internal Revenue Code.
27. Intoxicating Liquors.
28. Judiciary and Judicial Procedure.
29. Labor.
30. Mineral Lands and Mining.
31. Money and Finance.
32. National Guard.
33. Navigation and Navigable Waters.
34. Navy (*See Title 10, Armed Forces*).
35. Patents.
36. Patriotic and National Observances, Ceremonies, and Organizations.
37. Pay and Allowances of the Uniformed Services.
38. Veterans' Benefits.
39. Postal Service.
40. Public Buildings, Property, and Works.
41. Public Contracts.
42. The Public Health and Welfare.
43. Public Lands.
44. Public Printing and Documents.
45. Railroads.
46. Shipping.
47. Telegraphs, Telephones, and Radiotelegraphs.
48. Territories and Insular Possessions.
49. Transportation.
50. War and National Defense.

UNITED STATES CODE ANNOTATED

TITLE 41

Public Contracts

Comprising All Laws of a General
and Permanent Nature
Under Arrangement of the Official Code of
the Laws of the United States
with
Annotations from Federal Courts

Mat #40624120

Copyright is not claimed as to any part of the original work prepared by a United States Government officer or employee as part of that person's official duties.

This publication was created to provide you with accurate and authoritative information concerning the subject matter covered; however, this publication was not necessarily prepared by persons licensed to practice law in a particular jurisdiction. The publisher is not engaged in rendering legal or other professional advice, and this publication is not a substitute for the advice of an attorney. If you require legal or other expert advice, you should seek the services of a competent attorney or other professional.

© 2008 Thomson/West

UNITED STATES CODE ANNOTATED, U.S.C.A. and USCA
are registered in the U.S. Patent and Trademark Office.

West's and Westlaw are registered in the U.S. Patent and Trademark Office.

TABLE OF CONTENTS

---

*

EXPLANATION

This volume, comprising Title 41 of the United States Code, contains laws of a general and permanent nature relating to Public Contracts, including all amendments and enactments through Public Law 110–180, approved January 8, 2008.

Historical and Statutory Notes

This volume contains complete historical and statutory notes relating to amendments, effective dates, legislative reports, repeals, prior provisions, reorganization plans, executive orders and other matters.

References

This volume contains cross references to constitutional and code provisions. Guidance to related materials in other publications is also provided, including references to the Code of Federal Regulations (CFR), the digest system collating judicial decisions from all jurisdictions, American Law Reports (ALR), encyclopedias, law review articles, forms and texts.

Notes of Decisions

The case annotations or constructions of the courts are arranged under numbered catchlines so that the user, by referring to the same catchline number in the supplementary pamphlets and pocket parts, can readily locate the latest decisions on any phase of the law. The catchlines are themselves collated and indexed to facilitate access to the judicial and administrative decisions classified to each section.

The annotations cover decisions of the Federal courts, the Comptroller General, the United States Merit Systems Protection Board, formal opinions of the Attorney General, and the informal opinions of the Office of Legal Counsel of the Department of Justice.

The annotations close with the following:

Reports	Abbreviations
Supreme Court Reporter	127 S.Ct. 3078
Federal Reporter, Third Series	498 F.3d 482
Federal Supplement, Second Series	501 F.Supp.2d 1385
Federal Rules Decisions	243 F.R.D. 483
United States Merit Systems Protection Board Reporter	106 M.S.P.R. 501
Federal Claims Reporter	78 Fed.Cl. 335
Military Justice Reporter	65 M.J.
	#10 C.M.A. 294
	#10 C.M.R. 761

EXPLANATION

Index to Text

A complete index to the text of the laws contained in Title 41 appears at the end of this volume.

THE PUBLISHER

March 2008

RELATED PRODUCTS IN
FEDERAL LAW FROM WEST

FEDERAL PRACTICE
COURTROOM HANDBOOK ON FEDERAL EVIDENCE
Steven Goode and Olin Guy Wellborn III
FEDERAL CIVIL RULES HANDBOOK
Steven Baicker–McKee, William Janssen and John B. Corr
FEDERAL CRIMINAL RULES HANDBOOK
Laurie L. Levenson
MODERN SCIENTIFIC EVIDENCE
David L. Faigman, David H. Kaye, Michael J. Saks,
Joseph Sanders, and Edward K. Cheng
FEDERAL JURY PRACTICE AND INSTRUCTIONS
Kevin F. O'Malley, Jay E. Grenig and William C. Lee
[Also available in CD–ROM]
FEDERAL PRACTICE AND PROCEDURE
Charles Alan Wright, Arthur R. Miller, Mary Kay Kane, Edward H. Cooper,
Richard L. Marcus, Kenneth W. Graham, Victor James Gold, Richard D.
Freer, Vikram David Amar, Joan E. Steinman, Andrew D. Leipold, Peter
J. Henning, Sarah H. Welling, Nancy J. King, Susan R. Klein, Charles H.
Koch, Jr., Catherine T. Struve, and Michael H. Graham
[Also available in CD–ROM]
WEST'S FEDERAL ADMINISTRATIVE PRACTICE
Authored by Federal Practice Experts
WEST'S FEDERAL FORMS
Authored by Federal Practice Experts
[Also available in CD–ROM]
FEDERAL COURT OF APPEALS MANUAL
David G. Knibb
FEDERAL PRACTICE AND PROCEDURE—
FEDERAL PRACTICE DESKBOOK
Charles Alan Wright and Mary Kay Kane
HANDBOOK OF FEDERAL EVIDENCE
Michael H. Graham
TREATISE ON CONSTITUTIONAL LAW
Ronald D. Rotunda and John E. Nowak
THE JUDGE'S EVIDENCE BENCHBOOK
Leo H. Whinery, Theodore P. Roberts, and Robert B. Smith
ADMINISTRATIVE LAW AND PRACTICE
Charles H. Koch, Jr.

IX

RELATED PRODUCTS

FEDERAL TRIAL OBJECTIONS
Charles B. Gibbons

BUSINESS AND COMMERCIAL LITIGATION IN FEDERAL COURTS
Robert L. Haig, Editor–In–Chief

NEWBERG ON CLASS ACTIONS, 3rd
Herbert Newberg and Alba Conte

HANDBOOK OF FEDERAL CIVIL DISCOVERY AND DISCLOSURE
Jay E. Grenig and Jeffrey S. Kinsler
[Includes forms on Disk]

ANNOTATED MANUAL FOR COMPLEX LITIGATION
David F. Herr

MULTIDISTRICT LITIGATION MANUAL
David F. Herr

FEDERAL STANDARDS OF REVIEW
Hon. Harry T. Edwards and Linda A. Elliott

United States Code Annotated
West's Federal Practice Digest 4th
United States Code Congressional and Administrative News

CRIMINAL PRACTICE

SEARCH AND SEIZURE
Wayne R. LaFave

SUBSTANTIVE CRIMINAL LAW
Wayne R. LaFave

CRIMINAL LAW DEFENSES
Paul H. Robinson

CRIMINAL PROCEDURE
Wayne R. LaFave, Jerold H. Israel, and Nancy J. King

FEDERAL SENTENCING LAW AND PRACTICE
Thomas W. Hutchison, Peter B. Hoffman, Deborah
Young, and Sigmund G. Popko

FEDERAL SENTENCING GUIDELINES HANDBOOK
Roger W. Haines, Jr., Frank O. Bowman III, and Jennifer C. Woll

---

Corpus Juris Secundum
West's Federal Case News
Federal Civil Judicial Procedure and Rules
Federal Criminal Code and Rules

X

RELATED PRODUCTS

Federal Environmental Laws
Federal Immigration Laws and Regulations
Federal Labor Laws
Federal Sentencing Guidelines
Federal Social Security Laws, Selected Statutes and Regulations
Federal Intellectual Property Laws and Regulations
Federal Litigator
Reference Manual on Scientific Evidence, Second
Manual for Complex Litigation, Fourth

TAX PUBLICATIONS

Federal Tax Regulations
Internal Revenue Code
Internal Revenue Acts

Westlaw®
WestCheck.com™
West CD–ROM Libraries™

To order any of these Federal practice tools, call your
West Representative or **1–800–328–9352**.

NEED RESEARCH HELP?

You can get quality research results with free help—call the West
Reference Attorneys when you have questions concerning
Westlaw or West Publications at **1-800-733-2889**.

INTERNET ACCESS

Contact the West Editorial Department directly with your
questions and suggestions by e-mail at west.editor@thomson.com.
Visit West's home page at
west.thomson.com.

*

WESTLAW ELECTRONIC RESEARCH GUIDE

Westlaw—Expanding the Reach of Your Library

Westlaw is West's online legal research service. With Westlaw, you experience the same quality and integrity that you have come to expect from West books, plus quick, easy access to West's vast collection of statutes, case law materials, public records, and other legal resources, in addition to current news articles and business information. For the most current and comprehensive legal research, combine the strengths of West books and Westlaw.

When you research with westlaw.com you get the convenience of the Internet combined with comprehensive and accurate Westlaw content, including exclusive editorial enhancements, plus features found only in westlaw.com such as ResultsPlus™ or StatutesPlus.™

Accessing Databases Using the Westlaw Directory

The Westlaw Directory lists all databases on Westlaw and contains links to detailed information relating to the content of each database. Click **Directory** on the westlaw.com toolbar. There are several ways to access a database even when you don't know the database identifier. Browse a directory view. Scan the directory. Type all or part of a database name in the Search these Databases box. The Find a Database Wizard can help you select relevant databases for your search. You can access up to ten databases at one time for user-defined multibase searching.

Retrieving a Specific Document

To retrieve a specific document by citation or title on westlaw.com click **Find&Print** on the toolbar to display the Find a Document page. If you are unsure of the correct citation format, type the publication abbreviation, e.g., **xx st** (where xx is a state's two-letter postal abbreviation), in the Find this document by citation box and click **Go** to display a fill-in-the-blank template. To retrieve a specific case when you know one or more parties' names, click **Find a Case by Party Name**.

KeyCite®

KeyCite, the citation research service on Westlaw, makes it easy to trace the history of your case, statute, administrative decision or regulation to determine if there are recent updates, and to find other documents that cite your document. KeyCite will also find pending legislation relating to federal or state statutes. Access the powerful features of KeyCite from the westlaw.com toolbar, the **Links** tab, or KeyCite flags in a document display. KeyCite's red and yellow warning flags tell you at a glance whether your document has negative history. Depth-of-treatment stars help you focus on the most important citing references. KeyCite Alert allows you to monitor the status of your case, statute or rule, and automatically sends you updates at the frequency you specify.

ResultsPlus™

ResultsPlus is a Westlaw technology that automatically suggests additional information related to your search. The suggested materials are accessible by a set of links that appear to the right of your westlaw.com search results:

- Go directly to relevant ALR® articles and Am Jur® annotations.

- Find on-point resources by key number.

- See information from related treatises and law reviews.

StatutesPlus™

When you access a statutes database in westlaw.com you are brought to a powerful Search Center which collects, on one toolbar, the tools that are most useful for fast, efficient retrieval of statutes documents:

- Have a few key terms? Click **Statutes Index**.

- Know the common name? Click **Popular Name Table**.

- Familiar with the subject matter? Click **Table of Contents**.

- Have a citation or section number? Click **Find by Citation**.

- Interested in topical surveys providing citations across multiple state statutes? Click **50 State Surveys**.

- Or, simply search with **Natural Language** or **Terms and Connectors**.

When you access a statutes section, click on the **Links** tab for all relevant links for the current document that will also include a KeyCite section with a description of the KeyCite status flag. Depending on your document, links may also include administrative, bill text, and other sources that were previously only available by accessing and searching other databases.

WESTLAW GUIDE

Additional Information

Westlaw is available on the Web at westlaw.com.

For search assistance, call the West Reference Attorneys at 1–800–REF–ATTY (1–800–733–2889).

For technical assistance, call West Customer Technical Support at 1–800–WESTLAW (1–800–937–8529).

*

PREFACE
UNITED STATES CODE 2000 EDITION

This fourth supplement to the 2000 edition of the United States Code has been prepared and published under the supervision of Peter G. LeFevre, Law Revision Counsel of the House of Representatives, pursuant to section 285b of Title 2 of the Code. It contains the additions to and changes in the general and permanent laws of the United States enacted during the One Hundred Eighth Congress, Second Session. This supplement together with the 2000 edition establishes prima facie those laws in effect on January 3, 2005, except for those titles of the Code that have been revised, codified, and enacted into positive law and are legal evidence of the law contained therein.

Speaker of the House of Representatives

Washington, D.C., *January 3, 2005.*

*

ABBREVIATIONS

A.B.A. J. E-Report	ABA Journal E-Report
Admin. & Reg. L. News	Administrative & Regulatory Law News
Admin. L. Rev.	Administration Law Review
ALI-ABA	American Law Institute-American Bar Association
ALR	American Law Reports
ALR2d	American Law Reports, Second Series
ALR3d	American Law Reports, Third Series
ALR4th	American Law Reports, Fourth Series
ALR5th	American Law Reports, Fifth Series
ALR, Fed	American Law Reports, Federal
Am. Bankr. Inst. J.	American Bankruptcy Institute Journal
Am. Bankr. Inst. L. Rev.	American Bankruptcy Institute Law Review
Am. Bankr. L.J.	American Bankruptcy Law Journal
Americans With Disab. Pract. & Compliance Manual	Americans With Disabilities Practice and Compliance Manual
Am. Jur. 2d	American Jurisprudence, Second Edition
Am. Jur. LF 2d	American Jurisprudence Legal Forms, Second Edition
Am. Jur. Pl. & Pr. Forms (Rev ed)	American Jurisprudence Pleading and Practice Forms, Revised Edition
Am. Jur. Proof of Facts	American Jurisprudence Proof of Facts
Am. Jur. Proof of Facts 2d	American Jurisprudence Proof of Facts, Second Series
Am. Jur. Proof of Facts 3d	American Jurisprudence Proof of Facts, Third Series
Am. Jur. Trials	American Jurisprudence Trials
Ann. Am. Acad. Pol. & Soc. Sci.	Annals of the American Academy of Political & Social Science
CFR	Code of Federal Regulations
CJS	Corpus Juris Secundum
Disclosures & Remedies Under the Securities Laws	Disclosures and Remedies Under the Securities Laws
Eckstrom's Licensing in Foreign & Domestic Ops.	Eckstrom's Licensing in Foreign and Domestic Operations

ABBREVIATIONS

Cite this Book

Thus: 41 U.S.C.A. § —

*

UNITED STATES CODE ANNOTATED

TITLE 41

PUBLIC CONTRACTS

CHAPTER 1—GENERAL PROVISIONS

1

2

EXECUTIVE ORDERS
EXECUTIVE ORDER NO. 10925

Ex. Ord. No. 10925, Mar. 6, 1961, 26 F.R. 1977, which related to nondiscrimination provisions in Government contracts and established the President's Committee on Equal Employment Opportunity, was revoked by section 403 of Ex. Ord. No. 11246, Sept. 24, 1965, 30 F.R. 12319, set out as a note under section 2000e of Title 42, The Public Health and Welfare.

CROSS REFERENCES

Contracting agency, kickback, prime contractor, subcontractor, etc. defined, see 41 USCA § 52.
Defense contractor defined, see 41 USCA § 50.
Department, continental United States, Government, and appropriation defined, see 41 USCA § 5a.
Honorable discharge from land and naval forces as substitute for birth certificate required for defense employment, see 41 USCA § 49.

WESTLAW COMPUTER ASSISTED LEGAL RESEARCH

Westlaw supplements your legal research in many ways. Westlaw allows you to

• update your research with the most current information

- expand your library with additional resources
- retrieve current, comprehensive history citing references to a case with KeyCite

For more information on using Westlaw to supplement your research, see the Westlaw Electronic Research Guide, which follows the Explanation.

---

§§ 1 to 4a.   Repealed. Oct. 21, 1941, c. 452, 55 Stat. 743

HISTORICAL AND STATUTORY NOTES

Section 1, R.S. § 512; Act Feb. 4, 1929, c. 146, §§ 1, 3, 45 Stat. 1147, established a return office for filing returns of contracts made by the Secretaries of War, Navy and Interior and appointed a clerk for this office.

Section 2, R.S. § 513, required the clerk to file all returns.

Section 3, R.S. § 514, required the clerk to keep an index book.

Section 4, R.S. § 515, required the clerk to provide certified copies of any returns for an established fee.

Section 4a, Act Feb. 4, 1929, c. 146, §§ 1, 3, 45 Stat. 1147, transferred returns office to the General Accounting Office and imposed duties relating thereto upon the Comptroller General.

§ 5.   Advertisements for proposals for purchases and contracts for supplies or services for Government departments; application to Government sales and contracts to sell and to Government corporations

Unless otherwise provided in the appropriation concerned or other law, purchases and contracts for supplies or services for the Government may be made or entered into only after advertising a sufficient time previously for proposals, except (1) when the amount involved in any one case does not exceed $25,000, (2) when the public exigencies require the immediate delivery of the articles or performance of the service, (3) when only one source of supply is available and the Government purchasing or contracting officer shall so certify, or (4) when the services are required to be performed by the contractor in person and are (A) of a technical and professional nature or (B) under Government supervision and paid for on a time basis.   Except (1) as authorized by section 1638 of Appendix to Title 50, (2) when otherwise authorized by law, or (3) when the reasonable value involved in any one case does not exceed $500, sales and contracts of sale by the Government shall be governed by the requirements of this section for advertising.

In the case of wholly owned Government corporations, this section shall apply to their administrative transactions only.

(R.S. § 3709; Aug. 2, 1946, c. 744, § 9(a), (c), 60 Stat. 809; June 30, 1949, c. 288, Title VI, § 602(f), formerly Title V, § 502(e), 63 Stat. 400; renumbered § 602(f), Sept. 5, 1950, c. 849, §§ 6(a), (b), 8(c), 64 Stat. 583, 591, and amended Aug. 28, 1958, Pub.L. 85–800, § 7, 72 Stat. 967; July 25, 1974, Pub.L. 93–356, § 1, 88 Stat. 390; Dec. 1, 1983, Pub.L. 98–191, § 9(b), 97 Stat. 1332.)

HISTORICAL AND STATUTORY NOTES

Revision Notes and Legislative Reports
1949 Acts. House Report No. 670 and Conference Report No. 935, see 1949 U.S. Code Cong. Service, p. 1475.

1950 Acts. Senate Report No. 2140 and Conference Report No. 3001, see 1950 U.S. Code Cong. Service, p. 3547.

1958 Acts. Senate Report No. 2201, see 1958 U.S. Code Cong. and Adm. News, p. 4021.

1974 Acts. Senate Report No. 93–901, see 1974 U.S. Code Cong. and Adm. News, p. 3913.

1983 Acts. Senate Report No. 98–214, see 1983 U.S. Code Cong. and Adm. News, p. 2027.

References in Text
Section 1638 of Appendix to Title 50, referred to in text, was repealed by Act June 30, 1949, c. 288, Title VI, § 602(a)(1), formerly Title V, § 502(a)(1), 63 Stat. 399, eff. July 1, 1949, renumbered by Act Sept. 5, 1950, c. 849, § 6(a), (b), 64 Stat. 583.

Codifications
R.S. § 3709 derived from Act Mar. 2, 1861, c. 84, § 10, 12 Stat. 220.

Section is also set out in D.C.Code, § 1–808.

Amendments
1983 Amendments. Pub.L. 98–191 substituted "$25,000" for "$10,000".

1974 Amendments. Pub.L. 93–356 substituted "$10,000" for "$2,500".

1958 Amendments. Pub.L. 85–800 substituted "$2,500" for $500".

1949 Amendments. Act June 30, 1949, substituted "$500" for "$100".

1946 Amendments. Act Aug. 2, 1946, among other changes, inserted clauses (1), (3) and (4), made section applicable to sales and contracts of sale by the Government, except in certain cases, and added limitation on applicability to Government corporations.

Effective and Applicability Provisions
1949 Acts. Amendment by Act June 30, 1949, effective July 1, 1949, see provisions set out as a note under section 471 of Title 40, Public Buildings, Property, and Works.

Exemption of Functions
Functions authorized by Foreign Assistance Act of 1961, as amended, as exempt, see Ex. Ord. No. 11223, May 12, 1965, 30 F.R. 6635, set out as a note under section 2393 of Title 22, Foreign Relations and Intercourse.

Repeal of Exemptions
Section 9(b) of Act Aug. 2, 1946, provided that: "Exemptions from section 3709, Revised Statutes [this section], in other law in amounts of $100 or less are hereby repealed."

Section Inapplicable to Armed Services and National Aeronautics and Space Administration
Section inapplicable to procurement of supplies or services by Armed Services and National Aeronautics and Space Administration, see section 2314 of Title 10, Armed Forces.

CROSS REFERENCES

AIDS research, contracts and cooperative agreements, expedite and coordinate research, see 42 USCA § 300cc–41.

Air pollution control research and contracts, see 42 USCA §§ 7403, 7405.

Architect of Capitol, purchasing supplies and procuring services not in excess of $25,000, see 41 USCA § 6a–1.

Armed services procurement of supplies and services, see 10 USCA §§ 2302 et seq., 2381.

Bonneville power project, purchase of supplies and services without advertisement, see 16 USCA § 832g.

Conservation, National Park Service—
    Hiring of work animals and equipment not required to comply with this section in certain cases, see 16 USCA § 17i.

Conservation, National Park Service——Cont'd

 Seeding and tree planting within national forests, open purchases without advertisement, see 16 USCA § 504.

 Services and accommodations for public in national parks and national monuments, see 16 USCA § 17b.

Contracts for engraving, lithographing, and photolithographing, without advertisement for proposals, see 16 USCA § 825k.

Contracts for transportation of moneys, bullion, coin, etc., see 41 USCA § 24.

Control of coal mine fires, employment of equipment without regard to this section, see 30 USCA § 556.

Definitions of terms employed in this section, see 41 USCA § 5a.

Detention and removal of aliens ordered removed and places of detention, see 8 USCA § 1231.

Executive agencies, section inapplicable to procurement of property or services by, see 41 USCA § 260.

Farm Credit Administration, maintenance and disposal of properties by, see 12 USCA § 1141b.

Farm housing, service and supply contracts not exceeding $300 unaffected by provisions of this section, see 42 USCA § 1480.

Federal Deposit Insurance Corporation, employment of certified public accountants without regard to this section, see 12 USCA § 1827.

Fishery resources, utilization of certain State facilities and services without regard to this section, see 16 USCA § 757.

Fort Peck power project, purchase of supplies and services without advertisement, see 16 USCA § 833f.

Government traffic by pipeline carriers, see 49 USCA § 15504.

Group life and accident and dismemberment insurance policies, purchase by Office of Personnel Management without regard to this section, see 5 USCA § 8709.

Health benefits plans for government employees, power of Office of Personnel Management to contract without regard to this section, see 5 USCA § 8902.

Housing—

 Contracts for hazard insurance and purchases by Secretary of Housing and Urban Development, see 12 USCA §§ 1703, 1710, 1713.

 Funds available to public agencies, educational institutions, or nonprofit organizations, use of by Secretary of Housing and Urban Development and Federal Home Loan Bank Board without regard to this section, see 12 USCA § 1701c.

 National defense housing, purchases and supplies under $1,000 excepted from this section, see 12 USCA § 1750c.

Indian Self-Determination Act contracts and construction, see 25 USCA § 450j.

International Health Research Act of 1960, authority of President to contract with public and nonprofit private institutions and agencies and individuals in participating foreign countries without regard to provisions of this section, see 22 USCA § 2103.

Jefferson National Expansion Memorial, payment for services and facilities used with respect to construction of, without regard to this section, see 16 USCA § 450jj-1.

Menominee Indian Reservation, supplies for operations on reservation, and sale of Indian-produced forest products, see 41 USCA § 6b.

National Fisheries Center and Aquarium, provision of vessels for specimen collection purposes without regard to this section, see 16 USCA § 1052.

National Science Foundation contracts and other arrangements, see 42 USCA § 1870.

National Transportation Safety Board powers and duties, see 49 USCA § 1113.

Procurement procedures, see 41 USCA § 251 et seq.

Public printing—

 Authority required to authorize publication of advertisements, notices, or proposals for any executive department, see 44 USCA § 3702.

Public printing——Cont'd
    Purchase of paper and materials for Government Printing Office, see 44 USCA § 501 et seq.
    Purchases and contracts, Government Printing Office, see 44 USCA § 311.
Railroad unemployment insurance administration fund, appropriation of moneys for administrative expenses without regard to this section, see 45 USCA § 361.
Rates and through routes for United States Government, see 49 USCA § 13712.
Reconditioning of foreign merchant vessels acquired under emergency authority without regard to provisions of this section, see 50 USCA § 198.
Small Business Administrator, power to pursue assigned claims to final collection in connection with loans, see 15 USCA § 634.
State Department—
    Foreign Service Institute, acquisition of real and personal property and equipment without regard to this section, see 22 USCA § 4024.
    International Labour Conference, printing and binding for without regard to this section, see 22 USCA § 272a.
    International Refugee Organization, funds available for expenditure without regard to this section, see 22 USCA § 289c.
    South Pacific Commission, printing and binding for without regard to this section, see 22 USCA § 280b.
    United Nations, payment of expenses without regard to this section, see 22 USCA § 287e.
Stationery for Senate, advertisement for sealed proposals, see 2 USCA § 106.
Training of uniformed services at non–Government facilities and authority to enter into agreements, see 10 USCA § 2013.
Use of nongovernment facilities for training of agency employees without regard to this section, see 5 USCA § 4105.
Water resources research and technology institutes coordination, see 42 USCA § 10303.

CODE OF FEDERAL REGULATIONS

Disposition of property, Navy Department, see 32 CFR § 736.1 et seq.

LIBRARY REFERENCES

American Digest System
    United States ⟂64, 70, 73, 74.
    Key Number System Topic No. 393.

Corpus Juris Secundum
    CJS Carriers § 146, Government Traffic.
    CJS United States § 113, Advertising and Proposals or Bids.

Research References

ALR Library
    99 ALR 173, Aeroplanes and Aeronautics.
    83 ALR 333, Aeroplanes and Aeronautics.
    71 ALR 173, What Is an "Emergency" Within Charter or Statutory Provision Excepting Emergency Contract or Work from Requirement of Bidding on Public Contracts.
    65 ALR 835, Bidder's Variation from Specifications on Bid for Public Work.
Encyclopedias
    Am. Jur. 2d Aliens and Citizens § 2166, Aliens May Not Bid on Exclusive Privileges at Immigrant Stations.
    Am. Jur. 2d Public Works and Contracts § 3, Authorization and Regulation, Generally--Federal Statutes and Regulations, Generally; Grants to States and Municipalities.

Am. Jur. 2d Public Works and Contracts § 9, Generally; Power or Authority of Public Body--United States.

Am. Jur. 2d Public Works and Contracts § 17, Federal Procurement and Contracts.

Am. Jur. 2d Public Works and Contracts § 18, Federal Procurement and Contracts--By Negotiation or in Open Market.

Am. Jur. 2d Public Works and Contracts § 34, Federal Contracts.

Am. Jur. 2d Public Works and Contracts § 38, Circumstances Dispensing with Bidding; Emergencies.

Am. Jur. 2d Public Works and Contracts § 42, Personal Service Contracts.

Am. Jur. 2d Public Works and Contracts § 52, Generally; Invitation and Advertisement for and Solicitation of Bids.

70 Am. Jur. Proof of Facts 3d 97, Proof That a Government Agency Was Liable for Improperly Granting a Bid Award to a Bid Applicant.

Forms

30 West's Legal Forms § 30:37, Release of Claims Under Government Construction Contract.

Treatises and Practice Aids

Immigration Law Service 2d PSD INA § 241, Detention and Removal of Aliens Ordered Removed.

Immigration Law Service 2d PSD INA § 285, Disposal of Privileges at Immigrant Stations.

West's Federal Administrative Practice § 2010, Duties and Powers--Experts and Consultants.

West's Federal Administrative Practice § 5414, Administrative Powers.

WESTLAW ELECTRONIC RESEARCH

See Westlaw guide following the Explanation pages of this volume.

Notes of Decisions

3 1833 05545 8134

I. ADVERTISING FOR CONTRACTS

Subdivision Index

1. Advertising for contracts generally

It is a sufficient objection to a naked unexecuted contract, made by an officer of the Government, that he has neglected to comply with this section, requiring that proposals shall precede the letting of the contract. 1862, 10 Op.Atty.Gen. 416.

2. Purpose, advertising for contracts

The purpose of this section and regulations promulgated under it is to give all persons equal right to compete for Government contracts, to prevent unjust favoritism, or collusion or fraud in the letting of contracts for the purchase of supplies, and to secure for the Government the benefits which arise from competition. U.S. v. Brookridge Farm, C.C.A.Colo.1940, 111 F.2d 461. See, also, 1937, 39 Op.Atty.Gen. 71.

3. Policy, advertising for contracts

The provisions of this section are in the line of a wise public policy, insuring to the Government the advantage of competition in making contracts for supplies. 1897, 22 Op.Atty.Gen. 1.

4. Mandatory nature of section, advertising for contracts

In absence of any exigency of fact or of one determined by the officer in charge of a public work, or of one that can be judicially inferred, the provision of this section, requiring advertisement for supplies, is mandatory and contracts made in violation thereof are void. Schneider v. U.S., Ct.Cl.1884, 19 Ct.Cl. 547. See, also, Clark v. U.S., Ct.Cl.1877, 95 U.S. 539, 5 Otto. 539, 24 L.Ed. 518; U.S. v. Speed, Ct.Cl.1869, 75 U.S. 77, 8 Wall. 77, 19 L.Ed. 449; Wentworth v. U.S., 1869, 5 Ct.Cl. 302; Henderson v. U.S., 1868, 4 Ct.Cl. 75. United States ☞ 64

5. Persons or entities protected, advertising for contracts

This section was not enacted for the protection of sellers and confers no enforceable rights upon prospective bidders. Perkins v. Lukens Steel Co., U.S.Dist.Col.1940, 60 S.Ct. 869, 310 U.S. 113, 84 L.Ed. 1108. See, also, Friend v. Lee, 1955, 221 F.2d 96, 95 U.S.App.D.C. 224; Brookfield Const. Co. v. Stewart, D.C.D.C.1964, 234 F.Supp. 94, affirmed 339 F.2d 753, 119 U.S.App.D.C. 254. United States ☞ 64.55(1)

The requirements in this section of advertising for Government contracts are for the protection of the United States and not those dealing with it. American Smelting & Refining Co. v. U.S., U.S.

1922, 42 S.Ct. 420, 259 U.S. 75, 66 L.Ed. 833. United States ☞ 64.10

Fundamental government procurement statutes for general public contracts, or for military procurements, were designed not to protect bidders but rather to protect the government. Gary Aircraft Corp. v. U.S., W.D.Tex.1972, 342 F.Supp. 473. United States ☞ 64.5

6. Departments required to advertise, advertising for contracts

The Columbia Institution for the Deaf was formerly in the Department of the Interior, in the sense that its expenditures of public money were under the supervision of the head of that Department and subject to the provisions of this section in making purchases and contracts for supplies or services. 1897, 22 Op.Atty.Gen. 1. See, also, 1896, 21 Op.Atty.Gen. 349.

Contracts for supplies or services in any of the departments of the Government, except for personal services, or when the public exigency requires the same immediately, must be made after advertisement for proposals in accordance with this section. 1894, 21 Op. Atty.Gen. 59. See, also, 1897, 22 Op. Atty.Gen. 11.

7. Contracts required to be advertised, advertising for contracts—Generally

Contracts for the purchase of seals by the United States used to secure packages while being transported in bond must be awarded upon advertisement, but this section did not apply where the seals or fastenings were paid for and owned by common carriers. 1896, 21 Op.Atty.Gen. 304.

It is competent for the Secretary of Agriculture to purchase seeds for distribution under this section, the right to reject any and all bids being reserved. 1895, 21 Op.Atty.Gen. 162.

This section did not apply to paper and materials for the Government Printing Office for Acts Jan. 27, 1894, c. 22, 28 Stat. 33, and Apr. 21, 1894, c. 61, 28 Stat. 58, 62, which amended this section but are superseded, enlarged it in respect to that Office only so as to apply to fuel, ice, stationery, and miscellaneous supplies. 1895, 21 Op.Atty.Gen. 137.

The object of this section, in requiring advertisement for proposals before making purchases and contracts for supplies, is to invite competition among bidders, and it contemplates only those purchases and contracts where competition as to the article needed is possible, which is not the case with the postal guide. 1881, 17 Op.Atty.Gen. 84.

Executory contracts for supplies and materials for the departments must be duly advertised. 1853, 6 Op.Atty.Gen. 99.

8. —— Intergovernmental transfers of property, contracts required to be advertised, advertising for contracts

The provisions of this section, and similar statutes, requiring that all purchases and contracts for Government supplies shall be made by advertising for proposals, are inapplicable to a transfer of property from one Government establishment to another. 1922, 33 Op.Atty.Gen. 327.

9. —— Modified contracts, contracts required to be advertised, advertising for contracts

Where one contract is to furnish sandstone for a public building at a designated price, and another is to substitute marble at a different price, the material being the sole subject-matter of either agreement, the latter contract cannot be regarded as a modification of the former and it requires a new advertisement. Schneider v. U.S., Ct.Cl.1884, 19 Ct.Cl. 547. United States ☞ 64; United States ☞ 72(2)

Where an advertisement for proposals for furnishing the Government with stamped envelopes, etc., stated a definite term, and did not provide for any extension of the contract beyond the terms, but the contract contained a provision that it might be extended or modified by mutual agreement, and it was subsequently modified and extended repeatedly so as to embrace several successive years, such extensions were each new contracts which should have been preceded by advertisements for proposals. 1895, 21 Op. Atty.Gen. 207. See, also, 1869, 13 Op. Atty.Gen. 174.

Where the Commissioner of Patents [now Commissioner of Patents and Trademarks], without previous advertisement, contracted with P. to furnish certain photolithographic copies of patent drawings and without advertising extended the contract so as to cover another appropriation and P. thereupon made, in good faith, large expenditures to enable him to execute the contract thus extend-ed, the extension of the original contract, having been made without due advertisement, was not valid and binding upon the Government. 1876, 15 Op.Atty.Gen. 539.

10. Persons to whom advertisements addressed, advertising for contracts

While there was no express provision as to the persons with whom the Postmaster General should contract, or to whom he should by advertisement address his proposals, he was justified in doing so to those who were able to do the work or furnish supplies which he needed in his Department and in such a matter he would exercise his own discretion as to that which should be for the best interests of the public, and would carry out the policy of this section by thus limiting his advertisements, when he would deem it expedient to do so. 1877, 15 Op.Atty. Gen. 226.

11. Exceptions from advertising requirement generally, advertising for contracts

The validity of a contract did not depend on the degree of skill or wisdom with which an officer's discretion as to dispensing with advertising was exercised. U.S. v. Speed, U.S.Ct.Cl.1868, 75 U.S. 77, 19 L.Ed. 449, 8 Wall. 77.

Where expenditure of appropriation was specially confided to discretion of Secretary of Interior Department, he had discretionary power to award contracts without advertising under this section. Fowler v. U.S., Ct.Cl.1867, 3 Ct.Cl. 43.

This section, while requiring such advertisement as the general rule, invests the officer charged with the duty of procuring supplies or services with a discretion to dispense with advertising if the exigencies of the public service require immediate delivery or performance and it is too well settled to admit of dispute at this day that where there is a discretion of this kind conferred on an officer or board of officers, and a contract is made in which they have exercised that discretion, the validity of the contract cannot be made to depend on the degree of wisdom or skill which may have accompanied its exercise. Staab's Case, 1882, 17 Op.Atty. Gen. 384. See, also, U.S. v. Speed, 1868, 75 U.S. 77, 8 Wall. 77, 19 L.Ed. 449.

12. Public exigencies, advertising for contracts—Generally

A "public exigency" demanding immediate delivery of Government supplies and obviating necessity, under this section, of advertising for competitive bids is a sudden and unexpected happening, an unforeseen occurrence or condition, a perplexing contingency or complication of circumstances, or a sudden or unexpected occasion for action. Good Roads Machinery Co. of New England v. U.S., D.C.Mass.1937, 19 F.Supp. 652. United States ⊙ 64.10

A vendor contracting with the Government in an alleged emergency is bound to inquire and know whether the required order declaring it has been made. Cobb, Blasdell & Co. v. U.S., Ct.Cl.1883, 18 Ct.Cl. 514. United States ⊙ 64

Contracts made in emergencies need not await advertising for bids. Brady v. U.S., Ct.Cl.1867, 3 Ct.Cl. 203.

The "public exigency" contemplated by this section is one of time only. 1877, 15 Op.Atty.Gen. 254.

The "public exigency," contemplated by this section, is one of time only and while the officer intrusted with making the contract may be entitled himself to adjudicate whether or not the facts are such as to require immediate delivery of the articles contracted for, or the immediate rendering of the service desired, yet the exigency cannot be extended beyond that of time only, and if he adjudicates any other state of facts to be an exigency he is not proceeding within the authority given him by this section. 1877, 15 Op. Atty.Gen. 253.

13. —— Immediate delivery or performance, public exigencies, advertising for contracts

A contract made by the acceptance on Apr. 11, 1918, of the Government's offer of Mar. 28, 1918, to purchase 30,000 metric tons of copper, deliveries to be completed on or before June 1, 1918, could hardly be said not to be for a delivery as immediate as was practicable for the subject-matter, within the exception in this section, in favor of Government contracts not made by advertising, when the public exigencies require immediate delivery. American Smelting & Refining Co. v. U.S., U.S.1922, 42 S.Ct. 420, 259 U.S. 75, 66 L.Ed. 833. United States ⊙ 64.10

Purchases of material and equipment for civil works project by administrator who had authority to make purchases were made under "public exigency" requiring immediate delivery, and hence seller's right to recover purchase price was not barred because of failure to advertise for competitive bids, especially where Government had paid for other purchases from same seller. Good Roads Machinery Co. of New England v. U.S., D.C.Mass.1937, 19 F.Supp. 652. United States ⊙ 64.10

Circumstances showed emergency authorizing War Department to purchase, without readvertising for proposals after rejecting unsatisfactory proposals, caskets for reburial of soldiers who died in World War service in France. U.S. v. Heller, D.C.Md.1932, 1 F.Supp. 1. United States ⊙ 64.10

Where the service required was under a statute making an appropriation to relieve a suffering condition of the people of the territory, it intended immediate execution, and contracts thereunder would be valid though not reduced to writing. Pacific Steam Whaling Co. v. U.S., Ct.Cl.1901, 36 Ct.Cl. 105.

A contract made by a navy agent in compliance with a requisition from the naval storekeeper, marked "open purchase requisition," with the added words "immediate use," without sufficient time to enable the parties to learn the place of the manufacture of the article contracted for or the manufacturer's price, the bills approved by the inspecting officer, and certified by the commandant of the yard, that the public exigency required the immediate delivery of the articles, and, there not being time to advertise, they were obtained by open purchase, and the same is therefore approved, was not in violation of Act Mar. 2, 1861, c. 84, § 10, 12 Stat. 220, from which this section is derived, and the contractor was entitled to the contract price of the article delivered, although he did not deal in it or possess it at the time of sale, but if a contract be made with ample time from the date of the requisition to enable the contractor and purchasing agent to inform themselves of the place where the article is manufactured, and of the manufacturer's price, and they do not avail themselves of the opportunity for obtaining this information, the contractor can only recover its fair and reasonable value, without regard to the sums named in the contract. Wentworth v. U.S., Ct.Cl.1869, 5 Ct.Cl. 302.

Under former provision of this section automobile tires immediately needed in an exigency may have been procured by open purchase. 1937, 39 Op.Atty.Gen. 111.

Where the public exigency requires the immediate delivery of envelopes, they may be purchased by the head of the Department in which the exigency arises. 1895, 21 Op.Atty.Gen. 181.

The power given by this section to make contracts, without advertisement, plainly contemplates only such contracts as the urgent necessities of the service may demand and in cases where the public interests would suffer by the delay attendant upon advertising and the only exception is when "immediate performance" is required by the public exigency, and that is the test by which the necessity of advertising is to be determined. 1861, 10 Op.Atty.Gen. 28.

Purchases in open market cannot be resorted to, except in cases of and in reference to such articles as are wanted for use so immediate as not to permit of contracts by advertisement, but such immediate want cannot usually occur in reference to hemp. 1846, 4 Op.Atty.Gen. 475.

Where the public exigencies do not require the immediate delivery of the articles, or performance of the service, it is necessary to advertise previously for proposals respecting the same, but where immediate delivery is necessary the article must be obtained by open purchase. 1829, 2 Op.Atty.Gen. 257.

14. —— War contracts, public exigencies, advertising for contracts

The World War created a public exigency, within the meaning of the exception in this section, in favor of Government contracts not made by advertising, when the public exigencies require immediate delivery and the Government's delay in sending shipping orders until after the time fixed by the contract for completing delivery did not entitle the contractor to recover the difference between the contract price and a fair price for goods thereafter delivered, where the contractor, whatever its motives, patriotic or otherwise, instead of refusing to proceed on that account, kept the contract

on foot, even requesting to be allowed to continue deliveries. American Smelting & Refining Co. v. U.S., U.S.1922, 42 S.Ct. 420, 259 U.S. 75, 66 L.Ed. 833.

This section relieved from necessity of advertising in case of war contract with packing company. Swift & Co. v. U.S., Ct.Cl.1924, 59 Ct.Cl. 364, affirmed as modified on other grounds 46 S.Ct. 308, 270 U.S. 124, 70 L.Ed. 497.

15. Personal service contracts, advertising for contracts

Exception (4) of this section from competitive bidding procedures for personal service contracts confers no right upon those seeking government contracts to demand that competitive bidding not be used. Goldhaber v. Foley, E.D.Pa.1981, 519 F.Supp. 466. United States ☞ 64.10

Although a contract may require in some of its details personal service, this does not make the whole contract one for personal service within the meaning of this section. 1876, 15 Op.Atty.Gen. 538.

Cutting and dressing stone itself is not within the exception of personal services. 1879, 15 Op.Atty.Gen. 253.

A contract for personal service is one by which the individual contracted with renders his personal service to the Government through its agents, thus himself becoming the servant of the Government. 1877, 15 Op.Atty.Gen. 235.

A contract for surveying Indian reservations is a contract for "personal services," and, therefore, may be made without previous advertisement for proposals. 1862, 10 Op.Atty.Gen. 261.

16. Impossibility of competition, advertising for contracts

If the Secretary of the Treasury determined that competition was not possible, this section was inapplicable and articles may have been procured by open purchases or negotiated contract. 1937, 39 Op.Atty.Gen. 111.

17. Reletting of contracts, advertising for contracts

Statutory provisions requiring the advertising for competitive bids in connection with Government contracts are for the protection of the Government and not those dealing with it and in reletting a contract which had been terminated for default, the Government need not advertise for competitive bids. H & H Mfg.

Co. Inc. v. U.S., Ct.Cl.1964, 168 Ct.Cl. 873. United States ☞ 64.10; United States ☞ 72.1(6)

United States, in awarding contract to build facility for housing National Park Service's museum collection, did not violate the competitive bidding provision of the Competition in Contracting Act (CICA) by failing to re-bid contract after modifications to original solicitation for offers (SFO) were made, where government had encouraged bidders to submit suggested modifications to the solicitation so as to create a state of the art facility, so the scope of the contract was understood to embrace changes or modifications to the original contract requirements for the facility. H.G. Properties A, L.P. v. U.S., C.A.Fed.2003, 68 Fed.Appx. 192, 2003 WL 21421629, Unreported. United States ☞ 64.25

18. Form or content of advertisement, advertising for contracts

Under circumstances, government's failure to include qualifying word "approximate" in description of figures set forth in request for proposals for microfilming of obsolete engineering documents for the Air Force, after it had been included in earlier requests for estimates, was an inadvertent omission on the government's part, and contractor's attempt to attach critical importance to such error was not justified, for it necessitated an overly literal interpretation of language of request for proposals—an interpretation which would in effect ignore the essential realities of the bargain made by the parties. Microcord Corp. v. U.S., Ct.Cl.1966, 361 F.2d 1000, 176 Ct.Cl. 46. United States ☞ 73(22)

Under this section, invitations and specifications must be such as to permit competitors to compete on common basis, and conditions or limitations which have no reasonable relation to actual needs of service and which are designed to limit bidding to one of several sources of supply are interdicted and render the award of a contract made under such circumstances voidable. U.S. v. Brookridge Farm, C.C.A.10 (Colo.) 1940, 111 F.2d 461. United States ☞ 64.15

Where Government's invitation for bids stated that contract was not, necessarily, to be let to lowest bidder, but was to be negotiated after study of bids and permitted bids to be made upon basis of use of several materials differing greatly in cost,

it meant that resulting contract should require contractor to use one of the materials upon which the bid and negotiated contract would be based, and it did not mean that the contractor could be required, without extra compensation, to furnish the costlier material if the cheaper material agreed upon became unavailable. Olson Const. Co. v. U.S., Ct.Cl. 1948, 75 F.Supp. 1014, 110 Ct.Cl. 249. Contracts ☞ 232(1); United States ☞ 70(27)

Where the plaintiffs entered into three separate contracts with the Government dated respectively March 30, and March 30, and April 18, 1943, whereby the plaintiffs agreed to build three war housing projects according to specifications, schedules and drawings made a part of the contracts and the "Instructions to Bidders" accompanying the Specifications for each project contained a statement calling the attention of bidders to Ex.Ord. No. 9301 (8 F.R. 1825) and to the regulations and directives, if any, issued under such executive order by the War Manpower Commission, or the Chairman thereof, and the "Form of Contract" received by plaintiffs along with the Invitation for Bids also contained a statement that "this contract is subject to Executive Order 9301" and the Executive Order, which was issued in February 1943 had the force and effect of law and at the time the bids on the three projects were submitted no exception was taken by plaintiffs to the references to such executive order, plaintiffs were not entitled to recover for overtime costs incurred by reason of compliance with the provisions of such Executive Order 9301. Beuttas v. U.S., Ct.Cl.1952, 122 Ct.Cl. 295. United States ☞ 70(27)

An advertisement by the Secretary of the Treasury for seal locks to be used on railroad cars in the revenue service is a sufficient compliance with section 5 of this title to authorize a contract by a subsequent Secretary for locks to be used on the cars and on bonded warehouses. International S.S. & Ry. Supply Co. of N.Y. v. U.S., Ct.Cl.1877, 13 Ct.Cl. 209. United States ☞ 64

Where an advertisement was published, calling for proposals for performance of certain work for the Government, with the specification that it be begun on or before Oct. 1, 1892, and be concluded on or before Dec. 31, 1893, and where one of the proposals stated that the bid was that the entire work was to be completed on or before June 1, 1894, and provided for stopping that work in certain contingencies, such modifications in the proposals were inconsistent with the specifications and with the spirit and intent of this section. 1892, 20 Op.Atty.Gen. 496.

The manner of advertising is left by the law to the discretion of the department advertising, no particular form being prescribed. 1877, 15 Op.Atty.Gen. 226.

A Standard Form 33 solicitation provision which provides that a 60-day bid acceptance period will apply unless the bidder specifies a different number of days should have been cross-referenced with another solicitation provision which provides that bids with acceptance periods of fewer than 45 days would be considered nonresponsive; the failure to cross-refer was not in this case grossly misleading and, therefore, the cancellation of the solicitation is not required. 1983, 62 Op.Comp.Gen. 31.

19. Incorporation of advertisement into contract, advertising for contracts

A bid form which was expressly made a part of specifications became part of construction contract, and stipulation in bid form that concrete floor slabs not on earth or gravel would be included in lump sum price bid for each building prevented contractor from recovering additional amount in respect to such concrete, notwithstanding that various provisions of bid form were not set out in full in specifications. Pfotzer v. U.S., Ct.Cl. 1948, 77 F.Supp. 390, 111 Ct.Cl. 184, certiorari denied 69 S.Ct. 237, 335 U.S. 885, 93 L.Ed. 424. United States ⬬ 70(27)

The advertisement for proposals for Government work required by this section and the proposals in response thereto form no part of the contract, and cannot be admitted to contradict or vary its terms. Harvey v. U.S., Ct.Cl.1872, 8 Ct. Cl. 501.

20. Open market purchases, advertising for contracts

There is a distinction in administrative law of United States between purchase in open market, and by contract. 1853, 6 Op.Atty.Gen. 99.

21. Effect of failure to comply, advertising for contracts

An officer who, in giving out a contract, has failed to comply with this section requiring advertisement previous to letting the contract, cannot, by permitting performance thereunder to proceed to any extent, make such contract obligatory upon the Government. 1876, 15 Op.Atty. Gen. 539.

II. CONSTRUCTION AND INTERPRETATION OF CONTRACTS
Subdivision Index

**51. Law governing, construction and in-
    terpretation of contracts**

Prime contracts to which the United
States is a party are governed by federal
common law.   U.S. Fidelity & Guaranty
Co. v. Hendry Corp., C.A.5 (Fla.) 1968,
391 F.2d 13, certiorari denied 89 S.Ct.
446, 393 U.S. 978, 21 L.Ed.2d 439.   Federal Courts ⬤ 413

Contracts with the United States Government are governed by the uniform federal "common law."   Padbloc Co. v.
U.S., Ct.Cl.1963, 161 Ct.Cl. 369, 137
U.S.P.Q. 224.   United States ⬤ 70(1)

**52. Discretion of officials, construction
    and interpretation of contracts**

Procurement policies set by higher government authority are not to be avoided
or evaded deliberately or negligently by
lesser officials, or by concert of contractor and contracting officer.   G.L. Christian and Associates v. U.S., Ct.Cl.1963,
320 F.2d 345, 160 Ct.Cl. 58.   United
States ⬤ 59

**53. Rules of construction or interpreta-
    tion, construction and interpreta-
    tion of contracts—Generally**

Where Congress has not adopted a different standard, it is customary to apply
to construction of Government contracts

the principles of general contract law.
Priebe & Sons v. U.S., U.S.1947, 68 S.Ct.
123, 332 U.S. 407, 92 L.Ed. 32.   United
States ⬤ 70(2.1)

A government contract must be read as
a whole and, if reasonably possible, interpreted in a manner which gives meaning
to all its parts and in such a fashion the
provisions do not conflict with each other.   B.D. Click Co., Inc. v. U.S., Ct.Cl.
1980, 614 F.2d 748, 222 Ct.Cl. 290.
United States ⬤ 70(4)

An instrument must be viewed in its
entirety and language contained therein
given that meaning which would be derived by a reasonably intelligent contractor acquainted with contemporaneous
circumstances.   J.B. Williams Co. v. U.S.,
Ct.Cl.1971, 450 F.2d 1379, 196 Ct.Cl.
491.   Contracts ⬤ 147(3)

In construing contract, court will first
resort to its words, not to one or a few of
them but to all of them as associated, and
as well to the conditions to which they
are addressed and intended to provide
for.   Ambrose-Augusterfer Corp. v. U.S.,
Ct.Cl.1968, 394 F.2d 536, 184 Ct.Cl. 18.
Contracts ⬤ 143(1)

In choosing between conflicting interpretations of government indefinite delivery requirements type contract, court
would look both to the written terms and
surrounding circumstances and avail itself of same light which parties possessed
when contract was made.   Franklin Co.
v. U.S., Ct.Cl.1967, 381 F.2d 416, 180
Ct.Cl. 666.   United States ⬤ 70(2.1)

Each government contract and set of
specifications must be individually interpreted.   Gelco Builders & Burjay Const.
Corp. v. U.S., Ct.Cl.1966, 369 F.2d 992,
177 Ct.Cl. 1025.   United States ⬤
70(2.1)

Government contracts should be construed, wherever possible, to avoid foreclosing exercise of sovereign power.
Acacia Villa v. Kemp, C.D.Cal.1990, 774
F.Supp. 1240, affirmed 955 F.2d 1382,
certiorari granted 113 S.Ct. 490, 506 U.S.
984, 121 L.Ed.2d 429, reversed 113 S.Ct.
1898, 508 U.S. 10, 123 L.Ed.2d 572, on
remand 995 F.2d 948.   United States ⬤
70(1)

The contracts of the Government with
one of its citizens are construed according to the ordinary rules of contracts applying between individuals.   Lundstrom
v. U.S., D.C.Or.1941, 53 F.Supp. 709, af-

firmed 139 F.2d 792. See, also, Hughes Transp. v. U.S., 1954, 121 F.Supp. 212, 128 Ct.Cl. 221; U.S. v. State of Minn., D.C.Minn.1953, 113 F.Supp. 488; Refining Associates v. U.S., 1953, 109 F.Supp. 259, 124 Ct.Cl. 115; David J. Joseph Co. v. U.S., 1949, 82 F.Supp. 345, 113 Ct.Cl. 3. United States ⟜ 70(1)

In the absence of some statutory direction, the principles of general contract law are applied in the interpretation of Government contracts and this involves the consideration of the language of the agreement, the purpose of the agreement and the circumstances of its making. Societe Anonyme Des Ateliers Brillie Freres v. U.S., Ct.Cl.1963, 160 Ct.Cl. 192. United States ⟜ 70(2.1)

54. —— Drafter, interpretation against, rules of construction or interpretation, construction and interpretation of contracts

Latent ambiguities in government contracts are construed against the government. Chemical Technology, Inc. v. U.S., Ct.Cl.1981, 645 F.2d 934, 227 Ct.Cl. 120. Public Contracts ⟜ 16

If drafters of plans and specifications for government project failed to convey true intent to bidders and instead wrote ambiguously so that another interpretation was reasonably possible, then given reliance on such alternative reasonable interpretation, contract must be construed against writer. Troup Bros., Inc. v. U.S., Ct.Cl.1980, 643 F.2d 719, 224 Ct.Cl. 594. United States ⟜ 70(3)

Where searchlight contract, taken at its best for the Government, was ambiguous as to whether it required the prime contractor or the Government to pay for testing of xenon lamps furnished as "first articles," doctrine of contra proferentem applied so as to require the Government, rather than the prime contractor, to pay for testing. Varo, Inc. v. U.S., Ct.Cl. 1977, 548 F.2d 953, 212 Ct.Cl. 432. United States ⟜ 70(32)

The "contra proferentem" rule that all doubts should be resolved against the Government who drafted contract does not apply where contractor knew of alleged ambiguity before it submitted its bid. James A. Mann, Inc. v. U.S., Ct.Cl. 1976, 535 F.2d 51, 210 Ct.Cl. 104. United States ⟜ 70(3)

Under the "contra proferentem" rule, if a discrepancy in contract language creates an ambiguity, and if the contractor's interpretation falls within the zone of reasonableness, the ambiguity will be construed against the Government as the author of the ambiguous document. Merando, Inc. v. U.S., Ct.Cl.1973, 475 F.2d 601, 201 Ct.Cl. 23. United States ⟜ 70(3)

When there is a contract that has been written by the government which is ambiguous, the ambiguity will be resolved against the drafter of the document and in favor of the other party, if that party's interpretation can be reasonably sustained by the contract. Max Drill, Inc. v. U.S., Ct.Cl.1970, 427 F.2d 1233, 192 Ct. Cl. 608. United States ⟜ 70(3)

Conflict between government contract specification requiring that walls be plastered or wallboarded, latter only on wood framed walls, and drawing showing use of door in masonry block wall consistent with painted wall was of such nature as to require contractor to submit matter to contracting officer for determination, and he could not later rely on principle that ambiguities should be construed against government. D & L Const. Co. and Associates v. U.S., Ct.Cl.1968, 402 F.2d 990, 185 Ct.Cl. 736. United States ⟜ 70(8)

Ambiguity in contracts written by government is resolved in favor of contractor. Sternberger v. U.S., Ct.Cl.1968, 401 F.2d 1012, 185 Ct.Cl. 528. United States ⟜ 70(3)

The rule that contract provisions will be construed against draftee presupposes that a reasonable interpretation is being given to the alleged ambiguous language, and the fact that by giving words strained or unusual connotations a certain interpretation might or could be considered is not a proper basis for application of the rule. Dittmore-Freimuth Corp. v. U.S., Ct.Cl.1968, 390 F.2d 664, 182 Ct.Cl. 507. Contracts ⟜ 155

Rule that an ambiguous contract susceptible of several possible meanings must be construed against party which, drew it had no applicability where language of contract was not susceptible to an intelligent meaning other than that which was given to it by the parties. A.R.F. Products, Inc. v. U.S., Ct.Cl.1967, 388 F.2d 692, 181 Ct.Cl. 1176. Contracts ⟜ 155

Government, as author of agreement, must shoulder the major task of seeing that, within zone of reasonableness, words of agreement communicate proper notions, as well as main risk of failure to carry that responsibility. Kraus v. U.S., Ct.Cl.1966, 366 F.2d 975, 177 Ct.Cl. 108. See, also, United Pac. Ins. Co. v. U.S., 1974, 497 F.2d 1402, 204 Ct.Cl. 686. United States ☞ 70(3)

A contract drafted by the government must be construed against it. Roberts v. U.S., Ct.Cl.1966, 357 F.2d 938, 174 Ct.Cl. 940. See, also, U.S. v. Pickett's Food Service, C.A.La.1966, 360 F.2d 338; Freedman v. U.S., 1963, 320 F.2d 359, 162 Ct.Cl. 390; Guyler v. U.S., 1963, 314 F.2d 506, 161 Ct.Cl. 159. United States ☞ 70(3)

Any doubt as to whether, under terms of construction contract, certain work fell into one price or another, should be resolved in favor of contractor, where United States prepared the contract. Pfotzer v. U.S., Ct.Cl.1948, 77 F.Supp. 390, 111 Ct.Cl. 184, certiorari denied 69 S.Ct. 237, 335 U.S. 885, 93 L.Ed. 424. United States ☞ 70(3)

Where contract for sale of milled rice to Federal Government was drawn up by the Government, ambiguities therein should be resolved against the Government. Standard Rice Co. v. U.S., Ct.Cl. 1944, 53 F.Supp. 717, 101 Ct.Cl. 85, certiorari granted 64 S.Ct. 1285, 322 U.S. 725, 88 L.Ed. 1561, affirmed 65 S.Ct. 145, 323 U.S. 106, 89 L.Ed. 104. Sales ☞ 54; United States ☞ 70(3)

"Patent ambiguity doctrine" calls for construing ambiguities in a government contract against the contractor, not the government as drafter, where the ambiguities are so patent and glaring that it is unreasonable for the contractor not to discover and inquire about them. Sunshine Const. & Engineering, Inc. v. U.S., Fed.Cl.2005, 64 Fed.Cl. 346. United States ☞ 70(30)

In context of a government contract, essential ingredients of the rule of contra proferentem, which requires that ambiguities be construed against the drafter, are: (1) that the contract specifications were drawn by the government; (2) that language was used therein which is susceptible of more than one interpretation; (3) that the intention of the parties does not otherwise appear; and (4) that the contractor actually and reasonably construed the specifications in accordance with one of the meanings of which the language

was susceptible. Record Steel and Const., Inc. v. U.S., Fed.Cl.2004, 62 Fed. Cl. 508. United States ☞ 70(3)

Where government, during negotiations of a contract whereby plaintiff was to prepare and furnish drawings of an item developed by plaintiff, insisted on its right to employ the drawings fully for subsequent procurements of the item from others, and where plaintiff notified government by telegram so worded that the Government could readily and reasonably think that plaintiff was willing to comply with the requirement as to the drawings themselves, reserving only such patent or other rights which it might possess independent of the drawings, plaintiff as the creator of the ambiguity (if such it was) is responsible for its own failure to clarify the meaning of the contract in definitive fashion before the government was bound. Canadian Commercial Corp. v. U.S., Ct.Cl.1973, 202 Ct.Cl. 65. United States ☞ 70(3)

In interpreting an ambiguous provision in a contract drafted by the Government, the ambiguity will be resolved against the drafter of the document where the other party's interpretation is reasonable. Ray D. Bolander Co., Inc. v. U.S., Ct.Cl.1968, 186 Ct.Cl. 398. United States ☞ 70(3)

Where doubt arises as to the meaning of a contract provision, that doubt will be resolved against the party who drafted the language in question. Western Contracting Corp. v. U.S., Ct.Cl.1958, 144 Ct.Cl. 318. Contracts ☞ 155

Where one of the parties to a contract draws the document and uses language which is susceptible of more than one meaning, and the intention of the parties does not otherwise appear, that meaning will be given the document which is more favorable to the party who did not draw it, and this rule is especially applicable to a Government contract where the contractor has nothing to say as to its provisions. Peter Kiewit Sons' Co. v. U.S., Ct.Cl.1947, 109 Ct.Cl. 390. Contracts ☞ 155; United States ☞ 70(3)

55. —— Reasonableness, rules of construction or interpretation, construction and interpretation of contracts

Where government contractor intended, and its contract price was based upon, vertical stacking of supplemental refreshment areas, and government reserved right to designate "the location of the refreshment areas," contractor reasonably read such reservation as referring only to designations conforming to a normal industry practice, and doctrine of contra proferentem also supported trial judge's decision that government's reserved power did not include power to designate where each supplemental refreshment area was to be located without regard to location of any other. Haney v. U.S., Ct.Cl.1982, 676 F.2d 584, 230 Ct.Cl. 148. United States ☞ 70(6.1)

In construing provisions of a contract, court is under a duty to give a reasonable meaning to all parts of the instrument rather than leaving a portion of it useless; the word "and" should be read as "or" if the contract so indicates. Monroe M. Tapper & Associates v. U.S., Ct.Cl.1979, 602 F.2d 311, 221 Ct.Cl. 27. Contracts ☞ 143.5; Contracts ☞ 159

Where there was no showing that methods of packaging axles sold to Post Office Department by contractor had been dependent upon outcome of final design and development of the installation procedures or that Post Office Department so believed, and Post Office was responsible for damage in transit, even if contractor's proposal, containing three prices for different methods of packaging, had not been intended to offer Post Office Department a choice between the three prices, Post Office Department's interpretation that proposal offered such choice was reasonable, for purposes of determining whether Government was liable for cost of packaging utilized that was allegedly in excess of contract requirements. Dana Corp. v. U.S., Ct.Cl.1972, 470 F.2d 1032, 200 Ct.Cl. 200. United States ☞ 70(27)

Government contractor's interpretation of procurement contract as contemplating that each waist size of groin armor would be cut from pattern size bearing corresponding number was unreasonable where, inter alia, such interpretation left one portion of contract useless and meaningless and where an explicit allusion to pattern sizes in one paragraph would, under contractor's interpretation, require government to furnish pattern sizes nowhere mentioned. Martin Lane Co. v. U.S., Ct.Cl.1970, 432 F.2d 1013, 193 Ct. Cl. 203. United States ☞ 70(30)

Contractor's interpretation of ambiguous contract provision will be adopted if reasonable. HRH Const. Corp. v. U.S., Ct.Cl.1970, 428 F.2d 1267, 192 Ct.Cl. 912. United States ☞ 70(3)

Parties to a contract drafted by government do not bear burden of correctly interpreting the same, only of reasonably interpreting it. Max Drill, Inc. v. U.S., Ct.Cl.1970, 427 F.2d 1233, 192 Ct.Cl. 608. United States ☞ 70(1)

Where contractor knew government's intended meaning of changes clause in contract when it willingly signed contract, contractor's interpretation was unreasonable and contractor was bound by the interpretation of the government. Perry & Wallis, Inc. v. U.S., Ct.Cl.1970, 427 F.2d 722, 192 Ct.Cl. 310. United States ☞ 70(25.1)

Only reasonable interpretation of provisions of contract, according to which plaintiff, suing to recover for fill material it has to supply after excavated materials had been exhausted, was to construct for United States a creek channel, levees and appurtenances, and according to which plaintiff was also to fill in designated "waste areas" with excavated materials, was that the United States was not required to make original field surveys of the construction site, including waste areas. Ace Const. Co. v. U.S., Ct.Cl.1968, 401 F.2d 816, 185 Ct.Cl. 487. United States ☞ 70(8)

A contract for microfilming of obsolete engineering documents for the Air Force should not be construed in such a manner as to contradict the reasonable, mutual, and manifested understanding of signatories, such as by giving undue significance to a careless recital contained therein or by divorcing language employed from relevant factual environment. Micrecord Corp. v. U.S., Ct.Cl. 1966, 361 F.2d 1000, 176 Ct.Cl. 46. United States ☞ 70(2.1)

Court should not so interpret agreement as to make a contract for the parties which it is satisfied that they would not have knowingly made for themselves. Pressed Steel Car Co. v. U.S., Ct.Cl.1958, 157 F.Supp. 950, 141 Ct.Cl. 318, certiorari denied 78 S.Ct. 1007, 356 U.S. 967, 2 L.Ed.2d 1074. Contracts ☞ 143(3)

Provision in highway construction contracts for deviation from drawings is not to be availed of by Government beyond reasonable limits, or in such fashion as to place upon contractor a burden of performance which may not be regarded as being fairly and reasonably within contemplation of parties when they entered into the contract. First Citizens Bank & Trust Co. v. U.S., Ct.Cl.1948, 76 F.Supp. 250, 110 Ct.Cl. 280. Highways ☞ 113(4); Contracts ☞ 314; United States ☞ 73(17)

An interpretation which gives a reasonable meaning to all parts of an instrument will be preferred to one which leaves a portion of it meaningless. Blake Const. Co., Inc. v. U.S., Ct.Cl.1973, 202 Ct.Cl. 794. Contracts ☞ 153

56. ── Practical interpretations, rules of construction or interpretation, construction and interpretation of contracts

Practical interpretation which parties gave to government contract before it became the subject of controversy is to be accorded great weight. Centre Mfg. Co. v. U.S., Ct.Cl.1968, 392 F.2d 229, 183 Ct.Cl. 115. United States ☞ 70(2.1)

57. ── Duty to request clarification, rules of construction or interpretation, construction and interpretation of contracts

Where bid documents regarding ductwork in hospital renovation project did not supply information about above-ceiling conditions, and contractor and its mechanical subcontractor were unable to perform site inspection of those conditions because maze of pipes and ducts blocked view of space above ceilings from access panel, patent ambiguity was created, triggering contractor's duty to inquire, and its failure to do so precluded equitable adjustment for alleged extra work related to connection of new diffusers and grills to hospital's HVAC system. Conner Brothers Const. Co., Inc. v. U.S., Fed.Cl.2005, 65 Fed.Cl. 657. United States ☞ 70(22.1)

Contractor whose proprietary cost information was disclosed by Government in contract solicitation had duty to inquire into any ambiguity as to length of time that directed subcontract would last at time contractor entered into settlement agreement with Government, if Government drafted the agreement and there were any ambiguity as to duration of subcontract in terms of date certain or time after prime contract's performance commenced. Blackstone Consulting Inc. v. U.S., Fed.Cl.2005, 65 Fed.Cl. 463, af-

firmed 170 Fed.Appx. 128, 2006 WL 618805. United States ☞ 70(30)

Government construction contractor was not entitled to additional compensation for adding columns at planters and terraces, based on contention that drawings were ambiguous as to whether columns were indicated; any ambiguity in the drawings was patent due to the glaring ambiguity of the meaning of certain vertical lines, as indicating either masonry control joints or columns, and failure of contractor to inquire as to the meaning of the vertical lines forfeited its claims. Sunshine Const. & Engineering, Inc. v. U.S., Fed.Cl.2005, 64 Fed.Cl. 346. United States ☞ 70(30)

Exception to general rule that ambiguities in government contracts are to be construed against the government as drafter is the " patent ambiguity doctrine," which mandates resolving ambiguities against the contractor where the ambiguities are so patent and glaring that it is unreasonable for a contractor not to discover and inquire about them. Record Steel and Const., Inc. v. U.S., Fed.Cl. 2004, 62 Fed.Cl. 508. United States ☞ 70(30)

If, in the opinion of the contractor, a Government contract or its specifications contain a patent ambiguity, the contractor is under a duty to request clarification. Bishop Engineering Co., Inc. v. U.S., Ct.Cl.1967, 180 Ct.Cl. 411. United States ☞ 70(2.1)

58. ── Reference to clause as whole, rules of construction or interpretation, construction and interpretation of contracts

Where ambiguity of word within government contract was resolved by reference to clause as a whole, there was no basis for invocation of canons of construction based on ambiguities in government-drafted contracts. Rice v. U.S., Ct. Cl.1970, 428 F.2d 1311, 192 Ct.Cl. 903. United States ☞ 70(3)

59. ── Time of actions or interpretations, rules of construction or interpretation, construction and interpretation of contracts

Forward pricing agreement entered into between Government and contractor in 1970, in which Government approved system of nonupdating of direct labor factors, was not admission against interest which would bar Government from seeking recovery for defective pricing due to use of noncurrent direct labor factor data in connection with contract for which certificate was executed in 1968; only actions and interpretations which occur before controversy arises are relevant in determining and interpreting meaning of contract. Singer Co., Librascope Div. v. U.S., Ct.Cl.1978, 576 F.2d 905, 217 Ct.Cl. 225. United States ⇒ 70(18)

60. —— Conduct of parties, rules of construction or interpretation, construction and interpretation of contracts

Any deficiency of vagueness in language of government contract was remedied by course of conduct in which both parties acted from common premise that development of test program was as much contractor's responsibility as was identification and conduct of tests themselves. Singer Co. Librascope Div. v. U.S., Ct.Cl.1977, 568 F.2d 695, 215 Ct.Cl. 281. United States ⇒ 70(32)

Government's acquiescence in contractor's removal of pillow tanks was significant contemporaneous interpretation of contract language indicating contractor's right to remove steel storage tanks installed pursuant to same contractual provision covering pillow tanks. Norcoast Constructors, Inc. v. U.S., Ct.Cl.1971, 448 F.2d 1400, 196 Ct.Cl. 1. United States ⇒ 70(3)

If contract is not clear, conduct of parties is given great weight in construing it. Hensel Phelps Const. Co. v. U.S., C.A.10 (Colo.) 1969, 413 F.2d 701. Contracts ⇒ 170(1)

Evidence of the surrounding circumstances and of the conduct of the parties to a contract is relevant in the ascertainment of the intention of the parties when their minds met. Cave Const., Inc. v. U.S. for Use and Benefit of Angell Bros., Inc., C.A.10 (Wyo.) 1967, 387 F.2d 760. Contracts ⇒ 175(1)

Contractor did not establish that government waived requirements of formal written work order and notice to proceed for creating express contracts to perform work orders under two indefinite quantity contracts (IQCs), absent showing of a consistent prior course of dealing under which government compensated it for performing work orders without a written work order signed by the contracting officer and a notice to proceed. L.P.

Consulting Group, Inc. v. U.S., Fed.Cl. 2005, 66 Fed.Cl. 238. United States ⇒ 65

Ambiguity in government construction contract as to whether over-excavation was required or merely recommended was not patent, where government did not explicitly raise its competing interpretation of the contract until the briefing of the pending dispositive motions in suit brought by contractor, and its actions in implementing the contract left uncertain its position on contractual interpretation. Record Steel and Const., Inc. v. U.S., Fed.Cl.2004, 62 Fed.Cl. 508. United States ⇒ 70(30)

The action of the parties in performing and accepting performance of a contract before a controversy arises is highly relevant in determining what the parties intended, particularly when their intention is not expressed in writing. Northbridge Electronics, Inc. v. U.S., Ct.Cl.1966, 175 Ct.Cl. 426. United States ⇒ 70(3)

61. —— Conflicting provisions of contracts, rules of construction or interpretation, construction and interpretation of contracts

Rule that contract provisions should not be construed as conflicting unless no other reasonable interpretation is possible was particularly applicable when provision sought to be eliminated, or subordinated, was a standard mandatory clause of broad application, whereby the government stipulated that if property furnished was not received in condition suitable for intended use contractor might have an equitable adjustment of delivery or performance dates or contract price or both. Thompson Ramo Wooldridge Inc. v. U.S., Ct.Cl.1966, 361 F.2d 222, 175 Ct.Cl. 527. United States ⇒ 70(4)

62. —— Custom and practice, rules of construction or interpretation, construction and interpretation of contracts

Trade practice could not override clear and unambiguous provision of government contract. Merando, Inc. v. U.S., Ct.Cl.1973, 475 F.2d 603, 201 Ct.Cl. 28. Customs And Usages ⇒ 17

Trade usage and custom in business community within which agreement was framed is factor to be considered in ascertaining meaning intended for contractual provision. Kenneth Reed Const.

Corp. v. U.S., Ct.Cl.1973, 475 F.2d 583, 201 Ct.Cl. 282. Customs And Usages ⊙ 15(1)

Where contract specifications were clear and unambiguous, trade practice could not override contract provisions. Northwestern Indus. Piping, Inc. v. U.S., Ct.Cl.1972, 467 F.2d 1308, 199 Ct.Cl. 540. Customs And Usages ⊙ 17

In interpreting terms of a contract, trade usage should be considered. Bromion, Inc. v. U.S., Ct.Cl.1969, 411 F.2d 1020, 188 Ct.Cl. 31. Customs And Usages ⊙ 15(1)

Government contract for installation of tile floor in powerhouse of federal dam was required to be read as including requirement for bond between setting bed and slab, where, during entire time of performance, contractor and all government representatives were of opinion that bond was required and attainment of such bond was acknowledged trade practice or custom. Stoeckert v. U.S., Ct.Cl. 1968, 391 F.2d 639, 183 Ct.Cl. 152. United States ⊙ 70(8)

A contract must be construed in the light of the previous practice of the department, and the Secretary, by ordering a test after being notified of the contractor's construction of the contract, and without objecting thereto, impliedly accepted such construction, and bound the Government to pay the additional expense of such test. U.S. v. Newport News Shipbuilding & Dry Dock Co., C.C.A.4 (Va.) 1910, 178 F. 194, 101 C.C.A. 514.

A trade practice in the building construction industry of using Masonite doors on paint-grade cabinets cannot properly be permitted to overcome an unambiguous contract provision requiring the use of wood doors. WRB Corp. v. U.S., Ct.Cl.1968, 183 Ct.Cl. 409.

63. —— Intent or understanding of parties, rules of construction or interpretation, construction and interpretation of contracts

Where contractor knew of Government's erroneous reference to armed services procurement regulation at time contracting officer was drafting liquidated damages clause, and said nothing about it, contractor accepted error for its own purposes with knowledge that reference in clause ran contrary to agreement, and contractor could not later disavow mutu-

al understanding by claiming invalidity of clause. Simmonds Precision Products, Inc. v. U.S., Ct.Cl.1976, 546 F.2d 886, 212 Ct.Cl. 305. United States ⊙ 74(12.1)

The understanding of parties to government contract that paragraph relating to submission of shop drawing of equipment must be interpreted to apply to special designs for switchboards and panelboards but not to automatic transfer switches of different manufacturer should be given great weight. Sherwin v. U.S., Ct.Cl.1971, 436 F.2d 992, 193 Ct.Cl. 962. United States ⊙ 70(3)

Where contract between United States and contractor for construction of dam contained provision that increase in cost of performance brought about by changed condition would be remediable under the contract disputes procedure, parties contemplated that latent subsurface condition might be discovered and that contractor's method of operation could be affected as consequence. Paul Hardeman, Inc. v. U.S., Ct.Cl.1969, 406 F.2d 1357, 186 Ct.Cl. 743. United States ⊙ 70(22.1)

Fact that neither electronics firm nor Air Force knew for certainty that antenna couplers with single knob control could be produced which would meet performance requirements of firm's contract to supply couplers to Air Force did not mean that this was not objective intended by parties. A.R.F. Products, Inc. v. U.S., Ct.Cl.1967, 388 F.2d 692, 181 Ct.Cl. 1176. United States ⊙ 70(9)

If in the judgment of the court the contract when considered by the whole of its parts clearly and unmistakably expresses the intention of the parties, extrinsic inquiry is unwarranted. Cave Const., Inc. v. U.S. for Use and Benefit of Angell Bros., Inc., C.A.10 (Wyo.) 1967, 387 F.2d 760. Contracts ⊙ 169

64. —— Judicial and administrative interpretations, rules of construction or interpretation, construction and interpretation of contracts

Reference to judicial and administrative decisions subsequent to making of contract was justified in many cases, in determining scope of disputes clause, as practical construction of clause by government (which frequently urged narrow construction) and in any event as showing construction on which innumerable other government contractors may have relied in not presenting breach of contract claims to contracting officer, which claims would be forever barred under government's broad interpretation by contractual time limitations on presentation of claims and appeals. U.S. v. Utah Const. & Min. Co., U.S.Ct.Cl.1966, 86 S.Ct. 1545, 384 U.S. 394, 16 L.Ed.2d 642. United States ⊙ 70(3); United States ⊙ 73(14)

Where the fiscal officers of the Navy allowed the plaintiff to retain the cash discounts up to one percent from the beginning of performance of its first contract on Oct. 29, 1940, until Sept. 2, 1942, at which time plaintiff was advised that under a new interpretation of T.D. 5000 such retention would no longer be permitted, a provision written into an administrative regulation and from the regulation incorporated by reference into a contract could not be eliminated from the contract by one of the parties by changing its interpretation of the regulation. Cramp Shipbuilding Co. v. U.S., Ct.Cl. 1952, 122 Ct.Cl. 72. United States ⊙ 73(12)

65. —— Official statements, rules of construction or interpretation, construction and interpretation of contracts

Official statements by representative of Government should be taken into account in ascertaining joint understanding of parties to contract. Macke Co. v. U.S., Ct.Cl.1972, 467 F.2d 1323, 199 Ct.Cl. 552. United States ⊙ 70(3)

A subordinate Government employee or one not concerned with the negotiation of the contract cannot render contract interpretations binding on the parties and consequently, an employee of The Alaska Railroad who was not involved in the preparation of bid invitations relating to the Railroad's sale of scrap and having no responsibility for the making of the contract, who informed one of the bidders concerning the applicability of the Railroad's tariffs to the transportation of goods for hire, would not be held to have been interpreting the delivery provisions of the contract for the information of the bidders. Commercial Metals Co. v. U.S., Ct.Cl.1966, 176 Ct.Cl. 343. United States ⊙ 70(3)

66. —— Prior agreements, rules of construction or interpretation, construction and interpretation of contracts

Where manufacturer knew, when preparing its bid on contract for production of certain radiological survey meters, that government had previously contracted for and accepted full delivery of a large number of survey meters manufactured under exactly the same specification requirements, and where there was never any indication that previously manufactured meters were in any way deficient or not acceptable to government, conclusion of manufacturer that previous product fully satisfied government and that producing an equivalent product necessarily implied conformance with specifications was justified and reasonable. J.B. Williams Co. v. U.S., Ct.Cl.1971, 450 F.2d 1379, 196 Ct.Cl. 491. United States ⊙ 70(3)

Prior contract calling for painting of entire area of specified portion of government building could not be used as aid in interpreting subsequent contract entered into with same contractor, which contract called for painting of another portion of same building but which omitted reference to entire area, for purpose of determining whether work rooms as well as corridors and rest rooms were to be painted. Jamsar, Inc. v. U.S., Ct.Cl.1971, 442 F.2d 930, 194 Ct.Cl. 819. United States ⊙ 70(4)

Experience of contractor under somewhat similar government contracts could be considered in determining reasonableness of contractor's interpretation of contract documents. Singer-General Precision, Inc. v. U.S., Ct.Cl.1970, 427 F.2d 1187, 192 Ct.Cl. 435. United States ⊙ 70(3)

Government contractor's experience, under somewhat similar contracts, may be considered in determining reasonableness of his interpretation of contract documents. D & L Const. Co. and Associates v. U.S., Ct.Cl.1968, 402 F.2d 990, 185 Ct.Cl. 736. United States ⊙ 70(3)

67. —— Proprietorship principles, rules of construction or interpretation, construction and interpretation of contracts

In determining whether government contractor's constructive compensation claim is allowable, it is the parties' contract rather than any commonsense principles of proprietorship which governs. Norman M. Giller and Associates v. U.S., Ct.Cl.1976, 535 F.2d 37, 210 Ct.Cl. 80. United States ☞ 70(15.1)

68. —— Obsolete provisions, rules of construction or interpretation, construction and interpretation of contracts

Where contract contained alternatives which, useful and rational in negotiation stage when bids were being received, became obsolete and irrational as terms of a definite contract, the failure to strike out the alternatives did not indicate that they were intended to remain a part of the contract, and the inadvertence did not lay contractor open to being required, merely because of the letter of the contract, to perform what he had not promised. Olson Const. Co. v. U.S., Ct.Cl. 1948, 75 F.Supp. 1014, 110 Ct.Cl. 249. Contracts ☞ 172

69. —— Omissions, rules of construction or interpretation, construction and interpretation of contracts

When a government contractor is presented with an obvious omission, inconsistency or discrepancy of significance in the contract documents, he must consult the government's representatives if he intends to bridge the crevasse in his own favor. Blake Const. Co., Inc. v. U.S., Ct.Cl.1973, 202 Ct.Cl. 794. See, also, HRH Const. Corp. v. U.S., 1970, 428 F.2d 1267, 192 Ct.Cl. 912. United States ☞ 70(4)

There is no rigid requirement that a Government-Furnished Property clause apply only to property listed *eo nomine* in the contract; if the contract specifications elsewhere provide that the Government will make available certain facilities, including by collateral reference the use of a pier then under construction, such reference supplies the omission. Koppers/Clough, v. U.S., Ct.Cl.1973, 201 Ct.Cl. 344. United States ☞ 70(12.1)

70. Access to records provisions, construction and interpretation of contracts

Where access-to-records provisions of contract entered into between government and pharmaceutical company permitted government access to information that was a significant input in the cost of products purchased in contract, government's inquiry was not limited to only those items specifically assigned by com-

pany as costs of contract or to information relating to possible impropriety of negotiating process, and therefore, Comptroller General was entitled to information relating to costs of research and development, marketing, promotion, distribution and administration in order to conduct a review of the procurement of drugs by agencies of federal government, including the pricing of drugs and pharmaceuticals procured under negotiated contracts. U.S. v. Abbott Laboratories, C.A.7 (Ill.) 1979, 597 F.2d 672. United States ☞ 70(12.1); United States ☞ 75(1)

71. Intended use provisions, construction and interpretation of contracts

On issue whether making of prints was an "intended use" for which the government furnished microfilm to manufacturer of radio transmitters, a contract amendment eliminating requirement with respect to certain parts was evidence that the government's representatives agreed that without something more than the bare microfilm the government-furnished property was not adequate to enable contractor to meet the interchangeability standard with respect to parts affected by the amendment. Thompson Ramo Wooldridge Inc. v. U.S., Ct.Cl.1966, 361 F.2d 222, 175 Ct.Cl. 527. United States ☞ 72(5)

72. Limitation of cost provisions, construction and interpretation of contracts

Under limitation of cost clause in military contract requiring contractor to notify contracting officer if contractor has reason to believe that cost overrun is imminent, contractor was excused from giving notice where at no time during performance of contract did contractor have reason to know of its overrun. General Elec. Co. v. U.S., Ct.Cl.1971, 440 F.2d 420, 194 Ct.Cl. 678. United States ☞ 70(36)

73. Suitability for use provisions, construction and interpretation of contracts

Government-furnished property "suitable for use" does not mean merely that article conforms to technical specifications but that it is suitable for use in process of manufacturing the items called for in government contract. Thompson Ramo Wooldridge Inc. v. U.S., Ct.Cl.

1966, 361 F.2d 222, 175 Ct.Cl. 527. United States ☞ 70(9)

Under government contract specification for generators requiring a "suitable opening for the engine system radiator, with thermostatically operated shutters having auxiliary manual control" thermostatically operated shutters were required by the plain language of specifications. Hol-Gar Mfg. Corp. v. U.S., Ct.Cl.1965, 351 F.2d 972, 169 Ct.Cl. 384. United States ☞ 70(9)

Under a Government contract for the manufacture of jackets for the Government which was to furnish cloth "suitable for use", suitability was an additional obligation assumed by the Government, a primary obligation, and was to be determined by reference to the contract as a whole and not by mere reference to the technical wording of the specifications only. Topkis Bros. Co. v. U.S., Ct.Cl. 1962, 299 F.2d 952, 155 Ct.Cl. 648. United States ☞ 70(9)

74. Employment contracts, construction and interpretation of contracts

Employment contracts, the performance of which involves the procurement of public contracts, are closely scrutinized by the courts, and, where compensation is contingent on the success of the person specially employed to procure the public contract, the employment contract is against public policy and unenforceable. Bradley v. American Radiator & Standard Sanitary Corp., S.D.N.Y.1946, 6 F.R.D. 37, affirmed 159 F.2d 39. Contracts ☞ 123(1)

75. Reprocurement contracts, construction and interpretation of contracts

Government need not, in all cases, consider defaulting contractor for reprocurement, but contractor may be permitted to bid on repurchase solicitations and, if defaulted contractor is found to be responsible and capable of performance, is responsive to the solicitation, and is the lowest bidder, it may receive the repurchase contract, but on reprocurement, defaulted contractor, notwithstanding its submission of lowest bid, may not receive more than initial contract price for its reprocurement performance. Churchill Chemical Corp. v. U.S., Ct.Cl.1979, 602 F.2d 358, 221 Ct.Cl. 284. United States ☞ 64.45(2); United States ☞ 72.1(6)

Where government on reprocurement is not in fact replacing contract between it and terminated contractor but instead is placing a new contract calling for different items, former contractor is not chargeable for excess costs. Meinberg v. U.S., W.D.Mo.1969, 310 F.Supp. 86. United States ☞ 75(5)

Where a Government contractor objects to the price of a reprocurement contract, he has the burden of proof of making such a showing. General Ship Contracting Corp. v. U.S., D.C.N.J.1962, 205 F.Supp. 658. United States ☞ 74(10)

76. Miscellaneous provisions ambiguous, construction and interpretation of contracts

Provision of contract whereby government would make capital advances required to construct nickel smelter and such replacements or improvements agreed upon and other necessary agreed upon expenditures which, in accordance with generally accepted accounting practices, were capitalized, was ambiguous as to whether replacements and improvements should be treated as included within capital advance provisions or as repair and maintenance expenses for purpose of fixing delivery price of nickel to government to be based on contractor's actual cost of production and amount sufficient to amortize government's capital advances plus interest. U.S. v. Hanna Nickel Smelting Co., D.C.Or.1966, 253 F.Supp. 784, affirmed 400 F.2d 944. United States ☞ 70(19)

Contract for construction of dormitory at Air Force base was ambiguous with respect to whether over-excavation was required as contended by the government, or merely recommended as contended by the contractor, as both interpretations were within the zone of reasonableness. Record Steel and Const., Inc. v. U.S., Fed.Cl.2004, 62 Fed.Cl. 508. United States ☞ 70(8)

77. Miscellaneous provisions not ambiguous, construction and interpretation of contracts

Government contract which stated, inter alia, as to preproduction equipment, that "1 equipment * * * conforming in every respect to the requirements set forth under the heading 'PRODUCTION EQUIPMENT' and manufactured with tools, materials and methods which are the same as or representative of those which will be used in the manufacture of the equipment to be furnished * *.*, shall be submitted by the Contractor for approval by the Government * * *," was not ambiguous and required both that the sample conform to the specifications in every respect for the production units and that the samples be manufactured with tools, materials and methods which were the same or representative of those which would be used in the manufacture of the production units. Burnett Electronics Lab, Inc. v. U.S., Ct.Cl.1973, 479 F.2d 1329, 202 Ct.Cl. 463. United States ☞ 70(14)

Provision of government contract calling for painting of portion of federal building and describing portion of building that contractor was to "repair, clean and paint" as "second story: all work spaces or rooms and public areas such as corridors and rest rooms" and "third story: all work spaces or rooms and public area such as corridors and rest rooms" was not ambiguous and did not, in view of provisions that contractor cover all furniture and equipment, require contractor to paint only corridors and rest rooms but required that contractor paint all work spaces or rooms in addition to corridors and rest rooms. Jamsar, Inc. v. U.S., Ct.Cl.1971, 442 F.2d 930, 194 Ct.Cl. 819. United States ☞ 70(6.1)

Government contract for rehabilitation of Government railroad which required track to be lifted twice for over-all raise of 6 inches and ballast to be spread for average depth of 6 inches, was, under circumstances, susceptible of only one interpretation, that is, that two lifts had to be made on new ballast as required by contracting officer. Wm. A. Smith Contracting Co. v. U.S., Ct.Cl.1961, 292 F.2d 854, 155 Ct.Cl. 44. United States ☞ 70(8)

Bid condition that payment be made in full prior to removal of any of property purchased from Government was clear and unambiguous and meant that payment must be made in full amount of bid, and not merely for property removed. Fay v. U.S., C.A.5 (Fla.) 1958, 253 F.2d 936. United States ☞ 58(4)

III.   CREATION OR FORMATION OF CONTRACTS

Subdivision Index

---

101. Consideration, creation or formation of contracts

The rule that every contract, legal on its face, imports a consideration, and is presumed to be obligatory until the contrary is shown, if the parties be ostensibly able to contract, applies to Government contracts. U.S. v. Maurice, C.C.Va.1823, 26 F.Cas. 1211, No. 15747.

102. Intent or knowledge, creation or formation of contracts—Generally

A government contractor, regardless of its size, locality or experience, is bound to understand the complexities and consequences of its undertaking. Tony Downs Foods Co. v. U.S., Ct.Cl.1976, 530 F.2d 367, 209 Ct.Cl. 31. Public Contracts ☞ 23

Postal service was not required to advise bidders on construction contract of the possibility of waiver of prohibition contained in postal service regulation that no construction contract shall be awarded to designer of project except by approval of named individual, in that regulation itself put bidders on notice that requirement might be waived. Morgan Associates v. U.S. Postal Service, C.A.2 (N.Y.) 1975, 511 F.2d 1223. United States ☞ 64.5

Unexpressed, subjective, unilateral intent of one party to contract is insufficient to bind other contracting party, especially when latter reasonably believes otherwise. Firestone Tire & Rubber Co. v. U.S., Ct.Cl.1971, 444 F.2d 547, 195 Ct.Cl. 21. Contracts ☞ 147(1)

103. —— Authority of government agent, intent or knowledge, creation or formation of contracts

One who deals with a Government officer or agent must be held to have notice of the limits of the agent's authority, so that where the language of the contract and the circumstances surrounding its negotiation makes it clear that the Government had obligated itself to pay the unit prices prescribed in the contract and to pay for any additional stone required to repair hurricane damage but no other extra costs incurred from such damage, neither the extensive damage caused by a hurricane nor the oral assurance of some unauthorized Government agent regarding reimbursement, will serve to expand the Government's contract obligation beyond the terms of the contract. Richards & Associates v. U.S., Ct.Cl.1966, 177 Ct. Cl. 1037. United States ☞ 70(20)

104. Bids, creation or formation of contracts—Generally

To preserve integrity of bidding process, government contractors must bid on basis of meeting contract requirements. Troup Bros., Inc. v. U.S., Ct.Cl.1980, 643 F.2d 719, 224 Ct.Cl. 594. United States ☞ 64.30

United States should not require contractors to wade though maze of numbers, catalogs, cross-reference tables and other data resembling crossword puzzles in order to find out what the government requires in an invitation for bids, particularly where requirements can be clearly specified by use of ordinary words and figures. Gorn Corp. v. U.S., Ct.Cl.1970, 424 F.2d 588, 191 Ct.Cl. 560. United States ☞ 64.30

Federal Housing Administration's invitation for bids on leasehold interest was merely invitation for offers, and not an "offer" requiring Administration to accept highest bid. Trump v. Mason, D.C.D.C.1961, 190 F.Supp. 887. United States ☞ 64.25

A bidder on federal construction work is entitled to consider the information and data disclosed in the specifications and on the drawings, and to read and reasonably interpret such provisions in the light of the other provisions of the contract. Loftis v. U.S., Ct.Cl.1948, 76 F.Supp. 816, 110 Ct.Cl. 551. Contracts ☞ 164; United States ☞ 70(4)

Agency's failure to follow pertinent government bidding regulation raises doubt as to whether government is receiving items at lowest possible cost and whether integrity of competitive bidding system is being maintained and consequently contract entered into pursuant to such bidding should be terminated and the matter resolicited. (1979) 58 Comp. Gen. 586.

It is the duty of the Director of Procurement to reject all bids when convinced they result from bidders' collusion depriving the Government of the benefits conferred by section 5 of this title. 1937, 39 Op.Atty.Gen. 71.

105. —— Law governing, bids, creation or formation of contracts

Terms of plaintiff's answer to government's invitation for bids on surplus army trucks were construed according to federal general contract law. George Epcar Co. v. U.S., C.A.10 (Utah) 1967, 377 F.2d 225, certiorari denied 88 S.Ct. 473, 389 U.S. 973, 19 L.Ed.2d 466. United States ☞ 64.30

106. —— Form, bids, creation or formation of contracts

Where invitation for bids on government land stated that bids had to be submitted in duplicate in bid form accompanying invitation for bids, that bid submitted in any other form could be summarily rejected, and that telegraphic bids would not be considered, telephone call to General Services Administration Regional Headquarters on day before opening of bids could not constitute valid bid for three parcels as group or effect modification of pending separate bids for such parcels into bid for parcels as group. Ruggiero v. U.S., Ct.Cl.1970, 420 F.2d 709, 190 Ct.Cl. 327. United States ☞ 64.30

Solicitation was controlling document for determining submission deadline for price proposals, and not section of contracting agency's web site describing the solicitation; language in solicitation established that web site was the mechanism for offerors to access the solicitation and any amendments and notices but only potential amendments to the solicitation could become part of the solicitation, not a web site. Conscoop-Consorzia Fra Coop. Di Prod. E Lavoro v. U.S., Fed.Cl. 2004, 62 Fed.Cl. 219, affirmed 159 Fed. Appx. 184, 2005 WL 1368664. United States ☞ 64.30

It is customary, but not essential, that a telegraphed proposition or bid should be confirmed by letter. 1898, 22 Op.Atty. Gen. 45.

Where the advertisement requires the proposals to be made on blank forms furnished by the Department, the omission or erasure of immaterial words in the proposal of a bidder does not affect the validity of his bid. 1877, 15 Op.Atty. Gen. 226.

107. —— Amendment, bids, creation or formation of contracts

Bidder on a federally assisted construction contract who failed to submit with his bid the appropriate commitment required by the "Chicago Plan" for minority hiring, could not amend his bid submission subsequent to the opening of the bid so as to qualify as a responsive bidder, even though defect in commitment did not go to the price, quantity or quality of the services and even though error in commitment was a good-faith inadvertent error and bidder was in fact in current compliance with utilization goals. Rossetti Contracting Co., Inc. v. Brennan, C.A.7 (Ill.) 1974, 508 F.2d 1039. United States ☞ 64.30

Where invitation for bids on government property provided that modifications or withdrawals received after date for opening bids would not be considered unless received before award was made and late receipt was due to delay in mails or to mishandling by government, letters sent by bidder that were written after date set for opening bid could not affect either modification or withdrawal of bids previously submitted. Ruggiero v. U.S., Ct.Cl.1970, 420 F.2d 709, 190 Ct.Cl. 327. United States ☞ 64.30

Bid form which had to be filled out, signed and filed by construction contractor could not thereafter be altered as to terms and conditions by either contractor or United States. Pfotzer v. U.S., Ct.Cl. 1948, 77 F.Supp. 390, 111 Ct.Cl. 184, certiorari denied 69 S.Ct. 237, 335 U.S. 885, 93 L.Ed. 424. United States ☞ 64.30; Contracts ☞ 17

Where there was a request for proposals for design and manufacture of elec-

tronic air navigation equipment and subsequent amendment to such request made changes in equipment configuration, delivery schedule, and various technical specifications, such changes in requirements were not so substantial as to warrant cancellation and resolicitation. (1979) 58 Comp.Gen. 591.

108. —— Errors or mistakes, bids, creation or formation of contracts

Government is not liable to contractor for contractor's unilateral mistake unless it can be shown that government knew or should have known of mistake in interpretation of contract requirements. Astro-Space Laboratories, Inc. v. U.S., Ct. Cl.1972, 470 F.2d 1003, 200 Ct.Cl. 282. United States ☞ 70(29)

Where question of rental expense was being tried in Court of Claims at time of negotiations on later contracts with United States, contractor assumed risk of consequences of alleged mistake with regard to building overhead and could not subsequently be heard to complain. Loral Corp. v. U.S., Ct.Cl.1970, 434 F.2d 1328, 193 Ct.Cl. 473. United States ☞ 70(29)

Evidence, in action by bidders to recover forfeited deposits made in bidding for purchase of two parcels of government land, established that bidders had submitted separate bids for three parcels in mistaken belief that this was way to bid for such parcels as group, and not individually, and that contracting officer accepted two of such bids, though he should have known that they were mistaken, and thus bidders were entitled to recover deposits. Ruggiero v. U.S., Ct.Cl.1970, 420 F.2d 709, 190 Ct.Cl. 327. United States ☞ 64.40(4)

Evidence sufficiently sustained finding that contractor failed to prove either by preponderance of the evidence or by clear and convincing proof as required by armed services procurement regulations that mistake had been made in submission of bid on government contract for construction of bridge for United States Army. Burtz-Durham Const. Co. v. U.S., C.A.5 (Ga.) 1967, 384 F.2d 913, certiorari denied 88 S.Ct. 1046, 390 U.S. 953, 19 L.Ed.2d 1146. Bridges ☞ 20(6)

Where Government should have known at time it awarded contract that a gross mistake had been made by bidder, it would be inequitable to hold bidder to terms of contract. C.N. Monroe Mfg. Co.

v. U.S., E.D.Mich.1956, 143 F.Supp. 449. United States ⟶ 74(4)

Bid for sale of lumber to the United States, based on F.O.B. mill price instead of price free alongside vessel in designated vicinity, as specified in invitation for bids, was so obviously erroneous that the United States had no right to accept such bid and hold bidder liable for breach of contract, where bidder's representative disclosed error to United States representative immediately upon discovery thereof and sought to withdraw or correct bid before execution of formal contract. West v. U.S., N.D.Fla.1956, 143 F.Supp. 167. United States ⟶ 64.40(4)

Even if contractual relationship existed between subcontractor furnishing lumber millwork to prime contractors constructing facilities for Marine Corps and Federal Government, an error by subcontractor in submitting its bid could not be relied upon by subcontractor to recover amount in addition to contract price after the bid had ripened into a contract. Brister & Koester Lumber Corp. v. U.S., Ct.Cl. 1950, 90 F.Supp. 695, 116 Ct.Cl. 824. United States ⟶ 74.2

Manufacturer which negligently failed to notice provision in invitation to bid for contract for manufacture of army uniforms that cloth to be furnished by United States was unshrunk rather than shrunk, so that manufacturer made a miscalculation in bid and was required to obtain additional allowance of cloth from the United States, was not entitled to recover charge for additional cloth. Hyde Park Clothes v. U.S., Ct.Cl.1949, 84 F.Supp. 589, 114 Ct.Cl. 424. United States ⟶ 70(29)

The Government is entitled to contract for transportation even under unreasonable classifications, and if the bidder miscalculates the price he must bear the loss, but such classification must have been incorporated in the contract before it becomes binding upon the bidder. Lundstrom v. U.S., D.C.Or.1941, 53 F.Supp. 709, affirmed 139 F.2d 792. United States ⟶ 70(1)

109. —— Solicited or unsolicited bids, creation or formation of contracts

Whether proposal based on licensing arrangement, submitted after date for receipt of initial proposals under ongoing request for proposals, was solicited or unsolicited is immaterial because procurement activity is entitled to receive information concerning procurement at any time and utilize that information to assess or reassess its procurement needs. (1979) 58 Comp.Gen. 575.

110. —— Time of opening, bids, creation or formation of contracts

Whether plaintiff contractor's bid on federal housing rehabilitation contract was opened first or last did not affect its sufficiency. Northeast Const. Co. v. Romney, C.A.D.C.1973, 485 F.2d 752, 157 U.S.App.D.C. 381. United States ⟶ 64.40(4)

111. —— Withdrawal, bids, creation or formation of contracts

Where bid was made subject to provisions that it might not be withdrawn after opening of bids, attempted revocation after opening of bids was ineffective, notwithstanding bidder's contention that it was not, after advising Government that it wished to withdraw its bid, a "responsible bidder". Refining Associates v. U.S., Ct.Cl.1953, 109 F.Supp. 259, 124 Ct.Cl. 115. United States ⟶ 64.40(4)

The agents of the Government must be allowed reasonable time for the examination of proposals after the opening of bids before the bidders can be allowed to withdraw. Scott v. U.S., Ct.Cl.1909, 44 Ct.Cl. 524.

In the absence of any special statutory provision to the contrary, a bidder for a Government contract may withdraw his bid at any time until notice of acceptance. 1894, 21 Op.Atty.Gen. 56.

Where bidder requests permission only to correct bid price, bidder may alternatively be allowed to withdraw its bid if evidence is clear and convincing only as to the mistake but not as to the intended bid. (1979) 58 Comp.Gen. 583.

112. —— Recovery of costs, bids, creation or formation of contracts

Costs incurred in fabricating an aircraft in anticipation of future procurement by the government cannot be recovered by being charged to the contractor's overhead account as selling costs and allocated proportionately to its various defense contracts, for such costs are not bidding costs which ASPR § 15–205.3 allows as indirect costs, nor are they allowable selling costs under ASPR § 15–205.37 arising in the marketing of the contractor's products. General Dynamics Corp. v. U.S., Ct.Cl.1973, 202 Ct. Cl. 347. United States ⊗ 70(18)

113. Parol contracts, creation or formation of contracts

Where applicable procurement regulations required Government contracts to be in writing in order to be binding upon the parties, where evidence established that parties envisioned formal writing as only document which could establish binding contractual relationships between them, where private contractors never did anything in actual performance of supposed contracts, and where securing of approval of General Services Administration was understood to be condition to formation of contract and no such approval was given, no binding express oral contract existed between Government and private contractors who responded to solicitation by Government. American General Leasing, Inc. v. U.S., Ct.Cl.1978, 587 F.2d 54, 218 Ct.Cl. 367. United States ⊗ 63

114. Implied contracts, creation or formation of contracts

Implied contract with Government to pay more than contract price for hay delivered under protest was not established, where balance of contract price was accepted without protest. Early & Daniel Co. v. U.S., U.S.1926, 46 S.Ct. 457, 271 U.S. 140, 70 L.Ed. 874. United States ⊗ 69(7)

There is no implied contract of Government to pay for moving of oil storage tanks to provide storage for army transport fuel oil. Interocean Oil Co. v. U.S., U.S.1926, 46 S.Ct. 219, 270 U.S. 65, 70 L.Ed. 473. Armed Services ⊗ 27; United States ⊗ 69(2)

Where defense contract provided that contractor was to maintain, repair, protect, and preserve government property delivered in connection with the contract so long as such property was in its possession, and where, when contract was completed, government did not remove the property but inquired as to amount of storage space available at contractor's plant, there arose contract implied in fact for storage of the property by contractor, for which it would be reasonably compensated by the government. Algonac Mfg. Co. v. U.S., Ct.Cl.1970, 428 F.2d 1241, 192 Ct.Cl. 649, supplemented 458 F.2d 1373, 198 Ct.Cl. 258. United States ⊗ 69(7)

Where a Government employee, having property in his possession for a certain purpose, by consent of the owner, uses it by order of his superior officer for another purpose, there is no legal implied contract of hiring for Government use. Carpenter v. U.S., C.C.S.D.Ohio 1891, 45 F. 341. United States ⊗ 69(2)

Where Government contract required contractor to feed and house workers, but Government made facilities available at a charge to contractors, and contractor, in accord with Government's practice, cooperated in assigning employees to quarters, there was an implied contract that contractor would pay the usual charges. A.L.Coupe Const. Co. v. U.S., Ct.Cl.1956, 139 F.Supp. 61, 134 Ct.Cl. 392, certiorari denied 77 S.Ct. 52, 352 U.S. 834, 1 L.Ed.2d 53. United States ⊗ 69(2)

In action to recover compensation for services rendered to United States Army in connection with Army's hiring of longshoreman, an undertaking to compensate plaintiff for fair and reasonable value of its services furnished after its demand for payment could be fairly implied in fact from all of circumstances revealed, and especially from fact of Army's continued use of plaintiff's services subsequent to such demand. Pacific Maritime Ass'n v. U.S., Ct.Cl.1952, 108 F.Supp. 603, 123 Ct.Cl. 667, rehearing denied 117 F.Supp. 307, 125 Ct.Cl. 216. United States ⊗ 69(7)

Where plaintiff contracted with Government for employment of prisoner of war labor, even in absence of express condition in contract for reimbursement of plaintiff for cost of housing and utilities furnished at prisoner of war camp, contract requiring Government to reimburse plaintiff would be implied when furnishing of housing was not customary for free labor in similar work, and when plaintiff had paid Government an amount equivalent to cost of free labor for the prisoner of war labor. Tennessee Products & Chemical Corp. v. U.S., M.D.Tenn. 1952, 108 F.Supp. 271. United States ⊗ 70(21)

Where the plaintiff who had three contracts with the Government relative to high-energy fuel production, represented at contract negotiations and during the course of the contracts' performance that the expense of constructing and operating its own pilot plant would be met entirely by plaintiff and at no time was any reimbursement asked for such costs until months after the completion of such contracts, and where the contracts themselves contained no language indicating that such costs were to be related in any way to the three contracts, the plaintiff has failed to establish an express or implied obligation on the part of the Government to reimburse plaintiff for such costs. Olin Mathieson Chemical Corp. v. U.S., Ct.Cl.1967, 179 Ct.Cl. 368.

Where responsible officers of Government employ plaintiff to invent and perfect a device, with mutual understanding that, if it is patentable, Government will compensate plaintiff for its services, and device is completed, accepted, manufactured for, and used by Government in large quantities, and valid patent is thereafter issued to plaintiff, through its chief engineer, a contract will be implied to pay plaintiff for its services in inventing and perfecting said device. Cygnet Mfg. Co. v. U.S., Ct.Cl.1925, 60 Ct.Cl. 840. United States ⟶ 69(5)

Where United States leased land for aviation purposes, and lease provided lessor should close all roads on said land and put premises into good condition for aviation purposes, there was no implied promise to pay for such destruction. McLennan County, Tex., v. U.S., Ct.Cl. 1925, 60 Ct.Cl. 496. United States ⟶ 69(3)

Where agency of Government, without authority, suggested pledge from plaintiff to conserve war materials and speed up production, there was no implied agreement to reimburse plaintiff for any loss suffered by it in carrying out its pledge. Peerless Insulated Wire & Cable Co. v. U.S., Ct.Cl.1925, 60 Ct.Cl. 409. United States ⟶ 69(6)

Where Government, through an unnamed instrumentality, ordered plaintiff to secure yarn from one company, weave it into cloth, and deliver cloth to Government contractor, to be manufactured into puttees, and there was no averment that Government agreed to compensate plaintiff for labor and materials furnished, contract to make Government liable to plaintiff for goods furnished by it to contractor could not be implied. Roessler v. U.S., Ct.Cl.1925, 60 Ct.Cl. 405. United States ⟶ 69(4)

Where Government established training camp on creek, and obtained license from owners bordering thereon to enter on and drain their lands on said creek and its tributaries to improve sanitary condition of said camp and its surroundings, Government officer in charge of said work, claiming under said license, which was signed by party from whom plaintiff acquired title, entered on plaintiff's land, surveyed right of way 100 feet wide, cut canal through center thereof, diverted water from said creek, and thereby destroyed water power of plaintiff's mill, there was no implied promise on part of Government to pay for such damage. Livingston v. U.S., Ct.Cl.1925, 60 Ct.Cl. 114, affirmed 47 S.Ct. 245, 273 U.S. 648, 71 L.Ed. 821. United States ⟶ 69(2)

Where after filing his bid plaintiff was requested by the project manager not to wait for acceptance of his bid but to proceed with preparations for performance of his contract, and he thereupon purchased and assembled materials for the erection of the buildings, after which his bid was rejected, there was no implied contract on the part of the Government to pay him the difference between the cost price and salvage value of such materials in his hands. Horton v. U.S., Ct.Cl.1922, 57 Ct.Cl. 395. United States ⟶ 69(6)

Where a company, under threat that its property would be taken over if it refused, entered into three contracts in writing with the Government, with the option to renew the same yearly for not exceeding 5 years, to furnish cold storage space and to sharply freeze and place in cold storage a certain quantity of beef at prices fixed by itself, with a provision that said contracts might be terminated at any time by the Government giving 30 days' notice to the contractor, and it became necessary for said company to expend a large sum of money to increase its facilities for sharp freezing, which it did in the expectation that the cost would be absorbed in its profits if the war should continue 5 years, without having a provision for reimbursement incorporated in said contracts, there was no implied contract making the Government liable for the payment of the cost of such increased facilities. Chicago Cold Storage Warehouse Co. v. U.S., Ct.Cl.1922, 57 Ct.Cl. 220, affirmed 44 S.Ct. 32, 263 U.S. 677, 68 L.Ed. 502. United States ⟶ 69(6)

Where a steamer was seized by the proper military authorities during pendency of rebellion or insurrection upon the ground that it was the property of the enemy and was at the time being used in furtherance of the rebellion, and the vessel was subsequently used in the service of the United States, there was no implied contract to pay for the use thereof. Castelo v. U.S., Ct.Cl.1916, 51 Ct.Cl. 221. United States ⊕ 69(3)

___

IV. CONDITIONS OF CONTRACTS

Subdivision Index

___

141. Conditions of contracts generally

The Federal Government, after receiving benefits of a contract into which it has lawfully entered, cannot repudiate the conditions upon which the contract was made. U.S. v. Chicago, R.I. & P. R. Co., C.A.5 (Tex.) 1952, 200 F.2d 263. United States ⊕ 70(12.1)

142. Honesty and fairness, conditions of contracts

Government is required to maintain with those who contract with it same standard of fairness as an honest, fair-minded and reasonable man. C.N. Monroe Mfg. Co. v. U.S., E.D.Mich.1956, 143 F.Supp. 449. United States ⊕ 66

143. Excavation, conditions of contracts

In view of contract language, including provision that contractor "shall make

such surveys and computations as are necessary to determine the quantities of work performed or placed," and in view of fact that contractor performed the work necessary to balance excavation and fill, it could not be said that government, being sued for fill material contractor had to supply after excavated materials had been exhausted, had contractual responsibility to balance excavation and fill. Ace Const. Co. v. U.S., Ct.Cl.1968, 401 F.2d 816, 185 Ct.Cl. 487. United States ⊕ 70(8)

144. Facilities, labor and materials, conditions of contracts

Under contract provision to the effect that contractor shall furnish without additional charge all reasonable facilities, labor and materials necessary for safe and convenient inspection and test that might be required by contracting officer, contractor was not required merely to make the site safely and conveniently available to the government for testing purposes, but was required to furnish necessary labor and materials for testing reasonably requested by the government. Tecon Corp. v. U. S., Ct.Cl.1969, 411 F.2d 1262, 188 Ct.Cl. 15. United States ⊕ 70(14)

145. Inspections, conditions of contracts

Given provisions in contract for manufacture and delivery of artillery shell components to the United States of shipment at seller's risk and acceptance at point of destination, United States did not contractually bind itself to a situation whereby its origin inspections would preempt its right to reject nonconforming goods upon their latter tender. A. B. G. Instrument & Engineering, Inc. v. U.S., Ct.Cl. 1979, 593 F.2d 394, 219 Ct.Cl. 381. United States ⊕ 70(14)

Whether or not government contractor actually looked prior to bidding at microfilms which would be furnished to successful bidder on contract for radio sets whose parts were to be interchangeable with set previously procured, it was bound by what it would have seen if it had looked. Rixon Electronics, Inc. v. U.S., Ct.Cl.1976, 536 F.2d 1345, 210 Ct. Cl. 309. United States ⊕ 70(30)

Armed services was not required to inspect the manner in which glue in flashtube of ignition cartridge was applied by plaintiff experienced contractor who used an acceptable procedure, since inspections were for benefit of Government not the contractor and failure of Government to provide for inspection did not relieve contractor of its responsibilities under contract which was partially terminated because of excess glue in one lot. Penguin Industries, Inc. v. U.S., Ct.Cl.1976, 530 F.2d 934, 209 Ct.Cl. 121. United States ⟐ 70(14)

Where general conditions of contract provided that contractor should notify housing authority when work would be ready for final inspection and that authority would make inspection on date stated in notice and special conditions provided that authority could accept any part of work if it was reasonably fit for use, general contractor was obligated to notify authority when work was substantially completed but authority was not then obliged to accept. Wertheimer Const. Corp. v. U.S., Ct.Cl.1969, 406 F.2d 1071, 186 Ct.Cl. 836. United States ⟐ 70(14)

146. Investigation of consequences, conditions of contracts

Neither "cooperation" clause nor any other provision of contract under which contractor was to design, manufacture, test and supervise erection of hydraulic turbines for power plant units at dam project required contractor to investigate consequences of and make adjustments for switch to single-bearing generators, supplied by separate prime contractor. Baldwin-Lima-Hamilton Corp. v. U.S., Ct.Cl.1970, 434 F.2d 1371, 193 Ct.Cl. 556. United States ⟐ 70(14)

147. Reliability predictions, conditions of contracts

Under proper construction of contract as a whole, contractor was bound to furnish reliability predictions not only for its own equipment but also for such off-the-shelf equipment as it chose to use. Singer Co. Librascope Div. v. U.S., Ct.Cl. 1977, 568 F.2d 695, 215 Ct.Cl. 281. United States ⟐ 70(12.1)

148. Removal of fixtures, conditions of contracts

In view of fact that performance of contract for installation of air-conditioning system in post office required removal of ductwork to which light fixtures were attached, removal of fixtures was by implication an indispensable part of contractor's contractual obligation. Am-

brose-Augusterfer Corp. v. U.S., Ct.Cl. 1968, 394 F.2d 536, 184 Ct.Cl. 18. United States ⟐ 70(8)

149. Restoration or reconstruction, conditions of contracts

Provision of government contract calling for construction and lease of a post office facility and obligating lessor to keep demised premises in good repair and tenantable condition, except in case of damage arising from act or negligence of government's agents or employees, did not constitute an absolute undertaking by lessor to restore or reconstruct leased building in event of structural damage, thereby relieving government of its implied warranty that plans submitted by it were sufficient, but only required lessor to sustain burden of repairing premises if such repairs were not necessitated by damage caused by insufficient plans and specifications. Poorvu v. U.S., Ct.Cl. 1970, 420 F.2d 993, 190 Ct.Cl. 640. United States ⟐ 70(29)

150. Return of equipment, conditions of contracts

Under prime contract which required the United States to furnish barge transportation for removal of prime contractor's equipment and material from nuclear test site and which provided that on return trip transportation would be on a space available basis, United States had no obligation to make special effort outside its normal routines to return the prime contractor's equipment on certain barge when another barge was available early the next month with available space for all of the contractor's equipment. B-E-C-K Constructors v. U.S., Ct.Cl.1978, 571 F.2d 25, 215 Ct.Cl. 793. United States ⟐ 70(8)

151. Time for performance, conditions of contracts—Generally

Time is of the essence in any contract containing fixed dates for performance. DeVito v. U.S., Ct.Cl.1969, 413 F.2d 1147, 188 Ct.Cl. 979. Contracts ⟐ 211

152. —— Acceleration, time for performance, conditions of contracts

Letters to contractor on construction of a government building, though not couched in mandatory terms, could be found to constitute orders to accelerate, where the Government recognized some delays were validly excusable but did not say which and left it clear that it disagreed with contractor as to amount, so that contractor may have been required to accelerate the work beyond what it thought was the proper rate, allowing for excusable delays, to avoid the risk of liquidated damages. Norair Engineering Corp. v. U.S., Ct.Cl.1981, 666 F.2d 546, 229 Ct.Cl. 160. United States ☞ 74(1)

Where at no time did Government indicate, either expressly or by conduct, that it would agree to four to six-month extension requested by contractor but rather flatly rejected the request, there could be no acceleration without affirmative act by Government setting forth more lenient standard than the one eventually imposed. Simmonds Precision Products, Inc. v. U.S., Ct.Cl.1976, 546 F.2d 886, 212 Ct.Cl. 305. United States ☞ 70(34)

Where railroad line had to be relocated before contractor could complete construction of dam, and Government contracting officer had duty to co-ordinate the work of several contractors within the area to best advantage, officer's requirement that contractor finish dike construction at an earlier date than that required by contract in order to permit earlier resumption of operations in the same area by company engaged in relocation of railroad was not arbitrary, though construction of other work by contractor under dam contract was probably delayed. Wm. Eisenberg & Sons, to Use of Aetna Cas. & Sur. Co. v. U.S., Ct.Cl.1948, 75 F.Supp. 1006, 110 Ct.Cl. 388. Contracts ☞ 299(2); United States ☞ 73(9)

153. —— Extension, time for performance, conditions of contracts

Period of a little over two months during which epoxy resins necessary to complete fixed price contract for supply of parts for certain antipersonnel mines was one of such relatively short duration that contract did not lapse and was such as should have caused contractor to resort to time extension remedy granted under default clause. Consolidated Molded Products Corp. v. U.S., Ct.Cl.1979, 600 F.2d 793, 220 Ct.Cl. 594. United States ☞ 70(34)

Third parties who supplied government infringing devices under contracts obligating them to indemnify government and who claimed that extension of accounting period should not apply to them must make prompt application for such relief. Bowser, Inc. v. U.S., Ct.Cl.1970,

427 F.2d 740, 192 Ct.Cl. 377, 166 U.S.P.Q. 46. United States ☞ 97

Evidence warranted granting general contractor 15 days' extension for completion of group 2 buildings by reason of delay caused by paving contractor as to group 1 buildings with resultant delaying effect on group 2 buildings. Wertheimer Const. Corp. v. U.S., Ct.Cl.1969, 406 F.2d 1071, 186 Ct.Cl. 836. United States ☞ 74(11)

Grant of extension of time by government contracting officer carries with it administrative admission that delays in construction resulted through no fault of contractor. J.D. Hedin Const. Co. v. U.S., Ct.Cl.1965, 347 F.2d 235, 171 Ct.Cl. 70. Evidence ☞ 219(1)

Government was not chargeable with breach of construction contract because floods occurred, and contractor was not entitled to an extension of time because of occurrence of second flood, where occurrence of two floods in one winter was not unusual on river where work was to be done. E.J. Albrecht Co. v. U.S., Ct.Cl. 1959, 174 F.Supp. 942, 146 Ct.Cl. 299. United States ☞ 70(34)

Where Government contract provided that if changes were made and caused an increase or decrease in amount due under contract or in the time required for its performance an equitable adjustment would be made and the contract modified accordingly and Government changed plans and then unreasonably delayed in acting on contractor's proposal covering such change, denial of an extension of time was a breach of contract. Kirk v. U.S., Ct.Cl.1948, 77 F.Supp. 614, 111 Ct. Cl. 552. United States ☞ 73(22)

Provision in contract for construction of dam that, if there was a delay in relocation of railroad upon which completion of dam depended, contracting officer would extend date for completion of dam negatived promise by United States to cause relocation by any certain time, except for implied obligation not to cause unreasonable delay. Wm. Eisenberg & Sons, to Use of Aetna Cas. & Sur. Co. v. U.S., Ct.Cl.1948, 75 F.Supp. 1006, 110 Ct.Cl. 388. Contracts ☞ 299(2); United States ☞ 73(20)

A provision of standard Government construction contract providing for extension of time for completion of work on account of delays due to unforeseen causes, does not relieve Government of liability for damages for such delays. George A. Fuller Co. v. U.S., Ct.Cl.1947, 69 F.Supp. 409, 108 Ct.Cl. 70. Contracts ☞ 299(2); United States ☞ 73(20)

Under contract with United States for construction of auditorium providing for extension of time if work should be delayed on account of unforeseen causes beyond control of contractor, contractor's death resulting in delay constituted an "unforeseen cause". U.S. Cas. Co. v. U.S., Ct.Cl.1946, 67 F.Supp. 950, 107 Ct. Cl. 46. Contracts ☞ 300(1); United States ☞ 73(3)

Where plaintiff and defendant entered into a contract Dec. 27, 1933, for the construction of certain buildings at the military academy at West Point, said contract being expressly subject to the approval of the Quartermaster General, or his designee, and providing for the beginning of the work on or before Jan. 5, 1934, and its completion on or before July 5, 1934; and where said contract was not approved by the Quartermaster General until Feb. 8, 1934, the requirement that the work be completed by a certain time was not nullified by the unreasonable delay in approval since no more than was done by the contractor during said delay would have been done if such approval had been given within a reasonable time, and plaintiff was granted an extension of time because of inclement weather during said period of delay. Jacob Schlesinger, Inc. v. U.S., Ct.Cl.1941, 94 Ct.Cl. 289. United States ☞ 73(26)

Even assuming that contractor correctly allocated the burden on the Department of Army for obtaining approval from local water authority to narrow the river, in connection with contract with the Department of Army to replace and repair portions of existing retaining wall at water supply facility in Germany, contractor failed to establish that it likely could have completed the project by contract deadline had the Army timely secured requisite permission, as was required to establish that its delay was excusable. Bender GmbH v. Brownlee, C.A.Fed.2004, 106 Fed.Appx. 728, 2004 WL 1799402, Unreported. United States ☞ 73(26)

154. —— Waiver, time for performance, conditions of contracts

Defense supply agency, which complained of government contractor's deliveries only to extent of issuing three cure notices and took no other steps to complain or to terminate contract for failure to make delivery-time requirements, waived delay and could not raise contractor's delay as a retroactive default to excuse its own breach. Inland Container, Inc. v. U.S., Ct.Cl.1975, 512 F.2d 1073, 206 Ct.Cl. 478. United States ☞ 73(26)

If government contractor fails to deliver contracted-for item on agreed delivery date, and the government thereafter permits contractor to continue performance, government will be deemed to have waived the agreed-upon delivery date; and a termination for default cannot properly be effected until a new delivery date is set and the contractor fails to make delivery on or before the new date. Panoramic Studios, Inc. v. U.S., Ct.Cl. 1969, 413 F.2d 1156, 188 Ct.Cl. 1092. United States ☞ 72.1(3)

Following contractor's delivery default, the government's conduct, including a 48-days' delay in termination, over which period the government accepted certain deliveries from the contractor and also was aware of the contractor's considerable efforts to catch up on delivery requirements, constituted a waiver of the delivery schedule and a constructive election to permit continued performance by the contractor. DeVito v. U.S., Ct.Cl. 1969, 413 F.2d 1147, 188 Ct.Cl. 979. United States ☞ 72.1(3)

Under letter of September 20, 1957, by which plaintiff and United States amended their primary aluminum pig production contract, plaintiff did not waive its "most favored nation" right to compute contract production prior to April 1, 1957 in same way another purchaser was permitted to do, where definition of contract production contained in amendment pertained only to production after March 31, 1957. Kaiser Aluminum & Chemical Corp. v. U.S., Ct.Cl.1967, 388 F.2d 317, 181 Ct.Cl. 902, rehearing denied 409 F.2d 238, 187 Ct.Cl. 443. United States ☞ 70(4)

Where the Government has waived the time limitations contained in its contract with plaintiff and has permitted plaintiff to make late deliveries, it is not precluded from later terminating the contract for default where the plaintiff thereafter fails, within a reasonable time, to make delivery. Potter v. U.S., Ct.Cl.1964, 167 Ct.Cl. 28. United States ☞ 73(3)

The failure of the head of the department to approve the contract until after delivery had begun operated as a waiver of all the time limits specified in the contract, but left the contractor bound to deliver within a reasonable time. Little Falls Knitting Mill Co. v. U.S., Ct.Cl.1908, 44 Ct.Cl. 1. United States ☞ 70(11); United States ☞ 73(3)

155. Warranties, conditions of contracts—Generally

Government must warrant sufficiency of its specifications on government contract. Southwest Welding & Mfg. Co. v. U.S., Ct.Cl.1969, 413 F.2d 1167, 188 Ct. Cl. 925. United States ☞ 70(30)

Where plaintiff who agreed to manufacture radio transmitters for the government was required to satisfy standard of interchangeability and government agreed to supply "microfilm of manufacturing drawings" and warranted that government furnished property was suitable for intended use, and real utility of film lay in fact that it might be employed for making prints which could be used in workshop, passed around on the production line, or used in purchasing supplies, the making of the prints was an "intended use" for which film was furnished, rendering the government liable if microfilm was not suitable for making prints. Thompson Ramo Wooldridge Inc. v. U.S., Ct.Cl.1966, 361 F.2d 222, 175 Ct.Cl. 527. United States ☞ 73(17)

Contractor, in submitting bid and entering into contract with government agency, has right to rely on positive representations by agency regarding subsurface conditions; such representations amount to warranty and establish a predicate for a possible action for breach of contract if it is later discovered that representations are untrue. T.F. Scholes, Inc. v. U.S., Ct.Cl.1966, 357 F.2d 963, 174 Ct.Cl. 1215. United States ☞ 73(22)

Where bid form for purchase of war surplus scrap webbing material expressly stated that all property was sold "as is" without any express or implied warranty of any kind and invited inspection by the bidders, and scrap webbing sent to buyer contained pieces of metal and general trade practice recognized scrap webbing

as free of metal, buyer who had not inspected the goods prior to sale was not entitled to damages for breach of contract, and Federal Government was entitled to unpaid balance due on purchase price. U.S. v. Silverton, C.A.1 (Mass.) 1952, 200 F.2d 824. United States ☞ 73(22)

Building size specifications listed by government in its invitation to bid on cleaning contract were representations or warranties binding upon the government, and failure of government to include in the invitation space for lobbies, corridors, and rest rooms was breach of warranty entitling contractor to damages. Eastern Service Management Co. v. U.S., D.C.S.C.1965, 243 F.Supp. 302, decision affirmed in part and remanded on other grounds 363 F.2d 729. United States ☞ 74(3)

Genuine issue of material fact as to whether contracting agency required electrical contractor to install recloser switches in violation of manufacturer's warranty precluded summary judgment on contractor's claim that agency supplied defective specifications, requiring engineering work not contemplated by contractor's bid. Orlosky Inc. v. U.S., Fed.Cl.2005, 64 Fed.Cl. 63. Federal Courts ☞ 1120

Where plaintiffs in 1946 purchased from the War Assets Administration certain tire gauges, manufactured and sold under the name of "Schrader" and the gauges were sold subject to conditions stated in a "Memo Order and Contract" prepared by the War Assets Administration in which it was stated that all merchandise offered for sale "will meet U.S. Army issue specifications" and that "all merchandise will be new" and the specifications under which the Schrader gauges were built contained no requirement as to their accuracy, the War Assets Administration, in offering for sale as war surplus the Schrader gauges, also made no warranty of accuracy. Handler Motor Co. v. U.S., Ct.Cl.1952, 121 Ct.Cl. 845. United States ☞ 58(4)

156. —— Implied warranties, conditions of contracts

Where the government orders a structure built and in so doing prepares the project's specifications prescribing character, dimension, and location of construction work, the government implicitly warrants, nothing else appearing, that if specifications are complied with, satisfactory performance will result, and this implied warranty is not overcome by the general clauses requiring contractor to examine the site, check up on the plans, and assume responsibility for the work until completion and acceptance. Allied Contractors, Inc. v. U.S., Ct.Cl.1967, 381 F.2d 995, 180 Ct.Cl. 1057. See, also, J. D. Hedin Const. Co. v. U.S., 1965, 347 F.2d 235, 171 Ct.Cl. 70. United States ☞ 70(4); United States ☞ 70(1)

Provision of government contract for construction of flood control levee that contractor might construct low water crossings did not constitute an implied promise or guarantee that low water crossing, if constructed, would always be there and that government would pay damages for its destruction, and provision could not be construed as a promise not to perform a sovereign act such as Government's necessary release of water from upstream dam which destroyed contractor's low water crossing. Amino Bros. Co. v. U.S., Ct.Cl.1967, 372 F.2d 485, 178 Ct.Cl. 515, certiorari denied 88 S.Ct. 98, 389 U.S. 846, 19 L.Ed.2d 112. United States ☞ 69(2)

Implied warranty that if specifications prepared by government for construction project are complied with, satisfactory performance will result is not defeated by contract clause permitting prospective bidders to conduct independent subsurface investigations, if such explorations could not reasonably be completed before bids were to be submitted. J.D. Hedin Const. Co. v. U.S., Ct.Cl.1965, 347 F.2d 235, 171 Ct.Cl. 70. United States ☞ 70(4)

Requirements in Government contract that construction contractors determine availability of roads to construction site and use established roads and agreement by Government to compensate contractors for loss sustained by reason of unusual conditions did not constitute implied warranty of continued availability of access roads, and Government was not liable for additional costs incurred by contractors when hurricane destroyed parts of access roads. Lenry, Inc. v. U.S., Ct.Cl.1962, 297 F.2d 550, 156 Ct.Cl. 46. United States ☞ 70(30)

Standing alone, language in a Government construction contract setting forth that a pier then under construction by another contractor "when completed

* * * may be used by the [second-stage] contractor" for unloading of materials provided only for permissive use of the pier whenever available and did not constitute an implied warranty, nor did other language in the contract granting the second-stage contractor non-exclusive use of the pier (then under construction) for operations related to and for the life of the contract, constitute a guarantee that the pier would be available at any particular time so as to make deprivation of its use compensable under the contract, where the delayed availability was not attributable to the Government's fault or negligence. Koppers/Clough, v. U.S., Ct.Cl. 1973, 201 Ct.Cl. 344. United States ☞ 70(1); United States ☞ 70(12.1)

Where plaintiff granted a permit to the Government allowing Army personnel to engage in maneuvers on the former's rights-of-way, the permit specifically requiring defendant in installing communication lines on plaintiff's power transmission poles to observe minimum statutory clearances, there is an implied warranty in the permit that plaintiff would also observe the minimum statutory precautions. California-Pacific Utilities Co. v. U.S., Ct.Cl.1971, 194 Ct.Cl. 703. United States ☞ 70(12.1)

Where the Government has drawn specifications for use in the contract work, it impliedly warrants that if those specifications are followed by the plaintiff contractor a satisfactory performance will result. WRB Corp. v. U.S., Ct.Cl. 1968, 183 Ct.Cl. 409. United States ☞ 70(30); United States ☞ 74(14)

Where the Government has drawn specifications relating to the manufacture of an item by the contractor, there is an implied warranty that a satisfactory item may be made in accordance with such specifications and, when it eventuates that the specifications are so faulty that such an article or item may not be made in accordance with them, the contractor has a claim for damages for breach of the implied warranty. Ithaca Gun Co., Inc. v. U.S., Ct.Cl.1966, 176 Ct.Cl. 437. United States ☞ 73(22)

Where the plaintiff was performing work for the Government which required that the water in underground pipes be turned off and the Government agent assumed responsibility for having the municipality turn the water off and later assured the contractor that the water had been turned off, the Government is liable for damages incurred by the plaintiff contractor when it turned out that the water had not been turned off and plaintiff's attempt to work on the pipes caused a minor flood delaying plaintiff and causing it to incur extra costs and the circumstances of this incident require the conclusion that the Government had warranted that the water would be turned off and that plaintiff need not check into the matter itself. Dale Const. Co. v. U.S., Ct.Cl.1964, 168 Ct.Cl. 692.

157. Miscellaneous conditions, conditions of contracts

Provision of contract for public works that in case of its annulment the United States may, at a valuation to be fixed by the engineer, take over any equipment in use in the prosecution of the work, gave it no right to so take over the property of another engaged in the work. Ball Engineering Co. v. J.G. White & Co., U.S.Conn.1919, 39 S.Ct. 393, 250 U.S. 46, 63 L.Ed. 835. United States ☞ 75(1)

Where shirt manufacturer agreed to provision of contract with United States that swatches of contractor-furnished cloth would be evaluated for shade by United States in its laboratory and that, should any of the swatches be rejected, shirts made from the cloth would be rejected, manufacturer had not created independent shade range for military uniform shirts which would be binding on the United States. Doyle Shirt Mfg. Corp. v. U.S., Ct.Cl.1972, 462 F.2d 1150, 199 Ct.Cl. 150. United States ☞ 70(9)

Government's statement in settlement offer to contractor whose proprietary cost information was disclosed in contract solicitation, that Government hoped contractor's performance of directed subcontract to date certain would be of such quality that prime contractor would desire to continue relationship beyond date certain, was a "recital" and did not create obligation on Government's part to provide contractor with opportunity to develop relationship with prime contractor separate from obligation to provide directed subcontract through the date certain. Blackstone Consulting Inc. v. U.S., Fed.Cl.2005, 65 Fed.Cl. 463, affirmed 170 Fed.Appx. 128, 2006 WL 618805. United States ☞ 74(6)

Contracting agency violated solicitation for military housing privatization project when it relaxed six-month limitation on a mortgagee's right to postpone termination of lease for successful offeror after refusing to do so for unsuccessful offeror, and violation was prejudicial as unsuccessful bidder was unable to change its financial proposal and take advantage of decreased risk to its lender and concomitant decreased costs of financing afforded by the change. Hunt Building Co., Ltd. v. U.S., Fed.Cl.2004, 61 Fed.Cl. 243, modified 63 Fed.Cl. 141. United States ☞ 64.40(2); United States ☞ 64.55(1)

V. CHANGES, MODIFICATIONS OR ADJUSTMENTS OF CONTRACTS

Subdivision Index

---

181. Changes, modifications or adjustments of contracts generally

When extent of government contract work is not clearly set forth in that instrument, then an order to do the work is in legal effect a change. Max Drill, Inc. v. U.S., Ct.Cl.1970, 427 F.2d 1233, 192 Ct. Cl. 608. United States ☞ 70(27)

Regardless of technical soundness of requirements of United States in contract with contractor, contractor must comply with requirements and cannot substitute its own views for those of United States. Maxwell Dynamometer Co. V . U.S., Ct. Cl.1967, 386 F.2d 855, 181 Ct.Cl. 607. United States ☞ 70(12.1)

In its role as a party to a business contract, the United States is subject to the same but no greater liability than any other person would be under similar circumstances, and, therefore, the fact that a person who has contracted with the Government to furnish materials or services encounters unforeseen difficulties, and thereby incurs unexpected expenses in performance of contract, does not impose upon Government any legal obligation to relieve its contractor of the unexpected financial burden. Rolin v. U.S., Ct.Cl.1958, 160 F.Supp. 264, 142 Ct.Cl. 73. United States ☞ 70(2.1); United States ☞ 70(20)

182. Construction of change clause, changes, modifications or adjustments of contracts

Only in exceptional circumstances can an equitable adjustment be made for extra cost in performing one government contract, caused by government doing things it has a right to do, respecting other contracts. General Dynamics Corp. v. U.S., Ct.Cl.1978, 585 F.2d 457, 218 Ct.Cl. 40. United States ☞ 70(24)

In action by government contractor seeking equitable adjustment for alleged "change," question whether contract was susceptible to more than one reasonable interpretation was to be approached with due regard to principles that contract must be read as whole, that interpretation which gives reasonable meaning to all parts of instrument will be preferred to one which leaves portion of its useless, and that one contractual provision should be construed as being in conflict with another only where no other reasonable interpretation is possible. Martin Lane Co. v. U.S., Ct.Cl.1970, 432 F.2d 1013, 193 Ct.Cl. 203. United States ☞ 70(2.1)

Broad exculpatory contract clauses in behalf of the government cannot be given their full literal reach and do not relieve it of liability for changed conditions as the broad language would seem to indicate. Woodcrest Const. Co. v. U.S., Ct. Cl.1969, 408 F.2d 406, 187 Ct.Cl. 249, certiorari denied 90 S.Ct. 2164, 398 U.S. 958, 26 L.Ed.2d 542. United States ☞ 70(22.1)

A changes provision, incorporated in contract for construction of road, cannot lightly be read out of it, or deprived of most of its normal substance. Morrison-Knudsen Co. v. U.S., Ct.Cl.1968, 397 F.2d 826, 184 Ct.Cl. 661. Highways ☞ 113(4)

183. Authorization for extra work, changes, modifications or adjustments of contracts

United States could not impose on contractor duty to determine actual elevations of gravel strata in which footings were to be laid without first authorizing change order or proceed order assuring contractor compensation for such work which was beyond scope of original contract. J.D. Hedin Const. Co. v. U.S., Ct. Cl.1965, 347 F.2d 235, 171 Ct.Cl. 70. United States ⊕ 70(14)

Parties erecting buildings for Coast Guard under contract with United States could not recover compensation under contract or on quantum meruit for extra work done and materials furnished on direction of Government's civil engineer in charge of work, in absence of evidence of written order for changes in plans causing increase in costs, written approval of changes amounting to over $500 by department head or his representative, and claim for adjustment within 10 days or extended time after changes, as required by contract, though Government accepted benefits of such extras. Yuhasz v. U.S., C.C.A.7 (Ind.) 1940, 109 F.2d 467. United States ⊕ 70(21)

Where contract provides that there shall be no charges for extra work unless a written agreement is made therefor, owner is not liable either on quantum meruit or on the contract for changes or extras, unless they were authorized by the proper officials of the owner and were approved as provided by the contract. Blair v. U.S., M.D.Ala.1946, 66 F.Supp. 405, affirmed 164 F.2d 115, certiorari denied 68 S.Ct. 910, 333 U.S. 880, 92 L.Ed. 1155, rehearing denied 68 S.Ct. 1336, 334 U.S. 830, 92 L.Ed. 1758. Contracts ⊕ 232(4)

There can be no recovery for extra work or material where the contract provided that no charge for extra work or material would be allowed without written order from the contracting officer and no such order was given for the extra work done. James McHugh Sons, Inc., v. U.S., Ct.Cl.1943, 99 Ct.Cl. 414. Contracts ⊕ 232(4); United States ⊕ 70(28)

184. Consideration, changes, modifications or adjustments of contracts

Where plaintiff who had entered into contract with Federal Government for sale of honing and drilling machines agreed to give 5 percent discount in consideration of securing large additional order, but before Government ever entered into formal contract for the additional machines it canceled the informal order for them previously given, immediate cancellation of orders for additional machines constituted failure of consider-

ation for plaintiff's agreement to allow discount on machines purchased under prior contracts. Barnes Drill Co. v. U.S., Ct.Cl.1949, 84 F.Supp. 646, 114 Ct.Cl. 340. United States ⊕ 66

Where a production procedure requirement in a manufacturing contract was omitted in the performance of the work but another procedure fulfilling the same function was substituted with the approval of a Government official assigned to the contract and authorized to make changes in the contract requirements so long as the changes did not affect price or quality, and where the units so manufactured were accepted by the Government with full knowledge that the procedure requirement had been omitted there has been a modification of the contract which was deliberate and valid and since both sides obtained a benefit therefrom, it was not without consideration and the contractor was entitled to rely on it during the entire performance of the contract. Northbridge Electronics, Inc. v. U.S., Ct. Cl.1966, 175 Ct.Cl. 426. United States ⊕ 72(2); United States ⊕ 72(5)

The Secretary of the Treasury had no authority to change binding contracts entered into with the United States by responsible parties, secured by responsible sureties, in the interest of private parties thereto, without consideration inuring to the Government. 1895, 21 Op.Atty.Gen. 115.

185. Party responsible for change, changes, modifications or adjustments of contracts

That bidder, with best engineering and geological advice, could have determined that quarry was no better than a marginal source of armor rock required for riprap in highway repair project did not preclude recovery of equitable adjustment for changed condition where quarry fell far short of contract indications as stated in government memorandum provided to bidders. Stock & Grove, Inc. v. U.S., Ct.Cl.1974, 493 F.2d 629, 204 Ct.Cl. 103. Highways ⊕ 113(4)

Government contractor, who has underestimated his bid or encountered unanticipated expense or inefficiencies, may not properly use change order as a excuse to reform contract or to shift his own risks and losses to the Government. Pacific Architects & Engineers, Inc. v. U.S., Ct.Cl.1974, 491 F.2d 734, 203 Ct.Cl. 499. United States ⊕ 70(25.1)

While contractor's miscalculation may cause it to absorb some of costs over its original estimate, it does not automatically result in its recovering nothing on claim for adjustment based on changed condition. Roscoe-Ajax Const. Co. v. U.S., Ct.Cl.1972, 458 F.2d 55, 198 Ct.Cl. 133. United States ☜ 74(12.1)

Contractor was entitled to recover from government under changes clause on basis of delay-producing inability of government to furnish source of supply or material specifications for component of article to be produced under contract. Aerodex, Inc. v. U.S., Ct.Cl.1969, 417 F.2d 1361, 189 Ct.Cl. 344. United States ☜ 73(20)

In proceeding by excavation contractor to recover from the United States added costs allegedly incurred because of changed conditions, contractor's showing that certain decisions bearing signature of contracting officer were prepared by subordinate of contracting officer and were adopted by contracting officer without change was insufficient to call for further inquiry into question whether contracting officer put his mind to the problems and rendered his own decisions. J.A. Terteling & Sons, Inc. v. U.S., Ct.Cl.1968, 390 F.2d 926, 182 Ct.Cl. 691. United States ☜ 74(11)

Rule that standard changed conditions article in government contract does not protect party from result of its own miscalculations must be applied to government which is no more entitled to use faulty estimate as basis for invoking benefit of changed conditions article than is a careless contractor making an improvident bid. Perini Corp. v. U.S., Ct.Cl. 1967, 381 F.2d 403, 180 Ct.Cl. 768. United States ☜ 70(22.1)

Where the Government had misled a contractor in the drawings or specifications accompanying a contract, through error or misrepresentation, and as a result of this error or misrepresentation the contractor had to perform additional work, defendant was responsible and recovery could be had for the amount of extra work performed and no liquidated damages could be assessed under the terms of the contract. Lukens Dredging & Contracting Corporation v. U.S., Ct.Cl. 1940, 90 Ct.Cl. 184. Contracts ☜ 232(1); United States ☜ 70(30)

186. Intent or knowledge of parties, changes, modifications or adjustments of contracts

Where contractor estimated cost for weapons project to be about $327,000, and government advised contractor that only $250,000 was available and offered no-fee cost contract and substituted word "proposal" in portion of final contract for word "report" which had appeared in original statement, and both contractor and government knew that at least $327,000 would be spent on project and contractor had previously distributed certain expenses to general overhead account contractor reasonably assumed that it could allocate portion of work under project as indirect costs includable in overhead and government was liable for additional $156,639. Singer-General Precision, Inc. v. U.S., Ct.Cl.1970, 427 F.2d 1187, 192 Ct.Cl. 435. United States ☜ 70(15.1)

Where contract for installation of air-conditioning system in post office contained three specific admonitions to investigate and determine building conditions at site, contractor should have known that performance of contract involved problem of removing light fixtures attached to ductwork and that government would not make additional payment for such work. Ambrose-Augusterfer Corp. v. U.S., Ct.Cl.1968, 394 F.2d 536, 184 Ct.Cl. 18. United States ☜ 70(30)

187. Failure of government to disclose information, changes, modifications or adjustments of contracts

A failure by government to disclose pertinent information or misrepresentation by government concerning conditions at construction site will not enable contractor to obtain equitable adjustment for changed conditions if contractor has another source of information concerning conditions or if contractor is not misled by government's misrepresentation or failure to disclose. Wm. A. Smith Contracting Co. v. U.S., Ct.Cl.1969, 412 F.2d 1325, 188 Ct.Cl. 1062. United States ☜ 70(30)

Finding that contractor performing government project was actively misled by government in sense that it withheld or concealed information within its grasp is not essential to proof of changed condition within provision of contract allowing equitable adjustment of price if contractor encounters conditions materially different from those shown on plans or specifications. United Contractors v. U.S., Ct.Cl.1966, 368 F.2d 585, 177 Ct.Cl. 151. United States ⊙ 70(22.1)

Government contractor on project to supply the Army National Guard with a commercial aircraft converted to a military aircraft failed to establish contract should be equitably adjusted because the government failed to disclose superior knowledge; although expertise of contracting agency with regard to major aircraft overhauls was greater than contractor's, that did not compel finding that agency had superior knowledge about the full implications of the project. Short Bros., PLC v. U.S., Fed.Cl.2005, 65 Fed. Cl. 695. United States ⊙ 70(30)

Contractor who performed ductwork for hospital renovation did not establish that it was entitled to equitable adjustment on ground that government possessed superior knowledge concerning above-ceiling conditions which it failed to impart to contractor; there was no evidence that government possessed additional knowledge that was not shared with contractor, and contractor was on notice to inquire as to above-ceiling conditions. Conner Brothers Const. Co., Inc. v. U.S., Fed.Cl.2005, 65 Fed.Cl. 657. United States ⊙ 70(30)

Although the specifications submitted with the invitation for bids did not disclose that the building in which the work was to be done would be occupied by personnel and furniture, where the invitation to bidders warned that they should visit the site and inspect the character and extent of the work, and where such inspection, if made, would have revealed the occupancy of the building, the discovery of such occupancy after the execution of the contract without such an inspection does not give rise to a changed condition within the meaning of the contract and the Government is not liable for the cost of the extra work occasioned by such occupancy. Appalachian Floor Co. v. U.S., Ct.Cl.1958, 144 Ct.Cl. 11. United States ⊙ 70(22.1)

188. Limits on changes provided in contract, changes, modifications or adjustments of contracts

Although inclusion of article providing that, if contractor had reason to believe that total cost of contract would be substantially greater or less than estimated cost, contracting officer would decide whether to allow any excess costs and then notify contractor of that decision in writing normally made agreement a cost reimbursement contract, which by its nature did not specifically limit costs, inclusion of further article providing that contractor agreed to faithfully and diligently pursue and complete work specified in proposal at a maximum total cost converted what would have been a cost plus contract into a limited price contract, thereby precluding recovery of excess costs. Lsi Service Corp. v. U.S., Ct.Cl. 1970, 422 F.2d 1334, 191 Ct.Cl. 185. United States ⊙ 70(18); United States ⊙ 70(20)

Even though the Government's failure to provide a pier in promised time for a second-stage contractor to use in unloading supplies might normally create entitlement to an equitable adjustment under the Changes clause as an alteration in the work to be performed or in the method of performance, where a Government–Furnished Property clause limits administrative relief to changes in the property furnished and does not apply to delay in its delivery, the normal breadth of the Changes clause is curtailed and inapplicable, since scope of an equitable adjustment under the Changes clause of a Government contract can be limited by specific provisions elsewhere in the contract. Koppers/Clough, v. U.S., Ct.Cl. 1973, 201 Ct.Cl. 344. United States ⊙ 73(20)

189. Reservation of right to make changes, changes, modifications or adjustments of contracts

Where United States, which entered into contract with building contractor for construction of buildings, reserved right to make changes in design, United States was not liable to contractor because it changed design of buildings. Torres v. U.S., Ct.Cl.1953, 112 F.Supp. 363, 126 Ct.Cl. 76. United States ⊙ 73(17)

190. Prior negotiations, changes, modifications or adjustments of contracts

Prior negotiations between the contractor and the United States concerning contemplated changes of certain portions of creek relocation project did not preclude the United States from thereafter exercising its right under changes article of the contract to unilaterally order changes different from those previously agreed to by the parties. Carl M. Halvorson, Inc. v. U.S., Ct.Cl.1972, 461 F.2d 1337, 198 Ct. Cl. 882. United States ☞ 70(25.1)

191. Impossibility of performance, changes, modifications or adjustments of contracts

Where compaction of subgrade of taxiway shoulders to density required to contract for construction of air base was shown to have been practical impossibility, and it was undisputed that parties did not anticipate difficulty encountered, contractor was entitled to reimbursement for additional expenses, even though achievement of specified compaction was not literally and physically impossible. Tombigbee Constructors v. U. S., Ct.Cl.1970, 420 F.2d 1037, 190 Ct.Cl. 615. United States ☞ 70(22.1)

Where specifications, as interpreted by government, regarding placement of polyurethane foam were impossible of performance and subcontractors' interpretation of specification was the most reasonable interpretation according to understanding in trade, subcontractors, suing by and through use of prime contractor, were entitled to equitable adjustment. Owens-Corning Fiberglas Corp. v. U.S., Ct.Cl.1969, 419 F.2d 439, 190 Ct.Cl. 211. United States ☞ 70(30)

192. Nature of efforts to comply, changes, modifications or adjustments of contracts

Where Government contractor had made every effort toward compliance with change order, and had manufactured some of the articles from its steel supply and was in process of retooling, Government's action terminating contract was unwarranted. U.S. v. Lennox Metal Mfg. Co., E.D.N.Y.1954, 131 F.Supp. 717, affirmed 225 F.2d 302. United States ☞ 72.1(2)

193. Scope or extent of changes generally, changes, modifications or adjustments of contracts

Broad original competition for public contract may validate a broader range of later modifications without further bid procedures. AT&T Communications, Inc. v. Wiltel, Inc., C.A.Fed.1993, 1 F.3d 1201, rehearing denied, in banc suggestion declined, rehearing in banc declined. United States ☞ 70(35); United States ☞ 72(1.1)

There is no automatic or easy formula to determine whether a change of a government contract is beyond the scope of the contract or not and each case must be analyzed on its own facts and circumstances, giving just consideration to magnitude and quality of changes ordered and their cumulative effect upon project as a whole. General Dynamics Corp. v. U.S., Ct.Cl.1978, 585 F.2d 457, 218 Ct.Cl. 40. United States ☞ 73(17)

To be successful on a category changed conditions claim, actual conditions encountered must differ materially from those indicated on contract documents or reasonably to be expected from examination thereof. Arundel Corp. v. U.S., Ct. Cl.1975, 515 F.2d 1116, 207 Ct.Cl. 84. United States ☞ 70(22.1)

Where the 26 modifications issued by government to the original contract for channel improvement and levee construction did not result in project which when completed was substantially different from the project originally contracted for, the changes did not give rise to a new or different contract or give rise to implied contracts between government and subcontractor seeking additional compensation for extra work and for standby and delay costs. Seger v. U.S., Ct.Cl.1972, 469 F.2d 292, 199 Ct.Cl. 766. United States ☞ 74.2

Test for breach of government contract by a change order is whether the job, after the change order is essentially the same as that contracted for by the parties. Perry & Wallis, Inc. v. U.S., Ct.Cl. 1970, 427 F.2d 722, 192 Ct.Cl. 310. United States ☞ 73(17)

When changes ordered by contracting officer, either formally or constructively, amount to drastic modification beyond scope of contract, "changes" article is not applicable and such fundamental operation is breach of contract, which entitles the contractor to damages. Embassy Moving & Storage Co. v. U.S., Ct.Cl.1970, 424 F.2d 602, 191 Ct.Cl. 537. United States ☞ 70(27)

Recovery under adjustment clause of government contract requires only that actual conditions differ materially from those indicated on plans; there need be no finding of fault, that contractor was actively misled, or that government withheld, misconcealed, or misstated any information. Jefferson Const. Co. v. U.S., Ct.Cl.1968, 392 F.2d 1006, 183 Ct.Cl.

720, certiorari denied 89 S.Ct. 122, 393 U.S. 842, 21 L.Ed.2d 113.   United States ☞ 70(30); United States ☞ 74(7)

Point at which change in government contract must be considered to be beyond scope of contract and inconsistent with "changes" article is matter of degree varying from one contract to another. J.D. Hedin Const. Co. v. U.S., Ct.Cl.1965, 347 F.2d 235, 171 Ct.Cl. 70.   United States ☞ 72(2)

Clauses providing that equitable adjustment shall be made and that contract between government and contractor shall be modified in writing accordingly if changes cause increase or decrease in amount due under contract apply to variations in amount of work to be done because of differences in stated specifications and actual conditions.   Eastern Service Management Co. v. U.S., D.C.S.C. 1965, 243 F.Supp. 302, decision affirmed in part and remanded on other grounds 363 F.2d 729.   United States ☞ 72(1.1)

194. Cardinal changes, changes, modifications or adjustments of contracts

An ordered change determined to be outside scope of government contract is an abuse of contract right and is a "cardinal change."   General Dynamics Corp. v. U.S., Ct.Cl.1978, 585 F.2d 457, 218 Ct.Cl. 40.   United States ☞ 73(17)

A "cardinal change" in contract is a breach which occurs when government effects an alteration in work so drastic that it effectively requires the contractor to perform duties materially different from those originally bargained for.   Allied Materials & Equipment Co., Inc. v. U.S., Ct.Cl.1978, 569 F.2d 562, 215 Ct.Cl. 406.   United States ☞ 73(17)

Setoff threats against a contractor engaged in three contracts, based on default in one contract, did not constitute a cardinal change, redressable only in court, and not administratively, in view of fact exercise of right of set-off does not equal cardinal change excising progress payment provisions of the contract and, in any event, breach of such progress payment provision would not afford a remedy different from contract provided remedy for breach of progress payments clause.   William Green Const. Co., Inc. v. U.S., Ct.Cl.1973, 477 F.2d 930, 201 Ct.Cl. 616, certiorari denied 94 S.Ct. 2606, 417 U.S. 909, 41 L.Ed.2d 213.   United States ☞ 74(7)

The "cardinal change doctrine" is not a rigid one; its purpose is to provide a breach remedy for contractors who are directed by the government to perform work which is not within the general scope of the contract; in other words, a cardinal change is one which, because it fundamentally alters the contractual undertaking of the contractor, is not comprehended by the normal changes clause.   Edward R. Marden Corp. v. U.S., Ct.Cl. 1971, 442 F.2d 364, 194 Ct.Cl. 799.   United States ☞ 70(27)

Fact that armed forces board of contract appeals, whose administrative power flowed from government contract changes clause, which expressly limited modifications to those within general scope of contract and which impliedly excepted alteration which transformed nature of work to be done or item to be furnished, was willing to consider equitable adjustment under the changes clause did not preclude contractor from trial on issue of whether government changes constituted cardinal change.   Air-A-Plane Corp. v. U.S., Ct.Cl.1969, 408 F.2d 1030, 187 Ct.Cl. 269.   United States ☞ 74(7)

In determining whether change or series of changes is within contract changes clause derived from armed services procurement regulations, variance which cannot properly be considered a change is a breach of contract, a change not within language of changes clause is equally a breach of contract, and a cardinal change, which is so fundamental as to be beyond scope of contract, is also a breach of contract.   Westinghouse Elec. Corp. v. Garrett Corp., D.C.Md.1977, 437 F.Supp. 1301, affirmed 601 F.2d 155.   Contracts ☞ 312(1)

195. Constructive changes generally, changes, modifications or adjustments of contracts

In proceeding on equitable adjustments claims, claimant has burden of proving that costs incurred were due to constructive changes caused by defective specifications.   Teledyne McCormick-Selph v. U.S., Ct.Cl.1978, 588 F.2d 808, 218 Ct.Cl. 513.   United States ☞ 74(10)

196. Direct result of change, changes, modifications or adjustments of contracts

Under changes and changed conditions articles of government contract, equitable adjustment can include increased costs which are direct and necessary result of change or changed conditions, where that condition or change directly leads to disruption, extra work or new procedures. Merritt-Chapman & Scott Corp. v. U.S., Ct.Cl.1970, 429 F.2d 431, 192 Ct.Cl. 848. United States ☞ 70(22.1)

Where contractor's limited placement of concrete by first crane was caused by contractor's inability to use second crane because of changed condition, increased costs were direct result of changed condition. Paul Hardeman, Inc. v. U.S., Ct.Cl. 1969, 406 F.2d 1357, 186 Ct.Cl. 743. United States ☞ 70(22.1)

Where it is found that on the contract the excess performance costs were directly attributable to the delay caused by the defendant and to the changed conditions encountered, plaintiff is entitled to recover. Hirsch v. U.S., Ct.Cl.1941, 94 Ct.Cl. 602. Contracts ☞ 300(3); United States ☞ 70(34)

197. Acceleration of performance, changes, modifications or adjustments of contracts

In order to recover for increased costs of acceleration under a changes clause, contractor must establish that any delays giving rise to the order were excusable, that the contractor was ordered to accelerate, and that the contractor in fact accelerated performance and incurred extra costs. Norair Engineering Corp. v. U.S., Ct.Cl.1981, 666 F.2d 546, 229 Ct.Cl. 160. Public Contracts ☞ 23

Where initiative for acceleration of work on air base came from government, government benefited, and work was done in manner different than required by contract, subcontractor was entitled to equitable adjustment reimbursing it for increased costs. Tombigbee Constructors v. U.S., Ct.Cl.1970, 420 F.2d 1037, 190 Ct.Cl. 615. United States ☞ 70(25.1)

198. Design and planning changes, changes, modifications or adjustments of contracts

Army contractor was not entitled to equitable adjustment for having been required to demolish and reconstruct noncomplying intersections between interior and exterior beams; although contract was patently ambiguous, contractor failed to seek clarification of reinforcement bar requirements but, rather, exercised its own judgment, which was not in accordance with local trade practice for installing concrete distribution rib type of foundation. Fortec Constructors v. U.S., C.A.Fed.1985, 760 F.2d 1288. United States ☞ 70(31)

Where government furnished defective design specification for rotary switch incorporated into a radio receiving set for military aircraft the contractor was entitled to recover reasonable damages which flowed from the defective drawing and, thus, rework costs for repairing radios which were assembled prior to discovery of the defect were recoverable. S.W. Electronics & Mfg. Corp. v. U.S., Ct.Cl. 1981, 655 F.2d 1078, 228 Ct.Cl. 333. United States ☞ 70(30)

Fact that government contractor's bid was based on erroneous 1' = 200' scale provided on contract drawing did not entitle government contractor to contract price adjustment or time extension, where drawing also specified the correct 1" = 200' scale, creating a discrepancy and putting government contractor on notice of possible drawing error, and government contractor refused opportunity to withdraw its bid on basis of drawing error. Wickham Contracting Co., Inc. v. U.S., Ct.Cl.1976, 546 F.2d 395, 212 Ct.Cl. 318. United States ☞ 70(30); United States ☞ 70(34)

Where contractor initially followed mandatory, but not suggested, production techniques in producing preproduction guided missile warhead samples and, after samples were found to be unacceptable, contractor produced warheads in accordance with more costly design specifications suggested in contract, contractor transferred to government risk that product would not adequately perform under contract's ballistics revised standards, but contractor was not entitled to equitable price adjustment for following production techniques suggested by original design specifications and drawings of contract, as costs incurred in complying with suggested techniques were not extra costs under the contract. Gulf Western Precision Engineering Co. v. U.S., Ct. Cl.1976, 543 F.2d 125, 211 Ct.Cl. 207. United States ☞ 70(27)

Under contract for supply of quantities of 100 and 200-kilowatt diesel engine generator sets for Air Force, contractor was legally entitled, at its option, to utilize any of four engine combinations; Government, by prohibiting substitution of one type of engine for another, constructively changed contract. Consolidated Diesel Elec. Co. v. U.S., Ct.Cl.1976, 533 F.2d 556, 209 Ct.Cl. 521. United States ☞ 70(8); United States ☞ 72(2)

Where change order in relocation of creek was necessitated by the error on contract drawings prepared by the Corps of Engineers which indicated the location of sewer crossing to be upstream from the work area and the contractor's work in the priority work area was necessarily suspended for the performance of such extra work, the contractor was entitled to recover for any increased costs resulting from such suspension. Carl M. Halvorson, Inc. v. U.S., Ct.Cl.1972, 461 F.2d 1337, 198 Ct.Cl. 882. United States ☞ 70(29)

Where government drawings in connection with contract for manufacture of gas mask carriers were defective and caused plaintiff difficulties in production and defects caused delay and stoppage in plaintiff's operations for two weeks, plaintiff was entitled to equitable adjustment in amount of increased costs. La Crosse Garment Mfg. Co. v. U.S., Ct.Cl. 1970, 432 F.2d 1377, 193 Ct.Cl. 168. United States ☞ 70(29)

Fact that tolerance specifications for artillery fuzes resulted in arming failure in only 20% of fuzes rather than all of them did not mean that drawings specifying tolerance range for leaves at thickness which caused arming failure could not be deemed defective for liability purposes, and fact that contractor was unable to explain why reducing leaf thickness substantially eliminated arming test failure was not ground for denying equitable adjustment for extra costs incurred. R.E.D.M. Corp. v. U.S., Ct.Cl.1970, 428 F.2d 1304, 192 Ct.Cl. 891. United States ☞ 70(30)

Where government's design specifications for penstocks in power plant units of dam project required that every inch of every weld pass a 100% radiographic inspection, with no defects equal to or greater than two percent of thickness of base metal, so-called "defects" which had a thickness of less than two percent and which appeared in welding after inspection and acceptance were not "rejectable defects" for which government could deny contractor an equitable adjustment in contract price. Southwest Welding & Mfg. Co. v. U.S., Ct.Cl.1969, 413 F.2d

1167, 188 Ct.Cl. 925. United States ☞ 73(22)

A government contractor was entitled to an equitable adjustment under change clause of its contract for manufacture of parachutes based on additional supervisory salaries and travel expense incurred as a result of defective design by the government. Bell v. U.S., Ct.Cl.1968, 404 F.2d 975, 186 Ct.Cl. 189. United States ☞ 70(29)

Where prime contractor and United States agreed that contract called for "walls and roofs first" construction plan and oral directive required contractor to follow "floors first" construction plan, contractor could treat directive as constructive change order under "Changes" provision of contract and demand that written change order be issued retroactively to compensate for extra costs incurred, and dispute as to amount of equitable adjustment would be processed under "Disputes" provision of contract with armed services board of contract appeals determination which would be final if supported by substantial evidence and if it were not fraudulent, capricious, arbitrary or grossly erroneous. Turnbull, Inc. v. U.S., Ct.Cl.1967, 389 F.2d 1007, 180 Ct.Cl. 1010. United States ☞ 70(27)

Where contract between contractor and United States for the building by contractor of multiple wheel drive vehicle chassis dynamometers required that speed be measured from power roller rather than from idler roller, and contract required that rollers be no more than 8½ inches in diameter, so that it was factually impossible for dynamometer to comply with contract specification that it absorb 175 horsepower at 50 miles per hour for period of one hour, contractor was entitled to judgment for increased costs and expenses which contractor incurred in attempt to comply with impossible requirement. Maxwell Dynamometer Co. v. U.S., Ct.Cl.1967, 386 F.2d 855, 181 Ct.Cl. 607. United States ☞ 70(29)

Alleged errors in plans and specifications for construction of long, thin walls in that they were to stand completely unsupported on all sides except the rear until they became part of walls that would result after two-foot concrete walls were poured were so obvious that experienced contractor headed by competent engineer as active president knew or should have recognized those errors, and contractor was not entitled to recover from government the additional costs incurred as result of collapse of walls from hydrostatic pressure due to heavy rains. Allied Contractors, Inc. v. U.S., Ct.Cl. 1967, 381 F.2d 995, 180 Ct.Cl. 1057. United States ☞ 70(29)

199. Energy costs, changes, modifications or adjustments of contracts

Under contract between common carrier and Military Sea Transportation Service setting forth cost responsibilities of parties in a schedule nominating the responsibility of carrier for cost of specific services did not authorize carrier to escalate freight rates to compensate for increased cost of bunker fuel as measured by fixed claim surcharge or otherwise, since the appendix described cost only by nature, kind or character without regard to any dollar amount and without any warranty against exclusion of contingency factors in rates. Sea-Land Service, Inc. v. U.S., Ct.Cl.1977, 553 F.2d 651, 213 Ct.Cl. 555, certiorari denied 98 S.Ct. 724, 434 U.S. 1012, 54 L.Ed.2d 755. United States ☞ 70(22.1)

Where United States represented to contractor, before contract for construction of dam was entered into, that power company would deliver adequate electric power to site of work, and power company confirmed but both representation and confirmation were based upon Government's estimate that only about 200 kilowatts would be required, when in fact as much as 1250 kilowatts was needed, and contractor was forced to build power line to bring in such power, contractor, who had not included cost of running such power line in estimate, having been led to believe that no such cost would be incurred, was entitled to recover such cost from Government. Arcole Midwest Corp. v. U.S., Ct.Cl.1953, 113 F.Supp. 278, 125 Ct.Cl. 818. United States ☞ 70(30)

200. Equipment use, changes, modifications or adjustments of contracts

Fact that equipment of government contractor, who owned and operated equipment used in doing extra work that contract, pursuant to reasonable interpretation, did not call for, was subjected to greater abuse because of adverse circumstances under which it was used in performing extra work, did not warrant use of cost rates for such equipment more

liberal than average of equipment ownership rates published by Associated General Contractors of America. Bennett v. U.S., Ct.Cl.1967, 371 F.2d 859, 178 Ct.Cl. 61. United States ☞ 70(21)

Where invitation to bid on government contract provided that all new parts furnished should be those of named manufacturer but there was provision that reference in specifications to any article by name shall be interpreted as establishing standard of quality and that contractor may make substitutions equal to items specified, if approved in advance by contracting officer, contractor was not required to furnish equipment of named manufacturer but could supply articles equal to those of named manufacturer with consent of contracting officer. Jack Stone Co. v. U.S., Ct.Cl.1965, 344 F.2d 370, 170 Ct.Cl. 281. United States ☞ 70(9)

201. Excavation, changes, modifications or adjustments of contracts

That road construction project was in fact designed as balanced project with respect to cuts, fills and borrow pits and that contractor's use of borrow pits not mentioned in contract documents was necessary in performance did not establish changed conditions within standard Changed Conditions article of United States Government contract, where documents did not contain any express statement that project was designed as balanced within each of its successive segments for excavation and placement of materials and where specifications contained frequent reminders that estimated figures were to be viewed with great caution. Pacific Alaska Contractors, Inc. v. U.S., Ct.Cl.1971, 436 F.2d 461, 193 Ct.Cl. 850. United States ☞ 70(27)

Where basic cause of contractor's failure to obtain watertight cofferdam in construction of bridge was changed conditions, contractor was entitled to recover on claim for placing choker course or cover at bottom of excavation for one pier to make cofferdam watertight. Foster Const. C.A. & Williams Bros. Co. v. U.S., Ct.Cl.1970, 435 F.2d 873, 193 Ct.Cl. 587. United States ☞ 70(22.1)

Alaska road contractors were not entitled to equitable adjustment under "Changed Conditions" provision of contract with Department of Commerce for cost of excavating frozen material not indicated in the contract specifications. Wm. A. Smith Contracting Co. v. U.S., Ct.Cl.1969, 412 F.2d 1325, 188 Ct.Cl. 1062. Highways ☞ 113(4)

Action taken by road commission in designating substitute borrow pits to replace pits originally designated in drawings, ordering certain of original borrow pits enlarged, and ordering plaintiff road builder to perform borrow excavation and overhaul far in excess of quantities shown on contract drawings constituted compensable changes within changes clause of contract. Morrison-Knudsen Co. v. U.S., Ct.Cl.1968, 397 F.2d 826, 184 Ct.Cl. 661. Highways ☞ 113(4)

Department of Commerce Appeals Board had authority to give road contractor equitable adjustment for constructive change under "changes" clause of road construction contract for claim of necessity to excavate additional material and transport it for greater distances than called for by plans. Clack v. U.S., Ct.Cl. 1968, 395 F.2d 773, 184 Ct.Cl. 40. Highways ☞ 113(4)

Where conditions actually encountered during excavation differ materially from those indicated by plans and no fault in preparation of borings, drawings or plans is proved, change of conditions clause applies and remedies available thereunder are in equitable adjustment, non-assessment of liquidated damages, and extension of time. Jefferson Const. Co. v. U.S., Ct.Cl.1968, 392 F.2d 1006, 183 Ct. Cl. 720, certiorari denied 89 S.Ct. 122, 393 U.S. 842, 21 L.Ed.2d 113. United States ☞ 74(7)

Government contractor's interpretation of levee construction contract specifications, which set out fixed distance from center line of levee for excavation, as not requiring removal of material from beyond such point was reasonable, and thus contractor was entitled to recover additional compensation for extra excavation performed under protest beyond such point. Bennett v. U.S., Ct.Cl.1967, 371 F.2d 859, 178 Ct.Cl. 61. United States ☞ 70(27)

Where contractor entered into unit price contract with Government for grading, etc., of an airport, total consideration was to be based on quantity of work performed, contractor when excavating for particular ditch placed material as required in embankment for later grading and filling and it later developed that dirt

was not needed and contractor was directed to level embankment which bordered on runway to height of four feet, contractor was not entitled to extra compensation for such work, in view of fact that under contract contractor was obliged to do such leveling work. Palumbo v. U.S., Ct.Cl.1953, 113 F.Supp. 450, 125 Ct.Cl. 678. United States ☞ 70(27)

202. Financing costs, changes, modifications or adjustments of contracts

Where contractor failed to prove direct traceability of or necessity for borrowing to expenditures for change order work, no recovery of financing expense as against United States would be allowed, despite showing of history of business borrowings and courses dealing through various banks during time frame at issue. Dravo Corp. v. U.S., Ct.Cl.1979, 594 F.2d 842, 219 Ct.Cl. 416. United States ☞ 74(12.1)

Contractor could not charge United States for fluctuation of market prices in light of mutual amendments to the contract made by the parties which extended the closing date on eight different occasions, since market fluctuations affecting cost of financing are risks the bidder must assume just as he assumes the risk of higher labor and material costs. D & L Const. Co. & Associates v. U.S., Ct.Cl. 1967, 378 F.2d 675, 180 Ct.Cl. 366. United States ☞ 70(23)

203. Inspections, changes, modifications or adjustments of contracts

Given language of paragraph on resubmitted lots or batches in contract for manufacture and delivery of artillery shell components to the United States, contractor was not entitled to equitable adjustment due to Government's imposition of a 100% inspection requirement. A.B.G. Instrument & Engineering, Inc. v. U.S., Ct.Cl.1979, 593 F.2d 394, 219 Ct.Cl. 381. United States ☞ 70(14)

Under government contract requiring contractor to furnish and install vertical lift gates, providing for acceptance after completion and that all inspections, except shop inspections, were to be made at work site, Government reserving rights as to shop inspections, contractor could not recover additional costs of repairing defects in gates built by subcontractor, although Government did not take advantage of provision entitling it to be present during assembly and disassembly at subcontractor's plant, particularly since contractor did not inform Government when assembly and disassembly would take place. Kenneth Reed Const. Corp. v. U.S., Ct.Cl.1973, 475 F.2d 583, 201 Ct.Cl. 282. United States ☞ 70(31)

204. Labor or wages, changes, modifications or adjustments of contracts

Modification to contract to provide accounting services for the Department of Housing and Urban Development (HUD), under which contractor agreed to continue unfinished work, did not provide for retroactive pricing of work already performed; modification was directed toward extending the period of performance and repricing the continuing work, not repricing the work already performed, modification's statement of purpose said nothing about repricing work already performed for which the contractor had already been paid, and modification had an effective date. Gardiner, Kamya & Associates, P.C. v. Jackson, C.A.Fed.2006, 467 F.3d 1348. United States ☞ 72(5)

United States had to bear loss, if any, from breach of Air Force's duty to disclose, to contractor on federal construction project, its plans for high priority federal construction program which caused labor shortage requiring contractor, and its subcontractors, to pay higher wages than those anticipated in bid on project, in view of Air Force's knowledge, at time of award of contract to contractor, of the other program, its probable consequences, and contractor's ignorance thereof, and in view of contractor's lack of knowledge or reason to know. J.A. Jones Const. Co. v. U.S., Ct.Cl.1968, 390 F.2d 886, 182 Ct.Cl. 615. United States ☞ 70(30)

If United States agency at time it asked for construction bids computed at prevailing wage rates knew that another department was going to construct a project nearby which would have the effect of creating a severe labor shortage and cause an increase in wage rates, it would seem that United States agency in good faith was required to apprise bidder of that fact, and if United States caused increase over prevailing wages that contractor had to pay, United States would be liable for increase. Bateson-Stolte, Inc. v. U.S., Ct.Cl.1959, 172 F.Supp. 454, 145 Ct.Cl. 387. United States ☞ 70(24)

Under Government contract providing that total costs should be sum of all costs incurred by contractor incident to and necessary for performance of contract and properly chargeable thereto, Government contractor was entitled to recover amount of increase of unemployment compensation taxes paid to state of North Carolina due to adverse effect of contractor's employment and unemployment experience under Government contract. U.S. Rubber Co. v. U.S., Ct.Cl.1958, 160 F.Supp. 492, 142 Ct.Cl. 42. United States ☞ 70(33)

Where Presidential "freeze" order, Ex. Ord. No. 9328, made it impossible for construction contractor to secure necessary labor even after Wage Adjustment Board granted an increase over contract wage rate fixed by Secretary of Labor and freeze order was one of general application issued in exercise of sovereign power of the United States, construction contractor was not entitled to recover from the United States damages for excess costs resulting in failure to secure necessary labor, such loss being damnum absque injuria. J.B. McCrary Co. v. U.S., Ct.Cl.1949, 84 F.Supp. 368, 114 Ct.Cl. 12. United States ☞ 73(25)

Where contract required contractor to obtain labor locally and gave contractor choice of obtaining carpenters through local unions or through nearby offices of United States Employment Service, and contractor chose the latter method, but had complete freedom to employ or not to employ laborers referred by Employment Service, contractor was not entitled to labor claim against Government based on alleged inefficiency of carpenters supplied by Employment Service. Joseph Meltzer, Inc., of N.J. v. U.S., Ct.Cl.1948, 77 F.Supp. 1018, 111 Ct.Cl. 389. United States ☞ 73(25)

Where Federal Government in time of war assumed control of motor transportation system whose employees were on strike, Government was entitled to payment for services of drivers and dockmen furnished by Government pursuant to contract whereby carrier agreed to pay for such services at rates currently in effect on its system, though drivers and dockmen thus furnished were members of armed forces and compensation payable under contract would exceed amount paid soldiers by Government. U.S. v. Coordinated Transport, N.D.Ill.

1947, 73 F.Supp. 176. Automobiles ⊨ 109

Where a contractor incurs extra costs due to delays wrongfully caused by the Government's breach of its obligations to furnish proper specifications, the plaintiff is entitled to recover those direct and indirect extra costs which it can establish and which were the result of the breach, and such excess labor costs during a delay period will not be presumed but must be proved. Ithaca Gun Co., Inc. v. U.S., Ct.Cl.1966, 176 Ct.Cl. 437. United States ⊨ 70(30); United States ⊨ 74(10)

Where the plaintiffs, as joint venturers, in 1942, entered into a contract with the War Department to furnish the plant, labor, and certain materials and to perform the work to construct and complete certain buildings at Fort Leonard Wood and the progress of the work was delayed by unusually heavy rains and by the failure of lumber to arrive on schedule from Government suppliers and the plaintiffs did not make written requests for extensions of time because of these delays until after work had been completed and likewise did not protest in writing the orders of the contracting officer requiring them to work extra shifts, to work overtime and to employ additional carpenters, plaintiffs were not entitled to recover the increased costs representing wages paid to carpenters employed by order of the contracting officer. Dunnigan Const. Co. v. U.S., Ct.Cl.1952, 122 Ct.Cl. 262. United States ⊨ 73(14)

In a suit to recover the sum of $19,150 which plaintiff claimed for overtime on certain buildings he was required to construct under the original contract between the plaintiff and the Government at a unit price per building, where it was found that the claim was denied by the contracting officer in accordance with the provisions of the contract and it was found that neither the contracting officer nor other responsible officials of the Government acted arbitrarily or unreasonably in denying plaintiff's claim but on the contrary made an honest effort to adjust equitably the differences between the parties, the plaintiff was not entitled to recover. Slonk v. U.S., Ct.Cl.1952, 121 Ct.Cl. 246. United States ⊨ 73(14)

In a contract with the Government for the construction of a levee along the Illinois River and one of its tributaries, where the contract provided that labor

should first be secured from the relief rolls, and where it was not possible to secure skilled and semi-skilled labor from this source, and where it was found from the evidence that the contract provision did not cause the plaintiff to use unskilled labor uneconomically, plaintiff was not entitled to recover for excessive labor costs in the completion of the contract. Stiers Bros. Const. Co. v. U.S., Ct.Cl. 1947, 109 Ct.Cl. 353. Levees And Flood Control ⊨ 16; United States ⊨ 70(23)

Plaintiff paid the increased wages of common laborers as a result of the wrongful demand of defendant's representative in charge of the work, and hence defendant should pay the increased cost resulting therefrom. A.J. Paretta Contracting Co. v. U.S., Ct.Cl.1947, 109 Ct.Cl. 324. United States ⊨ 70(23); United States ⊨ 70(24)

Where the Government terminated a construction contract because of delay and default on the part of the contractor and completed the work, and where a regularly employed architect remained on the job continuously during the time the Government was actually engaged in completing the work, the salary of said architect for said period was properly included as a part of the excess costs of completing said work. Maryland Casualty Co. v. U.S., Ct.Cl.1941, 93 Ct.Cl. 247. Contracts ⊨ 306(3); United States ⊨ 75

205. Materials or components, changes, modifications or adjustments of contracts

Nature of two-month delay which ensued when necessary epoxy resins needed for performance of fixed price contract for supply of parts for certain antipersonnel mines became unavailable did not mean that an equitable adjustment could be had for increased costs due to disruption where, aside from fact that contract did not contain a changed condition or a suspension of work clause, changes clause applied in case of a change order as to which there was none. Consolidated Molded Products Corp. v. U.S., Ct.Cl. 1979, 600 F.2d 793, 220 Ct.Cl. 594. United States ⊨ 70(34)

Where specification clearly notified contractor that electric power receptacles to be supplied under contract to upgrade aircraft carrier berthing facilities were those described in qualified products list on which only one manufacturer had qualified, where contractor had failed to seek qualification of its product for qualified products list prior to bid opening, and where procedural irregularity did not injure contractor, contractor was not entitled to recover additional compensation representing difference in cost between its receptacles and approved receptacles, which it was forced to furnish. American Elec. Contracting Corp. v. U.S., Ct.Cl. 1978, 579 F.2d 602, 217 Ct.Cl. 338. United States ☞ 70(21)

Fact that Government's estimator, in making prebid estimate, calculated cost of paving which was subject of federal contract on basis that bank run gravel would be utilized for base course did not permit contractor to recover difference between cost of gravel base course and more expensive macadam course which it was required to use where estimator relied only on drawing indicating a gravel base course at time he made his estimate and was not familiar with pertinent contract specifications which required a macadam base course. William F. Klingensmith, Inc. v. U.S., Ct.Cl.1974, 505 F.2d 1257, 205 Ct.Cl. 651. United States ☞ 70(29)

Under federal highway repair contract designating quarry as a "type B source" (as distinguished from "type A source" as to which government assumed responsibility for adequacy) and indicating that government would not make equitable adjustment if contractor should elect to use type B source, contractor could claim equitable adjustment on account of inadequacy of quarry where it was the only source designated. Stock & Grove, Inc. v. U.S., Ct.Cl.1974, 493 F.2d 629, 204 Ct.Cl. 103. Highways ☞ 113(4)

Government contractor who entered contract on assumption that specifications for forms permitted tolerances which would have produced acceptable finished concrete structure and who was held by resident engineer to more restrictive standards than was customary could recover compensation for extra costs incurred in adjusting forms to comply with standards imposed by engineer. Kenneth Reed Const. Corp. v. U.S., Ct.Cl.1973, 475 F.2d 583, 201 Ct.Cl. 282. United States ☞ 70(28)

Evidence, including evidence that government laboratory personnel advised contractor that core samples taken from nearby borrow area did not satisfy contract fill requirement, whereupon contractor took fill only from further borrow area, did not establish entitlement to equitable adjustment under "changed conditions" provision. D.J. McQuestion and Sons v. U.S., Ct.Cl.1971, 439 F.2d 181, 194 Ct.Cl. 522, certiorari denied 92 S.Ct. 69, 404 U.S. 830, 30 L.Ed.2d 60. United States ☞ 74(11)

Requirement that contractor use friable materials only in air base construction was within terms of contract, which provided in part that "borrow material shall be selected to meet the requirements and conditions for the particular embankment or backfill for which it is to be used," precluding contractor's recovery of costs incurred when government insisted on approving borrow material used by contractor to use random material excavated from borrow pit. Tombigbee Constructors v. U.S., Ct.Cl.1970, 420 F.2d 1037, 190 Ct. Cl. 615. United States ☞ 70(27)

Where government construction contract contained standard "changes" provision and contracting officer, without issuing formal change order, requires contractor to perform work or utilize material which contractor regards as being beyond requirements of pertinent specifications or drawings, contractor may elect to treat officer's directive as constructive change order and prosecute claim for equitable adjustment. Ets-Hokin Corp. v. U.S., Ct.Cl.1970, 420 F.2d 716, 190 Ct.Cl. 668. United States ☞ 70(28)

Contractor, which had contract with United States for erection of dam, was not entitled to recover additional compensation for use of more expensive reinforced concrete in construction of spillway bucket rather than cheaper gravity concrete, where additions to contract made it clear that only spillway training walls, bucket training walls, and part of gatehouse were classified as reinforced concrete, and that all other portions of dam, including spillway bucket, were to be paid for as gravity concrete. Construction Service Co. v. U.S., Ct.Cl.1966, 357 F.2d 973, 174 Ct.Cl. 756. United States ☞ 70(26)

Government contractor who suffered losses on account of change requiring use of special tubing rather than commercial tubing would be allowed recovery for extra cost of special tubing, for additional engineering expense, and for increased manufacturing costs, but not for estimated profit paid to subcontractors. Kings Electronics Co. v. U.S., Ct.Cl.1965, 341 F.2d 632, 169 Ct.Cl. 433. United States ☞ 70(25.1)

In suit by contractor against the Government for extra costs because required to use more expensive material than called for by contract, plaintiff was entitled to recover on the ground that its interpretation of ambiguous provisions of contract drawn up by the Government permitted it to use gypsum tile instead of the more expensive hollow clay tiling in the construction of "furring" at exterior walls and around steel columns. Ring Const. Corp. v. U.S., Ct.Cl.1958, 162 F.Supp. 190, 142 Ct.Cl. 731. United States ☞ 70(27)

Where contractor offered to make plywood boxes contingent on required supply of fir plywood being made available through allocation by Government and Government's letter accepting bid in response to condition stated that if necessary, a release for contractor's suppliers would be obtained upon request, Government was not obligated to make allocation of plywood to contractor without regard to needs of other contractors and contractor could not recover additional costs in procuring plywood where delay in delivery after allocation was made was not fault of Government. Piggly Wiggly Corp. v. U.S., Ct.Cl.1949, 81 F.Supp. 819, 112 Ct.Cl. 391. United States ☞ 70(24)

Where contract called for stiff concrete mix, contractor was not entitled to compensation for extra expense incurred in distributing a stiff mix, notwithstanding that stiff mix produced a concrete of a strength in excess of minimum strength required by contract. Joseph Meltzer, Inc., of N.J. v. U.S., Ct.Cl.1948, 77 F.Supp. 1018, 111 Ct.Cl. 389. United States ☞ 70(27)

Where invitation for bids for construction of cold storage building stated that contract was not, necessarily, to be let to lowest bidder but was to be negotiated after study of bids and permitted bids to be made on basis of use of three types of insulation material differing greatly in cost, and before contract was signed both parties understood that the contractor proposed to use the cheapest insulation but by inadvertence the parties neglected to limit contractual provisions to the material intended, and, when such material

became unavailable, Government required contractor to use costlier insulation, the contractor was entitled to recover the additional cost. Olson Const. Co. v. U.S., Ct.Cl.1948, 75 F.Supp. 1014, 110 Ct.Cl. 249. Contracts ☞ 232(1); United States ☞ 70(27)

Where contract specifications authorized differences in construction if approved by competent authority, the submission by the contractor of a nonconforming sample and its approval by the contracting officer amounts to a request by the plaintiff for permission to use such nonconforming component, and the granting of such request by the contracting officer, despite the fact that the contract did not require the contractor to submit samples and if the contracting officer thereafter rejects the component because it does not conform to the specifications and requires the contractor to replace the component with another, the extra cost incurred in compliance with such order should be borne by the defendant and not the plaintiff. WRB Corp. v. U.S., Ct.Cl.1968, 183 Ct.Cl. 409. United States ☞ 70(28)

Where contract specifications describe in detail the performance requirements of certain components to be used by plaintiff in performing its contract, without naming any particular brand or giving any source of procurement, there is no assurance to bidders of the availability of commercial units ready-made and conformable to the stated performance requirements of the specifications with only minimal modification, and the risk of availability is on the bidder and not the Government and where the only components available required more than minimal adaptation to conform to the contract specifications, the Government does not become liable to the contractor for the extra costs of such modifications under the "changes" article of the contract since the contractor was not restricted to any one source of supply or any particular brand of component. Remler Co. v. U.S., Ct.Cl.1967, 179 Ct.Cl. 459, certiorari denied 88 S.Ct. 66, 389 U.S. 840, 19 L.Ed.2d 102. United States ☞ 70(26)

Where a contract prescribes the materials to be used in performing a contract to manufacture a particular item for the Government and also specifies the end result required but does not specify the method or technique of performance, a so-called change order permitting the contractor to perform the work in a certain manner, which technique had been devised by the contractor to overcome difficulties encountered in the method originally adopted, will not entitle the contractor to an equitable adjustment in the contract price to compensate him for the expense of performing the work by the new method; but such is not the case of a contract specifying performance methods which did not work and which required changes for which the Government was liable if the change in method turned out to be more costly or where, because of the defective method specified in the contract, the contractor incurred increased costs. Robertson Elec. Co., Inc. v. U.S., Ct.Cl.1966, 176 Ct.Cl. 1287. United States ☞ 70(27)

Where the record shows that the tests which defendant required plaintiff to apply to water pipe being made under the contract did not result in pipe any different or stronger than the pipe which plaintiff had agreed to construct, the testing requirement did not amount to a change within the meaning of the Changes Article of the contract. River Const. Corp. v. U.S., Ct.Cl.1962, 159 Ct.Cl. 254. United States ☞ 72(2)

In a suit to recover additional costs alleged by contractor to be due for extra work on ground that gravel which contracting officer required the contractor to use in constructing Fish and Wildlife rearing ponds was in excess of contract specifications, the order to use the gravel did not amount to a change and the decision of the head of the department to that effect was not arbitrary, capricious or unsupported by substantial evidence and was therefore binding on contractor. Anderson v. U.S., Ct.Cl.1958, 143 Ct.Cl. 729. United States ☞ 70(27); United States ☞ 73(14)

206. Method of performance, changes, modifications or adjustments of contracts

Where contract for installation of bituminous flashings on firewalls of project did not otherwise call for installation of flashings on tops of firewalls, and contractor's surety, having agreed to perform all work under contract by virtue of a take-over agreement, had option to either return-and-seal or cap-and-seal flashings, and chose cap-and-seal method by which

flashings on tops of firewalls were not required, surety was entitled to recover for extra work caused by government's demand that flashings be returned and sealed, which required removal of all existing terra cotta copings, installation of new flashings over tops of firewalls, and subsequent reinstallation of new coping over flashings. United Pac. Ins. Co. v. U.S., Ct.Cl.1974, 497 F.2d 1402, 204 Ct. Cl. 686, 204 Ct.Cl. 938. United States ☞ 70(24)

Where the contract prescribes the components to be used in manufacturing an item and the end result to be obtained but does not specify the method to be employed in achieving the desired result, a change in the method first employed by the contractor which did not produce the result desired is not a change within the meaning of the "Changes" article of the contract and does not obligate the contracting officer to issue a change order; however if the contracting officer does issue a change order permitting the contractor to employ the new method, this does not entitle the contractor to an equitable adjustment since the Government has not, within the meaning of the "Changes" article ordered a "change" in the scope of or the manner of performing the work specified in the contract. Robertson Elec. Co., Inc. v. U.S., Ct.Cl.1966, 176 Ct.Cl. 1287. United States ☞ 70(27)

207. Packaging, changes, modifications or adjustments of contracts

Where contractor's letter accompanying completed request for quotation form of Post Office Department showed three methods of packaging axles to be supplied and prices for each, Government's notice of award set out total price mathematically consistent with contractor's quotation for kits shipped loose and formal contract stated that Government was accepting such packaging, contract was not ambiguous as to packaging; thus Government was not liable for excess packaging costs prior to date that its finance office employee discovered that sufficient funds had not been authorized to pay invoices based on such costs. Dana Corp. v. U.S., Ct.Cl.1972, 470 F.2d 1032, 200 Ct.Cl. 200. United States ☞ 70(27)

208. Painting, changes, modifications or adjustments of contracts

Government contractor was not entitled to equitable adjustment for cost of painting on theory that, since contract was one for repair of earthquake damage to hospital, no painting should be required to areas which were not damaged by the earthquake. Chris Berg, Inc. v. U.S., Ct.Cl.1972, 455 F.2d 1037, 197 Ct. Cl. 503. United States ☞ 70(27)

Where only item listed under explicit specifications, in government contract, for construction of highrise apartment, for "surfaces not to be painted" was "prefinished elevator doors and frames," and finish schedule in some instances specifically directed that certain walls and ceilings made of disputed surfaces be painted, but in others named disputed surfaces while omitting directions to paint such surfaces, and where contracting officer was not consulted as to such discrepancy prior to bidding for such contract, contractor was not entitled to adjustment on the theory that requirement that it paint disputed surfaces constituted change in contract. HRH Const. Corp. v. U.S., Ct.Cl.1970, 428 F.2d 1267, 192 Ct.Cl. 912. United States ☞ 70(27)

Contract for repair, renovation and painting of dormitory buildings at air force base was ambiguous as to whether wood sashes beneath aluminum storm windows were to be painted, and contractor's interpretation that contract did not require such painting was reasonable, and United States order that sashes be painted constituted change for which contractor could be equitably compensated providing damages could be proved. Max Drill, Inc. v. U.S., Ct.Cl.1970, 427 F.2d 1233, 192 Ct.Cl. 608. United States ☞ 70(6.1); United States ☞ 70(27)

Where it appeared that post office builder was to paint only doors supplied by it, and that vault door was supplied by government and was wrong color and that builder was directed by post office department to change color, determination that such item was an "extra" for which builder was entitled to recover under theory of quantum meruit was not clearly erroneous. Leo A. Daly Co. v. Ray Smith Industries, Inc., C.A.5 (Tex.) 1968, 387 F.2d 899. Federal Courts ☞ 859

Contractor who claimed that he was required to paint and reglaze building for which contract with United States made no provision was not entitled to recover damages in excess of contract price for work he actually performed on building covered by the contract, which was unambiguous and clearly identified the building on which to work. Crowder v. U.S., N.D.Cal.1964, 255 F.Supp. 873, affirmed 362 F.2d 1011. United States ☞ 70(27)

209. Place of performance, changes, modifications or adjustments of contracts

In action by contractor against United States for sums allegedly due contractor under contract to manufacture and erect two 20-ton jib cranes at Philadelphia Navy Yard, evidence which did not reveal portion of work which should have been done in field and portion which should have been done in subcontractor's shop nor extra cost for completing at Navy Yard those portions which should have been completed in shop was not sufficient to establish reasonable basis for alleged additional costs to contractor of completing parts of crane at yard instead of at subcontractor's plant. Wagner Whirler & Derrick Corp. v. U.S., Ct.Cl.1954, 121 F.Supp. 664, 128 Ct.Cl. 382. United States ☞ 74(11)

210. Produce prices, changes, modifications or adjustments of contracts

While the termination of price freeze obstructed and made more costly plaintiff's performance under its June contract with the Department of Agriculture calling for plaintiff to supply the Department with canned turkey and chicken parts for the Department's school lunch program, the termination of the price freeze was a public and general act for the general good issued in the exercise of the sovereign power of the United States, and the government was contractually immune from liability for such a sovereign act; moreover, removal of the temporarily imposed price controls could not legitimately be viewed as unforeseeable or beyond reasonable anticipation. Tony Downs Foods Co. v. U.S., Ct.Cl.1976, 530 F.2d 367, 209 Ct.Cl. 31. United States ☞ 70(24)

Where, during the performance of a contract, which was satisfactorily completed, the defendant furnished the specified flour and tea called for in the preliminary agreement, and also furnished the sugar, except for a period of about three months in the middle of the contract, when the defendant's supply of sugar became low and plaintiff thereupon purchased the required amount of sugar in the market, but at a higher price, plaintiff was entitled to recover the amount of the excess cost. Chahroudi v. U.S., Ct.Cl. 1953, 124 Ct.Cl. 792. United States ☞ 70(23)

211. Production techniques, changes, modifications or adjustments of contracts

Contractor could not recover additional costs attributable to drilling difficulties in producing steel track shoes for armored personnel carriers where at the time it entered to its prime contract it was fully aware of those unresolved problems by virtue of its prior subcontracting activities on behalf of other prime contractors. Firestone Tire & Rubber Co. v. U.S., Ct. Cl.1977, 558 F.2d 577, 214 Ct.Cl. 457. United States ☞ 70(21)

Despite fact that performance requirements of contract for guided missile warheads could not have been met even if contractor had adhered to contract's suggested, as well as mandatory, production techniques, where contractor chose to ignore suggested production techniques and proceeded to employ less costly techniques of its own in fabricating initial set of preproduction samples, contractor assumed the risk that its own techniques would not yield acceptable result and contractor was not entitled to reimbursement for its additional costs incurred in producing unacceptable initial set of preproduction samples. Gulf Western Precision Engineering Co. v. U.S., Ct.Cl.1976, 543 F.2d 125, 211 Ct.Cl. 207. United States ☞ 70(31)

212. Quantity or volume, changes, modifications or adjustments of contracts

The government was negligent in preparing meal estimates for naval base in that it did not place in "Invitation for Bids" information that was reasonably available to it concerning requirement to feed four battalions of reservists who performed their two weeks' active duty at the base, and, as the meal estimate misled or did not adequately inform bidders as to scope of the contract, government could not use "volume variation" clause in the contract to limit successful bidder's equitable adjustment. Chemical Technology, Inc. v. U.S., Ct.Cl.1981, 645 F.2d 934, 227 Ct.Cl. 120. United States ☞ 70(24)

Where contracting navy officer's demand that supplier furnish 362 production-quality radio transmitters plus eight refurbished first-article samples was contrary to plain language of bid solicitation and was arbitrary and unlawful, supplier was entitled to compensation for additional eight units which it supplied, even though the supplier might have been remiss in failing to inform contracting navy officer forthrightly that extra compensation would be expected for the eight additional production-quality transmitters demanded by the officer. CRF - a Joint Venture of Cemco, Inc. v. U.S., Ct.Cl. 1980, 624 F.2d 1054, 224 Ct.Cl. 312. United States ☞ 70(24)

In action by government contractor to recover compensation for additional work performed by subcontractor at government's behest, contracting officer erred in treating excess portion of work as though it had been performed under retroactive type of fixed price redeterminable contract, thus permitting contract officer to reprice excess quantities on basis of contractor's average actual cost of providing entire quantities, both base and excess, of each item involved in excess, plus allowance for reasonable profit thereunder. Victory Const. Co., Inc. v. U.S., Ct.Cl.1975, 510 F.2d 1379, 206 Ct. Cl. 274. United States ☞ 74.2

Where government drawings were ambiguous as to whether three or four stitches were required in sewing waist strap to body of gas mask carrier and plaintiff's interpretation that only three stitches were required was reasonable and plaintiff's request for clarification was made but not answered until one contract had been all but performed and the second contract awarded and plaintiff's interpretation was concurred in by responsible representatives of government, plaintiff was entitled to costs incurred in complying with government directive requiring fourth stitch. La Crosse Garment Mfg. Co. v. U.S., Ct.Cl.1970, 432 F.2d 1377, 193 Ct.Cl. 168. United States ☞ 70(28)

Within provision of contract for cleaning Navy mess facilities that either party might "request" adjustment of contract price, "request" would properly be understood as "demand," founded on right, despite ambiguity of the word "request" and contention of contractor that purpose of clause was to allow adjustment in line with increases or decreases in his costs, where right to request adjustment arose on precisely stated condition and amount thereof was to be determined by mathematical formula, both related to number of meals served, and where contract contained no provision for discretionary disposition of any request. Rice v. U.S., Ct.Cl.1970, 428 F.2d 1311, 192 Ct.Cl. 903. United States ☞ 72(1.1)

Government contractor was not entitled to additional compensation due to requirement by contracting officer that contractor cover or insulate certain mixed air supply ducts in hung ceiling spaces where paragraph of standard specification relating to covering for air conditioning ducts was susceptible to only one reasonable interpretation, that being that all supply ducts must be covered. Paschen Contractors, Inc. v. U.S., Ct.Cl.1969, 418 F.2d 1360, 190 Ct.Cl. 177. United States ☞ 70(30)

Where facts established that a material variation from the erroneously computed estimated quantities was foreseeable, United States was not entitled to an equitable adjustment in government contract unit price on ground that a changed condition existed. Perini Corp. v. U.S., Ct. Cl.1967, 381 F.2d 403, 180 Ct.Cl. 768. United States ☞ 70(22.1)

Clause in government contract requiring completion of work at specified unit-price even when performance involves quantities greater or less than estimated quantities unless actual quantity work performed under any item varies from estimated quantity by more than 25% is not controlling when cost for doing extra work greatly differs from stated unit-price because of factors not foreseen by either party, and, in that event, the changed conditions clause comes into play and overrides the special condition. United Contractors v. U.S., Ct.Cl.1966, 368 F.2d 585, 177 Ct.Cl. 151. United States ☞ 70(20)

In view of fact that government's percentages of roll size drawings to be microfilmed were but estimates and that contractor agreeing to microfilm obsolete engineering documents for the Air Force must have known general condition of the drawings, the 6.5% variation between suggested estimates and actual number of roll size drawings filmed was a reasonable one under the circumstances and within scope of risk assumed by the contractor. Micrecord Corp. v. U.S., Ct.Cl. 1966, 361 F.2d 1000, 176 Ct.Cl. 46. United States ☞ 73(22)

Under Government contract providing that if alterations involve increase or decrease of more than 25 percent of any bid item then contractor or Government may request adjustment of unit bid price, overrun of 25 percent in volume does not ipso facto authorize re-examination of unit bid price for adjustment in contractor's favor. Wm. A. Smith Contracting Co. v. U.S., Ct.Cl.1961, 292 F.2d 854, 155 Ct.Cl. 44. United States ☞ 70(18)

Contractor who was misled by specifications and drawings contained in invitation of Government for bids to replace existing doors in Government buildings with brick, as to number of doors to be replaced, causing contractor to make a bid on basis of lower number of doors, and bid was made irrevocable and backed by substantial bond and exposed contractor to liability to Government for any increased costs resulting from performance by some other contractor if contractor refused to perform, was entitled to costs of extra work, notwithstanding contractor signed contract on basis of bid after discovery of mistake and finished work, where contractor signed contract but orally protesting against signing after Government threatened to forfeit the bond. Albert & Harrison v. U.S., Ct.Cl.1946, 68 F.Supp. 732, 107 Ct.Cl. 292, certiorari denied 67 S.Ct. 1199, 331 U.S. 810, 91 L.Ed. 1830. Contracts ☞ 232(2); United States ☞ 70(36)

Where Government contract for hauling "Lumber (Portable Knocked Down buildings and building material)" and "lumber" entitled the Government to increase the quantity of buildings and building materials hauled to the extent of 25 percent and the Government required the hauling of a vast increase in quantity of knocked down buildings and building materials and did not require the hauling of any lumber, Government was required to pay the reasonable value for hauling the excess quantity as an extra under the contract. Lundstrom v. U.S., D.C.Or. 1941, 53 F.Supp. 709, affirmed 139 F.2d 792. United States ☞ 70(2.1)

Where government requirements contract explicitly stated that quantities of items to be supplied by contractor, specified as "Best Estimated Quantities," were estimates only, there was no reference to minimum quantities in contract, and contractor was not reasonable in inferring that figures represented minimums, contractor was not entitled to equitable adjustment in contract price on basis that government failed to make minimum purchases; contention that absence of minimum figures exposed contractor to unpredictable requirements did not warrant change in contract terms to which parties had agreed. Solar Turbines Intern. v. U.S., Cl.Ct.1983, 3 Cl.Ct. 489. United States ⟶ 70(24)

Where plaintiff entered into a contract with the War Assets Administration for the purchase of whatever remained of the electrical distribution system at a discontinued Navy Yard and plaintiff's offer to purchase was based on the information contained in the invitation for bids as to the description and location of the remaining electrical equipment and after conference with the War Assets Administration office plaintiff was furnished copies of drawings showing the locations and plaintiff's representatives inspected the site and computed its bid upon the probable quantity of cable underground which might be obtained and the quantity of cable actually reclaimed fell short of the reasonable estimate made by the plaintiff, the plaintiff was entitled to recover. Industrial Salvage Corp. v. U.S., Ct.Cl.1952, 122 Ct.Cl. 611. United States ⟶ 66

Where the plaintiffs, in addition to their claim relating to Ex.Ord. No. 9301, also presented a claim for alleged excess cost of lumber because the Government did not provide them in time with the necessary priorities, due to the Government's error in calculation of the quantity of certain kinds of lumber needed, and plaintiffs failed to present proof that they could have bought the lumber cheaper if they had had the priorities earlier, plaintiffs were not entitled to recover. Beuttas v. U.S., Ct.Cl.1952, 122 Ct.Cl. 295. United States ⟶ 74(11)

213. Rents, changes, modifications or adjustments of contracts

Where, although contractor suffered economic detriment when it failed to receive rent it had expected during period of delay, such loss of income was not an additional cost of performance of contract and where the rent that the contractor did not receive did not impose any out-of-pocket expenses upon the contractor but merely reduced its income, con-

tractor was not entitled to an equitable adjustment under contract changes clause which covered changes that caused an increase in the cost of performance of the contract for rent it did not receive during periods of delay. Coley Properties Corp. v. U.S., Ct.Cl.1979, 593 F.2d 380, 219 Ct.Cl. 227. United States ⟶ 74(14)

214. Research and development, changes, modifications or adjustments of contracts

Experienced contractor which entered into supply contract containing fixed price incentive clause and which during performance of contract discovered various problems and spent substantial sum of money on research and development which resulted in far greater performance than parties had anticipated was not entitled to recover any part of its research and development costs. Sperry Rand Corp. v. U.S., Ct.Cl.1973, 475 F.2d 1168, 201 Ct.Cl. 169. United States ⟶ 70(21)

215. Restoration of land, changes, modifications or adjustments of contracts

Even assuming, arguendo, that issue of changed conditions had been properly raised and that plaintiff, which contracted with the United States to construct creek channel, levees and appurtenances, could prove that unexpected nature of waste area was result of subsurface, latent or unusual conditions, plaintiff still could not prevail on its claim in connection with extra fill it had to secure to complete filling of waste area since it was undisputed that there was no shortage of fill if overall project were considered, and since plaintiff had obligation under contract to fill to specification all required waste areas. Ace Const. Co. v. U.S., Ct. Cl.1968, 401 F.2d 816, 185 Ct.Cl. 487. United States ⟶ 70(27)

Where the United States leased for $1 a year land on which the plaintiff-owner had conducted a profitable kaolin mining operation, and where the defendant did not fulfill its covenant to restore the land to its original condition by removing from the ground live ammunition, with the result that the plaintiff's cost of using its land for its normal and usual mining purposes was materially increased and the cost of restoring the land was in excess of the fair market value of the land determined either at the time the lease was executed or at the time the land was returned to the plaintiff, equity and good conscience required that plaintiff be reimbursed for such additional cost. Georgia Kaolin Co. v. U.S., Ct.Cl.1959, 145 Ct.Cl. 39. United States ☞ 74(3)

216. Subcontractors, changes, modifications or adjustments of contracts

Where contractor agreed to supply quartermaster depot with brass buckles and subcontracted order for brass buckles, subcontractor became insolvent, and contractor did not seek and therefore was not denied permission to substitute subcontractors, provision in contract placing it within power of United States to refuse contractor permission to substitute subcontractors did not excuse contractor's performance. Whitlock Corp. v. U.S., Ct. Cl.1958, 159 F.Supp. 602, 141 Ct.Cl. 758, certiorari denied 79 S.Ct. 23, 358 U.S. 815, 3 L.Ed.2d 58. United States ☞ 73(1)

217. Suspension of work, changes, modifications or adjustments of contracts

Contractor, which had agreed to install mail handling equipment at new post office, was entitled to equitable adjustment under suspension of work clause because of 15-month delay in site availability, notwithstanding that Government was found without fault or negligence in causing the delay, especially since site conditions were described by all knowledgeable witnesses as the worst they had ever seen, with delay not attributable to fault or negligence of the contractor. Fruehauf Corp. v. U.S., Ct.Cl.1978, 587 F.2d 486, 218 Ct.Cl. 456. United States ☞ 70(34)

Equitable adjustment was available under "suspension of work" clause in government contract even though cause was an appropriation cutoff, whose possibility parties contemplated and whose consequences they dealt with in "funds available for payments" clause, even though Government's officers acted reasonably in allocating restricted funds available between plaintiff contractor's contract and other claimants against same appropriation item, and even though plaintiff contractor followed an accelerated schedule in spite of full knowledge of possible exhaustion of funds. C.H. Leavell & Co. v. U.S., Ct.Cl.1976, 530 F.2d 878, 208 Ct.Cl. 776. United States ☞ 70(24)

Construction corporation, which contracted with government to construct air traffic control center, was entitled, under suspension of work clause of contract, to damages over and above additional costs incurred in effecting change order with respect to underground fuel tank where resultant delay caused some increase in cost of performing contract, though contractor, in administrative proceeding on contractor's claim for such damages, may have overstated consequences in alleging that overall completion of building was delayed. Chaney & James Const. Co. v. U.S., Ct.Cl.1970, 421 F.2d 728, 190 Ct.Cl. 699. United States ☞ 74(8)

218. Time of completion or performance, changes, modifications or adjustments of contracts

Contracting officer's decision to grant contractor extension of time for completion of contract does not raise rebuttable presumption that government caused the delay. England v. Sherman R. Smoot Corp., C.A.Fed.2004, 388 F.3d 844. United States ☞ 73(20)

Army Corps of Engineers acted reasonably in sending letter to excavation contractor on flood-control project urging contractor to adhere to its schedule and advising that failure to diligently prosecute excavation would result in contract termination, precluding contractor's claim of constructive acceleration that was based on letter combined with Corps' allegedly improper non-recognition of high-water conditions as justifying extensions; at time of letter contractor had made only one claim for contract extension which plainly wrongly identified high water conditions as "differing site condition," and letter was partly precipitated by subcontractor's non-water-related refusal to haul materials. Fraser Const. Co. v. U.S., C.A.Fed.2004, 384 F.3d 1354. United States ☞ 70(34)

Where a reasonable interpretation of a contract permitted completion in 1951 and the contracting officer required the contractor to wait until 1952, such action amounted to a change in the refusal of the contracting officer to grant an equitable adjustment for increased costs of performance amounted to a breach of the "Changes" article of the contract. Western Contracting Corp. v. U.S., Ct.Cl.1958, 144 Ct.Cl. 318. United States ☞ 73(17)

Where the extra work under the change order prolonged performance into the winter, when working conditions were more difficult, the shifting of work was due to authorized changes and cannot be considered a breach of the contract. Irwin v. U.S., Ct.Cl.1945, 104 Ct.Cl. 84. United States ☞ 73(22)

219. Training, changes, modifications or adjustments of contracts

Where express contract existed between steel manufacturer and Department of Labor requiring Department to pay manufacturer specified amount for each day worked by hardcore unemployed individuals trained by manufacturer, such contract did not contain changes clause or any other clause providing for equitable adjustment of claims of manufacturer, and such contract authorized manufacturer to train individuals to work in only one department or division, manufacturer was not entitled to reimbursement for special additional training of certain individuals in a second department or division. U.S. Steel Corp. v. U.S., Ct.Cl.1976, 536 F.2d 921, 210 Ct.Cl. 228. United States ☞ 70(21)

220. Transportation, changes, modifications or adjustments of contracts

Where "delivery" was subject matter of contract between moving company and army joint household goods shipping office for transportation of unaccompanied baggage between points in Washington, D.C. and defined portions of Maryland and Virginia, place of delivery was not an incidental matter, "change" in contract to include delivery to points outside of specified area materially altered nature of moving company's performance and was not essentially same work as parties bargained for when contract was awarded and "changes" article of contract was not applicable. Embassy Moving & Storage Co. v. U.S., Ct.Cl.1970, 424 F.2d 602, 191 Ct.Cl. 537. Carriers ☞ 68

Where tramway contractor was given permission to use existing tramway in construction of new tramway, use was optional, United States made no warranty or representation as to tramway's condition and did not obligate itself to maintain the property in such condition as to enable contractor to use it in any manner it contemplated and contractor could have determined by site inspection that tramway was unsuitable for contemplated use, contractor was not entitled to equitable adjustment of contract price for in-

creased costs necessitating inability to use existing tramway. Chris Berg, Inc. v. U.S., Ct.Cl.1968, 389 F.2d 401, 182 Ct.Cl. 23. United States ☞ 70(30)

Clause in tramway construction contract that contractor assumed all liability in use of existing tramway for erection purposes applied to liability to third persons resulting from operation of tramway by contractor and did not preclude contractor from recovering from United States for additional costs incurred as result of inability to use existing tramway for construction purposes. S.S. Mullen, Inc. v. U.S., Ct.Cl.1968, 389 F.2d 390, 182 Ct.Cl. 1. United States ☞ 70(27)

The United States was not liable for increased cost of performance of contract to erect buildings in Canal Zone due to increase in ocean freight rates, in absence of provision in contract for payment of any such increase. McCarthy Bros. Const. Co. v. U.S., Ct.Cl.1947, 70 F.Supp. 124, 108 Ct.Cl. 366. Contracts ☞ 232(1); United States ☞ 70(31)

Contract providing that the price for cement should be adjusted in accordance with any change in freight rates on cement during life of contract did not include any increased freight rates on raw materials used in the manufacture of the cement. Bessemer Limestone & Cement Co. v. U.S., Ct.Cl.1943, 99 Ct.Cl. 195. Sales ☞ 77(2); United States ☞ 70(19)

221. Unknown physical conditions, changes, modifications or adjustments of contracts—Generally

Express representations as to nature of conditions to be encountered in performance of United States government contract are not essential to establish right to equitable adjustment under standard Changed Conditions article, at least insofar as subsurface or latent conditions are concerned, but there must be reasonably plain or positive indications in bid information or contract documents that such subsurface conditions would be otherwise than actually found in performance or that there were indications inducing reasonable reliance by successful bidder that subsurface conditions would be more favorable than those encountered. Pacific Alaska Contractors, Inc. v. U.S., Ct.Cl. 1971, 436 F.2d 461, 193 Ct.Cl. 850. United States ☞ 70(30)

For portion of changed conditions clause in standard government construction contract referring to conditions materially different from those indicated in contract to apply, it is not necessary that indications in the contract be explicit or specific but merely that there be enough of an indication on face of contract documents for bidder reasonably not to expect subsurface or latent physical conditions at site differing materially from those indicated in contract. Foster Const. C.A. & Williams Bros. Co. v. U.S., Ct.Cl.1970, 435 F.2d 873, 193 Ct.Cl. 587. United States ☞ 70(22.1)

Provision of road construction contract of United States pertaining to "changed conditions" was intended to authorize adjustment of contract price only with respect to physical conditions that were unknown to, and could not reasonably be anticipated by, the parties at the time they entered into the contract. Clack v. U.S., Ct.Cl.1968, 395 F.2d 773, 184 Ct.Cl. 40. Highways ☞ 113(4)

The unknown physical condition referred to in the changed conditions article of the standard form Government contract is one that could not be reasonably anticipated by the contractor after a study of the contract documents, inspection of the site, and general experience, if any, as a contractor in the area of the work. Fort Sill Associates v. U.S., Ct.Cl. 1968, 183 Ct.Cl. 301. United States ☞ 70(22.1)

Where the conditions (subsurface and surface boulders) encountered by a contractor at the site he had contracted to clear could have been readily ascertained by a site examination, there has been no changed condition within the meaning of the contract. National Concrete & Foundation Co. v. U.S., Ct.Cl.1965, 170 Ct.Cl. 470. United States ☞ 70(22.1)

222. —— Sea conditions, unknown physical conditions, changes, modifications or adjustments of contracts

Unanticipated adverse sea conditions existing at site of pier construction was not "changed condition" entitling contractor to equitable adjustment of contract. Hardeman-Monier-Hutcherson v. U.S., Ct.Cl.1972, 458 F.2d 1364, 198 Ct. Cl. 472. United States ☞ 70(22.1)

223. —— Weather conditions, unknown physical conditions, changes, modifications or adjustments of contracts

Where condition, which existed at time of execution of contract for reconstruc-

tion of road for Forest Service, did not reflect drought conditions, drought condition which occurred almost two months after execution of contract could not support a changed conditions claim under "Differing Site Conditions" article of contract, inasmuch as drought in question was unprecedented, unanticipated and unforeseeable in duration. Turnkey Enterprises, Inc. v. U.S., Ct.Cl.1979, 597 F.2d 750, 220 Ct.Cl. 179. United States ☞ 70(22.1)

That flood protection channel project plans were changed to eliminate catch basins, and that early construction of such basins would have protected Government contractor's work from rain damage, did not impose liability on Government for unforeseen results of heavy rain. Maxwell v. U.S., Ct.Cl.1962, 297 F.2d 554, 156 Ct.Cl. 72. United States ☞ 73(22)

Where contract for delivery of hay to United States provided that plaintiffs should not be liable for excess costs if any failure to perform arose out of unusually severe weather, plaintiffs who performed contract by buying hay at increased costs after hay-producing area was struck by severe drought could not recover such excess costs from United States. Dillon v. U.S., Ct.Cl.1957, 156 F.Supp. 719, 140 Ct.Cl. 508. United States ☞ 70(23)

There can be no recovery for extra expense incurred for temporary heat in accordance with an agreement made by an unauthorized representative of the Government. B-W Const. Co. v. U.S., Ct.Cl. 1945, 104 Ct.Cl. 608, certiorari denied 66 S.Ct. 704, 327 U.S. 785, 90 L.Ed. 1012. Contracts ☞ 232(2); United States ☞ 70(25.1)

224. —— Miscellaneous cases, unknown physical conditions, changes, modifications or adjustments of contracts

Court of Federal Claims did not clearly err by finding that grant by Army Corps of Engineers of 30 days' worth of extensions to excavation contractor on flood-control project, on account of high water flows and wet conditions, had not been untimely, precluding relief on contractor's claim of constructive acceleration; situation where contractor had to make judgment as to whether to incur additional expense by continuing work on days for which it had requested but not yet received extensions was inherent in any case where extension was not granted on spot, and Corps' allegedly improper non-recognition of high-water conditions as justifying extensions was mitigated by its willingness to consider granting extensions for "weather-related" wet conditions under contract's severe-weather clause. Fraser Const. Co. v. U.S., C.A.Fed.2004, 384 F.3d 1354. United States ☞ 70(34)

Government contractor was not entitled to recover from United States for damage resulting from explosion during production of igniters used in fire bombs, where, before the explosion, contractor had been told by government that artificial aging had been found to desensitize the atomized magnesium used in the igniters but that the contractor did not age the magnesium for the necessary length of time. Ordnance Research, Inc. v. U.S., Ct.Cl.1979, 609 F.2d 462, 221 Ct.Cl. 641. United States ☞ 74(1)

Where plaintiff contractor in performing contract for construction of earthen dam across creek incurred extra costs of performing work under unforeseen condition of unavailability of water in natural basin for construction purposes and costs of attempting to develop other sources of water and, if plaintiff had been permitted to use water in basin, pool would have been replenished from underground sources during applicable period, finding was justified that water hole would have provided half the water needed by plaintiff for construction purposes during applicable period and would have reduced by one-half plaintiff's expenditures during that period to develop other sources of supply and plaintiff would be entitled to recover that amount from defendant. Briscoe v. U.S., Ct.Cl.1971, 442 F.2d 953, 194 Ct.Cl. 866. United States ☞ 70(22.1)

Where contract drawings depicted cross section of floor that showed drain connected to P–trap below floor by nipple stated to be 6 inches long that extended from point just below bowl of drain, base of which was approximately even with bottom of concrete cross section, into joint on P–trap, such drawings, for purpose of changed conditions article of government contract that permitted equitable adjustment if contractor encountered subsurface or latent conditions differing materially from those indicated in contract, contained indication that concrete,

which was up to 24 inches thick, and portion of which contractor had contracted to remove, would be about 6 inches thick as contractor expected it to be. J.E. Robertson Co. v. U.S., Ct.Cl.1971, 437 F.2d 1360, 194 Ct.Cl. 289. United States ☞ 70(30)

Government contractor, hired to repair tower and light on a pipe pile foundation for Coast Guard, had established a change of conditions in that contract drawing showed, in accordance with general understanding, a rock bottom which was not dispelled by a reasonable prebid inspection by contractor and that bottom was spoils which prevented performance of contract whether by drilling or driving. Vann v. U.S., Ct.Cl.1970, 420 F.2d 968, 190 Ct.Cl. 546. United States ☞ 74(11)

Where facts established that estimated quantities of water to be pumped as recited in government dam construction contract had been grossly underestimated by government and that contractor which had submitted a unit bid for pumping of water as required by contract recognized that estimate was unduly low and did not rely thereon, government was not entitled to relief under standard changed conditions article allowing adjustments for discovery of subsurface and/or latent physical conditions which differ materially from those shown on drawings or indicated in specifications. Perini Corp. v. U.S., Ct.Cl.1967, 381 F.2d 403, 180 Ct.Cl. 768. United States ☞ 70(22.1)

Profiles of test borings indicated in drawings furnished to contractor performing work for government were particularly important in determining in contractor's action against government whether contractor had encountered changed conditions sufficient to allow equitable adjustment in price under contract provision authorizing such adjustment where, inter alia, subsurface and/or latent physical conditions are materially different from those shown on drawings. United Contractors v. U.S., Ct.Cl.1966, 368 F.2d 585, 177 Ct.Cl. 151. United States ☞ 70(22.1)

Contractor who performed ductwork for hospital renovation did not establish a Type I differing site condition claim which entitled it to equitable adjustment for demolition of old ductwork and installation of new ductwork associated with new diffusers and grilles, based on its contention that above-ceiling conditions actually encountered were different from those indicated in contract, where no affirmative representations concerning above-ceiling conditions were made in bid documents, and conditions encountered were reasonably foreseeable by experienced government contractor. Conner Brothers Const. Co., Inc. v. U.S., Fed. Cl.2005, 65 Fed.Cl. 657. United States ☞ 70(22.1)

Government contractor on project involving electrical work at naval facility was precluded from asserting differing site condition claim based on actual condition of recloser switches, by contractor's failure to attend pre-bid site visit conducted by contracting agency; actual condition of reclosers was reasonably foreseeable because a reasonable contractor would have conducted a site inspection before bidding. Orlosky Inc. v. U.S., Fed.Cl.2005, 64 Fed.Cl. 63. United States ☞ 70(22.1)

Where a contractor laying pipe underground for the Government encounters numerous underground obstructions not visible from above ground, shown on drawings or indicated in the specifications and where the presence of the obstructions could not have been discovered by any reasonable inspection, the extra time required to overcome these obstructions and the extra cost of doing the work by hand rather than by backhoe, is compensable to the contractor. Dale Const. Co. v. U.S., Ct.Cl.1964, 168 Ct.Cl. 692. United States ☞ 70(22.1)

In an action for damages for breach of a building construction contract based on the failure of the Government to make an equitable adjustment for extra work occasioned by alleged changed conditions in that the building in which the work was to be performed was, contrary to the expectations of the contractor, occupied by personnel and furniture during the entire course of the contract work, no liability arises on the part of the Government where the occupancy of the building could and should have been discovered by the plaintiff upon inspection of the premises prior to submission of its bid, in accordance with the instructions to bidders. Appalachian Floor Co. v. U.S., Ct. Cl.1958, 144 Ct.Cl. 11. United States ☞ 70(22.1)

Where contractor had no reason not to expect that it would encounter in the site which it contracted to excavate whatever

foundations, footings, or pillars may have been used to support the former brick building on said site, and where contractor, though having an unusual opportunity to do so, made no effort to ascertain what foundations the former building had, and where contractor had agreed to take the site as it found it and to remove such material as it might find there, plaintiff was not entitled to recover for loss on account of additional costs incurred by reason of encountering more difficult conditions than it had expected. James Stewart & Co. v. U.S., Ct.Cl.1941, 94 Ct.Cl. 95. Contracts ☞ 232(2); United States ☞ 70(22.1)

225. Weight, changes, modifications or adjustments of contracts

Fact that Government contracted to purchase tent pins by contract providing for shipping weight of 160 lbs. per 100 units, upon default of contractor who had agreed to furnish pins with shipping weight of only 124 lbs. per 100 units, would not preclude recovery by Government from defaulting contractor of resulting excess costs, where shipping weight was not a specification of the Government but merely an item of information used to evaluate transportation costs, and pins actually shipped by second contractor only weighed 124 lbs. per 100 units. U.S. v. Adams, W.D.Ark.1958, 160 F.Supp. 143. United States ☞ 75(2)

226. Miscellaneous changes, changes, modifications or adjustments of contracts

Where government did not clarify the base bid control points on energy monitoring and control system for Veterans' Administration Hospital prior to award of alternate as required by bidder's condition, government was bound by the interpretation bidder placed on the contract and bidder was therefore entitled to equitable adjustment as to award of the alternate; to extent that government's award of alternate required bidder to install 54 more points than bid, the action constituted a constructive change and the bidder was entitled to recover an equitable adjustment, covering those 54 points. Johnson Controls, Inc. v. U.S., Ct.Cl. 1982, 671 F.2d 1312, 229 Ct.Cl. 445. United States ☞ 70(21)

Contractor's claim for costs of building temporary trestle to provide work space for construction of bridge under standard government construction contract after bureau of public roads denied permission to build an earth ramp was claim for a constructive change only and had nothing to do with changed conditions and was properly denied in light of conflicting testimony as to propriety of discretionary denial of permission to build earth ramp. Foster Const. C.A. & Williams Bros. Co. v. U.S., Ct.Cl.1970, 435 F.2d 873, 193 Ct.Cl. 587.   United States ⚬═ 70(22.1)

Government construction contract provision relating to pile driving intended that specified unit price should apply only to first ten percent underrun, and that for underrun in excess of ten percent, equitable adjustment was called for.   Blount Bros. Corp. v. U.S., Ct.Cl.1970, 424 F.2d 1074, 191 Ct.Cl. 784.   United States ⚬═ 70(17)

Conclusion was required, in government contract dispute, that contractor's contractual obligation to supply exterior thermal covering to high pressure air supply ducts in basement was not increased by change order, so that contractor was not entitled to recover on such claim, but contractor was entitled to a fair reading of specification explicitly applicable to hot air ducts involved and was entitled to recover on claim relating to those ducts.   Paschen Contractors, Inc. v. U.S., Ct.Cl.1969, 418 F.2d 1360, 190 Ct. Cl. 177.   United States ⚬═ 70(25.1); United States ⚬═ 70(27)

Contracting agency violated solicitation for military housing privatization project which provided that terms of form legal documents agency executed with successful offeror (SO) after selection would be "substantially identical" to the form legal documents appended to solicitation, by permitting SO to make changes, postselection, to a number of terms of the form legal documents addressing termination of lease, pest control, excusable delay, contingency of base closure, default, and applicability of Hawaii law, in all cases relaxing or clarifying the terms such that they were not "substantially identical" to those in the solicitation, to the benefit of the SO and the prejudice of unsuccessful offeror. Hunt Building Co., Ltd. v. U.S., Fed.Cl.2004, 61 Fed.Cl. 243, modified 63 Fed.Cl. 141.   United States ⚬═ 64.40(2)

227. Administration costs, changes, modifications or adjustments of contracts

Where, judged both from standpoint of time of submission and purpose of submission, government contractor's requests for equitable adjustment were not performance related and bore no beneficial nexus either to contract production or to contract administration, costs, including attorney fees, technical consultants' fees and in-house personnel costs incurred incidentally to making of claim were not recoverable though claim was to contracting officer for equitable adjustment rather than to Armed Services Board of Contract Appeals.   Singer Co. Librascope Div. v. U.S., Ct.Cl.1977, 568 F.2d 695, 215 Ct.Cl. 281.   United States ⚬═ 147(12)

228. Interest, changes, modifications or adjustments of contracts

Government was required to pay interest to contractor on claims for extra work required by changes that government had ordered in its original contract if claims processing period was unreasonably lengthy.   General Ry. Signal Co. v. Washington Metropolitan Area Transit Authority, D.C.D.C.1979, 527 F.Supp. 359, affirmed 664 F.2d 296, 214 U.S.App.D.C. 170, certiorari denied 101 S.Ct. 3049, 452 U.S. 915, 69 L.Ed.2d 418.   United States ⚬═ 70(33)

229. Profits, changes, modifications or adjustments of contracts

Where contract for operation of food service facilities at air force base was a loss contract and contractor would have suffered loss even if 100% of Government's estimate of meals to be served had been served in months when meals actually served were less than 70% of estimated meals, equitable adjustment for those months based upon amount which contractor would have received if 100% of estimated meals had been served, less offset for additional costs contractor would have had to incur to serve the additional meals, was proper; contractor was not entitled to receive 6% profit on costs incurred for the months in dispute. Pacific Architects & Engineers, Inc. v. U.S., Ct.Cl.1974, 491 F.2d 734, 203 Ct.Cl. 499.   United States ⚬═ 70(18); United States ⚬═ 70(22.1)

Where changes clause of government contract specifically defined "actual necessary cost" as including all reasonable expenditures for material, labor and supplies and clause further stated in no case would actual and necessary costs include an allowance for any general expense not directly attributable to the extra work, contractor was not entitled to have included in base cost formula for cost changes ten percent for subcontractor's overhead plus ten percent of subcontractor's profits. Perry & Wallis, Inc. v. U.S., Ct.Cl.1970, 427 F.2d 722, 192 Ct.Cl. 310. United States ☞ 70(21)

Since no profit level had been agreed upon, Department of Defense regulation illustrating the "weighted guidelines method" of determining reasonable levels of contractor profits was to be applied to provision of defense contract authorizing contracting officer to deny any upward adjustment in contract price on finding that such adjustment was not required to enable contractor to earn a fair and reasonable profit, even though contract had been awarded to other than a low bidder for purpose of continuing existence of an essential defense facility. Bethlehem Steel Corp. v. U.S., Ct.Cl.1970, 423 F.2d 300, 191 Ct.Cl. 141. United States ☞ 73(12)

Government contractor who was delayed in performance of Government contract because of unsuitability of Government-furnished cloth was entitled to equitable adjustment for its increased costs but was not, because of contract provision to contrary, entitled to loss of profit. Topkis Bros. Co. v. U.S., Ct.Cl. 1961, 297 F.2d 536, 155 Ct.Cl. 648, motion denied 299 F.2d 952, 155 Ct.Cl. 648. United States ☞ 70(24); United States ☞ 74(15)

The Government is not necessarily liable because it directly or indirectly increases costs or decreases profit of a party contracting with the Government. Geo. H. Evans & Co. v. U.S., E.D.Pa. 1947, 74 F.Supp. 58. United States ☞ 70(24)

230. Termination costs, changes, modifications or adjustments of contracts

Electronics manufacturer, as party to multiyear procurement contract to supplier of aircraft carrier radar systems to United States Navy, was entitled to equitable reformation of "cancellation ceiling" provided for in contract and redetermination of proper cancellation charge with reformed ceiling percentage. Applied Devices Corp. v. U.S., Ct.Cl.1979, 591 F.2d 635, 219 Ct.Cl. 109. United States ☞ 72(1.1)

Where partial termination of government contract by United States eliminated entire unperformed section as to spare parts and left intact entire portion as to finished products, the preparatory nonabsorbed costs with respect to terminated portion, not absorbed by nonterminated portion, thereby became awardable as lump sum, without any need for their distribution among completed finished products, in determining amount awardable to contractor in equitable adjustment for increased costs as consequence of partial termination. Sternberger v. U.S., Ct.Cl.1968, 401 F.2d 1012, 185 Ct.Cl. 528. United States ☞ 74(12.1)

Excess costs should not have to be paid by government contractor where they are incurred as result of termination of contract without good faith. Meinberg v. U.S., W.D.Mo.1969, 310 F.Supp. 86. United States ☞ 75(5)

A prime Government contractor could bring action against United States on behalf of subcontractor, for subcontractor's damages for increased costs sustained upon termination of the prime contract, where the subcontract did not negate liability for increased costs occasioned by the acts of the Government. J.W. Bateson Co. v. U.S., Ct.Cl.1958, 163 F.Supp. 871, 143 Ct.Cl. 228. United States ☞ 74.2

Where, in awarding both original contract to plaintiff for supplying cots to the United States and substituted contract, which was entered into for balance of cots due after plaintiff's contract had been terminated, United States expressly took into consideration transportation costs from plant of bidder to designated Army stations, plaintiff, in determining amount it had owed United States for excess costs following termination of original contract, was entitled to credit for the transportation costs saving resulting from fact that successful bidder on substituted contract had plant which was closer to the Army stations to which the cots were transported than was plaintiff's plant. National Wood Products, Inc. v. U.S., Ct.Cl.1956, 146 F.Supp. 451, 137 Ct.Cl. 83. United States ☞ 75(5)

231. Discharge of claim, changes, modifications or adjustments of contracts

Document, entitled contract modification, which provided that contract was amended so that first aid boxes should be fabricated in accordance with drawing which was described in original contract and that delivery date should be extended three months since it had been determined that contractor had been excusably delayed did not constitute a discharge of contractor's claim under changes article of contract for equitable adjustment for alleged re-working of the boxes following prior rejection of them by Navy because they were not watertight. Emerson-Sack-Warner Corp. v. U.S., Ct.Cl.1969, 416 F.2d 1335, 189 Ct.Cl. 264. United States ☞ 70(35)

232. Oral modifications, changes, modifications or adjustments of contracts

A provision in a sales contract between defendant as seller and plaintiff as buyer which provides that any statements by any Government representative modifying or changing any conditions of the contract is an expression of opinion and confers no rights upon the purchaser, is a plain warning to both parties that the rights and obligations under the contract will be governed by the written language rather than oral negotiations which might precede the making of the contract. Commercial Metals Co. v. U.S., Ct.Cl. 1966, 176 Ct.Cl. 343. Sales ☞ 58; United States ☞ 58(5)

Where plaintiffs in 1946 entered into a contract with the Government through the War Assets Administration to protect, preserve, and maintain an ordinance plant which had been deactivated, the contract providing for a fixed fee of $850 per month reflecting five percent of the Government engineers' estimate of $17,000 per month as the over-all cost of performance and after work under the contract had begun plaintiffs were given oral orders by defendant to open and reactivate parts of the facility for active multiple occupancy by tenants leasing from defendant and the additional instructions issued and the additional services and changes or alterations in the services required by the defendant in the reactivation and the servicing of tenants resulted in a material increase in the amount or character of the services rendered by plaintiffs, plaintiffs were entitled to recover additional fees. Stiers v. U.S., Ct.Cl.1951, 121 Ct.Cl. 157. United States ☞ 70(25.1)

When offeror is orally informed of an agency's requirement during negotiation, notwithstanding its absence in solicitation, offeror is on notice of the requirement and General Accounting Office will deny protest based on failure to state it in the solicitation. 1983, 62 Op.Comp.Gen. 50.

233. Price escalation clauses, changes, modifications or adjustments of contracts

Price escalation clause of contract for purchase of tank track shoe assemblies by government required that price escalation be effected in accordance with comparative data derived from indexed prices of specific individual steel commodities specified for use in contract. Firestone Tire & Rubber Co. v. U.S., Ct.Cl.1971, 444 F.2d 547, 195 Ct.Cl. 21. United States ☞ 70(19)

234. Downward adjustment, changes, modifications or adjustments of contracts

The Army was not entitled to equitable adjustment downward of $30,000 in the price of searchlight contract on ground that prime contractor did not, in accordance with contract, perform first-article tests on three xenon lamps, and did not perform initial-production tests on two lamps, where tests were performed at beginning of production process by subcontractor in accordance with requirements of contract and subjection of the lamps to an additional series of first-article and initial-production tests not only would have failed to make "economic sense", but would also have failed to comply with contract requirements. Varo, Inc. v. U.S., Ct.Cl.1977, 548 F.2d 953, 212 Ct.Cl. 432. United States ☞ 72(5)

Government has burden of proving how much of downward equitable adjustment in price should be made on account of deletion of item from contract. Nager Elec. Co. v. U.S., Ct.Cl.1971, 442 F.2d 936, 194 Ct.Cl. 835. United States ☞ 74(10)

Where government ordered and received units of needed groin armor when it had no right to them under terms of original contract, and government, until filing of contractor's suit in Court of

Claims, did not question agreed price for the additional units government had no ground for counterclaim seeking downward price adjustment even if, by such order, contractor was spared some loss attributable to its misunderstanding of original contract. Martin Lane Co. v. U.S., Ct.Cl.1970, 432 F.2d 1013, 193 Ct. Cl. 203. United States ☞ 75(5)

Even if adjustment provision of government contract were intended to entitle United States to decrease in contract price only in event of decreased costs to contractor, contractor's operating losses had no necessary bearing on right to adjustment, as they could be product of inefficiency or improvident bid. Rice v. U.S., Ct.Cl.1970, 428 F.2d 1311, 192 Ct. Cl. 903. United States ☞ 74(11)

235. Amount of adjustment, changes, modifications or adjustments of contracts

Contractor was entitled to equitable adjustment in amount of extra costs associated with supplying concrete retainers instead of polystyrene retainers, in government contract for construction of vehicle maintenance facility, where government demanded that contractor use concrete retainers, in violation of choice provided in contract, and contractor used lower costs associated with polystyrene retainers in its bid for that contract. Medlin Const. Group, Ltd. v. Harvey, C.A.Fed.2006, 449 F.3d 1195. United States ☞ 70(26)

Government contractor, seeking equitable allowance, was not entitled to recover at least the sum which contracting officer awarded it as a contracting officer's allowance where such allowance was merely an offer which contractor rejected by its appeal. Fruehauf Corp. v. U.S., Ct.Cl. 1978, 587 F.2d 486, 218 Ct.Cl. 456. United States ☞ 73(9)

Plaintiff contractor was entitled to equitable adjustment in contract price relative to construction of earthen dam across creek sufficient to reimburse him for difference between what it actually cost him to do the work and what it would have cost him if unforeseen condition, the unavailability of water in natural basin for construction purposes had not been encountered. Briscoe v. U.S., Ct.Cl. 1971, 442 F.2d 953, 194 Ct.Cl. 866. United States ☞ 70(22.1)

Ascertainment of damages, or of equitable adjustment, is not exact science and where responsibility for damage is clear, it is not essential that amount thereof be ascertainable with absolute exactness or mathematical precision; it is enough that the evidence adduced is sufficient to enable court or jury to make fair and reasonable approximation. Electronic & Missile Facilities, Inc. v. U.S., Ct.Cl.1969, 416 F.2d 1345, 189 Ct.Cl. 237. Damages ☞ 6; United States ☞ 70(20)

Equitable adjustment allowable as result of changed condition is difference between what it cost contractor to do work and what it would have cost if unforeseen conditions had not been encountered. Paul Hardeman, Inc. v. U.S., Ct. Cl.1969, 406 F.2d 1357, 186 Ct.Cl. 743. United States ☞ 70(22.1)

Use of "total cost" method in computing prime contractor's losses on subcontracts occasioned by government caused delays was improper, where exact amount of excess costs incurred were subject to precise computation. J.D. Hedin Const. Co. v. U.S., Ct.Cl.1965, 347 F.2d 235, 171 Ct.Cl. 70. United States ☞ 73(21)

Upon determination that claimed delays were not attributable to government but that there had been contract change requiring equitable adjustment of contract price, Court of Claims must determine amount which would represent reasonable recovery of such losses as might be attributed to change. Kings Electronics Co. v. U.S., Ct.Cl.1965, 341 F.2d 632, 169 Ct.Cl. 433. United States ☞ 74(13)

Absent a fixed agreed price for portion of work covered by a lump-sum contract and subsequently eliminated from the project, proper measure of an equitable adjustment in the contract for the reduction of work is reasonable cost of performing the work, which is presumptively determined by a contractor's actual cost; bid pricing calculations, while useful in some instances in showing a contractor's own predispute estimate of actual cost, cannot be relied on when they vary widely from only estimates of actual cost in evidence. General Ry. Signal Co. v. Washington Metropolitan Area Transit Authority, D.C.D.C.1984, 598 F.Supp. 595.

Even if the government has caused an unreasonable delay to contract work, that delay will not be compensable if the contractor, or some other factor not chargeable to the government, has caused a delay concurrent with the government-caused delay. George Sollitt Const. Co. v. U.S., Fed.Cl.2005, 64 Fed.Cl. 229. United States ☞ 73(20)

Bilateral modification of government contract amended original contract which called for contractor to perform separate clearinghouse and database services by eliminating database project and selecting particular pricing rates for clearinghouse project, precluding contractor's claim for equitable adjustment based on contention that government breached contract by not paying at higher rate reflected in contractor's proposed pricing for performing either service. Cygnus Corp. v. U.S., Fed.Cl.2004, 63 Fed.Cl. 150, affirmed 177 Fed.Appx. 86, 2006 WL 1049326. United States ☞ 72(5)

In seeking to recover damages for overrun costs incurred because of alleged Government caused delays in plaintiff's contract work, plaintiff's "total time" method of estimating damages is unacceptable where it takes the original and extended completion dates, computes therefrom the intervening time or overrun, points to a host of individual delay incidents for which defendant was allegedly responsible and which allegedly contributed to the overall extended time, and concludes therefrom that the entire overrun time was attributable to defendant; such proof of delay is ordinarily as unsatisfactory as the "total cost" method of proving damages, and is no less susceptible to inaccuracies than the total cost theory. Law v. U.S., Ct.Cl.1971, 195 Ct. Cl. 370. United States ☞ 74(11)

A contractor suing for damages for breach of his right to an equitable adjustment for extra costs incurred as the result of an alleged constructive change in the contract specifications, must show that the alleged change actually damaged him in some degree even though the precise amount of damages may not be initially litigated. Midwest Spray & Coating Co. v. U.S., Ct.Cl.1966, 176 Ct.Cl. 1331. United States ☞ 74(10)

While ordinarily a contractor who incurs extra costs due to idle equipment during delays caused by the Government is entitled to damages measured by the fair rental value of such equipment, reduced by 50% [to reflect absence of ordi-nary wear and tear], in the absence of proof of a fair rental value which is appropriate for the particular contractor, depreciation should be used. H.R. Henderson & Co., Inc. v. U.S., Ct.Cl. 1965, 169 Ct.Cl. 228. United States ☞ 74(14)

Where on July 27, 1943, plaintiff, an experienced contractor, entered into a unit price contract with the Government, through the Army Corps of Engineers, whereby the plaintiff agreed to furnish the materials and perform the work for clearing, grading, and paving of four additional runways at an Army airfield in Georgia, in accordance with the specifications and drawings, and, being the low bidder, was awarded the contract on the basis of bid unit prices applied to the quantity of work done and the materials furnished and its claim for additional compensation in the amount of $125,545.72 for increased costs, plaintiff was entitled to recover $68,853.19. Mac-Dougald Const. Co. v. U.S., Ct.Cl.1952, 122 Ct.Cl. 210. United States ☞ 70(22.1)

Where the responsibility for excess costs is clearly established, and where the fact that plaintiff sustained damages is also clearly established, and where the amount of damages actually sustained by plaintiff is sufficiently proved, it is immaterial that each item making up the total excess cost is not proved with absolute accuracy. Hirsch v. U.S., Ct.Cl.1941, 94 Ct.Cl. 602. Courts ☞ 464(5)

236. Time of determining claim, changes, modifications or adjustments of contracts

Navy was in no way excused with respect to inordinate delay in handling government contractor's claim for equitable adjustment in contract price merely because the administrator originally handling matter left Navy employment shortly after filing of claim without informing anyone about the claim's pendency. Manpower, Inc. of Tidewater v. U.S., Ct. Cl.1975, 513 F.2d 1396, 206 Ct.Cl. 726. United States ☞ 73(13)

237. Time of issuance of change order, changes, modifications or adjustments of contracts

Where a Changes article of a Government construction contract authorized the making of changes "at any time or times," the timing of the issuance of a change order after the portion of the work involved has already been commenced and which may require redoing of the work, does not constitute a compensable breach of contract, where the contractor has been adequately compensated for the change which covers all resulting costs. Law v. U.S., Ct.Cl.1971, 195 Ct.Cl. 370. United States ⇒ 70(34)

238. Notice of changed condition, changes, modifications or adjustments of contracts

Contractor was not entitled to reimbursement for cost overrun incurred in the performance of a contract between it and the Department of Housing and Urban Development, where it failed to give notice as required by a limitation of cost clause which had been modified by imposition of an absolute ceiling on costs. National Civil Service League v. U.S., Ct. Cl.1981, 643 F.2d 768, 226 Ct.Cl. 478. United States ⇒ 70(36)

Contractor's failure to give prompt written notice of alleged changed condition as required by contract did not defeat claim where both contracting officer and board of contract appeals considered claim on merits without any point being made as to lack of notice. Blount Bros. Corp. v. U.S., Ct.Cl.1970, 424 F.2d 1074, 191 Ct.Cl. 784. United States ⇒ 74(8)

Lack of notice by contractor to government as required by contracts was no defense to proceeding on contractor's claim for equitable adjustment for additional costs in view of consideration of the claim on the merits by contracting officer and armed services board of contract appeals without any point being made as to lack of notice or protest. Dittmore-Freimuth Corp. v. U.S., Ct.Cl. 1968, 390 F.2d 664, 182 Ct.Cl. 507. United States ⇒ 74(8)

239. Necessity of raising issue, changes, modifications or adjustments of contracts

On record, change in contract specifications suggested by composite group consisting of industry members and government members, was not a change by governmental order, and in view also of contractor's opportunity to point out and claim additional compensation for any changes and fact that contractor did not raise claim before presentation to Armed Services Board of Contract Appeals, contractor was not entitled to extra compensation for change. Singer Co. Librascope Div. v. U.S., Ct.Cl.1977, 568 F.2d 695, 215 Ct.Cl. 281. United States ⇒ 70(25.1); United States ⇒ 70(36)

Where no protest in writing stating basis of landscape contractor's objection to inspector's requirements regarding planting was submitted either to inspector or contracting officer as required by contract, contractor could not recover amount of increased costs occasioned thereby even if work was outside contract requirements. Stafford v. U.S., Ct.Cl. 1947, 74 F.Supp. 155, 109 Ct.Cl. 479. Contracts ⇒ 232(1); United States ⇒ 70(36)

240. Waiver, changes, modifications or adjustments of contracts

Where work was done by government contractor without notice to contracting officer that contractor considered effort involved to be extra-contractual, failure to protest was evidentiary consideration which, under circumstances, was controlling, and whether contractor ultimately accepted government's interpretation as correct or whether contractor deliberately waived its right to assert claim under changes article of contract, contractor's right to press claim was extinguished. Singer Co. Librascope Div. v. U.S., Ct.Cl. 1977, 568 F.2d 695, 215 Ct.Cl. 281. United States ⇒ 70(36)

Where Government and contractor's meeting which resulted in modification of agreement to build "shock-hard" boilers took place after contractor had incurred costs which it subsequently claimed under "change clause" in contract, and contractor continued to incur costs until Government reneged on modification agreement several months later, contractor had not waived right to equitable adjustment under "change clause" by failing to assert claim within 30 days after meeting. Foster Wheeler Corp. v. U.S., Ct.Cl.1975, 513 F.2d 588, 206 Ct.Cl. 533. United States ⇒ 70(36)

Where the contracting officer receives and considers a claim under the "Changes" article of the contract without raising the issue of lack of protest or the timeliness of the asserting of the claim or the lack of a written order, and where the article provides that the contracting officer may receive and act upon such claim at any time prior to final payment, defendant may not, on suit in Court of Claims [now United States Court of Federal

Claims] defend on the ground that formal protest was not made at an earlier date. Fox Valley Engineering, Inc. v. U.S., Ct. Cl.1960, 151 Ct.Cl. 228. United States ⬡ 74(8)

241. Administrative findings, changes, modifications or adjustments of contracts

Contracting officer of department of army had no duty to make detailed findings of fact in denying plaintiff contractor's claim for upward equitable adjustment, and plaintiff was not entitled to mandamus to compel such findings. R.E.D.M. Corp. v. Lo Secco, S.D.N.Y. 1968, 291 F.Supp. 53, affirmed 412 F.2d 303. Mandamus ⬡ 101; United States ⬡ 73(13)

242. Admissions, changes, modifications or adjustments of contracts

Under government contract requiring piles to be driven to practical refusal at boring elevations indicating rock, with provision for adjustment in case of piling overrun or underrun, contracting officer's advice to contractor establishing new criteria for practical refusal was not an admission of changed condition within changed conditions article. Blount Bros. Corp. v. U.S., Ct.Cl.1970, 424 F.2d 1074, 191 Ct.Cl. 784. United States ⬡ 70(28)

VI.   BREACH OR TERMINATION OF CONTRACTS

Subdivision Index

Reasonableness, delay in performance 280
Refusal to accept work   299
Refusal to perform, default termination 315
Requirements contracts   300
Specifications, errors in   301
Strikes, delay in performance   287
Substantial performance   272
Threat of termination   318
Uncertainty of termination   302
Unforeseeable causes, delay in performance   283
Waiver, default termination   316
War conditions, delay in performance 288
Warranties   276
Worksite availability, delay in performance   289

---

271. Breach or termination of contracts generally

If the Government terminates a contract without justification, such termination is a breach of contract. Dale Const. Co. v. U.S., Ct.Cl.1964, 168 Ct.Cl. 692. United States ☞ 73(24)

272. Substantial performance, breach or termination of contracts

Where government issued request for proposals in which it stated it did not have the drawings and specifications and which contained general description which led to catalog which described switch that could come in variety of voltages and contractor issued proposal that clearly stated that contractor would furnish 28 volts direct current switches and government accepted the proposal, contractor was in substantial compliance with terms of bid specifications and contracts, and government wrongfully terminated contracts on ground that proposal called for 115 volts alternating current switches. Gorn Corp. v. U.S., Ct.Cl.1970, 424 F.2d 588, 191 Ct.Cl. 560. United States ☞ 72.1(2)

Where housing project was 99.6 per cent complete on completion date and only work remaining to be done would not have interfered with occupancy of houses by tenants, refusal of United States to accept project and assessment of liquidated damages was unjustified, and contractor was entitled to recover amount of liquidated damages assessed by Government. Continental Ill. Nat. Bank & Trust Co. v. U.S., Ct.Cl.1952, 101

F.Supp. 755, 121 Ct.Cl. 203, certiorari denied 72 S.Ct. 1057, 343 U.S. 963, 96 L.Ed. 1361.   Damages ☞ 85

273. Material breach, breach or termination of contracts

Government's handling of checks for two progress payments was not such material breach of levee repair contract with Corps of Engineers that plaintiff was justified in ending agreement, since government acted on oral instructions received from office of bankruptcy trustee of plaintiff's joint venturer, and letters which government sent to referees in bankruptcy and to trustee showed that Corps did not anticipate that trustee would refuse to permit proceeds of two checks to be used by plaintiff in performance of contract or to return them to the government. Allan Const. Co., Inc. v. U.S., Ct.Cl.1981, 646 F.2d 487, 227 Ct.Cl. 193.   Levees And Flood Control ☞ 18

Failure of contractor to deliver drawings and specifications and operation and maintenance manuals before hardware was delivered and installed did not constitute substantial impairment or material breach of whole contract with United States Postal Service, and thus, Service could not treat whole contract as broken and should have continued to perform its obligations under contract, reserving any claims for actual damages for later settlement. Burroughs Corp. v. U.S., Ct.Cl. 1980, 634 F.2d 516, 225 Ct.Cl. 63.   United States ☞ 73(22)

274. Cure of nonconformities, breach or termination of contracts

Right to cure nonconformities under government contract assumes that defects are of nature susceptible to correction within reasonable time. Astro Science Corp. v. U.S., Ct.Cl.1973, 471 F.2d 624, 200 Ct.Cl. 354.   United States ☞ 72.1(2)

275. Acts of God, breach or termination of contracts

Neither party to contract is responsible to other for damages caused by act of God, where contract is silent as to allocation of loss to one or other party. Tombigbee Constructors v. U.S., Ct.Cl.1970, 420 F.2d 1037, 190 Ct.Cl. 615.   Contracts ☞ 303(3)

Where housing authority hired contractor to disassemble, move and reassemble prefabricated houses and contractual provision that contractor should be liable for any loss, breakage or other damage did not mention acts of God, but provision dealing with liability for delay specifically excepted from those delays for which contractor would be liable, delays caused by "acts of God," contractor was liable for damages caused by hurricane. Blair v. U.S., C.C.A.5 (Ala.) 1947, 164 F.2d 115, certiorari denied 68 S.Ct. 910, 333 U.S. 880, 92 L.Ed. 1155, rehearing denied 68 S.Ct. 1336, 334 U.S. 830, 92 L.Ed. 1758. United States ☞ 73(22)

276. Breach of warranty, breach or termination of contracts

While the Government, in issuing a contract drawing upon which were listed the names of government-approved sources of supply, warranted that the listed suppliers had the ability to do the work contemplated by the contract, the Government did not thereby also warrant their willingness to do such work and within the time period contemplated by the contract; accordingly, no breach of contract could be imputed to the Government simply because the manufacturers that it listed as approved sources of supply declined to undertake the work for which they had been found qualified. Franklin E. Penny Co. v. U.S., Ct.Cl.1975, 524 F.2d 668, 207 Ct.Cl. 842. United States ☞ 73(22)

Financing arrangement whereby, instead of contracting to have post office facility constructed for it as owner, government assigned its option to purchase land to plaintiffs' assignor as low bidder, in return for which latter was to construct a building on premises and rent same to government for an initial period of 30 years, did not alter government's choices of method of construction and, where plans submitted by government proved inadequate, in that severe settlement occurred due to lack of pilings in maneuvering area, implied warranty that plans would be sufficient was breached, entitling plaintiffs to reimbursement for cost of repairs. Poorvu v. U.S., Ct.Cl. 1970, 420 F.2d 993, 190 Ct.Cl. 640. United States ☞ 70(29)

Under contract for manufacture of radio transmitters whereby the government agreed to furnish microfilm and warranted its use for making of prints, evidence supported finding that microfilm was so defective as to prevent print making, constituting breach of warranty and entitling contractor to monetary relief for extra expenses incurred because of such breach. Thompson Ramo Wooldridge Inc. v. U.S., Ct.Cl.1966, 361 F.2d 222, 175 Ct.Cl. 527. United States ☞ 74(11)

Where evidence established that primary cause of delays encountered in construction of hospital facility resulted from government's faulty specifications, contractor was entitled to recover delay damages as result of government's breach of its implied warranty that satisfactory performance would result if government's specifications were complied with. J.D. Hedin Const. Co. v. U.S., Ct.Cl.1965, 347 F.2d 235, 171 Ct.Cl. 70. United States ☞ 73(20)

Where after resale by plaintiffs of a large number of gauges, complaints were received from purchasers that the gauges had proved to be inaccurate and gauges were all finally offered for sale on an "as is" basis, the total receipts for all gauges sold being $76,727.44 and the plaintiffs sued for the difference between that amount and $140,000, which they alleged would have been the market value had the gauges been satisfactory, claiming a breach of warranty on the part of the defendant, the plaintiffs were not entitled to recover. Handler Motor Co. v. U.S., Ct.Cl.1952, 121 Ct.Cl. 845. United States ☞ 58(4)

277. Delay in performance, breach or termination of contracts—Generally

Where contract with Government for installation of plumbing, heating, and electrical equipment in veterans' hospital to be erected provided for liquidated damages for failure to complete work by time principal contract had been completed, and contractor was absolved from payment of liquidated damages for delay if it resulted from several causes including "acts of Government", and Government reserved right to make changes which might interrupt the work, and Government changed site and altered specifications because of unexpected discovery of unsuitable soil condition, and extended time of performance and waived any claim to liquidated damages, the delay in commencing construction did not constitute a "breach of contract" by the Government so as to entitle contractor to recover from Government damages due to such delay. U.S. v. Rice, U.S.1942, 63 S.Ct. 120, 317 U.S. 61, 87 L.Ed. 53. United States ☞ 74(3)

Contracting officer's decision to grant contractor extension of time for completion of contract does not raise rebuttable presumption that government caused the delay. England v. Sherman R. Smoot Corp., C.A.Fed.2004, 388 F.3d 844. United States ☞ 73(20)

Government, which had contracted for the assembly of military rations whose components were to be furnished by government, breached its contract in requiring contractor to delay for over a month in the assembly of rations for which the contractor had on hand the prescribed food components. Mulholland v. U.S., Ct.Cl.1966, 361 F.2d 237, 175 Ct.Cl. 832. United States ☞ 73(22)

Contractor could not recover from United States on ground that Government caused delay in performance of construction contract, unless contractor proved delay caused by Government employees, that such delay constituted breach, and that damage to contractor resulted. Metropolitan Paving Co. v. U.S., Ct.Cl.1963, 325 F.2d 241, 163 Ct.Cl. 420. United States ☞ 74(10)

Where the defendant is liable to plaintiff for unreasonable delays, plaintiff is entitled to recover the expense of supervision during such idle time. Cornell Wrecking Co. v. U.S., Ct.Cl.1968, 184 Ct. Cl. 289. United States ☞ 73(21)

In the exercise of its reserved right to make changes, the Government is permitted, without incurring damages, to hold up the project a reasonable period of time to consider the changes it desires to make, and where the change order is required as the result of the Government's breaching its implied obligation to provide workable specifications, delay damages for the breach will not be limited or reduced by allowing the Government a reasonable time for making the change. Ithaca Gun Co., Inc. v. U.S., Ct.Cl.1966, 176 Ct.Cl. 437. United States ☞ 73(21)

278. —— **Consent of parties, delay in performance, breach or termination of contracts**

Although contract for sale of property by the Department of Housing and Urban Development specifically provided that time was of the essence, purchaser could not claim breach of the contract to recover damages accruing during two extensions where such extensions were a result of mutual consent between the parties. Pinewood Realty Ltd. Partnership v. U.S., Ct.Cl.1980, 617 F.2d 211, 223 Ct.Cl. 98. United States ☞ 70(34)

279. —— **Disclosure of information, delay in performance, breach or termination of contracts**

Where the United States has information about conditions which may delay contract performance, not reasonably available to the contractor, it is under a duty to divulge such information or pay damages, under its implied duty not to do anything to delay contract performance. Broome Const., Inc. v. U.S., Ct.Cl.1974, 492 F.2d 829, 203 Ct.Cl. 521. United States ☞ 73(21)

280. —— **Reasonableness, delay in performance, breach or termination of contracts**

Where the record shows that during periods of delay in the contract work the parties were negotiating with reasonable speed and part of the time was being used by the plaintiff-contractor in formulating proposals, and where the delay was not unreasonable under the circumstances, there has been no breach of the contract by defendant. River Const. Corp. v. U.S., Ct.Cl.1962, 159 Ct.Cl. 254. United States ☞ 73(22)

281. —— **Government order, delay in performance, breach or termination of contracts**

A Government contractor engaged in installing a heating system for the post office building at Washington cannot recover damages from the United States, occasioned by delays attributable to the suspension of the work at the Government's request, where the contract expressly provides that no claim shall be made or allowed for any damages which may arise out of any delay caused by the United States,—especially where no protest was made against the suspension, and no claim of right to damages arising therefrom was made until asserted by suit. Wood v. U.S., U.S.1922, 42 S.Ct. 209, 258 U.S. 120, 66 L.Ed. 495.

A Government building contractor, whose contract authorized the United States to suspend the whole or any part of the work, and allowed additional time to the contractor for such suspension, but provided that no claim for damages on account of such delays should be made or allowed, cannot make claims for delays ordered until additional legislation affecting the building was enacted by Congress, especially where the first and longest delay was ordered before the contractor became bound by the approval of his bond. Wells Bros. Co. of New York v. U.S., U.S.1920, 41 S.Ct. 34, 254 U.S. 83, 65 L.Ed. 148. See, also, Poole Engineering & Machine Co. v. U.S., 1922, 57 Ct.Cl. 232. United States ☞ 74(3)

Where construction of postal service facility was intertwined with construction of an office tower and delays caused by change orders relating to the postal facility caused delays in constructing the tower and where the construction of the tower was part of the contract and it was envisioned that rentals from the tower would reduce the rental which the Postal Service would have to pay for its facility, government contractor was entitled to recover increased costs which it incurred in completing the tower, as well as those related to the postal facility, as a result of the changes. Coley Properties Corp. v. U.S., Ct.Cl.1979, 593 F.2d 380, 219 Ct.Cl. 227. United States ☞ 70(25.1)

Construction corporation, which contracted with government to construct air traffic control center, was entitled under suspension of work clause of contract to damages over and above additional costs incurred in effecting change orders with respect to elevation of roof leader drain pipe, location of fire pump drain, and roof washdown system where at least part of contractor's work was delayed by such change orders and delay was caused by defective specifications. Chaney & James Const. Co. v. U.S., Ct.Cl.1970, 421 F.2d 728, 190 Ct.Cl. 699. United States ☞ 70(29)

The lack of express contractual provision exempting Government from liability for delay not contemplated by contract would not justify holding Government liable in damages for increased expenses allegedly caused by delay in giving notice to proceed, in absence of showing that Government had unnecessarily interfered to prevent contractor's work from proceeding within a reasonable time. Stafford v. U.S., Ct.Cl.1947, 74 F.Supp. 155, 109 Ct.Cl. 479. United States ☞ 73(20)

Where the Government improvidently gave a stop order that interrupted contractor's work in Canal Zone on airfield, and later that day the Government revoked the stop order, but native workmen

could not be assembled again for four days, contractor was entitled to recover from the Government the cost of such delay. Froemming Bros. of Tex. v. U.S., Ct.Cl.1947, 70 F.Supp. 126, 108 Ct.Cl. 193. United States ☞ 73(20)

Where contractor (A) was delayed in performance of its work by a stop order on the ground that its work would interfere with certain scheduled installation work of contractor (B) provided for in B's contract but not contained in A's and of which provision A was unaware, and where the provision was included after defendant was assured by B that savings would result by adoption of its recommended sequence of work, such a saving to defendant should not fairly accrue at the expense of A who was equally protected by contrary provisions in its contract, and an unjustified stop order constitutes a breach of contract entitling a contractor to such damages as flow from it. Law v. U.S., Ct.Cl.1971, 195 Ct.Cl. 370. United States ☞ 73(20)

Where the specifications are defective and the Government unduly delays in giving permission to perform the work in the only way it could reasonably have been performed, it is liable to plaintiff for the expense caused by the delay and by the increased difficulties encountered because of the delay. WRB Corp. v. U.S., Ct.Cl.1968, 183 Ct.Cl. 409. United States ☞ 70(30); United States ☞ 74(14)

Where the contract expressly provides that the Government will give notice to proceed within a certain number of days after the date of award to the contractor and the Government gives such notice but also includes therein a notice of suspension of the contract work, there is a breach of an express covenant of the contract and plaintiff is entitled to recover damages representing the increased cost of performance resulting from the ensuing delays. A.S. Schulman Elec. Co. v. U.S., Ct.Cl.1959, 145 Ct.Cl. 399. United States ☞ 70(24); United States ☞ 73(22)

Where plaintiff entered into a contract with the Government to construct certain buildings within a stipulated period of time, and where plaintiff was, after beginning operations, ordered by the defendant to suspend work on account of litigation concerning the site, to which the Government had not acquired title prior to letting the contract, and where plaintiff was put to extra expenses on account of the delay, plaintiff is entitled to recover, as for a breach of contract. Fred R. Comb Co. v. U.S., Ct.Cl.1945, 103 Ct.Cl. 174. Contracts ☞ 313(2); United States ☞ 73(24)

Where, in pursuance to the Government's economy program, orders were given to the plaintiffs by the Government to discontinue work on a building with a view to the possible elimination of said building from the project, and work was accordingly stopped for 116 days, but ultimately, by order of Government, work on said building was resumed and completed, the delay so caused was not the fault of the contractor and plaintiffs were entitled to recover the actual and necessary costs thereby incurred. Herbert M. Baruch Corporation v. U.S., Ct.Cl.1941, 93 Ct.Cl. 107. Contracts ☞ 299(2); United States ☞ 73(20)

282. —— Fault or causation, delay in performance, breach or termination of contracts

The government is responsible to contractors working on government projects only for damages proved to be attributable to government's delay. United Contractors v. U.S., Ct.Cl.1966, 368 F.2d 585, 177 Ct.Cl. 151. United States ☞ 73(21)

Where government caused delays resulting in breaches of contract force contractor into more costly operations, government will have to respond in damages for resulting additional delays. J.D. Hedin Const. Co. v. U.S., Ct.Cl.1965, 347 F.2d 235, 171 Ct.Cl. 70. United States ☞ 73(20)

Government is responsible to contractor for damages for additional costs incurred because of unnecessary delay caused by Government. Helene Curtis Industries, Inc. v. U.S., Ct.Cl.1963, 312 F.2d 774, 160 Ct.Cl. 437. United States ☞ 70(24)

Contract and negotiations whereunder Government undertook only to conduct negotiations for utility owner's removal of facilities as prelude to contractor's work did not impose on Government, which diligently attempted to secure removal, liability to contractor for delay caused by owner's delayed performance. Maxwell v. U.S., Ct.Cl.1962, 297 F.2d 554, 156 Ct.Cl. 72. United States ☞ 70(12.1)

Fault of Government in causing delay in completion of Government contract is requisite to Government's liability for consequences of delay, and absent fault or negligence there is no liability. William A. Smith Contracting Co. of Mo. v. U.S., Ct.Cl.1961, 292 F.2d 847, 155 Ct.Cl. 1. United States ☞ 73(20)

A contractor on a Government project may not recover against the United States for the delays in completing the contract which were not attributable to the fault or misconduct of the Government. Northwestern Engineering Co. v. U.S., C.C.A.8 (S.D.) 1946, 154 F.2d 793. United States ☞ 73(20)

Where delay in compliance with contract was considerably and materially contributed to by inaction of government in failing timely to answer inquiry with respect to stock numbers and specifications and default on contract was due to inability of manufacturer timely to produce articles in question rather than to any financial inability on part of contractor and government refused request for continuances, fault or delay in completion could not be attributed to contractor or to manufacturer but instead fell on government. Meinberg v. U.S., W.D.Mo. 1969, 310 F.Supp. 86. United States ☞ 73(20)

In proceeding on petition by contractor for use and benefit of subcontractor and sureties on completion and performance bonds alleging Government's breach of contract for military airport construction project, evidence established that any delay caused subcontractor in commencing work because of absence of grading stakes was caused by subcontractor's surveyor in completing his check of Government's surveying team's results, and not by Government's delay in setting grading stakes. Hargrave v. U.S., Ct.Cl.1955, 130 F.Supp. 598, 132 Ct.Cl. 73. United States ☞ 74.2

Contractor on project to renovate naval training center was not entitled to award of delay-related extended overhead costs for Phase I of project, where delay was concurrently caused by contractor and the Navy, and it could not be apportioned with any certainty. George Sollitt Const. Co. v. U.S., Fed.Cl.2005, 64 Fed.Cl. 229. United States ☞ 73(21)

Genuine issue of material fact as to whether contacting agency actually caused some or all of the alleged delays precluded summary judgment on government contractor's claim for delay damages under the Eichleay formula. Orlosky Inc. v. U.S., Fed.Cl.2005, 64 Fed.Cl. 63. Federal Courts ⟊ 1120

Where a contractor is delayed by the delay in arrival of equipment to be furnished by the Government under contract with a third party, the Government itself is to be considered responsible for the delay even though it chose to operate through a third-party contractor. Law v. U.S., Ct.Cl.1971, 195 Ct.Cl. 370. United States ⟊ 73(20)

The Government cannot be held liable in damages for delay in completion of the original work called for by a construction contract, unless the Government abused its privilege to make changes or otherwise unreasonably delayed the prosecution of the work in such a way and under such circumstances as to constitute a breach of some express or implied provision of the contract. Magoba Const. Co. v. U.S., Ct.Cl.1943, 99 Ct.Cl. 662. Contracts ⟊ 299(2); United States ⟊ 73(20)

Where contractor is delayed in the completion of the work by the defendant, and put to extra expense, the rule is well settled that the Government is liable. G. Schwartz & Co. v. U.S., Ct.Cl.1939, 89 Ct.Cl. 82. Contracts ⟊ 300(3); United States ⟊ 70(34)

Where contractor, without fault on his part, is delayed by failure of Government to have other work completed in contract time, and time for completion was extended a corresponding number of days, Government is liable for actual damages sustained by contractor by reason of delays. H.E. Crook Co. v. U.S., Ct.Cl.1924, 59 Ct.Cl. 348. Damages ⟊ 124(1)

283. —— Unforeseeable causes, delay in performance, breach or termination of contracts

Purchaser of apartment building from Department of Housing and Urban Development was not entitled to recover, for breach of contract, any damages on account of delays in closing the contract resulting from circumstances beyond control of the parties even though purchaser conditioned acceptance of extension of the closing date on express reservation of rights for damages. Pinewood Realty Ltd. Partnership v. U.S., Ct.Cl. 1980, 617 F.2d 211, 223 Ct.Cl. 98. United States ⟊ 74(14)

Under sustainable findings of Army Corps of Engineers Board of Contract Appeals it was practically certain at time of plaintiff's bid for relocation of several miles of railroad line and highway as part of dam project that plaintiff would encounter spillage caused by blasting of rock and earth under another party's contract for relocation of some of the highway and hence plaintiff could not recover from the United States for delay or "impact" costs necessitated by the spillage. Donald M. Drake Co. v. U.S., Ct.Cl.1971, 439 F.2d 169, 194 Ct.Cl. 549. United States ⟊ 70(34)

Under provision of public contract relating to excusable causes of delay and declaring that contractor "shall not be * * * charged with resulting damage if: (1) The delay * * * arises from * * * delays of subcontractors * * * arising from unforeseeable causes beyond the control and without the fault or negligence of both the contractor and such subcontractors * * *," contractor was entitled to be excused for delay arising from unforeseeable causes beyond fault or negligence of contractor and subcontractor with which contractor was in privity of contract, even though delay lay was not from unforeseeable causes beyond control and without fault of subsubcontractor with which contractor was not in privity of contract. Schweigert, Inc. v. U.S., Ct.Cl.1967, 388 F.2d 697, 181 Ct.Cl. 1184. United States ⟊ 73(26)

Under contract for construction of buildings on army post on unit price basis providing that contractor should visit site before making proposal, and permitting additions only in event of changed conditions promptly called to attention of contracting officer, posting of signs at important intersections to warn that troop movements had right of way there and elsewhere on post did not constitute unforeseeable traffic regulations justifying claim for additional compensation as result of delays caused by trucks waiting on troop movements. Hallman v. U.S., Ct.Cl.1948, 80 F.Supp. 370, 112 Ct.Cl. 170. United States ⟊ 70(24)

Difficulties with reference to the dyeing and weaving of Army blankets were not "unforeseeable difficulties" to a contractor, manufacturer, who knew that the work was new to it, and would have to be started with the help of experts. Lebanon Woolen Mills v. U.S., Ct.Cl.1943, 99 Ct.Cl. 318. Sales ⟊ 172; United States ⟊ 73(6)

Where, in accordance with a contract with the Government, plaintiff performed work and completed buildings, but a delay was caused and a revision of plans necessitated by the discovery of unforeseen conditions in connection with the foundations of one of the buildings, the plaintiff was entitled to recover damages caused by such delay. Herbert M. Baruch Corporation v. U.S., Ct.Cl.1941, 93 Ct.Cl. 107.

Delays by subcontractors or suppliers of Government contractors to be regarded as unforeseeable causes beyond the control or without the fault or negligence of the contractor under the standard default provision excusing the prime contractor from performance must be due to causes which could not have been foreseen by either the contractor or the subcontractor or supplier. 1959, 39 Comp. Gen. 343.

284. —— Approval of samples or plans, delay in performance, breach or termination of contracts

Government's unforeseen difficulties in acting on preproduction samples due principally to fact that one of the components was a new device and the government could not be sure that existing test procedures were fully capable of measuring its performance did not excuse government from discharging plain obligation which it imposed upon itself as drafter of contract to approve or reject preproduction samples within stated number of days of submission. Specialty Assembling & Packing Co. v. U.S., Ct.Cl. 1966, 355 F.2d 554, 174 Ct.Cl. 153. United States ☞ 73(20)

Government contractor which utilized for packaging bags certified to pass Government required waterproofing standards was entitled to recover from Government for extra expenses incurred because of Government's 30 day stop order issued because bags were rejected as not sufficiently waterproof, in view of unreasonable duration of stop order due to ambiguity of bag specifications causing uncertainty among Government representatives and failure of Government officials to accept for almost a month a curative suggestion made by contractor. Helene Curtis Industries, Inc. v. U.S., Ct.Cl.1963, 312 F.2d 774, 160 Ct.Cl. 437. United States ☞ 70(34)

Government, in requesting a new estimate or bid for extra work to correct defect in expansion joint anchors for pipeline, rejecting the bid, and then accepting work done retroactively because Government thought the price was too high, did not thereby recognize that expansion joints were properly installed and contractor was not entitled to damages for delays allegedly resulting from Government's failure to accept work promptly after it was completed. Archie & Allan Spiers, Inc. v. U.S., Ct.Cl.1961, 296 F.2d 757, 155 Ct.Cl. 614. United States ☞ 70(28)

Contract provision that failure to inspect and accept or reject supplies should not impose liability on Government for supplies not in accordance with specifications could not absolve Government from liability for delay in notification of rejection of unfitness after inspection was actually made. Cudahy Packing Co. v. U.S., Ct.Cl.1948, 75 F.Supp. 239, 109 Ct. Cl. 833. United States ☞ 73(20)

Where construction contract required Government to furnish models to contractor, meticulosity of architect in passing on models was an insufficient excuse for delay in furnishing models, which resulted in damage to contractor, in absence of contract provision exempting Government from liability for delay. George A. Fuller Co. v. U.S., Ct.Cl.1947, 69 F.Supp. 409, 108 Ct.Cl. 70. Contracts ☞ 300(1); United States ☞ 73(20)

Where plans submitted by contractor for approval of chief architect in connection with construction of auditorium for United States were laid aside without action by associate architect under belief that they were plans he had previously reviewed, delay in project resulting from failure to approve plans within reasonable time was due to fault of United States. U.S. Cas. Co. v. U.S., Ct.Cl.1946, 67 F.Supp. 950, 107 Ct.Cl. 46. Contracts ☞ 299(2); United States ☞ 73(20)

Where a contractor claims that the Government caused delays in the performance of his contract by delaying the approval of submitted shop drawings, the length of time for approval is meaningful only in relation to the effect it had in delaying the project operations, and does not establish ipso facto an unreasonable delay on the part of the Government, and it is the contractor's burden to show where the work was delayed because of tardy approval. Law v. U.S., Ct.Cl.1971, 195 Ct.Cl. 370. United States ☞ 73(20)

Where the shop drawings for doors as originally submitted did not comply with the specifications, and for that reason were not originally approved, but upon plaintiff's insistence were finally approved in order to prevent further delay and the defendant was not responsible for this delay, plaintiff was not entitled to recover. Cauldwell-Wingate Co. v. U.S., Ct.Cl.1947, 109 Ct.Cl. 193. Contracts ☞ 299(2); United States ☞ 73(20)

285. —— **Delivery of material, delay in performance, breach or termination of contracts**

Where Government contract did not require Government to stock-pile lumber, although it was required to provide lumber, and, due to impossibility of keeping all grades and sizes of lumber on hand, Government requested that orders be made ahead of time, and any orders timely made would have been filled, contractor was not entitled to recover from Government on account of delays in work due to contractor's failure to make timely order for lumber and consequent delay in delivery of lumber. A. L. Coupe Const. Co. v. U.S., Ct.Cl.1956, 139 F.Supp. 61, 134 Ct.Cl. 392, certiorari denied 77 S.Ct. 52, 352 U.S. 834, 1 L.Ed.2d 53. United States ☞ 70(34)

Where the United States agreed with building contractor to furnish materials for buildings and represented that materials would be available when needed, and such representation induced contractor to reduce price to amount agreed on, contractor was entitled to recover damages from United States for failure to furnish required materials on time. Torres v. U.S., Ct.Cl.1953, 112 F.Supp. 363, 126 Ct.Cl. 76. United States ☞ 73(20)

Where construction contract required Government to furnish certain material for use by contractor in completion of construction, and Government diligently attempted to procure such material, Government did not breach its contractual obligation, though materials were not procured in time to prevent delay of construction work. Barling v. U.S., Ct.Cl. 1953, 111 F.Supp. 878, 126 Ct.Cl. 34. United States ☞ 73(20)

Where contractor was already delayed as a result of its inability to secure labor, delay of the United States in furnishing drawings for the roughing in of plumbing and in furnishing plumbing and heating material as required by contract caused

contractor no damage, hence, Government was not liable for such delay. J.B. McCrary Co. v. U.S., Ct.Cl.1949, 84 F.Supp. 368, 114 Ct.Cl. 12. United States ☞ 73(20)

The United States was not liable for delay in delivery of materials to contractor due to proper operation of the priority system. Ross Elec. Const. Co. v. U.S., Ct.Cl.1948, 77 F.Supp. 749, 111 Ct.Cl. 644. United States ☞ 73(22)

Unexplained or unjustified failure to make timely delivery of Government-furnished material resulting in delay to the contractor's operations, is a breach of contract. Law v. U.S., Ct.Cl.1971, 195 Ct.Cl. 370. United States ☞ 73(20)

Where a contract to sell tungsten to the Government obligated the seller to deliver the tungsten F.O.B. vessel South American West Coast Port and the Government to designate the vessel on which the tungsten was to be shipped, delivery of a lot of tungsten to the dock before the expiration date of the contract and after issuance of shipping instructions by defendant, was compliance with the delivery provisions of the contract even though the tungsten arrived too late to be loaded on the ship designated and could only be loaded on a ship departing after the expiration date of the contract; however tungsten arriving at the dock and offered for delivery after the expiration date of the contract, was a late delivery which defendant was not obligated to accept. Mauricio Hochschild, S.A. M. I. v. U.S., Ct.Cl.1966, 176 Ct.Cl. 808. Sales ☞ 150(3); United States ☞ 73(6)

286. —— **Inspection time, delay in performance, breach or termination of contracts**

Fact that contractor did not conduct independent subsurface investigation to determine whether government prepared specifications with respect to pilings to be used to support hospital facility were faulty did not preclude contractor from asserting breach of contract claim for delays encountered as result of alleged faulty piling specifications where it was determined that period of time between invitations to bid and opening of bids was insufficient for bidders to make adequate investigation of subsurface conditions. J.D. Hedin Const. Co. v. U.S., Ct.Cl.1965, 347 F.2d 235, 171 Ct.Cl. 70. United States ☞ 74(8)

287. —— Strikes, delay in perform-ance, breach or termination of contracts

Government would not be liable to construction contractor for damages caused by refusal of some workmen to cross picket line. D & L Const. Co. and Associates v. U.S., Ct.Cl.1968, 402 F.2d 990, 185 Ct.Cl. 736. United States ☞ 70(31)

Where government insisted upon using non-union labor on air force base in defiance of demands that only union labor be used, although government knew that strike would almost certainly result, contractor was entitled to equitable adjustment for any delay and additional expense stemming from the strike. Arthur Venneri Co. v. U.S., Ct.Cl.1967, 381 F.2d 748, 180 Ct.Cl. 920. United States ☞ 70(24)

Government was liable to contractor for increased overhead costs resulting from delays caused by strikes to extent that such increased costs were occasioned by government caused delays. J.D. Hedin Const. Co. v. U.S., Ct.Cl.1965, 347 F.2d 235, 171 Ct.Cl. 70. United States ☞ 70(34)

Government contract provision authorizing contracting officer to suspend work on dam-building project for "convenience of the Government" was inapplicable to situation where railroad strike threatened to cut off cement supply, and denial of contractors' request for suspension did not shift burden of additional costs occasioned by strike from contractors to Government. Ozark Dam Constructors v. U.S., Ct.Cl.1961, 288 F.2d 913, 153 Ct.Cl. 120. United States ☞ 70(34)

A strike which is in existence and known to the contracting parties at the time of an award of a Government construction contract which contains a clause excusing performance delays due to unforeseeable causes may not be regarded as an unforeseeable cause to justify an extension of time for performance of the contract. 1959, 39 Comp.Gen. 478.

288. —— War conditions, delay in performance, breach or termination of contracts

Contractor which had dredging contract with the United States was not entitled to recover from the United States because of hardships and difficulties en-countered because contractor was unable to secure repairs and replacements for dredging equipment due to priority systems then in effect because of the war. Guion v. U.S., Ct.Cl.1947, 69 F.Supp. 341, 108 Ct.Cl. 186. Navigable Waters ☞ 6; United States ☞ 73(22)

Contractor constructing decontamination building under contract with Federal Government could not recover damages from Government for delays caused by difficulties in securing materials due to priority system which was in effect during wartime, since Government, in enforcing priority system, was acting in its sovereign capacity. J.J. Kelly Co. v. U.S., Ct.Cl.1947, 69 F.Supp. 117, 107 Ct.Cl. 594. United States ☞ 73(20); War And National Emergency ☞ 10(1)

289. —— Worksite availability, delay in performance, breach or termination of contracts

Where contract for the construction of lighting equipment for airport runways contemplated that the work was to commence as the Government completed construction of the runways, but contract did not contain a warranty on the part of the Government to make the runways promptly available, and the work of constructing runways was performed with diligence but was delayed due to unforeseen causes, the Government was not liable to the contractor for damages caused by delay in completing contract. U.S. v. Howard P. Foley Co., U.S.1946, 67 S.Ct. 154, 329 U.S. 64, 91 L.Ed. 44. Contracts ☞ 300(1); United States ☞ 73(20)

Under circumstances, government's delay of four and one-half months in making part of excavation site available to contractor was unreasonably long, for purpose of determining contractor's claim for damages for delay. Merritt-Chapman & Scott Corp. v. U.S., Ct.Cl. 1971, 439 F.2d 185, 194 Ct.Cl. 461. United States ☞ 73(20)

Whether delay damages are recoverable by contractor from United States is determined by whether the government obligated itself to pay damages to contractor because of delay in making work available. Paul Hardeman, Inc. v. U.S., Ct.Cl.1969, 406 F.2d 1357, 186 Ct.Cl. 743. United States ☞ 74(14)

In action to recover alleged excess costs which plaintiff incurred in completing on time contract with the Government for construction of hydroelectric power plant and adjoining switchyard facilities, plaintiff was required to persuade court that it had been ready and willing to get to work on substructure of the powerhouse and in switchyard and that it had, against its will, been prevented from doing so by uncompleted work of another contractor; and, on record presented, such burden was not sustained, and it was established, to contrary, that plaintiff had had access to its worksite substantially as soon as it wanted it and could make use of it, and that it could not fairly charge Government with delaying its work. E.J. Albrecht Co. v. U.S., Ct.Cl. 1959, 174 F.Supp. 942, 146 Ct.Cl. 299. United States ☞ 74(10); United States ☞ 74(11)

Where United States entered into channel improvement contract providing that land, easements and rights-of-way would be provided by the Government without cost to contractor, United States knew or was chargeable with knowledge that certain realty owners were vigorously disputing right of a levee board of State to appropriate realty and realty owners forcibly caused work stoppage for period of 39½ days, the United States was liable for damages thereby incurred. Delta Equipment & Const. Co. v. U.S., Ct.Cl.1953, 113 F.Supp. 459, 125 Ct.Cl. 632. United States ☞ 73(20)

Where the Government unreasonably delays the plaintiff's contract performance by not making buildings available to plaintiff for demolition within the time provided for in the contract, and where the contract did not contemplate nor excuse the particular delays and no suspension of work clause was included in the contract to permit an administrative adjustment of the contract price for such delays, there has been a breach of contract for which the plaintiff is entitled to recover damages. Cornell Wrecking Co. v. U.S., Ct.Cl.1968, 184 Ct.Cl. 289. United States ☞ 73(20)

In the absence of an express warranty or its own fault, the Government is not liable for failing to make the worksite available to a contractor at a specified time where the delays are due to the work of another contractor. Fort Sill Associates v. U.S., Ct.Cl.1968, 183 Ct.Cl. 301. United States ☞ 73(20)

Where the Government, for the financial and operational convenience of itself and other contractors working on a large single project, delayed making plaintiff's worksite available for many months during which time plaintiff necessarily incurred increased costs and losses, such delays not being beyond the control of defendant or the result of the fault or negligence of the plaintiff, a constructive suspension of plaintiff's work has occurred within the meaning of the standard suspension of work clause of the Government contract. John A. Johnson and Sons, Inc. v. U.S., Ct.Cl.1967, 180 Ct.Cl. 969.

Contractor entitled to recover the excess costs of construction directly resulting from delay of 85 days in the removal of railroad tracks by another contractor, where it was provided in the specifications that the contractor would not be permitted to construct a certain portion of a dam until an existing railroad line, passing through the dam site, was relocated under the contract with said other contractor, and where such delay was due to the acts of the defendant. Rogers v. U.S., Ct.Cl.1943, 99 Ct.Cl. 393. Navigable Waters ☞ 22(2); United States ☞ 70(34)

290. —— Failure to object, delay in performance, breach or termination of contracts

Where plaintiff made no protest to the contracting officer that it was being unreasonably delayed and (except in one instance) made no claim to the contracting officer for any extra cost or unnecessary work or expense not contemplated by its contract, plaintiff was not entitled to recover. Hunter Steel Co. v. U.S., Ct.Cl.1943, 99 Ct.Cl. 692. Contracts ☞ 232(4); United States ☞ 70(36)

291. Demands of government, breach or termination of contracts

Under Government contract for hauling "Lumber (Portable Knocked Down buildings and building material)" and "lumber", Government's demand that panels of knocked down buildings containing no doors or windows be transported as lumber was a breach of the contract. Lundstrom v. U.S., D.C.Or. 1941, 53 F.Supp. 709, affirmed 139 F.2d 792. United States ☞ 73(21)

292. Fraud or misrepresentation, breach or termination of contracts

Mere governmental failure to disclose each and every bit of information it has is not, in and of itself, enough to serve as a basis for contractor recovery. Piasecki Aircraft Corp. v. U.S., Ct.Cl.1981, 667 F.2d 50, 229 Ct.Cl. 208. United States ⊂⇒ 74(1)

Evidence in action against United States to recover for loss sustained on hydrographic survey ship building contract by corporation which acquired successful bidder and entered into novation with Government established that Government did not act fraudulently or in bad faith toward the purchaser with respect to financial disclosures concerning the contract during the period when purchaser was contemplating the shipyard purchase. Aerojet-General Corp. v. U.S., Ct.Cl.1972, 467 F.2d 1293, 199 Ct.Cl. 422. United States ⊂⇒ 74(11)

As government was not possessed of any pertinent information not available to plaintiff, which contracted to construct creek channel, levees and appurtenances, and as plaintiff did not allege that its representatives were in any way directed or urged to rely on alleged consensus with government that waste area would necessitate only 20,000 cubic yards of fill, plaintiff, in support of its claim for damages in connection with extra fill needed, could not reasonably claim it was misled by government's acquiescence in conclusion that only 20,000 yards of fill would be needed. Ace Const. Co. v. U.S., Ct.Cl. 1968, 401 F.2d 816, 185 Ct.Cl. 487. United States ⊂⇒ 70(30)

Where contractor which undertook to install air-conditioning system in post office should have known of necessity of removing and replacing lighting fixtures attached to ductwork, contractor was not misled by government's failure to furnish contractor all knowledge government possessed, nor was contractor damaged thereby. Ambrose-Augusterfer Corp. v. U.S., Ct.Cl.1968, 394 F.2d 536, 184 Ct.Cl. 18. United States ⊂⇒ 74(4)

The language of contract for microfilming obsolete engineering documents for the Air Force and course of conduct between the parties failed to reveal such a misrepresentation or mistake on the government's part as would amount to a breach of contract. Microcord Corp. v. U.S., Ct.Cl.1966, 361 F.2d 1000, 176 Ct. Cl. 46. United States ⊂⇒ 73(22)

Essential prerequisite for recovery on cause of action for breach of contract against government on account of mis-

representation of subsurface conditions by contracting agency was proof that contractor was misled by misrepresentations. T.F. Scholes, Inc. v. U.S., Ct.Cl.1966, 357 F.2d 963, 174 Ct.Cl. 1215. United States ⊂⇒ 74(10)

Where government's acceptance of photographic processing tray sets manufactured by plaintiff was induced by such gross mistake as to amount to fraud, government was not barred from reopening contract under inspection clause providing that final acceptance was not conclusive in case of fraud or such gross mistakes as amount to fraud, and, in view of concession that units failed to meet specifications and evidence establishing that no change of specifications was authorized, contracting officer had authority to determine that plaintiff was obligated to government for purchase price of such units for which payment had been made. Bar Ray Products, Inc. v. U.S., Ct.Cl. 1964, 340 F.2d 343, 167 Ct.Cl. 839. United States ⊂⇒ 72.1(2)

In action against the United States for delays in delivering materials to plaintiff, constituting breach of a contract which provided that all disputes involving questions of fact would be decided by contracting officer, where Government admitted that it failed to consider prefabrication costs in its computation, in absence of a showing what amount prefabrication cost was, court cannot hold that it is such an amount as indicates a mistake so gross as to warrant an inference of fraud. Lindsay v. U.S., C.A.9 (Cal.) 1950, 181 F.2d 582. United States ⊂⇒ 73(14)

That contract price for cleaning regional service center was for cleaning the entire building regardless of its size did not relieve government of its responsibility for misleading contractor in invitation to bid as to what the various components consisted of in view of material effect on cost of contractor's performance by composition of those components. Eastern Service Management Co. v. U.S., D.C.S.C.1965, 243 F.Supp. 302, decision affirmed in part and remanded on other grounds 363 F.2d 729. United States ⊂⇒ 74(4)

Where the contract places upon the contractor the responsibility for locating suitable borrow areas and requires that the contractor secure permission of the contracting officer for the obtaining of any borrow material within the limits of the project site, the gratuitous act of the contracting officer (in response to the contractor's specific request) of suggesting possible borrow areas within the project site limits cannot be characterized as actionable misrepresentation even if the information in the contracting officer's letter was not accurate in all respects regarding the availability of suitable borrow material in one of the areas suggested and since the contract placed on the contractor the duty of locating suitable borrow areas, it could not have been misled by defendant in the preparation of its bid or entering into the contract under these circumstances. WRB Corp. v. U.S., Ct.Cl.1968, 183 Ct.Cl. 409. United States ☞ 70(30)

Plaintiff may not recover for defendant's misrepresentation unless he can show that he was actually misled thereby, and where the damage to plaintiff was caused not by defendant's representations but by plaintiff's own failure to examine pertinent data made available to him by defendant prior to bidding, plaintiff has established no ground for recovery. L.M. Jones Co., Inc. v. U.S., Ct.Cl.1967, 178 Ct.Cl. 636. United States ☞ 74(4)

Where, even if contractor did not have complete knowledge of the facts at the time its bid was submitted but did have complete knowledge before bid was accepted and contract was signed, there can be no recovery on the ground of misrepresentation of conditions by the defendant. Ross Engineering Co. v. U.S., Ct.Cl.1945, 103 Ct.Cl. 185, certiorari denied 66 S.Ct. 45, 326 U.S. 735, 90 L.Ed. 438. United States ☞ 73(1)

Where the Government in the invitation for bids or in specifications makes a misrepresentation of material fact or conceals material facts and information known to it but not available to or known to the bidder, damages by way of excess costs may under the implied terms of the contract be recovered in a suit on the contract. Frazier-Davis Const. Co. v. U.S., Ct.Cl.1943, 100 Ct.Cl. 120. Contracts ☞ 4; United States ☞ 74(12.1)

Where contractor had ample notice and was warned in the specifications to visit the site of the proposed building and inspect the conditions, and where contractor failed to make such visit and inspection before submitting bid, there was no misrepresentation on the part of defendant and the plaintiff was not entitled to recover. Blauner Const. Co. v. U.S., Ct.Cl.1941, 94 Ct.Cl. 503. Contracts ☞ 323(2); United States ☞ 70(30)

293. Interference with performance, breach or termination of contracts

Government contractor was not entitled to maintain claim for breach of contract for United States' alleged interference with work where suspension clause of contract granted necessary remedy under the contract. Hoel-Steffen Const. Co. v. U.S., Ct.Cl.1972, 456 F.2d 760, 197 Ct.Cl. 561. United States ☞ 74(7)

Under facts presented, neither time taken by government to remove its personal property and equipment from premises being sold, i.e., 39 days after date of closing, nor manner of removal or in-place sale of property, constituted a violation of clause in purchase agreement wherein government reserved the right to remove its personal property or to hold sales thereof for a period of 120 days after closing of title, with provision that any such removal or in-place sale would be conducted in such a manner as to cause the least possible interference with successful bidder's use and occupancy of premises. Review Co. v. U.S., Ct.Cl. 1970, 425 F.2d 1227, 192 Ct.Cl. 259. United States ☞ 58(4)

United States is obligated to prevent interference with orderly and reasonable progress of a contractor's work by other contractors over whom government has control. L.L. Hall Const. Co. v. U.S., Ct.Cl.1966, 379 F.2d 559, 177 Ct.Cl. 870. United States ☞ 73(22)

Plaintiff who contracted to construct concrete roadway for government could not recover for government's unwarranted interference with plaintiff's performance even though the government's control of the work was a breach of the contract where plaintiff failed to produce satisfactory proof to enable court to determine, with reasonable accuracy, the extent of claimed losses and delays that were due to the breach of the contract. Roberts v. U.S., Ct.Cl.1966, 357 F.2d 938, 174 Ct.Cl. 940. Highways ☞ 113(4)

The duty resting on Government's engineer to abstain from unnecessarily or unreasonably interfering with contractor's performance of his work on his contract with Government does not preclude exercise of reasonable judgment on engineer's part as to how work should be carried out, whenever contractor may be of opinion that he can employ a different method in discharging his overall obligation under the contract with no additional cost to Government and with some possible saving of expense to himself. First Citizens Bank & Trust Co. v. U.S., Ct.Cl. 1948, 76 F.Supp. 250, 110 Ct.Cl. 280. United States ☞ 73(9); Contracts ☞ 314; United States ☞ 73(17)

It is an implied condition of every Government construction contract that neither party will do anything to hinder the performance of the other. Law v. U.S., Ct.Cl.1971, 195 Ct.Cl. 370. United States ☞ 70(12.1)

Where the Government contracting officer or his representative improperly imposed a non-tolerance standard of construction upon the plaintiff although the contract specifications did not require such perfection and the method used by the contractor was in accordance with accepted trade and industry practices, the Government has breached its implied obligation not to do anything to hinder or prevent the contractor from performing the contract. WRB Corp. v. U.S., Ct.Cl. 1968, 183 Ct.Cl. 409. United States ☞ 73(22)

Where the contractor could not perform his pipe laying work until the Government required its employees to cease parking their cars in the area, the refusal of the Government to have the parked cars removed for a week when the plaintiff was ready to work in the area was a breach of implied obligation not to do anything to hinder, delay or prevent performance for which the Government must respond in damages. Dale Const. Co. v. U.S., Ct.Cl.1964, 168 Ct.Cl. 692.

Where a contract to repair and rehabilitate a central heating plant in a Government building did not specify whether or not the plant would have to be completely shut down for a reasonable period while the repairs were being made, but where certain clauses of the contract and the work requirements clearly contemplated a complete closing of the boiler plant for an appreciable period if the clauses were to be complied with, the Government's refusal to permit such shutdown of the plant was a breach of its implied obligation not to hinder or delay the performance of the other party. W.H. Edwards

Engineering Corp. v. U.S., Ct.Cl.1963, 161 Ct.Cl. 322. United States ☞ 73(22)

For an improper interference with the work of a contractor the Government, like an individual, is liable. Houston Const. Co. v. U.S., Ct.Cl.1903, 38 Ct.Cl. 724. United States ☞ 73(1)

294. Negligence, breach or termination of contracts

Provision in Government contract that contractor shall be responsible for loss to the Government that occurs as result of the contractor's fault or negligence meant the sole fault of the contractor or its agents or employees, and did not include fault of third parties or fault of the Government's own agents or employees. Douglass Bros., Inc. v. U.S., Ct.Cl.1963, 319 F.2d 872, 162 Ct.Cl. 289. United States ☞ 70(17)

Plaintiff's failure to maintain its high voltage power lines on its right-of-way in accordance with the National Electrical Safety Code standards constituted negligence and breach of its contract (i.e. a permit allowing the Government to conduct military maneuvers on said right-of-way), as well as a breach of the license (contract) granting plaintiff its right-of-way. California-Pacific Utilities Co. v. U.S., Ct.Cl.1971, 194 Ct.Cl. 703. United States ☞ 73(22)

295. Nonpayment, breach or termination of contracts

Prolonged failure of United States to pay large amounts due on contract for purchase of helium was a "material breach" of the contract where, at time suit was filed, $8,671,632 was owing to plaintiff corporation. Northern Helex Co. v. U.S., Ct.Cl.1972, 455 F.2d 546, 197 Ct.Cl. 118. United States ☞ 73(16)

Notwithstanding prior practice of government agency, which loaned contractor money and took assignment of proceeds of sales to government, to release most of funds received, agency's failure to release funds did not breach any contract with supplier of materials to contractor. Meriden Industries Co. v. U.S., Ct.Cl.1967, 386 F.2d 885, 181 Ct.Cl. 438. United States ☞ 74.2

Where Government agent's appraisal of building, which Government intended to lease, followed standards then in effect and lease entered into between plaintiff and Government was valid and binding on both parties, plaintiff was entitled to damages for breach of lease by Government amounting to sum of rentals as agreed upon from first day upon which Government refused to pay rent, up to and through date when Government filed declaration of taking in condemnation proceeding. Meyer v. U.S., Ct.Cl.1958, 159 F.Supp. 333, 141 Ct.Cl. 537. United States ☜ 74(13)

Where Government contractor's delays in delivery were entirely excused, and Government recognized that contractor's costs shown on invoice requesting advances were good costs, Government's failure to make partial payments on invoices constituted violation of agreements. U.S. v. Lennox Metal Mfg. Co., E.D.N.Y.1954, 131 F.Supp. 717, affirmed 225 F.2d 302. United States ☜ 73(16)

Where after plaintiffs' offer to purchase the 39 cabinet assemblies had been accepted, the War Assets Administration wrote to plaintiffs that the cabinet assemblies had been sold to another buyer and to this letter, which constituted a breach of the contract by anticipatory repudiation, plaintiffs did not reply and the statement of repudiation was withdrawn by defendant in a subsequent letter before the plaintiffs changed their position in any way and defendant delivered the cabinet assemblies in accordance with their agreement, and plaintiffs accepted them, in the circumstances there was a valid and subsisting contract of sale of the control cabinets by defendant to plaintiffs and plaintiffs are liable to defendant for the agreed price. Zink v. U.S., Ct.Cl. 1952, 123 Ct.Cl. 85. United States ☜ 58(4)

Under an agreement to pay for material, whether used or not, contractor is entitled to recover for material ordered by direction of Government agent but not used where the Government receipted for the material and retained it. James McHugh Sons, Inc., v. U.S., Ct.Cl.1943, 99 Ct.Cl. 414. Sales ☜ 179(1); United States ☜ 70(17)

Failure by the Government to pay an obligation under a valid contract is a breach of the contract for which the Government is liable in damages. Seatrain Lines v. U.S., Ct.Cl.1943, 99 Ct.Cl. 272. Contracts ☜ 312(3); United States ☜ 73(22)

296. Notice to contractor, breach or termination of contracts

Where United States agency in an attempt to comply with terms of contract requiring notices to proceed to be sent to contractors within a certain time sent letter giving notice to proceed but also at the same time invoked section of contract allowing Government to suspend operations, notices constituted breach of the contract and rendered Government liable to contractor for actual damages caused by delay as result of failure of Government to give proper notices to proceed. Abbett Elec. Corp. v. U.S., Ct.Cl.1958, 162 F.Supp. 772, 142 Ct.Cl. 609. United States ☜ 73(20)

For purposes of damages award, government's breach of contract occurred on date contracting agency cancelled solicitation during pendency of contract awardee's appeal of decision of General Services Board of Contract Appeals (GSBCA) holding that contract was void ab initio, notwithstanding government's contention that breach could not have occurred prior or to subsequent date when contracting officer issued notice of termination; contract did not go out of existence merely because of GSBCA's ruling, and cancellation of solicitation was clear indication of government's refusal to perform the contract. Marketing and Management Information, Inc. v. U.S., Fed.Cl.2004, 62 Fed. Cl. 126. United States ☜ 73(24)

Where contractor, having complied with the terms of the contract and having carried the work to a point where it would have been possible to complete it within the time limit, was notified that the funds appropriated for the purpose were exhausted and work would have to be suspended, and work was accordingly suspended, the necessity of such suspension constituted a breach of the contract on the part of the Government. Joplin v. U.S., Ct.Cl.1939, 89 Ct.Cl. 345. Contracts ☜ 313(2); United States ☜ 73(23)

297. Orders of government, breach or termination of contracts

The United States was not liable for breach of contract because of the effect of an executive order of general application issued in exercise of sovereign power of the United States. J.B. McCrary Co. v. U.S., Ct.Cl.1949, 84 F.Supp. 368, 114 Ct. Cl. 12. United States ☜ 73(22)

The Government's unjustified stop order, after accepting contractor's proposal to use different kind of stone in constructing post office, was breach of contract, entitling contractor to damages occasioned by the delay. Brand Inv. Co. v. U.S., Ct.Cl.1944, 58 F.Supp. 749, 102 Ct. Cl. 40, certiorari denied 65 S.Ct. 684, 324 U.S. 850, 89 L.Ed. 1410. Postal Service ⊚ 6; United States ⊚ 73(20)

The orders of the Area Engineer, as contracting officer, requiring plaintiffs to hire additional carpenters, without regard for the excusable delays which had occurred, did not constitute a breach of the contract. Dunnigan Const. Co. v. U.S., Ct.Cl.1952, 122 Ct.Cl. 262. United States ⊚ 73(9)

298. Procurement from non-party, breach or termination of contracts

Defense supply agency's procurement of boxes from General Services Administration amounted to a breach of agency's contracts which obligated agency to order from government contractor all of its requirements of boxes to be purchased, notwithstanding Government's argument that boxes available on shelves of a sister agency, when obtained by requisition, were not "purchased." Inland Container, Inc. v. U.S., Ct.Cl.1975, 512 F.2d 1073, 206 Ct.Cl. 478. United States ⊚ 73(22)

299. Refusal to accept work, breach or termination of contracts

Where it is found that the cracks developed as a direct result of the defendant's faulty design and defendant supervised the original work, its refusal to accept the work was a breach of the contract, entitling plaintiff to recovery of damages. Joseph A. Holpuch Co. v. U.S., Ct.Cl. 1945, 104 Ct.Cl. 58. United States ⊚ 73(22)

300. Requirements contracts, breach or termination of contracts

Government contractor assumed risk of any premature termination of primary source contract which was not for a fixed supply, but rather was a "requirement" contract which could in good faith be terminated as soon as Government's requirements ceased. Kalvar Corp., Inc. v. U.S., Ct.Cl.1976, 543 F.2d 1298, 211 Ct. Cl. 192, certiorari denied 98 S.Ct. 112, 434 U.S. 830, 54 L.Ed.2d 89. United States ⊚ 74(5)

Wording of indefinite delivery requirements type contract for production of technical manuals as a part of program carried out by government with two contractors and actions of parties showed that it was their understanding that government, which plaintiff contractor claimed shortchanged it in assignment of work, had responsibility to make a good faith attempt to assign to plaintiff contractor that part of whole program normally performed at particular army depot, notwithstanding the insertion of a dollar amount of estimated requirements under contract. Franklin Co. v. U.S., Ct. Cl.1967, 381 F.2d 416, 180 Ct.Cl. 666. United States ⊚ 70(6.1)

301. Specifications, errors in, breach or termination of contracts

Although government personnel were chargeable with faulty administration of contract in rejecting negative master mold without actually inspecting it and on basis of conclusion that the mold was necessarily defective because relief mold, which had been cast from the mold, failed to meet the contract specifications, the poor administrative practice of the government could not excuse contractor from complying with the contract by producing within prescribed period, as extended, a negative master mold that met the contract requirements. Panoramic Studios, Inc. v. U.S., Ct.Cl.1969, 413 F.2d 1156, 188 Ct.Cl. 1092. United States ⊚ 73(1)

The government is liable for damages resulting from issuance of faulty or inadequate plans, specifications, or designs or for misleading contractor by erroneous statements contained therein. Allied Contractors, Inc. v. U.S., Ct.Cl.1967, 381 F.2d 995, 180 Ct.Cl. 1057. United States ⊚ 70(29); United States ⊚ 70(30)

Fact that government prepared specifications contained errors with respect to elevations of gravel strata constituted faulty specifications and established predicate to breach of contract claimed by contractor. J.D. Hedin Const. Co. v. U.S., Ct.Cl.1965, 347 F.2d 235, 171 Ct.Cl. 70. United States ⊚ 73(22)

Contractor could not place upon government responsibility for time contractor expended in reaching solution to problem presented by conflicts in drawings and specifications, where contractor, rather than apprising Government of conflicts within reasonable time after discovery, sought to work matters out for itself. Kings Electronics Co. v. U.S., Ct.Cl.1965, 341 F.2d 632, 169 Ct.Cl. 433. United States ☞ 70(30)

Clauses in Government contract for rehabilitation of old existing piers warning bidders not to rely on specifications and to inspect work site and verify all dimensions at site could not be disregarded, and Government contractor could not recover for alleged erroneous contract drawing and alleged delays by Government in taking corrective measures when contractor did not make his own measurements and when delays were occasioned through late delivery of materials. Archie & Allan Spiers, Inc. v. U.S., Ct.Cl. 1961, 296 F.2d 757, 155 Ct.Cl. 614. United States ☞ 70(31)

Faulty contract specifications alone will not necessarily render the Government liable for breach of contract particularly where any delays incurred were occasioned by factors outside the Government's control and not related to the faulty specifications and the mere fact that the Government made changes in the specifications does not prove that they were faulty or that, if faulty, they were the cause of delay and extra expense for the contractor. Remler Co. v. U.S., Ct.Cl. 1967, 179 Ct.Cl. 459, certiorari denied 88 S.Ct. 66, 389 U.S. 840, 19 L.Ed.2d 102. United States ☞ 70(25.1)

Where the contract drawings or plans contain material errors in designating the size of pipes and valves to be replaced so that the materials procured by the contractor were of no use and other materials had to be procured to perform the work, and where the contractor was justified in relying on the representations contained in the specifications and plans which did not contain any caveat regarding the possibility of incorrectness, plaintiff is entitled to recover damages caused by the misrepresentations in the plans. Dale Const. Co. v. U.S., Ct.Cl.1964, 168 Ct.Cl. 692. United States ☞ 70(29)

Where the drawings which the War Assets Administration had furnished to plaintiff showed the course and the length of the distribution system and from these drawings and from an inspection of the ends of cables sticking out of the ground, the location of which was in accord with the drawings, plaintiff was able to compute with reasonable accuracy the amount of pounds of copper it

would be able to secure from the underground cables, but when the cables were exhumed by machinery, it was discovered that the cable underground extended but a few feet from the ends projecting above ground, the balance having been removed, plaintiff's contention that it had been misled was sustained by the court, although the misrepresentation was not intentional. Industrial Salvage Corp. v. U.S., Ct.Cl.1952, 122 Ct.Cl. 611. United States ☞ 66

302. Uncertainty of termination, breach or termination of contracts

Uncertainty in July 1965 and thereafter as to whether government contract would be terminated respecting relief model did not constitute any justification for contractor's failure to proceed with work on projection slide set in response to contracting officer's specific advice of July 7, 1965 that contractor should continue with such work, particularly in view of fact that prior to April 29, 1966, the termination date, five of the separate items under the contract had been produced by contractor and had been inspected, accepted, and paid for by the government. Panoramic Studios, Inc. v. U.S., Ct.Cl. 1969, 413 F.2d 1156, 188 Ct.Cl. 1092. United States ☞ 73(1)

303. Miscellaneous breaches, breach or termination of contracts

Although United States did specify requirement that contractor use certain equipment in order to qualify for contract award, where this was not a matter of whim or caprice on its part and where fact that United States had insisted upon certain machines, in lieu of accepting contractor's choice of equipment, was apparently not a matter of much concern to contractor at time it was seeking contract award, fact that machines which contractor purchased did not perform adequately would not excuse nonperformance of contract for delivery and manufacture of artillery shell components. A.B.G. Instrument & Engineering, Inc. v. U.S., Ct. Cl.1979, 593 F.2d 394, 219 Ct.Cl. 381. United States ☞ 73(1)

Where, after nuclear detonation, a period was required to determine that island and facilities were safe from radiation, and, as a consequence, there was no barge transportation in October, no breach of contract could be based on United States' failure to load and return in October prime contractor's remaining equipment on island. B-E-C-K Constructors v. U.S., Ct.Cl.1978, 571 F.2d 25, 215 Ct.Cl. 793. United States ☞ 73(22)

Where contract between International Cooperation Administration and predecessor of plaintiff for development of Korean handicraft industry provided a provisional overhead rate of 65% of base salaries, and rate was to be revised at end of each of fiscal years, and revision was to reimburse plaintiff for actual overhead costs determined on basis of such annual or other audits as Administration might make, but United States did no auditing until more than one year after performance had been completed by plaintiff, United States violated its contractual duty. Scherr & McDermott, Inc. v. U.S., Ct.Cl.1966, 360 F.2d 966, 175 Ct.Cl. 440. United States ☞ 73(22)

Where supplier contracted with United States to supply axles, and supplier informed United States where some of axles could be found, Government's failure to purchase axles because the same had been sold to supplier's president rather than to supplier itself, was unreasonable. U.S. v. Elliott Truck Parts, Inc., E.D.Mich.1957, 149 F.Supp. 52, affirmed 261 F.2d 835. Damages ☞ 62(4)

Where United States contracted to take and pay for 80,000 tons of scrap iron and there was no reservation of power to cancel contract and no complaint was made concerning performance by seller, cancellation of contract by United States on ground that the British Purchasing Commission had advised that they were withdrawing from the present scrap market and had requested that the United States cancel undelivered balances of all scrap contracts was wrongful and entitled seller to damages as to undelivered 26,570 tons under the contract. David J. Joseph Co. v. U.S., Ct.Cl.1949, 82 F.Supp. 345, 113 Ct.Cl. 3. United States ☞ 72.1(2)

304. Cure of breach, breach or termination of contracts

Failure to furnish property the government promised to furnish would sometimes be remediable under the contract and therefore would not always be a breach. Allied Materials & Equipment Co., Inc. v. U.S., Ct.Cl.1978, 569 F.2d 562, 215 Ct.Cl. 406. United States ☞ 73(22)

Where contract entered into between steel manufacturer and Department of Labor called for filling of job slots with manufacturer by training of an average of 48 hard-core unemployed individuals per week, and further provided for reimbursement to manufacturer of specified amount for each day worked by such individuals, and such contract provided that the furnishing of recruits was to be joint responsibility of manufacturer and state agencies, and not Department of Labor, Department of Labor, which provided referrals at the rate of 80 per week, resulting in 47.5 trainees per week selected by manufacturer, did not breach such contract by failing to furnish manufacturer with 48 trainees per week, and even if Department of Labor had breached original contract, subsequent extension of time for performance of contract, resulting in additional compensation to manufacturer, cured such alleged breach. U.S. Steel Corp. v. U.S., Ct.Cl.1976, 536 F.2d 921, 210 Ct.Cl. 228. United States ☞ 73(25)

Affirmative wrongful action or failure of United States to discharge its obligation under government contract may not be cured simply by waiving liquidated damages. L.L. Hall Const. Co. v. U.S., Ct.Cl.1966, 379 F.2d 559, 177 Ct.Cl. 870. United States ☞ 74(6)

305. Constructive termination, breach or termination of contracts

Doctrine of constructive termination, pursuant to which government may defend against a breach of contract claim on ground there existed a legal excuse for nonperformance unknown to the government at time of alleged breach, was not applicable to suspension of timber sale contracts by the Forest Service, since Forest Service did not breach the contracts by attempting to terminate; moreover, Forest Service was aware it had legal right to terminate contracts under contract clause, and chose not to exercise that right. Scott Timber Co. v. U.S., Fed. Cl.2005, 64 Fed.Cl. 130, reconsideration denied 65 Fed.Cl. 131. United States ☞ 73(24)

306. Convenience termination, breach or termination of contracts

Increase in estimated cost of asbestos removal portion of demolition contract from 10% of total cost of contract, or $40,000, to just under 50% of total contract, or $320,000, constituted change of circumstances sufficient to justify terminating contract for government's convenience under Competition in Contracting Act, where contract had no clause which would have accounted for additional cost of asbestos removal. Krygoski Const. Co., Inc. v. U.S., C.A.Fed.1996, 94 F.3d 1537, rehearing denied, in banc suggestion declined, certiorari denied 117 S.Ct. 1691, 520 U.S. 1210, 137 L.Ed.2d 819. United States ☞ 72.1(2)

Prime contract amendment which changed basic specifications of vehicle to be furnished by contractor and which provided that ceiling cost did not include costs relative to inventory made obsolete by amendment or include costs relative to subcontract cancellations necessitated by amendment but which did not contain standard termination for convenience clause was a sub silentio incorporation by reference of federal procurement regulations relating to termination of contracts. Universal Fiberglass Corp. v. U.S., Ct.Cl. 1976, 537 F.2d 400, 210 Ct.Cl. 220. United States ☞ 72(5)

Convenience-termination clause in a government contract is designed to provide a mechanism whereby the government may end its obligation on the contract and yet limit its liability to the contractor's costs and profits on the preparations made and work done. Colonial Metals Co. v. U.S., Ct.Cl.1974, 494 F.2d 1355, 204 Ct.Cl. 320. United States ☞ 72.1(2)

Factual situations do not always demand exclusive use of either termination for convenience or changes clause to exclusion of other. Nager Elec. Co. v. U.S., Ct.Cl.1971, 442 F.2d 936, 194 Ct.Cl. 835. United States ☞ 72(1.1); United States ☞ 72.1(1)

Provision in Government contract authorizing "termination for convenience" of Government does not authorize cancellation which violates contract. G.L. Christian and Associates v. U.S., Ct.Cl. 1963, 320 F.2d 345, 160 Ct.Cl. 58. United States ☞ 72.1(2)

Where decision to terminate contract "for the convenience of the government" was result of agency's conclusion that no valid grounds for debarment could be found, court would not allow government to hide behind the cloak of conclusory terms such as "convenience" and "responsibility" to justify its actions. Art-

Metal-USA, Inc. v. Solomon, D.C.D.C. 1978, 473 F.Supp. 1. United States ☞ 72.1(2)

Contractor failed to establish by clear and convincing evidence that government's termination of contract for convenience was in bad faith because it was based on gender discrimination; contractor offered only speculative and uncorroborated allegations of its female president that she was treated unprofessionally at kick-off meeting by male government employee who was chief administrator of contract because of her gender, and that same employee forced her to hire a male as co-principal investigator on project to keep the contract. Rice Systems, Inc. v. U.S., Fed.Cl.2004, 62 Fed.Cl. 608. United States ☞ 74(11)

307. Default termination, breach or termination of contracts—Generally

If contracting officer does not decide to terminate contractor for default within reasonable time, any new delivery schedule unilaterally set by contracting officer must be reasonable. Burroughs Corp. v. U.S., Ct.Cl.1980, 634 F.2d 516, 225 Ct.Cl. 63. Public Contracts ☞ 16

Whether default of federal contractor is excusable is most often a question of fact. Marley v. U.S., Ct.Cl.1970, 423 F.2d 324, 191 Ct.Cl. 205. United States ☞ 74(7)

Default terminations—as a species of forfeiture—are to be strictly construed. DeVito v. U.S., Ct.Cl.1969, 413 F.2d 1147, 188 Ct.Cl. 979. United States ☞ 72.1(1)

308. —— Assurances, default termination, breach or termination of contracts

Contract for construction of campground in national forest was justifiably terminated for default where, despite a 10-day cure notice demanding that work be resumed so as to ensure project's completion before expiration of total contractual time remaining, no more than piddling construction activities were begun at campground, and contractor not only failed to assure Government that completion deadline would be met, but even failed to undertake any substantial work thereafter. Discount Co. v. U.S., Ct.Cl.1977, 554 F.2d 435, 213 Ct.Cl. 567, certiorari denied 98 S.Ct. 428, 434 U.S. 938, 54 L.Ed.2d 298. United States ☞ 72.1(2)

Upon failure of contractor not only to assure attempts to perform or secure performance in delivering requested gyro motors but also to reply to naval ordnance plant's warning letter inquiring about performance, plant was justified in terminating contract for default even though plant could have terminated contract previously, contract could have been reissued to purported assignee by novation or otherwise and plant knew that contractor had not been maintaining any manufacturing facility but had been relying exclusively on purported assignee. U.S. v. Russell Elec. Co., S.D.N.Y.1965, 250 F.Supp. 2.   United States ☞ 72.1(3)

309. —— Conversion to convenience termination, default termination, breach or termination of contracts

In proceeding on claim that default termination of contract should be converted to termination for convenience of the government, record supported conclusion that the government had not so interfered with performance so as to entitle contractor to additional time in which to submit acceptable first articles. Piasecki Aircraft Corp. v. U.S., Ct.Cl.1981, 667 F.2d 50, 229 Ct.Cl. 208. United States ☞ 74(11)

Where contract was improperly terminated for default and contract for delivery of preproduction communications system model contained a termination for convenience of government clause, wrongful termination for default would be treated by courts as if contract had been terminated for convenience of the government. International Tel. & Tel. Corp., ITT Defense Communication Division v. U.S., Ct.Cl.1975, 509 F.2d 541, 206 Ct.Cl. 37. United States ☞ 72.1(6)

Termination for default clause in government contract did not, by incorporating clause for termination for convenience of government or otherwise, convert an improper default termination into one for which an administrative remedy was provided under disputes clause. Vann v. U.S., Ct.Cl.1970, 420 F.2d 968, 190 Ct.Cl. 546. United States ☞ 73(9)

Where subcontractor was equally at fault in events leading to termination of subcontract under which it was to design, manufacture, test and deliver 250 cooling systems to be incorporated into electronic countermeasure pods prime contractor was producing for the United States Air Force, failure of prime contractor to sea-

sonably deliver final source control drawings, which constituted material breach of subcontract and failure of condition precedent to prime contractor's right to require counterperformance by subcontractor, did not entitle subcontractor to have its termination converted to one for convenience so as to entitle it to recover its costs. Westinghouse Elec. Corp. v. Garrett Corp., D.C.Md.1977, 437 F.Supp. 1301, affirmed 601 F.2d 155. Contracts ☞ 274

Portions of work under government contract for modernization of hydroelectric power plant were not severable, and thus default termination could not be converted to one of convenience with respect to one portion of the contract; considering interdependent nature of the several tasks, and the unified purpose of which they were a part, contract was not divisible. Aptus Co. v. U.S., Fed.Cl.2004, 62 Fed.Cl. 808. United States ☞ 72.1(6)

310. —— Equitable adjustments, default termination, breach or termination of contracts

Contractor's failure to seek equitable adjustment was required to be considered in determining whether, within meaning of exculpatory provision in standard default clause of government contract, contractor's ability to proceed was frustrated by financial hardship resulting from any underpayments by government. Johnson v. U.S., Ct.Cl.1980, 618 F.2d 751, 223 Ct.Cl. 210. United States ☞ 70(35)

311. —— Fault or negligence, default termination, breach or termination of contracts

Contractor's inability to continue work, as result of financial incapacity caused by government's wrongful failure to make progress payments falls within the scope of exculpatory provision of standard default clause in government contract forbidding involuntary termination if contractor's delay in completion is caused by circumstances that are beyond his control and not the product of his own fault or negligence. Johnson v. U.S., Ct.Cl.1980, 618 F.2d 751, 223 Ct.Cl. 210. United States ☞ 70(35)

Under contract for design, manufacture, and delivery of cooling systems to be incorporated into electronic countermeasure pods which prime contractor was producing for United States Air Force, burden was on prime contractor who had terminated subcontract to show that subcontractor was responsible for default so that contractor could recover amount paid in excess of subcontract price to procure cooling system after termination of subcontractor. Westinghouse Elec. Corp. v. Garrett Corp., C.A.4 (Md.) 1979, 601 F.2d 155. Contracts ⬦ 322(1)

Where government had not unilaterally established new contract completion date and contractor had not officially tendered delivery of preproduction model of communications system, government's termination of contract for default was improper. International Tel. & Tel. Corp., ITT Defense Communication Division v. U.S., Ct.Cl.1975, 509 F.2d 541, 206 Ct.Cl. 37. United States ⬦ 72.1(2)

Death of officer of government contractor in September, 1966, could not be held to have been the sole proximate cause of contractor's failure to perform, where officer had agreed in letter of December, 1965 to transfer realty and machinery to contractor at beginning of new year but failed to do so, and where, while it might have been preferable had a personal guarantee of performance by the official been requested by the United States, absence of guarantee was not a matter beyond control and without the fault or negligence of contractor within meaning of the "Default" clause since it could have been executed by the parties on their own initiative and without an invitation from the United States. National Eastern Corp. v. U.S., Ct.Cl.1973, 477 F.2d 1347, 201 Ct.Cl. 776. United States ⬦ 74(4)

Where a contractor's delay in delivering items contracted for by the Government is not the fault of the Government but is due to the contractor's own acts and mistakes, the Government is not at fault in terminating the contract for default. Lester Bros., Inc. v. U.S., Ct.Cl. 1960, 151 Ct.Cl. 536. United States ⬦ 73(24)

312. ——— **Fraud, default termination, breach or termination of contracts**

Government contractor's fraud with respect to one change order on contract for construction of animal disease research facility was sufficient to taint entire contract so as to warrant termination of contract by default. Joseph Morton Co., Inc. v. U.S., C.A.Fed.1985, 757 F.2d 1273. United States ⬦ 72.1(2)

313. ——— **Nondelivery, default termination, breach or termination of contracts**

Where contractor fails to comply with government contract delivery schedule, contract may be terminated, pursuant to default clause, except where government has waived contract delivery schedules or where contractor has tendered supplies which substantially comply with contract requirements. Churchill Chemical Corp. v. U.S., Ct.Cl.1979, 602 F.2d 358, 221 Ct.Cl. 284. United States ⬦ 72.1(2)

Where United States refused to accept certain lots of defective military uniform shirts from the beginning, after last date for delivery had passed, 19,040, shirts due under contract were undelivered and the manufacturer did not respond to the contracting officer's ten-day ultimatum of November 27, 1968, United States did not waive its right to terminate the contract for default by waiting until January 2, 1969, to issue the default. Doyle Shirt Mfg. Corp. v. U.S., Ct.Cl.1972, 462 F.2d 1150, 199 Ct.Cl. 150. United States ⬦ 72.1(3)

Where the dates set for delivery of each installment of goods by contractor fell on Saturdays but the Form of Bid, which was a part of the contract, gave notice that the Government depot where the goods were to be delivered would not be open on Saturdays or Sundays and that no deliveries would be accepted there on those days, the contractor was not in default in his deliveries until the Mondays following the Saturdays on which deliveries would have been due but for this notice, and the number of days of default for each delivery is computed from Monday, rather than from Saturday. Lebanon Woolen Mills v. U.S., Ct.Cl.1943, 99 Ct.Cl. 318. Sales ⬦ 170; United States ⬦ 73(26)

314. ——— **Progress, default termination, breach or termination of contracts**

Where there was no reliance by contractor on United States' alleged waiver of contract delivery schedule, and where default termination was not for failure to deliver but for failure to make satisfactory progress so as to endanger the delivery of quantities remaining to be shipped, United States could terminate for default, despite claim that it had waived delivery schedule and at time of termination, no other enforceable delivery schedule was in existence. A.B.G. Instrument & Engineering, Inc. v. U.S., Ct.Cl.1979, 593 F.2d 394, 219 Ct.Cl. 381. United States ⊆ 72.1(3)

That time for completion of contract to construct a campground in a national forest had not as yet run was insufficient to preclude termination of contract for default where a demonstrated lack of diligence on part of contractor indicated that Government could not be assured of timely completion and, under contract provisions, default termination was appropriate in event of a demonstrated lack of diligence. Discount Co., Inc. v. U.S., Ct.Cl.1977, 554 F.2d 435, 213 Ct.Cl. 567, certiorari denied 98 S.Ct. 428, 434 U.S. 938, 54 L.Ed.2d 298. United States ⊆ 72.1(2)

Government contractor's lack of production, inadequate financial condition, failure to employ an adequate labor force and failure to manufacture any vehicle under new specifications justified Government's termination of contract for failure to make progress. Universal Fiberglass Corp. v. U.S., Ct.Cl.1976, 537 F.2d 393, 210 Ct.Cl. 206. United States ⊆ 72.1(2)

Proportion of total contract value allocated by contractor to a contract line item (CLIN) provided a valid estimation of the amount of progress attributable to the completion of the CLIN, and thus provided a valid method of measuring contractor's overall progress toward completion of government contract for modernization of hydroelectric power plant. Aptus Co. v. U.S., Fed.Cl.2004, 62 Fed.Cl. 808. United States ⊆ 73(1)

Contracting officer for United States Navy reasonably determined that contractor hired to build electrical testing devices for refurbished electrical generators on ships would not deliver complying devices by due date specified in contract or at any time thereafter and, therefore, could default terminate contract before its completion date for failure to make progress, even though contractor had nearly completed performance; devices built by contractor were so large as to be untransportable, and contractor's response to Navy's cure notice indicated that it was unable or unwilling to comply with size requirement. Hannon Elec. Co. v. U.S., Fed.Cl.1994, 31 Fed.Cl. 135, affirmed 52 F.3d 343. United States ⊆ 72.1(2)

315. ⸺ **Refusal to perform, default termination, breach or termination of contracts**

Government contractor's obligation to provide "16 man-months level of effort" did not require the contractor to employ 16 different individuals, but such language referred to performance level, and thus contractor could not be found to have defaulted on basis that he failed to employ 16 different technicians to perform contract for calibration, preventive maintenance and repair of test, measuring, and diagnostic equipment at government sites located in foreign country. International Electronics Corp. v. U.S., Ct.Cl.1981, 646 F.2d 496, 227 Ct.Cl. 208. United States ⊆ 70(6.1)

Termination of government tile installation contract for default was proper where contractor refused to follow contracting officer's directive to remove and replace tile floor and instead elected to abandon work and refuse to proceed with removal and replacement of floor except at government expense and by method of installation specified by government. Stoeckert v. U.S., Ct.Cl.1968, 391 F.2d 639, 183 Ct.Cl. 152. United States ⊆ 72.1(2)

Contracting officer of General Services Administration was reasonable in interpreting message from successful bidder stating that authorization was received too late to comply with terms and conditions on invitation to bid as refusal to perform rather than as offer to perform at time later than that specified in invitation and government's termination of contract was lawful. National Movers Co. v. U.S., Ct.Cl.1967, 386 F.2d 999, 181 Ct.Cl. 419. United States ⊆ 64.50

Termination of contract with the Department of Army to replace and repair portions of existing retaining wall at water supply facility in Germany for default was justified; contracting officers testified that because of contractor's repeated delays extending over two years, inability or unwillingness to protect the work site from flooding damage, and unwillingness to continue work on other areas of the project after the Army issued the partial suspension, they felt justifiably insecure whether contractor would complete the project either by contract deadline or date to which contractor sought an extension, and contractor proffered no record evidence to show it could have completed project by contract deadline. Bender GmbH v. Brownlee, C.A.Fed.2004, 106 Fed.Appx. 728, 2004 WL 1799402, Unreported. United States ☞ 73(24)

316. —— Waiver, default termination, breach or termination of contracts

Conduct of government when, instead of terminating contractor for default for failure to deliver a conforming system on delivery date, it sent contractor a letter stating that it was not waiving any rights under contract and that liquidated damages would be assessed against contractor until project was completed did not operate to preclude the government from exercising its right to terminate contract for default until a new delivery date had been set in absence of evidence that contractor was denied right to make an informed decision to continue or to terminate. Olson Plumbing & Heating Co. v. U.S., Ct.Cl.1979, 602 F.2d 950, 221 Ct.Cl. 197. United States ☞ 72.1(3)

Letter from contracting officer asking government contractor to submit revised delivery schedule constituted waiver of default for nondelivery and an implied waiver of default for failure to make progress. Universal Fiberglass Corp. v. U.S., Ct.Cl.1976, 537 F.2d 393, 210 Ct.Cl. 206. United States ☞ 73(3)

Where show cause letter was issued by procurement contracting officer immediately on contractor's failure to deliver television transmitters on delivery date of October 29, 1969, and all that occurred during period between passage of delivery date and issuance of default notice on November 18 were contractor's efforts to obtain FCC approval and testing of transmitters to show compliance with contract specifications, and tests regarding compliance with the more stringent contract requirements were never successful, Government did not waive the delivery date of October 29 so as to lose its right to terminate for default. Pelliccia v. U.S., Ct.Cl.1975, 525 F.2d 1035, 208 Ct.Cl. 278. United States ☞ 73(3)

In a waiver after breach situation, time may again become essential to a contract and the government may regain the right to terminate a delinquent contractor for default if (1) the government unilaterally issues a notice under the contractor's default clause establishing a reasonable and specific time for performance on pain of default termination or (2) the parties bilaterally agree upon a new delivery date.

International Tel. & Tel. Corp., ITT Defense Communication Division v. U.S., Ct.Cl.1975, 509 F.2d 541, 206 Ct.Cl. 37. United States ☞ 72.1(5)

Language of agreement between seller of helium and United States was evidence that seller could continue to deliver helium without waiving government's breach, where agreement provided "No waiver by either party for any one or more defaults by the other in the performance of any provisions of this contract shall operate or be construed as a waiver of any future default or defaults, whether of a like or of a different character.", which indicated that even an express waiver would be limited, and would operate only as to the particular defaults mentioned. Northern Helex Co. v. U.S., Ct.Cl.1972, 455 F.2d 546, 197 Ct.Cl. 118. United States ☞ 74(6)

317. —— Miscellaneous default terminations, breach or termination of contracts

That the Government never took the further step of unilaterally ordering contractor to use the alternative site designated by it for use of contractor in completing its contract for construction of a campground in a national forest was not such as to justify a failure on part of contractor to make progress on campground work, a failure that led to termination of a contract for default, notwithstanding whether designation of an alternative borrow site was merely a government proposal or a fully operative and effective change order, where contractor not only knew that new site was available, but was aware, or should have known, that it could have protected its right to an equitable adjustment by simply saying so. Discount Co., Inc. v. U. S., Ct.Cl.1977, 554 F.2d 435, 213 Ct.Cl. 567, certiorari denied 98 S.Ct. 428, 434 U.S. 938, 54 L.Ed.2d 298. United States ☞ 72.1(2)

318. Threat of termination, breach or termination of contracts

Where armed services contracting officer believed that two to three-month extension was reasonable, specific time for performance of fixed price supply contract and where there was no evidence to contradict such belief, he acted well within scope of his responsibility in threatening termination and listing contractor on contractor experience list. Simmonds

Precision Products, Inc. v. U.S., Ct.Cl. 1976, 546 F.2d 886, 212 Ct.Cl. 305. United States ☞ 72.1(2)

Even if government contract officer, in course of hard bargaining with contractors who were behind schedule, bluntly made threat of termination of contract, such action, absent more, was not improper where officer had already written several letters to contractors threatening termination for default. Johnson, Drake & Piper, Inc. v. U.S., Ct.Cl.1976, 531 F.2d 1037, 209 Ct.Cl. 313. United States ☞ 74(5)

319. Notice of termination, breach or termination of contracts

The government, which terminated contract for sale and removal of smokeless gunpowder after expiration of second extension period of the contract, was not required to give notice contemplated in provision of the contract governing posttermination rights to seek storage and resale charges against contractor in event contractor failed to remove the powder pursuant to removal schedule of the contract. Petrofsky v. U.S., Ct.Cl.1980, 616 F.2d 494, 222 Ct.Cl. 450, certiorari denied 101 S.Ct. 1488, 450 U.S. 968, 67 L.Ed.2d 618. United States ☞ 72.1(5)

Notice given to contractor under MA–4 jobs contract by government was insufficient to work partial default termination where it was not preceded by ten-day cure letter required by contract and was insufficient under applicable procurement regulations; evidence failed to support contention that parties had agreed to bilateral modification of contract, and notice therefore gave rise to partial termination of contract for convenience of government, thus permitting recovery by contractor in accordance with contract terms relating to such terminations. Kisco Co., Inc. v. U.S., Ct.Cl.1979, 610 F.2d 742, 221 Ct.Cl. 806. United States ☞ 72.1(5)

Under contract which provided for termination by the United States by notice upon breach by contractor and for liability of contractor in amount of excess cost occasioned Government by such breach, the United States could recover increased cost of construction where there was refusal even to begin the work, notwithstanding lack of notice of termination. Conti v. U.S., C.C.A.1 (Mass.) 1946, 158 F.2d 581. United States ☞ 70(20)

Where notice actually sent fulfilled requisites of show cause notice under default termination clause and termination itself was likewise sufficient, prime contractor's default termination of subcontract was not procedurally improper nor was such termination rendered improper because prime contractor decided to fabricate cooling systems for prime contract electronic countermeasure pods for the Air Force in-house, and to procure some from another subcontractor, prior to termination. Westinghouse Elec. Corp. v. Garrett Corp., D.C.Md.1977, 437 F.Supp. 1301, affirmed 601 F.2d 155. Contracts ☞ 267; Contracts ☞ 271

Notification given by Government to Government contractor that contract was "terminated" when contractor fell behind schedule constituted only a poorly expressed election by the Government of its alternative of terminating contractor's rights and assigning another to finish the jobs, and did not bring to an end Government's claim under liquidated damages provision of contract. U.S. v. Continental Cas. Co., S.D.N.Y.1962, 210 F.Supp. 433. United States ☞ 72.1(6)

Where plaintiff contracted with United States to supply rock and gravel in such quantities and at such times as ordered, order placed under such contract was subject to cancellation to whatever extent it had not been acted upon by plaintiff at time notice of cancellation was given by United States. Ready-Mix Concrete Co. v. U.S., Ct.Cl.1958, 158 F.Supp. 571, 141 Ct.Cl. 168. United States ☞ 72.1(1)

VII.   ACTIONS FOR BREACH

Subdivision Index

---

341. Actions for breach generally

When the Government contracts, it divests itself of its sovereign character as to the particular transaction, and assumes that of an ordinary citizen, and therefore cannot recede from its obligations. Cooke v. U.S., U.S.N.Y.1875, 91 U.S. 389, 1 Otto 389, 23 L.Ed. 237. See, also, England Nat. Bank v. U.S., C.C.A.Ark. 1922, 282 F. 121; Lyons v. U.S., 1895, 30 Ct.Cl. 352; Jones v. U.S., 1865, 1 Ct.Cl. 28, 2 Ct.Cl. 605; Gilbert v. U.S., 1863, 1 Ct.Cl. 28, 2 Ct.Cl. 550, affirmed 75 U.S. 358, 8 Wall. 358, 19 L.Ed. 303; Simonsen v. Barth, 1922, 208 P. 938, 64 Mont. 95.

If acts of United States taken in relationship to contract as such cause a loss, it is subject to same liability as any private contracting party in same situation. Shedd-Bartush Foods of Ill. v. Commodity Credit Corp., N.D.Ill.1955, 135 F.Supp. 78, affirmed 231 F.2d 555. United States ⊂⊃ 74(3)

342. Elements of action, actions for breach

Plaintiff's burden in breach of contract case is to demonstrate its willingness and ability to perform. National Movers Co. v. U.S., Ct.Cl.1967, 386 F.2d 999, 181 Ct.Cl. 419. Contracts ⊂⊃ 348

In actions brought upon contracts, plaintiff must shoulder the burden of establishing the fundamental facts of liability, causation and resultant injury relating to claim for which he seeks recovery, and such requirement applies with equal efficacy to counterclaims brought by the government. Roberts v. U.S., Ct.Cl.1966, 357 F.2d 938, 174 Ct.Cl. 940. United States ⊂⊃ 74(10); United States ⊂⊃ 75(4)

In order to recover damages for breach of contract where the defendant's resident engineer wrongfully attempted to impose unauthorized requirements on the plaintiff in connection with the contract work, the plaintiff must show that it actually sustained some injury from defendant's error and where the plaintiff successfully protested the imposition of the unauthorized requirements and the delays encountered during this process were compensated, plaintiff has failed to prove that it sustained any further injury from defendant's error. WRB Corp. v. U.S., Ct.Cl.1968, 183 Ct.Cl. 409. United States ☞ 74(10); United States ☞ 74(11)

343. Implied contract liability, actions for breach—Generally

Telephone company could not recover under alleged implied contract for installation of large telephone switchboard for war use, where installation was covered by written contract with Secretary of Treasury. Chesapeake & Potomac Telephone Co. v. U.S., U.S.1930, 50 S.Ct. 343, 281 U.S. 385, 74 L.Ed. 921. United States ☞ 69(4)

Implication of a contract that the United States would pay for B.'s implements, which must be the basis of its liability under Fifth Amendment, is rebutted, and its liability, if any, is in tort, for which it has not consented to be sued, where on annulment of contract with H. for public works, and making of contract with W. for completion thereof, it at request of W., knowing of B.'s claim of ownership of implements on the grounds, but not conceding B.'s title, took them under a clause in its contract with H., and turned them over to W., crediting their value on its contract with H., and advising W. that the United States would not, under any circumstances, be held liable for the seizure. Ball Engineering Co. v. J.G. White & Co., U.S.Conn.1919, 39 S.Ct. 393, 250 U.S. 46, 63 L.Ed. 835. United States ☞ 69(3)

Under government contract obligating government to order certain minimum quantities of generators and obligating manufacturer to deliver quantities in excess thereof if government, at its option, should order them within the 18-month contract period, government orders mailed before expiration of the 18-month period but received by manufacturer after the expiration of that period were not a valid exercise of option, and manufacturer which furnished generators in accordance with those invalid orders at insistence of government was entitled to the reasonable value thereof rather than the contract price. Dynamics Corp. of America v. U.S., Ct.Cl.1968, 389 F.2d 424, 182 Ct.Cl. 62. United States ☞ 70(27)

Even though contract be unenforceable against United States because not properly advertised, not authorized, or for some other reason, it is only just that Government pay for goods delivered or services rendered and accepted, and in limited fact situations courts will grant relief of quasi-contractual nature when Government rescinds invalid contract. Prestex Inc. v. U.S., Ct.Cl.1963, 320 F.2d 367, 162 Ct.Cl. 620. United States ☞ 69(7)

If an officer of the United States takes the property of a private person for public use without compensation, he is liable in tort for the trespass, although the Government may also be liable on an implied contract. O'Reilly De Camara v. Brooke, S.D.N.Y.1905, 135 F. 384. United States ☞ 50

Where Government wrongfully rejected automatic packing machine made for it by manufacturer when Government was unable to procure the proper type of corrugated paper necessary to be used in machine, and manufacturer thereafter expended certain sums of money in attempting to reconstruct the machine to use paper that was available to the Government, manufacturer could not recover the amount of such expenditures from the Government on ground of an implied contract. Standard-Knapp Corp. v. U.S., Ct.Cl.1947, 70 F.Supp. 132, 108 Ct.Cl. 270. Sales ☞ 33; United States ☞ 69(6)

Where goods have been actually sold and delivered for the use and benefit of our Government, an action may be maintained for the value thereof, though the contract under which they were delivered was irregular or void. Belt's Ex'x v. U.S., Ct.Cl.1879, 15 Ct.Cl. 92. United States ☞ 74(7)

Where the proper officers of the Government receive services or property under a contract made by one who was not an authorized agent of the Government, and they use it for a lawful purpose, so that the Government derives a legal benefit therefrom, the contractor may recover the actual value of the property sold or service rendered. Reeside v. U.S., Ct.Cl.

1866, 2 Ct.Cl. 1, affirmed 7 Ct.Cl. 82, 19 L.Ed. 391.

344. —— Quantum meruit, implied contract liability, actions for breach

If and to extent that Corps of Engineers breached levee repair contract, plaintiff, which decided to continue work, believing and hoping that it might recoup its losses by seeking recovery on quantum meruit basis, was paid full amount of damages it was entitled to recover, by having been paid full amount of contract price, except for $100, which was retained to keep contract open for administration. Allan Const. Co., Inc. v. U.S., Ct.Cl.1981, 646 F.2d 487, 227 Ct.Cl. 193. Levees And Flood Control ☞ 18

Government contractor was not entitled to recover on theory of quantum meruit costs incurred by it in completing contract beyond cost estimates at its own expense, where there was no way to balance detriment to Government occasioned by contractor's silence after learning of a competing project against any benefit Government may have obtained from contractor's development work under contract and record did not contain any evidence on basis of which value derived from developmental work could be expressed in financial terms. Ling-Temco-Vought, Inc. v. U.S., Ct.Cl.1973, 475 F.2d 630, 201 Ct.Cl. 135. United States ☞ 74(11)

Post office builder was not entitled to recover under a theory of quantum meruit for alleged "extra" item which was thought necessary by builder who departed voluntarily and without authorization from contract specifications in an exercise of its own judgment. Leo A. Daly Co. v. Ray Smith Industries, Inc., C.A.5 (Tex.) 1968, 387 F.2d 899. Implied And Constructive Contracts ☞ 64

In action to recover on quantum meruit basis for reasonable value of concrete roadway constructed by plaintiff for Smithsonian Institution, claims were not proven either because their appearance on plaintiff's damage schedule did not by itself amount to probative evidence in absence of anything else, or because suppliers' discounts earned by plaintiff were not allowable as costs of performance, or because an allocation of home office overhead to contract was of no probative value if no basis for allocation was shown. Roberts v. U.S., Ct.Cl.1966, 357

F.2d 938, 174 Ct.Cl. 940. Highways ☞ 113(4)

Where written contracts between contractor and Federal Housing Agencies provided that no charge for extra work could be valid unless extra work was ordered in writing and price was stated in such order, alleged oral agreement between the regional director of housing agencies and contractor's representative concerning repair by contractor of damage caused by hurricane was not binding on housing agencies, and therefore contractor could not recover for additional work performed either on contract or on quantum meruit. Blair v. U.S., M.D.Ala. 1946, 66 F.Supp. 405, affirmed 164 F.2d 115, certiorari denied 68 S.Ct. 910, 333 U.S. 880, 92 L.Ed. 1155, rehearing denied 68 S.Ct. 1336, 334 U.S. 830, 92 L.Ed. 1758. United States ☞ 70(28)

Judgment on the basis of quantum meruit can not be allowed where there is a valid contract between the parties. Frazier-Davis Const. Co. v. U.S., Ct.Cl.1943, 100 Ct.Cl. 120. Contracts ☞ 4; United States ☞ 74(7)

Where the diversions were not shown by the evidence adduced to have been authorized and were made without the knowledge or approval of the duly authorized official, and where no agreement, express or implied, was made to make payment at a rate in excess of that stipulated in the contract, there was no basis for a recovery on the theory of quantum meruit. Walter C. Reediger, Inc., v. U.S., Ct.Cl.1941, 94 Ct.Cl. 120. Sales ☞ 77(2); United States ☞ 70(28)

There can be no recovery on a quantum meruit for extra work where the officer ordering it was without authority. J. & J. Stolts Association v. U.S., Ct.Cl.1928, 66 Ct.Cl. 1. See, also, Goetz v. U.S., 1928, 66 Ct.Cl. 17.

Where a contractor, without agreement as to compensation, has been employed by the Government to raise a sunken dredge and tow it into a dry dock, and the contractor has performed the work without fault or negligence, such contractor is entitled to payment on the basis of quantum meruit. Reid Wrecking Co. v. U.S., Ct.Cl.1920, 55 Ct.Cl. 453. Implied And Constructive Contracts ☞ 62

Where work not provided for in a contract is ordered to be done, and no compensation is agreed on, the plaintiff is entitled to compensation on the basis of quantum meruit. Snare & Triest Co. v. U.S., Ct.Cl.1920, 55 Ct.Cl. 386. Implied And Constructive Contracts ⚖ 62

345. Defenses, actions for breach—Generally

An action could not be maintained against the Government in the Court of Claims [now United States Court of Federal Claims] upon a contract for secret services during a war, made between the President and the claimant, the publicity produced by an action being itself a breach of a contract of that kind and thus defeating a recovery. Totten v. U.S., U.S.Ct.Cl.1875, 92 U.S. 105, 2 Otto 105, 23 L.Ed. 605. United States ⚖ 131

Where Government contract was "terminated" by the Government when contractor fell behind schedule and where Government sought recovery under contract's liquidated damages provisions, contractor was entitled to litigate its defense that Government had not exercised due diligence in completing the project after termination. U.S. v. Continental Cas. Co., S.D.N.Y.1962, 210 F.Supp. 433. United States ⚖ 129

346. —— Accord and satisfaction, defenses, actions for breach

Provision of Navy contract modifications, that acceptance of modification by contractor would constitute accord and satisfaction, did not bar contractor's claim for equitable adjustment for delays caused by such modifications, where Navy continued to consider contractor's claim after contractor signed release, and actually paid contractor compensation on the claim as well. England v. Sherman R. Smoot Corp., C.A.Fed.2004, 388 F.3d 844. United States ⚖ 74(6)

Disclaimer contained in contract for design and manufacture of radio transceivers did not relieve government from liability when it delivered to contractor an outdated drawing set, and government's waiver of certain specifications was not an accord and satisfaction of contractor's electromagnetic interference claims; thus, contractor was entitled to recover costs, including delay costs, of review it undertook when it discovered it had an outdated drawing set and costs it incurred in trying unsuccessfully to eliminate the electromagnetic interference difficulty which persisted despite conformance to control plan approved by the

government. Teledyne Lewisburg v. U.S., C.A.Fed.1983, 699 F.2d 1336. United States ⚖ 70(29)

Where government contractor claimed that amount of loss with respect to government-furnished property destroyed in fire on contractor's premises had been greatly increased by government's delay in delivery and thereafter contractor agreed to accept stated amount to settle its claim for increased labor and overhead costs caused by government's delay in delivery without reserving any other claim against government arising from delay in delivery, there was an accord and satisfaction with respect to delay claim precluding contractor from asserting government's delay as defense to government's claim for loss of government-furnished property in fire. Fraass Surgical Mfg. Co., Inc. v. U.S., Ct.Cl.1974, 505 F.2d 707, 205 Ct.Cl. 585. United States ⚖ 74(6)

Modification extending time for completion, under "termination for default-damages for delay-time extensions" clause of government contract did not constitute accord and satisfaction of contractor's claim for delay damages under "suspension of work" clause for causes of delay other than those recited in modification. Merritt-Chapman & Scott Corp. v. U.S., Ct.Cl.1971, 439 F.2d 185, 194 Ct.Cl. 461. United States ⚖ 72(5)

Doctrine of accord and satisfaction barred government construction contractor's claims that it was entitled to damages for an early completion delay caused by waterline relocation and for the cumulative impact of numerous changes required by contracting agency during the course of performance, where the parties executed bilateral modifications that covered items on which contractor's delay claims were based, and all the modifications contained release provision which settled claims. Jackson Const. Co., Inc. v. U.S., Fed.Cl.2004, 62 Fed.Cl. 84. United States ⚖ 74(6)

347. —— Appropriations, defenses, actions for breach

Where Congress had appropriated sufficient legally unrestricted funds, via general appropriation to Indian Health Service (IHS), to pay specific contracts made pursuant to Self-Determination and Education Assistance Act (ISDEAA) under which tribes provided health services otherwise providable by IHS, government could not, on grounds of "insufficient appropriations," avoid its contractual promise to pay full contract support costs, even though Act made provision of funds "subject to availability of appropriations," and even if IHS' total lump-sum appropriation was insufficient to pay all contracts IHS had made. Cherokee Nation of Oklahoma v. Leavitt, U.S.2005, 125 S.Ct. 1172, 543 U.S. 631, 161 L.Ed.2d 66, on remand 404 F.3d 1263. Indians ⟅ 139

348. —— Contributory negligence, defenses, actions for breach

Evidence established that corporation which acquired shipyard and entered into novation which replaced contract to build two hydrographic survey ships for the maritime administration was contributorily negligent in its preacquisition investigation by failure to exercise due care and was barred from recovery from United States for $7,000,000 loss on the ship building contract. Aerojet-General Corp. v. U.S., Ct.Cl.1972, 467 F.2d 1293, 199 Ct.Cl. 422. United States ⟅ 74(11)

Where notwithstanding defendant's fault the contractor's loss was caused by the contractor's own negligence, recovery of damage is precluded and the fact that the plaintiff contractor could have operated negligently and not have been delayed in its work if the Government had performed certain acts required of it, is not a ground for recovery. L.M. Jones Co., Inc. v. U.S., Ct.Cl.1967, 178 Ct.Cl. 636. United States ⟅ 74(8)

349. —— Disagreement with contracting officer, defenses, actions for breach

Government contractor could not justifiably abandon work simply because of disagreement with contracting officer. Stoeckert v. U.S., Ct.Cl.1968, 391 F.2d 639, 183 Ct.Cl. 152. United States ⟅ 73(1)

350. —— Duress, defenses, actions for breach

Evidence that contractors were behind schedule, that government contract officer inspected construction site and was convinced that contractors' excuses for delay were invalid, that counsel and corporate officers represented contractors at meeting with government officer, and that officer reminded contractors of loss of reputation which would result if their contract were terminated for default, was insufficient to support contractors' contention that release of all claims against Government, signed by them at such meeting in exchange for extension of time to complete contract, was result of duress and was invalid, especially where contractors failed to raise issue of duress for at least one and a half years after such meeting. Johnson, Drake & Piper, Inc. v. U.S., Ct.Cl.1976, 531 F.2d 1037, 209 Ct. Cl. 313. United States ⟅ 74(11)

Even though contractor was under a great deal of pressure from government to deliver preproduction communications system's model which was nine months behind initial contract completion date, such pressure which included the threat of considerable financial loss to contractor was not the equivalent of duress for purpose of allowing contractor to avoid representations as to its contract completion potential. International Tel. & Tel. Corp., ITT Defense Communication Division v. U.S., Ct.Cl.1975, 509 F.2d 541, 206 Ct.Cl. 37. United States ⟅ 74(4)

Where Government did not withhold progress payments on airfield construction contract in order to coerce contractor's acquiescence in supplemental agreements providing that grades should be raised to eliminate necessity for excavating ledge rock, contractor's silence and inaction negatived duress and precluded recovery for excavation of ledge rock inconsistent with the supplemental agreements. John Arborio, Inc. v. U.S., Ct.Cl. 1948, 76 F.Supp. 113, 110 Ct.Cl. 432. Contracts ⟅ 238(1); United States ⟅ 72(4)

In order to establish that a contract modification was entered into by the plaintiff under duress from the Government, the plaintiff must show at a minimum that the fear driving him to agreement had some foundation in the other party's conduct or in other external circumstances. WRB Corp. v. U.S., Ct.Cl. 1968, 183 Ct.Cl. 409. United States ⟅ 72(4)

Where a supplemental agreement was entered into providing that plaintiff should be paid at the rate fixed in the contract for all work done up to that time and that plaintiff and its surety should be relieved from any further liability under the contract, and where under such agreement the plaintiff released defendant from any and all claims under the contract, and supplemental agreement, plaintiff did not enter into the supplemental agreement under duress and the said supplemental agreement would be a complete bar to any recovery by plaintiff in a suit based on its contract. Canal Dredging Co. v. U.S., Ct.Cl.1943, 99 Ct.Cl. 235.

351. —— Estoppel, defenses, actions for breach

Representation which an officer of the Army Corps of Engineers made to contractor and which was to effect that sandbags to be procured under invitation for bid would be the same type of bags which contractor was supplied under a previous contract did not operate to estop the Corps from demanding compliance with requirement in bid that only "new" sandbags be furnished by contractor where officer did not intend for contractor to interpret description of bags furnished under previous contract to be the full and complete description of the bags to be procured under the bid and, in any event, the contractor did not have a reasonable right to believe that officer intended his representation to be a full and complete description. Northwestern Bag Corp. v. U.S., Ct.Cl.1980, 619 F.2d 896, 223 Ct.Cl. 333. Estoppel ☞ 62.2(3)

Government was not estopped from denying that it had exercised option to extend agreement pertaining to site for construction of leased post office, in absence of any showing that officials who made statements upon which plaintiff allegedly relied had authority to bind Government. Thanet Corp. v. U.S., Ct.Cl.1979, 591 F.2d 629, 219 Ct.Cl. 75. Estoppel ☞ 62.2(4)

In absence of any proof that the Government had actual and contemporaneous notice that ordnance contractor's work stoppage and changeover in procedures were activities prompted by anticipated issuance of a change order, Government was not estopped from denying responsibility for costs incurred by the contractor in making changes in the method of production which the contractor believed were necessitated by the change order. Manufacturers Hanover Trust Co. v. U.S., Ct.Cl.1978, 590 F.2d 893, 218 Ct.Cl. 563. Estoppel ☞ 62.2(4)

Doctrines of waiver and estoppel applied to prevent successful bidder under Department of Army contract for manufacture of fuses from contending that "option" provision in contract was improperly invoked in violation of Armed Services Procurement Regulations. E. Walters & Co., Inc. v. U.S., Ct.Cl.1978, 576 F.2d 362, 217 Ct.Cl. 254. United States ☞ 70(36)

Where all of an injured party's actions are inconsistent with the reservation of right to end a contract for material breach and where the injured party's expressed declaration of material breach comes long after the acts complained of and after the parties have both continued performance, a prior general and undifferentiated reservation of rights is insufficient to preserve the right to declare the contract breached and terminated; the reservation must plainly and explicitly assert the right to claim a breach ending the contract unless adequate warning has otherwise been given. Cities Service Helex, Inc. v. U.S., Ct.Cl.1976, 543 F.2d 1306, 211 Ct.Cl. 222. Contracts ☞ 262

Prime contractor, which failed to go over contracting officer's head administratively, was not estopped by acquiescence from maintaining that Government breached contract for construction of transmission line by refusing to permit prime contractor to substitute another subcontractor for one listed by prime contractor in its successful bid as subcontractor who had performed clearing and footings work. Meva Corp. v. U.S., Ct.Cl. 1975, 511 F.2d 548, 206 Ct.Cl. 203. United States ☞ 74(8)

Assuming arguendo that contractor relied on erroneous statement made by contract administrator for Navy that no other large screen display system for plotting data revealed by ship's radar was being considered by Navy other than that being developed by contractor, and assuming arguendo that statement constituted an affirmative and actionable misrepresentation, where contractor was aware that another organization within Navy was interested in procuring a display system utilizing an electronic or photochromic technique and, instead of stopping work, protesting to Navy, or reserving its right to bring suit or file a claim, continued to perform its contract and to spend its own funds on cost overruns, contractor was barred by its own conduct after discovery of competing project from recovering on its breach claim expenses incurred by it in completing contract beyond estimated cost at its own expense. Ling-Temco-Vought, Inc. v. U.S., Ct.Cl.1973, 475 F.2d

630, 201 Ct.Cl. 135. United States ⊙ 70(36)

Where Government employee who knew that Government contractor was performing in excess of contract requirements and expected to be paid therefor was both contract administrator and contracting officer on the job and her authority extended to change orders not exceeding $10,000 and interpretation of contract insofar as it was not substantial interpretation, decision of employee to continue payment without informing contractor of the problem was within scope of her authority and Government was estopped from denying the effects thereof, for purposes of determining whether Government was liable to contractor for the excess performance. Dana Corp. v. U.S., Ct.Cl.1972, 470 F.2d 1032, 200 Ct. Cl. 200. Estoppel ⊙ 62.2(4); United States ⊙ 70(28)

United States' previous acceptance of military uniform shirts under shade waivers did not estop United States from refusing to grant waivers for other shirts where manufacturer knew of only three prior waivers, United States did not have any consistent practice of granting waivers in every case and manufacturer knew that waivers would not be granted when deficiencies affected serviceability or appearance of shirts. Doyle Shirt Mfg. Corp. v. U.S., Ct.Cl.1972, 462 F.2d 1150, 199 Ct.Cl. 150. Estoppel ⊙ 62.2(4)

Fact that plaintiffs' assignor as low bidder on government contract knew of architect's misgivings about plans submitted by government before construction began did not serve to destroy government's implied warranty that plans would be sufficient, nor did it estop plaintiffs from invoking warranty, where misgivings occurred after bids were opened and at a time when plaintiffs' assignor was already obligated to construct a building in accordance with government's plans. Poorvu v. U.S., Ct.Cl.1970, 420 F.2d 993, 190 Ct.Cl. 640. United States ⊙ 70(29); United States ⊙ 70(36)

Contractor who knew or should have known facts on conditions at site is estopped to claim change of conditions. Vann v. U.S., Ct.Cl.1970, 420 F.2d 968, 190 Ct.Cl. 546. United States ⊙ 70(36)

Contractor, which would have been without possibility of relief if it had bypassed armed forces board of contract appeals and proceeded directly to Court of Claims and received adverse decision on claim that government's changes in contract were cardinal, did not estop itself from arguing that changes were cardinal by its invocation of contract procedure affording equitable relief by armed forces board of contract appeals even though contractor had not given notice that it deemed modifications to be cardinal and that it was merely exhausting administrative remedies. Air-A-Plane Corp. v. U.S., Ct.Cl.1969, 408 F.2d 1030, 187 Ct.Cl. 269. United States ⊙ 74(6)

In view of conduct of government's representative at administrative level, asserting that termination of contract based on default alleged by plaintiff contractors to have been justifiable was a "breach" beyond jurisdiction of administrative tribunal, government was estopped from claiming that issue of plaintiff's right of recovery under contract arose under contract and thus was determinable solely by administrative tribunal. Nager Elec. Co. v. U.S., Ct.Cl.1968, 396 F.2d 977, 184 Ct.Cl. 390. Estoppel ⊙ 62.2(3)

Where losses sustained by plaintiff who agreed to construct concrete roadway for government were occasioned by errors in bidding resulting from failure to notice that quantity of fill would be required in order to grade existing gravel road to required elevations, and omitted elevation data were available from contracting officer if asked for, the plaintiff having made no complaint during contract performance of such alleged omission in drawing was precluded from recovering such losses since he had the opportunity to avoid error in bidding period but failed to take reasonable precautions. Roberts v. U.S., Ct.Cl.1966, 357 F.2d 938, 174 Ct.Cl. 940. Highways ⊙ 113(4)

Subcontractor by act of performance lost its right to rescission as well as its right to deny existence of subcontract under which subcontractor was to design, manufacture, test and deliver 250 cooling systems to be incorporated into electronic countermeasure pods prime contractor was producing for the United States Air Force. Westinghouse Elec. Corp. v. Garrett Corp., D.C.Md.1977, 437 F.Supp. 1301, affirmed 601 F.2d 155. Contracts ⊙ 262; Estoppel ⊙ 78(6)

Where government knew in 1957 of government contractor's accounting practices which would result in increase of cost of product to government under contract and contract was ambiguous, government should have informed company of its objections to the accounting practices in 1957 and was estopped by waiting until 1963 to recover from contractor on basis of such practices. U.S. v. Hanna Nickel Smelting Co., D.C.Or. 1966, 253 F.Supp. 784, affirmed 400 F.2d 944. Estoppel ⬚ 62.2(3)

Where supplier of materials under contract with Government overcharged the Government and sued for overpayments, the fact that the supplier tendered an invoice each time a shipment was made and that Government accepted the material and made payment did not permit supplier to invoke the doctrine of estoppel against the Government. Fansteel Metallurgical Corp. v. U.S., Ct.Cl.1959, 172 F.Supp. 268, 145 Ct.Cl. 496. Estoppel ⬚ 62.2(4)

United States is neither bound nor estopped by acts of its officers or agents in entering into an arrangement or agreement to do or cause to be done that which the law does not sanction or permit. U.S. v. City and County of San Francisco, N.D.Cal.1953, 112 F.Supp. 451, affirmed 223 F.2d 737, certiorari denied 76 S.Ct. 181, 350 U.S. 903, 100 L.Ed. 793. Estoppel ⬚ 62.2(3); United States ⬚ 40

Where the United States never complained of performance of seller before cancellation by United States of contract, the United States was estopped from asserting that seller was guilty of breach of contract. David J. Joseph Co. v. U.S., Ct.Cl.1949, 82 F.Supp. 345, 113 Ct.Cl. 3. Estoppel ⬚ 62.2(4)

Under contract for construction of buildings on army post on unit price basis providing that contractor should visit site before making proposal, and permitting additions only in event of changed conditions promptly called to attention of contracting officer, failure of contractor to inform officer that trucks were not being allowed to pass moving troops under any circumstances, with resulting delay and increased costs, or to claim additional compensation therefor until contract was 98 percent completed, and facts necessary to decision on claim could not be ascertained, barred recovery of additional compensation. Hallman v. U.S., Ct.Cl.1948, 80 F.Supp. 370, 112 Ct.Cl. 170. United States ⬚ 70(25.1); United States ⬚ 70(36)

Where the Government has undertaken a substantive obligation extending beyond the narrow administrative remedy prescribed in a public contract, the contractor is not estopped, by having sought unsuccessfully to recover all its damages through an equitable adjustment under the Government–Furnished Property and Changes clauses, to seek relief by way of a breach suit in the Court of Claims. Koppers/Clough, v. U.S., Ct.Cl.1973, 201 Ct.Cl. 344. United States ⬚ 74(8)

Where the contracting officer approved the contractor's use of a particular catalogue item in performing work under an electrical installation contract, no mention being made in the communications of the number of bolts to be used to fasten the fixture in question, but where the fixtures submitted for approval actually had four mounting (bolt) holes, the Government is not estopped to require four-bolt installation of the fixtures. J.D. Steele, Inc. v. U.S., Ct.Cl.1967, 180 Ct.Cl. 1213. United States ⬚ 70(28)

Estoppel applicable to a prime contractor is equally applicable to the subcontractor on whose behalf the prime is suing, there being no privity between the United States and the subcontractor. H.R. Henderson & Co., Inc. v. U.S., Ct.Cl. 1965, 169 Ct.Cl. 228. United States ⬚ 74.2

352. —— **Exhaustion of administrative remedies, defenses, actions for breach**

Federal contractor, whose contract was terminated for default, recognized that he had administrative remedy under contract by claiming that termination should be treated as a convenience-termination under default clause, and costs awarded, and he could not sue for breach of contract. Marley v. U.S., Ct.Cl.1970, 423 F.2d 324, 191 Ct.Cl. 205. United States ⬚ 74(7)

That contractor with respect to government defaults which were outside scope of changes provisions made untimely effort to obtain from administrative agency relief unavailable anyway under changes provision did not preclude contractor from instituting and maintaining legal action based on breaches. Specialty Assembling & Packing Co. v. U.S., Ct.Cl. 1966, 355 F.2d 554, 174 Ct.Cl. 153. United States ⬚ 74(8)

353. —— **Failure to appeal, defenses, actions for breach**

Where plaintiffs, a partnership, on June 19, 1942, entered into a contract with the Government, represented by the Corps of Engineers, U.S.A., to furnish the materials and perform the work for grading, paving, draining and fencing an airport at Beaumont, Texas, the work to be completed within 120 days after the date of receipt of notice to proceed, which was June 27, 1942, and by reason of excessive rainfall and inadequate equipment performance was delayed and defendant on Dec. 2, 1942, gave plaintiffs notice denying their request for an extension of time and terminating the contract, effective December 15, because of plaintiffs' failure to complete the contract within the required time and plaintiffs did not appeal either from the denial of the request for an extension of time or from the order of termination, plaintiffs were not entitled to recover. Kilgore v. U.S., Ct.Cl.1952, 121 Ct.Cl. 340. United States ⚮ 73(14); United States ⚮ 73(24)

354. —— **Fault, absence of, defenses, actions for breach**

Fact that electronics firm in producing antenna couplers with single knob control which met performance requirements of its contract with Air Force incurred unanticipated costs did not entitle it to recover from the government where there was no fault on part of government. A.R.F. Products, Inc. v. U.S., Ct.Cl.1967, 388 F.2d 692, 181 Ct.Cl. 1176. United States ⚮ 70(21)

Evidence disclosed that contractor which had agreed to microfilm obsolete engineering documents for the Air Force could not reasonably have been misled by any statement of the government, and that major causes of contractor's unexpectedly high costs and attendant loss could not be attributed to any action on the government's part, and hence contractor failed to establish essential elements of either liability or damages. Microcord Corp. v. U.S., Ct.Cl.1966, 361 F.2d 1000, 176 Ct.Cl. 46. United States ⚮ 74(11)

355. —— **Illegality, defenses, actions for breach**

Where law in effect at time Foreign Liquidation Commissioner entered into contract on behalf of United States to sell portable sawmill to plaintiff was that contract was void and of no effect if sawmill was in fact nonexistent because beyond power conferred by law on Foreign Liquidation Commissioner, contract was entered into in view of existing law and plaintiff was not entitled to recover damages for breach of contract if in fact sawmill was nonexistent at time contract was made. Meads v. U.S., Ct.Cl.1957, 156 F.Supp. 938, 140 Ct.Cl. 526, certiorari denied 78 S.Ct. 1149, 357 U.S. 905, 2 L.Ed.2d 1155, rehearing denied 79 S.Ct. 91, 358 U.S. 870, 3 L.Ed.2d 102. United States ⚮ 74(1)

The Government, as a contractor, is excused from performance of its contracts if the Government as a sovereign, makes laws, regulations, or orders preventing performance. Froemming Bros. of Tex. v. U.S., Ct.Cl.1947, 70 F.Supp. 126, 108 Ct.Cl. 193. Contracts ⚮ 303(2); United States ⚮ 73(22)

Where a contract has been mutually performed, and the contractor sues to recover a part of his compensation erroneously withheld for some minor details, it is not a defense that the contract was illegal because not founded upon advertisement and proposals, the price allowed being reasonable. Mudgett v. U.S., Ct.Cl. 1873, 9 Ct.Cl. 467. Contracts ⚮ 41

356. —— **Impossibility of performance, defenses, actions for breach**

Stipulation by government that, during period of two months, epoxy resins needed for performance of fixed price contract for supply of parts for certain antipersonnel mines were in fact unavailable did not amount to a concession that there was impossibility of performance so as to preclude contractor from resorting to time extension remedy granted under default clause. Consolidated Molded Products Corp. v. U.S., Ct.Cl.1979, 600 F.2d 793, 220 Ct.Cl. 594. Stipulations ⚮ 14(10)

Where contractor which was late in delivering processed turkeys pursuant to supply contracts under Department of Agriculture commodity support and domestic food consumption programs due to its major supplier's experiencing disease problems with turkeys did not document its assertion that substitute healthy turkeys were unavailable within reasonable geographical area, contractor failed to meet burden of establishing that performance was anything more than an unanticipated economic hardship and failed to prove impossibility of performance. Jennie-O Foods, Inc. v. U.S., Ct.Cl.1978, 580 F.2d 400, 217 Ct.Cl. 314. United States ⊘ 75(4)

Where contractor agreed to supply quartermaster depot with brass buckles and subcontracted entire order for buckles, subsequent insolvency of subcontractor did not make contract impossible of performance under default clause of contract to effect that contractor should not be liable for any excess costs if failure to perform contract arose out of causes beyond control or without fault or negligence of contractor, and increased expense in obtaining buckles elsewhere alone did not render performance impossible. Whitlock Corp. v. U.S., Ct.Cl.1958, 159 F.Supp. 602, 141 Ct.Cl. 758, certiorari denied 79 S.Ct. 23, 358 U.S. 815, 3 L.Ed.2d 58. United States ⊘ 73(1)

Where firm executed contract with United States to supply axles and firm's source of supply was surplus property in Europe, the freezing of such surplus property by Germany at request of United States which did not render performance by firm impossible but only less profitable and more difficult, did not excuse failure of performance. U.S. v. Elliott Truck Parts, Inc., E.D.Mich.1957, 149 F.Supp. 52, affirmed 261 F.2d 835. United States ⊘ 73(1)

Government's performance of settlement agreement with Marine messhall contractor that provided for awarding contractor directed subcontract to date certain was excused under doctrine of impossibility, where numerous bid protests were filed that delayed award and performance of prime contract, Government was prohibited from awarding contract while protests were pending, contractor did not argue that performance could have commenced sooner, and contractor agreed that neither Government nor contractor could have anticipated protests or resultant delay when settlement agreement was entered into. Blackstone Consulting Inc. v. U.S., Fed. Cl.2005, 65 Fed.Cl. 463, affirmed 170 Fed.Appx. 128, 2006 WL 618805. United States ⊘ 74(6)

357. —— Impracticability, defenses, actions for breach

Doctrine of impracticable performance is not invoked merely because costs have become more expensive than originally contemplated, but may be utilized only when promisor has exhausted all its alternatives, when in fact it is determined that all means of performance are commercially senseless, and the burden of proof in this respect is on the contractor. Piasecki Aircraft Corp. v. U.S., Ct.Cl.1981, 667 F.2d 50, 229 Ct.Cl. 208. Contracts ⊘ 309(1)

Doctrine of commercial impracticability may be utilized to avoid liability on a contract only when promisor has exhausted all its alternatives, when in fact it is determined that all means of performance are commercially senseless. Jennie-O Foods, Inc. v. U.S., Ct.Cl.1978, 580 F.2d 400, 217 Ct.Cl. 314. Contracts ⊘ 309(1)

Government contractor on project to supply the Army National Guard with a commercial aircraft converted to a military aircraft failed to establish claims of commercial impracticability or impossibility; contractor had reason to know that its estimates for the effort that the conversion required potentially could be inadequate, and cost overrun of approximately 40% did not suffice to support finding of impracticability. Short Bros., PLC v. U.S., Fed.Cl.2005, 65 Fed.Cl. 695. United States ⊘ 70(29)

358. —— Inexperience of subcontractor, defenses, actions for breach

Where difficulties in manufacturing stainless steel canteens were to be expected and contractor was expressly put on notice of such difficulties when it bound itself to delivery dates called for in contract with Government, but contractor obligated itself to embark on work new to it with no dies and with no facilities to produce those dies, subcontractor's failure to produce adequate dies due to its inexperience was not excuse for contractor's failure to meet delivery schedule. Poloron Products, Inc. v. U.S., Ct.Cl. 1953, 116 F.Supp. 588, 126 Ct.Cl. 816. United States ⊘ 73(26)

359. —— Laches, defenses, actions for breach

Where contractor fails to bring conflicts or discrepancies in government contract to attention of the United States in timely manner as required by contract terms, contractor cannot thereafter "bridge the crevasse in his own favor." William F. Klingensmith, Inc. v. U.S., Ct. Cl.1974, 505 F.2d 1257, 205 Ct.Cl. 651. United States ⊘ 70(36)

Where it was contractors' own employee who caused "short" to occur, government's failure to give notice for 11 months before asserting claim for damage done to installation as result of employee's act and simultaneously deducting amount of such claim from amount due contractors for construction of certain improvements at air base did not deprive contractors of opportunity effectively to defend themselves against claim and did not defeat government's right to retain money. Delta Elec. Const. Co. v. U.S., C.A.5 (Tex.) 1971, 436 F.2d 547. United States ⟜ 73(16)

It was too late for claimant against United States to amend its petition after two years to ask for reformation of contract. Leopold Morse Tailoring Co. v. U.S., Ct.Cl.1969, 408 F.2d 739, 187 Ct.Cl. 304. Federal Courts ⟜ 1111

Evidence in breach of contract action against United States failed to establish that United States' ability to make its case was materially harmed by lapse of time before action was begun. Kaiser Aluminum & Chemical Corp. v. U.S., Ct.Cl. 1967, 388 F.2d 317, 181 Ct.Cl. 902, rehearing denied 409 F.2d 238, 187 Ct.Cl. 443. United States ⟜ 74(11)

Where plaintiff sued for damages for alleged excess costs, extra work and delays under a contract in connection with a flood control project, which involved the construction of a number of dams, reservoirs and levees in the Muskingum river valley in Ohio, as well as the relocation of parts of nine different railroad lines and several utility lines and the contract was for the relocation of certain railroad lines, recovery denied on all of the claims because of failure of proof, laches and failure to proceed with appeals in accordance with the provisions of the contract. Arundel Corp. v. U.S., Ct.Cl.1952, 121 Ct.Cl. 741. United States ⟜ 74(7)

360. —— Release, defenses, actions for breach

A contractor who executes a general release is thereafter barred from maintaining a suit for damages or for additional compensation under the contract based upon events that occurred prior to the execution of the release. B.D. Click Co., Inc. v. U.S., Ct.Cl.1980, 614 F.2d 748, 222 Ct.Cl. 290. United States ⟜ 74(6)

Where the government warned in its invitation for bids that microfilms to be furnished might not be complete or legible in whole or in any particular and that model furnished to be used in meeting interchangeability requirements was not represented to meet the requirements of the contract in every respect, and otherwise warned of the difficulty of the contract, and further warned the low bidder that it should carefully review and verify its cost estimates in that a substantial loss appeared likely, there was no such flagrant wrong by the government in connection with a contractor's claim with respect to defective microfilms under government-furnished property clause as to render invalid a general release, given by contractor in exchange for increase in progress payment limitation, on theory of economic duress. Rixon Electronics, Inc. v. U.S., Ct.Cl.1976, 536 F.2d 1345, 210 Ct.Cl. 309. United States ⟜ 74(6)

Evidence that Government and contractors renegotiated contract, that contractors agreed to release "all claims" against Government in exchange for extension of time to complete contract, and that prior letter written by contractors set forth contractors' excuses for delays but did not describe such excuses as claims against Government, was sufficient to show that contractors had agreed to release all claims against Government, including possible claims arising out of fact situations set forth in contractors' prior letter. Johnson, Drake & Piper, Inc. v. U.S., Ct.Cl.1976, 531 F.2d 1037, 209 Ct. Cl. 313. United States ⟜ 74(11)

Irrespective of government contractor's dire financial predicament at time it executed release in which contractor with certain exceptions discharged government from liability for claims contractor may have had, no conceivable economic coercion could invalidate release, where there was no evidence that contractor was restricted in scope of his exceptions to the release and allegation that government contractor lacked sufficient information at time it executed release in favor of government to frame proper exceptions to reserve his subsequent claims against government and that he obtained necessary data only in course of discovery proceedings in a subsequent action against government did not excuse his failure to state his exceptions covering the subsequent claims in general terms which would have sufficed purpose of preserving his right to pursue them. Adler Const. Co. v. U.S., Ct.Cl. 1970, 423 F.2d 1362, 191 Ct.Cl. 607, certiorari denied 91 S.Ct. 461, 400 U.S. 993, 27 L.Ed.2d 441, rehearing denied 91 S.Ct. 923, 401 U.S. 949, 28 L.Ed.2d 233.

Where facts were available as to excess unemployment compensation taxes required to be paid by Government contractor to state of North Carolina for years 1944, 1945 and 1946 due to adverse effect of contractor's employment and unemployment experience under Government contract but not for the years 1948 and 1949 when contractor in 1947 executed release stating that contract was completed and finally accepted, release was bar to contractor's claim for excess taxes for years 1944–1946, even though contractor failed to recognize significance of the data, but the claim for excess taxes for years 1948 and 1949 were within the "unknown claim" exception to the release and not barred on that account. U.S. Rubber Co. v. U.S., Ct.Cl.1958, 160 F.Supp. 492, 142 Ct.Cl. 42. United States ⟳ 74(6)

Where Government contractor executed release which excepted claims for additional costs incurred in transporting and handling lumber requirements, contractor's claim against Government for alleged breach of contract provision to provide lumber was limited by the exception and by the amounts set out in the exception. A.L. Coupe Const. Co. v. U.S., Ct.Cl.1956, 139 F.Supp. 61, 134 Ct.Cl. 392, certiorari denied 77 S.Ct. 52, 352 U.S. 834, 1 L.Ed.2d 53. United States ⟳ 74(6)

Where building contractor, at conclusion of contract with United States, signed release of United States from all claims under contract except those reserved, and claim for damages because United States failed to stake site of buildings in time was not reserved, contractor was not entitled to recover from the United States on such claim. Torres v. U.S., Ct.Cl.1953, 112 F.Supp. 363, 126 Ct.Cl. 76. Release ⟳ 36

Novation agreement providing that "all payments and reimbursements previously made by the Government to the Transferor, and all other previous actions taken by the Government under the contracts, shall be considered to have discharged those parts of the Government's obligations under the contracts" did not re-

lease government from liability for all claims relating to pre-novation services; rather, plain meaning of agreement was limited to discharging government for paying twice for the same service. Cygnus Corp. v. U.S., Fed.Cl.2004, 63 Fed.Cl. 150, affirmed 177 Fed.Appx. 86, 2006 WL 1049326. Novation ⟳ 10

Government contractor did not explicitly reserve its rights to assert an additional delay or impact claim due to waterline relocation when it inserted language underneath release in two modifications stating its belief that time for performance was extended 120 days due to delays, as reservation of rights was not done in a timely manner; contractor executed the modifications after it had accepted full payment for the waterline work and numerous other changes that had allegedly impacted its progress. Jackson Const. Co., Inc. v. U.S., Fed.Cl.2004, 62 Fed.Cl. 84. United States ⟳ 74(6)

A release executed by a person leasing property to the Government is enforceable even though it is the product of unilateral mistake on the part of the lessor and is not subject to reformation as it would be in the case of mutual mistake. Rocky River Co., Inc. v. U.S., Ct.Cl.1965, 169 Ct.Cl. 203. United States ⟳ 113

Where the parties to a contract to produce an item have indicated by their conduct and negotiations that the Government might approve the incurring of costs by the contractor prior and preparatory to the time the contract would be released for production, and where, before the contract was released for production, the plaintiff sought and obtained permission to procure a raw material for future production in order to take advantage of prices that were expected to go up in the near future, the Government's letter permitting such prior procurement could not be construed to amount to a release of the contract for production as the parties clearly intended that release of prior procurement and release for production were two separate and distinct matters. Universal Match Corp. v. U.S., Ct.Cl.1963, 161 Ct.Cl. 418. United States ⟳ 70(11)

361. —— Unauthorized agreements, defenses, actions for breach

Doctrine of estoppel cannot be applied against government on account of unauthorized statements or acts of officer or employee who is without authority in his individual capacity to bind the government. L.B. Samford, Inc. v. U.S., Ct.Cl. 1969, 410 F.2d 782, 187 Ct.Cl. 714. Estoppel ➾ 62.2(3)

Government was not estopped to deny limitation of authority of its contracting officer. Schoenbrod v. U.S., Ct.Cl.1969, 410 F.2d 400, 187 Ct.Cl. 627. Estoppel ➾ 62.2(3)

Contracting officer, as agent of executive department, has only that authority actually conferred on him by statute or regulation and if he exceeds his actual authority, Government is not estopped to deny limitations on his authority even though private contractor may have relied on contracting officer's apparent authority to his detriment. Prestex Inc. v. U.S., Ct.Cl.1963, 320 F.2d 367, 162 Ct.Cl. 620. Estoppel ➾ 62.2(3); United States ➾ 59

Where a Government agent acts outside the scope of the authority actually held by him, the United States is not estopped to deny his unauthorized or misleading representations, commitments, or acts, because those who deal with a Government agent, officer, or employee are deemed to have notice of limitations on his authority and the public should not suffer for the act or representation of a single Government agent, especially when the representation in question (the purported intention to include an absolute save harmless or indemnity clause in a contract (permit)), would encourage an act proscribed by law. California-Pacific Utilities Co. v. U.S., Ct.Cl. 1971, 194 Ct.Cl. 703. Estoppel ➾ 62.2(3); United States ➾ 40; United States ➾ 59

362. —— Waiver, defenses, actions for breach

Under contract with Government for installation of plumbing, heating, and electrical equipment in veterans' hospital to be erected, consequential damages resulting from delay in commencing construction made necessary by Government's change of site and alteration of specifications because of unexpected discovery of unsuitable soil condition were not recoverable under clauses of contract which essentially provided that, if changes were made causing an increase or decrease of cost or affecting the length of time of performance, an equitable adjustment should be made, where the Government extended the time of performance and waived any claim to liquidated damages for the period of the extension. U.S. v. Rice, U.S.1942, 63 S.Ct. 120, 317 U.S. 61, 87 L.Ed. 53. United States ➾ 74(14)

Inspection which an officer of the Army Corps of Engineers made of a facility which was to supply the contractor with the sandbags which were subject of the invitation for bid did not constitute a waiver by the Corps of its objections to the bags not being "new" within the meaning of the invitation for bid where both the officer and the contractor understood that, notwithstanding officer's inspection of the facility, contractor would be furnishing "new" bags if awarded the contract. Northwestern Bag Corp. v. U.S., Ct.Cl.1980, 619 F.2d 896, 223 Ct.Cl. 333. United States ➾ 73(3)

Government's failure to object to contractor's plan of endeavoring to meet Federal Communications Commission's requirements in fabricating television transmitters did not entitle contractor to conclude that it had been relieved from its obligation to comply with the more stringent contractual requirement. Pelliccia v. U.S., Ct.Cl.1975, 525 F.2d 1035, 208 Ct.Cl. 278. United States ➾ 72(2)

Contractor for jamming antennas for use on Air Force bombers could not, without knowledge of full impossibility of defective specifications, waive claims of contract impossibility. Dynalectron Corp. (Pacific Division) v. U.S., Ct.Cl. 1975, 518 F.2d 594, 207 Ct.Cl. 349. United States ➾ 70(30)

To determine whether waiver of government's breach of contract had occurred, in relation to actions of plaintiff seller of helium which continued to furnish helium to United States under the contract after the breach, a more complex inquiry would have to be made than merely noting that performance continued; the guiding principle would be whether in the individual circumstances the seller exercised reasonable commercial judgment in continuing to manufacture and deliver helium, in an effort to mitigate damages, although its obligation to perform had been discharged by total breach of contract by the United States. Northern Helex Co. v. U.S., Ct.Cl.1972, 455 F.2d 546, 197 Ct.Cl. 118. United States ➾ 74(6)

In view of disputes clause of government contract requiring performance of contract pending final decision of any dispute, contractor which delivered generators pursuant to invalid exercises of options by government under contract had not waived right to obtain more than the contract price therefor after having made a timely protest and indicated an intention to file claim in accordance with disputes clause. Dynamics Corp. of America v. U.S., Ct.Cl.1968, 389 F.2d 424, 182 Ct.Cl. 62. United States ⟜ 73(3)

In absence of showing that government engineers, who stated that if performance requirements of electronic firm's contract to supply antenna couplers to Air Force could not be realized with single knob tuning, then trimming adjustments would be required, were authorized to bind the government, there was no waiver of government's contract right. A.R.F. Products, Inc. v. U.S., Ct.Cl.1967, 388 F.2d 692, 181 Ct.Cl. 1176. United States ⟜ 73(3)

Where Government did not finally reject pillows, which it contracted to purchase, for nonconformity to specifications, as authorized by contract, until 141 days after delivery date specified therein, and did nothing to secure pillows from another source, as permitted by contract, until 25 days after expiration of extended time which Government offered to grant seller for delivery, Government "waived" delivery within contract time and could not recover liquidated damages from seller at rate stipulated in contract for delay in delivery. U.S. v. Kanter, C.C.A.8 (Mo.) 1943, 137 F.2d 828. Damages ⟜ 85

Where contractor during work under Government contract, except in one instance, did not comply with contract provisions relative to time extensions for delays but contractor did file requests for time extensions, remission of liquidated damages assessed for inexcusable delay in completing work and filed claims for certain extra work after completion of work and such requests and claims were considered on merits by contracting officer and head of department, contracting officer and head of department had waived failure to make timely protest. Palumbo v. U.S., Ct.Cl.1953, 113 F.Supp. 450, 125 Ct.Cl. 678. United States ⟜ 73(9)

Where contract with United States for construction of auditorium prohibited transfer of contract without consent of sureties, action of United States upon death of contractor in giving administratrix opportunity to complete contract without notifying surety, which was eventually compelled to complete contract, constituted a waiver by United States of liquidated damages for delay in completing contract by surety. U.S. Cas. Co. v. U.S., Ct.Cl.1946, 67 F.Supp. 950, 107 Ct. Cl. 46. Damages ⟜ 85

363.   Damages, actions for breach—Generally

In estimating damages under a convenience-termination clause in a government contract, the Court of Claims occupies the position of a jury under like circumstances. Inland Container, Inc. v. U.S., Ct.Cl.1975, 512 F.2d 1073, 206 Ct.Cl. 478. United States ⟜ 74(7)

Government contractor could not recover for alleged breaches of contract without offering evidence to support allegations that he was adversely affected by alleged breaches. T.F. Scholes, Inc. v. U.S., Ct.Cl.1966, 357 F.2d 963, 174 Ct.Cl. 1215. United States ⟜ 74(10)

Willful and unjustified breach by United States of contract to sell surplus Army tanks to highest bidder did not come within provision of contract restricting liability of United States to refund of purchase price, and normal damage rules were applicable in action by highest bidder against United States for breach of contract. Freedman v. U.S., Ct.Cl.1963, 320 F.2d 359, 162 Ct.Cl. 390. United States ⟜ 74(13)

Rights, duties and liabilities of United States and of contractor sued by United States for money damages arising from an alleged breach of contract for production of gyro motors were to be determined under federal law. U.S. v. Russell Elec. Co., S.D.N.Y.1965, 250 F.Supp. 2. Federal Courts ⟜ 413

Where there is clear proof that a contractor plaintiff was injured by some act of defendant and there is no more reliable method for computing damages, the court may enter a jury verdict on the basis of that evidence which it considers sufficient for the purpose. WRB Corp. v. U.S., Ct.Cl.1968, 183 Ct.Cl. 409. United States ⟜ 74(7)

The Government is liable for damages which are the direct and foreseeable result of its breach of the plaintiff's contract. Dale Const. Co. v. U.S., Ct.Cl. 1964, 168 Ct.Cl. 692. United States ⬆ 74(13)

Where plaintiff, a contractor with the Government, sues for damages sustained by contractor as a result of the Government's breach of contract and also for damages sustained by another person, a subcontractor, who in his contract with plaintiff had absolved plaintiff from any liability to him for delays caused by the Government, recovery may be had only for the loss proved to have been incurred by contractor. Severin v. U.S., Ct.Cl. 1943, 99 Ct.Cl. 435, certiorari denied 64 S.Ct. 1045, 322 U.S. 733, 88 L.Ed. 1567. Contracts ⬆ 330(2); United States ⬆ 74(12.1)

364. —— Authority of agency or department, damages, actions for breach

Unless authorized by Congress the head of a Department has no power to adjust and pay claims for unliquidated damages, even when arising from the breach of a contract, except where such claims are for work and labor done or materials furnished under a contract silent as to price and the amount thereof unliquidated. 1899, 22 Op.Atty.Gen. 437.

365. —— Consequential or incidental, damages, actions for breach

Government was liable to contractor for increased costs for temporary heating and snow removal occasioned by government's breach of contract with respect to foundation and sewers for hospital under construction by contractor. J.D. Hedin Const. Co. v. U.S., Ct.Cl.1965, 347 F.2d 235, 171 Ct.Cl. 70. United States ⬆ 70(24)

Timber purchaser who prevailed on claim that the Forest Service breached timber sale contracts when it suspended them pending its compliance with the Endangered Species Act (ESA) in the matter of the Mexican spotted owl was not entitled to consequential damages in form of increased logging costs; purchaser presenting no written contracts, correspondence or other contemporaneous documents establishing that its logging subcontractor increased the price for logging after suspensions were lifted. Precision Pine & Timber, Inc. v. U.S., Fed.Cl.

2004, 63 Fed.Cl. 122, reconsideration denied 64 Fed.Cl. 165. United States ⬆ 74(13)

Where it was found on the evidence that plaintiff was definitely caused damages on account of wages paid, payroll and other taxes, insurance on buildings and machinery, depreciation and use of facilities and gas and electricity and incidentals, the portion of the damage attributable to the defendant was $5,100. Langoma v. U.S., Ct.Cl.1953, 125 Ct.Cl. 366. United States ⬆ 74(14)

366. —— Equipment costs, damages, actions for breach

Wrapping machine which was in fact purchased for performance of terminated portion of contract with United States was not so unique that it could not be useful to the contractor for other than "Item 0003" work and was clearly not a "special tool" and, thus, contractor, upon United States' termination of contract for convenience, would not be entitled to cost of wrapping machine. Dairy Sales Corp. v. U.S., Ct.Cl.1979, 593 F.2d 1002, 219 Ct.Cl. 431. United States ⬆ 74(12.1)

367. —— Measure, damages, actions for breach

In situations in which contract performance has not yet begun, but the government terminates the contract for convenience after a period of delay, a contractor may recover unabsorbed overhead costs as part of its termination for convenience settlement if a reasonable method of allocation can be determined on the facts of the case and the contractor can otherwise satisfy the strict prerequisites for recovery of unabsorbed overhead costs. Nicon, Inc. v. U.S., C.A.Fed.2003, 331 F.3d 878. United States ⬆ 73(21)

Where Defense Logistics Agency (DLA) was aware several months before award of requirements contract that purchased quantity would be only about 10% of that estimated in request for proposals (RFP), but negligently failed to inform contractor of that fact until after beginning of contract term, proper methodology for determining contractor's damages was via equitable adjustment in price of units delivered to DLA to account for contractor's increased costs resulting from change plus allowance for profit on that cost. Rumsfeld v. Applied Companies, Inc., C.A.Fed.2003, 325 F.3d 1328, certiorari denied 124 S.Ct. 462, 540 U.S. 981, 157 L.Ed.2d 370, on remand 2004 WL 1616167. United States ⟋ 74(12.1); United States ⟋ 74(15)

Stipulation entitling government contractor to compensation at agreed daily rate if it was entitled to damages under contract's suspension of work (SOW) clause required contractor to only prove entitlement to damages under SOW clause to establish entitlement to all types of damages, including unabsorbed home office overhead; contractor was not required to prove it satisfied prerequisites to *Eichleay* damages. P.J. Dick Inc. v. Principi, C.A.Fed.2003, 324 F.3d 1364, on remand. United States ⟋ 73(21)

When the government contractor seeks equitable adjustment for overhead expenses incurred as the result of disruption, delay or suspension caused by the government, only proper method of calculating unabsorbed home office overhead is *Eichleay* formula, which allocates pro rata share of overhead expenses to delayed contract by multiplying total overhead cost incurred during contract period times ratio of billings from delayed contract to total billings of the firm during contract period. Wickham Contracting Co., Inc. v. Fischer, C.A.Fed. 1994, 12 F.3d 1574. United States ⟋ 70(24); United States ⟋ 73(21)

Under cost-reimbursement termination clause of contract with Federal Aviation Administration to produce airport radar systems and antennae, contractor was entitled to retain payments it had received and recover its additional costs under the contract. General Dynamics Corp. v. U.S., Ct.Cl.1982, 671 F.2d 474, 229 Ct.Cl. 399. United States ⟋ 70(35)

Armed services procurement regulations, which were specifically incorporated by references into contracts under review, rather than cost accounting standards relied on by contractor, applied in determining contractor's claims under two navy cost reimbursement research and development contracts, which turned entirely on elusive accounting principles, and only utility of CAS was for analogical purposes should the ASPR and advice of the experts leave answers to accounting issues inconclusive and vague. Hercules Inc. v. U.S., Ct.Cl. 1980, 626 F.2d 832, 224 Ct.Cl. 465. United States ⟋ 70(18)

Where government contractor established a plant on strength of award of contract which obligated defense supply agency to order from contractor all of its requirements of boxes to be purchased, the contract, which contained a termination-for-convenience clause, was breached by agency by procuring boxes from another source, and the new plant closed in less than six months for lack of orders, amount of first year operating loss of plant was a fair and reasonable approximation of the damages. Inland Container, Inc. v. U.S., Ct.Cl.1975, 512 F.2d 1073, 206 Ct.Cl. 478. United States ⟋ 74(13)

On basis of application of costs estimated in estimate of plaintiff, whose right to proceed on project was improperly terminated, to amount of work remaining to be accomplished as of termination date and a June, 1957 completion date, had there been no termination, plaintiff's completion costs would have amounted to $848,131.99 and, where successor contractor's completion costs totaled $1,267,929.02, plaintiff against whom completion cost components were charged back was entitled to recover $419,797.03 for excess completion costs. J.D. Hedin Const. Co. v. U.S., Ct.Cl.1972, 456 F.2d 1315, 197 Ct.Cl. 782. United States ⟋ 74(13)

Proper measure of damages for breach of contract by government is amount of contractor's extra costs directly attributable to breaches. J.D. Hedin Const. Co. v. U.S., Ct.Cl.1965, 347 F.2d 235, 171 Ct.Cl. 70. United States ⟋ 73(13)

Ordinarily, with respect to Government procurement contracts, measure of damages of United States when contractor breaches contract is sum by which reasonable cost of having work done by another contractor exceeds contractor's contract price, but not where second contract materially deviates from first contract. American Sur. Co. of New York v. U.S., C.A.8 (Mo.) 1963, 317 F.2d 652. United States ⟋ 75(2)

In determining plaintiff's damage caused by Government's breach of contract to purchase rock, Government was entitled to credit for proceeds of sale to third persons of some of rock which Government failed to take less necessary expenses incurred by plaintiff in so disposing of rock. Ready-Mix Concrete Co. v.

U.S., Ct.Cl.1958, 158 F.Supp. 571, 141 Ct.Cl. 168. United States ⟶ 74(13)

Where plaintiff was willing to make one year lease of building, which was being built as apartment building, to Government for office space, and certain changes were made in construction of building to make it adaptable for office use, but lease was never consummated, plaintiff's loss for failure of Government to accept contemplated lease was difference in rentals between amount provided in lease and amount which would have been received from private tenants during period of lease, and plaintiff was not entitled to recover cost of conversion and reconversion of building and loss of rentals during conversion. State House, Inc. v. U.S., Ct.Cl.1958, 157 F.Supp. 853, 141 Ct.Cl. 51. United States ⟶ 74(13)

Where contract between supplier and United States provided that upon failure of performance the United States would hold supplier liable for excess costs incurred and provided that United States might procure upon such terms and in such manner deemed appropriate the supplies and services similar to those terminated, fact that original contract did not limit source of supply did not prevent use of relet contracts as a measure of damages merely because such relet contracts limited source of supply to United States. U.S. v. Elliott Truck Parts, Inc., E.D.Mich.1957, 149 F.Supp. 52, affirmed 261 F.2d 835. United States ⟶ 73(4)

Where ceiling price regulation of Office of Price Stabilization provided that ceiling on potatoes should go into effect on certain date, and deliveries of potatoes by seller to the army took place after such date, seller was entitled to recover from the United States only the ceiling price and not the higher contract price, though Government representatives, who were involved in the purchase of the potatoes, allegedly told seller when contracts were entered into that contract and not ceiling price would govern, since such representatives had no right to waive ceiling price or contract out of it. Nick Delis Co. v. U.S., Ct.Cl.1953, 113 F.Supp. 442, 126 Ct.Cl. 133. War And National Emergency ⟶ 166

"Total cost method" of computing damages suffered by government contractor is based on the formula that a contractor is owed the difference between the actual cost of the contract and the contractor's bid, whereas a "modified total cost method" adjusts the total cost method for a contractor's lack of proof in the requirements of the total cost method. Sunshine Const. & Engineering, Inc. v. U.S., Fed.Cl.2005, 64 Fed.Cl. 346. United States ⟶ 74(12.1)

Contractor who prevailed on claim that government breached contact by improperly terminating during its three-year base period was not entitled to damages for two one-year option periods following the base period, as breach damages for the two option years would be inherently speculative, given that government was under no contractual obligation to extend performance beyond the base period. Marketing and Management Information, Inc. v. U.S., Fed.Cl.2004, 62 Fed.Cl. 126. United States ⟶ 74(13)

In determining the damages recoverable from the breach by the Government of plaintiff's contract right to strip-mine coal on Government-owned land, the court will take into consideration the number of acres in the leased area, the depth to which coal could be strip-mined, how much of the coal would be unrecoverable because of the necessity for leaving a plug to permit the later recovery of deeper deposits by underground mining, other coal unrecoverable because of the presence of roads and of faulting, the average price per ton of recoverable coal and the cost of recovery. Neely v. U.S., Ct.Cl.1964, 167 Ct.Cl. 407. Mines And Minerals ⟶ 5.1(9.1)

368. —— Mitigation, damages, actions for breach

Government's duty to mitigate damages does not necessarily require, although it may authorize, Government to permit defaulted contractor to bid on procurement or reletting of sales contract. Siller Bros., Inc. v. U.S., Ct.Cl.1981, 655 F.2d 1039, 228 Ct.Cl. 76, certiorari denied 102 S.Ct. 1970, 456 U.S. 925, 72 L.Ed.2d 440. United States ⟶ 75(5)

In effecting procurement after default of contractor, government must fulfill its duties to mitigate its damages. Churchill Chemical Corp. v. U.S., Ct.Cl.1979, 602 F.2d 358, 221 Ct.Cl. 284. Damages ⟶ 62(4)

Contractor which entered into four contracts with United States for manufacture of rocket launcher adapters and spare parts had duty to mitigate damages which contractor sought to recover for government's authorization or compelling of changes in applicable drawings and performance requirements. Dittmore-Freimuth Corp. v. U.S., Ct.Cl.1968, 390 F.2d 664, 182 Ct.Cl. 507. Damages ⚍ 62(4)

In action brought by government in 1963 to recover for breach of accounting provisions in government contract, evidence established that government learned in 1957 of contractor's accounting practices principally in dispute, but failed to protest at any time during the contract period, leading contractor to continue accounting practices and increase its exposure in action by $750,000. U.S. v. Hanna Nickel Smelting Co., D.C.Or.1966, 253 F.Supp. 784, affirmed 400 F.2d 944. United States ⚍ 75(4)

369. —— Overhead expenses, damages, actions for breach

Government contractor whose contract was terminated for convenience was not entitled to reimbursement for unabsorbed overhead for period during which performance was delayed, where delay was concurrently caused by contractor's failure to furnish certificate of insurance at preconstruction conference as required by contract and government's presentation of flawed construction plans at conference. Singleton Contracting Corp. v. Harvey, C.A.Fed.2005, 395 F.3d 1353. United States ⚍ 73(21)

Evidence that government contractor billed 53% less than month before during one delay period was insufficient to establish that contractor was on standby during period of government-caused delay, as required to support award of unabsorbed home office overhead damages; evidence indicated that contractor was able to progress other parts of the work during alleged suspensions, and there was no evidence that contractor's direct billings were less than they would have been absent the suspensions. P.J. Dick Inc. v. Principi, C.A.Fed.2003, 324 F.3d 1364, on remand. United States ⚍ 74(11)

United States, which was sued for overhead under contract between International Cooperation Administration and plaintiff's predecessor for development of Korean handicraft industry, and which was required by contract to make annual audits so that plaintiff could determine actual overhead, had burden of proving

that plaintiff waived requirement that United States make annual audits. Scherr & McDermott, Inc. v. U.S., Ct.Cl. 1966, 360 F.2d 966, 175 Ct.Cl. 440. United States ⚍ 74(10)

Where contract time for construction of buildings by building contractor for the United States was five months, and the United States breached its agreement to furnish contractor required materials on time, and that time spent by contractor in excess of the five months was forty-three days, contractor was entitled to recover from the United States additional overhead only for the forty-three days. Torres v. U.S., Ct.Cl.1953, 112 F.Supp. 363, 126 Ct.Cl. 76. United States ⚍ 73(21)

Under contract between United States and contractor for completion of post office building after original contract with another had been terminated by the United States, where union lathers employed by subcontractor refused to work until subcontractor was paid balance due him for work performed under original contract, the contractor was not entitled to recover, as for damages for breach of contract, his job and office overhead expense incurred on account of alleged unreasonable delay resulting from the refusal of the United States to pay unsatisfied claim of original contractor. Holton v. U.S., Ct.Cl.1946, 65 F.Supp. 903, 106 Ct. Cl. 477. Postal Service ⚍ 6; United States ⚍ 73(21)

Government construction contractor could not recover under the Eichleay formula for unabsorbed office overhead for 180 days of delay, absent evidence that all work under the contract was ever suspended during any particular time period. Sunshine Const. & Engineering, Inc. v. U.S., Fed.Cl.2005, 64 Fed.Cl. 346. United States ⚍ 73(21)

Government contractor was not entitled to award of delay-related extended overhead costs on Phase II and III of project to renovate naval training center caused by need for foundation stabilization; delays were caused both by Navy and contractor, and amount of delay attributable to each party was uncertain. George Sollitt Const. Co. v. U.S., Fed.Cl. 2005, 64 Fed.Cl. 229. United States ⚍ 73(21)

Government construction contractor failed to meet it burden of proof on its claim for Eichleay damages for an early completion delay; contractor failed to prove the exact number of days of delay to the project's critical path arising from difficulties in waterline relocation, and incorrectly calculated the daily contract overhead portion of its Eichleay calculation. Jackson Const. Co., Inc. v. U.S., Fed.Cl.2004, 62 Fed.Cl. 84. United States ☞ 74(11)

In determining the proper allocation of overhead expense in computing a contractor's recoverable damages incurred during a period of delay or wrongful suspension of its Government contract, the overhead expense must be allocated between the contract work suspended and the contract work not suspended; furthermore, damages are not properly measurable solely on the basis of the additional work which the plaintiff could have performed had the delay not occurred or the suspension not been ordered, since overhead costs would have increased with the increase in work. Blount Bros. Const. Co. v. U.S., Ct.Cl. 1967, 180 Ct.Cl. 35. United States ☞ 74(12.1)

370. —— Profits, damages, actions for breach

Contractor on Defense Logistics Agency (DLA) requirements contract was not entitled to anticipatory profits damages based on DLA's negligent overstatement, in its request for proposals (RFP), of quantity that it would order during contract term; DLA did not divert existing business from contractor, but rather had much lower requirement for contracted item than estimated, and contractor would not have sold overstated quantity to other parties if DLA had informed contractor of overstatement before awarding contract. Rumsfeld v. Applied Companies, Inc., C.A.Fed.2003, 325 F.3d 1328, certiorari denied 124 S.Ct. 462, 540 U.S. 981, 157 L.Ed.2d 370, on remand 2004 WL 1616167. United States ☞ 74(15)

Upon breach of contract by government, government contractor is entitled to recover full measure of bargain it made with the government, including any particular values the plant constructed under the contract had for it, but it cannot make a profit from the breach. Northern Helex Co. v. U.S., Ct.Cl.1980, 634 F.2d 557, 225 Ct.Cl. 194. United States ☞ 74(13)

Under contract with United States for butter-printing services, limiting any re-

covery of profits on terminated contract to profits on work actually performed prior to termination, contractor who performed no work on terminated portion of contract would not be entitled to recovery of any anticipated profits. Dairy Sales Corp. v. U.S., Ct.Cl.1979, 593 F.2d 1002, 219 Ct.Cl. 431. United States ☞ 74(15)

If contractor has been prevented from performing, as in any breach case, award of anticipatory profits may be an appropriate remedy. Allied Materials & Equipment Co., Inc. v. U.S., Ct.Cl.1978, 569 F.2d 562, 215 Ct.Cl. 406. Damages ☞ 124(3)

In view of termination for convenience clause in government contract for supply of film, contractor was not entitled to recover from Government the difference between price of film under contract and price contractor obtained when it subsequently sold the terminated inventory to others, or the cost of financing contractor's inventory which had been prepared for meeting anticipated contract demands for film, or to equitable adjustment to compensate contractor for higher unit costs in its subsequent sales to Government, brought about by lower production runs for Government's decreased demand, inasmuch as such asserted costs pertained only to anticipatory profits. Kalvar Corp., Inc. v. U.S., Ct.Cl.1976, 543 F.2d 1298, 211 Ct.Cl. 192, certiorari denied 98 S.Ct. 112, 434 U.S. 830, 54 L.Ed.2d 89. United States ☞ 70(35)

A profit factor could not be taken into account in assessing damage sustained by prime contractor as result of Government's breach of contract for construction of transmission line by refusing to permit prime contractor to substitute another subcontractor for one listed by prime contractor in its successful bid as subcontractor who would perform clearing and footings work. Meva Corp. v. U.S., Ct.Cl.1975, 511 F.2d 548, 206 Ct.Cl. 203. United States ☞ 74(15)

Difference between Government contract price of $.7838 per pound for copper ingot which was to be supplied by plaintiff, and plaintiff's own purchase price of $.7225, constituted anticipatory profit within meaning of regulation, incorporated into contract clause on convenience termination, providing that anticipatory profit would not be allowed in the settlement of termination costs, since the "profit" was unearned unrealized and contingent on the completion of the transaction, notwithstanding plaintiff's claim that its lost profit was fixed and certain once it had placed its order to buy the copper at $.7225. Colonial Metals Co. v. U.S., Ct.Cl.1974, 494 F.2d 1355, 204 Ct.Cl. 320. United States ⊕ 74(15)

In dispute arising out of contract by which plaintiff obtained right to supply extensive and exclusive food services for employees and others at Kennedy Space Center, plaintiff was entitled to recover for period after June, 1965 losses specified by Board of Contract Appeals for which defendant was directly responsible and also losses inherent in operating at Kennedy Space Center and beyond plaintiff's control, but losses due to contractor's inefficiency, other fault within its control or of kind that any food service enterprise would incur were to be excluded, and plaintiff was also entitled to recover a reasonable profit, not in excess of 6% taking into account compensable losses as calculated under that standard. Macke Co. v. U.S., Ct.Cl.1972, 467 F.2d 1323, 199 Ct.Cl. 552. United States ⊕ 74(12.1)

Where government failed to exercise option to renew plaintiff's contract, which contained standard "Termination for Convenience" clause, for next fiscal year under circumstances that warranted application of doctrine of equitable estoppel which, in effect, resulted in an amendment that renewed contract for next fiscal year, plaintiff was entitled to recover only in accordance with the "termination for convenience" clause, and not as if a common-law breach of contract had occurred, and thus plaintiff could not recover lost profits or consequential damages. Manloading & Management Associates, Inc. v. U.S., Ct.Cl. 1972, 461 F.2d 1299, 198 Ct.Cl. 628. United States ⊕ 74(12.1); United States ⊕ 74(15)

Where government contract could properly have been terminated under termination-for-convenience provisions, termination would be considered convenience termination rather than breach, though contracting officer had mistakenly deemed contract illegal, and contractor's recovery was accordingly to be determined in accordance with formula specified in termination-for-convenience article, which precluded compensation for loss of prospective profits. Albano Clean-

ers, Inc. v. U.S., Ct.Cl.1972, 455 F.2d 556, 197 Ct.Cl. 450. United States ⊕ 74(12.1)

Recovery of contractor seeking damages upon cancellation, pursuant to comptroller general's decision, of valid government contract awarded by contracting officer is limited to amount collectible if contract had formally been terminated pursuant to termination for convenience article; contractor is not entitled to anticipated profits. Warren Bros. Roads Co. v. U.S., Ct.Cl.1965, 355 F.2d 612, 173 Ct.Cl. 714. United States ⊕ 74(12.1)

Profit made by Government contractor was irrelevant to issue of whether contractor sustained damages for delays, erroneous contract drawing relied on by contractor, and increased cost in sustaining pipelines after Government took possession thereof. Archie & Allan Spiers, Inc. v. U.S., Ct.Cl.1961, 296 F.2d 757, 155 Ct.Cl. 614. United States ⊕ 74(10)

Where contractor entered into agreement with the United States whereby contractor was to furnish trousers, Government, in breaching contract by ordering disproportionate quantity of larger sizes contrary to tariff of such sizes, could not deprive contractors of profit that they were entitled to upon basis of original contract based on the tariff, and, therefore, contractors would be entitled to compensation for costs of extra cloth required by Government's deviation from the tariff. Burstein v. U.S., C.A.8 (Mo.) 1956, 232 F.2d 19. United States ⊕ 70(26)

In action by manufacturer of overcoats against the United States to recover balance allegedly due on overcoats manufactured pursuant to contract for the Army, evidence established that manufacturer was entitled to unit price of $17.2915, which included a profit allowance of $3.06 an overcoat. Rainier v. U.S., Ct.Cl. 1957, 147 F.Supp. 709, 137 Ct.Cl. 210. United States ⊕ 74(11)

Genuine issue of material fact as to whether Forest Service's suspension of timber purchase contracts caused lost profits precluded summary judgment on purchaser's claim for lost profits in its suit for breach of the contracts. Precision Pine & Timber, Inc. v. U.S., Fed.Cl. 2005, 64 Fed.Cl. 165. Federal Courts ⊕ 1120

Genuine issues of material fact as to whether Forest Service's suspension of timber purchase contracts was a "substantial factor" in causing purchaser's lost profits precluded summary judgment on purchaser's claim for lost profits in its suit for breach of the contracts. Precision Pine & Timber, Inc. v. U.S., Fed.Cl. 2004, 63 Fed.Cl. 122, reconsideration denied 64 Fed.Cl. 165.   Federal Courts ⟝ 1120

Where the plaintiff, in 1942, entered into a contract with the Government to supply water to a Government installation near Nashville, Tenn., plaintiff was entitled to recover in its suit for profits lost by reason of the fact that during the period that the contract was in effect the Government did not take from the plaintiff all of the water which was used, as the plaintiff claimed the Government was obligated to do, but took most of its water for the project from another supplier. First Suburban Water Utility Dist. of Davidson County, Tennessee v. U.S., Ct. Cl.1954, 129 Ct.Cl. 8.   United States ⟝ 74(15)

371. —— Reprocurement costs, damages, actions for breach

Where only requirement prescribed in invitation to bid was that adhesive should conform to specifications set out, and both surplus material which contractor delivered and material repurchased by Government after contractor defaulted met those specifications, there was sufficient similarity, for purposes of contract provision making contractor liable for any excess costs for "similar" supplies the Government was required to procure upon contractor's default; and even though there was no surplus material available, contractor was liable for excess costs, where Government made every reasonable effort to procure adhesive at lowest obtainable price.   Associated Traders, Inc. v. U.S., Ct.Cl.1959, 169 F.Supp. 502, 144 Ct.Cl. 744.   United States ⟝ 75(2)

After terminating a contract for default, the Government may procure the contract items or performance elsewhere and charge the defaulting contractor for the excess cost of such procurement unless the reprocurement was carried out improperly and unreasonably.   H & H Mfg. Co. Inc. v. U.S., Ct.Cl.1964, 168 Ct.Cl. 873.   United States ⟝ 72.1(6)

372. —— Setoffs, damages, actions for breach

Government which proved in counterclaim to contractor's suit for adjustment in contract price that contractor did actually realize savings in performance of contract by virtue of deviation from specifications allowed by contracting officer was entitled to recover the amount of such savings.   Topkis Bros. Co. v. U.S., Ct.Cl.1961, 297 F.2d 536, 155 Ct.Cl. 648, motion denied 299 F.2d 952, 155 Ct.Cl. 648.   United States ⟝ 75(5)

Provision in Government contract calling for Government set-off, in the discretion of the contracting officer, in case of unsettled claims for labor and materials, deduction for defects, and any other claim which Government might have against contractor under or in connection with contract, did not serve to contract away Government's rights to keep back from partial payment an internal revenue claim against the contractor for withholding taxes not arising out of the contract. U.S. v. Continental Cas. Co., S.D.N.Y. 1962, 210 F.Supp. 433.   United States ⟝ 130(5)

Where United States terminated for convenience of the Government contract to manufacture and erect two 20-ton jib cranes at Philadelphia Navy Yard, Government was entitled to deduct from contract price whatever it cost it to complete the work.   Wagner Whirler & Derrick Corp. v. U.S., Ct.Cl.1954, 121 F.Supp. 664, 128 Ct.Cl. 382.   United States ⟝ 70(17)

Where liability under bid bond was only $1800, and on lowest bidder's inability to furnish performance bonds the contract was cancelled by the Government which subsequently accepted much higher bid from same bidder who did the work, provision in first contract fixing liability if contractor refused or failed to perform, did not apply and Government's set-off was limited to $1800 under the first bid bond.   Winters v. U.S., Ct.Cl. 1949, 84 F.Supp. 756, 114 Ct.Cl. 394, certiorari denied 70 S.Ct. 305, 338 U.S. 903, 94 L.Ed. 556.   United States ⟝ 67(15)

Under contract for construction of earthen dam, contractor was entitled to payment at higher rate for excavation of trenches for concrete footings rather than at rate provided for ordinary rock excavation, but against amount so recoverable by contractor United States was entitled to recover unpaid social security taxes, penalty and interest. Wm. Eisenberg & Sons, to Use of Aetna Cas. & Sur. Co. v. U.S., Ct.Cl.1948, 75 F.Supp. 1006, 110 Ct.Cl. 388. Contracts ☞ 299(2); United States ☞ 73(1)

Where plaintiff sued to recover amount alleged to be due as rent for the period from July 1, 1935, to Dec. 31, 1938, inclusive, for certain premises described in a lease for a postal station, dated Dec. 8, 1923, said premises having been vacated by the Government on Mar. 1, 1935, and recovery having been had in a prior action, 87 Ct.Cl. 531, for the period from Mar. 1, 1935, to June 30, 1935, and the lease was valid, (1) the defendant was entitled to deduct from the rent due for the period stated the amount plaintiff would have been required, under the lease, to spend for heat, light, power and other services had the defendant continued to occupy the premises, during the period of the claim, (2) the plaintiff was under no legal obligation to the defendant to rerent the building after the defendant surrendered possession, (3) the lease in question having been entered into under the express authorization of an act of Congress, the obligation of the Government to pay the rent stipulated in the lease was not dependent on an annual appropriation by Congress to pay the rent as it accrued. Twin Cities Properties, Inc. v. U.S., Ct.Cl.1939, 90 Ct.Cl. 119. Postal Service ☞ 6

373. —— Miscellaneous damages, actions for breach

Contractor was entitled to recover unanticipated costs incurred in measuring, marking, and sequencing panels for fuel storage tanks after panels bowed as result of flaw in Government's design specification; sequencing process used to minimize impact of bowing required far more precision throughout process than was contemplated at time of contracting. Neal & Co., Inc. v. U.S., C.A.Fed.1991, 945 F.2d 385. United States ☞ 70(30)

Where plaintiff entered into contract with defendant in connection with Great Plains Conservation Program which required plaintiff to carry out specified conservation practices on farm owned by plaintiff and plaintiff received cost-share payments totalling $2,496 from defendant under contract but failed to carry out all of practices required by contract and con-

tract was terminated by defendant because of such failure, defendant was entitled to recover the $2,496 which was paid to plaintiff under terms of contract. Briscoe v. U.S., Ct.Cl.1971, 442 F.2d 953, 194 Ct.Cl. 866. United States ☞ 75(2)

United States was not liable for cost of travel by contractor's president from Milwaukee to Washington in attempt to obtain certain drawings because of discrepancies in government drawings already furnished, where president encountered contrariety only after he had secured transportation and was physically in Washington and contractor had no intention of filing claim when the expense was originally incurred, and where delay was not of unreasonable duration and did not occasion significant delay or extra cost in performance of the contracts. Dittmore-Freimuth Corp. v. U.S., Ct.Cl.1968, 390 F.2d 664, 182 Ct.Cl. 507. United States ☞ 70(21)

In action for United States' breach of contracts by which plaintiff was to produce specified amounts of primary aluminum pig and United States made market guaranty commitments, evidence established that plaintiff was damaged in sum of $6,951,088.59 on off-grade and alloy aluminum not purchased by United States and in sum of $247,566.96 for shutdown, standby, and startup costs. Kaiser Aluminum & Chemical Corp. v. U.S., Ct.Cl.1967, 388 F.2d 317, 181 Ct.Cl. 902, rehearing denied 409 F.2d 238, 187 Ct.Cl. 443. United States ☞ 74(13)

Under construction contract designating two distinct areas, one in which there was to be clearing and grubbing and the other clearing only, and providing that all timber of certain size within limits specified to be cleared and grubbed should remain property of government and that all other merchantable timber should be property of contractor, merchantable timber in area that was cleared only did not belong to government and contractor was entitled to recover value thereof from government which had retained it. Blanchard v. U.S., Ct.Cl.1965, 347 F.2d 268, 171 Ct.Cl. 559. United States ☞ 70(10)

Under federal government contract for grading, drainage and paving work in providing for normal trench excavation and backfill operation at unit price of $3.93 per cubic yard but also allowing $6 per cubic yard for removal of unsuitable soil, contractor was entitled to recover $6 per cubic yard for removal of all unsuitable soil and not just that portion of such soil which was beneath excavation depth stated in contract drawings. C.J. Langenfelder & Son, Inc. v. U.S., Ct.Cl.1965, 341 F.2d 600, 169 Ct.Cl. 465. United States ☞ 70(17)

Where provision of contract with Government whereby plaintiff employed prisoner of war labor required Government to furnish transportation of prisoners from prisoner of war camp to scene of work, but Government failed to furnish transportation and same was done by plaintiff, Government's breach of contract entitled plaintiff to recover amount expended in such transportation. Tennessee Products & Chemical Corp. v. U.S., M.D.Tenn.1952, 108 F.Supp. 271. United States ☞ 74(13)

Government construction contractor was not entitled to additional compensation for loss of productivity costs, based on its contentions that defective specifications, contracting agency's failure to provide corrected drawings, and its subsequent attempts to mitigate damages as delays occurred entitled it to compensation; contractor did not sustain predicate for loss of productivity by showing that the Corps was responsible for the underlying causes of delay due to defective plans and specifications. Sunshine Const. & Engineering, Inc. v. U.S., Fed. Cl.2005, 64 Fed.Cl. 346. United States ☞ 74(12.1)

Timber contractor who prevailed on claim that the Forest Service breached timber sales contracts when it suspended them to protect endangered bird species was not entitled to damages during period of suspension when the Forest Service was consulting with the Fish and Wildlife Service (FWS) concerning the species pursuant to section of the Endangered Species Act (ESA); because contractor was an "applicant" under the ESA during period of consultation, it was barred by the ESA from harvesting timber, and thus breach was not a "but for" cause of damages. Scott Timber Co. v. U.S., Fed.Cl. 2005, 64 Fed.Cl. 130, reconsideration denied 65 Fed.Cl. 131. United States ☞ 74(13)

Contractor who entered into contract with the FBI to operate legitimate business as cover for undercover operation was entitled to reimbursement from the FBI for the expense of hiring salesman at urging of targets of investigation; contractor consulted with the FBI concerning the expense as required by the contract, and FBI did not advise contractor that salesman's employment would not be in furtherance of the investigation or that he would not be reimbursed for salesman's salary. Forman v. U.S., Fed.Cl. 2004, 61 Fed.Cl. 665. United States ☞ 70(21)

Where on Aug. 31, 1944, when the defendant had finished all the work it considered necessary to restore the premises to good condition and had cleaned the premises, its offer to turn over possession to plaintiff was refused, and plaintiff did not resume occupancy until Nov. 11, 1944, plaintiff was not entitled to recover for the expense incurred for further cleaning the property when it resumed possession, where it was shown that the necessity for further cleaning was almost wholly due to the activities of plaintiff's employees. Vinoy Park Hotel Co. v. U.S., Ct.Cl.1953, 125 Ct.Cl. 336. United States ☞ 74(11)

Where plaintiff's claim was that under the applicable provisions of the contracts it was entitled to retain discounts, not in excess of one percent, which it obtained from suppliers by paying cash for supplies, the plaintiff was entitled to recover $61,594.07. Cramp Shipbuilding Co. v. U.S., Ct.Cl.1952, 122 Ct.Cl. 72. United States ☞ 70(15.1)

Where plaintiff, at request of two army officers, not authorized to bind Government, furnished copper to manufacturing company which had contracts with Government, on promise of such officers that Government would return to it same amount of copper furnished to said company, and Government returned same amount of equal quality, but at time when copper had fallen in price, there was no liability on Government to pay to plaintiff difference between selling price of copper when furnished and when returned. Rome Brass & Copper Co. v. U.S., Ct.Cl. 1925, 60 Ct.Cl. 280. United States ☞ 68

374. Sharing of costs, actions for breach

Where Air Force contractor weighed some but not all of multiple, independent impossibility claims arising out of defective specifications and contractor was deficient in contract administration, with result that there was fault on both sides, contractor, which was wrongfully default-ed, was not entitled to shift all of losses to Government and formula of shared costs as in a joint venture was applicable so that parties were to share equally the allowable and reasonable costs normally recoverable by contractor in a conven-ience termination. Dynalectron Corp. (Pacific Division) v. U.S., Ct.Cl.1975, 518 F.2d 594, 207 Ct.Cl. 349. United States ⊕ 74(13)

375. Attorney fees and costs, actions for breach

Legal accounting and secretarial ex-penses, and other costs not connected with performance of government contract are not compensable as a part of dam-ages for breach of contract. L.L. Hall Const. Co. v. U.S., Ct.Cl.1966, 379 F.2d 559, 177 Ct.Cl. 870. United States ⊕ 74(13)

Contractor was not entitled to attorney fees and overhead since United States could not be made to bear the initial incidental expenses incurred by lowest bidder when it failed to perform because of financial problems. D & L Const. Co. & Associates v. U.S., Ct.Cl.1967, 378 F.2d 675, 180 Ct.Cl. 366. United States ⊕ 74(1)

Legal costs incurred by general build-ing contractor in its state court suit against contractor who did project design for renovation of government building were not recoverable as damages in building contractor's suit against the gov-ernment for breach of renovation con-tract, as building contractor's decision to bring suit against design contractor broke chain of causation between government's alleged breach and the state court litiga-tion; moreover, claims against design contractor existed independently of gov-ernment's alleged breach, and did not arise directly from government's breach. SAB Const., Inc. v. U.S., Fed.Cl.2005, 66 Fed.Cl. 77, affirmed 206 Fed.Appx. 992, 2006 WL 3358391. United States ⊕ 74(13)

Timber purchaser who prevailed on claim that the Forest Service breached timber sale contracts when it suspended them pending its compliance with the Endangered Species Act (ESA) in the matter of the Mexican spotted owl was not entitled to recover attorney fees in-curred in connection with claim prepara-tion and litigation, under contract provi-sion providing for recovery of out-of-

pocket expenses incurred as a direct re-sult of purchaser's inability to harvest timber because of government delay. Precision Pine & Timber, Inc. v. U.S., Fed.Cl.2004, 63 Fed.Cl. 122, reconsidera-tion denied 64 Fed.Cl. 165. Federal Courts ⊕ 1101

376. Interest, actions for breach

Contract established right of govern-ment to interest on repayment of unliqui-dated progress payments upon default termination of contract. Piasecki Air-craft Corp. v. U.S., Ct.Cl.1981, 667 F.2d 50, 229 Ct.Cl. 208. United States ⊕ 72.1(6)

Under termination for convenience clause of government contract which in-corporated by reference subpart of feder-al procurement regulations specifically prohibiting interest on borrowings, how-ever represented, bond discounts and costs of financing or refinancing opera-tions, even if cost of inventory and sup-plies were allowable upon termination of portion of contract by Government, inter-est costs of financing inventory and sup-plies could not be reimbursed. Kalvar Corp., Inc. v. U.S., Ct.Cl.1976, 543 F.2d 1298, 211 Ct.Cl. 192, certiorari denied 98 S.Ct. 112, 434 U.S. 830, 54 L.Ed.2d 89. United States ⊕ 70(35)

Where neither contract nor statute pro-vided for interest, plaintiff was not enti-tled to recover interest in its suit against United States to recover on contract for payment of legal fees. Contra Costa County Flood Control and Water Conser-vation Dist. v. U.S., Ct.Cl.1975, 512 F.2d 1094, 206 Ct.Cl. 413. United States ⊕ 110

A government contractor was entitled to an allowance of interest as an addition-al cost under an equitable adjustment of its contract for manufacture of para-chutes where such additional costs and expenses were incurred as a result of faulty design by the government. Bell v. U.S., Ct.Cl.1968, 404 F.2d 975, 186 Ct.Cl. 189. United States ⊕ 70(33)

Court of Claims, in proceeding to re-view decision of Corps of Engineers Board of Contract Appeals relating to government contract for installation of tile floor in powerhouse of federal dam, refused to award government interest, under its counterclaim, on excess cost assessment allowed by Board in view of plaintiff contractor's financial condition, long time taken to bring case to final judgment, and contractor's good faith even though he acted erroneously. Stoeckert v. U.S., Ct.Cl.1968, 391 F.2d 639, 183 Ct.Cl. 152. United States ☞ 75(5)

Where from dates of overpayments to government contractor, contractor had use of government's money and amounts of overpayments, as well as dates, were always subject to ready calculation when existence of breach was determined, government was entitled to interest at rate of 6% per annum from dates of overpayments. U.S. v. Hanna Nickel Smelting Co., D.C.Or.1966, 253 F.Supp. 784, affirmed 400 F.2d 944. Interest ☞ 31; Interest ☞ 39(1)

Where contractor's liability was based on breach of contract for production of gyro motors and where full economic ramifications of breach, resulting in non-use by United States of principal sum, were incapable of precise determination, United States was entitled to annual six per cent interest rate on principal sum as element of damages even though interest rates on obligation of United States during period in question were less than six per cent. U.S. v. Russell Elec. Co., S.D.N.Y.1965, 250 F.Supp. 2. Interest ☞ 31

In action by Federal Government against one who contracted to purchase wooden boxes from Government through its ordnance district office for breach of the contract by failing to pay the agreed price, where judgment was entered for Government, allowance to Government of interest as part of the damages would be limited to a four per cent interest rate, rather than to the local statutory rate of six per cent, in view of Government's ability to borrow money at very low rates of interest. U.S. v. Barowsky, D.C.Mass. 1950, 91 F.Supp. 149. United States ☞ 110

377. Specific performance, actions for breach

Where Government and shipyard stipulated, in Government's action for specific performance of construction contract, they would negotiate in good faith to reach an agreement as rapidly as possible to modify contract provisions or to take other appropriate action, and thereafter purported settlement was reached although ultimately disapproved by Attorney General, there was a genuine dispute as to the meaning of the ambiguous clause "to take other appropriate action" so that summary disposition of specific performance case on basis of claim that the Government had unclean hands was inappropriate. U.S. v. Newport News Shipbuilding & Dry Dock Co., C.A.4 (Va.) 1978, 571 F.2d 1283, certiorari denied 99 S.Ct. 212, 439 U.S. 875, 58 L.Ed.2d 189. Federal Civil Procedure ☞ 2492

Generally, the United States cannot be compelled to specific performance under public contracts by private contractors. Tennessee Valley Authority v. Mason Coal, Inc., E.D.Tenn.1974, 384 F.Supp. 1107, affirmed 513 F.2d 632. Specific Performance ☞ 19

378. Reformation, actions for breach

Contractor who was awarded fixed price contract to provide mess attendant services at navy base was not entitled to reformation on basis of unilateral mistake in its bid where mistake in bid resulted from mistake in judgment on part of contractor's president and not from mistake which would entitle it to reformation. U.S. v. Hamilton Enterprises, Inc., C.A.Fed.1983, 711 F.2d 1038. United States ☞ 74(4)

Where government's ground for seeking to reform contract for production of airport radar systems and antennae was not presented to Department of Transportation Contract Appeals Board and therefore court has no basis for disagreeing with factual determination made by Board finding no misrepresentation, reformation would not be ordered. General Dynamics Corp. v. U.S., Ct.Cl.1982, 671 F.2d 474, 229 Ct.Cl. 399. United States ☞ 73(15)

Reformation is not a proper remedy for the enforcement of terms to which the defendant never assented; it is a remedy the purpose of which is to make mistake in writing conform to antecedent expressions on which the parties agreed. Bromion, Inc. v. U.S., Ct.Cl.1969, 411 F.2d 1020, 188 Ct.Cl. 31. Reformation Of Instruments ☞ 1

Evidence was insufficient to establish mutual mistake which would entitle contractor to reformation of contract with the United States for the manufacture by contractor of napalm fire bombs. Evans Reamer & Mach. Co. v. U.S., Ct.Cl.1967, 386 F.2d 873, 181 Ct.Cl. 539, certiorari denied 88 S.Ct. 1102, 390 U.S. 982, 19 L.Ed.2d 1279. United States ⬭ 74(11)

Government contract should be reformed so as to allow contractor to recover extra amounts spent for steel where, at time contract was written, both contractor and government shared mistaken notion that $7.53 per hundred pounds was contractor's steel procurement cost, and it was not until approximately one week later that contractor learned that its acquisition cost was $7.98 per hundred pounds, and the agreement, as written, conferred benefits upon government which neither party desired or intended. Southwest Welding & Mfg. Co. v. U.S., Ct.Cl.1967, 373 F.2d 982, 179 Ct.Cl. 39. United States ⬭ 74(4)

Liability on a construction contract entered into by the United States may be established only by strict compliance with its conditions, and the courts have no power to make a new and different contract for the parties. U.S. v. Cunningham, C.A.D.C.1941, 125 F.2d 28, 75 U.S.App.D.C. 95. United States ⬭ 70(12.1)

Government contractor on project to supply the Army National Guard with a commercial aircraft converted to a military aircraft failed to establish that contract should be reformed on ground of mutual mistake concerning the estimate of work required under the contract, as contractor assumed the risk that the manner in which it performed would be erroneous; moreover, even if contractor had not assumed the risk, the putative mistake was not about an existing fact. Short Bros., PLC v. U.S., Fed.Cl.2005, 65 Fed.Cl. 695. Reformation Of Instruments ⬭ 19(2)

Government contractor did not establish that it was entitled to reformation of dredging contract due to mutual mistake that contractor would be able to obtain local permission to conduct its dredging operations within particular county, absent proof that government knew, at time of the contract, that contractor would face difficulty obtaining the required permits; moreover, contract clearly and expressly assigned to contractor the risk of local compliance. L.W. Matteson, Inc. v. U.S., Fed.Cl.2004, 61 Fed.Cl. 296. Reformation Of Instruments ⬭ 19(2)

The court cannot reform a Government contract to include an indemnification provision proscribed by statute. Califor-nia-Pacific Utilities Co. v. U.S., Ct.Cl. 1971, 194 Ct.Cl. 703. United States ⬭ 74(4)

379. Rescission, actions for breach

Under cost-reimbursement termination clause of contract with Federal Aviation Administration to produce airport radar systems and antennae, government would not be entitled to rescission of contract and amount it had paid to contractor on ground that contractor breached contract by abandoning performance as government would not be permitted to use rescission theory to obtain measure of damages it would have obtained under termination provision that it agreed to eliminate from contract. General Dynamics Corp. v. U.S., Ct.Cl.1982, 671 F.2d 474, 229 Ct.Cl. 399. United States ⬭ 70(35)

Assuming arguendo that a mutual mistake occurred in respect to fact that Navy organization for which contractor was developing a display system for plotting data revealed by ship's radar was only organization within Navy seeking such a system, where contractor not only remained silent after learning of a competing system being developed for another organization within Navy, but evidence failed to establish that, if truth had been known, Navy would have agreed to pay for cost overruns, contractor was not entitled to recover on its reformation-rescission claim for costs incurred by it in completing contract beyond cost estimates at its own expense. Ling-Temco-Vought, Inc. v. U.S., Ct.Cl.1973, 475 F.2d 630, 201 Ct.Cl. 135. United States ⬭ 70(36)

By act of performance government contractor lost his right to rescission, as well as his right to deny existence of the contract. Adler Const. Co. v. U.S., Ct.Cl. 1970, 423 F.2d 1362, 191 Ct.Cl. 607, certiorari denied 91 S.Ct. 461, 400 U.S. 993, 27 L.Ed.2d 441, rehearing denied 91 S.Ct. 923, 401 U.S. 949, 28 L.Ed.2d 233. United States ⬭ 72.1(3)

Mutual mistake on which contract is premised ordinarily serves to rescind contract, but contract is not challengeable at instance of party who assumed risk of mistake; loss may not be shifted by one upon whom contract put risk. Tombigbee Constructors v. U.S., Ct.Cl.1970, 420 F.2d 1037, 190 Ct.Cl. 615. Contracts ⬭ 93(5)

Where it was learned on or about May 25 that contract between purchaser and United States for sale of former Air Force station did not, because of mutual mistake of fact, reflect real intention of parties, and when mutual mistake was first discovered purchaser indicated desire to have contract reformed so that it would express true intention, if that could be accomplished with reasonable promptness, but in early part of July purchaser learned that procedure proposed by United States to effect reformation would involve long period of delay, and purchaser then insisted that contract be rescinded, purchaser acted promptly in seeking to have contract rescinded, and was entitled to rescission on restoration of station and reconveyance to United States. Rash v. U.S., Ct.Cl.1966, 360 F.2d 940, 175 Ct.Cl. 797. United States ☞ 72.1(3)

Provision in bid-invitation and contract for sale of surplus Army tanks for scrap authorizing cancellation by United States for serious mistake justified cancellation of contract when it was discovered that valuable twin diesel engines in tanks did not have to be demilitarized and that it would be wasteful to sell them as scrap. Freedman v. U.S., Ct.Cl.1963, 320 F.2d 359, 162 Ct.Cl. 390. United States ☞ 58(4)

380. Persons protected, actions for breach

Corporation which purchased shipyard which was successful bidder on contract to build hydrographic survey ships and which entered into novation with Government did not have same status as that of a successful bidder, solicited by the Government, who relies to his detriment on representations in contract documents and was not within the rule that holds the United States liable either as absolute warrantor of its specifications and representations or for lack of appropriate due care toward the other contracting party. Aerojet-General Corp. v. U.S., Ct.Cl.1972, 467 F.2d 1293, 199 Ct.Cl. 422. United States ☞ 70(30)

381. Settlements, actions for breach

Where Navy sought specific performance of contract by shipbuilder and thereafter parties entered into negotiations for settlement of dispute and reached what the negotiators considered to be an oral agreement in principle followed by several drafts of the final one which was accepted by navy negotiator subject to certain conditions and accompanied by a letter indicating that ultimate approval must be received from the Deputy Secretary of Defense, parties did not intend to commit themselves irrevocably to an oral settlement of case. U.S. v. Newport News Shipbuilding & Dry Dock Co., C.A.4 (Va.) 1978, 571 F.2d 1283, certiorari denied 99 S.Ct. 212, 439 U.S. 875, 58 L.Ed.2d 189. Compromise And Settlement ☞ 5(1)

Fact that claim is seen, by hindsight, to be entirely meritorious does not mean that agreement to compromise such claim is in any way improper, for party who settles his claim may not avoid it by proof that his claim was just, and release of claim for lawful consideration is binding even though party receives only what was otherwise due him. Johnson, Drake & Piper, Inc. v. U.S., Ct.Cl.1976, 531 F.2d 1037, 209 Ct.Cl. 313. Compromise And Settlement ☞ 8(4)

Stipulation of settlement which constituted basis of dismissal with prejudice by Armed Services Board of Contract Appeals of appeals by government contractor from decisions by government contracting officer directing contractor to pay specified sums as damages for loss of hydrophone array in connection with contract to make marine installations was not a nullity on theory that money to effectuate the settlement could only have been obtained by contract modification and that government attorney who signed the stipulation was not a contract officer and had no authority to sign a contract modification. U.S. v. Bissett-Berman Corp., C.A.9 (Cal.) 1973, 481 F.2d 764. United States ☞ 113

Where post office and court house contractor submitted claim for additional work in construction of caissons beyond depths shown on drawing, contractor revised its claim and full amount of revised claim was paid and contractor in filing its further claim for extra payment confined such claim to cost of temporary heating which was not within terms of settlement, the contractor was not entitled to additional payment for equipment rentals, hoisting, engineer service and field force expense. Continental Ill. Nat. Bank & Trust Co. v. U.S., Ct.Cl.1946, 65 F.Supp. 908, 106 Ct.Cl. 503. Postal Service ☞ 6; United States ☞ 70(36)

382. Scope of judicial review, actions for breach—Generally

Where interdepartmental board of contracts and adjustments had construed standard government construction contract provision for extension of time for completion of work on account of delays as not denying contractor right to reasonable expenses due to delays, Court of Claims would not give contract provision a contrary construction in contractor's suit for damages for delay. George A. Fuller Co. v. U.S., Ct.Cl.1947, 69 F.Supp. 409, 108 Ct.Cl. 70.   United States ☞ 73(20); Contracts ☞ 299(2)

383. —— Questions of law, scope of judicial review, actions for breach

Although presiding member of armed services board of contract appeals passed away prior to rendering decision in case wherein contractor sought equitable adjustment for additional costs incurred in performance of four contracts with United States, the board's version of a certain conversation in which contractor claimed it gave notice of conflict between drawings and tests could not be discarded by Court of Claims.   Dittmore-Freimuth Corp. v. U.S., Ct.Cl.1968, 390 F.2d 664, 182 Ct.Cl. 507.   United States ☞ 73(15)

Interpretation of language of contract is a question of law, not a question of fact, and prior administrative determination on such question is not final or binding on court.   Dynamics Corp. of America v. U.S., Ct.Cl.1968, 389 F.2d 424, 182 Ct.Cl. 62.   United States ☞ 73(14)

Where ultimate question of government's liability under contract terms on proper interpretation of contract provision, issue is one of law to be resolved independently by court.   Schweigert, Inc. v. U.S., Ct.Cl.1967, 388 F.2d 697, 181 Ct.Cl. 1184.   United States ☞ 74(7)

Interpretation of contract documents, as basis of contractor's claim against United States, was question of law and was to be resolved independently by court even though sole record before court was administrative record.   Merritt-Chapman & Scott Corp. v. U.S., Ct.Cl.1966, 355 F.2d 622, 174 Ct.Cl. 250.   United States ☞ 73(14)

384. Standard of proof, actions for breach

Allegations of bad faith, prejudice, and personal malice on part of government representatives, in connection with performance of government contract, must be founded on clear and convincing proof.   Stoeckert v. U.S., Ct.Cl.1968, 391 F.2d 639, 183 Ct.Cl. 152.   United States ☞ 74(11)

It was incumbent on building owner, which had leased three floors thereof to United States for office space, to establish by preponderance of evidence in suit for breach of restoration clause in lease that fair market value of building in condition in which United States had covenanted to restore it, was greater than its fair market value in unrestored state at termination of lease, and evidence sustained finding of Commissioner that owner failed to sustain that burden.   Dodge St. Bldg. Corp. v. U.S., Ct.Cl.1965, 341 F.2d 641, 169 Ct.Cl. 496.   United States ☞ 74(10); United States ☞ 74(11)

§ 5a. Definitions

The word "department" as used in this Act shall be construed to include independent establishments, other agencies, wholly owned Government corporations (the transactions of which corporations shall be subject to the authorizations and limitations of this Act, except that section 5 of this title shall apply to their administrative transactions only), and the government of the District of Columbia, but shall not include the Senate, House of Representatives, or office of the Architect of the Capitol, or the officers or employees thereof. The words "continental United States" as used herein shall be construed to mean the forty-eight States and the District of Columbia. The word "Government" shall be construed to include the government of the District of Columbia. The word "appropriation" shall be construed as including funds made available by legislation under section 9104 of Title 31.

(Aug. 2, 1946, c. 744, § 18, 60 Stat. 811.)

HISTORICAL AND STATUTORY NOTES

References in Text

This Act, referred to in text, means Act Aug. 2, 1946, c. 744, 60 Stat. 806. For complete classification of this Act to the Code, see Tables.

Codifications

"Section 9104 of Title 31" was substituted in text for "section 104 of the Government Corporation Control Act, approved December 6, 1945 [31 U.S.C.

849]" on authority of Pub.L. 97–258, § 4(b), Sept. 13, 1982, 96 Stat. 1067, the first section of which enacted Title 31, Money and Finance.

Section was formerly classified to section 73b–4 of Title 5 prior to the general revision and reenactment of Title 5, Government Organization and Employees, by Pub.L. 89–554, Sept. 6, 1966 80 Stat. 378.

LAW REVIEW AND JOURNAL COMMENTARIES

Byrd shot: Congress takes a broad aim at government contract lobbyists. Thomas M. Susman and Clayton S. Marsh, 37 Fed.B.News & J. 387 (1990).

WESTLAW ELECTRONIC RESEARCH

See Westlaw guide following the Explanation pages of this volume.

§ 6.　Repealed. Oct. 31, 1951, c. 654, § 1(98) to (105), 65 Stat. 705

HISTORICAL AND STATUTORY NOTES

Section, Acts Oct. 10, 1940, c. 851, § 1, 54 Stat. 1109; June 28, 1941, c. 258, Titles II, III, IV, 55 Stat. 281, 289, 292, 302; June 8, 1942, c. 396, § 1, 56 Stat. 347; July 2, 1942, c. 472, Titles II, III, IV, 56 Stat. 483, 500, 505; June 28, 1943, c. 173, Titles I, II, 57 Stat. 236, 243; June 26, 1944, c. 277, Title I, § 101, 58 Stat. 351, Title II, § 201, 58 Stat. 358; June 13, 1945, c. 189, § 1, 59 Stat. 256; July 1, 1946, c. 530, § 101, 60 Stat. 405; June 30, 1947, c. 166, Title II, § 204, 61 Stat. 208; June 30, 1949, c. 288, Title I, §§ 103, 104(a), 63 Stat. 380, excepted from the provisions of section 5 of this title a number of specified government departments and agencies when purchases or services were not in excess of certain specified amounts up to $500.

Another provision of Title III of Act July 2, 1942, c. 472, 56 Stat. 493, which also had been shown as one of the sources of this former section, made an exception with respect to purchases or

services rendered for the Office of the Administrator of Civil Aeronautics, when the aggregate amount involved did not exceed $100. That provision was not repealed, but, if it did not expire with that Act, which was an appropriation Act, it was superseded by section 5 of this title, as amended.

A prior section 6, Acts Feb. 27, 1893, c. 168, 27 Stat. 485; Mar. 1, 1899, c. 325, 30 Stat. 957; Mar. 2, 1911, c. 192, 36 Stat. 975; May 18, 1916, c. 125, § 1, 39 Stat. 126; Mar. 1, 1919, c. 86, § 1, 40 Stat. 1262; May 29, 1920, c. 214, § 1, 41 Stat. 677; June 12, 1922, c. 218, 42 Stat. 638; Feb. 13, 1923, c. 72, 42 Stat. 1244; Feb. 15, 1934, c. 13, § 1, 48 Stat. 351, which related to exceptions to the requirements of section 5 of this title, was repealed by Act Oct. 10, 1940, c. 851, § 4, 54 Stat. 1111. Subject matter is now covered by sections 5, 6a, and 6b of this title.

§ 6a.   Advertisements for proposals for purchases and contracts for supplies or services for Government departments; limited to particular agencies under specified circumstances

Section 5 of this title shall not be construed to apply under any appropriation Act to the following departments and independent offices under the circumstances specified herein:

(a) American Battle Monuments Commission—to any leases in foreign countries for office or garage space.

(b) to (e) Repealed. Oct. 31, 1951, c. 654, § 1(107), 65 Stat. 705.

(f) The Bureau of Interparliamentary Union for Promotion of International Arbitration—to stenographic reporting services by contract if deemed necessary.

(g) Repealed. Oct. 31, 1951, c. 654, § 1(107), 65 Stat. 705.

(h) Department of State—when the purchase or service relates to the packing of personal and household effects of Diplomatic, Consular, and Foreign Service officers and clerks for foreign shipment.

(i) Repealed. Oct. 31, 1951, c. 654, § 1(107), 65 Stat. 705.

(j) The International Committee of Aerial Legal Experts—to stenographic and other service by contract as deemed necessary.

(June 12, 1917, c. 27, § 1, 40 Stat. 144; May 13, 1926, c. 294, § 1, 44 Stat. 547; Oct. 10, 1940, c. 851, § 2, 54 Stat. 1110; June 28, 1941, c. 259, § 1, 55 Stat. 344; Oct. 31, 1951, c. 654, §§ 1(106–108), 3(8, 9), 4(9), 65 Stat. 705, 708, 709; July 1, 1957, Pub.L. 85–75, § 101, 71 Stat. 251.)

HISTORICAL AND STATUTORY NOTES

Codifications

Opening par., and subsecs. (a), (f), (h), and (j) of this section are from Act Oct. 10, 1940, § 2, opening par., and pars. (a), (f), (h) and (j). Remainder of paragraphs of section 2 were repealed. See 1951 Amendment note below.

Subsec. (o), which was from Act May 13, 1926, c. 294, § 1, 44 Stat. 547, made section 5 of this title inapplicable to the Architect of the Capitol in the purchase of supplies and equipment and procurement of services when the aggregate amount thereof did not exceed $1,000 in any instance and was omitted as superseded by section 6a–1 of this title.

Subsec. (p) of this section, which was from Act June 12, 1917, c. 27, § 1, 40 Stat. 144, made section 5 of this title inapplicable to expenditures not exceeding $50 by the United States Geological Survey, and was repealed by Act Oct. 31, 1951, c. 654, § 1(106), 66 Stat. 705.

Amendments

1957   Amendments. Subsec. (o). Pub.L. 85–75 substituted "$1,000" for "$500".

1951 Amendments. Subsec. (a). Act Oct. 31, 1951, § 3(8), struck out "to any purchases when the aggregate amount involved does not exceed $500, nor" preceding "to any leases".

Subsecs. (b), (c). Act Oct. 31, 1951, § 1(107), repealed subsecs. (b) and (c), both of which related to the Botanic Garden.

Subsec. (d). Act Oct. 31, 1951, § 1(107), repealed subsec. (d), which related to the Bureau of the Budget.

Subsec. (e). Act Oct. 31, 1951, § 1(107), repealed subsec. (e), which related to the Bureau of Foreign and Domestic Commerce.

Subsec. (g). Act Oct. 31, 1951, § 1(107), repealed subsec. (g), which related to the Department of the Interior.

Subsec. (h). Act Oct. 31, 1951, § 3(9), struck out "to any purchase or service when the aggregate amount does not exceed $100, or with respect to articles, materials, or supplies for use outside the United States when the aggregate amount involved does not exceed $300; or" preceding "when the purchase".

Subsec. (i). Act Oct. 31, 1951, § 1(107), repealed subsec. (i), which related to the Federal Communications Commission.

Subsec. (k). Act Oct. 31, 1951, § 1(107), repealed subsec. (k), which related to the Medical Department of the Army.

Subsec. (*l*). Act Oct. 31, 1951, § 1(107), repealed subsec. (*l*), which related to the Social Security Board.

Subsec. (m). Act Oct. 31, 1951, § 1(107), repealed subsec. (m), which related to the Bureau of Mines.

Subsec. (n). Act Oct. 31, 1951, § 1(107), repealed subsec. (n), which related to the Bureau of Reclamation.

Subsec. (*o*). Act Oct. 31, 1951, § 4(9), increased the maximum from $200 to $500.

1941 Amendments. Subsec. (m). Act June 28, 1941, reaffirmed the provision respecting the Bureau of Mines.

Repeals

Section 1(108) of Act Oct. 31, 1951, repealed the proviso in section 1 of Act June 28, 1941, c. 259, 55 Stat. 344, cited as a credit to this section, which excepted expenditures not exceeding $500 by the Bureau of Mines from section 5 of this title.

Section 1(106) of Act Oct. 31, 1951, repealed the proviso in section 1 of Act June 12, 1917, c. 27, 40 Stat. 144, cited as a credit to this section, which excepted expenditures not exceeding $50 by the United States Geological Survey from section 5 of this title.

Section 4(a) of Act Oct. 10, 1940, provided for repeal of all prior laws, which are covered by that Act, and that any rights or liabilities existing under such repealed sections or parts of sections shall not be affected by their repeal.

Prior Provisions

A prior section 6a, Acts Jan. 25, 1929, c. 102, Title IV, 45 Stat. 1136; Apr. 18, 1930, c. 184, Title IV, 46 Stat. 215; Feb. 23, 1931, c. 280, Title IV, 46 Stat. 1352; July 1, 1932, c. 361, Title IV, 47 Stat. 520; Mar. 1, 1933, c. 144, Title IV, 47 Stat. 1409; Apr. 7, 1934, c. 104, Title IV, 48 Stat. 568; Mar. 22, 1935, c. 39, § 1, 49 Stat. 102; May 15, 1936, c. 405, § 1, 49 Stat. 1347; June 16, 1937, c. 359, § 1, Title IV, 50 Stat. 298; Apr. 27, 1938, c. 180, Title IV, § 1, 52 Stat. 285; June 29, 1939, c. 249, § 1, 53 Stat. 921; June 26, 1940, c. 428, Title I, 54 Stat. 575, which excepted the Department of Labor from the provisions of section 5 of this title, was repealed by Act Oct. 10, 1940, c. 851, § 4, 54 Stat. 1111.

Bureau of Employees' Compensation

Section 5 of this title shall not apply to any purchase or service of the Bureau of Employees' Compensation outside continental United States when the aggregate amount involved does not exceed $500 under Acts July 8, 1947, c. 210, Title II, § 201, 61 Stat. 264; June 14, 1948, c. 465, Title II, § 201, 62 Stat. 396; June 29, 1949, c. 275, Title II, § 201, 63 Stat. 284. This Bureau, with its functions, was transferred from the Federal Security Agency to the Department of Labor by Reorg. Plan No. 19, of 1950, § 1, eff. May 24, 1950, 15 F.R. 3178, 64 Stat. 1271, set out in the Appendix to Title 5, Government Organization and Employees.

Government-Owned Furniture Removed to Washington, D.C.

Act July 30, 1947, c. 359, Title I, § 101, 61 Stat. 594, provided in part: "That removal to the seat of government of Government-owned or leased furniture, equipment, supplies, and other property and household goods and personal effects of employees, and costs of restoration of leased office space when required, may be accomplished without regard to section 3709 of the Revised Statutes [section 5 of this title]".

Section Inapplicable to Armed Services and National Aeronautics and Space Administration

Section inapplicable to procurement or sale of property or services by Armed Services and National Aeronautics and

Space Administration, see 10 U.S.C.A. § 2314.

Leases for Foreign Service Offices
Provisions contained in annual appropriation Acts for the Department of State authorizing the Secretary of State to enter into leases for Foreign Service offices and grounds for periods not exceeding ten years without regard to section 5 of this title were made permanent, and are covered by section 2670 of Title 22, Foreign Relations and Intercourse.

CROSS REFERENCES

Exemption of all purchases and contracts when amount involved does not exceed $25,000, see 41 USCA § 5.

LIBRARY REFERENCES

American Digest System
United States ⬬64.10.
Key Number System Topic No. 393.

WESTLAW ELECTRONIC RESEARCH

See Westlaw guide following the Explanation pages of this volume.

§ 6a-1. Architect of the Capitol, exception from advertisement requirements

On and after July 27, 1965, the purchase of supplies and equipment and the procurement of services for all branches under the Architect of the Capitol may be made in the open market without compliance with section 5 of this title in the manner common among businessmen, when the aggregate amount of the purchase or the service does not exceed $25,000 in any instance.

(Pub.L. 89–90, § 101, July 27, 1965, 79 Stat. 276; Pub.L. 93–356, § 2, July 25, 1974, 88 Stat. 390; Pub.L. 98–191, § 9(c), Dec. 1, 1983, 97 Stat. 1332.)

HISTORICAL AND STATUTORY NOTES

Revision Notes and Legislative Reports
1974 Acts. Senate Report No. 93–901, see 1974 U.S.Code Cong. and Adm.News, p. 3913.
1983 Acts. Senate Report No. 98–214, see 1983 U.S.Code Cong. and Adm.News, p. 2027.

Amendments
1983 Amendments. Pub.L. 98–191 substituted "$25,000" for "$10,000".

1974 Amendments. Pub.L. 93–356 substituted "$10,000" for "$2,500".

Prior Provisions
A prior section 6a–1, Acts June 25, 1910, c. 431, § 23, 36 Stat. 861; May 18, 1916, c. 125, § 1, 39 Stat. 126; Jan. 12, 1927, c. 27, 44 Stat. 936, which related to the purchase of Indian supplies, was repealed by Act Oct. 10, 1940, c. 851, § 4, 54 Stat. 1111.

LIBRARY REFERENCES

American Digest System
United States ⬬64.10.
Key Number System Topic No. 393.

WESTLAW ELECTRONIC RESEARCH

See Westlaw guide following the Explanation pages of this volume.

§ 6a–2. Architect of the Capitol, authority for personal services contracts with legal entities

Notwithstanding any other provision of law, the Architect of the Capitol is authorized to contract for personal services with any firm, partnership, corporation, association, or other legal entity in the same manner as he is authorized to contract for personal services with individuals under the provisions of section 5 of this title.

(Pub.L. 96–558, Dec. 19, 1980, 94 Stat. 3263.)

HISTORICAL AND STATUTORY NOTES

Revision Notes and Legislative Reports
1980 Acts. Architectural and engineering services, as well as other services of a technical or professional nature, required in connection with major construction and other projects carried out by the Architect of the Capitol are now procured on the basis of personal service contracts with individual professionals, and have been so procured since amendment of R.S. 3709, by section 9 of Public Law 600 of August 2, 1946, 79th Congress, 2d session, 60 Stat. 809, 41 U.S.C. 5.

In the last two decades, the form of practice of professionals, throughout the Nation, has undergone substantial change. There has been an ever-widening trend to practice in the form of asso-

ciations and professional corporations. The Congress has recognized this trend by authorizing executive branch agencies engaged in construction projects for the Government to contract with architectural and engineering firms, associations and corporations for such services, rather than solely with individuals. ...

*   *   *

Enactment of the proposed legislation would simplify contract administration by the Architect of the Capitol and authorize him to contract with the best qualified professionals whether they practice as individuals or as members of a professional firm or corporation. Senate Report No. 96–442.

LIBRARY REFERENCES

American Digest System
United States ⊜17.
Key Number System Topic No. 393.

WESTLAW ELECTRONIC RESEARCH

See Westlaw guide following the Explanation pages of this volume.

§ 6a–3. Applicability of section 5 of this title [1]

Section 5 of this title does not apply to purchases and contracts for supplies or services for any office of the House of Representatives in any fiscal year.

(Pub.L. 108–7, Div. H, Title I, § 104, Feb. 20, 2003, 117 Stat. 354.)

[1] Section catchline was editorially supplied.

HISTORICAL AND STATUTORY NOTES

Revision Notes and Legislative Reports
2003 Acts. House Conference Report No. 108–10 and Statement by President,

see 2003 U.S. Code Cong. and Adm. News, p. 4.

LIBRARY REFERENCES

American Digest System
United States ☞64.10.
Key Number System Topic No. 393.

WESTLAW ELECTRONIC RESEARCH

See Westlaw guide following the Explanation pages of this volume.

§ 6a–4. Director of Congressional Budget Office; authority to contract [1]

(a) Contract authority

The Director of the Congressional Budget Office may enter into agreements or contracts without regard to section 5 of this title.

(b) Effective date

This section shall apply to fiscal year 2003 and each fiscal year thereafter.

(Pub.L. 108–7, Div. H, Title I, § 1102, Feb. 20, 2003, 117 Stat. 370.)

[1] Section catchline was editorially supplied.

HISTORICAL AND STATUTORY NOTES

Revision Notes and Legislative Reports
2003 Acts. House Conference Report No. 108–10 and Statement by President, see 2003 U.S. Code Cong. and Adm. News, p. 4.

LIBRARY REFERENCES

American Digest System
United States ☞64.10.
Key Number System Topic No. 393.

WESTLAW ELECTRONIC RESEARCH

See Westlaw guide following the Explanation pages of this volume.

§ 6b. Miscellaneous exceptions from advertisement requirements

(a) Control of insects, pests, and grass diseases

Materials and equipment for the control of incipient or emergency outbreaks of insects, pests, or grass diseases, including grasshoppers, Mormon crickets, and chinch bugs, may be procured with any sums appropriated to carry out the provisions of sections 148 to 148e of Title 7 without regard to the provisions of section 5 of this title, and the transportation thereof may be under such conditions and means as shall be determined by the Secretary of Agriculture to be most advantageous.

(b) Omitted

(c) Operations on Menominee Indian Reservation

All contracts for labor or supplies necessary for the carrying on of operations on the Menominee Indian Reservation pursuant to the Act of March 28, 1908 (35 Stat. 51), as amended, shall be exempt from the requirements of section 5 of this title.

(d) Sale of Indian produced forest products

The lumber and other forest products produced by Indian enterprises from the forests on Indian reservations may be sold under such regulations as the Secretary of the Interior may prescribe, without compliance with section 5 of this title.

(June 24, 1940, c. 412, 54 Stat. 504; Oct. 10, 1940, c. 851, § 3(a), (c), 54 Stat. 1111.)

HISTORICAL AND STATUTORY NOTES

References in Text

Section 148b of Title 7, included within the reference to sections 148 to 148e of Title 7 in subsec. (a), was repealed by Act Oct. 10, 1940, c. 851, § 4, 54 Stat. 1111, and is covered by this section.

Act of March 28, 1908 (35 Stat. 51), referred to in subsec. (c), probably means Act Mar. 28, 1908, c. 111, 35 Stat. 51, which is not classified to the Code.

Codifications

Subsec. (a) is from Act Oct. 10, 1940.

Subsec. (b), Act Oct. 10, 1940, relating to the obligations of the Civilian Conservation Corps, was omitted, because the Corps was liquidated June 30, 1944.

Subsec. (c) is from Act Oct. 10, 1940.

Subsec. (d) is from Act June 24, 1940, which was formerly classified to section 6mm of this title.

Subsec. (e), which related to the employment of experts or consultants in the Canal Zone, was from the General Government Matters Appropriation Act, 1962, Pub.L. 87–125, Title III, § 301, Aug. 3, 1961, 75 Stat. 279, and was omitted as not repeated in subsequent appropriation Acts.

Transfer of Functions

All functions of all officers, agencies and employees of the Department of Agriculture were transferred, with certain exceptions, to the Secretary of Agriculture by Reorg. Plan No. 2 of 1953, § 1, eff. June 4, 1953, 18 F.R. 3219, 67 Stat. 633, set out in the Appendix to Title 5, Government Organization and Employees.

Similar Provisions

Provisions similar to former subsec. (e) were contained in the following prior Appropriation Acts:

Pub.L. 86–451, Title II, § 201, May 13, 1960, 74 Stat. 101.

Pub.L. 86–88, Title II, § 201, July 13, 1959, 73 Stat. 208.

Pub.L. 85–469, Title II, § 203, June 25, 1958, 72 Stat. 236.

Pub.L. 85–52, Title II, § 203, June 13, 1957, 71 Stat. 79, as amended by Pub.L. 85–352, c. II, § 201, Mar. 28, 1958, 72 Stat. 52.

June 20, 1956, c. 415, Title II, § 203, 70 Stat. 324.

June 30, 1955, c. 253, Title II, § 203, 69 Stat. 236.

June 30, 1954, c. 425, § 104, 68 Stat. 335.

July 27, 1953, c. 245, § 104, 67 Stat. 202.

July 11, 1952, c. 669, § 104, 66 Stat. 584.

Oct. 24, 1951, c. 556, § 104, 65 Stat. 622.

Sept. 6, 1950, c. 896, ch. IX, § 103, 64 Stat. 730.

Oct. 13, 1949, c. 688, § 4, 63 Stat. 852.

June 25, 1948, c. 655, § 4, 62 Stat. 1026.

July 31, 1947, c. 411, § 4, 61 Stat. 694.

May 2, 1946, c. 247, § 4, 60 Stat. 167.

Mar. 31, 1945, c. 45, § 4, 59 Stat. 45.

June 26, 1944, c. 275, § 4, 58 Stat. 333.

June 2, 1943, c. 115, § 4, 57 Stat. 99.

Apr. 28, 1942, c. 246, § 5, 56 Stat. 225.

June 24, 1940, c. 412, 54 Stat. 504.

Prior Provisions

A prior section 6b, Acts Feb. 23, 1931, c. 281, § 1, 46 Stat. 1363; June 30, 1932,

c. 330, § 1, 47 Stat. 460; June 16, 1933, c. 101, § 1, 48 Stat. 292; Mar. 28, 1934, c. 102, Title I, § 1, 48 Stat. 514; Feb. 2, 1935, c. 3, § 1, 49 Stat. 11; Mar. 19, 1936, c. 156, § 1, 49 Stat. 1173; June 28, 1937, c. 396, 50 Stat. 336; May 23, 1938, c. 259, § 1, 52 Stat. 418; Mar. 16, 1939, c. 11, § 1, 53 Stat. 532; Apr. 18, 1940, c. 107, § 1, 54 Stat. 131, which excepted the General Accounting Office from the provisions of section 5 of this title, was repealed by Act Oct. 10, 1940, c. 851, § 4, 54 Stat. 1111.

LIBRARY REFERENCES

American Digest System

United States ⬯64.10.

Key Number System Topic No. 393.

Research References

Encyclopedias

70 Am. Jur. Proof of Facts 3d 97, Proof That a Government Agency Was Liable for Improperly Granting a Bid Award to a Bid Applicant.

WESTLAW ELECTRONIC RESEARCH

See Westlaw guide following the Explanation pages of this volume.

§§ 6c to 6jj. Repealed. Oct. 10, 1940, c. 851, § 4, 54 Stat. 1111

HISTORICAL AND STATUTORY NOTES

Section 6c, Acts June 22, 1936, c. 689, § 1, 49 Stat. 1604; June 28, 1937, c. 396, § 1, 50 Stat. 341; May 23, 1938, c. 259, § 1, 52 Stat. 424; Mar. 16, 1939, c. 11, § 1, 53 Stat. 539; June 25, 1940, c. 421, § 1, 54 Stat. 566, excepted the Rural Electrification Administration from the provisions of section 5 of this title when the aggregate amount involved did not exceed $100.

Section 6d, Acts June 22, 1936, c. 689, § 1, 49 Stat. 1605; June 28, 1937, c. 396, § 1, 50 Stat. 341; May 23, 1938, c. 259, § 1, 52 Stat. 426; Mar. 16, 1939, c. 11, § 1, 53 Stat. 540, excepted the Social Security Board from the provisions of section 5 of this title when the aggregate amount involved did not exceed $100.

Section 6e, Acts May 14, 1937, c. 180, Title I, § 1, 50 Stat. 139; Mar. 28, 1938, c. 55, § 1, 52 Stat. 123; May 6, 1939, c. 115, § 1, Title I, 53 Stat. 656; Mar. 25, 1940, c. 71, Title I, 54 Stat. 56, excepted the Treasury Department from the provisions of section 5 of this title when the

aggregate amount involved did not exceed $50.

Section 6f, Acts June 16, 1937, c. 359, Title I, 50 Stat. 273; Apr. 27, 1938, c. 180, Title I, § 1, 52 Stat. 258; June 29, 1939, c. 248, Title I, 53 Stat. 896; May 14, 1940, c. 189, Title I, 54 Stat. 192, excepted the Department of State from the provisions of section 5 of this title when the aggregate amount involved did not exceed certain specified amounts.

Section 6g, Acts June 16, 1937, c. 359, Title II, 50 Stat. 275; Apr. 27, 1938, c. 180, Title II, § 1, 52 Stat. 260; June 29, 1939, c. 248, Title II, 53 Stat. 898; May 14, 1940, c. 189, Title III, 54 Stat. 201, 202, excepted the Federal Bureau of Investigation from the provisions of section 5 of this title when the aggregate amount did not exceed $50.

Section 6h, Acts June 16, 1937, c. 359, Title III, 50 Stat. 285; Apr. 27, 1938, c. 180, Title III, § 1, 52 Stat. 272, excepted the Bureau of Air Commerce from the provisions of section 5 of this title when the aggregate amount involved did not exceed $100.

Section 6i, Acts June 28, 1937, c. 396, § 1, 50 Stat. 335; May 23, 1938, c. 259, § 1, 52 Stat. 417; Mar. 16, 1939, c. 11, § 1, 53 Stat. 532; Apr. 18, 1940, c. 107, § 1, 54 Stat. 124, excepted the Federal Trade Commission from the provisions of section 5 of this title when the aggregate amount involved did not exceed $50.

Section 6j, Acts June 28, 1937, c. 396, § 1, 50 Stat. 338; May 23, 1938, c. 259, § 1, 52 Stat. 420; Mar. 16, 1939, c. 11, § 1, 53 Stat. 534; Apr. 18, 1940, c. 107, § 1, 54 Stat. 133, excepted the Interstate Commerce Commission from the provisions of section 5 of this title when the aggregate amount involved did not exceed $50.

Section 6k, Acts June 28, 1937, c. 396, § 1, 50 Stat. 339; May 23, 1938, c. 259, § 1, 52 Stat. 421; Mar. 16, 1939, c. 11, § 1, 53 Stat. 536; Apr. 18, 1940, c. 107, § 1, 54 Stat. 135, excepted the National Archives from the provisions of section 5 of this title when the aggregate amount did not exceed $50.

Section 6l, Acts June 28, 1937, c. 396, § 1, 50 Stat. 339; May 23, 1938, c. 259, § 1, 52 Stat. 422; Mar. 16, 1939, c. 11, § 1, 53 Stat. 537; June 26, 1940, c. 428, Title IV, 54 Stat. 595, excepted the National Labor Relations Board from the provisions of section 5 of this title when the aggregate amount involved did not exceed $50.

Section 6m, Acts June 28, 1937, c. 396, § 1, 50 Stat. 341; May 23, 1938, c. 259, § 1, 52 Stat. 423; Mar. 16, 1939, c. 11, § 1, 53 Stat. 538; June 26, 1940, c. 428, Title VI, 54 Stat. 596, excepted the Railroad Retirement Board from the provisions of section 5 of this title when the aggregate amount involved did not exceed $50.

Section 6n, Acts June 28, 1937, c. 396, § 1, 50 Stat. 342; May 23, 1938, c. 259, § 1, 52 Stat. 425; Mar. 16, 1939, c. 11, § 1, 53 Stat. 539; Apr. 18, 1940, c. 107, § 1, 54 Stat. 136, excepted the Securities and Exchange Commission from the provisions of section 5 of this title when the aggregate amount involved did not exceed $50.

Section 6o, Act Apr. 6, 1937, c. 69, § 3, as added May 9, 1938, c. 192, 52 Stat. 344, excepted control of insects and plant diseases from the provisions of section 5 of this title.

Section 6p, Act May 23, 1938, c. 259, § 1, 52 Stat. 417, Mar. 16, 1939, c. 11, § 1, 53 Stat. 531; Apr. 18, 1940, c. 107, § 1, 54 Stat. 124, excepted the Federal Power Commission from the provisions of section 5 of this title when the aggregate amount involved did not exceed $50.

Section 6q, Acts June 25, 1938, c. 681, Title I, 52 Stat. 1117; Mar. 16, 1939, c. 11, § 1, 53 Stat. 535; Apr. 18, 1940, c. 107, § 1, 54 Stat. 134, excepted the Maritime Labor Board from the provisions of section 5 of this title when the aggregate amount involved did not exceed $100.

Section 6r, Acts Mar. 16, 1939, c. 11, § 1, 53 Stat. 527; Apr. 18, 1940, c. 107, § 1, 54 Stat. 116, excepted the Civil Aeronautics Authority from the provisions of section 5 of this title when the aggregate amount involved did not exceed $100.

Section 6s, Acts Aug. 7, 1935, c. 455, 49 Stat. 540; Feb. 11, 1936, c. 49, 49 Stat. 1123; May 15, 1936, c. 405, 49 Stat. 1316; June 16, 1937, c. 359, 50 Stat. 267; Apr. 27, 1938, c. 180, 52 Stat. 254; June 29, 1939, c. 248, Title I, 53 Stat. 892; May 14, 1940, c. 189, Title I, 54 Stat. 188, excepted the International Technical Committee of Aerial Legal Experts from the provisions of section 5 of this title.

Section 6t, Acts May 15, 1936, c. 405, 49 Stat. 1315; June 16, 1937, c. 359, 50 Stat. 267; Apr. 27, 1938, c. 180, 52 Stat. 253; June 29, 1939, c. 248, Title I, 53 Stat. 891, excepted the Bureau of Interparliamentary Union for Promotion of International Arbitration from the provisions of section 5 of this title.

Section 6u, Acts Feb. 20, 1929, c. 270, § 1, 45 Stat. 1243; Apr. 19, 1930, c. 201, § 1, 46 Stat. 243; Feb. 23, 1931, c. 281, § 1, 46 Stat. 1370; Feb. 2, 1935, c. 3, § 1, 49 Stat. 16; Mar. 19, 1936, c. 156, § 1, 49 Stat. 1180; June 28, 1937, c. 396, § 1, 50 Stat. 345; May 23, 1938, c. 259, § 1, 52 Stat. 427; Mar. 16, 1939, c. 11, § 1, 53 Stat. 542; Apr. 18, 1940, c. 107, § 1, 54 Stat. 137, excepted the Tariff Commission (now the International Trade Commission) from the provisions of section 5 of this title when the aggregate amount involved did not exceed $50.

Section 6v, Acts June 28, 1937, c. 396, § 1, 50 Stat. 331; May 23, 1938, c. 259, § 1, 52 Stat. 412; Mar. 16, 1939, c. 11, § 1, 53 Stat. 525; Apr. 18, 1940, c. 107,

§ 1, 54 Stat. 113, excepted the American Battle Monuments Commission from the provisions of section 5 of this title when the aggregate amount involved did not exceed $500.

Section 6v–1, Act Apr. 18, 1940, c. 107, § 1, 54 Stat. 113, excepted the American Battle Monuments Commission, when entering into leases in foreign countries, from the provisions of section 5 of this title.

Section 6w, Acts June 16, 1938, c. 464, 52 Stat. 750; June 30, 1939, c. 253, Title II, § 1, 53 Stat. 978; June 25, 1940, c. 421, § 1, 54 Stat. 568, excepted the Farm Credit Administration from the provisions of section 5 of this title when the aggregate amount did not exceed $50.

Section 6x, Act Aug. 25, 1937, c. 757, Title I, 50 Stat. 759, excepted the United States Maritime Commission from the provisions of section 5 of this title when the aggregate amount did not exceed $100.

Section 6y, Acts Aug. 9, 1939, c. 633, Title I, § 1, 53 Stat. 1318; June 18, 1940, c. 395, § 1, 54 Stat. 443, excepted the Bureau of Mines from the provisions of section 5 of this title when the aggregate amount did not exceed $500.

Section 6z, Act Apr. 18, 1940, c. 107, § 1, 54 Stat. 112, excepted the Bureau of the Budget (now the Office of Management and Budget) from the provisions of section 5 of this title when the aggregate amounts involved did not exceed certain specified sums.

Section 6aa, Act Apr. 18, 1940, c. 107, 54 Stat. 118, excepted the Federal Communications Commission from the provisions of section 5 of this title when the aggregate amount did not exceed $50.

Section 6bb, Act Apr. 18, 1940, c. 107, 54 Stat. 119, excepted the Federal Loan Agency from the provisions of section 5 of this title when the aggregate amounts involved did not exceed certain specified sums.

Section 6cc, Act Apr. 18, 1940, c. 107, 54 Stat. 120, excepted the Federal Home Loan Bank from the provisions of section 5 of this title when the aggregate amounts involved did not exceed certain specified sums.

Section 6dd, Act Apr. 18, 1940, c. 107, 54 Stat. 131, excepted the General Accounting Office from the provisions of section 5 of this title when the aggregate amount involved did not exceed $50.

Section 6ee, Acts Feb. 11, 1927, c. 104, § 1, 44 Stat. 1081; Apr. 18, 1940, c. 107, § 1, 54 Stat. 137, excepted the Tariff Commission (now the International Trade Commission) from the provisions of section 5 of this title when the aggregate amount involved did not exceed $50.

Section 6ff, Act May 14, 1940, c. 189, Title I, 54 Stat. 189, excepted the International Boundary Commission, United States and Mexico, from the provisions of section 5 of this title when the aggregate amount involved did not exceed $500.

Section 6gg, Act May 14, 1940, c. 189, Title IV, 54 Stat. 211, excepted the Administrative Office of the United States Courts from the provisions of section 5 of this title when the aggregate amount involved did not exceed $50.

Section 6hh, Act June 11, 1940, c. 313, Title I, 54 Stat. 290, excepted the Navy Department from the provisions of section 5 of this title when the aggregate amount involved did not exceed $50.

Section 6ii, Acts Jan. 25, 1929, c. 102, Title III, 45 Stat. 1119; Apr. 18, 1930, c. 184, Title III, 46 Stat. 198; Feb. 23, 1931, c. 280, Title III, 46 Stat. 1334; July 1, 1932, c. 361, Title III, 47 Stat. 502; Mar. 1, 1933, c. 144, Title III, 47 Stat. 1393; Apr. 7, 1934, c. 104, Title III, 48 Stat. 551; Mar. 22, 1935, c. 39, § 1, 49 Stat. 90; May 15, 1936, c. 405, § 1, 49 Stat. 1336; June 16, 1937, c. 359, Title III, § 1, 50 Stat. 287; Apr. 27, 1938, c. 180, Title III, § 1, 52 Stat. 273; June 29, 1939, c. 248, Title III, 53 Stat. 909, excepted the Bureau of Foreign and Domestic Commerce from the provisions of section 5 of this title when the aggregate amount involved did not exceed $100.

Section 6jj, Acts May 13, 1926, c. 294, § 1, 44 Stat. 548; Feb. 23, 1927, c. 168, § 1, 44 Stat. 1157; May 14, 1928, c. 551, § 1, 45 Stat. 528; Feb. 28, 1929, c. 367, § 1, 45 Stat. 1397; June 6, 1930, c. 407, § 1, 46 Stat. 516; Feb. 20, 1931, c. 234, § 1, 46 Stat. 1186; June 30, 1932, c. 314, § 1, 47 Stat. 393; Feb. 28, 1933, c. 134, § 1, 47 Stat. 1362; May 30, 1934, c. 372, § 1, 48 Stat. 828; July 8, 1935, c. 374, § 1, 49 Stat. 471; Apr. 17, 1936, c. 233, § 1, 49 Stat. 1226; May 18, 1937, c. 223, 50 Stat. 181; May 17, 1938, c. 236, § 1, 52 Stat. 392; June 16, 1939, c. 208, § 1, 53 Stat. 834; June 18, 1940, c. 396, § 1,

54 Stat. 474, excepted the Botanic Garden, in the purchase of trees and plants, from the provisions of section 5 of this

title when the aggregate amount involved did not exceed $300.

§ 6kk. Omitted

HISTORICAL AND STATUTORY NOTES

Codifications

Section, Acts Apr. 17, 1936, c. 233, § 1, 49 Stat. 1226; May 18, 1937, c. 223, 50 Stat. 181; May 17, 1938, c. 236, § 1, 52 Stat. 393; June 16, 1939, c. 208, § 1, 53 Stat. 834; June 18, 1940, c. 396, § 1, 54 Stat. 474, which excepted the Botanic

Garden, in the purchase of supplies and equipment, from the provisions of section 5 of this title when the aggregate amount did not exceed $50, was superseded by subsection (b) of section 6a of this title which was itself repealed by Act Oct. 31, 1951, c. 654, § 1(107), 65 Stat. 705.

§ 6*ll*. Repealed. Oct. 10, 1940, c. 851, § 4, 54 Stat. 1111

HISTORICAL AND STATUTORY NOTES

Section, Act Apr. 22, 1926, c. 171, § 1, 44 Stat. 314, excepted the National Advisory Committee for Aeronautics from the

provisions of section 5 of this title when the aggregate amount involved did not exceed $50.

§ 6mm. Transferred

HISTORICAL AND STATUTORY NOTES

Codifications

Section, Act June 24, 1940, c. 412, 54 Stat. 504, which excepted forest products

by Indian enterprises from the forests on Indian reservations, was transferred to subsec. (d) of section 6b of this title.

§§ 7 to 7d. Repealed. June 30, 1949, c. 288, Title VI, § 602(a)(29) to (31), formerly Title V, § 502(a)(29 to (31), 63 Stat. 401, renumbered Sept. 5, 1950, c. 849, § 6(a), (b), 64 Stat. 583

HISTORICAL AND STATUTORY NOTES

Section 7, Act June 17, 1910, c. 297, § 4, 36 Stat. 531; Ex. Ord. No. 6166, § 1, June 10, 1933, as amended by Ex. Ord. No. 6623, Mar. 1, 1934, related to advertisements and contracts for miscellaneous supplies for executive departments and other government establishments in Washington; Procurement Division in Department of Treasury; bond of contractor; and purchase or drawing of supplies.

Section 7a, Act Feb. 27, 1929, c. 354, § 1, 45 Stat. 1341; Ex. Ord. No. 6166, § 1, eff. June 10, 1933, as amended by Ex. Ord. No. 6623, eff. Mar. 1, 1934,

related to the consolidation and coordination of government purchases.

Section 7b, Act Feb. 27, 1929, c. 354, § 2, 45 Stat. 1342; Ex. Ord. No. 6166, § 1, June 10, 1933, as amended by Ex. Ord. No. 6623, Mar. 1, 1934, provided for requisition of supplies and reimbursement.

Section 7c, Act Feb. 27, 1929, c. 354, § 3, 45 Stat. 1342; Ex. Ord. No. 6166, § 1, eff. June 10, 1933, as amended by Ex. Ord. No. 6623, eff. Mar. 1, 1934, provided for a general supply fund and reports and audits.

Section 7c–1, Act May 14, 1935, c. 110, § 1, 49 Stat. 234; Ex. Ord. No. 6166, § 1, June 10, 1933, as amended by Ex. Ord. No. 6623, Mar. 1, 1934, related to expenditures incidental to operation of government fuel yards.

Section 7d, Act Feb. 27, 1929, c. 354, § 4, 45 Stat. 1342, related to Secretary of

Treasury's authority to prescribe regulations.

Effective Date of Repeal
Repeal of sections effective July 1, 1949, see section 505 of Act June 30, 1949.

§ 8.   Opening bids

Whenever proposals for supplies have been solicited, the parties responding to such solicitation shall be duly notified of the time and place of opening the bids, and be permitted to be present either in person or by attorney, and a record of each bid shall then and there be made.

(R.S. § 3710.)

HISTORICAL AND STATUTORY NOTES

Codifications
R.S. § 3710 derived from Res. Jan. 31, 1868, No. 8, 15 Stat. 246.

Exemption of Functions
Functions authorized by Foreign Assistance Act of 1961, as amended, as ex-

empt, see Ex. Ord. No. 11223, May 12, 1965, 30 F.R. 6635, set out as a note under section 2393 of Title 22, Foreign Relations and Intercourse.

LIBRARY REFERENCES

American Digest System
United States ⚖64.40(4).
Key Number System Topic No. 393.

Research References

Encyclopedias
Am. Jur. 2d Public Works and Contracts § 64, Receipt, Opening, and Recording of Bids; Time of Bid and of Acceptance or Award; Postponement.

WESTLAW ELECTRONIC RESEARCH

See Westlaw guide following the Explanation pages of this volume.

§ 9.   Repealed. Feb. 19, 1948, c. 65, § 11(a), 62 Stat. 25

HISTORICAL AND STATUTORY NOTES

Section, R.S. § 3717, related to separate proposals for works or material or labor.   See sections 2301 and 2303 to 2305 of Title 10, Armed Forces.

Effective Date of Repeal
Repeal of section effective 90 days after Feb. 19, 1948, see section 13 of Act Feb. 19, 1948, c. 65, 62 Stat. 26.

§ 10. Omitted

HISTORICAL AND STATUTORY NOTES

Codifications

Section, Act Mar. 3, 1875, c. 133, § 2, 18 Stat. 455, which related to preferential treatment of American material in con-tracts for public improvements, was superseded. See sections 10a to 10d of this title.

§ 10a. American materials required for public use

(a) In general

Notwithstanding any other provision of law, and unless the head of the department or independent establishment concerned shall determine it to be inconsistent with the public interest, or the cost to be unreasonable, only such unmanufactured articles, materials, and supplies as have been mined or produced in the United States, and only such manufactured articles, materials, and supplies as have been manufactured in the United States substantially all from articles, materials, or supplies mined, produced, or manufactured, as the case may be, in the United States, shall be acquired for public use. This section shall not apply with respect to articles, materials, or supplies for use outside the United States, or if articles, materials, or supplies of the class or kind to be used or the articles, materials, or supplies from which they are manufactured are not mined, produced, or manufactured, as the case may be, in the United States in sufficient and reasonably available commercial quantities and of a satisfactory quality. This section shall not apply to manufactured articles, materials, or supplies procured under any contract the award value of which is less than or equal to the micro-purchase threshold under section 428 of this title.

(b) Reports

(1) In general

Not later than 180 days after the end of each of fiscal years 2007 through 2011, the head of each Federal agency shall submit to the Committee on Homeland Security and Governmental Affairs of the Senate and the Committee on Oversight and Government Reform of the House of Representatives a report on the amount of the acquisitions made by the agency in that fiscal year of articles, materials, or supplies purchased from entities that manufacture the articles, materials, or supplies outside of the United States.

(2) Contents of report

The report required by paragraph (1) shall separately include, for the fiscal year covered by such report—

(A) the dollar value of any articles, materials, or supplies that were manufactured outside the United States;

(B) an itemized list of all waivers granted with respect to such articles, materials, or supplies under this Act, and a citation to the treaty, international agreement, or other law under which each waiver was granted;

(C) if any articles, materials, or supplies were acquired from entities that manufacture articles, materials, or supplies outside the United States, the specific exception under this section that was used to purchase such articles, materials, or supplies; and

(D) a summary of—

(i) the total procurement funds expended on articles, materials, and supplies manufactured inside the United States; and

(ii) the total procurement funds expended on articles, materials, and supplies manufactured outside the United States.

(3) Public availability

The head of each Federal agency submitting a report under paragraph (1) shall make the report publicly available to the maximum extent practicable.

(4) Exception for intelligence community

This subsection shall not apply to acquisitions made by an agency, or component thereof, that is an element of the intelligence community as specified in, or designated under, section 401a(4) of Title 50.

(Mar. 3, 1933, c. 212, Title III, § 2, 47 Stat. 1520; Aug. 23, 1988, Pub.L. 100–418, Title VII, § 7005(b), 102 Stat. 1553; Oct. 13, 1994, Pub.L. 103–355, Title IV, § 4301(b), 108 Stat. 3347; May 25, 2007, Pub.L. 110–28, Title VIII, § 8306, 121 Stat. 211.)

HISTORICAL AND STATUTORY NOTES

Revision Notes and Legislative Reports
  1988 Acts. House Conference Report No. 100–576, see U.S. Code Cong. and Adm. News, p. 1547.

  1994 Acts. Senate Report Nos. 103–258 and 103–259, and House Conference Report No. 103–712, see 1994 U.S. Code Cong. and Adm. News, p. 2561.

Codifications
  Section is set out to reflect that amendment by Pub.L. 100–418 has ceased to be effective. See Effective and Applicability

Provisions note of 1988 Acts under this section.

Amendments
  2007 Amendments. Subsec. (a). Pub.L. 110–28, § 8306(1), struck out "Notwithstanding" and inserted the following:
  "(a) In general
  "Notwithstanding".
  Subsec. (b). Pub.L. 110–28, § 8306(2), added subsec. (b).

1994 Amendments. Pub.L. 103–355, § 4301(b), enacted provision declaring this section inapplicable to manufactured articles, materials, or supplies procured under any contract the award value of which is less than or equal to the micropurchase threshold under section 428 of this title.

1988 Amendments. Pub.L. 100–418, § 7005(b), substituted "head of the Federal agency" for "head of the department or independent establishment".

Effective and Applicability Provisions
1994 Acts. Section 4301(c) of Pub.L. 103–355 provided that: "Notwithstanding any other provision of law—

"(1) section 32 of the Office of Federal Procurement Policy Act, as added by subsection (a) [section 428 of this title]; and

"(2) the amendment made by subsection (b) [amending this section];

shall take effect on the date of the enactment of this Act [Oct. 13, 1994] and shall be implemented in the Federal Acquisition Regulation not later than 60 days after such date of enactment."

1988 Acts. Section 7004 of Pub.L. 100–418 provided that: "The amendments made by this title [enacting section 10b–1 of this title, amending sections 10a, 10b, 10c, and 10d of this title, and sections 2511 and 2515 of title 19, and enacting provisions set out as notes under section 10a of this title, and amending provisions set out as notes under section 10c of this title] shall cease to be effective on April 30, 1996, unless the Congress, after reviewing the report required by section 305(k) of the Trade Agreements Act of 1979 [section 2515(k) of Title 19], and other relevant information, extends such date. After such date, the President may modify or terminate any or all actions taken pursuant to such amendments."

Section 7005(f) of Pub.L. 100–418 provided that: "The amendments made by this section [amending sections 10a, 10b, 10c, and 10d of this title, and section 2511 of Title 19, Customs Duties] shall take effect upon enactment [August 23, 1988]."

Short Title
1988 Acts. Section 7001 of Pub.L. 100–418 provided that: "This title [enacting section 10b–1 of this title, amending

sections 10a, 10b, 10c, and 10d of this title, and sections 2511 and 2515 of Title 19, Customs Duties, and enacting provisions set out as notes under section 10a of this title, and amending provisions set out as notes under section 10c of this title] may be cited as the 'Buy American Act of 1988'."

1933 Acts. Section 7, formerly § 5, of Act Mar. 3, 1933, as added Pub.L. 103–355, Title X, § 10005(f)(4), Oct. 13, 1994, 108 Stat. 3409, renumbered § 7 and amended Pub.L. 104–106, Div. D, Title XLIII, § 4321(a)(11), Feb. 10, 1996, 110 Stat. 671, provided that: "This title [enacting this section and sections 10b through 10c of this title] may be cited as the 'Buy American Act'."

[Amendment by Pub.L. 104–106 effective Oct. 13, 1994, see section 4321(a) of Pub.L. 104–106, set out as a note under section 2306a of Title 10, Armed Forces.]

Exemption of Functions
Functions authorized by Foreign Assistance Act of 1961, as amended, as exempt, see Ex. Ord. No. 11223, May 12, 1965, 30 F.R. 6635, set out as a note under section 2393 of Title 22, Foreign Relations and Intercourse.

Water Resource Projects; Cofferdam
Pub.L. 100–371, Title V, § 508, July 19, 1988, 102 Stat. 875, provided that:

"(a) **General Rule**.—For purposes of title III of the Act of March 3, 1933 (47 Stat. 1520; 41 U.S.C. 10a–10c) [sections 10a to 10c of this title], commonly known as the Buy American Act, a cofferdam or any other temporary structure to be constructed by the Secretary of the Army, acting through the Chief of Engineers, shall be treated in the same manner as a permanent dam constructed by the Secretary of the Army.

"(b) **Applicability**.—Subsection (a) shall only apply to contracts entered into after the date of the enactment of this Act [July 19, 1988]."

Applicability of Buy American Act With Respect to European Community
For applicability of Buy American Act to procurements covered by agreement with the European Community on government procurement, see Ex. Ord. No. 12849, May 25, 1993, 58 F.R. 30931, set out as a note under 19 U.S.C.A. § 2511.

CROSS REFERENCES

National education reform appropriation expenditures compliance with this Act, see 20 USCA § 6067.

Procedures applicable to purchases below micro-purchase threshold and exclusion from Buy American Act, see 41 USCA § 428.

CODE OF FEDERAL REGULATIONS

Special responsibilities, employment service system, see 20 CFR § 654.1 et seq.

LAW REVIEW AND JOURNAL COMMENTARIES

Department of defense balance of payments program: A brief history and critique. Robert F. Stamps, 18 Pub.Cont.L.J. 528 (1989).

LIBRARY REFERENCES

American Digest System
United States ⊂64.15.
Key Number System Topic No. 393.

Corpus Juris Secundum
CJS Territories § 36, Competitive Bidding; Buy American Act.

Research References

ALR Library
185 ALR, Fed. 253, Validity, Construction, and Operation of Buy American Act (41 U.S.C.A. § 10a-10d).

107 ALR 5th 673, Validity, Construction, and Application of State "Buy American" Acts.

84 ALR 4th 419, Validity, Construction, and Effect of State and Local Laws Requiring Governmental Units to Give "Purchase Preference" to Goods Manufactured or Services Performed in State.

131 ALR 878, Restitution as Remedy for Wrongful Injunction.

21 ALR 180, False Pretense: Presentation of and Attempt to Establish Fraudulent Claim Against Governmental Agency.

Encyclopedias
70 Am. Jur. Proof of Facts 3d 97, Proof That a Government Agency Was Liable for Improperly Granting a Bid Award to a Bid Applicant.

Forms
Nichols Cyclopedia of Legal Forms Annotated § 7:2518, Supply Contract with United States--General Provisions.

Treatises and Practice Aids
Federal Procedure, Lawyers Edition § 43:76, "Buy American" Rule--Waiver Application.

Restatement (Third) of Foreign Relations § 805, Indirect Barriers to Imports.

West's Federal Administrative Practice § 612, Laws Applicable--Buy American.

WESTLAW ELECTRONIC RESEARCH

See Westlaw guide following the Explanation pages of this volume.

Notes of Decisions

Administration of statute 12	Foreign supplies 6
Construction with other laws 1	Place of manufacture 5
Exemptions 7, 8	Policy 3
Generally 7	Public use 4
Time of request 8	

___

1. Construction with other laws

It was within authority of Navy to reject hollow metal doors as failing to conform to Navy specifications as result of their foreign manufacture, based upon "Buy American" clause in Navy contract; purchasing requirements imposed by the Buy American Act had not been supplanted by Trade Agreements Act of 1979. U.S. for Use and Ben. of A. Hollow Metal Warehouse, Inc. v. U.S. Fidelity & Guar. Co., N.D.Ill.1988, 700 F.Supp. 410.

2. Purpose

Central purpose of sections 10a to 10d of this title was to protect the American worker. Allis-Chalmers Corp., Hydro-Turbine Division v. Friedkin, C.A.3 (Pa.) 1980, 635 F.2d 248. United States ☞ 64.15

Sections 10a to 10d of this title were designed during depression as device to foster and protect American industry, American workers and American invested capital. Textron, Inc., Bell Helicopter Textron Division v. Adams, D.C.D.C.1980, 493 F.Supp. 824. United States ☞ 64.15

3. Policy

Buy American Act (BAA) evidences significant or deeply ingrained strand of public procurement policy that is required, under "Christian doctrine," to be included in federal construction contract by operation of law. S.J. Amoroso Const. Co., Inc. v. U.S., C.A.Fed.1993, 12 F.3d 1072. United States ☞ 70(6.1)

4. Public use

Sections 10a to 10d of this title do not apply to Bureau of Mint purchases of metal for use in manufacturing coins for foreign government because such acquisitions are not for public use under terms of such sections. 1979, 58 Comp.Gen. 327.

5. Place of manufacture

Finding that claims for payment from the Government for products delivered were knowingly made, if false, was supported by evidence that supplier thought that blanks were "components" of the hacksaw blades which he was selling to the Government and that the blades were not domestic end products for purposes of the Buy American Act, that one employee of the supplier falsely told a GSA official that supplier would be using domestic steel to make the blades, and that it destroyed packaging of foreign hacksaw blanks which contained the wording "Made in Sweden." U.S. v. Rule Industries, Inc., C.A.1 (Mass.) 1989, 878 F.2d 535. United States ☞ 122

Upon identification of contract components, this section et seq. requires cost analysis only of components themselves and not their constituent parts in order to determine place of their "manufacture." Textron, Inc., Bell Helicopter Textron Division v. Adams, D.C.D.C.1980, 493 F.Supp. 824. United States ☞ 64.40(1)

Government was not entitled to deduct cost of fire sprinkler piping on ground that it had not been manufactured in United States; de minimis use of short span of pipe in one room did not violate Buy American Act. Mega Const. Co., Inc. v. U.S., Fed.Cl.1993, 29 Fed.Cl. 396. United States ☞ 75(5)

Bid stating country of manufacture as "USA/England" was correctly evaluated as offering foreign end product, since bid could reasonably be construed to permit bidder to furnish either domestic or foreign product, in event of award. 1983, 62 Op.Comp.Gen. 154.

This section is concerned with place of manufacture, mining, or production, and not with nationality of contract bidders; consequently, waiver of this section depends upon place of production, and not upon ownership or control of bidding firms. 1982, 61 Comp.Gen. 431.

6. Foreign supplies

Use of foreign supplies as basis for brand name or as basis for equal procurement does not violate this section. 1980, 59 Comp.Gen. 678.

7. Exemptions—Generally

Contractor did not make timely request for waiver of statute requiring government to give preference to domestic construction materials, though contractor requested postaward approval of foreign wire material, where it did not make formal request for waiver; remark by contracting officer that nothing could be done about higher cost of domestic product could not reasonably be understood as formal denial of formal request for waiver. C. Sanchez and Son, Inc. v. U.S., C.A.Fed.1993, 6 F.3d 1539. United States ☞ 70(21); United States ☞ 70(36)

Navy's failure to grant waiver of Buy American Act's domestic buying requirements to construction contractor at Naval center was abuse of discretion, and thus Navy's actions constituted constructive change entitling contractor to equitable adjustment under contract; contractor originally bid panel fabrication at $165,500, contractor later found that it could not obtain panels domestically at that price, contractor obtained foreign bid of $120,000, and contractor ultimately obtained panels from domestic source for $200,000 due to Navy's denial of waiver. John C. Grimberg Co., Inc. v. U.S., C.A.Fed.1989, 869 F.2d 1475, rehearing denied.

Exemption from this section and section 10d of this title existed for British defense products, with exception of those products specifically excluded by memorandum of understanding between United States and United Kingdom, and thus award to British corporation of procurement contract for sight-post assembly for use on a rifle did not violate this section and section 10d of this title. Self-Powered Lighting, Ltd. v. U.S., S.D.N.Y.1980, 492 F.Supp. 1267. United States ☞ 64.15

Where waiver was appropriate under terms of this section, and had been granted, contractor's bid was based on cost of the foreign material in question, contractor's cost of performance was not affected by waiver, and contractor's bid would have remained the low bid even if it had been based entirely on domestic materials, imposition of a credit, under changes clause of contract in question, for contractor's use of nondomestic structural steel, was inappropriate. L.G. Lefler, Inc. v. U.S., Cl.Ct.1984, 6 Cl.Ct. 514, affirmed 801 F.2d 387. United States ☞ 70(17)

Agency head has authority to waive application of this section after government contract bid opening, if that action would be in public interest. 1985, 64 Op.Comp. Gen. 452.

In negotiated procurements, award to firm offering foreign product at higher price can properly be made, if foreign offer is evaluated as best offer, considering combination of price, applicable price differential, and technical approach. 1984, 63 Op.Comp.Gen. 585.

8. —— Time of request, exemptions

Appropriate time to request waiver of Buy American Act is in first instance before contract award, or at least before contract has been performed, so that grant of waiver, if warranted, will avoid increased construction costs. C. Sanchez and Son, Inc. v. U.S., C.A.Fed.1993, 6 F.3d 1539. United States ☞ 70(36)

Exceptions to sections 10a to 10d of this title can be granted after contract has been awarded. John T. Brady & Co. v. U.S., C.A.Fed.1982, 693 F.2d 1380. United States ☞ 64.45(4)

Exception to Buy American Act did not have to be requested at time of bid submission; exception could be granted by means of change order. Blinderman Const. Co., Inc. v. U.S., Cl.Ct.1988, 15 Cl.Ct. 121. United States ☞ 70(26)

9. Surcharge on foreign bid

Under sections 10a to 10d of this title, surcharge is not applied automatically to entire price of foreign bid when it is determined that bid is foreign, and post-delivery expenses are excluded. Allis-Chalmers Corp., Hydro-Turbine Division v. Friedkin, C.A.3 (Pa.) 1980, 635 F.2d 248. United States ☞ 64.40(1)

10. Substitution of materials

Contractor's failure, if any, to delineate "changes" clause of contract with Veterans Administration for general architectural work associated with construction of building as basis for recovery on account of contracting officer's refusal, pursuant to this section, to permit substitution of Japanese aluminum for domestic aluminum after award of contract did not bar right to recover, where relief sought was clearly described and well understood. John T. Brady & Co. v. U.S., C.A.Fed.1982, 693 F.2d 1380. United States ☞ 74(1)

11. Unresponsive bid

Bidder's failure to complete Buy American Certificate or check foreign source certificate in connection with its bid for contract from Washington Metropolitan Area Transit Authority (WMATA) rendered bid unresponsive; had bidder checked second option of foreign source certificate, either before or after opening of bids, WMATA would have been required by regulations to increase plaintiff's bid price by 10%, and allowing contractor to make choice after bids were submitted would thus have permitted material alteration of bid by allowing post-bidding manipulation based on bids of other competitors. Seal and Co., Inc. v. Washington Metropolitan Area Transit Authority, E.D.Va.1991, 768 F.Supp. 1150. Urban Railroads ☞ 8

12. Administration of statute

Administration of the Buy American Act is responsibility of government. C. Sanchez and Son, Inc. v. U.S., C.A.Fed.

1993, 6 F.3d 1539. United States ☞ 64.15

13. Quantitative requirement

Provision of Buy American Act (BAA), stating that manufactured articles acquired for public use must be manufactured substantially all from articles, materials, or supplies produced in United States, required that cost of domestic components of manufactured articles exceed 50% of cost of end product, pursuant to standard set forth in Federal Acquisition Regulations. U.S. ex rel. Made in the USA Foundation v. Billington, D.Md.1997, 985 F.Supp. 604. United States ☞ 64.45(3)

§ 10b. Contracts for public works; specification for use of American materials; blacklisting contractors violating requirements

(a) Every contract for the construction, alteration, or repair of any public building or public work in the United States growing out of an appropriation heretofore made or hereafter to be made shall contain a provision that in the performance of the work the contractor, subcontractors, material men, or suppliers, shall use only such unmanufactured articles, materials, and supplies as have been mined or produced in the United States, and only such manufactured articles, materials, and supplies as have been manufactured in the United States substantially all from articles, materials, or supplies mined, produced, or manufactured, as the case may be, in the United States except as provided in section 10a of this title: *Provided, however,* That if the head of the department or independent establishment making the contract shall find that in respect to some particular articles, materials, or supplies it is impracticable to make such requirement or that it would unreasonably increase the cost, an exception shall be noted in the specifications as to that particular article, material, or supply, and a public record made of the findings which justified the exception.

(b) If the head of a department, bureau, agency, or independent establishment which has made any contract containing the provision required by subsection (a) of this section finds that in the performance of such contract there has been a failure to comply with such provisions, he shall make public his findings, including therein the name of the contractor obligated under such contract, and no other contract for the construction, alteration, or repair of any public building or public work in the United States or elsewhere shall be awarded to such contractor, subcontractors, material men, or suppliers with which such contractor is associated or affiliated, within a period of three years after such finding is made public.

(Mar. 3, 1933, c. 212, Title III, § 3, 47 Stat. 1520; Aug. 23, 1988, Pub.L. 100–418, Title VII, § 7005(c), 102 Stat. 1553.)

HISTORICAL AND STATUTORY NOTES

Revision Notes and Legislative Reports.
1988 Acts. House Conference Report No. 100–576, see U.S. Code Cong. and Adm. News, p. 1547.

Codification
Section is set out to reflect that amendment by Pub.L. 100–418 has ceased to be effective. See Effective and Applicability Provisions note of 1988 Acts under this section.

Amendments
1988 Amendments. Subsec. (a). Pub.L. 100–418, § 7005(c)(1), temporarily substituted "head of the Federal agency" for "head of the department or independent establishment". See Effective and Applicability Provisions for 1988 Acts under this section.

Subsec. (b). Pub.L.100–418, § 7005(c)(2), substituted "head of a Federal agency" for "head of a department, bureau, agency, or independent establishment".

Effective and Applicability Provisions
1988 Acts. Amendment by Title VII, §§ 7001 to 7005, of Pub.L. 100–418 shall cease to be effective on April 30, 1996, unless Congress, after reviewing report required by section 2515(k) of Title 19, extends such date, see Effective and Applicability Provisions note set out under 41 U.S.C.A. § 10a.

Amendment by section 7005 of Pub.L. 100–418 effective August 23, 1988, see Effective and Applicability Provisions note set out under 41 U.S.C.A. § 10a.

Contractors and Suppliers From Foreign Countries Which Deny Fair and Equitable Market Opportunities for United States Products and Services
Pub.L. 101–514, Title V, § 511, Nov. 5, 1990, 104 Stat. 2098, provided that:

"(a)(1) None of the funds appropriated by this Act may be obligated or expended to enter into any contract for the construction, alteration, or repair of any public building or public work in the United States or any territory or possession of the United States with any contractor or subcontractor of a foreign country, or any supplier of products of a foreign country, during any period in which such foreign country is listed by the United States Trade Representative under subsection (c) of this section.

"(2) The President or the head of a Federal agency administering the funds for the construction, alteration, or repair may waive the restrictions of paragraph (1) of this subsection with respect to an individual contract if the President or the head of such agency determines that such action is necessary for the public interest. The authority of the President or the head of a Federal agency under this paragraph may not be delegated. The President or the head of a Federal agency waiving such restrictions shall, within 10 days, publish a notice thereof in the Federal Register describing in detail the contract involved and the reason for granting the waiver.

"(b)(1) Not later than May 1, 1991, the United States Trade Representative shall make a determination with respect to each foreign country of whether such foreign country—

"(A) denies fair and equitable market opportunities for products and services of the United States in procurement, or

"(B) denies fair and equitable market opportunities for products and services of the United States in bidding, for construction projects that cost more than $500,000 and are funded (in whole or in part) by the government of such foreign country or by an entity controlled directly or indirectly by such foreign country.

"(2) In making determinations under paragraph (1), the United States Trade Representative shall take into account information obtained in preparing the report submitted under section 181(b) of the Trade Act of 1974 [19 U.S.C.A. § 2241(b)] and such other information or evidence concerning discrimination in construction projects against United

States products and services that are available.

"(c)(1) The United States Trade Representative shall maintain a list of each foreign country which—

　"(A) denies fair and equitable market opportunities for products and services of the United States in procurement, or

　"(B) denies fair and equitable market opportunities for products and services of the United States in bidding,

for construction projects that cost more than $500,000 and are funded (in whole or in part) by the government of such foreign country or by an entity controlled directly or indirectly by such foreign country.

"(2) Any foreign country that is initially listed or that is added to the list maintained under paragraph (1) shall remain on the list until—

　"(A) such country removes the barriers in construction projects to United States products and services;

　"(B) such country submits to the United States Trade Representative evidence demonstrating that such barriers have been removed; and

　"(C) the United States Trade Representative conducts an investigation to verify independently that such barriers have been removed and submits, at least 30 days before granting any such waiver, a report to each House of the Congress identifying the barriers and describing the actions taken to remove them.

"(3) The United States Trade Representative shall publish in the Federal Register the entire list required under paragraph (1) and shall publish in the Federal [sic] Register any modifications to such list that are made after publication of the original list.

"(d) For purposes of this section—

　"(1) The term 'foreign country' includes any foreign instrumentality. Each territory or possession of a foreign country that is administered separately for customs purposes shall be treated as a separate foreign country.

　"(2) Any contractor or subcontractor that is a citizen or national of a foreign country, or is controlled directly or indirectly by citizens or nationals of a foreign country, shall be considered to be a contractor or subcontractor of such foreign country.

　"(3) Subject to paragraph (4), any product that is produced or manufactured (in whole or in substantial part) in a foreign country shall be considered to be a product of such foreign country.

　"(4) The restrictions of subsection (a)(1) shall not prohibit the use, in the construction, alteration, or repair of a public building or public work, of vehicles or construction equipment of a foreign country.

　"(5) The terms 'contractor' and 'subcontractor' include any person performing any architectural, engineering, or other services directly related to the preparation for or performance of the construction, alteration, or repair.

"(e) Paragraph (a)(1) of this section shall not apply to contracts entered into prior to the date of enactment of this Act [Nov. 5, 1990].

"(f) The provisions of this section are in addition to, and do not limit or supersede, any other restrictions contained in any other Federal law."

Prohibition on Use of Funds for Construction Contracts with Contractors of Foreign Countries Denying United States Contractors Fair Opportunities in Government Construction Projects
Pub.L. 101–516, Title III, § 340, Nov. 5, 1990, 104 Stat. 2187, provided that:

"(a)(1) None of the funds appropriated by this Act [Pub.L. 101–516, Nov. 5, 1990, 104 Stat. 2155] may be obligated or expended to enter into any contract for the construction, alteration, or repair of any public building or public work in the United States or any territory or possession of the United States with any contractor or subcontractor of a foreign country, or any supplier of products of a foreign country, during any period in which such foreign country is listed by the United States Trade Representative under subsection (c) of this section.

"(2) The President or the head of a Federal agency administering the funds for the construction, alteration, or repair may waive the restrictions of paragraph (1) of this subsection with respect to an individual contract if the President or the head of such agency determines that such action is necessary for the public interest. The authority of the President or the head of a Federal agency under this paragraph may not be delegated. The President or the head of a Federal agency waiving such restrictions shall, within 10 days, publish a notice thereof in the Federal Register describing in detail the contract involved and the reason for granting the waiver.

"(b)(1) Not later than 30 days after the date of enactment of this Act [Nov. 5, 1990], the United States Trade Representative shall make a determination with respect to each foreign country of whether such foreign country—

"(A) denies fair and equitable market opportunities for products and services of the United States in procurement, or

"(B) denies fair and equitable market opportunities for products and services of the United States in bidding,

for construction projects that cost more than $500,000 and are funded (in whole or in part) by the government of such foreign country or by an entity controlled directly or indirectly by such foreign country.

"(2) In making determinations under paragraph (1), the United States Trade Representative shall take into account information obtained in preparing the report submitted under section 181(b) of the Trade Act of 1974 [section 2241(b) of Title 19, Customs Duties] and such other information or evidence concerning discrimination in construction projects against United States products and services that are available.

"(c)(1) The United States Trade Representative shall maintain a list of each foreign country which—

"(A) denies fair and equitable market opportunities for products and services of the United States in procurement, or

"(B) denies fair and equitable market opportunities for products and services of the United States in bidding,

for construction projects that cost more than $500,000 and are funded (in whole or in part) by the government of such foreign country or by an entity controlled directly or indirectly by such foreign country.

"(2) Any foreign country that is initially listed or that is added to the list maintained under paragraph (1) shall remain on the list until—

"(A) such country removes the barriers in construction projects to United States products and services;

"(B) such country submits to the United States Trade Representative evidence demonstrating that such barriers have been removed; and

"(C) the United States Trade Representative conducts an investigation to verify independently that such barriers have been removed and submits, at least 30 days before granting any such waiver, a report to each House of the Congress identifying the barriers and describing the actions taken to remove them.

"(3) The United States Trade Representative shall publish in the Federal Register the entire list required under paragraph (1) and shall publish in the Federal Register any modifications to such list that are made after publication of the original list.

"(d) For purposes of this section—

"(1) The term 'foreign country' includes any foreign instrumentality. Each territory or possession of a foreign country that is administered separately for customs purposes shall be treated as a separate foreign country.

"(2) Any contractor or subcontractor that is a citizen or national of a foreign country, or is controlled directly or indirectly by citizens or nationals of a foreign country, shall be considered to be a contractor or subcontractor of such foreign country.

"(3) Subject to paragraph (4), any product that is produced or manufactured (in whole or in substantial part) in a foreign country shall be considered to be a product of such foreign country.

"(4) The restrictions of subsection (a)(1) shall not prohibit the use, in the construction, alteration, or repair of a public building or public work, of vehicles or construction equipment of a foreign country.

"(5) The terms 'contractor' and 'subcontractor' includes any person performing any architectural, engineering, or other services directly related to the preparation for or performance of the construction, alteration, or repair.

"(e) Paragraph (a)(1) of this section shall not apply to contracts entered into prior to the date of enactment of this Act [Nov. 5, 1990].

"(f) The provisions of this section are in addition to, and do not limit or supersede, any other restrictions contained in any other Federal law."

Restrictions on Expenditure of Funds Appropriated for Fiscal Year 1988 for Construction, Alteration or Repair of Public Buildings or Works by Foreign Contractors; Waiver of Restrictions

Provisions prohibiting the obligation or expenditure of funds to enter into any contract for construction, alteration, or repair of any public building or public work in the United States or any territory or possession of the United States with any contractor or subcontractor of a foreign country, or any supplier of products of a foreign country, during any period in which such foreign country denies fair and equitable market opportunities for products and services of the United States in procurement or bidding for construction projects that cost more than $500,000 and are funded in whole or in part by the government of such foreign country or by an entity controlled directly or indirectly by such foreign country were contained in the following appropriation Acts:

Pub.L. 101–516, Title III, § 340, Nov. 5, 1990, 104 Stat. 2187.

Pub.L. 101–514, Title V, § 511, Nov. 5, 1990, 104 Stat. 2098.

Pub.L. 100–202, § 109, Dec. 22, 1987, 101 Stat. 1329–434; Pub.L. 105 –362, Title XIV, § 1401(d), Nov. 10, 1998, 112 Stat. 3294.

LAW REVIEW AND JOURNAL COMMENTARIES

Debarment and suspension revisited: Fewer eggs in the basket? Brian D. Shannon, 44 Cath.U.L.Rev. 363 (1995).

LIBRARY REFERENCES

American Digest System

United States ⚎64.20.
Key Number System Topic No. 393.

Research References

ALR Library

185 ALR, Fed. 253, Validity, Construction, and Operation of Buy American Act (41 U.S.C.A. § 10a-10d).

108 ALR 5th 189, Validity of State and Local Statutes Allegedly Infringing on Federal Government's Exclusive Power Over Foreign Affairs--Nonalien Cases.

107 ALR 5th 673, Validity, Construction, and Application of State "Buy American" Acts.

21 ALR 180, False Pretense: Presentation of and Attempt to Establish Fraudulent Claim Against Governmental Agency.

Encyclopedias

70 Am. Jur. Proof of Facts 3d 97, Proof That a Government Agency Was Liable for Improperly Granting a Bid Award to a Bid Applicant.

Treatises and Practice Aids

West's Federal Administrative Practice § 659, Debarment and Suspension.

WESTLAW ELECTRONIC RESEARCH

See Westlaw guide following the Explanation pages of this volume.

Notes of Decisions

1. Contracts within section

Buy American Act (BAA) provision mandating that each individual component delivered to construction site be at least 50% domestic material applied to contract, even though parties erroneously included clause that would have governed supply contract, rather than construction contract, whether error was advertent or inadvertent. S.J. Amoroso Const. Co., Inc. v. U.S., Cl.Ct.1992, 26 Cl.Ct. 759, affirmed 12 F.3d 1072. United States ☞ 70(9)

Architect's approval of certain vinyl flooring for use in government construction project was not decisive; architect did not have authority to override requirements of Buy American Act, as incorporated in government contract, minimum size requirements of Veterans Administrative specification or contracting officer's authority to approve submittal pursuant to contract. Blinderman Const. Co., Inc. v. U.S., Cl.Ct.1988, 15 Cl.Ct. 121. United States ☞ 70(6.1)

Grants from funds appropriated by J.Res. Apr. 8, 1935, c. 48, 49 Stat. 115, to the Governors of the several States for emergency relief purposes were "projects" within the meaning of section 13 of that Resolution, whether for construction work or for the purchase of such items as food and clothing, and such grants were subject to provisions of this section. 1935, 38 Op.Atty.Gen. 207.

This section, implemented by defense acquisition regulation, provides preference for suppliers of domestic end products, but does not require that contract bidders offering foreign end products be rejected as nonresponsive. 1982, 61 Op. Comp.Gen. 431.

2. Construction materials

Each steel beam brought to construction site for incorporation into building had to satisfy domestic content requirements of Buy American Act (BAA), even though beams were later combined with other materials. S.J. Amoroso Const.

Co., Inc. v. U.S., C.A.Fed.1993, 12 F.3d 1072. United States ☞ 70(8)

3. Domestic or foreign bids

All or none government contract bid cannot be used to characterize as domestic, bid items that are clearly foreign, on ground that particular contract items represent less than half of total bid. 1984, 63 Op.Comp.Gen. 503.

4. Adjustment in price

Where agency concedes violation by contractor of Buy American certification but it is impractical to remove foreign materials in question, contract price should be adjusted by difference in costs of similar domestic and foreign products. 1980, 59 Comp.Gen. 405.

5. Case or controversy

Neither American turbine manufacturer's claim that Secretary of Defense did not validly waive applicable provisions of section 10a et seq. of this title nor claim that Army Corps of Engineers incorrectly interpreted phrase "defense articles and services" in Swiss "Memorandum of Understanding" to include fishwater turbines such as those purchased by the Corps for installation in dam presented live controversy where decision by Defense Logistics Agency that such turbines could no longer be purchased from foreign countries under "Memoranda of Understanding" and substantial completion of the contract concerning the Swiss turbines had mooted the American manufacturer's claim for injunctive relief, and same issues were bound to arise, in more concrete setting, in the American manufacturer's suit for money damages in Court of Claims. Allis-Chalmers Corp. v. Arnold, C.A.9 (Or.) 1980, 619 F.2d 44. Federal Courts ☞ 13

6. Injunction

Refusal of federal agency, which awarded contract for manufacture and installation of turbines for a power plant to lowest foreign bidder rather than sole domestic bidder, to apply differential to bid price of foreign bidder to bid prices for services and installation after delivery was not clearly illegal under sections 10a to 10d of this title and interpretative executive orders and federal procurement regulations; thus, sole domestic bidder was not entitled to the grant of a preliminary injunction halting performance of procurement contract notwithstanding fact that agency's refusal to review domestic bidder's allegations regarding its status as a labor surplus area concern was clearly illegal. Allis-Chalmers Corp. v. Friedkin, M.D.Pa.1980, 481 F.Supp. 1256, affirmed 635 F.2d 248. Injunction ⊂⇒ 138.63

In proceeding by petroleum corporation to enjoin cancellation of Government procurement contracts and any discrimination in future in sales to Government because of importation of oil above its allotted quota under voluntary oil import program, evidence established that refusal of administrator of voluntary oil import program to revise corporation's quota to include imported oil which was not included in corporation's estimate of oil to be imported was not so arbitrary as to warrant granting of preliminary injunction. Eastern States Petroleum & Chemical Corp. v. Seaton, D.C.D.C.1958, 165 F.Supp. 363. Injunction ⊂⇒ 147

§ 10b–1. Omitted

HISTORICAL AND STATUTORY NOTES

Codification

Section, Mar. 3, 1933, c. 212, Title III, § 4, as added Aug. 23, 1988, Pub.L. 100–418, Title VII, § 7002(2), 102 Stat. 1545, and amended Oct. 13, 1994, Pub.L. 103–355, Title VII, § 7206(a), 108 Stat. 3382, which related to prohibition on procurement contracts for products or services connected with certain foreign countries, was omitted in view of section 7004 of Pub.L. 100–418 which provided that the amendment by Pub.L. 100–418, enacting this section, ceased to be effective on April 30, 1996. See section 7004 of Pub.L. 100–418, set out as an Effective and Applicability Provisions note under 41 U.S.C.A. § 10a.

§ 10b–2. Waiver of Buy American Act

(a) Buy American Act waiver rescissions

(1) If the Secretary of Defense, after consultation with the United States Trade Representative, determines that a foreign country which is party to an agreement described in paragraph (2) has violated the terms of the agreement by discriminating against certain types of products produced in the United States that are covered by the agreement, the Secretary of Defense shall rescind the Secretary's blanket waiver of the Buy American Act with respect to such types of products produced in that foreign country.

(2) An agreement referred to in paragraph (1) is any reciprocal defense procurement memorandum of understanding between the United States and a foreign country pursuant to which the Secretary of Defense has prospectively waived the Buy American Act for certain products in that country.

(b) Definition

For purposes of this section, the term "Buy American Act" means Title III of the Act entitled "An Act making appropriations for the Treasury and Post Office Departments for the fiscal year ending June 30, 1934, and for other purposes", approved March 3, 1933 (41 U.S.C. 10a et seq.).

(Pub.L. 103–160, Div. A, Title VIII, § 849(c), (d), Nov. 30, 1993, 107 Stat. 1725.)

HISTORICAL AND STATUTORY NOTES

Revision Notes and Legislative Reports
1989 Acts. House Report No. 101–121, House Conference Report No. 101–331, and Statement by President, see 1989 U.S. Code Cong. and Adm. News, p. 838.

1991 Acts. House Report No. 102–60 and House Conference Report No. 102–311, see 1991 U.S. Code Cong. and Adm. News, p. 918.

1993 Acts. House Report No. 103–200 and House Conference Report No. 103–357, see 1993 U.S. Code Cong. and Adm. News, p. 2013.

1997 Acts. House Conference Report No. 105–265 and Statement by President, see 1997 U.S. Code Cong. and Adm. News, p. 1703.

1998 Acts. House Conference Report No. 105–746 and Statement by President, see 1998 U.S. Code Cong. and Adm. News, p. 514.

2002 Acts. Statement by President, see 2001 U.S. Code Cong. and Adm. News, p. 1776.

Statement by President, see 2002 U.S. Code Cong. and Adm. News, p. 1030.

2004 Acts. House Conference Report No. 108–622, see 2004 U.S. Code Cong. and Adm. News, p. 873.

Statement by President, see 2004 U.S. Code Cong. and Adm. News, p. S23.

2005 Acts. House Conference Report No. 109–359, see 2005 U.S. Code Cong. and Adm. News, p. 1446.

Statement by President, see 2005 U.S. Code Cong. and Adm. News, p. S50.

References in Text
The Buy American Act, referred to in text, is Act Mar. 3, 1933, c. 212, Title III, §§ 1 to 3, 47 Stat. 1520, which are classified to 41 U.S.C.A. §§ 10a, 10b, 10b–1, and 10c. For complete classification, see Short Title note set out under 41 U.S.C.A. § 10a and Tables.

Codifications
Section is from the National Defense Authorization Act for Fiscal Year 1994 not as part of the Buy American Act which consists of 41 U.S.C.A. §§ 10a, 10b, 10b–1, and 10c.

Subsections (a) and (b) of this section were subsections (c) and (d) in the original and were editorially renumbered for purposes of codification.

The text of this section was formerly set out as a note under this section.

Similar Provisions
Provisions similar to those in this section and 41 U.S.C.A. § 10b–3 were contained in the following Acts:

Pub.L. 110–116, Div. A, Title VIII, § 8029, Nov. 13, 2007, 121 Stat. 1321.

Pub.L. 109–289, Div. A, Title VIII, § 8027, Sept. 29, 2006, 120 Stat. 1279.

Pub.L. 109–148, Div. A, Title VIII, § 8030, Dec. 30, 2005, 119 Stat. 2705.

Pub.L. 108–287, Title VIII, § 8032, Aug. 5, 2004, 118 Stat. 977.

Pub.L. 108–87, Title VIII, § 8033, Sept. 30, 2003, 117 Stat. 1079.

Pub.L. 107–248, Title VIII, § 8033, Oct. 23, 2002, 116 Stat. 1544.

Pub.L. 107–117, Div. A, Title VIII, § 8036, Jan. 10, 2002, 115 Stat. 2255.

Pub.L. 106–259, Title VIII, § 8036, Aug. 9, 2000, 114 Stat. 682.

Pub.L. 106–79, Title VIII, § 8038, Oct. 25, 1999, 113 Stat. 1239.

Pub.L. 105–262, Title VIII, § 8038, Oct. 17, 1998, 112 Stat. 2305.

Pub.L. 105–56, Title VIII, § 8040, Oct. 8, 1997, 111 Stat. 1229.

Pub.L. 104–208, Div. A, Title I, § 101(b) [Title VIII, § 8042], Sept. 30, 1996, 110 Stat. 3009–97.

Pub.L. 104–61, Title VIII, § 8051, Dec. 1, 1995, 109 Stat. 662.

Pub.L. 103–335, Title VIII, § 8058, Sept. 30, 1994, 108 Stat. 2631.

Pub.L. 103–139, Title VIII, § 8069, Nov. 11, 1993, 107 Stat. 1455.

Pub.L. 102–396, Title IX, § 9096, Oct. 6, 1992, 106 Stat. 1924.

Pub.L. 102–190, Div. A, Title VIII, § 833, Dec. 5, 1991, 105 Stat. 1447.

Pub.L. 102–172, Title VIII, § 8123, Nov. 26, 1991, 105 Stat. 1205.

Pub.L. 101–189, Div. A, Title VIII, § 823, Nov. 29, 1989, 103 Stat. 1504.

[Section 9096(b) of Pub.L. 102–396 was repealed by Pub.L. 103–355, Title VII, § 7206(b), Title X, § 10001, Oct. 13, 1994, 108 Stat. 3382, 3404, effective Oct. 13, 1994, and applicable on and after such date.]

LIBRARY REFERENCES

American Digest System
United States ☞64.15.
Key Number System Topic No. 393.

Research References

ALR Library
185 ALR, Fed. 253, Validity, Construction, and Operation of Buy American Act (41 U.S.C.A. § 10a-10d).

WESTLAW ELECTRONIC RESEARCH

See Westlaw guide following the Explanation pages of this volume.

§ 10b–3.   Annual report relating to Buy American Act

The Secretary of Defense shall submit to Congress, not later than 60 days after the end of each fiscal year, a report on the amount of purchases by the Department of Defense from foreign entities in that fiscal year. Such report shall separately indicate the dollar value of items for which the Buy American Act (41 U.S.C. 10a et seq.) was waived pursuant to any of the following:

(1) Any reciprocal defense procurement memorandum of understanding described in section 10b–2(a)(2) of this title.

(2) The Trade Agreements Act of 1979 (19 U.S.C. 2501 et seq.)

(3) Any international agreement to which the United States is a party.

(Pub.L. 104–201, Div. A, Title VIII, § 827, Sept. 23, 1996, 110 Stat. 2611, and amended Pub.L. 105–85, Div. A, Title VIII, § 846, Nov. 18, 1997, 111 Stat. 1845; Pub.L. 105–261, Div. A, Title VIII, § 812, Oct. 17, 1998, 112 Stat. 2086.)

HISTORICAL AND STATUTORY NOTES

Revision Notes and Legislative Reports
1996 Acts. House Report No. 104–563 and House Conference Report No. 104–724, see 1996 U.S. Code Cong. and Adm. News, p. 2948.

1997 Acts. House Conference Report No. 105–340 and Statement by President, see 1997 U.S. Code Cong. and Adm. News, p. 2251.

1998 Acts. House Conference Report No. 105–736 and Statement by President, see 1998 U.S. Code Cong. and Adm. News, p. 513.

References in Text
The Buy American Act, referred to in text, is Act Mar. 3, 1933, c. 212, Title III, §§ 1 to 3, 47 Stat. 1520, which are classi-

fied to 41 U.S.C.A. §§ 10a, 10b, 10b–1, and 10c. For complete classification, see Short Title note set out under 41 U.S.C.A. § 10a and Tables.

The Trade Agreements Act of 1979, referred to in par. (2), is Pub.L. 96–39, July 26, 1979, 93 Stat. 144, as amended, which is classified principally to chapter 13 (section 2501 et seq.) of Title 19, Customs Duties. For complete classification of this Act to the Code, see References in Text note set out under section 2501 of Title 19 and Tables.

Codifications
This section was enacted as part of the National Defense Authorization Act for Fiscal Year 1997 and not as part of the

Buy American Act which consists of 41 U.S.C.A. §§ 10a, 10b, 10b–1, and 10c.

Amendments

1998 Amendments. Pub.L. 105–261, § 812, substituted "60 days" for "90 days" in provisions preceding par. (1).

1997 Amendments. Pub.L. 105–85, § 846, substituted "90 days" for "120 days".

Similar Provisions

Provisions similar to those in this section were contained in the Acts listed in the Similar Provisions note set out under 41 U.S.C.A. § 10b–2.

Research References

ALR Library

185 ALR, Fed. 253, Validity, Construction, and Operation of Buy American Act (41 U.S.C.A. § 10a-10d).

WESTLAW ELECTRONIC RESEARCH

See Westlaw guide following the Explanation pages of this volume.

§ 10c. Definition of terms used in sections 10a, 10b, and 10c

When used in sections 10a, 10b, and 10c of this title—

(a) The term "United States", when used in a geographical sense, includes the United States and any place subject to the jurisdiction thereof;

(b) The terms "public use", "public building", and "public work" shall mean use by, public building of, and public work of, the United States, the District of Columbia, Puerto Rico, American Samoa, the Canal Zone, and the Virgin Islands.

(c) Omitted.

(Mar. 3, 1933, c. 212, Title III, § 1, 47 Stat. 1520; 1946 Proc. No. 2695, eff. July 4, 1946, 11 F.R. 7517, 60 Stat. 1352; June 25, 1959, Pub.L. 86–70, § 43, 73 Stat. 151; July 12, 1960, Pub.L. 86–624, § 28, 74 Stat. 419; Aug. 23, 1988, Pub.L. 100–418, Title VII, § 7005(a), 102 Stat. 1552.)

HISTORICAL AND STATUTORY NOTES

Revision Notes and Legislative Reports

1959 Acts. Senate Report No. 331, see 1959 U.S. Code Cong. and Adm. News, p. 1675.

1960 Acts. Senate Report No. 1681, see 1960 U.S. Code Cong. and Adm. News, p. 2963.

1988 Acts. House Conference Report No. 100–576, see U.S. Code Cong. and Adm. News, p. 1547.

References in Text

For definition of Canal Zone, referred to in subsec. (b), see section 3602(b) of Title 22, Foreign Relations and Intercourse.

Codifications

Words "the Philippine Islands" in subsec. (b) were deleted as obsolete in view of recognition of independence of the Philippines by Proc. No. 2695, which was issued pursuant to section 1394 of Title 22, Foreign Relations and Intercourse, and is set out as a note under said section 1394.

Section is set out to reflect that amendment by Pub.L. 100–418, temporarily adding subsec. (c) to this section, has ceased to be effective. See Effective and Applicability Provisions note of 1988 Acts under this section.

Amendments

1988 Amendments. Subsec. (c). Pub.L. 100–418, § 7005(a), temporarily added subsec. (c), which read: "The term 'Federal agency' has the meaning given such term by section 472 of Title 40, which includes the Departments of the Army, Navy, and Air Force." See Effective and Applicability Provisions note of 1988 Acts under this section.

1960 Amendments. Subsec. (b). Pub.L. 86–624 eliminated Hawaii.

1959 Amendments. Subsec. (b). Pub.L. 86–70 eliminated Alaska.

Effective and Applicability Provisions
1988 Acts. Amendment by Title VII, §§ 7001 to 7005, of Pub.L. 100–418 shall cease to be effective on April 30, 1996, unless Congress, after reviewing report required by section 2515(k) of Title 19, extends such date, see Effective and Applicability Provisions note set out under 41 U.S.C.A. § 10a.

Amendment by section 7005 of Pub.L. 100–418 effective Aug. 23, 1988, see Effective and Applicability Provisions note set out under 41 U.S.C.A. § 10a.

1933 Acts. Section 5, formerly section 4, of Act Mar. 3, 1933, renumbered Pub.L. 100–418, Title VII, § 7002(1), Aug. 23, 1988, 102 Stat. 1545, provided that: "This title [enacting this section and sections 10a and 10b of this title] shall take effect on the date of its enactment [Mar. 3, 1933], but shall not apply to any contract entered into prior to such effective date."

Separability of Provisions
Section 6, formerly section 5, of Act Mar. 3, 1933, renumbered Pub.L. 100–418, Title VII, § 7002(1), Aug. 23, 1988, 102 Stat. 1545, provided that: "If any provision of this Act [enacting this section and sections 10a and 10b of this title] or the application thereof to any person or circumstances, is held invalid, the remainder of the Act, and the application thereof to other persons or circumstances, shall not be affected thereby."

LIBRARY REFERENCES

Corpus Juris Secundum
CJS Territories § 36, Competitive Bidding; Buy American Act.

Research References

ALR Library
185 ALR, Fed. 253, Validity, Construction, and Operation of Buy American Act (41 U.S.C.A. § 10a-10d).
21 ALR 180, False Pretense: Presentation of and Attempt to Establish Fraudulent Claim Against Governmental Agency.

WESTLAW ELECTRONIC RESEARCH

See Westlaw guide following the Explanation pages of this volume.

Notes of Decisions

Puerto Rico　1
──────────

1. Puerto Rico
Buy American Act, which provides that American made articles and supplies be preferred in government contracts over bids containing foreign manufactured materials unless inconsistent with public interest, applies to procurements and purchases made by government of Commonwealth of Puerto Rico. Caribbean Tubular Corp. v. Fernandez Torrecillas, D.Puerto Rico 1986, 67 B.R. 172, appeal dismissed and remanded on other grounds 813 F.2d 533. Territories ⚭ 25

§ 10d. Clarification of Congressional intent regarding sections 10a and 10b(a)

In order to clarify the original intent of Congress, hereafter, section 10a of this title and that part of section 10b(a) of this title preceding the words *"Provided, however,"* shall be regarded as requiring the purchase, for public use within the United States, of articles, materials, or supplies manufactured in the United States in sufficient and reasonably available commercial quantities and of a satisfactory quality, unless the head of the department or independent establishment concerned shall determine their purchase to be inconsistent with the public interest or their cost to be unreasonable.

(Oct. 29, 1949, c. 787, Title VI, § 633, 63 Stat. 1024; Aug. 23, 1988, Pub.L. 100–418, Title VII, § 7005(d), 102 Stat. 1553.)

HISTORICAL AND STATUTORY NOTES

Revision Notes and Legislative Reports
1988 Acts. House Conference Report No. 100–576, see U.S. Code Cong. and Adm. News, p. 1547.

Codification
This section was not enacted as part of the Buy American Act.

Section is set out to reflect that amendment by Pub.L. 100–418 has ceased to be effective. See Effective and Applicability Provisions note of 1988 Acts under this section.

Amendments
1988 Amendments. Pub.L. 100–418, § 7005(d), substituted "head of the Fed-

eral agency" for "head of the department or independent establishment".

Effective and Applicability Provisions
1988 Acts. Amendment by Title VII, §§ 7001 to 7005, of Pub.L. 100–418 shall cease to be effective on April 30, 1996, unless Congress, after reviewing report required by section 2515(k) of Title 19, extends such date, see Effective and Applicability Provisions note set out under section 10a of this title.

Amendment by section 7005 of Pub.L. 100–418 effective August 23, 1988, see Effective Date note set out under section 10a of this title.

EXECUTIVE ORDERS
EXECUTIVE ORDER NO. 10582

Dec. 17, 1954, 19 F.R. 8723, as amended by Ex.Ord. No. 11051, Sept. 27, 1962, 27 F.R. 9683; Ex.Ord. No. 12148, July 20, 1979, 44 F.R. 43239; Ex.Ord. No. 12608, Sept. 9, 1987, 52 F.R. 34617

UNIFORM PROCEDURES FOR DETERMINATIONS

Section 1. As used in this order, (a) the term "materials" includes articles and supplies, (b) the term "executive agency" includes executive department, independent establishment, and other instrumentality of the executive branch of the Government, and (c) the term "bid or offered price of materials of foreign origin" means the bid or offered price of such materials delivered at the place specified in the invitation to bid including applicable duty and all costs incurred after arrival in the United States.

Sec. 2. (a) For the purposes of this order materials shall be considered to be of foreign origin if the cost of the foreign products used in such materials consti-

tutes fifty per centum or more of the cost of all the products used in such materials.

(b) For the purposes of the said act of March 3, 1933 [enacting sections 10a to 10c of this title], and the other laws referred to in the first paragraph of the preamble of this order, the bid or offered price of materials of domestic origin shall be deemed to be unreasonable, or the purchase of such materials shall be deemed to be inconsistent with the public interest, if the bid or offered price thereof exceeds the sum of the bid or offered price of like materials of foreign origin and a differential computed as provided in subsection (c) of this section.

(c) The executive agency concerned shall in each instance determine the amount of the differential referred to in subsection (b) of this section on the basis of one of the following-described formulas, subject to the terms thereof:

(1) The sum determined by computing six per centum of the bid or offered price of materials of foreign origin.

(2) The sum determined by computing ten per centum of the bid or offered price of materials of foreign origin exclusive of applicable duty and all costs incurred after arrival in the United States: provided that when the bid or offered price of materials of foreign origin amounts to less than $25,000, the sum shall be determined by computing ten per centum of such price exclusive only of applicable duty.

Sec. 3. Nothing in this order shall affect the authority or responsibility of an executive agency:

(a) To reject any bid or offer for reasons of the national interest not described or referred to in this order; or

(b) To place a fair proportion of the total purchases with small business concerns in accordance with section 302(b) of the Federal Property and Administrative Services Act of 1949, as amended [section 252(b) of this title], section 2(b) of the Armed Services Procurement Act of 1947, as amended [former section 151(b) of this title; now covered by sections 2301, 2303–2305 of Title 10, Armed Forces], and section 202 of the Small Business Act of 1953 [section 631 of Title 15, Commerce and Trade]; or

(c) To reject a bid or offer to furnish materials of foreign origin in any situation in which the domestic supplier offering the lowest price for furnishing the desired materials undertakes to produce substantially all of such materials in areas of substantial unemployment, as determined by the Secretary of Labor in accordance with such appropriate regulations as he may establish and during such period as the President may determine that it is in the national interest to provide to such areas preference in the award of Government contracts:

Provided, that nothing in this section shall prevent the rejection of a bid or offered price which is excessive; or

(d) To reject any bid or offer for materials of foreign origin if such rejection is necessary to protect essential national-security interests after receiving advice with respect thereto from the President or from the Director of the Federal Emergency Management Agency. In providing this advice the Director shall be governed by the principle that exceptions under this section shall be made only upon a clear showing that the payment of a greater differential than the procedures of this section generally prescribe is justified by consideration of national security.

Sec. 4. The head of each executive agency shall issue such regulations as may be necessary to insure that procurement practices under his jurisdiction conform to the provisions of this order.

Sec. 5. This order shall apply only to contracts entered into after the date hereof. In any case in which the head of an executive agency proposing to purchase domestic materials determines that a greater differential than that provided in this order between the cost of such materials of domestic origin and materials of foreign origin is not unreasonable or that the purchase of materials of domestic origin is not inconsistent with the public interest, this order shall not apply. A written report of the facts of each case in which such a determination is made shall be submitted to the President through the Director of the Office of Management and Budget by the official making the determination within 30 days thereafter.

[For transfer of functions of the Federal Emergency Management Agency, including existing responsibilities for emergency alert systems and continuity of operations and continuity of government plans and programs as constituted on June 1, 2006, including all of its personnel, assets, components, authorities, grant programs, and liabilities, and including the functions of the Under Secretary for Federal Emergency Management relating thereto, see 6 U.S.C.A. § 315.]

LIBRARY REFERENCES

American Digest System
  United States ⬤64.15.
  Key Number System Topic No. 393.

Research References

ALR Library

185 ALR, Fed. 253, Validity, Construction, and Operation of Buy American Act (41 U.S.C.A. § 10a-10d).

107 ALR 5th 673, Validity, Construction, and Application of State "Buy American" Acts.

84 ALR 4th 419, Validity, Construction, and Effect of State and Local Laws Requiring Governmental Units to Give "Purchase Preference" to Goods Manufactured or Services Performed in State.

131 ALR 878, Restitution as Remedy for Wrongful Injunction.

Forms

Nichols Cyclopedia of Legal Forms Annotated § 7:2518, Supply Contract with United States--General Provisions.

Treatises and Practice Aids

Federal Procedure, Lawyers Edition § 43:76, "Buy American" Rule--Waiver Application.

Restatement (Third) of Foreign Relations § 805, Indirect Barriers to Imports.

West's Federal Administrative Practice § 612, Laws Applicable--Buy American.

WESTLAW ELECTRONIC RESEARCH

See Westlaw guide following the Explanation pages of this volume.

Notes of Decisions

Mandatory nature of section   1

1. Mandatory nature of section

Under Buy American Act (BAA), only domestic construction materials are to be used in public construction contracts in the United States unless agency head, after timely application for waiver, determines that use of only domestic construction materials would be inconsistent with public interest or that cost of those materials is unreasonable. S.J. Amoroso Const. Co., Inc. v. U.S., C.A.Fed.1993, 12 F.3d 1072. United States ⟜ 70(8)

§ 11. No contracts or purchases unless authorized or under adequate appropriation; report to the Congress

(a) No contract or purchase on behalf of the United States shall be made, unless the same is authorized by law or is under an appropriation adequate to its fulfillment, except in the Department of Defense and in the Department of Homeland Security with respect to the Coast Guard when it is not operating as a service in the Navy, for clothing, subsistence, forage, fuel, quarters, transportation, or medical and hospital supplies, which, however, shall not exceed the necessities of the current year.

(b) The Secretary of Defense and the Secretary of Homeland Security with respect to the Coast Guard when it is not operating as a service in the Navy shall immediately advise the Congress of the exercise of the authority granted in subsection (a) of this section, and shall report quarterly on the estimated obligations incurred pursuant to the authority granted in subsection (a) of this section.

(R.S. § 3732; June 12, 1906, c. 3078, 34 Stat. 255; Oct. 15, 1966, Pub.L. 89–687, Title VI, § 612(e), 80 Stat. 993; Oct. 30, 1984, Pub.L. 98–557, § 17(e), 98 Stat. 2868; Feb. 10, 1996, Pub.L. 104–106, Div. D, Title XLIII, § 4322(b)(4), 110 Stat. 677; July 11, 2006, Pub.L. 109–241, Title IX, § 902(c), 120 Stat. 566.)

HISTORICAL AND STATUTORY NOTES

Revision Notes and Legislative Reports

1984 Acts. Senate Report No. 98–454, see 1984 U.S. Code Cong. and Adm. News, p. 4831.

1996 Acts. House Conference Report No. 104–450, see 1996 U.S. Code Cong. and Adm. News, p. 238.

2006 Acts. House Conference Report No. 109–43, see 2006 U.S. Code Cong. and Adm. News, p. 579.

Statement by President, see 2006 U.S. Code Cong. and Adm. News, p. S29.

Codifications

R.S. § 3732 derived from Act Mar. 2, 1861, c. 84, § 10, 12 Stat. 220.

The Department of the Air Force was inserted under the authority of section 207(a), (f) of Act July 26, 1947, c. 343, Title II, 61 Stat. 501, and Secretary of Defense Transfer Orders No. 6, eff. Jan. 15, 1948; No. 12 [§ 1(13)], May 14, 1948; No. 39, May 18, 1949, and No. 40 [App. B(115)], July 22, 1949. The Department of War was designated the Department of the Army and the title of the Secretary of War was changed to Secretary of the Army by section 205(a) of such Act July 26, 1947. Sections 205(a) and 207(a), (f) of Act July 26, 1947, were repealed by section 53 of Act Aug. 10, 1956, c. 1041, 70A Stat. 641. Section 1 of Act Aug. 10, 1956, enacted "Title 10, Armed Forces", which in sections 3010 to 3013 and 8010 to 8013 continued the Departments of the Army and Air Force under the administrative supervision of a Secretary of the Army and a Secretary of the Air Force, respectively.

Amendments

2006 Amendments. Subsec. (a). Pub.L. 109–241, § 902(c), struck out "of Transportation" and inserted "of Homeland Security" following "Department".

Subsec. (b). Pub.L. 109–241, § 902(c), struck out "of Transportation" and inserted "of Homeland Security" following "Secretary".

1996 Amendments. Subsec. (a). Pub.L. 104–106, § 4322(b)(4), struck out the second comma following "quarters".

1984 Amendments. Subsec. (a). Pub.L. 98–557, § 17(e)(1)(A), substituted "except in the Department of Defense and in the Department of Transportation with respect to the Coast Guard when it is not operating as a service in the Navy" for "except in the War and Navy Departments".

Pub.L. 98–557, § 17(e)(1)(B), substituted ", transportation, or medical and hospital supplies" for "or transportation", such change having been made by Act June 12, 1906, thereby requiring no further change in text. See Repeals note below.

Subsec. (b). Pub.L. 98–557, § 17(e)(2), added provisions relating to the Secretary of Transportation with respect to the Coast Guard when it is not operating as a service in the Navy.

1966 Amendments. Pub.L. 89–687 designated existing provisions as subsec. (a) and added subsec. (b).

1906 Amendments. Act June 12, 1906, inserted "medical and hospital supplies".

Effective and Applicability Provisions

1996 Acts. Amendment by Pub.L. 104–106 effective Feb. 10, 1996, except as otherwise provided, see section 4401 of Pub.L. 104–106, set out as a note under section 251 of this title.

Termination of Reporting Requirements

Reporting requirement of this section excepted from termination under Pub.L. 104–66, § 3003(a)(1), as amended, set out in a note under 31 U.S.C.A. § 1113, see Pub.L. 106–65, Div. A, § 1031, set out as a note under 31 U.S.C.A. § 1113.

Transfer of Functions

For transfer of authorities, functions, personnel, and assets of the Coast Guard, including the authorities and functions of the Secretary of Transportation relating thereto, to the Department of Homeland Security, and for treatment of related references, see 6 U.S.C.A. §§ 468(b), 551(d), 552(d) and 557, and the Department of Homeland Security Reorganization Plan of November 25, 2002, as modified, set out as a note under 6 U.S.C.A. § 542.

Repeals

The first proviso under the heading "MEDICAL DEPARTMENT" in Act June 12, 1906, c. 3078, 34 Stat. 255, cited to text, was repealed by Pub.L. 98–557, § 17(e)(3), Oct. 30, 1984, 98 Stat. 2868.

CROSS REFERENCES

Alien smuggling and undercover investigation authority and sums appropriated used for leasing space, see 8 USCA § 1363a.

Contracts for Indian supplies in advance of appropriations, see 25 USCA § 99.

Expenditure by any department in excess of appropriations prohibited, see 31 USCA § 1341.

Printing appropriations not to be exceeded, see 44 USCA § 1102.

Projects under Mexican treaties, authority to enter into contracts beyond amount appropriated, notwithstanding this section, see 22 USCA § 277d–3.

LAW REVIEW AND JOURNAL COMMENTARIES

Risk analysis of financing federal government equipment leases. Gregg A. Day and Patrick J. Keogh, 18 Pub.Cont.L.J. 544 (1989).

LIBRARY REFERENCES

American Digest System

United States ⊕62.
Key Number System Topic No. 393.

Corpus Juris Secundum

CJS United States § 108, Authority of Boards or Officers to Bind Government.
CJS United States § 114, Appropriation or Provision for Payment as Prerequisite to Validity of Contract.

Research References

ALR Library

19 ALR 408, Liability for Work Done or Materials Furnished, Etc., for State or Federal Governments in Excess of Appropriations.

Encyclopedias

14 Am. Jur. Trials 437, Representing the Government Contractor.

Treatises and Practice Aids

Immigration Law Service 2d PSD INA § 294, Undercover Investigation Authority.
West's Federal Administrative Practice § 603, Differences from Private Contracts.

WESTLAW ELECTRONIC RESEARCH

See Westlaw guide following the Explanation pages of this volume.

Notes of Decisions

Generally 1
Affirmative nature of section 3
Appropriation authority 15-23
  Generally 15
  Authority of law 16
  Duration 20
  Exhaustion of appropriation 21

Appropriation authority—Cont'd
  Failure to appropriate 23
  Future appropriations 19
  General appropriation 18

1. Generally

Contracts to be valid must be shown to come under one or the other of provisions of this section. Shipman v. U.S., Ct.Cl.1883, 18 Ct.Cl. 138.

2. Construction with other laws

The exception contained in this section in favor of contracts or purchases in the Army and Navy Departments for clothing, subsistence, forage, fuel, etc., withdraws such contracts or purchases from the operation of the prohibition in former section 665 of Title 31 [now section 1341 of Title 31]. Floyd Acceptances, Ct.Cl.1869, 74 U.S. 666, 7 Wall. 666, 19 L.Ed. 169. The Floyd Acceptances, U.S.Ct.Cl.1868, 74 U.S. 666, 19 L.Ed. 169, 7 Wall. 666.

These provisions apply to the public service in general, and must yield to special provisions relating to a particular department. New York Cent. & H.R.R.R. v. U.S., Ct.Cl.1886, 21 Ct.Cl. 468.

This section and former section 665 of Title 31 [now section 1341 of Title 31] should have been construed together. 1877, 15 Op.Atty.Gen. 209. See, also, 1890, 19 Op.Atty.Gen. 650.

3. Affirmative nature of section

Although exceptional and negative in its form this provision in regard to contracts for clothing, etc., is to be deemed affirmative in its character. Floyd Acceptances, Ct.Cl.1869, 74 U.S. 666, 7 Wall. 666, 19 L.Ed. 169. See, also, 1877, 15 Op.Atty.Gen. 209.

4. Purpose

The object of this section was to prevent executive officers from involving the Government in expenditures and liabilities beyond those authorized by the Legislature. 1895, 21 Op.Atty.Gen. 248.

Purpose of this section is to prevent government officers from contracting beyond legislative authorization. 1981, 60 Comp.Gen. 311.

5. Contracts or purchases within section—Generally

Former section 665 of Title 31 [now section 1341 of Title 31], and this section, relating to contracts involving payments from future appropriations, do not apply to license agreements permitting the Government to use patented inventions. Semple v. U.S., Ct.Cl.1924, 59 Ct.Cl. 664. United States ☞ 62

The appointment of a special agent for the protection of timber on public land at a designated salary per annum, where no such office exists by law, is subject to the provisions of this section and former section 665 of Title 31 [now section 1341 of Title 31]. Peden v. U.S., Ct.Cl.1886, 21 Ct.Cl. 189. United States ☞ 39(1)

6. —— Implied contracts, contracts or purchases within section

The limitation on power of Government officers, who make contracts for the Government not to exceed the amounts appropriated therefor, applies to implied contracts as well as express contracts, so that no contract can be implied from the acts or omissions of a Government officer, if an express contract by him would have been unauthorized. Sutton v. U.S., U.S.1921, 41 S.Ct. 563, 256 U.S. 575, 65 L.Ed. 1099. United States ☞ 69(1)

This section undoubtedly applies to express contracts and prohibits the making of such contracts except as therein provided but it has no application to that class of implied contracts which arise from the acts of public officers in the performance of their duties, in carrying on the business of the Government intrusted to them by law in their respective spheres. Semmes v. U.S., Ct.Cl.1891, 26 Ct.Cl. 119.

7. Procedural irregularities

This section is not violated by mere procedural irregularities in award of authorized contract. 1981, 60 Comp.Gen. 311.

8. Capacity of government to contract generally

The United States, being a body politic, may within the sphere of the constitutional powers confided to it, and through the instrumentality of the proper department to which those powers are confided, enter into contracts not prohibited by law, and appropriate to the just exercise of those powers. U.S. v. Tingey, U.S.Dist.Col. 1831, 30 U.S. 115, 5 Pet. 115, 8 L.Ed. 66.

Both parties to government contract are presumed to be endowed with at least a modicum of business acumen. Fire-

stone Tire & Rubber Co. v. U.S., Ct.Cl. 1971, 444 F.2d 547, 195 Ct.Cl. 21. United States ☞ 70(2.1)

The United States Government has capacity to contract which is coextensive with its duties and powers. U.S. v. Salon, C.A.7 (Ill.) 1950, 182 F.2d 110. United States ☞ 59

9. Authority of government to contract generally

Contracts with the Government must be in strict conformity with the authority conferred before they are enforceable. Wildermuth v. U.S., C.A.7 (Ind.) 1952, 195 F.2d 18. United States ☞ 66

To be "authorized by law," within the meaning of this section, a contract must appear to have been made either in pursuance of express authority given by statute, or of authority necessarily inferable from some duty imposed upon, or from some power given to, the person assuming to contract on behalf of the Government. 1877, 15 Op.Atty.Gen. 236.

10. Authority of contracting officers— Generally

No cases have been found which hold that a person who is not an officer or a representative of the government occupies in dealing with it the position of or a position akin to that of a guardian or trustee. U.S. v. A. Bentley & Sons Co., S.D.Ohio 1923, 293 F. 229, 2 Ohio Law Abs. 243.

An agent without authority so to do cannot make United States liable for its contracts. Pulaski Cab Co. v. U.S., Ct.Cl. 1958, 157 F.Supp. 955, 141 Ct.Cl. 160. United States ☞ 59

The Government is not bound by the acts of its agents when such acts are beyond the scope of their authority. Potter v. U.S., Ct.Cl.1964, 167 Ct.Cl. 28. United States ☞ 59

In actions on contract, express or implied, the Government is to be regarded as the principal, and its officers as its agents, and no acts of theirs can bind the Government for a greater amount than that to which it has limited its liability by statute. Curtis v. U.S., Ct.Cl.1866, 2 Ct. Cl. 144. United States ☞ 68

11. —— Miscellaneous cases officers lacking authority, authority of contracting officers

Recovery upon contractor's claim that elimination of duplexer had been unilaterally ordered by government and that it therefore became necessary to substitute more complex and more expensive distributed switching system was properly disallowed in view of lack of evidence that change was directed by any official of the government authorized to do so. Singer Co. Librascope Div. v. U.S., Ct.Cl. 1977, 568 F.2d 695, 215 Ct.Cl. 281. United States ☞ 70(25.1)

United States was not liable to owner for expense of maintaining crews on tug and barge prior to requisitioning of title by Government on ground that he did so at direction of War Shipping Administration official, in absence of showing that official had authority to bind United States. U.S. v. Willis, C.C.A.4 (Va.) 1947, 164 F.2d 453. War And National Emergency ☞ 14

United States was not liable to plaintiff for injuries to mules, resulting from failure to exercise extra care for them, where contract with an agent for such care was not binding on United States. Occidental Const. Co. v. U.S., C.C.A.9 (Cal.) 1917, 245 F. 817, 158 C.C.A. 157, error dismissed 39 S.Ct. 390, 249 U.S. 623, 63 L.Ed. 806. United States ☞ 68; United States ☞ 78(10)

Even if Government's representative, who was not contracting officer, gave warranty to contractor that certain materials would be provided by Government as needed by contractor in construction work, such warranty would be ineffectual because made without authority. Barling v. U.S., Ct.Cl.1953, 111 F.Supp. 878, 126 Ct.Cl. 34. United States ☞ 60

In absence of any appeal within 30 days from action of contracting officer approving change orders and assessing liquidated damages, or of any action until 16 months after issuance of final voucher, when contractor wrote letter requesting review of items reserved in its release, contracting officer was then without authority to change ruling and allow such items on their merits. Centaur Const. Co. v. U.S., Ct.Cl.1947, 69 F.Supp. 217, 107 Ct.Cl. 498, certiorari denied 68 S.Ct. 56, 332 U.S. 757, 92 L.Ed. 343. United States ☞ 73(14); United States ☞ 73(15)

Where a Government representative advised a prospective bidder for the purchase of scrap from The Alaska Railroad to be delivered to the purchaser "F.O.B. Cars, The Alaska Railroad * * * Seward, Alaska," that the Railroad's Tariff 3–A

would be applicable to the switching of the scrap-loaded cars onto the Railroad's dock in Seward, the Government representative acted without authority and his statements were not binding on either party to the contract. Commercial Metals Co. v. U.S., Ct.Cl.1966, 176 Ct.Cl. 343.

Where officers of Government, without authority to bind Government, give verbal assurances to subcontractor that, if it would furnish contractor with certain gauges and said contractor should fail to pay for them, the United States would pay the said subcontractor, there is no liability on United States to pay for said gauges. Industrial Engineering Co. v. U.S., Ct.Cl.1925, 60 Ct.Cl. 766, affirmed 47 S.Ct. 345, 273 U.S. 659, 71 L.Ed. 827. United States ☞ 68

Where officers of Ordnance Department, without authority to place orders with him or to bind United States by contract, promised plaintiff order would be placed and contract made with him by Government to manufacture and deliver to Ordnance Department certain machinery, and on faith of such promises, plaintiff incurred great expenditures in preparation for performance of orders promised, he could not recover his losses occasioned thereby from Government. Wright v. U.S., Ct.Cl.1925, 60 Ct.Cl. 519. United States ☞ 68

Where army officer, without authority from Secretary of the Army, assured plaintiff that he would have contracts awarded him in future, there was no liability on part of United States to pay plaintiff loss occasioned by cancellation of lease entered into with third party in consequence of such assurance. Burney Axe v. U.S., Ct.Cl.1925, 60 Ct.Cl. 493. United States ☞ 69(6)

12. —— **Miscellaneous cases officers not lacking authority, authority of contracting officers**

Contract whereby federal government agreed to furnish drivers and dockmen to enable motor carrier whose transportation system had been seized by Government in time of war because its employees were on strike to carry on its transportation service, and carrier agreed to pay Government for such services at rates currently in effect on transportation system, was valid and not ultra vires the power of the Government to make. U.S. v. Coordinated Transport,

N.D.Ill.1947, 73 F.Supp. 176. Automobiles ☞ 109

Purchasing agent of Interior Department had authority to contract with freight forwarder for transportation of freight, with provision for unloading and storage at destination. National Carloading Corp. v. U.S., Ct.Cl.1946, 64 F.Supp. 150, 105 Ct.Cl. 479. United States ☞ 40

13. Delegation of authority of contracting officers

In carrying out his obligation to assure that the contractor will comply with the contract plans and specifications, and as a part of his power to order the work done in a reasonable and proper manner, the contracting officer has authority to delegate certain duties and power to others; where a contracting officer designates a resident engineer as his representative to assure compliance with the terms of all contracts within that official's assigned area and specifically delegated to that engineer the obligation to inspect, examine and test workmanship, reject defective workmanship, and require replacement of defective material or workmanship, the resident engineer in exercising this authority acted for the contracting officer, and the contractor to whom the resident engineer gave orders within the scope of this delegated authority was not obligated to appeal from those orders to the contracting officer; and if the resident engineer, acting within the scope of his delegated authority, misconstrued the contract the Government is liable therefor. WRB Corp. v. U.S., Ct.Cl.1968, 183 Ct.Cl. 409. United States ☞ 70(28)

Where an official of the contracting agency is not the contracting officer but has been sent to the plaintiff's plant by the contracting officer for the express purpose of giving guidance and instructions in connection with the contract work, the contractor is justified in relying on his representations as having been made with full authority. Fox Valley Engineering, Inc. v. U.S., Ct.Cl.1960, 151 Ct.Cl. 228. United States ☞ 70(30)

Subordinate unauthorized Government employees cannot give contract interpretations which may be safely relied on by contractors. Jefferson Const. Co. v. U.S., Ct.Cl.1960, 151 Ct.Cl. 75. United States ☞ 70(3)

14. Statutory authority

Where statute under which Government contracting officers or agents act contains no prohibition against a particular type of purchase contract and no direction to use a particular type, the contracting officers are free to follow business practices. Kern-Limerick v. Scurlock, U.S.Ark.1954, 74 S.Ct. 403, 347 U.S. 110, 98 L.Ed. 546, conformed to 266 S.W.2d 298, 223 Ark. 464. United States ☞ 63

Government agency cannot contract in derogation of its statutory powers. Associated Elec. Co-op., Inc. v. Morton, C.A.D.C.1974, 507 F.2d 1167, 165 U.S.App.D.C. 344, certiorari denied 96 S.Ct. 49, 423 U.S. 830, 46 L.Ed.2d 47. United States ☞ 53(6.1)

Government contracting officer has only that authority actually conferred by statute or regulation. Schoenbrod v. U.S., Ct.Cl.1969, 410 F.2d 400, 187 Ct.Cl. 627. United States ☞ 59

The executive officers of the government have no power to bind it by contract, unless there be statutes expressly or by clear implication authorizing them to do so. Chase v. U.S., C.C.Ind.1890, 44 F. 732, affirmed 15 S.Ct. 174, 155 U.S. 489, 39 L.Ed. 234.

Where Government official purports to bind United States to agreement which official has no statutory authority to execute, his act is nugatory and void. U.S. v. City and County of San Francisco, N.D.Cal.1953, 112 F.Supp. 451, affirmed 223 F.2d 737, certiorari denied 76 S.Ct. 181, 350 U.S. 903, 100 L.Ed. 793. United States ☞ 40

No person can make a valid contract in behalf of the United States unless expressly or impliedly authorized by statute to do so, but, if so authorized, the right to make such a contract is not necessarily limited to contracts with persons who are not enemies of the United States and whether the right to make the contract is a right to make it with an enemy depends upon the true construction of the statutes authorizing the making of the contract and not upon any general principles of law. 1870, 13 Op.Atty.Gen. 314.

15. Appropriation authority—Generally

An agency of government cannot create a binding contract without authority of an appropriation of funds from Congress to cover contract; if such an unautho-

rized contract is entered into it is a nullity. Robert F. Simmons and Associates v.
U.S., Ct.Cl.1966, 360 F.2d 962, 175 Ct.Cl.
510. United States ⟶ 62

If an officer is clothed with authority to
do a piece of work, without limitation as
to cost, the contracts made by him therefor are binding on the Government,
whether money is appropriated for the
purpose or not. Shipman v. U.S., Ct.Cl.
1883, 18 Ct.Cl. 138. United States ⟶ 59

Two classes of contracts are authorized
by this section: One where the contract is
authorized and an appropriation sufficient for its fulfillment is provided for;
the other where no appropriation sufficient to the completion of the contract is
made. 1877, 15 Op.Atty.Gen. 235.

**16. —— Authority of law, appropria-
tion authority**

Where an Act of Congress authorizes
an enlargement of the Library of Congress according to a certain specified
plan, and prescribes the length and
breadth and position of the enlargement,
it is "a law authorizing" a contract, even
though the contract slightly exceeds the
appropriation made for that purpose.
Fowler v. U.S., Ct.Cl.1867, 3 Ct.Cl. 43.
United States ⟶ 60

In view of former sections 436 [now
6402, 6405], 483 [now 6101, 6106], 486
[now 6101, 6402], and 493 [now 6402] of
Title 39, expressly authorizing Postmaster
General to contract for carrying mails for
term not to exceed four years, regardless
of appropriations therefor, he may contract for star route service for current
year in excess of the appropriation, since
former section 665 of Title 31 [now section 1341 of Title 31], and this section,
prohibiting expenditures without appropriation, expressly except "contracts authorized by law." 1913, 30 Op.Atty.Gen.
186.

**17. —— Specificity, appropriation au-
thority**

Congress is not required to set out with
particularity each item in an appropriation as a requisite of validity, but it is
sufficient if the appropriation be identifiable sufficiently to make clear the intent
of Congress. U.S. v. State Bridge Commission of Mich., E.D.Mich.1953, 109
F.Supp. 690. United States ⟶ 85

Where contract between city and the
United States, relative to money ad-

vanced by the city towards expenses of
investigating proposed dam project, provided that in event Congress made sufficient appropriations for reimbursement
of sums advanced then refunds would be
made, and thereafter Congress appropriated money for the "continued investigation" of the project without expressly providing for reimbursement, the contract, if
interpreted to bind the Government to
make refund, was invalid as in violation
of this section. City of Los Angeles v.
U.S., Ct.Cl.1946, 68 F.Supp. 974, 107 Ct.
Cl. 315. Contracts ⟶ 123(1); Municipal
Corporations ⟶ 244(1); United States ⟶
66

Contract with the Government to supply all labor and material and to construct bathhouse, swimming pool, and
other playground structures on high
school grounds in the city of Washington,
D.C., was illegal inasmuch as the appropriation for the work stipulated that the
pools, etc., should be located "upon lands
acquired or hereafter acquired for park,
parkway, or playground purposes".
Loehler v. U.S., Ct.Cl.1940, 90 Ct.Cl. 158.
Contracts ⟶ 123(1); United States ⟶ 66

The Secretary of the Navy cannot legally contract with the patentee for the purchase of his patent, or for a license to use
it, under an appropriation limited to the
purchase of material and the employment
of labor in the manufacture of such article out of it. 1889, 19 Op.Atty.Gen. 407.

**18. —— General appropriation, appro-
priation authority**

Though an executive department has
no authority to bind the Government in
excess of appropriations, yet, where an
appropriation has been made by Congress for a general purpose contemplating a multitude of acts to be done by the
department, its agency is general within
those limits, and where persons act in
good faith under orders of the department, no excess of authority in giving
orders above the prescribed limits will be
presumed, and the burden of proving this
defense is upon the Government, when
the facts are peculiarly within its power,
and the creditor was not in circumstances to ascertain them. Leavitt v.
U.S., S.D.N.Y.1888, 34 F. 623. United
States ⟶ 141(1.1)

Fact that appropriation for rent paid to
bridge commission for use of premises at
international bridge as a customs office
was not ear-marked by Congress for par-

ticular disbursement to commission did not render lease of such premiums invalid under provision of this section that no contract on behalf of United States shall be made unless authorized by law or under appropriation adequate to its fulfillment, where Congressional intent that the appropriation was for payment of rent for use of facilities at international bridges was clearly established. U.S. v. State Bridge Commission of Mich., E.D.Mich.1953, 109 F.Supp. 690. United States ⊕ 62

Where service was performed under a general appropriation, the contractor is not bound to know the condition of the appropriation account at the Treasury. Myerle v. U.S., Ct.Cl.1897, 33 Ct.Cl. 1. United States ⊕ 63

A contractor, building a vessel under general appropriations, is not chargeable with a knowledge of the condition of the fund. Myerle v. U.S., Ct.Cl.1896, 31 Ct. Cl. 105. United States ⊕ 74(1)

Persons contracting with the Government for partial service, under general appropriations, are not bound to know the condition of the appropriation or the contract books of the department. Dougherty, for Use of Slavens v. U.S., Ct.Cl.1883, 18 Ct.Cl. 496.

19. —— Future appropriations, appropriation authority

A contract for postal car facilities which makes the liability of the Government conditional upon future appropriations is valid, and becomes operative if appropriations be subsequently made. New York Cent. & H.R.R.R. v. U.S., Ct. Cl.1886, 21 Ct.Cl. 468. Postal Service ⊕ 21(1)

When all that is done is the appropriation of a certain sum to be expended on a certain structure, the plan of which has been determined on, the authority to contract for the completion of the whole structure cannot be inferred; nor can such a contract be binding so as to affix itself to future appropriations even if it is subject to the contingency that such appropriations shall be made. 1877, 15 Op.Atty.Gen. 235.

20. —— Duration, appropriation authority

The power of the Postmaster General to lease buildings for post office use is limited by this section to leases for a period

not exceeding that covered by the appropriations of the year for which the contract is made. Abbott v. U.S., C.C.Wash. 1895, 66 F. 447. See, also, Chase v. U.S., Ind.1894, 15 S.Ct. 174, 155 U.S. 489, 39 L.Ed. 284. Postal Service ⊕ 6

The annual appropriations which are made by Congress to defray the expenses of the executive departments do not authorize heads of those departments to bind the government by contract beyond the time for which such appropriations are made applicable. Chase v. U.S., C.C.Ind.1890, 44 F. 732, affirmed 15 S.Ct. 174, 155 U.S. 489, 39 L.Ed. 234.

Provisions of this section clearly limit the liability of the Government by the appropriation made for each fiscal year, and a lease of a building is included thereunder, and, although for a term of years, is binding on the Government only until the end of the fiscal year in which it is made, with a future option from year to year until the end of the term. Smoot v. U.S., Ct.Cl.1903, 38 Ct.Cl. 418.

Leases entered into under an appropriation of one fiscal year, though for a term of years, are binding on the lessee, the Government, only for the year covered by the appropriation Act, but the extended term named in the lease in effect gives an option to the Government to continue it, if subsequent appropriations be made, until the expiration of the designated term. McCollum v. U.S., Ct.Cl.1881, 17 Ct.Cl. 92. United States ⊕ 70(11)

21. —— Exhaustion of appropriation, appropriation authority

Lease of office space for federal agencies for term of years was in violation of law, in so far as terms extended beyond existing appropriation, precluding recovery for balance after being vacated in accordance with due notice. Leiter v. U.S., U.S.1926, 46 S.Ct. 477, 271 U.S. 204, 70 L.Ed. 906. United States ⊕ 62

Under former section 184 of Title 18 [now section 435 of Title 18], section 12 of this title, this section, and former section 627 of Title 31 [now section 1341 of Title 31], denying authority to make contracts on behalf of the United States in excess of appropriations therefor, Acts making appropriations for a harbor channel improvement did not authorize the Secretary of War [now Secretary of Defense] to contract for the completion of the improvement at a cost exceeding the amount appropriated. Sutton v. U.S., U.S.1921, 41 S.Ct. 563, 256 U.S. 575, 65 L.Ed. 1099.

By express understanding and agreement of the parties the substance of this section forbidding any department from involving the Government in any contract for the future payment of money in excess of the appropriation therefor was incorporated in the instrument, and that the fact that the appropriations for two years of the term were made by Congress was not such recognition of the validity of the contract as to bind the United States to pay the stipulated rental for the third year, and that the lessor had sufficient notice that a smaller amount would be paid as rental for the third year, and by not demanding possession of the premises, he must be held to have assented to the terms offered by that Act of appropriation. Bradley v. U.S., U.S.Ct.Cl.1878, 98 U.S. 104, 8 Otto 104, 25 L.Ed. 105.

The fact that an appropriation is exhausted justifies an officer in stopping a contractor's work, but does not constitute a defense in a suit for breach of contract. Ferris v. U.S., Ct.Cl.1892, 27 Ct.Cl. 542. United States ☞ 73(23)

If a contract, dependent upon an appropriation for its validity, does not exceed the appropriation, it will be deemed valid, though the appropriation be exhausted. New York Cent. & H.R.R.R. v. U.S., Ct.Cl.1886, 21 Ct.Cl. 468. United States ☞ 62

Where the Secretary of the Interior is authorized to expend a certain amount in protecting the timber on the public lands, and he has done so, his authority is exhausted and the Government is not liable to his agents in excess of the expenditure authorized. Peden v. U.S., Ct.Cl.1886, 21 Ct.Cl. 189. United States ☞ 39(9)

Where the authority to enter into a contract for a particular work in behalf of the United States depends wholly upon the appropriation made for that purpose, no officer of the Government has power to create a liability therefor beyond the amount appropriated and the contractor cannot recover more than the amount appropriated, whatever may be the extent of the work. Shipman v. U.S., Ct.Cl. 1883, 18 Ct.Cl. 138. United States ☞ 62

Under this section the Secretary of the Navy has no authority to incur any obligation for work on an uncompleted dry dock when the appropriation has been exhausted, even though immediate action is very important. 1896, 21 Op.Atty.Gen. 288.

Executive officers are prohibited from continuing the employment of the contractors and involving the Government in expenditures or liabilities beyond those contemplated by Congress, or authorized by law, and, if further appropriations are made, there must be a new contract for their expenditure. 1895, 21 Op.Atty.Gen. 244.

22. —— Notice of extent of appropriation, appropriation authority

Section 12 of this title, this section, and former section 627 of Title 31 [now section 1341 of Title 31], prohibit the making of a contract with the United States for work in excess of a specific appropriation therefor by Congress, and where a contractor enters into an agreement for such work he must be held to have notice of the law, especially where the contract itself provides that the work shall be done "within the limits of available funds." Sutton v. U.S., Ct.Cl.1920, 55 Ct.Cl. 193, affirmed as modified 41 S.Ct. 563, 256 U.S. 575, 65 L.Ed. 1099. United States ☞ 62

The contractor is bound to know the restrictions imposed by statute. Sanger & Moody v. U.S., Ct.Cl.1904, 40 Ct.Cl. 47.

Where one contract on its face assumes to provide for all the work authorized by an appropriation, the contractor is bound to know the amount of the appropriation, and cannot recover beyond it. Dougherty, for Use of Slavens v. U.S., Ct.Cl.1883, 18 Ct.Cl. 496. United States ☞ 70(15.1)

A statute limiting the amount of an expenditure is notice in law and in fact to the contractor that the officers of the Government cannot exceed the prescribed bounds and if they are exceeded, the claimant must be deemed to have gone beyond the fixed limit at his own risk. Curtis v. U.S., Ct.Cl.1866, 2 Ct.Cl. 144.

23. —— Failure to appropriate, appropriation authority

Where Congress in an appropriation Act denied to a department funds for payment for services rendered to the Government under a valid contract, there was no attempt by Congress to repudiate the contract. Seatrain Lines v. U.S., Ct.Cl.1943,

99 Ct.Cl. 272.   Contracts ☞ 272; United
States ☞ 72.1(4)

A failure by Congress to appropriate
the full amount of the rent reserved in a
valid lease does not imply a new lease,
nor relieve the Government from liability
for the rent reserved in the old lease.
Freedman's Savings & Trust Co. v. U.S.,
Ct.Cl.1880, 16 Ct.Cl. 19.   United States
☞ 62

The absence of an appropriation out of
which payment can be made is no defense to a valid claim.   Collins' Case,
1879, 15 Ct.Cl. 35.

24. Oral or written authority

Where plaintiff agreed, under purchase
agreements with the United States, to deliver top soil to several parks and park-
ways in New York State at stipulated
prices for delivery at stated locations, and
where the major portion of top soil contracted for delivery to one location was
diverted to other more distant locations,
and where such diversions were made on
oral orders of unauthorized persons and
without written authority from authorized agents of the defendant, plaintiff was
not entitled to recover.   Walter C. Reediger, Inc., v. U.S., Ct.Cl.1941, 94 Ct.Cl.
120.   Sales ☞ 77(2); United States ☞
70(28)

25. Implied authority

Under contract authorizing War Shipping Administration as purchasing agent
for buyer to procure eggs for buyer
through use of priorities or in any manner whatsoever, the Administration had
implied authority to engage the Department of the Army as a subagent to obtain
eggs.   John Minder & Son v. L.D.
Schreiber Co., S.D.N.Y.1947, 73 F.Supp.
477.   United States ☞ 40

Where the Government departed from
its usual practice of providing a naval
officer with funds in advance to purchase
liquor for the Naval Mission in a foreign
country and instead authorized the officer to receive delivery of the liquor before
payment was made, some form of credit
extension by the liquor dealer was required and the Government impliedly authorized the officer to pledge the Government's credit to make the purchase and
in such a case the Government must bear
the loss of plaintiff on that particular
transaction.   Henriquez & Gornell, Inc.
v. U.S., Ct.Cl.1967, 180 Ct.Cl. 1040.

26. Notice of extent of authority

Persons dealing with Government must
take notice of extent of its agents' authority, and Government or public authority
is not bound by such agents' acts or declarations, in absence of showing that they
acted within scope of their authority or
were held out as authorized to do acts or
make declarations for or on behalf of
public authorities.   Kelly v. U.S., Ct.Cl.
1950, 91 F.Supp. 305, 116 Ct.Cl. 811,
certiorari denied 71 S.Ct. 78, 340 U.S.
850, 95 L.Ed. 623, rehearing denied 71
S.Ct. 236, 340 U.S. 898, 95 L.Ed. 651.
United States ☞ 40

Anyone who contracts with the Government must accurately ascertain the extent
of the authority of the Government official with whom he contracts since the
Government may be held liable only for
the authorized acts of its agents.   Henriquez & Gornell, Inc. v. U.S., Ct.Cl.1967,
180 Ct.Cl. 1040.   United States ☞ 68

Persons dealing with the United States
Government must take notice of the extent of the authority of the particular
agent with whom they may be dealing
because the Government is not bound by
the acts or representations of an agent
acting beyond the scope of his actual
authority.   Miami Metropolitan Bldg.
Corp. v. U.S., Ct.Cl.1967, 180 Ct.Cl. 503.
United States ☞ 40

Plaintiff was bound to know and take
notice of limited authority of officer with
whom it was dealing, and court will not
imply that such officer was acting under
proper authority.   Jacob Reed's Sons v.
U.S., Ct.Cl.1925, 60 Ct.Cl. 97, affirmed 47
S.Ct. 339, 273 U.S. 200, 71 L.Ed. 608.
See, also, Ferguson v. U.S., 1925, 60 Ct.
Cl. 649, affirmed 47 S.Ct. 345, 273 U.S.
660, 71 L.Ed. 827.   United States ☞ 68

A contractor dealing with the Government is chargeable with notice of all statutory limitations placed upon the powers
of public officers, but there is a difference
between those powers expressly defined
by statute and those which rest upon the
discretion confided by law to an officer
and where a statute expressly defines the
power it is notice to all the world, but
where it confides a discretion to an officer the party dealing with him, in good
faith, may assume that the discretion is
properly exercised and if the discretion
be vested in a superior while the transaction is with his subordinate the contractor may assume that the discretion has

been properly exercised, and that the subordinate is acting in accordance with his superior's orders. Thompson v. U.S., Ct. Cl.1873, 9 Ct.Cl. 187. United States ⊕ 59

27. Ratification—Generally

Where a service, additional to that required by an express contract, is accepted by an executive department with the understanding that compensation must be dependent upon the future action of Congress, and Congress passes an act referring the claim to the Court of Claims [now United States Claims Court] and directing the manner in which damages, if any, shall be computed, the effect of the statute is to validate the service. Wightman v. U.S., Ct.Cl.1888, 23 Ct.Cl. 144.

Ratification by the head of an executive department, or other responsible officer, will render an unauthorized contract effective and valid. Ford v. U.S., Ct.Cl. 1881, 17 Ct.Cl. 60.

The rule of the common law relative to the ratification of the unauthorized acts of an agent is as applicable to the obligations of the Government as of individuals. Fremont, for Use of Jackson, v. U.S., Ct.Cl.1866, 2 Ct.Cl. 461.

28. ⸺ Appropriation of funds, ratification

While appropriations in some instances may constitute ratification of committee reports, ratification by appropriation will not be found unless prior knowledge of the specific disputed action can be clearly demonstrated. Associated Elec. Co-op., Inc. v. Morton, C.A.D.C.1974, 507 F.2d 1167, 165 U.S.App.D.C. 344, certiorari denied 96 S.Ct. 49, 423 U.S. 830, 46 L.Ed.2d 47. Statutes ⊕ 220

Where a contractor does work of which Congress is cognizant, and for which payments are authorized by legislative appropriation, a contract existed. Myerle v. U.S., Ct.Cl.1897, 33 Ct.Cl. 1. United States ⊕ 63

A contract repeatedly brought to the attention of Congress by reports of a department, and recognized legislatively, as binding upon the United States, by repeated appropriations, must be deemed to have been ratified by legislative authority. Myerle v. U.S., Ct.Cl.1896, 31 Ct.Cl. 105. United States ⊕ 68

Where Congress authorizes an executive officer to procure suitable rooms for

a newly established executive department and subsequently appropriates for the rent of the building, the precise rent reserved in the lease, it must be deemed a ratification. Freedman's Savings & Trust Co. v. U.S., Ct.Cl.1880, 16 Ct.Cl. 19. United States ⊕ 68

29. Bond sales

In view of section 5 of this title there was no existing authority, except as to two of the bond issues involved, to negotiate a sale of the bonds to the issuing agencies at less than par and accrued interest. 1955, 41 Op.Atty.Gen. 33.

30. Indemnification of carriers

The Federal Aviation Administration and the Federal Bureau of Investigation do not have, with certain limited exceptions, the authority to indemnify a carrier for its liability in connection with the management of a hijacking. 1978 (Counsel-Inf.Op.) 2 Op.O.L.C. 219.

31. Lease of buildings

It was in view of former section 665 of Title 31 [now section 1341 of Title 31], and this section, and in the absence of statutory authority that the Secretary of the Treasury had no power to make on behalf of the Government a contract to lease for a term of years a building for the use of the customs service, and such a contract was without authority of law and not binding upon the United States. U.S. v. Doullut, C.C.A.5 (La.) 1914, 213 F. 729, 130 C.C.A. 243.

Where War Assets Administration Officer, who executed 21-month office building lease with plaintiff, did not have authority to obligate United States credit for period of time in excess of the then fiscal year, United States was not legally obligated under lease for period beyond end of the fiscal year, and, therefore, plaintiff would not be entitled to judgment, as matter of law, against United States for breach of lease as of end of such fiscal year. Gay Street Corp. of Baltimore, MD v. U.S., Ct.Cl.1955, 127 F.Supp. 585, 130 Ct.Cl. 341. United States ⊕ 70(11)

Where Congress authorized an executive officer to procure suitable rooms for a new executive department, and he entered into a lease for the term of one year with the right reserved to the Government of continuing the occupancy for a term of years, it was a proper exercise of his discretion. Freedman's Savings &

Trust Co. v. U.S., Ct.Cl.1880, 16 Ct.Cl. 19. United States ☞ 59

32. Liquor purchases

United States was not liable for liquor purchased by a naval officer for the personal use of U.S. Naval Mission personnel despite the fact that an official airplane was used for its transportation, that the liquor dealer was given a consolidated order including separate orders by the Government agency (the Naval Mission) and its personnel, and the fact that a checking account in the name of the U.S. Naval Mission was established in a local Panamanian bank for payment of the wine and liquor purchased from plaintiff, inasmuch as the officer was not authorized to open such an account for payment of personal liquor purchases. Henriquez & Gornell, Inc. v. U.S., Ct.Cl.1967, 180 Ct.Cl. 1040.

33. Measure of damages

In suit against United States to recover money withheld by defendant for contamination of aviation gasoline transported by barge by plaintiff for defendant under contract, record did not establish that defendant's representatives who entered into oral agreement with plaintiff regarding measure of plaintiff's damages lacked authority to enter into such agreement, and such lack of authority would not be presumed, and agreement was binding upon parties as to measure of plaintiff's damages. Southeastern Oil Florida v. U.S., Ct.Cl.1953, 115 F.Supp. 198, 127 Ct.Cl. 480. United States ☞ 60; United States ☞ 74(11)

34. Modification or waiver of provisions

Government contract provision for presence of government inspector during assembly and disassembly work simply gave Government right to be present, was for Government's benefit, and could be waived by contracting officer. Kenneth Reed Const. Corp. v. U.S., Ct.Cl.1973, 475 F.2d 583, 201 Ct.Cl. 282. United States ☞ 70(14); United States ☞ 73(3)

Under government contract providing that inspectors employed by government were not authorized to waive or alter in any respect any of terms or requirements of contract, government inspector lacked authority to bind government by agreeing with excavation contractor to change method of measuring boulders in excavated materials pursuant to contract from

the method prescribed in the specifications. L.B. Samford, Inc. v. U.S., Ct.Cl. 1969, 410 F.2d 782, 187 Ct.Cl. 714. United States ☞ 70(28)

Only such Governmental officials as are authorized by law may modify or waive the provisions of a Governmental contract and persons dealing with Government officials must at their peril inquire into authority of the officials. Bayboro Marine Ways Co. v. U.S., S.D.Fla. 1947, 72 F.Supp. 728. United States ☞ 40; United States ☞ 68; United States ☞ 72(3)

The contract fixed the rights and obligations of the parties and vested in the Government the right to have performance in accordance with its terms, and no unauthorized officer of the Government could waive the terms of the contract. Walter C. Reediger, Inc., v. U.S., Ct.Cl. 1941, 94 Ct.Cl. 120. Sales ☞ 77(2); United States ☞ 73(3)

35. Option contracts

Under this section and former section 665 of Title 31 [now section 1341 of Title 31], no contract for the rental of property can be entered into by the Government for more than 1 year and where a contract is made for a longer term of years, an option has to be exercised before the beginning of the next fiscal year. Brownstein-Lewis Co. v. U.S., Ct.Cl.1939, 90 Ct.Cl. 1.

36. Personal liability of contracting officer

A public agent of the Government contracting for it under his own seal is not personally liable. Hodgson v. Dexter, U.S.Dist.Col.1803, 1 Cranch 345, 5 U.S. 345, 2 L.Ed. 130. United States ☞ 47

When a commissioned officer or other agent of the United States makes a contract with any person for their use and benefit, and with due authority of law, such officer or other public agent is not responsible to the party, whose only remedy is against the Government, but, in making contracts with any one claiming to act for the Government, it is the duty of the party contracting to inquire as to the authority of such agent or officer, without which it is doubtful whether the contract affects the Government and if a public officer, make a Government contract without authority, and which, therefore, does not bind the Government, such officer is himself personally responsible to the contracting party, but a public officer or other agent, though contracting for the Government, may, if he see fit, make himself the responsible party, either exclusively or in addition to the Government. 1855, 7 Op.Atty.Gen. 88.

37. Persons entitled to maintain action

The rule of the law of agency that, when a contract is made by an agent, the principal may maintain an action upon it in his own name, although it was not disclosed to the Government at the time of making the contract, could not be upheld in suits against the Government since section 15 and former section 16 of this title required public contracts to be signed by the contracting parties, and forbade their transfer. Gill v. U.S., Ct.Cl. 1871, 7 Ct.Cl. 522.   United States ☞ 135

§ 11a. Contracts for fuel by Secretary of the Army without regard to current fiscal year

When, in the opinion of the Secretary of the Army, it is in the interest of the United States so to do, he is authorized to enter into contracts and to incur obligations for fuel in sufficient quantities to meet the requirements for one year without regard to the current fiscal year, and payments for supplies delivered under such contracts may be made from funds appropriated for the fiscal year in which the contract is made, or from funds appropriated or which may be appropriated for such supplies for the ensuing fiscal year.

(June 30, 1921, c. 33, § 1, 42 Stat. 78.)

HISTORICAL AND STATUTORY NOTES

Codifications

This section was formerly classified to section 668 of Title 31 prior to the general revision and enactment of Title 31, Money and Finance, by Pub.L. 97–258, § 1, Sept. 13, 1982, 96 Stat. 877.

Change of Name

The Department of War was designated the Department of the Army and the title of the Secretary of War was changed to Secretary of the Army by section 205(a) of Act July 26, 1947, c. 343, Title II, 61 Stat. 501.   Section 205(a) of Act July 26, 1947, was repealed by section 53 of Act Aug. 10, 1956, c. 1041, 70A Stat. 641. Section 1 of Act Aug. 10, 1956, enacted "Title 10, Armed Forces" which in sections 3010 to 3013 continued the Department of the Army under the administrative supervision of a Secretary of the Army.

Any reference in any provision of law to the Federal Supply Service deemed a reference to the Federal Acquisition Service, see Pub.L. 109–313, § 2(c)(1), Oct. 6, 2006, 120 Stat. 1734, set out as a note under 40 U.S.C.A. § 303.

Transfer of Functions

For transfer of certain procurement and related functions and property, and functions relating to finance and fiscal matters, insofar as they pertain to the Air Force, from the Secretary of the Army to the Secretary of the Air Force, see Secretary of Defense Transfer Order Nos. 6, eff. Jan. 15, 1948; 25, Oct. 14, 1948; 39, May 18, 1949; and 40 [App.B. (93)], July 22, 1949.

Public Buildings Administration was abolished by Act June 30, 1949, c. 288, Title I, § 103, 63 Stat. 380, and functions were transferred to General Services Administration. See generally 40 U.S.C.A. § 303(b).

Public Buildings Branch of Procurement Division [Bureau of Federal Supply] of Treasury Department transferred to Public Buildings Administration within Federal Works Agency, see 1939 Reorg. Plan No. 1, §§ 301, 303, eff. July 1, 1939, 4 F.R. 2729, 53 Stat. 1426, 1427, set out in the Appendix to Title 5, Government Organization and Employees.

Functions of procurement of supplies, services, stores, etc., exercised by any other agency were transferred to the Procurement Division in the Treasury Department by Ex. Ord. No. 6166, § 1, June 10, 1933, set out as a note under section 901 of Title 5. The name of the Procurement Division was changed to Bureau of Federal Supply by Treasury Department Order 73 dated Nov. 19, 1946. The Bureau was transferred on July 1, 1949, to the General Services Administration, where it functions as the Federal Supply Service, pursuant to Act June 30, 1949, c. 288, § 102, 63 Stat. 380.

CROSS REFERENCES

Federal Acquisition Service, establishment, functions and regional executives, see 40 U.S.C.A. § 303.

LIBRARY REFERENCES

American Digest System
United States ⊶62.
Key Number System Topic No. 393.

WESTLAW ELECTRONIC RESEARCH

See Westlaw guide following the Explanation pages of this volume.

§ 12. No contract to exceed appropriation

No contract shall be entered into for the erection, repair, or furnishing of any public building, or for any public improvement which shall bind the Government to pay a larger sum of money than the amount in the Treasury appropriated for the specific purpose. (R.S. § 3733.)

HISTORICAL AND STATUTORY NOTES

Codifications
R.S. § 3733 derived from Act July 25, 1868, c. 233, § 3, 15 Stat. 177.

CROSS REFERENCES

Contracting officer paying larger amount than specific appropriation, punishment for, see 18 USCA § 435.
Foreign military personnel, furnishing facilities for training without regard to this section, see 22 USCA § 2396.
Projects under Mexican treaties, authority to enter into contracts beyond amount appropriated notwithstanding this section, see 22 USCA § 277d–3.

LIBRARY REFERENCES

American Digest System
United States ⊶62.
Key Number System Topic No. 393.

Research References

Encyclopedias
Am. Jur. 2d Public Works and Contracts § 20, Necessity of Availability, Appropriation, and Certification of Funds--For Federal Purchases or Contracts.
Am. Jur. 2d Public Works and Contracts § 141, Right to Contract Price--Limitation of Recovery to Amounts Appropriated or Certified.
14 Am. Jur. Trials 437, Representing the Government Contractor.

Treatises and Practice Aids
 West's Federal Administrative Practice § 603, Differences from Private Contracts.

WESTLAW ELECTRONIC RESEARCH

See Westlaw guide following the Explanation pages of this volume.

Notes of Decisions

1. Purpose

The object of this section is to prevent executive officers from involving the Government in expenditures or liabilities beyond those contemplated and authorized by the law making power. 1895, 21 Op. Atty.Gen. 244.

2. Implied provision of contract

In every Government contract it is implied that the amount to be paid shall not exceed the appropriation. U.S. v. McMullen, U.S.Cal.1912, 32 S.Ct. 128, 222 U.S. 460, 56 L.Ed. 269.

3. Scope of appropriation

Where an Act of Congress limited the expenditure for the erection of a mint and its machinery, the limitation did not extend to a contract for planking the street in front of the mint, consequent to the street being regraded after the premises had been conveyed to the Government. Curtis v. U.S., Ct.Cl.1866, 2 Ct.Cl. 144. United States ⊕ 85

4. Exhaustion of appropriations

Where Congress authorized the Secretary of the Treasury to erect a building, but expressly limited the costs to a fixed amount, and the whole of that amount was paid to one contractor, he could not charge the defendants with any further liability for a contractor doing all the work under such a statute was chargeable with notice of the restriction set upon the cost of the building by Congress, and could not set up a breach of contract which would in effect do away with the restriction. Trenton Locomotive & Ma-

chine Mfg. Co. v. U.S., Ct.Cl.1876, 12 Ct.Cl. 147. United States ⊕ 62

After an appropriation is exhausted, a contract not for the completion of any specific work is at an end, because executive officers are prohibited from continuing the employment of the contractors. 1857, 9 Op.Atty.Gen. 18. See, also, 1895, 21 Op.Atty.Gen. 244.

5. Unrestricted authorization with inadequate appropriation

In cases where Congress passes an Act authorizing officers to construct a building or to do other specified work without restriction as to cost, and then makes an appropriation inadequate to do the whole of it, or makes none at all, the authority to cause the work to be done and to make contracts therefor is complete and unrestricted and all work, therefore, done under the direction of the officers thus charged with the execution of the law creates a liability on the part of the Government to pay for it, and if a written contract be made and work be done in excess of the contract specifications, or entirely outside of or in addition to the written contract, and such work inures to the benefit of the United States, in the execution of the law, or is accepted by the proper public officers, a promise to pay its reasonable value is implied and will be enforced. Shipman v. U.S., Ct.Cl.1883, 18 Ct.Cl. 138.

6. Future appropriations

The amount appropriated limits the liability of the Government, but the contract may provide for an extension or continuation of the work if Congress shall subsequently appropriate therefor. Smith v. U.S., Ct.Cl.1913, 48 Ct.Cl. 235. United States ⊕ 108

Authority to contract for the completion of an entire structure, the plan of which has been determined on, cannot be inferred from the mere fact that an appropriation of a certain sum to be expended on the structure has been made, hence a contract, though it might be good to the extent of such appropriation, could not be made to affix itself to future appropriations and control their expenditure and a contract of this character would be in violation of the spirit of this section if not of its express terms. 1877, 15 Op. Atty.Gen. 236.

7. Assumption of risk

Where a contractor with the Government for excavation at a specified rate per yard was notified that the appropriation was only enough for 60,000 cubic yards, further excavations were at its own risk. San Francisco Bridge Co. v. U.S., N.D.Cal.1913, 209 F. 135. Contracts ☞ 232(3); United States ☞ 70(27)

8. Miscellaneous contracts exceeding appropriations

Where Congress appropriates a certain sum to be expended by the Secretary of the Army for the improvement of a river

the Secretary exceeds his power when he makes a contract for more work than the appropriation will pay. 1857, 9 Op.Atty. Gen. 18.

Road betterments which are requested by a State to be incorporated in relocated highways constructed by the Corps of Engineers under section 701r–1 of Title 33, which merely requires the Engineers to replace the highway to existing standards rather than to superior standards to meet future needs, must be regarded as the sole financial responsibility of the State and unless the cost of additional work is provided by the State in advance of construction, any attempt by the Corps of Engineers to undertake the work with Federal funds would be contrary to the prohibitions of former sections 628 and 665 of Title 31 [now sections 1301 and 1341, respectively, of Title 31] and this section. 1961, 41 Comp.Gen. 255.

§ 13. Contracts limited to one year

Except as otherwise provided, it shall not be lawful for any of the executive departments to make contracts for stationery or other supplies for a longer term than one year from the time the contract is made.

(R.S. § 3735.)

HISTORICAL AND STATUTORY NOTES

Codifications

R.S. § 3735 derived from Res. Jan. 31, 1868, No. 8, 15 Stat. 246; Res. Mar. 24, 1874, No. 6, 18 Stat. 286.

"Except as otherwise provided," was first inserted by the Revisers of the 1934 edition of the Code.

Exemption of Functions

Functions authorized by Foreign Assistance Act of 1961, as amended, as exempt, see Ex. Ord. No. 11223, May 12,

1965, 30 F.R. 6635, set out as a note under section 2393 of Title 22, Foreign Relations and Intercourse.

Section Inapplicable to Armed Services and National Aeronautics and Space Administration

Section inapplicable to procurement or sale of property or services by Armed Services and National Aeronautics and Space Administration, see 10 U.S.C.A. § 2314.

CROSS REFERENCES

Armed Services and National Aeronautics and Space Administration, section inapplicable to procurement of supplies or services by, see 10 USCA § 2314.

Contracts by Secretary of Treasury for manufacture of distinctive paper for United States securities, see 31 USCA § 5114.

Executive agencies, section inapplicable to procurement of property or services by, see 41 USCA § 260.

LIBRARY REFERENCES

American Digest System
United States ☞70(11).
Key Number System Topic No. 393.

Research References

Encyclopedias
Am. Jur. 2d Public Works and Contracts § 24, Time Limits.

WESTLAW ELECTRONIC RESEARCH

See Westlaw guide following the Explanation pages of this volume.

Notes of Decisions

Generally 1

1. Generally

It is unlawful for an executive department to make a contract for supplies for a longer term than one year from the time the contract was made. 1896, 21 Op.Atty.Gen. 304.

§ 13a. Repealed. Pub. L. 86–682, § 12(c), Sept. 2, 1960, 74 Stat. 710

HISTORICAL AND STATUTORY NOTES

Section, Joint Res. Mar. 24, 1874, No. 6, 18 Stat. 286, excepted mail bags, mail locks, and keys from the provisions of section 13 of this title.

§ 14. Restriction on purchases of land

No land shall be purchased on account of the United States, except under a law authorizing such purchase.

(R.S. § 3736.)

HISTORICAL AND STATUTORY NOTES

Codifications
R.S. 3736 derived from Act May 1, 1820, c. 52, § 7, 3 Stat. 568.

CODE OF FEDERAL REGULATIONS

Military reservations and national cemeteries, see 32 CFR § 552.16 et seq.

LIBRARY REFERENCES

American Digest System
United States ☞55.
Key Number System Topic No. 393.

Corpus Juris Secundum
CJS United States § 96, Acquisition and Ownership, Generally.

WESTLAW ELECTRONIC RESEARCH

See Westlaw guide following the Explanation pages of this volume.

Notes of Decisions

---

1. Generally

This section negatives any idea that Congress claims power to take to the Government of the United States dry lands, or soil covered by water, for the purpose of commerce or navigation, or naval or military purposes, or for the construction of any kind of public buildings or public improvements without a cession from the state, or a purchase from an individual who may have title to the property desired for the site of the public works intended by the United States. 1853, 6 Op.Atty.Gen. 172.

2. Purchases within section—Generally

The acquisition of land at a receiver's sale when it is taken as security for a debt is not a "purchase" within this section. 1928, 35 Op.Atty.Gen. 474.

3. —— Corporate purchases, purchases within section

Land purchased, by nonstock, nonprofit corporations officered by employees of the Government as temporary directors,

with the proceeds of loans made to them by Farm Security Administration was not purchased in violation of this section. 1942, 40 Op.Atty.Gen. 193.

4. —— Exchange of lands, purchases within section

The Secretary of the Treasury may, if authorized by the President, accept a site for a Federal building in Honolulu acquired in exchange for public land in Hawaii and assume the custody and control thereof, no objection thereto arising under this section. 1903, 24 Op.Atty. Gen. 600.

5. —— Leases, purchases within section

The leasing of State-owned lands within grazing districts established pursuant to sections 315 et seq. of Title 43, is not authorized by said sections and is therefore prohibited by this section. 1937, 39 Op.Atty.Gen. 56.

The acquiring of a leasehold interest in a mine, for purposes of experimentations in mine rescue work, constitutes a purchase of land within the meaning of this section and if it be broadly held that it does not apply to the acquiring of an interest in land by lease, then its provisions could, in a large measure, be avoided by the taking of long-term leases instead of acquiring the fee simple title by purchase, and if an attempt were made to distinguish between a temporary and permanent acquisition, which is in fact not authorized by this section, a new difficulty would be met in endeavoring to determine what length of time should be considered as temporary. 1910, 28 Op.Atty. Gen. 463.

6. —— Mortgages or other security interests, purchases within section

The United States has the capacity within the sphere of its constitutional powers, and through the instrumentality of the proper department, to take mortgages of real estate to secure the payment of debts due to it, notwithstanding this section. Van Brocklin v. Anderson (U.S. Reports Title: Van Brocklin v. Tennessee), U.S.Tenn.1886, 6 S.Ct. 670, 117 U.S. 151, 29 L.Ed. 845.

A deed to trustees to pay a debt due the United States, being an authority to sell so much of the land as might be necessary to pay the debt, is not such a purchase as is forbidden by this section, but it does not prohibit the acquisition directly by the United States of the legal title to land, when it is taken by way of security for a debt. Neilson v. Lagow, U.S.Ind. 1851, 53 U.S. 98, 12 How. 98, 13 L.Ed. 909.

The compromise of a suit, receiving real and other property in discharge of the debt in trust, and selling the same, does not come under any authority to purchase lands. U.S. v. Lane, C.C.Ind. 1844, 26 F.Cas. 861, 3 McLean 365, No. 15559. See, also, U.S. v. Hudson, C.C.Ind.1843, 26 Fed.Cas.No.15,413. United States ⊶ 55; United States ⊶ 58(1); United States ⊶ 75.5

7. Executed contracts

This section should not be construed to apply to executed contracts so as to defeat the title of the United States to land it has paid for. Burns v. U.S., C.C.A.2 (N.Y.) 1908, 160 F. 631, 87 C.C.A. 533.

8. Authority for purchase—Generally

A conveyance of lands to the United States is void and inoperative unless the purchase is authorized by Congress. U.S. v. Tichenor, C.C.Or.1882, 12 F. 415, 8 Sawy. 142. United States ⊶ 55

The general effect of this section is to render the exercise by an executive department of a power to purchase land on account of the United States illegal, unless the intention of Congress that such power should be exercised has been so clearly expressed as to amount to an express authority. 1865, 11 Op.Atty.Gen. 201.

9. —— Implied authority, authority for purchase

Under this section, providing that "no land shall be purchased on account of the United States, except under a law authorizing such purchase," authority to purchase land need not be conferred by express statutory provision but may be implied. 1941, 40 Op.Atty.Gen. 69.

When Congress has made an appropriation, and one of the objects for which the appropriation is to be used, specially designated in the Act, is the construction of wharves, it necessarily follows that the right to purchase land upon which to build such wharves is implied. 1899, 22 Op.Atty.Gen. 665.

10. —— Improvements contracts, authority for purchase

Under this section an Act authorizing a public improvement and appropriating money therefor is sufficient authority for the purchase of land necessary or proper to such improvement. Burns v. U.S., C.C.A.2 (N.Y.) 1908, 160 F. 631, 87 C.C.A. 533.

11. —— Appropriation authority, authority for purchase

An appropriation for repairs, improvements, and new machinery at an armory, could not, nor could any portion of it, be applied to the purchase of the lands described in the estimate made at the ordnance office, although a portion of the appropriation was asked for with a view to the purchase of lands, if Congress saw fit to specify the purposes for which it granted it, among which the purchase of lands was not included. 1846, 4 Op.Atty. Gen. 533.

§ 15.   Transfers of contracts; assignments; assignee not subject to reduction or setoff

(a) Transfer

No contract or order, or any interest therein, shall be transferred by the party to whom such contract or order is given to any other party, and any such transfer shall cause the annulment of the contract or order transferred, so far as the United States is concerned. All rights of action, however, for any breach of such contract by the contracting parties, are reserved to the United States.

(b) Assignment

The provisions of subsection (a) of this section shall not apply in any case in which the moneys due or to become due from the United States or from any agency or department thereof, under a contract providing for payments aggregating $1,000 or more, are assigned to a bank, trust company, or other financing institution, including any Federal lending agency, provided:

(1) That, in the case of any contract entered into after October 9, 1940, no claim shall be assigned if it arises under a contract which forbids such assignment.

(2) That, unless otherwise expressly permitted by such contract, any such assignment shall cover all amounts payable under such contract and not already paid, shall not be made to more than one party, and shall not be subject to further assignment, except that any such assignment may be made to one party as agent or trustee for two or more parties participating in such financing.

(3) That, in the event of any such assignment, the assignee thereof shall file written notice of the assignment together with a true copy of the instrument of the assignment with—

(A) the contracting officer or the head of his department or agency;

(B) the surety or sureties upon the bond or bonds, if any, in connection with such contract; and

(C) the disbursing officer, if any, designated in such contract to make payment.

(c) Validity of assignment

Notwithstanding any law to the contrary governing the validity of assignments, any assignment pursuant to this section shall constitute a valid assignment for all purposes.

(d) Assignee liability

In any case in which moneys due or to become due under any contract are or have been assigned pursuant to this section, no liability of any nature of the assignor to the United States or any department or agency thereof, whether arising from or independently of such contract, shall create or impose any liability on the part of the assignee to make restitution, refund, or repayment to the United States of any amount heretofore since July 1, 1950, or hereafter received under the assignment.

(e) Amendment of contract

Any contract of the Department of Defense, the General Services Administration, the Department of Energy, or any other department or agency of the United States designated by the President, except any such contract under which full payment has been made, may, upon a determination of need by the President, provide or be amended without consideration to provide that payments to be made to the assignee of any moneys due or to become due under such contract shall not be subject to reduction or setoff. Each such determination of need shall be published in the Federal Register.

(f) Assignor liability arising independent of contract

If a provision described in subsection (e) of this section or a provision to the same general effect has been at any time heretofore or is hereafter included or inserted in any such contract, payments to be made thereafter to an assignee of any moneys due or to become due under such contract shall not be subject to reduction or setoff for any liability of any nature of the assignor to the United States or any department or agency thereof which arises independently of such contract, or hereafter for any liability of the assignor on account of—

(1) renegotiation under any renegotiation statute or under any statutory renegotiation article in the contract;

(2) fines;

(3) penalties (which term does not include amounts which may be collected or withheld from the assignor in accordance with or for failure to comply with the terms of the contract); or

(4) taxes, social security contributions, or the withholding or non withholding of taxes or social security contributions, whether arising from or independently of such contract.

(g) Accrued rights and obligations

Except as herein otherwise provided, nothing in this section shall be deemed to affect or impair rights or obligations heretofore accrued.

(R.S. § 3737; Oct. 9, 1940, c. 779, § 1, 54 Stat. 1029; May 15, 1951, c. 75, 65 Stat. 41; Oct. 13, 1994, Pub.L. 103–355, Title II, § 2451, 108 Stat. 3324; Feb. 10, 1996, Pub.L. 104–106, Div. D, Title XLIII, § 4321(i)(9), 110 Stat. 676.)

HISTORICAL AND STATUTORY NOTES

Revision Notes and Legislative Reports
1951 Acts. Senate Report No. 217, see 1951 U.S.Code Cong. and Adm.News, p. 1414.

1994 Acts. Senate Reports Nos. 103–258 and 103–259, and House Conference Report No. 103–712, see 1994 U.S. Code Cong. and Adm. News, p. 2561.

1996 Acts. House Conference Report No. 104–450, see 1996 U.S. Code Cong. and Adm. News, p. 238.

Codifications
R.S. § 3737 derived from Act July 17, 1862, c. 200, § 14, 12 Stat. 596.

Amendments
1996 Amendments. Subsec. (g). Pub.L. 104–106, § 4321(i)(9), substituted

"rights or obligations" for "rights of obligations".

1994 Amendments. Subsec. (a). Pub.L. 103–355, § 2451, designated the first paragraph as subsec. (a) and substituted "is concerned" for "are concerned".

Subsec. (b). Pub.L. 103–355, § 2451, designated the second paragraph as subsec. (b); substituted in introductory text "provisions of subsection (a) of this section" for "provisions of the preceding paragraph" and "lending agency, provided:" for "lending agency: Provided," and paragraph and subparagraph (1)-(3)(A), (B), and (C) designations for prior numerical and alphabetical designations, "That," for "That" and a period for semicolons in the paragraph designations; and struck out "1. That in the case of any contract entered into prior to October 9, 1940, no claim shall be assigned without the consent of the head of the department or agency concerned;".

Subsec. (c). Pub.L. 103–355, § 2451, designated the third paragraph as subsec. (c) and substituted "this section" for "this section,".

Subsec. (d). Pub.L. 103–355, § 2451, designated the fourth paragraph as subsec. (d).

Subsec. (e). Pub.L. 103–355, § 2451, designated the first part of the fifth paragraph as subsec. (e), substituted "Department of Energy" for "Atomic Energy Commission", "may, upon a determination of need by the President, provide" for "may, in time of war or national emergency proclaimed by the President (including the national emergency proclaimed December 16, 1950) or by Act or joint resolution of the Congress and until such was or national emergency has been terminated in such manner, provide", and "setoff." for "set-off,", and added provision for publication in the Federal Register the President's determination of need.

Subsec. (f). Pub.L. 103–355, § 2451, designated the last part of the fifth paragraph as subsec. (f), substituted "If a provision described in subsection (e) of this section or a provision to the same general effect" for "and if such provision or one to the same general effect", "setoff" for "set-off", "moneys due or to become due under such contract shall not be subject" for "moneys due or to become due under

such contract, whether during or after such war or emergency, shall not be subject", "on account of—" for "on account of", paragraph arrangement for items (1) to (4) ending in semicolons instead of commas and "non withholding" for "nonwithholding" in item (4).

Subsec. (g). Pub.L. 103–355, § 2451, designated the sixth paragraph as subsec. (g).

1951 Amendments. Act May 15, 1951, made it clear that a bank or other financing institution taking an assignment of claims pursuant to this section would not be subject to later recovery by the Government of amounts previously paid to the bank by the assignee except in cases of fraud.

1940 Amendments. Act Oct. 9, 1940, added the second and third paragraphs.

Effective and Applicability Provisions

1996 Acts. Amendment by Pub.L. 104–106 effective Feb. 10, 1996, except as otherwise provided, see section 4401 of Pub.L. 104–106, set out as a note under section 251 of this title.

1994 Acts. Amendment by section 2451 of Pub.L. 103–355 effective Oct. 13, 1994, except as otherwise provided, see section 10001 of Pub.L. 103–355, set out as a note under section 251 of this title.

Transfer of Functions

The Atomic Energy Commission was abolished and all functions were transferred to the Administrator of the Energy Research and Development Administration (unless otherwise specifically provided) by section 5814 of Title 42, The Public Health and Welfare. The Energy Research and Development Administration was terminated and functions vested by law in the Administrator thereof were transferred to the Secretary of Energy (unless otherwise specifically provided) by sections 7151(a) and 7293 of Title 42.

Non-Applicability of National Emergencies Act

The provisions of the National Emergencies Act, Pub.L. 94–412, Sept. 14, 1976, 90 Stat. 1255, not applicable to the powers and authorities conferred by this section and actions taken hereunder, see 50 U.S.C.A. § 1651.

Moneys Due Under Letters of Commitment Issued in Connection With Disposition of Surplus Agricultural Commodities

Moneys due under letters of commitment issued against funds or guaranties of funds supplied by Commodity Credit Corporation in connection with disposition of surplus agricultural commodities to foreign countries, as assignable under the Assignment of Claims Act of 1940, which constitutes this section and former section 203 of Title 31, see 7 U.S.C.A. § 1702.

MEMORANDA OF PRESIDENT
DELEGATION OF AUTHORITY UNDER THE ASSIGNMENT OF CLAIMS ACT

Oct. 3, 1995, 60 F.R. 52289

Memorandum for the Heads of Executive Departments and Agencies

Section 2451 of the Federal Acquisition Streamlining Act of 1994, Public Law 103–355 (41 U.S.C. 15) ("Act") [this section], provides, in part, that "[a]ny contract of the Department of Defense, the General Services Administration, the Department of Energy or any other department or agency of the United States designated by the President, except [contracts where] ... full payment has been made, may, upon a determination of need by the President, provide or be amended without consideration to provide that payments to be made to the assignee of any moneys due or to become due under [the] contract shall not be subject to reduction or set-off."

By the authority vested in me as President by the Constitution and the laws of the United States of America, including section 301 of title 3, United States Code [section 301 of Title 3, The President], I hereby designate all other departments and agencies of the United States as subject to this provision. Furthermore, I hereby delegate to the Secretaries of Defense and Energy, the Administrator of General Services, and the heads of all other departments and agencies, the authority under section 2451 of the Act [this section] to make determinations of need for their respective agency's contracts, subject to such further guidance as issued by the Office of Federal Procurement Policy.

The authority delegated by this memorandum may be further delegated within the departments and agencies.

This memorandum shall be published in the **Federal Register.**

WILLIAM J. CLINTON

CROSS REFERENCES

Assignment of claims, generally, see 31 USCA § 3727.
National Emergencies Act not applicable to powers and authorities conferred by this section and actions taken hereunder, see 50 USCA § 1651.

LAW REVIEW AND JOURNAL COMMENTARIES

Federal assignment-backed securities (FAst–BackS): Financing federal accounts receivable through securitization. 27 Loy.L.A.L.Rev. 1195 (1994).
Financing American health care security: The securitization of healthcare receivables. Charles E. Harrell & Mark D. Folk, 50 Bus.Law. 47 (1994).

LIBRARY REFERENCES

American Digest System

United States ☞71, 111, 130(2).
Key Number System Topic No. 393.

Corpus Juris Secundum

CJS United States § 124, Transfer or Assignment.

Research References

ALR Library

44 ALR, Fed. 775, Modern Status and Application of Rule That Only Voluntary Transfer or Assignment of Claim Against United States Is Within Assignment of Claims Act (31 U.S.C.A. § 203, 41 U.S.C.A. § 15).

75 ALR 3rd 1184, Agency: Anti-Assignment Clause in Contract as Precluding Enforcement by Undisclosed Principal.

175 ALR 1119, Validity and Construction of Legislation Forbidding Assignment of Contract with State or Municipality or of Claim Arising Therefrom.

135 ALR 695, Allowance or Rejection of Claim in Bankruptcy Proceedings as Res Judicata in Independent Action or Proceeding Between the Claimant and Another Creditor.

135 ALR 1509, Priority in Bankruptcy Proceedings of Claims for Contributions Under Unemployment or Social Security Acts.

76 ALR 917, Right as Between Surety on Contractor's Bond and Assignee of Money to Become Due on Contract.

64 ALR 611, Contract to Pay for Legal Services as an Assignment Within Statute Relating to Assignment of Claims Against the Government.

Encyclopedias

Am. Jur. 2d Assignments § 101, Particular Transfers or Assignments Not Subject to Statute.

Am. Jur. 2d Assignments § 104, Particular Transfers or Assignments Not Subject to Statute--Transfer in Connection with Bankruptcy.

Am. Jur. 2d Bankruptcy § 2347, Nonassignable and Nonassumable Contracts and Leases--Where Applicable Law Excuses Performance.

Am. Jur. 2d Federal Tort Claims Act § 118, Assignment.

Am. Jur. 2d Secured Transactions § 407, Particular Federal Statutes as Displacing Uniform Commercial Code Filing Requirements.

70 Am. Jur. Proof of Facts 3d 97, Proof That a Government Agency Was Liable for Improperly Granting a Bid Award to a Bid Applicant.

14 Am. Jur. Trials 437, Representing the Government Contractor.

Forms

Nichols Cyclopedia of Legal Forms Annotated § 2:04, Contents, Form, and Recording Assignment--Statutory Provisions.

Nichols Cyclopedia of Legal Forms Annotated § 7:2518, Supply Contract with United States--General Provisions.

Nichols Cyclopedia of Legal Forms Annotated § 7:2530, United States Lessee--General Clauses.

Nichols Cyclopedia of Legal Forms Annotated § 7:2536, Construction Contract with United States--General Provisions.

Nichols Cyclopedia of Legal Forms Annotated § 8:2719, Accounts Receivable Security Agreement--Assignment of Specific Accounts.

Nichols Cyclopedia of Legal Forms Annotated § 8:2720, Accounts Receivable and Contract Rights Security Agreement.

Nichols Cyclopedia of Legal Forms Annotated § 8:2721, Contract Rights Security Agreement--Specific Contract.

14A West's Legal Forms § 20:43, Notice of Assignment (Federal Assignment of Claims Act).

15 West's Legal Forms § 25:5 Form 4, Trust Receipt Used with Letter of Credit--For Documents Turned Over to Bank's Customer/Applicant--Another Form.

27 West's Legal Forms § 3:136, Notice of Assignment of Claim Against United States.

27 West's Legal Forms § 3:137, Notice of Release of Assignment of Claims Against United States.

27 West's Legal Forms § 4:126, Notice of Assignment of Claim Against United States.

27 West's Legal Forms § 4:127, Notice of Release of Assignment of Claims Against United States.

Treatises and Practice Aids

Bankruptcy Law Fundamentals § 9:9, Assuming or Rejecting Executory Contracts--Bankruptcy Code § 365--Defining the Executory Contract.

Bankruptcy Service Lawyers Edition § 19:906, Assumption or Rejection of Executory Contract or Unexpired Lease.

Bankruptcy Service Lawyers Edition § 19:1028, Contract Matters, Generally--Assumption or Rejection.

Bankruptcy Service Lawyers Edition § 21:47, Termination of Contract or Lease.

Bankruptcy Service Lawyers Edition § 21:237, Other Particular Applications.

Bankruptcy Service Lawyers Edition § 21:285, "Hypothetical" and "Actual" Tests.

Bankruptcy Service Lawyers Edition § 21:287, Necessity of Governmental Consent or Approval.

Bankruptcy Service Lawyers Edition § 21:290, Statute as Limited or Not Limited to Personal Service Contracts.

Bankruptcy Service Lawyers Edition § 21:293, Illustrative Particular Determinations.

Bankruptcy Service Lawyers Edition § 21:301, Real Estate Sales and Financing.

Bankruptcy Service Lawyers Edition § 21:313, Land Sales and Financing.

Bankruptcy Service Lawyers Edition § 31:45, In Chapter 11.

Bankruptcy Service Lawyers Edition § 33:636, Executory Contracts.

Bankruptcy Service Lawyers Edition § 45:470, Relationship to Other Federal Laws or Regulations.

Bankruptcy Service Lawyers Edition § 45:499, Other Particular Applications of Res Judicata.

West's Federal Administrative Practice § 660, Financing.

WESTLAW ELECTRONIC RESEARCH

See Westlaw guide following the Explanation pages of this volume.

Notes of Decisions

1. Construction

In order to accomplish purposes of this section, in preventing possible multiple payment of claims and making unnecessary the investigation of alleged assignments, requirements of notice to contracting officer as well as to disbursing officer, must be strictly construed. American Financial Associates, Ltd. v. U.S., Cl.Ct.1984, 5 Cl.Ct. 761, affirmed 755 F.2d 912. United States ☞ 111(10)

2. Construction with other laws

This section, prohibiting assignment of Government contracts, is given a construction similar to that given former section 203 of Title 31 [now section 3727 of Title 31], which declared void the assignment of claims against the United States. Ozanic v. U.S., S.D.N.Y.1949, 83 F.Supp. 4, affirmed 188 F.2d 228. United States ☞ 111(7)

Provision in this section that, notwithstanding any law to contrary governing validity of assignments, any assignment pursuant to this section shall constitute a valid assignment for all purposes, was intended by Congress to mean that an assignee shall stand in the assignor's shoes, to avoid a technical construction, that an assignment made in conformity with this section should not be declared invalid because of former section 203 of Title 31 [now section 3727 of Title 31], which made certain assignments of claims on the United States void. Hardin County Sav. Bank v. U.S., Ct.Cl.1946, 65 F.Supp. 1017, 106 Ct.Cl. 577. Assignments ☞ 1; United States ☞ 111(2)

Assignment of Claims Act, which generally prohibits the assignment of claims against the United States, was not applicable to bar nuclear utility's assignment of its claims for breach of standard contract for disposal of spent nuclear fuel (SNF) to purchaser of its nuclear power facility, as section of the Nuclear Waste Policy Act (NWPA) created exception to the Assignment of Claims Act . Vermont Yankee Nuclear Power Corp. v. U.S., Fed. Cl.2006, 73 Fed.Cl. 236. United States ☞ 111(4)

3. Purpose

This section and former section 203 of Title 31 [now section 3727 of Title 31], were passed for the protection of the government, in order that the government might not be harassed by multiplying the number of persons with whom it had to deal and might always know with whom it was dealing until the contract was completed and a settlement made; their purpose was not to dictate to the contractor what he should do with the money received on his contract after the contract had been performed.   Hobbs v. McLean, U.S.Iowa 1886, 6 S.Ct. 870, 117 U.S. 567, 29 L.Ed. 940.

Purpose of this section and former section 203 of Title 31 [now section 3727 of Title 31] was to make it easier for government contractors to secure financing for carrying out obligations to the government to the end that government contracts may be speedily and effectively performed; additionally, these sections implemented the congressional preference that federal contracts be financed by private rather than public capital.   Produce Factors Corp. v. U.S., Ct.Cl.1972, 467 F.2d 1343, 199 Ct.Cl. 572.   United States ☞ 111(2)

The interdiction of this section against transfer of Government contracts was passed in order that Government might not be harassed by multiplying number of persons with whom it had to deal and so that it might always know with whom it was dealing until contract was completed and settlement made; and was designed to secure to Government personal attention and services of contractor, and to render him liable to punishment for fraud or neglect of duty, and prevent parties from acquiring mere speculative interests and thereafter selling contracts at profit to bona fide bidders and contractors. Thompson v. C.I.R., C.A.3 1953, 205 F.2d 73.   See, also, Chemicals Recovery Co. v. U.S., 1952, 103 F.Supp. 1012, 122 Ct.Cl. 166; Francis v. U.S., 1875, 11 Ct.Cl. 638, affirmed 96 U.S. 354, 6 Otto. 354, 24 L.Ed. 663, 13 Ct.Cl. 543.   United States ☞ 71

The prohibition found in this section is intended to prevent such assignments of public contracts as would relieve the original contractor from the obligation of the contract with the Government.   U.S. v. Farley, C.C.N.D.Iowa 1899, 91 F. 474.

This section was designed to protect the United States from the assertion by parties other than the contracting party of rights under Government contracts. Maffia v. U.S., Ct.Cl.1956, 142 F.Supp. 891, 135 Ct.Cl. 604.

Purpose of this section and former section 203 of Title 31 [now section 3727 of Title 31] was to assist Government contractors in financing their operations, and under this section, contractor may assign his payments under particular contract to bank as security for advances made in connection with such contract or, when contractor is performing a number of Government contracts, may assign his payments under a particular contract as security for money advanced by bank in connection with his whole operation of performing other Government contracts as well as the particular contract.   Peterman Lumber Co. v. Adams, W.D.Ark. 1955, 128 F.Supp. 6.   United States ☞ 111(3)

Purpose of the setoff clause in this section was to insure that an assignee within the terms of this section, would not by virtue of the assignment, become subject to setoff or reduction by reason of an indebtedness of the assignor to the Government.   Hadden v. U.S., Ct.Cl.1952, 105 F.Supp. 1010, 123 Ct.Cl. 246.   United States ☞ 130(2.1)

Anti-Assignment Act was intended for benefit of Government and serves two purposes: first, to prevent persons of influence from buying up claims against United States, which might then be properly urged upon officers of Government, and second, to enable United States to deal exclusively with original claimant instead of several parties.   Monchamp Corp. v. U.S., Cl.Ct.1990, 19 Cl.Ct. 797. United States ☞ 111(1)

Purpose of this section is to secure to the United States the personal attention and services of the contractor and to assure that the government might also know with whom it is dealing until the contract is completed and settlement made.   In re Adana Mortg. Bankers, Inc., Bkrtcy.N.D.Ga.1980, 12 B.R. 977.   United States ☞ 71

One of the purposes of this section was to secure integrity in bidding for contracts, by preventing a bidder or contractor from making several bids, one by himself and others by his friends and employees, to be afterwards consummated by assignments of the contract by them to the real bidder, for whom they all acted and another was to prevent those who bid for and obtain contracts for mere speculation, and who have neither the intention nor the ability to perform them, from selling the contracts at a profit to bona fide bidders or contractors.   1888, 19 Op.Atty.Gen. 187.

4. Law governing

In proceedings in federal district court in New Jersey for reorganization, under former section 501 et seq. of Title 11, a New York corporation authorized to do business in New Jersey, New Jersey law was presumed to determine the effectiveness of assignment by debtor under this section and former section 203 of Title 31 [now section 3727 of Title 31], executed and delivered prior to filing of reorganization proceedings. In re Italian Cook Oil Corp., C.A.3 (N.J.) 1951, 190 F.2d 994. Bankruptcy ⟐ 2574

5. Persons or entities protected

This section is for the protection of the United States only, and does not affect the rights of the parties to such a transfer. Hegness v. Chilberg, C.C.A.9 (Alaska) 1915, 224 F. 28, 139 C.C.A. 492.

A stipulation in a contract in conformity with this section is for the sole benefit of the Government. Tinker & Scott v. U.S. Fidelity & Guaranty Co., C.C.Or. 1909, 169 F. 211.

A valid assignment of a government contract may be enforceable between the parties even though it might be challenged by the United States. United Pac. Ins. Co. v. Timber Access Industries Co., D.C.Or.1967, 277 F.Supp. 925. United States ⟐ 71

This section is intended for the protection of the Government, which may treat a contract as annulled thereunder by an assignment, or recognize the assignment. Dulaney v. Scudder, Miss.1899, 94 F. 6, 36 C.C.A. 52. See, also, Federal Manufacturing & Printing Co. v. U.S., 1906, 41 Ct.Cl. 318; 1879, 16 Op.Atty.Gen. 278; 1877, 15 Op.Atty.Gen. 236; 1821, 5 Op. Atty.Gen. 738.

Under the provisions of this section a transfer operated to annul the contract so far as the United States are concerned, but these provisions were not made to enable a contractor to avoid his agreement with the Government and relieve himself from his obligations by a mere transfer. 1884, 18 Op.Atty.Gen. 88. See, also, 1863, 10 Op.Atty.Gen. 523.

6. Persons against whom assignments void

Assuming that persons carrying on work under a Government contract in the name of the contractor were the contractor's assignees, where they never agreed, either with the Government or the contractor, to do any work, the Government could not enforce the contract against them, especially as, under this section, it was not obliged to recognize an assignee, and did not in fact recognize them. Ball Engineering Co. v. J.G. White, Inc., D.C.Conn.1922, 283 F. 496, affirmed 298 F. 709, certiorari denied 44 S.Ct. 639, 265 U.S. 596, 68 L.Ed. 1198. United States ⟐ 71

In view of this section, an assignment by a public contractor of a claim against the United States for money accruing on a building contract was void, both as against the United States, the contractor's surety, the laborers, and materialmen. Henningsen v. U.S. Fidelity & Guar. Co., C.C.A.9 (Wash.) 1906, 143 F. 810, 74 C.C.A. 484, affirmed 28 S.Ct. 389, 208 U.S. 404, 52 L.Ed. 547.

In view of this section, a person having a contract with the United States cannot transfer or assign any part of the money coming to him thereunder so as to affect any one but himself, and the acceptance by a disbursing agent of the United States of an order on such fund has no validity against third persons. Greenville Sav. Bank v. Lawrence, C.C.A.4 (S.C.) 1896, 76 F. 545, 22 C.C.A. 646. United States ⟐ 71

As between the South Boston Iron Works and the United States no privity existed by reason of the transfer, and in the absence of any agreement between that company and the United States, importing an undertaking by the former to perform the contract referred to, such contract could not be enforced against it by the latter. 1884, 18 Op.Atty.Gen. 88.

7. Personal performance

The policy expressed by this section is broader than general rule of contract law, requiring personal performance of some types of contract, and therefore mere fact that there was nothing in nature of contract which called for its personal performance by one or more individuals would not justify assignment in contravention of this section. Chemicals Recovery Co. v. U.S., Ct.Cl.1952, 103 F.Supp. 1012, 122 Ct.Cl. 166. United States ⟐ 71

8. Capacity of party to contract

Contracts are to be performed by those who make them, and are not to be the subjects of traffic or transfer and it is, therefore, necessary that they should be made with those who from their capacity are competent to render their service to be performed or from their business are able to furnish from its resources that which they contract to supply. 1877, 15 Op. Atty.Gen. 226.

9. Intent of parties to be bound

Where the Government declined to recognize persons carrying on work under a Government contract in the name of the contractor as parties to the contract, the fact that it permitted them to perform the work was no consideration for their promise to subject their property to the operation of the contract, and their intent to be bound by the contract did not create an implied agreement to subject their property to a provision authorizing the Government, upon annulment of the contract, to take over all materials, tools, etc., at a valuation to be determined. Ball Engineering Co. v. J.G. White, Inc., D.C.Conn.1922, 283 F. 496, affirmed 298 F. 709, certiorari denied 44 S.Ct. 639, 265 U.S. 596, 68 L.Ed. 1198. United States ☞ 71

10. Transfers or assignments within section—Generally

In applying interdiction of this section against transfer of Government contracts, court will not mechanically define "transfer" in terms of mere change of legal identity, but will pragmatically test each situation by extent to which change deprives Government of particular management and financial responsibility which rendered contractor a responsible bidder. Thompson v. C.I.R., C.A.3 1953, 205 F.2d 73. United States ☞ 71

No technical, formal, or written transfer of a Government contract by the contractor is necessary to bring the case within the prohibition of this section and it is sufficient to annul the contract that the facts disclose a substantial transfer of it or of an interest therein by whatever means attempted, or however much disguised, as where the contractor made a power of attorney authorizing another to receive and collect the vouchers, and to receive and receipt for payments, and the nominal agent performed and subsequently procured an assignment of the nominal contractor's claim, with authority to bring suit in his name, the contract was thereby annulled, and no suit could be maintained on it. Francis, for Use of

Myrick, v. U.S., Ct.Cl.1875, 11 Ct.Cl. 638, affirmed 96 U.S. 354, 6 Otto 354, 24 L.Ed. 663. United States ☞ 71

Key to assignability of a United States government contract is whether the assignment is within the mischief Congress intended to prevent in enactment of this section and if the contract is of the sort where the government depends on certain characteristics or abilities of the contractor, the statutory prohibition will apply. In re Adana Mortg. Bankers, Inc., Bkrtcy.N.D.Ga.1980, 12 B.R. 977. United States ☞ 71

11. —— Bankruptcy executory contracts, transfers or assignments within section

Where the Anti-Assignment Act prohibited assignment of Chapter 11 debtor's government contracts, debtor, in its capacity as debtor-in-possession, was barred from assuming those contracts over the government's objection, even though debtor did not intend to assign them. In re TechDyn Systems Corp., Bkrtcy.E.D.Va.1999, 235 B.R. 857. Bankruptcy ☞ 3105.1

Factor who received assignments of Chapter 11 debtors' rights to proceeds of reforestation contracts with United States Department of Agriculture (USDA) established all statutory conditions of exception to prohibition against assignment of interests in government contracts, and thus, assignments were valid and factor's claim to payment from proceeds of contracts had priority over Internal Revenue Service's (IRS') claim seeking to set off contract proceeds against debtors' tax debt; factor was "financing institution," within meaning of exception in federal statute prohibiting assignment of government contracts, contracts provided for aggregate payments in excess of $1,000 and expressly permitted assignment, contracts were not assigned to more than one party and were not further assigned, and written notice of assignment was properly filed. In re Medina, Bkrtcy. D.Or.1994, 177 B.R. 335, affirmed in part, reversed in part 205 B.R. 216. United States ☞ 71

Despite Non-Assignment Act, which provides that no contract can be transferred by party to whom such contract is given to another party, debtor-in-possession had right to assume its prepetition, executory government contract to build ship, even though postpetition DIP was not same entity as prepetition debtor that entered into the contract. Matter of American Ship Bldg. Co., Inc., Bkrtcy. M.D.Fla.1994, 164 B.R. 358. Bankruptcy ☞ 3105.1

United States Air Force was entitled to administratively terminate fixed price defense contracts with debtor manufacturer for supply of parachutes and related items, with timing of Government's motion for modification of stay to terminate contracts, debtor's performance under contracts, and financial status of debtor being irrelevant factors; statute precludes assumption if applicable law excuses party other than debtor from accepting performance from entity other than debtor or debtor in possession and Federal Nonassignment Act prohibits assignment of government contract without Government's consent. In re Carolina Parachute Corp., M.D.N.C.1989, 108 B.R. 100, affirmed in part, vacated in part on other grounds 907 F.2d 1469. Bankruptcy ☞ 3105.1; United States ☞ 70(35)

Federal statute, 41 U.S.C.A. § 15, prohibiting assignment of government contracts, prohibited assignment of contract for review of health care services provided under Medicare Program, so that contract for such review between government and debtor could not be assumed by debtor-in-possession. In re Pennsylvania Peer Review Organization, Inc., Bkrtcy. M.D.Pa.1985, 50 B.R. 640. Bankruptcy ☞ 3102.1

12. —— Contingent fee arrangements, transfers or assignments within section

A contract by a claimant, employing an attorney to prosecute a claim against the United States in the Court of Claims [now United States Court of Federal Claims] on a contingent fee of 50 percent of the amount recovered, and stipulating that the fee shall be a lien on any draft issued by the Government in payment of the claim, is not an assignment of a claim against the United States within this section. Roberts v. Consaul, App.D.C.1905, 24 App.D.C. 551. United States ☞ 111(6)

13. —— Corporate formations, transfers or assignments within section

A corporation formed to carry out a Government contract was not an assignee of the contract, but a mere agent of the contractor. U.S. ex rel. Giant Powder

Co. v. Axman, C.C.N.D.Cal.1906, 152 F. 816.

Where owner of capital stock of corporation to which war contracts had been awarded transferred stock to corporation in exchange for its assets, including uncompleted contracts, and thereafter sold assets to a newly organized corporation which took formal assignment of the contracts, transfer was a nullity as to Government under this section prohibiting transfer of Government contracts. U.S. v. Star Const. Co., W.D.Okla.1948, 77 F.Supp. 758, affirmed 186 F.2d 666. United States ☞ 71

14. —— Joint ventures, transfers or assignments within section

A joint agreement to procure and perform a public contract is not within the prohibition of this section though the public contract when procured is made in the names of a part only of the joint adventurers. Anderson v. Blair, Ala. 1918, 80 So. 31, 202 Ala. 209.

15. —— Leases, transfers or assignments within section

Whatever may be the scope and effect of section 3737 [this section] it does not embrace a lease of real estate to be used for public purposes, under which the lessor is not required to perform any service for the government, and has nothing to do in respect to the lease except to receive from time to time the rent agreed to be paid: the assignment of such a lease is not within the mischief which Congress intended to prevent. Freedman's Saving & Trust Co. v. Shepherd, U.S.Dist.Col. 1888, 8 S.Ct. 1250, 127 U.S. 494, 32 L.Ed. 163.

16. —— Partnership formations, transfers or assignments within section

This section does not invalidate a partnership formed between a party to whom the Government has given a contract and other persons whose means are required to carry it out, and written promises to such moneyed partners by the other to pay back out of the contract money his portion of the fund advanced does not bring the case within this section. Hobbs v. McLean, U.S.Iowa 1886, 6 S.Ct. 870, 117 U.S. 567, 29 L.Ed. 940. See, also, Burck v. Taylor, Tex.1894, 14 S.Ct. 696, 152 U.S. 634, 38 L.Ed. 578. Limitation Of Actions ☞ 43; Limitation Of Actions ☞ 49(1)

This section providing that no contract or order shall be transferred by party to whom Government contract or order is given to any other party and that any such transfer annuls Government contract does not apply where contractor enters into a partnership agreement with another to share the profits and losses under Government contract. McPhail v. U.S., Ct.Cl.1960, 181 F.Supp. 251, 149 Ct.Cl. 179. United States ☞ 71

An agreement amounting to a partnership arrangement entered into before the execution of contracts with the Government, made in good faith and not for the purpose of influencing bidding or in any way otherwise to prejudice the United States, is not a transfer of a contract such as will annul the contract under the provisions of this section. Field v. U.S., Ct. Cl.1880, 16 Ct.Cl. 434.

The formation of a partnership by persons holding a contract with the Government for the erection of public buildings does not necessarily effect an annulment of the contract. North Pacific Lumber Co. v. Spore, Or.1904, 75 P. 890, 44 Or. 462.

17. —— Power of attorney, transfers or assignments within section

Where plaintiffs were allegedly awarded Government contract for feeding of Mexican laborers, plaintiffs' management agreement under which third party was given all powers necessary for performance, and by which plaintiffs retained no right to control such third party since they had given him power of attorney to act in their place and stead, was within this section providing that any transfer of Government contract or order to any other party should cause annulment of contract or order transferred so far as United States was concerned. McPhail v. U.S., Ct.Cl.1960, 181 F.Supp. 251, 149 Ct.Cl. 179. United States ☞ 71

A shipbuilding company having contracts with the Federal Government for the building of several vessels, by depositing the contracts in a bank with power of attorney authorizing it to collect payments by the Government on the contract, on the faith of which the bank made loans to the company, effectuated a valid equitable assignment of the contracts. S.H. Hawes & Co. v. Wm. R. Trigg Co., Va.1909, 65 S.E. 538, 110 Va. 165, modified on other grounds 31 S.Ct.

49, 218 U.S. 452, 54 L.Ed. 1107. United States ☞ 71

S., having a contract with the Engineer Department for dredging in the Occoquan River, by the terms of which the compensation named therein was to be paid to him from time to time, gave to I. a power of attorney (declared in the instrument to be irrevocable) "to demand, receive, and receipt for, to the proper disbursing officer of the United States, all moneys, warrants, drafts, vouchers, and checks that may become due and payable to me (S.) from the United States", which instrument did not amount to a transfer of an interest in the contract so as to authorize the annulment thereof under this section. 1879, 16 Op.Atty.Gen. 261.

O. having given a power of attorney to S., coupled with an interest in the performance of the contract, by which power S. was to sign and receipt for all moneys due under the contract, this was a transfer of the contract within this section, yet although the Government may avail itself of such transfer to annul the contract under this section, it is not compelled to do so. 1877, 15 Op.Atty.Gen. 236.

Where one having a contract awarded him by the State Department gives a power of attorney to another, coupled with an interest in the performance of the contract by which power the second party is to sign and receipt for all moneys due under the contract, it constitutes a transfer of the contract within the meaning of this section. 1877, 15 Op.Atty. Gen. 235.

18. —— Preliminary capital arrangements, transfers or assignments within section

The provisions of this section do not apply to a preliminary arrangement for the honest purpose of uniting capital to obtain the necessary means to fulfill a public contract, there being no intent to influence bidding or to evade the duties and responsibilities of a public contractor. Field v. U.S., Ct.Cl.1880, 16 Ct.Cl. 434. United States ☞ 71

19. —— Subcontracts, transfers or assignments within section

Even if contract modification making subcontractor joint payee on all payments made by government to contractor was considered assignment of contractor's claims, record established that contracting officer clearly assented to such assignment, thereby waiving statutory prohibition against assignments. D & H Distributing Co. v. U.S., C.A.Fed.1996, 102 F.3d 542, rehearing denied. United States ⌖ 71

A contractor with the United States for the construction of a public improvement does not, by contracting with a third party to furnish material for such work, make an assignment or a transfer of his contract. U.S. v. Farley, C.C.N.D.Iowa 1899, 91 F. 474. United States ⌖ 71

An agreement by a sculptor that, in the event of an award to him by a Congressional commission of a contract for a certain statue for which he had submitted designs, he would enter into a contract with a contractor for stone work for the erection by the latter of a granite pedestal for such statute, and that, to the amount of such pedestal, the contractor should be made a party to the contract between the commission and the sculptor, is not void under this section. Manning v. Ellicott, App.D.C.1896, 9 App.D.C. 71. United States ⌖ 71

A contractor has a right to perform by ordinary business methods, provided he does not assign his contract and does retain his personal responsibility and he may make subcontracts and perform through the agency of others. Manning v. Ellicott, App.D.C.1896, 9 App.D.C. 71. See, also, Stout, Hall & Bangs v. U.S., 1892, 27 Ct.Cl. 385.

As between naval ordnance plant and contractor, purported assignment of invoices for delivery of gyro motors by contractor to purported assignee was of no binding effect and in no way obligated plant to honor them particularly where plant accepted purported assignee as subcontractor to contractor. U.S. v. Russell Elec. Co., S.D.N.Y.1965, 250 F.Supp. 2. United States ⌖ 71

This section providing that no contract or order shall be transferred by party to whom Government contract or order is given to any other party and that any such transfer annuls Government contract does not apply where contractor merely subcontracts duty to Government, so long as contractor remains primarily liable to Government and retains power to perform duty under contract or to require performance. McPhail v. U.S., Ct. Cl.1960, 181 F.Supp. 251, 149 Ct.Cl. 179. United States ⌖ 71

In action by subcontractor against prime contractor's assignee bank for receipts, which arose under prime contract with Government from shipment of materials under subcontract, and which were credited by assignee on debts arising from other prime Government contracts, evidence was sufficient to establish that prime contractor and assignee had effected a valid assignment of such receipts as security for all advances made by assignee to prime contractor to finance his complete operations in performing various Government contracts. Peterman Lumber Co. v. Adams, W.D.Ark.1955, 128 F.Supp. 6. United States ⌖ 111(10)

Where the United States was not a party to Government construction subcontract, no contractual rights other than a beneficial interest existed or could be implied as between subcontractor and the Government. Evans Elec. Const. Co. v. Wm. S. Lozier, Inc., W.D.Mo.1946, 68 F.Supp. 256, appeal dismissed 162 F.2d 717. United States ⌖ 74.2

Under Assignment of Claims Act, Government and coal broker could not enter into settlement agreement which required Government to pay settlement figure directly to broker, where broker, broker's subcontractors and government had entered into agreement giving subcontractors payment priority. D & S Universal Min. Co., Inc. v. U.S., Cl.Ct.1986, 10 Cl. Ct. 707. United States ⌖ 111(13)

The fact that a Government contractor contracted with another to do certain work on articles which he had agreed to furnish the Government did not constitute an assignment of the contract. White v. McNulty, N.Y.A.D. 1 Dept.1898, 49 N.Y.S. 903, 26 A.D. 173, affirmed 58 N.E. 1094, 164 N.Y. 582.

20. ―― **Sublets, transfers or assignments within section**

"Sublet" is included by the word "transfer". U.S. v. A. Bentley & Sons Co., S.D.Ohio 1923, 293 F. 229, 2 Ohio Law Abs. 243.

21. ―― **Surety agreements, transfers or assignments within section**

Federal government contractor's assignment of claims to surety in general indemnity agreement was not valid as against federal government under Anti–Assignment Act, since no claims had been allowed at time assignment was made and surety did not fit within exception to

Act because surety was not "financing institution." Fireman's Fund Ins. Co. v. England, C.A.Fed.2002, 313 F.3d 1344.

A contract with the Government is not annulled by the fact that the contractor makes an agreement with one of the sureties on his bond to the Government by which the surety furnishes the money necessary for carrying out the contract, and the contractor agrees to divide the profits with him. Bowe v. U.S., C.C.N.D.Ga.1890, 42 F. 761.

Where as further protection for surety on contractor's performance bond of contract for the Government, a joint control agreement was executed by the contractor under which he assigned to the surety all payments including retained percentages to become due under the contracts, the assignment was invalid, and a bank loaning funds to the contractor to complete the contract was not obligated to take notice thereof. U.S. Cas. Co. v. First Nat. Bank of Columbus, M.D.Ga.1957, 157 F.Supp. 789. United States ☞ 111(10)

22. —— **Miscellaneous transfers or assignments, transfers or assignments within section**

Where, after the members of a firm had obtained a contract for the performance of public work for the United States, two of the members of the firm assigned their interest therein to the third, who agreed to assume all the debts of the firm and to prosecute the work at his own risk and for his own benefit, such assignment, while valid as between the parties, could not affect the rights of the United States, and operated only as an assumption by the assignee of the debts of the firm in consideration of the receipt of the benefits to be derived from the execution of the agreement. Hardaway & Prowell v. National Sur. Co., C.C.A.6 (Ky.) 1907, 150 F. 465, 80 C.C.A. 283, affirmed 29 S.Ct. 202, 211 U.S. 552, 53 L.Ed. 321, 6 Ohio Law Rep. 647. United States ☞ 71

There is nothing in this section to prevent a sugar planter from pledging bounty to become payable on his crop, before his claims have been presented and allowed and a Treasury warrant issued. Barrow v. Milliken, C.C.A.5 (La.) 1896, 74 F. 612, 20 C.C.A. 559, certiorari denied 17 S.Ct. 991, 167 U.S. 746, 42 L.Ed. 1210.

An agreement between a Government contractor and one of the sureties on his bond, by which the surety agrees to furnish the money necessary for carrying out the contract, and the contractor agrees to divide the profits with him, does not amount to a transfer of the contract. Bowe v. U.S., C.C.N.D.Ga.1890, 42 F. 761. United States ☞ 71

Escrow agent under escrow agreement between government contractor and subcontractor, pursuant to which agent would receive contract funds for dispersal to contractor and subcontractor, sufficiently alleged that government recognized assignment of payment to establish jurisdiction under the Assignment of Claims Act and the Assignment of Contracts Act over his suit to recover purchase order payment for subcontractor which government sent directly to contractor; agent pleaded an assignment of the right to payment under purchase order, recognition of the assignment by the government, and wrongful payment by the government to contractor. Kawa v. U.S., Fed.Cl.2007, 77 Fed.Cl. 294. Federal Courts ☞ 1111

Corporation was successor-in-interest of entity awarded government contract, and thus corporation did not lack privity to advance claim against United States in Claims Court, even if entity awarded contract continued to exist in some form after name change agreement was incorporated into government contract, where successor assumed all contractual duties, and no evidence indicated that successor was subcontractor or that government was prejudiced. United Intern. Investigative Services v. U.S., Cl.Ct.1992, 26 Cl. Ct. 892. United States ☞ 70(5)

Forest Service's approval of assignment of a contract by bidder which received a contract award to fourth highest bidder was reasonable and permissible; Government permissibly waived provisions of Anti-Assignment Act by including a clause in contract explicitly providing for transfer of contractual rights or obligations upon notice to and written approval from Forest Service. Monchamp Corp. v. U.S., Cl.Ct.1990, 19 Cl.Ct. 797. United States ☞ 71

A transfer of the legal title of real property by virtue of the decree of a court of equity, carrying with it the right to rents accrued, is not an assignment of a claim against the Government within the prohibition of this section. Mills v. U.S., Ct.Cl. 1884, 19 Ct.Cl. 79. United States ⌕ 111(7)

Where suit is brought on a contract, and the petition alleges that a third person became the owner of one-third interest in the contract before performance, and seeks to recover to his use, but the transfer is not produced on the trial, the assignment will be regarded as related to the contract itself, and not to moneys due under it, and that it was void. Chouteau v. U.S., Ct.Cl.1873, 9 Ct.Cl. 155, affirmed 95 U.S. 61, 5 Otto 61, 24 L.Ed. 371. United States ⌕ 71

Assignment, as security by contractor with the United States, of its interest in a special fund created by contract by it with others, and consisting of money borrowed to carry on contract with the United States and money received from the United States on account of the government contract, was not a transfer or assignment of a contract with or claim on the United States, in violation of former section 203 of Title 31 [now section 3727 of Title 31], and this section. Irwin's Bank v. Fletcher Savings & Trust Co., Ind.1924, 145 N.E. 869, 195 Ind. 669, modified on other grounds 146 N.E. 909, 195 Ind. 669.

Where S., having a contract with the Engineer Department to perform certain dredging, entered into an agreement with G., by which it was stipulated that S. should furnish two-thirds and G. one-third of the money, material, or labor necessary for the execution of the contract, that in case of loss by reason of such execution the loss should be borne in the proportion of two-thirds thereof by S. and one-third by G., and that the net proceeds should be divided between them in the same proportion, such agreement was an assignment of an interest in the contract, and fell within the provision of this section. 1879, 16 Op.Atty.Gen. 278.

23. Financing institutions—Generally

That portion of the 1940 Assignment of Claims Act, this section and former section 203 of Title 31 [now section 3727 of Title 31], which permitted assignment to financial institutions was entirely written in terms of a single government contract which was being financed by a lender or group of lenders, not in government-wide terms; statutory concept was that of financing a specific government contract, not of the financing of government con-

tracts in general or across the board, or financing of all of a contractor's contracts as a lump; immediate context of phrase "participating in such financing" related to financing the particular contract on which the statutory provision centers. First Nat. City Bank v. U.S., Ct.Cl.1977, 548 F.2d 928, 212 Ct.Cl. 357. United States ⌕ 111(3)

This section as it applies to contracts with United States, provides that proceeds of such contracts may be assigned only to a bank, trust company or other financing institution. U.S. v. Russell Elec. Co., S.D.N.Y.1965, 250 F.Supp. 2. United States ⌕ 111(10)

Government was not required to pay financier of alleged assignee of Navy paving contract, after alleged assignor had dissipated payment made to it, even though Government was aware of intended assignment and had accepted assignee's work, absent compliance with financing institution exception of Assignment of Contracts Act; Government's knowledge was limited to fact that assignment had been unsuccessfully attempted, Government had explicitly rejected attempted assignment, and no authorized contracting officer had ever assured assignee that assignment would be recognized or had taken any other action indicating acceptance of assignment. Trust Co. Bank of Middle Georgia, N.A. v. U.S., Cl.Ct.1992, 24 Cl.Ct. 710. United States ⌕ 71

Government contractor's secured note, assigning accounts receivable to financial institution, which was executed during the period the instant government contract was being performed, should be recognized under this section. (1979) 58 Comp.Gen. 619.

24. —— Farm credit association, financing institutions

Debtor-farmers' assignment to farm credit association of right to payment in kind under contract with Commodity Credit Corporation pursuant to special program of payment in kind for acreage diversion for 1983 crops was valid and not precluded by general antiassignment statutes. Matter of Sunberg, Bkrtcy. S.D.Iowa 1983, 35 B.R. 777, affirmed 729 F.2d 561. United States ⌕ 111(3)

25. —— Insurance carrier, financing institutions

This section, and former section 203 of Title 31 [now section 3727 of Title 31], authorized an assignment by a contractor to an insurance company of moneys due or to become due under a contract with the Government. 1943, 40 Op.Atty.Gen. 269.

26. —— **Trustee or agent, financing institutions**

Under this section permitting assignment to only one financing institution but providing that such institution may be trustee for two or more parties participating in financing, bank, which knew that middleman was borrowing from it in order to lend to contractor and which agreed with contractor and middleman that money received under assignments and not necessary to satisfaction of middleman's obligations to bank would be turned over to middleman, became a trustee for middleman, which had bound itself absolutely to pay bank regardless of outcome of contractor's transaction with Government; and it was not necessary, in order that middleman's loans to contractor be secured by assignments, that bank's notices to Government advise it of arrangements which the bank had with middleman. Chelsea Factors, Inc. v. U.S., Ct.Cl.1960, 181 F.Supp. 685, 149 Ct.Cl. 202. United States ☞ 111(10)

27. Recognition of transfer or assignment—Generally

Nothing in takeover agreement between government and surety for defaulting contractor showed government's recognition of contractor's assignment to surety, under their indemnity agreement, of claims arising under construction contract between contractor and government in the event of default, and therefore claim of contract illegality that surety sought to assert did not come within exception under Anti-Assignment Act for situations in which government chose to recognize assignment, and claim was barred by Act's invalidation of assignment. United Pacific Ins. Co. v. Roche, C.A.Fed.2004, 380 F.3d 1352, rehearing denied. United States ☞ 111(4)

Where contracting officer for Department of Housing and Urban Development was contacted prior to each assignment of contracts for purchase of mobile homes for his advice on validity of proposed assignments and officer assured assignees that despite this section and former section 203 of Title 31 [now section 3727 of Title 31], the assignments were

proper and would be recognized by Department, and where officer made signed acknowledgment, there was recognition of assignments by the government. Tuftco Corp. v. U.S., Ct.Cl.1980, 614 F.2d 740, 222 Ct.Cl. 277. United States ☞ 111(10)

This section prohibiting assignment of government contracts was enacted for benefit of the United States and if the United States recognizes the assignment parties are not in a position to object. United Pac. Ins. Co. v. Timber Access Industries Co., D.C.Or.1967, 277 F.Supp. 925. United States ☞ 71

Despite this section providing against transfer of government contract or order by party to whom such contract or order was given, government may, if it chooses to do so, recognize assignment of a contract between itself and another. U.S. v. Russell Elec. Co., S.D.N.Y.1965, 250 F.Supp. 2. See, also, Maffia v. U.S., 1958, 163 F.Supp. 859, 143 Ct.Cl. 198. United States ☞ 71

Plaintiffs who received payments for janitorial services rendered in name of original government contractor and who rejected opportunity to surrender contract and negotiate a new one failed to establish that United States recognized assignment of contract and thereby waived strict provisions of R.C.W.A. 63.16.030 and this section and accordingly contracting party had better title than plaintiffs to money in hands of United States for janitorial services rendered and plaintiffs could not recover such money impounded for contracting party's default in tax payments. Bullock v. U.S., E.D.Wash.1964, 247 F.Supp. 370. United States ☞ 71

The defendants having recognized the relation of landlord and tenant between them and the plaintiff, they cannot assert the defense that the lease in suit was not assignable under this section. Musselman v. U.S., Ct.Cl.1917, 52 Ct.Cl. 436. United States ☞ 71

The contract may still be treated by the Government as obligatory upon the contractor notwithstanding the transfer. 1884, 18 Op.Atty.Gen. 88.

28. —— **Notice of assignment, recognition of transfer or assignment**

Before government contracting officer has authority to recognize an assignment so as to preclude bar of this section and former section 203 of Title 31 [now section 3727 of Title 31], assignee need not comply with notice provisions applicable to financing institutions. Tuftco Corp. v. U.S., Ct.Cl.1980, 614 F.2d 740, 222 Ct.Cl. 277. United States ⬥ 111(10)

If, at time government receives notification of an assignment, it knows that the assignee's collateral is worthless, the government must convey that information to the assignee so that he will not advance funds on the strength of government contract proceeds that will never come due; and if the government fails to discover such information solely because of its own lack of diligence, it may become liable to the assignee where the contractor could not have recovered any proceeds. Produce Factors Corp. v. U.S., Ct.Cl.1972, 467 F.2d 1343, 199 Ct.Cl. 572. United States ⬥ 111(12)

Assignee of government contract did not comply with requirement of the Assignment of Claims Act and the Assignment of Contract Act that assignee "file written notice of the assignment together with a true copy of the instrument of the assignment" with the contracting officer and the disbursing officer, by sending notice of assignment and invoice to contracting agency, as notice and invoice were not a "true copy" of assignment instrument. Riviera Finance of Texas, Inc. v. U.S., Fed.Cl.2003, 58 Fed.Cl. 528. United States ⬥ 71; United States ⬥ 111(10)

Assignee of payment under government contract did not violate Assignment of Claims Act by sending notice of assignment to government with incorrect identification of contract; correct contract had been attached to notice, and correspondence indicated that government knew true nature of contract. Merchants' Funding Group v. U.S., Fed.Cl. 1995, 33 Fed.Cl. 445. United States ⬥ 111(10)

Financing institution that received assignment of proceeds of government contract failed to comply with notice provisions of Anti-Assignment Acts, precluding institution from recovering contract proceeds withheld by Government; copy of assignment was not filed either with contracting official or disbursing official before contract was terminated. United California Discount Corp. v. U.S., Cl.Ct. 1990, 19 Cl.Ct. 504. United States ⬥ 71

29. Consent or waiver

United States could properly waive limitations of this section where there was nothing to indicate that assignment of surplus cruiser by high bidder to a third party was not an outright sale. Benjamin v. U.S., Ct.Cl.1963, 318 F.2d 728, 162 Ct.Cl. 47. United States ⬥ 111(1)

Where principal was insolvent and unable to pay its obligations under government contracts containing nonassignment clauses and surety was therefore exposed to claims by the United States under bonds given in connection with contracts, but principal and sole owners of its capital stock were liable to surety on indemnity agreement, surety was given two weeks in which to obtain consent of the United States to assignment of contracts before court would determine what further action to take with respect to enforcing indemnity agreement. United Pac. Ins. Co. v. Timber Access Industries Co., D.C.Or.1967, 277 F.Supp. 925. Principal And Surety ⬥ 190(1)

In view of surrounding correspondence, beginning of deliveries of gyro motors under contract, and failure of contractor and alleged assignee to provide information had by them and regarded as a necessary prelude to novation discussions, consent to contract assignment could not be implied from naval ordnance plant's acceptance of delivered motors or approval of alleged assignee's written proposal to establish itself as contractor's subcontractor. U.S. v. Russell Elec. Co., S.D.N.Y.1965, 250 F.Supp. 2. United States ⬥ 71

Where Department of the Army permitted assignment of contract for purchase of caskets from Government and joined in making new contract with new buyer, contract did not violate this section forbidding assignment. U.S. v. Heller, D.C.Md.1932, 1 F.Supp. 1. United States ⬥ 71

Government waived requirements of the Assignment of Claims Act and the Assignment of Contract Act for assignment of payment rights under government contract, where both assignor and assignee sent notice of assignment to the government, contracting officer assistant signed notice of assignment, contracting officer modified the contract according to the assignment, and the government sent a payment to the assignee pursuant to the assignment. Riviera Finance of Texas,

Inc. v. U.S., Fed.Cl.2003, 58 Fed.Cl. 528. United States ☞ 71; United States ☞ 111(1)

Transaction by which buyer acquired commercial nuclear fuels assets, including facility where subcontractor performed government contract work, did not constitute a corporate reorganization, whereby buyer assumed seller's government contract rights by operation of law, where entire entity responsible for performance of contract was not sold to buyer; thus, even if seller transferred to buyer its contractual right to seek contamination cleanup costs, such transfer was void under the Anti-Assignment Act, because the transfer occurred without government consent. Westinghouse Elec. Co. v. U.S., Fed.Cl.2003, 56 Fed.Cl. 564, affirmed 97 Fed.Appx. 931, 2004 WL 1153023. United States ☞ 71

Government did not waive requirements of the Anti–Assignment Act with respect to government contractor's assignment of contract proceeds to bank, where the government did not affirmatively acknowledge the assignment in writing or make payments consistent with the assignment. Banco Bilbao Vizcaya-Puerto Rico v. U.S., Fed.Cl.2000, 48 Fed.Cl. 29. United States ☞ 71

Lessor's assignment of rents from building leased by the United States Postal Service (USPS) was valid under lease provision requiring acknowledgement of assignment of rents by the USPS, where USPS received notification of the assignment in a letter sent by lessor to agency's real estate manager, and the USPS acknowledged the assignment of rents in two letters addressed to assignee. Spodek v. U.S., Fed.Cl.2000, 46 Fed.Cl. 819. United States ☞ 71

When contracting officer modified contract for the government's lease of housing facility to name bank as assignee of rent payments and to incorporate the notice of assignment document, the government expressly agreed to the lessor's assignment directing payments to the bank, thereby waiving any defects with the requirements of the Assignment of Claims Act and Assignment of Contracts Act. Summerfield Housing Ltd. Partnership v. U.S., Fed.Cl.1998, 42 Fed.Cl. 160, affirmed 217 F.3d 860, rehearing denied, certiorari denied 120 S.Ct. 2691, 530 U.S. 1244, 147 L.Ed.2d 963. United States ☞ 111(10)

Government did not assent to assignment of proceeds of government contract to financing institution when institution's representative met with government officials, where institution did not seek assent by responsible officials such as contracting officer or disbursing officer until after contract had been terminated. United California Discount Corp. v. U.S., Cl.Ct.1990, 19 Cl.Ct. 504. United States ☞ 71

Although assignee failed to give required notice of assignment of accounts receivable respecting government contract to disbursing officer at any time, government's actions with respect to contract evinced recognition of assignment sufficient to constitute waiver of this section, where responsible government officials had knowledge of assignment at time of payment, and government assented to assignment, taking action to comply therewith. American Financial Associates, Ltd. v. U.S., Cl.Ct.1984, 5 Cl.Ct. 761, affirmed 755 F.2d 912. United States ☞ 111(10)

A contract for transporting the mails cannot be transferred or assigned, in whole or in part, without the consent of the Postmaster General, and such transfer being illegal it is not a valid consideration to support a promise to pay for a half interest in such contract. Nix v. Bell, Ga.1881, 66 Ga. 664. Postal Service ☞ 21(2); Contracts ☞ 105

A manufacturing company, after having entered into a contract with the Navy Department to deliver a large quantity of steel castings to be used in the construction of an armoured cruiser, proposed to transfer the contract to another manufacturing company, which contemplated fulfilling the covenants of the former company with the Government, and asked the approval of such transfer by the Secretary of the Navy, but in view of the prohibition in this section the proposed transfer could not lawfully be approved and recognized by the Navy Department. 1888, 19 Op.Atty.Gen. 186.

Contractors with the Government may transfer with the assent of Government, and when such transfers are made and assented to the assignees take the place of the original party. 1823, 5 Op.Atty.Gen. 747. See, also, 1861, 10 Op.Atty.Gen. 4.

30. Voiding of transferred contracts

This section avoids the liability of the United States on a contract after the transfer of any interest therein to another person by the party with whom the contract was made. St. Paul & D.R. Co. v. U.S., 1885, 5 S.Ct. 366, 112 U.S. 733, 28 L.Ed. 861. St. Paul & D.R. Co. v. U.S., U.S.1885, 5 S.Ct. 366, 112 U.S. 733, 28 L.Ed. 861. United States ☞ 71

The interdiction of this section against transfer of Government contracts merely enables Government, at its option, to annul assigned contract, and does not act as self-executing nullification in all cases where Government contracts are assigned. Thompson v. C.I.R., C.A.3 1953, 205 F.2d 73. United States ☞ 71

The transfer of a contract is not by this section declared null and void. Dulaney v. Scudder, C.C.A.5 (Miss.) 1899, 94 F. 6, 36 C.C.A. 52.

Corporation to whom government contract was assigned in violation of Anti-Assignment Act did not have necessary privity of contract with United States to bring claim for alleged changed conditions on contract; assignment of contract in violation of Act was void and nullified contract. NGC Inv. and Development, Inc. v. U.S., Fed.Cl.1995, 33 Fed.Cl. 459. United States ☞ 71

31. Novation agreements

Where Government asserted in good faith that intercorporate transfer was barred by this section and former section 203 of Title 31 [now section 3727 of Title 31] and insisted on provision, in novation agreement, that neither corporation would present claim to Government for any costs, etc., attributable to assignment, there was consideration for such provision in assignment. ITT Gilfillan, Inc. v. U.S., Ct.Cl.1973, 471 F.2d 1382, 200 Ct. Cl. 367. United States ☞ 71

32. Recovery by assignee against assignor

The express declaration that, so far as the United States are concerned, a transfer shall work an annulment of the contract carries, by clear implication, the declaration that it shall have no such effect as between the contractor and his transferee. Burck v. Taylor, U.S.Tex. 1894, 14 S.Ct. 696, 152 U.S. 634, 38 L.Ed. 578.

Contractor's assignee had right to rely upon its assignment as security, and not having been party to contractor's bankruptcy proceedings was not bound by allowance therein of Government's claim against contractor. Chelsea Factors, Inc. v. U.S., Ct.Cl.1960, 181 F.Supp. 685, 149 Ct.Cl. 202. Bankruptcy ☞ 2928

Where Government contract was validly assigned to bank advancing funds to contractor to complete performance of the contract and held by bank as security for loans made by it to the contractor in connection with the Government contracts, and a check was received in part payment by the bank for work under the contract, bank was authorized to apply the proceeds of the check so far as need be towards liquidating its debt and was under no obligation to inquire into the contractor's accounts with the contractee. U.S. Cas. Co. v. First Nat. Bank of Columbus, M.D.Ga.1957, 157 F.Supp. 789. United States ☞ 111(12)

Where assignment, which was absolute on its face and had been made by prime contractor to assignee bank prior to execution of subcontract, constituted an assignment of all receipts under prime contract and security for all advances made by assignee to prime contractor to finance his complete operation in performing various Government contracts, bank's application of receipts from shipment of materials under subcontract to payment of prime contractor's indebtedness under another Government contract was proper. Peterman Lumber Co. v. Adams, W.D.Ark.1955, 128 F.Supp. 6. United States ☞ 111(12)

Underlying contract could not limit creditor's rights under assignment of federal government contract only to amount of its loan to Chapter 7 debtor, where such limitation could not be found in Assignment of Claims Act or Anti-Assignment Act. In re Computer Engineering Associates, Inc., D.Mass.2002, 278 B.R. 665, affirmed 337 F.3d 38. United States ☞ 71

Assignment of Claims Act, which was designed to protect United States government, did not apply to invalidate creditor's recorded security interest in general intangibles as applied to federal tax refund to debtor, based on failure to comply with the Act; the Act did not affect the rights of contracting parties inter se. Matter of Palmetto Pump & Irr., Inc.,

Bkrtcy.M.D.Fla.1987, 81 B.R. 109. United States ⊶ 111(11)

33. Recovery by assignee against government—Generally

Pursuant to regulation incorporated by construction contract, surety that completed performance under contract following contractor's default was not entitled to receive balance due under contract until it provided required release of all claims against government except those specifically excepted from operation of release, notwithstanding surety's contention that it would be unable to pursue other claims against government if it provided release. United Pacific Ins. Co. v. Roche, C.A.Fed.2004, 380 F.3d 1352, rehearing denied. United States ⊶ 74.1

Government contractor's liability to Small Business Administration (SBA) on promissory note was independent of defense contracts and therefore contractor's assignee was entitled to recover amount due under government's settlement with contractor; although notes were intended to finance performance of contracts, and security agreements expressly listed rights to contract payments as collateral, liability on notes did not arise from defense contracts but was imposed by loan documents, and government had conceded any defense to payment based on inadequate performance of contracts by settling contractor's contract claims. Bank of America Nat. Trust and Sav. Ass'n v. U.S., C.A.Fed.1994, 23 F.3d 380, rehearing denied. United States ⊶ 111(12)

Under this section, the assignee who finances a transaction assumes the risk of nonperformance by the assignor. Merchants Nat. Bank of Mobile v. U.S., Ct.Cl. 1982, 689 F.2d 181, 231 Ct.Cl. 563. United States ⊶ 111(10)

Rights of assignee of a government contractor are limited to the right to receive money under the contract; the assignee has only a limited interest in the financing aspects of the contract, not the performance aspects. Produce Factors Corp. v. U.S., Ct.Cl.1972, 467 F.2d 1343, 199 Ct.Cl. 572. United States ⊶ 111(12)

This section does not give contractor's assignee rights in retainages held by United States superior to those of contractor's surety. Royal Indem. Co. v. U.S., Ct.Cl. 1967, 371 F.2d 462, 178 Ct.Cl. 46, certio-

rari denied 88 S.Ct. 33, 389 U.S. 833, 19 L.Ed.2d 93. United States ⊶ 111(13)

Where a government officer who received payment of balance of purchase price on certain tugs sold under a contract, was advised that payment was being made by an assignee of buyer under the contract, subject to assignment of the contract of purchase to such assignee but such officer failed to inform contracting officer of the condition upon which such payment was made, and Government transferred title to the tugs to the original buyer, instead of his assignee, under such circumstances, assignee was entitled to a return of his money following original buyer's dishonor of the assignment, since had the contracting officer been advised of the conditions attached to the payment he would have been compelled to either recognize the assignment, or return the money to assignee. Maffia v. U.S., Ct.Cl. 1958, 163 F.Supp. 859, 143 Ct.Cl. 198. United States ⊶ 71

Even if financing institution that received assignment of proceeds of government contract had properly complied with notice provisions of Anti-Assignment Acts, or if Government had waived compliance with those provisions, institution could not recover assignment contract after Government withheld contract proceeds for violation of federal labor laws. United California Discount Corp. v. U.S., Cl.Ct.1990, 19 Cl.Ct. 504.

Under this section and former section 203 of Title 31 [now section 3727 of Title 31], plaintiff by its assignment from the contractor could acquire no greater rights in respect of payments or claims arising under the assigned contract than its assignor, the contractor, had, and it may not, therefore, recover any more than the contractor could have recovered in the absence of the assignment. Modern Indus. Bank v. U.S., Ct.Cl.1944, 101 Ct.Cl. 808. Assignments ⊶ 94; United States ⊶ 71

The parties to an assignment may suffer damage, but can derive no benefit from an assignment of a Government contract. 1888, 19 Op.Atty.Gen. 186.

34. —— Damages, recovery by assignee against government

Where assignee of contract to purchase surplus tugs from Government under Surplus Property Act, 50 App. § 1611 et seq., sent check for $10,800, the balance due on purchase price, to the Government, and the Government accepted the payment but, through mistake, delivered title documents to original purchaser instead of to assignee, and assignee was required to expend $92,000 to secure title documents, assignee was barred from recovering the $92,000 by this section, providing that no Government contract or order, or any interest therein, shall be transferred by party to whom such contract or order is given to any other party, and any such transfer shall cause annulment of contract or order transferred, so far as the United States are concerned, but assignee was entitled to recover the $10,800 received by the United States. Maffia v. U.S., Ct.Cl.1956, 142 F.Supp. 891, 135 Ct.Cl. 604. United States ⊶ 71

35. —— Priority, recovery by assignee against government

Financing institution that received assignment of proceeds of government contract did not have priority over funds withheld by Government under either security interest theory or equitable lien theory after contract proceeds were withheld by Government due to violation of federal labor laws. United California Discount Corp. v. U.S., Cl.Ct.1990, 19 Cl.Ct. 504. United States ⊶ 71

36. —— Quantum meruit, recovery by assignee against government

Theory of quantum meruit did not apply to financing institution's action against Government to recover proceeds of government contract allegedly assigned to it, where there was never any contract between institution and Government. United California Discount Corp. v. U.S., Cl.Ct.1990, 19 Cl.Ct. 504. United States ⊶ 71

Where an express contract is void, the person who had delivered his goods to the Government, the Government having used them, may recover on the implied contract in quantum meruit. Heathfield v. U.S., Ct.Cl.1872, 8 Ct.Cl. 213. United States ⊶ 69(1)

A suit cannot be maintained for damages for the breach by the United States of a transferred contract, but where there has been a delivery of goods under the contract, duly accepted by the United States, an action may be maintained by the contractor for the use of the assignee in quantum meruit. Wheeler v. U.S., Ct. Cl.1869, 5 Ct.Cl. 504.

37. —— Royalties, recovery by assignee against government

The Government is liable to the assignee of a patent for royalties, notwithstanding the provisions of this section. Federal Manufacturing & Printing Co. v. U.S., Ct.Cl.1907, 42 Ct.Cl. 479.

38. Recovery by government against assignee

Under amendment to this section providing that notwithstanding any law to contrary governing validity of assignments, any assignment pursuant to this section shall constitute a valid assignment for all purposes, United States cannot recover from assignee progress payments once it has made them except for fraud, even if the payments were erroneously made. American Fidelity Co. v. National City Bank of Evansville, C.A.D.C.1959, 266 F.2d 910, 105 U.S.App.D.C. 312. United States ⊶ 111(10)

This section and former section 203 of Title 31 [now section 3727 of Title 31] were enacted for purpose of protecting rights of contractor's assignee in "moneys due or to become due under any contract", and only funds earned under contract and not committed to payment for labor and materials could "become due" to contractor and its assignee, and therefore even if Government had mistakenly paid money to assignee after receiving notice that laborers and materialmen had not been paid, former section 203 of Title 31, which provided that no liability of any nature of assignor to the United States should impose any liability on part of assignee to make restitution, refund or repayment to United States, would not preclude Government from recovering over from assignee if Government was held liable to contractor's surety. Newark Ins. Co. v. U.S., Ct.Cl.1960, 181 F.Supp. 246, 149 Ct.Cl. 170. United States ⊶ 111(10)

Failure of government, in setting off $1.9 million owed in termination settlement for preexisting debts of contractor as result of overpayments on another contractor, to issue a Contracting Officer's final decision pursuant to Contracts Disputes Act, did not invalidate government's setoff; government's right to recover funds paid under a mistake of fact was inherent right supported by case law and not subject to that Act. Applied Companies v. U.S., Fed.Cl.1997, 37 Fed.

Cl. 749, affirmed 144 F.3d 1470. United States ☜ 130(3)

39. Set-off against assignee

Under Assignment of Claims Act, government contractor's assignment to bank of amounts owed by government under settlement agreement for terminated contract did not prohibit government from making setoff of overpayment debt owed by contractor against amounts owed under settlement, where contractor fully repaid outstanding balance owed bank, thus releasing assignment in favor of bank; with extinguishment of bank's interest in collateral as assignee, Act's prohibitions against setoffs became unenforceable. Applied Companies v. U.S., C.A.Fed.1998, 144 F.3d 1470. United States ☜ 111(1)

Tennessee Valley Authority was barred by this section and former section 203 of Title 31 [now section 3727 of Title 31] from recovering from factor that had been assigned proceeds of coal mining contract amounts previously paid out to assignor mining company for reclamation work by a setoff against unpaid invoices for delivered coal. Sigmon Fuel Co. v. Tennessee Valley Authority, C.A.6 (Tenn.) 1983, 709 F.2d 440. United States ☜ 111(12)

Where proceeds of defense contract were assigned by contractor to lender to secure anticipated performance loans, contract was terminated for convenience of government, all of contractor's obligations thereunder were fulfilled, all advances made by lender for performance of contract were repaid, but contractor was indebted to lender on other loans secured by assignment, the government was not entitled to set off contractor's indebtedness to it under other defense contracts against sums admittedly due under terms of convenience termination. Continental Bank & Trust Co. v. U.S., Ct.Cl.1969, 416 F.2d 1296, 189 Ct.Cl. 99. United States ☜ 130(4)

Claim of surety to retainages in hands of United States is subordinate and inferior to right of United States to set off amount of taxes owed it by contractor against contract retainages. Royal Indem. Co. v. U.S., Ct.Cl.1967, 371 F.2d 462, 178 Ct.Cl. 46, certiorari denied 88 S.Ct. 33, 389 U.S. 833, 19 L.Ed.2d 93. Internal Revenue ☜ 4775

If loans to finance borrower's performance of contracts with Government were secured by borrower's assignment of proceeds of those contracts, which contained "no setoff" provisions, lender would be entitled to contract price for goods received by Government and not yet paid for, even though Government had offsets in larger amount against borrower for excess costs of replacing defectively packed shipment and for overpayments made on other shipments. Chelsea Factors, Inc. v. U.S., Ct.Cl.1960, 181 F.Supp. 685, 149 Ct.Cl. 202. United States ☜ 130(3)

In action by trustee in bankruptcy of assignee of a claim against the Government of a war contractor, Government had the right of setoff of claims against the assignee itself arising independently and not by virtue of the assignment even though the contractor might also be liable to the Government for the same debt. Hadden v. U.S., Ct.Cl.1952, 105 F.Supp. 1010, 123 Ct.Cl. 246. United States ☜ 130(4)

40. Subrogation

Where, although Government's payment to assignee of contractor of part of retained contract funds had been erroneous and had resulted in double liability because of priority of contractor's surety to such funds, Government was prevented by this section from recovering payment thus made to assignee, Government would be subrogated to debt of assignee which was satisfied by payment. Great American Ins. Co. v. U.S., Ct.Cl.1974, 492 F.2d 821, 203 Ct.Cl. 592. Subrogation ☜ 26

Where assignment of Government contractor to surety on payment and performance bond, even if not invalid as in contravention of this section was effective only upon the contractor's default and there was no showing that such default occurred before deduction by bank advancing funds to the contractor to complete contracts of the amount in dispute from the check received by contractor, no right of subrogation in the surety against the bank existed. U.S. Cas. Co. v. First Nat. Bank of Columbus, M.D.Ga.1957, 157 F.Supp. 789. United States ☜ 74.1

41. Surety, rights of

Sureties on bond of defaulting Government contractor who had assigned rights to progress payment to bank in consideration of loan could not recover from bank which had received progress payments before default sums sureties were required to pay under performance bond unless the progress payments to bank had been induced by fraud. American Fidelity Co. v. National City Bank of Evansville, C.A.D.C.1959, 266 F.2d 910, 105 U.S.App.D.C. 312. United States ☞ 74.1

Surety that issued performance and payment bond for project under government contract had equitable right to recover progress payments that had been assigned by contractor to his bank; bank applied payments to reduce contractor's indebtedness on loans unrelated to government project, and bank never provided surety with notice of assignment. Central Nat. Ins. Co. of Omaha v. Tri-County State Bank, D.Minn.1993, 823 F.Supp. 652. United States ☞ 111(10)

Where contractor entered into construction contract with the United States Government with bonding company as surety for performance of contract, and bank loaned contractor certain sums and received an assignment from contractor under this section of all funds due or to become due under the contract, and thereafter on failure of contractor to complete the work, bonding company, at a time when no amount was due to contractor on the contract, completed work on the contract, bonding company, and not the bank, was entitled to funds due from Government for work done under the contract, though Government had never formally declared the contractor in default. Hardin County Sav. Bank v. U.S., Ct.Cl.1946, 65 F.Supp. 1017, 106 Ct.Cl. 577. Subrogation ☞ 36

General agreement of indemnity in which government contractor voluntarily subrogated its rights under prime contract to surety which issued performance and payment bonds did not provide surety with standing to appeal final decision of contracting officer (CO) finding contractor in default, as statutory provisions of Assignment of Contracts Act and the Assignment of Claims Act precluded such assignment of contract rights. Nova Cas. Co. v. U.S., Fed.Cl.2006, 69 Fed.Cl. 284. United States ☞ 71; United States ☞ 73(15)

Completion contractor did not have standing as assignee of surety to bring suit for alleged omitted home office overhead on construction contract under As-

signment of Claims Act since completion contractor was not bank, trust company, other financial institution, or surety. George W. Kane, Inc. v. U.S., Cl.Ct.1992, 26 Cl.Ct. 655. United States ☞ 71

42. Notice of default

If the assignee of a public contract can be held to the liabilities of the contractor, he must nevertheless be put in default by proper notice. Hersch v. U.S., Ct.Cl. 1879, 15 Ct.Cl. 385.

43. Jurisdiction

This section and former section 203 of Title 31 [now section 3727 of Title 31] did not contain grants of jurisdiction, either express or implied. Sterling Nat. Bank & Trust Co. of New York v. Teltronics Services, Inc., S.D.N.Y.1979, 471 F.Supp. 182. United States ☞ 131

44. Persons entitled to maintain action

As assignee under Assignment of Claims Act, Bank of America's security interest in government contractor's contract receivables included right to bring suit against government to recover any contract payment made to another, which Bank had not relinquished in transfer of portion of security interest to Small Business Administration (SBA) in return for payment on loan guaranty, and thus Bank had right to payment under Act; government's payment to contractor/assignor in settlement of contract dispute was payment under contract that should have gone to Bank under assignment. Bank of America Nat. Trust and Sav. Ass'n v. U.S., C.A.Fed.1994, 23 F.3d 380, rehearing denied. United States ☞ 111(12)

A contractor who assigns his claim to the Small Business Administration under this section in order to secure a loan, is still the proper party to bring suit on the claim in the Court of Claims [now United States Claims Court] for any amounts still due, provided that any recovery be first applied to the payment of any balance due on the contractor's obligation to the Small Business Administration. Keco Industries, Inc. v. U.S., Ct.Cl.1962, 157 Ct. Cl. 691. Federal Courts ☞ 1110

Under this section, assignee of contract for construction of a ship cannot maintain a suit thereon against the United States. New York Shipbuilding Corporation v. U.S., Ct.Cl.1925, 61 Ct.Cl. 357.

An action by the transferee of a Government contract ought not to fail merely because the assignor does not appear as nominal plaintiff suing for the use and benefit of the transferee. Federal Mfg. & Printing Co. v. U.S., Ct.Cl.1906, 41 Ct.Cl. 318. United States ☞ 135

Where a quartermaster and the assignee of a contract both treat the contract as a nullity, the assignee actually furnishing the goods, and the quartermaster dealing with him, giving him vouchers in his own name and certifying that he purchased the goods from him, an action on the vouchers is properly brought in the name of the party in interest. Heathfield v. U.S., Ct.Cl.1872, 8 Ct.Cl. 213. Assignments ☞ 121

This section is imperative and absolute, and bars any action by the assignor as well as the assignee. Wanless v. U.S., Ct.Cl.1870, 6 Ct.Cl. 123.

45. Counterclaims

In action by trustee in bankruptcy as assignee of claim against the Government under a war contract, where Government asserted a counterclaim for taxes on ground that plaintiff was successor in interest to the contractor, if the Government could prove that the contractor was the transferee of tax debtors and that subsequently the plaintiff became the transferee of the contractor, the counterclaim could properly be asserted. Hadden v. U.S., Ct.Cl.1952, 105 F.Supp. 1010, 123 Ct.Cl. 246. Federal Civil Procedure ☞ 779

46. Defenses—Generally

Where the Government treats a person as a contractor, and responsible as such, all through the work, and until its completion, and accepts the entire work as satisfactory and makes a final settlement with him, it may not make the objection that he was not a lawful contractor on the ground of a transfer by the contractor to one of his sureties of an interest in the contract. Bowe v. U.S., C.C.N.D.Ga. 1890, 42 F. 761.

In action by trustee in bankruptcy of claim against the Government under a war contract that counterclaim of the Government for taxes arose independently of the contract within the meaning of this section was no defense to liability asserted against the trustee as successor in interest to the contractor and not as assignee. Hadden v. U.S., Ct.Cl.1952,

105 F.Supp. 1010, 123 Ct.Cl. 246. Federal Civil Procedure ☞ 779

An attempted assignment which the parties do not set up or claim under cannot, after a full performance, be set up by the Government to prevent a recovery for service performed and the provisions of this section do not apply to such a case. Dougherty, for Use of Slavens v. U.S., Ct.Cl.1883, 18 Ct.Cl. 496. United States ☞ 71

Where a party brings his action in his own name and upon the implied contract arising from the taking of his own property for public use, it is no defense that he had been acting as assignee of a contract for the sale of similar goods, and that the transfer of such contracts renders them void under this section. Hersch v. U.S., Ct.Cl.1879, 15 Ct.Cl. 385.

Subcontractor cannot defend breach of contract on ground that it was not assignable without having attempted to secure approval of assignment. Mullen & Junkin v. Byrd & Clopton, Miss.1929, 122 So. 485, 154 Miss. 215. United States ☞ 71

47. —— Estoppel, defenses

Assignee's claim of equitable estoppel, predicated on charge that government, knowing of assignee's interest in government contract invoices, should not have permitted assignor to retrieve some of them without at least informing assignee, was unavailing, since, inter alia, it could not be reasonably asserted that the government should have prevented contractor-assignor from recalling invoices for allegedly needed correction, and since assignee's endorsement on the invoices, stating that assignee should receive notice of "merchandise returns or claims for shortage, nondelivery, or for other grounds," was only intended as a safeguard against nonnotification regarding faulty performance. Produce Factors Corp. v. U.S., Ct.Cl.1972, 467 F.2d 1343, 199 Ct.Cl. 572. Estoppel ☞ 62.6

48. —— Fraud in the inducement, defenses

Government could not assert defense of contractor's alleged fraud in the inducement in obtaining contract against innocent assignee of contract proceeds; "no setoff" provision in contract precluded government from reducing amount paid to assignee when contractor's liability was based on reasons independent of contract. In re Gulf Apparel Corp., M.D.Ga.1992, 140 B.R. 593. United States ☞ 111(12)

49. —— Laches, defenses

Where contracting officer of Department of Housing and Urban Development recognized assignments and yet failed to act consistent with their terms, United States could not invoke doctrine of laches as bar against assignee's claim. Tuftco Corp. v. U.S., Ct.Cl.1980, 614 F.2d 740, 222 Ct.Cl. 277. Equity ☞ 84

Although there was a considerable lapse of time before assignee of buyer of certain tugs under a contract with the Government called to the attention of the Government, buyer's repudiation of the assignment, such fact was not sufficient to charge assignee with laches in view of fact that under assignee's agreement with buyer, buyer was to take delivery of the tugs and arrange for making of necessary

repairs and provide for their eventual sale, and assignee, therefore, had no reason for complaint because the Government delivered the tugs to buyer rather than assignee. Maffia v. U.S., Ct.Cl.1958, 163 F.Supp. 859, 143 Ct.Cl. 198. United States ☞ 71

50. —— Mitigation of damages, defenses

Naval ordnance plant's refusal to pay purported assignee directly, which resulted in purported assignee's refusal to continue manufacturing gyro motors for contractor, did not constitute failure to mitigate damages and did not bar government from recovering against defaulting contractor where plant did not by affirmative conduct hinder performance by contractor or purported assignee. U.S. v. Russell Elec. Co., S.D.N.Y.1965, 250 F.Supp. 2. United States ☞ 75(5)

§ 16.   Repealed.   Oct. 21, 1941, c. 452, 55 Stat. 743

HISTORICAL AND STATUTORY NOTES

Section, R.S. § 3744; Acts June 15, 1917, c. 29, § 1, 40 Stat. 198; Feb. 4, 1929, c. 146, § 1, 45 Stat. 1147, related to requirement that contracts made by

the Secretaries of War, Navy, and Interior be in writing, and that copies thereof be filed in the returns of the office of the Interior Department.

§§ 16a to 16d.   Omitted

HISTORICAL AND STATUTORY NOTES

Codifications

Section 16a, Acts June 25, 1910, c. 431, § 23, 36 Stat. 861; May 18, 1916, c. 125, § 1, 39 Stat. 126; Jan. 12, 1927, c. 27, 44 Stat. 936, authorized purchases by Department of Interior without compliance with former section 16 of this title.

Section 16b, Acts Apr. 17, 1936, c. 233, § 1, 49 Stat. 1226; May 18, 1937, c. 223, 50 Stat. 181; May 17, 1938, c. 236, § 1, 52 Stat. 393; June 16, 1939, c. 208, § 1, 53 Stat. 834; June 18, 1940, c. 396, § 1,

54 Stat. 474, authorized purchases by Botanic Garden without compliance with former section 16 of this title.

Section 16c, Act May 13, 1926, c. 294, § 1, 44 Stat. 547 authorized purchases by Architect of Capitol without compliance with former section 16 of this title.

Section 16d, Act Aug. 4, 1939, c. 418, § 13, 53 Stat. 1197, authorized purchases by Bureau of Reclamation without compliance with former section 16 of this title.

§§ 17 to 19.   Repealed.   Oct. 21, 1941, c. 452, 55 Stat. 743

HISTORICAL AND STATUTORY NOTES

Section 17, R.S. § 3745, provided that an affidavit be affixed to the return of

contract required by former section 16 of this title.

Section 18, R.S. § 3746, provided punishment for failure to make returns of contracts as required by former sections 16 and 17 of this title.

Section 19, R.S. § 3747, imposed duty on Secretaries of War, Navy, and Interior to furnish officers with letters of instruction relating to their duties under former sections 17 and 18 of this title, contract forms, and affidavits, to insure uniformity.

§ 20. Repealed. Pub.L. 103–355, Title II, § 2452, Oct. 13, 1994, 108 Stat. 3326

HISTORICAL AND STATUTORY NOTES

Section, R.S. § 3743; Feb. 27, 1877, c. 69, § 1, 19 Stat. 249; July 31, 1894, c. 174, § 18, 28 Stat. 210; June 10, 1921, c. 18, §§ 304, 310, 42 Stat. 24, 25, related to the deposit of all contracts which required advance money or the settlement of public accounts in the General Accounting Office.

Effective Date of Repeal

Repeal of section effective Oct. 13, 1994, except as otherwise provided, see section 10001 of Pub.L. 103–355, set out as a note under section 251 of this title.

§ 20a. Repealed. Pub.L. 104–106, Div. D, Title XLIII, § 4321(i)(10), Feb. 10, 1996, 110 Stat. 676

HISTORICAL AND STATUTORY NOTES

Section 20a, Act June 15, 1940, c. 367, 54 Stat. 398, exempted from the provisions of former section 20 of this title deposit of contracts concerning national-forest lands, when the permit or other instrument did not require payment to the Government in excess of $300 in any one fiscal year.

Effective Date of Repeal

Repeal of sections by Pub.L. 104–106 effective Feb. 10, 1996, except as otherwise provided, see section 4401 of Pub.L. 104–106, set out as a note under section 251 of this title.

§ 20b. Repealed. Pub.L. 104–106, Div. D, Title XLIII, § 4321(i)(11), Feb. 10, 1996, 110 Stat. 676

HISTORICAL AND STATUTORY NOTES

Section 20b, Act Nov. 28, 1943, c. 328, 57 Stat. 592, exempted from the provisions of former section 20 of this title deposit of leases, contracts, etc., concerning use of lands or waters under jurisdiction of the Department of the Interior, when the lease or other instruments did not require payment to the Government in excess of $300 in any one fiscal year.

Effective Date of Repeal

Repeal of sections by Pub.L. 104–106 effective Feb. 10, 1996, except as otherwise provided, see section 4401 of Pub.L. 104–106, set out as a note under section 251 of this title.

§ **21.**   Repealed.   Pub.L.   97–258,   §   5(b),   Sept.   13,   1982,   96 Stat. 1069

HISTORICAL AND STATUTORY NOTES

Section, Acts July 31, 1894, c. 174, § 22, 28 Stat. 210; June 10, 1921, c. 18, §§ 304, 310, 42 Stat. 24, 25, provided that the heads of the several executive departments and the proper officers of other Government establishments, not within the jurisdiction of any executive department, make appropriate rules and regulations to secure a proper adminis-trative examination of all accounts sent to them before their transmission to the General Accounting Office, and for the execution of other requirements of section 20 of this title, insofar as the same related to the several departments or establishments. See section 3521(a) of Title 31, Money and Finance.

§ 22.   Interest of Member of Congress

No Member of Congress shall be admitted to any share or part of any contract or agreement made, entered into, or accepted by or on behalf of the United States, or to any benefit to arise thereupon. Nor shall the provisions of this section apply to any contracts or agreements heretofore or hereafter entered into under the Agricultural Adjustment Act [7 U.S.C.A. § 601 et seq.], the Federal Farm Loan Act, the Emergency Farm Mortgage Act of 1933, the Federal Farm Mortgage Corporation Act, the Farm Credit Act of 1933, and the Home Owners' Loan Act of 1933 [12 U.S.C.A. § 1461 et seq.], and shall not apply to contracts or agreements of a kind which the Secretary of Agriculture may enter into with farmers: *Provided,* That such exemption shall be made a matter of public record.

(R.S. § 3741; Feb. 27, 1877, c. 69, § 1, 19 Stat. 249; Jan. 25, 1934, c. 5, 48 Stat. 337; June 27, 1934, c. 847, Title V, § 510, 48 Stat. 1264; Aug. 26, 1937, c. 821, 50 Stat. 838; Oct. 13, 1994, Pub.L. 103–355, Title VI, § 6004, 108 Stat. 3364; Feb. 10, 1996, Pub.L. 104–106, Div. D, Title XLIII, § 4321(i)(12), 110 Stat. 676.)

HISTORICAL AND STATUTORY NOTES

Revision Notes and Legislative Reports
1994   Acts. Senate   Reports   Nos. 103–258 and 103–259, and House Conference Report No. 103–712, see 1994 U.S. Code Cong. and Adm. News, p. 2561.

1996 Acts. House Conference Report No. 104–450, see 1996 U.S. Code Cong. and Adm. News, p. 238.

References in Text
The Agricultural Adjustment Act, referred to in text, is Act May 12, 1933, c. 25, Title I, 48 Stat. 31, as amended, which is classified generally to chapter 26 of Title 7, 7 U.S.C.A. § 601 et seq. For complete classification, see Short Title

note set out under 7 U.S.C.A. § 601 and Tables.

The Federal Farm Loan Act, referred to in text, is Act July 17, 1916, c. 245, 39 Stat. 360, as amended, and was classified principally to 12 U.S.C.A. § 641 et seq. The Federal Farm Loan Act, as amended, was repealed by the Farm Credit Act of 1971, Pub.L. 92–181, § 5.26(a), Dec. 10, 1971, 85 Stat. 624. Section 5.26(a) of the Farm Credit Act of 1971 also provided that all references in other legislation to the Acts repealed thereby "shall be deemed to refer to comparable provisions of this Act". For further details, see notes set out under 12 U.S.C.A. § 2001. For complete classification of the Federal

Farm Loan Act to the Code prior to such repeal, see Tables.

The Emergency Farm Mortgage Act of 1933, referred to in text, is Act May 12, 1933, c. 25, Title II, 48 Stat. 31, which was substantially repealed by Act June 30, 1947, ch. 166, Title II, § 206(c), 61 Stat. 208; Act Aug. 6, 1953, c. 335, § 19, 67 Stat. 400; Oct. 4, 1961, Pub.L. 87–353, § 3(a), (b), (w), 75 Stat. 773, 774; Act Dec. 10, 1971, Pub.L. 92–181, Title V, § 5.26(a), 85 Stat. 624. For complete classification, see Tables.

The Federal Farm Mortgage Corporation Act, referred to in text, is Act Jan. 31, 1934, ch. 7, 48 Stat. 344, which enacted 12 U.S.C.A. § 992a, and amended 12 U.S.C.A. §§ 347, 355, 723, 772, 781, 897, 1016, 1020, 1020a, 1020b, 1020c, 1020d to 1020h, 1061, 1131i, 1138b and 1138d, has been substantially repealed. For complete classification, see Tables.

The Farm Credit Act of 1933, referred to in text, is Act June 16, 1933, ch. 98, 48 Stat. 2, as amended, and was classified principally to subchapter IV of chapter 7 of Title 12, 12 U.S.C.A. § 1131 et seq. The Farm Credit Act of 1933, as amended, was repealed by section 5.26(a) of the Farm Credit Act of 1971, Pub.L. 92–181, Dec. 10, 1971, 85 Stat. 624. Section 5.26(a) of the Farm Credit Act of 1971 also provided that all references in other legislation to the Acts repealed thereby "shall be deemed to refer to comparable provisions of this Act". For further details, see notes set out under 12 U.S.C.A. § 2001. For complete classification of the Farm Credit Act of 1933 to the Code prior to such repeal, see Tables.

The Home Owners' Loan Act of 1933, referred to in text, is Act June 13, 1933, ch. 64, 48 Stat. 128, as amended, now known as the Home Owners' Loan Act, which is classified generally to chapter 12 of Title 12, 12 U.S.C.A. § 1461 et seq. For complete classification, see 12 U.S.C.A. § 1461 and Tables.

Codifications

R.S. § 3741 derived from Act Apr. 21, 1808, c. 48, § 3, 2 Stat. 484.

Amendments

1996 Amendments. Pub.L. 104–106, § 4321(i)(12), made technical changes substituting "Sec. 3741. No Member" for "No member", which, for purposes of codification, required no further changes in text.

1994 Amendments. Pub.L. 103–355, § 6004, in revising the section, substituted "No member of Congress shall be admitted to any share or part of any contract or agreement made, entered into, or accepted by or on behalf of the United States, or to any benefit to arise thereupon." for "In every contract or agreement to be made or entered into, or accepted by or on behalf of the United States, there shall be inserted an express condition that no member of or delegate to Congress shall be admitted to any share or part of such contract or agreement, or to an benefit to arise thereupon."

1937 Amendments. Act Aug. 26, 1937, added the provision at the end beginning with "and shall not apply".

1934 Amendments. Act June 27, 1934, inserted "the Federal Farm Loan Act, the Emergency Farm Mortgage Act of 1933, the Federal Farm Mortgage Corporation Act, the Farm Credit Act of 1933, and the Home Owners' Loan Act of 1933".

Act Jan. 25, 1934, added "Nor shall the provision of this section apply to any contracts or agreements heretofore or hereafter entered into under the Agricultural Adjustment Act".

1877 Amendments. Act Feb. 27, 1877, inserted "or delegate to" after "that no member of".

Effective and Applicability Provisions

1996 Acts. Amendment by Pub.L. 104–106 effective Feb. 10, 1996, except as otherwise provided, see section 4401 of Pub.L. 104–106, set out as a note under section 251 of this title.

1994 Acts. Amendment by Pub.L. 103–355 effective Oct. 13, 1994, except as otherwise provided, see section 10001 of Pub.L. 103–355, set out as a note under section 251 of this title.

CROSS REFERENCES

Acquisition of land for flood control, applicability to, see 33 USCA § 702m.
Alien smuggling and undercover investigation authority and sums appropriated used for leasing space, see 8 USCA § 1363a.
Commodity Credit Corporation agreements, applicability to, see 15 USCA § 714*l.*

Contracts by Members of Congress and exemptions with respect to certain contracts, see 18 USCA §§ 431 and 433.

Crop-insurance agreements pursuant to the Federal Crop Insurance Act, inapplicability to, see 7 USCA § 1514.

Loans or payments pursuant to the Agricultural Adjustment Act of 1938, inapplicability to, see 7 USCA § 1386.

United States exchange program, contracts with foreign or domestic agencies without regard to this section, see 22 USCA § 1472.

LAW REVIEW AND JOURNAL COMMENTARIES

Enhancing the value of the thrift franchise: A possible solution for the dilemma of the FSLIC? C. Thomas Long, William J. Schilling, and Carol R. Van Cleef, 37 Cath.U.L.Rev. 385 (1988.)

LIBRARY REFERENCES

American Digest System

United States ☞12, 66.

Key Number System Topic No. 393.

Research References

Encyclopedias

Am. Jur. 2d Public Works and Contracts § 25, Officials Not to Have Interest in Contract or Benefit Therefrom.

70 Am. Jur. Proof of Facts 3d 97, Proof That a Government Agency Was Liable for Improperly Granting a Bid Award to a Bid Applicant.

Forms

Nichols Cyclopedia of Legal Forms Annotated § 145:223, Federal Offshore Oil and Gas Lease Under Outer Continental Shelf Lands Act.

Treatises and Practice Aids

Immigration Law Service 2d PSD INA § 294, Undercover Investigation Authority.

WESTLAW ELECTRONIC RESEARCH

See Westlaw guide following the Explanation pages of this volume.

Notes of Decisions

Contracts within section   1
Partnerships   2
Sureties   3

---

1. Contracts within section

This section is applicable to executory contracts only and a receipt or release by a landowner on the taking of his property for military purposes is not within its scope. U.S. v. McIntosh, E.D.Va.1932, 2 F.Supp. 244, rehearing denied 3 F.Supp. 715, appeal dismissed 70 F.2d 507, certiorari denied 55 S.Ct. 101, 293 U.S. 586, 79 L.Ed. 682, certiorari denied 55 S.Ct. 111, 293 U.S. 587, 79 L.Ed. 682, rehearing denied 55 S.Ct. 140, 293 U.S. 631, 79 L.Ed. 716.

The express condition that no Member of Congress has an interest in the con-

tract need not be inserted in those contracts made with railroad corporations. 1885, 18 Op.Atty.Gen. 112.

Although the employment of members of Congress as assistant counsel to the attorneys of the United States was not within the view of Congress at the passage of this section, yet the language thereof is so broad as to include and forbid a contract for professional services in such a case. 1826, 2 Op.Atty.Gen. 39.

2. Partnerships

A partnership of which a member of Congress is a member cannot enter into a contract with the Government, but, if he withdraw from it, the contract may be concluded with the other partners. 1842, 4 Op.Atty.Gen. 47.

3. Sureties
  Under this section a member of Congress may be lawfully accepted as a sure- ty on the bond of a contractor with the United States. 1885, 18 Op.Atty.Gen. 286.

§ 23. Orders or contracts for material placed with Government-owned establishments deemed obligations

All orders or contracts for work or material or for the manufacture of material pertaining to approved projects heretofore or hereafter placed with Government-owned establishments shall be considered as obligations in the same manner as provided for similar orders or contracts placed with commercial manufacturers or private contractors, and the appropriations shall remain available for the payment of the obligations so created as in the case of contracts or orders with commercial manufacturers or private contractors.

(June 5, 1920, c. 240, 41 Stat. 975; July 1, 1922, c. 259, 42 Stat. 812; June 2, 1937, c. 293, 50 Stat. 245.)

HISTORICAL AND STATUTORY NOTES

Codifications
  Section is a composite of acts June 5, 1920, ch. 240, and July 1, 1922, ch. 259. The words for work or material" after All orders or contracts", or contracts" after similar orders", and or private contractors" after commercial manufacturers" in two places are based on act July 1, 1922.

Amendments
1937 Amendments. Act June 2, 1937, continued this section in effect.

1922 Amendments. Act July 1, 1922, inserted "for work or material or" preceding "for the manufacture of", "or contracts" following "similar orders", and "or private contractors" following "commercial manufacturers" in two places.

LIBRARY REFERENCES

American Digest System
  United States ☞62.
  Key Number System Topic No. 393.

WESTLAW ELECTRONIC RESEARCH

  See Westlaw guide following the Explanation pages of this volume.

§ 24. Contracts for transportation of moneys, bullion, coin, and securities

Whenever it is practicable contracts for the transportation of moneys, bullion, coin, notes, bonds, and other securities of the United States, and paper shall be let to the lowest responsible bidder therefor, after notice to all parties having means of transportation.

(July 7, 1884, c. 332, 23 Stat. 204.)

HISTORICAL AND STATUTORY NOTES

Codifications

Section is from the Sundry Civil Appropriation Act, July 7, 1884.

LIBRARY REFERENCES

American Digest System

United States ⚖64.45(1).

Key Number System Topic No. 393.

WESTLAW ELECTRONIC RESEARCH

See Westlaw guide following the Explanation pages of this volume.

§ 24a. Omitted

HISTORICAL AND STATUTORY NOTES

Codifications

Section, Acts June 16, 1933, c. 101, § 5, 48 Stat. 305; Apr. 24, 1935, c. 78, 49 Stat. 161; Aug. 29, 1935, c. 816, 49 Stat. 991, provided for cancellation on or before Mar. 31, 1936, of contracts for transportation entered into prior to June 16, 1933.

§ 25. Repealed. Feb. 19, 1948, c. 65, § 11(a), 62 Stat. 25

HISTORICAL AND STATUTORY NOTES

Section, R.S. § 3729, related to contracts for bunting, and is now covered generally by section 2301 et seq. of Title 10, Armed Forces.

§ 26. Repealed. June 30, 1949, c. 288, Title VI, § 602 (a)(26), 63 Stat. 401, renumbered Sept. 5, 1950, c. 849, § 6(a), (b), 64 Stat. 583

HISTORICAL AND STATUTORY NOTES

Section, Acts Mar. 4, 1915, c. 147, § 5, 38 Stat. 1161; May 29, 1928, c. 901, § 1(5), 45 Stat. 986, related to exchange of typewriters and adding machines in part payment for new machines.

Effective Date of Repeal

Repeal of section effective July 1, 1949, see section 605 of Act June 30, 1949.

§ 27. Repealed. Oct. 31, 1951, c. 654, § 1(109), 65 Stat. 705

HISTORICAL AND STATUTORY NOTES

Section, Act June 5, 1920, c. 235, § 7, 41 Stat. 947, related to disposition of typewriting machines by Government departments and establishments.

§§ 28 to 34. Omitted

HISTORICAL AND STATUTORY NOTES

Codifications

Section 28, Act June 16, 1934, c. 553, § 1, 48 Stat. 974, related to adjustment and settlement of claims by persons who entered into contracts with the United States prior to Aug. 10, 1933 and claim loss due to compliance with codes of fair competition.

Section 29, Act June 16, 1934, c. 553, § 2, 48 Stat. 975, related to the amount allowed for settlement.

Section 30, Act June 16, 1934, c. 553, § 3, 48 Stat. 975, related to limitation on the amount of profits.

Section 31, Act June 16, 1934, c. 553, § 4, 48 Stat. 975, related to the time for presentment of claims.

Section 32, Act June 16, 1934, c. 553, § 5, 48 Stat. 975, authorized appropriations for the settlement of claims.

Section 33, Act June 16, 1934, c. 553, § 6, 48 Stat. 975, related to the procedure for settlement of claims and reservation of the right to prosecute for fraud and criminal conduct.

Section 34, Act Aug. 29, 1935, c. 815, 49 Stat. 990, provided that bids made subject to codes of fair competition prior to Aug. 29, 1935 should not be rejected where bidder agreed to be subject to Acts of Congress requiring observance of minimum wages, maximum hours, or limitations as to age of employees in performance of contracts, with Federal agencies.

§ 35. Contracts for materials, etc., exceeding $10,000; representations and stipulations

In any contract made and entered into by any executive department, independent establishment, or other agency or instrumentality of the United States, or by the District of Columbia, or by any corporation all the stock of which is beneficially owned by the United States (all the foregoing being hereinafter designated as agencies of the United States), for the manufacture or furnishing of materials, supplies, articles, and equipment in any amount exceeding $10,000, there shall be included the following representations and stipulations:

(a) That all persons employed by the contractor in the manufacture or furnishing of the materials, supplies, articles, or equipment used in the performance of the contract will be paid, without subsequent deduction or rebate on any account, not less than the minimum wages as determined by the Secretary of Labor to be the prevailing minimum wages for persons employed on similar work or in the particular or similar industries or groups of industries currently operating in the locality in which the materials, supplies, articles, or equipment are to be manufactured or furnished under said contract;

(b) That no person employed by the contractor in the manufacture or furnishing of the materials, supplies, articles, or equipment used in the performance of the contract shall be permitted to work in excess of forty hours in any one week: *Provided*, That the provisions of this subsection shall not apply to any employer who shall have entered into an agreement with his employees pursuant to the provisions of paragraphs (1) or (2) of subsection (b) of section 207 of Title 29;

(c) That no male person under sixteen years of age and no female person under eighteen years of age and no convict labor will be employed by the contractor in the manufacture or production or furnishing of any of the materials, supplies, articles, or equipment included in such contract, except that this section, or any other law or Executive order containing similar prohibitions against purchase of goods by the Federal Government, shall not apply to convict labor which satisfies the conditions of section 1761(c) of Title 18; and

(d) That no part of such contract will be performed nor will any of the materials, supplies, articles, or equipment to be manufactured or furnished under said contract be manufactured or fabricated in any plants, factories, buildings, or surroundings or under working conditions which are unsanitary or hazardous or dangerous to the health and safety of employees engaged in the performance of said contract.   Compliance with the safety, sanitary, and factory inspection laws of the State in which the work or part thereof is to be performed shall be prima-facie evidence of compliance with this subsection.

(June 30, 1936, c. 881, § 1, 49 Stat. 2036; May 13, 1942, c. 306, 56 Stat. 277; Pub.L. 90–351, Title I, § 819(b), formerly § 827(b), as added Dec. 27, 1979, Pub.L. 96–157, § 2, 93 Stat. 1215, and renumbered Oct. 12, 1984, Pub.L. 98–473, Title II, § 609B(f), 98 Stat. 2093; Nov. 8, 1985, Pub.L. 99–145, Title XII, § 1241(b), 99 Stat. 734, and amended Oct. 13, 1994, Pub.L. 103–355, Title VII, § 7201(1), 108 Stat. 3378.)

HISTORICAL AND STATUTORY NOTES

Revision Notes and Legislative Reports
1979 Acts. Senate Report No. 96–695, see 1979 U.S.Code Cong. and Adm.News, p. 2471.

1985 Acts. House Report No. 99–235, see 1985 U.S.Code Cong. and Adm.News, p. 472.

1994 Acts. Senate Report Nos. 103–258 and 103–259, and House Conference Report No. 103–712, see 1994 U.S. Code Cong. and Adm. News, p. 2561.

Amendments
1994 Amendments. Subsec. (a). Pub.L. 103–355, § 7201(1), struck out subsec. (a), which required contracts for materials, etc., exceeding $10,000, to include representations and stipulations that the contractor is the manufacturer of or a regular dealer in the materials, supplies, articles, or equipment to be manufactured or used in the performance of

the contract, and redesignated subsec. (b) as subsec. (a).

Subsecs. (b) to (e). Pub.L. 103–355, § 7201(1), redesignated subsecs. (b) to (e) as subsecs. (a) to (d), respectively.

1985 Amendments. Subsec. (c). Pub.L. 99–145 struck out "eight hours in any one day or in excess of" preceding "forty hours".

1979 Amendments. Subsec. (d). Pub.L. 90–351, § 827(b), as added by 96–157, added provisions relating to convict labor which satisfies the conditions of Section 1761(c) of Title 18.

1942 Amendments. Subsec. (c). Act May 13, 1942, added proviso.

Effective and Applicability Provisions
1994 Acts. Amendment by section 7201(1) of Pub.L. 103–355 effective Oct. 13, 1994, except as otherwise provided,

see section 10001 of Pub.L. 103–355, set out as a note under section 251 of this title.

1985 Acts. Section 1241(c) of Pub.L. 99–145 provided that: "The amendments made by this section [amending subsec. (c) of this section and former 40 U.S.C.A. § 328] shall take effect on January 1, 1986."

Short Title
1936 Acts. Section 14, formerly § 12, of Act June 30, 1936, as added Pub.L. 103–355, Title X, § 10005(f)(5), Oct. 13, 1994, 108 Stat. 3409, and renumbered § 14 by Pub.L. 104–106, Div. D, Title XLIII, § 4321(f)(1)(B), Feb. 10, 1996, 110 Stat. 675, provided that: "This Act [enacting this section and sections 36 to 45 of this title] may be cited as the 'Walsh–Healey Act'."

Contracting Authority of Government Agencies in Connection with National Defense Functions
Provisions of sections 35 to 45 of this title as applicable to Government agencies exercising certain contracting authority in connection with national-defense functions, see section 13 of Ex. Ord. No. 10789, set out as a note under section

1431 of Title 50, War and National Defense.

Exceptions and Exemptions
7 F.R. 9399 (amending Exemption Order Apr. 21, 1942, 7 F.R. 3003), which exempted female persons under 18 years of age from the provisions of subsec. (d) of this section, was superseded by 10 F.R. 10438.

Exemptions to Federal Restrictions on Marketability of Prison–Made Goods
Amendment of this section by Pub.L. 96–157 not applicable unless representatives of local union central bodies or similar labor union organizations have been consulted prior to the initiation of any project qualifying of any exemption created by the amendment and such paid inmate employment will not result in the displacement of employed workers, or be applied in skills, crafts, or trades in which there is a surplus of available gainful labor in the locality, or impair existing contracts for services, see section 827(c) of Pub.L. 90–351, as added Pub.L. 96–157, set out as a note under section 1761 of Title 18, Crimes and Criminal Procedure.

EXECUTIVE ORDERS
EXECUTIVE ORDER NO. 13126
June 12, 1999, 64 F.R. 32383

PROHIBITION OF ACQUISITION OF PRODUCTS PRODUCED BY FORCED OR INDENTURED CHILD LABOR

By the authority vested in me as President by the Constitution and the laws of the United States of America, and in order to continue the executive branch's commitment to fighting abusive child labor practices, it is hereby ordered as follows:

Section 1. Policy. It shall be the policy of the United States Government, consistent with the Tariff Act of 1930, 19 U.S.C. 1307, the Fair Labor Standards Act, 29 U.S.C. 201 et. seq., and the Walsh–Healey Public Contracts Act, 41 U.S.C. 35 et seq., that executive agencies shall take appropriate actions to enforce the laws prohibiting the manufacture or importation of goods, wares, articles, and merchandise mined, produced, or manufactured wholly or in part by forced or indentured child labor.

Sec. 2. Publication of List. Within 120 days after the date of this order, the Department of Labor, in consultation and cooperation with the Department of the Treasury and the Department of State, shall publish in the **Federal Register** a list of products, identified by their country of origin, that those Departments have a reasonable basis to believe might have been mined, produced, or manufactured by forced or indentured child labor. The Department of Labor may conduct hearings to assist in the identification of those products.

Sec. 3. Procurement Regulations. Within 120 days after the date of this order, the Federal Acquisition Regulatory Council shall issue proposed rules to implement the following:

(a) **Required Solicitation Provisions.** Each solicitation of offers for a contract for the procurement of a product included on the list published under section 2 of this order shall include the following provisions:

(1) A provision that requires the contractor to certify to the contracting officer that the contractor or, in the case of an incorporated contractor, a responsible official of the contractor has made a good faith effort to determine whether forced or indentured child labor was used to mine, produce, or manufacture any product furnished under the contract and that, on the basis of those efforts, the contractor is unaware of any such use of child labor; and

(2) A provision that obligates the contractor to cooperate fully in providing reasonable access to the contractor's records, documents, persons, or premises if reasonably requested by authorized officials of the contracting agency, the Department of the Treasury, or the Department of Justice, for the purpose of determining whether forced or indentured child labor was used to mine, produce, or manufacture any product furnished under the contract.

(b) **Investigations.** Whenever a contracting officer of an executive agency has reason to believe that forced or indentured child labor was used to mine, produce, or manufacture a product furnished pursuant to a contract subject to the requirements of subsection 3(a) of this order, the head of the executive agency shall refer the matter for investigation to the Inspector General of the executive agency and, as the head of the executive agency or the Inspector General determines appropriate, to the Attorney General and the Secretary of the Treasury.

(c) **Remedies.**

(1) The head of an executive agency may impose remedies as provided in this subsection in the case of a contractor under a contract of the executive agency if the head of the executive agency finds that the contractor:

(i) Has furnished under the contract products that have been mined, produced, or manufactured by forced or indentured child labor or uses forced or indentured child labor in the mining, production, or manufacturing operations of the contractor;

(ii) Has submitted a false certification under subsection 3(a)(1) of this order; or

(iii) Has failed to cooperate in accordance with the obligation imposed pursuant to subsection 3(a)(2) of this order.

(2) The head of an executive agency, in his or her sole discretion, may terminate a contract on the basis of any finding described in subsection 3(c)(1) of this order for any contract entered into after the date the regulation called for in section 3 of this order is published in final.

(3) The head of an executive agency may debar or suspend a contractor from eligibility for Federal contracts on the basis of a finding that the contractor has engaged in an act described in subsection 3(c)(1) of this order. The provision for debarment may not exceed 3 years.

(4) The Administrator of General Services shall include on the List of Parties Excluded from Federal Procurement and Nonprocurement Programs (maintained by the Administrator as described in the Federal Acquisition Regulation) each party that is debarred, suspended, proposed for debarment or suspension, or declared ineligible by the head of an agency on the basis that the person has engaged in an act described in subsection 3(c)(1) of this order.

(5) This section shall not be construed to limit the use of other remedies available to the head of an executive agency or any other official of the Federal Government on the basis of a finding described in subsection 3(c)(1) of this order.

Sec. 4.   Report.   Within 2 years after implementation of any final rule under this order, the Administrator of General Services, with the assistance of other executive agencies, shall submit to the Office of Management and Budget a report on the actions taken pursuant to this order.

Sec. 5.   Scope. (a)   Any proposed rules issued pursuant to section 3 of this order shall apply only to acquisitions for a total amount in excess of the micropurchase threshold as defined in section 32(f) of the Office of Federal Procurement Policy Act (41 U.S.C. 428(f)).

(b) This order does not apply to a contract that is for the procurement of any product, or any article, material, or supply contained in a product that is mined, produced, or manufactured in any foreign country if:

(1) the foreign country is a party to the Agreement on Government Procurement annexed to the WTO Agreement or a party to the North American Free Trade Agreement ("NAFTA"); and

(2) the contract is of a value that is equal to or greater than the United States threshold specified in the Agreement on Government Procurement annexed to the WTO Agreement or NAFTA, whichever is applicable.

Sec. 6. Definitions. (a) "Executive agency" and "agency" have the meaning given to "executive agency" in section 4(1) of the Office of Federal Procurement Policy Act (41 U.S.C. 403(1)).

(b) "WTO Agreement" means the Agreement Establishing the World Trade Organization, entered into on April 15, 1994.

(c) "Forced or indentured child labor" means all work or service (1) exacted from any person under the age of 18 under the menace of any penalty for its nonperformance and for which the worker does not offer himself voluntarily; or (2) performed by any person under the age of 18 pursuant to a contract the enforcement of which can be accomplished by process or penalties.

Sec. 7. Judicial Review. This order is intended only to improve the internal management of the executive branch and does not create any rights or benefits, substantive or procedural, enforceable by law by a party against the United States, its agencies, its officers, or any other person.

WILLIAM J. CLINTON

CROSS REFERENCES

Construction, repair, alteration, furnishing and equipping of Naval vessels, see 10 USCA § 7299.

Fair Labor Standards Act, see 29 USCA § 201 et seq.

Indian Self–Determination Act contracts and construction, see 25 USCA § 450j.

Purchases or contracts for armed forces treated as made with sealed bid procedures for purposes of §§ 35 to 45 of this title, see 10 USCA § 2304.

Wage determinations and interpretations of terms, review of, see 41 USCA § 43a.

CODE OF FEDERAL REGULATIONS

Federal Acquisition Regulations System, see 48 CFR § 1.000 et seq.

General enforcement statements, see 29 CFR §§ 775.0, 775.1; 41 CFR §§ 50–210.0, 50–210.1.

Minimum wage determinations, see 41 CFR § 50–202.1 et seq.

Occupational safety and health standards, see 29 CFR § 1910.1 et seq.

Policy and interpretation, wages and hours, see 29 CFR § 775.0 et seq.

Procedural rules for modification, etc., of occupational safety or health standards, see 29 CFR § 1911.1 et seq.

Safety and health standards—
Enforcement by State officers and employees, see 41 CFR § 50–205.1 et seq.
Promulgation and applicability, see 41 CFR § 50–204.1 et seq.

LAW REVIEW AND JOURNAL COMMENTARIES

Debarment and suspension revisited: Fewer eggs in the basket? Brian D. Shannon, 44 Cath.U.L.Rev. 363 (1995).

Interest groups, political freedom, and antitrust: A modern reassessment of the Noerr–Pennington doctrine. Gary Minda, 41 Hastings L.J. 905 (1990).

Sister sovereign states: Preemption and the Second Twentieth Century Revolution in the law of the American workplace. Henry H. Drummonds, 62 Fordham L.Rev. 469 (1993).

LIBRARY REFERENCES

American Digest System
Labor and Employment ⬤2243, 2304, 2350, 2563, 2838.
United States ⬤64.15.
Key Number System Topic Nos. 231H, 393.

Corpus Juris Secundum
  CJS Labor Relations § 1103, Public Employees; Employees on Public Works.
  CJS Labor Relations § 1129, Work Under Public Contracts or on Public Works--
    Federal Statutes.
  CJS Labor Relations § 1272, Quasi-Legislative Powers; Promulgation of Rules and
    Regulations--United States Department of Labor.
  CJS Labor Relations § 1292, Walsh-Healey Public Contracts Act.
  CJS Labor Relations § 1302, Under Federal Law.
  CJS United States § 113, Advertising and Proposals or Bids.
  CJS United States § 120, Extra Work or Expenses.

Research References

ALR Library
  196 ALR, Fed. 507, Validity, Construction, and Application of Fair Labor Stan-
    dards Act--Supreme Court Cases.
  185 ALR, Fed. 253, Validity, Construction, and Operation of Buy American Act (41
    U.S.C.A. § 10a-10d).
  80 ALR, Fed. 246, Employee Training Time as Exempt from Minimum Wage and
    Overtime Requirements of Fair Labor Standards Act.
  43 ALR, Fed. 159, Validity, Construction, and Application of OSHA General
    Industry Standard Regulating Exposure to Occupational Noise (29 CFR
    § 1910.95).
  31 ALR, Fed. 348, What Limitation Periods Apply Under 28 U.S.C.A. § 2415 to
    Government Suits.
  16 ALR, Fed. 982, Judicial Review Under § 10(C) of Walsh-Healey Act (41
    U.S.C.A. § 43a(C)) of Legal Questions Involved in Award of Government
    Contracts Under Such Act.
  2 ALR, Fed. 637, What Contracts Are Subject to Wage and Hour Requirements of
    Walsh-Healey Act (41 U.S.C.A. § 35).
  73 ALR 4th 582, Tort Liability for Nonmedical Radiological Harm.
  20 ALR 2nd 600, Income Tax: Deductibility of Amount Paid or Expense Incurred
    by Taxpayer on Account of His Liability or Alleged Liability for Tort, Crime,
    or Statutory Violation.
  18 ALR 3rd 944, Validity of Statute, Ordinance, or Charter Provision Requiring
    That Workmen on Public Works Be Paid the Prevailing or Current Rate of
    Wages.
  15 ALR 2nd 500, Effect of Fraud to Toll the Period for Bringing Action Prescribed
    in Statute Creating the Right of Action.
  3 ALR 2nd 1097, Portal-to-Portal Act.
  169 ALR 1307, Provision of Fair Labor Standards Act for Increased Compensation
    for Overtime.
  163 ALR 1300, Validity, Construction, and Effect of Statutory or Contractual
    Provision in Government Construction Contract Referring to Secretary of
    Labor Questions Respecting Wage Rates or Classification of Employees of
    Contractor.
  162 ALR 237, Statute of Limitations Applicable to Action to Recover Minimum
    Wage, Overtime Compensation, or Liquidated Damages Under Fair Labor
    Standards Act.
  154 ALR 1255, What Amounts to "Penalty or Forfeiture" Within Provision of
    Bankruptcy Act Against Allowance of Claim of that Character Made by
    Governmental Body.
  151 ALR 1481, Judicial Decisions Involving Rationing.
  132 ALR 1297, Constitutionality of Statute or Ordinance Relating to Rate of Wages
    of Persons Employed on Public Work.
  132 ALR 1443, Judicial Questions Regarding Federal Fair Labor Standards Act
    (Wage and Hours Act) and State Acts in Conformity Therewith.
  107 ALR 705, Servant's Right to Compensation for Extra Work or Overtime.
  96 ALR 1351, What Is a "Manufacturing Establishment" Within Meaning of
    Regulatory Statutes.

82 ALR 808, Conflict Between Federal and State Statutes of Limitations.

61 ALR 412, State Statute of Limitations as Affecting Action or Proceeding by Federal Government or Its Officials.

50 ALR 1408, Consent to Suit Against State.

Encyclopedias

Am. Jur. 2d Public Works and Contracts § 216, The Walsh-Healey Act.

Am. Jur. 2d Public Works and Contracts § 224, The Walsh-Healey Act.

Am. Jur. 2d Public Works and Contracts § 237, Contract Work Hours Standards Act.

Am. Jur. 2d Public Works and Contracts § 239, Application of Act--Walsh-Healey Act.

Am. Jur. 2d Public Works and Contracts § 240, Exception in Case of Emergency and Meaning Thereof.

70 Am. Jur. Proof of Facts 3d 97, Proof That a Government Agency Was Liable for Improperly Granting a Bid Award to a Bid Applicant.

14 Am. Jur. Trials 437, Representing the Government Contractor.

Forms

Am. Jur. Pl. & Pr. Forms Public Works & Contracts § 118, Petition--For Administrative Review--Of Decision of Administrative Law Judge.

Am. Jur. Pl. & Pr. Forms Public Works & Contracts § 119, Decision--Of Administrator--Department of Labor--Upholding Decision of Administrative Law Judge--Denying Relief from Imposition of Ineligible List Sanction.

Am. Jur. Pl. & Pr. Forms Public Works & Contracts § 121, Complaint in Federal Court--By United States--To Recover Liquidated Damages--Violations of Walsh-Healey Act.

Am. Jur. Pl. & Pr. Forms Public Works & Contracts § 122, Complaint in Federal Court--By Deputy Solicitor--Department of Labor--Violation of Walsh-Healey Act.

Am. Jur. Pl. & Pr. Forms Public Works & Contracts § 123, Complaint in Federal Court--By U.S. Department of Labor--Against Contractor--Violations of Walsh-Healey Act.

Am. Jur. Pl. & Pr. Forms Public Works & Contracts § 124, Complaint in Federal Court--By U.S. Department of Labor--Against Contractor--Violations of Walsh-Healey Act--Another Form.

Am. Jur. Pl. & Pr. Forms Public Works & Contracts § 125, Answer--By Contractor--To Complaint by U.S. Department of Labor--Denying Violations of Walsh-Healey Act.

Am. Jur. Pl. & Pr. Forms Public Works & Contracts § 128, Answer--By Contractor--Reliance on Administrative Ruling Precludes Liquidated Damages Under Walsh-Healey Act--Under Portal-to-Portal Act.

Am. Jur. Pl. & Pr. Forms Public Works & Contracts § 129, Answer--By Contractor--Contracts Failed to Contain Representations and Stipulations Required by Walsh-Healey Act.

Am. Jur. Pl. & Pr. Forms Public Works & Contracts § 133, Petition in Federal Court--For Review of Minimum Wage Determination Under Walsh-Healey Act.

Am. Jur. Pl. & Pr. Forms Public Works & Contracts § 134, Motion--For Temporary Injunction--To Stay Execution of Minimum Wage Determination Under Walsh-Healey Act.

Am. Jur. Pl. & Pr. Forms Public Works & Contracts § 136, Findings of Fact and Conclusions of Law--By Federal Court--Favoring Review of Minimum Wage Determination Under Walsh-Healey Act.

Am. Jur. Pl. & Pr. Forms Public Works & Contracts § 137, Order--Granting Stay of Minimum Wage Determination Under Walsh-Healey Act--Pending Review.

Federal Procedural Forms § 34:349, Introduction.

Federal Procedural Forms § 34:359, Reports of Breach or Violation of the Walsh-Healey Act.

Federal Procedural Forms § 34:388, Complaint--Against Contractor--Failure to Pay Employees Proper Wages [41 U.S.C.A. §§ 35 to 45; 41 C.F.R. § 50-203.2].

Federal Procedural Forms § 34:389, Complaint--Against Contractor--Failure to Pay Employees Proper Wages--Another Form [41 U.S.C.A. §§ 35 to 45; 41 C.F.R. § 50-203.2].

Federal Procedural Forms § 34:390, Answer--To Complaint--Denying Violation of Walsh-Healey Act [41 U.S.C.A. §§ 35 to 45; 41 C.F.R. § 50-203.2].

Federal Procedural Forms § 34:392, Complaint--To Recover Liquidated Damages Under Walsh-Healey Act [41 U.S.C.A. §§ 35 to 45; Fed. R. Civ. P. Rule 8].

Federal Procedural Forms § 34:393, Complaint--For Review of Minimum Wage Determination Under Walsh-Healey Act [5 U.S.C.A. §§ 701 to 706; 28 U.S.C.A. §§ 2201, 2202; 41 U.S.C.A. §§ 35 to 45; Fed. R. Civ. P. Rule 8(A), 57, 65].

Federal Procedural Forms § 34:394, Complaint--By Deputy Solicitor--Department of Labor--Violation of Walsh-Healey Act.

Federal Procedural Forms § 34:395, Complaint--By U.S. Department of Labor--Against Contractor--Violations of Walsh-Healey Act.

Federal Procedural Forms § 34:395.50, Complaint--For Injunctive Relief and Declaratory Judgment--Violation of Walsh-Healey Act--Contract Wrongfully Awarded to Unqualified Bidder [41 U.S.C.A. §§ 35, 43a; 28 U.S.C.A. §§ 1346, 1391; 4 C.F.R. § 21; 5 U.S.C.A. § 706(2)].

Federal Procedural Forms § 34:397, Order--For Stay of Judicial Proceedings Pending Administrative Proceedings [41 U.S.C.A. §§ 35 to 45; Fed. R. Civ. P. Rule 8].

Federal Procedural Forms § 34:398, Motion--For Preliminary Injunction--To Stay Execution of Minimum Wage Determination Under Walsh-Healey Act [5 U.S.C.A. §§ 701 to 706; 41 U.S.C.A. §§ 35 to 45; Fed. R. Civ. P. Rules 7(B), 65(a)].

Federal Procedural Forms § 34:399, Order--Granting Stay of Minimum Wage Determination Under Walsh-Healey Act--Pending Judicial Review [5 U.S.C.A. §§ 701 to 706; 41 U.S.C.A. §§ 35 to 45; Fed. R. Civ. P. Rule 65(a)].

Federal Procedural Forms § 34:402, Answer--By Contractor--To Complaint by U.S. Department of Labor--Denying Violations of Walsh-Healey Act.

Federal Procedural Forms § 34:403, Answer--By Contractor--Contracts Failed to Contain Representations and Stipulations Required by Walsh-Healey Act.

Federal Procedural Forms § 34:405, Defense in Answer--Defense Under Section 10 of Portal-to-Portal Act of Good Faith Reliance on Administrative Ruling [29 U.S.C.A. § 259; 41 U.S.C.A. §§ 35 to 45; Fed. R. Civ. P. Rule 8(C)].

Federal Procedural Forms § 34:406, Order--Judicial Review of Agency Order--Exclusive Seller Not Regular Dealer Under Walsh-Healey Act [41 U.S.C.A. §§ 35 to 45; 48 C.F.R. §§ 22.601, 22.606-2; 41 C.F.R. § 50-206.53(a)].

Federal Procedural Forms § 37:96, Preemption--Federal Laws.

Nichols Cyclopedia of Legal Forms Annotated § 7:2518, Supply Contract with United States--General Provisions.

24A West's Legal Forms § 4.7, Prevailing Wage Laws.

Treatises and Practice Aids

Callmann on Unfair Compet., TMs, & Monopolies § 3:9, Private Interests Influencing Government Action--Public Officials Taking Anticompetitive Action.

Callmann on Unfair Compet., TMs, & Monopolies § 16:11, Violation of Contractual Obligations--Contracts of Coordination--Noncompetitive Contracts.

Federal Procedure, Lawyers Edition § 39:139, Introduction.

Federal Procedure, Lawyers Edition § 39:195, Institution of Enforcement Action.

Federal Procedure, Lawyers Edition § 39:425, Nonconsideration or Dismissal of Protests.

Federal Procedure, Lawyers Edition § 42:2298, Laws Which OSHA Supersedes.

Federal Procedure, Lawyers Edition § 42:2310, Government Contracting.

WESTLAW ELECTRONIC RESEARCH

See Westlaw guide following the Explanation pages of this volume.

Notes of Decisions

----

1. Generally

In enacting this section, Congress did no more than instruct its agents who were selected and granted final authority to fix the terms and conditions under which the Government would permit goods to be sold to it. Perkins v. Lukens Steel Co., U.S.Dist.Col.1940, 60 S.Ct. 869, 310 U.S. 113, 84 L.Ed. 1108.

2. Constitutionality

The minimum wage provision of subsec. (b) of this section does not represent an exercise by Congress of regulatory power over private business or employ-ment. Perkins v. Lukens Steel Co., U.S.Dist.Col.1940, 60 S.Ct. 869, 310 U.S. 113, 84 L.Ed. 1108.

3. Construction

Sections 35 to 45 of this title are reme-dial wage and hour legislation and will be construed liberally to effectuate congres-sional policy that federal government should procure and use only goods pro-duced under safe and fair working condi-tions. U.S. v. Davison Fuel & Dock Co., C.A.4 (W.Va.) 1967, 371 F.2d 705. Labor And Employment ☞ 2243

4. Construction with other laws

The Fair Labor Standards Act of 1938, section 201 et seq. of Title 29, and sec-tions 35 to 45 of this title are not mutual-ly exclusive, but mutually supplementary, and applicability of sections 35 to 45 of this title to cost-plus-fixed-fee contracts does not preclude application of Fair La-bor Standards Act to employees under such contracts. Powell v. U.S. Cartridge Co., U.S.Mo.1950, 70 S.Ct. 755, 339 U.S. 497, 94 L.Ed. 1017. Labor And Employ-ment ☞ 2240

Manufacturer which had purchase no-tice agreement with government but which failed to use procedure available for determining applicability of sections 35 to 45 of this title to the agreement could not rely on defense department's or its own interpretation of sections 35 to 45 of this title as a defense to action charg-ing manufacturer with violations of over-time provisions of Portal-to-Portal Act of 1947, section 251 et seq. of Title 29. United Biscuit Co. of America v. Wirtz, C.A.D.C.1965, 359 F.2d 206, 123 U.S.App.D.C. 222, certiorari denied 86 S.Ct. 1861, 384 U.S. 971, 16 L.Ed.2d 682. Labor And Employment ☞ 2366

The restrictions of sections 35 to 45 of this title, relative to hours to be worked, applying to contracts between contrac-tors and Government and providing its own penalties, have no application to an action by an employee under Fair Labor Standards Act, section 201 et seq. of Title 29. Harrington v. Empire Const. Co., C.C.A.4 (Md.) 1948, 167 F.2d 389. Labor And Employment ☞ 2292(3)

Contract Work Hours Standard Act, McNamara-O'Hara Service Contracts Act, and sections 35 to 45 of this title, incorporated into Air Force contracts did not provide exclusive remedies for any wage and hour violations committed with respect to defendant's contract with United States Air Force and did not exclude application of Fair Labor Standards Act of 1938, section 201 et seq. of Title 29. Dowd v. Blackstone Cleaners, Inc., N.D.Tex.1969, 306 F.Supp. 1276. Labor And Employment ☞ 2292(3)

The Portal-to-Portal Act, section 251 et seq. of Title 29, is not applicable to action by United States against public contractor to recover, as liquidated damages for violation of sections 35 to 45 of this title, the unpaid overtime wages which public contracts require contractor to pay employees. U.S. v. Hudgins-Dize Co., E.D.Va.1949, 83 F.Supp. 593. Labor And Employment ☞ 2217(3)

A work schedule under which employee had a different day off in each calendar week, was not violation of Fair Labor Standards Act, section 207 of Title 29, or this section, as construed by Labor Department, so that employee was not entitled to overtime compensation for last day of each period of seven consecutive days worked by him. Barclay v. Magnolia Petroleum Co., Tex.Civ.App.-Beaumont 1947, 203 S.W.2d 626, ref. n.r.e.. Labor And Employment ☞ 2313

5. Purpose

Sections 35 to 45 of this title are not of general applicability to industry, but only to contractors who voluntarily enter into competition to obtain Government business, and their purpose is to use the leverage of the Government's immense purchasing power to raise labor standards. Endicott Johnson Corp. v. Perkins, U.S.N.Y.1943, 63 S.Ct. 339, 317 U.S. 501, 87 L.Ed. 424. See, also, United Biscuit Co. of America v. Wirtz, 1965, 359 F.2d 206, 123 U.S.App.D.C. 222, certiorari denied 86 S.Ct. 1861, 384 U.S. 971, 16 L.Ed.2d 682; McGraw-Edison Co. v. U.S., 1962, 300 F.2d 453, 156 Ct.Cl. 590; Ruth Elkhorn Coals, Inc. v. Mitchell, 1957, 248 F.2d 635, 101 U.S.App.D.C. 313, certiorari denied 78 S.Ct. 539, 355 U.S. 953, 2 L.Ed.2d 530; U.S. v. Westland Oil Co., D.C.N.D.1964, 228 F.Supp. 85. Labor And Employment ☞ 2243

The purpose of this section was to impose obligations upon those favored with Government business and to obviate the possibility that any part of the tremendous national expenditures would go to forces tending to depress wages and purchasing power and offending fair social standards of employment. Perkins v. Lukens Steel Co., U.S.Dist.Col.1940, 60 S.Ct. 869, 310 U.S. 113, 84 L.Ed. 1108. See, also, United Biscuit Co. of America v. Wirtz, 1965, 359 F.2d 206, 123 U.S.App.D.C. 222, certiorari denied 86 S.Ct. 1861, 384 U.S. 971, 16 L.Ed.2d 682.

Purpose of this section authorizing Secretary of Labor to determine prevailing minimum wages paid employees in industry so that such wages may be required by government in supply contracts within that industry is to avoid competitive advantages for firms which pay substandard labor wages. Industrial Union Dept., AFL-CIO v. Barber-Colman Co., C.A.D.C. 1965, 348 F.2d 787, 121 U.S.App.D.C. 175. Labor And Employment ☞ 2217(1)

Purpose of sections 35 to 45 of this title is to make certain that United States, in contracting for materials for its own use, does not patronize firms which pay wages lower than those being generally paid in industry. Wirtz v. Baldor Elec. Co., C.A.D.C.1963, 337 F.2d 518, 119 U.S.App.D.C. 122. Labor And Employment ☞ 2243

Purpose of sections 35 to 45 of this title was to prevent use of public funds to depress working conditions, and instead to use leverage of Government's immense purchasing power to raise labor standards. U.S. v. New England Coal & Coke Co., C.A.1 (Mass.) 1963, 318 F.2d 138. Labor And Employment ☞ 2243

Sections 35 to 45 of this title represent a general public policy that the Federal Government should procure and use only goods produced under safe and fair working conditions, and the $10,000 minimum was designed both to enable small manufacturers to obtain Government contracts and to avoid administrative burdens. George v. Mitchell, C.A.D.C.1960, 282 F.2d 486, 108 U.S.App.D.C. 324. Labor And Employment ☞ 2243

Sections 35 to 45 of this title are intended to regulate Governmental conduct in entering into contracts, and not to confer enforceable rights on private parties contracting under their aegis. U.S. v.

Warsaw Elevator Co., C.A.2 (N.Y.) 1954, 213 F.2d 517. United States ☞ 74(1)

Purpose of Congress in enacting requirement of Walsh-Healey Act that contractor be a regular manufacturer or dealer was to restrict bounty of government contracts to established manufacturers and dealers because they are most likely to effect the Act's goals of maintaining high labor standards in connection with wages and conditions. Ulstein Maritime, Ltd. v. U.S., D.R.I.1986, 646 F.Supp. 720, affirmed 833 F.2d 1052. United States ☞ 64.15

This section providing that contract by instrumentality of United States for furnishing of supplies exceeding $10,000 shall contain stipulation that all persons employed by contractor will be paid not less than minimum wages expresses congressional intent that employees of persons supplying United States are to be paid minimum wages prevailing for persons employed on similar work. Jno. McCall Coal Co. v. U.S., D.C.Md.1965, 248 F.Supp. 253, affirmed 374 F.2d 689. Labor And Employment ☞ 2243

Purpose of sections 35 to 45 of this title was to insure that persons employed by Government contractors would be paid not less than minimum wages as determined by Secretary of Labor. U.S. v. Continental Cas. Co., E.D.Pa.1949, 85 F.Supp. 573, affirmed 182 F.2d 941. United States ☞ 74.2

6. Rules and regulations

Regulations such as the armed services procurement regulations, including regulation governing exchange of purchase information, are deemed terms of contract between government and contractor even if not specifically set out therein. SCM Corp. v. U.S., Ct.Cl.1981, 645 F.2d 893, 227 Ct.Cl. 12. United States ☞ 70(2.1)

Under section 259(b) of Title 29, designating Secretary of Labor or any federal officer utilized by him as the agency of United States whose rulings can be relied upon by Government contractor, Administrator of Wage and Hour and Public Contracts Divisions, who had been designated by Secretary of Labor as person to administer this chapter, was the person who had authority to issue rulings and a field office supervisor had no authority to issue an authoritative ruling with respect to this chapter and was not an agency on which a contractor could rely. U.S. v. Stocks Lincoln-Mercury, Inc., C.A.10 (Utah) 1962, 307 F.2d 266. United States ☞ 70(28)

7. Mandatory nature of section

Subsec. (d) of this section is mandatory. U.S. v. Smoler Bros., C.A.7 (Ill.) 1951, 187 F.2d 29.

8. Exclusiveness of section

The remedy provided by sections 35 to 45 of this title is exclusive except for fact that there is a right to assess damages on bonds issued in connection with injunction to restrain Secretary from enforcing order made pursuant to such sections. Alabama Mills v. Mitchell, D.C.D.C.1958, 159 F.Supp. 637. Labor And Employment ☞ 2362

9. Duty of Secretary

Congress submitted administration of sections 35 to 45 of this title to judgment of the Secretary of Labor, not the courts, and one of Secretary's principal functions is conclusive determination of questions of fact for guidance of procurement officers in withholding Government contracts from violators. Endicott Johnson Corp. v. Perkins, U.S.N.Y.1943, 63 S.Ct. 339, 317 U.S. 501, 87 L.Ed. 424. Labor And Employment ☞ 2350(3)

10. Persons or entities subject to section

This section setting forth representations and stipulations required of contractor for government contracts was enacted for benefit of government and is spent when contract is awarded. U.S. v. Russell Elec. Co., S.D.N.Y.1965, 250 F.Supp. 2. United States ☞ 64.15

The Federal Reserve Banks are subject to the provisions of this chapter. 1978 (Counsel-Inf.Op.) 2 Op.O.L.C. 211.

11. Contracts within section—Generally

Stipulations and representations required by sections 35 to 45 of this title and liability for their violation are applicable only to any contract made and entered into by any executive department, independent establishment, or other agency or instrumentality of the United States. U.S. v. Davison Fuel & Dock Co., C.A.4 (W.Va.) 1967, 371 F.2d 705. Labor And Employment ☞ 2243

In determining whether particular contract between government and supplier was subject to provisions of sections 35 to

45 of this title, court must start with presumption that Congress intended sections 35 to 45 of this title to cover all regular and institutionalized methods of purchase used by government resulting in large scale acquisitions of materials and supplies from the private sector of our economy. United Biscuit Co. of America v. Wirtz, C.A.D.C.1965, 359 F.2d 206, 123 U.S.App.D.C. 222, certiorari denied 86 S.Ct. 1861, 384 U.S. 971, 16 L.Ed.2d 682. Labor And Employment ☞ 2243

12. —— Public or private contracts, contracts within section

This section applies only to manufacturers of or regular dealers in materials, supplies, articles or equipment to be manufactured or used in the performance of a public contract. Miller v. Lummus Co., Tex.Civ.App.-Beaumont 1948, 215 S.W.2d 227, ref. n.r.e.. Labor And Employment ☞ 2243; Labor And Employment ☞ 2500

13. —— Service contracts, contracts within section

Government contract requiring both furnishing of materials, supplies and articles and the performance of services by Government contractor was not a "contract exclusively for services" nor was it a contract primarily for services and such contract was covered by sections 35 to 45 of this title concerning hours of labor and overtime. U.S. v. Stocks Lincoln-Mercury, Inc., C.A.10 (Utah) 1962, 307 F.2d 266. Labor And Employment ☞ 2243

14. Amounts exceeding $10,000

Purchase notice agreement under which manufacturer offered to sell specified items to government at prices listed, or any lower price that it might offer to any other purchaser, and under which government in return distributed list to all its commissaries and other military installations was a contract for furnishing of supplies to government within meaning of sections 35 to 45 of this title, and was a contract in amount exceeding $10,000 under sections 35 to 45 of this title, although no single order under agreement had exceeded that amount. United Biscuit Co. of America v. Wirtz, C.A.D.C.1965, 359 F.2d 206, 123 U.S.App.D.C. 222, certiorari denied 86 S.Ct. 1861, 384 U.S. 971, 16 L.Ed.2d 682. Labor And Employment ☞ 2243

Where Atomic Energy Commission issued offer to purchase 50,000 tons of coal

in one or more lots, minimum bid to be 1,800 tons, and in response corporation, with the intention of avoiding requirements of sections 35 to 45 of this title, submitted six bids for 1,800 tons each, each of which named different mine as source of coal to be supplied, and held out corporation as the prime contractor and as a regular dealer in coal, and the six bids totalled more than $10,000, the six bids and agreement based thereon would be treated as one contract for more than $10,000, which was within terms of sections 35 to 45 of this title, and corporation, its owner and president, and individual mine owners who supplied the coal might be properly blacklisted for violations of terms of this section. George v. Mitchell, C.A.D.C.1960, 282 F.2d 486, 108 U.S.App.D.C. 324. Labor And Employment ☞ 2243

Where defendant entered into contract with Department of the Army to supply lumber at total price exceeding $10,000, but in order to conform with Office of Price Administration regulations a lower unit price was agreed upon by parties, making total price less than $10,000, final amount agreed upon was controlling amount of contract, and sections 35 to 45 of this title, providing for federal regulation of wages and working conditions of employees of public contractor when amount of contract, exceeded $10,000, were not applicable, notwithstanding provision in contract allowing for a ten percent overage or underage in loading and shipping. U.S. v. Ozmer, C.A.5 (Ga.) 1950, 181 F.2d 508. United States ☞ 75(1)

15. Regular dealer or manufacturer— Generally

Where the Government terminated contract with company for failure of performance and relet it to another at higher price, company could not rely on alleged fact that contract was not relet to a "manufacturer" or "regular dealer" within sections 35 to 45 of this title to avoid liability under contract provision making company liable for excess costs in obtaining similar supplies or services elsewhere. U S v. Warsaw Elevator Co, C.A.2 (N.Y.) 1954, 213 F.2d 517. United States ☞ 73(4)

Requirement of this section that government contractors qualify as "regular dealers" in materials to be used in performance of contract is intended to restrict bounty of government contracts to established dealers because they are most likely to effect Walsh–Healey goals of maintaining high labor standards in connection with wages and conditions. Steuart Petroleum Co. v. U.S., D.C.D.C.1977, 438 F.Supp. 527. United States ☞ 64.15

Where contractor was eligible supplier of gyro motors at time contract for production of gyro motors was entered into, its failure to maintain manufacturing facility did not under this section relating to government contract requirements invalidate contract or require naval ordnance plant to terminate contract, and plant by its failure to immediately terminate contract accordingly was not precluded from recovery of full damages for default. U.S. v. Russell Elec. Co., S.D.N.Y.1965, 250 F.Supp. 2. United States ☞ 66; United States ☞ 72.1(3)

Secretary of Labor acted reasonably and within delegated power necessary to carry out provisions of sections 35 to 45 of this title where Secretary adopted regulation defining the term "regular dealer" within this section as one having stock in trade and thereafter adopting regulation permitting coal dealer not qualified as regular dealer to become supplier to United States on condition of liability for observance of all labor standards under the Act in the mines. Jno. McCall Coal Co. v. U.S., D.C.Md.1965, 248 F.Supp. 253, affirmed 374 F.2d 689. Labor And Employment ☞ 2338

16. —— Newly entering manufacturers

With regard to Walsh-Healey Act regulation requiring that bidder, in order to be considered "newly entering" into manufacturing activity, enter into written, legally binding arrangements and commitments to acquire for itself plant, equipment and personnel if awarded a government contract, regulation does not preclude arrangements contingent upon award but does require that bidder be a genuine manufacturer and not a mere subcontractor. Ulstein Maritime, Ltd. v. U.S., D.R.I.1986, 646 F.Supp. 720, affirmed 833 F.2d 1052. United States ☞ 64.15

17. Minimum wages—Generally

This section commanding that employees of government suppliers in contracts exceeding $10,000 be paid not less than the minimum wages as determined by Secretary of Labor does not permit the Secretary or courts to weigh equities in determining when to enforce the mandate. Jno. McCall Coal Co. v. U.S., C.A.4 (Md.) 1967, 374 F.2d 689. Labor And Employment ☞ 2298

Under provision of this section that certain Government contracts should include stipulation that contractors pay employees not less than minimum wages as determined by Secretary of Labor, to be prevailing minimum wage for persons employed in the particular or similar industries or groups of industries currently operating in the locality, Secretary could determine minimum wage for textile workers on industry-wide basis. Mitchell v. Covington Mills, Inc., C.A.D.C.1955, 229 F.2d 506, 97 U.S.App.D.C. 165, certiorari denied 76 S.Ct. 546, 350 U.S. 1002, 100 L.Ed. 865, rehearing denied 76 S.Ct. 787, 351 U.S. 934, 100 L.Ed. 1462. Labor And Employment ☞ 2350(2)

Under contract requiring the furnishing of coal to TVA and compliance with this section, obligations of company furnishing coal did not cease with delivery of coal but included payment of minimum wages as determined by Department of Labor. U.S. v. Glens Falls Ins. Co., E.D.Tenn.1967, 279 F.Supp. 236. United States ☞ 70(12.1)

Secretary of Labor had no authority under this section to impose two different prevailing minimum wages, one for blueprint machine operators or craftsmen and other for employees engaged in other occupations for machine tool manufacturers. Barber-Colman Co. v. Wirtz, D.C.D.C.1963, 224 F.Supp. 137, remanded 348 F.2d 787, 121 U.S.App.D.C. 175. Labor And Employment ☞ 2350(2)

18. —— Persons subject to limitation, minimum wages

Interpretation of Secretary that coal wholesaler which contracted to supply coal to United States on four different contracts but which was not a regular dealer within meaning of this section requiring payment of minimum wage and overtime compensation was under administrative regulations adopted pursuant to section 38 of this title the party responsible for failure to pay wages to miners who mined coal for wholesaler's supplier was both correct and reasonable. Jno. McCall Coal Co. v. U.S., C.A.4 (Md.) 1967, 374 F.2d 689. Labor And Employment ☞ 2338

Coal dealer who agreed to supply coal to Government under this section, contracted with representation as to wage rates of his employees, and who supplied coal from stockpile produced in part by his own employees and in part by suppliers, was not liable for labor standards of his suppliers. U.S. v. New England Coal & Coke Co., D.C.Mass.1962, 228 F.Supp. 414, affirmed 318 F.2d 138. Labor And Employment ☞ 2243

19. —— Employees of contractor, minimum wages

Term "employed by the contractor," as used in sections 35 to 45 of this title should be construed so that persons who are employed by prime contractor may be, in certain carefully defined situations, persons other than those on prime contractor's payroll. U.S. v. Davison Fuel & Dock Co., C.A.4 (W.Va.) 1967, 371 F.2d 705. Labor And Employment ☞ 2243

20. —— Locality, minimum wages

Under minimum wage provision of this section, that the Secretary of Labor is charged with an erroneous interpretation of the term "locality" as an element in her wage determination is not sufficient to entitle prospective bidders on Government purchasing contracts to maintain action to restrain Government officials from applying the Secretary's wage determination in awarding contracts. Perkins v. Lukens Steel Co., U.S.Dist.Col.1940, 60 S.Ct. 869, 310 U.S. 113, 84 L.Ed. 1108.

Under this section, authorizing Secretary of Labor to determine prevailing minimum wages for (1) persons employed in similar work, or (2) persons employed in particular or similar industry, or (3) persons employed in groups of industries "currently operating in locality" in which materials, supplies, articles or equipment are to be manufactured or furnished under Government contract, quoted phrase relates back to all three preceding groups and not merely to persons employed in group of industries in locality. Covington Mills v. Mitchell, D.C.D.C.1955, 129 F.Supp. 740. Labor And Employment ☞ 2350(2)

21. Convict labor

This section, requiring the insertion of a provision in certain Government con-

tracts that no convict labor shall be employed by the contractor, was inapplicable to contracts for war materials because such contracts were exempted under an order of the Secretary of Labor dated May 26, 1942. 1942, 40 Op.Atty.Gen. 207.

22. Incorporation by reference

Government contracts' incorporation by reference of provisions of sections 35 to 45 of this title, is reasonable and not inconsistent with terms of those sections. U.S. v. Davison Fuel & Dock Co., C.A.4 (W.Va.) 1967, 371 F.2d 705. Labor And Employment ☞ 2243

23. Review

Where employees' action for overtime compensation was predicated squarely on Fair Labor Standards Act, section 201 et seq. of Title 29, and after adoption of Portal-to-Portal Act, section 251 et seq. of Title 29, on section 252 of the same title, and was tried and disposed of on theory that court was without jurisdiction under section 252 of Title 29, appellate court need not consider contention advanced by defendant for the first time on appeal that employees' rights were governed by sections 35 to 45 of this title rather than Fair Labor Standards Act. Adkins v. E.I. Du Pont De Nemours & Co., C.A.10 (Okla.) 1949, 176 F.2d 661, certiorari denied 70 S.Ct. 234, 338 U.S. 895, 94 L.Ed. 550, certiorari denied 70 S.Ct. 661, 339 U.S. 935, 94 L.Ed. 1353. Appeal And Error ☞ 172(1)

24. Remand

Where it appeared possible that in further proceedings under this section before Secretary of Labor or court only one minimum wage would be established for machine tool industry, for which Secretary had established two minimum wages, and that single wage would most likely be calculated at some figure different from either of two wages previously determined, Secretary's determination of one wage could not be affirmed and case could not be remanded merely for consideration of the other wage. Industrial Union Dept., AFL-CIO v. Barber-Colman Co., C.A.D.C.1965, 348 F.2d 787, 121 U.S.App.D.C. 175. Labor And Employment ☞ 2358

§ 36. Liability for contract breach; cancellation; completion by Government agency; employee's wages

Any breach or violation of any of the representations and stipulations in any contract for the purposes set forth in section 35 of this title shall render the party responsible therefor liable to the United States of America for liquidated damages, in addition to damages for any other breach of such contract, the sum of $10 per day for each male person under sixteen years of age or each female person under eighteen years of age, or each convict laborer knowingly employed in the performance of such contract, and a sum equal to the amount of any deductions, rebates, refunds, or underpayment of wages due to any employee engaged in the performance of such contract; and, in addition, the agency of the United States entering into such contract shall have the right to cancel same and to make open-market purchases or enter into other contracts for the completion of the original contract, charging any additional cost to the original contractor. Any sums of money due to the United States of America by reason of any violation of any of the representations and stipulations of said contract set forth in section 35 of this title may be withheld from any amounts due on any such contracts or may be recovered in suits brought in the name of the United States of America by the Attorney General thereof. All sums withheld or recovered as deductions, rebates, refunds, or underpayments of wages shall be held in a special deposit account and shall be paid, on order of the Secretary of Labor, directly to the employees who have been paid less than minimum rates of pay as set forth in such contracts and on whose account such sums were withheld or recovered: *Provided*, That no claims by employees for such payments shall be entertained unless made within one year from the date of actual notice to the contractor of the withholding or recovery of such sums by the United States of America.

(June 30, 1936, c. 881, § 2, 49 Stat. 2037.)

CROSS REFERENCES

Conduct and argument of cases by Attorney General, see 28 USCA § 518.
Construction, repair, alteration, furnishing and equipping of Naval vessels, see 10 USCA § 7299.
Power of Solicitor General to assist Attorney General, see 28 USCA § 505.
Statute of limitations, action to enforce any cause of action under § 35 et seq. of this title, see 29 USCA § 255.

LIBRARY REFERENCES

American Digest System

Labor and Employment ⚷2388.
United States ⚷73(16), 75(2).
Key Number System Topic Nos. 231H, 393.

Research References

ALR Library

162 ALR 237, Statute of Limitations Applicable to Action to Recover Minimum Wage, Overtime Compensation, or Liquidated Damages Under Fair Labor Standards Act.

107 ALR 705, Servant's Right to Compensation for Extra Work or Overtime.

82 ALR 808, Conflict Between Federal and State Statutes of Limitations.

61 ALR 412, State Statute of Limitations as Affecting Action or Proceeding by Federal Government or Its Officials.

Encyclopedias

Am. Jur. 2d Public Works and Contracts § 216, The Walsh-Healey Act.

Am. Jur. 2d Public Works and Contracts § 224, The Walsh-Healey Act.

Am. Jur. 2d Public Works and Contracts § 239, Application of Act--Walsh-Healey Act.

Forms

Am. Jur. Pl. & Pr. Forms Public Works & Contracts § 121, Complaint in Federal Court--By United States--To Recover Liquidated Damages--Violations of Walsh-Healey Act.

Am. Jur. Pl. & Pr. Forms Public Works & Contracts § 122, Complaint in Federal Court--By Deputy Solicitor--Department of Labor--Violation of Walsh-Healey Act.

Federal Procedural Forms § 34:388, Complaint--Against Contractor--Failure to Pay Employees Proper Wages [41 U.S.C.A. §§ 35 to 45; 41 C.F.R. § 50-203.2].

Federal Procedural Forms § 34:392, Complaint--To Recover Liquidated Damages Under Walsh-Healey Act [41 U.S.C.A. §§ 35 to 45; Fed. R. Civ. P. Rule 8].

Federal Procedural Forms § 34:394, Complaint--By Deputy Solicitor--Department of Labor--Violation of Walsh-Healey Act.

Treatises and Practice Aids

Federal Procedure, Lawyers Edition § 39:195, Institution of Enforcement Action.

WESTLAW ELECTRONIC RESEARCH

See Westlaw guide following the Explanation pages of this volume.

Notes of Decisions

Burden of proof   19
Defenses   17, 18
    Generally   17
    Limitations   18
Exhaustion of administrative remedies   11
Indemnification   5
Interest   8
Joint and several liability   4
Jurisdiction   13
Knowledge of violation   1
Limitations, defenses   18
Liquidated damages   6
Nature of action   10
Necessary parties   16
Parties responsible or liable   2, 3
    Generally   2
    Sureties   3
Persons entitled to maintain action   15
Service of process   14
Standard of review   21

Stay pending administrative proceeding   12
Sureties, parties responsible or liable   3
Tax deductibility of damages   9
Trial de novo   20
Withholding of money due   7

---

1. Knowledge of violation

Where navy contract for supplies contained stipulation that no female person under age of 18 years would be employed by contractor, and Secretary of Labor granted conditional exemption as to such stipulation, one condition being that no female between ages of 16 and 18 years could be employed for more than 8 hours in any one day, and record of plant, which was located in city other than city in which contractor's home office was located, clearly showed violation of conditional exemption for 630 days, contractor could not avoid liability for such violation by asserting that officials at contractor's home office had no personal knowledge of violation. U.S. v. Smoler Bros., C.A.7 (Ill.) 1951, 187 F.2d 29. Infants ⬧ 14

In action by United States under sections 35 to 45 of this title, to recover liquidated damages for breach of contract for knowingly employing minors, evidence that contractor who had contracted to furnish shoes to federal Government in an amount exceeding $10,000 did not knowingly employ minors, and that on several occasions, after receiving information that employees were in fact under age, he investigated such cases and discharged employee, sustained judgment for contractor. U.S. v. Craddock-Terry Shoe Corp., C.A.4 (Va.) 1949, 178 F.2d 760. United States ⬧ 75(4)

Employer which knowingly employed five minors, or should have known he was doing so, under 18 years of age, in the performance of certain contracts subject to sections 35 to 45 of this title was liable therefor to pay sums of money to United States in accordance with sections 35 to 45 of this title. U.S. v. Southland Mfg. Corp., D.C.Puerto Rico 1967, 264 F.Supp. 174. Infants ⬧ 14

A person has "reason to know," within meaning of term "knowingly", when he has such information as would lead person exercising reasonable care to acquire knowledge of fact or infer its existence. U.S. v. Sweet Briar, Inc., W.D.S.C.1950, 92 F.Supp. 777.

"Knowingly" with reference to employment of minors, under this section, means intentionally or with actual knowledge, including evil intent or bad purpose. U.S. v. Loveknit Mfg. Co., N.D.Tex. 1950, 90 F.Supp. 679. United States ⬧ 75(1)

2. Parties responsible or liable—Generally

Fact that fuel and dock company and its subsidiaries were separate legal entities would not preclude consideration of them as an integrated production structure for purpose of enforcing sections 35 to 45 of this title since, in applying regulatory statutes such as sections 35 to 45 of this title, separate corporate entities are not inviolate. U.S. v. Davison Fuel & Dock Co., C.A.4 (W.Va.) 1967, 371 F.2d 705. Labor And Employment ⬧ 2243

Coal wholesaler which did not qualify as regular dealer within section 35 of this title nevertheless rendered itself liable for payment of minimum wages in mine of its supplier of coal it sold to United States under four contracts and became "party responsible therefor" within this section that breach or violation of contract stipulation required by sections 35 to 45 of this title shall render party responsible therefor liable to the United States. Jno. McCall Coal Co. v. U.S., D.C.Md.1965, 248 F.Supp. 253, affirmed 374 F.2d 689. Labor And Employment ⬧ 2227

In action by the Government under this section for damages for underpayment of wages on a Government contract against the corporate contracting party and the president of the corporation who was not a signatory thereon but whose liability was predicated upon the finding that he was in effect a "party responsible" for breach of the contract, where in reality, corporation was the individual defendant's alter ego or agent, he could be held liable as the "party responsible" by disregarding the corporate fiction and considering him the actual party to the contract. U.S. v. Islip Mach. Works, Inc., E.D.N.Y. 1959, 179 F.Supp. 585. Corporations ⬧ 1.6(4)

The word "party" in this section, providing that breach of stipulation in public contract shall render liable the "party" responsible therefor, is a word of art and refers only to a promisor or covenantor of the contract. U.S. v. Hudgins-Dize Co., E.D.Va.1949, 83 F.Supp. 593. United States ⬧ 75(2)

3. —— Sureties, parties responsible or liable

Where court, temporarily enjoining Secretary of Labor from enforcing minimum wage determination, had ordered that any plaintiff who entered into a contract otherwise covered by determination should post bond to make good overpayments of wages, up to amount of bond, in case Secretary's minimum wage determination were ultimately upheld, liability of sureties was limited to amount of bonds that had been posted, but plaintiffs were liable for entire amount of their underpayments, that is, for the difference between the wages they had paid while the injunction against the Secretary was in effect and the minimum wages which he had fixed. Mitchell v. Riegel Textile, Inc., C.A.D.C.1958, 259 F.2d 954, 104

U.S.App.D.C. 139. Injunction ⟜ 239; Labor And Employment ⟜ 2435

Surety on coal company's performance bond, conditioned on company's compliance with contract which required company to furnish coal to TVA and to comply with federal minimum wage and overtime compensation statute, was obligated not only to TVA but also to the United States which sought to recover minimum wages and overtime compensation due company's employees. U.S. v. Glens Falls Ins. Co., E.D.Tenn.1967, 279 F.Supp. 236. Principal And Surety ⟜ 66(2)

Where surety bond of contractor engaged in work for United States provided that employees of contractor would be paid an amount not less than minimum wages as determined by Secretary of Labor, surety would be liable for contractor's failure to pay that amount and could not deny liability on ground that provision in bond meant that contractor would agree in good faith to endeavor to maintain minimum wages as determined by Secretary of Labor. U.S. v. Continental Cas. Co., E.D.Pa.1949, 85 F.Supp. 573, affirmed 182 F.2d 941. United States ⟜ 67(7.1)

4. Joint and several liability

Where corporation was small, closely held family corporation, and complete control over all affairs including hiring and firing of help and establishing wage scales, time schedules and working conditions was exercised by president and by her husband as general manager, and work was done in performance of government contract, they were charged with obligation of carrying out working conditions set forth in this section, and failure to perform statutory public duty was not only corporate liability but also personal liability of each officer, and president and general manager were jointly liable with corporation for failure to pay overtime. U.S. v. Sancolmar Industries, Inc., E.D.N.Y.1972, 347 F.Supp. 404. Corporations ⟜ 306

Coal producing company, which supplied coal under government contract, and coal selling company, which, as exclusive sales agents of producing company, contracted with government agency and was under nondelegable duty to assure compliance with sections 35 to 45 of this title establishing minimum wage requirements applicable to contracts with

United States, were jointly and severally liable to United States for producing company's failure to pay its employees minimum wage scale specified by such sections. Southern Coal & Coke Co. v. Beech Grove Min. Co., Tenn.App.1963, 381 S.W.2d 299, 53 Tenn.App. 108. Labor And Employment ⟜ 2243

5. Indemnification

Coal selling company, which, as exclusive sales agent of coal producing company, contracted with government agency to supply coal for atomic energy plant, and which therefore was under nondelegable duty to assure compliance with sections 35 to 45 of this title establishing minimum wage requirements applicable to contracts with United States, was entitled to indemnification from producing corporation for payment made to government for failure of producing company to comply with minimum wage requirements. Southern Coal & Coke Co. v. Beech Grove Min. Co., Tenn.App.1963, 381 S.W.2d 299, 53 Tenn.App. 108. Principal And Agent ⟜ 77

6. Liquidated damages

Liquidated damages, imposed by this section on Government contractors, for knowingly employing under-age minors, are not penalties or forfeitures. U.S. v. Sweet Briar, Inc., W.D.S.C.1950, 92 F.Supp. 777. Damages ⟜ 76

7. Withholding of money due

Since the withholding provision of this section would be pure surplusage if the usual power to set off mutual debts were intended to be left intact, Congress would be deemed to have intended that only withholding to be permitted was that provided therein, and even though Secretary of Labor had determined that contractor had violated sections 35 to 45 of this title and that contractor should pay to Government amount fixed by Secretary, pursuant to provisions of said sections, Government could not pay itself by withholding money otherwise due contractor on contracts not covered by said sections. Unexcelled Chemical Corp. v. U.S., Ct.Cl.1957, 149 F.Supp. 383, 137 Ct.Cl. 681. United States ⟜ 73(16)

The provision of this section, that sums due United States because of violation of representations and stipulations in contracts named therein may be withheld from amounts due from United States on such contracts, gave Government right to withhold amount owing by it under its contract to purchase crushed stone and gravel for Navy installation because of corporate seller's failure to pay overtime wages required by sections 35 to 45 of this title in performance of all of 17 contracts with Government to furnish stone products to Army and Navy. Ready-Mix Concrete Co. v. U.S., Ct.Cl.1955, 130 F.Supp. 390, 131 Ct.Cl. 204. United States ☞ 73(16)

Where certain amounts were withheld from plaintiff on account of an alleged underpayment by plaintiff of its employees, it was incumbent on plaintiff to prove that it had complied with the provisions of the contract as to the rate of wages paid and that in the absence of such proof plaintiff was not entitled to recover. Continental Contracting Co. v. U.S., Ct.Cl.1941, 94 Ct.Cl. 244. Contracts ☞ 322(1); United States ☞ 73(20)

Where plaintiff leased plant to defendants for manufacture of coats for which defendants held a Government contract for one-half defendants' profits thereunder upon payment by the Government, and defendants admitted contract with the Government had been performed and that defendants had received final payment thereunder, for a net profit of a specified sum, plaintiff was entitled to one-half of such profits, as against contention that defendants had been orally informed the Department of Labor would make an assessment for alleged violations of section 35 et seq. of this title and that defendants would be entitled to hold plaintiff's share as reimbursement for such assessment. Kingsley Clothing Mfg. Co. v. Jacobs, Pa.1942, 26 A.2d 315, 344 Pa. 551. Joint Adventures ☞ 5(1)

This section does not purport to make employer liable to employee for a failure to pay overtime rates for overtime work, since it only prescribes administrative procedure whereby funds may be withheld by the United States from sums due employer to employee if claim therefor is timely made. Greenstein v. Pan Am. Airways, N.Y.Sup.1945, 57 N.Y.S.2d 178, 185 Misc. 429. Labor And Employment ☞ 2362

8. Interest

As soon as underpayments of wages were made, unjust enrichment of employer was completed, and interest could be allowed from dates of underpayments. Mitchell v. Riegel Textile, Inc., C.A.D.C.

1958, 259 F.2d 954, 104 U.S.App.D.C. 139. Interest ☞ 44

Under this section, directing that sums recovered by the United States from contractors as underpayment of wages be paid directly to the employees, Congress intended to give employees what they would have been entitled to get had they been able to sue their employer in their own right, including interest. Philadelphia Joint Bd. Amalgamated Clothing Workers of America v. U.S., E.D.Pa.1952, 106 F.Supp. 534. United States ☞ 75(2)

9. Tax deductibility of damages

Damages provided for in a Government contract for knowingly employing underaged persons were in fact penalties designed to insure that child labor would not be used in performance of the Government contract, and as such are not a deductible expense for income tax purposes. McGraw-Edison Co. v. U.S., Ct. Cl.1962, 300 F.2d 453, 156 Ct.Cl. 590. Internal Revenue ☞ 3353

10. Nature of action

Action by United States under sections 35 to 45 of this title, for liquidated damages for failure of employer to pay overtime compensation and knowingly employing child labor is action for penalty or forfeiture for violation of law, since it is not sovereign who has been damaged, but employee. In re Thrift Packing Co., N.D.Tex.1951, 100 F.Supp. 907. Labor And Employment ☞ 2409

11. Exhaustion of administrative remedies

Institution of an action for recovery of liquidated damages under this section for unpaid overtime compensation is not conditioned upon the making of findings by the Secretary of Labor, and the making of administrative findings of that kind is not a prerequisite to the right of United States to maintain and institute the action. U.S. v. Winegar, C.A.10 (Utah) 1958, 254 F.2d 693. Labor And Employment ☞ 2363

Administrative hearings and findings under this section are not a prerequisite to a suit under this section by the United States. U.S. v. Lovknit Mfg. Co., C.A.5 (Tex.) 1951, 189 F.2d 454, certiorari denied 72 S.Ct. 229, 342 U.S. 896, 96 L.Ed. 671, rehearing denied 72 S.Ct. 287, 342 U.S. 915, 96 L.Ed. 684. See, also, U.S. v. W.H. Kistler Stationery Co., C.A.Colo.

1952, 200 F.2d 805.   Administrative Law And Procedure ☞ 230; United States ☞ 75(3)

The remedy at law afforded by sections 35 to 45 of this title to public contractors charged by the Secretary of Labor with overtime, child labor and record-keeping violations, is adequate, and action to enjoin administrative proceedings under said sections would not lie where plaintiffs had not exhausted their administrative remedies. Anderson v. Schwellenbach, N.D.Cal. 1947, 70 F.Supp. 14.   Injunction ☞ 108; Labor And Employment ☞ 2416

12. Stay pending administrative proceeding

Where federal district court which had original jurisdiction of suit by United States Attorney General Under sections 35 to 45 of this title to recover alleged underpayment of wages by government contractor waited two years for the Department of Labor to complete administrative proceedings with respect to same matter, failure of district court to continue to stay the lawsuit and to determine same could not be termed an abuse of discretion.   U.S. v. Gulf States Asphalt Co., Inc., C.A.5 (Tex.) 1973, 472 F.2d 933. Labor And Employment ☞ 2399

When action is instituted during pendency of administrative proceeding but before findings of fact therein, whether judicial action should be stayed for reasonable time to await completion of administrative proceeding is question addressed to sound judicial discretion of court.   U.S. v. Pine Tp. Coal Co., W.D.Pa. 1962, 201 F.Supp. 441. See, also, U.S. v. Winegar, C.A.Utah 1958, 254 F.2d 693. Action ☞ 69(7)

13. Jurisdiction

District court, in which suit was instituted by United States Attorney General to recover alleged underpayment of wages by government contractor, had original jurisdiction of suit and was not required to wait for an administrative determination to be made by the Secretary of Labor with respect to the same matter.   U.S. v. Gulf States Asphalt Co., Inc., C.A.5 (Tex.) 1973, 472 F.2d 933. Labor And Employment ☞ 2367

Under Fulbright Amendment to sections 35 to 45 of this title, District Court for the District of Columbia had jurisdiction over action by corporation and individuals against Secretary of Labor and Comptroller General for declaratory judgment that contracts to sell coal to Atomic Energy Commission were not within provisions of sections 35 to 45 of this title, and for injunction to restrain Secretary and Comptroller General from placing plaintiffs' names on list of persons ineligible, because of violation of such sections 35 to 45, to be awarded Government contracts, and plaintiffs had standing to bring such suit.   George v. Mitchell, C.A.D.C.1960, 282 F.2d 486, 108 U.S.App.D.C. 324.   Declaratory Judgment ☞ 274.1; Declaratory Judgment ☞ 301; Labor And Employment ☞ 2428; Labor And Employment ☞ 2429

The district court had jurisdiction of action by United States to recover liquidated damages for employment of girls under 16 years of age and girls between ages of 16 and 18 for more than eight hours per day on work under Government contracts in violation of sections 35 to 45 of this title.   U.S. v. Harp, W.D.Okla.1948, 80 F.Supp. 236, affirmed 173 F.2d 761, certiorari denied 70 S.Ct. 56, 338 U.S. 816, 94 L.Ed. 494.   Federal Courts ☞ 192

14. Service of process

In action by the Government for breach of contract arising out of underpayment of wages on a Government contract, where defendants were a corporation which was the contracting party and president of corporation who was not a signatory on the contract and whose liability was predicated upon a finding that he was the "party responsible" as used in this section for the breach of contract, where, in addition to the prior service by mail of the administrative complaint and notice, there was personal service of the complaint on both defendants followed by service by registered mail of a supplemental notice of the date of the administrative hearing, requirements of due process were sufficiently complied with.   U.S. v. Islip Mach. Works, Inc., E.D.N.Y. 1959, 179 F.Supp. 585.   Constitutional Law ☞ 3975

15. Persons entitled to maintain action

Under minimum wage provision of section 35 of this title, the responsibility of the Secretary of Labor is to superior executive and legislative authority, and prospective bidders on Government purchasing contracts have no standing in court to enforce that responsibility or to represent the public's interest in the Secretary's compliance with section 35 of this title. Perkins v. Lukens Steel Co., U.S.Dist.Col. 1940, 60 S.Ct. 869, 310 U.S. 113, 84 L.Ed. 1108.

Sections 35 to 45 of this title relate only to Government business, and the right of action granted under such sections belongs to Government alone. U.S. v. W.H. Kistler Stationery Co., C.A.10 (Colo.) 1952, 200 F.2d 805. Labor And Employment ⟐ 2362

No one may sue for breach of contracts under this section except the United States through the Attorney General, since the contracts are public contracts to which only United States and the contractors are parties. U.S. v. Lovknit Mfg. Co., C.A.5 (Tex.) 1951, 189 F.2d 454, certiorari denied 72 S.Ct. 229, 342 U.S. 896, 96 L.Ed. 671, rehearing denied 72 S.Ct. 287, 342 U.S. 915, 96 L.Ed. 684. United States ⟐ 75(1)

Under contract requiring the furnishing of coal to TVA and compliance with federal minimum wage and overtime provisions of section 35 of this title, TVA was empowered to sue in its own name or withhold payment upon matters of particular concern to it, but Attorney General, representing other branches of federal government, was empowered to bring suit in name of the United States on matters of concern to them. U.S. v. Glens Falls Ins. Co., E.D.Tenn.1967, 279 F.Supp. 236. Attorney General ⟐ 7; United States ⟐ 53(14)

An action on a contract of employment to perform services in Brazil for a contractor engaged in a project for the United States Government, brought by an employee of the contractor, which only prescribes administrative procedure whereby funds may be withheld by the Government from sums due the employer and which gives no right to an employee to bring suit against the employer under this section. Greenstein v. Pan Am. Airways, N.Y.Sup. 1945, 57 N.Y.S.2d 178, 185 Misc. 429. Labor And Employment ⟐ 2362

Sections 35 to 45 of this title gave no right of action to employees, but expressly limited the action to be brought in the name of the United States by the Attorney General for damages to the United States plus unpaid wages to be held and paid out by Secretary of Labor to those mak-

ing claim against him within one year, and hence such sections were not applicable to suit by former employee of a prime contractor with the United States to recover overtime compensation. Todd v. Roane-Anderson Co., Tenn.App.1952, 251 S.W.2d 132, 35 Tenn.App. 687. Labor And Employment ⟐ 2361

16. Necessary parties

The United States was a necessary party defendant to suit for declaratory judgment that Government's right, under sections 35 to 45 of this title, to sue plaintiff for liquidated damages for breach of contract with Government or deny future contracts to plaintiff was barred by limitations, and suit could not be maintained against officials of Labor Department in their individual capacity. Reynolds Corp. v. Morse, D.C.D.C.1948, 81 F.Supp. 137, affirmed 174 F.2d 159, 84 U.S.App.D.C. 420. Declaratory Judgment ⟐ 304

17. Defenses—Generally

Liability of government contractor as party responsible for payment of minimum wages to workers of contractor's supplier attached whether employees went unpaid because of bankruptcy of supplier or from any other cause beyond direct control of contractor, or whether they went unpaid because of inadvertence or because of a willful act. Jno. McCall Coal Co. v. U.S., C.A.4 (Md.) 1967, 374 F.2d 689. Labor And Employment ⟐ 2301

Oil refinery, which had contracted with Government for delivery of semi-processed and processed petroleum, was entitled to combine for purposes of asserting stock pile defense to action by United States for recovery of damages for alleged violation of section 35 et seq. of this title stocks of crude petroleum with stocks of semi-processed or processed petroleum. U.S. v. Westland Oil Co., D.C.N.D.1964, 228 F.Supp. 85. Labor And Employment ⟐ 2243

18. —— Limitations, defenses

Initiation of administrative proceedings with the Secretary of Labor under sections 35 to 45 of this title to recover from government contractor for underpayment of wages does not toll two-year statute of limitations so far as bringing of judicial proceedings for the same type of relief by United States Attorney General. U.S. v. Gulf States Asphalt Co., Inc., C.A.5 (Tex.)

1973, 472 F.2d 933. Limitation Of Actions ☞ 105(2)

Government's cause of action for liquidated damages for unpaid overtime wages, under this section, accrues upon failure of contractor who has entered into a contract with the Government to pay applicable rates of compensation for overtime work on performance of the contracts, and the Government has the right at any time thereafter within the applicable period of limitations to institute and maintain the action. U.S. v. Winegar, C.A.10 (Utah) 1958, 254 F.2d 693. Limitation Of Actions ☞ 58(1)

Where defendant violated section 35 et seq. of this title by knowingly employing underage minors in 1945, action, instituted in 1949 by United States for liquidated damages determined to be due by Secretary of Labor, was barred by section 255 of Title 29. Lance, Inc. v. U.S., C.A.4 (N.C.) 1951, 190 F.2d 204, certiorari denied 72 S.Ct. 229, 342 U.S. 896, 96 L.Ed. 671, rehearing denied 72 S.Ct. 287, 342 U.S. 915, 96 L.Ed. 684. Limitation Of Actions ☞ 11(1)

The limitation provisions of the Portal-to-Portal Act, section 255 of Title 29, are applicable to an action by the United States under this section. U.S. v. Lovknit Mfg. Co., C.A.5 (Tex.) 1951, 189 F.2d 454, certiorari denied 72 S.Ct. 229, 342 U.S. 896, 96 L.Ed. 671, rehearing denied 72 S.Ct. 287, 342 U.S. 915, 96 L.Ed. 684. See, also, U.S. v. W.H. Kistler Stationery Co., C.A.Colo.1952, 200 F.2d 805. Limitation Of Actions ☞ 11(1)

Provision of the Portal-to-Portal Act, section 255 of Title 29, stating that a cause of action which has accrued prior to date of enactment of that Act shall not be barred by two-year time limit if commenced within 120 days after date of enactment unless barred at commencement by applicable state statute of limitations, did not make previously inapplicable Oklahoma statute of limitations apply so as to bar suit instituted by the United States within required 120 days for recovery of liquidated damages for breach of contract made with Oklahoma poultry packer under section 35 et seq. of this title. Harp v. U.S., C.A.10 (Okla.) 1949, 173 F.2d 761, certiorari denied 70 S.Ct. 56, 338 U.S. 816, 94 L.Ed. 494. Limitation Of Actions ☞ 11(1)

The provision of this section, authorizing United States to withhold sums due it

because of violation of representations and stipulations in contracts named therein from amounts due from it on any such contracts, extends common-law withholding right beyond particular contract to other contracts of same species, so that limitations of Portal-to-Portal Act, section 251 et seq. of Title 29, as to times for commencement of actions for overtime compensation do not apply to withholding or recoupment authorized by sections 35 to 45 of this title, as such withholding is not an action to enforce a cause of action. Ready-Mix Concrete Co. v. U.S., Ct.Cl.1955, 130 F.Supp. 390, 131 Ct.Cl. 204. United States ☞ 73(16)

The two-year limitation period prescribed by section 255 of Title 29, began to run at time of alleged violation of section 35 of this title and not from time of completion of administrative proceedings by Labor Department, and therefore action for damages instituted by United States over two years after defendant had allegedly employed minors in violation of section 35(d) of this title was barred, though such action was brought within two years after Administrator of Wage and Hour and Public Contract Division of the Department of Labor had found that defendant had employed such minors and was liable in a certain sum as liquidated damages. U.S. v. W.H. Kistler Stationery Co., D.C.Colo.1952, 104 F.Supp. 16, affirmed 200 F.2d 805. Limitation Of Actions ☞ 58(1)

An action by United States, under this section, to recover damages from Government contractors for breach of contracts by employment of minor females under prescribed minimum ages for more than permitted maximum number of hours a day, was not barred by statute of limitations, where it was filed within two years after date of decision of Secretary of Labor, in administrative proceeding, that defendants were subject to sections 35 to 45 of this title and indebted to United States for liquidated damages in specified amounts. U.S. v. Sweet Briar, Inc., W.D.S.C.1950, 92 F.Supp. 777. Limitation Of Actions ☞ 65(3)

Limitation of Portal-to-Portal Act, section 255 of Title 29, began to run against action under this section by United States against contractor for liquidated damages for breach of contract by knowingly employing minors in manufacture and production of articles contracted for, when

Secretary of Labor determined occurrence of violations and adjudged liability against contractor, and not when the minors allegedly were knowingly employed. U.S. v. Craddock-Terry Shoe Corp., W.D.Va.1949, 84 F.Supp. 842, affirmed 178 F.2d 760. Limitation Of Actions ⇐ 46(6)

An action by United States against public contractor to recover as liquidated damages for violation of section 35 et seq. of this title the unpaid overtime wages which public contracts require contractor to pay employees was not barred by two year limitations prescribed by Portal-to-Portal Act, section 255 of Title 29, if Act was applicable where action was instituted within one year of termination of Department of Labor proceedings determining that overtime wages were due and unpaid. U.S. v. Hudgins-Dize Co., E.D.Va.1949, 83 F.Supp. 593. Limitation Of Actions ⇐ 58(1)

19. Burden of proof

Administrative findings were presumptively correct, and burden was on defendant employer to show that such findings were not supported by preponderance of evidence, in action under sections 35 to 45 of this title to recover sums of money due United States by reason of underpayment of wages and the employment of female minors under 18 years of age. U.S. v. Southland Mfg. Corp., D.C.Puerto Rico 1967, 264 F.Supp. 174. Labor And Employment ⇐ 2245; Labor And Employment ⇐ 2355

Corporation and its officers and directors sued by United States for liquidated damages for failure to pay minimum wages and overtime rates while fulfilling Government coal contracts had burden of establishing perishability of lignite coal to come within exception in section 43 of this title, and to show that all hours were not worked in manufacturing or furnishing materials used in performing contracts to rebut presumption that all employees engaged in performing contracts. U.S. v. Sawyer Fuels, Inc., D.C.N.D.1961, 199 F.Supp. 876, appeal dismissed 313 F.2d 637. Commerce ⇐ 62.67; Labor And Employment ⇐ 2385(4)

Fact findings of Secretary of Labor in administrative proceeding under sections 35 to 45 of this title to determine Government contractors' liability for liquidated damages for employment of under-age minors are presumptively correct, and burden is on contractors in action by United States for such damages to show that findings were not supported by evidence. U.S. v. Sweet Briar, Inc., W.D.S.C.1950, 92 F.Supp. 777. Administrative Law And Procedure ⇐ 749; United States ⇐ 75(4)

20. Trial de novo

Defendant employers in action under sections 35 to 45 of this title to recover sums of money due United States were not entitled to a trial de novo, but were entitled to a determination as to whether findings of fact, conclusions of law, and decision of hearing examiner, as affirmed by administrator of Wage and Hour and Public Contracts Divisions, were supported by the preponderance of the evidence. U.S. v. Southland Mfg. Corp., D.C.Puerto Rico 1967, 264 F.Supp. 174. Labor And Employment ⇐ 2355

Employer against which Under Secretary of Labor had initiated administrative proceeding for failure to pay minimum wages and overtime rates under sections 35 to 45 of this title was not entitled to trial de novo before federal district court in suit by United States to recover liquidated damages for failure to pay such wages and rates. U.S. v. Sawyer Fuels, Inc., D.C.N.D.1961, 199 F.Supp. 876, appeal dismissed 313 F.2d 637. Labor And Employment ⇐ 2347

21. Standard of review

In determining the preponderance of the evidence, only that evidence presented to hearing examiner and reviewed by administrator of Wage and Hour and Public Contracts Divisions was to be considered by court in action under sections 35 to 45 of this title to recover sums of money due United States, particularly where court had by exercise of its judicial discretion stayed the judicial proceeding pending completion of the administrative proceedings. U.S. v. Southland Mfg. Corp., D.C.Puerto Rico 1967, 264 F.Supp. 174. Labor And Employment ⇐ 2357

§ 37. Distribution of list of persons breaching contract; future contracts prohibited

The Comptroller General is authorized and directed to distribute a list to all agencies of the United States containing the names of persons or firms found by the Secretary of Labor to have breached any of the agreements or representations required by sections 35 to 45 of this title. Unless the Secretary of Labor otherwise recommends no contracts shall be awarded to such persons or firms or to any firm, corporation, partnership, or association in which such persons or firms have a controlling interest until three years have elapsed from the date the Secretary of Labor determines such breach to have occurred.

(June 30, 1936, c. 881, § 3, 49 Stat. 2037.)

CROSS REFERENCES

Construction, repair, alteration, furnishing and equipment of Naval vessels, see 10 USCA § 7299.

LIBRARY REFERENCES

American Digest System
Labor and Employment ⊗2296.
Key Number System Topic No. 231H.

Research References

Encyclopedias
Am. Jur. 2d Public Works and Contracts § 216, The Walsh-Healey Act.
Am. Jur. 2d Public Works and Contracts § 224, The Walsh-Healey Act.
Am. Jur. 2d Public Works and Contracts § 239, Application of Act--Walsh-Healey Act.

Forms
Am. Jur. Pl. & Pr. Forms Public Works & Contracts § 119, Decision--Of Administrator--Department of Labor--Upholding Decision of Administrative Law Judge--Denying Relief from Imposition of Ineligible List Sanction.
Am. Jur. Pl. & Pr. Forms Public Works & Contracts § 120, Decision--Of Secretary of Labor--Denying Relief from Imposition of Ineligible List Sanction.
Am. Jur. Pl. & Pr. Forms Public Works & Contracts § 122, Complaint in Federal Court--By Deputy Solicitor--Department of Labor--Violation of Walsh-Healey Act.
Federal Procedural Forms § 34:372, Decision of Administrative Law Judge.
Federal Procedural Forms § 34:388, Complaint--Against Contractor--Failure to Pay Employees Proper Wages [41 U.S.C.A. §§ 35 to 45; 41 C.F.R. § 50-203.2].
Federal Procedural Forms § 34:394, Complaint--By Deputy Solicitor--Department of Labor--Violation of Walsh-Healey Act.

Treatises and Practice Aids
Federal Procedure, Lawyers Edition § 39:139, Introduction.

WESTLAW ELECTRONIC RESEARCH

See Westlaw guide following the Explanation pages of this volume.

Notes of Decisions

1. Rules and regulations

Secretary of Labor's regulation providing that any government contractor or subcontractor found to have willfully violated overtime pay provisions of certain acts relating to federally financed or assisted construction would be ineligible for three-year period from doing business with government was not a penal measure but was regulation for effecting compliance with and furthering public policy represented by labor acts and was valid under Reorganization Plan No. 14 of 1950, set out in the Appendix to Title 5, Government Organization and Employees. Copper Plumbing & Heating Co. v. Campbell, C.A.D.C.1961, 290 F.2d 368, 110 U.S.App.D.C. 177. Labor And Employment ☞ 2338

2. Period of ineligibility

Violations of representations and stipulations in government contracts by government suppliers and manufacturers renders contracting party liable for damages and, possibly, for black-listing from government contracts for three-year period. United Biscuit Co. of America v. Wirtz, C.A.D.C.1965, 359 F.2d 206, 123 U.S.App.D.C. 222, certiorari denied 86 S.Ct. 1861, 384 U.S. 971, 16 L.Ed.2d 682. Labor And Employment ☞ 2296; Labor And Employment ☞ 2361

3. Injunction

Where plaintiffs were parties in proceeding in Labor Department and as result of findings and decisions therein plaintiffs had been subjected to payment of liquidated damages pursuant to section 36 of this title, which it was alleged was not applicable to their contracts, and pursuant to this section the plaintiffs' names had been submitted to Comptroller General for inclusion on list of those ineligible to contract with agencies of the Government, plaintiffs were entitled to maintain action to restrain Government officials from taking any further action to cause the publication of ineligibility pending the determination. Capitol Coal Sales v. Mitchell, D.C.D.C.1958, 164 F.Supp. 161, affirmed 282 F.2d 486, 108 U.S.App.D.C. 324. Labor And Employment ☞ 2423

4. Stay of proceedings

In future situations where dispute arises over applicability of sections 35 to 45 of this title and blacklisting of contractors for violation of such sections, courts should be careful to guard against a multiplicity of litigation, and ordinarily the district court having jurisdiction over suit for declaratory relief should stay its proceedings until United States has had opportunity to institute and complete enforcement proceedings, although temporary restraining order to prevent blacklisting pending outcome of enforcement action may be appropriate, but where district court with jurisdiction over enforcement proceedings had stayed its proceedings to permit completion of declaratory judgment suit, and district court had already considered administrative record and issues raised in declaratory judgment suit, court of appeals would, rather than staying its proceedings pending enforcement proceedings, rule on legal questions presented by the appeal. George v. Mitchell, C.A.D.C.1960, 282 F.2d 486, 108 U.S.App.D.C. 324. Federal Courts ☞ 742

§ 38. Administration of Walsh–Healey provisions; officers and employees; appointment; investigations; rules and regulations

The Secretary of Labor is authorized and directed to administer the provisions of sections 35 to 45 of this title and to utilize such Federal officers and employees and, with the consent of the State, such State and local officers and employees as he may find necessary to assist in the administration of said sections and to prescribe rules and regulations with respect thereto. The Secretary shall appoint, subject to chapter 51 and subchapter III of chapter 53 of Title 5, an administrative officer, and such attorneys and experts, and other employees with regard to existing laws applicable to the employment and compensation of officers and employees of the United States, as he may from time to time find necessary for the administration of sections 35 to 45 of this title. The Secretary of Labor or his authorized representatives shall have power to make investigations and findings as provided in sections 35 to 45 of this title, and prosecute any inquiry necessary to his functions in any part of the United States. The Secretary of Labor shall have authority from time to time to make, amend, and rescind such rules and regulations as may be necessary to carry out the provisions of sections 35 to 45 of this title.

(June 30, 1936, c. 881, § 4, 49 Stat. 2038; Oct. 28, 1949, c. 782, Title XI, § 1106(a), 63 Stat. 972.)

HISTORICAL AND STATUTORY NOTES

Codifications

Provisions of second sentence of this section that authorized the Secretary to appoint an administrative officer and such attorneys and experts "without regard to the provisions of the civil service laws" were omitted as obsolete. Such appointments are subject to the civil service laws unless specifically excepted by such laws or by laws enacted subsequent to Executive Order 8743, Apr. 23, 1941, issued by the President pursuant to the Act of Nov. 26, 1940, c. 919, Title I, § 1, 54 Stat. 1211, which covered most excepted positions into the classified (competitive) civil service. The Order is set out as a note under section 3301 of Title 5, Government Organization and Employees.

"Chapter 51 and subchapter III of chapter 53 of Title 5" were substituted in text for "the Classification Act of 1949, as amended" on authority of Pub.L. 89–554, § 7(b), Sept. 6, 1966, 80 Stat. 631, the first section of which enacted Title 5,

Government Organization and Employees.

Amendments

1949 Amendments. Act Oct. 28, 1949, substituted "Classification Act of 1949" for "Classification Act of 1923".

Transfer of Functions

For transfer of functions of all other officers, employees, and agencies of the Department of Labor, with certain exceptions, to the Secretary of Labor, with power to delegate, see Reorg. Plan No. 6 of 1950, §§ 1, 2, eff. May 24, 1950, 15 F.R. 3174, 64 Stat. 1263, set out in the Appendix to Title 5, Government Organization and Employees.

Repeals

Act Oct. 28, 1949, c. 782, Title XI, § 1106(a), 63 Stat. 972, cited as a credit to this section, was repealed (subject to a savings clause) by Pub.L. 89–554, Sept. 6, 1966, § 8, 80 Stat. 632, 655.

CROSS REFERENCES

Construction, repair, alteration, furnishing and equipping of Naval vessels, see 10 USCA § 7299.
This section as governing Secretary's authority to enforce Service Contract Act of 1965, see 41 USCA § 353.

CODE OF FEDERAL REGULATIONS

Investigations and inspections by State agencies, see 29 CFR § 515.1 et seq.
Labor standards for federal service contracts, see 29 CFR § 4.1 et seq.

Procedural rules for modification, etc., of occupational safety or health standards, see 29 CFR § 1911.1 et seq.
Public Contracts, generally, see 41 CFR § 50-201.1 et seq.

LIBRARY REFERENCES

American Digest System
Labor and Employment ⟂2336 to 2351.
Key Number System Topic No. 231H.

Research References

Encyclopedias
70 Am. Jur. Proof of Facts 3d 97, Proof That a Government Agency Was Liable for Improperly Granting a Bid Award to a Bid Applicant.

Forms
Federal Procedural Forms § 34:406, Order--Judicial Review of Agency Order--Exclusive Seller Not Regular Dealer Under Walsh-Healey Act [41 U.S.C.A. §§ 35 to 45; 48 C.F.R. §§ 22.601, 22.606-2; 41 C.F.R. § 50-206.53(a)].

Treatises and Practice Aids
Federal Procedure, Lawyers Edition § 39:139, Introduction.

WESTLAW ELECTRONIC RESEARCH

See Westlaw guide following the Explanation pages of this volume.

Notes of Decisions

Action against Secretary 5
Constitutionality 1
Duty or authority of Secretary 2-4
  Generally 2
  Exemptions 3
  Rules and regulations 4
Exemptions, duty or authority of Secretary 3
Rules and regulations, duty or authority of Secretary 4

1. Constitutionality

Authority given Secretary of Labor to make, amend, and rescind rules and regulations which are to have force and effect of law and are necessary to carry out provisions of sections 35 to 45 of this title was not unconstitutional delegation of legislative power. U.S. v. Sawyer Fuels, Inc., D.C.N.D.1961, 199 F.Supp. 876, appeal dismissed 313 F.2d 637. Constitutional Law ⟂ 2424(1); Labor And Employment ⟂ 2218(2)

2. Duty or authority of Secretary—Generally

Determination of whether sections 35 to 45 of this title and contracts for manufacture of shoes for the United States covered separate plants wherein parts only of the shoes were manufactured was primarily duty of the Secretary of Labor, not of courts. Endicott Johnson Corp. v. Perkins, U.S.N.Y.1943, 63 S.Ct. 339, 317 U.S. 501, 87 L.Ed. 424. Labor And Employment ⟂ 2357

3. ——— **Exemptions, duty or authority of Secretary**

The Secretary of Labor had authority under this section to grant exemptions from operation of sections 35 to 45 of this title upon such conditions as may be reasonable, include the terms of such sections in contracts by reference or practice and require employers securing Government contracts to keep a separate record of the time for work performed under Government contract, or, in the alternative, sustain the burden of proof that employees were working on other than Government contracts, and such regulations have the force of law. U.S. v. Harp, W.D.Okla.1948, 80 F.Supp. 236, affirmed 173 F.2d 761, certiorari denied 70 S.Ct. 56, 338 U.S. 816, 94 L.Ed. 494. Administrative Law And Procedure ⟂ 390.1; Administrative Law And Procedure ⟂ 417; United States ⟂ 75(1)

4. ——— **Rules and regulations, duty or authority of Secretary**

Interpretation of Secretary that coal wholesaler which contracted to supply coal to United States on four different contracts but which was not a regular dealer within meaning of section 35 of this title requiring payment of minimum wage and overtime compensation was under administrative regulations adopted pursuant to this section the party responsible for failure to pay wages to miners who mined coal for wholesaler's supplier was both correct and reasonable. Jno. McCall Coal Co. v. U.S., C.A.4 (Md.) 1967, 374 F.2d 689. Labor And Employment ⟜ 2338

Administrative rulings under sections 35 to 45 of this title which impose joint liability on one with a government contract for the manufacture of materials for failure of another manufacturer to which work has been shifted to comply with the standards of sections 35 to 45 of this title represent reasonable interpretation of statutory policy and are well within authority of Secretary of Labor to make such rules and regulations as are necessary to carry out provisions of said sections. U.S. v. Davison Fuel & Dock Co., C.A.4 (W.Va.) 1967, 371 F.2d 705. Labor And Employment ⟜ 2243

Regulation which was issued by Secretary of Labor for purpose of directing contracting officers as to what to incorporate into Government contracts so far as sections 35 to 45 of this title were concerned and which were incorporated into contract for purpose of notifying contractor that any violation of such sections in performance of contract would result in contractor's pay under contract being reduced by amount necessary to compensate for violation did not affect the Government's right under such sections to withhold amounts owed by contractor for violations committed in performance of other contracts. Ready-Mix Concrete Co. v. U.S., Ct.Cl.1958, 158 F.Supp. 571, 141 Ct.Cl. 168. United States ⟜ 73(16)

5. Action against Secretary

An action for injunctive relief based on assertion that Secretary of Labor exceeded his authority under this section in determining that contracts might be grouped for purpose of meeting jurisdictional minimum limitation of $10,000 when entered into in response to a single invitation to bid did not constitute a suit against the United States so as to preclude maintenance of the action because United States had not consented to be sued since if court should determine, when case was heard on merits, that section 35 et seq. of this title did not contemplate the grouping of such contracts it would not then be declaring the rights of the United States, but rather it would declare that the Secretary of Labor had acted in violation of section 35 et seq. of this title and that such action was void. Capitol Coal Sales v. Mitchell, D.C.D.C. 1958, 164 F.Supp. 161, affirmed 282 F.2d 486, 108 U.S.App.D.C. 324. United States ⟜ 125(28.1)

§ 39. Hearings on Walsh–Healey provisions by Secretary of Labor; witness fees; failure to obey order; punishment

Upon his own motion or on application of any person affected by any ruling of any agency of the United States in relation to any proposal or contract involving any of the provisions of sections 35 to 45 of this title, and on complaint of a breach or violation of any representation or stipulation as provided in said sections, the Secretary of Labor, or an impartial representative designated by him, shall have the power to hold hearings and to issue orders requiring the attendance and testimony of witnesses and the production of evidence under oath. Witnesses shall be paid the same fees and mileage that are paid witnesses in the courts of the United States. In case of contumacy, failure, or refusal of any person to obey such an order, any District Court of the United States or of any Territory or possession within the jurisdiction of which the inquiry is carried on, or within the jurisdiction of which said person who is guilty of contumacy, failure, or refusal is found, or resides or transacts business, upon the application by the Secretary of Labor or representative designated by him, shall have jurisdiction to issue to such person an order requiring such person to appear before him or representative designated by him, to produce evidence if, as, and when so ordered, and to give testimony relating to the matter under investigation or in question; and any failure to obey such order of the court may be punished by said court as a contempt thereof; and shall make findings of fact after notice and hearing, which findings shall be conclusive upon all agencies of the United States, and if supported by the preponderance of the evidence, shall be conclusive in any court of the United States; and the Secretary of Labor or authorized representative shall have the power, and is authorized, to make such decisions, based upon findings of fact, as are deemed to be necessary to enforce the provisions of sections 35 to 45 of this title.

(June 30, 1936, c. 881, § 5, 49 Stat. 2038; June 25, 1948, c. 646, § 32(b), 62 Stat. 991; May 24, 1949, c. 139, § 127, 63 Stat. 107.)

HISTORICAL AND STATUTORY NOTES

Codifications

As originally enacted, the words ", or the district court of the United States for the District of Columbia," were set out following "Territory or possession". Act June 25, 1948, as amended by Act May 24, 1949, substituted "United States District Court for the District of Columbia" for "district court of the United States for the District of Columbia". The words "United States District Court for the District of Columbia" have been deleted entirely as superfluous in view of section 132(a) of Title 28, Judiciary and Judicial Procedure, which states that "There shall be in each judicial district a district court which shall be a court of record known as the United States District Court for the district", and section 88 of Title 28 which states that "the District of Columbia constitutes one judicial district".

CROSS REFERENCES

Construction, repair, alteration, furnishing and equipping of Naval vessels, see 10 USCA § 7299.

Criminal contempt, see 18 USCA §§ 401, 402, 3285, and 3691; Fed.Rules Cr.Proc. Rule 42, 18 USCA.

Findings by court, Fed.Rules Civ.Proc. Rule 52, 28 USCA.

Per diem and mileage of witnesses, see 28 USCA § 1821.

Subpoena, Fed.Rules Civ.Proc. Rule 45, 28 USCA and Fed.Rules Cr.Proc. Rule 17, 18 USCA.

This section as governing Secretary's authority to enforce Service Contract Act of 1965, see 41 USCA § 353.

CODE OF FEDERAL REGULATIONS

Rules of practice, see 41 CFR § 50–203.1 et seq.

LIBRARY REFERENCES

American Digest System

Labor and Employment ⬥2336 to 2351.
Key Number System Topic No. 231H.

Research References

Forms

Federal Procedural Forms § 34:365, Subpoenas--Failure to Comply with a Subpoena.

Federal Procedural Forms § 34:368, Conduct of Evidentiary Hearing.

Federal Procedural Forms § 34:370, Conduct of Evidentiary Hearing--Witnesses.

Federal Procedural Forms § 34:372, Decision of Administrative Law Judge.

Federal Procedural Forms § 34:386, Scope of Review.

3B West's Federal Forms § 3981, Rule 45--Subpoena.

Treatises and Practice Aids

Federal Procedure, Lawyers Edition § 29:331, Authority of Secretary of Labor; Jurisdiction of District Courts.

Federal Procedure, Lawyers Edition § 39:179, Witnesses--Enforcement of Obligation to Appear and Testify.

Federal Procedure, Lawyers Edition § 39:182, Finality and Conclusiveness.

Federal Procedure, Lawyers Edition § 39:190, Scope and Standard of Review.

Federal Procedure, Lawyers Edition § 39:197, Standard of Review.

Federal Procedure, Lawyers Edition § 39:198, Institution of Enforcement Action.

Federal Procedure, Lawyers Edition § 52:6, Department of Labor Proceedings Governed by the Act.

12A Wright & Miller: Federal Prac. & Proc. App. C, Advisory Committee Notes for the Federal Rules of Civil Procedure for the United States District Courts.

WESTLAW ELECTRONIC RESEARCH

See Westlaw guide following the Explanation pages of this volume.

Notes of Decisions

Burden of proof, judicial review   7
Enforcement of subpoenas   3
Evidence considered, judicial review   6
Injunction   4
Issuance of subpoenas   1
Judicial review   5-9
   Generally   5
   Burden of proof   7
   Evidence considered   6
   Remand   9
   Weight and conclusiveness of administrative findings   8
Quashing of subpoenas   2
Remand, judicial review   9
Weight and conclusiveness of administrative findings, judicial review   8

---

1. Issuance of subpoenas

The power to issue subpoenas delegated to Secretary of Labor by this section is within limits of Congressional authority. Endicott Johnson Corp. v. Perkins, U.S.N.Y.1943, 63 S.Ct. 339, 317 U.S. 501, 87 L.Ed. 424. Labor And Employment ⟜ 2341

2. Quashing of subpoenas

Where action was brought by Government against employer for breach of contract on violations of sections 35 to 45 of this title, and subpoena duces tecum was served on employer with respect to records of employment, no cause of action was available to Government prior to two years preceding start of administrative hearings by Department of Labor on violations of those sections; however, subpoena would not be quashed in its entirety but modified to comply with regulations requiring employer to maintain records for period of four years. Billera v. Mitchell, E.D.Pa.1958, 166 F.Supp. 701. Witnesses ⟜ 16; Limitation Of Actions ⟜ 58(1)

3. Enforcement of subpoenas

The Secretary of Labor was entitled to enforcement of subpoena seeking evidence that manufacturer having Government contract underpaid employees in plants where parts only were made, without having first determined that such plants were covered by sections 35 to 45 of this title and the contracts in question. Endicott Johnson Corp. v. Perkins, U.S.N.Y.1943, 63 S.Ct. 339, 317 U.S. 501, 87 L.Ed. 424. Labor And Employment ⟜ 2342

4. Injunction

Paper manufacturer and union were entitled to preliminary injunction against

Secretary of Labor enjoining him from directly or indirectly debarring manufacturer from further business with the government by means of formal debarment, temporary suspension, or otherwise, and from interfering with manufacturer's collective bargaining agreement with union, prior to administrative hearing in which question of whether manufacturer was in compliance with Executive Order relating to equal employment opportunity clauses in government contracts and subcontracts could be resolved. Crown Zellerbach Corp. v. Wirtz, D.C.D.C.1968, 281 F.Supp. 337. Injunction ☞ 138.63

5. Judicial review—Generally

Scope of review of administrative decision holding that government contractor violated minimum wage and fringe benefits provisions of Service Contract Act, section 351 et seq. of this title, is limited to legal question whether the administrative law judge applied and satisfied the standard of proof required to find a violation and the Administrative law judge's findings are conclusive in any court of the United States if supported by a preponderance of the evidence. American Waste Removal Co. v. Donovan, C.A.10 (N.M.) 1984, 748 F.2d 1406. Labor And Employment ☞ 2357

Scope of judicial review in action under sections 35 to 45 of this title was that provided by sections 35 to 45 of this title, i.e., findings if supported by preponderance of evidence were conclusive in any court of the United States. U.S. v. Sancolmar Industries, Inc., E.D.N.Y.1972, 347 F.Supp. 404. Labor And Employment ☞ 2357

Credibility of witnesses relied upon by hearing examiner in arriving at his findings in proceeding under sections 35 to 45 of this title arising out of alleged underpayment of wages to employees and alleged employment of female minors under 18 years of age was function of hearing examiner, and his findings could be overruled only where, on basis of record, they were clearly incorrect. U.S. v. Southland Mfg. Corp., D.C.Puerto Rico 1967, 264 F.Supp. 174. Labor And Employment ☞ 2245; Labor And Employment ☞ 2357

6. —— Evidence considered, judicial review

In determining the preponderance of the evidence, only that evidence present-

ed to hearing examiner and reviewed by administrator of Wage and Hour and Public Contracts Divisions was to be considered by court in action under sections 35 to 45 of this title to recover sums of money due United States, particularly where court had by exercise of its judicial discretion stayed the judicial proceeding pending completion of the administrative proceedings. U.S. v. Southland Mfg. Corp., D.C.Puerto Rico 1967, 264 F.Supp. 174. Labor And Employment ☞ 2357

In an action by the United States under this section based upon findings and conclusions of a hearing examiner of the Department of Labor for underpayment of wages on a contract, only evidence that the court could consider was the evidence submitted to the hearing examiner and the "preponderance of the evidence" described in this section referred to that evidence and no other. U.S. v. Islip Mach. Works, Inc., E.D.N.Y.1959, 179 F.Supp. 585. Labor And Employment ☞ 2357; Labor And Employment ☞ 2387(3)

7. —— Burden of proof, judicial review

Findings made by the Department of Labor in a proceeding under sections 35 to 45 of this title that particular employees were underpaid by determined amounts were not deficient for failure to contain supporting evidence in as much as party taking an exception to such findings had burden of showing wherein administrative determination was wrong. Ready-Mix Concrete Co. v. U.S., Ct.Cl. 1958, 158 F.Supp. 571, 141 Ct.Cl. 168. Labor And Employment ☞ 2349; Labor And Employment ☞ 2351

Fact findings of Secretary of Labor in administrative proceeding under this section to determine Government contractors' liability for liquidated damages for employment of under-age minors are presumptively correct, and burden is on contractors in action by United States for such damages to show that findings were not supported by evidence. U.S. v. Sweet Briar, Inc., W.D.S.C.1950, 92 F.Supp. 777. Administrative Law And Procedure ☞ 749; United States ☞ 75(4)

Findings made in Department of Labor administrative proceedings charging violations of section 35 et seq. of this title that public contractor had not paid employees engaged in performance of contracts the overtime compensation required by the contracts and such sections were presumptively correct, and burden was on contractor and its sureties sued by United States for recovery, as liquidated damages, of amount of overtime wages which Department found had not been paid, to show that such findings were not supported by the evidence. U.S. v. Hudgins-Dize Co., E.D.Va.1949, 83 F.Supp. 593. Administrative Law And Procedure ☞ 499; Labor And Employment ☞ 2355; United States ☞ 67(20)

8.   —— Weight and conclusiveness of administrative findings, judicial review

Hearing examiner's findings of facts supported by preponderance of evidence are conclusive. U.S. v. Sawyer Fuels, Inc., D.C.N.D.1961, 199 F.Supp. 876, appeal dismissed 313 F.2d 637.

In action by the Government to recover damages for breach of contract for underpayment of wages by defendants who were the corporate contracting party and the president of the corporation whose liability was predicated upon a finding that he was a "party responsible" for breach of the contract, where the individual defendant made no point of the jurisdictional question, he must be deemed to have consented to the binding effect of the findings in the administrative hearing if supported by a preponderance of the evidence. U.S. v. Islip Mach. Works, Inc., E.D.N.Y.1959, 179 F.Supp. 585. Labor And Employment ☞ 2350(3)

Where section 40 of this title authorized Secretary of Labor to set rate of pay for overtime in the event the Secretary should permit increase in maximum hours of labor stipulated in public contract, and public contract contained overtime stipulation, such stipulation was an undertaking within condition of contractor's bond for faithful performance of contract, the Secretary could make finding with respect to overtime in administrative proceeding charging violation of such section, and such finding was enforceable against the bond. U.S. v. Hudgins-Dize Co., E.D.Va.1949, 83 F.Supp. 593. Labor And Employment ☞ 2350(2); United States ☞ 67(7.1)

9.   —— Remand, judicial review

There was no impropriety in district court's remanding of case to Secretary of Labor for further findings on question of whether funds used in connection with purchase notice agreement between government and manufacturer were appropriated funds since manufacturer, claiming that agreement was not subject to sections 35 to 45 of this title, had not argued applicability of open market exception of sections 35 to 45 of this title before the administrative agency. United Biscuit Co. of America v. Wirtz, C.A.D.C.1965, 359 F.2d 206, 123 U.S.App.D.C. 222, certiorari denied 86 S.Ct. 1861, 384 U.S. 971, 16 L.Ed.2d 682. Labor And Employment ☞ 2358

§ 40.   Exceptions from Walsh–Healey provisions; modification of contracts; variations; overtime; suspension of representations and stipulations

Upon a written finding by the head of the contracting agency or department that the inclusion in the proposal or contract of the representations or stipulations set forth in section 35 of this title will seriously impair the conduct of Government business, the Secretary of Labor shall make exceptions in specific cases or otherwise when justice or public interest will be served thereby. Upon the joint recommendation of the contracting agency and the contractor, the Secretary of Labor may modify the terms of an existing contract respecting minimum rates of pay and maximum hours of labor as he may find necessary and proper in the public interest or to prevent injustice and undue hardship. The Secretary of Labor may provide reasonable limitations and may make rules and regulations allowing reasonable variations, tolerances, and exemptions to and from any or all provisions of sections 35 to 45 of this title respecting minimum rates of pay and maximum hours of labor or the extent of the application of said sections to contractors, as hereinbefore described. Whenever the Secretary of Labor shall permit an increase in the maximum hours of labor stipulated in the contract, he shall set a rate of pay for any overtime, which rate shall be not less than one and one-half times the basic hourly rate received by any employee affected: *Provided*, That whenever in his judgment such course is in the public interest, the President is authorized to suspend any or all of the representations and stipulations contained in section 35 of this title.

(June 30, 1936, c. 881, § 6, 49 Stat. 2038; June 28, 1940, c. 440, Title I, § 13, 54 Stat. 681.)

HISTORICAL AND STATUTORY NOTES

Amendments
1940 Amendments. Act June 28, 1940, added the proviso.

CROSS REFERENCES

Construction, repair, alteration, furnishing and equipping of Naval vessels, see 10 USCA § 7299.

CODE OF FEDERAL REGULATIONS

Contract provisions, see 41 CFR § 50–201.1 et seq.
Enforcement of safety and health standards by state officers and employees, see 41 CFR § 50–205.1 et seq.
Rules of practice, see 41 CFR § 50–203.13 et seq.

LIBRARY REFERENCES

American Digest System
Labor and Employment ☞2292(3).
United States ☞75(1).
Key Number System Topic Nos. 231H, 393.

Research References

Encyclopedias
Am. Jur. 2d Public Works and Contracts § 237, Contract Work Hours Standards Act.
Am. Jur. 2d Public Works and Contracts § 239, Application of Act--Walsh-Healey Act.
Am. Jur. 2d Public Works and Contracts § 240, Exception in Case of Emergency and Meaning Thereof.

Forms
Am. Jur. Pl. & Pr. Forms Public Works & Contracts § 122, Complaint in Federal Court--By Deputy Solicitor--Department of Labor--Violation of Walsh-Healey Act.
Federal Procedural Forms § 34:350, How to Obtain Exemption from Coverage.
Federal Procedural Forms § 34:388, Complaint--Against Contractor--Failure to Pay Employees Proper Wages [41 U.S.C.A. §§ 35 to 45; 41 C.F.R. § 50-203.2].

Federal Procedural Forms § 34:394, Complaint--By Deputy Solicitor--Department of Labor--Violation of Walsh-Healey Act.

Nichols Cyclopedia of Legal Forms Annotated § 7:2518, Supply Contract with United States--General Provisions.

Treatises and Practice Aids

Federal Procedure, Lawyers Edition § 39:140, Suspension; Exceptions or Exemptions.

WESTLAW ELECTRONIC RESEARCH

See Westlaw guide following the Explanation pages of this volume.

Notes of Decisions

Conditions of exemption order   1
Overtime   3
Stockpile exemption   2

---

1. Conditions of exemption order

A Government contractor's full compliance with conditions of exemption order, issued by Secretary of Labor, permitting employment of sixteen and seventeen year old girls in performance of contract, is condition of such employment, not a mere privilege to be exercised in employer's discretion. U.S. v. Sweet Briar, Inc., W.D.S.C.1950, 92 F.Supp. 777. United States ☞ 75(1)

2. Stockpile exemption

Where government contract for supply of asphalt products in steel drums was an indefinite amount requirements contract reciting 300,000 as the general estimate of the number of drums needed and contract contained a specified delivery requirement on drums for the first 45-day period, contractor which had on hand a sufficient number of drums in stock during duration of contract to meet the specified delivery schedule but not the general estimate of 300,000 drums, was entitled to exemption from the overtime provisions of sections 35 to 45 of this title under the stockpile exemption with respect to work of its employees in making delivery to stockpile of different drums which were commingled with those on hand. U.S. v. Gulf States Asphalt Co., Inc., C.A.5 (Tex.) 1973, 472 F.2d 933. Labor And Employment ☞ 2292(3)

3. Overtime

Where this section authorized Secretary of Labor to set rate of pay for overtime in the event the Secretary should permit increase in maximum hours of labor stipulated in public contract, and public contract contained overtime stipulation, such stipulation was an undertaking within condition of contractor's bond for faithful performance of contract, and Secretary could make finding with respect to overtime in administrative proceeding charging violation of this section, and such finding was enforceable against the bond. U.S. v. Hudgins-Dize Co., E.D.Va.1949, 83 F.Supp. 593. Labor And Employment ☞ 2350(2); United States ☞ 67(7.1)

§ 41.   "Person" defined in Walsh–Healey provisions

Whenever used in sections 35 to 45 of this title, the word "person" includes one or more individuals, partnerships, associations, corporations, legal representatives, trustees, trustees in cases under Title 11, or receivers.

(June 30, 1936, c. 881, § 7, 49 Stat. 2039; Nov. 6, 1978, Pub.L. 95–598, Title III, § 326, 92 Stat. 2679.)

HISTORICAL AND STATUTORY NOTES

Revision Notes and Legislative Reports
1978 Acts. House Report No. 95–595 and Senate Report No. 95–589, see 1978 U.S.Code Cong. and Adm.News, p. 5787.

Amendments
1978 Amendments. Pub.L. 95–598 substituted "trustees in cases under Title 11" for "trustees in bankruptcy".

Effective and Applicability Provisions
1978 Acts. Amendment by Pub.L. 95–598 effective Oct. 1, 1979, see section 402(a) of Pub.L. 95–598, set out as an Effective Date note preceding section 101 of Title 11, Bankruptcy.

CROSS REFERENCES

Construction, repair, alteration, furnishing and equipping of Naval vessels, see 10 USCA § 7299.

Research References

Encyclopedias
14 Am. Jur. Trials 437, Representing the Government Contractor.
31 Am. Jur. Trials 317, Wrongful Discharge of At-Will Employee.

WESTLAW ELECTRONIC RESEARCH

See Westlaw guide following the Explanation pages of this volume.

§ 42. Effect of Walsh–Healey provisions on other laws

The provisions of sections 35 to 45 of this title shall not be construed to modify or amend Title III of the Act entitled "An Act making appropriations for the Treasury and Post Office Departments for the fiscal year ending June 30, 1934, and for other purposes", approved May 3, 1933 (commonly known as the Buy American Act) [41 U.S.C.A. § 10a et seq.], nor shall the provisions of sections 35 to 45 of this title be construed to modify or amend sections 3141 to 3144, 3146, 3147 of Title 40, nor the labor provisions of Title II of the National Industrial Recovery Act, approved June 16, 1933, as extended, or of section 7 of the Emergency Relief Appropriation Act, approved April 8, 1935; nor shall the provisions of sections 35 to 45 of this title be construed to modify or amend chapter 307 and section 4162 of Title 18.

(June 30, 1936, c. 881, § 8, 49 Stat. 2039.)

HISTORICAL AND STATUTORY NOTES

References in Text
Title III of the Act entitled "An Act making appropriations for the Treasury and Post Office Departments for the fiscal year ending June 30, 1934, and for other purposes", approved May 3, 1933 (commonly known as the Buy American Act), referred to in text, is Act Mar. 3, 1933, c. 212, Title III, 47 Stat. 1520, as amended, popularly known as the Buy American Act, which enacted sections 10a to 10c of this title and enacted provisions set out as notes under section 10c of this title. For complete classification of this Act to the Code, see Short Title note set out under section 10a of this title and Tables.

The National Industrial Recovery Act, referred to in text, is Act June 16, 1933, c. 90, 48 Stat. 195, Title II of which was classified principally to subchapter I of chapter 8 of former Title 40, former 40 U.S.C.A. § 401 et seq., prior to being terminated on June 30, 1943, by Act June 27, 1942, c. 450, § 1, 56 Stat. 410.

Section 7 of the Emergency Relief Appropriation Act, approved April 8, 1935, referred to in text, is Act Apr. 8, 1935, c. 48, § 7, 49 Stat. 115, which is not classified to the Code.

Section 4162 of Title 18, referred to in text, was repealed by Pub.L. 98–473, Title II, § 218(a)(4), Oct. 12, 1984, 98 Stat. 2027.

Codifications

In text, "sections 3141 to 3144, 3146, 3147 of Title 40" substituted for "the Act entitled 'An Act relating to the rate of wages for laborers and mechanics employed on public buildings of the United States and the District of Columbia by contractors and subcontractors, and for other purposes', approved March 3, 1931 (commonly known as the Bacon–Davis Act), as amended from time to time [40 U.S.C.A. § 276a et seq.]" on authority of Pub.L. 107–217, § 5(c), Aug. 21, 2002,

116 Stat. 1301, which is set out as a note preceding 40 U.S.C.A. § 101. Pub.L. 107–217, § 1, enacted Title 40 into positive law. The Davis–Bacon Act is Act Mar. 3, 1931, c. 411, 46 Stat. 1494, which was classified to former 40 U.S.C.A. §§ 276a, 276a–1 to 276a–6, prior to being repealed by Pub.L. 107–217, § 6(b), Aug. 21, 2002, 116 Stat. 1308, and its substance reenacted as 40 U.S.C.A. §§ 3141 to 3144, 3146, 3147.

"Chapter 307 and section 4162 of Title 18" was substituted for "the Act entitled 'An Act to provide for the diversification of employment of Federal prisoners, for their training and schooling in trades and occupations, and for other purposes', approved May 27, 1930, as amended and supplemented by the Act approved June 23, 1934" on authority of Act June 25, 1948, c. 645, 62 Stat. 683, the first section of which enacted Title 18, Crimes and Criminal Procedure. Prior to the enactment of Title 18, the Act of May 27, 1930, as amended, had been classified to sections 744a to 744n of Title 18.

CROSS REFERENCES

Construction, repair, alteration, furnishing and equipping of Naval vessels, see 10 USCA § 7299.

WESTLAW ELECTRONIC RESEARCH

See Westlaw guide following the Explanation pages of this volume.

§ 43. Walsh–Healey provisions not applicable to certain contracts

Sections 35 to 45 of this title shall not apply to purchases of such materials, supplies, articles, or equipment as may usually be bought in the open market; nor shall they apply to perishables, including dairy, livestock and nursery products, or to agricultural or farm products processed for first sale by the original producers; nor to any contracts made by the Secretary of Agriculture for the purchase of agricultural commodities or the products thereof. Nothing in said sections shall be construed to apply to carriage of freight or personnel by vessel, airplane, bus, truck, express, or railway line where published tariff rates are in effect or to common carriers subject to the Communications Act of 1934 [47 U.S.C.A. § 151 et seq.].

(June 30, 1936, c. 881, § 9, 49 Stat. 2039.)

HISTORICAL AND STATUTORY NOTES

References in Text

The Communications Act of 1934, referred to in text, is Act June 19, 1934, c. 652, 48 Stat. 1064, as amended, which is classified principally to chapter 5 (section 151 et seq.) of Title 47, Telegraphs, Telephones, and Radiotelegraphs. For complete classification of this Act to the Code see section 609 of Title 47 and Tables.

CROSS REFERENCES

Construction, repair, alteration, furnishing and equipping of Naval vessels, see 10 USCA § 7299.

LIBRARY REFERENCES

American Digest System

Labor and Employment ☞2292(3).
Key Number System Topic No. 231H.

Research References

ALR Library

16 ALR, Fed. 982, Judicial Review Under § 10(C) of Walsh-Healey Act (41 U.S.C.A. § 43a(C)) of Legal Questions Involved in Award of Government Contracts Under Such Act.

2 ALR, Fed. 637, What Contracts Are Subject to Wage and Hour Requirements of Walsh-Healey Act (41 U.S.C.A. § 35).

Encyclopedias

Am. Jur. 2d Public Works and Contracts § 216, The Walsh-Healey Act.

Am. Jur. 2d Public Works and Contracts § 239, Application of Act--Walsh-Healey Act.

WESTLAW ELECTRONIC RESEARCH

See Westlaw guide following the Explanation pages of this volume.

Notes of Decisions

Open market purchases 1
Perishables 2

_____

1. Open market purchases

Fact that purchase notice agreement entered into between manufacturer and government had been entered into pursuant to Armed Services Procurement Act of 1947, section 2301 et seq. of Title 10, took agreement out of the ambit of exception of sections 35 to 45 of this title provision relating to purchases of supplies as may usually be bought in the open market. United Biscuit Co. of America v. Wirtz, C.A.D.C.1965, 359 F.2d 206, 123 U.S.App.D.C. 222, certiorari denied 86 S.Ct. 1861, 384 U.S. 971, 16 L.Ed.2d 682. Labor And Employment ☞ 2243

Provision of this section that sections 35 to 45 of this title "shall not apply to purchases of such materials, supplies, articles or equipment as may usually be bought in the open market" did not exempt bituminous coal from sections 35 to 45 of this title even though it could be purchased in the open market, such exemption excluding from coverage of sections 35 to 45 of this title only purchases the Government itself was authorized to make in the open market. Ruth Elkhorn Coals, Inc. v. Mitchell, C.A.D.C.1957, 248 F.2d 635, 101 U.S.App.D.C. 313, certiorari denied 78 S.Ct. 539, 355 U.S. 953, 2 L.Ed.2d 530. Labor And Employment ☞ 2292(3)

2. Perishables

Corporation and its officers and directors sued by United States for liquidated damages for failure to pay minimum wages and overtime rates while fulfilling Government coal contracts had burden of establishing perishability of lignite coal to come within exception in this section, and to show that all hours were not worked in manufacturing or furnishing materials used in performing contracts to rebut presumption that all employees engaged in performing contracts. U.S. v. Sawyer Fuels, Inc.,

D.C.N.D.1961, 199 F.Supp. 876, appeal dismissed 313 F.2d 637. Commerce ⌾ 62.67; Labor And Employment ⌾ 2385(4)

§ 43a. Administrative procedure provisions

(a) Applicability

Notwithstanding any provision of section 553 of Title 5, subchapter II of chapter 5, and chapter 7, of Title 5 shall be applicable in the administration of sections 35 to 39 and 41 to 43 of this title.

(b) Wage determination; administrative review

All wage determinations under section 35(a) of this title shall be made on the record after opportunity for a hearing. Review of any such wage determination, or of the applicability of any such wage determination, may be had within ninety days after such determination is made in the manner provided in chapter 7 of Title 5 by any person adversely affected or aggrieved thereby, who shall be deemed to include any supplier of materials, supplies, articles or equipment purchased or to be purchased by the Government from any source, who is in any industry to which such wage determination is applicable.

(c) Judicial review

Notwithstanding the inclusion of any stipulations required by any provision of sections 35 to 45 of this title in any contract subject to said sections, any interested person shall have the right of judicial review of any legal question which might otherwise be raised, including, but not limited to, wage determinations and the interpretation of the terms "locality" and "open market".

(June 30, 1936, c. 881, § 10, as added June 30, 1952, c. 530, Title III, § 301, 66 Stat. 308, and amended Oct. 13, 1994, Pub.L. 103–355, Title VII, § 7201(2), (3), 108 Stat. 3378; Feb. 10, 1996, Pub.L. 104–106, Div. D, Title XLIII, § 4321(f)(2), 110 Stat. 675.)

HISTORICAL AND STATUTORY NOTES

Revision Notes and Legislative Reports
1952 Acts. Subsection (a) of section 10 makes the provisions of the Administrative Procedure Act applicable to sections 1 to 5 and 7 to 9 of the Walsh–Healey Act. Section 4 of the Administrative Procedure Act now excepts matters relating to public contracts from the requirements of the act pertaining to rule making. The effect of the amendment made by subsection (a) is to make rules (as defined in the Administrative Procedure Act) which are pro-

mulgated by the Secretary of Labor in the administration of sections 1 to 5 and 7 to 9 of the Walsh–Healey Act subject to certain minimum procedural requirements applicable to agencies generally in exercising rule making powers. Such requirements include (1) adequate notice of the proposed rule making with a clear statement of the terms or substance of the proposed rule, (2) opportunity for interested persons to participate in the proposed rule making by submission of views or arguments, and (3) the right of interested persons to petition for the issuance, amendment, or repeal of a rule. It is to be noted that compliance with the procedural requirements of the Administrative Procedure Act is not required in the case of rules promulgated under section 6 of the Walsh–Healey Act. Section 6 provides statutory authority for the Secretary of Labor to make exceptions under certain conditions with respect to contracts which would otherwise be subject to the provisions of the act.

Subsection (b) of section 10 provides that all wage determinations by the Secretary of Labor under section 1(b) of the Walsh–Healey Act shall be made on the record after opportunity for an agency hearing. The effect of this language is to compel compliance by the Secretary of Labor with the requirements of sections 7 and 8 of the Administrative Procedure Act (relating to hearings and decisions) as a prerequisite to the making of a determination of the prevailing minimum wages in an industry. The full force of the procedural safeguards contained in the Administrative Procedure Act is thereby brought into play insofar as these controversial determinations are concerned. The subsection further assures the right to obtain judicial review of these determinations in the manner provided in section 10 of the Administrative Procedure Act by any person adversely affected or aggrieved thereby, who shall be deemed to include any manufacturer of, or regular dealer in, materials, supplies, articles, or equipment purchased or to be purchased by the Government from any source, who is in any industry to which the wage determination is applicable. The language assuring judicial review makes it clear that the court may consider the applicability of the wage determination to any person as well as the amount arrived at by the Secretary of Labor. Any such review may be sought, however, only by a proceeding instituted within 90 days after the determination is made.

Subsection (c) of section 10 is designed to permit any Government contractor whose contract contains stipulations required by the Walsh–Healey Act to obtain a judicial determination in any appropriate proceeding of any legal question (including the applicability of the act) to the same extent as any such question could be raised if the stipulations were not contained in the contract. Without the language contained in subsection (c) there would be some doubt as to whether any Government contractor who had signed a contract containing "Walsh–Healey stipulations" could later in any legal proceeding raise questions concerning (1) the applicability of the act to his particular contract, or (2) the legality of any such stipulation. Under subsection (c) the court and not the Secretary of Labor may ultimately decide whether, in respect to any particular Government contract, the Walsh–Healey Act is being properly applied. The House amendment did not contain a similar provision. The conference substitute contains the provisions of the Senate bill. Conference Report No. 2352.

1994 Acts. Senate Report Nos. 103–258 and 103–259, and House Conference Report No. 103–712, see U.S. Code Cong. and Adm. News, p. 2561.

1996 Acts. House Conference Report No. 104–450, see 1996 U.S. Code Cong. and Adm. News, p. 238.

Codifications

"Section 553 of Title 5", "subchapter II of chapter 5, and chapter 7, of Title 5", and "chapter 7 of Title 5" were substituted for "section 1003 of Title 5", "such Act [meaning the Administrative Procedure Act]", and "section 1009 of Title 5", respectively, on authority of Pub.L. 89–554, § 7(b), Sept. 6, 1966, 80 Stat. 631, the first section of which enacted Title 5, Government Organization and Employees.

Amendments

1996 Amendments. Subsec. (b). Pub.L. 104–106, § 4321(f)(2)(A), substituted "section 35(a)" for "section 35(b)".

1994 Amendments. Subsec. (b). Pub.L. 103–355, § 7201(2), substituted "supplier of materials" for "manufacturer of, or regular dealer in, materials".

Subsec. (c). Pub.L. 103–355, § 7201(3), struck out from the enumeration of reviewable legal questions references to interpretation of the terms regular dealer and manufacturer.

Effective and Applicability Provisions

1996 Acts. Amendment by Pub.L. 104–106 effective Feb. 10, 1996, except as otherwise provided, see section 4401 of Pub.L. 104–106, set out as a note under section 251 of this title.

1994 Acts. Amendment by section 7201(2) and (3) of Pub.L. 103–355 effective Oct. 13, 1994, except as otherwise provided, see section 10001 of Pub.L. 103–355, set out as a note under section 251 of this title.

Prior Provisions

A prior section 10 of act June 30, 1936, was renumbered section 12, and is classified to section 44 of this title.

CROSS REFERENCES

Construction, repair, alteration, furnishing and equipping of Naval vessels, see 10 USCA § 7299.

CODE OF FEDERAL REGULATIONS

Minimum wage determinations, see 41 CFR § 50–202.1 et seq.

LIBRARY REFERENCES

American Digest System
Labor and Employment ⚯2336 to 2352.
Key Number System Topic No. 231H.

Research References

ALR Library
16 ALR, Fed. 982, Judicial Review Under § 10(C) of Walsh-Healey Act (41 U.S.C.A. § 43a(C)) of Legal Questions Involved in Award of Government Contracts Under Such Act.

Forms
Am. Jur. Pl. & Pr. Forms Public Works & Contracts § 130, Answer and Counterclaim--By Contractor--To Action by United States Seeking Liquidated Damages Under Walsh-Healey Act.

Am. Jur. Pl. & Pr. Forms Public Works & Contracts § 133, Petition in Federal Court--For Review of Minimum Wage Determination Under Walsh-Healey Act.

Am. Jur. Pl. & Pr. Forms Public Works & Contracts § 134, Motion--For Temporary Injunction--To Stay Execution of Minimum Wage Determination Under Walsh-Healey Act.

Am. Jur. Pl. & Pr. Forms Public Works & Contracts § 135, Motion in Federal Court--For Leave to Intervene in Proceeding for Review of Minimum Wage Determination Under Walsh-Healey Act--By Member of Industry Affected--As Respondent.

Am. Jur. Pl. & Pr. Forms Public Works & Contracts § 136, Findings of Fact and Conclusions of Law--By Federal Court--Favoring Review of Minimum Wage Determination Under Walsh-Healey Act.

Federal Procedural Forms § 34:349, Introduction.
Federal Procedural Forms § 34:352, Introduction.
Federal Procedural Forms § 34:374, Overview.
Federal Procedural Forms § 34:375, Availability of Review.
Federal Procedural Forms § 34:376, Standing.
Federal Procedural Forms § 34:382, Jurisdiction.
Federal Procedural Forms § 34:383, Selecting the Remedy.
Federal Procedural Forms § 34:384, Standing.
Federal Procedural Forms § 34:386, Scope of Review.
Federal Procedural Forms § 34:387, Scope of Review--Administrative Interpretation of Statutory Terms.
Federal Procedural Forms § 34:393, Complaint--For Review of Minimum Wage Determination Under Walsh-Healey Act [5 U.S.C.A. §§ 701 to 706; 28 U.S.C.A. §§ 2201, 2202; 41 U.S.C.A. §§ 35 to 45; Fed. R. Civ. P. Rule 8(A), 57, 65].

Federal Procedural Forms § 34:395.50, Complaint--For Injunctive Relief and Declaratory Judgment--Violation of Walsh-Healey Act--Contract Wrongfully Awarded to Unqualified Bidder [41 U.S.C.A. §§ 35, 43a; 28 U.S.C.A. §§ 1346, 1391; 4 C.F.R. § 21; 5 U.S.C.A. § 706(2)].

Federal Procedural Forms § 34:398, Motion--For Preliminary Injunction--To Stay Execution of Minimum Wage Determination Under Walsh-Healey Act [5 U.S.C.A. §§ 701 to 706; 41 U.S.C.A. §§ 35 to 45; Fed. R. Civ. P. Rules 7(B), 65(a)].

Federal Procedural Forms § 34:400, Motion--For Leave to Intervene as Defendant in Proceeding to Review Minimum Wage Determination Under Walsh-Healey Act--By Member of Industry Affected [5 U.S.C.A. §§ 701 to 706; 41 U.S.C.A. §§ 35 to 45; Fed. R. Civ. P. Rules 7(b), 24].

Federal Procedural Forms § 34:401, Answer and Counterclaim--To Action by United States Seeking Liquidated Damages Under Walsh-Healey Act [5 U.S.C.A. §§ 701 to 706; 28 U.S.C.A. § 2201; 41 U.S.C.A. §§ 35 to 45; Fed. R. Civ. P. Rules 8, 13].

Treatises and Practice Aids

Federal Procedure, Lawyers Edition § 2:103, Formal Rulemaking Must Be Specified in the Regulatory Statute.

Federal Procedure, Lawyers Edition § 39:139, Introduction.

Federal Procedure, Lawyers Edition § 39:140, Suspension; Exceptions or Exemptions.

Federal Procedure, Lawyers Edition § 39:156, Who May Obtain Review.

Federal Procedure, Lawyers Edition § 39:157, Timeliness of Filing.

Federal Procedure, Lawyers Edition § 39:160, Stay of Secretary's Determination Pending Review.

Federal Procedure, Lawyers Edition § 39:185, Jurisdiction.

Federal Procedure, Lawyers Edition § 39:187, Standing.

Federal Procedure, Lawyers Edition § 39:188, Indispensable Parties.

Federal Procedure, Lawyers Edition § 39:190, Scope and Standard of Review.

Federal Procedure, Lawyers Edition § 39:191, Scope and Standard of Review--Administrative Interpretation of Statutory Terms.

WESTLAW ELECTRONIC RESEARCH

See Westlaw guide following the Explanation pages of this volume.

Notes of Decisions

Admissibility of evidence   13
Conditional nature of incorporating clauses   1
Conditions for administrative review   5
Conditions for judicial review   7
Exhaustion of administrative remedies   8
Inspection records, disclosure of   3
Interested persons, persons entitled to judicial review   10
Intervention   11
Issues reviewable   12
Persons entitled to judicial review   9, 10
    Generally   9
    Interested persons   10
Right to administrative review   4
Supplementation of administrative record   6

Wage determinations   2

1. Conditional nature of incorporating clauses

Conditional nature, in government contracts, of incorporating clauses referring to sections 35 to 45 of this title is proper since this section itself provides for administrative proceedings to determine applicability of sections 35 to 45 of this title to any particular contract. U.S. v. Davison Fuel & Dock Co., C.A.4 (W.Va.) 1967, 371 F.2d 705. Labor And Employment ⬅ 2243

2. Wage determinations

While Secretary of Labor could conduct proceedings to determine present prevailing minimum wage if he abandoned old determination which had not been supported by sufficient evidence, he could not keep the old determination in effect until he superseded it. Wirtz v. Baldor Elec. Co., C.A.D.C.1963, 337 F.2d 518, 119 U.S.App.D.C. 122. Labor And Employment ☞ 2350(3)

3. Inspection records, disclosure of

Documents, which were prepared by inspectors employed by Secretary of Labor and other officials in connection with their inspection of plants subject to sections 35 to 45 of this title, were subject to disclosure under the Freedom of Information Act, section 552 of Title 5. Wecksler v. Shultz, D.C.D.C.1971, 324 F.Supp. 1084. Records ☞ 54

4. Right to administrative review

The fact that judicial review of a wage determination under sections 35 to 45 of this title is available in an appropriate case, under subsec. (c) of this section, does not preempt the right of review available under subsec. (b) of this section. Ruth Elkhorn Coals, Inc. v. Mitchell, C.A.D.C.1957, 248 F.2d 635, 101 U.S.App.D.C. 313, certiorari denied 78 S.Ct. 539, 355 U.S. 953, 2 L.Ed.2d 530. Labor And Employment ☞ 2353

5. Conditions for administrative review

An administrative body should not begin proceeding to determine whether sections 35 to 45 of this title have been violated unless the body has made at least a tacit tentative determination that the data already before it is sufficient to justify the institution of such an inquiry. Perkins v. Endicott Johnson Corp., C.C.A.2 (N.Y.) 1942, 128 F.2d 208, certiorari granted 63 S.Ct. 35, 317 U.S. 607, 87 L.Ed. 492, affirmed 63 S.Ct. 339, 317 U.S. 501, 87 L.Ed. 424. Labor And Employment ☞ 2341

6. Supplementation of administrative record

Proposals of Secretary of Labor to supplement record of wage determination hearing under sections 35 to 45 of this title in order to correct noted deficiencies were properly rejected as neither strengthening evidence nor affording any semblance of required procedures, as information on 1964 wages could not reflect wages paid in 1960 or support determinations based solely on summary tabulations of 1960 wages. Wirtz v. Baldor Elec. Co., C.A.D.C.1963, 337 F.2d

518, 119 U.S.App.D.C. 122. Labor And Employment ☞ 2347

7. Conditions for judicial review

Electric companies which alleged that they paid minimum wages less than those found by Secretary of Labor to be prevailing minimums in motors and generators industry, but who did not submit any affidavits or other facts in support of allegations, could not maintain actions for review of minimum wage determination by Secretary of Labor. Baldor Elec. Co. v. Wirtz, D.C.D.C.1964, 228 F.Supp. 210. Labor And Employment ☞ 2355

8. Exhaustion of administrative remedies

Issue of whether bid for Army procurement contract was unresponsive because bidder did not qualify as "manufacturer" under Walsh-Healey Act could not be considered by courts before Army made final determination as to whether the corporation met Act's requirements. Honeywell, Inc. v. U.S., C.A.Fed.1989, 870 F.2d 644. United States ☞ 64.60(1)

Paper manufacturer and union had adequate administrative remedy under procedures contemplated by executive order relating to equal employment opportunity clauses in government contracts and subcontracts, so that manufacturer and union were not entitled to an injunction restraining defendant Secretary of Labor from instituting administrative proceedings to debar manufacturer from eligibility for government contracts. Crown Zellerbach Corp. v. Wirtz, D.C.D.C.1968, 281 F.Supp. 337. Injunction ☞ 83

Where pursuant to section 36 of this title the Government had instituted an action for recovery of liquidated damages determined in administrative proceedings to be due, defendants in such action proclaimed that Secretary of Labor exceeded his authority in determining that contracts might be grouped for purpose of meeting jurisdictional minimum limitation of $10,000 when entered into in response to a single invitation to bid, did not have an adequate remedy as respects their liability on the contracts and hence they were entitled to review provided by the Administrative Procedure Act [repealed], former section 1009 of Title 5 [now covered by sections 701 to 706 of Title 5], unless dismissal of their action was required because of other reasons. Capitol Coal Sales v. Mitchell, D.C.D.C.

1958, 164 F.Supp. 161, affirmed 282 F.2d 486, 108 U.S.App.D.C. 324. Administrative Law And Procedure ☞ 701; Labor And Employment ☞ 2354

9. Persons entitled to judicial review—Generally

Plaintiffs alleging that they were paying wages equal to or greater than those set by Secretary of Labor as prevailing wage determination under sections 35–45 of this title had no standing to seek review of determination as their interests were not adversely affected, but plaintiffs alleging they paid wages less than the amount determined by Secretary prima facie had standing to review determination. Wirtz v. Baldor Elec. Co., C.A.D.C.1963, 337 F.2d 518, 119 U.S.App.D.C. 122. Labor And Employment ☞ 2355

Question of whether open market exemption provision of section 43 of this title put the bituminous coal industry as such entirely out of the operation of sections 35 to 45 of this title could be judicially reviewed in proceedings under subsec. (b) of this section, seeking invalidation of a determination by the Secretary of Labor made under section 35(b) of this title of prevailing minimum wages in the industry, by plaintiffs, who were regular dealers in supplies of the bituminous coal industry, even though they had not entered into a contract with the Government to supply the bituminous coal. Ruth Elkhorn Coals, Inc. v. Mitchell, C.A.D.C.1957, 248 F.2d 635, 101 U.S.App.D.C. 313, certiorari denied 78 S.Ct. 539, 355 U.S. 953, 2 L.Ed.2d 530. Labor And Employment ☞ 2354

That some complaining Government contractors had standing, under Fulbright Amendment to subsec. (b) of this section, to seek review of Secretary of Labor's determination of minimum wages conferred no standing on other contractors, and district court must decide which contractors have standing to complain. Mitchell v. Covington Mills, Inc., C.A.D.C.1955, 229 F.2d 506, 97 U.S.App.D.C. 165, certiorari denied 76 S.Ct. 546, 350 U.S. 1002, 100 L.Ed. 865, rehearing denied 76 S.Ct. 787, 351 U.S. 934, 100 L.Ed. 1462. Labor And Employment ☞ 2355

Electric companies, which paid minimum wages equal to or greater than those prescribed by Secretary of Labor in his minimum wage determination for motors and generators industry, and whose only allegation of injury was that general level of wages in industry would rise as result of minimum wage determination and that they would be forced to compete for labor in higher cost market, were not adversely affected or aggrieved by minimum wage determination and had no standing to bring actions for review of determination. Baldor Elec. Co. v. Wirtz, D.C.D.C.1964, 228 F.Supp. 210. Labor And Employment ☞ 2355

10. —— Interested persons, persons entitled to judicial review

Under Fulbright Amendment to this section, providing that any interested person has right of judicial review of any legal question which might otherwise be raised, the standard by which persons are entitled to sue is changed from the "legal wrong" criterion to the "any interested person" criterion and the right to judicial review of any legal question is established once a dispute arises under a Government contract covered or alleged to be covered by sections 35 to 45 of this title. George v. Mitchell, C.A.D.C.1960, 282 F.2d 486, 108 U.S.App.D.C. 324. Labor And Employment ☞ 2355

Losing bidder was "interested person" entitled to contest award of government contract. City Chemical Corp. v. Shreffler, S.D.N.Y.1971, 333 F.Supp. 46. United States ☞ 64.60(2)

11. Intervention

Fact that amendment to section 35 et seq. of this title requiring seller to agree to pay employees engaged in producing goods sold to United States not less than minimum wage determined by Secretary of Labor, which grants persons aggrieved by such determinations judicial review, makes no reference to intervention in judicial proceeding does not preclude intervention by persons who would be aggrieved if the determinations were set aside, but amendment only creates right of action which brings case into court and once there case is governed by principles which control all litigation. Textile Workers Union of America, CIO v. Allendale Co., C.A.D.C.1955, 226 F.2d 765, 96 U.S.App.D.C. 401. Federal Civil Procedure ☞ 315

12. Issues reviewable

Where challenge to decisions made by government procurement officers is leveled against administrative action peculiarly within competence of procurement authorities, judicial review is unavailable. Steuart Petroleum Co. v. U.S., D.C.D.C. 1977, 438 F.Supp. 527.   United States ⬦ 55

13. Admissibility of evidence

Under this section making applicable to wage determinations under sections 35 to 45 of this title, the Administrative Procedure Act [repealed], former section 1001 et seq. of Title 5 [now covered by sections 701 to 706 of Title 5], admission of wage tables compiled by Secretary of Labor from confidential replies without production of underlying data to protesting industry members failed to accord right of rebuttal and cross-examination prescribed by Congress. Wirtz v. Baldor Elec. Co., C.A.D.C.1963, 337 F.2d 518, 119 U.S.App.D.C. 122.   Administrative Law And Procedure ⬦ 355; Labor And Employment ⬦ 2348

§ 43b. Manufacturers and regular dealers

(a) The Secretary of Labor may prescribe in regulations the standards for determining whether a contractor is a manufacturer of or a regular dealer in materials, supplies, articles, or equipment to be manufactured or used in the performance of a contract entered into by any executive department, independent establishment, or other agency or instrumentality of the United States, or by the District of Columbia, or by any corporation all the stock of which is beneficially owned by the United States, for the manufacture or furnishing of materials, supplies, articles, and equipment.

(b) Any interested person shall have the right of judicial review of any legal question regarding the interpretation of the terms "regular dealer" and "manufacturer", as defined pursuant to subsection (a) of this section.

(June 30, 1936, c. 881, § 11, as added Oct. 13, 1994, Pub.L. 103–355, Title VII, § 7201(4), 108 Stat. 3378, and amended Feb. 10, 1996, Pub.L. 104–106, Div. D, Title XLIII, § 4321(f)(1)(A), 110 Stat. 675.)

HISTORICAL AND STATUTORY NOTES

Revision Notes and Legislative Reports
1994   Acts. Senate Report Nos. 103–258 and 103–259, and House Conference Report No. 103–712, see 1994 U.S. Code Cong. and Adm. News, p. 2561.

1996 Acts. House Conference Report No. 104–450, see 1996 U.S. Code Cong. and Adm. News, p. 238.

Amendments
1996 Amendments. Pub.L. 104–106, § 4321(f)(1)(A), made technical changes which, for purposes of codification, required no further changes in text.

Effective and Applicability Provisions
1994 Acts. Section effective Oct. 13, 1994, except as otherwise provided, see section 10001 of Pub.L. 103–355, set out as a note under section 251 of this title.

Prior Provisions
A prior section 11 of act June 30, 1936, was renumbered section 12, and is classified to section 44 of this title.

Another prior section 11 of act June 30, 1936, was renumbered section 13, and is classified to section 45 of this title.

CROSS REFERENCES

Construction, repair, alteration, furnishing and equipping of Naval vessels, see 10 USCA § 7299.

LIBRARY REFERENCES

American Digest System
United States ☞75(1).
Key Number System Topic No. 393.

Research References

Treatises and Practice Aids
West's Federal Administrative Practice § 2094, Government Contract Procurement for Disadvantaged Businesses--Product Supply Contracts.

WESTLAW ELECTRONIC RESEARCH
See Westlaw guide following the Explanation pages of this volume.

§ 44. Separability of Walsh–Healey provisions

If any provision of sections 35 to 45 of this title, or the application thereof to any persons or circumstances, is held invalid, the remainder of said sections, and the application of such provisions to other persons or circumstances, shall not be affected thereby.

(June 30, 1936, c. 881, § 12, formerly § 10, 49 Stat. 2039; renumbered § 11, June 30, 1952, c. 530, Title III, § 301, 66 Stat. 308; renumbered § 12, Feb. 10, 1996, Pub.L. 104–106, Div. D, Title XLIII, § 4321(f)(1)(B), 110 Stat. 675.)

HISTORICAL AND STATUTORY NOTES

Revision Notes and Legislative Reports
1996 Acts. House Conference Report No. 104–450, see 1996 U.S. Code Cong. and Adm. News, p. 238.

Prior Provisions
A prior section 12 of act June 30, 1936, was renumbered section 13, and is classified to section 45 of this title.

Another prior section 12 of act June 30, 1936, was renumbered section 14, and is set out as a Short Title note under section 35 of this title.

CROSS REFERENCES

Construction, repair, alteration, furnishing and equipping of Naval vessels, see 10 USCA § 7299.

WESTLAW ELECTRONIC RESEARCH
See Westlaw guide following the Explanation pages of this volume.

§ 45. Effective date of Walsh–Healey provisions; exception as to representations with respect to minimum wages

Sections 35 to 45 of this title shall apply to all contracts entered into pursuant to invitations for bids issued on or after ninety days from June 30, 1936: *Provided, however,* That the provisions requiring the inclusion of representations with respect to minimum wages shall apply only to purchases or contracts relating to such industries as have been the subject matter of a determination by the Secretary of Labor.

(June 30, 1936, c. 881, § 13, formerly § 11, 49 Stat. 2039; renumbered § 12, June 30, 1952, c. 530, Title III, § 301, 66 Stat. 308; renumbered § 13, Feb. 10, 1996, Pub.L. 104–106, Div. D, Title XLIII, § 4321(f)(1)(B), 110 Stat. 675.)

HISTORICAL AND STATUTORY NOTES

Revision Notes and Legislative Reports
1996 Acts. House Conference Report No. 104–450, see 1996 U.S. Code Cong. and Adm. News, p. 238.

CROSS REFERENCES

Applicability to Postal Service, see 39 USCA § 410.
Construction, repair, alteration, furnishing and equipping of Naval vessels, see 10 USCA § 7299.

LIBRARY REFERENCES

Corpus Juris Secundum
CJS Labor Relations § 1129, Work Under Public Contracts or on Public Works-- Federal Statutes.
CJS Labor Relations § 1272, Quasi-Legislative Powers; Promulgation of Rules and Regulations--United States Department of Labor.
CJS Labor Relations § 1292, Walsh-Healey Public Contracts Act.
CJS Labor Relations § 1302, Under Federal Law.

Research References

ALR Library
185 ALR, Fed. 253, Validity, Construction, and Operation of Buy American Act (41 U.S.C.A. § 10a-10d).
80 ALR, Fed. 246, Employee Training Time as Exempt from Minimum Wage and Overtime Requirements of Fair Labor Standards Act.
31 ALR, Fed. 348, What Limitation Periods Apply Under 28 U.S.C.A. § 2415 to Government Suits.
3 ALR 2nd 1097, Portal-to-Portal Act.
151 ALR 1481, Judicial Decisions Involving Rationing.
107 ALR 705, Servant's Right to Compensation for Extra Work or Overtime.
82 ALR 808, Conflict Between Federal and State Statutes of Limitations.
Encyclopedias
Am. Jur. 2d Public Works and Contracts § 216, The Walsh-Healey Act.
Am. Jur. 2d Public Works and Contracts § 224, The Walsh-Healey Act.
Am. Jur. 2d Public Works and Contracts § 237, Contract Work Hours Standards Act.
Am. Jur. 2d Public Works and Contracts § 239, Application of Act--Walsh-Healey Act.
70 Am. Jur. Proof of Facts 3d 97, Proof That a Government Agency Was Liable for Improperly Granting a Bid Award to a Bid Applicant.
14 Am. Jur. Trials 437, Representing the Government Contractor.
Forms
Am. Jur. Pl. & Pr. Forms Public Works & Contracts § 119, Decision--Of Administrator--Department of Labor--Upholding Decision of Administrative Law Judge--Denying Relief from Imposition of Ineligible List Sanction.
Am. Jur. Pl. & Pr. Forms Public Works & Contracts § 121, Complaint in Federal Court--By United States--To Recover Liquidated Damages--Violations of Walsh-Healey Act.

Am. Jur. Pl. & Pr. Forms Public Works & Contracts § 123, Complaint in Federal Court--By U.S. Department of Labor--Against Contractor--Violations of Walsh-Healey Act.

Am. Jur. Pl. & Pr. Forms Public Works & Contracts § 124, Complaint in Federal Court--By U.S. Department of Labor--Against Contractor--Violations of Walsh-Healey Act--Another Form.

Am. Jur. Pl. & Pr. Forms Public Works & Contracts § 125, Answer--By Contractor--To Complaint by U.S. Department of Labor--Denying Violations of Walsh-Healey Act.

Am. Jur. Pl. & Pr. Forms Public Works & Contracts § 129, Answer--By Contractor--Contracts Failed to Contain Representations and Stipulations Required by Walsh-Healey Act.

Am. Jur. Pl. & Pr. Forms Public Works & Contracts § 133, Petition in Federal Court--For Review of Minimum Wage Determination Under Walsh-Healey Act.

Am. Jur. Pl. & Pr. Forms Public Works & Contracts § 134, Motion--For Temporary Injunction--To Stay Execution of Minimum Wage Determination Under Walsh-Healey Act.

Am. Jur. Pl. & Pr. Forms Public Works & Contracts § 136, Findings of Fact and Conclusions of Law--By Federal Court--Favoring Review of Minimum Wage Determination Under Walsh-Healey Act.

Am. Jur. Pl. & Pr. Forms Public Works & Contracts § 137, Order--Granting Stay of Minimum Wage Determination Under Walsh-Healey Act--Pending Review.

Federal Procedural Forms § 34:349, Introduction.

Federal Procedural Forms § 34:359, Reports of Breach or Violation of the Walsh-Healey Act.

Federal Procedural Forms § 34:388, Complaint--Against Contractor--Failure to Pay Employees Proper Wages [41 U.S.C.A. §§ 35 to 45; 41 C.F.R. § 50-203.2].

Federal Procedural Forms § 34:389, Complaint--Against Contractor--Failure to Pay Employees Proper Wages--Another Form [41 U.S.C.A. §§ 35 to 45; 41 C.F.R. § 50-203.2].

Federal Procedural Forms § 34:390, Answer--To Complaint--Denying Violation of Walsh-Healey Act [41 U.S.C.A. §§ 35 to 45; 41 C.F.R. § 50-203.2].

Federal Procedural Forms § 34:392, Complaint--To Recover Liquidated Damages Under Walsh-Healey Act [41 U.S.C.A. §§ 35 to 45; Fed. R. Civ. P. Rule 8].

Federal Procedural Forms § 34:393, Complaint--For Review of Minimum Wage Determination Under Walsh-Healey Act [5 U.S.C.A. §§ 701 to 706; 28 U.S.C.A. §§ 2201, 2202; 41 U.S.C.A. §§ 35 to 45; Fed. R. Civ. P. Rule 8(A), 57, 65].

Federal Procedural Forms § 34:394, Complaint--By Deputy Solicitor--Department of Labor--Violation of Walsh-Healey Act.

Federal Procedural Forms § 34:395, Complaint--By U.S. Department of Labor--Against Contractor--Violations of Walsh-Healey Act.

Federal Procedural Forms § 34:397, Order--For Stay of Judicial Proceedings Pending Administrative Proceedings [41 U.S.C.A. §§ 35 to 45; Fed. R. Civ. P. Rule 8].

Federal Procedural Forms § 34:398, Motion--For Preliminary Injunction--To Stay Execution of Minimum Wage Determination Under Walsh-Healey Act [5 U.S.C.A. §§ 701 to 706; 41 U.S.C.A. §§ 35 to 45; Fed. R. Civ. P. Rules 7(B), 65(a)].

Federal Procedural Forms § 34:399, Order--Granting Stay of Minimum Wage Determination Under Walsh-Healey Act--Pending Judicial Review [5 U.S.C.A. §§ 701 to 706; 41 U.S.C.A. §§ 35 to 45; Fed. R. Civ. P. Rule 65(a)].

Federal Procedural Forms § 34:402, Answer--By Contractor--To Complaint by U.S. Department of Labor--Denying Violations of Walsh-Healey Act.

Federal Procedural Forms § 34:403, Answer--By Contractor--Contracts Failed to Contain Representations and Stipulations Required by Walsh-Healey Act.

Federal Procedural Forms § 34:406, Order--Judicial Review of Agency Order--Exclusive Seller Not Regular Dealer Under Walsh-Healey Act [41 U.S.C.A. §§ 35 to 45; 48 C.F.R. §§ 22.601, 22.606-2; 41 C.F.R. § 50-206.53(a)].

Nichols Cyclopedia of Legal Forms Annotated § 7:2518, Supply Contract with United States--General Provisions.

24A West's Legal Forms § 4.7, Prevailing Wage Laws.

Treatises and Practice Aids

Callmann on Unfair Compet., TMs, & Monopolies § 3:9, Private Interests Influencing Government Action--Public Officials Taking Anticompetitive Action.

Federal Procedure, Lawyers Edition § 39:139, Introduction.

Federal Procedure, Lawyers Edition § 39:195, Institution of Enforcement Action.

Federal Procedure, Lawyers Edition § 39:425, Nonconsideration or Dismissal of Protests.

WESTLAW ELECTRONIC RESEARCH

See Westlaw guide following the Explanation pages of this volume.

§ 46. Committee for Purchase From People Who Are Blind or Severely Disabled

(a) Establishment

There is established a committee to be known as the Committee for Purchase From People Who Are Blind or Severely Disabled (hereafter in sections 46 to 48c of this title referred to as the "Committee"). The Committee shall be composed of fifteen members appointed as follows:

(1) The President shall appoint as a member one officer or employee from each of the following: The Department of Agriculture, the Department of Defense, the Department of the Army, the Department of the Navy, the Department of the Air Force, the Department of Health and Human Services, the Department of Commerce, the Department of Veterans Affairs, the Department of Justice, the Department of Labor, and the General Services Administration. The head of each such department and agency shall nominate one officer or employee in his department or agency for appointment under this paragraph.

(2)(A) The President shall appoint one member from persons who are not officers or employees of the Government and who are conversant with the problems incident to the employment of the blind.

(B) The President shall appoint one member from persons who are not officers or employees of the Government and who are conversant with the problems incident to the employment of other severely handicapped individuals.

(C) The President shall appoint one member from persons who are not officers or employees of the Government and who represent blind individuals employed in qualified nonprofit agencies for the blind.

(D) The President shall appoint one member from persons who are not officers or employees of the Government and who represent severely handicapped individuals (other than blind individuals) employed in qualified nonprofit agencies for other severely handicapped individuals.

(b) Vacancy

A vacancy in the membership of the Committee shall be filled in the manner in which the original appointment was made.

(c) Chairman

The members of the Committee shall elect one of their number to be Chairman.

(d) Terms

(1) Except as provided in paragraphs (2), (3), and (4), members appointed under paragraph (2) of subsection (a) of this section shall be appointed for terms of five years. Any member appointed to the Committee under such paragraph may be reappointed to the Committee if he meets the qualifications prescribed by that paragraph.

(2) Of the members first appointed under paragraph (2) of subsection (a) of this section—

(A) one shall be appointed for a term of three years,

(B) one shall be appointed for a term of four years, and

(C) one shall be appointed for a term of five years,

as designated by the President at the time of appointment.

(3) Any member appointed under paragraph (2) of subsection (a) of this section to fill a vacancy occurring prior to the expiration of the term for which his predecessor was appointed shall be appointed only for the remainder of such term. A member appointed under such paragraph may serve after the expiration of his term until his successor has taken office.

(4) The member first appointed under paragraph (2)(B) of subsection (a) of this section shall be appointed for a term of three years.

(e) Pay and travel expenses

(1) Except as provided in paragraph (2), members of the Committee shall each be entitled to receive the daily equivalent of the annual rate of basic pay in effect for grade GS–18 of the General Schedule for each day (including traveltime) during which they are engaged in the actual performance of services for the Committee.

(2) Members of the Committee who are officers or employees of the Government shall receive no additional pay on account of their service on the Committee.

(3) While away from their homes or regular places of business in the performance of services for the Committee, members of the Committee shall be allowed travel expenses, including per diem in lieu of subsistence, in the same manner as persons employed intermittently in the Government service are allowed expenses under section 5703(b) of Title 5.

(f) Staff

(1) Subject to such rules as may be adopted by the Committee, the Chairman may appoint and fix the pay of such personnel as the Committee determines are necessary to assist it in carrying out its duties and powers under sections 46 to 48c of this title.

(2) Upon request of the Committee, the head of any entity of the Government is authorized to detail, on a reimbursable basis, any of the personnel of such entity to the Committee to assist it in carrying out its duties and powers under sections 46 to 48c of this title.

(3) The staff of the Committee appointed under paragraph (1) shall be appointed subject to the provisions of Title 5 governing appointments in the competitive service, and shall be paid in accordance with the provisions of chapter 51 and subchapter III of chapter 53 of such Title 5 relating to classification and General Schedule pay rates.

(g) Obtaining official data

The Committee may secure directly from any entity of the Government information necessary to enable it to carry out sections 46 to 48c of this title. Upon request of the Chairman of the Committee, the head of such Government entity shall furnish such information to the Committee.

(h) Administrative support services

The Administrator of General Services shall provide to the Committee on a reimbursable basis such administrative support services as the Committee may request.

(i) Annual report

The Committee shall, not later than December 31 of each year, transmit to the President and to the Congress a report which shall include the names of the Committee members serving in the preceding fiscal year, the dates of Committee meetings in that year, a description of its activities under sections 46 to 48c of this title in that year, and any recommendations for changes in sections 46 to 48c of this title which it determines are necessary.

(June 25, 1938, c. 697, § 1, 52 Stat. 1196; June 23, 1971, Pub.L. 92–28, § 1, 85 Stat. 77; July 25, 1974, Pub.L. 93–358, § 1(1), (2), 88 Stat. 392, 393; Apr. 21, 1976, Pub.L. 94–273, § 8(2), 90 Stat. 378; Oct. 17, 1979, Pub.L. 96–88, Title V, § 509(b), 93 Stat. 695; June 13, 1991, Pub.L. 102–54, § 13(p), 105 Stat. 278; Oct. 29, 1992, Pub.L. 102–569, Title IX, § 911(a), 106 Stat. 4486; Aug. 11, 1993, Pub.L. 103–73, Title III, § 301, 107 Stat. 736.)

HISTORICAL AND STATUTORY NOTES

Revision Notes and Legislative Reports

1971 Acts. House Report No. 92–228, see 1971 U.S.Code Cong. and Adm.News, p. 1079.

1974 Acts. Senate Report No. 93–908, see 1974 U.S.Code Cong. and Adm.News, p. 3940.

1976 Acts. House Report No. 94–1000, see 1976 U.S.Code Cong. and Adm.News, p. 690.

1992 Acts. Senate Report No. 102–357 and House Conference Report No. 102–973, see 1992 U.S. Code Cong. and Adm. News, p. 3712.

References in Text

The General Schedule, referred to in subsecs. (e)(1) and (f)(3), is set out under section 5332 of Title 5, Government Organization and Employees.

Section 5703 of Title 5, referred to in subsec. (e)(3), was amended generally by Pub.L. 94–22, § 4, May 19, 1975, 89 Stat. 85, and as so amended does not contain a subsec. (b).

Amendments

1993 Amendments. Subsec. (a). Pub.L. 103–73, § 301, substituted "Committee for Purchase From People Who Are Blind or Severely Disabled" for "Committee for Purchase From People Who Are Blind and Severely Disabled".

1992 Amendments. Catchline. Pub.L. 102–569, Title IX, § 911(a), substituted "From People Who Are Blind and Severely Disabled" for "from the Blind and Other Severely Handicapped".

Subsec. (a). Pub.L. 102–569, Title IX, § 911(a), substituted "From People Who Are Blind and Severely Disabled" for "from the Blind and Other Severely Handicapped".

1991 Amendments. Subsec. (a)(1). Pub.L. 102–54 substituted "Department

of Veterans Affairs" for "Veterans' Administration".

1976 Amendments. Subsec. (i). Pub.L. 94–273 substituted "December 31" for "September 30".

1974 Amendments. Subsec. (a). Pub.L. 93–358, § 1(1)(A), (B), substituted "Committee for Purchase from the Blind and Other Severely Handicapped" for "Committee for Purchase of Products and Services of the Blind and Other Severely Handicapped" and "fifteen" for "fourteen" in provisions preceding par. (1).

Subsec. (a)(2). Pub.L. 93–358, § 1(1)(C), (D), struck out "and other severely handicapped individuals" following "employment of the blind" in subpar. (A), added subpar. (B), and redesignated former subpars. (B) and (C) as (C) and (D), respectively.

Subsec. (d)(1). Pub.L. 93–358, § 1(2)(A), substituted "paragraphs (2), (3), and (4)" for "paragraphs (2) and (3)".

Subsec. (d)(4). Pub.L. 93–358, § 1(2)(B), added par. (4).

1971 Amendments. Pub.L. 92–28, in substituting subsecs. (a) to (i) for former paragraph, among other changes: renamed Committee on Purchases of Blind-made Products as Committee for Purchase of Products and Services of the Blind and Other Severely Handicapped; increased membership of Committee from seven to fourteen members; provided for appointments from Departments of Defense, Air Force, Health, Education, and Welfare, Justice, and Labor and from Veterans' Administration and General Services Administration; eliminated appointments from Treasury Department and Department of Interior; substituted appointment from Department of the Army for appointment from War Department; required one appointee to be also conversant with problems incident to employment of other severely handicapped individuals; substituted requirement that such appointment be from persons not officers or employees of the Government for requirement that appointee be a private citizen; reenacted provision for Presidential appointment; substituted subsec. (e) pay and travel expenses provisions for former requirement for service of Committee members without additional compensation; incorporated in subsec. (c) provision for selection of a Chairman, substituting "election" for "designation"; and added provisions incorporated in subsecs. (a)(1) (for nomination by head of each department and agency of one officer or employee of the department or agency for appointment under par. (1), (a)(2)(B), (C), (b), (d), and (f) to (i).

Effective and Applicability Provisions
1971 Acts. Section 2 of Pub.L. 92–28 provided that: "The amendment made by the first section of this Act [amending sections 46 to 48 and enacting sections 48a to 48c of this title] shall take effect on the first day of the first month which begins more than thirty days after the date of enactment of this Act [June 23, 1971]."

Termination of Reporting Requirements
For termination, effective May 15, 2000, of provisions in subsec. (i) of this section relating to the requirement that the Committee transmit a report to Congress each year, see Pub.L. 104–66, § 3003, as amended, set out as a note under 31 U.S.C.A. § 1113, and page 199 of House Document No. 103–7.

Change of Name
"Department of Health and Human Services" was substituted for "Department of Health, Education, and Welfare" in subsec. (a)(1) pursuant to section 509(b) of Pub.L. 96–88 which is classified to section 3508(b) of Title 20, Education.

Short Title
1938 Acts. Section 7 of Act June 25, 1938, as added Pub.L. 103–355, Title X, § 10005(f)(6), Oct. 13, 1994, 108 Stat. 3409, provided that: "This Act [enacting this section and sections 47 through 48c of this title] may be cited as the 'Javits-Wagner-O'Day Act'."

Contracting with Employers of Persons with Disabilities
Pub.L. 109–364, Div. A, Title VIII, § 856(a), (d), Oct. 17, 2006, 120 Stat. 2347, 2349, provided that:

"(a) **Inapplicability of certain laws.**—

"(1) **Inapplicability of the Randolph-Sheppard Act to contracts and subcontracts for military dining facility support services covered by Javits-Wagner-O'Day Act.**—The Randolph-Sheppard Act (20 U.S.C. 107 et seq.) does not apply to full food services, mess attendant services, or services supporting the operation of a military dining facility that, as of the date of the enactment of this Act, were services on the procurement list established under section 2 of the Javits-Wagner-O'Day Act (41 U.S.C. 47).

"(2) **Inapplicability of the Javits-Wagner-O'Day Act to contracts for the operation of a military dining facility.**—(A) The Javits-Wagner-O'Day Act (41 U.S.C. 46 et seq.) does not apply at the prime contract level to any contract entered into by the Department of Defense as of the date of the enactment of this Act with a State licensing agency under the Randolph-Sheppard Act (20 U.S.C. 107 et seq.) for the operation of a military dining facility.

"(B) The Javits-Wagner-O'Day Act shall apply to any subcontract entered into by a Department of Defense contractor for full food services, mess attendant services, and other services supporting the operation of a military dining facility.

"(3) [Omitted]"

"(d) **Definitions.**—In this section [this note]:

"(1) The term 'State licensing agency' means any agency designated by the Secretary of Education under section 2(a)(5) of the Randolph-Sheppard Act (20 U.S.C. 107a(a)(5)).

"(2) The term 'military dining facility' means a facility owned, operated, leased, or wholly controlled by the Department of Defense and used to provide dining services to members of the Armed Forces, including a cafeteria, military mess hall, military troop dining facility, or any similar dining facility operated for the purpose of providing meals to members of the Armed Forces."

Statement of Policy; Report
Pub.L. 109–163, Div. A, Title VIII, § 848(b), (c), Jan. 6, 2006, 119 Stat. 3395, provided that:

"**(b) Statement of policy.**—The Secretary of Defense, the Secretary of Education, and the Chairman of the Committee for Purchase From People Who Are Blind or Severely Disabled shall jointly issue a statement of policy related to the implementation of the Randolph–Sheppard Act (20 U.S.C. 107 et seq.) and the Javits–Wagner–O'Day Act (41 U.S.C. 48) [Act June 25, 1938, c. 697, 52 Stat. 1196, which enacted this section; see Tables for complete classification] within the Department of Defense and the Department of Education. The joint statement of policy shall specifically address the application of those Acts to both operation and management of all or any part of a military mess hall, military troop dining facility, or any similar dining facility operated for the purpose of providing meals to members of the Armed Forces, and shall take into account and address, to the extent practicable, the positions acceptable to persons representing programs implemented under each Act.

"**(c) Report.**—Not later than April 1, 2006, the Secretary of Defense, the Secretary of Education, and the Chairman of the Committee for Purchase From People Who Are Blind or Severely Disabled shall submit to the Committees on Armed Services of the Senate and the House of Representatives, the Committee on Health, Education, Labor and Pensions of the Senate, and the Committee on Education and the Workforce of the House of Representatives a report describing the joint statement of policy issued under subsection (b) [of this note], with such findings and recommendations as the Secretaries consider appropriate."

LIBRARY REFERENCES

American Digest System
> United States ⚷64.10.
> Key Number System Topic No. 393.

Research References

ALR Library
> 197 ALR, Fed. 435, Construction and Application of Historically Underutilized Business Zone (Hubzone) Act, Pub. L. No. 105-135, §§ 601 to 607, 111 Stat. 2592, 2627-36.
> 160 ALR, Fed. 483, Construction and Application of Federal Advisory Committee Act (5 U.S.C.A. App. 2 §§ 1-15).

Treatises and Practice Aids
> West's Federal Administrative Practice § 606, Procurement Agencies.
> West's Federal Administrative Practice § 2158, Government Contract Procurement for Businesses of Service-Disabled Veterans.

WESTLAW ELECTRONIC RESEARCH

See Westlaw guide following the Explanation pages of this volume.

Notes of Decisions

Construction with other laws 1
___

1. Construction with other laws
   As more specific statute dealing explicitly with issue of contracting priority for operation of cafeterias on federal property, Randolph–Sheppard Act, authorizing Secretary of Department of Education to secure operation of cafeterias on federal property by blind licensees, was controlling as to granting of contract for military base's mess hall services, rather than Javits Wagner O'Day Act, which was general federal procurement statute favoring commodities and services produced by nonprofit agencies for the blind and disabled. NISH v. Cohen, C.A.4 (Va.) 2001, 247 F.3d 197. United States ⚷ 57

§ 47.   Duties and powers of the Committee

(a)   Procurement list: publication in Federal Register;   additions and removals

(1) The Committee shall establish and publish in the Federal Register a list (hereafter in sections 46 to 48c of this title referred to as the "procurement list") of—

(A) the commodities produced by any qualified nonprofit agency for the blind or by any qualified nonprofit agency for other severely handicapped, and

(B) the services provided by any such agency,

which the Committee determines are suitable for procurement by the Government pursuant to sections 46 to 48c of this title.   Such list shall be established and published in the Federal Register before the expiration of the thirty-day period beginning on Aug. 1, 1971, and shall initially consist of the commodities contained, on such date, in the schedule of blind-made products issued by the former Committee on Purchases of Blind-Made Products under its regulations.

(2) The Committee may, by rule made in accordance with the requirements of subsections (b), (c), (d), and (e) of section 553 of Title 5, add to and remove from the procurement list commodities so produced and services so provided.

(b)   Fair market price;   price revisions

The Committee shall determine the fair market price of commodities and services which are contained on the procurement list and which are offered for sale to the Government by any qualified nonprofit agency for the blind or any such agency for other severely handicapped.   The Committee shall also revise from time to time in accordance with changing market conditions its price determinations with respect to such commodities and services.

(c)   Central nonprofit agency;   designation

The Committee shall designate a central nonprofit agency or agencies to facilitate the distribution (by direct allocation, subcontract, or any other means) of orders of the Government for commodities and services on the procurement list among qualified nonprofit agencies for the blind or such agencies for other severely handicapped.

(d)   Rules and regulations;   blind-made products, priority

(1) The Committee may make rules and regulations regarding (A) specifications for commodities and services on the procurement list,

(B) the time of their delivery, and (C) such other matters as may be necessary to carry out the purposes of sections 46 to 48c of this title.

(2) The Committee shall prescribe regulations providing that—

    (A) in the purchase by the Government of commodities produced and offered for sale by qualified nonprofit agencies for the blind or such agencies for other severely handicapped, priority shall be accorded to commodities produced and offered for sale by qualified nonprofit agencies for the blind, and

    (B) in the purchase by the Government of services offered by nonprofit agencies for the blind or such agencies for other severely handicapped, priority shall, until the end of the calendar year ending December 31, 1976, be accorded to services offered for sale by qualified nonprofit agencies for the blind.

(e) Problems and production methods; study and evaluation

The Committee shall make a continuing study and evaluation of its activities under sections 46 to 48c of this title for the purpose of assuring effective and efficient administration of sections 46 to 48c of this title. The Committee may study (on its own or in cooperation with other public or nonprofit private agencies) (1) problems related to the employment of the blind and of other severely handicapped individuals, and (2) the development and adaptation of production methods which would enable a greater utilization of the blind and other severely handicapped individuals.

(June 25, 1938, c. 697, § 2, 52 Stat. 1196; June 23, 1971, Pub.L. 92–28, § 1, 85 Stat. 79.)

HISTORICAL AND STATUTORY NOTES

Revision Notes and Legislative Reports
1971 Acts. House Report No. 92–228, see 1971 U.S.Code Cong. and Adm.News, p. 1079.

Amendments
1971 Amendments. Pub.L. 92–28, in substituting subsecs. (a) to (e) for former paragraph, among other changes: extended the provisions to cover commodities and services of agencies for the blind and other severely handicapped, previously limited to brooms and mops and other suitable commodities manufactured by agencies for the blind; added provisions incorporated in subsecs. (a) and (e); incorporated in subsec. (b) provisions for determination of fair market price and price revisions; incorporated in subsec. (c) provisions for designation of a central nonprofit agency, providing for distribution by direct allocation, subcontract, or

any other means; incorporated existing provisions in subsec. (d)(1), adding par. (2) thereof; and deleted provision that no change in price shall become effective prior to expiration of fifteen days from date on which such change is made by the Committee.

Effective and Applicability Provisions
1971 Acts. Amendment by Pub.L. 92–28 effective Aug. 1, 1971, see section 2 of Pub.L. 92–28, set out as a note under section 46 of this title.

Termination of Reporting Requirements
For termination effective May 15, 2000 of provisions in subsec. (i) of this section relating to the requirement that the Committee transmit a report to Congress each year, see section 3003 of Pub.L. 104–66, as amended, set out as a note under section 31 U.S.C.A. § 1113 and page 199 of House Document No. 103–7.

CROSS REFERENCES

Treatment under subcontracting plan of purchases from qualified nonprofit agencies for blind or severely disabled, see 10 USCA § 2410d.

CODE OF FEDERAL REGULATIONS

Committee for Purchase from Blind and Other Severely Handicapped, see 41 CFR § 51–1.1 et seq.

LIBRARY REFERENCES

American Digest System
United States ⬡64.10.
Key Number System Topic No. 393.

WESTLAW ELECTRONIC RESEARCH

See Westlaw guide following the Explanation pages of this volume.

Notes of Decisions

Persons entitled to maintain action   2
Procurement list   3
Suitable commodities and services   1

_____

1. Suitable commodities and services

Record was insufficient to support conclusion, if any, of committee for purchase from the blind and other severely handicapped that it could add computer tabulating machine paper to list of commodities to be procured from workshop for the blind even if workshop could not produce paper at fair market price; former supplier presented evidence that workshop could produce paper only at a loss even if it sold paper at calculated fair market price.   McGregor Printing Corp. v. Kemp, C.A.D.C.1994, 20 F.3d 1188, 305 U.S.App.D.C. 324.   United States ⬡ 64.10

The Committee acting pursuant to this section and sections 46 and 48 of this title, did not act arbitrarily or capriciously in determining that involved floor wax product was "suitable," that the blind workshop was capable of producing acceptable floor wax, and that the adverse impact on competitive bidder was not so serious as to preclude the Committee's action of adding floor wax to procurement list for mandatory government purchase from qualified blind workshops. Barrier Industries, Inc. v. Eckard, C.A.D.C.1978, 584 F.2d 1074, 190 U.S.App.D.C. 93.   United States ⬡ 64.10

2. Persons entitled to maintain action

Corporations, which for past few years had supplied federal government with ball point pens, had standing to challenge allegedly illegal actions of Committee on Purchases of Blind–Made Products and General Services Administration in adding ball point pens and refills to Schedule of Blind–Made Products and in issuing a letter of commitment to National Industries for the Blind which guaranteed purchases from it of 70% of estimated annual requirements for ball point pens and refills.   Ballerina Pen Co. v. Kunzig, C.A.D.C.1970, 433 F.2d 1204, 140 U.S.App.D.C. 98, dismissed 91 S.Ct. 1186, 401 U.S. 950, 28 L.Ed.2d 234.   Administrative Law And Procedure ⬡ 668; United States ⬡ 55

3. Procurement list

Under the contracting scheme established by Javits-Wagner-O'Day (JWOD) Act, until a service is placed on the procurement list for qualified nonprofit agencies which employ blind or severely disabled persons, a federal agency may, under various contracting authorities, contract with any provider, including a qualified nonprofit agency for the severely disabled, even before the qualified nonprofit agency becomes a mandatory sole-source for those services; once a service is added to the procurement list, however, an agency must contract with one of the qualified providers.   Brothers Cleaning Service, Inc. v. Chair, Committee for Purchase from People Who are Blind or Severely Disabled, D.D.C.1998, 26 F.Supp.2d 1.   United States ⬡ 64.10

§ 48. Procurement requirements for the Government; nonapplication to prison-made products

If any entity of the Government intends to procure any commodity or service on the procurement list, that entity shall, in accordance with rules and regulations of the Committee, procure such commodity or service, at the price established by the Committee, from a qualified nonprofit agency for the blind or such an agency for other severely handicapped if the commodity or service is available within the period required by that Government entity; except that this section shall not apply with respect to the procurement of any commodity which is available for procurement from an industry established under chapter 307 of Title 18, and which, under section 4124 of such Title 18, is required to be procured from such industry.

(June 25, 1938, c. 697, § 3, 52 Stat. 1196; June 23, 1971, Pub.L. 92–28, § 1, 85 Stat. 80.)

HISTORICAL AND STATUTORY NOTES

Revision Notes and Legislative Reports
1971 Acts. House Report No. 92–228, see 1971 U.S.Code Cong. and Adm.News, p. 1079.

Amendments
1971 Amendments. Pub.L. 92–28 extended provisions to cover any commodity or service on the procurement list from provisions covering brooms and mops and other suitable commodities, excepted the section from application to prison-made products, and deleted provision for nonapplicability of sections 46 to 48 of this title to cases where brooms and mops were available for procurement from any Federal department or agency and procurement therefrom was required under provisions of any law in effect on June 25, 1938, or to cases where brooms and mops were procured outside continental United States.

Effective and Applicability Provisions
1971 Acts. Amendment by Pub.L. 92–28 effective Aug. 1, 1971, see section 2 of Pub.L. 92–28, set out as a note under section 46 of this title.

LIBRARY REFERENCES

American Digest System
United States ☞64.45.
Key Number System Topic No. 393.

Research References

Treatises and Practice Aids
West's Federal Administrative Practice § 606, Procurement Agencies.

WESTLAW ELECTRONIC RESEARCH

See Westlaw guide following the Explanation pages of this volume.

§ 48a. Audit

The Comptroller General of the United States, or any of his duly authorized representatives, shall have access, for the purpose of audit and examination, to any books, documents, papers, and other records of the Committee and of each agency designated by the Committee under section 47(c) of this title. This section shall also apply to any qualified nonprofit agency for the blind and any such agency for other severely handicapped which have sold commodities or services under sections 46 to 48c of this title but only with respect to the books, documents, papers, and other records of such agency which relate to its activities in a fiscal year in which a sale was made under sections 46 to 48c of this title.

(June 25, 1938, c. 697, § 4, as added June 23, 1971, Pub.L. 92–28, § 1, 85 Stat. 81.)

HISTORICAL AND STATUTORY NOTES

Revision Notes and Legislative Reports
1971 Acts. Under authority not contained in existing law, the Comptroller General is authorized to audit and examine the books and other records of the Committee and of each agency designated by the Committee under section 2(c) to distribute orders of the Government. The Comptroller General is also authorized to audit and examine the books and other records of agencies for the blind and

agencies for the other severely handicapped which relate to the activities of such agencies in any fiscal year in which a sale is made under the Act. House Report No. 92–228.

Effective and Applicability Provisions
1971 Acts. Section effective Aug. 1, 1971, see section 2 of Pub.L. 92–28, set out as a note under section 46 of this title.

LIBRARY REFERENCES

American Digest System
United States ⏥44.
Key Number System Topic No. 393.

WESTLAW ELECTRONIC RESEARCH

See Westlaw guide following the Explanation pages of this volume.

§ 48b. Definitions

For purposes of sections 46 to 48c of this title—

(1) The term "blind" refers to an individual or class of individuals whose central visual acuity does not exceed 20/200 in the better eye with correcting lenses or whose visual acuity, if better than 20/200, is accompanied by a limit to the field of vision in the better eye to such a degree that its widest diameter subtends an angle of no greater than 20 degrees.

(2) The terms "other severely handicapped" and "severely handicapped individuals" mean an individual or class of individuals under a physical or mental disability, other than blindness, which (according to criteria established by the Committee after consultation with appropriate entities of the Government and taking into account the views of non-Government entities representing the handicapped) constitutes a substantial handicap to

employment and is of such a nature as to prevent the individual under such disability from currently engaging in normal competitive employment.

(3) The term "qualified nonprofit agency for the blind" means an agency—

  (A) organized under the laws of the United States or of any State, operated in the interest of blind individuals, and the net income of which does not inure in whole or in part to the benefit of any shareholder or other individual;

  (B) which complies with any applicable occupational health and safety standard prescribed by the Secretary of Labor; and

  (C) which in the production of commodities and in the provision of services (whether or not the commodities or services are procured under sections 46 to 48c of this title) during the fiscal year employs blind individuals for not less than 75 per centum of the man-hours of direct labor required for the production or provision of the commodities or services.

(4) The term "qualified nonprofit agency for other severely handicapped" means an agency—

  (A) organized under the laws of the United States or of any State, operated in the interest of severely handicapped individuals who are not blind, and the net income of which does not inure in whole or in part to the benefit of any shareholder or other individual;

  (B) which complies with any applicable occupational health and safety standard prescribed by the Secretary of Labor; and

  (C) which in the production of commodities and in the provision of services (whether or not the commodities or services are procured under sections 46 to 48c of this title) during the fiscal year employs blind or other severely handicapped individuals for not less than 75 per centum of the man-hours of direct labor required for the production or provision of the commodities or services.

(5) The term "direct labor" includes all work required for preparation, processing, and packing of a commodity, or work directly relating to the performance of a service, but not supervision, administration, inspection, or shipping.

(6) The term "fiscal year" means the twelve-month period beginning on October 1 of each year.

(7) The terms "Government" and "entity of the Government" include any entity of the legislative branch or the judicial branch,

any executive agency or military department (as such agency and department are respectively defined by sections 102 and 105 of Title 5), the United States Postal Service, and any nonappropriated fund instrumentality under the jurisdiction of the Armed Forces.

(8) The term "State" includes the District of Columbia, the Commonwealth of Puerto Rico, the Virgin Islands, Guam, American Samoa, and the Trust Territory of the Pacific Islands.

(June 25, 1938, c. 697, § 5, as added June 23, 1971, Pub.L. 92–28, § 1, 85 Stat. 81, and amended July 25, 1974, Pub.L. 93–358, § 1(3), 88 Stat. 393; Apr. 21, 1976, Pub.L. 94–273, § 3(22), 90 Stat. 377.)

HISTORICAL AND STATUTORY NOTES

Revision Notes and Legislative Reports
1971 Acts. This section adds to the Act definitions of certain key terms used in the Act. The standard definition of a blind person is contained in paragraph (1). Paragraph (2) defines severely handicapped individuals to mean individuals or classes of individuals under a physical or mental disability (other than blindness) which (according to criteria established by the Committee after consultation with appropriate Government agencies and after taking into account the views of private agencies representing the handicapped) constitutes a substantial handicap to employment and is of such a nature as to prevent the individual under such disability from engaging in normal competitive employment.

Paragraph (3) establishes three criteria for the definition of a qualified nonprofit agency for the blind. These are (1) incorporation as a nonprofit agency under State or Federal law, (2) compliance with such occupational health and safety standards as may be prescribed by the Secretary of Labor, and (3) specification that 75 percent of the man hours of direct labor on commodities and services of the agency during the fiscal year must be performed by blind persons. As used in this paragraph and paragraph (4), the term "service" does not include any rehabilitative or other training service.

Paragraph (4) establishes similar criteria to define a qualified nonprofit agency for the other severely handicapped, but permits 75 percent of the man hours of direct labor on commodities and services during the fiscal year to be performed by blind or other severely handicapped individuals.

The requirement of 75 percent of the man hours of direct labor by blind persons in the production of commodities is in the regulations, and the existing law has been administered on this basis since the beginning of its operation in 1938. It is necessary to specify this requirement in the amended law for qualified nonprofit agencies for the blind and to also state a requirement for qualified nonprofit agencies for the other severely handicapped to assure that this preferential procurement program is, in fact, used to provide employment opportunities for blind and other severely handicapped individuals who are incapable of engaging in regular competitive employment. As has been the practice, the 75 percent criterion is to be applied during the fiscal year in which the commodities or services are procured under the Act. The percentage of blind or other severely handicapped labor on a given commodity may be slightly higher or lower in any given fiscal year owing to a variety of factors, including training of personnel for the manufacture of a new product or absence of blind or other severely handicapped workers on account of illness. However, the overall average of man hours of direct labor during the entire fiscal year should meet the 75 percent requirement.

Paragraph (8) defines the terms "Government" and "entity of the Government" to include the United States Postal Service and nonappropriated fund instrumentalities under the jurisdiction of the Armed Forces.

Paragraph (9) defines the term "State" to include the District of Columbia, the Commonwealth of Puerto Rico, the Virgin Islands, Guam, American Samoa, and the Trust Territory of the Pacific Islands. House Report No. 92–228.

1974 Acts. Senate Report No. 93–908, see 1974 U.S.Code Cong. and Adm.News, p. 3940.

1976 Acts. House Report No. 94–1000, see 1976 U.S.Code Cong. and Adm.News, p. 690.

Amendments

1976 Amendments. Par. (6). Pub.L. 94–273 substituted "October" for "July".

1974 Amendments. Pars. (5) to (8). Pub.L. 93–358 added par. (5), redesignated former pars. (7), (8), and (9) as pars.

(6), (7), and (8), respectively, and struck out former par. (6), which defined "direct labor" without reference to work directly relating to the performance of a service.

Effective and Applicability Provisions

1971 Acts. Section effective Aug. 1, 1971, see section 2 of Pub.L. 92–28, set out as a note under section 46 of this title.

Termination of Trust Territory of the Pacific Islands

For termination of Trust Territory of the Pacific Islands, see note set out preceding 48 U.S.C.A. § 1681.

WESTLAW ELECTRONIC RESEARCH

See Westlaw guide following the Explanation pages of this volume.

Notes of Decisions

Qualified nonprofit agency   1

---

1. Qualified nonprofit agency

Interpretation by the Committee for Purchase From the Blind and Other Severely Handicapped of term "qualified nonprofit agency" for blind or others severely handicapped from which government may procure item without competitive bidding as employing blind or other severely handicapped individuals for not less than 75% of the man-hours of direct labor required for the production or provisions of the commodities or services and not requiring application of 75% rule to the production of all components of an item placed on procurement list was neither arbitrary nor capricious for congressional intent mandated more liberal application of 75% requirement. HLI Lordship Industries, Inc. v. Committee for Purchase from the Blind & Other Severely Handicapped, E.D.Va.1985, 615 F.Supp. 970, reversed 791 F.2d 1136. United States ⊙⇒ 64.60(4)

§ 48c. Authorization of appropriations

There are authorized to be appropriated to the Committee to carry out sections 46 to 48c of this title $240,000 for the fiscal year ending June 30, 1974, and such sums as may be necessary for the succeeding fiscal years.

(June 25, 1938, c. 697, § 6, as added June 23, 1971, Pub.L. 92–28, § 1, 85 Stat. 82, and amended July 30, 1973, Pub.L. 93–76, 87 Stat. 176; July 25, 1974, Pub.L. 93–358, § 1(4), 88 Stat. 393.)

HISTORICAL AND STATUTORY NOTES

Revision Notes and Legislative Reports

1971 Acts. House Report No. 92–228, see 1971 U.S.Code Cong. and Adm.News, p. 1079.

1974 Acts. Senate Report No. 93–908, see 1974 U.S.Code Cong. and Adm.News, p. 3940.

Amendments

1974 Amendments. Pub.L. 93–358 substituted "$240,000 for the fiscal year ending June 30, 1974, and such sums as may be necessary for the succeeding fiscal years" for "$200,000 each for the fiscal year ending June 30, 1972, and the next succeeding fiscal year, and $240,000 for the fiscal year ending June 30, 1974".

1973 Amendments. Pub.L. 93–76 increased the authorization of appropriation to $240,000 for the fiscal year ending June 30, 1974.

Effective and Applicability Provisions
1971 Acts. Section effective Aug. 1, 1971, see section 2 of Pub.L. 92–28, set out as a note under section 46 of this title.

Research References

Treatises and Practice Aids
   West's Federal Administrative Practice § 606, Procurement Agencies.

WESTLAW ELECTRONIC RESEARCH
   See Westlaw guide following the Explanation pages of this volume.

§ 49. Defense employment; honorable discharge from land and naval forces as equivalent to birth certificate

No defense contractor shall deny employment, on account of failure to produce a birth certificate, to any person who submits, in lieu of a birth certificate, an honorable discharge certificate or certificate issued in lieu thereof from the Army, Air Force, Navy, Marine Corps, or Coast Guard of the United States, unless such honorable discharge certificate shows on its face that such person may have been an alien at the time of its issuance.

(June 22, 1942, c. 432, § 1, 56 Stat. 375.)

HISTORICAL AND STATUTORY NOTES

Change of Name
   Air Force was inserted under the authority of section 207(a), (f) of Act July 26, 1947, c. 343, Title II, 61 Stat. 502, 503. The Department of War was designated the Department of the Army and the title of the Secretary of War was changed to Secretary of the Army by section 205(a) of such Act July 26, 1947. Sections 205(a) and 207(a), (f) of Act July 26, 1947 were repealed by section 53 of Act Aug. 10, 1956, c. 1041, 70A Stat. 641. Section 1 of Act Aug. 10, 1956, enacted "Title 10, Armed Forces", which in sections 3010 to 3013 and 8010 to 8013 continued the military Departments of the Army and Air Force under the administrative supervision of a Secretary of the Army and a Secretary of the Air Force, respectively.

Transfer of Functions
   For transfer of authorities, functions, personnel, and assets of the Coast Guard, including the authorities and functions of the Secretary of Transportation relating thereto, to the Department of Homeland Security, and for treatment of related references, see 6 U.S.C.A. §§ 468(b), 551(d), 552(d) and 557, and the Department of Homeland Security Reorganization Plan of November 25, 2002, as modified, set out as a note under 6 U.S.C.A. § 542.

LIBRARY REFERENCES

American Digest System
   Aliens, Immigration, and Citizenship ⊙124.
   Key Number System Topic No. 24.

WESTLAW ELECTRONIC RESEARCH

See Westlaw guide following the Explanation pages of this volume.

§ 50. "Defense contractor" defined

As used in sections 49 and 50 of this title the term "defense contractor" means an employer engaged in—

(1) the production, maintenance, or storage of arms, armament, ammunition, implements of war, munitions, machinery, tools, clothing, food, fuel, or any articles or supplies, or parts or ingredients of any articles or supplies; or

(2) the construction, reconstruction, repair, or installation of a building, plant, structure, or facility;

under a contract with the United States or under any contract which the President, the Secretary of the Army, the Secretary of the Air Force, the Secretary of the Navy, or the Secretary of Transportation certifies to such employer to be necessary to the national defense.

(June 22, 1942, c. 432, § 2, 56 Stat. 376; Aug. 6, 1981, Pub.L. 97–31, § 12(16), 95 Stat. 154.)

HISTORICAL AND STATUTORY NOTES

Revision Notes and Legislative Reports

1981 Acts. House Report No. 97–199, see 1981 U.S.Code Cong. and Adm.News, p. 92.

Amendments

1981 Amendments. Pub.L. 97–31 substituted "Secretary of Transportation" for "United States Maritime Commission".

Change of Name

The Secretary of the Air Force was inserted under the authority of section 207(a), (f) of Act July 26, 1947, c. 343, Title II, 61 Stat. 502, 503. The Department of War was designated the Department of the Army and the title of the Secretary of War was changed to Secretary of the Army by section 205(a) of Act July 26, 1947. Sections 205(a) and 207(a), (f) of Act July 26, 1947, were repealed by section 53 of Act Aug. 10, 1956, c. 1041, 70A Stat. 641. Section 1 of Act Aug. 10, 1956 enacted "Title 10, Armed Forces", which in sections 3010 to 3013 and 8010 to 8013 continued the military Departments of the Army and Air Force under the administrative supervision of a Secretary of the Army and a Secretary of the Air Force, respectively.

Research References

ALR Library

140 ALR 1518, Validity and Construction of War Enactments in United States Suspending Operation of Statute of Limitations.

WESTLAW ELECTRONIC RESEARCH

See Westlaw guide following the Explanation pages of this volume.

§ 51. Short title

Sections 51 to 58 of this title may be cited as the "Anti–Kickback Act of 1986".

(Mar. 8, 1946, c. 80, § 1, 60 Stat. 37; Sept. 2, 1960, Pub.L. 86–695, 74 Stat. 740; Nov. 7, 1986, Pub.L. 99–634, § 2(a), 100 Stat. 3523.)

HISTORICAL AND STATUTORY NOTES

Revision Notes and Legislative Reports

1946 Acts. The purpose of the bill is to eliminate the practice of subcontractors of paying fees or kick-backs, or of granting gifts or gratuities, to employees of cost-plus-a-fixed-fee or cost-reimbursable prime contractors, or of higher tier subcontractors, for the purpose of securing the award of subcontracts or orders.

Legislation of this character and in substantially the form of the present bill was recommended in a report of the Comptroller General of the United States to the Congress under date of October 5, 1943, which report, explaining in detail the need for such legislation, is set forth hereinafter.

The practice which the bill would prohibit was revealed in the audit of payments under certain cost-plus-a-fixed-fee contracts by the General Accounting Office and was brought to the attention of the chairman, Special Committee to Investigate the National Defense Program, United States Senate, and to the chairman, Military Affairs Committee, House of Representatives, by the Comptroller General of the United States by letters dated April 24, 1943. Thereafter the matter was investigated by representatives of the said Senate committee and later was the subject of hearings conducted by a subcommittee thereof on May 20, 21, and 22, 1943. It was revealed that gratuities or gifts in the form of money, War bonds, and entertainment had been given by certain concerns to individuals employed in the purchasing departments of the prime contractors in acknowledgment for orders previously given to the concerns through the influence of said individuals, or for the purpose of inducing the award of future orders by their influence. Since cost-plus-a-fixed-fee or cost-reimbursable prime contractors are reimbursed by the United States for the cost of all subcontracts and purchase orders performed thereunder, the Government undoubtedly bears the ultimate cost of such fees, commissions, and gratuities without receiving any benefit therefrom.

Section 1 of the bill would prohibit the granting of such fees, gratuities, etc., and would authorize the recovery thereof by the United States by withholding amounts otherwise due the subcontractor who pays such fees or gratuities, or the recipient thereof, either directly by the United States, or by a prime contractor, or by an action in an appropriate court of the United States. There is no existing statutory or other authority of law under which it may be said that the United States clearly has a right to recover the amounts of any such fees or gratuities.

Section 2 of the bill merely defines the terms "subcontractor" and "person" as used therein.

Section 3 of the bill authorizes the General Accounting Office to inspect the plants and to audit the books and records of any prime contractor or subcontractor engaged in the performance of a cost-plus-a-fixed-fee or other cost reimbursable contract for the purpose of ascertaining whether fees, commissions, gifts, etc., have been paid or granted by subcontractors. The General Accounting Office has no clear right to make such inspections and audits under existing law but such authority is imperative if the bill is to be fully effective.

Section 4 of the bill would authorize the fine or imprisonment, or both, of any person who knowingly, directly or indirectly, makes or receives any such payments as are prohibited by the bill.

The Comptroller General of the United States appeared before this committee, at its request, and strongly urged enactment of legislation prohibiting the payment or granting of fees, gratuities, etc., under the circumstances indicated. Also, representatives of the War Department, the Navy Department, and the Maritime Commission appeared before the committee and expressed the need and desirability of legislation which would prohibit such practices. House Report No. 212.

1960 Acts. House Report No. 1880, see 1960 U.S.Code Cong. and Adm.News, p. 3292.

1986 Acts. H.R. 4783, the Anti–Kickback Enforcement Act of 1986, amends the Anti–Kickback Act of 1946, 41 U.S.C. 51–54, to clarify its meaning, expand its coverage, and increase its criminal and civil sanctions. The text of the 1946 Anti–Kickback Act is completely rewritten in H.R. 4783 to both modernize and clarify its provisions. New definitions of important terms are added or substituted to clear up ambiguities which exist under the text of the Act. A six-year statute of limitations provision for civil suits is included in the bill because the Act does not fix a limitation period.

The Anti–Kickback Act pertains to kickbacks made in connection with contracts of the Federal Government. H.R. 4783 extends its coverage in several ways. The bill would prohibit the acceptance of a kickback, or the inclusion of its cost in a contract, as well as its payment; only the payment or granting of a kickback is presently actionable under the Act. The bill would prohibit attempted, as well as completed, kickbacks; the Act now applies only to completed kickbacks. Coverage also is extended to kickbacks made in connection with all Federal contracts, not just in connection with "negotiated contracts" as the Act currently provides. Further, the bill prohibits kickbacks made to induce any favorable treatment in contracting; the Act is presently limited to inducements for the award of a subcontract or order.

In addition to expanding the prohibited conduct, the bill includes new requirements for government prime contractors designed to prevent kickbacks. All government contracts must specify that the prime contractor will use internal procedures to prevent and detect kickbacks in its operations and those of its direct business relations. Government contracts must contain agreements that the prime contractor shall cooperate with government kickback investigations. Further, prime contractors are required to report a suspected kickback to the government whenever they have reasonable grounds to believe one has occurred.

Along with broadening the scope of the Anti–Kickback Act, H.R. 4783 would increase its penalties. Criminal penalties are increased from a maximum two-year prison term and a $10,000 fine to a maximum 10-year prison term and a $250,000 fine ($1,000,000 for business entities). Civil penalties are increased, in cases of knowing violations, from the amount of the kickback to twice that amount plus up to $10,000.

These changes are made to the Anti–Kickback Act by H.R. 4783 to enhance the government's ability to prevent and prosecute kickback practices. These practices have become a pervasive problem in Federal procurement. This form of commercial bribery has tremendous impact. Kickbacks directly inflate contract costs paid by the taxpayer. Kick-

backs destroy competition and they foster corruption. H.R. 4783 is intended to provide the statutory provisions needed to stop kickbacks. House Report No. 99–964.

Amendments

1986 Amendments. Pub.L. 99–634, § 2(a), substituted provision that this Act may be cited as the Anti–Kickback Act of 1986 for provisions relating to fees or kick-backs by subcontractors on negotiated contracts, recovery thereof by the United States, conclusive presumption that such payments by such subcontractors were included in the price of the subcontract or order and ultimately borne by the United States, and withholding by the prime contractor of such amounts from sums otherwise due a subcontractor.

1960 Amendments. Pub.L. 86–695 inserted "negotiated" preceding "contract" and deleted ", on a cost-plus-a-fixed-fee or other cost-reimbursable basis" following "whatsoever" in clause (1), and substituted "setoff" for "set-off" and "contract" for "cost-plus-a-fixed-fee or cost-reimbursable contract," preceding "or by an action".

Effective and Applicability Provisions

1986 Acts. Section 3 of Pub.L. 99–634 provided that:

"**(a)** Except as provided in subsection (b), the Anti–Kickback Act of 1986 (as set out in section 2(a)) [enacting sections 55, 56, 57(c), and 58 and amending sections 51 to 54 of this title] shall take effect with respect to conduct described in section 3 of such Act [section 53 of this title] which occurs on or after the date of the enactment of this Act [Nov. 7, 1986].

"**(b)** Subsections (a) and (b) of section 7 of the Anti–Kickback Act of 1986 (as set out in section 2(a)) [section 57(a) and (b) of this title] shall take effect with respect to contract solicitations issued by an agency, department, or other establishment of the Federal Government on or after the date which is 90 days after the date of the enactment of this Act [Nov. 7, 1986]."

Short Title

1986 Amendments. Section 1 of Pub.L. 99–634 provided: "That this Act [enacting sections 55 to 58, amending sections 51 to 54 of this title and enacting provision set out as a note under this section] may be cited as the 'Anti–Kickback Enforcement Act of 1986'.''

FEDERAL SENTENCING GUIDELINES

See Federal Sentencing Guidelines § 2B4.1, 18 USCA.

Research References

ALR Library

41 ALR, Fed. 10, Propriety and Prejudicial Effect of Prosecutor's Argument to Jury Indicating His Belief or Knowledge as to Guilt of Accused--Federal Cases.

19 ALR, Fed. 545, Validity, Construction, and Application of Federal Anti-Kickback Act (41 U.S.C.A. §§ 51-54).

19 ALR, Fed. 709, State or Federal Law as Governing Applicability of Doctrine of Res Judicata or Collateral Estoppel in Federal Court Action.

1 ALR 3rd 1350, Validity and Construction of Statutes Punishing Commercial Bribery.

162 ALR 495, Constitutionality of Statutes or Ordinances Making One Fact Presumptive or Prima Facie Evidence of Another.

149 ALR 495, Constitutionality, Construction, and Application of Statutes Prohibiting Agreements to Refund Wages Under Employment Contracts "Kickback" Agreements.

148 ALR 768, Validity of Contract to Influence Administrative or Executive Officer or Department.

69 ALR 377, Constitutionality of Corrupt Practices Acts.

Encyclopedias

Am. Jur. 2d Federal Courts § 2022, Accounts of Officers, Agents, or Contractors.

Am. Jur. 2d Public Works and Contracts § 129, Kickbacks.

14 Am. Jur. Trials 437, Representing the Government Contractor.

Forms

Nichols Cyclopedia of Legal Forms Annotated § 7:2530, United States Lessee--General Clauses.

Treatises and Practice Aids

Federal Procedure, Lawyers Edition § 39:1371, Introduction.

West's Federal Administrative Practice § 613, Laws Applicable--Contract Solicitation.

21B Wright & Miller: Federal Prac. & Proc. § 5123.1, Scope of Rule 301--Exceptions.

WESTLAW ELECTRONIC RESEARCH

See Westlaw guide following the Explanation pages of this volume.

Notes of Decisions

Policy   1
Preemption   2

1. Policy

Public policy requires that United States be able to rid itself of prime contracts tainted by kickbacks. U.S. v. Acme Process Equipment Co., U.S.Ct.Cl.1966, 87 S.Ct. 350, 385 U.S. 138, 17 L.Ed.2d 249, rehearing denied 87 S.Ct. 738, 385 U.S. 1032, 17 L.Ed.2d 680. United States ⊕ 72.1(2)

2. Preemption

The Anti-Kickback Act did not preempt remedies available to the United States under the False Claims Act and federal common law with respect to shipbuilder's construction differential subsidy applications that included cost data tainted by kickback payments, which remedies were not limited to amount of kickbacks, but extended to, consequential damages resulting from payment of kickbacks. U.S. v. General Dynamics Corp., C.A.2 (N.Y.)

1994, 19 F.3d 770. United States ☞ 120.1

If defense contractor was not found vicariously liable for its supplier's violations of False Claims Act (FCA) or Anti–Kickback Act (AKA), it could assert independent damages claims against supplier under Massachusetts unfair trade practices statute; however, if contractor was found liable, Massachusetts statutory claim would be preempted by the FCA or AKA because, in such scenario, that claim would have the effect of providing for indemnification prohibited under federal statutes. U.S. v. Dynamics Research Corp., D.Mass.2006, 441 F.Supp.2d 259. Antitrust And Trade Regulation ☞ 132; States ☞ 18.84

Government could not use False Claims Act and federal common law to sue shipbuilder for injuries that government sustained as result of kickback scheme between shipbuilder and subcontractor; Anti-Kickback Act preempted False Claims Act and federal common-law remedies. U.S. v. Davis, S.D.N.Y.1992, 803 F.Supp. 830, affirmed in part, reversed in part 19 F.3d 770. United States ☞ 120.1

§ 52. Definitions

As used in sections 51 to 58 of this title:

(1) The term "contracting agency", when used with respect to a prime contractor, means any department, agency, or establishment of the United States which enters into a prime contract with a prime contractor.

(2) The term "kickback" means any money, fee, commission, credit, gift, gratuity, thing of value, or compensation of any kind which is provided, directly or indirectly, to any prime contractor, prime contractor employee, subcontractor, or subcontractor employee for the purpose of improperly obtaining or rewarding favorable treatment in connection with a prime contract or in connection with a subcontract relating to a prime contract.

(3) The term "person" means a corporation, partnership, business association of any kind, trust, joint-stock company, or individual.

(4) The term "prime contract" means a contract or contractual action entered into by the United States for the purpose of obtaining supplies, materials, equipment, or services of any kind.

(5) The term "prime contractor" means a person who has entered into a prime contract with the United States.

(6) The term "prime contractor employee" means any officer, partner, employee, or agent of a prime contractor.

(7) The term "subcontract" means a contract or contractual action entered into by a prime contractor or subcontractor for the purpose of obtaining supplies, materials, equipment, or services of any kind under a prime contract.

(8) The term "subcontractor"—

(A) means any person, other than the prime contractor, who offers to furnish or furnishes any supplies, materials, equipment, or services of any kind under a prime contract or a subcontract entered into in connection with such prime contract; and

(B) includes any person who offers to furnish or furnishes general supplies to the prime contractor or a higher tier subcontractor.

(9) The term "subcontractor employee" means any officer, partner, employee, or agent of a subcontractor.

(Mar. 8, 1946, c. 80, § 2, 60 Stat. 38; Sept. 2, 1960, Pub.L. 86–695, 74 Stat. 740; Nov. 7, 1986, Pub.L. 99–634, § 2(a), 100 Stat. 3523.)

HISTORICAL AND STATUTORY NOTES

Revision Notes and Legislative Reports

1946 Acts. See House Report No. 212, set out in part as a note under section 51 of this title.

1960 Acts. House Report No. 1880, see 1960 U.S.Code Cong. and Adm.News, p. 3292.

1986 Acts. The Anti–Kickback Act defines three terms—"subcontractor," "person", and "negotiated contract." 41 U.S.C. 52. Section 2 of the amendment provided by H.R. 4783 deletes the definition of "negotiated contract" and changes the other two. It also adds six new definitions, including a definition for "kickback".

Section 2(1) defines "contracting agency", a term which is not used in the current Act. "Contracting agency" is defined as "any department, agency, or establishment of the United States which enters into a prime contract with a prime contractor." This definition borrows language from the existing Act which refers to contracts "entered into by any department, agency, or establishment of the United States". 41 U.S.C. 51.

Section 2(2) defines "kickback". This term does not appear in the existing Act. The definition of "kickback" serves to broaden the coverage of the Act. First, Section 2(2) defines "kickback" to mean "any money, fee, commission, credit, gift, gratuity, thing of value, or compensation of any kind. . . ." This generally tracks the existing Act, which prohibits the "payment of any fee, commission, or compensation of any kind or the granting of any gift or gratuity of any kind," 41 U.S.C. 51, but adds the terms "money," "credit," and "thing of value" to clarify the law's application to all forms of kickback exchanges.

Second, the definition continues "which is provided, directly or indirectly, to any prime contractor, prime contractor employee, subcontractor, or subcontractor employee . . ." This portion of the definition incorporates provisions in the current law. These terms are defined in later subsections of Section 2.

Third, the definition of kickback continues, "for the purpose of improperly obtaining or acknowledging favorable treatment . . ." This portion is intended to expand the coverage of the existing Act to kickbacks made in the Federal procurement process for any improper purpose. The existing Act only includes kickbacks made "as an inducement for the award of a subcontract or order . . . or as an acknowledgement of a subcontract or order previously awarded." 41 U.S.C. 51.

Some examples of the "favorable treatment" covered under H.R. 4783 include receiving confidential information on competitors' bids such as prices, specifications, suppliers, delivery schedules, etc.; obtaining placement on the bidders list without meeting the requisite qualifications, or obtaining the removal of competitors who do meet them; obtaining the unwarranted waiver of bidding or contracting deadlines; obtaining the acceptance of substandard goods; obtaining undeserved price increases or the recovery of improper expenses; and obtaining the award of the subcontract itself or of orders under it. These are just a few of the purposes covered under the definition.

The Committee intends that the definition of "favorable treatment" used in the definition of "kickback" provided in Section 2(2) be construed broadly to reach all instances of behavior which constitute a commercial bribe in connection with a government contract. The Committee has, however, included the term "improperly" to ensure that exchange[s] made which are authorized by the contract itself, such as additional payments made under acceleration provisions, or for other permissible purposes, such as innocent or incidental favors, are not included under the definition of "kickback".

Finally, the definition of "kickback" concludes, "in connection with a prime contract or in connection with a subcontract relating to a prime contract." This portion of the definition is intended to ensure the Act's broad coverage over kickbacks that may be made by subcontractors who are in any contractual relationship related to the performance of the government's prime contract.

Section 2(3) defines "person" as "a corporation, partnership, business association of any kind, trust, joint-stock company, or individual." It mirrors the existing Act and is meant to cover any individual or business entity.

Section 2(4) defines "prime contract" as "a contract or contractual action entered into by the United States for the purpose of obtaining supplies, materials, equipment, or services of any kind." This term extends the coverage of the Act by replacing "negotiated contract" in the existing definition.

The term "prime contract" is intended to be construed broadly. The phrase "contractual action" has been included to ensure that all contracts, including but not limited to written and oral agreements, purchase orders, telephone orders, change orders, etc., of any amount, are covered.

Section 2(5) defines "prime contractor" as "a person who has entered into a prime contract with the United States." The term "prime contractor" is not defined in the existing Act. This definition is to be used in conjunction with the definitions of "prime contract" and "person".

Section 2(6) defines "prime contractor employee" as "any officer, partner, employee, or agent of a prime contractor". This definition borrows general language from the existing Act which prohibits payments to any "officer, partner, employee, or agent of a prime contractor." The definition is meant to include, *inter*

alia, owners, directors, trustees, or independent sales representatives of the prime contractor.

Section 2(7) defines "subcontract" as "a contract or contractual action entered into by a prime contractor or subcontractor for the purposes of obtaining supplies, materials, equipment, or services of any kind under a prime contract." The term applies to contractual arrangements between a prime contractor and subcontractor and to contractual arrangements between higher and lower tier subcontractors who are performing tasks related to a prime contract. The portion of the definition—"a contract or contractual action"—is to be construed broadly as in the definition of "prime contract", to include written and oral contracts, purchase orders, telephone orders, letter agreements, change orders, etc., of any amount.

Section 2(8) defines "subcontractor" as "any person, other than the prime contractor, who offers to furnish or furnishes any supplies, materials, equipment, or services of any kind under a prime contract or a subcontract entered into in connection with such prime contract." The definition includes "any person who offers to furnish or furnishes general supplies to the prime contractor or a higher tier subcontractor." The definition would replace the definition of "subcontractor" in the existing Act. "Subcontractor" is defined in the existing Act as "any person, including a corporation, partnership, or business association of any kind, who holds an agreement or purchase order to perform all or any part of the work or to make or to furnish any article or service required for the performance of a negotiated contract or of a subcontract entered into thereunder."

The definition in Section 2(8) is meant to expand the current definition in two ways. First, it covers persons acting under any type of contract, not just a negotiated contract. It also covers persons who "offer" to perform under a prime contract, not just those who "hold" an agreement or purchase order. This change makes it clear that the bill is meant to cover all persons who bid on a subcontract, whether or not they win the award. The definition also explicitly includes companies who furnish general supplies to prime contractors or related subcontractors.

Section 2(9) defines "subcontractor employee" and "any officer, partner, employee, or agent of a subcontractor." This definition parallels that of "prime contractor employee" and is also meant to be construed broadly to include the owners, directors, trustees, or independent sales representatives of a subcontractor. House Report No. 99–964.

Amendments

1986 Amendments. Pub.L. 99–634, § 2(a), designated existing provisions in part as pars. (3) and (8), in par. (3), as so designated, substituted definition of "person" as meaning a corporation, partnership, business association of any kind, trust, joint-stock company, or individual for provision defining such term as meaning any subcontractor, corporation, association, trust, joint-stock company, partnership, or individual, in par. (8), as so designated, substituted definition of "subcontractor" as any person, other than the prime contractor, who offers to furnish or furnishes any supplies, materials, equipment or services under a prime contract or subcontract entered into in connection therewith, and including persons furnishing or offering to furnish supplies to the prime contractor or a higher tier subcontractor, for any person, including a corporation, partnership, or business association of any kind, who held an agreement or purchase order to perform all or any part of the work or to make or to furnish any article or service required for the performance of a negotiated contract or of a subcontract entered into thereunder, added pars. (1), (2) (4) to (7), and (9), and struck out provision which defined "negotiated contract" as meaning one made without formal advertising.

1960 Amendments. Pub.L. 86–695 substituted "negotiated contract" for "cost-plus-a-fixed-fee or cost-reimbursable contract" in the definition of "subcontractor" and defined the term "negotiated contract."

Effective and Applicability Provisions

1986 Acts. Amendment by Pub.L. 99–634 effective with respect to conduct described in section 53 of this title which occurs on or after Nov. 7, 1986, see section 3(a) of Pub.L. 99–634, set out as a note under section 51 of this title.

Research References

ALR Library
149 ALR 495, Constitutionality, Construction, and Application of Statutes Prohibiting Agreements to Refund Wages Under Employment Contracts "Kickback" Agreements.

Encyclopedias
Am. Jur. 2d Public Works and Contracts § 129, Kickbacks.

Treatises and Practice Aids
Federal Procedure, Lawyers Edition § 39:1371, Introduction.

WESTLAW ELECTRONIC RESEARCH

See Westlaw guide following the Explanation pages of this volume.

Notes of Decisions

Kickback   1
Prime contract   2
Prime contractor   3
Prime contractor employee   4
Subcontractor   5

---

1. Kickback

Public Contracts Anti–Kickback Act (AKA) encompassed pharmacy benefit manager's (PBM) alleged payment to health plan in exchange for favorable treatment, even though health plan had entered into agreement with Medicare program to provide managed care services. U.S. v. Merck-Medco Managed Care, L.L.C., E.D.Pa.2004, 336 F.Supp.2d 430. United States ☞ 75(6)

Illegal Medicare payments allegedly received by physicians were not "kickbacks" within meaning of Anti-Kickback Act, where alleged payments were not made to intermediaries/carriers in return for favorable treatment. U.S. v. Kensington Hosp., E.D.Pa.1991, 760 F.Supp. 1120. Health ☞ 980

In action by United States to recover amounts paid by subcontractors to prime contractors having cost-plus contracts with War Shipping Administration, or to employees of one of the prime contractors, evidence disclosed that payments were made either as inducements for awards of subcontracts or as acknowledgment of subcontracts previously awarded in violation of section 51 et seq. of this title. U.S. v. Gemmell, E.D.Pa.1958, 160 F.Supp. 792. United States ⌑ 75(6)

2. Prime contract

Relationship between Pennsylvania Department of Public Welfare and the medicaid trust funds did not constitute a "prime contract" within meaning of Anti-Kickback Act that could form basis for liability under Act in medicare fraud case. U.S. v. Kensington Hosp., E.D.Pa. 1991, 760 F.Supp. 1120. Health ⌑ 980

3. Prime contractor

Subsidiary which entered into prime contract with the United States and parent which owned 50% of subsidiary were "prime contractors" subject to the Anti-Kickback Act. Morse Diesel Intern., Inc.

v. U.S., Fed.Cl.2005, 66 Fed.Cl. 788. United States ⌑ 75(6)

4. Prime contractor employee

Where prime contractor selected agents to carry on its business in obtaining and performing government contracts, agents' conduct in that field should be considered as prime contractor's conduct, particularly where it touched the all-important subject of kickbacks from subcontractors. U.S. v. Acme Process Equipment Co., U.S.Ct.Cl.1966, 87 S.Ct. 350, 385 U.S. 138, 17 L.Ed.2d 249, rehearing denied 87 S.Ct. 738, 385 U.S. 1032, 17 L.Ed.2d 680. Principal And Agent ⌑ 159(1)

5. Subcontractor

Relationship between medicare intermediaries/carriers and physician did not create prime contractor/subcontractor relationship required for Anti-Kickback Act to apply to alleged medicare fraud; any contract between intermediaries/carriers and physicians existed for benefit of government, not for benefit of intermediaries/carriers. U.S. v. Kensington Hosp., E.D.Pa.1991, 760 F.Supp. 1120. Health ⌑ 980

§ 53. Prohibited conduct

It is prohibited for any person—

(1) to provide, attempt to provide, or offer to provide any kickback;

(2) to solicit, accept, or attempt to accept any kickback; or

(3) to include, directly or indirectly, the amount of any kickback prohibited by clause (1) or (2) in the contract price charged by a subcontractor to a prime contractor or a higher tier subcontractor or in the contract price charged by a prime contractor to the United States.

(Mar. 8, 1946, c. 80, § 3, 60 Stat. 38; Sept. 2, 1960, Pub.L. 86–695, 74 Stat. 741; Nov. 7, 1986, Pub.L. 99–634, § 2(a), 100 Stat. 3524.)

HISTORICAL AND STATUTORY NOTES

Revision Notes and Legislative Reports
1946 Acts. See House Report No. 212 set out in part as a note under section 51 of this title.

1960 Acts. House Report No. 1880, see 1960 U.S.Code Cong. and Adm.News, p. 3292.

1986 Acts. Section 3 specifies the exact conduct which is to be prohibited under the Act. The existing law directly prohibits the "payment" or "granting" of a kickback. It also indicates that the amount of any kickback "shall not be charged" as a part of the contract price. Further, the existing statute provides, "Upon a showing" of a kickback that "it shall be conclusively presumed that the cost of such expense was included in the price of the subcontract or order and ultimately borne by the United States.".....

Section 3, while shortening and simplifying the language, generally tracts the existing statute except in two important regards. Section 3(a), unlike the existing Act, prohibits attempted as well as completed kickbacks. Secondly, by employing the new definition of kickback from section 2, section 3 prohibits payments to obtain or acknowledge any type of favorable treatment in connection with any prime contract. House Report No. 99–964.

Amendments
1986 Amendments. Pub.L. 99–634, § 2(a), substituted provisions specifying

prohibited conduct for provisions empowering the General Accounting Office to inspect the plants and to audit the books and records of any prime contractor or subcontractor engaged in the performance of a negotiated contract. See section 58 of this title.

1960 Amendments. Pub.L. 86–695 substituted "negotiated contract" for "cost-plus-a-fixed-fee or cost-reimbursable contract".

Effective and Applicability Provisions
1986 Acts. Amendment by Pub.L. 99–634 effective with respect to conduct described in this section which occurs on or after Nov. 7, 1986, see section 3(a) of Pub.L. 99–634, set out as a note under section 51 of this title.

FEDERAL SENTENCING GUIDELINES

See Federal Sentencing Guidelines § 2B4.1, 18 USCA.

LIBRARY REFERENCES

American Digest System
United States ⊂⊃75(6).
Key Number System Topic No. 393.

Corpus Juris Secundum
CJS United States § 136, Rights and Remedies of United States.

Research References

ALR Library
1 ALR 3rd 1350, Validity and Construction of Statutes Punishing Commercial Bribery.
Encyclopedias
70 Am. Jur. Proof of Facts 3d 97, Proof That a Government Agency Was Liable for Improperly Granting a Bid Award to a Bid Applicant.

Treatises and Practice Aids
Federal Procedure, Lawyers Edition § 39:1371, Introduction.
Federal Procedure, Lawyers Edition § 39:1374, Criminal Prosecution.

WESTLAW ELECTRONIC RESEARCH

See Westlaw guide following the Explanation pages of this volume.

Notes of Decisions

Generally 1
Contracts within prohibition 2
Financial harm 4
Payments considered kickbacks 3

Time of kickback 5

1. Generally
The vice which section 51 et seq. of this title was designed to correct was not only the improper awarding of subcontracts but also the corruption of judgment of officers, employees or agents of prime

contractors who are in some manner participating in the awarding of subcontracts involving the use of government funds. Howard v. U.S., C.A.1 (Mass.) 1965, 345 F.2d 126, certiorari denied 86 S.Ct. 86, 382 U.S. 838, 15 L.Ed.2d 80. United States ☞ 75(6)

2.   Contracts within prohibition

Section 51 et seq. of this title does not prohibit making or receiving of so called "kickback" payments, except in connection with contracts with Federal Government on a cost-plus-a-fixed-fee or other cost reimbursable basis, and such payments made in connection with a nonfederal cost-plus-a-fixed-fee contract are not prohibited by this section. U.S. v. Dobar, M.D.Fla.1963, 223 F.Supp. 8. United States ☞ 75(6)

Where treasurer of corporation requested second corporation to take assignment of Government contract and second corporation declined but made oral contract to pay treasurer of first corporation commission of 5 percent if he could obtain contract for second corporation directly, and as result of treasurer's efforts, second corporation received a "negotiable Marine Corps contract", payment of commission under oral contract was not illegal under section 51 et seq. of this title prohibiting payments by subcontractor to any officer, partner, employee or agent of prime contractor. Gilbert v. Merrimac Development Corp., Mass. 1956, 133 N.E.2d 491, 333 Mass. 758. Contracts ☞ 123(1)

3.   Payments considered kickbacks

Gift of corporate stock to procure subcontract from prime contractor which held a negotiated government contract was a prohibited payment within meaning of section 51 et seq. of this title. U.S. v. Grossman, C.A.4 (N.C.) 1968, 400 F.2d 951, certiorari denied 89 S.Ct. 453, 393 U.S. 982, 21 L.Ed.2d 443. Bribery ☞ 1(1)

Public Contracts Anti–Kickback Act (AKA) encompassed pharmacy benefit manager's (PBM) alleged payment to health plan in exchange for favorable treatment, even though health plan had entered into agreement with Medicare program to provide managed care services. U.S. v. Merck-Medco Managed Care, L.L.C., E.D.Pa.2004, 336 F.Supp.2d 430. United States ☞ 75(6)

Interest free loans made to officer of government contractor were "kickbacks," under Anti-Kickback Act, even though repayment of principal was expected. U.S. v. Kruse, E.D.Va.2000, 101 F.Supp.2d 410. United States ☞ 75(6)

"Commission splitting" arrangements between parent of prime contractor and surety brokers who provided performance and payment bonds for government construction projects violated the Anti-Kickback Act, as they were "for the purpose of improperly obtaining or rewarding favorable treatment" for the brokers. Morse Diesel Intern., Inc. v. U.S., Fed.Cl. 2005, 66 Fed.Cl. 788. United States ☞ 75(6)

4.   Financial harm

In order to constitute violation of Anti-Kickback Act, section 51 et seq. of this title, it is not necessary that government be financially harmed. Travers v. U.S., C.A.1 (Mass.) 1966, 361 F.2d 753, certiorari denied 87 S.Ct. 76, 385 U.S. 834, 17 L.Ed.2d 68. Bribery ☞ 1(1)

5.   Time of kickback

Although kickbacks from subcontractors to three principal employees of prime contractor took place after prime contract had been awarded, where kickback arrangements existed either at time prime contract was awarded or shortly thereafter, one of kickbacking contractors actually participated in negotiation of prime contract, and prime contract contained price redetermination feature, there was great likelihood that cost of prime contract to government and reliability of prime contractor's performance under it would be directly affected by fact that prime contract was to be performed largely through subcontracts obtained by kickbacks and government was entitled to cancel prime contract. U.S. v. Acme Process Equipment Co., U.S.Ct.Cl.1966, 87 S.Ct. 350, 385 U.S. 138, 17 L.Ed.2d 249, rehearing denied 87 S.Ct. 738, 385 U.S. 1032, 17 L.Ed.2d 680. United States ☞ 72.1(2)

Kickbacks made at any point in government procurement process for purpose of improperly obtaining favorable treatment are prohibited by Anti-Kickback Act, regardless of whether or not offender knew of government involvement. U.S. v. Purdy, C.A.2 (Conn.) 1998, 144 F.3d 241, certiorari denied 119 S.Ct. 548, 525 U.S. 1020, 142 L.Ed.2d 455, post-conviction

relief denied 245 F.Supp.2d 411. Bribery ☞ 1(1)

§ 54.   Criminal penalties

Any person who knowingly and willfully engages in conduct prohibited by section 53 of this title shall be imprisoned for not more
than 10 years or shall be subject to a fine in accordance with Title 18,
or both.

(Mar. 8, 1946, c. 80, § 4, 60 Stat. 38; Sept. 2, 1960, Pub.L. 86–695, 74 Stat.
741; Nov. 7, 1986, Pub.L. 99–634, § 2(a), 100 Stat. 3524.)

HISTORICAL AND STATUTORY NOTES

Revision Notes and Legislative Reports
1946 Acts. See House Report No. 212,
set out in part as a note under section 51
of this title.

1960 Acts. House Report No. 1880, see
1960 U.S.Code Cong. and Adm.News, p.
3292.

1986 Acts. Section 4 would increase
the criminal penalties provided in the existing Act from a maximum prison term
of two years and a maximum criminal
fine of $10,000, 41 U.S.C. 54, to a maxi-
mum prison term of 10 years and a maximum criminal fine of $250,000 for indi-
viduals and $1 million for persons other
than individuals. These penalties apply
to any person who "willfully" engages in
the conduct prohibited by Section 3. The
existing Act's criminal penalties apply to
anyone who "knowingly" makes or receives a prohibited payment.

Thus, H.R. 4783 both broadens and
tightens application of the criminal sanctions. The bill broadens the criminal
provisions by applying them to persons
who include kickback costs in the price of
a contract, as well as those who pay (or
solicit) or offer (or receive) a kickback.
The criminal provisions would only apply, however, to those who "willfully"

engage in such conduct. In light of the
bill's stiff criminal penalties and broad
scope, the Committee believes the high
standard of conscious culpability—will-
fulness—must be shown to impose the
criminal sanctions. House Report No.
99–964.

Amendments
1986 Amendments. Pub.L. 99–634,
§ 2(a), substituted penalties of not more
than 10 years' imprisonment and/or a
fine in accordance with Title 18 in the
case of persons knowingly and willfully
violating section 53 of this title for penalties of not more than 2 years' imprisonment and/or a fine of not more than
$10,000 in the case of persons knowingly,
directly or indirectly, making or receiving
any prohibited payment.

1960 Amendments. Pub.L. 86–695 reenacted section without change.

Effective and Applicability Provisions
1986 Acts. Amendment by Pub.L.
99–634 effective with respect to conduct
described in section 53 of this title which
occurs on or after Nov. 7, 1986, see section 3(a) of Pub.L. 99–634, set out as a
note under section 51 of this title.

FEDERAL SENTENCING GUIDELINES

See Federal Sentencing Guidelines § 2B4.1, 18 USCA.

LIBRARY REFERENCES

American Digest System
United States ☞75(6).
Key Number System Topic No. 393.

Research References

ALR Library

41 ALR, Fed. 10, Propriety and Prejudicial Effect of Prosecutor's Argument to Jury Indicating His Belief or Knowledge as to Guilt of Accused--Federal Cases.

19 ALR, Fed. 545, Validity, Construction, and Application of Federal Anti-Kickback Act (41 U.S.C.A. §§ 51-54).

1 ALR 3rd 1350, Validity and Construction of Statutes Punishing Commercial Bribery.

149 ALR 495, Constitutionality, Construction, and Application of Statutes Prohibiting Agreements to Refund Wages Under Employment Contracts "Kickback" Agreements.

Encyclopedias

Am. Jur. 2d Public Works and Contracts § 129, Kickbacks.

70 Am. Jur. Proof of Facts 3d 97, Proof That a Government Agency Was Liable for Improperly Granting a Bid Award to a Bid Applicant.

14 Am. Jur. Trials 437, Representing the Government Contractor.

37 Am. Jur. Trials 273, Handling the Defense in a Bribery Prosecution.

Treatises and Practice Aids

Federal Procedure, Lawyers Edition § 39:1374, Criminal Prosecution.

WESTLAW ELECTRONIC RESEARCH

See Westlaw guide following the Explanation pages of this volume.

Notes of Decisions

Knowing and willful conduct 1
Subsequent conduct 2

1. Knowing and willful conduct

That none of officers of prime contractor were aware of kickbacks by subcontractors did not preclude government from cancelling prime contract on basis of the kickbacks, where those of prime contractor's employees and agents who did know were in the upper echelon of its managers, one of guilty employees was general manager of one of company's chief plants and son of president of prime contractor, and the other two kickback receivers were in charge of operations, sales and government contracts. U.S. v. Acme Process Equipment Co., U.S.Ct.Cl. 1966, 87 S.Ct. 350, 385 U.S. 138, 17 L.Ed.2d 249, rehearing denied 87 S.Ct. 738, 385 U.S. 1032, 17 L.Ed.2d 680. United States ☞ 72.1(2)

Knowledge by subcontractor's employee of terms of prime contract was not essential to constitute a violation of sections 51 to 54 of this title where such employee was charged with having given gifts to employee of prime contractor as inducement for award of subcontract. U.S. v. Grossman, C.A.4 (N.C.) 1968, 400 F.2d 951, certiorari denied 89 S.Ct. 453,

393 U.S. 982, 21 L.Ed.2d 443. Bribery ☞ 1(1)

Sections 51 to 54 of this title do not require a showing of a specific criminal intent to induce or influence the award of particular subcontracts, but criminal intent is an essential element of offense and conviction cannot be had on mere appearance of guilt. Howard v. U.S., C.A.1 (Mass.) 1965, 345 F.2d 126, certiorari denied 86 S.Ct. 86, 382 U.S. 838, 15 L.Ed.2d 80. Bribery ☞ 1(1)

In prosecution of buyer employed by prime Government contractor operating under cost-reimbursable contract, and others, for conspiracy to violate section 51 et seq. of this title precluding the payment of gratuities by subcontractors to officers or agents of persons operating under such contracts, evidence showing requisite criminal intent supported finding that buyer and at least one co-conspirator entered into illegal plan and that overt acts were committed to carry it into effect. Hanis v. U.S., C.A.8 (Mo.) 1957, 246 F.2d 781. Conspiracy ☞ 47(6)

2. Subsequent conduct

Crime of bribery stands by itself and does not depend on subsequent actions. Travers v. U.S., C.A.1 (Mass.) 1966, 361 F.2d 753, certiorari denied 87 S.Ct. 76,

385 U.S. 834, 17 L.Ed.2d 68. Bribery ☞ 1(1)

A purpose of section 51 et seq. of this title is basically the same as that of section 201 of Title 18 and should be construed according to the same principles;

the crime of bribery is complete upon acceptance of bribe regardless of whether or not improper action is thereafter taken. Howard v. U.S., C.A.1 (Mass.) 1965, 345 F.2d 126, certiorari denied 86 S.Ct. 86, 382 U.S. 838, 15 L.Ed.2d 80. Bribery ☞ 2

§ 55. Civil actions

(a)(1) The United States may, in a civil action, recover a civil penalty from any person who knowingly engages in conduct prohibited by section 53 of this title. The amount of such civil penalty shall be—

    (A) twice the amount of each kickback involved in the violation; and

    (B) not more than $10,000 for each occurrence of prohibited conduct.

(2) The United States may, in a civil action, recover a civil penalty from any person whose employee, subcontractor or subcontractor employee violates section 53 of this title by providing, accepting, or charging a kickback. The amount of such civil penalty shall be the amount of that kickback.

(b) A civil action under this section shall be barred unless the action is commenced within 6 years after the later of (1) the date on which the prohibited conduct establishing the cause of action occurred, and (2) the date on which the United States first knew or should reasonably have known that the prohibited conduct had occurred.

(Mar. 8, 1946, c. 80, § 5, as added Nov. 7, 1986, Pub.L. 99–634, § 2(a), 100 Stat. 3524.)

HISTORICAL AND STATUTORY NOTES

Revision Notes and Legislative Reports
  1986 Acts. Section 5(a)(1) creates a cause of action for the United States to bring a civil suit "against any person who violates section 3(a)." The existing Act provides that a kickback "shall be recoverable on behalf of the United States from the subcontractor or the recipient thereof . . . by an action in an appropriate court of the United States."

  Read in conjunction with Section 3, Section 5(a)(1) provides the United States with a cause of action directly against a prime contractor or a higher tier subcontractor when a kickback has occurred at any lower subcontracting level. Under the terms of the existing Act, the govern-

ment could proceed in civil court against the "subcontractor or the recipient" of kickback to recover its amount.

  In providing a civil cause of action against a prime or subcontractor that has not paid or received a kickback, Section 5(a)(1)—in combination with section 3(b), which provides a conclusive presumption that all kickbacks are included the price of a contract and ultimately borne by the United States—creates a no-fault, vicarious civil liability.

  Section 5(a) and Section 3(b) together allow the government to sue a prime contractor or higher tier subcontractor and receive an automatic judgment upon showing a payment or acceptance by a lower tier subcontractor. Under Section 5(a), the government may sue the prime contractor or a higher tier subcontractor for violating Section 3(a)(3) by including the amount of a kickback in the contract price. In that suit, upon a showing that a payment or acceptance has been made by a lower tier subcontractor, Section 3(b) provides an automatic conclusion that the prime contractor or higher tier subcontractor has violated section 3(a)(3) and that the cost has been borne by the government. Hence, the prime contractor or higher tier subcontractor may be held liable for kickbacks involving lower tier subcontractors without regard to its own behavior. The Committee believes that such liability would provide a strong incentive for contractors to scrutinize their subcontracting arrangements to ensure kickbacks do not occur.

Section 5(a)(2) sets forth the amounts the government may recover in civil suits. The existing Act limits the government's award to the amount of the kickback itself. Section 5(a)(2) provides civil awards for "knowing" violations of the Act equal to twice the kickback amount plus up to $10,000. For violations which are not "knowing," the government may be awarded the kickback amount.

The no-fault vicarious liability imposed upon prime contractors and higher tier subcontractors for the kickbacks paid by lower tier subcontractors is limited, therefore, to the amount of the kickback. To prove that a contractor "knowingly" included a cost in a contract price under 3(a)(3), the government must prove that that cost was actually included. The conclusive presumption in 3(b) will not substitute for proof that the prohibited conduct actually occurred, which is inherent in proving it was done "knowingly".

In providing for recovery by the government of double the kickback amount and up to $10,000 in civil cases involving a knowing violation of section 3, the bill fixes an amount which reasonably relates to the actual costs the government suffers when kickbacks occur. As has been indicated, kickbacks often end up costing the government more than the amount of the kickback that is passed along through the contract. In addition to increased prices the government may suffer increased costs from the delivery of substandard goods or by poor performance under the contract. Further, the government incurs expenses in investigating and prosecuting kickback cases.

Doubling the kickback payment compensates for these greater costs but keeps the award tied to the size of the kickback itself. In allowing for an additional award of up to $10,000, the court is given discretion to provide greater recovery when it is due. The additional award can also provide a sufficient deterrent amount when the kickback amount itself is small. The Committee believes that these amounts are reasonable in light of the serious harm caused the government by kickbacks and the need to prevent such misbehavior.

Section 5(b) specifies a statute of limitations applicable to civil suits under the Act. It would ban any civil suit brought under the Act which is not brought within six years from the date the conduct occurred or from the date the government became aware or should have become aware that it had occurred. This provision is patterned after 28 U.S.C. 2416, a general Federal statute government contract actions. House Report No. 99–964.

Effective and Applicability Provisions

1986 Acts. Section effective with respect to conduct described in section 53 of this title which occurs on or after Nov. 7, 1986, see section 3(a) of Pub.L. 99–634, set out as a note under section 51 of this title.

LIBRARY REFERENCES

American Digest System
> United States ☞75(6).
> Key Number System Topic No. 393.

Research References

ALR Library
> 26 ALR 1523, Right to Recover Back Fine or Penalty Paid in Criminal Proceeding.

Encyclopedias
> Am. Jur. 2d Public Works and Contracts § 129, Kickbacks.
> 70 Am. Jur. Proof of Facts 3d 97, Proof That a Government Agency Was Liable for Improperly Granting a Bid Award to a Bid Applicant.

Treatises and Practice Aids
   Federal Procedure, Lawyers Edition § 39:1376, Limitation of Actions.
   West's Federal Administrative Practice § 613, Laws Applicable--Contract Solicitation.

WESTLAW ELECTRONIC RESEARCH
See Westlaw guide following the Explanation pages of this volume.

Notes of Decisions

Annulment of contract   2
Constitutionality   1
Contribution or indemnity   3
Joint and several liability   5
Persons liable   4
Persons or entities entitled to maintain action   6
Summary judgment   7

1. Constitutionality
   Penalty provision of Anti-Kickback Act does not violate Excessive Fines provision of Eighth Amendment, to extent that amounts assessed roughly reimbursed government. U.S. v. Kruse, E.D.Va.2000, 101 F.Supp.2d 410.

2. Annulment of contract
   That Anti-Kickback Act, section 51 et seq. of this title, provided for fine or imprisonment for one who made or received kickback and recovery of kickback by United States but did not provide for contract annulment did not preclude government from cancelling contract on basis that three of prime contractor's principal employees had accepted compensation for awarding subcontracts. U.S. v. Acme Process Equipment Co., U.S.Ct.Cl.1966, 87 S.Ct. 350, 385 U.S. 138, 17 L.Ed.2d 249, rehearing denied 87 S.Ct. 738, 385 U.S. 1032, 17 L.Ed.2d 680. United States ⊕ 72.1(2)

3. Contribution or indemnity
   Anti–Kickback Act (AKA) did not provide an implied right of action for indemnification or contribution. U.S. v. Dynamics Research Corp., D.Mass.2006, 441 F.Supp.2d 259. Contribution ⊕ 5(6.1); Indemnity ⊕ 64

4. Persons liable
   Where money paid to induce award of purchase orders and subcontracts to payer was shared by four persons, two of whom were not connected with first-tier subcontractor which awarded the orders and subcontracts, only money received by two who were proscribed by this section could be recovered by United States. Jensen v. U.S., C.A.9 (Cal.) 1964, 326 F.2d 891. United States ⊕ 75(6)

5. Joint and several liability
   Where subcontractor made payments to employees of prime contractor having cost-plus contract with War Shipping Administration, in violation of section 51 et seq. of this title, payees and payor were jointly and severally liable to the United States for amount of payments made. U.S. v. Gemmell, E.D.Pa.1958, 160 F.Supp. 792. United States ⊕ 75(6)

6. Persons or entities entitled to maintain action
   United States, although not a direct party to contract between subcontractor and sub-subcontractor, was ultimate beneficiary of contract and could recover from sub-subcontractor amount of kickback given subcontractor's employee to obtain contract. U.S. v. Davio, E.D.Mich.1955, 136 F.Supp. 423. Contracts ⊕ 187(1)

   Government contractor sued by the United States for receiving fees from subcontractors in connection with award of subcontract was not entitled to maintain third-party complaint against subcontractors even though he returned the "kickback" payments after receiving them. U.S. v. Hutchins, D.C.Or.1969, 47 F.R.D. 340. Federal Civil Procedure ⊕ 287

7. Summary judgment
   In action by government to recover under section 51 et seq. of this title certain payments made by subcontractor to agents of a higher tier subcontractor allegedly in violation of section 51 et seq. of this title affidavits disclosed that there were genuine issues of fact as to whether agents who received payments in fact influenced award of contracts, whether payments to agents were made with the full knowledge and approval of higher tier subcontractor and whether the pay-

ments were lawful at time made, precluding summary judgment.   U.S. v. Perry,
C.A.9 (Cal.) 1970, 431 F.2d 1020.   Federal Civil Procedure ☞ 2539

§ 56. Administrative offsets

(a) Offset authority

A contracting officer of a contracting agency may offset the amount
of a kickback provided, accepted, or charged in violation of section
53 of this title against any moneys owed by the United States to the
prime contractor under the prime contract to which such kickback
relates.

(b) Duties of prime contractor

(1) Upon direction of a contracting officer of a contracting agency
with respect to a prime contract, the prime contractor shall withhold
from any sums owed to a subcontractor under a subcontract of the
prime contract the amount of any kickback which was or may be
offset against that prime contractor under subsection (a) of this
section.

(2) Such contracting officer may order that sums withheld under
paragraph (1)—

   (A) be paid over to the contracting agency; or

   (B) if the United States has already offset the amount of such
   sums against that prime contractor, be retained by the prime
   contractor.

(3) The prime contractor shall notify the contracting officer when
an amount is withheld and retained under paragraph (2)(B).

(c) Claim of Government

An offset under subsection (a) of this section or a direction or order
of a contracting officer under subsection (b) of this section is a claim
by the Government for the purposes of the Contract Disputes Act of
1978 [41 U.S.C.A. § 601 et seq.].

(d) "Contracting officer" defined

As used in this section, the term "contracting officer" has the
meaning given that term for the purposes of the Contract Disputes
Act of 1978 [41 U.S.C.A. § 601 et seq.].

(Mar. 8, 1946, c. 80, § 6, as added Nov. 7, 1986, Pub.L. 99–634, § 2(a), 100
Stat. 3524.)

HISTORICAL AND STATUTORY NOTES

Revision Notes and Legislative Reports
   1986 Acts. The existing Act provides a
limited right of offset to recover the
amount of any kickback. It states that
the kickback amount "shall be recovera-

ble on behalf of the United States from the subcontractor or the recipient thereof by setoff of moneys otherwise owing to the subcontractor either directly by the United States, or by a prime contractor under any contract or by an action in an appropriate court of the United States." Further, it indicates, "Upon the direction of the contracting department or agency or of the General Accounting Office, the prime contractor shall withhold from sums otherwise due a subcontractor any amount reported to have been found to have been paid by a subcontractor" as a kickback. Thus, the kickback amount may be recoverable by the United States from the subcontractor or the kickback recipient through an offset of moneys owed directly to the United States or the kickback amount may be offset by a prime contractor under a contract upon the direction of the contracting agency or the General Accounting Office. Section 6 of H.R. 4783 preserves and extends this right of offset.

Section 6(a) provides the United States the general authority to offset kickback amounts. It extends the existing Act to allow the United States to offset kickback amounts from moneys owed the prime contractor, any higher-tier subcontractor, and certain involved employees thereof. Section 6(a) provides "The United States may recover the amount of any kickback paid, accepted, or charged in violation of section 3(a) by offsetting such amount against any moneys owed by the United States—(1) to the prime contractor, prime contractor employee, subcontractor, or subcontractor employee which included such amount in a contract price, or (2) to the recipient or recipients of such kickback." The offset right, therefore, is not restricted, as in the existing Act, to offset recovery from the subcontractor or kickback recipients. Further, reading section 6(a) in conjunction with the conclusive presumption provided in Section 3(b), this offset right is automatically established against the prime contractor or a higher-tier subcontractor whenever a kickback occurs at a lower tier. The offset, however, does not apply to attempted kickbacks, but only when a kickback has actually been paid, accepted, or charged in violation of the Act.

Section 6(b) generally reflects the provision in the existing law allowing the government to direct a prime contractor to withhold kickback amounts from mon-

ey owed to a subcontractor. As in the existing Act, Section 6(b) gives the United States the right to exercise an offset through a prime contractor.

Section 6(b)(2) extends this existing provision to allow the government to recoup such an offset directed to be made by a prime contractor under section 6(b)(1). The government may direct the prime contractor to pay to the contracting agency any or all of the amount offset from a subcontractor by the prime contractor. Under Section 6(b)(2)(B), the government may direct the prime contractor to retain such sums when the government has already recovered the kickback amount from the prime contractor under Section 6(a).

Sections 6(b)(1) and 6(b)(2) are designed to work together to provide both the government and the prime contractor, at the government's direction, a full recoupment of any kickback amounts. For example, read together, subsections 6(b)(1) and 6(b)(2)(A) will cover situations when the United States does not owe the subcontractor sufficient sums to seek a direct offset under Section 6(a). Under Section 6(b)(1), the government may direct the prime contractor to withhold the necessary amount from moneys the prime contractor owes the subcontractor, and under subsection 6(b)(2)(A), to pay that amount to the contracting agency.

Read together, subsections 6(b)(1) and 6(b)(2)(B) cover situations when the government has already offset against a prime contractor under subsection 6(a) but wants to authorize the prime contractor to recover that amount from the subcontractor. Under subsection 6(b)(1), the government may direct the prime contractor to withhold from moneys it owes the subcontractor the amount of kickback and, on direction of the government under subsection 6(b)(2)(B), the prime contractor retains the money offset since the government has already collected that amount directly from the prime contractor. When funds are actually retained by the prime contractor under Section 6(b)(2)(B), the prime contractor must notify the contracting officer.

Section 6(b) is intended to benefit those prime contractors who have had sums offset by the United States under Section 6(a) for violating Section 3(a)(3). As explained above, Section 3(a)(3), in conjunction with the conclusive presumption in Section 3(b) imposes vicarious liability for kickbacks made by lower-tier subcontractors without regard to knowledge or actual harm to the government. Section 6(b) is intended to allow prime contractors recoupment of the amount of the kickback which the government has recovered from them through an offset. This section 6(b) remedy is provided in addition to any other legal rights a prime contractor or higher tier subcontractor may pursue to recoup such losses.

Section 6(b) predicates the authority of the prime contractor to offset against moneys it owes a subcontractor on the "written direction of the contracting officer." This is an important safeguard against the prime contractor's using these provisions unilaterally. It is intended that a contracting officer will not authorize a prime contractor to retain funds under subsection 6(b)(2)(B) when the prime contractor was a knowing participant in a kickback scheme. Further, the Committee intends that the contracting officer's actions and decisions under section 6(b) be governed by the Contract Disputes Act of 1978, in cases of offsets against the contract connected with the kickback or the Debt Collection Act of 1982 in all other circumstances. A prime contractor may seek review under the Contract Disputes Act when it disagrees with a contracting officer's decisions or actions under Section 6(b). House Report No. 99–964.

References in Text

The Contract Disputes Act of 1978, referred to in subsecs. (c) and (d), is Pub.L. 95–563, Nov. 1, 1978, 92 Stat. 2383, which is classified principally to chapter 9 (section 601 et seq.) of this title. For complete classification of this Act to the Code, see Short Title note set out under section 601 of this title and Tables.

Effective and Applicability Provisions

1986 Acts. Section effective with respect to conduct described in section 53 of this title which occurs on or after Nov. 7, 1986, see section 3(a) of Pub.L. 99–634, set out as a note under section 51 of this title.

LIBRARY REFERENCES

American Digest System
United States ⬦75(6).
Key Number System Topic No. 393.

Corpus Juris Secundum
CJS United States § 136, Rights and Remedies of United States.

Research References

Encyclopedias
70 Am. Jur. Proof of Facts 3d 97, Proof That a Government Agency Was Liable for Improperly Granting a Bid Award to a Bid Applicant.

Treatises and Practice Aids
Federal Procedure, Lawyers Edition § 39:1372, Setoff.

WESTLAW ELECTRONIC RESEARCH

See Westlaw guide following the Explanation pages of this volume.

Notes of Decisions

1. Subcontractor offsets

Where subcontractor made illegal payments to employee of prime contractor having contract with War Shipping Administration as an inducement for award of subcontracts, subcontractor making payments was entitled to set off against total amount of liability to United States for the amount of such payments, amount paid by him to employee of prime contractor in co-operation with and at request of agents of the Federal Bureau of Investigation. U.S. v. Gemmell, E.D.Pa. 1958, 160 F.Supp. 792. United States ⬦ 75(6)

2. Persons entitled to maintain action

Where substantial question existed as to whether third party owed any sum to bankrupt estate and United States asserted claim against third party which was substantial and not merely colorable, and United States, prior to bankruptcy, had notified third party, pursuant to provisions of section 51 et seq. of this title, to withhold any moneys claimed to be due bankrupt, both parties were entitled to have their rights adjudicated in plenary suit. Goggin v. Consolidated Liquidating Corp., C.A.9 (Cal.) 1951, 190 F.2d 553. Bankruptcy ⟾ 2045

§ 57.   Contractor responsibilities

(a) Procedural requirements for prevention and detection of violations

Each contracting agency shall include in each prime contract awarded by such agency a requirement that the prime contractor shall have in place and follow reasonable procedures designed to prevent and detect violations of section 53 of this title in its own operations and direct business relationships.

(b) Cooperation in investigations requirement

Each contracting agency shall include in each prime contract awarded by such agency a requirement that the prime contractor shall cooperate fully with any Federal Government agency investigating a violation of section 53 of this title.

(c) Reporting requirement; supplying information as favorable evidence of responsibility

(1)(A) Whenever a prime contractor or subcontractor has reasonable grounds to believe that a violation of section 53 of this title may have occurred, the prime contractor or subcontractor shall promptly report the possible violation in writing.

(B) A contractor shall make the reports required by subparagraph (A) to the inspector general of the contracting agency, the head of the contracting agency if the agency does not have an inspector general, or the Department of Justice.

(2) In the case of an administrative or contractual action to suspend or debar any person who is eligible to enter into contracts with the Federal Government, evidence that such person has supplied information to the United States pursuant to paragraph (1) shall be favorable evidence of such person's responsibility for the purposes of Federal procurement laws and regulations.

(d) Partial inapplicability to small contracts

Subsections (a) and (b) of this section do not apply to a prime contract that is not greater than $100,000 or to a prime contract for the acquisition of commercial items (as defined in section 403(12) of this title).

(e) Cooperation in investigations regardless of contract amount

Notwithstanding subsection (d) of this section, a prime contractor shall cooperate fully with any Federal Government agency investigating a violation of section 53 of this title.

(Mar. 8, 1946, c. 80, § 7, as added Nov. 7, 1986, Pub.L. 99–634, § 2(a), 100 Stat. 3525, and amended Oct. 13, 1994, Pub.L. 103–355, Title IV, § 4104(a), Title VIII, 8301(c)(1), 108 Stat. 3341, 3397; Feb. 10, 1996, Pub.L. 104–106, Div. D, Title XLIII, § 4321(g), 110 Stat. 675.)

HISTORICAL AND STATUTORY NOTES

Revision Notes and Legislative Reports
1986 Acts. Section 7 of H.R. 4783 places new requirements on prime contractors and subcontractors designed to elicit their efforts in detecting and deterring subcontractor kickbacks. The existing Act does not contain similar provision.

Section 7(a) states that all government contracts must have provisions requiring prime contractors to "have in place and follow reasonable procedures designed to prevent and detect violations" of the Act, "in its own operations and direct business relationships." This provision is intended to require prime contractors to institute formal procedures to detect and eliminate kickbacks.

Examples of such procedures include, *inter alia*, education programs for employees and subcontractors, policy manuals regarding kickback indicators and company rules, special procurement and audit procedures, company ethics policies which address kickback activities, applicant screening processes to detect kickback violators, and reporting procedures to notify company and law enforcement officials of suspected kickbacks.

Such procedures are not required by this provision to be imposed upon a company's subcontractors. Rather, these need only be internal company procedures designed to detect kickbacks whenever they occur and to prevent kickbacks involving their own company.

Section 7(b) states that all Federal contracts must contain a requirement that the "prime contractor shall cooperate fully with any Federal government agency investigating" a kickback violation. The Committee intends that full cooperation mean, at a minimum that the prime contractor will promptly report kickback activities to Federal law enforcement officials as provided in subsection 7(c) and

will provide reasonable access to relevant company documents.

Subsection 7(c)(1)(a) requires prime contractors and subcontractors to report in writing to the appropriate government official when they have "reasonable grounds to believe" a violation of the Act has occurred. The Committee intends that the prime or subcontractor only report well-founded suspicions of kickbacks activity. It is not intended that suspicions based only on rumor be reported.

Subsection 7(c)(1)(B) specifies that these written reports be made to "the inspector general of the contracting agency, the head of the contracting agency if the agency does not have an inspector general, or the Department of Justice."

Subsection 7(c)(2) provides that the act of reporting potential violations of the Act under subsection 7(c) must be viewed as favorable evidence of a contractor's present responsibility to contract with the Federal government in a suspension and debarment proceeding based upon the kickbacks reported. This provision is not conclusive as to the issue of a contractor's present responsibility in such a proceeding and it does not immunize contractors from suspension and debarment proceedings. It is only favorable evidence on that issue. House Report No. 99–964.

1994 Acts. Senate Report Nos. 103–258 and 103–259, and House Conference Report No. 103–712, see 1994 U.S. Code Cong. and Adm. News, p. 2561.

1996 Acts. House Conference Report No. 104–450, see 1996 U.S. Code Cong. and Adm. News, p. 238.

Amendments
1996 Amendments. Subsec. (d). Pub.L. 104–106, § 4321(g), struck out the second period at end of sentence and made technical changes which, for pur-

poses of codification, required no further changes in text.

1994   Amendments. Subsec.   (d). Pub.L. 103–355, §§ 4104(a), 8301(c)(1), added subsec. (d) and amended such subsection to declare subsecs. (a) and (b) inapplicable to a prime contract for the acquisition of commercial items defined in section 403(12) of this title.

Subsec. (e). Pub.L. 103–355, § 4101(a) added subsec. (e).

Effective and Applicability Provisions
1996 Acts. Amendment by Pub.L. 104–106 effective Feb. 10, 1996, except as otherwise provided, see section 4401 of Pub.L. 104–106, set out as a note under section 251 of this title.

1994   Acts. Amendment by sections 4104(a) and 8301(c)(1) of Pub.L. 103–355 effective Oct. 13, 1994, except as otherwise provided, see section 10001 of Pub.L. 103–355, set out as a note under section 251 of this title.

1986 Acts. Subsecs. (a) and (b) effective with respect to contract solicitations issued by an agency, department, or other establishment of the Federal Government on or after the date which is 90 days after Nov. 7, 1986; and subsec. (c) effective with respect to conduct described in section 53 of this title which occurs on or after Nov. 7, 1986, see section 3 of Pub.L. 99–634, set out as a note under section 51 of this title.

LIBRARY REFERENCES

American Digest System
United States ☞75(6).
Key Number System Topic No. 393.

WESTLAW ELECTRONIC RESEARCH

See Westlaw guide following the Explanation pages of this volume.

§ 58. Inspection authority

For the purpose of ascertaining whether there has been a violation of section 53 of this title with respect to any prime contract, the Government Accountability Office and the inspector general of the contracting agency, or a representative of such contracting agency designated by the head of such agency if the agency does not have an inspector general, shall have access to and may inspect the facilities and audit the books and records, including any electronic data or records, of any prime contractor or subcontractor under a prime contract awarded by such agency. This section does not apply with respect to a prime contract for the acquisition of commercial items (as defined in section 403(12) of this title).

(Mar. 8, 1946, c. 80, § 8, as added Nov. 7, 1986, Pub.L. 99–634, § 2(a), 100 Stat. 3525, and amended Oct. 13, 1994, Pub.L. 103–355, Title VIII, § 8301(c)(2), 108 Stat. 3397; July 7, 2004, Pub.L. 108–271, § 8(b), 118 Stat. 814.)

HISTORICAL AND STATUTORY NOTES

Revision Notes and Legislative Reports
1986 Acts. The existing Act authorizes the General Accounting Office "to inspect the plants and to audit the books and records of any prime contractor or subcontractor engaged in the performance of

a negotiated contract" when investigating a possible kickback. 41 U.S.C. 53.

Section 8 of H.R. 4783 retains this authority and expands it in two aspects. First, in accordance with the general provisions of the bill, the authority is expanded to include contractors under all types of government contracts, not just negotiated contracts.

Second, Section 8 provides this authority to inspect and audit to the inspectors general of the contracting agencies, or, in the case of agencies without inspectors general, to representatives designated by the agency head. The inspectors general were created after the enactment of the existing law. It is the Committee's understanding that the authority granted in this section to the inspectors general is merely duplicative of authority under other existing statutes. The inspectors general are included in this Section to ensure that it does not diminish, by inference, that authority. House Report No. 99–964.

1994 Acts. Senate Report Nos. 103–258 and 103–259, and House Conference Report No. 103–712, see 1994 U.S. Code Cong. and Adm. News, p. 2651.

Amendments

1994 Amendments. Pub.L. 103–355, § 8301(c)(2), provided that this section does not apply with respect to a prime contract for the acquisition of commercial items as defined in section 403(12) of this title.

Subsec. (b). Pub.L. 103–355, § 4103(a), added subsec. (b).

Effective and Applicability Provisions

1994 Acts. Amendment by section 8301(c)(2) of Pub.L. 103–355 effective Oct. 13, 1994, except as otherwise provided, see section 10001 of Pub.L. 103–355, set out as a note under section 251 of this title.

1986 Acts. Section effective with respect to conduct described in section 53 of this title which occurs on or after Nov. 7, 1986, see section 3(a) of Pub.L. 99–634, set out as a note under section 51 of this title.

Change of Name

"Government Accountability Office" substituted for "General Accounting Office" in text on authority of Pub.L. 108–271, § 8(b), cited in the credit to this section and set out as a note under 31 U.S.C.A. § 702, which provided that any reference to the General Accounting Office in any law, rule, regulation, certificate, directive, instruction, or other official paper in force on July 17, 2004, to refer and apply to the Government Accountability Office.

LIBRARY REFERENCES

American Digest System

United States ☞75(1).
Key Number System Topic No. 393.

Research References

Encyclopedias

70 Am. Jur. Proof of Facts 3d 97, Proof That a Government Agency Was Liable for Improperly Granting a Bid Award to a Bid Applicant.

Forms

Nichols Cyclopedia of Legal Forms Annotated § 7:2530, United States Lessee--General Clauses.

Treatises and Practice Aids

Federal Procedure, Lawyers Edition § 39:1371, Introduction.

West's Federal Administrative Practice § 613, Laws Applicable--Contract Solicitation.

WESTLAW ELECTRONIC RESEARCH

See Westlaw guide following the Explanation pages of this volume.

CHAPTER 2—TERMINATION OF WAR CONTRACTS

WESTLAW COMPUTER ASSISTED LEGAL RESEARCH

Westlaw supplements your legal research in many ways. Westlaw allows you to

- update your research with the most current information
- expand your library with additional resources
- retrieve current, comprehensive history citing references to a case with KeyCite

For more information on using Westlaw to supplement your research, see the Westlaw Electronic Research Guide, which follows the Explanation.

---

§ 101. Declaration of policy

The Congress declares that the objectives of this chapter are—

(a) to facilitate maximum war production during the war, and to expedite reconversion from war production to civilian production as war conditions permit;

(b) to assure to prime contractors and subcontractors, small and large, speedy and equitable final settlement of claims under terminated war contracts, and adequate interim financing until such final settlement;

(c) to assure uniformity among Government agencies in basic policies and administration with respect to such termination settlements and interim financing;

(d) to facilitate the efficient use of materials, manpower, and facilities for war and civilian purposes by providing prime contractors and subcontractors with notice of termination of their war contracts as far in advance of the cessation of work thereunder as is feasible and consistent with the national security;

(e) to assure the expeditious removal from the plants of prime contractors and subcontractors of termination inventory not to be retained or sold by the contractor;

(f) to use all practicable methods compatible with the foregoing objectives to prevent improper payments and to detect and prosecute fraud.

(July 1, 1944, c. 358, § 1, 58 Stat. 649.)

HISTORICAL AND STATUTORY NOTES

Revision Notes and Legislative Reports
  1944 Acts. Senate Report No. 836 and House Report No. 1590, see 1944 U.S.Code Cong.Service, p. 1161.

Separability of Provisions
  Section 26 of Act July 1, 1944, provided that: "If any provision of this Act [enacting this chapter], or the application of such provision to any person or circumstance, is held invalid, the remainder of this Act or the application of such provision to persons or circumstances other than those as to which it is held invalid, shall not be affected thereby."

Short Title
  1944 Acts. Section 27 of Act July 1, 1944, provided that "This Act [enacting this chapter] may be cited as the 'Contract Settlement Act of 1944'."

Settlement of Claims for War Contract Losses Incurred Between September 16, 1940, and August 14, 1945
  See Act Aug. 7, 1946, c. 864, §§ 1–6, 60 Stat. 902, set out as a note under section 106 of this title.

LIBRARY REFERENCES

American Digest System
  United States ⏀74(16).
  Key Number System Topic No. 393.

Corpus Juris Secundum
  CJS Federal Courts § 778, Jurisdiction--Claims Against United States--Under General Jurisdiction Statute.

Research References

ALR Library

68 ALR, Fed. 842, What Is "Agency" Within Meaning of Federal Sunshine Act (5 U.S.C.A. § 552b).

28 ALR 2nd 867, Measure and Items of Compensation of Contractor Under Cost-Plus Contract Which Is Terminated, Without Breach, Before Completion.

175 ALR 1366, What Amounts to Conditional Sale.

140 ALR 1518, Validity and Construction of War Enactments in United States Suspending Operation of Statute of Limitations.

76 ALR 268, Right of Public Contractor to Allowance of Extra Expense Over What Would Have Been Necessary if Conditions Had Been as Represented by the Plans and Specifications.

51 ALR 233, Extent of Liability in Respect to Property Seized by Alien Property Custodian Under Trading with the Enemy Act.

Forms

30 West's Legal Forms § 30:22, Mutual Release on Termination of Contract.

Treatises and Practice Aids

Federal Procedure, Lawyers Edition § 2:4, What Is an Agency?

WESTLAW ELECTRONIC RESEARCH

See Westlaw guide following the Explanation pages of this volume.

Notes of Decisions

Constitutionality   1
Construction   2
Construction with other laws   3
Purpose   4

-----

1. Constitutionality

The provisions of this chapter and the War Mobilization and Reconversion Act [repealed], 50 App. former § 1651 et seq., for termination of war contracts and payment of fair compensation to war contractors, were war measures enacted under war powers of Congress and reasonably necessary and proper for carrying into execution these war powers, and to prevent a complete disruption of the economy following end of war. Monolith Portland Midwest Co. v. R.F.C., S.D.Cal. 1955, 128 F.Supp. 824. United States ☞ 72.1(7); United States ☞ 74(16)

Congress exercised its constitutional war powers in enactment of this chapter. Monolith Portland Midwest Co. v. R.F.C., S.D.Cal.1951, 95 F.Supp. 570. War And National Emergency ☞ 35; War And National Emergency ☞ 43

2. Construction

This chapter superseded any provisions in conflict with it and stands for interpretation on its own language. Johnson v. R.F.C., E.D.Tenn.1950, 94 F.Supp. 214. United States ☞ 74(16)

3. Construction with other laws

Neither the law of specific performance or breach of contract applied in cases under this chapter and the War Mobilization and Reconversion Act [repealed], 50 App. former § 1651 et seq., on termination of war contracts. Monolith Portland Midwest Co. v. R.F.C., S.D.Cal.1955, 128 F.Supp. 824. United States ☞ 72.1(7); United States ☞ 74(16)

The War Mobilization and Reconversion Act [repealed], 50 App. former § 1651 et seq., and this chapter had to be read together. Monolith Portland Midwest Co. v. R.F.C., S.D.Cal.1951, 95 F.Supp. 570. Statutes ☞ 223.2(32)

4. Purpose

This chapter plainly shows that the prime purpose of Congress in enacting it was to eliminate all red tape and to provide a means for the expeditious settlement of war contracts which had been abruptly terminated at the conclusion of the war. U.S. v. Erie Basin Metal Products, Inc., C.A.7 (Ill.) 1957, 244 F.2d 809. United States ☞ 74(16)

The objective of this chapter is the speedy and final settlement of claims of contractors against agencies of the United States. Condenser Service & Engineering Co. v. U.S., Ct.Cl.1955, 128 F.Supp. 148, 130 Ct.Cl. 714. United States ☞ 74(16)

The purpose of this chapter was to set up a procedure for dealing with the termination of war contracts by arranging for payment to contractors when the Government cancelled the contract because it no longer wanted the article contracted for. U.S. v. Sack, S.D.N.Y.1954, 125 F.Supp. 633. United States ☞ 74(16)

Purpose of this chapter is to provide quick, efficient and equitable method of settling terminated war contracts and expediting reconversion and to achieve uniformity not only among Governmental agencies charged with termination settlement and interim financing, but also among instrumentalities of Government which Congress appointed to hear and decide such claims. Monolith Portland Midwest Co. v. R.F.C., S.D.Cal.1952, 102 F.Supp. 951. United States ☞ 74(16)

In enacting this chapter, Congress intended to fully and fairly compensate war contractors whose contracts had been terminated, as a result of termination of active hostilities, for all costs and expenses reasonably incurred by war contractors in the prosecution of their contract, including a fair profit in accordance with established sound accounting practices. U.S. v. Leyde & Leyde, D.C.Md.1950, 89 F.Supp. 256. United States ☞ 74(16)

§ 102. Surveillance by Congress

(a) To assist the Congress in appraising the administration of this chapter and in developing such amendments or related legislation as may further be necessary to accomplish the objectives of this chapter, the appropriate committees of the Senate and the House of Representatives shall study each report submitted to the Congress under this chapter and shall otherwise maintain continuous surveillance of the operations of the Government agencies under this chapter.

(b) Repealed. Oct. 31, 1951, c. 654, § 1(110), 65 Stat. 705.

(July 1, 1944, c. 358, § 2, 58 Stat. 649; Oct. 31, 1951, c. 654, § 1(110), 65 Stat. 705.)

HISTORICAL AND STATUTORY NOTES

Amendments
1951 Amendments. Subsec. (b). Act Oct. 31, 1951, repealed subsec. (b), which related to reports to Congress.

LIBRARY REFERENCES

American Digest System
    United States ☞74(16).
    Key Number System Topic No. 393.

WESTLAW ELECTRONIC RESEARCH

See Westlaw guide following the Explanation pages of this volume.

§ 103. Definitions

As used in this chapter—

(a) The term "prime contract" means any contract, agreement, or purchase order heretofore or hereafter entered into by a contracting agency and connected with or related to the prosecution of the war; and the term "prime contractor" means any holder of one or more prime contracts.

(b) The term "subcontract" means any contract, agreement, or purchase order heretofore or hereafter entered into to perform any work, or to make or furnish any material to the extent that such work or material is required for the performance of any one or more prime contracts or of any one or more other subcontracts; and the term "subcontractor" means any holder of one or more subcontracts.

(c) The term "war contract" means a prime contract or a subcontract; and the term "war contractor" means any holder of one or more war contracts.

(d) The terms "termination", "terminate" and "terminated" refer to the termination or cancellation, in whole or in part, of work under a prime contract for the convenience or at the option of the Government (except for default of the prime contractor) or of work under a subcontract for any reason except the default of the subcontractor.

(e) The term "material" includes any article, commodity, machinery, equipment, accessory, part, component, assembly, work in process, maintenance, repair, and operating supplies, and any product of any kind.

(f) The term "Government agency" means any executive department of the Government, or any administrative unit or subdivision thereof, any independent agency or any corporation owned or controlled by the United States in the executive branch of the Government, and includes any contracting agency.

(g) The term "contracting agency" means any Government agency, which has been or hereafter may be authorized to make contracts pursuant to section 611 of Appendix to Title 50, and includes the Reconstruction Finance Corporation and any corporation organized pursuant to the Reconstruction Finance Corporation Act, and the Secretary of Commerce.

(h) The term "termination claim" means any claim or demand by a war contractor for fair compensation for the termination of any war contract and any other claim under a terminated war contract, which regulations prescribed under this chapter authorize to be asserted and settled in connection with any termination settlement.

(i) The term "interim financing" includes advance payments, partial payments, loans, discounts, advances, and commitments in connection therewith, and guaranties of loans, discounts, advances, and commitments in connection therewith and any other type of financing made in contemplation of or related to termination of war contracts.

(j) The term "Administrator" means the Administrator of General Services.

(k) The term "person" means any individual, corporation, partnership, firm, association, trust, estate, or other entity.

(l) The term "termination inventory" means any materials (including a proper part of any common materials), properly allocable to the terminated portion of a war contract, except any machinery or equipment subject to a separate contract specifically governing the use or disposition thereof.

(m) The term "final and conclusive", as applied to any settlement, finding, or decision, means that such settlement, finding, or decision shall not be reopened, annulled, modified, set aside, or disregarded by any officer, employee, or agent of the United States or in any suit, action, or proceeding except as provided in this chapter.

(July 1, 1944, c. 358, § 3, 58 Stat. 650; Ex. Ord. No. 9638, § 1, eff. Oct. 4, 1945, 10 F.R. 12591; Ex. Ord. No. 9809, §§ 1, 8, eff. Dec. 12, 1946, 11 F.R. 14281; Ex. Ord. No. 9841, §§ 101, 203, eff. Apr. 23, 1947, 12 F.R. 2645; June 30, 1947, c. 166, Title II, § 207, 61 Stat. 209; 1947 Reorg. Plan No. 1, § 201, eff. July 1, 1947, 12 F.R. 4534, 61 Stat. 951; June 30, 1949, c. 288, Title I, § 102(b), 63 Stat. 380.)

HISTORICAL AND STATUTORY NOTES

References in Text

Section 611 of Appendix to Title 50, referred to in subsec. (g), was repealed by Pub.L. 89–554, § 8(a), Sept. 6, 1966, 80 Stat. 651. See section 1431 et seq. of Title 50, War and National Defense.

The Reconstruction Finance Corporation Act, referred to in subsec. (g), is Act Jan. 22, 1932, c. 8, 47 Stat. 5, as amended, which was classified to chapter 14 (section 601 et seq.) of Title 15, Commerce and Trade, and has been eliminated from the Code. For complete classification of this Act to the Code prior to its elimination from the Code, see Tables.

Codifications

The Smaller War Plants Corporation was omitted from the definition of the term "contracting agency," in subsec. (g) of this section on the authority of section 207 of Act June 30, 1947, which provided: "The liquidation of the affairs of the Smaller War Plants Corporation administered by the Reconstruction Finance Corporation pursuant to Executive Order 9665 shall be carried out by

the Reconstruction Finance Corporation, notwithstanding the provisions of the last paragraph of section 5 of the First War Powers Act, 1941 [section 605 of Appendix to Title 50, War and National Defense]. The Smaller War Plants Corporation is hereby abolished."

Transfer of Functions

In subsec. (g) "Secretary of Commerce" was substituted for "War Production Board" in view of transfer of War Production Board functions to the Civilian Production Administration, then to the Office of Temporary Controls, and then to the Secretary of Commerce by Ex. Ord. Nos. 9638, 9809, and 9841, respectively.

In subsec. (j), functions of Director of Contract Settlement were transferred to Secretary of the Treasury by Executive Order No. 9809, § 8, and Reorg. Plan No. 1 of 1947, § 201, were retransferred to Administrator of General Services by Act June 30, 1949, c. 288, § 102(b), 63 Stat. 380, which was classified to former 40 U.S.C.A. § 752(b), prior to repeal by

Pub.L. 107–217, § 6(b), Aug. 21, 2002, 116 Stat. 1304.

Effective Date of Transfer of Functions

Act June 30, 1949, § 605, which set July 1, 1949, as the effective date for the transfer of functions by that Act, was repealed by Pub.L. 107–217, § 6(b), Aug. 21, 2002, 116 Stat. 1313.

Abolition of Reconstruction Finance Corporation

Reorg. Plan No. 1 of 1957, § 6(a), eff. June 30, 1957, 22 F.R. 4633, 71 Stat. 647, set out in the Appendix to Title 5, Government Organization and Employees, abolished the Reconstruction Finance Corporation.

CROSS REFERENCES

War contracts penal provision as comprehending definitions of terms used in this section, see 18 USCA § 443.

Wartime suspension of limitations, applicability of definitions, see 18 USCA § 3287.

WESTLAW ELECTRONIC RESEARCH

See Westlaw guide following the Explanation pages of this volume.

Notes of Decisions

Construction with other laws 1
Final and conclusive 4
Prime contract 2
Private right of action 5
Termination 3

1. Construction with other laws

Anti–Deficiency Act did not bar war contractor's recovery under Contract Settlement Act (CSA) of environmental cleanup costs arising from performance of contract during World War II. Ford Motor Co. v. U.S., C.A.Fed.2004, 378 F.3d 1314, rehearing and rehearing en banc denied. United States ⬅ 62; United States ⬅ 74(16)

Amendment of the War Time Suspension of Limitations Act of 1942, section 3287 of Title 18, by this section did not manifest an intent to deal solely with offenses growing out of the subject matter of this section, where the amendment did not confine itself to termination of contracts but applied to any offense against the laws of the United States committed in connection with war contracts including those involving renegotiation. U.S. v. Sack, S.D.N.Y.1954, 125 F.Supp. 633. Criminal Law ⬅ 151.1

2. Prime contract

A contract between a cement company and Defense Plant Corporation for the construction and operation of a test plant to determine the feasibility of commercially extracting alumina from certain ores by method developed by the company was a "prime contract" within this

section, defining a prime contract for war production and could be validly terminated by the Reconstruction Finance Corporation upon an order issued pursuant to 50 App. former § 1651 et seq. Monolith Portland Midwest Co. v. Reconstruction Fin. Corp., C.A.9 (Cal.) 1949, 178 F.2d 854, certiorari denied 70 S.Ct. 668, 339 U.S. 932, 94 L.Ed. 1352, rehearing denied 70 S.Ct. 839, 339 U.S. 954, 94 L.Ed. 1367. United States ⬅ 72.1(7)

3. Termination

Provision in termination agreement between war contractor and Air Force for reimbursement of costs 'which are not now known" was not limited to liability that existed at time of termination of contract, but rather, extended to later-arising environmental cleanup costs; there was no temporal limit as to when claims would become known, provided their origin was performance of the war contract. Ford Motor Co. v. U.S., C.A.Fed.2004, 378 F.3d 1314, rehearing and rehearing en banc denied. United States ⬅ 74(16)

Where Government cancels contract therewith because of other party's default, such party has no rights under this chapter, as sole basis for contractor's recovery thereunder is Government's violation of contract by terminating or cancelling it. Glade Mountain Corp. v. R.F.C., C.A.3 (N.J.) 1952, 200 F.2d 815. United States ⬅ 74(16)

Under subsec. (d) of this section providing that term "termination" refers to termination or cancellation in whole or in part of work under principal contract for convenience of Government, supplemental agreement to Government contract providing that because it was advantageous and in best interest of United States to modify contract to terminate production activities under contract and allowing contractor to place plant in standby condition, terminated contract within meaning of said subsection. Houdaille Industries, Inc. v. U.S., Ct.Cl. 1957, 151 F.Supp. 298, 138 Ct.Cl. 301. United States ⚍ 74(16)

Contracts for sale of manganese ore to Metals Reserve Company, which expired automatically by their own terms, were not "terminated" within meaning of subsec. "(d) of this section, and hence contractors had no cause of action under section 106 of this title for fair compensation. Haberle v. R.F.C., D.C.D.C.1951, 104 F.Supp. 636. United States ⚍ 74(16)

Under subsec. (d) of this section, differentiating between terminations which are for convenience or at option of Government and which are covered by this chapter and those which are for default of contractor and which are excluded, contracting agencies are required to provide fair compensation for termination only in cases of termination for convenience. Johnson v. R.F.C., E.D.Tenn.1950, 94 F.Supp. 214. United States ⚍ 74(16)

4. Final and conclusive

Because war contractor's claim for reimbursement of environmental cleanup costs was exempted from settlement by terms of termination agreement between contractor and Air Force, government's liability under Contract Settlement Act (CSA) was not released. Ford Motor Co. v. U.S., C.A.Fed.2004, 378 F.3d 1314, rehearing and rehearing en banc denied. United States ⚍ 74(16)

Settlement of premiums between insurer and Maritime Commission in 1950 was final settlement within meaning of Contract Settlement Act of 1944, so that insurer could not seek additional premium payments to cover subsequently filed claims for injuries said to arise from asbestos exposure; there was no evidence that settlement was anything other than full settlement of all claims, plan's own terms set out procedure for final determination of premium, and insurer never requested that reserve be set aside for future claims that might be filed after final settlement was reached. American Employers Ins. Co. v. U.S., C.A.Fed.1987, 812 F.2d 700. United States ⚍ 74(16)

5. Private right of action

Contract Settlement Act creates a private right of action for disputes arising from the government's failure to enter into settlement agreements; however, the Act does not create a private right of action for alleged violations of provision prohibiting government from modifying or disregarding any final and conclusive settlement entered into under Act. Tucson Airport Authority v. General Dynamics Corp., D.Ariz.1996, 922 F.Supp. 273, affirmed 136 F.3d 641. United States ⚍ 74(16)

§ 104. Administration of chapter

(a) Repealed. Pub.L. 89–554, § 8(a), Sept. 6, 1966, 80 Stat. 652

(b) Rules and regulations

In order to insure uniform and efficient administration of the provisions of this chapter, the Administrator of General Services, subject to such provisions, by general orders or general regulations—

(1) shall prescribe policies, principles, methods, procedures, and standards to govern the exercise of the authority and discretion and the performance of the duties and functions of all Government agencies under this chapter; and

(2) may require or restrict the exercise of any such authority and discretion, or the performance of any such duty or function,

to such extent as he deems necessary to carry out the provisions of this chapter.

(c) Compliance

The exercise of any authority or discretion and the performance of any duty or function, conferred or imposed on any Government agency by this chapter, shall be subject to such orders and regulations prescribed by the Administrator of General Services pursuant to subsection (b) of this section. Each Government agency shall carry out such orders and regulations of the Administrator of General Services expeditiously, and shall issue such regulations with respect to its operations and procedures as may be necessary to carry out the policies, principles, methods, procedures, and standards prescribed by the Administrator of General Services. Any Government agency may issue such further regulations not inconsistent with the general orders or regulations of the Administrator of General Services as it deems necessary or desirable to carry out the provisions of this chapter.

(d) Personnel; supplies, facilities, and services

The Administrator of General Services may, within the limits of funds which may be made available, employ and fix the compensation of necessary personnel in accordance with the provisions of the civil-service laws and chapter 51 and subchapter III of chapter 53 of Title 5, and make expenditures for supplies, facilities, and services necessary for the performance of his functions under this chapter. Without regard to the provisions of the civil-service laws, he may employ certified public accountants, qualified cost accountants, industrial engineers, appraisers, and other experts, and contract with certified public accounting firms and qualified firms of engineers in the discharge of the duties imposed upon him and in furtherance of the objectives and policies of this chapter. The Administrator of General Services shall perform the duties imposed upon him through the personnel and facilities of the contracting agencies and other established Government agencies, to the extent that this does not interfere with the function of the Administrator of General Services to insure uniform and efficient administration of the provisions of this chapter.

(e) Publication in Federal Register

All orders and regulations prescribed by the Administrator of General Services or any Government agency under this chapter shall be published in the Federal Register.

(July 1, 1944, c. 358, § 4, 58 Stat. 651; Ex. Ord. No. 9809, § 8, eff. Dec. 12, 1946, 11 F.R. 14281; 1947 Reorg. Plan No. 1, § 201, eff. July 1, 1947, 12 F.R. 4534, 61 Stat. 951; June 30, 1949, c. 288, Title I, § 102(b), 63 Stat. 380; Oct. 28, 1949, c. 782, Title XI, § 1106(a), 63 Stat. 972; Sept. 6, 1966, Pub.L. 89–554, § 8(a), 80 Stat. 652.)

HISTORICAL AND STATUTORY NOTES

References in Text

The civil-service laws, referred to in subsec. (d), are set forth in Title 5, Government Organization and Employees. See, particularly, section 3301 et seq. of that Title.

Codifications

In subsec. (d) of this section, "chapter 51 and subchapter III of chapter 53 of Title 5" was substituted for "the Classification Act of 1949" on authority of Pub.L. 89–554, § 7(b), Sept. 6, 1966, 80 Stat. 631, the first section of which enacted Title 5, Government Organization and Employees.

In the second sentence of subsec. (d) of this section, provisions that authorized the appointment of a Deputy Director and that authorized the employment of certified public accountants, qualified cost accountants, industrial engineers, appraisers, and other experts without regard to "the Classification Act of 1923", were omitted as obsolete. Sections 1202 and 1204 of the Classification Act of 1949, 63 Stat. 972, 973, repealed the 1923 Act and all laws or parts of laws inconsistent with the 1949 Act. While section 1106(a) of the 1949 Act provided that references in other laws to the 1923 Act should be held and considered to mean the 1949 Act, it did not have the effect of continuing the exceptions contained in this sentence because of section 1106(b) which provided that the application of the 1949 Act to any position, officer, or employee shall not be affected by section 1106(a). The Classification Act of 1949 was repealed by Pub.L. 89–554, Sept. 6, 1966, § 8(a), 80 Stat. 632 (of which section 1 revised and enacted Title 5, Government Organization and Employees, into law). Section 5102 of Title 5 contains the applicability provisions of the 1949 Act, and section 5103 of Title 5 authorizes the Office of Personnel Management to determine the applicability to specific positions and employees.

Amendments

1966 Amendments. Subsec. (a). Pub.L. 89–554 repealed subsec. (a), which provided for the appointment, pay, and term of the Director of Contract Settlement. This office was abolished previously by Reorg. Plan No. 1 of 1947.

1949 Amendments. Subsec. (d). Act Oct. 28, 1949, substituted "Classification Act of 1949" for "Classification Act of 1923".

Transfer of Functions

The functions of Director of Contract Settlement were transferred to Secretary of the Treasury by Executive Order No. 9809, § 8, and Reorg. Plan No. 1 of 1947, § 201, were retransferred to Administrator of General Services by Act June 30, 1949, c. 288, § 102(b), 63 Stat. 380, which was classified to former 40 U.S.C.A. § 752(b), prior to repeal by Pub.L. 107–217, § 6(b), Aug. 21, 2002, 116 Stat. 1304.

Subsec. (a), establishing the Office of Contract Settlement to be headed by the Director of Contract Settlement and providing for the appointment of the Director by the President with the advice and consent of the Senate with compensation of $12,000 per year and a term of two years, was omitted and references in the remainder of this section to "Director" were changed to "Secretary of the Treasury" by Ex. Ord. No. 9809 and section 201 of Reorg. Plan No. 1 of 1947. Reorg. Plan No. 1 of 1947 is set out in the Appendix to Title 5, Government Organization and Employees.

Effective Date of Transfer of Functions

Act June 30, 1949, § 605, which set July 1, 1949, as the effective date for the transfer of functions by that Act, was repealed by Pub.L. 107–217, § 6(b), Aug. 21, 2002, 116 Stat. 1313.

Repeals

Act Oct. 28, 1949, c. 782, Title XI, § 1106(a), 63 Stat. 972, cited as a credit to this section, was repealed (subject to a savings clause) by Pub.L. 89–554, Sept. 6, 1966, § 8, 80 Stat. 632, 655.

CROSS REFERENCES

Additional duties of Administrator and delegation of authority by him, see 41 USCA §§ 121 and 123.

LIBRARY REFERENCES

American Digest System
United States ☞74(16).
Key Number System Topic No. 393.

WESTLAW ELECTRONIC RESEARCH

See Westlaw guide following the Explanation pages of this volume.

Notes of Decisions

Protection of United States interests 1

---

1. Protection of United States interests
It was the responsibility of former Director, now Administrator, to decide what administrative steps should be taken by the contracting agencies to protect the interests of the United States. 1945, 40 Op.Atty.Gen. 357.

§ 105. Contract Settlement Advisory Board; composition; duties

There is created a Contract Settlement Advisory Board, with which the Administrator of General Services shall advise and consult. The Board shall be composed of the Administrator of General Services who shall act as its Chairman, and of the Secretary of the Army, the Secretary of the Navy, the Secretary of Transportation, the Secretary of State, the chairman of the board of directors of the Reconstruction Finance Corporation, Secretary of Commerce, and the Attorney General or any alternate or representative designated by any of them. The Administrator of General Services shall request other Government agencies to participate in the deliberations of the Board whenever matters specially affecting them are under consideration.

(July 1, 1944, c. 358, § 5, 58 Stat. 651; Ex. Ord. No. 9630, § 1, eff. Sept. 27, 1945, 10 F.R. 12245; Ex. Ord. No. 9638, § 1, eff. Oct. 4, 1945, 10 F.R. 12591; Ex. Ord. No. 9665, § 2, eff. Dec. 27, 1945, 10 F.R. 15365; Ex. Ord. No. 9730, § 1, eff. May 27, 1946, 11 F.R. 5777; Ex. Ord. No. 9809, § 8, eff. Dec. 12, 1946, 11 F.R. 14281; Ex. Ord. No. 9841, §§ 101, 203, eff. Apr. 23, 1947, 12 F.R. 2645; 1947 Reorg.Plan No. 1, § 201, eff. July 1, 1947, 12 F.R. 4534, 61 Stat. 951; June 30, 1949, c. 288, Title I, § 102(b), 63 Stat. 380; Aug. 6, 1981, Pub.L. 97–31, § 12(17), 95 Stat. 154.)

HISTORICAL AND STATUTORY NOTES

Revision Notes and Legislative Reports
1981 Acts. House Report No. 97–199, see 1981 U.S.Code Cong. and Adm.News, p. 92.

Amendments
1981 Amendments. Pub.L. 97–31 substituted "Secretary of Transportation" for "Chairman of the Maritime Commission".

Change of Name
The Department of War was designated the Department of the Army and the title of the Secretary of War was changed to Secretary of the Army by section 205(a) of Act July 26, 1947, c. 343, Title II, 61 Stat. 501. Section 205(a) of Act July 26, 1947 was repealed by section 53 of Act Aug. 10, 1956, c. 1041, 70A Stat. 641. Section 1 of Act Aug. 10, 1956, enacted Title 10, Armed Forces, which in sections

3010 to 3013 continued the Department of the Army under the administrative supervision of a Secretary of the Army.

Transfer of Functions

Contract Settlement Advisory Board and all its property, records, etc., were transferred to the General Services Administration, but with the functions of the Board to be performed by the Board under conditions and limitations prescribed by law, by Act June 30, 1949, c. 288, § 102(b), 63 Stat. 380, which was classified to former 40 U.S.C.A. § 752(b), prior to repeal by Pub.L. 107–217, § 6(b), Aug. 21, 2002, 116 Stat. 1304.

Functions of Secretary of the Treasury were transferred to Administrator of General Services by Act June 30, 1949, c. 288, § 102(b), 63 Stat. 380, which was classified to former 40 U.S.C.A. § 752(b), prior to repeal by Pub.L. 107–217, § 6(b), Aug. 21, 2002, 116 Stat. 1304.

The Contract Settlement Advisory Board was transferred to the Department of the Treasury by section 8 of Ex. Ord. No. 9809 and section 201 of Reorg. Plan No. 1 of 1947. Reorg. Plan No. 1 of 1947 is set out in the Appendix to Title 5, Government Organization and Employees.

In text of this section, references to "Director" were changed to "Secretary of the Treasury" and phrase "the Secretary of the Treasury" following reference to Secretary of the Navy was omitted by section 8 of Ex. Ord. No. 9809, and section 201 of Reorg. Plan No. 1 of 1947.

The Administrator of the Foreign Economic Administration was changed to Secretary of State in view of Ex. Ord. No. 9630, as amended by Ex. Ord. No. 9730.

"Secretary of Commerce" was substituted for references to the Chairman of the War Production Board and the chairman and board of directors of the Smaller War Plants Corporation. War Production Board functions were transferred successively to the Civilian Production Administration, to the office of Temporary Controls and then to the Secretary of Commerce by Ex. Ord. Nos. 9638, 9809, and 9841, respectively. Functions of the chairman and Board of Directors of the Smaller War Plants Corporation were transferred to the Secretary of Commerce by Ex. Ord. No. 9665.

Effective Date of Transfer of Functions

Transfer of functions by Act June 30, 1949, as effective July 1, 1949, see section 605 of Act June 30, 1949, set out as an Effective Date note under section 471 of Title 40, Public Buildings, Property, and Works.

Abolition of Reconstruction Finance Corporation

Reorg. Plan No. 1 of 1957, § 6(a), eff. June 30, 1957, 22 F.R. 4633, 71 Stat. 647, set out in the Appendix to Title 5, Government Organization and Employees, abolished the Reconstruction Finance Corporation.

Secretary of the Air Force

For transfer of certain procurement and related functions and property, insofar as they pertain to the Air Force, from the Secretary of the Army and Department of the Army, to the Secretary of the Air Force and Department of the Air Force, see Secretary of Defense Transfer Order No. 6, eff. Jan. 15, 1948.

Termination of Advisory Boards

Advisory boards in existence on Jan. 5, 1973, to terminate not later than the expiration of the two-year period following Jan. 5, 1973, unless, in the case of a board established by the President or an officer of the Federal Government, such board is renewed by appropriate action prior to the expiration of such two-year period, or in the case of a board established by the Congress, its duration is otherwise provided by law, see sections 3(2), and 14 of Pub.L. 92–463, Oct. 6, 1972, 86 Stat. 770, 776, set out in Appendix 2 to Title 5, Government Organization and Employees.

LIBRARY REFERENCES

American Digest System

United States ⚖74(16).
Key Number System Topic No. 393.

WESTLAW ELECTRONIC RESEARCH

See Westlaw guide following the Explanation pages of this volume.

§ 106. Basis for settlement of termination claims

(a) Priority to private contractors

It is the policy of the Government, and it shall be the responsibility of the contracting agencies and the Administrator of General Services to provide war contractors with speedy and fair compensation for the termination of any war contract, in accordance with and subject to the provisions of this chapter, giving priority to contractors whose facilities are privately owned or privately operated. Such fair compensation for the termination of subcontracts shall be based on the same principles as compensation for the termination of prime contracts.

(b) Establishment of methods and standards

Each contracting agency shall establish methods and standards, suitable to the conditions of various war contractors, for determining fair compensation for the termination of war contracts on the basis of actual, standard, average, or estimated costs, or of a percentage of the contract price based on the estimated percentage of completion of work under the terminated contract, or on any other equitable basis, as it deems appropriate. To the extent that such methods and standards require accounting, they shall be adapted, so far as practicable, to the accounting systems used by war contractors, if consistent with recognized commercial accounting practice.

(c) Conclusiveness of settlement

Any contracting agency may settle all or any part of any termination claim under any war contract by agreement with the war contractor, or by determination of the amount due on the claim or part thereof without such agreement, or by any combination of these methods. Where any such settlement is made by agreement, the settlement shall be final and conclusive, except (1) to the extent otherwise agreed in the settlement; (2) for fraud; (3) upon renegotiation to eliminate excessive profits under section 1191 of Appendix to Title 50, unless exempt or exempted under such section; or (4) by mutual agreement before or after payment. Where any such settlement is made by determination without agreement, it shall likewise be final and conclusive, subject to the same exceptions as if made by agreement, unless the war contractor appeals or brings suit in accordance with section 113 of this title: *Provided*, That no settlement agreement hereunder involving payment to a war contractor of an amount in excess of $50,000 (or such lesser amount as the Administrator of General Services may from time to time determine) shall become binding upon the Government until the agreement has been reviewed and approved by a settlement review board of three or more members established by the contracting agency in the bureau, division, regional or district office, or other unit of the contracting agency authorized to make such settlement, or in the event of disapproval by the settlement review board, unless approved by the head of such bureau, division, regional or district office, or other unit. Failure of the settlement review board to act upon any settlement within thirty days after its submission to the board shall operate as approval by the board. The sole function of settlement review boards shall be to determine the over-all reasonableness of proposed settlement agreements from the point of view of protecting the interests of the Government. In determining, for purposes of this subsection, whether review of any settlement agreement is required because of the amounts involved, no deduction shall be made on account of credits for property chargeable to the Government or for advance or partial payments, but amounts payable under such settlement agreement for completed articles or work at the contract price and for the discharge of the termination claims of subcontractors shall be deducted.

(d) Allowable costs

Except as hereinafter provided, the methods and standards established under subsection (b) of this section for determining fair compensation for termination claims which are not settled by agreement shall be designed to compensate the war contractor fairly for the termination of the war contract, taking into account—

(1) the direct and indirect manufacturing, selling and distribution, administrative and other costs and expenses incurred by the war contractor which are reasonably necessary for the performance of the war contract and properly allocable to the terminated portion thereof under recognized commercial accounting practices; and

(2) reasonable costs and expenses of settling termination claims of subcontractors related to the terminated portion of the war contract; and

(3) reasonable accounting, legal, clerical, and other costs and expenses incident to termination and settlement of the terminated war contract; and

(4) reasonable costs and expenses of removing, preserving, storing and disposing of termination inventories; and

(5) such allowance for profit on the preparations made and work done for the terminated portion of the war contract as is reasonable under the circumstances; and

(6) interest on the termination claim in accordance with subsection (f) of this section; and

(7) the contract price and all amounts otherwise paid or payable under the contract.

The following shall not be included as elements of cost:

(i) Losses on other contracts, or from sales or exchanges of capital assets, fees and other expenses in connection with reorganization or recapitalization, antitrust or Federal income-tax litigation, or prosecution of Federal income-tax claims or other claims against the Government (except as provided in paragraph (3) of this subsection); losses on investments; provisions for contingencies; and premiums on life insurance where the contractor is the beneficiary.

(ii) The expense of conversion of the contractor's facilities to uses other than the performance of the contract.

(iii) Expenses due to the negligence or willful failure of the contractor to discontinue with reasonable promptness the incurring of expenses after the effective date of the termination notice.

(iv) Costs incurred in respect to facilities, materials, or services purchased or work done in excess of the reasonable quantitative requirements of the entire contract.

The failure specifically to mention in this subsection any item of cost is not intended to imply that it should be allowed or disallowed. The Administrator of General Services may interpret the provisions of this subsection and may provide for the inclusion or exclusion of other costs in accordance with recognized commercial accounting practice.

Where the small size of claims or the nature of production or performance or other factors make it impracticable to apply the principles stated in this subsection to any class of settlements which are subject to this subsection, the contracting agencies may establish alternative methods and standards for determining fair compensation for that class of termination claims. The aggregate amount of compensation allowed in accordance with this subsection (excluding amounts allowed under paragraphs (3) and (4) of this subsection) shall not exceed the total contract price reduced by the amount of payments otherwise made or to be made under the contract.

(e) Settlement by agreement

In order to carry out the objectives of this chapter, termination claims shall be settled by agreement to the maximum extent feasible and the methods and standards established under subsection (b) of this section shall be designed to facilitate such settlements. To the extent that he deems it practicable to do so without impeding expeditious settlements, the Administrator of General Services shall require the contracting agencies to take into account the factors enumerated in subsection (d) of this section in establishing methods and standards for determining fair compensation in the settlement of termination claims by agreement.

(f) Interest

Each contracting agency shall allow and pay interest on the amount due and unpaid from time to time on any termination claim under a prime contract at the rate of 2½ per centum per annum for the period beginning thirty days after the date fixed for termination and ending with the date of final payment, except that (1) if the prime contractor unreasonably delays the settlement of his claim, interest shall not accrue for the period of such delay, (2) if interest for the period after termination on any advance payment or loan, made or guaranteed by the Government, has been waived for the benefit of the contractor, the amount of the interest so waived allocable to the terminated contract or the terminated part of the contract shall be deducted from the interest otherwise payable hereunder, and (3) if after delivery of findings by a contracting agency, the contractor appeals or sues as provided in section 113 of this title, interest shall not accrue after the thirtieth day following the delivery of the findings on any amount allowed by such findings, unless such amount is increased upon such appeal or suit.   In approving, ratifying, authorizing, or making termination settlements with subcontractors, each contracting agency shall allow interest on the termination claim of the subcontractor on the same basis and subject to the same conditions as are applicable to a prime contractor.

(g) Amendment of contracts

Where any war contract does not provide for or provides against such fair compensation for its termination, the contracting agency, either before or after its termination, shall amend such war contract by agreement with the war contractor, or shall authorize, approve, or ratify an amendment of such war contract by the parties thereto, to provide for such fair compensation.

(July 1, 1944, c. 358, § 6, 58 Stat. 652; Ex. Ord. No. 9809, § 8, eff. Dec. 12, 1946, 11 F.R. 14281; 1947 Reorg.Plan No. 1, § 201, eff. July 1, 1947, 12 F.R. 4534, 61 Stat. 951; June 30, 1949, c. 288, Title I, § 102(b), 63 Stat. 380.)

HISTORICAL AND STATUTORY NOTES

References in Text
Section 1191 of the Appendix to Title 50, referred to in subsec. (c), was omitted from the Code. See note set out under section 1191 of the Appendix to Title 50, War and National Defense.

Transfer of Functions

Functions of Secretary of the Treasury were transferred to Administrator of General Services by Act June 30, 1949, c. 288, § 102(b), 63 Stat. 380, which was classified to former 40 U.S.C.A. § 752(b), prior to repeal by Pub.L. 107–217, § 6(b), Aug. 21, 2002, 116 Stat. 1304. "Secretary of the Treasury" was substituted for "Director" by section 8 of Ex. Ord. No. 9809 and section 201 of Reorg. Plan No. 1 of 1947. Reorg. Plan No. 1 of 1947 is set out in the Appendix to Title 5, Government Organization and Employees.

Effective Date of Transfer of Functions

Act June 30, 1949, § 605, which set July 1, 1949, as the effective date for the transfer of functions by that Act, was repealed by Pub.L. 107–217, § 6(b), Aug. 21, 2002, 116 Stat. 1313.

Application to Terminated War Contracts

For application of this section to war contracts terminated at or before July 21, 1944, see section 124(a) of this title.

Settlement of Claims for War Contract Losses Incurred Between September 16, 1940, and August 14, 1945

Act Aug. 7, 1946, c. 864, §§ 1 to 6, 60 Stat. 902, as amended June 25, 1948, c. 646, § 37, 62 Stat. 992; Aug. 30, 1954, c. 1076, § 1(2), 68 Stat. 966, provided that if work, supplies, or services were provided for any department or agency of the Government, under a contract or subcontract, between Sept. 16, 1940, and Aug. 14, 1945, and a loss was incurred by the contractors or subcontractors without fault or negligence on their part, then those departments or agencies were authorized to adjust and settle these losses on a fair and equitable basis, if claims were filed within six months after Aug. 7, 1946, and granted claimants dissatisfied with the settlement the right of judicial review.

LIBRARY REFERENCES

American Digest System

United States ⬠74(16).
Key Number System Topic No. 393.

Research References

ALR Library

126 ALR 837, Constitutionality, Construction, and Application of Statute Providing for Correction or Relief from Consequences of Error or Mistake in Bids for Public Contract.

99 ALR 173, Aeroplanes and Aeronautics.

WESTLAW ELECTRONIC RESEARCH

See Westlaw guide following the Explanation pages of this volume.

Notes of Decisions

---

1. Construction with Constitutional provisions

It would be assumed that Congress, in employing the words "fair compensation" in this section, was familiar with Fifth Amendment and the term "just compensation" used therein, and the judicial interpretation placed upon the term "just compensation". Monolith Portland Midwest Co. v. R.F.C., S.D.Cal. 1955, 128 F.Supp. 824. Statutes ⟐ 212.1

2. Purpose

The general purpose of this chapter is to reimburse a contractor for his proper costs and to allow such profit on the preparations made for work done for terminated portion of contract as is reasonable under the circumstances but not to pay for work not done, or to pay profits to contractor, which would have accrued had contract not been terminated. Mac-Cluney v. Kelsey-Hayes Wheel Co., E.D.Mich.1949, 87 F.Supp. 58, 83 U.S.P.Q. 203, affirmed 186 F.2d 552, 88 U.S.P.Q. 274. United States ⟐ 74(16)

3. Remedial nature of section

Although the record submitted by plaintiff is not complete a liberal view is taken of the evidence presented because of the remedial nature of this section. Worth Engineering Co., Inc. v. U.S., Ct. Cl.1956, 135 Ct.Cl. 843. United States ⟐ 74(17)

4. Authority of contracting agency

A contracting officer has no authority to determine or settle liability to Government of a contractor under War Frauds Act, former sections 231–235 of Title 31 [now sections 3729 to 3731 of Title 31], but his authority is limited to administrative settlement of disputes of fact arising in execution of contract, not crimes in nature of frauds of fact resulting from its execution. U.S. v. U.S. Cartridge Co., E.D.Mo.1948, 78 F.Supp. 81. Administrative Law And Procedure ⟐ 315; United States ⟐ 75.5

This section authorized former Director of Contract Settlement, now the Administrator of General Services, and the contracting agencies, subject to former Director's regulations, to settle finally, subject to the exceptions stated in subsec. (c) of this section, all matters which are or may be in dispute relating to the performed part of a war contract as well as all claims arising under the terminated part of the contract. 1944, 40 Op.Atty. Gen. 328.

5. Actions constituting termination— Generally

Government's amendment to prime contract changing basic specifications of vehicle to be supplied by contractor, resulting in contractor terminating subcontracts with supplier of parts, amounted to a constructive partial termination of prime contract and a total termination of subcontracts for Government's convenience, entitling subcontractor to termination costs. Universal Fiberglass Corp. v. U.S., Ct.Cl.1976, 537 F.2d 400, 210 Ct.Cl. 220. United States ⟐ 72.1(4)

6. —— Default cancellation, actions constituting termination

Where contract for sale of manganese ore to Metals Reserve Company was cancelled for failure of seller to make delivery in full under contract, contract was cancelled for "default" of seller and was not "terminated" within meaning of section 103 of this title, and hence seller had no cause of action under this section for fair compensation. Haberle v. R.F.C., D.C.D.C.1951, 104 F.Supp. 636. United States ⟐ 74(16)

7. Actions constituting settlement

An agreement between a trustee in bankruptcy of a war contractor and the Government releasing the Government from all claims, demands, etc., under war contracts and reciting that many of the amounts were unliquidated with respect to such contracts, compromised unliquidated claims due under the contracts and was not a settlement in the sense of a unilateral administrative determination of the amount due. Fogarty v. U.S., D.C.Minn.1948, 80 F.Supp. 90, affirmed 176 F.2d 599, certiorari granted 70 S.Ct. 572, 339 U.S. 909, 94 L.Ed. 1336, affirmed 71 S.Ct. 5, 340 U.S. 8, 95 L.Ed. 10. United States ☞ 74(16)

Where war fraud action was pending against defendant munitions manufacturer at time Government and defendant entered into supplemental contract terminating prime contract, and supplemental contract made no mention of pending action, supplemental contract did not show a settlement or attempted settlement of war fraud claims. U.S. v. U.S. Cartridge Co., E.D.Mo.1948, 78 F.Supp. 81. United States ☞ 75.5

8. Contractual cancellation provisions

Contractual right of officer of United States to direct omission of any portion of work covered by contract for construction of emergency housing units gave such officer right to cancel further work on such units. Reiss & Weinsier v. U.S., Ct.Cl.1953, 116 F.Supp. 562, 126 Ct.Cl. 713. United States ☞ 72(2)

Where plaintiff's contract with Government agency was by its terms subject to cancellation and was canceled for default, plaintiff was not entitled to relief under this section. Johnson v. R.F.C., E.D.Tenn.1950, 94 F.Supp. 214. United States ☞ 74(16)

Under war contract with the United States Government which provided for suspension of time of performance during periods of force majeure, and which provided that notwithstanding other provisions, Government could cancel contract without payment of damages with respect to material remaining undelivered after Jan. 1, 1946, cancellation provision was valid, and Government could cancel contracts on Jan. 4, 1946, although contract performance time as extended by operation of force majeure clause had not expired. Jardine Min. Co. v. U.S., Ct.Cl.

1950, 88 F.Supp. 265, 115 Ct.Cl. 279. United States ☞ 73(24)

Where in a suit under this chapter to recover certain "distribution services" rendered in connection with ten prime contracts entered into with the Department of the Navy for the furnishing of certain machine tools and for legal and clerical expenses, where the contracts were terminated in accordance with the provisions of the contracts, plaintiff was not entitled to recover. Byrns v. U.S., Ct.Cl.1952, 121 Ct.Cl. 266. United States ☞ 74(16)

9. Convenience of government

Where corporation, contracting with Government Metals Reserve Company for delivery of low grade manganese thereto, violated contract by failing to deliver last installment of manganese on delivery date fixed therein, whereupon such company cancelled contract as to undelivered portion pursuant to its terms, and second contract for delivery of high grade ore ended by its own terms without any performance by corporation neither contract was terminated solely for convenience or at option of Government, as required to authorize compensation of corporation under this chapter. Glade Mountain Corp. v. R.F.C., D.C.N.J.1952, 104 F.Supp. 695, affirmed 200 F.2d 815. United States ☞ 74(16)

10. Fraud

The "fraud" referred to in this section that settlement shall be final and conclusive except for "fraud," includes "fraudulent * * * statement[s]" and "fraudulent trick[s]," as used in section 119 of this title, and contemplates that settlement may not release contractor from liability under such later section. U.S. v. Dinerstein, C.A.2 (N.Y.) 1966, 362 F.2d 852. United States ☞ 74(16)

A contract settlement agreement entered into between the Government and a contractor pursuant to this chapter, like a court judgment, is open to attack if procured by fraud, but fraud must be alleged and proved. U.S. v. Erie Basin Metal Products, Inc., C.A.7 (Ill.) 1957, 244 F.2d 809. United States ☞ 74(16)

Where process of fabricating canteens from stainless steel was comparatively new process and because of that fact quartermaster personnel favored award of contract to experienced firms, contractor was afforded opportunity to withdraw from its bid but declined and was warned from beginning that failure to meet delivery schedule would result in termination action, Government's adherence strictly to delivery date requirements of contract and termination of contract for failure to meet delivery schedule did not amount to fraud. Poloron Products, Inc. v. U.S., Ct.Cl.1953, 116 F.Supp. 588, 126 Ct.Cl. 816. United States ⟋ 73(24)

11. Allowable costs or items—Generally

Under terms of research contract which Government terminated for its own benefit, contracting officer acted unreasonably in failing to approve reimbursement for termination costs actually paid by contractor. North Am. Philips Co. v. U.S., Ct.Cl.1961, 292 F.2d 861, 154 Ct.Cl. 754. United States ⟋ 73(9)

Where the Reconstruction Finance Corporation had terminated contract of war contractor for construction and operation of alumina extraction plant, war contractor's claims for cost of completion of plant and readying plant for operation, for cost of managing and operating plant during an experimental test period, and for general damages were not proper under this chapter. Monolith Portland Midwest Co. v. R.F.C., C.A.9 (Cal.) 1957, 240 F.2d 444, certiorari denied 77 S.Ct. 1379, 354 U.S. 921, 1 L.Ed.2d 1435. United States ⟋ 74(16)

A manufacturer's "cost" to be included in determining fair compensation to be paid on termination of war contract must be liberally construed as including all legitimate costs and expenses incurred in conduct of business. Allis-Chalmers Mfg. Co. v. U.S., C.C.A.7 (Wis.) 1948, 165 F.2d 495. War And National Emergency ⟋ 42; United States ⟋ 74.2

The fair compensation allowed under this chapter does not include benefits lost as a result of termination of contract. Monolith Portland Midwest Co. v. R.F.C., S.D.Cal.1955, 128 F.Supp. 824. United States ⟋ 74(16)

In action by petitioners against United States to recover for alleged losses suffered in performance of war contracts, petitioners could not recover in amount of "repair and over, short and damage" claims held against petitioners by United States Maritime Commission, in absence of evidence as to petitioners' liability on such claims. McGann Mfg. Co. v. U.S.,

M.D.Pa.1951, 98 F.Supp. 225. United States ⟋ 74(10)

12. —— Administrative costs, allowable costs or items

In terminating Government war contract for plywood boxes contractor was entitled to allowance for administrative expenses applicable to uncompleted portion of contract determined by applying ratio of administrative expenses to total manufacturing costs to manufacturing costs of uncompleted portion of contract. Piggly Wiggly Corp. v. U.S., Ct.Cl.1949, 81 F.Supp. 819, 112 Ct.Cl. 391. United States ⟋ 73(24)

13. —— Attorney fees, allowable costs or items

Contractor, which in behalf of its excavation contractor and its attorney, sought to recover equitable adjustment for changed conditions encountered when subcontractor removed part of concrete floor of building at Air Force base, was not entitled, under this chapter, to recover sum for legal services rendered in negotiations concerning proposed partial termination for convenience by government where contract had not been terminated. J.E. Robertson Co. v. U.S., Ct.Cl. 1971, 437 F.2d 1360, 194 Ct.Cl. 289. United States ⟋ 74(12.1)

In enacting this chapter and removing the bar of sovereign immunity to proceedings on appeal from findings on war contractors' claims, Congress had right to omit provisions for allowance of attorneys' fees and legal costs. Monolith Portland Midwest Co. v. R.F.C., S.D.Cal.1955, 128 F.Supp. 824. United States ⟋ 74(16)

In action against United States to recover costs allegedly resulting from termination by defendant of a war contract whereunder plaintiff was to reclaim used Signal Corps wire furnished to plaintiff by defendant, claim for attorney's fee for services rendered by attorney in prosecuting appeal to Appeal Board from decision of officer who entered into war contract with plaintiff, rendered on plaintiff's claim for termination expenses and for work in progress when contract was terminated, and claim for traveling expenses and hotel bills incurred in connection with a trip for prosecution of appeal, were not allowable as termination expenses. Hanson v. U.S., Ct.Cl.1950, 92

F.Supp. 972, 117 Ct.Cl. 605. United States ☞ 74(16)

Where Government sent check for benefit of subcontractor to assignee of prime contractor in accordance with contract of assignment, and upon refusal of prime contractor to allow assignee to make payment, subcontractor hired legal counsel to arbitrate dispute over first partial payment, subcontractor's claim for alleged costs of settlement of terminated contract, the major portion of which were incurred as result of arbitration, without evidence as to portion of such expenses allowable to preparation and presentation of settlement proposals, would not be allowed. Edelman v. U.S., Ct.Cl.1950, 91 F.Supp. 729, 117 Ct.Cl. 400. United States ☞ 74.2

In action at common law by subcontractor against prime contractor to recover damages upon cancellation of subcontract for war materials, subcontractor was not entitled to recover trial expenses as an element of damages. Rumsey Mfg. Corp. v. U.S. Hoffman Machinery Corp., W.D.N.Y.1949, 88 F.Supp. 394, modified on other grounds 187 F.2d 927. Damages ☞ 71.5

Contractor could not recover reasonable accounting and legal fees incurred in connection with suit against United States in Court of Claims [now United States Claims Court] as part of Government war contract termination claim. Piggly Wiggly Corp. v. U.S., Ct.Cl.1949, 81 F.Supp. 819, 112 Ct.Cl. 391. See, also, Byrns v. U.S., 1952, 121 Ct.Cl. 266. United States ☞ 73(24)

Where attorneys for appellees had collected three payments from defendants prior to suit for unsettled portion of claim under this chapter, collections were partial payments and were not voluntary settlements and attorneys' fees for such collections would be allowed. Walsh Const. Co. v. Davis, Miss.1948, 37 So.2d 757, 204 Miss. 509. United States ☞ 74(16)

14. —— Buildings, allowable costs or items

Under war contract whereunder plaintiff was to reclaim used Signal Corps wire furnished to plaintiff by United States, inclusion of costs of buildings and improvements acquired and paid for by plaintiff in connection with performance of contract, in amount used to determine fair and reasonable unit cost, did not make the improvements the property of United States. Hanson v. U.S., Ct.Cl. 1950, 92 F.Supp. 972, 117 Ct.Cl. 605. United States ☞ 70(10)

Under the regulations, where it was shown that plaintiff's building and its equipment in the form to which it was converted were acquired solely for the performance of the terminated contracts and other war contracts and where it was shown that after termination the building and equipment were not reasonably capable of use in the other business of the plaintiff, plaintiff was entitled to recover the residual value of the building and equipment, after deducting the net sum for which plaintiff sold the building. Preload Corporation v. U.S., Ct.Cl.1950, 115 Ct.Cl. 596. United States ☞ 74(16)

15. —— Environmental clean-up, allowable costs or items

Provision in termination agreement between war contractor and Air Force for reimbursement of costs "which are not now known" was not limited to liability that existed at time of termination of contract, but rather, extended to later-arising environmental cleanup costs; there was no temporal limit as to when claims would become known, provided their origin was performance of the war contract. Ford Motor Co. v. U.S., C.A.Fed.2004, 378 F.3d 1314, rehearing and rehearing en banc denied. United States ☞ 74(16)

Because war contractor's claim for reimbursement of environmental cleanup costs was exempted from settlement by terms of termination agreement between contractor and Air Force, government's liability under Contract Settlement Act (CSA) was not released. Ford Motor Co. v. U.S., C.A.Fed.2004, 378 F.3d 1314, rehearing and rehearing en banc denied. United States ☞ 74(16)

Termination settlement procedures of the Contract Settlement Act of 1944, which was enacted to effectuate speedy and final settlement of claims for World War II contracts, were not applicable to claims of contractor seeking to recover under wartime contract the costs of environmental cleanup of site where contract was performed, where contract was terminated and a final settlement negotiated that expressly covered the circumstances that contractor asserted entitled it to relief under the contract. Ford Motor Co. v. U.S., Fed.Cl.2003, 56 Fed.Cl. 85, reversed 378 F.3d 1314, rehearing and re-

hearing en banc denied. United States
☞ 74(16)

16. —— Equipment, allowable costs or items

Under 10-year Government research contract which provided that contractor should pay certain percent of costs and that property should revert to Government on termination, contractor was entitled, upon Government's termination after three and one-half years, to reimbursement for that part of its share of investment in capital equipment representing the contractor's loss of use of equipment for remaining six and one-half years. North Am. Philips Co. v. U.S., Ct.Cl.1961, 292 F.2d 861, 154 Ct.Cl. 754. United States ☞ 74(16)

Where war contractor let subcontract, whereunder it agreed to provide certain equipment, amount which contractor paid for equipment which it shipped to subcontractor prior to termination and for which contractor was not paid was includable in termination claim under this chapter. Arlington Trust Co., Inc. v. U.S., Ct.Cl.1956, 139 F.Supp. 556, 134 Ct.Cl. 251. United States ☞ 74(16)

Where airplane manufacturer had secured a fixed price Government contract and it was necessary that certain tooling be purchased to fulfill contract and much of the same tooling was available when the manufacturer started on cost-plus-a-fixed-fee contract for Government, pro rated portion of production tooling expense carried in deferred account of manufacturer was properly a part of cost of producing airplanes under cost-plus contracts. Bell Aircraft Corp. v. U.S., Ct.Cl.1951, 100 F.Supp. 661, 120 Ct.Cl. 398, certiorari granted 72 S.Ct. 646, 343 U.S. 913, 96 L.Ed. 1329, affirmed 73 S.Ct. 102, 344 U.S. 860, 97 L.Ed. 668. United States ☞ 70(18)

17. —— Extra costs, allowable costs or items

Where contract for construction of army hospital provided that disputes under contract concerning questions of fact should be decided by contracting officer but when dispute arose and contractor requested extension of time, officer refused to grant extension, not himself deciding question but deferring responsibility to superior, and later officer held that contract was terminated at fault of contractor, not because of merits of case but

because army lawyers had told him that legal complications might otherwise ensue, decisions were nullity and contractor was not chargeable with excess cost Government incurred in having project completed by another contractor. John A. Johnson Contracting Corp. v. U.S., Ct.Cl. 1955, 132 F.Supp. 698, 132 Ct.Cl. 645. United States ☞ 73(14); United States ☞ 75(1)

Where Reconstruction Finance Corporation issued stop work order in connection with war contract, and contract was subsequently terminated, contractor could recover for expenditures after stop work order only to the extent that these expenditures had been authorized by the Corporation. Monolith Portland Midwest Co. v. R.F.C., S.D.Cal.1955, 128 F.Supp. 824. United States ☞ 74(16)

Contractor was entitled, upon termination of contract for convenience of administration, to recover amount which it had expended above amount which it was paid for units manufactured. Elastic Stop Nut Corp. v. U.S., Ct.Cl.1953, 113 F.Supp. 446, 126 Ct.Cl. 100. United States ☞ 70(35)

Act of Office of Price Administration in increasing price of plywood after plaintiff had contracted with United States to construct plywood boxes was a "sovereign act" so that contractor could not recover increased cost from United States. Piggly Wiggly Corp. v. U.S., Ct.Cl.1949, 81 F.Supp. 819, 112 Ct.Cl. 391. United States ☞ 70(23)

18. —— Insurance, allowable costs or items

Where contract with United States provided that additional insurance coverages determined to be necessary by contractor should be approved by Government agent prior to the obtaining of such insurance, in absence of such approval of purchase of additional insurance which was not included in insurance as to which United States was to reimburse contractor for premiums, contractor was not entitled to reimbursement for cost of such insurance. Reiss & Weinsier v. U.S., Ct.Cl. 1953, 116 F.Supp. 562, 126 Ct.Cl. 713. United States ☞ 70(21)

19. —— Interest, allowable costs or items

Under this chapter, Government contractor was entitled to interest at 2½ percent on termination costs due, commencing 30 days after Government terminated contract for its own convenience. North Am. Philips Co. v. U.S., Ct.Cl.1961, 292 F.2d 861, 154 Ct.Cl. 754. See, also, Preload Corporation v. U.S., 1950, 115 Ct.Cl. 596. United States ☞ 74(16)

In action at common law by subcontractor against prime contractor to recover damages upon cancellation of contract for war materials where subcontractor sued without invoking procedure provided by this chapter, rate of interest on the judgment would be fixed at that which state law allowed in such case, and would not be limited to 2½ percent under subsec. (f) of this section. Rumsey Mfg. Corp. v. U.S. Hoffman Machinery Corp., C.A.2 (N.Y.) 1951, 187 F.2d 927. Interest ☞ 38(1)

Where Government contract was terminated within purview of this section, contractor was entitled to interest on amount of increase of unemployment taxes paid to state of Illinois by reason of adverse effect of contractor's employment and unemployment experience under Government contractor from date on which each of payments of unemployment taxes became due. Houdaille Industries, Inc. v. U.S., Ct.Cl.1957, 151 F.Supp. 298, 138 Ct.Cl. 301. United States ☞ 110

Where there was a formal termination of contract between Government and manufacturer for manufacture of shell fuzes, and manufacturer's petition was based on a termination claim, and from Government writing and testimony of a Government expert it appeared that claim was a termination claim, claim would be deemed a termination claim within meaning of provision of subsec. (f) of this section, providing for payment of interest on any termination claim. Elastic Stop Nut Corp. of America v. U.S., Ct.Cl.1955, 132 F.Supp. 466, 132 Ct.Cl. 631. United States ☞ 110

Where war contractor, in proceeding attacking Reconstruction Finance Corporation's determination as to sum due on termination claim, obtained a material decrease in Corporation's counterclaim or offset claim, contractor was entitled to claim interest, notwithstanding this section, providing that interest prior to suit should not be allowed unless amount of award is increased upon appeal or suit, even though contractor had been unsuccessful in increasing amount of its award. Monolith Portland Midwest Co. v. R.F.C.,

S.D.Cal.1955, 128 F.Supp. 824. United States ☞ 110

War contractor could not recover interest on amount refused from date of such refusal. Piggly Wiggly Corp. v. U.S., Ct. Cl.1949, 81 F.Supp. 819, 112 Ct.Cl. 391.

The record being confused as to which party was responsible for the delay in handling the termination claims, interest under subsec. (f) of this section was not allowed plaintiffs. Schultz v. U.S., Ct.Cl. 1958, 142 Ct.Cl. 551. United States ☞ 110

20. —— Materials, allowable costs or items

Where war contractor and subcontractor, both of whom made termination claims, agreed that certain material which contractor had shipped for use by subcontractor belonged to contractor, contractor was entitled to make claim on account of such material, even though Government had insisted that subcontractor make claim therefor and had paid subcontractor. Arlington Trust Co., Inc. v. U.S., Ct.Cl.1956, 139 F.Supp. 556, 134 Ct.Cl. 251. United States ☞ 74(16)

Where United States, with permission of company which had contracted with United States to construct certain emergency housing projects, had stored surplus materials on company's equipment and material yard, though original contract did not give United States the right to do so, and United States paid all expenses of operation of the yard, allowance of $2400, which represented six per cent of the amount of the expenses incurred, was reasonable. Reiss & Weinsier v. U.S., Ct.Cl.1953, 116 F.Supp. 562, 126 Ct.Cl. 713. United States ☞ 74(12.1)

21. —— Overhead, allowable costs or items

Where company, which had contracted with United States to construct certain emergency housing projects, was entitled, upon cancellation of contract by United States, to recover home office overhead, but company had a contract with another party and time of home office was spent about equally on both contracts, company was entitled to recover from United States one-half of its home office overhead. Reiss & Weinsier v. U.S., Ct.Cl. 1953, 116 F.Supp. 562, 126 Ct.Cl. 713. United States ☞ 74(13)

"Factory burden" or "factory overhead" for purposes of making allowances to contractors upon termination of Government war contracts represents expenses of production which are not identified with a product with sufficient certainty to warrant including them as part of costs of material or labor. Piggly Wiggly Corp. v. U.S., Ct.Cl.1949, 81 F.Supp. 819, 112 Ct.Cl. 391. United States ⚯ 73(24)

22. —— Profit, allowable costs or items

Where government contract contained termination for convenience of government clause, contractor's recovery must be calculated in accordance with that clause and should not include anticipated profits. International Tel. & Tel. Corp., ITT Defense Communication Division v. U.S., Ct.Cl.1975, 509 F.2d 541, 206 Ct.Cl. 37. United States ⚯ 74(15)

Where termination clause of Government war contract provided that contractor was entitled to proportionate profit on uncompleted portion of contract, in computing amount of compensation due contractor for inventory on hand, contractor was entitled to net cost of his purchases plus discount taken on such purchases prior to termination of contract. Piggly Wiggly Corp. v. U.S., Ct.Cl.1949, 81 F.Supp. 819, 112 Ct.Cl. 391. United States ⚯ 73(24)

23. —— Research and development, allowable costs or items

Amount which war contractor spent in experimentation to develop item before he had a contract or promise of a contract was not includable in his termination claim. Arlington Trust Co., Inc. v. U.S., Ct.Cl.1956, 139 F.Supp. 556, 134 Ct.Cl. 251. United States ⚯ 74(16)

In action by a plane manufacturer against United States to recover sum alleged to be reimbursable items of cost incurred in performance of four cost-plus-a-fixed-fee contracts, evidence established that true measure of value of experimental work on three previous models of airplanes to production of planes for one type of plane under cost-plus contracts was represented by excess of cost on experimental contracts over and above recoveries under contracts and that sum was fair and reasonable value of general experimental and development work in benefits and savings on later production contracts. Bell Aircraft Corp. v. U.S.,

Ct.Cl.1951, 100 F.Supp. 661, 120 Ct.Cl. 398, certiorari granted 72 S.Ct. 646, 343 U.S. 913, 96 L.Ed. 1329, affirmed 73 S.Ct. 102, 344 U.S. 860, 97 L.Ed. 668. United States ⚯ 74(16)

24. —— Taxes, allowable costs or items

Wisconsin income taxes paid by manufacturer should be included as a cost item in determining fair compensation to be paid to manufacturer on termination of war sub-contract. Allis-Chalmers Mfg. Co. v. U.S., C.C.A.7 (Wis.) 1948, 165 F.2d 495. War And National Emergency ⚯ 42

War contractor whose contract was terminated but who had been requested by R.F.C. to perform shutdown work was not entitled to recover for payroll taxes paid in connection with salaries and wages of employees, recovery for whose salaries and wages was disallowed. Monolith Portland Midwest Co. v. R.F.C., S.D.Cal.1955, 128 F.Supp. 824. United States ⚯ 74(16)

25. —— Wages, allowable costs or items

War contractor whose contract had been terminated and who had been requested by Reconstruction Finance Corporation to perform shutdown operations was not entitled to recover for salaries which were not direct expenses or salaries in connection with the program and which would have been normal expenses incurred regardless of the program. Monolith Portland Midwest Co. v. R.F.C., S.D.Cal.1955, 128 F.Supp. 824. United States ⚯ 74(16)

Where company contracted with United States to construct certain emergency housing projects in consideration for reimbursement for costs and fixed fee plus fixed overhead and United States directed company to suspend operations on certain projects pending further legislative appropriations and stated that such appropriations were expected soon, and authorized agent of United States thereafter told company representative that contract would not be continued and that lump-sum bids would be invited for completion of projects, and contract was subsequently canceled, company was entitled to recover wage expenditures necessary to maintain ability to resume work on projects from time of winding up work on projects which had not suspended until time of such notification by agent. Reiss

& Weinsier v. U.S., Ct.Cl.1953, 116 F.Supp. 562, 126 Ct.Cl. 713. United States ☞ 74(13)

26. Valuation of cost or items allowable

In action against Government for taking of trucks constituting part of war contractor's termination inventory and allegedly diverted by Government subsequent to their sale to plaintiff, evidence, on damages issue, would not sustain Government's contention that market price at time of taking was less than that fixed by price control regulations then in existence. L.B. Smith, Inc. v. U.S., Ct.Cl. 1956, 145 F.Supp. 216, 136 Ct.Cl. 587, 81 Ohio Law Abs. 561, 9 O.O.2d 177. United States ☞ 74(16)

In action against United States to recover costs allegedly resulting from termination by defendant of a war contract whereunder plaintiff was to reclaim used Signal Corps wire furnished to plaintiff by defendant, finding that at time of termination of contract total cost of wire in process but not completely reclaimed was $3,192.48, was not unreasonable under circumstances. Hanson v. U.S., Ct.Cl. 1950, 92 F.Supp. 972, 117 Ct.Cl. 605. United States ☞ 74(16)

In terminating Government war contract for plywood boxes contractor was entitled to salvage value of oil drums. Piggly Wiggly Corp. v. U.S., Ct.Cl.1949, 81 F.Supp. 819, 112 Ct.Cl. 391. United States ☞ 73(24)

27. Payment in full

Contractor who had received payment from Government of full contract price of contract with Army, could not recover on termination claim under provision of this chapter restricting aggregate amount of compensation allowed on termination claim to total contract price reduced by amount of payments made. Lawrance Aeronautical Corp. v. U.S., Ct.Cl.1955, 130 F.Supp. 603, 133 Ct.Cl. 1. United States ☞ 74(16)

28. Overpayments

Under this chapter the United States has a right to institute an independent suit in federal district court upon a claim based upon an alleged overpayment to contractor under a war contract. Hadden v. U.S., Ct.Cl.1952, 105 F.Supp. 1010, 123 Ct.Cl. 246. United States ☞ 75(1)

29. Set-off

In action by war contractor under this chapter, Government could assert set-off without pleading it. Arlington Trust Co., Inc. v. U.S., Ct.Cl.1956, 139 F.Supp. 556, 134 Ct.Cl. 251. Federal Civil Procedure ☞ 772.1

30. Reorganization proceedings

In reorganization proceeding district court did not, under the evidence, abuse its discretion in authorizing trustee to accept compromise settlement of a terminated contract offered the debtor by the United States under this chapter. Daniel Hamm Drayage Co. v. Willson, C.A.8 (Mo.) 1949, 178 F.2d 633. Bankruptcy ☞ 3033

31. Waiver

Execution of agreement by mine owner and Reconstruction Finance Corporation purporting to be a settlement of all rights under this chapter which created owner's only legal rights, waived claim for lost profits. Teutsch v. U.S., Ct.Cl.1961, 288 F.2d 920, 153 Ct.Cl. 86. United States ☞ 74(16)

Where officers and directors of subcontractor decided to reject Navy Department offer of direct settlement and to encourage informal negotiations after cancellation of prime contract and subcontractor brought action against prime contract for war materials, and subcontractor for damages subcontractor waived its right to recover damages under formula provided by this chapter. Rumsey Mfg. Corp. v. U.S. Hoffman Machinery Corp., W.D.N.Y.1949, 88 F.Supp. 394, modified on other grounds 187 F.2d 927. Damages ☞ 124(1)

32. Admissibility of evidence

Under provision of this section that where any war contract does not provide for fair compensation for its termination contracting agency shall amend war contract by agreement with war contractor or shall authorize an amendment of such war contract to provide for such fair compensation, parol evidence rule is not applicable. Daubendick v. U.S., Ct.Cl. 1950, 88 F.Supp. 1008, 116 Ct.Cl. 209. Evidence ☞ 465

33. Weight and sufficiency of evidence

Where plaintiff was entitled to be paid for cost of services plaintiff had performed on work in progress when war contract whereunder plaintiff was to reclaim used Signal Corps wire for defendant United States was terminated, but plaintiff was not paid, fact that evidence relative to how much work was in progress when contract was terminated was contradictory did not relieve court of responsibility of arriving at some measure of relief for plaintiff. Hanson v. U.S., Ct.Cl.1950, 92 F.Supp. 972, 117 Ct.Cl. 605. United States ☞ 74(16)

§ 107. Settlement of subcontractors' claims

(a) Conclusiveness of settlement

Where, in connection with the settlement of any termination claim by a contracting agency, any war contractor makes settlements of the termination claims of his subcontractors, the contracting agency shall limit or omit its review of such settlements with subcontractors to the maximum extent compatible with the public interest. Any contracting agency (1) may approve, ratify, or authorize such settlements with subcontractors upon such evidence, terms, and conditions as it deems proper; (2) shall vary the scope and intensity of its review of such settlements according to the reliability of the war contractor, the size, number, and complexity of such claims, and other relevant factors; and (3) shall authorize war contractors to make such settlements with subcontractors without review by the contracting agency, whenever the reliability of the war contractor, the amount or nature of the claims, or other reasons appear to the contracting agency to justify such action. Any such settlement of a subcontract approved, ratified, or authorized by a contracting agency shall be final and conclusive as to the amount due to the same extent as a settlement under subsection (c) of section 106 of this title, and no war contractor shall be liable to the United States on account of any amounts paid thereon except for his own fraud.

(b) Supervision of payments to war contractors

Whenever any contracting agency is satisfied of the inability of a war contractor to meet his obligations it shall exercise supervision or control over payments to the war contractor on account of termination claims of subcontractors of such war contractor to such extent and in such manner as it deems necessary or desirable for the purpose of assuring the receipt of the benefit of such payments by the subcontractors.

(c) Group settlements

The Administrator of General Services shall prescribe policies and methods for the settlement as a group, or otherwise, by any contracting agency of some or all of the termination claims of a war contractor under war contracts with one or more (1) bureaus or divisions within a contracting agency, (2) contracting agencies, or (3) prime contractors and subcontractors, to the extent he deems such action necessary or desirable for expeditious and equitable settlement of such claims. After consulting with the contracting agencies concerned, the Administrator of General Services may provide for assigning any war contractor to a contracting agency for such settlement, and such agency shall have authority to settle, on behalf of any other contracting agency, some or all of the termination claims of such war contractor.

(d) Direct settlement by contracting agency

Any contracting agency may settle directly termination claims of subcontractors to the extent that it deems such action necessary or desirable for the expeditious and equitable settlement of such claims. In making such termination settlements any contracting agency may discharge the claim of the subcontractor by payment or may purchase such claim, and may agree to assume, or indemnify the subcontractor against, any claims by any person in connection with such claim or the termination settlement. Any contracting agency undertaking to settle the termination claim of any subcontractor shall deliver to the subcontractor and the war contractor liable to him written notice stating its acceptance of responsibility for settling his claim and the conditions applicable thereto, which may include the release, or assignment to the contracting agency, of his claim against the war contractor liable to him; upon consent thereto by the subcontractor, the Government shall become liable for the settlement of his claims upon the conditions specified in the notice.

(e) Amount of settlement

Any contracting agency may make settlements with subcontractors in accordance with any of the provisions of this chapter without regard to any limitation on the amount payable by the Government to the prime contractor.

(f) Equitable payments

If any contracting agency determines that in the circumstances of a particular case equity and good conscience require fair compensation for the termination of a war contract to be paid to a subcontractor who has been deprived of and cannot otherwise reasonably secure such fair compensation, the contracting agency concerned may pay such compensation to him although such compensation already has been included and paid as part of a settlement with another war contractor.

(July 1, 1944, c. 358, § 7, 58 Stat. 654; Ex. Ord. No. 9809, § 8, eff. Dec. 12, 1946, 11 F.R. 14281; 1947 Reorg. Plan No. 1, § 201, eff. July 1, 1947, 12 F.R. 4534, 61 Stat. 951; June 30, 1949, c. 288, Title I, § 102(b), 63 Stat. 380.)

HISTORICAL AND STATUTORY NOTES

Transfer of Functions

Functions of Secretary of the Treasury were transferred to Administrator of General Services by Act June 30, 1949, c. 288, § 102(b), 63 Stat. 380, which was classified to former 40 U.S.C.A. § 752(b), prior to repeal by Pub.L. 107–217, § 6(b), Aug. 21, 2002, 116 Stat. 1304.

"Secretary of the Treasury" was substituted for "Director" by section 8 of Ex. Ord. No. 9809 and section 201 of Reorg. Plan No. 1 of 1947. Reorg. Plan No. 1 of 1947 is set out in the Appendix to Title 5,

Government Organization and Employees.

Effective Date of Transfer of Functions

Act June 30, 1949, § 605, which set July 1, 1949, as the effective date for the transfer of functions by that Act, was repealed by Pub.L. 107–217, § 6(b), Aug. 21, 2002, 116 Stat. 1313.

Application to Terminated War Contracts

For application of this section to war contracts terminated at or before July 21, 1944, see section 124(a) of this title.

LIBRARY REFERENCES

American Digest System
United States ⟋74.2.
Key Number System Topic No. 393.

WESTLAW ELECTRONIC RESEARCH

See Westlaw guide following the Explanation pages of this volume.

Notes of Decisions

Assumption of obligation by government
  7
Bankruptcy 10
Conclusiveness of settlement 4
Direct settlements 6
Duty of contracting agency to settle 2
Failure of primary contractor's right to recover 9
Prime contractor liability 8
Privity of contract 3
Subcontracts within section 1
Supervision of payments 5

1. Subcontracts within section

Where contract whereby plaintiff was to steam clean trucks of defendant was evidenced merely by invitation to bid, bid by plaintiff, and acceptance of bid by defendants, and there was no reference whatever to any prime contract between defendants and the Federal Government for construction work, court, in action for breach of contract, properly held that this section was inapplicable. Truck-Trailer Equipment Co. v. S. Birch & Sons Const. Co., Wash.1951, 231 P.2d 304, 38 Wash.2d 583. Automobiles ⟋ 368

2. Duty of contracting agency to settle

Under this section, a contracting agency is not required to settle the termination claims of subcontractors and

where it elects not to do so in a particular case, that subcontractor has no claim against the United States within the jurisdiction of the Court of Claims [now United States Court of Federal Claims]. Somerset Mach. & Tool Co. v. U.S., Ct.Cl. 1959, 144 Ct.Cl. 481, certiorari denied 80 S.Ct. 73, 361 U.S. 825, 4 L.Ed.2d 69. United States ⟋ 74(16)

3. Privity of contract

Except for this section, a subcontractor whose contract was canceled after United States canceled contract with contractor had no right of action against United States for want of privity of contract. Kal Mach. Works v. U.S., Ct.Cl.1946, 68 F.Supp. 436, 107 Ct.Cl. 202. Contracts ⟋ 186(1); United States ⟋ 74.2

Plaintiff had no valid claim against the Submarine Signal Company since it had agreed to do the work at fixed prices and a person contracting on such a basis takes the chance that unanticipated difficulties may increase the cost of performance and result in losses; there is no basis for a claim against the Navy because plaintiff had no contract with the Navy. Palmer-Bee Co. v. U.S., Ct.Cl. 1958, 142 Ct.Cl. 485. Contracts ⟋ 232(1); United States ⟋ 74.2

4. Conclusiveness of settlement

Subsec. (a) of this section, that any settlement of a subcontractor approved, ratified, or authorized by a contracting agency shall be final and conclusive as to the amount due, refers to final settlements on a subcontractor's termination claims and not to partial payments made by way of interim financing. Commercial Credit Corp. v. California Shipbuilding Corp., S.D.Cal.1947, 71 F.Supp. 936. United States ☞ 74.2

5. Supervision of payments

Under subsec. (b) of this section, requiring contracting agency when satisfied of inability of war contractor to meet obligation to supervise payments to war contractor on account of termination claims of subcontractors, contracting agency is obliged rather than permitted to exercise required supervision and control when war contractor is unable to meet obligations. Erie Basin Metal Products v. U.S., Ct.Cl.1953, 109 F.Supp. 402, 124 Ct.Cl. 95, certiorari denied 74 S.Ct. 29, 346 U.S. 831, 98 L.Ed. 355. United States ☞ 74.2

6. Direct settlements

Under this section, subcontract termination claims arising from termination for Government's convenience of prime contract are to be paid to prime contractor and by him in turn paid to deserving subcontractors except to the extent that contracting agency elects to settle or pay subcontract termination claims directly. Universal Fiberglass Corp. v. U.S., Ct.Cl. 1976, 537 F.2d 400, 210 Ct.Cl. 220. United States ☞ 74.2

Former Director of Contract Settlement, now Administrator of General Services, was authorized to provide by regulations that direct settlement of certain subcontractors' termination claims may be made under this chapter without deduction for claims the Government may have against the prime contractor or other higher tier contractor and without regard to insolvency or bankruptcy of higher tier contractors or set-offs between contractors in the contractual chain. 1945, 40 Op.Atty.Gen. 357.

7. Assumption of obligation by government

Subcontractor did not have vested right in termination claim at moment subcontract was terminated by government contractor due to specification amendments

in prime contract but enjoyed no vested right in such claim unless and until contracting agency assumed obligation to pay claim; until that transpired subcontractor's claim was solely against prime contractor which had obligation under this section to pay claim and seek reimbursement from contracting agency. Universal Fiberglass Corp. v. U.S., Ct.Cl. 1976, 537 F.2d 400, 210 Ct.Cl. 220. United States ☞ 74.2

Suggestion of official of contracting agency that subcontractor who received an order from corporation which had a prime contract for production of equipment for war purposes by the United States file claim under subsec. (f) of this section against the United States for compensation following termination of the prime contract and subcontract did not justify implying an undertaking on part of United States to accept responsibility for settling claim. Aerovox Corp. v. U.S., D.C.Mass.1950, 89 F.Supp. 873. United States ☞ 69(4)

To establish liability of the United States under subsecs. (a) and (d) of this section for damages sustained by subcontractor incident to cancellation of subcontract, United States must not only agree with the subcontractor on the amount which should be paid in settlement of such claim, but must also agree to pay such amount. Precision Metal & Mach. Co. v. U.S., Ct.Cl.1946, 68 F.Supp. 437, 107 Ct.Cl. 219. Compromise And Settlement ☞ 5(1); United States ☞ 74.2

The United States is not liable for damages incident to carbine manufacturer's cancellation of contract with subcontractor after United States canceled contract with contractor, where United States did not accept responsibility for settlement of claim but denied responsibility by virtue of disapproval of Award Board of Chicago Ordinance District of settlement between subcontractor and negotiator for such district. Kal Mach. Works v. U.S., Ct.Cl.1946, 68 F.Supp. 436, 107 Ct.Cl. 202. Compromise And Settlement ☞ 8(1); United States ☞ 74.2

8. Prime contractor liability

Where Government representatives, plaintiff and prime contractor cancelled plaintiff's subcontracts and prime contractor executed new subcontracts directly to plaintiff with parol understanding that former contract and new contracts would be treated by Government as one for settlement purposes, parol agreement did not contradict or vary prime contractor's written agreement to plaintiff which provided that prime contractor was not to assume responsibility for plaintiff's past commitments or debts. Daubendick v. U.S., Ct.Cl.1950, 88 F.Supp. 1008, 116 Ct.Cl. 209. Evidence ☞ 465

The United States was not liable for damages incident to carbine manufacturer's cancellation of contract with subcontractor after United States canceled contract with contractor, notwithstanding that Award Board of Chicago Ordinance District approved settlement between subcontractor and negotiator for such district, where settlement agreement provided, not that the Government would pay the claim, but that the prime contractor would be authorized to do so. Precision Metal & Mach. Co. v. U.S., Ct.Cl. 1946, 68 F.Supp. 437, 107 Ct.Cl. 219. Compromise And Settlement ☞ 15(1); United States ☞ 74.2

9. Failure of primary contractor's right to recover

Where it was held that plaintiffs were not entitled to recover and the petition was dismissed, the claim of the subcontractor, presented by plaintiffs, also failed and the subcontractor had no independent right of action against the defendant. Kilgore v. U.S., Ct.Cl.1952, 121 Ct.Cl. 340. United States ☞ 74.2

10. Bankruptcy

Where bankrupt subcontractor had assigned all of its rights to moneys due and to become due under subcontract for war materials as collateral security for a loan, and assignees presented their claims against subcontractor to bankruptcy court, and trustee was a party, subcontractor as assignor could maintain action against prime contractor for damages upon cancellation of the subcontract. Rumsey Mfg. Corp. v. U.S. Hoffman Machinery Corp., W.D.N.Y.1949, 88 F.Supp. 394, modified on other grounds 187 F.2d 927. Assignments ☞ 117

§ 108. Interim financing

(a) Prime contractors

It is the policy of the Government, and it shall be the responsibility of the contracting agencies and the Administrator of General Services, in accordance with and subject to the provisions of this chapter, to provide war contractors having any termination claim or claims, pending their settlement, with adequate interim financing, within thirty days after proper application therefor.

(b) Method of financing; amounts payable

Each contracting agency shall, to the greatest extent it deems practicable, make available interim financing through loans and discounts, and commitments and guaranties in connection therewith, in contemplation of or related to termination of war contracts. Where interim financing is made by advance payments or partial payments, it shall, insofar as practicable, consist of the following:

(1) An amount equal to 100 per centum of the amount payable, at the contract price, on account of acceptable items completed prior to the termination date under the terms of the contract, or completed thereafter with the approval of the contracting agency; plus

(2) An amount equal to 90 per centum of the cost of raw materials, purchased parts, supplies, direct labor, and manufac-

turing overhead allocable to the terminated portion of the war contract; plus

(3) A reasonable percentage of other allowable costs, including administrative overhead, allocable to the terminated portion of the war contract not included in the foregoing; plus

(4) Such additional amounts, if any, as the contracting agency deems necessary to provide the war contractor with adequate interim financing.

(5) In lieu of the costs referred to in clauses (2) and (3) of this subsection, where a detailed ascertainment of such costs is not suitable to the conditions of any war contractor and is apt to cause delay in the obtaining of interim financing by him, that portion of such interim financing shall be equal to an amount not greater than 90 per centum of the estimated costs which are allocable to the terminated part or parts of the war contract or group of war contracts, and are ascertained in accordance with such methods and standards as the Administrator of General Services shall prescribe.

(6) There shall be deducted from the amount of such interim financing any unliquidated balances of advance and partial payments theretofore made to such war contractor, which are allocable to the terminated war contract or the terminated part of the war contract.

(c) Evidence to support financing

The Administrator of General Services shall prescribe (1) the types of estimates, certificates, or other evidence to be required to support such interim financing; (2) the terms and conditions upon which such interim financing shall be made including the use of standard forms for agreements with respect to such interim financing to the extent practicable; (3) the classes of cases in which such interim financing shall be refused; and (4) such methods of supervision and control over such interim financing as he deems necessary or desirable to assure adequate and speedy interim financing to subcontractors of the war contractor.

(d) Penalty for overstatement of claims

In case of an overstatement by any war contractor of the amount due on his termination claim or claims in connection with any interim financing under this chapter, such contractor shall pay to the United States, as a penalty, an amount equal to 6 per centum of the amount of the overstatement, but the Administrator of General Services may suspend or modify any such penalty if in his opinion the imposition thereof would be inequitable. Any penalty may be deducted from any amounts due the war contractor upon such termination claim or claims, or otherwise, or may be collected from the war contractor by suit. The obligation to pay any penalty imposed and to repay any interim financing made or assumed by the United States under this chapter shall constitute a debt due to the United States within the meaning of section 3713(a) of Title 31.

(e) Advance payments as part of termination settlement

Any contracting agency may allow any advance payments, previously made or authorized by it in connection with the performance of a war contract, to be used for payments and expenses related to the termination settlement of such contract, upon such terms and conditions as it deems necessary or appropriate to protect the interest of the Government.

(f) Liquidation of loans, etc., prior to final settlement

No interim financing shall be made by any contracting agency under this chapter unless the terms of such financing provide for the liquidation by the war contractor of all loans, discounts, advance payments, or partial payments thereunder not later than the time of final payment of the amount due on the settlement of the termination claim or claims of the war contractor involved or such time thereafter as the contracting agency deems necessary for the liquidation of such interim financing in an orderly manner.

(g) Settlement of claims; validation of prior financing

Any contracting agency may settle, upon such terms and conditions as it deems proper, any claim or obligation due by or to the Government arising from or related to any interim financing made, acquired, or authorized by it. Any interim financing made, acquired, or authorized by any contracting agency before July 21, 1944, shall be valid to the extent it would be authorized under the provisions of this chapter if made after its effective date.

(July 1, 1944, c. 358, § 8, 58 Stat. 655; Ex. Ord. No. 9809, § 8, eff. Dec. 12, 1946, 11 F.R. 14281; 1947 Reorg. Plan No. 1, § 201, eff. July 1, 1947, 12 F.R. 4534, 61 Stat. 951; June 30, 1949, c. 288, Title I, § 102(b), 63 Stat. 380.)

HISTORICAL AND STATUTORY NOTES

Codifications

In subsec. (d), "section 3713(a) of Title 31" was substituted for "Revised Statutes, section 3466 (31 U.S.C., sec. 191)" on authority of Pub.L. 97–258, § 4(b), Sept. 13, 1982, 96 Stat. 1067, the first section of which enacted Title 31, Money and Finance.

Transfer of Functions

Functions of Secretary of the Treasury were transferred to Administrator of General Services by Act June 30, 1949, c. 288, § 102(b), 63 Stat. 380, which was classified to former 40 U.S.C.A. § 752(b), prior to repeal by Pub.L. 107–217, § 6(b), Aug. 21, 2002, 116 Stat. 1304.

"Secretary of the Treasury" was substituted for "Director" by section 8 of Ex.

Ord. No. 9809 and section 201 of Reorg. Plan No. 1 of 1947. Reorg. Plan No. 1 of 1947 is set out in the Appendix to Title 5, Government Organization and Employees.

Effective Date of Transfer of Functions

Act June 30, 1949, § 605, which set July 1, 1949, as the effective date for the transfer of functions by that Act, was repealed by Pub.L. 107–217, § 6(b), Aug. 21, 2002, 116 Stat. 1313.

Application to Terminated War Contracts

For application of this section to war contracts terminated at or before July 21, 1944, see section 124(a) of this title.

LIBRARY REFERENCES

American Digest System

United States ⊙74(16).
Key Number System Topic No. 393.

WESTLAW ELECTRONIC RESEARCH

See Westlaw guide following the Explanation pages of this volume.

§ 109. Advance or partial payments to subcontractors; excessive payments, interest, liability of war contractor

(a) Any contracting agency may make advance or partial payments to any war contractor on account of any termination claim or claims, and may authorize, approve, or ratify any such advance or partial payments by any war contractor to his subcontractors, upon such conditions as it deems necessary to insure compliance with the provisions of subsection (b) of this section. Each contracting agency shall make final payments from time to time on partial settlements or on settlements fixing a minimum amount due before complete settlement, or as tentative payments before any settlement of the claim or claims.

(b) Where any such advance or partial payment is made to any war contractor by any contracting agency or by another war contractor under this section, except a final payment on a partial settlement, any amount in excess of the amount finally determined to be due on the termination claim shall be treated as a loan from the Government to the war contractor receiving it, and shall be payable upon demand together with a penalty computed at the rate of 6 per centum per annum, for the period from the date such excess advance or partial payment is received to the date on which such excess is repaid or extinguished. Where the advance or partial payment was made by a war contractor and authorized, approved, or ratified by any contracting agency, the war contractor making it shall not be liable for any such excess payment in the absence of fraud on his part and shall receive payment or credit from the Government for the amount of such excess payment.

(July 1, 1944, c. 358, § 9, 58 Stat. 657.)

HISTORICAL AND STATUTORY NOTES

Application to Terminated War Contracts

For application of this section to war contracts terminated at or before July 21, 1944, see section 124(a) of this title.

LIBRARY REFERENCES

American Digest System

United States ☜74(16).
Key Number System Topic No. 393.

WESTLAW ELECTRONIC RESEARCH

See Westlaw guide following the Explanation pages of this volume.

Notes of Decisions

Effect of approval   2
Mandatory nature of payment   1

1. Mandatory nature of payment

Under subsec. (a) of this section, that contracting agency may make partial payments, partial payments are not mandatory upon Government agency involved, and the same is true as to approval of partial payments by prime contractor to his subcontractor in view of provision that contracting agency "may approve" such payments. Commercial Credit Corp. v. California Ship-building Corp., S.D.Cal.1947, 71 F.Supp. 936. United States ☜ 74.2

2. Effect of approval

Under this section, the only legal significance of an approval by the Maritime Commission [now Department of Transportation] or other Government contracting agency, of a partial payment by a prime contractor to his subcontractor, is that the former will be protected, if not guilty of fraud, in the event the amount finally determined to be due is less than the partial payment. Commercial Credit Corp. v. California Shipbuilding Corp., S.D.Cal.1947, 71 F.Supp. 936. United States ☜ 74.2

§ 110.   Guarantee of loans, advances, etc.

(a) By contract

Any contracting agency is authorized—

   (1) to enter into contracts with any Federal Reserve bank, or other public or private financing institution, guaranteeing such financing institution against loss of principal or interest on loans, discounts, or advances or on commitments in connection therewith, which such financing institution may make to any war contractor or to any person who is or has been engaged in performing any operation deemed by such contracting agency to be connected with or related to war production, for the purpose of financing such war contractor or other person in connection with or in contemplation of the termination of one or more such war contracts or operations; and

   (2) to make, enter into contracts to make, or to participate with any Government agency, any Federal Reserve bank or public or private financing institution in making loans, discounts, or advances, or commitments in connection therewith, for the purpose of financing any such war contractor or other person in connection with or in contemplation of the termination of such war contracts or operations.

(b) By assignment

Any such loan, discount, advance, guaranty, or commitment in connection therewith may be secured by assignment of, or covenants to assign, some or all of the rights of such war contractor or other person in connection with the termination of such war contracts or operations, or in such other manner as the contracting agency may prescribe.

(c) Federal Reserve bank as fiscal agent

Subject to such regulations as the Board of Governors of the Federal Reserve System may prescribe with the approval of the Administrator of General Services, any Federal Reserve bank is authorized to act, on behalf of the contracting agencies, as fiscal agent of the United States in carrying out the purposes of this chapter.

(d) Application of other laws

This section shall not limit or affect any authority of any contracting agency, under any other statute, to make loans, discounts, or advances, or commitments in connection therewith or guaranties thereof.

(July 1, 1944, c. 358, § 10, 58 Stat. 657; Ex. Ord. No. 9809, § 8, eff. Dec. 12, 1946, 11 F.R. 14281; 1947 Reorg. Plan No. 1, § 201, eff. July 1, 1947, 12 F.R. 4534, 61 Stat. 951; June 30, 1949, c. 288, Title I, § 102(b), 63 Stat. 380.)

HISTORICAL AND STATUTORY NOTES

Revision Notes and Legislative Reports
1949 Acts. House Report No. 670 and Conference Report No. 935, see 1949 U.S.Code Cong.Service, p. 1475.

Transfer of Functions
Functions of Secretary of the Treasury were transferred to Administrator of General Services by Act June 30, 1949, c. 288, § 102(b), 63 Stat. 380, which was classified to former 40 U.S.C.A. § 752(b), prior to repeal by Pub.L. 107–217, § 6(b), Aug. 21, 2002, 116 Stat. 1304.

"Secretary of the Treasury" was substituted for "Director" by section 8 of 1946 Ex. Ord. No. 9809 and section 201 of

Reorg. Plan No. 1 of 1947. Reorg. Plan No. 1 of 1947 is set out in the Appendix to Title 5, Government Organization and Employees.

Effective Date of Transfer of Functions
Act June 30, 1949, § 605, which set July 1, 1949, as the effective date for the transfer of functions by that Act, was repealed by Pub.L. 107–217, § 6(b), Aug. 21, 2002, 116 Stat. 1313.

Application to Terminated War Contracts
For application of this section to war contracts terminated at or before July 21, 1944, see section 124(a) of this title.

LIBRARY REFERENCES

American Digest System
United States ☞74(16).
Key Number System Topic No. 393.

WESTLAW ELECTRONIC RESEARCH
See Westlaw guide following the Explanation pages of this volume.

§ 111.   Termination of contracts

(a) Advance notice; prime contracts

In order to facilitate the efficient use of materials, manpower, and facilities for war and civilian purposes, each contracting agency—

   (1) shall provide its prime contractors with notice of termination of their prime contracts as far in advance of the cessation of work thereunder as is feasible and consistent with the national security without permitting unneeded production or performance;

   (2) shall establish procedures whereby prime contractors shall provide affected subcontractors with immediate notice of termination; and

   (3) shall permit the continuation of some or all of the work under a terminated prime contract whenever the agency deems that such continuation will benefit the Government or is necessary to avoid substantial injury to the plant or property.

(b) Cessation of work without termination

Whenever a contracting agency hereafter directs a prime contractor to cease or suspend all or a substantial part of the work under a prime contract, without terminating the contract, then, unless the contract provides otherwise, (1) the contracting agency shall compensate the contractor for reasonable costs and expenses resulting from such cessation or suspension, and (2) if the cessation or suspension extends for thirty days or more, the contractor may elect to treat it as a termination by delivering written notice of his election so to do to the contracting agency, at any time before the contracting agency directs the prime contractor to resume work under the contract.

(c) Authority of Administrator of General Services; classes of contracts

The Administrator of General Services shall have no authority under this chapter to regulate or control the classes of contracts to be terminated by the contracting agencies.

(July 1, 1944, c. 358, § 11, 58 Stat. 658; Ex. Ord. No. 9809, § 8, eff. Dec. 12, 1946, 11 F.R. 14281; 1947 Reorg. Plan No. 1, § 201, eff. July 1, 1947, 12 F.R. 4534, 61 Stat. 951; June 30, 1949, c. 288, Title I, § 102(b), 63 Stat. 380.)

HISTORICAL AND STATUTORY NOTES

Transfer of Functions

Functions of Secretary of the Treasury were transferred to Administrator of General Services by Act June 30, 1949, c. 288, § 102(b), 63 Stat. 380, which was classified to former 40 U.S.C.A. § 752(b), prior to repeal by Pub.L. 107–217, § 6(b), Aug. 21, 2002, 116 Stat. 1304.

"Secretary of the Treasury" was substituted for "Director" by section 8 of Ex. Ord. No. 9809 and section 201 of Reorg.

Plan No. 1 of 1947. Reorg. Plan No. 1 of 1947 is set out in the Appendix to Title 5, Government Organization and Employees.

Effective Date of Transfer of Functions

Act June 30, 1949, § 605, which set July 1, 1949, as the effective date for the transfer of functions by that Act, was repealed by Pub.L. 107–217, § 6(b), Aug. 21, 2002, 116 Stat. 1313.

LIBRARY REFERENCES

American Digest System

United States ⊂⇒74(16).
Key Number System Topic No. 393.

WESTLAW ELECTRONIC RESEARCH

See Westlaw guide following the Explanation pages of this volume.

Notes of Decisions

Suspension of contract   1

---

1.   Suspension of contract

Where a contractor who had entered into a contract for the assembly of combat rations for the armed forces received a directive to suspend final assemblies until further notice on June 5, 1951, and received authorization to start assembly on July 16, by a telegram received on July 9, contractor under this chapter could not thereafter treat the suspension as a termination even though it notified the contracting agency of its election to treat the suspension as a termination on July 10.   Oliver-Finnie Co. v. U.S., Ct.Cl.1960, 279 F.2d 498, 150 Ct.Cl. 189.   United States ⊂⇒ 74(16)

§ 112.   Removal and storage of materials

(a)   Termination inventory

It is the policy of the Government, upon the termination of any war contract, to assure the expeditious removal from the plant of the war contractor of the termination inventory not to be retained or sold by the war contractor.

(b)   Statement on material of inventory

Any war contractor may submit to the contracting agency concerned or to any other Government agency designated by the Administrator of General Services, one or more statements showing the materials which such war contractor claims to be termination inventory under one or more war contracts and desires to have removed by the Government.   Such statements shall be prepared in such form and detail, shall be submitted in such manner, through the prime contractor or otherwise, and shall be supported by such certificates or other data, as may be prescribed under this chapter.

(c) Removal and storage by Government agency

Within sixty days after the submission of any such statement by a war contractor, or such shorter period as may be prescribed under this chapter, or within such longer period as the war contractor may agree, the Government agency concerned (1) shall arrange, upon such terms and conditions as may be agreed, for the storage by the war contractor on his own premises or elsewhere of all such claimed termination inventory which the war contractor does not retain or dispose of, except any part which may be determined not to be allocable to the terminated war contract or contracts, or (2) shall remove from the plant or plants of the war contractor all of such claimed termination inventory not retained, disposed of, or stored by the war contractor or determined not to be allocable to the terminated war contract or contracts.

(d) Removal and storage by war contractor

Upon the failure of the Government so to arrange for storage by the war contractor or to remove any termination inventory within the period specified under subsection (c) of this section, the war contractor, subject to regulations prescribed under this chapter, may remove some or all of such termination inventory from his plant or plants and may store it on his own premises or elsewhere for the account and at the risk and expense of the Government, using reasonable care for its transportation and preservation. If any war contractor intends so to remove any claimed termination inventory, he shall deliver to the Government agency concerned written notice of the date fixed for removal and a statement showing the quantities and condition of the materials so to be removed, certified on behalf of the war contractor to have been prepared in accordance with a concurrent physical inventory of such materials. Such notice and statement shall be delivered at least twenty days in advance of the date fixed for removal and may be delivered before or after the expiration of the period specified under subsection (c) of this section. If the Government agency fails to check such materials, at or before the time of their removal by the war contractor, a certificate of the war contractor specifying the materials shown on such statement which were so removed, and filed with the Government agency concerned within thirty days after the date fixed for removal, shall constitute prima facie evidence against the United States as to the quantities and condition of the materials so removed, and the fact of their removal.

(e) Acquisition by Government agency of inventory material; liability

Notwithstanding any other provisions of law, but subject to subsection (h) of this section, the contracting agency concerned or the

Administrator of General Services, or any Government agency designated by him, on behalf of the United States, may, by the exercise of any contract rights or otherwise, acquire and take possession of any termination inventory of any war contractor, and any materials removed by the Government or stored for its account under subsections (c) and (d) of this section, whether or not such materials are finally determined not to constitute termination inventory.   With respect to any such materials, the Government shall be liable to any war contractor concerned only for their return to such war contractor or for their disposal value at the time of their removal or for the proceeds realized by the Government from their disposal, at the election of the Government agency concerned, unless the Government agency and the war contractor agree or have agreed on a different basis.   Any amount so paid or payable to a war contractor for materials allocable to a terminated war contract shall be credited against the termination claim under such contract but shall not otherwise affect the amount due on the claim, unless the Government agency concerned and the war contractor agree or have agreed otherwise.   Any materials to which the Administrator of General Services takes title under this section shall be delivered for disposal to any appropriate Government agency authorized to make such disposal.

(f) Postponement or delay of termination settlement

No contracting agency shall postpone or delay any termination settlement beyond the period specified in subsection (c) of this section for the purpose of awaiting disposal by the war contractor or the Government of any termination inventory reported in accordance with subsection (b) of this section.

(g) Government-owned machinery

Whenever any war contractor no longer requires, for the performance of any war contract, any Government-owned machinery, tools, or equipment installed in his plant for the performance of one or more war contracts, the Government agency concerned, upon written demand by the war contractor, and within sixty days after such demand or such other period as may be prescribed under this chapter, and upon such conditions as may be so prescribed, shall remove or provide for the removal of such machinery, tools, or equipment from such plant, unless the Government agency concerned and the war contractor, by facilities contract or otherwise, have made or make other provisions for the retention, storage, maintenance, or disposition of such machinery, tools or equipment. The Government agency concerned may waive or release on behalf of the United States any obligation of the war contractor with respect to such machinery, tools, or equipment upon such terms and conditions as the agency deems appropriate. Upon the failure of the Government so to remove or provide for removal of any such machinery, tools, or equipment, the war contractor, subject to regulations prescribed under this chapter, may remove all or part of such machinery, tools, or equipment from his plant and may store it on his own premises or elsewhere, for the account and at the risk and expense of the Government, using reasonable care for its transportation and preservation.

(h) Limitation on Government acquisition of inventories

Nothing in this chapter shall limit or affect the authority of the Department of the Army, Department of the Air Force, Navy Department, or the Department of Transportation, respectively, to take over any termination inventories and to retain them for their use for any purpose or to dispose of such termination inventories for the purpose of war production, or to authorize any war contractor to retain or dispose of such termination inventories for the purpose of war production.

(i) Removal and storage by war contractor at own risk

Nothing in this section shall be construed to prevent the removal and storage of any termination inventory by any war contractor, at his own risk, at any time after termination of any war contract to which it is allocable.

(July 1, 1944, c. 358, § 12, 58 Stat. 658; Ex. Ord. No. 9809, § 8, eff. Dec. 12, 1946, 11 F.R. 14281; 1947 Reorg. Plan No. 1, § 201, eff. July 1, 1947, 12 F.R. 4534, 61 Stat. 951; June 30, 1949, c. 288, Title I, § 102(b), 63 Stat. 380; Aug. 6, 1981, Pub.L. 97–31, § 12(18), 95 Stat. 154.)

HISTORICAL AND STATUTORY NOTES

Revision Notes and Legislative Reports
1981 Acts. House Report No. 97–199, see 1981 U.S.Code Cong. and Adm.News, p. 92.

Amendments
1981 Amendments. Subsec. (h). Pub.L. 97–31 substituted "the Department of Transportation" for "Maritime Commission".

Change of Name
The Department of the Air Force was inserted under the authority of section 207(a), (f) of Act July 26, 1947, c. 343, Title II, 61 Stat. 502, 503. The Department of War was designated the Department of the Army and the title of the Secretary of War was changed to Secretary of the Army by section 205(a) of Act July 26, 1947. Sections 205(a) and

207(a), (f) of Act July 26, 1947 were repealed by section 53 of Act Aug. 10, 1956, c. 1041, 70A Stat. 641. Section 1 of Act Aug. 10, 1956 enacted Title 10, Armed Forces, which in sections 3010 to 3013 and 8010 to 8013 continued the military Departments of the Army and Air Force under the administrative supervision of a Secretary of the Army and a Secretary of the Air Force, respectively.

Transfer of Functions
Functions of Secretary of the Treasury were transferred to Administrator of General Services by Act June 30, 1949, c. 288, § 102(b), 63 Stat. 380, which was classified to former 40 U.S.C.A. § 752(b), prior to repeal by Pub.L. 107–217, § 6(b), Aug. 21, 2002, 116 Stat. 1304.

"Secretary of the Treasury" was substituted for "Director" by section 8 of Ex.

Ord. No. 9809 and section 201 of Reorg. Plan No. 1 of 1947. Reorg. Plan No. 1 of 1947 is set out in the Appendix to Title 5, Government Organization and Employees.

All executive and administrative functions of the Maritime Commission were transferred to the Chairman of the Maritime Commission by 1949 Reorg. Plan No. 6, set out under section 1111 of Title 46, Shipping.

Effective Date of Transfer of Functions

Act June 30, 1949, § 605, which set July 1, 1949, as the effective date for the transfer of functions by that Act, was repealed by Pub.L. 107–217, § 6(b), Aug. 21, 2002, 116 Stat. 1313.

Application to Terminate War Contracts

For application of subsecs. (b) to (e) of this section to war contracts terminated at or before July 21, 1944, see section 124(a) of this title.

LIBRARY REFERENCES

American Digest System
    United States ⟲74(16).
    Key Number System Topic No. 393.

Research References

ALR Library
    175 ALR 1366, What Amounts to Conditional Sale.

WESTLAW ELECTRONIC RESEARCH

See Westlaw guide following the Explanation pages of this volume.

Notes of Decisions

Acquisition by government agency of inventory material   2-4
    Generally   2
    Contracting agency   3
    Termination inventory   4
Contracting agency, acquisition by government agency of inventory material   3
Disposition of inventory   5
Removal and storage by government agency   1
Termination inventory, acquisition by government agency of inventory material   4

---

1.   Removal and storage by government agency

Where war contract whereunder plaintiff was to reclaim used Signal Corps wire was terminated before all wire furnished to plaintiff by defendant United States had been reclaimed, and defendant removed wire in normal course of winding up operations and without design or purpose to defeat plaintiff's claim for costs of services plaintiff had performed on work in progress when contract was terminated, and removal was accomplished under erroneous belief of defendant that claim of plaintiff for work in progress at time of termination was unallowable as matter of law, removal did not give rise to an estoppel against the United States which satisfied plaintiff's burden of proof as to accuracy of plaintiff's inventory of wire on hand when removal was accomplished. Hanson v. U.S., Ct.Cl.1950, 92 F.Supp. 972, 117 Ct.Cl. 605.   Estoppel ⟲ 62.2(4)

2.   Acquisition by government agency of inventory material—Generally

Subsec. (e) of this section discloses a plan for concerted action by contracting agency and war contractor for disposition of war surplus assets to best interests of the Government and for the hastening of reconversion of manufacturing plant to peacetime production, and war contractors' authority is restricted to sales of surplus inventories for not less than cost for which Government would otherwise be liable under its contract. L.B. Smith, Inc. v. Aetna-Standard Engineering Co., Ohio App.1949, 92 N.E.2d 818, 86 Ohio App. 418, 42 O.O. 16, appeal dismissed 89 N.E.2d 476, 152 Ohio St. 452, 40 O.O. 482.   United States ⟲ 74(16)

3.   —— Contracting agency, acquisition by government agency of inventory material

Under subsec. (e) of this section, providing that "contracting agency" on behalf of the United States may by exercise of contract rights or otherwise acquire termination inventory of any war contractor, quoted phrase included army officers sent to manufacturer's factory to take charge of disposition of trucks which had been manufactured for Federal Government under war contract but had become surplus because they were no longer needed in prosecution of war. L.B. Smith, Inc. v. Aetna-Standard Engineering Co., Ohio App.1949, 92 N.E.2d 818, 86 Ohio App. 418, 42 O.O. 16, appeal dismissed 89 N.E.2d 476, 152 Ohio St. 452, 40 O.O. 482. United States ☞ 74(16)

4. —— Termination inventory, acquisition by government agency of inventory material

Under subsec. (e) of this section, providing that federal contracting agency may by exercise of contract rights or otherwise acquire "termination inventory" of any war contractor, quoted phrase included trucks produced by manufacturer for the Government under war contract even after contract for sale of trucks had been entered into between manufacturer and private buyer, and such inventory included trucks until they were actually removed from possession of manufacturer. L.B. Smith, Inc. v. Aetna-Standard Engineering Co., Ohio App.1949, 92 N.E.2d 818, 86 Ohio App. 418, 42 O.O. 16, appeal dismissed 89 N.E.2d 476, 152 Ohio St. 452, 40 O.O. 482. United States ☞ 74(16)

5. Disposition of inventory

Under subsec. (c) of this section, governing disposition of termination inventories of war contractors, contractor, whose power so to do had not been revoked, had authority to sell trucks constituting part of its termination inventory; and actual delivery to buyer was not essential to severance of trucks from termination inventory. L.B. Smith, Inc. v. U.S., Ct.Cl. 1956, 145 F.Supp. 216, 136 Ct.Cl. 587, 81 Ohio Law Abs. 561, 9 O.O.2d 177. United States ☞ 74(16)

§ 113. Appeals

(a) Failure to settle claims by agreement; preparation of findings; notice to war contractor

Whenever the contracting agency responsible for settling any termination claim has not settled the claim by agreement or has so settled only a part of the claim, (1) the contracting agency at any time may determine the amount due on such claim or such unsettled part, and prepare written findings indicating the basis of the determination, and deliver a copy of such findings to the war contractor, or (2) if the termination claim has been submitted in the manner and substantially the form prescribed under this chapter, the contracting agency, upon written demand by the war contractor for such findings, shall determine the amount due on the claim or unsettled part and prepare and deliver such findings to the war contractor within ninety days after the receipt by the agency of such demand. In preparing such findings, the contracting agency may require the war contractor to furnish such information and to submit to such audits as may be reasonably necessary for that purpose. Within thirty days after the delivery of any such findings, the contracting agency shall pay to the war contractor at least 90 per centum of the amount thereby determined to be due, after deducting the amount of any outstanding interim financing applicable thereto.

(b) Rights of war contractor

Whenever any war contractor is aggrieved by the findings of a contracting agency on his claim or part thereof or by its failure to make such findings in accordance with subsection (a) of this section, he may bring suit against the United States for such claim or such part thereof, in the United States Court of Federal Claims or in a United States district court, in accordance with sections 1346, 2401, and 2402 of Title 28, except that, if the contracting agency is the Reconstruction Finance Corporation, or any corporation organized pursuant to the Reconstruction Finance Corporation Act, or any corporation owned or controlled by the United States, the suit shall be brought against such corporation in any court of competent jurisdiction in accordance with existing law.

(c) Procedure

Any proceeding under subsection (b) of this section shall be governed by the following conditions:

(1) When any contracting agency provides a procedure within the agency for protest against such findings or for other appeal therefrom by the war contractor, the war contractor, before proceeding under subsection (b) of this section, (i) in his discretion may resort to such procedure within the time specified in his contract or, if no time is specified, within thirty days after the delivery to him of the findings; and (ii) shall resort to such procedure for protest or other appeal to the extent required by the Administrator of General Services, but failure of the contracting agency to act on any such required protest or appeal within thirty days shall operate as a refusal by the agency to modify its findings. Any revision of the findings by the contracting agency, upon protest or appeal within the agency, shall be treated as the findings of the agency for the purpose of appeal or suit under subsection (b) of this section. Notwithstanding any contrary provision in any war contract, no war contractor shall be required to protest or appeal from such findings within the contracting agency except in accordance with this paragraph.

(2) A war contractor may initiate proceedings in accordance with subsection (b) of this section (i) within ninety days after delivery to him of the findings by the contracting agency, or (ii) in case of protests or appeal within the agency, within ninety days after the determination of such protest or appeal, or (iii) in case of failure to deliver such findings, within one year after his demand therefor. If he does not initiate such proceedings within the time specified, he shall be precluded thereafter from initiating any proceedings in accordance with subsection (b) of this section, and the findings of the contracting agency shall be final

and conclusive, or if no findings were made, he shall be deemed to have waived such termination claim.

(3) Notwithstanding any contrary provision in any war contract, the court shall not be bound by the findings of the contracting agency, but shall treat such findings as prima facie correct, and the burden shall be on the war contractor to establish that the amount due on his claim or part thereof exceeds the amount allowed by the findings of the contracting agency. Whenever the court finds that the war contractor failed to negotiate in good faith with the contracting agency for the settlement of his claim or part thereof before appeal or suit thereon, or failed to furnish to the agency any information reasonably requested by it regarding his termination claim or part thereof, or failed to prosecute diligently any protest or appeal required to be taken under subsection (c)(1)(ii) of this section, the court (i) may refuse to receive in evidence any information not submitted to the contracting agency; (ii) may deny interest on the claim or part thereof for such period as it deems proper; or (iii) may remand the case to the contracting agency for further proceedings upon such terms as the court may prescribe. Unless the case is remanded, the court shall enter the appropriate award or judgment on the basis of the law and facts, and may increase or decrease the amount allowed by the findings of the contracting agency.

(4) Any such proceedings shall not affect the authority of the contracting agency concerned to make a settlement of the termination claim, or any part thereof, by agreement with the war contractor at any time before such proceedings are concluded.

(d) Omitted

(e) Arbitration

The contracting agency responsible for settling any claim and the war contractor asserting the claim, by agreement, may submit all or any part of the termination claim to arbitration, without regard to the amount in dispute. Such arbitration proceedings shall be governed by the provisions of United States Arbitration Act to the same extent as if authorized by an effective agreement in writing between the Government and the war contractor. Any such arbitration award shall be final and conclusive upon the United States to the same extent as a settlement under subsection (c) of section 106 of this title, but shall not be subject to approval by any settlement review board.

(f) Conclusiveness of decisions

Whenever any dispute exists between any war contractor and a subcontractor regarding any termination claim, either of them, by agreement with the other, may submit the dispute to a contracting agency for mediation or arbitration whenever authorized by the agency or required by the Administrator of General Services.

Any award or decision in such proceedings shall be final and conclusive as to the parties so submitting any such dispute and shall not be questioned by the United States in settling any related claim, in the absence of fraud or collusion.

(July 1, 1944, c. 358, § 13, 58 Stat. 660; Ex. Ord. No. 9809, § 8, eff. Dec. 12, 1946, 11 F.R. 14281; 1947 Reorg. Plan No. 1, § 201, eff. July 1, 1947, 12 F.R. 4534, 61 Stat. 951; June 30, 1949, c. 288, Title I, § 102(b), 63 Stat. 380; July 14, 1952, c. 739, §§ 1, 2, 66 Stat. 627; Apr. 2, 1982, Pub.L. 97–164, Title I, § 160(a)(14), 96 Stat. 48; Oct. 29, 1992, Pub.L. 102–572, Title IX, § 902(b)(1), 106 Stat. 4516.)

HISTORICAL AND STATUTORY NOTES

Revision Notes and Legislative Reports

1982 Acts. Senate Report No. 97–275, see 1982 U.S.Code Cong. and Adm.News, p. 11.

1992 Acts. House Report No. 102–1006, see 1992 U.S. Code Cong. and Adm. News, p. 3921.

References in Text

The Reconstruction Finance Corporation Act, referred to in subsec. (b), is Act Jan. 22, 1932, ch. 8, 47 Stat. 5, as amended, which was classified to chapter 14 (section 601 et seq.) of Title 15, Commerce and Trade, and has been eliminated from the Code. For complete classification of this Act prior to its elimination from the Code, see Tables.

United States Arbitration Act, referred to in subsec. (e), is Act Feb. 12, 1925, c. 213, 43 Stat. 883, which is classified generally to Title 9, Arbitration.

Codifications

In subsec. (b) of this section, "sections 1346, 2401, and 2402 of Title 28" was substituted for "subsection (20) of section 41 of Title 28" on authority of Act June 25, 1948, c. 646, 62 Stat. 869, the first section of which enacted Title 28, Judiciary and Judicial Procedure.

Subsec. (d) of this section, which provided for appointment and duties of an Appeal Board, was omitted on authority of Act July 14, 1952, c. 739, §§ 1, 2, 66 Stat. 627, which abolished the Appeal Board and terminated all appeals, effective nine months after July 14, 1952. References in other subsections of this section to the Appeal Board were omitted

in view of Act July 14, 1952. As a result of these omissions, cl. (1) of subsec. (b), which authorized a war contractor to appeal to the Appeal Board, was deleted, and cl. (2), which permitted suits against the United States, became a part of subsec. (b) without numerical designation.

Amendments

1982 Amendments. Subsec. (b). Pub. L. 97–164 substituted "United States Claims Court" for "Court of Claims".

Effective and Applicability Provisions

1992 Acts. Amendment by section 902(b)(1) of Pub.L. 102–572 effective Oct. 29, 1992, see section 911 of Pub.L. 102–572, set out as a note under section 171 of Title 28, Judiciary and Judicial Procedure.

1982 Acts. Amendment by Pub.L. 97–164 effective Oct. 1, 1982, see section 402 of Pub.L. 97–164, set out as a note under section 171 of Title 28, Judiciary and Judicial Procedure.

Change of Name

References to United States Claims Court deemed to refer to United States Court of Federal Claims and references to Claims Court deemed to refer to Court of Federal Claims, see section 902(b) of Pub.L. 102–572, set out as a note under section 171 of Title 28, Judiciary and Judicial Procedure.

Transfer of Functions

Functions of Secretary of the Treasury were transferred to Administrator of General Services by Act June 30, 1949, c. 288, § 102(b), 63 Stat. 380, which was classified to former 40 U.S.C.A. § 752(b), prior to repeal by Pub.L. 107–217, § 6(b), Aug. 21, 2002, 116 Stat. 1304.

"Secretary of the Treasury" was substituted for "Director" by section 8 of Ex. Ord. No. 9809 and section 201 of Reorg. Plan No. 1 of 1947. Reorg. Plan No. 1 of 1947 is set out in the Appendix to Title 5, Government Organization and Employees.

Effective Date of Transfer of Functions

Act June 30, 1949, § 605, which set July 1, 1949, as the effective date for the transfer of functions by that Act, was repealed by Pub.L. 107–217, § 6(b), Aug. 21, 2002, 116 Stat. 1313.

Abolition of Reconstruction Finance Corporation

Reorg. Plan No. 1 of 1957, § 6(a), eff. June 30, 1957, 22 F.R. 4633, 71 Stat. 647, set out in the Appendix to Title 5, Government Organization and Employees, abolished the Reconstruction Finance Corporation.

Abolition of Appeals Board; Termination of Appeals; No Further Appeals Accepted; Return of Erroneous Filed Appeals

Act July 14, 1952, c. 739, 66 Stat. 627, provided:

"That the Appeal Board established under section 13(d) of the Contract Settlement Act of 1944 [subsec. (d) of this section] is hereby abolished: *Provided, however,* That said abolition shall not become effective until six months after the enactment of this Act [July 14, 1952] or such later date, nor more than nine months after the enactment of this Act, as may be fixed by written order of the Director of Contract Settlement published in the Federal Register. Such an order shall be made only in case the Director finds that it is impracticable for the Appeal Board to dispose of its pending business before the date fixed for abolition of the Board by this Act or a previous order of the Director. No such order shall be made less than thirty days prior to the date theretofore fixed for abolition of the Appeal Board.

"Sec. 2. (a) Upon the effective date of the abolition of the Appeal Board all appeals and disputes pending therein shall be terminated without prejudice and the right of the parties to pursue such other remedies as are provided by law shall not be affected thereby.

"(b) In any such terminated appeal, timely initiated in the Appeal Board, where the period for pursuit of any other remedy pursuant to section 13(b)(2) of the Contract Settlement Act of 1944 [subsec. (b)(2) of this section] shall have expired or would expire within sixty days after the effective date of the abolition of the Appeal Board, the period within which proceedings may be initiated in accordance with the said section shall be extended to sixty days after said effective date.

"(c) Effective thirty days after the enactment of this Act [July 14, 1952] no further appeals or submitted disputes shall be accepted for determination by said Appeal Board.

"(d) Where an attempt is erroneously made to file an appeal with the Appeal Board after the time limited therefor by section 1(c) of this Act but prior to the effective date of the abolition of the Appeal Board, said Board shall forthwith return the papers to the person therein named as appellant together with a notice in writing that, pursuant to the terms of section 1(c) of this Act, it can no longer accept such an appeal. Where such an attempt is made in good faith and the appeal would, except for the provisions of section 1(c) of this Act, have been timely and the period for pursuit of any other remedy pursuant to section 13(b)(2) of the Contract Settlement Act of 1944 [subsec. (b)(2) of this section] expires or would expire prior to the expiration of sixty days after the receipt of such notice, the period within which proper proceedings may be initiated in accordance with said section 13(b)(2) shall be extended to sixty days after the receipt of such notice."

Application to Terminated War Contracts

For application of this section to war contracts terminated at or before July 21, 1944, see section 124(a) of this title.

LIBRARY REFERENCES

American Digest System

Federal Courts ⟜1076.

United States ☞74(16).
Key Number System Topic Nos. 170B, 393.

Research References

ALR Library
    106 ALR 1241, Right to Set-Off, Counterclaim, or Recoupment Against the United States or a Sovereign Foreign State.
    27 ALR 48, Construction of "Cost Plus" Contracts.
Treatises and Practice Aids
    West's Federal Administrative Practice § 837, Subject Matter Jurisdiction--Termination of War Contracts.
    17 Wright & Miller: Federal Prac. & Proc. § 4101, The Claims Court.
    20 Wright & Miller: Federal Prac. & Proc. § 23, Civil Actions to Which the United States Is a Party.

WESTLAW ELECTRONIC RESEARCH

See Westlaw guide following the Explanation pages of this volume.

Notes of Decisions

Acceptance of award   1
Accrual of action   6
Admissibility of evidence   19
Appellate review   24
Attempt to settle   2
Burden of proof   18
Compromise of claim   3
Counterclaims   12
Denial of claim   4
Exhaustion of administrative remedies   7
Interest   22
Judgment on pleadings   16
Jurisdiction   10
Jury trial   17
Laches   14
Limitations   13
Notice of contracting officer's decision   8
Pleadings   11
Res judicata   15
Scope of claim   5
Specific performance   23
Time of filing appeal   9
Weight and conclusiveness of administrative findings   21
Weight and sufficiency of evidence   20

1. Acceptance of award

Under subsec. (a) of this section, authorizing Government contracting agency settling a termination claim to pay war contractor 90 percent of amount determined to be due, contractor would not lose right to appeal by accepting award of contracting agency on termination of Government war contract. Piggly Wiggly Corp. v. U.S., Ct.Cl.1949, 81 F.Supp. 819,

112 Ct.Cl. 391.   Administrative Law And Procedure ☞ 665.1;   United States ☞ 74(16);   United States ☞ 110

2. Attempt to settle

An attempt by a war contractor to settle his claim against the federal government is a condition precedent to bringing of an action in the Court of Claims [now United States Claims Court] based on provisions of this chapter.   Jardine Min. Co. v. U.S., Ct.Cl.1950, 88 F.Supp. 265, 115 Ct.Cl. 279.   United States ☞ 74(16)

The intention of Congress in passing this chapter was to make an attempt to settle contract claims thereunder a condition precedent to bringing of action, both for prime contractors and for subcontractors, and it is mandatory for subcontractors to file their claims against prime contractors under this chapter on forms prescribed by regulations passed thereunder as a condition precedent to commencement of action.   Stevens v. Federal Cartridge Corp., Minn.1948, 32 N.W.2d 312, 226 Minn. 148.   War And National Emergency ☞ 67

3. Compromise of claim

Negotiated agreement between subcontractor and Government representative, as to amount due subcontractor under preliminary decision of appeal board of the office of contracts settlement sustaining portion of subcontractor's claim, was not a compromise of that part of subcontractor's claim which had been denied by the appeal board in its preliminary decision and would not prevent subcontractor suing for such portion of its claim as had been denied by the preliminary decision. Condenser Service & Engineering Co. v. U.S., Ct.Cl.1954, 120 F.Supp. 262, 128 Ct.Cl. 1.   United States ☞ 74.2

4. Denial of claim

Where plaintiff requested Maritime [now Department of Transportation] Commission to make payment for machine parts shipped to subsidiary of company which had contract with Maritime Commission, according to alleged guarantee made by agent of Commission, but Commission stated it had no authority to authorize payment and recommended filing of claim under this chapter, original refusal of payment did not constitute denial of claim under this section precluding plaintiff from bringing suit for payment of claim within 90 days after denial of plaintiff's formal claim by Commission. Rice Barton Corp. v. U.S., Ct.Cl.1950, 88 F.Supp. 271, 115 Ct.Cl. 575.   United States ☞ 74(16)

5. Scope of claim

Where war contract between contractor and the Government is terminated by the Government, the contractor is limited to the scope and extent of his filed claim in any action that he may bring in district courts following findings and determination by the contracting agency, and the filed claim in turn is limited as to its allowable scope and extent by provisions of this chapter and by its specific reference to fair compensation. Monolith Portland Midwest Co. v. R.F.C., S.D.Cal. 1951, 95 F.Supp. 570.   United States ☞ 74(16)

6. Accrual of action

War contractor's letters to Air Force, which were written before cost of cleanup of factory site was assessed and did not contain demand for written findings, were not claims under Contract Settlement Act (CSA), and thus Air Force's subsequent denial of reimbursement did not commence limitations period for contractor's suit against government. Ford Motor Co. v. U.S., C.A.Fed.2004, 378 F.3d 1314, rehearing and rehearing en banc denied.   United States ☞ 74(16)

Where cause of action arose in 1949, and action was filed in 1956, claim was necessarily predicated on this chapter. North Am. Philips Co. v. U.S., Ct.Cl.1961, 292 F.2d 861, 154 Ct.Cl. 754.   United States ☞ 74(16)

7. Exhaustion of administrative remedies

The right to recover in an action at law any of the items classified in section 106(d) of this title is limited to an action brought after Government agency, responsible for settlement of the claim, has passed upon it by findings under this section.   Rumsey Mfg. Corp. v. U.S. Hoffman Machinery Corp., C.A.2 (N.Y.) 1951, 187 F.2d 927.   United States ☞ 74(16)

Remedy of a contractor under this chapter must be exhausted before recourse may be had to any court other than as prescribed in this chapter. Daniel Hamm Drayage Co. v. Willson, C.A.8 (Mo.) 1949, 178 F.2d 633.   United States ☞ 74(16)

Where war contractor, whose contract for construction and operation of an alumina extraction plant was terminated after war, failed to include in its claim against contracting agency claim for loss of value of the contract, it could not, without exhausting administrative proceeding by filing a claim for this amount, claim the amount in court. Monolith Portland Midwest Co. v. R.F.C., S.D.Cal. 1955, 128 F.Supp. 824.   United States ☞ 74(16)

Reformation of instrument appeals to equitable jurisdiction of courts, which jurisdiction has not been granted to any other branch of government or any agency thereof, and therefore distiller seeking, as against Reconstruction Finance Corporation, reformation of contract for lease of defense plant was not obliged to first proceed under this chapter. Belvidere Distilling Co. v. R.F.C., N.D.Ill.1949, 109 F.Supp. 298.   United States ☞ 53(13.1)

8. Notice of contracting officer's decision

Where individual to whom findings of Contract Settlement Board were mailed was agent for both corporation which originally filed claim and individual to whom claim had been assigned, delivery was effective to commence running of time for appeal, even though findings were addressed to individual as agent for corporation rather than as agent for assignee. Doggett v. U.S., E.D.N.Y.1956, 142 F.Supp. 636.   United States ☞ 74(16)

Under contract with Government providing that all disputes should be decided by contracting officer who should reduce decision to writing and mail copy thereof to contractor and giving contractor 30 days within which to appeal, contracting officer's notices of terminations because of contractor's failure to meet delivery schedule and letters making it clear why contractor's excuses for delays had been rejected constituted sufficient notice of contracting officer's decisions, and failure to appeal within 30 days thereafter barred recovery for alleged loss resulting from termination of contract. Poloron Products, Inc. v. U.S., Ct.Cl.1953, 116 F.Supp. 588, 126 Ct.Cl. 816. United States ☞ 73(15)

9. Time of filing appeal

Letters of war contractor to the Reconstruction Finance Corporation after receiving instructions to suspend work on a test plant, prior to date it was notified that contract was terminated, if construable as a termination settlement proposal and a demand for findings indicating basis of termination of contract were insufficient to constitute a compliance with this chapter which allows the Government agency 90 days after receipt of demand for findings in which to make its determination, where the contractor filed a court action less than 60 days after the contract was terminated, and less than 90 days after the second letter was mailed. Monolith Portland Midwest Co. v. Reconstruction Fin. Corp., C.A.9 (Cal.) 1949, 178 F.2d 854, certiorari denied 70 S.Ct. 668, 339 U.S. 932, 94 L.Ed. 1352, rehearing denied 70 S.Ct. 839, 339 U.S. 954, 94 L.Ed. 1367. United States ☞ 74(16)

Where it was shown that the petition was received by the Court of Claims [now United States Claims Court] on Sunday, July 15, which was the last day for the filing of the petition under this section, the petition was timely filed. Schultz v. U.S., Ct.Cl.1955, 132 F.Supp. 953, 132 Ct.Cl. 618. Courts ☞ 463

Where contractor appealed to Appeal Board, Office of Contract Settlement from decision of Army rejecting claim for amount of expenditures made by it on contract over contract price, which Government had paid, and board affirmed Army's decision, action on claim in Court of Claims [now United States Claims Court] was one of review of board's action, not an appeal from Army directly to court, and failure to file claim in Court of Claims within 90 days after board's decision barred claim. Lawrance Aeronautical Corp. v. U.S., Ct.Cl.1955, 130 F.Supp. 603, 133 Ct.Cl. 1. Federal Courts ☞ 1105

Suit upon informal war contract under this chapter, which was appealed to the Court of Claims [now United States Court of Federal Claims] within 90 days after adverse decision by Appeal Board of the Office of Contract Settlement was not subject to the defense of the specific statute of limitations contained in this chapter. Gonzolez v. U.S., Ct.Cl.1952, 106 F.Supp. 180, 123 Ct.Cl. 222. United States ☞ 74(16)

Where no appeal was filed and no suit brought within time provided by this section, upon partial denial of claim for additional compensation under this chapter, suit based upon denial of subsequent claim concerning matter disallowed under original claim would be dismissed. S. Buchsbaum & Co. v. U.S., Ct.Cl.1952, 105 F.Supp. 821, 123 Ct.Cl. 262, certiorari denied 73 S.Ct. 829, 345 U.S. 939, 97 L.Ed. 1365. United States ☞ 74(16)

Where contractor failed to timely file with appeal board an appeal from findings of contracting agency, and appeal board dismissed appeal because it was filed too late, no judicial appeal from appeal board's dismissal would lie, even though attempted appeal from such decision were filed within 90 days. Luff v. U.S., Ct.Cl.1951, 100 F.Supp. 925, 120 Ct.Cl. 682. United States ☞ 73(15)

Contractor's claim that the government failed to pay "fair compensation" under World War II contract, in violation of the Contract Settlement Act of 1944, afforded no basis for recovery of its share of cost of environmental cleanup of site where contract was performed; contractor set forth no evidence that it did not receive "fair compensation" in 1946 termination settlement of contract, and time to contest any recovery pursuant to the termination agreement had long since passed. Ford Motor Co. v. U.S., Fed.Cl.2003, 56 Fed.Cl. 85, reversed 378 F.3d 1314, rehearing and rehearing en banc denied. Environmental Law ☞ 447; United States ☞ 74(16)

Where a claim based on alleged wrongful denial of a termination claim under this chapter is brought more than 90 days after such denial by the contracting agency, the claim in Court of Claims [now United States Court of Federal Claims] is barred by this section. Somerset Mach.

& Tool Co. v. U.S., Ct.Cl.1959, 144 Ct.Cl. 481, certiorari denied 80 S.Ct. 73, 361 U.S. 825, 4 L.Ed.2d 69. United States ☞ 74(16)

10. Jurisdiction

Contracts of conventional non-appropriated-fund instrumentalities of armed forces, such as post exchanges, ships' stores, and officers' clubs, do not bind appropriated funds, do not create a United States debt, and may not be vindicated in the Court of Claims [now United States Court of Federal Claims] even though made by Government officers. G.L. Christian and Associates v. U.S., Ct.Cl. 1963, 312 F.2d 418, 160 Ct.Cl. 1, reargument denied 320 F.2d 345, 160 Ct.Cl. 58, certiorari denied 84 S.Ct. 444, 375 U.S. 954, 11 L.Ed.2d 314, rehearing denied 84 S.Ct. 657, 376 U.S. 929, 11 L.Ed.2d 627, rehearing denied 84 S.Ct. 1906, 377 U.S. 1010, 12 L.Ed.2d 1059. Federal Courts ☞ 1074; United States ☞ 60

Federal district court, which had jurisdiction of any suit by Army supplier under its contract with the United States, had jurisdiction of action by supplier's attorney against United States to enforce his alleged lien for attorney's services on funds due supplier, even though supplier had, before attorney performed services, assigned any and all moneys due or which might accrue under contract to a factors corporation. Malman v. U.S., C.A.2 (N.Y.) 1953, 202 F.2d 483, rehearing denied 207 F.2d 897. Federal Courts ☞ 263

Where suit involving claim under this chapter involved an amount in excess of $10,000, although plaintiff waived all damages in excess of that amount, federal district court did not have jurisdiction of suit. Pioneer Gen-E-Motor Corp. v. Department of the Army, N.D.Ill.1955, 135 F.Supp. 871. Federal Courts ☞ 979

This chapter does not take from contractor his right to bring suit under court's general jurisdiction, and does not prevent him from invoking court's general jurisdiction, and in alternative, court's jurisdiction under this chapter. Pacific Maritime Ass'n v. U.S., Ct.Cl.1953, 117 F.Supp. 307, 125 Ct.Cl. 216. United States ☞ 74(16)

Under subsec. (b) of this section, authorizing suit against United States in Court of Claims [now United States Court of Federal Claims] or in district court, ex-

cept that, if contracting agency is Reconstruction Finance Corporation, suit shall be brought against such corporation in any court of competent jurisdiction, Court of Claims had jurisdiction over suit under this section where contracting agency was the Reconstruction Finance Corporation acting merely as agent for United States and not in its corporate capacity. National Cored Forgings Co. v. U.S., Ct.Cl.1953, 115 F.Supp. 469, 126 Ct.Cl. 250. Federal Courts ☞ 1076

Where war contractor filed with Maritime Commission [now Department of Transportation] a claim for $20,326.15 damages on account of cancellation of contract and Commission made finding allowing claimant $10,493.90 and paid claimant 90 per cent. thereof within 30 days thereafter, district court was without jurisdiction of action against United States for balance of $9,832.25, the difference between amount claimed and amount allowed, though claimant offered to waive right to recover any greater sum than such balance, since subsec. (b) of this section, giving district court concurrent jurisdiction with Court of Claims to try claims not exceeding $10,000, has reference to the original claim filed with the contracting agency. Thompson Foundry & Machine Co. v. U.S., M.D.Ga.1946, 67 F.Supp. 121. Federal Courts ☞ 976

In a suit by a sub-subcontractor under a prime contract between the United States and a private corporation, based on the denial of its termination claim under this chapter, unless suit is filed within 90 days after denial of the termination claim by the contracting agency as required by this section, Court of Claims [now United States Court of Federal Claims] lacks jurisdiction to entertain the claim. Somerset Mach. & Tool Co. v. U.S., Ct.Cl.1959, 144 Ct.Cl. 481, certiorari denied 80 S.Ct. 73, 361 U.S. 825, 4 L.Ed.2d 69. United States ☞ 74(16)

State circuit and chancery courts were courts of "competent jurisdiction" to adjudicate suit against federal public housing authority under this section, authorizing suit in any court of competent jurisdiction. Walsh Const. Co. v. Davis, Miss.1948, 37 So.2d 757, 204 Miss. 509. United States ☞ 74(16)

11. Pleadings

In action for fair compensation due on a war contract, complaint which alleged that plaintiff failed to produce manganese ore because ore did not meet specifications which both parties assumed it would, did not show plaintiff was in default or that he was barred from relief under this chapter, and was sufficient. Collord v. R.F.C., W.D.Pa.1950, 94 F.Supp. 828. United States ☞ 74(16)

12. Counterclaims

Where contractor presented claim to Department of the Army, which was the contracting agency, and claim was denied, and contractor appealed to Appeal Board, Office of Contract Settlement, pursuant to this chapter and Appeal Board awarded contractor $110,000 on its total claim of $285,340.08, and the $110,000 was paid to contractor, and contractor then brought action in the Court of Claims for amount which Appeal Board had not awarded it, the United States had no right to file a counterclaim to recover the $110,000, on ground that allowance of the $110,000 was error. Condenser Service & Engineering Co. v. U.S., Ct.Cl.1955, 128 F.Supp. 148, 130 Ct.Cl. 714. Federal Courts ☞ 1087

Parties suing United States in Court of Claims [now United States Court of Federal Claims] under this chapter for sums due on terminated war contracts were not required to wait until defendant prosecuted to conclusion in district courts its claims under this chapter against contractors for fraud in contract settlements, as Government may assert rights given it by this chapter by counterclaims in Court of Claims actions. Erie Basin Metal Products, Inc. v. U.S., Ct.Cl.1952, 107 F.Supp. 588, 123 Ct.Cl. 433. Federal Courts ☞ 1087

13. Limitations

War contractor's letters to Air Force, which were written before cost of cleanup of factory site was assessed and did not contain demand for written findings, were not claims under Contract Settlement Act (CSA), and thus Air Force's subsequent denial of reimbursement did not commence limitations period for contractor's suit against government. Ford Motor Co. v. U.S., C.A.Fed.2004, 378 F.3d 1314, rehearing and rehearing en banc denied. United States ☞ 74(16)

Any claim that plaintiff has against United States for relief from losses sustained under contract to produce mahogany lumber for United States during Second World War involved no mutual and open accounts and no trust on part of Government, so that claim was barred by statute of limitations where more than 14 years elapsed between time that plaintiff abandoned its contract and filed its petition in Court of Claims [now United States Claims Court]. Kraemer Mills, Inc. v. U.S., Ct.Cl.1963, 319 F.2d 535, 162 Ct.Cl. 367. Federal Courts ☞ 1107

Petition against United States for loss of profits resulting from producing item for war use was barred where petition was filed more than six years after date on which production ceased and more than six years after settlement agreement had been entered into with Reconstruction Finance Corporation. Teutsch v. U.S., Ct.Cl.1961, 288 F.2d 920, 153 Ct.Cl. 86. Limitation Of Actions ☞ 58(1)

Where district court for the Territory of Alaska entered an order dismissing first amended complaint in action against the United States under this chapter to recover $35,000, on ground that court did not have jurisdiction because damages sought exceed $10,000, filing of second amended complaint seeking recovery of only $10,000, without leave of court or consent of adverse party was the institution of a new action, and statute of limitations with respect to the second amended complaint was not tolled by the first amended complaint. Fern v. U.S., C.A.9 (Alaska) 1954, 213 F.2d 674, 15 Alaska 31. Limitation Of Actions ☞ 130(7)

Cause of action against United States for rent due under written contract of rental of drilling equipment used by United States until Dec. 1, 1942, accrued on that date and action thereon commenced in 1949 was barred by Alaskan six-year statute of limitations relative to actions on sealed instruments and by six-year statute of limitations in respect of civil actions against the United States, in absence of allegation of any termination claim under this chapter, permitting suit within 90 days after rejection of such claim. Erceg v. United States, C.A.9 (Alaska) 1950, 179 F.2d 510, 12 Alaska 569. Limitation Of Actions ☞ 22(2); United States ☞ 133

This chapter imposes civil penalties, and an action or counterclaim therefore is barred if not brought within statutory period. Erie Basin Metal Products, Inc. v. U.S., Ct.Cl.1957, 150 F.Supp. 561, 138 Ct.Cl. 67. Limitation Of Actions ☞ 5(3)

Where Maritime Commission [now Department of Transportation] refused to take action on inter-agency appeal by war contractor asserting contract termination claim until civil fraud aspect of case had been cleared by department, and Commission made no findings, the one year limitation period in which contractor could bring suit in Court of Claims [now United States Court of Federal Claims] commenced to run on date when contractor made written demand for final determination by Commission. Arlington Trust Co. v. U.S., Ct.Cl.1953, 109 F.Supp. 722, 124 Ct.Cl. 309. Limitation Of Actions ⊂⊃ 105(2)

14. Laches

Where plaintiff's war contract was canceled by Government agency on Oct. 8, 1943, and only response or steps taken thereafter was plaintiff's letter of Oct. 17, 1943, explaining that he expected to be ready to commence deliveries by the first of the month, and nothing was done thereafter by either plaintiff or Government agency until Dec. 29, 1949, when plaintiff filed claim with agency for reformation of contract and award of fair compensation, and plaintiff failed to comply with regulation issued by defendant for handling termination settlements, plaintiff was guilty of such delay and laches as would bar his suit. Johnson v. R.F.C., E.D.Tenn.1950, 94 F.Supp. 214. United States ⊂⊃ 74(16)

15. Res judicata

Where assignee of claim of war contractor against the Government was adjudicated a bankrupt and the Government filed its claim for alleged overpayments under the contract in the bankruptcy court, district court had jurisdiction to determine the claim and where the referee's order of disallowance of the claim was affirmed by the district court and the court of appeals, the court of appeals decision was res judicata. Hadden v. U.S., Ct.Cl.1952, 105 F.Supp. 1010, 123 Ct.Cl. 246. Judgment ⊂⊃ 744

16. Judgment on pleadings

In action under this chapter against United States and based on alleged wrongs committed by Reconstruction Finance Corporation as agent of United States, whether the Reconstruction Finance Corporation acted in its corporate capacity and not as agent for United States was a mixed question of law and fact, and would not be disposed of on motion for judgment on pleadings. National Cored Forgings Co. v. U.S., Ct.Cl. 1953, 115 F.Supp. 469, 126 Ct.Cl. 250. Federal Civil Procedure ⊂⊃ 1063

17. Jury trial

In action by war contractor against the Reconstruction Finance Corporation for damages sustained as result of corporation's termination of contractor's contract, contractor, which had made timely request for jury trial, should have been granted a jury trial. Monolith Portland Midwest Co. v. R.F.C., C.A.9 (Cal.) 1957, 240 F.2d 444, certiorari denied 77 S.Ct. 1379, 354 U.S. 921, 1 L.Ed.2d 1435. Jury ⊂⊃ 12(1.2)

Actions brought under provision of subsec. (b) of this section, providing methods by which war contractor may obtain review of claims against United States, or corporations owned or controlled thereby, are primarily in nature of appeal to review findings of administrative agency and are not ordinary actions for breach of contracts, since action is expressly limited to action on "claim or part thereof", and nature of action is not one, therefore, which demands granting of jury trial. Monolith Portland Midwest Co. v. R.F.C., S.D.Cal.1952, 102 F.Supp. 951. Jury ⊂⊃ 19(1)

18. Burden of proof

In proceeding by war contractor on appeal from Reconstruction Finance Corporation's findings on contractor's claims upon termination, burden was on contractor to show for what services legal fees claimed had been paid. Monolith Portland Midwest Co. v. R.F.C., S.D.Cal. 1955, 128 F.Supp. 824. United States ⊂⊃ 74(16)

19. Admissibility of evidence

In contractor's action against Government to recover balance due after termination of war contract, sworn testimony given by Government officer before Board of Contract Appeals to effect that he requested that contracting officer sign letter of termination, which was introduced through another witness who was present at that hearing, and which related to statements of fact material and relevant to issues before the court, was properly received as evidence of admissions by the Government. Climatic Rainwear Co. v. U.S., Ct.Cl.1950, 88 F.Supp. 415, 115 Ct.Cl. 520. Evidence ⊂⊃ 203

In action by subcontractor against prime contractor to recover damages upon cancellation of subcontract for war materials, settlement proposals which were objected to as self-serving declarations but which were received subject to proper connection being made were properly received in view of subsequent proof. Rumsey Mfg. Corp. v. U.S. Hoffman Machinery Corp., W.D.N.Y.1949, 88 F.Supp. 394, modified on other grounds 187 F.2d 927. Trial ⊂⊃ 51

20. Weight and sufficiency of evidence

Evidence established that United States was not directly responsible for restraint on miner's production of ceramic talc or for loss of market for that item although Government urged him to concentrate his efforts on production of lava talc during war. Teutsch v. U.S., Ct.Cl.1961, 288 F.2d 920, 153 Ct.Cl. 86. United States ⊂⊃ 74(16)

In action for compensation for Government's termination of war contract for plaintiff's delivery of manganese to Metals Reserve Company, affidavit of plaintiff's representative in negotiations for contract that company's negotiator said that contract was being cancelled, as stated in company's letter to plaintiff, merely as routine thing to clear books for following year, was insufficient to show company's waiver of delivery expiration date in contract, as required by court's order permitting amendment of complaint to allege such fact, in absence of substantial competent evidence that company held out its negotiator as authorized to bind it on contract. Glade Mountain Corp. v. R.F.C., D.C.N.J.1952, 104 F.Supp. 695, affirmed 200 F.2d 815. United States ⊂⊃ 74(16)

Where plaintiff, a subcontractor, brings suit against the United States under this section for materials and supplies furnished to the prime contractor, Frontier Machine and Tool Corporation, which in April 1942 had agreed to furnish and deliver to defendant certain materials including a large quantity of shot, the evidence was insufficient to establish that any authorized representative of the defendant had guaranteed to the plaintiff, as claimed, that Frontier's indebtedness to plaintiff would be assumed and paid by the defendant in the event of default by Frontier, and plaintiff was not entitled to

recover. General Elevator Co. v. U.S., Ct.Cl.1952, 122 Ct.Cl. 467. United States ⊂⊃ 74.2

21. Weight and conclusiveness of administrative findings

Under contract with Government providing that all disputes concerning questions of fact should be decided by contracting officer and allowing appeal within 30 days from mailing of notice of decision, decision of War Department Board of Contract Appeals as to facts is binding on Court of Claims [now United States Court of Federal Claims] but Board's decision as to whether a timely appeal has been perfected is question of law and can be determined by the court. Poloron Products, Inc. v. U.S., Ct.Cl. 1953, 116 F.Supp. 588, 126 Ct.Cl. 816. United States ⊂⊃ 73(14)

22. Interest

Despite provision of this section, that when it appears that war contractor failed to negotiate in good faith for settlement of claim, appeal board or court may deny interest, court in its discretion refused to deny interest even though it appeared that contractor had not negotiated in good faith. Monolith Portland Midwest Co. v. R.F.C., S.D.Cal.1955, 128 F.Supp. 824. United States ⊂⊃ 110

23. Specific performance

Contractor, whose war contracts with the Government were terminated by the Government, was not entitled to remedy of specific performance or remedy of injunction. Monolith Portland Midwest Co. v. R.F.C., S.D.Cal.1951, 95 F.Supp. 570. Injunction ⊂⊃ 106; Specific Performance ⊂⊃ 19

24. Appellate review

On appeal by general creditors of debtor in reorganization proceeding from an order authorizing trustee to accept compromise settlement of a terminated contract offered by the United States under this chapter, court of appeals would not be warranted in reversing order unless it clearly appeared that district court acted arbitrarily and in abuse of a judicial discretion, or that compromise itself was not for best interests of the estate. Daniel Hamm Drayage Co. v. Willson, C.A.8 (Mo.) 1949, 178 F.2d 633. Bankruptcy ⊂⊃ 3836

§ 114. Court of Federal Claims

(a) Appointment of auditors

For the purpose of expediting the adjudication of termination claims, the United States Court of Federal Claims is authorized to appoint not more than ten auditors.

(b) Procedure

The United States Court of Federal Claims, on motion of either of the parties, or on its own motion, may summon any and all persons with legal capacity to be sued to appear as a party or parties in any suit or proceeding of any nature whatsoever pending in said court to assert and defend their interests, if any, in such suits or proceedings, within such period of time prior to judgment as the United States Court of Federal Claims shall prescribe. If the name and address of any such person is known or can be ascertained by reasonable diligence, and if he resides within the jurisdiction of the United States, he shall be summoned to appear by personal service; but if any such person resides outside of the jurisdiction of the United States, or is unknown, or if for any other good and sufficient reason appearing to the court personal service cannot be had, he may be summoned by publication, under such rules as the court may adopt, together with a copy of the summons mailed by registered mail to such person's last known address. The United States Court of Federal Claims may, upon motion of the Attorney General, in any suit or proceeding where there may be any number of persons having possible interests therein, notify such persons to appear to assert and defend such interests. Upon failure so to appear, any and all claims or interests in claims of any such person against the United States, in respect of the subject matter of such suit or proceeding, shall forever be barred and the court shall have jurisdiction to enter judgment pro confesso upon any claim or contingent claim asserted on behalf of the United States against any person who, having been duly served with summons, fails to respond thereto, to the same extent and with like effect as if such person had appeared and had admitted the truth of all allegations made on behalf of the United States. Upon appearance by any person pursuant to any such summons or notice, the case as to such person shall, for all purposes, be treated as if an independent proceeding has been instituted by such person pursuant to sections 1491, 1496, 1501, 1503, and 2501 of Title 28, and as if such independent proceeding had then been consolidated, for purposes of trial and determination, with the case in respect of which the summons or notice was issued, except that the United States shall not be heard upon any counterclaims, claims for damages or other

346

demands whatsoever against such person, other than claims and contingent claims for the recovery of money hereafter paid by the United States in respect of the transaction or matter which constitutes the subject matter of such case, unless and until such person shall assert therein a claim, or an interest in a claim, against the United States, and the United States Court of Federal Claims shall have jurisdiction to adjudicate, as between any and all adverse claimants, their respective several interests in any matter in suit and to award several judgments in accordance therewith.

(c) Jurisdiction

The jurisdiction of the United States Court of Federal Claims shall not be affected by this chapter except to the extent necessary to give effect to this chapter, and no person shall recover judgment on any claim, or on any interest in any claim, in said court which such person would not have had a right to assert in said court if this section had not been enacted.

(July 1, 1944, c. 358, § 14, 58 Stat. 663; July 28, 1953, c. 253, § 5, 67 Stat. 226; Apr. 2, 1982, Pub.L. 97–164, Title I, § 160(a)(14), 96 Stat. 48; Oct. 29, 1992, Pub.L. 102–572, Title IX, § 902(b)(1), 106 Stat. 4516.)

HISTORICAL AND STATUTORY NOTES

Revision Notes and Legislative Reports

1953 Acts. House Report No. 695, see 1953 U.S.Code Cong. and Adm.News, p. 2006.

1982 Acts. Senate Report No. 97–275, see 1982 U.S.Code Cong. and Adm.News, p. 11.

1992 Acts. House Report No. 102–1006, see 1992 U.S. Code Cong. and Adm. News, p. 3921.

Codifications

In subsec. (b) of this section, "sections 1491, 1496, 1501, 1503, and 2501 of Title 28" were substituted for "section 250 of Title 28" on authority of June 25, 1948, c. 646, 62 Stat. 869, the first section of which enacted Title 28, Judiciary and Judicial Procedure.

Amendments

1982 Amendments. Pub. L. 97–164 substituted "United States Claims Court" for "Court of Claims" wherever appearing.

1953 Amendments. Subsec. (a). Act July 28, 1953, struck out provisions relating to the appointment of a maximum of twenty commissioners for the purpose of expediting the adjudication of termination claims.

Effective and Applicability Provisions

1992 Acts. Amendment by section 902(b)(1) of Pub.L. 102–572 effective Oct. 29, 1992, see section 911 of Pub.L. 102–572, set out as a note under section 171 of Title 28, Judiciary and Judicial Procedure.

1982 Acts. Amendment by Pub. L. 97–164 effective Oct. 1, 1982, see section 402 of Pub. L. 97–164, set out as a note under section 171 of Title 28, Judiciary and Judicial Procedure.

Change of Name

References to United States Claims Court deemed to refer to United States Court of Federal Claims and references to Claims Court deemed to refer to Court of Federal Claims, see section 902(b) of Pub.L. 102–572, set out as a note under section 171 of Title 28, Judiciary and Judicial Procedure.

Commissioners; Termination of Appointing Authority

Section 4(b) of Act July 28, 1953, provided that the authority contained in subsec. (a) of this section respecting the appointment of commissioners "is hereby terminated".

Section Unaffected by Revised Title 28
Act June 25, 1948, c. 646, § 2(d), 62
Stat. 985, provided that nothing in Title

28, Judiciary and Judicial Procedure,
should be construed as repealing any of
the provisions of this section.

LIBRARY REFERENCES

American Digest System
Federal Courts ⊕1076, 1101, 1110.
Key Number System Topic No. 170B.

Corpus Juris Secundum
CJS Federal Courts § 827, Parties.
CJS Federal Courts § 828, Process and Appearance.

Research References

ALR Library
106 ALR 1241, Right to Set-Off, Counterclaim, or Recoupment Against the United
States or a Sovereign Foreign State.
65 ALR 1134, Rendition of Judgment Against One Not a Formal Party, Who Has
Assumed the Defense.

Treatises and Practice Aids
Patent Law Fundamentals § 18:18, Government Access to Privately Owned Inven-
tions--Adjudication of Claims Against the United States for Intellectual
Property Infringement.
West's Federal Administrative Practice § 811, Parties Right to Appear; Representation by Attorney.
West's Federal Administrative Practice § 816, Set-Offs and Counterclaims; Forfeiture of Claims.
West's Federal Administrative Practice § 837, Subject Matter Jurisdiction--Termi-
nation of War Contracts.
14 Wright & Miller: Federal Prac. & Proc. § 3657, Statutory Exceptions to
Sovereign Immunity--Actions Under the Tucker Act.
17 Wright & Miller: Federal Prac. & Proc. § 4101, The Claims Court.

WESTLAW ELECTRONIC RESEARCH

See Westlaw guide following the Explanation pages of this volume.

Notes of Decisions

1. Constitutionality

Statute giving claims court jurisdiction to adjudicate Government's claims against third parties is not unconstitutional on ground it allows claims court, an Article I court, to exercise the judicial power of the United States vested in Article III courts. U.S. v. Rush, C.A.Fed. 1986, 804 F.2d 645. Federal Courts ⊕ 1087

2. Purpose

This section permitting Court of Claims to summon any and all interested persons to appear in any proceeding before it had as its principal purpose not to provide for adjudication of all possible rights and obligations which stem, however remotely, from transaction involved in principal suit, but to permit parties to bring in others who might later show that they had interest in claim and whose rights, if not foreclosed could be used as a defense by United States, and to permit United States to bring in parties who are all under duty to save it harmless and to recover money from parties to which it had paid money which it might be adjudged to have to pay plaintiff. Richfield Oil Corp. v. U.S., Ct.Cl.1957, 151 F.Supp. 333, 138 Ct.Cl. 520. Federal Courts ⟜ 1110

3. Claims within section—Generally

This section authorizes Court of Claims, on motion of government, to summon or notify a third-party indemnitor to appear and assert its interest in patent infringement suit against government, and jurisdiction of Court of Claims over third party is not restricted by Act to claims arising from terminated war contracts. Bowser, Inc. v. U.S., Ct.Cl.1970, 420 F.2d 1057, 190 Ct.Cl. 441, 164 U.S.P.Q. 460, on reconsideration 427 F.2d 740, 192 Ct.Cl. 377, 166 U.S.P.Q. 46. Federal Courts ⟜ 1110

The third party practice authorized in Court of Claims under this section is limited to situations where any interest which would-be third parties may have against the Government or the Government against them is derived through contract or claim upon which plaintiff's suit is instituted. Oliver-Finnie Co. v. U.S., Ct.Cl.1956, 137 F.Supp. 719, 133 Ct.Cl. 555. Federal Courts ⟜ 1110

4. —— Contingent claims, claims within section

Court of Federal Claims had jurisdiction over Government's third-party contingent claims against public utility power purchasers in action seeking refund of portion of amounts two utilities paid Western Area Power Authority under long-term contract for purchase of electricity generated at Hoover Dam; although each of parties had a separate contract with the government, contingent claims had same subject matter, relating to proper distribution of the over-collection of excess revenues. Southern California Edison Co. v. U.S., C.A.Fed.2000, 226 F.3d 1349. Federal Courts ⟜ 1087

Where oyster grower brought action against United States to recover for damage allegedly arising from dredging oper-

ations in making river and harbor improvements, and parish council, which had given an act of assurance to save United States free from damages, had not asserted any claim against United States, and United States did not seek to recover from parish council money which United States once had but had paid out to parish council in respect to subject matter of suit, contingent claim of United States against parish council was required to be dismissed by Court of Claims. Petrovich v. U.S., Ct.Cl.1970, 421 F.2d 1364, 190 Ct.Cl. 760. Federal Courts ⟜ 1087

Portion of this section relating to contingent claims for recovery of money paid by government to defendant indemnitor is intended to apply to third-party indemnitor when government is sued for money which it had in its hands at one time but which it has disbursed to third-party indemnitor under mistake of fact or law. Bowser, Inc. v. U.S., Ct.Cl.1970, 420 F.2d 1057, 190 Ct.Cl. 441, 164 U.S.P.Q. 460, on reconsideration 427 F.2d 740, 192 Ct. Cl. 377, 166 U.S.P.Q. 46. United States ⟜ 74(16)

That portion of this section relating to contingent claims of the government is intended to apply to a third party when government is sued for money which it had in its hands at one time but which it has disbursed to third party under mistake of law or fact. Christy Corp. v. U.S., Ct.Cl.1967, 387 F.2d 395, 181 Ct.Cl. 768. United States ⟜ 74(16)

Federal government's third-party contingent claims against other public utility power purchasers, on basis that any monetary liability against government in electric utility's favor was incorrectly paid to purchasers, were contingent claims for money paid in respect of transaction or matter which constituted subject matter of utility's case for purposes of jurisdictional statute so as to render Court of Federal Claims with jurisdiction over contingent claims, in utility's action against government alleging insufficient rate refund upon completion of long-term contract for purchase of electricity generated at Hoover Dam; if utility prevailed in its claim, then government had to prevail in its demands against purchasers, for matter involved one pool of money to be distributed among all eligible Dam electricity sales participants according to single set of rules provided by regulations incorporated in all of parties' contracts. Southern California Edison Co. v. U.S., Fed.Cl.1997, 38 Fed.Cl. 54, affirmed 226 F.3d 1349. Federal Courts ⚬ 1087

5. —— Counterclaims, claims within section

Where foreign manufacturer of aircraft engines filed claim against United States for patent infringement on basis that, without license or consent of plaintiff, government procured engines from domestic aircraft corporations containing blades fabricated from alloys alleged to be protected by plaintiff's patent and one of manufacturers was permitted to intervene as third-party defendant on ground that it had pecuniary interest, Court of Claims did not have jurisdiction of intervenor's counterclaim against plaintiff to recover for breach of contract, even though counterclaim might have had questions of fact in common with defense to main action. Rolls-Royce Ltd., Derby, England v. U.S., Ct.Cl.1966, 364 F.2d 415, 176 Ct.Cl. 694, 150 U.S.P.Q. 460. Federal Courts ⚬ 1110

Once the jurisdiction of Court of Claims [now United States Court of Federal Claims] has been invoked by contractor as original party plaintiff the United States has right to assert by way of counterclaim against plaintiff contractor such claims as may have arisen out of terminated contracts. Hadden v. U.S., Ct.Cl. 1952, 105 F.Supp. 1010, 123 Ct.Cl. 246. Federal Courts ⚬ 1087

6. Election of remedies

A plaintiff who institutes an action in Court of Claims under this chapter is not precluded thereby from also invoking, in the alternative, general jurisdiction of Court of Claims, provided the limitations of this chapter as to time within which suit must be brought are complied with. National Cored Forgings Co. v. U.S., Ct. Cl.1953, 115 F.Supp. 469, 126 Ct.Cl. 250. Federal Courts ⚬ 1139

Where contractor had elected to pursue remedies accorded him by this chapter, he was bound by limitations therein, and having been unsuccessful in those proceedings because of failure to timely invoke remedies given by this chapter, he was thereby foreclosed from later claiming right of action under general jurisdiction of Court of Claims. Luff v. U.S., Ct.Cl.1951, 100 F.Supp. 925, 120 Ct.Cl. 682. Limitation Of Actions ⚬ 17

7. Summons

In oil company's Court of Claims suit to recover compensation allegedly due because of removal of a pipeline in flood control project, wherein the Government interposed contingent claim against state Flood Control District involved on basis of alleged liability to save United States harmless from costs, the provision of this section authorizing Court of Claims to summon all interested persons to appear in any proceeding could not be invoked by District to bring in the State Controller and Director of Water Resources as allegedly contingently liable to the District. Richfield Oil Corp. v. U.S., Ct.Cl. 1957, 151 F.Supp. 333, 138 Ct.Cl. 520. Federal Courts ⚬ 1110

This section, providing that Court of Claims may summon persons to appear as parties in any suit or proceeding of any nature whatsoever pending in said court to assert and defend their interest, if any, did not apply merely to cases arising under this chapter, but also applied to situations in which a third party's right to retain money paid by the Government to it was in dispute. Maryland Cas. Co. v. U.S., Ct.Cl.1956, 141 F.Supp. 900, 135 Ct.Cl. 428. Federal Courts ⚬ 1110

In action on claim against United States by assignee of contractor, Government's motion for summons against the contractor to whom partial payment had been made to appear as a party would not be denied on ground that testimony of contractor had already been taken, and claim had been pending for over two years. Central Nat. Bank of Richmond, Va. v. U.S., Ct.Cl.1949, 84 F.Supp. 654, 114 Ct.Cl. 390. Federal Courts ⚬ 1110

Under statute authorizing Court of Federal Claims to summon third party to appear in suit to defend its interests, Court would issue summons to the Prairie Island, and Shakopee Indian Communities of Minnesota to appear and defend their interests in trust management case brought against the United States by lineal descendants of Mdewakanton Sioux who were loyal to the United States during the Sioux Outbreak in Minnesota during 1862, as interests involved control over, and a custodial interest in, the trust property that was subject of plaintiffs' breach of trust claim. Wolfchild v. U.S., Fed.Cl.2006, 72 Fed.Cl. 511. Federal Courts ⚬ 1110

8. Notice

Under the provisions of subsec. (b) of this section, a notice gives the one notified an opportunity to enter his appearance and participate in the pending proceedings, if he thinks he has an interest and desires to protect it; he need not appear and participate but if he does not, said subsection provides that his interest in the subject matter of the suit "shall be forever barred." Hardin County Sav. Bank v. U.S., Ct.Cl.1945, 102 Ct.Cl. 815. Courts ☞ 460; Courts ☞ 470

9. Failure to appear or respond

If third-party indemnitor fails to appear in response to summons or notice when patent infringement suit is brought against government for using apparatus of third-party defendant, it may not, in later litigation for enforcement of indemnity against it, assert that Court of Claims incorrectly decided that plaintiff's patent is valid and was infringed by apparatus of third party. Bowser, Inc. v. U.S., Ct.Cl. 1970, 420 F.2d 1057, 190 Ct.Cl. 441, 164 U.S.P.Q. 460, on reconsideration 427 F.2d 740, 192 Ct.Cl. 377, 166 U.S.P.Q. 46. Indemnity ☞ 85

In action by assignee of claim under public contract to recover against Government, where assignor of claim had been summoned and had failed to appear, Court of Claims had jurisdiction to enter judgment pro confesso against such assignor after recovery in favor of assignee against Government had been allowed. Central Nat. Bank of Richmond, Va. v. U.S., Ct.Cl.1950, 91 F.Supp. 738, 117 Ct. Cl. 389. United States ☞ 75(1)

Where trustee in bankruptcy of defaulting contractor was given due notice under subsec. (b) of this section and an opportunity to be heard in proceedings in Court of Claims concerning disposition of money due on construction contract from the United States Government after completion of the contract by surety for performance of the contract, but trustee in bankruptcy did not file a petition or a claim, any interest which estate of contractor in bankruptcy might have to the money was forever barred under this section. Hardin County Sav. Bank v. U.S., Ct.Cl.1946, 65 F.Supp. 1017, 106 Ct.Cl. 577. United States ☞ 74(16); Bankruptcy ☞ 2553

10. Standing

Where in an action by the surety on the performance and payment bonds of a contractor which had a contract to construct a building for the Government, to recover moneys earned by the contractor and paid by the Government to the contractor's assignee, a bank, the assignee bank filed a motion to dismiss the Government's cross-claim against it on the grounds that the court lacks jurisdiction over the plaintiff's suit and that, in any event, the court has no jurisdiction over defendant's cross-claim against the assignee bank, the motion must be denied since the third-party defendant has no standing to question the court's jurisdiction of plaintiff's suit and the court does have jurisdiction of the defendant's cross-claim against the assignee bank. Seaboard Sur. Co. v. U.S., Ct.Cl.1959, 144 Ct.Cl. 686.

11. Jurisdiction

Claims court had jurisdiction to adjudicate Government's cross claim against third-party defendant for recovery of money it paid out to third-party defendant in respect of transaction or matter which constituted subject matter of principal action. U.S. v. Rush, C.A.Fed.1986, 804 F.2d 645. Federal Courts ☞ 1087

Where surety under sections 270a–270d of Title 40 sued United States in Court of Claims, alleging that surety had completed contract and had paid creditors of defaulting joint venture $91,319.16, and that it had thereby acquired equitable rights to $52,000.74 held by United States as unpaid balance due on contract, and that bank claimed that same fund, and that notice had been served on bank pursuant to subsection (b) of this section, jurisdiction of Court of Claims extended to claim asserted by surety against bank, and Court of Claims had jurisdiction to determine whether surety or bank was entitled to recover fund. Great Am. Ins. Co. v. U.S., Ct.Cl. 1968, 397 F.2d 289, 184 Ct.Cl. 520. Federal Courts ☞ 1080

Court of Claims lacked jurisdiction of United States' contingent counterclaim against third-party defendant, who had prepared plans and specifications for vessel to be built for United States, for amount of any judgment awarded shipbuilder against United States for breach of implied warranty that plans and specifications would be correct and complete.

Christy Corp. v. U.S., Ct.Cl.1967, 387 F.2d 395, 181 Ct.Cl. 768. Federal Courts ⟜ 1087

This chapter enlarged jurisdiction of Court of Claims to cover certain aspects of third-party practice, but it does not embrace actions by plaintiff against third parties or by third parties against plaintiff to recover on causes of action not cognizable by Court of Claims. Rolls-Royce Ltd., Derby, England v. U.S., Ct.Cl.1966, 364 F.2d 415, 176 Ct.Cl. 694, 150 U.S.P.Q. 460. Federal Courts ⟜ 1110

Court of Claims has no jurisdiction of a suit on a contract implied in law. Gazda v. U.S., Ct.Cl.1952, 108 F.Supp. 516, 123 Ct.Cl. 760, 95 U.S.P.Q. 329. Federal Courts ⟜ 1077

Court of Federal Claims lacked jurisdiction to grant third party's motion to intervene as defendant, since third party did not have any claim against government, despite court rule authorizing third-party intervention and authority to award injunctive relief on a government contractor's claim against government; third party's own bid protest claim had been settled by agreement. Orion Scientific Systems v. U.S., Fed.Cl.1993, 28 Fed. Cl. 669. Federal Courts ⟜ 1110

12. Complaint

In order for subcontractors to maintain actions against United States under this chapter to recover money allegedly owing to subcontractors, subcontractors were required to allege and prove that United States gave written notice to both prime contractor and subcontractors that United States was assuming responsibility for settling subcontractors' claims upon conditions set out in notice, and that subcontractors consented thereto, and allegation that United States agreed upon amounts by which subcontractors' claims were to be settled, was insufficient. Erie Basin Metal Products v. U.S., Ct.Cl.1953, 109 F.Supp. 402, 124 Ct.Cl. 95, certiorari denied 74 S.Ct. 29, 346 U.S. 831, 98 L.Ed. 355. United States ⟜ 74.2

13. Parties

When government is sued for patent infringement for using apparatus of third-party indemnitor, the third-party indemnitor, summoned or noticed, may be made a party to the suit and has a right to participate in order to protect its interest, and it may assist the government in the defense of the case, or it may offer additional evidence on its own behalf and advance such legal contentions as it deems appropriate in protection of its interest. Bowser, Inc. v. U.S., Ct.Cl. 1970, 420 F.2d 1057, 190 Ct.Cl. 441, 164 U.S.P.Q. 460, on reconsideration 427 F.2d 740, 192 Ct.Cl. 377, 166 U.S.P.Q. 46. United States ⟜ 135

14. Jury trial

Where surety under sections 270a–270d of Title 40 sued United States in Court of Claims, alleging that it had completed contract and had paid creditors of defaulting joint venture $91,319.16, and that it had thereby acquired equitable rights to $52,000.74 held by United States as unpaid balance due on contract, and that bank claimed that same fund, and that notice had been served on bank pursuant to subsection (b) of this section, bank could not complain that it was denied its right to jury trial under Seventh Amendment. Great Am. Ins. Co. v. U.S., Ct.Cl.1968, 397 F.2d 289, 184 Ct.Cl. 520. Jury ⟜ 31.2(1)

The Court of Claims has jurisdiction of cross-claims by defendant against third parties under this section, although the right to a jury trial guaranteed by Seventh Amendment is not available to parties before Court of Claims. Seaboard Sur. Co. v. U.S., Ct.Cl.1959, 144 Ct.Cl. 686.

15. Res judicata

Where oyster grower brought action in Court of Claims against United States to recover for damage allegedly arising from dredging operations, and both parish council, against which United States asserted contingent claim, and State not only assisted United States in its defense, but interrogated witnesses on their own behalf, they had their day in court, though Court of Claims did not have jurisdiction over contingent claim of United States against parish council, and could not in future relitigate any of issues of fact or law decided by Court of Claims. Petrovich v. U.S., Ct.Cl.1970, 421 F.2d 1364, 190 Ct.Cl. 760. Judgment ⟜ 675(1)

16. Remedies or relief

A noticed third party may present any defense to claims in the Court of Claims it wishes; however, it is not entitled to seek any affirmative judgment, either monetary or declaratory, against plaintiff, including award of costs, expenses and at-

torney's fees. Lemelson v. U.S., Cl.Ct.
1985, 8 Cl.Ct. 789, 227 U.S.P.Q. 562.
Federal Courts ☞ 1110

§ 115. Personal financial liability of contracting officers

(a) Whenever any payment is made from Government funds to any war contractor or other person as an advance, partial or final payment on any termination claim, or pursuant to any loan, guaranty, or agreement for the purchase of any loan, or any commitment in connection therewith, entered into by the Government, no officer or other Government agent authorizing or approving such payment or settlement, or certifying the voucher for such payment, or making the payment in accordance with a duly certified voucher, shall be personally liable for such payment, in the absence of fraud on his part. In settling the accounts of any disbursing officer the Government Accountability Office shall allow any such disbursements made by him notwithstanding any other provisions of law.

(b) For the purpose of making termination settlements or interim financing any Government agency is authorized to rely upon such certificates of war contractors as it deems proper and to permit war contractors and other persons to rely upon such certificates without financial liability in the absence of fraud on their part.

(July 1, 1944, c. 358, § 15, 58 Stat. 664; July 7, 2004, Pub.L. 108–271, § 8(b), 118 Stat. 814.)

HISTORICAL AND STATUTORY NOTES

Change of Name
"Government Accountability Office" substituted for "General Accounting Office" in subsec. (a) on authority of Pub.L. 108–271, § 8(b), cited in the credit to this section and set out as a note under 31 U.S.C.A. § 702, which provided that any reference to the General Accounting Office in any law, rule, regulation, certificate, directive, instruction, or other official paper in force on July 17, 2004, to refer and apply to the Government Accountability Office.

LIBRARY REFERENCES

American Digest System
United States ☞127(1).
Key Number System Topic No. 393.

WESTLAW ELECTRONIC RESEARCH

See Westlaw guide following the Explanation pages of this volume.

§ 116. Repealed. Pub.L. 104–316, Title I, § 121(a), Oct. 19, 1996, 110 Stat. 3836

HISTORICAL AND STATUTORY NOTES

Section, Act July 1, 1944, c. 358, § 16, 58 Stat. 664; Ex. Ord. No. 9809, § 8, eff. Dec. 12, 1946, 11 F.R. 14281; 1947 Reorg. Plan No. 1, § 201, eff. July 1, 1947, 12 F.R. 4534, 61 Stat. 951; June 30, 1949, c. 288, Title I, § 102(b), 63 Stat. 380, related to the functions and jurisdiction of General Accounting Office: in reviewing final settlements made by a contracting agency, in certifying settlements suspected of being fraudulent to the De-

partment of Justice, the Administrator of General Services, and the contracting agency, and in reporting on the efficacy of settlement methods and procedures to Congress.

Effective Date of Repeal

Repeal of section effective Oct. 19, 1996, see section 101(e) of Pub.L. 104–316, set out as a note under section 130c of Title 2, The Congress.

§ 117. Defective, informal, and quasi contracts

(a) Lack of formalized contract

Where any person has arranged to furnish or furnished to a contracting agency or to a war contractor any materials, services, or facilities related to the prosecution of the war, without a formal contract, relying in good faith upon the apparent authority of an officer or agent of a contracting agency, written or oral instructions, or any other request to proceed from a contracting agency, the contracting agency shall pay such person fair compensation therefor.

(b) Technical defects or omissions

Whenever any formal or technical defect or omission in any prime contract, or in any grant of authority to an officer or agent of a contracting agency who ordered any materials, services, and facilities might invalidate the contract or commitment, the contracting agency (1) shall not take advantage of such defect or omission; (2) shall amend, confirm, or ratify such contract or commitment without consideration in order to cure such defect or omission; and (3) shall make a fair settlement of any obligation thereby created or incurred by such agency, whether expressed or implied, in fact or in law, or in the nature of an implied or quasi contract.

(c) Failure to settle

Where a contracting agency fails to settle by agreement any claim asserted under this section, the dispute shall be subject to the provisions of section 113 of this title.

(d) Formalization of obligations; termination date for filing claim

The Administrator of General Services shall require each contracting agency to formalize all such obligations and commitments within such period as the Administrator of General Services deems appropriate. No person shall be entitled to recover compensation, to receive a settlement of any alleged obligation, or to obtain the benefit of any amendment, confirmation, ratification, or formalization of any alleged contract or commitment under the provisions of subsection (a), (b), (c), or (d) of this section, unless such person shall, on or before one hundred and eighty days after June 28, 1954, have filed a claim therefor with the contracting agency.

(July 1, 1944, c. 358, § 17, 58 Stat. 665; Ex. Ord. No. 9809, § 8, eff. Dec. 12, 1946, 11 F.R. 14281; 1947 Reorg. Plan No. 1, § 201, eff. July 1, 1947, 12 F.R. 4534, 61 Stat. 951; June 30, 1949, c. 288, Title I, § 102(b), 63 Stat. 380; June 28, 1954, c. 403, § 1, 68 Stat. 300.)

HISTORICAL AND STATUTORY NOTES

Revision Notes and Legislative Reports
1954 Acts. Senate Report No. 1445, see 1954 U.S.Code Cong. and Adm.News, p. 2425.

Amendments
1954 Amendments. Subsec. (d). Act June 28, 1954, added the sentence providing a termination date for filing claims.

Transfer of Functions
Functions of Secretary of the Treasury were transferred to Administrator of General Services by Act June 30, 1949, c. 288, § 102(b), 63 Stat. 380, which was classified to former 40 U.S.C.A. § 752(b), prior to repeal by Pub.L. 107–217, § 6(b), Aug. 21, 2002, 116 Stat. 1304.

"Secretary of the Treasury" was substituted for "Director" by section 8 of Ex. Ord. No. 9809 and section 201 of Reorg. Plan No. 1 of 1947. Reorg. Plan No. 1 of 1947 is set out in the Appendix to Title 5, Government Organization and Employees.

Effective Date of Transfer of Functions
Act June 30, 1949, § 605, which set July 1, 1949, as the effective date for the transfer of functions by that Act, was repealed by Pub.L. 107–217, § 6(b), Aug. 21, 2002, 116 Stat. 1313.

Nonaccrual of Liability
Section 2 of Act June 28, 1954, provided that no liability shall accrue by reason of the enactment of section 1 of such Act (amending subsec. (d) of this section) which would not otherwise have accrued.

LIBRARY REFERENCES

American Digest System
United States ⬡74(16).
Key Number System Topic No. 393.

Research References

ALR Library
106 ALR 1241, Right to Set-Off, Counterclaim, or Recoupment Against the United States or a Sovereign Foreign State.
99 ALR 173, Aeroplanes and Aeronautics.
70 ALR 1326, Adverse Inference from Failure of Party to Produce Available Witness or Evidence, as Affirmative or Substantive Proof.
64 ALR 611, Contract to Pay for Legal Services as an Assignment Within Statute Relating to Assignment of Claims Against the Government.

WESTLAW ELECTRONIC RESEARCH

See Westlaw guide following the Explanation pages of this volume.

Notes of Decisions

1. Request

Under subsec. (a) of this section, the contractor must prove existence of a request by a contracting agency to furnish materials or services, request must have been relied upon by contractor, reliance must have been in good faith, arrangement must have been in strict compliance with request and circumstances must be such that basic principles of justice require that contracting agency be held liable. Electronic Enterprises v. U.S., Ct.Cl. 1951, 100 F.Supp. 944, 120 Ct.Cl. 578. United States ☞ 74(16)

Following defendant's several requests for "all-out production" because of the extremely critical character of the shells being manufactured, where the contractor increased its work schedule in order to comply with these requests, plaintiff was entitled to recover for the increased costs due to overtime pay. Maryland Sanitary Mfg. Corp. v. U.S., Ct.Cl.1951, 119 Ct.Cl. 100. United States ☞ 70(23)

2. Promises

Where the Government denied that any of its representatives agreed to purchase all or any part of plaintiffs' graphite production; and where the Government insisted that the purchase of the ore-bearing properties and the erection of the mill was done on plaintiffs' own initiative, although with the Government's encouragement in order to meet war time needs for graphite, but without any promise on its part to purchase plaintiffs' output or any of it; the evidence produced by plaintiffs failed to establish, as required by this section, that an agent of the Government expressly or impliedly promised to purchase plaintiffs' output or any certain part of it, and failed to establish that any agent of the Government had apparent authority to make such agreement which would entitle the plaintiffs to recover. Alabama Flake Graphite Co. v. U.S., Ct.

Cl.1953, 125 Ct.Cl. 635. United States ☞ 74(16)

Where evidence showed that plaintiff sought a contract with the Government at a time when plaintiff did not have the plant and equipment to manufacture the products on which it proposed to bid, and that the Government gave plaintiff a small contract so that it could get into production and show what it could do, there was no informal promise on the part of the Government nor any obligation, express or implied, which entitled plaintiff to recover either under this section. Preload Corporation v. U.S., Ct.Cl. 1950, 115 Ct.Cl. 596. United States ☞ 74(16)

3. Reliance

Where contractor had received payment of full contract price from Government on contract with Navy, and contractor did not allege that extra costs were spent in accomplishing work done outside the contract at request of contracting agency, contractor could not bring claim under this section, permitting contracting agency to pay fair compensation to any person who has furnished material or services without formal contract to contracting agency in good faith. Lawrance Aeronautical Corp. v. U.S., Ct.Cl.1955, 130 F.Supp. 603, 133 Ct.Cl. 1. United States ☞ 74.2

In action by mine operator against Government to recover a fair compensation on its mining facilities which allegedly were furnished to the Government pursuant to a contract, evidence was insufficient to establish that operator furnished its mining facilities to a contracting agency of the Government or to a war contractor pursuant to any contract, or that its mining operations were undertaken because of its reliance in good faith upon the apparent authority of an officer or agent of a contracting agency. Victoria Mines v. U.S., Ct.Cl.1954, 126 F.Supp. 205, 130 Ct.Cl. 277. United States ☞ 74(11)

Where pursuant to written contract plaintiff furnished machine parts to subsidiary of corporation which had contract with Maritime Commission [now Department of Transportation], and on default in credit terms ceased deliveries until responsible officer of Maritime Commission gave plaintiff assurance of payment on behalf of Government on which plaintiff relied in making further deliveries and materials furnished ultimately found their way into engines for liberty ships for use in prosecution of war, plaintiff's claim was within subsec. (a) of this section for parts shipped after guarantee was given. Rice Barton Corp. v. U.S., Ct.Cl.1950, 88 F.Supp. 271, 115 Ct.Cl. 575. United States ☞ 74(16)

Where after Frontier became involved in financial difficulties, the prime contract was terminated in May 1944, for failure to perform and in July 1946 plaintiff filed a claim with the Rochester Ordnance District under this section for $33,057.83, the balance due to plaintiff from Frontier, on the grounds that it would not have accepted the Frontier purchase orders except that it did so at the request of and in reliance upon the representatives of the United States Government, "acting through the officers and agents of its representative, the Rochester Ordnance District" and it was claimed that Gorman gave assurance to the plaintiff that the United States Government, through its agent, the Rochester Ordnance District, was behind the prime contractor and it requested the proposed work to be undertaken by plaintiff and guaranteed that plaintiff's invoices would be paid, claim under this section filed by plaintiff was denied, and on appeal the decision was sustained. General Elevator Co. v. U.S., Ct.Cl.1952, 122 Ct.Cl. 467. United States ☞ 74.2

Where it was not alleged in plaintiff's petition that he relied upon any promise, express or implied, by any agency of the United States or any war contractor, to pay plaintiff on account of the manufacture of the guns, there was no cause of action set forth within the provisions of this section. Oerlikon Mach. Tool Works Buehrle & Co. v. U.S., Ct.Cl.1951, 118 Ct.Cl. 614. United States ☞ 74(16)

According to the allegations of plaintiff's petition the negotiations and transactions with respect to the use of plaintiff's invention, while carried on with the knowledge and consent of the United States Government, were between plaintiff and the British Purchasing Commission, and the United States Government was not a party to any contract, express or implied, with plaintiff. Oerlikon Mach. Tool Works Buehrle & Co. v. U.S.,

Ct.Cl.1951, 118 Ct.Cl. 614. United States ☞ 63; United States ☞ 69(5)

4. Ability to complete contract

Where it was shown by the evidence adduced that no contract, either oral or written, was entered into by the responsible officers of the Government, that the proposed pipe line was never constructed and that plaintiff was not at any time in position to build the pipe line nor to supply the gas, plaintiff was not entitled to recover. General Gas Pipe Line Corp. v. U.S., Ct.Cl.1949, 115 Ct.Cl. 1.

5. Subsequent different formal contract

Termination supplement by which government and contractor terminated contract for operation of ordnance plant, including supplement provision that preserved indemnification clause in plant operation contract, enjoyed benefit of any dispensation of Anti-Deficiency Act (ADA) restrictions on open-ended indemnification clauses conferred by Contract Settlement Act (CSA), which was enacted after parties signed termination supplement, even though indemnification commitment being preserved by termination supplement arose before CSA was enacted, in that, by expressly exempting covenants of indemnity from rights and liabilities being released by termination supplement, government ratified its earlier indemnification promise, as permitted by CSA. E.I. Du Pont de Nemours and Co., Inc. v. U.S., C.A.Fed.2004, 365 F.3d 1367, rehearing and rehearing en banc denied. United States ☞ 62

Where contractor, who had been producing certain tubes for the Army and Navy, received a notice of award to produce 4,400 tubes of the particular type offered with request that manufacture begin at once even though formal contract would be prepared at a later date, and the contractor stopped production immediately when the formal contract contained certain specifications not a part of offer or notice of award, contractor was entitled to recover for tubes produced before knowledge of formal contract at price per tube as specified in notice of award and offer, and contractor was not limited to the actual cost incurred by him. Electronic Enterprises v. U.S., Ct. Cl.1951, 100 F.Supp. 944, 120 Ct.Cl. 578. United States ☞ 74(16)

6. Technical defects or omissions

Provision of this section for certain adjustments whenever any formal or technical defect or omission in any prime contract may invalidate contract or commitment did not authorize recovery by manufacturer from the United States for cost of additional development work on supersensitive electronic device designed for television cameras in connection with guided missile weapons, where alleged defect or omission was one of substance rather than technical or formal. Remington Rand Inc., v. U.S., Ct.Cl.1954, 120 F.Supp. 912, 128 Ct.Cl. 722. United States ☞ 74(16)

7. Exhaustion of administrative remedies

If claim by contractor against Government arising out of contract with Army was based on subsec. (a) of this section, permitting contracting agency to pay fair compensation to any person furnishing material without formal contract to a contracting agency in good faith, where contractor had made claim to Army un-

der this chapter, contractor had not exhausted its administrative remedies and claim could not be considered under this chapter. Lawrance Aeronautical Corp. v. U.S., Ct.Cl.1955, 130 F.Supp. 603, 133 Ct.Cl. 1. United States ☞ 74(16)

8. Inferences

Where officer of Maritime Commission [now Department of Transportation] who urged plaintiff to continue shipment of machine parts for liberty ships to subsidiary of corporation which had contract with Maritime Commission and who told plaintiff that Government would guarantee plaintiff full payment of parts shipped, was not called to testify on behalf of Government in suit to recover value of shipments, failure to call officer as witness, or offer explanation why he was not called, authorized conclusion that had he been called, officer would not have given testimony more favorable to Government. Rice Barton Corp. v. U.S., Ct.Cl.1950, 88 F.Supp. 271, 115 Ct.Cl. 575. Evidence ☞ 77(1)

§ 118. Administration

(a) Records and forms

The Administrator of General Services shall establish policies for such supervision and review within the contracting agencies of termination settlements and interim financing as he deems necessary and appropriate to prevent and detect fraud and to assure uniformity in administration and to provide for expeditious settlements. For this purpose he shall prescribe such records to be prepared by the contracting agencies and by war contractors as he deems necessary in connection with such settlements and interim financing. He shall seek to reduce the amount of record keeping, reporting, and accounting in connection with the settlement of termination claims and interim financing to the minimum compatible with the reasonable protection of the public interest. Each contracting agency shall prescribe forms for use by war contractors in connection with termination settlements and interim financing to the extent it deems necessary and feasible.

(b) Repealed. Oct. 31, 1951, c. 654, § 1(111), 65 Stat. 705

(c) Advance notice on cut-backs

The Administrator of General Services, by regulation, shall provide for making available to any interested Government agency such advance notice and other information on cut-backs in war production resulting from terminations or failures to renew or extend war contracts, as he deems necessary and appropriate.

(d) Investigations

The Administrator of General Services shall make such investigations as he deems necessary or desirable in connection with termination settlements and interim financing. For this purpose he may utilize the facilities of any existing agencies and if he determines that the facilities of existing agencies are inadequate, he may establish a unit in the General Services Administration to supplement and facilitate the work of existing agencies. He shall report to the Department of Justice any information received by him indicating any fraudulent practices, for appropriate action.

(e) Certification of fraudulent settlements to Department of Justice

Whenever any contracting agency or the Administrator of General Services believes that any settlement was induced by fraud, the agency or Administrator of General Services shall report the facts to the Department of Justice. Thereupon, (1) the Department of Justice shall make an investigation to determine whether such settlement was induced by fraud, and (2) until the Department of Justice notifies the contracting agency that in its opinion the facts do not support the belief that the settlement was induced by fraud, the contracting agency, by set-off or otherwise, may withhold, from amounts owing to the war contractor by the United States under such settlement or otherwise, the amount of the settlement, or the portion thereof, which, in its opinion, was affected by the fraud. In any such case the Department of Justice shall take such action as it deems appropriate to recover payments made to such war contractor.

(July 1, 1944, c. 358, § 18, 58 Stat. 666; Ex. Ord. No. 9809, § 8, eff. Dec. 12, 1946, 11 F.R. 14281; 1947 Reorg.Plan No. 1, § 201, eff. July 1, 1947, 12 F.R. 4534, 61 Stat. 951; June 30, 1949, c. 288, Title I, § 102(b), 63 Stat. 380; Oct. 31, 1951, c. 654, § 1(111), 65 Stat. 705; Oct. 19, 1996, Pub.L. 104–316, Title I, § 121(b), 110 Stat. 3836.)

HISTORICAL AND STATUTORY NOTES

Amendments

1996   Amendments. Subsec.   (a). Pub.L. 104–316, § 121(b), struck out "(1)" following "For this purpose he shall prescribe" and struck out "; and (2) the records in connection therewith to be transmitted to the General Accounting Office" following "connection with such settlements and interim financing".

1951 Amendments. Subsec. (b). Act Oct. 31, 1951, repealed provisions which related to preparation of information and reports regarding termination of war con-

tracts, settlements of termination claims, interim financing, etc.

Effective and Applicability Provisions

1996   Acts. Amendment by Pub.L. 104–316 effective Oct. 19, 1996, see section 101(e) of Pub.L. 104–316, set out as a note under section 130c of Title 2, The Congress.

Transfer of Functions

Functions of Secretary of the Treasury were transferred to Administrator of General Services and reference to the Department of Treasury in subsec. (d) was changed to "General Services Administration" by Act June 30, 1949, c. 288, § 102(b), 63 Stat. 380, which was classified to former 40 U.S.C.A. § 752(b), prior to repeal by Pub.L. 107–217, § 6(b), Aug. 21, 2002, 116 Stat. 1304.

"Department of the Treasury" was substituted for "Office of Contract Settlement" in subsec. (d) and references to "Director" were changed to "Secretary of the Treasury" throughout this section by

section 8 of Ex. Ord. No. 9809 and section 201 of Reorg. Plan No. 1 of 1947. Reorg. Plan No. 1 is set out in the Appendix to Title 5, Government Organization and Employees.

Effective Date of Transfer of Functions

Act June 30, 1949, § 605, which set July 1, 1949, as the effective date for the transfer of functions by that Act, was repealed by Pub.L. 107–217, § 6(b), Aug. 21, 2002, 116 Stat. 1313.

LIBRARY REFERENCES

American Digest System
United States ☞74(16).
Key Number System Topic No. 393.

WESTLAW ELECTRONIC RESEARCH

See Westlaw guide following the Explanation pages of this volume.

Notes of Decisions

Certification of fraudulent settlements
1

---

1. Certification of fraudulent settlements

Subsec. (e) of this section, prohibiting contracting agency of United States from paying any amount to contractor suspected of fraud until Justice Department notifies agency that no fraud has been com-

mitted, did not deprive Court of Claims [now United States Court of Federal Claims] of jurisdiction to entertain claims under this chapter against United States for sums due claimants on terminated war contracts until Justice Department gave such notice. Erie Basin Metal Products, Inc. v. U.S., Ct.Cl.1952, 107 F.Supp. 588, 123 Ct.Cl. 433. Federal Courts ☞ 1076

§ 119. Fraudulent claims, vouchers, statements, etc.; jurisdiction

Every person who makes or causes to be made, or presents or causes to be presented to any officer, agent, or employee of any Government agency any claim, bill, receipt, voucher, statement, account, certificate, affidavit, or deposition, knowing the same to be false, fraudulent, or fictitious or knowing the same to contain or to be based on any false, fraudulent, or fictitious statement or entry, or who shall cover up or conceal any material fact, or who shall use or engage in any other fraudulent trick, scheme, or device, for the purpose of securing or obtaining, or aiding to secure or obtain, for any person any benefit, payment, compensation, allowance, loan, advance, or emolument from the United States or any Government agency in connection with the termination, cancelation, settlement, payment, negotiation, renegotiation, performance, procurement, or award of a contract with the United States or with any other person, and every person who enters into an agreement, combination, or conspiracy so to do, (1) shall pay to the United States an amount equal to 25 per centum of any amount thereby sought to be wrongfully secured or obtained but not actually received, and (2) shall forfeit and refund any such benefit, payment, compensation, allowance, loan, advance, and emolument received as a result thereof and (3) shall in addition pay to the United States the sum of $2,000 for each such act, and double the amount of any damage which the United States may have sustained by reason thereof, together with the costs of suit.

The several district courts of the United States, the several district courts of the Territories of the United States, within whose jurisdictional limits the person, or persons, doing or committing such act, or any one of them, resides or shall be found, shall, wheresoever such act may have been done or committed, have full power and jurisdiction to hear, try, and determine such suit, and such person or persons as are not inhabitants of or found within the district in which suit is brought may be brought in by order of the court to be served personally or by publication or in such other reasonable manner as the court may direct.

(July 1, 1944, c. 358, § 19(a), (c)–(e), 58 Stat. 667; June 25, 1948, c. 645, § 21, 62 Stat. 862.)

HISTORICAL AND STATUTORY NOTES

Codifications

As originally enacted, the second undesignated paragraph of this section contained the words, ", the District of Columbia" following "The several district courts of the United States". The words "District of Columbia" have been deleted entirely as superfluous in view of section 132(a) of Title 28, Judiciary and Judicial Procedure, which states that "There shall be in each judicial district a district court which shall be a court of record known as the United States District Court for the district", and section 88 of Title 28 which states that "the District of Columbia constitutes one judicial district".

Section was comprised of subsecs. (a) and (c) to (e) of section 19 of Act July 1, 1944. Subsec. (b) of section 19 was classified to section 590a of Title 18, Criminal Code and Criminal Procedure, prior to

the general revision and enactment of Title 18, Crimes and Criminal Procedure, by Act June 25, 1948, c. 645, 62 Stat. 683. Subsecs. (a), (d), and (e) of section 19 were repealed by Act June 25, 1948, leaving only subsec. (c) of section 19, which comprises this section. Subject matter of former subsecs. (a), (d), and (e) of section 19 is covered by sections 201, 287, 443, and 1001 of Title 18.

Amendments

1948 Amendments. Act June 25, 1948, repealed first, second, fifth, and sixth undesignated paragraphs. See Codifications note set out above.

Effective and Applicability Provisions

1948 Acts. Section 20 of Act June 25, 1948, provided that the amendment of this section should be effective Sept. 1, 1948.

CROSS REFERENCES

False, fictitious or fraudulent claims, see 18 USCA § 287.
False statements or entries generally, see 18 USCA § 1001.
Penal provisions, destruction of war contracts records, see 18 USCA § 443.
Wartime suspension of limitations, see 18 USCA § 3287.

LIBRARY REFERENCES

American Digest System
United States ☞74(16), 122.
Key Number System Topic No. 393.

Corpus Juris Secundum
CJS United States § 214, Informer's Rights.

Research References

ALR Library
42 ALR 2nd 634, Conviction or Acquittal in Criminal Prosecution as Bar to Action for Statutory Damages or Penalty.
127 ALR 909, Commencement of Action as Suspending Running of Limitation Against Claim Which Is Subject of Setoff, Counterclaim, or Recoupment.

WESTLAW ELECTRONIC RESEARCH

See Westlaw guide following the Explanation pages of this volume.

Notes of Decisions

Admissibility of evidence 9
Benefit received 3
Construction with other laws 1
Limitations 6
Persons or entities entitled to maintain action 4
Reliance 2
Res judicata 8
Standard of proof 7
Summary judgment 5
Weight and sufficiency of evidence 10

---

1. Construction with other laws

The "fraud" referred to, in section 106 of this title that settlement shall be final and conclusive except for "fraud," includes "fraudulent * * * statement[s]" and "fraudulent trick[s]," as used in this section, and contemplates that settlement may not release contractor from liability under such later section. U.S. v. Dinerstein, C.A.2 (N.Y.) 1966, 362 F.2d 852. United States ☞ 74(16)

2. Reliance

Purpose of quoted words, in provision of this section for forfeiture of any payment received "as a result thereof", was solely to limit forfeiture to that portion of payment not properly due and not to require reliance or causation, and government need not have relied on contractor's false claim in order to recover payment made as result thereof. U.S. v. Dinerstein, C.A.2 (N.Y.) 1966, 362 F.2d 852. United States ☞ 120.1

3. Benefit received

The provision of this section stating that one who practices fraud shall forfeit any refund or benefit received as a result thereof could not be invoked to allow Government recovery on counterclaim in action involving termination claims arising out of Government contract where no benefit had been received as a result of alleged fraud. Goggin v. U.S., Ct.Cl. 1957, 152 F.Supp. 78, 138 Ct.Cl. 279. United States ☞ 74(16)

4. Persons or entities entitled to maintain action

This section applies to suits by United States and not by informers. U.S. v. Rippetoe, C.A.4 (S.C.) 1949, 178 F.2d 735. United States ☞ 122

5. Summary judgment

In an action by the Government to recover on the ground that Smaller War Plants Corporation made loans to a partnership in which defendant was a partner on the basis of false representations, prior decree in action by the Reconstruction Finance Corporation against defendant did not warrant summary judgment for Government in view of the differences in the nature of the two actions in that a corporation was the chief actor in the present transaction which was not a defendant in the former suit. U.S. v. Temple, N.D.Ill.1956, 147 F.Supp. 118. Federal Civil Procedure ☞ 2515

6. Limitations

The provisions of this section stating that one who has made fraudulent claims shall forfeit $2,000 for each fraudulent act and pay an amount equal to 25 percent of any amount sought to be wrongfully secured provide civil penalties within section 2462 of Title 28 imposing five year limitation on assertion of such and making the bringing of suit within such time a condition precedent of right to sue, and section 2462 of Title 28 was not tolled by contractor's trustee in bankruptcy's filing suit based on same transaction as Government's counterclaim for such penalty. Goggin v. U.S., Ct.Cl.1957, 152 F.Supp. 78, 138 Ct.Cl. 279. Limitation Of Actions ☞ 1; Limitation Of Actions ☞ 35(1); Limitation Of Actions ☞ 129

In action by contractor against the United States under this chapter, counterclaim of the United States under this section for damages for alleged fraud or defense thereunder was barred by five year statute of limitations as to all acts of alleged fraud committed within five years of filing of counterclaim, and counterclaim under former False Claims Act, section 231 et seq. of Title 31 [now covered by section 3729 of Title 31], or defense thereunder was barred by six year statute of limitations as to all acts of alleged fraud committed within six years of the filing of the counterclaim, whether alleged fraudulent acts were committed in connection with termination or renegotiation proceedings. Erie Basin Metal Products, Inc. v. U.S., Ct.Cl.1957, 150 F.Supp. 561, 138 Ct.Cl. 67. Limitation Of Actions ☞ 40(2); Limitation Of Actions ☞ 41

An action seeking to recover for the presentation to the Government of a fraudulent claim brought by the Government under this section, allowing recovery for presenting to the Government a false document for the purpose of obtaining money, is subject to no specific statutory limitation and is not subject to the limitations imposed by section 2462 of Title 28, limiting the time for recovery of "penalties". U.S. v. Temple, N.D.Ill. 1956, 147 F.Supp. 118. Limitation Of Actions ☞ 35(1)

7. Standard of proof

In action for alleged fraudulent claims submitted to the Maritime Commission [now Department of Transportation] with respect to amount claimed to be payable by United States because of cancellation of war contracts, United States was not obliged to prove the charge of fraud beyond a reasonable doubt, but in establishing charge the proof would be required to be clear, unequivocal and convincing. U.S. v. Leyde & Leyde, D.C.Md.1950, 89 F.Supp. 256. United States ☞ 120.1

8. Res judicata

Where former action by Reconstruction Finance Corporation was solely to recover for unpaid loans and fraud was not alleged or mentioned but fraud was the gist of the counts in subsequent action on ground that Smaller War Plants Corporation made loans to a partnership in which defendant was a partner on the basis of false representations, and the issue of fraud was not adjudicated in the prior suit, it was not adjudicated by the prior judgment. U.S. v. Temple, N.D.Ill.1956, 147 F.Supp. 118. Judgment ☞ 588

In action by Government to recover civil penalties provided in this section, judgment of conviction entered upon guilty plea by same defendant in prosecution under former False Claims Act, section 231 et seq. of Title 31 [now covered by section 3729 et seq. of Title 31], was res judicata of all issues settled by it and operated as complete estoppel by judgment authorizing directed verdict against defendant as to those issues. U.S. v. Bower, E.D.Tenn.1951, 95 F.Supp. 19. Judgment ☞ 648

Former acquittal of defendant in prosecution for filing fraudulent claims with respect to amounts claimed to be payable by United States because of cancellation of war contracts for manufacture and equipment of life rafts, did not bar prosecution of civil action by United States because of same alleged fraudulent claims, on grounds of res judicata or double jeopardy. U.S. v. Leyde & Leyde, D.C.Md.1950, 89 F.Supp. 256. Double Jeopardy ☞ 23; Judgment ☞ 559

9. Admissibility of evidence

In civil action by Government to recover civil penalties provided in this chapter, transcript of record in criminal prosecution of same defendant under section 117 of this title would be admissible. U.S. v. Bower, E.D.Tenn.1951, 95 F.Supp. 19. Evidence ☞ 577.5

10. Weight and sufficiency of evidence

In action under this chapter, there was ample evidence that defendant falsely stated that facilities were exclusively devoted to five contracts in July and August and falsely claimed direct labor costs of $15,989.70 in negotiating settlement when actually costs were only $746.02. U.S. v. Dinerstein, C.A.2 (N.Y.) 1966, 362 F.2d 852. United States ⇔ 74(16)

In action for alleged fraudulent claims submitted to the Maritime Commission [now Department of Transportation] with respect to amount claimed to be payable by United States because of cancellation of war contracts, evidence would be required to exclude reasonable hypothesis of good faith to extent the evidence was circumstantial. U.S. v. Leyde & Leyde, D.C.Md.1950, 89 F.Supp. 256. United States ⇔ 120.1

§ 120. Powers and duties of contracting agencies

(a) Limitation

Each contracting agency shall have authority, notwithstanding any provisions of law other than contained in this chapter, (1) to make any contract necessary and appropriate to carry out the provisions of this chapter; (2) to amend by agreement any existing contract, either before or after notice of its termination, on such terms and to such extent as it deems necessary and appropriate to carry out the provisions of this chapter; and (3) in settling any termination claim, to agree to assume, or indemnify the war contractor against, any claims by any person in connection with such termination claims or settlement. This subsection shall not limit or affect in any way any authority of any contracting agency under the First War Powers Act, 1941, or under any other statute.

(b) Evidence required; conclusiveness of determinations

Any contracting agency may prescribe the amount and kind of evidence required to identify any person as a war contractor, or any contract, agreement, or purchase order as a war contract for any of the purposes of this chapter. Any determination so made that any person is a war contractor, or that any contract, agreement, or purchase order is a war contract, shall be final and conclusive for any of the purposes of this chapter.

(c) Appropriations

There are authorized to be appropriated such sums as may be necessary for administering the provisions of this chapter.

(d) Validation of prior settlements

All policies and procedures relating to termination of war contracts, termination settlements, and interim financing, prescribed by the Secretary of the Treasury or any contracting agency, in effect on July 21, 1944, and not inconsistent with this chapter, shall remain in full force and effect unless and until superseded by the Administrator of General Services in accordance with this chapter, or by regulations of the contracting agency not inconsistent with this chapter or the policies prescribed by the Administrator of General Services.

(e) Impairment of contract

Nothing in this chapter shall be deemed to impair or modify any war contract or any term or provision of any war contract or any assignment of any claim under a war contract, without the consent of the parties thereto, if the war contract, or the term, provision, or assignment thereof, is otherwise valid.

(f) Aid to war contractors

Any contracting agency may authorize or direct its officers and employees, as a part of their official duties, to advise, aid, and assist war contractors in preparing and presenting termination claims, in obtaining interim financing, and in related matters, to such extent as it deems desirable.   Such advice, aid, or assistance shall not constitute a violation of section 205 of Title 18 or of any other law, provided the officer or employee does not receive therefor benefit or compensation of any kind, directly or indirectly, from any war contractor.

(July 1, 1944, c. 358, § 20, 58 Stat. 668; Ex. Ord. No. 9809, § 8, eff. Dec. 12, 1946, 11 F.R. 14281; June 30, 1947, c. 166, Title II, § 207, 61 Stat. 209; 1947 Reorg.Plan No. 1, § 201, eff. July 1, 1947, 12 F.R. 4534, 61 Stat. 951; June 30, 1949, c. 288, Title I, § 102(b), 63 Stat. 380.)

HISTORICAL AND STATUTORY NOTES

References in Text

The First War Powers Act, 1941, referred to in subsec. (a), is Act Dec. 18, 1941, c. 593, 55 Stat. 838, which enacted sections 32 to 37 and 601 to 605, 611, and 616 to 622 of the Appendix to Title 50, War and National Defense, and amended section 95a of Title 12, Banks and Banking, and section 5 of the Appendix to Title 50.   The First War Powers Act, 1941, was substantially repealed, with certain exceptions, by Pub.L. 89–554, § 8(a), Sept. 6, 1966, 80 Stat. 651.   For complete classification of this Act to the Code, see Tables.

Codifications

In subsec. (f) of this section, "section 205 of Title 18" was substituted for "section 109 of the Criminal Code (18 U.S.C. 198)" on authority of Act June 25, 1948, c. 645, 62 Stat. 683, the first section of which enacted Title 18, Crimes and Criminal Procedure, and on authority of Pub.L. 87–849, § 2, Oct. 23, 1962, 76 Stat. 1126.

Subsec. (g) of this section, relating to the duties of Smaller War Plants Corporation, was omitted on the authority of section 207 of act June 30, 1947, which provided: "The liquidation of the affairs of the Smaller War Plants Corporation administered by the Reconstruction Finance Corporation pursuant to Executive Order 9665 shall be carried out by the Reconstruction Finance Corporation, notwithstanding the provisions of the last paragraph of section 5 of the First War Powers Act, 1941 [section 605 of the Appendix to Title 50, War and National Defense].   The Smaller War Plants Corporation is hereby abolished."

Transfer of Functions

Functions of Secretary of the Treasury were transferred to Administrator of General Services and reference to the Department of Treasury in subsec. (d) was changed to "General Services Administration" by Act June 30, 1949, c. 288, § 102(b), 63 Stat. 380, which was classified to former 40 U.S.C.A. § 752(b), prior to repeal by Pub.L. 107–217, § 6(b), Aug. 21, 2002, 116 Stat. 1304.

"Secretary of the Treasury" was substituted for "Director" by section 8 of Ex. Ord. No. 9809 and section 201 of Reorg. Plan No. 1 of 1947. Reorg. Plan No. 1 of 1947 is set out in the Appendix to Title 5,

Government Organization and Employees.

Effective Date of Transfer of Functions

Act June 30, 1949, § 605, which set July 1, 1949, as the effective date for the transfer of functions by that Act, was repealed by Pub.L. 107–217, § 6(b), Aug. 21, 2002, 116 Stat. 1313.

LIBRARY REFERENCES

American Digest System

United States ⊕74(16).
Key Number System Topic No. 393.

WESTLAW ELECTRONIC RESEARCH

See Westlaw guide following the Explanation pages of this volume.

Notes of Decisions

Indemnification   1

___

1. Indemnification

Contract Settlement Act (CSA) authorized War Department to confirm, in "settlement" represented by termination supplement by which government and contractor terminated contract for operation of World War II ordnance plant, broad indemnification commitment first made by government in plant operation contract. E.I. Du Pont de Nemours and Co., Inc. v. U.S., C.A.Fed.2004, 365 F.3d 1367, rehearing and rehearing en banc denied. United States ⊕ 74(16)

§ 121. Administrator of General Services; additional duties

In addition to his other functions under this chapter, the Administrator of General Services shall—

(a) promote the training of personnel for termination settlement and interim financing by contracting agencies, war contractors, and financing institutions;

(b) Omitted.

(c) promote decentralization of the administration of termination settlements and interim financing by fostering delegation of authority within contracting agencies and to war contractors, to the extent he deems necessary and feasible; and

(d) consult with war contractors through advisory committees or such other methods as he deems appropriate.

(July 1, 1944, c. 358, § 21, 58 Stat. 669; Ex. Ord. No. 9809, § 8, eff. Dec. 12, 1946, 11 F.R. 14281; June 30, 1947, c. 166, Title II, § 207, 61 Stat. 209; 1947 Reorg.Plan No. 1, § 201, eff. July 1, 1947, 12 F.R. 4534, 61 Stat. 951; June 30, 1949, c. 288, Title I, § 102(b), 63 Stat. 380.)

HISTORICAL AND STATUTORY NOTES

Codifications

Subsec. (b), providing for Administrators' collaboration with Smaller War Plants Corporation in protecting interests of smaller war contractors, was omitted on authority of section 207 of Act June 30, 1947, which provided: "The liquidation of the affairs of the Smaller War Plants Corporation administered by the Reconstruction Finance Corporation pursuant to Executive Order 9665 shall be carried out by the Reconstruction Finance Corporation, notwithstanding the provisions of the last paragraph of section 5 of the First War Powers Act, 1941 [former section 605 of Appendix to Title 50, War and National Defense]. The Smaller War Plants Corporation is hereby abolished."

Transfer of Functions

Functions of Secretary of the Treasury were transferred to Administrator of General Services and reference to the Department of Treasury in subsec. (d) was changed to "General Services Administration" by Act June 30, 1949, c. 288, § 102(b), 63 Stat. 380, which was classified to former 40 U.S.C.A. § 752(b), prior to repeal by Pub.L. 107–217, § 6(b), Aug. 21, 2002, 116 Stat. 1304.

"Secretary of the Treasury" was substituted for "Director" by section 8 of Ex. Ord. No. 9809 and section 201 of Reorg. Plan No. 1 of 1947. Reorg. Plan No. 1 of 1947 is set out in the Appendix to Title 5, Government Organization and Employees.

Effective Date of Transfer of Functions

Act June 30, 1949, § 605, which set July 1, 1949, as the effective date for the transfer of functions by that Act, was repealed by Pub.L. 107–217, § 6(b), Aug. 21, 2002, 116 Stat. 1313.

Termination of Advisory Committees

Advisory committees in existence on Jan. 5, 1973, to terminate not later than the expiration of the two-year period following Jan. 5, 1973, unless, in the case of a committee established by the President or an officer of the Federal Government, such committee is renewed by appropriate action prior to the expiration of such two-year period, or in the case of a committee established by the Congress, its duration is otherwise provided by law. Advisory committees established after Jan. 5, 1973, to terminate not later than the expiration of the two-year period beginning on the date of their establishment, unless, in the case of a committee established by the President or an officer of the Federal Government, such committee is renewed by appropriate action prior to the expiration of such two-year period, or in the case of a committee established by the Congress, its duration is otherwise provided by law. See section 14 of Pub.L. 92–463, Oct. 6, 1972, 86 Stat. 776, set out in the Appendix to Title 5, Government Organization and Employees.

LIBRARY REFERENCES

American Digest System

United States ☞74(16).

Key Number System Topic No. 393.

WESTLAW ELECTRONIC RESEARCH

See Westlaw guide following the Explanation pages of this volume.

§ 122. Use of appropriated funds

Any contracting agency is authorized—

(a) to use for interim financing, the payment of claims, and for any other purposes authorized in this chapter any funds which have heretofore been appropriated or allocated or which may hereafter be appropriated or allocated to it, or which are or may become available to it, for such purposes or for the purposes of war production or war procurement;

(b) to use any such funds appropriated, allocated, or available to it for expenditures for or in behalf of any other contracting agency for the purposes authorized in this chapter; and

(c) to determine by agreement, joint estimate, or any other method authorized by the Administrator of General Services, the part of any expenditure made pursuant to subsection (b) of this section to be paid by each contracting agency concerned and to make transfers of funds between such contracting agencies accordingly. Transfers of funds between appropriations carried upon the books of the Treasury shall be made by the Administrator of General Services in accordance with joint requests of the contracting agencies involved.

(July 1, 1944, c. 358, § 22, 58 Stat. 670; Ex. Ord. No. 9809, § 8, eff. Dec. 12, 1946, 11 F.R. 14281; 1947 Reorg.Plan No. 1, § 201, eff. July 1, 1949, 12 F.R. 4534, 61 Stat. 951; June 30, 1949, c. 288, Title I, § 102(b), 63 Stat. 380.)

HISTORICAL AND STATUTORY NOTES

Transfer of Functions

Functions of Secretary of the Treasury were transferred to Administrator of General Services and reference to the Department of Treasury in subsec. (d) was changed to "General Services Administration" by Act June 30, 1949, c. 288, § 102(b), 63 Stat. 380, which was classified to former 40 U.S.C.A. § 752(b), prior to repeal by Pub.L. 107–217, § 6(b), Aug. 21, 2002, 116 Stat. 1304.

"Secretary of the Treasury" was substituted for "Director" by section 8 of Ex.

Ord. No. 9809 and section 201 of Reorg. Plan No. 1 of 1947. Reorg. Plan No. 1 of 1947 is set out in the Appendix to Title 5, Government Organization and Employees.

Effective Date of Transfer of Functions

Act June 30, 1949, § 605, which set July 1, 1949, as the effective date for the transfer of functions by that Act, was repealed by Pub.L. 107–217, § 6(b), Aug. 21, 2002, 116 Stat. 1313.

LIBRARY REFERENCES

American Digest System

United States ⚷62.
Key Number System Topic No. 393.

WESTLAW ELECTRONIC RESEARCH

See Westlaw guide following the Explanation pages of this volume.

Notes of Decisions

Indemnification 1

___

1. Indemnification

Provision of Contract Settlement Act (CSA) addressing appropriations to be used by contracting agency did not limit contracting authority conferred by CSA so as to deny government authority to

make or ratify its obligation to indemnify contractor for liability incurred from operation of World War II ordnance plant that did not result from contractor's lack of good faith or due care. E.I. Du Pont de Nemours and Co., Inc. v. U.S., C.A.Fed.2004, 365 F.3d 1367, rehearing and rehearing en banc denied. United States ⚷ 74(16)

§ 123. Delegation of authority by Administrator of General Services

(a) Officers and agencies of General Service Administration and other governmental agencies

The Administrator of General Services may delegate any authority and discretion conferred upon him by this chapter to such officers and agencies of the General Services Administration as he may designate, and may delegate such authority and discretion, upon such terms and conditions as he may prescribe, to the head of any Government agency to the extent necessary to the handling and solution of problems peculiar to that agency.

(b) Authority delegated to other governmental agencies

The head of any Government agency may delegate any authority and discretion conferred upon him or his agency by or pursuant to this chapter to any officer, agent, or employee of such agency or to any other Government agency, and may authorize successive redelegations of such authority and discretion.

(c) Joint exercise of delegated authority

Any two or more Government agencies may exercise jointly any authority and discretion conferred upon each of them individually by or pursuant to this chapter.

(d) Application to other laws

Nothing in this chapter shall prevent the Administrator of General Services from exercising any authority conferred upon him by any other statute.

(July 1, 1944, c. 358, § 23, 58 Stat. 670; Ex.Ord. No. 9809, § 8, eff. Dec. 12, 1946, 11 F.R. 14281; 1947 Reorg.Plan No. 1, § 201, eff. July 1, 1947, 12 F.R. 4534, 61 Stat. 951; June 30, 1949, c. 288, Title I, § 102(b), 63 Stat. 380.)

HISTORICAL AND STATUTORY NOTES

Codifications

The phrase "such officers and agencies of the General Services Administration as he may designate" was substituted for "any Deputy Director" on the authority of section 102(b) of Act June 30, 1949, which is classified to section 752(b) of Title 40, Public Buildings, Property, and Works.

Transfer of Functions

Functions of Secretary of the Treasury were transferred to Administrator of General Services and reference to the Department of Treasury in subsec. (d) was changed to "General Services Administration" by Act June 30, 1949, c. 288, § 102(b), 63 Stat. 380, which was classified to former 40 U.S.C.A. § 752(b), prior to repeal by Pub.L. 107–217, § 6(b), Aug. 21, 2002, 116 Stat. 1304.

"Secretary of the Treasury" was substituted for "Director" by section 8 of Ex. Ord. No. 9809 and section 201 of Reorg. Plan No. 1 of 1947. Reorg. Plan No. 1 of 1947 is set out in the Appendix to Title 5, Government Organization and Employees.

Effective Date of Transfer of Functions

Act June 30, 1949, § 605, which set July 1, 1949, as the effective date for the transfer of functions by that Act, was repealed by Pub.L. 107–217, § 6(b), Aug. 21, 2002, 116 Stat. 1313.

LIBRARY REFERENCES

American Digest System
> United States ☞74(16).
> Key Number System Topic No. 393.

WESTLAW ELECTRONIC RESEARCH

See Westlaw guide following the Explanation pages of this volume.

§ 124. Effective date; applicability to lend lease contracts

(a) This chapter shall become effective twenty days after July 1, 1944. With the exception of the provisions of paragraphs (b), (c), (d), and (e) of section 112 of this title, and sections 106 to 110, and 113 of this title, this chapter shall be applicable in the case of any terminated war contract which has been finally settled at or before the effective date of this chapter.

(b) Nothing in this chapter shall limit or affect any authority conferred by sections 411 to 419 of Title 22, or Acts supplemental thereto.

(July 1, 1944, c. 358, § 24, 58 Stat. 670.)

HISTORICAL AND STATUTORY NOTES

References in Text
Sections 411 to 419 of Title 22, referred to in subsec. (b), have been omitted from the Code.

LIBRARY REFERENCES

American Digest System
> United States ☞74(16).
> Key Number System Topic No. 393.

WESTLAW ELECTRONIC RESEARCH

See Westlaw guide following the Explanation pages of this volume.

Notes of Decisions

Retroactive effect   1

1. Retroactive effect

The War Mobilization and Reconversion Act, 50 App. former § 1651 et seq., and this chapter were applicable to contracts entered into before passage of the Acts. Monolith Portland Midwest Co. v. R.F.C., S.D.Cal.1951, 95 F.Supp. 570. United States ☞ 72.1(7); United States ☞ 74(16)

§ 125.   Exemption of certain contracts outside continental United States or in Alaska

Subject to policies prescribed by the Administrator of General Services, any contracting agency may exempt from some or all of the provisions of this chapter (a) any war contract made or to be performed outside the continental limits of the United States or in Alaska, or (b) any termination inventory situated outside of the continental limits of the United States or in Alaska, or (c) any modification of a war contract pursuant to its terms for the purpose of changing plans or specifications applicable to the work without substantially reducing its extent.

(July 1, 1944, c. 358, § 25, 58 Stat. 670; Ex.Ord. No. 9809, § 8, eff. Dec. 12, 1946, 11 F.R. 14281; 1947 Reorg.Plan No. 1, § 201, eff. July 1, 1947, 12 F.R. 4534, 61 Stat. 951; June 30, 1949, c. 288, Title I, § 102(b), 63 Stat. 380.)

HISTORICAL AND STATUTORY NOTES

Transfer of Functions

Functions of Secretary of the Treasury were transferred to Administrator of General Services and reference to the Department of Treasury in subsec. (d) was changed to "General Services Administration" by Act June 30, 1949, c. 288, § 102(b), 63 Stat. 380, which was classified to former 40 U.S.C.A. § 752(b), prior to repeal by Pub.L. 107–217, § 6(b), Aug. 21, 2002, 116 Stat. 1304.

"Secretary of the Treasury" was substituted for "Director" by section 8 of Ex.

Ord. No. 9809 and section 201 of Reorg. Plan No. 1 of 1947. Reorg. Plan No. 1 of 1947 is set out in the Appendix to Title 5, Government Organization and Employees.

Effective Date of Transfer of Functions

Act June 30, 1949, § 605, which set July 1, 1949, as the effective date for the transfer of functions by that Act, was repealed by Pub.L. 107–217, § 6(b), Aug. 21, 2002, 116 Stat. 1313.

LIBRARY REFERENCES

American Digest System
   United States ⊙→74(16).
   Key Number System Topic No. 393.

WESTLAW ELECTRONIC RESEARCH

See Westlaw guide following the Explanation pages of this volume.

CHAPTER 3—PROCUREMENT OF SUPPLIES AND SERVICES BY ARMED SERVICES

§§ 151 to 162. Repealed. Aug. 10, 1956, c. 1041, § 53, 70A Stat. 641

HISTORICAL AND STATUTORY NOTES

Section 151, Act Feb. 19, 1948, c. 65, § 2, 62 Stat. 21, related to purchases and contracts for supplies and services for the Armed Services, stated the Congressional declaration of policy, provided for advertising requirements, excepted certain purchases and contracts, authorized reference to Attorney General where there is any evidence of violation of antitrust laws, and excluded certain authorizations and contracts, and is now covered by sections 2301, and 2303 to 2305 of Title 10, Armed Forces.

Section 152, Acts Feb. 19, 1948, c. 65, § 3, 62 Stat. 22; Aug. 9, 1955, c. 628, § 15, 69 Stat. 551, related to advertisements for bids, opening of bids, and award or rejection of bids, and is now covered by section 2305 of Title 10. Act Aug. 9, 1955, c. 628, § 15, 69 Stat. 551, which amended former section 152 of this title, was repealed by Pub.L. 85–861, § 36A, Sept. 2, 1958, 72 Stat. 1569.

Section 153, Acts Feb. 19, 1948, c. 65, § 4, 62 Stat. 23; Oct. 31, 1951, c. 652, 65 Stat. 700, provided for types of contracts and examination of books, records, etc., of contractors, and is now covered by sections 2306 and 2313 of Title 10.

Section 154, Act Feb. 19, 1948, c. 65, § 5, 62 Stat. 24, authorized advance payments under negotiated contracts, and is now covered by section 2307 of Title 10.

Section 155, Act Feb. 19, 1948, c. 65, § 6, 62 Stat. 24, provided for remission of liquidated damages, and is now covered by section 2312 of Title 10.

Section 156, Act Feb. 19, 1948, c. 65, § 7, 62 Stat. 24, provided for determinations and decisions, powers of agency head, finality of decisions, delegation of powers, non-delegable powers, written decisions, and preservation of data, and is now covered by sections 2304, 2310, and 2311 of Title 10.

Section 157, Act Feb. 19, 1948, c. 65, § 8, 62 Stat. 24, related to exemption of purchases or contracts from certain other provisions of law, and is now covered by section 2304 of Title 10.

Section 158, Act Feb. 19, 1948, c. 65, § 9, 62 Stat. 24, defined the terms "agency head" and "supplies", and is now covered by sections 2302 and 2303 of Title 10.

Section 159, Act Feb. 19, 1948, c. 65, § 10, 62 Stat. 25, related to assignment and delegation of joint procurement responsibilities by agency head, and allocation of appropriations, and is now covered by sections 2308 and 2309 of Title 10.

Section 160, Act Feb. 19, 1948, c. 65, § 11(b), 62 Stat. 25, provided that sections 5, 6, 6a, and 13 of this title should be inapplicable to procurement of supplies and services, and is now covered by section 2314 of Title 10.

Section 161, Act Feb. 19, 1948, c. 65, § 12, 62 Stat. 26, related to concurrent authority of Secretaries of Army, Navy and Air Force, and is now covered by sections 2381 of Title 10.

Section 162, Act July 10, 1952, c. 630, Title VI, § 638, 66 Stat. 537, related to obligation of funds by Department of Defense for procurement and distribution of supplies or equipment, and is now covered by section 2202 of Title 10.

CHAPTER 4—PROCUREMENT PROCEDURES

WESTLAW COMPUTER ASSISTED LEGAL RESEARCH

Westlaw supplements your legal research in many ways. Westlaw allows you to

• update your research with the most current information

• expand your library with additional resources

• retrieve current, comprehensive history citing references to a case with KeyCite

For more information on using Westlaw to supplement your research, see the Westlaw Electronic Research Guide, which follows the Explanation.

SUBCHAPTER I—GENERAL PROVISIONS

§§ 201 to 205. Transferred

HISTORICAL AND STATUTORY NOTES

Codifications

Section 201, Act June 30, 1949, c. 288, § 2, 63 Stat. 378, which related to Congressional declaration of policy, was transferred to former 40 U.S.C.A. § 471 prior to being repealed by Pub.L.

107–217, § 6(b), Aug. 21, 2002, 116 Stat. 1313 and its substance reenacted as 40 U.S.C.A. § 101.

Section 202, Acts June 30, 1949, c. 288, § 3, 63 Stat. 378; Sept. 5, 1950, c. 849,

§§ 7(a), 8(a), 64 Stat. 590, which related to definitions, was transferred to former 40 U.S.C.A. § 472 prior to being repealed by Pub.L. 107–217, § 6(b), Aug. 21, 2002, 116 Stat. 1313 and its substance reenacted as 40 U.S.C.A. § 102.

Section 203, Acts June 30, 1949, c. 288, Title VI, § 601, formerly Title V, § 501, 63 Stat. 399, renumbered Sept. 5, 1950, c. 849, § 6(a), (b), 64 Stat. 583, which related to applicability of existing provisions, was transferred to former 40 U.S.C.A. § 473 prior to being repealed by Pub.L. 107–217, § 6(b), Aug. 21, 2002, 116 Stat. 1313 and its substance reenacted as 40 U.S.C.A. § 112.

Section 204, Acts June 30, 1949, c. 288, Title VI, § 602(c), (d), formerly Title V, § 502(c), (d), 63 Stat. 401, renumbered and amended Sept. 5, 1950, c. 849,

§§ 6(a), (b), 7(e), (f), 8(c), 64 Stat. 583, 590, which related to exemptions for Congress, departments, agencies, corporations, and persons, was transferred to former 40 U.S.C.A. § 474 of Title 40 prior to being repealed by Pub.L. 107–217, § 6(b), Aug. 21, 2002, 116 Stat. 1313 and its substance reenacted as 40 U.S.C.A. § 113.

Section 205, Acts June 30, 1949, c. 288, Title VI, § 603, formerly Title V, § 503, 63 Stat. 403, renumbered and amended Sept. 5, 1950, c. 849, §§ 6(a), (b), 7(g), 64 Stat. 583, 590, which related to authorization of appropriations and fund transfer authority, was transferred to former 40 U.S.C.A. § 475 prior to being repealed by Pub.L. 107–217, § 6(b), Aug. 21, 2002, 116 Stat. 1313 and its substance reenacted as 40 U.S.C.A. §§ 124, 125.

SUBCHAPTER II—GENERAL SERVICES ADMINISTRATION

§§ 211 to 219.   Transferred

HISTORICAL AND STATUTORY NOTES

Codifications

Section 211, Act June 30, 1949, c. 288, Title I, § 101, 63 Stat. 379, which related to General Services Administration, was transferred to former 5 U.S.C.A. § 630, and subsequently transferred to former 40 U.S.C.A. § 751 prior to being repealed by Pub.L. 107–217, § 6(b), Aug. 21, 2002, 116 Stat. 1313 and its substance reenacted as 40 U.S.C.A. §§ 301, 302.

Section 212, Act June 30, 1949, c. 288, Title I, § 102, 63 Stat. 380, which related to transfer of functions, was transferred to former 5 U.S.C.A. § 630a, and subsequently transferred to former 5 U.S.C.A. § 752 prior to being repealed by Pub.L. 107–217, § 6(b), Aug. 21, 2002, 116 Stat. 1313 and its substance reenacted as 40 U.S.C.A. § 303(a).

Section 213, Act June 30, 1949, c. 288, Title I, § 103, 63 Stat. 380, which related to transfer of affairs of Federal Works Agency, was transferred to former 5 U.S.C.A. § 630b, and subsequently transferred to former 40 U.S.C.A. § 753 prior to being repealed by Pub.L. 107–217, § 6(b), Aug. 21, 2002, 116 Stat. 1313 and its substance reenacted as 40 U.S.C.A. § 303(b).

Section 214, Act June 30, 1949, c. 288, Title I, § 104, 63 Stat. 381, which related

to records management, was transferred to former 44 U.S.C.A. § 391 prior to being repealed by Pub.L. Pub.L. 90–620, § 3, Oct. 22, 1968, 82 Stat. 1309 and its substance reenacted as 44 U.S.C.A. §§ 1506, 2102, 2301, 2501, 2902.

Section 215, Act June 30, 1949, c. 288, Title I, § 105, 63 Stat. 381, which related to transfer and liquidation of War Assets Administration, was transferred to former 5 U.S.C.A. § 630c, prior to being repealed by Pub.L. 89–554, § 8(a) Sept. 6, 1966, 80 Stat. 632.

Section 216, Act June 30, 1949, c. 288, Title I, § 106, 63 Stat. 381, which related to redistribution of Administrator's functions, was transferred to former 5 U.S.C.A. § 630d, and subsequently transferred to former 40 U.S.C.A. § 754 prior to being repealed by Pub.L. 107–217, § 6(b), Aug. 21, 2002, 116 Stat. 1313 and its substance reenacted as 40 U.S.C.A. § 121.

Section 217, Act June 30, 1949, c. 288, Title I, § 107, 63 Stat. 382, which related to transfer of funds, was transferred to former 5 U.S.C.A. § 630e, and subsequently transferred to former 40 U.S.C.A. § 755 prior to being repealed by Pub.L. 107–217, § 6(b), Aug. 21, 2002, 116 Stat. 1313.

Section 218, Act June 30, 1949, c. 288, Title I, § 108, 63 Stat. 382, which related to status of transferred employees, was transferred to former 5 U.S.C.A. § 630f, prior to being repealed by Pub.L. 89–554, § 8(a) Sept. 6, 1966, 80 Stat. 632.

Section 219, Acts June 30, 1949, c. 288, Title I, § 109, 63 Stat. 382; Sept. 5, 1950, c. 849, §§ 1, 2(a), (b), 3, 64 Stat. 578, which related to the General Supply Fund, was transferred to former 5 U.S.C.A. § 630g, and subsequently transferred to former 40 U.S.C.A. § 756 prior to being repealed by Pub.L. 107–217, § 6(b), Aug. 21, 2002, 116 Stat. 1313 and its substance reenacted as 40 U.S.C.A. §§ 313, 321.

SUBCHAPTER III—PROPERTY MANAGEMENT

§§ 231 to 240. Transferred

HISTORICAL AND STATUTORY NOTES

Codifications

Section 231, Acts June 30, 1949, c. 288, Title II, § 201, 63 Stat. 383; Aug. 10, 1949, c. 412, § 12(a), 63 Stat. 591; Sept. 5, 1950, c. 849, § 8(b), 64 Stat. 591, which related to procurement, warehousing, and related activities, was transferred to former 40 U.S.C.A. § 481 prior to being repealed by Pub.L. 107–217, § 6(b), Aug. 21, 2002, 116 Stat. 1313 and its substance reenacted as 40 U.S.C.A. §§ 501 to 505.

Section 231a, Act Oct. 26, 1949, c. 737, 63 Stat. 920, which related to clarification of status of Architect of the Capitol under this chapter, was transferred to former 40 U.S.C.A. § 482 prior to being repealed by Pub.L. 107–217, § 6(b), Aug. 21, 2002, 116 Stat. 1313.

Section 232, Acts June 30, 1949, c. 288, Title II, § 202, 63 Stat. 384; Aug. 10, 1949, c. 412, § 12(a), 63 Stat. 591, which related to property utilization, was transferred to former 40 U.S.C.A. § 483 prior to being repealed by Pub.L. 107–217, § 6(b), Aug. 21, 2002, 116 Stat. 1313 and its substance reenacted as 40 U.S.C.A. §§ 521 to 527, 529.

Section 233, Acts June 30, 1949, c. 288, Title II, § 203, 63 Stat. 385; Aug. 10, 1949, c. 412, § 12(a), 63 Stat. 591; Sept. 5, 1950, c. 849, § 4, 64 Stat. 579, which related to disposal of surplus property, was transferred to former 40 U.S.C.A. § 484 prior to being repealed by Pub.L. 107–217, § 6(b), Aug. 21, 2002, 116 Stat. 1313 and its substance reenacted as 40 U.S.C.A. §§ 541 to 555.

Section 234, Act June 30, 1949, c. 288, Title I, § 204, 63 Stat. 388, which related to proceeds from transfer, sale, etc., of property, was transferred to former 40 U.S.C.A. § 485 prior to being repealed by Pub.L. 107–217, § 6(b), Aug. 21, 2002, 116 Stat. 1313 and its substance reenacted as 40 U.S.C.A. §§ 571 to 574.

Section 235, Acts June 30, 1949, c. 288, Title II, § 205, 63 Stat. 389; Sept. 5, 1950, c. 849, § 9, 64 Stat. 591, which related to policies, regulations, and delegations, was transferred to former 40 U.S.C.A. § 486 prior to being repealed by Pub.L. 107–217, § 6(b), Aug. 21, 2002, 116 Stat. 1313 and its substance reenacted as 40 U.S.C.A. § 121.

Section 236, Acts June 30, 1949, c. 288, Title II, § 206, 63 Stat. 390; Aug. 10, 1949, c. 412, § 12(a), 63 Stat. 591, which related to surveys of government property and property management practices, was transferred to former 40 U.S.C.A. § 487 prior to being repealed by Pub.L. 107–217, § 6(b), Aug. 21, 2002, 116 Stat. 1313 and its substance reenacted as 40 U.S.C.A. § 506.

Section 237, Act June 30, 1949, c. 288, Title II, § 207, 63 Stat. 391, which related to applicability of antitrust laws to property disposal, was transferred to former 40 U.S.C.A. § 488 prior to being repealed by Pub.L. 107–217, § 6(b), Aug. 21, 2002, 116 Stat. 1313 and its substance reenacted as 40 U.S.C.A. § 559.

Section 238, Acts June 30, 1949, c. 288, Title II, § 208, 63 Stat. 391; Sept. 5, 1950, c. 849, § 7(b), (c), 64 Stat. 590, which related to appointment and compensation of personnel, was transferred to former 5 U.S.C.A. § 630h, and was subsequently transferred to former 40 U.S.C.A. § 758 prior to being repealed by Pub.L. 107–217, § 6(b), Aug. 21, 2002, 116 Stat. 1313 and its substance reenacted as 40 U.S.C.A. § 311.

Section 239, Act June 30, 1949, c. 288, Title II, § 209, 63 Stat. 392, which related to civil remedies and penalties, was transferred to former 40 U.S.C.A. § 489 prior to being repealed by Pub.L. 107–217, § 6(b), Aug. 21, 2002, 116 Stat. 1313 and its substance reenacted as 40 U.S.C.A. § 123.

Section 239a, Act June 30, 1949, c. 288, Title II, § 210, as added Sept. 5, 1950, c. 849, § 5(c), 64 Stat. 580, which related to operation of buildings and related activities by the Administrator, was transferred to former 40 U.S.C.A. § 490 prior to being repealed by Pub.L. 107–217, § 6(b), Aug. 21, 2002, 116 Stat. 1313 and its substance reenacted as 40 U.S.C.A. §§ 581 to 587.

Section 239b, Act June 30, 1949, c. 288, Title II, § 211, as added Sept. 5, 1950, c. 849, § 5(c), 64 Stat. 580, which related to motor vehicle identification, was transferred to former 40 U.S.C.A. § 491 prior to being repealed by Pub.L. 107–217, § 6(b), Aug. 21, 2002, 116 Stat. 1313 and its substance reenacted as 40 U.S.C.A. §§ 601 to 611.

Section 240, Act June 30, 1949, c. 288, Title II, § 212, formerly § 210, 63 Stat. 393, renumbered Sept. 5, 1950, c. 849, § 5(a), 64 Stat. 580, which related to reports to Congress, was transferred to former 40 U.S.C.A. § 492 prior to being repealed by Pub.L. 107–217, § 6(b), Aug. 21, 2002, 116 Stat. 1313 and its substance reenacted as 40 U.S.C.A. § 126.

SUBCHAPTER IV—PROCUREMENT PROVISIONS

CROSS REFERENCES

Government Printing Office purchases made without reference to this subchapter, see 44 USCA § 311.

Indian Self-Determination Act contracts and construction, see 25 USCA § 450j.

Metric conversion implementation of construction services and materials for Federal facilities, see 15 USCA § 205l.

§ 251. Declaration of purpose of this subchapter

The purpose of this subchapter is to facilitate the procurement of property and services.

(June 30, 1949, c. 288, Title III, § 301, 63 Stat. 393; July 12, 1952, c. 703, § 1(m), 66 Stat. 594.)

HISTORICAL AND STATUTORY NOTES

Revision Notes and Legislative Reports

1952 Acts. Senate Report No. 2075, see 1952 U.S.Code Cong. and Adm.News, p. 2121.

Amendments

1952 Amendments. Act July 12, 1952, substituted "property" for "supplies".

Effective and Applicability Provisions

1996 Acts. Section 4401 of Pub.L. 104–106 provided that:

"(a) **Effective date.**—Except as otherwise provided in this division, this division and the amendments made by this division [Division D of Pub.L. 104–106, Feb. 10, 1996, 110 Stat. 642, as amended Pub.L. 104–208, Title I, § 101(f) [Title VIII, § 808(c)], Sept. 30, 1996, 110 Stat.

3009–394, the Clinger-Cohen Act of 1996, for classification of which to the Code, see Short Title note set out under this section] shall take effect on the date of the enactment of this Act [Feb. 10, 1996].

"(b) **Applicability of amendments.—**

"(1) **Solicitations, unsolicited proposals, and related contracts.**—An amendment made by this division shall apply, in the manner prescribed in the final regulations promulgated pursuant to section 4402 [section 4402 of Pub.L. 104–106, set out as a note under this section] to implement such amendment, with respect to any solicitation that is issued, any unsolicited proposal that is received, and any contract entered into pursuant to such a solicitation or proposal, on or after the date described in paragraph (3).

"(2) Other matters.—An amendment made by this division shall also apply, to the extent and in the manner prescribed in the final regulations promulgated pursuant to section 4402 to implement such amendment, with respect to any matter related to—

"(A) a contract that is in effect on the date described in paragraph (3);

"(B) an offer under consideration on the date described in paragraph (3); or

"(C) any other proceeding or action that is ongoing on the date described in paragraph (3).

"(3) Demarcation date.—The date referred to in paragraphs (1) and (2) is the date specified in such final regulations. The date so specified shall be January 1, 1997, or any earlier date that is not within 30 days after the date on which such final regulations are published."

1994 Acts. Pub.L. 103–355, Title X, § 10001, Oct. 13, 1994, 108 Stat. 3404, provided that:

"(a) Effective date.—Except as otherwise provided in this Act, this Act and the amendments made by this Act [Pub.L. 103–355, Oct. 13, 1994, 108 Stat. 3243, the Federal Acquisition Streamlining Act of 1994, for classification of which to the Code, see Short Title note set out under this section and Tables] shall take effect on the date of the enactment of this Act [Oct. 13, 1994].

"(b) Applicability of amendments.—**(1)** An amendment made by this Act [Pub.L. 103–355, Oct. 13, 1994, 108 Stat. 3243, for classification of which to the Code, see Short Title note set out under this section and Tables] shall apply, in the manner prescribed in the final regulations promulgated pursuant to section 10002 [section 10002 of Pub.L. 103–355, set out as a note under this section] to implement such amendment, with respect to any solicitation that is issued, any unsolicited proposal that is received, and any contract entered into pursuant to such a solicitation or proposal, on or after the date described in paragraph (3).

"(2) An amendment made by this Act [Pub.L. 103–355, Oct. 13, 1994, 108 Stat. 3243, for classification of which to the

Code, see Short Title note set out under this section and Tables] shall also apply, to the extent and in the manner prescribed in the final regulations promulgated pursuant to section 10002 [section 10002 of Pub.L. 103–355, set out as a note under this section] to implement such amendment, with respect to any matter related to—

"(A) a contract that is in effect on the date described in paragraph (3);

"(B) an offer under consideration on the date described in paragraph (3); or

"(C) any other proceeding or action that is ongoing on the date described in paragraph (3).

"(3) The date referred to in paragraphs (1) and (2) is the date specified in such final regulations. The date so specified shall be October 1, 1995, or any earlier date that is not within 30 days after the date on which such final regulations are published.

"(c) Immediate applicability of certain amendments.— Notwithstanding subsection (b), the amendments made by the following provisions of this Act [Pub.L. 103–355, Oct. 13, 1994, 108 Stat. 3243, for classification of which to the Code, see Short Title note set under this section and Tables] apply on and after the date of the enactment of this Act [Oct. 13, 1994]: sections 1001, 1021, 1031, 1051, 1071, 1092, 1201, 1506(a), 1507, 1554, 2002(a), 2191, 3062(a), 3063, 3064, 3065(a)(1), 3065(b), 3066, 3067, 6001(a), 7101, 7103, 7205, and 7206, the provisions of subtitles A, B, and C of title III, and the provisions of title V [enacting section 263 of this title and sections 2220 and 2401a of Title 10, Armed Forces, amending sections 10b–1, 253, 254, 405, and 418b of this title, sections 139, 2304, 2306, 2306a, 2318, 2366, 2381, 2386, 2388, 2400, 2424, 2431, 2432, 2433, 2434, 2435, and 2539b of Title 10, section 644 of Title 15, Commerce and Trade, and section 3321 of Title 31, Money and Finance, and section 6962 of Title 42, The Public Health and Welfare, repealing sections 258, 419, and 420 of this title, sections 2329, 2355, 2369, 2438, 2439, 7203, 7299, and 7302 of Title 10, section 2516 of Title 19, Customs Duties, and section 801 of Title 37, Pay and Allowances, enacting provisions set out as notes under sections 263, 405, and 413 of this title, sections 2220, 2430, 2435, and 10212 of Title 10, section 2473 of Title 42, and section 40110 of Title 49,

Transportation, amending provisions set out as notes under section 10b-2 of this title, section 2430 of Title 10, and section 637 of Title 15, and repealing provisions set out as notes under sections 2305, 2401, and 2430 of Title 10, and section 6962 of Title 42]."

1984 Acts. Pub.L. 98–369, Title VII, § 2751, July 18, 1984, 98 Stat. 1203, provided that:

"**(a)** Except as provided in subsection (b), the amendments made by this title [see Short Title note below] shall apply with respect to any solicitation for bids or proposals issued after March 31, 1985.

"**(b)** The amendments made by section 2713 [amending section 759 of former Title 40 and enacting provision set out as a note under former section 759 of Title 40] and subtitle D [enacting sections 3551 to 3556 of Title 31, Money and Finance] shall apply with respect to any protest filed after January 14, 1985."

1949 Acts. Section effective July 1, 1949, see section 605 of Act June 30, 1949, set out as a note under section 471 of Title 40, Public Buildings, Property, and Works.

Transfer of Functions

For transfer of authorities, functions, personnel, and assets of the Coast Guard, including the authorities and functions of the Secretary of Transportation relating thereto, to the Department of Homeland Security, and for treatment of related references, see 6 U.S.C.A. §§ 468(b), 551(d), 552(d) and 557, and the Department of Homeland Security Reorganization Plan of November 25, 2002, as modified, set out as a note under 6 U.S.C.A. § 542.

Severability of Provisions

Act June 30, 1949, 63 Stat. 403, § 604, formerly 504, renumbered by Act Sept. 5, 1950, c. 849, 6(a), (b), 64 Stat. 583, provided that: "If any provision of this Act or the application thereof to any person or circumstances, is held invalid, the remainder of this Act, and the application of such provision to other persons or circumstances, shall not be affected thereby."

Short Title

1996 Amendments. Pub.L. 104–106, Div. D, § 4001, Feb. 10, 1996, 110 Stat. 642, as amended Pub.L. 104–208, Div. A, Title I, § 101(f) [Title VIII, § 808(a)], Sept. 30, 1996, 110 Stat. 3009–393, provided that: "This division [enacting sections 253m, 431, 432, and 433 of this title, and section 2305a of Title 10, Armed Forces, amending sections 11, 15, 22, 43a, 57, 253, 253a, 253b, 254b, 254d, 257, 264a, 265, 403, 404, 405, 410, 416, 421, 422, 423, 425, 427, 428, 601, 605, 612, and 701 of this title, section 11 of Appendix 3 of Title 5, Government Organization & Employees, sections 2220, 2302, 2304, 2305, 2306a, 2323, 2324, 2350b, 2372, 2384, 2400, 2405, 2410b, 2410d, 2410g, 2424, 2431, 2461, 2533, 2539b, 2662, and 2701 of Title 10, sections 637 and 644 of Title 15, Commerce and Trade, section 799 of Title 16, Conservation, section 2761 of Title 22, Foreign Relations and Intercourse, section 721 of Title 29, Labor, and sections 1352, 3551, 3553, and 3554 of Title 31, Money and Finance, redesignating sections 2247 and 2304a as 2249 and 2304e of Title 10, respectively, repealing sections 20a, 20b, 401, 402, 407, and 409 of this title, sections 2397, 2397a, 2397b, and 2397c of Title 10, section 789 of Title 15, section 281 of Title 18, Crimes and Criminal Procedure, and sections 5816a, 5918, 6392, 7211, 7212 and 7218 of Title 42, Public Health and Welfare, enacting provisions set out as notes under sections 251 and 425 of this title, section 11 of Appendix 3 of Title 5, sections 1701, 2304, and 2306a of Title 10, section 2761 of Title 22, and section 481 of Title 40, Public Buildings, Property, and Works, amending provisions set out as notes under sections 10a, 254b, and 413 of this title, section 571 of Title 5, sections 2326, 2401, and 2431 of Title 10, and section 270a of Title 40, and repealing provisions set out as a note under section 2432 of Title 10] and division E [enacting chapter 25 (section 1401 et seq.) of Title 40, Public Buildings, Property, and Works, and section 434 of this title, amending section 5315 of Title 5, Government Organization and Employees, sections 2305, 2306b, and 2315 of Title 10, Armed Forces, section 278g–3 of Title 15, Commerce and Trade, section 612 of Title 28, Judiciary and Judicial Procedure, sections 1558, 3552, 3553, and 3554 of Title 31, Money and Finance, section 310 of Title 38, Veterans' Benefits, sections 253b and 405 of Title 41, section 8287 of Title 42, The Public Health and Welfare, sections 3502, 3504, 3506, 3507, and 3518 of Title 44, Public Printing and Documents, section 40112 of Title 49, Transportation, and section

403c of Title 50, War and National Defense, repealing section 759 of this title, enacting provisions set out as notes under this section] may be cited as the 'Clinger-Cohen Act of 1996'."

1994 Amendments. Pub.L. 103–355, § 1, Oct. 13, 1994, 108 Stat. 3243, provided that: "This Act [see Tables for classification] may be cited as the 'Federal Acquisition Streamlining Act of 1994'."

1984 Amendments. Pub.L. 98–577, § 1, Oct. 30, 1984, 98 Stat. 3066 provided, in part, that this Act [enacting sections 253c to 253g, 414a, 418a and 418b of this title, repealing section 2303a of Title 10, Armed Forces, amending sections 253, 253b, 259, 403, and 416 of this title, sections 637 and 644 of Title 15, Commerce and Trade and sections 2302, 2304, 2311 and 2320 of Title 10, Armed Forces, and enacting provisions set out as notes under sections 251 and 416 of this title and sections 637 and 644 of Title 15, Commerce and Trade] may be cited as the "Small Business and Federal Procurement Competition Enhancement Act of 1984".

Pub.L. 98–369, Title VII, § 2701, July 18, 1984, 98 Stat. 1175, provided that: "This title [enacting sections 253a, 253b, 416–419 of this title and sections 3551–3556 of Title 31, Money and Finance, amending sections 252, 253, 254, 257, 258, 259, 260, 403, 405, and 414 of this title, sections 2301–2306, 2310, 2311, 2313 and 2356 of Title 10, Armed Forces, and section 759 of Title 40, Public Buildings, Property, and Works, and enacting provisions set out as notes under this section and sections 253, 403, and 407 of this title and section 2304 of Title 10, Armed Forces, and section 759 of Title 40, Public Buildings, Property, and Works] may be cited as the 'Competition in Contracting Act of 1984'."

1949 Acts. Act, June 30, 1949, c. 288, § 1(a), 63 Stat. 377, amended Oct. 13, 1994, Pub.L. 103–355, Title X, § 10005(a)(2), 108 Stat. 3406, provided that: "This Act may be cited as the 'Federal Property and Administrative Services Act of 1949'." Title III of the Act is currently classified to this subchapter while the remainder was formerly classified to chapter 10 of former Title 40, 40 U.S.C.A. § 471 et seq., prior to being repealed by Pub.L. 107–217, § 6(b), Aug. 21, 2002, 116 Stat. 1313; see now generally chapter 1 of Title 40, 40 U.S.C.A. § 101 et seq.

[The repeal of section 1(a) by Pub.L. 107–217, § 6(b), Aug. 21, 2002, 116 Stat. 1313, was repealed and "revived to read as if section 6(b) had not been enacted" by Pub.L. 108–178, § 2(b)(1), Dec. 19, 2003, 117 Stat. 2640.]

[Amendments by Pub.L. 108–178 effective August 21, 2002, see Pub.L. 108–178, § 5, set out as a note under 5 U.S.C.A. § 5334.]

Application to Federal Property and Administrative Services Act of 1949

The words "this subtitle" in certain provisions of Title 40 of the United States Code deemed to refer also to Title III of the Federal Property and Administrative Services Act of 1949 (this subchapter), see 40 U.S.C.A. § 111.

Commission on Government Procurement

Pub.L. 91–129, Nov. 26, 1969, 83 Stat. 269, as amended Pub.L. 92–47, July 9, 1971, 85 Stat. 102, established the Commission on Government Procurement, which was to study and investigate statutes, rules, regulations, procedures, and practices affecting Government procurement and to submit a final report to Congress on or before Dec. 31, 1972, on the results of this study, including recommendations for changes designed to promote economy, efficiency, and effectiveness in the procurement of goods, services, and facilities by and for the executive branch of the Government. The Commission terminated 120 days after submission of the final report.

Congressional Statement of Purpose

Pub.L. 98–577, Title I, § 101, Oct. 30, 1984, 98 Stat. 3066, provided that: "The purposes of this Act [see Short Title note above] are to—

"**(1)** eliminate procurement procedures and practices that unnecessarily inhibit full and open competition for contracts;

"**(2)** promote the use of contracting opportunities as a means to expand the industrial base of the United States in order to ensure adequate responsive capability of the economy to the increased demands of the Government in times of national emergency; and

"**(3)** foster opportunities for the increased participation in the competitive procurement process of small business concerns and small business concerns owned and controlled by socially and economically disadvantaged individuals."

Definitions

The definitions in 40 U.S.C.A. § 102 apply to terms appearing in this subchapter.

Evaluation by the Comptroller General

Pub.L. 103–355, Title X, § 10003, Oct. 13, 1994, 108 Stat. 3405, provided that:

"(a) **Evaluation relating to issuance of regulations.**—Not later than 180 days after the issuance in final form of revisions to the Federal Acquisition Regulation pursuant to section 10002 [section 10002 of Pub.L. 103–355, set out as a note under this section], the Comptroller General shall submit to Congress a report evaluating compliance with such section.

"(b) **Evaluation of implementation of regulations.**—Not later than 18 months after issuance in final form of revisions to the Federal Acquisition Regulation pursuant to section 10002 [section 10002 of Pub.L. 103–355, set out as a note under this section], the Comptroller General shall submit to the committees referred to in subsection (c) a report evaluating the effectiveness of the regulations implementing this Act in streamlining the acquisition system and fulfilling the other purposes of this Act [Pub.L. 103–355, Oct. 13, 1994, 108 Stat. 3243, the Federal Acquisition Streamlining Act of 1994, for classification of which to the Code, see Short Title note set out under this section and Tables].

"(c) **Committees designated to receive the reports.**—The Comptroller General shall submit the reports required by this section to—

"(1) the Committees on Governmental Affairs, on Armed Services, and on Small Business of the Senate; and

"(2) the Committees on Government Operations, on Armed Services, and on Small Business of the House of Representatives."

[Any reference in any provision of law enacted before Jan. 4, 1995, to the Committee on Government Operations of the House of Representatives treated as referring to the Committee on Government Reform and Oversight of the House of Representatives, except that any reference in any provision of law enacted before Jan. 4, 1995, to the Committee on Government Operations of the House of Representatives treated as referring to the Committee on the Budget of the House of Representatives in the case of a provision of law relating to the establishment, extension, and enforcement of special controls over the Federal budget, see section 1(a)(6) and (c)(2) of Pub.L. 104–14, set out as a note preceding section 21 of Title 2, The Congress.]

Implementing Regulations for Pub.L. 104–106

Section 4402 of Pub.L. 104–106 provided that:

"(a) **Proposed revisions.**—Proposed revisions to the Federal Acquisition Regulation and such other proposed regulations (or revisions to existing regulations) as may be necessary to implement this Act [the National Defense Authorization Act for Fiscal Year 1996, Pub.L. 104–106, Feb. 10, 1996, 110 Stat. 186, for classification of which to the Code, see Tables] shall be published in the Federal Register not later than 210 days after the date of the enactment of this Act [Feb. 10, 1996].

"(b) **Public comment.**—The proposed regulations described in subsection (a) shall be made available for public comment for a period of not less than 60 days.

"(c) **Final regulations.**—Final regulations shall be published in the Federal Register not later than 330 days after the date of enactment of this Act [Feb. 10, 1996].

"(d) **Modifications.**—Final regulations promulgated pursuant to this section to implement an amendment made by this Act may provide for modification of an existing contract without consideration upon the request of the contractor.

"(e) **Savings provisions.—**

"(1) **Validity of prior actions.**—Nothing in this division [Division D of Pub.L. 104–106, Feb. 10, 1996, 110 Stat. 642, as amended Pub.L. 104–208, Title I, § 101(f) [Title VIII, § 808(c)], Sept. 30, 1996, 110 Stat. 3009–394, the Clinger-Cohen Act of 1996, for classification of which to the Code, see Short Title note set out under this section] shall be construed to affect the validity of any action taken or any contract entered into before the date specified in the regulations pursuant to section 4401(b)(3) [section 4401(b)(3) of Pub.L.

104–106, set out as a note under this section] except to the extent and in the manner prescribed in such regulations.

"**(2) Renegotiation and modification of preexisting contracts.**—Except as specifically provided in this division, nothing in this division shall be construed to require the renegotiation or modification of contracts in existence on the date of the enactment of this Act [Feb. 10, 1996].

"**(3) Continued applicability of preexisting law.**—Except as otherwise provided in this division [Division D of Pub.L. 104–106, Feb. 10, 1996, 110 Stat. 642, as amended Pub.L. 104–208, Title I, § 101(f) [Title VIII, § 808(c)], Sept. 30, 1996, 110 Stat. 3009–394, the Clinger-Cohen Act of 1996, for classification of which to the Code, see Short Title note set out under this section], a law amended by this division shall continue to be applied according to the provisions thereof as such law was in effect on the day before the date of the enactment of this Act [Feb. 10, 1996] until—

"**(A)** the date specified in final regulations implementing the amendment of that law (as promulgated pursuant to this section); or

"**(B)** if no such date is specified in regulations, January 1, 1997."

Implementing Regulations for Pub.L. 103–355

Pub.L. 103–355, Title X, § 10002, Oct. 13, 1994, 108 Stat. 3404, provided that:

"**(a) Proposed revisions.**—Proposed revisions to the Federal Acquisition Regulation and such other proposed regulations (or revisions to existing regulations) as may be necessary to implement this Act [Pub.L. 103–355, Oct. 13, 1994, 108 Stat. 3243, the Federal Acquisition Streamlining Act of 1994, for classification of which to the Code, see Short Title note set out under this section and Tables] shall be published in the Federal Register not later than 210 days after the date of the enactment of this Act.[Oct. 13, 1994].

"**(b) Public comment.**—The proposed regulations described in subsection (a) shall be made available for public comment for a period of not less than 60 days.

"**(c) Final regulations.**—Final regulations shall be published in the Federal Register not later than 330 days after the date of enactment of this Act [Oct. 13, 1994].

"**(d) Modifications.**—Final regulations promulgated pursuant to this section to implement an amendment made by this Act [Pub.L. 103–355, Oct. 13, 1994, 108 Stat. 3243, for classification of which to the Code, see Short Title note set out under this section and Tables] may provide for modification of an existing contract without consideration upon the request of the contractor.

"**(e) Requirement for clarity.**—Officers and employees of the Federal Government who prescribe regulations to implement this Act and the amendments made by this Act [Pub.L. 103–355, Oct. 13, 1994, 108 Stat. 3243, for classification of which to the Code, see Short Title note set out under this section and Tables] shall make every effort practicable to ensure that the regulations are concise and are easily understandable by potential offerors as well as by Government officials.

"**(f) Savings provisions.**—(1) Nothing in this Act [Pub.L. 103–355, Oct. 13, 1994, 108 Stat. 3243, for classification of which to the Code, see Short Title note set out under this section and Tables] shall be construed to affect the validity of any action taken or any contract entered into before the date specified in the regulations pursuant to section 10001(b)(3) [section 10001(b)(3) of Pub.L. 103–355, set out as a note under this section] except to the extent and in the manner prescribed in such regulations.

"**(2)** Except as specifically provided in this Act, nothing in this Act [Pub.L. 103–355, Oct. 13, 1994, 108 Stat. 3243, for classification of which to the Code, see Short Title note set out under this section and Tables] shall be construed to require the renegotiation or modification of contracts in existence on the date of the enactment of this Act [Oct. 13, 1994].

"**(3)** Except as otherwise provided in this Act, a law amended by this Act [Pub.L. 103–355, Oct. 13, 1994, 108 Stat. 3243, for classification of which to the Code, see Short Title note set out under this section and Tables] shall continue to be applied according to the provisions thereof as such law was in effect on the day before the date of the enactment of this Act [Oct. 13, 1994] until—

"**(A)** the date specified in final regulations implementing the amendment of that law (as promulgated pursuant to this section); or

"**(B)** if no such date is specified in regulations, October 1, 1995."

EXECUTIVE ORDERS
EXECUTIVE ORDER NO. 13005

May 21, 1996, 61 F.R. 26069

EMPOWERMENT CONTRACTING

In order to promote economy and efficiency in Federal procurement, it is necessary to secure broad-based competition for Federal contracts. This broad competition is best achieved where there is an expansive pool of potential contractors capable of producing quality goods and services at competitive prices. A great and largely untapped opportunity for expanding the pool of such contractors can be found in this Nation's economically distressed communities.

Fostering growth of Federal contractors in economically distressed communities and ensuring that those contractors become viable businesses for the long term will promote economy and efficiency in Federal procurement and help to empower those communities. Fostering growth of long-term viable contractors will be promoted by offering appropriate incentives to qualified businesses.

Accordingly, by the authority vested in me as President by the Constitution and the laws of the United States, including section 486(a) of title 40, United States Code [see now 40 U.S.C.A. § 121(a)], and section 301 of title 3, United States Code [3 U.S.C.A. § 301], it is hereby ordered as follows:

Section 1. Policy. The purpose of this order is to strengthen the economy and to improve the efficiency of the Federal procurement system by encouraging business development that expands the industrial base and increases competition.

Sec. 2. Empowerment Contracting Program. In consultation with the Secretaries of the Departments of Housing and Urban Development, Labor, and Defense; the Administrator of General Services; the Administrator of the National Aeronautics and Space Administration; the Administrator of the Small Business Administration; and the Administrator for Federal Procurement Policy, the Secretary of the Department

of Commerce shall develop policies and procedures to ensure that agencies, to the extent permitted by law, grant qualified large businesses and qualified small businesses appropriate incentives to encourage business activity in areas of general economic distress, including a price or an evaluation credit, when assessing offers for government contracts in unrestricted competitions, where the incentives would promote the policy set forth in this order. In developing such policies and procedures, the Secretary shall consider the size of the qualified businesses.

Sec. 3. Monitoring and Evaluation. The Secretary shall:

(a) monitor the implementation and operation of the policies and procedures developed in accordance with this order;

(b) develop a process to ensure the proper administration of the program and to reduce the potential for fraud by the intended beneficiaries of the program;

(c) develop principles and a process to evaluate the effectiveness of the policies and procedures developed in accordance with this order; and

(d) by December 1 of each year, issue a report to the President on the status and effectiveness of the program.

Sec. 4. Implementation Guidelines. In implementing this order, the Secretary shall:

(a) issue rules, regulations, and guidelines necessary to implement this order, including a requirement for the periodic review of the eligibility of qualified businesses and distressed areas;

(b) draft all rules, regulations, and guidelines necessary to implement this order within 90 days of the date of this order; and

(c) ensure that all policies and procedures and all rules, regulations, and guidelines adopted and implemented in accordance with this order minimize the administrative burden on affected agencies and the procurement process.

Sec. 5. Definitions. For purposes of this Executive order:

(a) "Agency" means any authority of the United States that is an "agency" under 44 U.S.C. 3502(1), other than those considered to be independent regulatory agencies, as defined in 44 U.S.C. 3502(10).

(b) "Area of general economic distress" shall be defined, for all urban and rural communities, as any census tract that has a poverty rate of at least 20 percent or any designated Federal Empowerment Zone, Supplemental Empowerment Zone, Enhanced Enterprise Community, or Enterprise Community. In addition, the Secretary may designate as an area of general economic distress any additional rural or Indian reservation area after considering the following factors:

(1) Unemployment rate;

(2) Degree of poverty;

(3) Extent of outmigration; and

(4) Rate of business formation and rate of business growth.

(c) "Qualified large business" means a large for-profit or not-for-profit trade or business that (1) employs a significant number of residents from the area of gen-eral economic distress; and (2) either has a significant physical presence in the area of general economic distress or has a direct impact on generating significant economic activity in the area of general economic distress.

(d) "Qualified small business" means a small for-profit or not-for-profit trade or business that (1) employs a significant number of residents from the area of general economic distress; (2) has a significant physical presence in the area of general economic distress; or (3) has a direct impact on generating significant economic activity in the area of general economic distress.

(e) "Secretary" means the Secretary of Commerce.

Sec. 6. Agency Authority. Nothing in this Executive order shall be construed as displacing the agencies' authority or responsibilities, as authorized by law, including specifically other programs designed to promote the development of small or disadvantaged businesses.

Sec. 7. Judicial Review. This Executive order does not create any right or benefit, substantive or procedural, enforceable at law or equity by a party against the United States, its agencies or instrumentalities, its officers or employees, or any other person.

WILLIAM J. CLINTON

EXECUTIVE ORDER NO. 13202

Feb. 17, 2001, 66 F.R. 11225, as amended by Ex.Ord. No. 13208, 66 F.R. 18717, Apr. 6, 2001

PRESERVATION OF OPEN COMPETITION AND GOVERNMENT NEUTRALITY TOWARDS GOVERNMENT CONTRACTORS' LABOR RELATIONS ON FEDERAL AND FEDERALLY FUNDED CONSTRUCTION PROJECTS

By the authority vested in me as President by the Constitution and laws of the United States of America, including the Federal Property and Administrative Services Act, 40 U.S.C. 471 et seq. [currently classified to subchapter IV of chapter 4 of Title 41, 41 U.S.C.A. § 251 et seq., and formerly classified to chapter 10 of former Title 40, 40 U.S.C.A. § 471 et seq., which was repealed by Pub.L. 107–217, § 6(b), Aug. 21, 2002, 116 Stat. 1313; see now generally chapter 1 of Title 40, 40 U.S.C.A. § 101 et seq.], and in order to (1) promote and ensure open competi-tion on Federal and federally funded or assisted construction projects; (2) maintain Government neutrality towards Government contractors' labor relations on Federal and federally funded or assisted construction projects; (3) reduce construction costs to the Federal Government and to the taxpayers; (4) expand job opportunities, especially for small and disadvantaged businesses; and (5) prevent discrimination against Government contractors or their employees based upon labor affiliation or lack thereof; thereby promoting the economical, nondiscriminatory, and efficient administration and completion of Federal and federally funded or assisted construction projects, it is hereby ordered that:

Section 1. To the extent permitted by law, any executive agency awarding any construction contract after the date of this order, or obligating funds pursuant to such a contract, shall ensure that neither the awarding Government authority nor any construction manager acting on behalf of the Government shall, in its bid specifications, project agreements, or other controlling documents:

(a) Require or prohibit bidders, offerors, contractors, or subcontractors to enter into or adhere to agreements with one or more labor organizations, on the same or other related construction project(s); or

(b) Otherwise discriminate against bidders, offerors, contractors, or subcontractors for becoming or refusing to become or remain signatories or otherwise to adhere to agreements with one or more labor organizations, on the same or other related construction project(s).

(c) Nothing in this section shall prohibit contractors or subcontractors from voluntarily entering into agreements described in subsection (a).

Sec. 2. Contracts awarded before the date of this order, and subcontracts awarded pursuant to such contracts, whenever awarded, shall not be governed by this order.

Sec. 3. To the extent permitted by law, any executive agency issuing grants, providing financial assistance, or entering into cooperative agreements for construction projects, shall ensure that neither the bid specifications, project agreements, nor other controlling documents for construction contracts awarded after the date of this order by recipients of grants or financial assistance or by parties to cooperative agreements, nor those of any construction manager acting on their behalf, shall contain any of the requirements or prohibitions set forth in section 1(a) or (b) of this order.

Sec. 4. In the event that an awarding authority, a recipient of grants or financial assistance, a party to a cooperative agreement, or a construction manager acting on behalf of the foregoing, performs in a manner contrary to the provisions of sections 1 or 3 of this order, the executive agency awarding the contract, grant, or assistance shall take such action, consistent with law and regulation, as the agency determines may be appropriate.

Sec. 5. (a) The head of an executive agency may exempt a particular project, contract, subcontract, grant, or cooperative agreement from the requirements of any or all of the provisions of sections 1 and 3 of this order, if the agency head finds that special circumstances require an exemption in order to avert an imminent threat to public health or safety or to serve the national security.

(b) A finding of "special circumstances" under section 5(a) may not be based on the possibility or presence of a labor dispute concerning the use of contractors or subcontractors who are nonsignatories to, or otherwise do not adhere to, agreements with one or more labor organizations, or concerning employees on the project who are not members of or affiliated with a labor organization.

(c) The head of an executive agency, upon application of an awarding authority, a recipient of grants or financial assistance, a party to a cooperative agreement, or a construction manager acting on behalf of the foregoing, may exempt a particular project from the requirements of any or all of the provisions of sections 1 and 3 of this order, if the agency head finds: (i) that the awarding authority, recipient of grants or financial assistance, party to a cooperative agreement, or construction manager acting on behalf of the foregoing had issued or was a party to, as of the date of this order, bid specifications, project agreements, agreements with one or more labor organizations, or other controlling documents with respect to that particular project, which contained any of the requirements or prohibitions set forth in sections 1(a) or (b) of this order; and (ii) that one or more construction contracts subject to such requirements or prohibitions had been awarded as of the date of this order.

Sec. 6. (a) The term "construction contract" as used in this order means any contract for the construction, rehabilitation, alteration, conversion, extension, or repair of buildings, highways, or other improvements to real property.

(b) The term "executive agency" as used in this order shall have the same meaning it has in 5 U.S.C. 105, excluding the General Accounting Office [now Government Accountability Office].

(c) The term "labor organization" as used in this order shall have the same meaning it has in 42 U.S.C. 2000e(d).

Sec. 7. With respect to Federal contracts, within 60 days of the issuance of this order, the Federal Acquisition Regulatory Council shall take whatever action is required to amend the Federal Acquisition Regulation in order to implement the provisions of this order.

Sec. 8. As it relates to project agreements, Executive Order 12836 of February 1, 1993 [41 U.S.C.A. § 401 note], which, among other things, revoked Executive Order 12818 of October 23, 1992 [41 U.S.C.A. § 401 note], is revoked.

Sec. 9. The Presidential Memorandum of June 5, 1997, entitled "Use of Project Labor Agreements for Federal Construction Projects" (the "Memorandum"), is also revoked.

Sec. 10. The heads of executive departments and agencies shall revoke expeditiously any orders, rules, regulations, guidelines, or policies implementing or enforcing the Memorandum or Executive Order 12836 of February 1, 1993, as it relates to project agreements, to the extent consistent with law.

Sec. 11. This order is intended only to improve the internal management of the executive branch and is not intended to, nor does it, create any right to administrative or judicial review, or any right, whether substantive or procedural, enforce able by any party against the United States, its agencies or instrumentalities, its officers or employees, or any other person.

GEORGE W. BUSH

LAW REVIEW AND JOURNAL COMMENTARIES

Free speech and due process in the workplace. Cynthia L. Estlund, 71 Ind.L.J. 101 (1995).

LIBRARY REFERENCES

American Digest System

United States ☞55, 59.
Key Number System Topic No. 393.

Research References

ALR Library

30 ALR, Fed. 355, Recovery from United States of Costs Incurred by Unsuccessful Bidder in Preparing and Submitting Contract Bid in Response to Government Solicitation.

23 ALR, Fed. 301, Standing of Unsuccessful Bidder for Federal Procurement Contract to Seek Judicial Review of Award.

Encyclopedias

Am. Jur. 2d Public Works and Contracts § 17, Federal Procurement and Contracts.

14 Am. Jur. Trials 437, Representing the Government Contractor.

Forms

Federal Procedural Forms § 34:1, Introduction to the Far.

Federal Procedural Forms § 34:4, Procedures to Promote Competition--Contracting Without Open Competition.

Treatises and Practice Aids

Federal Procedure, Lawyers Edition § 14:297, Who May Condemn; When and What Property May Be Condemned.

Federal Procedure, Lawyers Edition § 39:1, Introduction to the Federal Acquisition Regulations System.

West's Federal Administrative Practice § 607, Procurement Regulations.

WESTLAW ELECTRONIC RESEARCH

See Westlaw guide following the Explanation pages of this volume.

§ 252. Purchases and contracts for property

(a) Applicability of subchapter; delegation of authority

Executive agencies shall make purchases and contracts for property and services in accordance with the provisions of this subchapter and implementing regulations of the Administrator; but this subchapter does not apply—

    (1) to the Department of Defense, the Coast Guard, and the National Aeronautics and Space Administration; or

    (2) when this subchapter is made inapplicable pursuant to section 113(e) of Title 40 or any other law, but when this subchapter is made inapplicable by any such provision of law, sections 5 and 8 of this title shall be applicable in the absence of authority conferred by statute to procure without advertising or without regard to said section 5 of this title.

(b) Small business concerns; share of business

It is the declared policy of the Congress that a fair proportion of the total purchases and contracts for property and services for the Government shall be placed with small business concerns.

(c) Authorization of erection, repair, or furnishing of public buildings or improvements; contracts for construction or repair of buildings, roads, sidewalks, sewers, mains, etc.; Federal Lands Highway Program

(1) This subchapter does not (A) authorize the erection, repair, or furnishing of any public building or public improvement, but such authorization shall be required in the same manner as heretofore, or (B) permit any contract for the construction or repair of buildings, roads, sidewalks, sewers, mains, or similar items using procedures other than sealed-bid procedures under section 253(a)(2)(A) of this title, if the conditions set forth in section 253(a)(2)(A) of this title apply or the contract is to be performed outside the United States.

(2) Section 253(a)(2)(A) of this title does not require the use of sealed-bid procedures in cases in which section 204(e) of Title 23 applies.

(June 30, 1949, c. 288, Title III, § 302, 63 Stat. 393; July 12, 1952, c. 703, § 1(m), 66 Stat. 594; Aug. 28, 1958, Pub.L. 85–800, §§ 1–3, 72 Stat. 966; Nov. 8, 1965, Pub.L. 89–343, §§ 1, 2, 79 Stat. 1303; Nov. 8, 1965, Pub.L. 89–348, § 1(2), 79 Stat. 1310; Mar. 16, 1968, Pub.L. 90–268, § 4, 82 Stat.

50; July 25, 1974, Pub.L. 93–356, § 3, 88 Stat. 390; Dec. 1, 1983, Pub.L. 98–191, § 9(a)(1), 97 Stat. 1331; July 18, 1984, Pub.L. 98–369, Div. B, Title VII, § 2714(a)(1), 98 Stat. 1184.)

HISTORICAL AND STATUTORY NOTES

Revision Notes and Legislative Reports

1958 Acts. Senate Report No. 2201, see 1958 U.S.Code Cong. and Adm.News, p. 4021.

1965 Acts. House Report No. 1169, see 1965 U.S.Code Cong. and Adm.News, p. 4243.

House Report No. 1166, see 1965 U.S.Code Cong. and Adm.News, p. 4217.

1968 Acts. House Report No. 991, see 1968 U.S.Code Cong. and Adm.News, p. 1747.

1974 Acts. Senate Report No. 93–901, see 1974 U.S.Code Cong. and Adm.News, p. 3913.

1983 Acts. Senate Report No. 98–214, see 1983 U.S.Code Cong. and Adm.News, p. 2027.

1984 Acts. House Report No. 98–432, Pt. II, Senate Report Nos. 98–50 and 98–297, and House Conference Report No. 98–861, see 1984 U.S.Code Cong. and Adm.News, p. 697.

Codifications

In subsec. (a)(2), "section 113(e) of Title 40" substituted for "section 474(d) of Title 40", which originally read "section 602(d) of this Act", on authority of Pub.L. 107–217, § 5(c), Aug. 21, 2002, 116 Stat. 1301, which is set out as a note preceding 40 U.S.C.A. § 101. Pub.L. 107–217, § 1, enacted Title 40 into positive law. Section 602(d) of this Act means June 30, 1949, c. 288, Title VI, § 602d), formerly Title V, § 502(d), 63 Stat. 399, which was classified to former 40 U.S.C.A. § 474(d), prior to being repealed by Pub.L. 107–217, § 6(b), Aug. 21, 2002, 116 Stat. 1313, and its substance reenacted as 40 U.S.C.A. § 113(e).

Amendments

1984 Amendments. Subsec. (b). Pub.L. 98–369, § 2714(a)(1)(A), struck out provisions that whenever it was proposed to make a contract or purchase in excess of $10,000 by negotiation and without advertising, pursuant to the authority of subsec. (c)(7), of this section, suitable advance publicity, as determined by the agency head with due regard to the type of property involved and other relevant considerations, had to be given for a period of at least fifteen days, wherever practicable, as determined by the agency head.

Subsec. (c)(1). Pub.L. 98–369, § 2714(a)(1)(B), redesignated former subsec. (e) as (c)(1), and in subsec. (c)(1) as so redesignated substituted reference to this subchapter for reference to this section in provisions preceding subpar. (A), in subpar. (B), substituted provisions relating to contracts using procedures other than sealed-bid procedures under section 253(a)(2)(A) of this title for provisions relating to contracts negotiated without advertising as required by section 253 of this title, and struck out former subsec. (c), which related to conditions for negotiated purchases and contracts for property.

Subsec. (c)(2). Pub.L. 98–369, § 2714(a)(1)(B), added par. (2).

Subsec. (d). Pub.L. 98–369, § 2714(a)(1)(B), struck out subsec. (d), which related to bids in violation of the antitrust laws.

Subsec. (e). Pub.L. 98–369, § 2714(a)(1)(B), redesignated former subsec. (e) as (c)(1).

Subsec. (f). Pub.L. 98–369, § 2714(a)(1)(B), struck out subsec. (f), which related to specification of container size in contracts for the carriage of Government property in other than Government-owned cargo containers.

1983 Amendments. Subsec. (c)(3). Pub.L. 98–191 substituted "$25,000" for "$10,000".

1974 Amendments. Subsec. (c)(3). Pub.L. 93–356 substituted "$10,000" for "$2,500".

1968 Amendments. Subsec. (f). Pub.L. 90–268 added subsec. (f).

1965 Amendments. Subsec. (a). Pub.L. 89–343, § 1, substituted provisions requiring executive agencies to make purchases and contracts for property and services in accordance with the provisions of this subchapter and implementing regulations of the Administrator, exempting the Department of Defense, the Coast Guard, and the National Aeronautics and Space Administration from the application of this subchapter, and making this subchapter inapplicable when it is so made by law, for provisions which made this subchapter applicable to purchases and contracts for property or services made by the General Services Administration for the use of such agency or otherwise, or by any other executive agency (except the departments and activities specified in section 2303(a) of Title 10) in conformity with authority to apply such provisions delegated by the Administrator in his discretion.

Subsec. (c)(11). Pub.L. 89–348 deleted the proviso which required a semiannual report to be furnished to the Congress setting forth the name of each contractor with whom a contract has been entered into pursuant to this paragraph, the amount of the contract, and, with due consideration given to the national security, a description of the work required to be performed thereunder.

Subsec. (c)(15). Pub.L. 89–343, § 2, inserted "except that section 254 of this title shall apply to purchases and contracts made without advertising under this paragraph".

1958   Amendments. Subsec.   (a). Pub.L. 85–800, § 1, among other changes, substituted "or" for "and" in par. (1), substituted provisions excepting application of subchapter to departments and activities in section 2303(a) of Title 10, for provisions which excepted agencies named in section 151(a) of this title, substituted provisions applying subchapter to agencies in conformity with authority delegated by Administrator in his discretion for provisions which applied subchapter in conformity with authority delegated him pursuant to this subsection, and eliminated provisions authorizing Administrator to delegate authority for use of two or more agencies, and other cases where delegation is advantageous to Government in par. (2).

Subsec. (c). Pub.L. 85–800, § 2, substituted in par. (3) "$2,500" for "$1,000", eliminated proviso barring agencies other than General Services Administration from making purchases in excess of $500 except under authority to procure for two or more agencies, added par. (9), and renumbered former pars. (9) to (14) as pars. (10) to (15).

Subsec. (e). Pub.L. 85–800, § 3, substituted "(10) to (12), or (14)" for "(9) to (11), or (13)".

1952 Amendments. Subsecs. (a) to (c). Act July 12, 1952 substituted "property" for "supplies" wherever appearing.

Effective and Applicability Provisions

1984   Acts. Amendment   by   Pub.L. 98–369 applicable with respect to any solicitation for bids or proposals issued after Mar. 31, 1985, see section 2751(a) of Pub.L. 98–369, set out as a note under section 251 of this title.

1949 Acts. Act June 30, 1949, § 605, which set July 1, 1949, as the effective date for this section, was repealed by Pub.L. 107–217, § 6(b), Aug. 21, 2002, 116 Stat. 1313.

Definitions

The definitions in 40 U.S.C.A. § 102 apply to terms appearing in this subchapter.

Non-Applicability of National Emergencies Act

The provisions of the National Emergencies Act, Pub.L. 94–412, Sept. 14, 1976, 90 Stat. 1255, not applicable to the powers and authorities conferred by this section and actions taken hereunder, see 50 U.S.C.A. § 1651.

Emergency Relief for Small Business Concerns with Government Contracts

Pub.L. 94–190, Dec. 31, 1975, 89 Stat. 1095, provided:

"SHORT TITLE

"**Section 1.**   This Act may be cited as the 'Small Business Emergency Relief Act'.

"POLICY

"**Sec. 2.**   It is the policy of Congress to provide relief to small business concerns which have fixed-price Government contracts in cases where such concerns have suffered or can be expected to suffer serious financial loss because of significant and unavoidable difficulties during performance because of the energy crises or rapid and unexpected escalations of contract costs.

"DEFINITIONS

"**Sec. 3.**   As used in this Act—

"(1) the term 'executive agency' means an executive department, a military department, and an independent establishment within the meaning of sections 101, 102, and 104(1) respectively, of title 5, United States Code, and also a wholly owned Government corporation within the meaning of section 101 of the Government Corporation Control Act [section 9101(3) of Title 31, Money and Finance]; and

"(2) the term 'small business concern' means any concern which falls under the size limitations of the 'Small Business Administrator's Definitions of Small Business for Government Procurement'.

"AUTHORITY

"Sec. 4. (a) Pursuant to an application by a small business concern, the head of any executive agency may terminate for the convenience of the Government any fixed-price contract between that agency and such small business concern, upon a finding that—

"(1) during the performance of the contract, the concern has suffered or can be expected to suffer serious financial loss due to significant unanticipated cost increases directly affecting the cost of contract compliance; and

"(2) the conditions which have caused or are causing such cost increases were, or are being, experienced generally by other small business concerns in the market, at the same time and are not caused by negligence, underbidding, or other special management factors peculiar to that small business concern.

"(b) Upon application under subsection (a) by a small business concern to terminate a fixed-price contract between an executive agency and such small business concern, the head of the executive agency may modify the terms of the contract in lieu of termination for the convenience of the Government only if he finds after review of the application that—

"(1)(a) the agency would reprocure the supplies or services in the event that the contract was terminated for the convenience of the Government; and

"(b) the cost of terminating the contract for the convenience of the Government plus the cost of reprocurement would exceed the amount of the contract as modified; and

"(2) Any such modification shall be made in compliance with cost comparison and compensation guidelines to be issued by the Administrator of the Office of Federal Procurement Policy. Such cost comparison and compensation guidelines shall be promulgated by the Administrator not later than 10 days after enactment of this Act [December 31, 1975].

"(c) If a small business concern in performance of a fixed-price Government contract experiences or has experienced shortages of energy, petroleum products, or products or components manufactured or derived therefrom or impacted thereby, and such shortages result in a delay in the performance of a contract, the head of the agency, or his designee, shall provide by modification to the contract for an appropriate extension of the contract delivery date or period of performance.

"(d) A small business concern requesting relief under subsection (a) shall support that request with the following documentation and certification:

"(1) a brief description of the contract, indicating the date of execution and of any amendment thereto, the items being procured, the price and delivery schedule, and any revision thereof, and any other special contractual provision as may be relevant to the request;

"(2) a history of performance indicating when work under the contract or commitment was begun, the progress made as of the date of the application, an exact statement of the contractor's remaining obligations, and the contractor's expectations regarding completion thereof;

"(3) a statement of the factors which have caused the loss under the contract;

"(4) a statement as to the course of events anticipated if the request is denied;

"(5) a statement of payments received, payments due and payments yet to be received or to become due, including advance and progress payments, and amounts withheld by the Government, and information as to other obligations of the Government, if any, which are yet to be performed under the contract;

"(6) a statement and evidence of the contractor's original breakdown of estimated costs, including contingency allowances and profit;

"(7) a statement and evidence of the contractor's present estimate of total costs under the contract if enabled to complete, broken down between costs accrued to date of request, and runout costs, and as between costs for which the contractor has made payment and those for which he is indebted at the time of the request;

"(8) a statement and evidence of the contractor's estimate of the final price of the contract, giving effect to all escalation, changes, extras, and other comparable factors known or contemplated by the contractor;

"(9) a statement of any claims known or contemplated by the contractor against the Government involving the contract in question, other than those referred to under (8) above;

"(10) an estimate of the contractor's total profit or loss under the contract if required to complete at the original contract price;

"(11) an estimate of the total profits from other Government business, and all other sources, during the period from the date of the first contract involved to the latest estimated date of completion of any other contracts involved;

"(12) balance sheets, certified by a certified public accountant, as of the end of the contractor's fiscal year first preceding the date of the first contract, as of the end of each subsequent fiscal year, and as of the date of the request together with income statements for annual periods subsequent to the date of the first balance sheet; and

"(13) a list of all salaries, bonuses, and all other forms of compensation of the principal officers or partners and of all dividends and other withdrawals, and all payments to stockholders in any form since the date of the first contract involved.

"DELEGATION

"Sec. 5.   The head of each executive agency shall delegate authority conferred by this Act, to the extent practicable, to an appropriate level that will permit the expeditious processing of applications under this Act and to insure the uniformity of its application.

"LIMITATIONS

"Sec. 6.   (a) The authority prescribed in section 4(a) shall apply only to contracts which have not been completely performed or otherwise terminated and which were entered into during the period from August 15, 1971, through October 31, 1974.

"(b) The authority conferred by section 4(a) of this Act shall terminate September 30, 1976."

EXECUTIVE ORDERS

EXECUTIVE ORDER NO. 10936

Ex. Ord. No. 10936, Apr. 24, 1961, 26 F.R. 355, which provided for the reporting and investigation of identical bids in connection with the procurement of goods or services, was revoked by Ex. Ord. No. 12430, July 6, 1983, 48 F.R. 31371.

CROSS REFERENCES

Armed services procurement generally, see 10 USCA § 2302 et seq.
Bonneville Dam Project, purchase of supplies and services for, see 16 USCA § 832g.
Laws not applicable to procurement of property or services made pursuant to this subchapter, see 41 USCA § 260.
National Emergencies Act not applicable to powers and authorities conferred by this section and actions taken hereunder, see 50 USCA § 1651.
Small business concerns, availability of information, see 15 USCA § 637b.

CODE OF FEDERAL REGULATIONS

Emergency relief program, Federal Highway Administration, see 23 CFR § 668.101 et seq.

LIBRARY REFERENCES

American Digest System
   United States ⊙55, 59, 64.15.
   Key Number System Topic No. 393.

Research References

ALR Library
   60 ALR, Fed. 263, Requirement Under Defense Procurement and General Procurement Statutes (10 U.S.C.A. § 2306(B); 41 U.S.C.A. § 254(A)) and Regulations Promulgated Thereunder (32 CFR §§ 1-1500 et seq.; 41 CFR
   §§ 1-1.500 et seq.) That Government Contract for Property and Services
   Contain Warranty Against Commissions or Contingent Fees.

Encyclopedias
   Am. Jur. 2d Public Works and Contracts § 52, Generally; Invitation and Advertisement for and Solicitation of Bids.
   14 Am. Jur. Trials 437, Representing the Government Contractor.

Forms
   Federal Procedural Forms § 34:1, Introduction to the FAR.

Treatises and Practice Aids
   West's Federal Administrative Practice § 618, Small Business--Contract Award
   Preference.

WESTLAW ELECTRONIC RESEARCH

See Westlaw guide following the Explanation pages of this volume.

Notes of Decisions

Construction with other laws 1
Contracts within section 3
Department of Defense exemption 5
Duty of agency 2
Executive agency 4
Social or economic objectives 6
Trust as procurement agent 7

1. Construction with other laws

Procurements for prestige proof coin set containing Statue of Liberty-related and regular coins was governed by the Statue of Liberty-Ellis Island Commemorative Coin Act rather than by the Competition in Contracting Act, and thus, federal court did not have subject matter jurisdiction over action to enjoin execution of sole-source contract for packaging of the prestige proof sets, where contract number that was related to Statue of Liberty program, marketing emphasis, and allocation of funds received established overwhelmingly that prestige proof set was special proof set containing regular coins rather than regular proof set that contained special coins. Design Pak, Inc. v. Baker, D.Mass.1986, 639 F.Supp. 301. Federal Courts ⊙ 232

2. Duty of agency

Secretary of the Air Force is required to follow procedures and practices prescribed by Congress in making procurement contracts. Hayes Intern. Corp. v. McLucas, C.A.5 (Ala.) 1975, 509 F.2d 247, certiorari denied 96 S.Ct. 123, 423 U.S. 864, 46 L.Ed.2d 92. United States ⊙ 63

3. Contracts within section

Trust formed by Federal Aviation Administration, as operator of airport, to purchase ground transportation buses for use at airport with funds contributed by airlines in return for Administration's waiver of landing and mobile fees, was public in character, and contract for supply of buses was subject to federal procurement guidelines. Motor Coach Industries, Inc. v. Dole, C.A.4 (Va.) 1984, 725 F.2d 958.

Broad concession granting authority of the Secretary of the Interior did not relieve the National Park Service of the duty of complying with this section and implementing regulations in contracting with concessioner for transportation services within national park. Yosemite Park and Curry Co. v. U.S., Ct.Cl.1978,

582 F.2d 552, 217 Ct.Cl. 360. United States ☞ 66

Health Care Financing Administration (HCFA) did not procure any goods or services, so as to become subject to competition in Contracting Act (CICA), when it directed subcontractors providing accounting services for Medicare to standardize on single software system; HCFA was using previously granted license rights to use software, rather than seeking to acquire anything new. Health Systems Architects, Inc. v. Shalala, D.Md. 1998, 992 F.Supp. 804. United States ☞ 64.10

Veterans Administration's involvement in 1990 Advanced Technology Medical Equipment Shared Acquisition Program was subject to Competition in Contracting Act. Rapides Regional Medical Center v. Derwinski, W.D.La.1991, 783 F.Supp. 1006, reversed 974 F.2d 565, rehearing denied 979 F.2d 211, certiorari denied 113 S.Ct. 2413, 508 U.S. 939, 124 L.Ed.2d 636. United States ☞ 64.10

4. Executive agency

Army and Air Force Exchange Service is an "executive agency" and thus subject to this chapter, which provides for proper method of making purchases and contracts by such agencies, and subject to judicial review, at the behest of an unsuccessful contract seeker, of the manner in which it conducted such transactions. W.B. Fishburn Cleaners, Inc. v. Army and Air Force Exchange Service, N.D.Tex. 1974, 374 F.Supp. 162. United States ☞ 64.60(1)

Competition in Contracting Act (CICA) does not apply to the Administrative Office of the United States Courts (AOUSC), as the AOUSC is not an "executive agency" within meaning of the CICA. Novell, Inc. v. U.S., Fed.Cl.2000, 46 Fed.Cl. 601. United States ☞ 64.10

5. Department of Defense exemption

Army and Air Force Exchange Service was not required to procure goods and services in accordance with this section and therefore unsuccessful bidder on government contract had no standing under the Administrative Procedure Act, sections 551 et seq. and 701 et seq. of Title 5, to complain that the service had failed to do so. Ellsworth Bottling Co. v. U.S., W.D.Okla.1975, 408 F.Supp. 280. United States ☞ 64.60(2)

Since Army and Air Force Exchange Service is operated out of nonappropriated funds, it is not subject to Armed Services Procurement Act, section 2301 et seq. of Title 10, and thus not exempt from this chapter, which provides for the proper method by which executive agencies may make purchases and contracts for property and services. W.B. Fishburn Cleaners, Inc. v. Army and Air Force Exchange Service, N.D.Tex.1974, 374 F.Supp. 162. United States ☞ 53(6.1)

6. Social or economic objectives

Social or economic objectives may be sufficiently related to procurement considerations in broad sense and over long run to validate use of procurement power by Congress or the President. Northeast Const. Co. v. Romney, C.A.D.C.1973, 485 F.2d 752, 157 U.S.App.D.C. 381. United States ☞ 63

7. Trust as procurement agent

District Court did not abuse its discretion in enjoining enforcement of public contract for supply of ground transportation buses for airport operated by Federal Aviation Administration, where agency completely ignored substantive and procedural requirements of this chapter by using a trust as a purchasing agent. Motor Coach Industries, Inc. v. Dole, C.A.4 (Va.) 1984, 725 F.2d 958. Injunction ☞ 86

§ 252a. Simplified acquisition threshold

(a) Simplified acquisition threshold

For purposes of acquisitions by executive agencies, the simplified acquisition threshold is as specified in section 403(11) of this title.

(b) Inapplicable laws

No law properly listed in the Federal Acquisition Regulation pursuant to section 429 of this title shall apply to or with respect to a contract or subcontract that is not greater than the simplified acquisition threshold.

(June 30, 1949, c. 288, Title III, § 302A, as added and amended Oct. 13, 1994, Pub.L. 103–355, Title IV, §§ 4003, 4103(a), 108 Stat. 3338, 3341.)

HISTORICAL AND STATUTORY NOTES

Revision Notes and Legislative Reports
  1994 Acts. Senate Report Nos. 103–258 and 103–259, and House Conference Report No. 103–712, see 1994 U.S. Code Cong. and Adm. News, p. 2561.

Amendments
  1994 Amendments. Subsec. (b). Pub.L. 103–355, § 4103(a), added subsec. (b).

Effective and Applicability Provisions
  1994 Acts. Section, as added and amended by Pub.L. 103–355 effective Oct. 13, 1994, except as otherwise provided, see section 10001 of Pub.L. 103–355, set out as a note under section 251 of Title 41, Public Contracts.

LIBRARY REFERENCES

American Digest System
  United States ☞64.10.
  Key Number System Topic No. 393.

Research References

Forms
  Federal Procedural Forms § 34:11, Small Purchase and Other Simplified Procedures.

WESTLAW ELECTRONIC RESEARCH

See Westlaw guide following the Explanation pages of this volume.

§ 252b. Implementation of simplified acquisition procedures

The simplified acquisition procedures contained in the Federal Acquisition Regulation pursuant to section 427 of this title shall apply in executive agencies as provided in such section.

(June 30, 1949, c. 288, Title III, § 302B, as added Oct. 13, 1994, Pub.L. 103–355, Title IV, § 4203(b), 108 Stat. 3346.)

HISTORICAL AND STATUTORY NOTES

Revision Notes and Legislative Reports
  1994 Acts. Senate Report Nos. 103–258 and 103–259, and House Conference Report No. 103–712, see 1994 U.S. Code Cong. and Adm. News, p. 2561.

Effective and Applicability Provisions
  1994 Acts. Section effective Oct. 13, 1994, except as otherwise provided, see section 10001 of Pub.L. 103–355, set out as a note under section 251 of this title.

LIBRARY REFERENCES

American Digest System
  United States ☞64.10.
  Key Number System Topic No. 393.

WESTLAW ELECTRONIC RESEARCH

See Westlaw guide following the Explanation pages of this volume.

§ 252c. Implementation of electronic commerce capability

(a) Implementation of electronic commerce capability

(1) The head of each executive agency shall implement the electronic commerce capability required by section 426 of this title.

(2) In implementing the electronic commerce capability pursuant to paragraph (1), the head of an executive agency shall consult with the Administrator for Federal Procurement Policy.

(b) Designation of agency official

The head of each executive agency shall designate a program manager to implement the electronic commerce capability for that agency. The program manager shall report directly to an official at a level not lower than the senior procurement executive designated for the executive agency under section 414(3) of this title.

(June 30, 1949, c. 288, Title III, § 302C, as added Oct. 13, 1994, Pub.L. 103–355, Title IX, § 9003, 108 Stat. 3403, and amended Nov. 18, 1997, Pub.L. 105–85, Div. A, Title VIII, § 850(f)(4)(A), 111 Stat. 1850.)

HISTORICAL AND STATUTORY NOTES

Revision Notes and Legislative Reports

1994   Acts. Senate Report Nos. 103–258 and 103–259, and House Conference Report No. 103–712, see 1994 U.S. Code Cong. and Adm. News, p. 2561.

1997 Acts. House Conference Report No. 105–340 and Statement by President, see 1997 U.S. Code Cong. and Adm. News, p. 2251.

Amendments

1997 Amendments. Pub.L. 105–85, § 850(f)(4)(A), substituted provisions relating to implementation of electronic commerce capability for provisions relating to implementation of FACNET capability. Prior to amendment by Pub.L. 105–85, section read as follows:

"**§ 252c. Implementation of FACNET capability**

"**(a) Implementation of FACNET capability**

"**(1)** The head of each executive agency shall implement the Federal acquisition computer network ('FACNET') capability required by section 426 of this title.

"**(2)** In implementing the FACNET capability pursuant to paragraph (1), the head of an executive agency shall consult with the Administrator for Federal Procurement Policy.

"**(b) Designation of agency official**

"The head of each executive agency shall designate a program manager to have responsibility for implementation of FACNET capability for that agency and otherwise to implement this section. Such program manager shall report directly to the senior procurement executive designated for the executive agency under section 414(3) of this title."

Effective and Applicability Provisions

1997 Acts. Amendment by section 850 of Pub.L. 105–85 to take effect 180 days after Nov. 18, 1997, see section 850(g) of Pub.L. 105–85, set out as a note under section 2302c of Title 10, Armed Forces.

1994 Acts. Section effective Oct. 13, 1994, except as otherwise provided, see section 10001 of Pub.L. 103–355, set out as a note under section 251 of this title.

LIBRARY REFERENCES

American Digest System
    United States ⊂⊃64.
    Key Number System Topic No. 393.

WESTLAW ELECTRONIC RESEARCH

See Westlaw guide following the Explanation pages of this volume.

§ 253. Competition requirements

(a) Procurement through full and open competition; competitive procedures

(1) Except as provided in subsections (b), (c), and (g) of this section and except in the case of procurement procedures otherwise expressly authorized by statute, an executive agency in conducting a procurement for property or services—

(A) shall obtain full and open competition through the use of competitive procedures in accordance with the requirements of this title and the Federal Acquisition Regulation; and

(B) shall use the competitive procedure or combination of competitive procedures that is best suited under the circumstances of the procurement.

(2) In determining the competitive procedures appropriate under the circumstance, an executive agency—

(A) shall solicit sealed bids if—

(i) time permits the solicitation, submission, and evaluation of sealed bids;

(ii) the award will be made on the basis of price and other price-related factors;

(iii) it is not necessary to conduct discussions with the responding sources about their bids; and

(iv) there is a reasonable expectation of receiving more than one sealed bid; and

(B) shall request competitive proposals if sealed bids are not appropriate under clause (A).

(b) Exclusion of particular source; restriction of solicitation to small business concerns

(1) An executive agency may provide for the procurement of property or services covered by this section using competitive procedures but excluding a particular source in order to establish or maintain any alternative source or sources of supply for that property or service if the agency head determines that to do so—

(A) would increase or maintain competition and would likely result in reduced overall costs for such procurement, or for any anticipated procurement, of such property or services;

(B) would be in the interest of national defense in having a facility (or a producer, manufacturer, or other supplier) available for furnishing the property or service in case of a national emergency or industrial mobilization;

(C) would be in the interest of national defense in establishing or maintaining an essential engineering, research, or development capability to be provided by an educational or other non-profit institution or a federally funded research and development center;

(D) would ensure the continuous availability of a reliable source of supply of such property or service;

(E) would satisfy projected needs for such property or service determined on the basis of a history of high demand for the property or service; or

(F) in the case of medical supplies, safety supplies, or emergency supplies, would satisfy a critical need for such supplies.

(2) An executive agency may provide for the procurement of property or services covered by this section using competitive procedures, but excluding other than small business concerns in furtherance of sections 638 and 644 of Title 15.

(3) A contract awarded pursuant to the competitive procedures referred to in paragraphs (1) and (2) shall not be subject to the justification and approval required by subsection (f)(1) of this section.

(4) A determination under paragraph (1) may not be made for a class of purchases or contracts.

(c) Use of noncompetitive procedures

An executive agency may use procedures other than competitive procedures only when—

(1) the property or services needed by the executive agency are available from only one responsible source and no other type of property or services will satisfy the needs of the executive agency;

(2) the executive agency's need for the property or services is of such an unusual and compelling urgency that the Government would be seriously injured unless the executive agency is permitted to limit the number of sources from which it solicits bids or proposals;

(3) it is necessary to award the contract to a particular source or sources in order (A) to maintain a facility, producer, manufac-

turer, or other supplier available for furnishing property or services in case of a national emergency or to achieve industrial mobilization, (B) to establish or maintain an essential engineering, research, or development capability to be provided by an educational or other nonprofit institution or a federally funded research and development center, or (C) to procure the services of an expert for use, in any litigation or dispute (including any reasonably foreseeable litigation or dispute) involving the Federal Government, in any trial, hearing, or proceeding before any court, administrative tribunal, or agency, or to procure the services of an expert or neutral for use in any part of an alternative dispute resolution or negotiated rulemaking process, whether or not the expert is expected to testify;

(4) the terms of an international agreement or treaty between the United States Government and a foreign government or international organization, or the written directions of a foreign government reimbursing the executive agency for the cost of the procurement of the property or services for such government, have the effect of requiring the use of procedures other than competitive procedures;

(5) subject to subsection (h) of this section, a statute expressly authorizes or requires that the procurement be made through another executive agency or from a specified source, or the agency's need is for a brand-name commercial item for authorized resale;

(6) the disclosure of the executive agency's needs would compromise the national security unless the agency is permitted to limit the number of sources from which it solicits bids or proposals; or

(7) the head of the executive agency—

(A) determines that it is necessary in the public interest to use procedures other than competitive procedures in the particular procurement concerned, and

(B) notifies the Congress in writing of such determination not less than 30 days before the award of the contract.

(d) Property or services deemed available from only one source; nondelegable authority

(1) For the purposes of applying subsection (c)(1) of this section—

(A) in the case of a contract for property or services to be awarded on the basis of acceptance of an unsolicited research proposal, the property or services shall be considered to be available from only one source if the source has submitted an unsolicited research proposal that demonstrates a unique and innovative concept the substance of which is not otherwise available to the United States and does not resemble the substance of a pending competitive procurement; and

(B) in the case of a follow-on contract for the continued development or production of a major system or highly specialized equipment when it is likely that award to a source other than the original source would result in (i) substantial duplication of cost to the Government which is not expected to be recovered through competition, or (ii) unacceptable delays in fulfilling the executive agency's needs, such property may be deemed to be available only from the original source and may be procured through procedures other than competitive procedures.

(2) The authority of the head of an executive agency under subsection (c)(7) of this section may not be delegated.

(e) Offer requests to potential sources

An executive agency using procedures other than competitive procedures to procure property or services by reason of the application of subsection (c)(2) or (c)(6) of this section shall request offers from as many potential sources as is practicable under the circumstances.

(f) Justification for use of noncompetitive procedures

(1) Except as provided in paragraph (2), an executive agency may not award a contract using procedures other than competitive procedures unless—

(A) the contracting officer for the contract justifies the use of such procedures in writing and certifies the accuracy and completeness of the justification;

(B) the justification is approved—

(i) in the case of a contract for an amount exceeding $500,000 (but equal to or less than $10,000,000), by the competition advocate for the procuring activity (without further delegation) or by an official referred to in clause (ii) or (iii); and

(ii) in the case of a contract for an amount exceeding $10,000,000 (but equal to or less than $50,000,000), by the head of the procuring activity or a delegate who, if a member of the armed forces, is a general or flag officer or, if a civilian, is serving in a position in grade GS–16 or above under the General Schedule (or in a comparable or higher position under another schedule); or

(iii) in the case of a contract for an amount exceeding $50,000,000, by the senior procurement executive of the agency designated pursuant to section 414(3) of this title (without further delegation); and

(C) any required notice has been published with respect to such contract pursuant to section 416 of this title and all bids or proposals received in response to such notice have been considered by such executive agency.

(2) In the case of a procurement permitted by subsection (c)(2), the justification and approval required by paragraph (1) may be made after the contract is awarded. The justification and approval required by paragraph (1) is not required—

(A) when a statute expressly requires that the procurement be made from a specified source;

(B) when the agency's need is for a brand-name commercial item for authorized resale;

(C) in the case of a procurement permitted by subsection (c)(7) of this section; or

(D) in the case of a procurement conducted under (i) the Javits–Wagner–O'Day Act (41 U.S.C. 46 et seq.), or (ii) section 637(a) of Title 15.

(3) The justification required by paragraph (1)(A) shall include—

(A) a description of the agency's needs;

(B) an identification of the statutory exception from the requirement to use competitive procedures and a demonstration, based on the proposed contractor's qualifications or the nature of the procurement, of the reasons for using that exception;

(C) a determination that the anticipated cost will be fair and reasonable;

(D) a description of the market survey conducted or a statement of the reasons a market survey was not conducted;

(E) a listing of the sources, if any, that expressed in writing an interest in the procurement; and

(F) a statement of the actions, if any, the agency may take to remove or overcome a barrier to competition before a subsequent procurement for such needs.

(4) The justification required by paragraph (1)(A) and any related information shall be made available for inspection by the public consistent with the provisions of section 552 of Title 5.

(5) In no case may an executive agency—

(A) enter into a contract for property or services using procedures other than competitive procedures on the basis of the lack of advance planning or concerns related to the amount of funds available to the agency for procurement functions; or

(B) procure property or services from another executive agency unless such other executive agency complies fully with the requirements of this subchapter in its procurement of such property or services.

The restriction set out in clause (B) is in addition to, and not in lieu of, any other restriction provided by law.

(g) Simplified procedures for small purchases

(1) In order to promote efficiency and economy in contracting and to avoid unnecessary burdens for agencies and contractors, the Federal Acquisition Regulation shall provide for—

   (A) special simplified procedures for purchases of property and services for amounts not greater than the simplified acquisition threshold; and

   (B) special simplified procedures for purchases of property and services for amounts greater than the simplified acquisition threshold but not greater than $5,000,000 with respect to which the contracting officer reasonably expects, based on the nature of the property or services sought and on market research, that offers will include only commercial items.

(2)(A) The Administrator of General Services shall prescribe regulations that provide special simplified procedures for acquisitions of leasehold interests in real property at rental rates that do not exceed the simplified acquisition threshold.

   (B) For purposes of subparagraph (A), the rental rate or rates under a multiyear lease do not exceed the simplified acquisition threshold if the average annual amount of the rent payable for the period of the lease does not exceed the simplified acquisition threshold.

(3) A proposed purchase or contract for an amount above the simplified acquisition threshold may not be divided into several purchases or contracts for lesser amounts in order to use the simplified procedures required by paragraph (1).

(4) In using the simplified procedures, an executive agency shall promote competition to the maximum extent practicable.

(5) An executive agency shall comply with the Federal Acquisition Regulation provisions referred to in section 427(f) of this title.

(h) Efficient implementation of requirement

The Federal Acquisition Regulation shall ensure that the requirement to obtain full and open competition is implemented in a manner that is consistent with the need to efficiently fulfill the Government's requirements.

(i) Merit-based award of contracts

(1) It is the policy of Congress that an executive agency should not be required by legislation to award a new contract to a specific non–Federal Government entity. It is further the policy of Congress that any program, project, or technology identified in legislation be procured through merit-based selection procedures.

(2) A provision of law may not be construed as requiring a new contract to be awarded to a specified non-Federal Government entity unless that provision of law—

(A) specifically refers to this subsection;

(B) specifically identifies the particular non-Federal Government entity involved; and

(C) specifically states that the award to that entity is required by such provision of law in contravention of the policy set forth in paragraph (1).

(3) For purposes of this subsection, a contract is a new contract unless the work provided for in the contract is a continuation of the work performed by the specified entity under a preceding contract.

(4) This subsection shall not apply with respect to any contract that calls upon the National Academy of Sciences to investigate, examine, or experiment upon any subject of science or art of significance to an executive agency and to report on such matters to the Congress or any agency of the Federal Government.

(June 30, 1949, c. 288, Title III, § 303, 63 Stat. 395; July 12, 1952, c. 703, § 1(m), 66 Stat. 594; Mar. 16, 1968, Pub.L. 90–268, § 2, 82 Stat. 49; July 18, 1984, Pub.L. 98–369, Div. B, Title VII, § 2711(a)(1), 98 Stat. 1175; Oct. 30, 1984, Pub.L. 98–577, Title V, § 504(a)(1), (2), 98 Stat. 3086; Nov. 8, 1985, Pub.L. 99–145, Title IX, § 961(a)(2), Title XIII, § 1304(c)(2), (3), 99 Stat. 703, 742; Nov. 5, 1990, Pub.L. 101–510, Div. A, Title VIII, § 806(c), 104 Stat. 1592; Oct. 13, 1994, Pub.L. 103–355, Title I, §§ 1051, 1052, 1053, 1055(a), Title IV, § 4402(a), Title VII, § 7203 (b)(1), 108 Stat. 3260, 3261, 3265, 3348, 3380; Feb. 10, 1996, Pub.L. 104–106, Div. D, Title XLI, §§ 4101(b), 4102(b), Title XLII, § 4202(b)(1), Title XLIII, § 4321(e)(2), 110 Stat. 642, 643, 653, 674; Oct. 19, 1996, Pub.L. 104–320, §§ 7(a)(2), 11(c)(2), 110 Stat. 3871, 3873; Nov. 18, 1997, Pub.L. 105–85, Div. A, Title VIII, § 850(f)(3)(B), 111 Stat. 1850.)

HISTORICAL AND STATUTORY NOTES

Revision Notes and Legislative Reports
1968 Acts. House Report No. 991, see 1968 U.S.Code Cong. and Adm.News, p. 1747.

1984 Acts. Senate Report No. 98–523, see 1984 U.S.Code Cong. and Adm.News, p. 5347.

House Report No. 98–432, Pt. II, Senate Report Nos. 98–50 and 98–297, and

House Conference Report No. 98–861, see 1984 U.S.Code Cong. and Adm.News, p. 697.

1985 Acts. House Report No. 99–81, see 1985 U.S.Code Cong. and Adm.News, p. 472.

1990 Acts. House Report No. 101–665 and House Conference Report No.

101–923, see 1990 Act U.S.Code Cong. and Adm.News, p. 2931.

1994 Acts. Senate Report Nos. 103–258 and 103–259, and House Conference Report No. 103–712, see 1994 U.S. Code Cong. and Adm. News, p. 2561.

1996 Acts. House Conference Report No. 104–450, see 1996 U.S. Code Cong. and Adm. News, p. 238.

1997 Acts. House Conference Report No. 105–340 and Statement by President, see 1997 U.S. Code Cong. and Adm. News, p. 2251.

References in Text

Subsection (h) of this section, referred to in subsec. (c)(5), was redesignated subsec. (i) and a new subsec. (h) was added by Pub.L. 104–106, Div. D, Title XLI, § 4101(b), Feb. 10, 1996, 110 Stat. 642.

The General Schedule, referred to in subsec. (f)(1)(B)(ii), is set out under section 5332 of Title 5, Government Organization and Employees.

The Javits-Wagner-O'Day Act (41 U.S.C. 46 et seq.), referred to in subsec. (f)(2)(D), is Act June 25, 1938, c. 697, 52 Stat. 1196, as amended, which is classified to sections 46 to 48c of this title. For complete classification of this Act to the Code, see Short Title note set out under section 46 of this title and Tables.

Amendments

1997 Amendments. Subsec. (g)(5). Pub.L. 105–85, § 850(f)(4)(B), substituted "31(f)" for "31(g)".

1996 Amendments. Subsec. (c)(3)(C). Pub.L. 104–320, § 7(a)(2), substituted "agency, or to procure the services of an expert or neutral for use" for "agency, or".

Pub.L. 104–320, § 11(c)(2), inserted "or negotiated rulemaking" after "alternative dispute resolution".

Subsec. (f)(1)(B)(i). Pub.L. 104–106, § 4102(b)(1), substituted "$500,000 (but equal to or less than $10,000,000)" for "$100,000 (but equal to or less than $1,000,000)", and "(ii) or (iii); and" for "(ii), (iii), or (iv);", respectively.

Subsec. (f)(1)(B)(ii). Pub.L. 104–106, § 4102(b)(2), substituted "$10,000,000 (but equal to or less than $50,000,000)" for "$1,000,000 (but equal to or less than $10,000,000)".

Subsec. (f)(1)(B)(iii). Pub.L. 104–106, § 4102(b)(3), substituted "$50,000,000" for "$10,000,000".

Subsec. (f)(2)(D). Pub.L. 104–106, § 4321(e)(2), substituted "the Javits-Wagner-O'Day Act (41 U.S.C. 46 et seq.)," for "the Act of June 25, 1938 (41 U.S.C. 46 et seq.), popularly referred to as the Wagner-O'Day Act,".

Subsec. (g)(1). Pub.L. 104–106, § 4202(b)(1)(A), restructured existing provisions into subpar. (A) and added subpar. (B).

Subsec. (g)(5). Pub.L. 104–106, § 4202(b)(1)(B), added par. (5).

Subsecs. (h), (i). Pub.L. 104–106, § 4101(b), added subsec. (h) and redesignated former subsec. (h) as subsec. (i).

1994 Amendments. Subsec. (a)(1)(A). Pub.L. 103–355, § 1051(1), substituted "Federal Acquisition Regulation" for "modifications to regulations promulgated pursuant to section 2752 of the Competition in Contracting Act of 1984 [41 U.S.C.A. § 403 note]".

Subsec. (b)(1). Pub.L. 103–355, § 1052(a)(1)-(3), struck "or" at the end of subpar. (B); substituted a semicolon for the period at the end of subpar. (C); and added subpars. (D) to (F), respectively.

Subsec. (b)(4). Pub.L. 103–355, § 1052(b), added par. (4).

Subsec. (c)(3). Pub.L. 103–355, § 1055(a)(1), (2), substituted "(B)" for "or (B)" and added cl. ", or (C)" provision.

Subsec. (c)(5). Pub.L. 103–355, § 7203(b)(1)(A), inserted "subject to subsection (h) of this section ," preceding "a statute".

Subsec. (g)(1). Pub.L. 103-355, §§ 1051(2), 4402(a)(1)(B), enacted identical amendments, substituting "Federal Acquisition Regulation" for "regulations modified, in accordance with section 2752 of the Competition in Contracting Act of 1984 [41 U.S.C.A. § 403 note],".

Pub.L. 103–355, § 4402(a)(1)(A), substituted "purchases of property and services for amounts not greater than the simplified acquisition threshold" for "small purchases of property and services".

Subsec. (g)(2). Pub.L. 103–355, § 4402(a)(2), enacted par. (2) and struck out former par. (2), which provided that

"For the purposes of this subchapter, a small purchase is a purchase or contract for an amount which does not exceed the small purchase threshold.".

Subsec. (g)(3). Pub.L. 103–355, § 4402(a)(3)(A), (B), substituted "simplified acquisition threshold" for "small purchase threshold" and "simplified procedures" for "small purchase procedures".

Subsec. (g)(4). Pub.L. 103–355, § 4402(a)(4), substituted "the simplified procedures" for "small purchase procedures".

Subsec. (g)(5). Pub.L. 103–355, § 4402(a)(5), struck out par. (5), which provided that "In this subsection [(g)], the term 'small purchase threshold' has the meaning given the term in section 403(11) of this title.".

Subsec. (h). Pub.L. 103–355, § 7203(b)(1)(B), added subsec. (h).

1990 Amendments. Subsec. (g)(2). Pub.L. 101–510, § 806(c)(1), substituted "the small purchase threshold" for "$25,000".

Subsec. (g)(3). Pub.L. 101–510, § 806(c)(2), substituted "the small purchase threshold" for "$25,000".

Subsec. (g)(5). Pub.L. 101–510, § 806(c)(3), added par. (5).

1985 Amendments. Subsec. (f)(1)(C). Pub.L. 99–145, § 1304(c)(2), substituted "any" for "Any".

Subsec. (f)(2). Pub.L. 99–145, § 961(a)(2), added subpars. (A) and (B), designated existing provision as subpar. (C), and redesignated as subpar. (D), cls. (i) and (ii) provisions previously designated subpars. (A) and (B), substituting in cl. (ii) "section 637(a) of Title 15" for "the authority of section 637(a) of Title 15".

Subsec. (g)(1). Pub.L. 99–145, § 1304(c)(3), inserted a comma after "1984".

1984 Amendments. Subsec. (a). Pub.L. 98–369, § 2711(a)(1), substituted provision requiring procurement through full and open competition for provision requiring advertisement for bids to be made a sufficient time prior to the purchase or contract and permitting full and free competition, and struck out provision that no advertisement or bid invitation for carriage of Government property in other than Government-owned cargo containers specify carriage in cargo containers of any stated length, height, or width.

Subsec. (b). Pub.L. 98–369, § 2711(a)(1), substituted provision regarding the exclusion of a particular source of property or services from competitive procedures for provision regarding the opening of bids and procedures for awards, and added provision that in fulfilling the statutory requirements relating to small business concerns and socially and economically disadvantaged small business concerns, an executive agency shall use competitive procedures but may restrict a solicitation to allow only such business concerns to compete.

Subsec. (b)(2). Pub.L. 98–577, § 504(a)(1), substituted provisions to the effect that executive agencies may provide for procurement of property or services covered by this section using competitive procedures but excluding other than small business concerns for former provisions which provided that executive agencies shall use competitive procedures but may restrict a solicitation to allow only such small business concerns to compete.

Subsec. (b)(3). Pub.L. 98–577, § 504(a)(1), added par. (3).

Subsecs. (c) to (g). Pub.L. 98–369, § 2711(a)(1), added subsecs. (c) to (g).

Subsec. (f)(2). Pub.L. 98–577, § 504(a)(2), designated final sentence as subpar. (A) and added subpar. (B).

1968 Amendments. Subsec. (a). Pub.L. 90–268 added provision that no advertisement or invitation to bid for the carriage of Government property in other than Government-owned cargo containers shall specify carriage of such property in cargo containers of any stated length, height, or width.

1952 Amendments. Subsec. (a). Act July 12, 1952, substituted "property" for "supplies".

Effective and Applicability Provisions

1997 Acts. Amendment by section 850 of Pub.L. 105–85 to take effect 180 days after Nov. 18, 1997, see section 850(g) of Pub.L. 105–85, set out as a note under section 2302c of Title 10, Armed Forces.

1996 Acts. Amendment by Pub.L. 104–106 effective Feb. 10, 1996, except as otherwise provided, see section 4401 of Pub.L. 104–106, set out as a note under section 251 of this title.

1994 Acts. Amendment by section 1051 of Pub.L. 103–355 effective Oct. 13, 1994, and applicable on and after such date, see section 10001 of Pub.L. 103–355, set out as a note under section 251 of this title.

Amendment by sections 1052, 1053, 1055(a), 4402(a), and 7203(b)(1) of Pub.L. 103–355 effective Oct. 13, 1994, except as otherwise provided, see section 10001 of Pub.L. 103–355, set out as a note under section 251 of this title.

1985 Acts. Amendment by section 961(a)(2) of Pub.L. 99–145 effective as if included in enactment of Competition in Contracting Act of 1984, Pub.L. 98–369, Div. B, Title VII, see section 961(e) of Pub.L. 99–145, set out as a note under section 2304 of Title 10, Armed Forces.

1984 Acts. Amendment by section 2711(a)(1) of Pub.L. 98–369 applicable with respect to any solicitation for bids or proposals issued after Mar. 31, 1985, see section 2751(a) of Pub.L. 98–369, set out as a note under section 251 of this title.

1949 Acts. Act June 30, 1949, § 605, which set July 1, 1949, as the effective date for this section, was repealed by Pub.L. 107–217, § 6(b), Aug. 21, 2002, 116 Stat. 1313.

Definitions
The definitions in 40 U.S.C.A. § 102 apply to terms appearing in this subchapter.

Public Disclosure of Noncompetitive Contracting for the Reconstruction of Infrastructure in Iraq
Pub.L 108–136, Div. A, Title XIV, § 1442, Nov. 24, 2003, 117 Stat. 1674, provided that:

"**(a) Disclosure required.**—

"**(1) Publication and public availability.**—The head of an executive agency of the United States that enters into a contract for the repair, maintenance, or construction of infrastructure in Iraq without full and open competition shall publish in the Federal Register or Commerce Business Daily and otherwise make available to the public, not later than 30 days after the date on which the contract is entered into, the following information:

"**(A)** The amount of the contract.

"**(B)** A brief description of the scope of the contract.

"**(C)** A discussion of how the executive agency identified, and solicited offers from, potential contractors to perform the contract, together with a list of the potential contractors that were issued solicitations for the offers.

"**(D)** The justification and approval documents on which was based the determination to use procedures other than procedures that provide for full and open competition.

"**(2) Inapplicability to contracts after fiscal year 2005.**—Paragraph (1) does not apply to a contract entered into after September 30, 2005.

"**(b) Classified information.**—

"**(1) Authority to withhold.**—The head of an executive agency may—

"**(A)** withhold from publication and disclosure under subsection (a) [of this note] any document that is classified for restricted access in accordance with an Executive order in the interest of national defense or foreign policy; and

"**(B)** redact any part so classified that is in a document not so classified before publication and disclosure of the document under subsection (a) [of this note].

"**(2) Availability to Congress.**—In any case in which the head of an executive agency withholds information under paragraph (1), the head of such executive agency shall make available an unredacted version of the document containing that information to the chairman and ranking member of each of the following committees of Congress:

"**(A)** The Committee on Governmental Affairs of the Senate and the Committee on Government Reform of the House of Representatives.

"**(B)** The Committees on Appropriations of the Senate and House of Representatives.

"**(C)** Each committee that the head of the executive agency determines has legislative jurisdiction for the operations of such department or agency to which the information relates.

"**(c) Fiscal year 2003 contracts.**—This section [this note] shall apply to contracts entered into on or after October 1, 2002, except that, in the case of a contract entered into before the date of the enactment of this Act [Nov. 24, 2003], subsection (a) [of this note] shall be applied as if the contract had been entered into on the date of the enactment of this Act [Nov. 24, 2003].

"(d) Relationship to other disclosure laws.—Nothing in this section [this note] shall be construed as affecting obligations to disclose United States Government information under any other provision of law.

"(e) Definitions.—In this section [this note], the terms 'executive agency' and 'full and open competition' have the meanings given such terms in section 4 of the Office of Federal Procurement Policy Act (41 U.S.C. 403)."

Termination of Reporting Requirements

Reporting requirement of subsec. (c)(7) of this section excepted from termination under Pub.L. 104–66, § 3003(a)(1), as amended, set out as a note under 31

U.S.C.A. § 1113, see Pub.L. 107–74, set out as a note under 31 U.S.C.A. § 1113.

Small Business Act

Section 2711(c) of Pub.L. 98–369 provided that: "The amendments made by this section [enacting sections 253a and 253b of this title and amending this section and section 259 of this title] do not supersede or affect the provisions of section 8(a) of the Small Business Act (15 U.S.C. 637(a))."

Termination of Authority to Issue Solicitations for Purchases of Commercial Items in Excess of Simplified Acquisition Threshold

Authority to issue solicitations for purchases of commercial items in excess of simplified acquisition threshold pursuant to special simplified procedures authorized by subsec. (g)(1) of this section expires Jan. 1, 2002, see section 4202(e) of Pub.L. 104–106, set out as a note under section 2304 of Title 10.

CROSS REFERENCES

Advertising for proposals for purchases and contracts for supplies or services, see 41 USCA § 5.

Armed services procurement contracts—
    Competition requirements, see 10 USCA § 2304.
    Planning, solicitation, evaluation, and award procedures, see 10 USCA § 2305.
    Regulations for bids, see 10 USCA § 2381.

Authority to secure health-care resources and written justification with required information in accordance with this section, see 38 USCA § 8153.

Aviation programs, general procurement authority, duties and powers of senior procurement executive, see 49 USCA § 40110.

Record requirements, procurement contracts, see 41 USCA § 417.

Special rules for commercial items, see 41 USCA § 427.

CODE OF FEDERAL REGULATIONS

Competition requirements, see 48 CFR § 2406.202 et seq.

LAW REVIEW AND JOURNAL COMMENTARIES

Enforcing competition through government contract claims. Michael K. Love, 20 U.Rich.L.Rev. 525 (1986).

Federal environmental remediation contractual and insurance-based risk allocation schemes: Are they getting the job done? Major Amy L. Momber, 58 A.F. L. Rev. 61 (2006).

LIBRARY REFERENCES

American Digest System

  United States ☞64.10.

  Key Number System Topic No. 393.

Corpus Juris Secundum

  CJS United States § 113, Advertising and Proposals or Bids.

Research References

ALR Library

9 ALR, Fed. 2nd Series 565, "Cardinal Change" Doctrine in Federal Contracts Law.

96 ALR 712, Alternation of Plans or Materials as Necessary or Proper Factor in Proposal for or Acceptance of Bids for Public Works.

64 ALR 1281, Subsequent Developments as Authorizing Increase of Amount of Succession Tax Fixed by Taxing Authorities.

Encyclopedias

Am. Jur. 2d Public Works and Contracts § 34, Federal Contracts.

14 Am. Jur. Trials 437, Representing the Government Contractor.

Forms

Federal Procedural Forms § 34:2, Procedures to Promote Competition.

Federal Procedural Forms § 34:3, Procedures to Promote Competition--Exclusion of Sources.

Federal Procedural Forms § 34:4, Procedures to Promote Competition--Contracting Without Open Competition.

Treatises and Practice Aids

Federal Information Disclosure § 14:84, Government Contractors' Data Exemption Claims.

Federal Procedure, Lawyers Edition § 39:3, Promotion of Competition.

Federal Procedure, Lawyers Edition § 39:4, Promotion of Competition--Exclusion of Sources.

Federal Procedure, Lawyers Edition § 39:5, Promotion of Competition--Noncompetitive Procurements.

West's Federal Administrative Practice § 603, Differences from Private Contracts.

West's Federal Administrative Practice § 622, Competition Requirements.

West's Federal Administrative Practice § 635, Types of Contracts.

West's Federal Administrative Practice § 640, Research and Development Contracting.

WESTLAW ELECTRONIC RESEARCH

See Westlaw guide following the Explanation pages of this volume.

Notes of Decisions

Competitive bids or offers 4
Construction with other laws 1
Injunctive relief denied 7
Injunctive relief granted 8
Modification 5
Notification of potential bidders 3
Procedures otherwise expressly authorized 2
Public interest 6
Review 9

---

1. Construction with other laws

Court of Federal Claims has discretion not to enter an injunction in a bid protest case in which it finds a violation of the Competition in Contracting Act (CICA); reference in the Tucker Act to section of the Administrative Procedures Act (APA) incorporates standard of review from the APA, but it does not require the Court to set aside any action it finds unlawful without consideration of the relative harms of such action. CW Government Travel, Inc. v. U.S., Fed.Cl.2005, 63 Fed. Cl. 459, affirmed 163 Fed.Appx. 853, 2005 WL 3292539. Injunction ⇔ 86

2. Procedures otherwise expressly authorized

Even if agreement between hospital and Veterans Affairs Medical Center for acquisition and use of piece of medical equipment was a "procurement" for purposes of the Competition in Contracting Act (CICA), statute authorizing the Veterans Administration to enter into such arrangements was a procurement procedure "expressly authorized by statute" and thus not subject to the full and open competition requirements of CICA. Rapides Regional Medical Center v. Secretary, Dept. of Veterans' Affairs, C.A.5 (La.) 1992, 974 F.2d 565, rehearing de-

nied 979 F.2d 211, certiorari denied 113
S.Ct. 2413, 508 U.S. 939, 124 L.Ed.2d
636. United States ☞ 64.10

Neither Competition in Contracting Act
(CICA) nor federal acquisition regulations
(FAR) applied to selection of designated
bonding authority (DBA) for historically
black colleges and universities (HBCU)
capital financing program, as statutory
instructions regarding Secretary of Education's selection of DBA brought selection within ambit of CICA's savings
clause and therefore supplanted requirements of CICA and FAR. Grigsby Brand-
ford & Co., Inc. v. U.S., D.D.C.1994, 869
F.Supp. 984. United States ☞ 64.5

Provisions of the Buy Indian Act did
not fall within the "otherwise authorized
by law" exception to the advertising requirements of the Federal Property and
Administrative Services Act of 1949 insofar as they were interpreted by the Bureau of Indian Affairs as authorizing contractual negotiations with wholly owned
Indian companies in regard to road construction without complying with the advertising requirements and as authorizing
negotiations with non-Indian contractors
only if there were no qualified Indian
contractors within the normal competitive area. Glover Const. Co. v. Andrus,
E.D.Okla.1978, 451 F.Supp. 1102, affirmed 591 F.2d 554, certiorari granted
100 S.Ct. 448, 444 U.S. 962, 62 L.Ed.2d
374, affirmed 100 S.Ct. 1905, 446 U.S.
608, 64 L.Ed.2d 548. Injunction ☞ 86

3. Notification of potential bidders

Trial court would not bar performance
of contract to provide Customs Service
with mobile x-ray for detection of contra-
band, even though Customs Service erroneously used Broad Agency Announcement (BAA) single source procurement
procedure to avoid competitive bidding
when BAA was available only for research or applied research contracts;
Customs Service had good faith belief
that BAA procedure could be used, and
protestor requesting relief was not prejudiced, as it was previous sole source for
x-ray equipment, and Customs Service
wanted second source and could have
legitimately requested bids from potential
suppliers excluding protestor. American
Science and Engineering, Inc. v. Kelly,
D.Mass.1999, 69 F.Supp.2d 227. United
States ☞ 64.60(5.1)

General Services Administration's efforts to notify potential bidders, including

publication in Commerce Business Daily,
a compendium of all federal government
contracting opportunities, mailing of several hundred preinvitation notice letters,
and posting of solicitation of paper towel
contract in General Services Administration's business centers was not sufficient
to put incumbent contractor which did
not receive copy of solicitation from General Services Administration on notice of
solicitation, and because incumbent was
not among small number of potential responsible bidders, General Service Administration's efforts were insufficient to
satisfy competition requirements of Competition in Contracting Act. Abel Converting, Inc. v. U.S., D.D.C.1988, 679
F.Supp. 1133. United States ☞ 64.25

Bid protestor proved that it was prejudiced by government's failure to properly
and promptly notify it of its removal as
an approved source, and its failure to
urge it to requalify at any point after its
removal; but for the failures, protestor
would have had more than 7-1/2 months
to requalify as a pre-approved supplier,
and if it had requalified, there was a
substantial chance it would have received
the contractor, as it was the incumbent
contractor who was awarded three of the
last four contracts. SAI Industries Corp.
v. U.S., Fed.Cl.2004, 60 Fed.Cl. 731.
United States ☞ 64.55(1)

4. Competitive bids or offers

Where a contract has been awarded,
but a bid protest has been sustained and
the recommended corrective action is to
make a new best value determination, the
standard competition rules of the Competition in Contracting Act (CICA) and the
Federal Acquisition Regulation (FAR) apply, and under such circumstances, if an
agency conducts discussions, it must do
so with all offerors in the competitive
range. Chapman Law Firm Co. v. U.S.,
Fed.Cl.2006, 71 Fed.Cl. 124, appeal filed.
United States ☞ 64.40(1)

5. Modification

Separate competitive procurement for
modification to government telecommunications contract before contractor
could begin improvements in dedicated
transmission service was not required;
improvements in service fell within service improvements clause of contract and
bidders' expectations were that such improvements fell within contract and were
not changes which required competitive

bidding. AT&T Communications, Inc. v. Wiltel, Inc., C.A.Fed.1993, 1 F.3d 1201, rehearing denied, in banc suggestion declined, rehearing in banc declined. United States ☞ 70(25.1); United States ☞ 73(17)

With regard to contract to establish centralized coordination of benefits (COB) operation for Medicare, contract modification which made COB contractor responsible for "crossover" function of transmitting Medicare adjudicated claims data to secondary supplemental insurer or payer did not constitute a cardinal change so as to invoke competition requirement of the Competition in Contracting Act (CICA), as modification did not materially change scope of contract, it did not significantly change performance period or cost of contract, and a reasonable offeror would have expected modification to fall within changes clause of contract. HDM Corp. v. U.S., Fed.Cl. 2005, 69 Fed.Cl. 243. United States ☞ 73(17)

Government materially changed contract for custodial services at Air Force base, where changes increased cost of the original contract by nearly eighty percent, and nature of the work was so substantially increased that the change provision of the contract had to be deleted to accomplish the modifications; by so doing without resoliciting the contract, government violated the Competition in Contracting Act (CICA). Cardinal Maintenance Service, Inc. v. U.S., Fed. Cl.2004, 63 Fed.Cl. 98. United States ☞ 73(17)

Addition of traditional travel services to contract to provide military travel services using a paperless automated travel management system to be known as the common user interface (CUI) was a cardinal change, and failure of contracting agency to issue a competitive solicitation for traditional travel services added by the modification violated the Competition in Contracting Act (CICA); potential contractor bidding on the original contract would not have anticipated that it could also be called upon under the changes clause to provide traditional travel services, as reflected in fact that no provider of traditional travel services bid on the original contract. CW Government Travel, Inc. v. U.S., Fed.Cl.2004, 61 Fed.Cl. 559, opinion corrected 2004 WL 2358246, opinion clarified on denial of

reconsideration 63 Fed.Cl. 459, affirmed 163 Fed.Appx. 853, 2005 WL 3292539. United States ☞ 64.10; United States ☞ 73(17)

Bid protestor did not establish that post-award modifications to government contract for lease of office space so exceeded scope of original procurement that they violated the Competition in Contracting Act (CICA), based on claim that the modifications increased the cash flow to awardee and shifted the risk of payment and performance to the government beyond what was permitted in the original solicitation. CESC Plaza Ltd. Partnership v. U.S., Fed.Cl.2002, 52 Fed.Cl. 91. United States ☞ 64.55(1)

Modification of government contract for employee assistance program (EAP) services to include EAP services for approximately 850,000 Postal Service employees was not beyond scope of original contract, so as to constitute a new procurement without competition in violation of the Competition in Contracting Act (CICA), where original solicitation contained statement that services to Postal Service might be added to the contract in the future. VMC Behavioral Healthcare Services, Div. of Vasquez Group, Inc. v. U.S., Fed.Cl.2001, 50 Fed.Cl. 328.

Government's providing awardee with government-furnished property not listed in invitation for bids was not material modification requiring termination and resolicitation of contract after awardee returned government-furnished property to Government and refused to sign proposed contract modification. Graphic-Data, LLC v. U.S., Fed.Cl.1997, 37 Fed. Cl. 771. United States ☞ 72.1(2)

United States, in awarding contract to build facility for housing National Park Service's museum collection, did not violate the competitive bidding provision of the Competition in Contracting Act (CICA) by failing to re-bid contract after modifications to original solicitation for offers (SFO) were made, where government had encouraged bidders to submit suggested modifications to the solicitation so as to create a state of the art facility, so the scope of the contract was understood to embrace changes or modifications to the original contract requirements for the facility. H.G. Properties A, L.P. v. U.S., C.A.Fed.2003, 68 Fed.Appx. 192, 2003 WL 21421629, Unreported. United States ☞ 64.25

6. Public interest

Contractor who protested award of sole source contract modification to incumbent contractor was not entitled to preliminary injunction enjoining performance of the modification; determination of head of contracting agency that sole source modification advanced the underlying public interest was clearly and convincingly justified, and thus protestor could not prevail on the merits. Spherix, Inc. v. U.S., Fed.Cl.2003, 58 Fed.Cl. 514. Injunction ☞ 138.63

7. Injunctive relief denied

Bid protestor was not entitled to reconsideration of denial of injunctive relief on its claim that contracting agency violated the Competition in Contracting Act (CICA) by not issuing a new solicitation when it modified military travel management contract by changing to a web-based customer user interface (CUI) and changing contract from firm fixed-price to cost reimbursement; although protestor presented new evidence that percentage of travel services transactions using CUI was small, decision was not dependent on the percentage of travel services then booked using CUI, though the court did consider that terminating the contract would impact current operations. CW Government Travel, Inc. v. U.S., Fed.Cl. 2005, 63 Fed.Cl. 459, affirmed 163 Fed. Appx. 853, 2005 WL 3292539. Federal Courts ☞ 1121

Even assuming success on the merits and irreparable harm, bid protestor was not entitled injunctive relief on its claim that contracting agency violated the Competition in Contracting Act (CICA) by not issuing a new solicitation when it modified military travel management contract by changing to a web-based customer user interface (CUI) and changing contract from firm fixed-price to cost reimbursement; balance of hardships tipped in favor of the government considering that contract was in its sixth year of performance, and overwhelming public interest was to avoid further delay to project. CW Government Travel, Inc. v. U.S., Fed.Cl.2004, 61 Fed.Cl. 559, opinion corrected 2004 WL 2358246, opinion clarified on denial of reconsideration 63 Fed.Cl. 459, affirmed 163 Fed.Appx. 853, 2005 WL 3292539. Injunction ☞ 86

8. Injunctive relief granted

Bid protestor which prevailed on its claim that government materially modified contract after its award in violation of the Competition in Contracting Act (CICA) was entitled to permanent injunctive relief in form of cancellation of contract and resolicitation; loss of opportunity to compete on level playing field constituted irreparable harm which outweighed harm to government from having to resolicit contract, and public interest in integrity of procurement process favored injunction. Cardinal Maintenance Service, Inc. v. U.S., Fed.Cl.2004, 63 Fed.Cl. 98. Injunction ☞ 86

Bid protestor who prevailed on the merits of claim that contracting agency violated the Competition in Contracting Act (CICA) by effecting cardinal change to rival contractor's contract to add traditional travel services to contract without competition was entitled to permanent injunction enjoining performance of such work and requiring agency to recompete the work; fact that protestor was unable to compete for the traditional travel services constituted irreparable harm, balance of hardships was in favor of protestor, and granting injunction served the public interest in preserving integrity of procurement process. CW Government Travel, Inc. v. U.S., Fed.Cl.2004, 61 Fed. Cl. 559, opinion corrected 2004 WL 2358246, opinion clarified on denial of reconsideration 63 Fed.Cl. 459, affirmed 163 Fed.Appx. 853, 2005 WL 3292539. Injunction ☞ 86

9. Review

With regard to statute establishing procedures for the use of noncompetitive contract awards, including when head of agency determines that noncompetitive procedures are in the public interest, agency head's public interest determination is not committed to agency discretion by law, so as to preclude judicial review; section of the Federal Acquisition Regulation (FAR) requiring agency head to adopt a written finding setting out facts and circumstances that clearly and convincingly justify such determination provides a meaningful standard of review. Spherix, Inc. v. U.S., Fed.Cl.2003, 58 Fed.Cl. 351. United States ☞ 64.10

§ 253a.   Planning and solicitation requirements

(a) Preparation; planning; specifications in solicitation

(1) In preparing for the procurement of property or services, an executive agency shall—

> **(A)** specify its needs and solicit bids or proposals in a manner designed to achieve full and open competition for the procurement;

> **(B)** use advance procurement planning and market research; and

> **(C)** develop specifications in such manner as is necessary to obtain full and open competition with due regard to the nature of the property or services to be acquired.

(2) Each solicitation under this subchapter shall include specifications which—

> **(A)** consistent with the provisions of this subchapter, permit full and open competition;

> **(B)** include restrictive provisions or conditions only to the extent necessary to satisfy the needs of the executive agency or as authorized by law.

(3) For the purposes of paragraphs (1) and (2), the type of specification included in a solicitation shall depend on the nature of the needs of the executive agency and the market available to satisfy such needs. Subject to such needs, specifications may be stated in terms of—

> **(A)** function, so that a variety of products or services may qualify;

> **(B)** performance, including specifications of the range of acceptable characteristics or of the minimum acceptable standards; or

> **(C)** design requirements.

(b) Contents of solicitation

In addition to the specifications described in subsection (a) of this section, each solicitation for sealed bids or competitive proposals (other than for a procurement for commercial items using special simplified procedures or a purchase for an amount not greater than the simplified acquisition threshold) shall at a minimum include—

> **(1)** a statement of—

>> **(A)** all significant factors and significant subfactors which the executive agency reasonably expects to consider in evaluating sealed bids (including price) or competitive proposals

(including cost or price, cost-related or price-related factors and subfactors, and noncost-related or nonprice-related factors and subfactors); and

(B) the relative importance assigned to each of those factors and subfactors; and

(2)(A) in the case of sealed bids—

(i) a statement that sealed bids will be evaluated without discussions with the bidders; and

(ii) the time and place for the opening of the sealed bids; or

(B) in the case of competitive proposals—

(i) either a statement that the proposals are intended to be evaluated with, and award made after, discussions with the offerors, or a statement that the proposals are intended to be evaluated, and award made, without discussions with the offerors (other than discussions conducted for the purpose of minor clarification) unless discussions are determined to be necessary; and

(ii) the time and place for submission of proposals.

(c) Evaluation factors

(1) In prescribing the evaluation factors to be included in each solicitation for competitive proposals, an executive agency—

(A) shall clearly establish the relative importance assigned to the evaluation factors and subfactors, including the quality of the product or services to be provided (including technical capability, management capability, prior experience, and past performance of the offeror);

(B) shall include cost or price to the Federal Government as an evaluation factor that must be considered in the evaluation of proposals; and

(C) shall disclose to offerors whether all evaluation factors other than cost or price, when combined, are—

(i) significantly more important than cost or price;

(ii) approximately equal in importance to cost or price; or

(iii) significantly less important than cost or price.

(2) The regulations implementing subparagraph (C) of paragraph (1) may not define the terms "significantly more important" and "significantly less important" as specific numeric weights that would be applied uniformly to all solicitations or a class of solicitations.

(d) Additional information in solicitation

Nothing in this section prohibits an executive agency from—

(1) providing additional information in a solicitation, including numeric weights for all evaluation factors and subfactors on a case-by-case basis; or

(2) stating in a solicitation that award will be made to the offeror that meets the solicitation's mandatory requirements at the lowest cost or price.

(e) Evaluation of purchase options

An executive agency, in issuing a solicitation for a contract to be awarded using sealed bid procedures, may not include in such solicitation a clause providing for the evaluation of prices for options to purchase additional property or services under the contract unless the executive agency has determined that there is a reasonable likelihood that the options will be exercised.

(June 30, 1949, c. 288, Title III, § 303A, as added July 18, 1984, Pub.L. 98–369, Div. B, Title VII, § 2711(a)(2), 98 Stat. 1178, and amended Oct. 13, 1994, Pub.L. 103–355, Title I, §§ 1061(a), (b), 1062, Title IV, § 4402(b), 108 Stat. 3266, 3267, 3348; Feb. 10, 1996, Pub.L. 104–106, Div. D, Title XLII, § 4202(b)(2), 110 Stat. 653.)

HISTORICAL AND STATUTORY NOTES

Revision Notes and Legislative Reports

1984 Acts. Section 101 amends the FPASA by adding after section 310 (41 U.S.C. § 260) the solicitation requirements for civilian procurements.

Section 311(a) establishes standards for drafting specifications. Executive agencies would be required to state their purchase specifications, which serve as the baseline for the evaluation of offers, in a manner which would permit effective competition. A second standard requires that agencies only include restrictive provisions or conditions in specifications to the extent necessary to meet their minimum needs.

Depending on the agency's needs and the market available to meet them, section 311(a) permits agencies to state their specifications in terms of functional, performance, or detailed design requirements.

Subsection 311(b)(1) requires agencies to include in their solicitations for sealed bids and competitive proposals, in addition to a description of their needs, a list of the evaluation factors—including price—which are reasonably expected to have a significant bearing on the selection for award. Agencies also are required to indicate the relative order of importance of these factors in the evaluation process.

Subsections 311(b)(2) and (3) require that agencies state in their solicitations how they intend to evaluate and award submissions—either with or without discussions. In the case of sealed bids, the statement includes information on the time and place for the opening of bids; for competitive proposals, the statement includes the time and the place for the submission of proposals. Senate Report No. 98–50.

1994 Acts. Senate Report Nos. 103–258 and 103–259, and House Conference Report No. 103–712, see 1994 U.S. Code Cong. and Adm. News p. 2561.

1996 Acts. House Conference Report No. 104–450, see 1996 U.S. Code Cong. and Adm. News, p. 238.

Amendments

1996 Amendments. Subsec. (b). Pub.L. 104–106, § 4202(b)(2), added "a procurement for commercial items using special simplified procedures or" following "(other than for".

1994   Amendments. Subsec.   (b).
Pub.L.   103–355,   §§ 1061(a)(1)(A),
4402(b), substituted in: subpar. (1)(A),
"all significant factors and significant
subfactors which the executive agency
reasonably expects to consider in evaluating sealed bids (including price) or competitive proposals (including cost or
price, cost-related or price-related factors
and subfactors, and noncost-related or
nonprice-related factors and subfactors)"
for "all significant factors (including
price) which the executive agency reasonably expects to consider in evaluating
sealed bids or competitive proposals";
and in the parenthetical matter preceding
par. (1), "a purchase for an amount not
greater than the simplified acquisition
threshold" for "small purchases", respectively.

Subsec. (b)(1)(B).   Pub.L. 103–355,
§ 1061(a)(1)(B), substituted "factors and
subfactors" for "factors".

Subsec. (b)(2)(B)(i).   Pub.L. 103–355,
§ 1061(a)(2), inserted the introductory
word "either" and substituted "or a statement that the proposals are intended to
be evaluated, and award made, without
discussions with the offerors (other than
discussions conducted for the purpose of
minor clarification) unless discussions
are determined to be necessary" for "but
might be evaluated and awarded without
discussion with the offerors".

Subsecs. (c), (d).   Pub.L. 103–355,
§ 1061(b), added subsecs. (c) and (d).

Subsec. (e).   Pub.L. 103–355, § 1062,
added subsec. (e).

Effective and Applicability Provisions
1996 Acts. Amendment by Pub.L.
104–106 effective Feb. 10, 1996, except as
otherwise provided, see section 4401 of
Pub.L. 104–106, set out as a note under
section 251 of this title.

1994 Acts. Amendment by sections
1061(a) and (b), 1062, and 4402(b) of
Pub.L. 103–355 effective Oct. 13, 1994,
except as otherwise provided, see section
10001 of Pub.L. 103–355, set out as a
note under section 251 of this title.

1984 Acts. Section applicable with respect to any solicitation for bids or proposals issued after Mar. 31, 1985, see
section 2751(a) of Pub.L. 98–369, set out
as a note under section 251 of this title.

Authorization of Telecommuting for Federal Contractors
Pub.L. 108–136, Div. A, Title XIV,
§ 1428, Nov. 24, 2003, 117 Stat. 1670,
provided that:

"**(a) Amendment to the Federal Acquisition Regulation.**—Not later than 180
days after the date of the enactment of
this Act [Nov. 24, 2003], the Federal Acquisition Regulatory Council shall amend
the Federal Acquisition Regulation issued
in accordance with sections 6 and 25 of
the Office of Federal Procurement Policy
Act (41 U.S.C. 405 and 421) to permit
telecommuting by employees of Federal
Government contractors in the performance of contracts entered into with executive agencies.

"**(b) Content of amendment.**—The regulation issued pursuant to subsection (a)
[of this note] shall, at a minimum, provide that solicitations for the acquisition
of property or services may not set forth
any requirement or evaluation criteria
that would—

"**(1)** render an offeror ineligible to
enter into a contract on the basis of the
inclusion of a plan of the offeror to
permit the offeror's employees to telecommute, unless the contracting officer
concerned first determines that the requirements of the agency, including security requirements, cannot be met if
the telecommuting is permitted and
documents in writing the basis for that
determination; or

"**(2)** reduce the scoring of an offer
on the basis of the inclusion in the
offer of a plan of the offeror to permit
the offeror's employees to telecommute, unless the contracting officer
concerned first determines that the requirements of the agency, including
security requirements, would be adversely impacted if telecommuting is
permitted and documents in writing
the basis for that determination.

"**(c) Definition.**—In this section [this
note], the term 'executive agency' has the
meaning given that term in section 4(1) of
the Office of Federal Procurement Policy
Act (41 U.S.C. 403(1))."

Small Business Act
This section not to affect or supersede
the provisions of section 637(a) of Title
15, Commerce and Trade, see section
2711(c) of Pub.L. 98–369, set out as a
note under section 253 of this title.

Definitions
The definitions in 40 U.S.C.A. § 102 apply to terms appearing in this subchapter.

LIBRARY REFERENCES

American Digest System
United States ⊕64.15, 64.25, 64.30.
Key Number System Topic No. 393.

Research References

Treatises and Practice Aids
West's Federal Administrative Practice § 625, Contracting by Negotiation.
West's Federal Administrative Practice § 632, Specification and Design Problems.

WESTLAW ELECTRONIC RESEARCH

See Westlaw guide following the Explanation pages of this volume.

Notes of Decisions

1. Generally

Government has right to specify terms on which it will let contracts; its specifications may relate to kind and quality of product, to potential contractor's ability to produce particular quantity of it, or to produce it in a certain period of time, and its specifications may also extend to forbidding contractor to produce product in a manner, that does not comply with government's policies, such as a prohibition against denying employment to females or against denying them a certain kind of seniority. Crown Zellerbach Corp. v. Marshall, E.D.La.1977, 441 F.Supp. 1110. Public Contracts ⊕ 7

2. Duty of contractor

Fact that electrical conduits could not be installed overhead in precise manner depicted by specification drawings for naval hospital electrical system, and had to be installed at some points outside corridor itself, did not automatically relieve contractor of duty to install conduits overhead. Blake Const. Co., Inc. v. U.S., C.A.Fed.1993, 987 F.2d 743, rehearing denied, in banc suggestion declined, certiorari denied 114 S.Ct. 438, 510 U.S. 963, 126 L.Ed.2d 372. United States ⊕ 73(17)

Fact that contracting officer failed to recognize that the United States was liable for contractor's earlier reliance on defective design specification which government had furnished for rotary switch that was incorporated into radio receiving set used in military aircraft and had refused to pay damages did not alter contractor's obligation to follow contracting officer's instructions to substitute another switch and contractor was not entitled to continue to manufacture radios with the defective switch and then seek additional recovery for the working of such radios to replace them with the proper switch. S.W. Electronics & Mfg. Corp. v. U.S., Ct.Cl.1981, 655 F.2d 1078, 228 Ct.Cl. 333. United States ⊗ 70(30)

In undertaking a government contract, contractor promises to perform according to the contract specifications, and Government has right to insist on contractor performance in compliance with them. Jet Const. Co., Inc. v. U.S., Ct.Cl. 1976, 531 F.2d 538, 209 Ct.Cl. 200. United States ⊗ 73(1)

The Government has the right to insist on the contractor's compliance with the contract specifications unless they are defective or unworkable; and the fact that a better manner of doing some particular part of the work exists or that no useful purpose is served by certain contract requirements, will not relieve the plaintiff of the duty of performing the work in the manner to which it has agreed. WRB Corp. v. U.S., Ct.Cl.1968, 183 Ct.Cl. 409. United States ⊗ 70(23); United States ⊗ 73(22)

3. Assumption of risk

A government contractor who submits his bid without reading all specifications does so at his peril; in such a case, the contractor assumes the risk of complying with the specifications and cannot complain later on if he is required to perform the contract in accordance with the specifications. Robert L. Guyler Co. v. U.S., Ct.Cl.1979, 593 F.2d 406, 219 Ct.Cl. 403, certiorari denied 100 S.Ct. 85, 444 U.S. 843, 62 L.Ed.2d 55, rehearing denied 100 S.Ct. 438, 444 U.S. 957, 62 L.Ed.2d 330. United States ⊗ 70(31)

Contractor which fails to submit to contracting officer the matter of discrepancy between drawing and specifications proceeds at his own risk and expense. James A. Mann, Inc. v. U.S., Ct.Cl.1976,

535 F.2d 51, 210 Ct.Cl. 104. United States ⊗ 74(6)

Where certain provisions of government contract were meaningless if interpretation propounded by government contract were adopted, government contractor voluntarily assumed all risks of incorrect interpretation in going ahead with its bid preparation without consulting with proper authorities and therefore contractor, seeking additional sum for additional work, could not rely on principle that ambiguities in government-drawn contracts were to be construed against the drafter. Jamsar, Inc. v. U.S., Ct.Cl.1971, 442 F.2d 930, 194 Ct.Cl. 819. United States ⊗ 70(27)

Dredging contract which provided that contractor could transport fill material to alternative private property site selected by contractor clearly and unequivocally assigned to contractor the burden of complying with all applicable local laws, imposing on contractor the inchoate obligation to research relevant local legal requirements, as well as any attending problems such as local opposition that might hinder contractor's compliance; thus, contractor bore the risk that local authorities would deny conditional use permit allowing disposal of dredged material on alternative private property site in county. L.W. Matteson, Inc. v. U.S., Fed.Cl.2004, 61 Fed.Cl. 296. United States ⊗ 70(22.1)

4. Reliance

To recover an equitable adjustment based upon an erroneous specification in government contract, contractor must show that it was misled by the error in the specification; conversely, when contractor is not misled by error in government contract specification, it cannot claim an equitable adjustment. E.L. Hamm & Associates, Inc. v. England, C.A.Fed.2004, 379 F.3d 1334. United States ⊗ 70(30)

Federal highway repair contract designation of certain quarry as source of armor stone for riprap, in connection with project engineer's memorandum indicating that official inspection led to conclusion that high ledge formation in quarry would produce substantial yield of armor stone, constituted an indication of site condition, entitling contractor to equitable adjustment when contractor was unable to obtain armor stone of contract quality from quarry, leading to relaxation of specifications; contractor was not required to make scientifically educated skeptical analysis of contract and the documents made available for bidders. Stock & Grove, Inc. v. U.S., Ct.Cl.1974, 493 F.2d 629, 204 Ct.Cl. 103. Highways ⟷ 113(4)

Government contractor hired to repair for Coast Guard a tower and light on pipe pile foundation resting on submerged knoll had right, after having made a reasonable inspection which gave him no additional knowledge, to continue to rely on contract drawing showing ocean bottom was rock and on the general understanding to same effect. Vann v. U.S., Ct.Cl.1970, 420 F.2d 968, 190 Ct.Cl. 546. United States ⟷ 70(30)

A contractor who bids for work has right to rely on plans and specifications submitted to him for bidding purposes. Hensel Phelps Const. Co. v. U.S., C.A.10 (Colo.) 1969, 413 F.2d 701. Contracts ⟷ 166

Generally, the contractor may rely on definitive contract representations of the government. Thompson Ramo Wooldridge Inc. v. U.S., Ct.Cl.1966, 361 F.2d 222, 175 Ct.Cl. 527. United States ⟷ 70(30)

Where Government makes positive statements in specifications or drawings for guidance of bidders, a contractor has right to rely on them regardless of contractual provisions requiring contractor to make investigations. Arcole Midwest Corp. v. U.S., Ct.Cl.1953, 113 F.Supp. 278, 125 Ct.Cl. 818. United States ⟷ 66

Unless some reason therefor is indicated, contractors are not usually required, prior to bidding, to undertake expensive and time-consuming tolerance checks with respect to every possible permitted dimension of every component in an article to be manufactured under the contract simply to verify the accuracy of the Government's drawings and their suitability for the production of a properly functioning end item, but they are entitled to assume that parts made in compliance with prescribed dimensions and permitted tolerances will, when joined, function properly. Ithaca Gun Co., Inc. v. U.S., Ct.Cl.1966, 176 Ct.Cl. 437. United States ⟷ 70(29)

Where the instructions to bidders expressly warned that any explanation desired concerning the meaning of the specifications and drawings must be requested in writing with sufficient time allowed for a reply to reach the bidder before the submission of bids, and that the Government would not be bound by any oral explanations given before the contract was awarded, the failure of a bidder to so proceed will preclude the bidders' subsequent reliance on an alleged oral explanation. Jefferson Const. Co. v. U.S., Ct.Cl.1960, 151 Ct.Cl. 75. United States ⟷ 70(3)

5. Disclosure by government

The government is under no duty to volunteer information regarding performance of a contract which the contractor can reasonably be expected to seek out himself, and such rule is applicable in situations where information at issue can readily be obtained from outside sources or where the contract itself contemplates a certain means by which the information might be acquired, such as by site investigation. Petrofsky v. U.S., Ct.Cl.1980, 616 F.2d 494, 222 Ct.Cl. 450, certiorari denied 101 S.Ct. 1488, 450 U.S. 968, 67 L.Ed.2d 618. United States ⟷ 70(30)

Fact that contract specifications, clear, reasonable, possible, complete and competitive call for a unique or specialty item rather than a shelf item imposes no duty on Government to either affirmatively disclose the novelty of the item or entitle contractor to additional compensation for any difficulty or unanticipated expense incurred in meeting the contract specifications. Jet Const. Co., Inc. v. U.S., Ct. Cl.1976, 531 F.2d 538, 209 Ct.Cl. 200. United States ⟷ 70(21)

Record failed to establish an awareness on part of government, during contracting process, that it possessed vital information concerning production of radar map sets—including factor of bow tolerance in relation to relief model—which bidders in general, or plaintiff in particular, did not know and could not reasonably be expected to show; hence, circumstances did not impose on government an implied obligation to furnish the bidders with information beyond scope of the contract specifications with respect to bow tolerance factor in relation to relief model. Panoramic Studios, Inc. v. U.S., Ct.Cl.1969, 413 F.2d 1156, 188 Ct.Cl. 1092. United States ⟷ 74(11)

Air Force procurement regulations did not authorize it to disclose "unit pricing information" involuntarily submitted by contractors.   Canadian   Commercial Corp. v. Department of Air Force, D.D.C. 2006, 442 F.Supp.2d 15. United States ⊱ 64.5

Contractor did not establish that government breached dredging contract under superior knowledge doctrine by failing to reveal its alleged prior knowledge of county's shoreline protection act and level of local hostility in county towards dredging operations; contractual obligation to uncover potential roadblocks to contractor's proposed disposal site in county was on the contractor, not the government, and contractor presented no evidence in the record that government affirmatively misled it regarding local opposition. L.W. Matteson, Inc. v. U.S., Fed.Cl.2004, 61 Fed.Cl. 296. United States ⊱ 70(30)

6. Construction of specifications

None of specifications of government contract are to be rejected as meaningless when it is possible to give them a meaning consistent with the specifications of the whole. Jamsar, Inc. v. U.S., Ct.Cl. 1971, 442 F.2d 930, 194 Ct.Cl. 819. United States ⊱ 70(4)

Where government draws specifications which are susceptible of a certain construction and the contractor actually and reasonably so construes them, justice and equity require that construction be adopted. Gorn Corp. v. U.S., Ct.Cl.1970, 424 F.2d 588, 191 Ct.Cl. 560. See, also, Kings Electronics Co. v. U.S., 1965, 341 F.2d 632, 169 Ct.Cl. 433; W.H. Edwards Engineering Corp. v. U.S., 1963, 161 Ct. Cl. 322; Peter Kiewit Sons' Co. v. U.S., 1948, 109 Ct.Cl. 390. United States ⊱ 70(3)

Where tramway contractor's interpretation of contract specification that existing tramway might be used in erecting new towers on tramway was not reasonable, Court of Claims would not adopt contractor's construction of clause. Chris Berg, Inc. v. U.S., Ct.Cl.1968, 389 F.2d 401, 182 Ct.Cl. 23. United States ⊱ 70(3)

Where United States draws contract specifications which are susceptible to more than one interpretation, and contractor's interpretation is both fair and reasonable, Court of Claims will uphold contractor's construction of the contract. Maxwell Dynamometer Co. v. U.S., Ct.Cl.

1967, 386 F.2d 855, 181 Ct.Cl. 607. United States ⊱ 70(3)

All parts of the specifications contained in government contracts must be read together and harmonized, if at all possible. Gelco Builders & Burjay Const. Corp. v. U.S., Ct.Cl.1966, 369 F.2d 992, 177 Ct.Cl. 1025. United States ⊱ 70(4)

7. Ambiguous or inconsistent specifications

Ambiguity in solicitation for government contract to provide facility maintenance and utility services at Marine Corps recruit facility, as to amount of ceramic tile maintenance called for under contract, was "patent ambiguity," thus triggering duty on part of bidder to inquire into ambiguity, and bidder's failure to inquire required interpretation of ambiguous provisions in favor of government, rather than bidder; line items at issue were expressed in manner different than majority of line items, and totals yielded under bidder's interpretation were disproportionate to remainder of solicitation. NVT Technologies, Inc. v. U.S., C.A.Fed.2004, 370 F.3d 1153. United States ⊱ 70(30)

Where Government bid documents contained diagram of plan for diversion of river during construction of locks and dams, but stated that diagram was "schematic and for the purpose of estimating only," such documents contained patent ambiguity as to binding nature of diagrams, and contractor which ignored inherent conflict in documents and submitted bid without attempting to resolve such ambiguity could not recover from Government for additional expenses allegedly incurred as result of Government's interpretation of contract specifications. S.O.G. of Arkansas v. U.S., Ct. Cl.1976, 546 F.2d 367, 212 Ct.Cl. 125. United States ⊱ 70(31)

Note on contractor's bid on contract for modernization of federal building did not give notice of ambiguity as to whether contractor was required to furnish and install a generator and, having failed to give notice of the alleged ambiguity before bidding, contractor was precluded from recovering cost of the generator on basis of the alleged ambiguity. James A. Mann, Inc. v. U.S., Ct.Cl.1976, 535 F.2d 51, 210 Ct.Cl. 104. United States ⊱ 74(8)

Contract specification susceptible to more than one interpretation, each interpretation found to be consistent with contract's language and parties' objectively ascertainable intentions, becomes convincing proof of ambiguity, and burden of such ambiguity falls solely upon party who drew specification. Bennett v. U.S., Ct.Cl.1967, 371 F.2d 859, 178 Ct.Cl. 61. Contracts ⬤ 199(1)

Any ambiguous government-drawn specification in contract must be construed against it. C.J. Langenfelder & Son, Inc. v. U.S., Ct.Cl.1965, 341 F.2d 600, 169 Ct.Cl. 465. United States ⬤ 70(3)

Where specifications stated that interior concrete masonry units were to be painted except where otherwise specified and that interior exposed masonry surfaces, indicated on the drawings to be painted, were to be painted in accordance with attached figure, and figure did not specify what surfaces were to be painted, and one drawing provided for painting of walls in operating room, contractor was required to paint only walls in operating room. Guyler v. U.S., Ct.Cl. 1963, 314 F.2d 506, 161 Ct.Cl. 159. United States ⬤ 70(8)

Defendant contractor was entitled to recover reduction in contract price effected by Government because of contractor's failure to use particular type of exterior shipping container where specifications were confusing at best and contractor relied on prior experience in packing for Government contracts did not unreasonably interpret specifications. Abe L. Greenberg Co. v. U.S., Ct.Cl.1962, 300 F.2d 443, 156 Ct.Cl. 434. United States ⬤ 70(30)

Inconsistency in the specifications, if any, would have been resolved by the bidder examining the work and deciding for himself. Central Dredging Co. v. U.S., Ct.Cl.1941, 94 Ct.Cl. 1. Navigable Waters ⬤ 6; United States ⬤ 70(30)

8. Interpretation, request for

Bidder's failure to inquire as to ambiguity in solicitation for government contract to provide facility maintenance and utility services at Marine Corps recruit facility, regarding amount of ceramic tile maintenance called for under contract, precluded bidder's subsequent "mistake in bid" claim alleging that the specification was defective and that solicitation

should thus be rebid. NVT Technologies, Inc. v. U.S., C.A.Fed.2004, 370 F.3d 1153. United States ⬤ 64.25

Bidder on energy monitoring and control system for Veterans' Administration Hospital was not entitled to any equitable adjustment recovery with regard to award of base contract on ground that government had provided defective drawings on which to bid where bidder, upon discovery of government's error, failed to inquire of the appropriate government official in a specific and forthright manner as to the discrepancies despite opportunities prior to the award. Johnson Controls, Inc. v. U.S., Ct.Cl.1982, 671 F.2d 1312, 229 Ct.Cl. 445. United States ⬤ 70(29)

Doctrine that before submitting its bids a prospective government contractor should attempt to have the Government resolve any patent conflict in contract terms is a major device of preventive hygiene; it is designed to avoid postaward disputes by encouraging contractors to seek clarification before anyone is legally bound. Robert L. Guyler Co. v. U.S., Ct.Cl.1979, 593 F.2d 406, 219 Ct.Cl. 403, certiorari denied 100 S.Ct. 85, 444 U.S. 843, 62 L.Ed.2d 55, rehearing denied 100 S.Ct. 438, 444 U.S. 957, 62 L.Ed.2d 330. United States ⬤ 70(30)

Where patent and glaring discrepancy exists in contract drawing, and such discrepancy would be recognized by reasonable bidder, there is burden imposed on such bidder to seek clarification of such discrepancy from appropriate government official before submitting bid, if bidder, subsequent to award to bid, hopes to rely on its unilateral resolution of discrepancy issue as basis for subsequent contract price adjustment claim, and this proposition is for application in situations where bidder knew, as well as in situations where bidder should have known, of the discrepancy. Wickham Contracting Co., Inc. v. U.S., Ct.Cl.1976, 546 F.2d 395, 212 Ct.Cl. 318. United States ⬤ 70(30)

Discrepancy between painting schedules, which did not include ceilings in category of "surfaces not to be painted," and finish schedules, which indicated that ceilings were to be of "exposed concrete," was not subtle but was obvious, imposing on contractor duty to inquire prior to submission of bid. Merando,

Inc. v. U.S., Ct.Cl.1973, 475 F.2d 598, 201 Ct.Cl. 19. United States ⇔ 70(4)

Where Government's instructions to bidders called for submission in writing by bidder of request for any explanation or interpretation of specifications and drawings before submission of bid, contractor's entitlement to rely upon its interpretation was to be tested on principle that if it was confronted with obvious ambiguity, it was required to consult Government concerning Government's intention with respect to ambiguity before relying upon its own interpretation in submission of bid. John McShain, Inc. v. U.S., Ct.Cl.1972, 462 F.2d 489, 199 Ct.Cl. 364. United States ⇔ 64.25

Where there was at least a patent ambiguity in agreement between government and carrier participating in mass movement of household goods of individual members of Air Force with respect to continued availability of carrier's previously filed rates, carrier had duty to inquire as to meaning of unexplained term in relationship to alternation clause and with respect to statement that volume rate was "an exception" to carrier's published rate and where carrier failed to do so carrier's previously existing rate remained in force and effect and pertinent transportation charges could correctly be computed on that basis if lowest available rate. Container Transport Intern., Inc. v. U.S., Ct.Cl.1971, 437 F.2d 1365, 194 Ct. Cl. 320. Carriers ⇔ 192

Where there was an obvious discrepancy between various sheets of government contract drawings relating to communication manholes, it was incumbent upon contractor, in connection with submission of its bid, to obtain a clarification from the government; and having failed to do so, Corps of Engineers Board of Contract Appeals reasonably concluded, under the circumstances, that the controlling drawing for construction of the manhole system was the sheet indicating that the two manholes in question, rather than being "existing" facilities, were to be constructed. Woodcrest Const. Co. v. U.S., Ct.Cl.1969, 408 F.2d 406, 187 Ct.Cl. 249, certiorari denied 90 S.Ct. 2164, 398 U.S. 958, 26 L.Ed.2d 542. United States ⇔ 70(30)

Although potential Government contractor may have some duty to inquire about major patent discrepancy, obvious omission, or drastic conflict in provisions

in contract, he is not normally required, in absence of clear warning in contract, to seek clarification of any and all ambiguities, doubts, or possible differences in interpretation. WPC Enterprises, Inc. v. U.S., Ct.Cl.1963, 323 F.2d 874, 163 Ct.Cl. 1. United States ⇔ 70(2.1)

Contractor had no claim against United States in respect to money withheld to pay substitute contractor for weather-stripping windows in defense housing project, where specifications and drawings which accompanied invitation for bids and which became part of contract raised uncertainty as to whether only entrance doors or windows as well were to be weather-stripped, and contractor was aware of uncertainty and did not seek interpretation from Government before submitting his bid but relied on his interpretation that windows did not have to be weather-stripped. Beacon Const. Co. of Mass. v. U.S., Ct.Cl.1963, 314 F.2d 501, 161 Ct.Cl. 1. United States ⇔ 70(30)

9. Drawings in conflict with specifications

Specification of government contract requiring a macadam base layer under bituminous concrete surface of roadway and other paved areas which contractor had agreed to construct was unambiguous and contractor was not entitled to recover difference between gravel base course and more expensive macadam base course even though contract contained drawings indicating a gravel base course, in view of contract provision that specifications would govern over drawings. William F. Klingensmith, Inc. v. U.S., Ct.Cl.1974, 505 F.2d 1257, 205 Ct. Cl. 651. United States ⇔ 70(4)

10. Deviations—Generally

Where changes in government construction contract were not submitted for approval in writing, contractor was bound by unambiguous language of specifications. Northwestern Indus. Piping, Inc. v. U.S., Ct.Cl.1972, 467 F.2d 1308, 199 Ct.Cl. 540. United States ⇔ 70(6.1)

Where government contracting officer advertised for bids for cloth meeting certain specifications and contractor returned bid with attached sample which appeared to meet but which materially varied from specifications as shown by later laboratory tests, and contract was awarded to bidder and incorporated specifications, contract was invalid and not binding on Government. Prestex Inc. v. U.S., Ct.Cl.1963, 320 F.2d 367, 162 Ct.Cl. 620. United States ⟳ 66

Offer in response to solicitation by the Department of Veterans Affairs (VA) for distribution of pharmaceutical products in 14 VA regions was an "all or none offer" within meaning of the Federal Acquisition Regulation (FAR), notwithstanding that offer recognized that the VA maintained the right to set aside three regions for small business concerns, where proposal limited acceptance to "all regions" contained in the offer. AmerisourceBergen Drug Corp. v. U.S., Fed.Cl. 2004, 60 Fed.Cl. 30. United States ⟳ 64.30

11. ——— Waiver by government, deviations

Deviations from advertised specifications for government contract may be waived by contracting officers provided they do not go to substance of bid or work an injustice to other bidders; question is whether bid represented "substantial deviation", i.e., one which affects either price, quantity or quality of article offered. Albano Cleaners, Inc. v. U.S., Ct.Cl.1972, 455 F.2d 556, 197 Ct.Cl. 450. United States ⟳ 64.30

12. Errors and deficiencies—Generally

Defect in specification for government maintenance contract, which understated acreage figure for which policing work was to be provided on yearly basis, was latent, such that contractor, having relied on defective specification in calculating its bid for policing work, was eligible for equitable adjustment; facial inspection of contract's mowing and policing figures did not reveal any glaring or obvious discrepancy, and even though daily mowing and policing acreages were the same, number of steps were necessary to reverse-engineer figures in solicitation to arrive at daily policing acreage for comparison with single mowing acreage, and nothing in contract or bidding process required or suggested that contractor perform such calculations. E.L. Hamm & Associates, Inc. v. England, C.A.Fed. 2004, 379 F.3d 1334. United States ⟳ 70(30)

Even assuming that government designs and specifications were deficient, contractor's act in notifying Government of alleged design deficiency discharged its duty not to knowingly produce defective

items without first contacting Government, and thereafter, in absence of either an order by Government immediately to suspend production or of a change order modifying designed specifications, it was contractor's right to go forward with production even though in doing so Government might incur liability for defective products. Switlik Parachute Co., Inc. v. U.S., Ct.Cl.1978, 573 F.2d 1228, 216 Ct. Cl. 362. United States ⟳ 74(1)

Bare showing that a functionally interchangeable end products of equal or superior utility can be produced from specifications different from those previously in force does not imply defectiveness of the prior specifications, particularly where the prior specifications have resulted in totally satisfactory production. Firestone Tire & Rubber Co. v. U.S., Ct. Cl.1977, 558 F.2d 577, 214 Ct.Cl. 457. United States ⟳ 64.25

The government cannot make a contractor the insurer of all government mistakes merely by insertion of contract clause requiring bidder or contractor to obtain verification of ambiguous provisions from contracting officers. Mountain Home Contractors v. U.S., Ct.Cl. 1970, 425 F.2d 1260, 192 Ct.Cl. 16. United States ⟳ 70(29)

13. ——— Waiver by contractor, errors and deficiencies

Government contractor's complaints about bad specifications can be waived if not promptly made known to the government. Rixon Electronics, Inc. v. U.S., Ct.Cl.1976, 536 F.2d 1345, 210 Ct.Cl. 309. United States ⟳ 74(6)

Contractor, by not communicating with Air Force causes of impossibility of which it had knowledge, thereby waived some of defects in specifications which Air Force might, if notified, have corrected to its own as well as contractor's advantage. Dynalectron Corp. (Pacific Division) v. U.S., Ct.Cl.1975, 518 F.2d 594, 207 Ct.Cl. 349. United States ⟳ 70(30)

14. Omissions

When contractor is faced with an obvious omission, inconsistency, or discrepancy of significance in government specification, he is obligated to bring the situation to the government's attention if he intends subsequently to resolve the issue in his own favor. E.L. Hamm & Associates, Inc. v. England, C.A.Fed.

2004, 379 F.3d 1334. United States 70(30)

If there are omissions or inconsistencies in provisions of a government contract that are obvious, contractor is required to make inquiry regarding them before submitting its bid. B.D. Click Co., Inc. v. U.S., Ct.Cl.1980, 614 F.2d 748, 222 Ct.Cl. 290. United States 70(30)

Where neither contract nor bid invitation expressly restricted or eliminated interim federal specification, incorporated by reference into the contract, which allowed supplier the option to furnish trims of wrought fabrication whenever cast fabrication was specified, government could not by an act of omission eliminate the option so as to require supplier to provide exclusively cast fabrication for locksets to be installed on doors of government building. Blake Const. Co., Inc. v. U.S., Ct.Cl.1979, 597 F.2d 1357, 220 Ct.Cl. 56. United States 70(9)

Where amendment to invitation for bids provided for additional work outside the contract limit line and did not move the limit line but did provide additional detailed drawing which described only the work outside the limit line, the discrepancy created more than a mere ambiguity subject to reasonable interpretation by the contractor; rather, it evidenced an obvious omission on the part of the Government which imposed upon contractor a duty to inquire if he intended to benefit from his interpretation in the future, and upon failure to do so, contractor was not entitled to recover damages for work outside the contract limit line. Merando, Inc. v. U.S., Ct.Cl.1973, 475 F.2d 601, 201 Ct.Cl. 23. United States 70(4)

Assuming arguendo that drawing was missing from bid package for government contract, where there was sufficient evidence to merit conclusion that plaintiff did in fact know that there was an omission in the request for quotations and it should have known that it was an omission of the type that required further inquiry, plaintiff did not act reasonably in preparing bid knowing that drawing was missing and not inquiring as to its contents. Space Corp. v. U.S., Ct.Cl.1972, 470 F.2d 536, 200 Ct.Cl. 1. United States 64.40(3)

Under contract for construction of post office, items not contained in final plans and specifications which builder had in its possession when it bid did not neces-sarily constitute extra work, but rather post office department publication 39, tentative drawings, and amendatory letters and the like were part of bid and contract. Leo A. Daly Co. v. Ray Smith Industries, Inc., C.A.5 (Tex.) 1968, 387 F.2d 899. Contracts 232(1)

Where original scope of work provision in government contract provided for installation of "all air conditioning new and existing supply ducts" and was subsequently modified to provide that "all air conditioning new and existing should be covered," a rational analysis of the amended sentence, including its relation to other specification provisions, showed that an inadvertent omission had been made and placed duty on contractor to make inquiry to bring matter to government's attention, and if contractor which did not do so was in fact misled, it was result of an unreasonable, unilateral mistake for which judicial relief was unavailable. Gelco Builders & Burjay Const. Corp. v. U.S., Ct.Cl.1966, 369 F.2d 992, 177 Ct.Cl. 1025. United States 70(29)

15. Incorporation of specification

Government contract gave contractor adequate notice that electric power receptacles to be supplied under contract to upgrade aircraft carrier berthing facilities were those described in qualified products list on which only one manufacturer had qualified, even though contract did not physically incorporate specifications and qualified products list but only referred bidders to them. American Elec. Contracting Corp. v. U.S., Ct.Cl.1978, 579 F.2d 602, 217 Ct.Cl. 338. United States 70(8)

16. Design specifications—Generally

"Design specifications" describe in precise detail materials to be employed and manner in which construction work is to be performed; contractor has no discretion to deviate from specifications, but must follow them as road map. Blake Const. Co., Inc. v. U.S., C.A.Fed.1993, 987 F.2d 743, rehearing denied, in banc suggestion declined, certiorari denied 114 S.Ct. 438, 510 U.S. 963, 126 L.Ed.2d 372. Public Contracts 19.1

17. —— Miscellaneous cases

Electrical subcontractor was not entitled to equitable adjustment for additional costs incurred as result of government's insistence that electrical conduits at naval hospital be installed overhead rather than in underground duct bank, as initially constructed, though specifications gave contractor some discretion to avoid conflict with other trades, where specification drawings depicted only overhead installation of electrical conduits, either exposed or concealed. Blake Const. Co., Inc. v. U.S., C.A.Fed. 1993, 987 F.2d 743, rehearing denied, in banc suggestion declined, certiorari denied 114 S.Ct. 438, 510 U.S. 963, 126 L.Ed.2d 372. United States ☞ 70(30)

18. Performance specifications—Generally

Mere fact that specification for construction project be performed precisely does not, by itself, indicate that it is "performance," providing discretion to contractor, and not "design," requiring strict compliance. Blake Const. Co., Inc. v. U.S., C.A.Fed.1993, 987 F.2d 743, rehearing denied, in banc suggestion declined, certiorari denied 114 S.Ct. 438, 510 U.S. 963, 126 L.Ed.2d 372. Public Contracts ☞ 19.1

"Performance specifications" for construction contracts set forth objective to be achieved, and successful bidder is expected to exercise his ingenuity in achieving that objective, selecting means and assuming responsibility for that selection. Blake Const. Co., Inc. v. U.S., C.A.Fed. 1993, 987 F.2d 743, rehearing denied, in banc suggestion declined, certiorari denied 114 S.Ct. 438, 510 U.S. 963, 126 L.Ed.2d 372. Public Contracts ☞ 19.1

19. ____ Miscellaneous cases

Bid protestor did not establish that contracting agency failed to properly evaluate past performance factor in conducting price/technical tradeoff determination, notwithstanding protestor's contention that the three pages devoted to past performance in the source selection decision document (SSDD) were insufficient because the SSDD did not contain a "head-to-head" comparison of the various strengths and weakness of the offerors and did not list any weaknesses for protestor or contract awardee. Dismas Charities, Inc. v. U.S., Fed.Cl.2004, 61 Fed.Cl. 191. United States ☞ 64.45(2)

20. Factors considered in evaluation—Generally

Every solicitation of a government contract must identify the evaluation factors and significant subfactors which will be used to evaluate proposals, as well as the relative importance of each factor and subfactor. PHT Supply Corp. v. U.S., Fed.Cl.2006, 71 Fed.Cl. 1. United States ☞ 64.25

21. ____ Price and value, factors considered in evaluation

Internal Revenue Service (IRS) sufficiently demonstrated that price was factor in its final decision to award contract for procurement of office automation systems, software, and maintenance services, even though successful proposal was double cost of competing bid and $500 million more than another proposal, where increased productivity of software, higher scores on workload performance tests, and nonquantified discriminators indicated that successful proposal offered substantially more value to government than other proposals. Lockheed Missiles & Space Co., Inc. v. Bentsen, C.A.Fed. 1993, 4 F.3d 955. United States ☞ 64.40(1)

22. ____ Geographic scope and location, factors considered in evaluation

Geographic scope of contract for local telecommunications services for federal agencies in an area consisting of the five boroughs of New York City and suburban locations in New York and New Jersey did not violate the Competition in Contracting Act (CICA) on theory that it gave unfair advantage to the incumbent, as the only company with sufficient facilities to service the entire area directly; boundary of the contract area was reasonably drawn, and size of the area did not preclude anyone from competing. WinStar Communications, Inc. v. U.S., Fed.Cl. 1998, 41 Fed.Cl. 748. United States ☞ 64.10

23. Time and place for submission

Policy by General Services Administration (GSA) of allowing submission of bids up to deadline for best and final offer (BAFO) does not conflict with statute requiring each solicitation for competitive proposals to include time and place for submission of proposals. 60 Key Centre Inc. v. Administrator of General Services Admin. (GSA), C.A.2 (N.Y.) 1995, 47 F.3d 55, certiorari denied 116 S.Ct. 50, 516 U.S. 806, 133 L.Ed.2d 15. United States ☞ 64.30

Timeliness rule of the Government Accountability Office (GAO) limiting ability of bidders to raise objections to a solicitation was not applicable to preclude the Court of Federal Claims from considering bid protestor's claim that solicitation was unduly restrictive, notwithstanding that protestor did not raise objection prior to time set for receipt of proposals. Wit Associates, Inc. v. U.S., Fed.Cl.2004, 62 Fed.Cl. 657. United States ⊕ 64.60(1)

Bidder did not establish that it was late in submitting its price proposal by e-mail only because contracting's agency's "affirmative direction" on its web site "instructing offerors to submit proposals by 2:00 PM U.S. Time Zones" materially contributed to its late bid, as record demonstrated that bidder did not actually rely on time zone designation on web site but attempted to comply with deadline in solicitation which was 2:00 p.m. local time, which was the time in Naples, Italy.

Conscoop-Consorzia Fra Coop. Di Prod. E Lavoro v. U.S., Fed.Cl.2004, 62 Fed.Cl. 219, affirmed 159 Fed.Appx. 184, 2005 WL 1368664. United States ⊕ 64.30

Decision of contracting officer for government lease to allow late submission of proposal after deadline for initial proposals was contrary to Competition in Contracting Act of 1984 (CICA) requirement for provision of notice of due date for initial proposals in solicitation for offers (SFO) and Federal Acquisition Regulation (FAR) requiring that bidders submit initial offers by deadline for initial proposals as established in SFO, and thus Court of Federal Claims would enjoin award of instant contract to late bidder. Aerolease Long Beach v. U.S., Fed.Cl.1994, 31 Fed. Cl. 342, affirmed 39 F.3d 1198. Injunction ⊕ 86; United States ⊕ 64.40(1)

§ 253b. Evaluation and award

(a) Basis

An executive agency shall evaluate sealed bids and competitive proposals, and award a contract, based solely on the factors specified in the solicitation.

(b) Rejection of bids or proposals

All sealed bids or competitive proposals received in response to a solicitation may be rejected if the agency head determines that such action is in the public interest.

(c) Opening of bids; promptness of award; written notice

Sealed bids shall be opened publicly at the time and place stated in the solicitation. The executive agency shall evaluate the bids in accordance with subsection (a) of this section without discussions with the bidders and, except as provided in subsection (b) of this section, shall award a contract with reasonable promptness to the responsible source whose bid conforms to the solicitation and is most advantageous to the United States, considering only price and the other price-related factors included in the solicitation. The award of a contract shall be made by transmitting, in writing or by electronic means, notice of the award to the successful bidder. Within 3 days after the date of contract award, the executive agency shall notify, in writing or by electronic means, each bidder not awarded the contract that the contract has been awarded.

(d) Discussions with offerors; written notification

(1) An executive agency shall evaluate competitive proposals in accordance with subsection (a) of this section and may award a contract—

    (A) after discussions with the offerors, provided that written or oral discussions have been conducted with all responsible offerors who submit proposals within the competitive range; or

    (B) based on the proposals received and without discussions with the offerors (other than discussions conducted for the purpose of minor clarification), if, as required by section 253a(b)(2)(B)(i) of this title, the solicitation included a statement that proposals are intended to be evaluated, and award made, without discussions, unless discussions are determined to be necessary.

  (2) If the contracting officer determines that the number of offerors that would otherwise be included in the competitive range under paragraph (1)(A) exceeds the number at which an efficient competition can be conducted, the contracting officer may limit the number of proposals in the competitive range, in accordance with the criteria specified in the solicitation, to the greatest number that will permit an efficient competition among the offerors rated most highly in accordance with such criteria.

  (3) Except as otherwise provided in subsection (b) of this section, the executive agency shall award a contract with reasonable promptness to the responsible source whose proposal is most advantageous to the United States, considering only cost or price and the other factors included in the solicitation. The executive agency shall award the contract by transmitting, in writing or by electronic means, notice of the award to such source and, within 3 days after the date of contract award, shall notify, in writing or by electronic means, all other offerors of the rejection of their proposals.

(e) Post-award debriefings

  (1) When a contract is awarded by the head of an executive agency on the basis of competitive proposals, an unsuccessful offeror, upon written request received by the agency within 3 days after the date on which the unsuccessful offeror receives the notification of the contract award, shall be debriefed and furnished the basis for the selection decision and contract award. The executive agency shall debrief the offeror within, to the maximum extent practicable, 5 days after receipt of the request by the executive agency.

  (2) The debriefing shall include, at a minimum—

    (A) the executive agency's evaluation of the significant weak or deficient factors in the offeror's offer;

    (B) the overall evaluated cost and technical rating of the offer of the contractor awarded the contract and the overall evaluated cost and technical rating of the offer of the debriefed offeror;

    (C) the overall ranking of all offers;

(D) a summary of the rationale for the award;

(E) in the case of a proposal that includes a commercial item that is an end item under the contract, the make and model of the item being provided in accordance with the offer of the contractor awarded the contract; and

(F) reasonable responses to relevant questions posed by the debriefed offeror as to whether source selection procedures set forth in the solicitation, applicable regulations, and other applicable authorities were followed by the executive agency.

(3) The debriefing may not include point-by-point comparisons of the debriefed offeror's offer with other offers and may not disclose any information that is exempt from disclosure under section 552(b) of Title 5.

(4) Each solicitation for competitive proposals shall include a statement that information described in paragraph (2) may be disclosed in post-award debriefings.

(5) If, within one year after the date of the contract award and as a result of a successful procurement protest, the executive agency seeks to fulfill the requirement under the protested contract either on the basis of a new solicitation of offers or on the basis of new best and final offers requested for that contract, the head of such executive agency shall make available to all offerors—

(A) the information provided in debriefings under this subsection regarding the offer of the contractor awarded the contract; and

(B) the same information that would have been provided to the original offerors.

(f) Preaward debriefings

(1) When the contracting officer excludes an offeror submitting a competitive proposal from the competitive range (or otherwise excludes such an offeror from further consideration prior to the final source selection decision), the excluded offeror may request in writing, within 3 days after the date on which the excluded offeror receives notice of its exclusion, a debriefing prior to award. The contracting officer shall make every effort to debrief the unsuccessful offeror as soon as practicable but may refuse the request for a debriefing if it is not in the best interests of the Government to conduct a debriefing at that time.

(2) The contracting officer is required to debrief an excluded offeror in accordance with subsection (e) of this section only if that offeror requested and was refused a preaward debriefing under paragraph (1) of this subsection.

(3) The debriefing conducted under this subsection shall include—

(A) the executive agency's evaluation of the significant elements in the offeror's offer;

(B) a summary of the rationale for the offeror's exclusion; and

(C) reasonable responses to relevant questions posed by the debriefed offeror as to whether source selection procedures set forth in the solicitation, applicable regulations, and other applicable authorities were followed by the executive agency.

(4) The debriefing conducted pursuant to this subsection may not disclose the number or identity of other offerors and shall not disclose information about the content, ranking, or evaluation of other offerors' proposals.

(g) Summary of debriefing

The contracting officer shall include a summary of any debriefing conducted under subsection (e) or (f) of this section in the contract file.

(h) Alternative dispute resolution

The Federal Acquisition Regulation shall include a provision encouraging the use of alternative dispute resolution techniques to provide informal, expeditious, and inexpensive procedures for an offeror to consider using before filing a protest, prior to the award of a contract, of the exclusion of the offeror from the competitive range (or otherwise from further consideration) for that contract.

(i) Antitrust violations

If the agency head considers that a bid or proposal evidences a violation of the antitrust laws, such agency head shall refer the bid or proposal to the Attorney General for appropriate action.

(j) Planning for future competition

(1)(A) In preparing a solicitation for the award of a development contract for a major system, the head of an agency shall consider requiring in the solicitation that an offeror include in its offer proposals described in subparagraph (B). In determining whether to require such proposals, the head of the agency shall give due consideration to the purposes for which the system is being procured and the technology necessary to meet the system's required capabilities. If such proposals are required, the head of the agency shall consider them in evaluating the offeror's price.

(B) The proposals that the head of an agency is to consider requiring in a solicitation for the award of a development contract are the following:

    (i) Proposals to incorporate in the design of the major system items which are currently available within the supply system of the Federal agency responsible for the major system, available elsewhere in the national supply system, or commercially available from more than one source.

    (ii) With respect to items that are likely to be required in substantial quantities during the system's service life, proposals to incorporate in the design of the major system items which the United States will be able to acquire competitively in the future.

(2)(A) In preparing a solicitation for the award of a production contract for a major system, the head of an agency shall consider requiring in the solicitation that an offeror include in its offer proposals described in subparagraph (B). In determining whether to require such proposals, the head of the agency shall give due consideration to the purposes for which the system is being procured and the technology necessary to meet the system's required capabilities. If such proposals are required, the head of the agency shall consider them in evaluating the offeror's price.

(B) The proposals that the head of an agency is to consider requiring in a solicitation for the award of a production contract are proposals identifying opportunities to ensure that the United States will be able to obtain on a competitive basis items procured in connection with the system that are likely to be reprocured in substantial quantities during the service life of the system. Proposals submitted in response to such requirement may include the following:

    (i) Proposals to provide to the United States the right to use technical data to be provided under the contract for competitive reprocurement of the item, together with the cost to the United States, if any, of acquiring such technical data and the right to use such data.

    (ii) Proposals for the qualification or development of multiple sources of supply for the item.

(3) If the head of an agency is making a noncompetitive award of a development contract or a production contract for a major system, the factors specified in paragraphs (1) and (2) to be considered in evaluating an offer for a contract may be considered as objectives in negotiating the contract to be awarded.

(k) Protest file

(1) If, in the case of a solicitation for a contract issued by, or an award or proposed award of a contract by, the head of an executive agency, a protest is filed pursuant to the procedures in subchapter V of chapter 35 of Title 31, and an actual or prospective offeror so requests, a file of the protest shall be established by the procuring activity and reasonable access shall be provided to actual or prospective offerors.

(2) Information exempt from disclosure under section 552 of Title 5 may be redacted in a file established pursuant to paragraph (1) unless an applicable protective order provides otherwise.

(*l*) Agency actions on protests

If, in connection with a protest, the head of an executive agency determines that a solicitation, proposed award, or award does not comply with the requirements of law or regulation, the head of such executive agency—

(1) may take any action set out in subparagraphs (A) through (F) of subsection (b)(1) of section 3554 of Title 31; and

(2) may pay costs described in paragraph (1) of section 3554(c) of such title within the limits referred to in paragraph (2) of such section.

(m) Prohibition on release of contractor proposals

(1) Except as provided in paragraph (2), a proposal in the possession or control of an executive agency may not be made available to any person under section 552 of Title 5.

(2) Paragraph (1) does not apply to any proposal that is set forth or incorporated by reference in a contract entered into between the agency and the contractor that submitted the proposal.

(3) In this subsection, the term "proposal" means any proposal, including a technical, management, or cost proposal, submitted by a contractor in response to the requirements of a solicitation for a competitive proposal.

(June 30, 1949, c. 288, Title III, § 303B, as added July 18, 1984, Pub.L. 98–369, Div. B, Title VII, § 2711(a)(2), 98 Stat. 1179, and amended Oct. 30, 1984, Pub.L. 98–577, Title II, § 201(a), 98 Stat. 3068; Oct. 13, 1994, Pub.L. 103–355, Title I, §§ 1061(c), 1063 to 1066, 108 Stat. 3267 to 3269; Feb. 10, 1996, Pub.L. 104–106, Div. D, Title XLI, §§ 4103(b), 4104(b), Div. E, Title LVI, § 5607(c), 110 Stat. 644, 645, 701; Sept. 23, 1996, Pub.L. 104–201, Div. A, Title VIII, § 821(b), Title X § 1074(b)(7), 110 Stat. 2609, 2660.)

HISTORICAL AND STATUTORY NOTES

Revision Notes and Legislative Reports
1984 Acts. Section 101 amends the FPASA by adding section 312 which establishes evaluation and award procedures for sealed bids and competitive proposals.

Section 312(a) requires that executive agencies evaluate sealed bids and competitive proposals based on the factors specified in the solicitation. Section 312(b) permits the agency head to reject all bids and proposals which are not in the public interest.

Section 312(c) sets forth the evaluation and award procedures for sealed bids. This section adopts provisions from the "Formal Advertising Requirements" section of current law (41 U.S.C. § 253). Sealed bids would be opened publicly at the time and place specified in the solicitation and would be evaluated without discussions with the bidders. In accordance with present procedures, furthermore, contracts would be awarded to the responsible bidder whose bid conforms to the solicitation and is most advantageous to the government, price and other factors (included in the solicitation) considered.

Section 312(d) establishes a framework for the conduct of competitive negotiations. Executive agencies would be permitted to discuss their requirements or the terms and conditions of the proposed contract with offerors after receipt of proposals and prior to the award of the contract. This section adopts provisions from the Armed Services Procurement Act (10 U.S.C. § 2304(g)), which require that military agencies conduct written or oral discussions with all responsible offerors in the competitive range, and extends it to apply to civilian procurements. The "competitive range" would be determined by the contracting officer based on price, technical, and other salient factors, and would include all proposals which have a reasonable change of being selected for award.

Section 312(d) also provides that proposals need not be evaluated with discussions where it can be demonstrated from either the existence of effective competition or accurate prior cost experience that the acceptance of a proposal without discussion would result in fair and reasonable prices. If discussions are not held, the solicitation must have notified all offerors of the possibility that award could be made without discussions.

Award of the contract under section 312(d) would be made to the responsible offeror whose proposal is most advantageous to the government on the basis of price and other factors included in the solicitation. Agencies would be required to notify all offerors of the rejection of their proposals, at the time of rejection, and award the contract by giving notice to the responsible offeror.

Section 312(e) states that the head of an executive agency is authorized to refer any sealed bid he or she considers to be in violation of the antitrust laws to the Attorney General. Senate Report No. 98–50.

1994 Acts. Senate Report No. 98–523, see 1984 U.S.Code Cong. and Adm.News, p. 5347.

Senate Report Nos. 103–258 and 103–259, and House Conference Report No. 103–712, see 1994 U.S. Code Cong. and Adm. News, p. 2561.

1996 Acts. House Conference Report No. 104–450, see 1996 U.S. Code Cong. and Adm. News, p. 238.

House Report No. 104–563 and House Conference Report No. 104–724, see 1996 U.S. Code Cong. and Adm. News, p. 2948.

References in Text
The antitrust laws, referred to in subsec. (i), are classified generally to chapter 1 (section 1 et seq.) of Title 15, Commerce and Trade.

Codifications
Section 5607(c) of Pub.L. 104–106, which directed that subsec. (h) of this section be amended by striking out par. (3), and which could not be executed to subsec. (h) due to earlier redesignation of subsec. (h) as subsec. (k) and addition of new subsec. (h) not containing paragraph designations, was executed instead to par. (3) of subsec. (k), as so redesignated, as the probable intent of Congress.

Amendments
1996 Amendments. Subsec. (d)(2), (3). Pub.L. 104–106, § 4103(b), added par. (2) and redesignated former par. (2) as par. (3).

Subsec. (e)(6). Pub.L. 104–106, § 4104(b)(1), struck out par. (6), which related to a summary of the debriefing.

Subsecs. (f), (g). Pub.L. 104–106, § 4104(b)(2), (3), added subsecs. (f) and (g) and redesignated former subsecs. (f) and (g) as subsecs. (i) and (j), respectively.

Subsec. (h). Pub.L. 104–201, § 1074(b)(7), amended Pub.L. 104–106, § 5607(c), by substituting "303B(k)" for "303B(h)" and "253b(k)" for "253b(h)", which required no change in the text.

Pub.L. 104–106, § 4104(b)(2), (3), added subsec. (h), and redesignated former subsec. (h) as subsec. (k).

Subsecs. (i), (j). Pub.L. 104–106, § 4104(b)(2), redesignated former subsecs. (f), (g), and (i) as subsecs. (i), (j), and (l), respectively.

Subsec. (k). Pub.L. 104–201, § 1074(b)(7), amended Pub.L. 104–106, § 5607(c), by substituting "303B(k)" for "303B(h)" and "253b(k)" for "253b(h)", which required no change in the text.

Pub.L. 104–106, § 4104(b)(2), redesignated former subsec. (h) as (k).

Subsec. (k)(3). Pub.L. 104–106, § 5607(c), struck out par. (3), which read as follows: "Regulations implementing this subsection shall be consistent with the regulations regarding the preparation and submission of an agency's protest file (the so-called 'rule 4 file') for protests to the General Services Board of Contract Appeals under section 759 of Title 40.". See Codifications note set out under this section.

Subsec. (l). Pub.L. 104–106, § 4104(b)(2), redesignated former subsec. (i) as (l).

Subsec. (m). Pub.L. 104–201, § 821(b), added subsec. (m).

1994 Amendments. Subsec. (a). Pub.L. 103–355, § 1061(c)(1), inserted after "competitive proposals" the phrase ", and award a contract,".

Subsec. (c). Pub.L. 103–355, § 1061(c)(2), inserted after "shall evaluate the bids" in the second sentence the phrase "in accordance with subsection (a) of this section."

Pub.L. 103–355, § 1063(a)(1), (2), substituted in the third sentence "transmitting, in writing or by electronic means, notice" for "transmitting written notice"

and added the end sentence "Within 3 days after the date of contract award, the executive agency shall notify in writing or by electronic means, each bidder not awarded the contract that the contract has been awarded."

Subsec. (d)(1). Pub.L. 103–355, § 1061(c)(3)(A), substituted "An executive agency shall evaluate competitive proposals in accordance with subsection (a) of this section and may award a contract—

"**(A)** after discussions with the offerors, provided that written or oral discussions have been conducted with all responsible offerors who submit proposals within the competitive range; or

"**(B)** based on the proposals received and without discussions with the offerors (other than discussions conducted for the purpose of minor clarification), if, as required by section 253a(b)(2)(B)(i) of this title, the solicitation included a statement that proposals are intended to be evaluated, and award made, without discussions are determined to be necessary."

for

"An executive agency shall evaluate competitive proposals in accordance with subsection (a) of this section and may award a contract—

"**(A)** after discussions with the offerors, provided that written or oral discussions have been conducted with all responsible offerors who submit proposals within the competitive range; or

"**(B)** based on the proposals received and without discussions with the offerors (other than discussions conducted for the purpose of minor clarification), if, as required by section 233a(b)(2)(B)(i) of this title, the solicitation included a statement that proposals are intended to be evaluated, and award made, without discussions, unless discussions are determined to be necessary."

Subsec. (d)(2). Pub.L. 103–355, §§ 1061(c)(3)(B), (C), 1063(b)(1), (2), struck out par. "(2) In the case of award of a contract under paragraph (1)(A), the executive agency shall conduct, before such award, written or oral discussions with all responsible sources who submit proposals within the competitive range, considering only price and the other factors included in the solicitation." and redesignated par. (4) as (2) and substituted therein "transmitting, in writing or by electronic means, notice" for "transmitting written notice" and ", within 3 days after the date of contract award, shall notify, in writing or by electronic means," for "shall promptly notify", respectively.

Subsec. (d)(3). Pub.L. 103–355, § 1061(c)(3)(B), struck out par. (3) "In the case of award of a contract under paragraph (1)(B), the executive agency shall award the contract based on the proposals as received (and as clarified, if necessary, in discussions conducted for the purpose of minor clarification)."

Subsec. (d)(4). Pub.L. 103–355, § 1061(c)(3)(B), redesignated par. (4) as (2).

Subsec. (e). Pub.L. 103–355, § 1064(2), added subsec. (e). Former subsec. (e) redesignated (f).

Subsecs. (f), (g). Pub.L. 103–355, § 1064(1), redesignated subsecs. (e) and (f) as subsecs. (f) and (g), respectively.

Subsec. (h). Pub.L. 103–355, § 1065, added subsec. (h).

Subsec. (i). Pub.L. 103–355, § 1066, added subsec. (i).

1984 Amendments. Subsec. (f). Pub.L. 98–577 added subsec. (f).

Effective and Applicability Provisions
1996 Acts. Section 1074(b)(7) of Pub.L. 104–201 provided in part that Pub.L. 104–106, § 5607(c), is amended, effective Feb. 10, 1996.

Amendments by sections 4103, 4104, and 4202(b)(2) of Pub.L. 104–106 effective Feb. 10, 1996, except as otherwise provided, see section 4401 of Pub.L. 104–106, set out as a note under section 251 of this title.

Pub.L. 104–106, Div. E, Title LVII, § 5701, Feb. 10, 1996, 110 Stat. 702, which provided that amendment by section 5607(c) of Pub.L. 104–106 was to be effective 180 days after Feb. 10, 1996, was repealed by Pub.L. 107–217, § 6(b), Aug. 21, 2002, 116 Stat. 1325.

1994 Acts. Amendment by sections 1061(c) and 1063 through 1066 of Pub.L. 103–355 effective Oct. 13, 1994, except as otherwise provided, see section 10001 of Pub.L. 103–355, set out as a note under section 251 of this title.

1984 Acts. Section 201(b) of Pub.L. 98–577 provided that: "The amendment made by subsection (a) [enacting subsec. (f) of this section] shall apply with respect to any solicitation issued more than 180 days after the date of enactment of this Act [Oct. 30, 1984]."

Section applicable with respect to any solicitation for bids or proposals issued after Mar. 31, 1985, see section 2751(a) of Pub.L. 98–369, set out as a note under section 251 of this title.

Small Business Act
This section not to affect or supersede the provisions of section 637(a) of Title 15, Commerce and Trade, see section 2711(c) of Pub.L. 98–369, set out as a note under section 253 of this title.

EXECUTIVE ORDERS
EXECUTIVE ORDER NO 12979
Oct. 25, 1995, 60 F.R. 55171
AGENCY PROCUREMENT PROTESTS

By the authority vested in me as President by the Constitution and the laws of the United States of America, and in order to ensure effective and efficient expenditure of public funds and fair and expeditious resolution of protests to the award of Federal procurement contracts, it is hereby ordered as follows:

Section 1. Heads of executive departments and agencies ("agencies") engaged in the procurement of supplies and services shall prescribe administrative procedures for the resolution of protests to the award of their procurement contracts as an alternative to protests in fora outside the procuring agencies. Procedures prescribed pursuant to this order shall:

(a) emphasize that whenever conduct of a procurement is contested, all parties should use their best efforts to resolve the matter with agency contracting officers;

(b) to the maximum extent practicable, provide for inexpensive, informal, procedurally simple, and expeditious resolution of protests, including, where appropriate and as permitted by law, the use of alternative dispute resolution techniques, third party neutrals, and another agency's personnel;

(c) allow actual or prospective bidders or offerors whose direct economic interests would be affected by the award or failure to award the contract to request a review, at a level above the contracting officer, of any decision by a contracting officer that is alleged to have violated a statute or regulation and, thereby, caused prejudice to the protester; and

(d) except where immediate contract award or performance is justified for urgent and compelling reasons or is determined to be in the best interest of the United States, prohibit award or performance of the contract while a timely filed protest is pending before the agency. To allow for the withholding of a contract award or performance, the agency must have received notice of the protest within either 10 calendar days after the contract award or 5 calendar days after the bidder or offeror who is protesting the contract

award was given the opportunity to be debriefed by the agency, whichever date is later.

Sec. 2. The Administrator for Federal Procurement Policy shall: **(a)** work with the heads of executive agencies to provide policy guidance and leadership necessary to implement provisions of this order; and

(b) review and evaluate agency experience and performance under this order, and report on any findings to the President within 2 years from the date of this order.

Sec. 3. The Administrator of General Services, the Secretary of Defense, and the Administrator of the National Aeronautics and Space Administration, in coordination with the Office of Federal Procurement Policy, shall amend the Federal Acquisition Regulation, 48 C.F.R. 1, within 180 days of the date of this order to further the purposes of this order.

WILLIAM J. CLINTON

CROSS REFERENCES

Commercially available off–the–shelf item acquisitions, see 41 USCA § 431.

LAW REVIEW AND JOURNAL COMMENTARIES

Negotiated procurements: Squandering the benefit of the bargain. David A. Whiteford, 32 Pub.Cont.L.J. 509 (2003).

LIBRARY REFERENCES

American Digest System
United States ☞64.40, 64.45.
Key Number System Topic No. 393.

Research References

ALR Library
52 ALR 4th 186, Public Contracts: Authority of State or Its Subdivision to Reject All Bids.
Encyclopedias
Am. Jur. 2d Freedom of Information Acts § 109, Other Federal Statutes.
Am. Jur. 2d Public Works and Contracts § 64, Receipt, Opening, and Recording of Bids; Time of Bid and of Acceptance or Award; Postponement.

Treatises and Practice Aids
Federal Procedure, Lawyers Edition § 39:110, Debriefing--Pre-Award.
West's Federal Administrative Practice § 611, Laws Applicable--Access to Government Procurement Records.

WESTLAW ELECTRONIC RESEARCH

See Westlaw guide following the Explanation pages of this volume.

Notes of Decisions

---

1. Construction with other laws

Quartermaster Corps in determining unit prices for partial small business set-aside pursuant to Small Business Act, section 631 et seq. of Title 15, could properly determine unit prices for set-aside portions on basis of individual destinations, and plaintiff which was lowest bidder under advertised portion of procurement was not entitled to award of entire set-aside portion of procurement at highest unit price of advertised portion. Abe L. Greenberg Co. v. U.S., Ct.Cl.1962, 300 F.2d 443, 156 Ct.Cl. 434. United States ⮕ 70(19)

2. Purpose

Purpose of statutes barring government from holding discussions with only one bidder for government contract is to prevent a bidder from gaining an unfair advantage over its competitors by making its bid more favorable to the government in a context where the other bidders have no opportunity to do so. Information Technology & Applications Corp. v. U.S., C.A.Fed.2003, 316 F.3d 1312, rehearing and rehearing en banc denied.

3. Rules and regulations

Amended regulations' definitions of terms "discussions" and "clarifications," which broadened scope of permitted "clarifications" to allow bidders to clarify certain aspects of their proposals, such as the relevance of bidder's past performance information and adverse past performance information to which bidder previously had no opportunity to respond, were reasonable interpretations of statutes barring government from holding discussions with only one bidder for government contract and thus were entitled to deference by court. Information Technology & Applications Corp. v. U.S., C.A.Fed.2003, 316 F.3d 1312, rehearing and rehearing en banc denied.

Regulations concerning contract awards create duty on part of government procurement officials running to bidders as well as to public. Scanwell Laboratories, Inc. v. Thomas, C.A.D.C. 1975, 521 F.2d 941, 172 U.S.App.D.C. 281, certiorari denied 96 S.Ct. 1507, 425 U.S. 910, 47 L.Ed.2d 761. United States ⮕ 64.5

Whether a procurement regulation can have retroactive application to contract previously awarded in the absence of an express provision is not to be decided by any established rules but rather by reference to the character and intent of the contract and of the regulation involved. Bethlehem Steel Corp. v. U.S., Ct.Cl. 1975, 511 F.2d 529, 206 Ct.Cl. 122, certiorari denied 96 S.Ct. 71, 423 U.S. 840, 46 L.Ed.2d 60.   United States ☞ 63

Where armed services procurement regulation which became effective after completion of government contract in question constituted clarification of meaning intended by predecessor provision in force when contract was entered into, not a change in such predecessor provision, subsequent effective date did not detract from later regulation's relevance to interpretation of antecedent clause in subject contract. Victory Const. Co., Inc. v. U.S., Ct.Cl.1975, 510 F.2d 1379, 206 Ct.Cl. 274.   United States ☞ 70(4)

Provision of federal procurement regulations treating defect in bid as immaterial and inconsequential if it lacks significance as to price, quantity, quality or delivery had to be read in conjunction with provision of former section 253 of this title [now this section], which provided that awards or bids shall be made to that responsible bidder, whose bid, conforming to invitation for bids, will be most advantageous to government, price and other factors considered.   Northeast Const. Co. v. Romney, C.A.D.C.1973, 485 F.2d 752, 157 U.S.App.D.C. 381.   United States ☞ 64.30

Justification and approval procedures in Federal Acquisition Regulations (FAR) applicable to acquisitions involving qualification requirements did not apply to amendment made by Forest Service to its specification for fire retardant; altering the fire-retardant ingredients for enhanced efficiency and safety did not substantially effect the character of the product.   Fire-Trol Holdings, LLC v. U.S., Fed.Cl.2005, 66 Fed.Cl. 36.   United States ☞ 64.25

4.   Authority of agency—Generally

Contracting officer has broad discretion in determining competitive range, and such decisions are not disturbed unless clearly unreasonable. Birch & Davis Intern., Inc. v. Christopher, C.A.Fed. 1993, 4 F.3d 970, on remand 1994 WL 43227.   United States ☞ 64.60(4)

A head of department, advertising according to law for proposals for stationery, was the competent and only judge of

the matters of fact involved in the acceptance or rejection of any of the proposals. 1853, 6 Op.Atty.Gen. 226.

5. —— Arbitrary or capricious actions, authority of agency

In order to recover for government's breach of its obligation to deal lawfully and in good faith with those who respond to its requests for bids or proposals, a disappointed bidder must prove that the government acted in an arbitrary or capricious manner in awarding the contract to another. Tidewater Management Services, Inc. v. U.S., Ct.Cl.1978, 573 F.2d 65, 216 Ct.Cl. 69.   United States ☞ 64.60(4)

Bid protestor did not establish that Army's evaluation of its offer for award of contract for meals and lodgings at applicant processing center was arbitrary and capricious, with respect to ratings for monthly inspections, facility quality, security, and transportation of applicants. Four Points By Sheraton v. U.S., Fed.Cl. 2005, 66 Fed.Cl. 776.   United States ☞ 64.40(1)

Army Corps of Engineers did not act in an arbitrary and capricious fashion in reviewing and then revising its original estimate for dredging contract to reflect higher diesel prices, after initial bidding revealed only one bid which fell with 25 percent of original estimate as required by statute for award of contract, even if Corps in deciding to revise estimate considered possibility that an unduly low original estimate might have had the effect of improperly depriving the only HubZone contractor of the award because its bid was more than 25 percent higher than the original estimate. Manson Const. Co. v. U.S., Fed.Cl.2005, 64 Fed.Cl. 746.   United States ☞ 64.40(1)

Decision of technical evaluation panel (TEP) to upgrade technical rating of successful offeror made by technical evaluation team (TET) was not arbitrary or capricious; TEP was not bound by TET's rating which it considered, and its consensus rating for successful offeror was adequately documented and supported by the administrative record. Portfolio Disposition Management Group LLC v. U.S., Fed.Cl.2005, 64 Fed.Cl. 1.   United States ☞ 64.45(2)

Contracting agency was not arbitrary or capricious in concluding that there was some doubt that bidder could successfully perform the work involved in construction project, and assigning it a corresponding risk rating, where only one of the prior ten projects completed by bidder was of the monetary magnitude contemplated in solicitation, and bidder failed to demonstrate that its specialized experience was of a similar scope as that required by the solicitation. Gulf Group Inc. v. U.S., Fed.Cl.2004, 61 Fed.Cl. 338. United States ⟨⟩ 64.45(2)

Government's evaluation of unsuccessful bidder's response to solicitation for database systems software development and portion of database restructuring for Social Security Administration was not arbitrary, capricious, or violative of law or regulation, notwithstanding fact that bidder may have been rated lower in some categories because of lack of experience with system as large as Social Security Administration's; prior work cited by bidder in its proposal did not meet request for proposal (RFP) requirements for "similar" size, complexity and experience. Shields Enterprises, Inc. v. U.S., Fed.Cl.1993, 28 Fed.Cl. 615. United States ⟨⟩ 64.40(2)

Authority "to reject any and all bids" does not confer the right to arbitrarily or capriciously reject any bid. 1910, 28 Op. Atty.Gen. 384.

6. Discussions with offerors

Disappointed bidder did not show that agency engaged in improper, or any, discussions with contract awardee, as required to prevail on argument that agency waived "without discussions" requirement for award of government contract; agency was allowed to receive clarifying information from offerors during bidding process. Galen Medical Associates, Inc. v. U.S., C.A.Fed.2004, 369 F.3d 1324, rehearing denied. United States ⟨⟩ 64.40(1)

Communications by which federal agency obtained additional information about subcontractors listed in bidder's proposal for professional services contract were "clarifications," rather than "discussions," under regulation that implemented statutes barring government from holding discussions with only one bidder for government contract; communications, through which bidder provided requested explanation as to which parts of project each subcontractor would support and detailed subcontractors' relevant experience regarding those tasks, did not

qualify as "discussions," which were intended to occur in the context of negotiations during which bidders would have opportunity to revise their proposals, and agency's requests merely sought clarification of subcontractors' relevant experience, as authorized by regulation, even though additional, new information was sought. Information Technology & Applications Corp. v. U.S., C.A.Fed.2003, 316 F.3d 1312, rehearing and rehearing en banc denied. United States ⟨⟩ 64.40(1)

Contracting agency's request for a subcontracting plan from successful offeror did not constitute "discussions" or require that revised proposals be solicited from all offerors; agency's action of requesting offeror's subcontracting plan, and negotiating with it to ensure that the subcontracting plan was acceptable, was required by section of the Federal Acquisition Regulation (FAR), and such negotiations were patently not of the type that would permit other offerors to revise their proposals. Consolidated Engineering Services, Inc. v. U.S., Fed.Cl.2005, 64 Fed.Cl. 617. United States ⟨⟩ 64.40(1)

Contracting agency did not abuse its discretion in solicitation for construction project by not seeking clarification from bidder concerning its past performance information after technical evaluation team (TET) determined that the information was inadequate to determine the scope of past projects, despite fact that the TET concluded that clarifications should be required, where source selection authority (SSA) subsequently explained that no clarification were sought because no discussions were conducted with any bidders. Gulf Group Inc. v. U.S., Fed.Cl.2004, 61 Fed.Cl. 338. United States ⟨⟩ 64.45(2)

7. Right to acceptance

No assurance exists that a contractor responding to United States Government solicitation will receive an award; Government retains, in its discretion, right to reject all bids without liability, even after there have been extensive negotiations with bidder. American General Leasing, Inc. v. U.S., Ct.Cl.1978, 587 F.2d 54, 218 Ct.Cl. 367. United States ⟨⟩ 64.50

Even if Civil Aeronautics Administrator and Director of Washington National Airport informed operator of automobile rental service that his bid for concession at airport would be kept confidential and even if they informed competitor of such bid and awarded concession to competitor without giving plaintiff operator opportunity to meet or better terms of competitor's revised bid, such facts did not give plaintiff operator right to attack contract which was awarded and he had no fixed right to be awarded contract as against competitor. Friend v. Lee, C.A.D.C.1955, 221 F.2d 96, 95 U.S.App. D.C. 224. United States ☞ 64.60(2)

While government contractors have right to reasonable treatment of their bids, they do not have vested interest in contract until agency accepts bid and, as against bidder, government has absolute right to reject all bids. City of Rochester v. U.S. Environmental Protection Agency, D.C.Minn.1980, 496 F.Supp. 751. United States ☞ 64.50

While no individual or corporation has a right to be awarded a specific government contract, one who has been dealing with the government on an ongoing basis may not be blacklisted from further contracting except for valid reasons and in conformity with procedural safeguards established by law. Art-Metal-USA, Inc. v. Solomon, D.C.D.C.1978, 473 F.Supp. 1. United States ☞ 64.20

8. Actions constituting acceptance

Where bidder refused Government's proffered award of contract varying from that on which it had bid, and Government never accepted bid, no contract resulted. Pacific Alaska Contractors, Inc. v. U.S., Ct.Cl.1958, 157 F.Supp. 844, 141 Ct.Cl. 303. United States ☞ 64.40(1)

Inspection of offered space and/or request for alternate offer does not constitute an acceptance or implied lease by the Government as acceptance of an offer must be clear and unconditioned. 1983, 62 Op.Comp.Gen. 50.

9. Implied acceptance

Where the owner of an invention promised the Government that it would make its secret process and plans for an article available to the Government for a particular limited purpose if the Government would amend its existing bid invitations to include therein plaintiff's article as an approved alternative, and where the Government did make such bid revision and then asked for and obtained the plaintiff's secret plans, the law will imply an assent on defendant's part to plaintiff's offer of its plans for the limited purpose only.

Padbloc Co. v. U.S., Ct.Cl.1963, 161 Ct. Cl. 369, 137 U.S.P.Q. 224. United States ☞ 69(5)

10. Binding effect of acceptance

A proposal to furnish stamped envelopes and newspaper wrappers in accordance with an advertisement by the Post Office Department [now United States Postal Service] for bids, followed by the acceptance by the Department of such proposal and the entry of a formal order to that effect, the bidder being the lowest, and having been found upon investigation to be financially responsible, created a contract of the same force and effect as though such contract were formally signed and the bond formally approved. U.S. v. Purcell Envelope Co., 1919, 39 S.Ct. 300, 249 U.S. 313, 63 L.Ed. 620. U.S. v. Purcell Envelope Co., U.S.Ct.Cl. 1919, 39 S.Ct. 300, 249 U.S. 313, 63 L.Ed. 620.

When a bid which binds a bidder to perform is accepted, and he is ready and able to perform, the Government cannot escape liability by refusing to enter into the formal written contract contemplated by the terms of its acceptance and it is liable to the same extent as it would have been had the formal contract been executed. Garfielde v. U.S., U.S.Ct.Cl.1876, 93 U.S. 242, 3 Otto 242, 23 L.Ed. 779.

Terms of contract for plaintiff to install boilers within specified time in Government ordnance plant became fixed when bid was accepted and notice to proceed issued, notwithstanding formal contract was not then executed, and provision relieving defendant from liability for damages resulting to plaintiff from defendant's failure to furnish necessary materials to install boilers within specified time as required by contract was operative, and rider attached to formal contract at request of plaintiff when formal contract was executed, if purporting to impose liability upon defendant for damages resulting from delay, was ineffective for want of consideration. Power Service Corp. v. Joslin, C.A.9 (Cal.) 1949, 175 F.2d 698. Contracts ☞ 32; Contracts ☞ 237(1)

Where the United States Coast Guard invited sealed bids for certain construction, incorporating by reference in the invitation an article of a P.W.A. form which provided for termination of contract by notice upon breach by contractor and for liability of contractor in amount of excess cost occasioned Government by such breach, a valid contract between the United States and contractor came into existence upon acceptance of contractor's bid by the United States. Conti v. U.S., C.C.A.1 (Mass.) 1946, 158 F.2d 581. United States ☞ 65

Where there is no mistake, unreasonable delay, or the like, there is no injustice in holding bidder to conditions of invitation for bids. Refining Associates v. U.S., Ct.Cl.1953, 109 F.Supp. 259, 124 Ct.Cl. 115. United States ☞ 64.40(4)

Where defendant made offer to purchase from Government through its ordnance district office 651 wooden boxes at price of $1.55 each on the boxes "f.o.b. Bridgeport", the location of the boxes was not a term of the offer, and Government's reply that it would accept defendant's offer for the boxes "located at Stratford * * * and Bridgeport," did not so vary from defendant's offer that there was no contract. U.S. v. Barowsky, D.C.Mass.1950, 91 F.Supp. 149. United States ☞ 63

War Department's acceptance of bid for coal after bid was withdrawn did not constitute contract. Nason Coal Co. v. U.S., Ct.Cl.1928, 64 Ct.Cl. 526. United States ☞ 64

Contract of claimant with defendants was legally made, and left the defendants liable thereon to the amount thereof, although other parties may have offered to furnish the goods at a less price, their bid being defective in security, etc. Thompson v. U.S., Ct.Cl.1867, 3 Ct.Cl. 433.

11. Public interest

Regulation relating to acceptance of bid by disqualified contractor if doing so was in the public interest did not require formal public interest determination. Siller Bros., Inc. v. U.S., Ct.Cl.1981, 655 F.2d 1039, 228 Ct.Cl. 76, certiorari denied 102 S.Ct. 1970, 456 U.S. 925, 72 L.Ed.2d 440. United States ☞ 64.20

Even strong public interest in avoiding disruption of procurement process must give way to public interest in requiring agencies to stick to their regulations. City of Rochester v. U.S. Environmental Protection Agency, D.C.Minn.1980, 496 F.Supp. 751. United States ☞ 64.5

12. Solicitation terms

Where successful bidder's proposal was not substantially equal to disappointed bidder's, selection authority's use of cost as most important factor in selection violated terms of solicitation which designated itself as "best value" procurement in which cost would be least important factor in determining award. Latecoere Intern., Inc. v. U.S. Dept. of Navy, C.A.11 (Fla.) 1994, 19 F.3d 1342, as amended. United States ☞ 64.40(1)

Forest Service did not violate the Competition in Contracting Act (CICA) when it amended its specification for fire retardant used to fight wildland fires, resulting in only one responsible source for procurement; Forest Service procurement was for products with qualification requirements, so that procurement procedures in CICA provision that did not have a requirement of full and open competition applied. Fire-Trol Holdings, LLC v. U.S., Fed.Cl.2005, 66 Fed.Cl. 36. United States ☞ 64.25

Law of the case doctrine barred bid protestor's claim that contracting agency's rejection of its offer for failure to submit a mobilization plan was arbitrary and capricious because agency was aware of its ability to mobilize due to its status as incumbent contractor; Court of Federal Claims previously ruled in denying protestor's motion for preliminary injunction that agency's knowledge about protestor's capability to mobilize did not displace solicitation's requirement that all offerors submit a mobilization plan, and there had been no supplemental evidence which altered Court's prior conclusion and no change in the law since denial of the motion. International Resource Recovery, Inc. v. U.S., Fed.Cl.2005, 64 Fed.Cl. 150. Federal Courts ☞ 950

Bid protestor did not establish that solicitation for warehouse storage of goods was unduly restrictive because it essentially required that an offeror already possess a warehouse conforming to the requirements for housing the goods; solicitation did not require an offeror to have actual possession or control of a compliant warehouse at the time it submitted its offer, only that offeror submit lease agreement or other documentation showing that it would have access to such a warehouse. Wit Associates, Inc. v. U.S., Fed.Cl.2004, 62 Fed.Cl. 657. United States ☞ 64.25

Government did not violate provision of request for proposals to furnish security services to federal courthouses, that proposed price would be determining factor in choosing between "substantially equal" technical proposals, by selecting bidder whose price was higher than protestor's price; while several proposals, including winning bidder's and protestor's, were found technically satisfactory there was never a finding of substantial equality, and there was basis for finding winning proposal superior, due to arrangements for background checks on prospective employees and in-house training programs. United Intern. Investigative Services v. U.S., Fed.Cl.1998, 42 Fed.Cl. 73, affirmed 194 F.3d 1335, rehearing denied, in banc suggestion declined. United States ☞ 64.45(3)

13. Most advantageous bid

Contracting officers of Federal Government have duty to select contract most advantageous to Government and advantage is not measured exclusively in terms of price but includes other factors such as judgment, skill, ability, capacity and integrity. Friend v. Lee, C.A.D.C.1955, 221 F.2d 96, 95 U.S.App.D.C. 224. United States ☞ 64.40(1)

Former section 5 of this title [now this section] required that proposal most advantageous to Government be accepted, provided that it was made by responsible person. O'Brien v. Carney, D.C.Mass. 1934, 6 F.Supp. 761. United States ☞ 64.10

These statutes [former section 5 of this title, now this section, and former section 1201 of Title 10, now sections 2301, 2303–2305 of Title 10] were enacted for the benefit of the Government, and imposed a duty upon the Department to accept the proposal most advantageous to the Government. 1937, 38 Op.Atty.Gen. 555.

Solicitation for maintenance of grounds equipment, which allowed bidders to offer special discounts for prompt payment and for off-season work, but which provided only for evaluation of prompt payment discount in determining low bid, resulted in award that did not reflect most favorable cost to government for total work performed, and thus violated former section 253 of this title [now this section]. 1981, 60 Comp.Gen. 495.

14. Highest or lowest bids

Government properly accepted bid which had been made only on item seven but was highest bid on item seven and also exceeded sum of highest bids received for each individual item, thus precluding award on individual items to bidder whose bid was lower than that of successful bidder, where property, consisting of excess property related to missile system was offered to highest bidder and bid form enabled government to accept bids for property from various bidders on individual items or from a single bidder on a lump-sum basis, whichever was greater, and item seven was "all of the above salvageable property as described in items numbers one through six." Gellner v. Department of Army, C.A.8 (N.D.) 1979, 595 F.2d 1125. United States ☞ 58(3)

Pennsylvania Avenue Development Corporation (PADC) did not abuse its discretion in violation of Administrative Procedure Act (APA), when it awarded development contract, even if contract was not awarded to lowest bidder; although unsuccessful bidder demonstrated "flaws" in successful proposal, unsuccessful bidder had limited experience in developing similar projects and PADC acted within its discretion when it balanced flaws of competing bids. Saratoga Development Corp. v. U.S., D.D.C.1991, 777 F.Supp. 29, affirmed 21 F.3d 445, 305 U.S.App. D.C. 351. United States ☞ 64.45(2)

Unsuccessful bidder, alleging that bid set by United States on contract was ambiguous in its designation of precise item sought as either a mast section or antenna element, failed to establish any impropriety in bidding procedures sufficient to warrant cancellation of award to low bidder where national stock number, which specifically identified precise item demanded, was included in all bids set, a number which unsuccessful bidder used to verify item before making its bid, and invitation for bid invited bidders with questions to contact government at a specific number, a procedure which was utilized by low bidder to confirm its understanding. Century Metal Parts Corp. v. U.S., E.D.N.Y.1979, 474 F.Supp. 436. United States ☞ 70(30)

Where, in awarding plaintiff the original contract for manufacturing cots for the United States and in awarding substituted contract between United States and another manufacturer for balance of cots due under original contract after it was terminated, United States stated that it had taken into consideration the cost of transportation of the cots to designated Army stations, United States, in awarding the substituted contract, was not required to award such contract to company whose bid for cots was less than that of plaintiff but whose bid plus transportation costs exceeded successful bidder's bid plus such costs, even though the bid was greater than plaintiff's. National Wood Products, Inc. v. U.S., Ct.Cl.1956, 146 F.Supp. 451, 137 Ct.Cl. 83. United States ☞ 73(4)

Amended complaint alleging that Federal Government had by-passed plaintiff's low bid for supplying arch supports was insufficient to state cause of action for money judgment or for declaration that such a judgment was appropriate, in view of fact that Government was not compelled to accept low bid. Royal Sundries Corp. v. U.S., E.D.N.Y.1953, 112 F.Supp. 244. United States ☞ 74(9)

Statute preventing the Army Corps of Engineers from awarding a dredging contract when the contract price is more than 25 percent in excess of its estimate did not require the Corps to award dredging contract to low bidder whose bid was the only one whose bid fell below 125 percent of the Corps estimate. Manson Const. Co. v. U.S., Fed.Cl.2005, 64 Fed. Cl. 746. United States ☞ 64.45(1)

Bid protestor did not establish that contracting agency's rescoring of technical and management factors in solicitation had the effect of changing the solicitation from a "best value" procurement to "lowest price technically acceptable" procurement. Dismas Charities, Inc. v. U.S., Fed.Cl.2004, 61 Fed.Cl. 191. United States ☞ 64.45(1)

Government agents must accept the lowest or highest responsible bid or reject all and readvertise. Scott v. U.S., Ct.Cl. 1909, 44 Ct.Cl. 524.

Public contract with the United States for construction of a dam could only be let to the lowest responsible bidder after advertisement for proposals. Constructors Ass'n of Western Pennsylvania v. Seeds, Pa.Super.1940, 15 A.2d 467, 142 Pa.Super. 59. United States ☞ 64.10

If the patentee of an article was the lowest bidder for furnishing it, the Secretary of the Navy might have accepted his proposal and contracted with him. 1889, 19 Op.Atty.Gen. 407.

Where proposals were received by the Chief Signal Officer from different parties to supply certain manifold forms, at rates greatly varying in amount, and that officer, before awarding the contract, was notified by the party making the highest bid that the manufacture of the manifold forms was covered by a patent owned by himself, and that no other bidder could supply them without infringing his patent, some of the other bidders, however, denying the validity of the patent, and claiming that they were not thereby precluded from supplying the article, under the circumstances presented, the contract should not be given to the lowest or any other bidder, if the article to be supplied was covered by the terms of a patent, unless the Chief Signal Officer was satisfied that the bidder had authority from the patentee to manufacture and sell it. 1875, 15 Op.Atty.Gen. 26.

The requirement that a sale of Government property be made only after advertising for competitive bids contemplates acceptance of the highest bid and, therefore, a contract for the sale of surplus Government property which, through administrative error, was awarded to other than the highest bidder must be cancelled and reawarded to the highest bidder. 1956, 36 Comp.Gen. 94.

15. Responsiveness of bid

While usually experience of public bidder is matter of responsibility, there are occasions when it rises to level of responsiveness of bid, provided this is made clear in invitation for bids. Northeast Const. Co. v. Romney, C.A.D.C.1973, 485 F.2d 752, 157 U.S.App.D.C. 381. United States ☞ 64.30

In appropriate case, United States may disclaim a contract on ground of voidness ab initio because of nonresponsiveness of bid. Albano Cleaners, Inc. v. U.S., Ct.Cl. 1972, 455 F.2d 556, 197 Ct.Cl. 450. United States ☞ 64.30

Successful bidder's cockpit video recording system (CVRS) videotape recorders to be installed in Navy aircraft met requests for proposal's (RFP) specifications requiring it to operate under harsh environmental conditions experienced by that type of aircraft in flight, although it was alleged that recorder had never been tested for performance under those conditions; specific pages in successful bidder's proposal and Navy's evaluation of that proposal demonstrated the product was designed to withstand each of environmental eventualities and that appropriate testing was performed in advance of successful bidder's having submitted its proposal. TEAC America, Inc. v. U.S. Dept. of Navy, D.D.C.1995, 876 F.Supp. 289. United States ⚯ 64.30

Since contractor has the burden to comply with specifications in contract and since invitation for bids on wastewater treatment plant did not require the bidder to list the specific equipment but only to name a manufacturer listed in the invitation, low bid which allegedly listed equipment which significantly differed from the specifications was properly found by regional administrator of the Environmental Protection Agency to be responsive. Albert Elia Bldg. Co., Inc. v. Sioux City, Iowa, N.D.Iowa 1976, 418 F.Supp. 176. Environmental Law ⚯ 179

A bid of a stated amount or $20,000 more than any other bid, whichever amount was lesser, was not a "firm bid," and Federal Housing Commissioner could reject it as not responsive to invitation. Trump v. Mason, D.C.D.C.1961, 190 F.Supp. 887. United States ⚯ 64.40(1)

Bidder's failure to include a subcontracting plan in its proposal did not render it non-responsive, where solicitation was ambiguous with respect to whether subcontracting plan had to be submitted with proposal as indicated in attachment or whether subcontracting plan was due "upon request by the Contracting Officer," as provided in addenda to solicitation; ambiguity had to be resolved in favor of addenda under clause setting forth order of preference in event of inconsistencies within solicitation. Consolidated Engineering Services, Inc. v. U.S., Fed.Cl.2005, 64 Fed.Cl. 617. United States ⚯ 64.30

Where the engineer in charge, being required by law to invite proposals by circulars and advertisement for furnishing pipes for a water main from the Washington Aqueduct in the District of Columbia, and to give the contract to the lowest responsible bidder, issued instructions stating that "no bid will be considered which does not comply with" certain directions, and the lowest bid afterward received failed to comply with those directions in material points, such

bid could not be considered. 1871, 13 Op.Atty.Gen. 510.

Compliance with a mandatory minimum bid acceptance period established in an invitation for bids is a material requirement because a bidder offering a shorter acceptance period has an unfair advantage since it is not exposed to market place risks and fluctuations for as long as its competitors are; therefore, a bid which takes exception to the requirement by offering a shorter acceptance period is nonresponsive and cannot be corrected. 1983, 62 Op.Comp.Gen. 31.

16. Integrity or responsibility of bidder

Detailed audit report, which raised the possibility that dairy products supplier had violated terms of an existing contract and overcharged the government, provided government contracting officers with a reasoned basis upon which to determine that the supplier lacked integrity and responsibility. Old Dominion Dairy Products, Inc. v. Secretary of Defense, C.A.D.C.1980, 631 F.2d 953, 203 U.S.App.D.C. 371. United States ⚯ 64.45(2)

Bidder responsibility is ultimately question of fact. Northeast Const. Co. v. Romney, C.A.D.C.1973, 485 F.2d 752, 157 U.S.App.D.C. 381. United States ⚯ 64.45(2)

In view of delinquencies of principals of government bidder on private contracts contracting officer reasonably could disqualify lowest bidder for lack of requisite integrity for performing government contracts and accordingly award of contract to another as lowest responsible bidder was valid, entitling contractor to damages upon cancellation of contract pursuant to comptroller general's decision. Warren Bros. Roads Co. v. U.S., Ct.Cl.1965, 355 F.2d 612, 173 Ct.Cl. 714. United States ⚯ 64.45(2); United States ⚯ 73(24)

United States Department of Housing and Urban Development (HUD) had no duty to contractor in connection with Puerto Rico Public Housing Authority's (PRPHA) decision to cancel contract following its determination that contractor's president was "nonresponsible bidder," and thus HUD was not subject to liability for PRPHA's actions, even though HUD had some overview of PRPHA's procurement process, and funds for contract were assigned by HUD to Puerto Rico,

where HUD's oversight was limited to
ensuring compliance with federal regulations, and HUD played no role in determination of president as nonresponsible
bidder or in disclosure of that determination. Celta Const. v. U.S. Dept. of Housing and Urban Development, D.Puerto
Rico 2004, 337 F.Supp.2d 396. United
States ⚭ 82(3.3)

Where agency considered not only
criminal conviction of president of government contractor, but also mitigating
factors submitted by contractor in debarment proceedings, decision to debar contractor for period of one year was not
arbitrary, capricious or abuse of discretion. Joseph Const. Co. v. Veterans Admin. of U.S., N.D.Ill.1984, 595 F.Supp.
448. United States ⚭ 64.20

Government did not act in bad faith in
its dealings with unsuccessful bidder for
centralized data-based computer system,
where contracting officer made independent and rational determination of "non-
responsibility" based on finding that bidder failed, as regulations required, to
demonstrate affirmatively that it had satisfactory record of integrity and based on
theory that taint of previous contract
passed on to contract at hand, and even
had bidder carried its burden of proof,
court would have denied it equitable relief in view of its plea of guilty to two
criminal counts in indictment returned
against it by grand jury and to criminal
information. General Research Corp. v.
U.S., E.D.Va.1982, 541 F.Supp. 442.
United States ⚭ 64.60(5.1)

Disappointed bidder for a government
contract had standing to claim that procurement agency erroneously determined
that it was nonresponsible and that the
specifications under which the award
was made were defective. Environmental Tectonics Corp. v. Robinson, D.C.D.C.
1975, 401 F.Supp. 814. United States ⚭
64.60(2)

Although concern as to responsibility of
"best" bidder for food and beverage concession at Washington National Airport
was a legitimate concern, such bidder
had been arbitrarily discriminated
against where government's reserved
right to object to any proposal if objection
were in the government's interest was
raised for first time over 13 months from
date of original solicitation, reversal of
recommendation of FAA's Evaluation and
Negotiation Board was had without com-

plying with procurement regulations and
bidder was competitively injured by government's disclosure of its bid details
contrary to express intent of the court
and the regulations. Air Terminal Services, Inc. v. Department of Transp.,
D.C.D.C.1973, 400 F.Supp. 1029, affirmed 515 F.2d 1014, 169 U.S.App.D.C.
297. Aviation ⚭ 224

If the officer in charge of awarding a
contract for Government work feels that
the acts of a certain bidder in the past
have been such that he can no longer be
considered as responsible, it is within the
power of such officer to reject his bid,
even though such bid is the lowest, but
the mere fact that the Government has
brought suit against a corporation charging it with being wrong in the performance of prior contracts is not of itself
sufficient to compel the rejection of any
and all bids for future Government work
submitted by such corporation. 1923, 33
Op.Atty.Gen. 453.

An adjudication that a person or corporation is a party to an unlawful trust or
monopoly, from which decree an appeal
has been taken, is not sufficient to exclude such person or corporation from
competition in the sale of supplies to the
Government. Opinion of April 19, 1910,
28 Op.Atty.Gen. 247. See, also, 1910, 28
Op.Atty.Gen. 384.

17. State regulation or control

Virginia could not require that contractors working solely for background investigation contract services program
(BICS) of Federal Bureau of Investigation
(FBI) comply with Virginia's licensing
and registration requirements concerning
private security services, inasmuch as, by
adding to qualifications necessary for
BICS contractors to work for FBI, Virginia's regulatory scheme impermissibly
frustrated objectives of federal procurement laws. U.S. v. Com. of Va., C.A.4
(Va.) 1998, 139 F.3d 984. Detectives ⚭
1; Detectives ⚭ 3; States ⚭ 18.15

18. Risk involved

Bid protestor did not establish that
contracting agency improperly neglected
to assess the risk of contract awardee's
price proposal; fact that awardee's prices
were within the acceptable range indicated that the government reasonably concluded that the risk would not material-
ize, and because the contract was firm-
fixed-price, any such risk would fall on

awardee, not the government. Dismas Charities, Inc. v. U.S., Fed.Cl.2004, 61 Fed.Cl. 191. United States ☞ 64.45(1)

Where complainant argued that it was not permitted to compete on equal basis with sole-source awardee, there was no method whereby any firm could compete because licensing arrangement offered by awardee was determined to be government's need and only available to awardee and consequently acceptance of sole-source bid in view of lower technical risk and schedule requirements was justified. (1979) 58 Op.Comp.Gen. 575.

19. Deviations or errors in bid

It is not every bid deviation or error which automatically compels a bid rejection. Excavation Const., Inc. v. U.S., Ct. Cl.1974, 494 F.2d 1289, 204 Ct.Cl. 299. United States ☞ 64.30

Bid on Government contract specifying article materially different from articles specified in invitation for bids is properly rejected, notwithstanding fact that bid is accompanied by statement to effect that in opinion of bidder article offered is in strict compliance with Government specifications and that deviation therefrom should be regarded as an error in bidder's specifications and not as exception to Government specifications. 1937, 38 Op.Atty.Gen. 555.

20. Time of bid

Fact that best and final offer (BAFO) materials submitted by successful bidder might have been received both before and after the BAFO "request" date did not prove bias on part of agency, as the deadline was not a hard and fast cut-off, and thus late receipt of the documents was not necessarily improper. Galen Medical Associates, Inc. v. U.S., C.A.Fed.2004, 369 F.3d 1324, rehearing denied. United States ☞ 64.30

Term "local time" in solicitation provision setting forth deadline for electronic transmission of offer referred to the time in Naples, Italy, which was the location of government office designated in the solicitation, and not to United States Eastern Standard Time as contended by bid protestor based on language on contracting agency's web site. Conscoop-Consorzia Fra Coop. Di Prod. E Lavoro v. U.S., Fed.Cl.2004, 62 Fed.Cl. 219, affirmed 159 Fed.Appx. 184, 2005 WL 1368664. United States ☞ 64.30

Contracting agency properly rejected bidder's price proposal as untimely, where proposal was received at designated e-mail address after the 2:00 p.m. Italian time deadline set forth in solicitation, and untimely proposal did not fall within any of the regulatory exceptions permitting acceptance of a late offer. Conscoop-Consorzia Fra Coop. Di Prod. E Lavoro v. U.S., Fed.Cl.2004, 62 Fed.Cl. 219, affirmed 159 Fed.Appx. 184, 2005 WL 1368664. United States ☞ 64.30

Where snowstorm closed the Navy Automatic Data Processing Selection Office which had requested proposals on the original closing date and such office extended closing date for 24 hours, even though debilitating conditions continued beyond such extension period, a proposal received after the extension period should not be rejected as late where the government office failed to act reasonably in extending the closing date by only 24 hours without providing adequate notice of such limited extension. (1979) 58 Comp.Gen. 573.

The object of the Government is to secure fairness and impartiality in awarding Government contracts, and where proper notice has been given by advertisement, and the time and the place for opening such proposals designated and published, one submitting his bid or proposal and forwarding the same by due course of mail, by which it should have been delivered before two o'clock p.m., should not be deprived of his right to participate in the competitive bidding because his letter containing the bid did not reach the board of award until a few minutes after two p.m. 1897, 21 Op.Atty. Gen. 546.

21. Bonds

Provisions for bid bond being for benefit of Government and it being expressly provided that Government could waive any informality in bids received when in interest of Government, Government would not be legally powerless to accept bid, notwithstanding that it was submitted without bid bond. Adelhardt Const. Co. v. U.S., Ct.Cl.1952, 107 F.Supp. 845, 123 Ct.Cl. 456. United States ☞ 64.35

Under invitations for bids which require bidders to submit bid bonds prior to bid opening, the bid bond requirement is a material part of the invitation which cannot be waived by contracting officers and noncompliance with the bid bond provision will require rejection of the bid as nonresponsive. 1959, 38 Comp.Gen. 532.

22. Persons who must meet requirements

Where American affiliate of successful British bidder on arms procurement contract was licensed by State of North Carolina to handle, store, or work with radioactive material involved in performance under the contract, alleged failure of the successful bidder to itself meet such licensing requirements did not render award void. Self-Powered Lighting, Ltd. v. U.S., S.D.N.Y.1980, 492 F.Supp. 1267. United States ⟶ 64.15

Sale of low bidder to another company did not provide grounds for Government Accounting Office's (GAO) recommendation of termination of contract between low bidder and Immigration and Naturalization Service (INS) to provide security guard services; bidder was an ongoing business with substantial tangible and intangible assets, bidder retained its pre–sale assets and employees after sale, and bidder continued to perform its contracts and to conduct business as it had for 14 years. Lyons Sec. Services, Inc. v. U.S., Fed.Cl.1997, 38 Fed.Cl. 783. United States ⟶ 72.1(2)

23. Conditional acceptance of award

Conditional acceptance of award by bidder is rejection of award as made, and there is no contract. Sequoia Mills v. U.S., Ct.Cl.1925, 60 Ct.Cl. 985. United States ⟶ 64

24. Time of award

Claimant waived any claim for delay of United States in making award of bid to claimant for overcoats for Air Force use, where plaintiff acquiesced in extensions of times for making bids by acceptance of contract. Leopold Morse Tailoring Co. v. U.S., Ct.Cl.1969, 408 F.2d 739, 187 Ct.Cl. 304. United States ⟶ 64.40(1)

Where Government advertisement for bids required bidders to deposit with their bid 25 percent of amount thereof and to pay balance "within 10 days from date of award," and contracting officer had right to reject all bids at any time prior to acceptance, the award was made on and the 10 day period for payment of balance was to be computed from, day when letter of award was signed and mailed, not when it was dated. Stebel v.

U.S., Ct.Cl.1947, 69 F.Supp. 221, 108 Ct. Cl. 35. United States ⟶ 64.35; Contracts ⟶ 17

25. Withdrawal subsequent to acceptance

Where bidder's letter, indicating its intent to accept contract in accord with Government's partial award, was written before partial award was withdrawn, but letter was not received until after Government sent telegram withdrawing such award, no contract resulted. Pacific Alaska Contractors, Inc. v. U.S., Ct.Cl. 1958, 157 F.Supp. 844, 141 Ct.Cl. 303. United States ⟶ 64.40(1)

Where Government advertisement for bids required bidders to deposit 25 per cent of amount of bid and to pay balance within 10 days from date of award and successful bidder complied therewith, the Government had no right to cancel the award to the successful bidder and in doing so it breached its contract and was liable for damages resulting therefrom. Stebel v. U.S., Ct.Cl.1947, 69 F.Supp. 221, 108 Ct.Cl. 35. United States ⟶ 64.35; Contracts ⟶ 17

Where the area director had endorsed his acceptance of plaintiffs' offer but later notified plaintiffs that such acceptance had been withdrawn, the original acceptance not having been communicated to plaintiffs, there was no valid contract for the purchase of the property in question. Slobojan v. U.S., Ct.Cl.1956, 136 Ct.Cl. 620. United States ⟶ 64.40(4)

After a bid for public works has been accepted, the bidders have not the right to withdraw their proposal because of errors in calculation on their part, which mistake was not mutual and was due to their negligence. 1895, 21 Op.Atty.Gen. 186.

The head of an executive department is not at liberty to allow a contractor to withdraw his bid after acceptance for an error in stating the amount he intended to bid. 1881, 17 Op.Atty.Gen. 70.

26. Compliance with law and regulations

Courts do have obligation to insure agency compliance with applicable statutes and regulations in awarding contracts, and interests which must be weighed include practical considerations of efficient procurement of supplies for continuing government operations, public interest in avoiding excessive costs and bidder's entitlement to fair treatment through adherence to statutes and regulations, and a showing of illegality is appropriate standard to impose on aggrieved bidder who seeks relief. Allis-Chalmers Corp., Hydro-Turbine Division v. Friedkin, C.A.3 (Pa.) 1980, 635 F.2d 248. United States ☞ 64.60(3.1)

Unsuccessful bidder's claim that it would have been awarded contract on public transportation project but for Federal Transit Administration's (FTA's) alleged failure to find successful bidder's offer non-compliant with FTA's Buy America regulations did not allege injury-in-fact sufficient to establish its standing to challenge FTA's determination; regulations did not provide that a second low bidder would necessarily be entitled to the contract if low bidder was non-compliant, but, rather, that non-compliant successful bidder would breach contract if it did not take necessary steps to become compliant. Cubic Transp. System, Inc. v. Mineta, D.D.C.2004, 357 F.Supp.2d 261. United States ☞ 64.60(2)

Pennsylvania Avenue Development Corporation (PADC) awarded development contract in violation of federal procurement law where PADC deleted its financing criterion and changed its affirmative action criteria just minutes before its final vote awarding contract; no bidder had time or opportunity to consider changes before contract was awarded. Saratoga Development Corp. v. U.S., D.D.C.1991, 777 F.Supp. 29, affirmed 21 F.3d 445, 305 U.S.App.D.C. 351. United States ☞ 64.40(2)

Disappointed offeror whose proposal was found to be technically unacceptable in solicitation to select private-sector service provider to compete against government service provider failed to establish that composition of source selection evaluation board (SSEB) violated selection criteria or applicable regulations, based on allegation that members of board held positions in the administrative and technical support function covered by the proposal, and thus had an inherent conflict of interest. Federal Management Systems, Inc. v. U.S., Fed.Cl.2004, 61 Fed.Cl. 364. United States ☞ 64.40(1)

Bid protestor did not establish that contracting agency violated procurement regulation requiring it to discuss "defi-ciencies, significant weaknesses, and adverse past performance information to which the offeror has not yet had an opportunity to respond" by not allowing protestor to address negative contractor evaluation forms (CEFs) regarding its performance of prior contracts; protestor cited no CEFs that were deemed "poor" or otherwise deficient, and protestor had the opportunity to respond to any CEFs that it considered adverse by submitting rebuttal comments with its proposals, but failed to do so. Bannum, Inc. v. U.S., Fed.Cl.2004, 60 Fed.Cl. 718. United States ☞ 64.45(2)

27. Disparate treatment or bias

Disappointed bidder did not show that agency was biased in favor of contract awardee, even though two of awardee's references were on evaluation panel; technical scores given to awardee by references were never highest given by any member of panel, and were roughly in line with average of what other members gave, and disappointed bidder consistently received low technical scores from majority of evaluators. Galen Medical Associates, Inc. v. U.S., C.A.Fed.2004, 369 F.3d 1324, rehearing denied. United States ☞ 64.40(2)

Bid protestor failed to establish bias on part of contracting officer (CO) based on CO's alleged inconsistent or wrong evaluations of its offer, allegations which were too vague to warrant discovery; moreover, there was no alleged conduct which might indicate a motivation for bias on the part of CO or evaluators. Four Points By Sheraton v. U.S., Fed.Cl.2005, 66 Fed.Cl. 776. United States ☞ 64.40(2)

Bid protestor did not establish that contracting agency engaged in disparate treatment of offerors on solicitation for trash pick-up services by imposing more stringent mobilization plan requirements on it rather than contract awardee; although protestor contended that neither its proposal nor that of awardee specified which containers were to be owned or leased, but agency overlooked the defect for awardee while employing omission to downgrade it, agency's conclusion that awardee would own its containers was not clearly erroneous. International Resource Recovery, Inc. v. U.S., Fed.Cl. 2005, 64 Fed.Cl. 150. United States ☞ 64.45(1)

Bid protestor did not establish that contracting agency disparately and unequally downgraded its technical and management scores when it rescored technical and management factors because chair of evaluation panel was concerned that panel members were incorrectly scoring the proposals; there was no indication that the panel applied different standards when re-scoring the proposals, and mere fact that the re-scoring resulted in protestor's score going down, a disparate result, does not mean that protestor was treated unfairly or differently. Dismas Charities, Inc. v. U.S., Fed.Cl.2004, 61 Fed.Cl. 191. United States ⟐ 64.45(1)

28. Past performance

Bid protest was not proper forum for contractor's claim that Bureau of Prisons (BOP) violated requirement that "[a]gencies shall provide for review at a level above the contracting officer to consider disagreements between the parties regarding the evaluation," contained in section of the Federal Acquisition Regulation (FAR) establishing requirements for past performance evaluations of contractors by failing to assess its rebuttals on prior contracts, when assessing its bid in connection with request for proposals on contract for operation of community correction centers. Bannum, Inc. v. U.S., C.A.Fed.2005, 404 F.3d 1346. United States ⟐ 64.45(2)

In taking corrective action based on comments of General Accountability Office (GAO) regarding evaluation of past performance of offerors, contracting agency's decision to expand the scope of corrective action to permit revisions to key personnel and subcontractors was reasonable, as was its decision to limit revisions to those areas, notwithstanding bid protestor's contention that agency could not impose a limit on discussions, or revisions it would accept, including new price proposals. Consolidated Engineering Services, Inc. v. U.S., Fed.Cl. 2005, 64 Fed.Cl. 617. United States ⟐ 64.45(2)

Unsuccessful offeror did not establish that contracting officer (CO) acted in bad faith when he did not instruct evaluators to reevaluate its past performance in light of a settlement agreement which converted prior default termination to a termination for convenience; although CO erred in not advising evaluators, error

was ameliorated at source selection level by CO who upgraded offeror's past performance and risk ratings, and CO's action did not demonstrate a specific intent to harm offeror. International Resource Recovery, Inc. v. U.S., Fed.Cl.2005, 64 Fed.Cl. 150. United States ⟐ 64.45(2)

Bid protestor did not establish it was the victim of disparate treatment in risk rating evaluations in solicitation for construction project, based on allegation that contract awardee was not held to the same strict standard regarding its past performance submission, with discrepancies or omissions overlooked by contracting agency. Gulf Group Inc. v. U.S., Fed.Cl.2004, 61 Fed.Cl. 338. United States ⟐ 64.45(2)

29. Notice of award

Where invitation to bid on contract to move furniture issued on May 28, 1964 provided that bids would be opened on June 3 and that work was anticipated to begin on June 8, and on day bids were opened contractor was notified it was low bidder and on June 5 contractor was informed of award, notice of award was timely and binding contract was made. National Movers Co. v. U.S., Ct.Cl.1967, 386 F.2d 999, 181 Ct.Cl. 419. United States ⟐ 64.45(1)

A period of nine days elapsing between the opening of bids and the notice sent to plaintiff constitutes no such unreasonable delay as to operate to relieve the contractor from liability for performance within the contract time. Fowler, for Use of Exeter Mach. Works Inc., v. U.S., Ct.Cl. 1916, 51 Ct.Cl. 52. United States ⟐ 64

30. Release of proposal information

Documents pertaining to contractors' proposals, as requested from National Park Service (NPS) pursuant to sale of tract adjacent to public land area, would be properly withheld under Freedom of Information Act (FOIA) exemption pertaining to documents specifically exempted from disclosure by statute, since such documents were precluded from disclosure by National Defense Authorization Act of 1997. Hornbostel v. U.S. Dept. of Interior, D.D.C.2003, 305 F.Supp.2d 21, as amended, affirmed 2004 WL 1900562. Records ⟐ 55

31. Judicial review

Refusal of local housing authority and Department of Housing and Urban Development to award contract on negotiated bid under Low Rent Housing Act, section 1401 et seq. of Title 42, was decision committed to agency discretion and not reviewable. Davis Associates, Inc. v. Secretary, U.S. Dept. of Housing and Urban Development, D.C.N.H.1974, 373 F.Supp. 1256, affirmed 498 F.2d 385. United States ☞ 64.60(3.1)

Underlying purpose of bringing bid protests into district court to challenge government irregularities in contract award system is to protect integrity of bid process. Keco Industries, Inc. v. Laird, D.C.D.C.1970, 318 F.Supp. 1361. United States ☞ 64.60(1)

32. Standard of judicial review

Unsuccessful bidder on government contract awarded with independent approval of source selection official and contracting officer faced substantial burden of demonstrating that neither official's decision was premised on rational basis. General Elec. Co. v. Kreps, D.C.D.C.1978, 456 F.Supp. 468. United States ☞ 64.60(4)

33. Persons entitled to maintain action

Unsuccessful bidder on contract for operation of community correction centers was not significantly prejudiced by the Bureau of Prisons's (BOP's) violations of requirement that "[a]gencies shall provide for review at a level above the contracting officer to consider disagreements between the parties regarding the evaluation," contained in section of the Federal Acquisition Regulation (FAR) establishing requirements for past performance evaluations of contractors, as required for bidder to prevail in bid protest, where bidder did not have substantial chance of receiving contract but for BOP's errors in bid process. Bannum, Inc. v. U.S., C.A.Fed. 2005, 404 F.3d 1346. United States ☞ 64.55(1)

Disappointed bidder had standing to bring bid protest, where it finished second to contract awardee and thus had a substantial chance of receiving the award and a direct economic interest. Galen Medical Associates, Inc. v. U.S., C.A.Fed. 2004, 369 F.3d 1324, rehearing denied. United States ☞ 64.60(2)

Disappointed bidder for professional services contract established prejudice required for standing to file bid protest action, inasmuch as bidder was qualified bidder whose proposal met minimum contract requirements and was deemed fundamentally sound, and thus bidder had greater than insubstantial chance of securing contract if it prevailed on the merits of its bid protest and contract award to competing bidder was set aside. Information Technology & Applications Corp. v. U.S., C.A.Fed.2003, 316 F.3d 1312, rehearing and rehearing en banc denied. United States ☞ 64.60(2)

Provisions setting out government procurement procedures protect not only the Government's interest in securing advantageous contracts but also the interests of those responding to the Government's invitation to do business with it, and thus unsuccessful bidder who alleged illegal award of contract for lease to government agency of office space was within the zone of interest protected by the applicable procurement provision, and had standing to bring action challenging the award. Merriam v. Kunzig, C.A.3 (Pa.) 1973, 476 F.2d 1233, certiorari denied 94 S.Ct. 233, 414 U.S. 911, 38 L.Ed.2d 149. United States ☞ 64.60(2)

Party, including bidder, who can make prima facie showing of arbitrary and capricious action on part of government in handling of bid situation, has standing to sue. Keco Industries, Inc. v. U.S., Ct.Cl. 1970, 428 F.2d 1233, 192 Ct.Cl. 773. United States ☞ 64.60(2)

Where operator of automobile rental service did not allege facts showing that Civil Aeronautics Administrator and Director of Washington National Airport had, through conspiracy, fraud, malice or coercion abused their discretion in awarding contract to competitor, operator had no standing to sue to invalidate contract. Friend v. Lee, C.A.D.C.1955, 221 F.2d 96, 95 U.S.App.D.C. 224. United States ☞ 140

A suit by highest bidder on levee enlargement project to restrain Government officer from accepting lower bid on theory that officer should have awarded contract to plaintiff or rejected both bids and readvertised was properly dismissed since plaintiff, being the high bidder, was without right to an award in its favor and hence was seeking action with respect to matters as to which plaintiff was without standing to sue. Walter P. Villere Co. v. Blinn, C.C.A.5 (La.) 1946, 156 F.2d 914. Injunction ☞ 129(1)

Unsuccessful bidder on public transportation project failed to show that it suffered an actual injury, in the form of a competitive disadvantage in procurement process, a denial of its right to a legally valid procurement process, and a hindrance to its ability to compete on a level playing field, sufficient to establish its standing to challenge Federal Transit Administration's (FTA's) alleged failure to find successful bidder's offer non-compliant with FTA's Buy America regulations. Cubic Transp. System, Inc. v. Mineta, D.D.C.2004, 357 F.Supp.2d 261. United States ☞ 64.60(2)

Unsuccessful bidder was not prejudiced by violations of federal procurement laws that occurred when Pennsylvania Avenue Development Corporation (PADC) changed two of eight selection criteria for awarding development contracts and, therefore, unsuccessful bidder was not entitled to relief; unsuccessful bidder did not show that it would have altered its proposal to its competitive advantage if it had been given opportunity to respond to altered selection criteria. Saratoga Development Corp. v. U.S., D.D.C.1991, 777 F.Supp. 29, affirmed 21 F.3d 445, 305 U.S.App.D.C. 351. United States ☞ 64.60(5.1)

Unsuccessful bidder for public contract has no standing to bring suit to challenge legality of bidding procedure. Self-Powered Lighting, Ltd. v. U.S., S.D.N.Y.1980, 492 F.Supp. 1267. United States ☞ 64.60(2)

Disappointed bidder who alleged that it was deprived of an opportunity to compete on an even playing field because the evaluation process was improper, its ratings were erroneous, and the contracting officer (CO) was biased against it, had standing to bring a bid protest, since if bidder's assertions were proven and re-evaluation ordered, it would have a substantial chance of securing the award on a level playing field. Four Points By Sheraton v. U.S., Fed.Cl.2005, 66 Fed.Cl. 776. United States ☞ 64.60(2)

34. Exhaustion of administrative remedies

Some opportunity must be given procurement agency to consider objection of disappointed bidder and question whether his proposal satisfies in regulatory needs; such opportunity is precondition to judicial intervention, under principle of exhaustion of administrative remedies. Northeast Const. Co. v. Romney, C.A.D.C.

1973, 485 F.2d 752, 157 U.S.App.D.C. 381. United States ☞ 64.55(2)

Bidder on government contracts could not maintain action for temporary restraining order precluding Department of Defense from awarding contracts until its protest of the disallowance of its bids could be ruled upon, absent prior exhaustion of available administrative remedies. ABC Management Services, Inc. v. Clements, C.D.Cal.1973, 378 F.Supp. 340. United States ☞ 64.55(2)

35. Moot questions

Disappointed bidder's allegations that government officials failed to provide statement advising offerors of post-award debriefing in pre-corrective action solicitation and failed to provide information about what documents were subject to disclosure was moot, where government officials ordered a new solicitation. Galen Medical Associates, Inc. v. U.S., C.A.Fed.2004, 369 F.3d 1324, rehearing denied. United States ☞ 64.60(3.1)

Where petition prayed not merely that award of levee enlargement contract be restrained but that, if contract had been awarded, from proceeding further under it, controversy was not moot notwithstanding large part of contract had been and whole would soon be, completed. Walter P. Villere Co. v. Blinn, C.C.A.5 (La.) 1946, 156 F.2d 914. Federal Courts ☞ 13

36. Waiver

Where decision by Army to conduct negotiated procurement for rifle sight-post assembly, rather than one by formal advertising, was apparent on face of solicitation, unsuccessful bidder failed timely to object to it as required by applicable regulations, and the unsuccessful bidder subsequently participated in procurement procedures, the unsuccessful bidder waived any objection to any impropriety in decision to conduct negotiated procurement. Self-Powered Lighting, Ltd. v. U.S., S.D.N.Y.1980, 492 F.Supp. 1267. United States ☞ 64.10

Where officer of Philadelphia branch of War Assets Administration received and telephoned to Washington office a written bid on surplus goods which should have been mailed to Washington, whereupon award was made to bidder contingent upon legal opinion as to validity of bid, and was made final by public and individual notice following receipt of such opinion from Administration's Philadelphia legal office, Administration had exercised its right to waive formality of delivering bids to Washington and transaction gave rise to binding contract of sale which could not thereafter be cancelled on ground that the bid was improperly filed. Miller v. U.S., Ct.Cl.1952, 107 F.Supp. 555, 123 Ct.Cl. 438. United States ☞ 58(4)

In specific cases the Secretary of War [now Secretary of Defense] was authorized to waive formal defects in bids and bonds in order to secure the public advantage resulting from competitive bidding. 1897, 21 Op.Atty.Gen. 469.

37. Judicial award of contract to bidder

Decision of federal district court requiring contract for food and beverage concession at Washington National Airport to be awarded to bidder subject to favorable decision as to its responsibility, rather than to permit the Government to obtain new proposals, was affirmed though Government had reserved right to reject all proposals upon determining that it would be in the best interest of the Government to do so. Air Terminal Services, Inc. v. Department of Transp., C.A.D.C.1975, 515 F.2d 1014, 169 U.S.App.D.C. 297. Aviation ☞ 225.1

38. Unjust enrichment

Where United States retained right to reject all bids, disappointed bidder was improper party to ask for restitution, and where, even if there was abuse of discretion in awarding contract to defendant it would not be unfair to allow defendant to retain fruits of contract as against plaintiff, there was no cause of action for unjust enrichment. Scanwell Laboratories, Inc. v. Thomas, C.A.D.C.1975, 521 F.2d 941, 172 U.S.App.D.C. 281, certiorari denied 96 S.Ct. 1507, 425 U.S. 910, 47 L.Ed.2d 761. United States ☞ 64.60(2)

39. Interference with contract

Where plaintiff's bid for supplying clothing to government was not accepted, there was no valid enforceable contract between government and plaintiff and therefore plaintiff could not maintain action for wrongful interference with contractual rights against defendant which had offered to produce clothing at stated price for plaintiff but which submitted to government its own bid and was awarded contract. Alice v. Robett Mfg. Co.,

N.D.Ga.1970, 328 F.Supp. 1377, affirmed 445 F.2d 316. Torts ☞ 242

40. Injunction

District court has jurisdiction to enjoin the performance of a government procurement contract if the award was the result of procedures not comporting with the law. Sea-Land Service, Inc. v. Brown, C.A.3 (N.J.) 1979, 600 F.2d 429. Injunction ☞ 88

Disappointed bidder on public contract for cockpit video recording system (CVRS) to be installed in Navy aircraft failed to demonstrate a likelihood of success in prevailing on merits of its claim that decision to award contract to successful bidder was either irrational or not in accord with applicable statutes and regulations, and therefore, disappointed bidder was not entitled to preliminary injunctive relief. TEAC America, Inc. v. U.S. Dept. of Navy, D.D.C.1995, 876 F.Supp. 289. Injunction ☞ 138.63

Injunction against General Services Administration solicitation of offers for office space would impose greater harm on the Administration, since the federal procurement process would be greatly disrupted, than would be suffered by one party claiming that it was being improperly excluded from bidding. Fairplain Development Co. v. Freeman, N.D.Ill. 1981, 512 F.Supp. 201. Injunction ☞ 86

In view of timetable for decision by general accounting office on complaint of disappointed bidder for a government contract, and other facts relative to possible disruptive effects and public interests, a preliminary injunction pending decision by the accounting office would not be granted. Environmental Tectonics Corp. v. Robinson, D.C.D.C.1975, 401 F.Supp. 814. Injunction ☞ 138.63

Preliminary injunction preventing implementation of contract for production and distribution of copies of educational documents would not issue pending action by comptroller general on protest of award by losing party in negotiated bidding process on contract where losing contractor had failed to show the flagrant disregard for the regularity of contracting procedures and other factors bearing on public interest which would justify extraordinary relief by way of injunction and injunction would change, not preserve, status quo since successful bidder had made plans and incurred expenses to commence work. National Cash Register Co. v. Richardson, D.C.D.C.1971, 324 F.Supp. 920. Injunction ⊂⊃ 138.3; Injunction ⊂⊃ 138.63

Unsuccessful bidders which alleged that government officers did not fairly conduct bidding procedures and thereby deprived plaintiffs of a fair opportunity to bid on the job did not show that they had standing to sue or that there was any strong likelihood that they would succeed in their action, and they were not entitled to preliminary injunction to restrain government from taking further action pursuant to the contract. Lind v. Staats, N.D.Cal.1968, 289 F.Supp. 182. Injunction ⊂⊃ 138.63

Unsuccessful lowest bidder for materials to be supplied to Federal Emergency Relief Administration was not entitled to injunction restraining carrying out of contract awarded to another, since discretion of officers awarding contract to lowest responsible bidder is not subject to judicial review. O'Brien v. Carney, D.C.Mass.1934, 6 F.Supp. 761. United States ⊂⊃ 91.9

Contracting agency was not required to suspend performance of blanket purchase agreement (BPA) awarded under Federal Supply Schedule (FSS) of the General Services Administration (GSA) pending review of post-award bid protest by the Government Accountability Office (GAO), under statute requiring such suspension if agency receives notice of protest within 5 days after debriefing offered to unsuccessful offeror if debriefing is required, as such debriefing was not required for an award under a multiple award schedule of the GSA, which is not awarded on the basis of a "competitive proposal." Systems Plus, Inc. v. U.S., Fed.Cl.2005, 68 Fed.Cl. 206. United States ⊂⊃ 64.55(2)

Post-award bid protestor was not entitled to temporary restraining order (TRO) to enjoin contract awardee from performing hardware supply contract, considering that protestor did not show a substantial likelihood of success on the merits of its claim that agency was arbitrary and capricious in its determination that awardee was responsible; moreover, balance of harms did not weigh in favor of TRO, and public interest weighed in favor of not interfering with procurement decision, especially where protestor arguments challenged the exercise of agency discretion. CC Distributors, Inc. v. U.S.,

Fed.Cl.2005, 65 Fed.Cl. 813. Injunction ⊂⊃ 150

Bid protestor was entitled to preliminary injunction enjoining performance of contract by contract awardee, considering that there was a reasonable likelihood of success on the merits of its claim that agency improperly normalized cost of photocopying, that protestor would suffer irreparable harm in form of loss of staff and leases if procurement was not enjoined, that such harm outweighed harm to government and awardee, and that granting injunction served public interest in integrity of the procurement process. University Research Co., LLC v. U.S., Fed.Cl.2005, 65 Fed.Cl. 500. Injunction ⊂⊃ 138.63

41. Damages—Generally

Monetary recovery against United States is not automatic consequence of any abuse of discretion in awarding contracts. Scanwell Laboratories, Inc. v. Thomas, C.A.D.C.1975, 521 F.2d 941, 172 U.S.App.D.C. 281, certiorari denied 96 S.Ct. 1507, 425 U.S. 910, 47 L.Ed.2d 761. United States ⊂⊃ 64.60(5.1)

Court of Claims will not award recovery of lost profits in an action by an unsuccessful bidder alleging that contract was improperly awarded to another bidder. Excavation Const., Inc. v. U.S., Ct. Cl.1974, 494 F.2d 1289, 204 Ct.Cl. 299. United States ⊂⊃ 64.60(5.1)

Federal procurement provisions, while providing several other remedies, do not confer a private cause of action for damages in favor of unsuccessful bidder against successful bidder. Northland Equities, Inc. v. Gateway Center Corp., E.D.Pa.1977, 441 F.Supp. 259. United States ⊂⊃ 64.60(1)

42. —— Preparation costs, damages

Private contractor which sought to recover bid preparation costs from United States Government, alleging that certain officials of Department of Commerce had acted arbitrarily and capriciously in rejecting contractor's bid for reasons wholly unrelated to merits of its proposal, but which failed to allege facts from which could be inferred specific intent to injure it, and which failed to controvert Government's affidavits that cancellation had reasonable basis, was not entitled to award of bid preparation costs. American General Leasing, Inc. v. U.S., Ct.Cl. 1978, 587 F.2d 54, 218 Ct.Cl. 367. United States ☞ 74(9); United States ☞ 74(11)

Unsuccessful bidder could recover costs incurred in preparing technical proposals and bid if it established that government acted arbitrarily and capriciously in awarding contract to another, but could not recover lost profits since contract under which bidder would have made such profits never came into existence. Keco Industries, Inc. v. U.S., Ct. Cl.1970, 428 F.2d 1233, 192 Ct.Cl. 773. United States ☞ 64.60(6)

Disappointed bidder on General Services Administration lease would be able to recover its costs incurred in the preparation of the bid if it were successful on the merits of its claim that a requirement of the bid that the office space be located within central business district was illegal, and thus had an adequate remedy at law so that it was not entitled to a preliminary injunction against the solicitation of offers for office space leased by the Administration. Fairplain Development Co. v. Freeman, N.D.Ill.1981, 512 F.Supp. 201. Injunction ☞ 138.63

In view of conclusion that cancellation of request for proposals and award of sole-source contract was proper, there was no arbitrary or capricious action toward complainant to support claim for proposal preparation costs. (1979) 58 Comp.Gen. 575.

43. Vacation of award

Vacation of award of contract for medical testing services was required with instructions to contracting agency to conduct a fair and proper procurement process was required, where neither bid protestor nor contract awardee complied with solicitation requirement that they accompany their proficiency panel test results with a certification, signed by a laboratory supervisor, certifying that the administration of the prescribed tests were accomplished in the precise manner that the offeror would employ in the performance of the contract. ViroMed Laboratories, Inc. v. U.S., Fed.Cl.2004, 62 Fed.Cl. 206. United States ☞ 64.60(5.1)

§ 253c.   Encouragement of new competition

(a) "Qualification requirement" defined

In this section, "qualification requirement" means a requirement for testing or other quality assurance demonstration that must be completed by an offeror before award of a contract.

(b) Agency head; functions; prior to enforcement of qualification requirement

Except as provided in subsection (c) of this section, the head of the agency shall, before enforcing any qualification requirement—

(1) prepare a written justification stating the necessity for establishing the qualification requirement and specify why the qualification requirement must be demonstrated before contract award;

(2) specify in writing and make available to a potential offeror upon request all requirements which a prospective offeror, or its product, must satisfy in order to become qualified, such requirements to be limited to those least restrictive to meet the purposes necessitating the establishment of the qualification requirement;

(3) specify an estimate of the costs of testing and evaluation likely to be incurred by a potential offeror in order to become qualified;

451

(4) ensure that a potential offeror is provided, upon request, a prompt opportunity to demonstrate at its own expense (except as provided in subsection (d) of this section) its ability to meet the standards specified for qualification using qualified personnel and facilities of the agency concerned or of another agency obtained through interagency agreement, or under contract, or other methods approved by the agency (including use of approved testing and evaluation services not provided under contract to the agency);

(5) if testing and evaluation services are provided under contract to the agency for the purposes of clause (4), provide to the extent possible that such services be provided by a contractor who is not expected to benefit from an absence of additional qualified sources and who shall be required in such contract to adhere to any restriction on technical data asserted by the potential offeror seeking qualification; and

(6) ensure that a potential offeror seeking qualification is promptly informed as to whether qualification is attained and, in the event qualification is not attained, is promptly furnished specific information why qualification was not attained.

(c) Applicability; waiver authority; referral of offers

(1) Subsection (b) of this section does not apply with respect to a qualification requirement established by statute prior to October 30, 1984.

(2) Except as provided in paragraph (3), if it is unreasonable to specify the standards for qualification which a prospective offeror or its product must satisfy, a determination to that effect shall be submitted to the advocate for competition of the procuring activity responsible for the purchase of the item subject to the qualification requirement. After considering any comments of the advocate for competition reviewing such determination, the head of the procuring activity may waive the requirements of paragraphs (2) through (5) of subsection (b) of this section for up to two years with respect to the item subject to the qualification requirement.

(3) The waiver authority contained in paragraph (2) shall not apply with respect to any qualified products list.

(4) A potential offeror may not be denied the opportunity to submit and have considered an offer for a contract solely because the potential offeror has not been identified as meeting a qualification requirement, if the potential offeror can demonstrate to the satisfaction of the contracting officer that the potential offeror or its product meets the standards established for qualification or can meet such standards before the date specified for award of the contract.

(5) Nothing contained in this subsection requires the referral of an offer to the Small Business Administration pursuant to section 637(b)(7) of Title 15 if the basis for the referral is a challenge by the offeror to either the validity of the qualification requirement or the offeror's compliance with such requirement.

(6) The head of an agency need not delay a proposed procurement in order to comply with subsection (b) of this section or in order to provide a potential offeror with an opportunity to demonstrate its ability to meet the standards specified for qualification.

(d) Number; qualified sources or products; fewer than two actual manufacturers; functions of agency head

(1) If the number of qualified sources or qualified products available to compete actively for an anticipated future requirement is fewer than two actual manufacturers or the products of two actual manufacturers, respectively, the head of the agency concerned shall—

> **(A)** periodically publish notice in the Commerce Business Daily soliciting additional sources or products to seek qualification, unless the contracting officer determines that such publication would compromise national security; and

> **(B)** bear the cost of conducting the specified testing and evaluation (excluding the costs associated with producing the item or establishing the production, quality control, or other system to be tested and evaluated) for a small business concern or a product manufactured by a small business concern which has met the standards specified for qualification and which could reasonably be expected to compete for a contract for that requirement, but such costs may be borne only if the head of the agency determines that such additional qualified sources or products are likely to result in cost savings from increased competition for future requirements sufficient to offset (within a reasonable period of time considering the duration and dollar value of anticipated future requirements) the costs incurred by the agency.

(2) The head of an agency shall require a prospective contractor requesting the United States to bear testing and evaluation costs under paragraph (1)(B) to certify as to its status as a small business concern under section 632 of Title 15.

(e) Examination; need for qualification requirement

Within seven years after the establishment of a qualification requirement, the need for such qualification requirement shall be examined and the standards of such requirement revalidated in accordance with the requirements of subsection (b) of this section.

The preceding sentence does not apply in the case of a qualification requirement for which a waiver is in effect under subsection (c)(2) of this section.

(f) Enforcement determination by agency head

Except in an emergency as determined by the head of the agency, whenever the head of the agency determines not to enforce a qualification requirement for a solicitation, the agency may not thereafter enforce that qualification requirement unless the agency complies with the requirements of subsection (b) of this section.

(June 30, 1949, c. 288, Title III, § 303C, formerly § 303D, as added Oct. 30, 1984, Pub.L. 98–577, Title II, § 202(a), 98 Stat. 3069, and renumbered § 303C, Nov. 8, 1985, Pub.L. 99–145, Title XIII, § 1304(c)(4)(A), 99 Stat. 742.)

HISTORICAL AND STATUTORY NOTES

Revision Notes and Legislative Reports

1984 Acts. Section 4 of S. 2489 also prescribes procedures which must be followed by a Federal agency before it may establish any prequalification requirement with which a prospective contractor must comply before his offer will even be considered by the agency for a contract award. Three basic requirements are prescribed.

First, the agency must examine the need for establishing the prequalification requirement, given its adverse impact on free and open competition. Having established that a need for a prequalification requirement exists, the agency must prepare a written justification which explains that need.

Second, the agency must specify the standards which a prospective contractor, or its product, must satisfy in order to become qualified. In developing these qualification standards, S. 2489 directs the agency to limit them to those essential to "meet the purposes necessitating the establishment of the prequalification requirement". The Committee made this modification to section 4 to make clear the nexus between the standards to be met and the agency's justification for the prequalification requirement.

Third, the executive agency imposing the prequalification requirement must promptly provide a prospective contractor with the opportunity to demonstrate its ability to meet the standards the agency has specified for qualification....

By placing a statutory obligation on the agency to afford a prospective contractor the opportunity to become prequalified, the Committee seeks to make clear that the testing and evaluation function for the purpose of prequalifying prospective contractors or their products should not be consistently accorded a low priority in the competition for the necessary agency resources. Consistent with the demands of the primary agency mission attainment, and the importance of procurement in the attainment of mission objectives, it is the Committee's intention that the agency must make every reasonable effort to afford the prospective contractor a fair and impartial chance to demonstrate its ability, or, that of its product, to fulfill the agency's prequalification standards....

In addition to prescribing procedures relating to the establishment of new prequalification requirements or the enforcement of existing ones, section 4 of S. 2489 also requires and executive agency responsible for the procurement of supplies or services covered by a prequalification requirement to take affirmative steps to encourage new competitors, and particularly small business competitors, to seek prequalification. If the number of currently prequalified sources is below the specified threshold, the agency is required to take two types of actions to encourage new sources to seek prequalification.

First, the agency is required to periodically place notices in the *Commerce Business Daily* soliciting additional contractors to seek prequalification for themselves or their products. Through these notices, new competitors will know that a sheltered market with few competitors exists and may be ripe for their competition.

Second, the agency is required to bear the cost of conducting the testing and evaluation necessary to demonstrate that a prospective contractor, or its product, meets the prequalification standards specified by the agency, only if the prospective contractor (a) is a small business concern which can reasonably be expected to compete for future procurements; (b) attains prequalification by fulfilling the agency's specified standards to the satisfaction of the cognizant agency; and (3) is able to attain prequalification while the number of prequalified sources on a list remains below the threshold established in the statute. This financial encouragement to small business competitors to seek prequalification is closely regulated and balanced against the potential benefit to the procuring agency in several ways.

First, only success is rewarded. To be eligible, the small business concern must have been successful in attaining prequalification. In addition, the agency has obtained a new qualified competitor, thus broadening the industrial base.

Second, only the limited direct costs of conducting the testing and evaluation specified by the agency would be borne by the agency or reimbursed to the contractor, for example, when the testing and evaluation are provided by an outside testing organization under direct agreement with the contractor seeking prequalification or the costs directly incurred by the contractor in conducting a supervised self-test. The contractor seeking qualification must bear the cost of producing the item to be tested or the cost of establishing the production, quality control, or other system to be evaluated. Basically, the contractor seeking qualification is required to make an investment in his firm or product, which in practical terms, will match or exceed the investment being made by the Government.

Third, the small business concern must be one that can reasonably be expected to compete for future procurements of the item or service subject to the prequalification. While this judgment is left to the discretion of the procuring agency, sub-

ject only to a standard of "reasonableness", it is the Committee's expectation that this test could be used to refuse to bear the cost of a small business competitor that has met all of the other requirements when there is substantial evidence indicating that prequalification has been sought for reasons other than gaining the opportunity to compete for agency contracts. This safeguard was added during Committee consideration of the bill to prevent an otherwise eligible contractor from seeking government-supported prequalification solely for the purpose of using the attainment of qualification as a commercial advantage in the conduct of its non-governmental business. However, there need not be an immediate contract requirement being solicited before a determination is made that a contractor could reasonably be expected to compete for future procurement opportunities....

The objective of the financial inducement provision in section 4 is to encourage new small business suppliers to enter the marketplace. In the Committee's view, this will have a salutory effect on enhancing competition, and will broaden the industrial base, a goal especially important to the Department of Defense. Second, given the fact that the financial inducement is only a partial reimbursement (restricted to testing and evaluation costs), a contractor seeking qualification is not likely to make the substantial investment in producing the item to be subjected to testing and evaluation without first making a business-like inquiry into the competition already existing in the marketplace. In the Committee's view, the more prevalent concern should be the general lack of competition for most prequalified items (with the exception of those on "Qualified Products List"), rather than the more remote prospect that an agency will find itself with too many competitors for some items subject to prequalification. Senate Report No. 98–523.

1985 Acts. House Report No. 99–81 and House Conference Report No. 99–235, see 1985 U.S.Code Cong. and Adm.News, p. 472.

Effective and Applicability Provisions
1984 Acts. Section 202(b) of Pub.L. 98–577 provided that: "The amendment made by subsection (a) [enacting this section] shall apply with respect to solicitations issued more than 180 days after the

date of enactment of this Act [Oct. 30, 1984]."

LIBRARY REFERENCES

American Digest System
    United States ☞64.15.
    Key Number System Topic No. 393.

WESTLAW ELECTRONIC RESEARCH

See Westlaw guide following the Explanation pages of this volume.

§ 253d. Validation of proprietary data restrictions

(a) Contracts; delivery of technical services; contents

A contract for property or services entered into by an executive agency which provides for the delivery of technical data, shall provide that—

> **(1)** a contractor or subcontractor at any tier shall be prepared to furnish to the contracting officer a written justification for any restriction asserted by the contractor or subcontractor on the right of the United States to use such technical data; and

> **(2)** the contracting officer may review the validity of any restriction asserted by the contractor or by a subcontractor under the contract on the right of the United States to use technical data furnished to the United States under the contract if the contracting officer determines that reasonable grounds exist to question the current validity of the asserted restriction and that the continued adherence to the asserted restriction by the United States would make it impracticable to procure the item competitively at a later time.

(b) Review; challenge; notice

If after such review the contracting officer determines that a challenge to the asserted restriction is warranted, the contracting officer shall provide written notice to the contractor or subcontractor asserting the restriction. Such notice shall state—

> **(1)** the grounds for challenging the asserted restriction; and

> **(2)** the requirement for a response within 60 days justifying the current validity of the asserted restriction.

(c) Written request; additional time; schedule of responses

If a contractor or subcontractor asserting a restriction subject to this section submits to the contracting officer a written request, showing the need for additional time to comply with the requirement to justify the current validity of the asserted restriction, additional time to adequately permit the submission of such justification shall be provided by the contracting officer as appropriate. If a party asserting a restriction receives notices of challenges to restrictions on technical data from more than one contracting officer, and notifies each contracting officer of the existence of more than one challenge, the contracting officer initiating the first in time challenge, after consultation with the party asserting the restriction and the other contracting officers, shall formulate a schedule of responses to each of the challenges that will afford the party asserting the restriction with an equitable opportunity to respond to each such challenge.

(d) Decision; validity of asserted restriction; failure to submit response

(1) Upon a failure by the contractor or subcontractor to submit any response under subsection (b) of this section, the contracting officer shall issue a decision pertaining to the validity of the asserted restriction.

(2) If a justification is submitted in response to the notice provided pursuant to subsection (b) of this section, a contracting officer shall within 60 days of receipt of any justification submitted, issue a decision or notify the party asserting the restriction of the time within which a decision will be issued.

(e) Claim; considered claim within Contract Disputes Act of 1978

If a claim pertaining to the validity of the asserted restriction is submitted in writing to a contracting officer by a contractor or subcontractor at any tier, such claim shall be considered a claim within the meaning of the Contract Disputes Act of 1978 (41 U.S.C. 601 et seq.).

(f) Challenge; use of technical data; sustained; liability of United States for costs and fees

(1) If, upon final disposition, the contracting officer's challenge to the restriction on the right of the United States to use such technical data is sustained—

(A) the restriction on the right of the United States to use the technical data shall be cancelled; and

(B) if the asserted restriction is found not to be substantially justified, the contractor or subcontractor, as appropriate, shall be liable to the United States for payment of the cost to the United States of reviewing the asserted restriction and the fees and other expenses (as defined in section 2412(d)(2)(A) of Title 28) incurred by the United States in challenging the asserted restriction, unless special circumstances would make such payment unjust.

457

(2) If, upon final disposition, the contracting officer's challenge to the restriction on the right of the United States to use such technical data is not sustained—

　(A) the United States shall continue to be bound by the restriction; and

　(B) the United States shall be liable for payment to the party asserting the restriction for fees and other expenses (as defined in section 2412(d)(2)(A) of Title 28) incurred by the party asserting the restriction in defending the asserted restriction if the challenge by the United States is found not to be made in good faith.

(June 30, 1949, c. 288, Title III, § 303D, formerly § 303E, as added Oct. 30, 1984, Pub.L. 98–577, Title II, § 203(a), 98 Stat. 3071, and renumbered § 303D, Nov. 8, 1985, Pub.L. 99–145, Title XIII, § 1304(c)(4)(A), 99 Stat. 742.)

HISTORICAL AND STATUTORY NOTES

Revision Notes and Legislative Reports

1949 Acts. Section 7 of S. 2489, as reported by the Committee, amends section 15 of the Small Business Act by adding a new subsection (p), which specifies procedures for reviewing the validity of restrictions on the Government's right to use for governmental purposes technical data furnished to the Government under a procurement contract. The section also provides sanctions to be applied against a contractor or subcontractor who is found, by a board of contract appeals or a court, to have asserted such a restriction when it has no justification for doing so.

If an executive agency is to conduct a competitive procurement, it must have technical data adequate to describe to all potential suppliers what it is the agency is seeking to procure and what is expected of the contractor receiving the contract award. If the agency is to be able to adequately specify the performance that will be expected of the contractor, the agency must generally have access to technical data that is complete, current and without restrictions as to its use by the Government. If the technical data the Government needs to conduct a competitive procurement has been delivered to the Government with restrictions as to its disclosure outside of the Government, the agency will be unable to solicit any source other than the source asserting the restriction. The agency then will be compelled to make a sole source award, negotiating a price which hopefully proves to be fair and reasonable....

The sponsors of S. 2489, and subsequently the Committee, approached the proprietary technical data issue from the basis that legitimately held property rights should not be violated merely because the context of the rights was the Federal procurement process. Efforts might be made during the early state of the acquisition of a major system to avoid acquiring components covered by limited rights data (without sacrificing the technical capabilities of the overall system) in order to enhance the potential for the competitive acquisition of those components, items of support equipment, and services expected to be needed in substantial quantities to maintain the major system. But having procured a system, including components covered by technical data asserted to be proprietary, the focus of the effort should be on reviewing the legitimacy of the proprietary data assertion—honoring those demonstrated to be valid and eliminating those found to be unjustified. Providing fair procedures for reviewing the validity of proprietary data claims is the focus of section 7 of S. 2489, as reported. Senate Report No. 98–523.

1985 Acts. House Report No. 99–81 and House Conference Report No. 99–235, see 1985 U.S.Code Cong. and Adm.News, p. 472.

References in Text
The Contract Disputes Act of 1978, referred to in subsec. (e), is Pub.L. 95–563, Nov. 1, 1978, 92 Stat. 2383, as amended, which is classified principally to chapter 9 (section 601 et seq.) of this title. For complete classification of this Act to the Code, see Short Title note set out under section 601 of this title and Tables.

Effective and Applicability Provisions
1984 Acts. Section 203(b) of Pub.L. 98–577 provided that: "The amendment made by subsection (a) [enacting this section] shall apply with respect to solicitations issued more than 60 days after the date of the enactment of this Act [Oct. 30, 1984]."

LIBRARY REFERENCES

American Digest System
United States ⬪64.15.
Key Number System Topic No. 393.

WESTLAW ELECTRONIC RESEARCH

See Westlaw guide following the Explanation pages of this volume.

§ 253e. Repealed. Pub.L. 103–355, Title I, § 1252, Oct. 13, 1994, 108 Stat. 3284

HISTORICAL AND STATUTORY NOTES

Section 253e, Act June 30, 1949, c. 288, Title III, § 303E, formerly § 303F, as added Oct. 30, 1984, Pub.L. 98–577, Title II, § 204(a), 98 Stat. 3072, and renumbered § 303E, Nov. 8, 1985, Pub.L. 99–145, Title XIII, § 1304(c)(4)(A), 99 Stat. 742, related to commercial pricing for supplies.

Effective Date of Repeal
Repeal of section to take effect Oct. 13, 1994, except as otherwise provided, see section 10001 of Pub.L. 103–355, set out as a note under section 251 of this title.

§ 253f. Economic order quantities

(a) Procurement of supplies; costs advantageous to United States

Each executive agency shall procure supplies in such quantity as (A) will result in the total cost and unit cost most advantageous to the United States, where practicable, and (B) does not exceed the quantity reasonably expected to be required by the agency.

(b) Opinions; economic advantage to United States

Each solicitation for a contract for supplies shall, if practicable, include a provision inviting each offeror responding to the solicitation to state an opinion on whether the quantity of the supplies proposed to be procured is economically advantageous to the United States and, if applicable, to recommend a quantity or quantities which would be more economically advantageous to the United States. Each such recommendation shall include a quotation of the total price and the unit price for supplies procured in each recommended quantity.

(June 30, 1949, c. 288, Title III, § 303F, formerly § 303G, as added Oct. 30, 1984, Pub.L. 98–577, Title II, § 205(a), 98 Stat. 3073, and renumbered § 303F, Nov. 8, 1985, Pub.L. 99–145, Title XIII, § 1304(c)(4)(A), 99 Stat. 742.)

HISTORICAL AND STATUTORY NOTES

Revision Notes and Legislative Reports
  1984 Acts. Senate Report No. 98–523, see 1984 U.S.Code Cong. and Adm.News, p. 5347.
  1985 Acts. House Report No. 99–81 and House Conference Report No. 99–235, see 1985 U.S.Code Cong. and Adm.News, p. 472.

Effective and Applicability Provisions
  1984 Acts. Section 205(b) of Pub.L. 98–577 provided that: "The amendment made by subsection (a) [enacting this section] shall take effect at the end of the 180-day period beginning on the date of the enactment of this Act [Oct. 30, 1984]."

LIBRARY REFERENCES

American Digest System
  United States ☞64.45(1).
  Key Number System Topic No. 393.

WESTLAW ELECTRONIC RESEARCH

See Westlaw guide following the Explanation pages of this volume.

§ 253g. Prohibition of contractors limiting subcontractor sales directly to United States

(a) Contract restrictions

Each contract for the purchase of property or services made by an executive agency shall provide that the contractor will not—

>   **(1)** enter into any agreement with a subcontractor under the contract that has the effect of unreasonably restricting sales by the subcontractor directly to the United States of any item or process (including computer software) made or furnished by the subcontractor under the contract (or any follow-on production contract); or

>   **(2)** otherwise act to restrict unreasonably the ability of a subcontractor to make sales to the United States described in clause (1).

(b) Rights under law

This section does not prohibit a contractor from asserting rights it otherwise has under law.

(c) Inapplicability to certain contracts

This section does not apply to a contract for an amount that is not greater than the simplified acquisition threshold.

(d) Inapplicability when Government treated similarly to other purchasers

An agreement between the contractor in a contract for the acquisition of commercial items and a subcontractor under such contract that restricts sales by such subcontractor directly to persons other than the contractor may not be considered to unreasonably restrict sales by that subcontractor to the United States in violation of the provision included in such contract pursuant to subsection (a) of this section if the agreement does not result in the Federal Government being treated differently with regard to the restriction than any other prospective purchaser of such commercial items from that subcontractor.

(June 30, 1949, c. 288, Title III, § 303G, formerly § 303H, as added Oct. 30, 1984, Pub.L. 98–577, Title II, § 206(a), 98 Stat. 3073, and renumbered § 303G, Nov. 8, 1985, Pub.L. 99–145, Title XIII, § 1304(c)(4)(A), 99 Stat. 742, and amended Oct. 13, 1994, Pub.L. 103–355, Title IV, § 4103(b), Title VIII, § 8204(a), 108 Stat. 3341, 3396.)

HISTORICAL AND STATUTORY NOTES

Revision Notes and Legislative Reports
 1984 Acts. Senate Report No. 98–523, see 1984 U.S.Code Cong. and Adm.News, p. 5347.

 1985 Acts. House Report No. 99–81 and House Conference Report No. 99–235, see 1985 U.S.Code Cong. and Adm.News, p. 472.

 1994 Acts. Senate Report Nos. 103–258 and 103–259, and House Conference Report No. 103–712, see 1994 U.S. Code Cong. and Adm. News, p. 2561.

Amendments
 1994 Amendments. Subsec. (c). Pub.L. 103–355 § 4103(b), added subsec. (c).

 Subsec. (d). Pub.L. 103–355, § 8204(a), added subsec. (d).

Effective and Applicability Provisions
 1994 Acts. Amendment by sections 4103(b) and 8204(a) of Pub.L. 103–355 effective Oct. 13, 1994, except as otherwise provided, see section 10001 of Pub.L. 103–355, set out as a note under section 251 of this title.

 1984 Acts. Section 206(b) of Pub.L. 98–577 provided that: "The amendment made by subsection (a) [enacting this section] shall apply with respect to solicitations made more than 180 days after the date of enactment of this Act [Oct. 30, 1984]."

Definitions
 The definitions in 40 U.S.C.A. § 102 apply to terms appearing in this subchapter.

LIBRARY REFERENCES

American Digest System
 United States ☞64.15.
 Key Number System Topic No. 393.

WESTLAW ELECTRONIC RESEARCH

See Westlaw guide following the Explanation pages of this volume.

§ 253h. Task and delivery order contracts: general authority

(a) Authority to award

Subject to the requirements of this section, section 253j of this title, and other applicable law, the head of an executive agency may enter into a task or delivery order contract (as defined in section 253k of this title) for procurement of services or property.

(b) Solicitation

The solicitation for a task or delivery order contract shall include the following:

(1) The period of the contract, including the number of options to extend the contract and the period for which the contract may be extended under each option, if any.

(2) The maximum quantity or dollar value of the services or property to be procured under the contract.

(3) A statement of work, specifications, or other description that reasonably describes the general scope, nature, complexity, and purposes of the services or property to be procured under the contract.

(c) Applicability of restriction on use of noncompetitive procedures

The head of an executive agency may use procedures other than competitive procedures to enter into a task or delivery order contract under this section only if an exception in subsection (c) of section 253 of this title applies to the contract and the use of such procedures is approved in accordance with subsection (f) of such section.

(d) Single and multiple contract awards

(1) The head of an executive agency may exercise the authority provided in this section—

(A) to award a single task or delivery order contract; or

(B) if the solicitation states that the head of the executive agency has the option to do so, to award separate task or delivery order contracts for the same or similar services or property to two or more sources.

(2) No determination under section 253(b) of this title is required for an award of multiple task or delivery order contracts under paragraph (1)(B).

(3) The regulations implementing this subsection shall—

(A) establish a preference for awarding, to the maximum extent practicable, multiple task or delivery order contracts for the same or similar services or property under the authority of paragraph (1)(B); and

(B) establish criteria for determining when award of multiple task or delivery order contracts would not be in the best interest of the Federal Government.

(e) Contract modifications

A task or delivery order may not increase the scope, period, or maximum value of the task or delivery order contract under which the order is issued. The scope, period, or maximum value of the contract may be increased only by modification of the contract.

(f) Inapplicability to contracts for advisory and assistance service

Except as otherwise specifically provided in section 253i of this title, this section does not apply to a task or delivery order contract for the acquisition of advisory and assistance services (as defined in section 1105(g) of Title 31).

(g) Relationship to other contracting authority

Nothing in this section may be construed to limit or expand any authority of the head of an executive agency or the Administrator of General Services to enter into schedule, multiple award, or task or delivery order contracts under any other provision of law.

(June 30, 1949, c. 288, Title III, § 303H, as added Oct. 13, 1994, Pub.L. 103–355, Title I, § 1054(a), 108 Stat. 3261.)

HISTORICAL AND STATUTORY NOTES

Revision Notes and Legislative Reports
1994 Acts. Senate Report Nos. 103–258 and 103–259, and House Conference Report No. 103–712, see 1994 U.S. Code Cong. and Adm. News, p. 2561.

Effective and Applicability Provisions
1994 Acts. Section effective Oct. 13, 1994, except as otherwise provided, see section 10001 of Pub.L. 103–355, set out as a note under section 251 of this title.

Guidance on Use of Task Order and Delivery Order Contracts
Pub.L. 106–65, Div. A, Title VIII, § 804, Oct. 5, 1999, 113 Stat. 704, provided that:

"**(a) Guidance in the Federal Acquisition Regulation.**—Not later than 180 days after the date of the enactment of this Act [Oct. 5, 1999], the Federal Acquisition Regulation issued in accordance with sections 6 and 25 of the Office of Federal Procurement Policy Act (41 U.S.C. 405 and 421) shall be revised to provide guidance to agencies on the appropriate use of task order and delivery order contracts in accordance with sections 2304a through 2304d of title 10, United States Code, and sections 303H through 303K of the Federal Property and Administrative Services Act of 1949 (41 U.S.C. 253h through 253k).

"**(b) Content of guidance.**—The regulations issued pursuant to subsection (a) shall, at a minimum, provide the following:

"**(1)** Specific guidance on the appropriate use of government wide and other multiagency contracts entered into in accordance with the provisions of law referred to in that subsection.

"**(2)** Specific guidance on steps that agencies should take in entering into and administering multiple award task order and delivery order contracts to ensure compliance with—

"**(A)** the requirement in section 5122 of the Clinger–Cohen Act (40 U.S.C. 1422) [see now 40 U.S.C.A. § 11312] for capital planning and investment control in purchases of information technology products and services;

"**(B)** the requirement in section 2304c(b) of title 10, United States Code, and section 303J(b) of the Federal Property and Administrative Services Act of 1949 (41 U.S.C. 253j(b)) to ensure that all contractors are afforded a fair opportunity to be considered for the award of task orders and delivery orders; and

"**(C)** the requirement in section 2304c(c) of title 10, United States Code, and section 303J(c) of the Federal Property and Administrative Services Act of 1949 (41 U.S.C. 253j(c)) for a statement of work in each task order or delivery order issued that clearly specifies all tasks to be performed or property to be delivered under the order.

"**(c) GSA Federal Supply Schedules program.**—The Administrator for Federal Procurement Policy shall consult with the Administrator of General Services to assess the effectiveness of the multiple awards schedule program of the General Services Administration referred to in section 309(b)(3) of the Federal Property and Administrative Services Act of 1949 (41 U.S.C. 259(b)(3)) that is administered as the Federal Supply Schedules program. The assessment shall include examination of the following:

"**(1)** The administration of the program by the Administrator of General Services.

"**(2)** The ordering and program practices followed by Federal customer agencies in using schedules established under the program.

"**(d) GAO report.**—Not later than one year after the date on which the regulations required by subsection (a) are published in the Federal Register, the Comptroller General shall submit to Congress an evaluation of—

"**(1)** executive agency compliance with the regulations; and

"**(2)** conformance of the regulations with existing law, together with any recommendations that the Comptroller General considers appropriate."

Provisions Not Affected by Pub.L. 103–355

Section 1054(b) of Pub.L. 103–355 provided that: "Nothing in section 303H, 303I, 303J, or 303K of the Federal Property and Administrative Services Act of 1949, as added by subsection (a) [this section or section 253i, 253j, or 253k of this title], shall be construed as modifying or superseding, or as intended to impair or restrict, authorities or responsibilities under—

"**(1)** the Brooks Automatic Data Processing Act (section 111 of the Federal Property and Administrative Services Act of 1949 (40 U.S.C. 759) [repealed by Pub.L. 104–106, Div. E, Title LI, § 5101, Feb. 10, 1996, 110 Stat. 680]); and

"**(2)** the Brooks Architect-Engineers Act (title IX of the Federal Property and Administrative Services Act of 1949 (40 U.S.C. 541 et seq.) [see now 40 U.S.C.A. § 1101 et seq.])."

LIBRARY REFERENCES

American Digest System
United States ☞59.
Key Number System Topic No. 393.

WESTLAW ELECTRONIC RESEARCH

See Westlaw guide following the Explanation pages of this volume.

§ 253i. Task order contracts: advisory and assistance services

(a) Authority to award

(1) Subject to the requirements of this section, section 253j of this title, and other applicable law, the head of an executive agency may enter into a task order contract (as defined in section 253k of this title) for procurement of advisory and assistance services.

(2) The head of an executive agency may enter into a task order contract for advisory and assistance services only under the authority of this section.

(b) Limitation on contract period

The period of a task order contract entered into under this section, including all periods of extensions of the contract under options, modifications, or otherwise, may not exceed five years unless a longer period is specifically authorized in a law that is applicable to such contract.

(c) Content of notice

The notice required by section 416 of this title and section 637(e) of Title 15 shall reasonably and fairly describe the general scope, magnitude, and duration of the proposed task order contract in a manner that would reasonably enable a potential offeror to decide whether to request the solicitation and consider submitting an offer.

(d) Required content of solicitation and contract

(1) The solicitation shall include the information (regarding services) described in section 253h(b) of this title.

(2) A task order contract entered into under this section shall contain the same information that is required by paragraph (1) to be included in the solicitation of offers for that contract.

(e) Multiple awards

(1) The head of an executive agency may, on the basis of one solicitation, award separate task order contracts under this section for the same or similar services to two or more sources if the solicitation states that the head of the executive agency has the option to do so.

(2) If, in the case of a task order contract for advisory and assistance services to be entered into under the authority of this section, the contract period is to exceed three years and the contract amount is estimated to exceed $10,000,000 (including all options), the solicitation shall—

    (A) provide for a multiple award authorized under paragraph (1); and

    (B) include a statement that the head of the executive agency may also elect to award only one task order contract if the head of the executive agency determines in writing that only one of the offerers is capable of providing the services required at the level of quality required.

(3) Paragraph (2) does not apply in the case of a solicitation for which the head of the executive agency concerned determines in writing that, because the services required under the contract are unique or highly specialized, it is not practicable to award more than one contract.

(f) Contract modifications

(1) A task order may not increase the scope, period, or maximum value of the task order contract under which the order is issued. The scope, period, or maximum value of the contract may be increased only by modification of the contract.

(2) Unless use of procedures other than competitive procedures is authorized by an exception in subsection (c) of section 253 of this title and approved in accordance with subsection (f) of such section, competitive procedures shall be used for making such a modification.

(3) Notice regarding the modification shall be provided in accordance with section 416 of this title and section 637(e) of Title 15.

(g) Contract extensions

(1) Notwithstanding the limitation on the contract period set forth in subsection (b) of this section or in a solicitation or contract pursuant to subsection (e) of this section, a contract entered into by the head of an executive agency under this section may be extended on a sole-source basis for a period not exceeding six months if the head of such executive agency determines that—

(A) the award of a follow-on contract has been delayed by circumstances that were not reasonably foreseeable at the time the initial contract was entered into; and

(B) the extension is necessary in order to ensure continuity of the receipt of services pending the award of, and commencement of performance under, the follow-on contract.

(2) A task order contract may be extended under the authority of paragraph (1) only once and only in accordance with the limitations and requirements of this subsection.

(h) Inapplicability to certain contracts

This section does not apply to a contract for the acquisition of property or services that includes acquisition of advisory and assistance services if the head of the executive agency entering into such contract determines that, under the contract, advisory and assistance services are necessarily incident to, and not a significant component of, the contract.

466

(i) "Advisory and assistance services" defined

In this section, the term "advisory and assistance services" has the meaning given such term in section 1105(g) of Title 31.

(June 30, 1949, c. 288, Title III, § 303I, as added Oct. 13, 1994, Pub.L. 103–355, Title I, § 1054(a), 108 Stat. 3262.)

HISTORICAL AND STATUTORY NOTES

Revision Notes and Legislative Reports
1994   Acts. Senate Report Nos. 103–258 and 103–259, and House Conference Report No. 103–712, see 1994 U.S. Code Cong. and Adm. News, p. 2561.

Effective and Applicability Provisions
1994 Acts. Section effective Oct. 13, 1994, except as otherwise provided, see section 10001 of Pub.L. 103–355, set out as a note under section 251 of this title.

Waivers to Extend Task Order Contracts for Advisory and Assistance Services Pub.L. 109–364, Div. A, Title VIII, § 834, Oct. 17, 2006, 120 Stat. 2332, provided that:

"(a) Defense contracts.—

"(1) Waiver authority.—The head of an agency may issue a waiver to extend a task order contract entered into under section 2304b of title 10, United States Code, for a period not exceeding 10 years, through five one-year options, if the head of the agency determines in writing—

"(A) that the contract provides engineering or technical services of such a unique and substantial technical nature that award of a new contract would be harmful to the continuity of the program for which the services are performed;

"(B) that award of a new contract would create a large disruption in services provided to the Department of Defense; and

"(C) that the Department of Defense would, through award of a new contract, endure program risk during critical program stages due to loss of program corporate knowledge of ongoing program activities.

"(2) Delegation.—The authority of the head of an agency under paragraph (1) may be delegated only to the senior procurement executive of the agency.

"(3) Report.—Not later than April 1, 2007, the Secretary of Defense shall submit to the Committees on Armed Services of the Senate and the House of Representatives a report on advisory and assistance services. The report shall include the following information:

"(A) The methods used by the Department of Defense to identify a contract as an advisory and assistance services contract, as defined in section 2304b of title 10, United States Code.

"(B) The number of such contracts awarded by the Department during the five-year period preceding the date of the enactment of this Act [Oct. 17, 2006].

"(C) The average annual expenditures by the Department for such contracts.

"(D) The average length of such contracts.

"(E) The number of such contracts recompeted and awarded to the previous award winner.

"(4) Prohibition on use of authority by Department of Defense if report not submitted.—The head of an agency may not issue a waiver under paragraph (1) if the report required by paragraph (3) is not submitted by the date set forth in that paragraph.

"(b) Civilian agency contracts.—

"(1) Waiver authority.—The head of an executive agency may issue a waiver to extend a task order contract entered into under section 303I of the Federal Property and Administrative Services Act of 1949 (41 U.S.C. 253i) [this section] for a period not exceeding 10 years, through five one-year options, if the head of the agency determines in writing—

"(A) that the contract provides engineering or technical services of such a unique and substantial technical nature that award of a new contract would be harmful to the continuity of the program for which the services are performed;

"**(B)** that award of a new contract would create a large disruption in services provided to the executive agency; and

"**(C)** that the executive agency would, through award of a new contract, endure program risk during critical program stages due to loss of program corporate knowledge of ongoing program activities.

"**(2) Delegation.**—The authority of the head of an executive agency under paragraph (1) may be delegated only to the Chief Acquisition Officer of the agency (or the senior procurement executive in the case of an agency for which a Chief Acquisition Officer has not been appointed or designated under section 16(a) of the Office of Federal Procurement Policy Act (41 U.S.C. 414(a))).

"**(3) Report.**—Not later than April 1, 2007, the Administrator for Federal Procurement Policy shall submit to the Committee on Homeland Security and Governmental Affairs of the Senate and the Committee on Government Reform of the House of Representatives a report on advisory and assistance services. The report shall include the following information:

"**(A)** The methods used by executive agencies to identify a contract as an advisory and assistance services contract, as defined in section 303I(i) of the Federal Property and Administrative Services Act of 1949 (41 U.S.C. 253i(i)).

"**(B)** The number of such contracts awarded by each executive agency during the five-year period preceding the date of the enactment of this Act [Oct. 17, 2006].

"**(C)** The average annual expenditures by each executive agency for such contracts.

"**(D)** The average length of such contracts.

"**(E)** The number of such contracts recompeted and awarded to the previous award winner.

"**(4) Prohibition on use of authority by executive agencies if report not submitted.**—The head of an executive agency may not issue a waiver under paragraph (1) if the report required by

paragraph (3) is not submitted by the date set forth in that paragraph.

"**(c) Termination of authority.**—A waiver may not be issued under this section after December 31, 2011.

"**(d) Comptroller general review.**—

"**(1) Report requirement.**—Not later than one year after the date of the enactment of this Act [Oct. 17, 2006], the Comptroller General shall submit to the committees described in paragraph (3) a report on the use of advisory and assistance services contracts by the Federal Government.

"**(2) Defense and civilian agency contracts covered.**—The report shall cover both of the following:

"**(A)** Advisory and assistance services contracts as defined in section 2304b of title 10, United States Code.

"**(B)** Advisory and assistance services contracts as defined in section 303I(i) of the Federal Property and Administrative Services Act of 1949 (41 U.S.C. 253i(i)).

"**(3) Matters covered.**—The report shall address the following issues:

"**(A)** The extent to which executive agencies and elements of the Department of Defense require advisory and assistance services for periods of greater than five years.

"**(B)** The extent to which such advisory and assistance services are provided by the same contractors under recurring contracts.

"**(C)** The rationale for contracting for advisory and assistance services that will be needed on a continuing basis, rather than performing the services inside the Federal Government.

"**(D)** The contract types and oversight mechanisms used by the Federal Government in contracts for advisory and assistance services and the extent to which such contract types and oversight mechanisms are adequate to protect the interests of the Government and taxpayers.

"**(E)** The actions taken by the Federal Government to prevent organizational conflicts of interest and improper personal services contracts in its contracts for advisory and assistance services.

"**(4) Committees.**—The committees described in this paragraph are the following:

"**(A)** The Committees on Armed Services and on Homeland Security and Governmental Affairs of the Senate.

"**(B)** The Committees on Armed Services and on Government Reform of the House of Representatives."

Provisions Not Affected by Pub.L. 103–355

This section not to be construed as modifying or superseding, or as intended to impair or restrict, specified authorities or responsibilities, see section 1054(b) of Pub.L. 103–355, set out as a note under 41 U.S.C.A. § 253h.

LIBRARY REFERENCES

American Digest System
United States ⊕59, 66.
Key Number System Topic No. 393.

WESTLAW ELECTRONIC RESEARCH

See Westlaw guide following the Explanation pages of this volume.

§ 253j. Task and delivery order contracts: orders

(a) Issuance of orders

The following actions are not required for issuance of a task or delivery order under a task or delivery order contract:

> **(1)** A separate notice for such order under section 416 of this title or section 637(e) of Title 15.

> **(2)** Except as provided in subsection (b) of this section, a competition (or a waiver of competition approved in accordance with section 253(f) of this title) that is separate from that used for entering into the contract.

(b) Multiple award contracts

When multiple contracts are awarded under section 253h(d)(1)(B) or 253i(e) of this title, all contractors awarded such contracts shall be provided a fair opportunity to be considered, pursuant to procedures set forth in the contracts, for each task or delivery order in excess of $2,500 that is to be issued under any of the contracts unless—

> **(1)** the executive agency's need for the services or property ordered is of such unusual urgency that providing such opportunity to all such contractors would result in unacceptable delays in fulfilling that need;

> **(2)** only one such contractor is capable of providing the services or property required at the level of quality required because the services or property ordered are unique or highly specialized;

> **(3)** the task or delivery order should be issued on a sole-source basis in the interest of economy and efficiency because it is a

logical follow-on to a task or delivery order already issued on a competitive basis; or

(4) it is necessary to place the order with a particular contractor in order to satisfy a minimum guarantee.

(c) Statement of work

A task or delivery order shall include a statement of work that clearly specifies all tasks to be performed or property to be delivered under the order.

(d) Protests

A protest is not authorized in connection with the issuance or proposed issuance of a task or delivery order except for a protest on the ground that the order increases the scope, period, or maximum value of the contract under which the order is issued.

(e) Task and delivery order ombudsman

The head of each executive agency who awards multiple task or delivery order contracts pursuant to section 253h(d)(1)(B) or 253i(e) of this title shall appoint or designate a task and delivery order ombudsman who shall be responsible for reviewing complaints from the contractors on such contracts and ensuring that all of the contractors are afforded a fair opportunity to be considered for task or delivery orders when required under subsection (b) of this section. The task and delivery order ombudsman shall be a senior agency official who is independent of the contracting officer for the contracts and may be the executive agency's competition advocate.

(f) Applicability

This section applies to task and delivery order contracts entered into under sections 253h and 253i of this title.

(June 30, 1949, c. 288, Title III, § 303J, as added Oct. 13, 1994, Pub.L. 103–355, Title I, § 1054(a), 108 Stat. 3264.)

HISTORICAL AND STATUTORY NOTES

Revision Notes and Legislative Reports
  1994 Acts. Senate Report Nos. 103–258 and 103–259, and House Conference Report No. 103–712, see 1994 U.S. Code Cong. and Adm. News, p. 2561.

Effective and Applicability Provisions
  1994 Acts. Section effective Oct. 13, 1994, except as otherwise provided, see section 10001 of Pub.L. 103–355, set out as a note under section 251 of this title.

Provisions Not Affected by Pub.L. 103–355
  This section not to be construed as modifying or superseding, or as intended to impair or restrict, specified authorities or responsibilities, see section 1054(b) of Pub.L. 103–355, set out as a note under 41 U.S.C.A. § 253h.

LIBRARY REFERENCES

American Digest System
United States ⊘64.40, 64.55.
Key Number System Topic No. 393.

Research References

Treatises and Practice Aids
West's Federal Administrative Practice § 635, Types of Contracts.
West's Federal Administrative Practice § 664, Protests and Appeals.
West's Federal Administrative Practice § 822, Subject Matter Jurisdiction--Contract Claim: Jurisdiction, Limitations, Appeals and Interest.

WESTLAW ELECTRONIC RESEARCH

See Westlaw guide following the Explanation pages of this volume.

Notes of Decisions

Protests   1
___

1. Protests
Contractor which was awarded an indefinite delivery-indefinite quantity (IDIQ) master contract as part of a multiple award IDIQ contract with the General Services Administration (GSA) was barred by statute from filing bid protest in the Court of Federal Claims of award of task order issued under the multiple contract. A & D Fire Protection, Inc. v. U.S., Fed.Cl.2006, 72 Fed.Cl. 126. United States ⊘ 64.60(1)

§ 253k. Task and delivery order contracts: definitions

In sections 253h, 253i, and 253j of this title:

(1) The term "task order contract" means a contract for services that does not procure or specify a firm quantity of services (other than a minimum or maximum quantity) and that provides for the issuance of orders for the performance of tasks during the period of the contract.

(2) The term "delivery order contract" means a contract for property that does not procure or specify a firm quantity of property (other than a minimum or maximum quantity) and that provides for the issuance of orders for the delivery of property during the period of the contract.

(June 30, 1949, c. 288, Title III, § 303K, as added Oct. 13, 1994, Pub.L. 103–355, Title I, § 1054(a), 108 Stat. 3265.)

HISTORICAL AND STATUTORY NOTES

Revision Notes and Legislative Reports
1994   Acts. Senate   Report   Nos. 103–258 and 103–259, and House Conference Report No. 103–712, see 1994 U.S. Code Cong. and Adm. News, p. 2561.

Effective and Applicability Provisions
1994 Acts. Section effective Oct. 13, 1994, except as otherwise provided, see

section 10001 of Pub.L. 103–355, set out as a note under section 251 of this title.

Provisions Not Affected by Pub.L. 103–355
This section not to be construed as modifying or superseding, or as intended to impair or restrict, authorities or responsibilities under section 759 of Title

40, Public Buildings, Property, and Works, or subchapter VI (section 541 et seq.) of chapter 10 of Title 40, see section 1054(b) of Pub.L. 103–355, set out as a note under section 253h of this title.

Provisions Not Affected by Pub.L. 103–355
This section not to be construed as modifying or superseding, or as intended

to impair or restrict, specified authorities or responsibilities, see section 1054(b) of Pub.L. 103–355, set out as a note under 41 U.S.C.A. § 253h.

WESTLAW ELECTRONIC RESEARCH

See Westlaw guide following the Explanation pages of this volume.

§ 253*l*. Severable services contracts for periods crossing fiscal years

(a) Authority

The head of an executive agency may enter into a contract for procurement of severable services for a period that begins in one fiscal year and ends in the next fiscal year if (without regard to any option to extend the period of the contract) the contract period does not exceed one year.

(b) Obligation of funds

Funds made available for a fiscal year may be obligated for the total amount of a contract entered into under the authority of subsection (a) of this section.

(June 30, 1949, c. 288, Title III, § 303L, as added Oct. 13, 1994, Pub.L. 103–355, Title I, § 1073, 108 Stat. 3271, and amended Feb. 10, 1996, Pub.L. 104–106, Div. D, Title XLIII, § 4321(a)(1), 110 Stat. 671.)

HISTORICAL AND STATUTORY NOTES

Revision Notes and Legislative Reports
  1994 Acts. Senate Report Nos. 103–258 and 103–259, and House Conference Report No. 103–712, see 1994 U.S. Code Cong. and Adm. News, p. 2561.
  1996 Acts. House Conference Report No. 104–450, see 1996 U.S. Code Cong. and Adm. News, p. 238.

Amendments
  1996 Amendments. Pub.L. 104–106, § 4321(a)(1), as amending Pub.L. 103–355, § 1073, made technical changes to directory language which, for purposes

of codification, required no further changes in text.

Effective and Applicability Provisions
  1996 Acts. Amendment by Pub.L. 104–106 effective Oct. 13, 1994, see section 4321(a) of Pub.L. 104–106, set out as a note under section 2306a of Title 10, Armed Forces.
  1994 Acts. Section effective Oct. 13, 1994, except as otherwise provided, see section 10001 of Pub.L. 103–355, set out as a note under section 251 of this title.

LIBRARY REFERENCES

American Digest System
  United States ⬮59.
  Key Number System Topic No. 393.

WESTLAW ELECTRONIC RESEARCH

See Westlaw guide following the Explanation pages of this volume.

§ 253*l*–1. Contract authority of Comptroller General

The Comptroller General may use available funds, now and hereafter, to enter into contracts for the acquisition of severable services for a period that begins in one fiscal year and ends in the next fiscal year and to enter in multiyear contracts for the acquisition of property and nonaudit-related services, to the same extent as executive agencies under the authority of sections 253*l* and 254c of Title 41.

(Pub.L. 105–18, Title II, § 7004, June 12, 1997, 111 Stat. 192.)

HISTORICAL AND STATUTORY NOTES

Revision Notes and Legislative Reports
1997 Acts. For Related Reports and Statements by President, see 1997 U.S. Code Cong. and Admin. News, p. 149.

Codifications
Section was not enacted as part of Title III of Act June 30, 1949, c. 288, 63 Stat. 393, which comprises this subchapter.

LIBRARY REFERENCES

American Digest System
United States ⚏60.
Key Number System Topic No. 393.

WESTLAW ELECTRONIC RESEARCH

See Westlaw guide following the Explanation pages of this volume.

§ 253*l*–2. Contract authority of Library of Congress

The Library of Congress may use available funds, now and hereafter, to enter into contracts for the lease or acquisition of severable services for a period that begins in one fiscal year and ends in the next fiscal year and to enter into multi-year contracts for the acquisition of property and services pursuant to sections 303L and 304B, respectively, of the Federal Property and Administrative Services Act (41 U.S.C. 253*l* and 254c).

(Pub.L. 106–57, Title II, § 207, Sept. 29, 1999, 113 Stat. 423.)

HISTORICAL AND STATUTORY NOTES

Revision Notes and Legislative Reports
1999 Acts. House Conference Report No. 106–290, see 1999 U.S. Code Cong. and Adm. News, p. 78.

Codifications
Section was not enacted as part of Title III of Act June 30, 1949, c. 288, 63 Stat. 393, which comprises this subchapter.

LIBRARY REFERENCES

American Digest System
United States ⚏60.
Key Number System Topic No. 393.

WESTLAW ELECTRONIC RESEARCH

See Westlaw guide following the Explanation pages of this volume.

§ 253*l*-3. Contract authority of Chief Administrative Officer of the House of Representatives

During fiscal year 2001 and any succeeding fiscal year, the Chief Administrative Officer of the House of Representatives may—

(1) enter into contracts for the acquisition of severable services for a period that begins in 1 fiscal year and ends in the next fiscal year to the same extent as the head of an executive agency under the authority of section 253*l* of this title; and

(2) enter into multiyear contracts for the acquisitions of property and nonaudit-related services to the same extent as executive agencies under the authority of section 254c of this title.

(Pub.L. 106–554, § 1(a)(2) [Title I, § 101], Dec. 21, 2000, 114 Stat. 2763, 2763A–100.)

HISTORICAL AND STATUTORY NOTES

Revision Notes and Legislative Reports
2000 Acts. House Report No. 106–645 and Statement by President, see 2000 U.S. Code Cong. and Adm. News, p. 2459.

Codifications
Section was not enacted as part of Title III of Act June 30, 1949, c. 288, 63 Stat. 393, which comprises this subchapter.

LIBRARY REFERENCES

American Digest System
United States ☞60.
Key Number System Topic No. 393.

WESTLAW ELECTRONIC RESEARCH

See Westlaw guide following the Explanation pages of this volume.

§ 253*l*-4. Contract authority of Congressional Budget Office

Beginning on December 21, 2000, and hereafter, the Congressional Budget Office may use available funds to enter into contracts for the procurement of severable services for a period that begins in one fiscal year and ends in the next fiscal year and may enter into multiyear contracts for the acquisition of property and services, to the same extent as executive agencies under the authority of section [1] 253*l* and 254c, respectively, of this title.

(Pub.L. 106–554, § 1(a)(2) [Title I, § 110], Dec. 21, 2000, 114 Stat. 2763, 2763A–108.)

[1] So in original. Probably should be "sections".

HISTORICAL AND STATUTORY NOTES

Revision Notes and Legislative Reports
  2000 Acts. House Report No. 106–669, see 2000 U.S. Code Cong. and Adm. News, p. 2313.

Codifications
  Section was not enacted as part of Title III of Act June 30, 1949, c. 288, 63 Stat. 393, which comprises this subchapter.

LIBRARY REFERENCES

American Digest System
  United States ☞60.
  Key Number System Topic No. 393.

WESTLAW ELECTRONIC RESEARCH

See Westlaw guide following the Explanation pages of this volume.

§ 253*l*–5. Multi-year contracting authority

(a) Subject to regulations prescribed by the Committee on Rules and Administration of the Senate, the Secretary and the Sergeant at Arms and Doorkeeper of the Senate may—

(1) enter into contracts for the acquisition of severable services for a period that begins in one fiscal year and ends in the next fiscal year to the same extent and under the same conditions as the head of an executive agency under the authority of section 253*l* of this title; and

(2) enter into multiyear contracts for the acquisition of property and services to the same extent and under the same conditions as the head of an executive agency under the authority of section 254c of this title.

(b) This section shall take effect on October 1, 2002, and shall apply in fiscal year 2003 and successive fiscal years.

(Pub.L. 108–7, Div. H, Title I, § 5, Feb. 20, 2003, 117 Stat. 350.)

HISTORICAL AND STATUTORY NOTES

Revision Notes and Legislative Reports
  2003 Acts. House Conference Report No. 108–10 and Statement by President, see 2003 U.S. Code Cong. and Adm. News, p. 4.

Codifications
  Section was not enacted as part of Title III of Act June 30, 1949, c. 288, 63 Stat. 393, which comprises this subchapter.

LIBRARY REFERENCES

American Digest System
  United States ☞60.
  Key Number System Topic No. 393.

WESTLAW ELECTRONIC RESEARCH

See Westlaw guide following the Explanation pages of this volume.

§ 253*l*–6. Capitol Police contract authority

(a) In general

The United States Capitol Police may—

(1) enter into contracts for the acquisition of severable services for a period that begins in 1 fiscal year and ends in the next fiscal year to the same extent as the head of an executive agency under the authority of section 253*l* of this title; and

(2) enter into multiyear contracts for the acquisitions of property and nonaudit-related services to the same extent as executive agencies under the authority of section 254c of this title.

(b) Effective date

This section shall apply to fiscal year 2003 and each fiscal year thereafter.

(Pub.L. 108–7, Div. H, Title I, § 1002, Feb. 20, 2003, 117 Stat. 357.)

HISTORICAL AND STATUTORY NOTES

Revision Notes and Legislative Reports
  2003 Acts. House Conference Report No. 108–10 and Statement by President, see 2003 U.S. Code Cong. and Adm. News, p. 4.

Codifications
  Section was not enacted as part of Title III of Act June 30, 1949, c. 288, 63 Stat. 393, which comprises this subchapter.

LIBRARY REFERENCES

American Digest System
  United States ⬯60.
  Key Number System Topic No. 393.

WESTLAW ELECTRONIC RESEARCH

See Westlaw guide following the Explanation pages of this volume.

§ 253*l*–7. Multi–year contract authority

(a) In general

The Architect of the Capitol may—

(1) enter into contracts for the acquisition of severable services for a period that begins in 1 fiscal year and ends in the next fiscal year to the same extent as the head of an executive agency under the authority of section 253*l* of this title; and

(2) enter into multiyear contracts for the acquisitions of property and nonaudit-related services to the same extent as executive agencies under the authority of section 254c of this title.

(b) Effective date

This section shall apply to fiscal year 2003 and each fiscal year thereafter.

(Pub.L. 108–7, Div. H, Title I, § 1202, Feb. 20, 2003, 117 Stat. 373.)

HISTORICAL AND STATUTORY NOTES

Revision Notes and Legislative Reports
2003 Acts. House Conference Report No. 108–10 and Statement by President, see 2003 U.S. Code Cong. and Adm. News, p. 4.

Codifications
Section was not enacted as part of Title III of Act June 30, 1949, c. 288, 63 Stat. 393, which comprises this subchapter.

LIBRARY REFERENCES

American Digest System
United States ☞60.
Key Number System Topic No. 393.

WESTLAW ELECTRONIC RESEARCH

See Westlaw guide following the Explanation pages of this volume.

§ 253*l*–8. Contracting authority of Secretary

(a) In general

The Secretary of the Smithsonian Institution may—

(1) enter into multi-year contracts for the acquisition of property and services under the authority of section 254c of this title; and

(2) enter into contracts for the acquisition of severable services for a period that begins in one fiscal year and ends in the next fiscal year under the authority of section 253*l* of this title.

(b) Effective date

This section shall apply to contracts entered into on or after August 15, 2003.

(Pub.L. 108–72, § 4, Aug. 15, 2003, 117 Stat. 889.)

LIBRARY REFERENCES

American Digest System
United States ☞60.
Key Number System Topic No. 393.

WESTLAW ELECTRONIC RESEARCH

See Westlaw guide following the Explanation pages of this volume.

§ 253m. Design-build selection procedures

(a) Authorization

Unless the traditional acquisition approach of design-bid-build established under chapter 11 of Title 40 is used or another acquisition procedure authorized by law is used, the head of an executive agency shall use the two-phase selection procedures authorized in this section for entering into a contract for the design and construction of a public building, facility, or work when a determination is made under subsection (b) of this section that the procedures are appropriate for use.

(b) Criteria for use

A contracting officer shall make a determination whether two-phase selection procedures are appropriate for use for entering into a contract for the design and construction of a public building, facility, or work when the contracting officer anticipates that three or more offers will be received for such contract, design work must be performed before an offeror can develop a price or cost proposal for such contract, the offeror will incur a substantial amount of expense in preparing the offer, and the contracting officer has considered information such as the following:

(1) The extent to which the project requirements have been adequately defined.

(2) The time constraints for delivery of the project.

(3) The capability and experience of potential contractors.

(4) The suitability of the project for use of the two-phase selection procedures.

(5) The capability of the agency to manage the two-phase selection process.

(6) Other criteria established by the agency.

(c) Procedures described

Two-phase selection procedures consist of the following:

(1) The agency develops, either in-house or by contract, a scope of work statement for inclusion in the solicitation that defines the project and provides prospective offerors with sufficient information regarding the Government's requirements (which may include criteria and preliminary design, budget parameters, and schedule or delivery requirements) to enable the offerors to submit proposals which meet the Government's needs. If the agency contracts for development of the scope of work statement, the agency shall contract for architectural and engineering services as defined by and in accordance with chapter 11 of Title 40.

(2) The contracting officer solicits phase-one proposals that—

(A) include information on the offeror's—

(i) technical approach; and

(ii) technical qualifications; and

(B) do not include—

(i) detailed design information; or

478

(ii) cost or price information.

(3) The evaluation factors to be used in evaluating phase-one proposals are stated in the solicitation and include specialized experience and technical competence, capability to perform, past performance of the offeror's team (including the architect-engineer and construction members of the team) and other appropriate factors, except that cost-related or price-related evaluation factors are not permitted. Each solicitation establishes the relative importance assigned to the evaluation factors and subfactors that must be considered in the evaluation of phase-one proposals. The agency evaluates phase-one proposals on the basis of the phase-one evaluation factors set forth in the solicitation.

(4) The contracting officer selects as the most highly qualified the number of offerors specified in the solicitation to provide the property or services under the contract and requests the selected offerors to submit phase-two competitive proposals that include technical proposals and cost or price information. Each solicitation establishes with respect to phase two—

(A) the technical submission for the proposal, including design concepts or proposed solutions to requirements addressed within the scope of work (or both), and

(B) the evaluation factors and subfactors, including cost or price, that must be considered in the evaluations of proposals in accordance with subsections (b), (c), and (d) of section 253a of this title.

The contracting officer separately evaluates the submissions described in subparagraphs (A) and (B).

(5) The agency awards the contract in accordance with section 253b of this title.

(d) **Solicitation to state number of offerors to be selected for phase-two requests for competitive proposals**

A solicitation issued pursuant to the procedures described in subsection (c) of this section shall state the maximum number of offerors that are to be selected to submit competitive proposals pursuant to subsection (c)(4) of this section. The maximum number specified in the solicitation shall not exceed 5 unless the agency determines with respect to an individual solicitation that a specified number greater than 5 is in the Government's interest and is consistent with the purposes and objectives of the two-phase selection process.

(e) **Requirement for guidance and regulations**

The Federal Acquisition Regulation shall include guidance—

(1) regarding the factors that may be considered in determining whether the two-phase contracting procedures authorized by

subsection (a) of this section are appropriate for use in individual contracting situations;

(2) regarding the factors that may be used in selecting contractors; and

(3) providing for a uniform approach to be used Government-wide.

(June 30, 1949, c.288, Title III, § 303M, as added Feb. 10, 1996, Pub.L. 104–106, Div. D, Title XLI, § 4105(b)(1), 110 Stat. 647.)

HISTORICAL AND STATUTORY NOTES

Revision Notes and Legislative Reports
1996 Acts. House Conference Report No. 104–450, see 1996 U.S. Code Cong. and Adm. News, p. 238.

References in Text
Chapter 11 of Title 40, referred to in subsec. (a), is 40 U.S.C.A. § 1101 et seq.

Codifications
In subsec. (a), "chapter 11 of Title 40" substituted for "the Brooks Architect–Engineers Act (Title IX of this Act) [40 U.S.C.A. § 541 et seq.]", and in subsec. (c)(1), "chapter 11 of Title 40" substituted for "the Brooks Architect–Engineers Act (40 U.S.C. 541 et seq.)", on authority of Pub.L. 107–217, § 5(c), Aug. 21, 2002, 116 Stat. 1301, which is set out as a note preceding 40 U.S.C.A. § 101. Pub.L.

107–217, § 1, enacted Title 40 into positive law. The Brooks Architect–Engineers Act is Act June 30, 1949, c. 288, Title IX, §§ 901 to 904, as added Oct. 27, 1972, Pub.L. 92–582, 86 Stat. 1278, as amended, which was classified generally to subchapter VI of chapter 10 of former Title 40, 40 U.S.C.A. § 541 et seq., prior to being repealed by Pub.L. 107–217, § 6(b), Aug. 21, 2002, 116 Stat. 1319, and its substance reenacted as chapter 11 of Title 40, 40 U.S.C.A. § 1101 et seq.

Effective and Applicability Provisions
1996 Acts. Section effective Feb. 10, 1996, except as otherwise provided, see section 4401 of Pub.L. 104–106, set out as a note under section 251 of this title.

LIBRARY REFERENCES

American Digest System
   United States ⟐64.25.
   Key Number System Topic No. 393.

WESTLAW ELECTRONIC RESEARCH

See Westlaw guide following the Explanation pages of this volume.

§ 254. Contract requirements

(a) Contracts awarded using procedures other than sealed-bid procedures

Except as provided in subsection (b) of this section, contracts awarded after using procedures other than sealed-bid procedures may be of any type which in the opinion of the agency head will promote the best interests of the Government. Every contract awarded after using procedures other than sealed-bid procedures shall contain a suitable warranty, as determined by the agency head, by the contractor that no person or selling agency has been employed or retained to solicit or secure such contract upon an agreement or understanding for a commission, percentage, brokerage, or contingent fee, excepting bona fide employees or bona fide established commercial or selling agencies maintained by the contractor for the purpose of securing business, for the breach or violation of which warranty the Government shall have the right to annul such contract without liability or in its discretion to deduct from the contract price or consideration the full amount of such commission, percentage, brokerage, or contingent fee. The preceding sentence does not apply to a contract for an amount that is not greater than the simplified acquisition threshold or to a contract for the acquisition of commercial items.

(b) Barred contracts; fee limitation; determination of use; advance notification

The cost-plus-a-percentage-of-cost system of contracting shall not be used, and in the case of a cost-plus-a-fixed-fee contract the fee shall not exceed 10 percent of the estimated cost of the contract, exclusive of the fee, as determined by the agency head at the time of entering into such contract (except that a fee not in excess of 15 percent of such estimated cost is authorized in any such contract for experimental, developmental, or research work and that a fee inclusive of the contractor's costs and not in excess of 6 percent of the estimated cost, exclusive of fees, as determined by the agency head at the time of entering into the contract, of the project to which such fee is applicable is authorized in contracts for architectural or engineering services relating to any public works or utility project). All cost and cost-plus-a-fixed-fee contracts shall provide for advance notification by the contractor to the procuring agency of any subcontract thereunder on a cost-plus-a-fixed-fee basis and of any fixed-price subcontract or purchase order which exceeds in dollar amount either the simplified acquisition threshold or 5 percent of the total estimated cost of the prime contract; and a procuring agency, through any authorized representative thereof, shall have the right to inspect the plans and to audit the books and records of any prime contractor or subcontractor engaged in the performance of a cost or cost-plus-a-fixed-fee contract.

(June 30, 1949, c. 288, Title III, § 304, 63 Stat. 395; Oct. 31, 1951, c. 652, 65 Stat. 700; July 12, 1952, c. 703, § 1(m), 66 Stat. 594; Sept. 27, 1966, Pub.L. 89–607, § 2, 80 Stat. 850; July 18, 1984, Pub.L. 98–369, Div. B, Title VII, §§ 2712, 2714(a)(2), (3), 98 Stat. 1181, 1184; Oct. 13, 1994, Pub.L. 103–355, Title I, §§ 1071, 1251(a)(1), Title II, § 2251(b), Title IV, §§ 4103(c), 4402(c), Title VIII, § 8204(b), Title X, § 10005(e), 108 Stat. 3270, 3278, 3320, 3341, 3349, 3396, 3408.)

HISTORICAL AND STATUTORY NOTES

Revision Notes and Legislative Reports
1951 Acts. Senate Report No. 603, see 1951 U.S. Code Cong. Service, p. 2569.

1984 Acts. House Report No. 98–432, Pt. II, Senate Report Nos. 98–50 and 98–297, and House Conference Report No. 98–861, see 1984 U.S. Code Cong. and Adm. News, p. 697.

1994 Acts. Senate Report Nos. 103–258 and 103–259, and House Conference Report No. 103–712, see 1994 U.S. Code Cong. and Adm. News, p. 2561.

Amendments
1994 Amendments. Subsec. (a). Pub.L. 103–355, §§ 4103(c), 8204(b), added provisions "The preceding sentence does not apply to a contract for an amount that is not greater than the simplified acquisition threshold." and "or to a contract for the acquisition of commercial items".

Subsec. (b). Pub.L. 103–355, § 1071, struck out the second sentence which provided that "Neither a cost nor a cost-plus-a-fixed-fee contract nor an incentive-type contract shall be used unless the agency head determines that such method of contracting is likely to be less costly than other methods or that it is impractical to secure property of services of the kind or quality required without the use of a cost or cost-plus-a-fixed-fee contract or an incentive-type contract."

Pub.L. 103–355, § 4402(c), substituted "either the simplified acquisition threshold" for "either $25,000".

Pub.L. 103–355, § 1005(e), substituted "percent" for "per centum" wherever appearing.

Subsec. (c). Pub.L. 103–355, § 2251(b), struck out subsec. (c) providing for examination of books, records, etc., of contractors; time limitation; exemptions; exceptional conditions; reports to Congress. See section 254d of this title.

Subsec. (d). Pub.L. 103–355, § 1251(a)(1), struck out subsec. (d), which provided for submission of cost or pricing data by contractors and subcontractors, certification, adjustment of price, inspection of books, records, etc., necessity of data, and exceptions. See section 254b of this title.

Subsec. (f)(1)(B)(i). Pub.L. 103–355, § 1053, provided for approval by an official referred to in cl. (ii), (iii) or (iv) of justification for use of noncompetitive procedures.

1984 Amendments. Pub.L. 98–369, § 2714(a)(2), substituted "Contract requirements" for "Negotiated contracts" in section catchline.

Subsec. (a). Pub.L. 98–369, § 2714(a)(3)(A), substituted "awarded after using procedures other than sealed-bid procedures" for "negotiated pursuant to section 252(c) of this title" preceding "may be of any type".

Pub.L. 98–369, § 2714(a)(3)(B), substituted "Every contract awarded after using procedures other than sealed-bid procedures" for "Every contract negotiated pursuant to section 252(c) of this title".

Subsec. (c). Pub.L. 98–369, § 2714(a)(3)(C), substituted "Awarded after using procedures other than sealed-bid procedures" for "Negotiated without advertising pursuant to authority contained in this Act".

Subsec. (d). Pub.L. 98–369, § 2712, added subsec. (d).

1966 Amendments. Subsec. (c). Pub.L. 89–607 provided for exemption of certain contracts with foreign contractors from the requirement for an examination-of-records clause, such determination to be reported to Congress.

1952 Amendments. Subsec. (b). Act July 12, 1952, substituted "property" for "supplies".

1951 Amendments. Subsec. (c). Act Oct. 31, 1951, added subsec. (c).

Effective and Applicability Provisions
1994 Acts. Amendment by section 1071 of Pub.L. 103–355 effective Oct. 13, 1994, and applicable on and after such date, see section 10001 of Pub.L. 103–355, set out as a note under section 251 of this title.

Amendment by sections 1251(a)(1), 2251(b), 4103(c), 4402(c), 8204(b), and 10005(e) of Pub.L. 103–355 effective Oct. 13, 1994, except as otherwise provided, see section 10001 of Pub.L. 103–355, set out as a note under section 251 of this title.

1984 Acts. Amendment by Pub.L. 98–369 applicable with respect to any solicitation for bids or proposals issued after Mar. 31, 1985, see section 2751(a) of Pub.L. 98–369, set out as a note under section 251 of this title.

1949 Acts. Act June 30, 1949, § 605, which set July 1, 1949, as the effective date for this section, was repealed by Pub.L. 107–217, § 6(b), Aug. 21, 2002, 116 Stat. 1313.

Definitions
The definitions in 40 U.S.C.A. § 102 apply to terms appearing in this subchapter.

Exemption of Functions
Functions authorized by Foreign Assistance Act of 1961, as amended, as exempt, see Ex. Ord. No. 11223, May 12, 1965, 30 F.R. 6635, set out as a note

under section 2393 of Title 22, Foreign Relations and Intercourse.

Foreign Contractors
Secretaries of Defense, Army, Navy, or Air Force, or their designees, to determine, prior to exercising the authority provided in the amendment of this section by Pub.L. 89–607 to exempt certain contracts with foreign contractors from the requirement of an examination-of-records clause, that all reasonable efforts have been made to include such examination-of-records clause, as required by par. (11) of Part I of Ex. Ord. No. 10789, and that alternate sources of supply are not reasonably available, see par. (11) of Part I of Ex. Ord. No. 10789, Nov. 14, 1958, 23 F.R. 8897, as amended, set out as a note under section 1431 of Title 50, War and National Defense.

EXECUTIVE ORDERS
EXECUTIVE ORDER NO. 12800

Ex. Ord. No. 12800, Apr. 13, 1992, 57 F.R. 12985, as corrected Apr. 16, 1992, 57 F.R. 13413, which related to notification of employee rights concerning payment of union dues or fees, and which was formerly set out as a note under this section, was revoked by Ex. Ord. No. 12836, Feb. 1, 1993, 58 F.R. 7045.

EXECUTIVE ORDER NO. 13201

Feb. 17, 2001, 66 F.R. 11221

NOTIFICATION OF EMPLOYEE RIGHTS CONCERNING PAYMENT OF UNION DUES OR FEES

By the authority vested in me as President by the Constitution and the laws of the United States of America, including the Federal Property and Administrative Services Act, 40 U.S.C. 471 et seq. [currently classified to subchapter IV of chapter 4 of Title 41, 41 U.S.C.A. § 251 et seq., and formerly classified to chapter 10 of former Title 40, 40 U.S.C.A. § 471 et seq., which was repealed by Pub.L. 107–217, § 6(b), Aug. 21, 2002, 116 Stat. 1313; see now generally chapter 1 of Title 40, 40 U.S.C.A. § 101 et seq.], and in order to ensure the economical and efficient administration and completion of Government contracts, it is hereby ordered that:

Section 1. (a) This order is designed to promote economy and efficiency in Government procurement. When workers are better informed of their rights,

including their rights under the Federal labor laws, their productivity is enhanced. The availability of such a workforce from which the United States may draw facilitates the efficient and economical completion of its procurement contracts.

(b) The Secretary of Labor (Secretary) shall be responsible for the administration and enforcement of this order. The Secretary shall adopt such rules and regulations and issue such orders as are deemed necessary and appropriate to achieve the purposes of this order.

Sec. 2. (a) Except in contracts exempted in accordance with section 3 of this order, all Government contracting departments and agencies shall, to the extent consistent with law, include the following provisions in every Government contract, other than collective bargaining agreements as defined in 5 U.S.C. 7103(a)(8) and purchases under the "Simplified Acquisition Threshold" as defined in the Office of Federal Procurement Policy Act (41 U.S.C. 403).

"1. During the term of this contract, the contractor agrees to post a notice, of such size and in such form as the Secretary of Labor shall prescribe, in conspicuous places in and about its plants and offices, including all places where notices to employees are customarily posted. The notice shall include the following information (except that the last sentence shall not be included in notices posted in the plants or offices of carriers subject to the Railway Labor Act, as amended (45 U.S.C. 151–188)):

"NOTICE TO EMPLOYEES

Under Federal law, employees cannot be required to join a union or maintain membership in a union in order to retain their jobs. Under certain conditions, the law permits a union and an employer to enter into a union-security agreement requiring employees to pay uniform periodic dues and initiation fees. However, employees who are not union members can object to the use of their payments for certain purposes and can only be required to pay their share of union costs relating to collective bargaining, contract administration, and grievance adjustment.

"If you do not want to pay that portion of dues or fees used to support activities not related to collective bargaining, contract administration, or grievance adjustment, you are entitled to an appropriate reduction in your payment. If you believe that you have been required to pay dues or fees used in part to support activities not related to collective bargaining, contract administration, or grievance adjustment, you may be entitled to a refund and to an appropriate reduction in future payments.

"For further information concerning your rights, you may wish to contact the National Labor Relations Board (NLRB) either at one of its Regional offices or at the following address:

National Labor Relations Board

Division of Information

1099 14th Street, N.W.

Washington, D.C. 20570

"To locate the nearest NLRB office, see NLRB's website at www.nlrb.gov."

"2. The contractor will comply with all provisions of Executive Order 13201 of February 17, 2001, and related rules, regulations, and orders of the Secretary of Labor.

"3. In the event that the contractor does not comply with any of the requirements set forth in paragraphs (1) or (2) above, this contract may be cancelled, terminated, or suspended in whole or in part, and the contractor may be declared ineligible for further Government contracts in accordance with procedures authorized in or adopted pursuant to Executive Order 13201 of February 17, 2001. Such other sanctions or remedies may be imposed as are provided in Executive Order 13201 of February 17, 2001, or by rule, regulation, or order of the Secretary of Labor, or as are otherwise provided by law.

"4. The contractor will include the provisions of paragraphs (1) through (3) herein in every subcontract or purchase order entered into in connection with this contract unless exempted by rules, regulations, or orders of the Secretary of Labor issued pursuant to section 3 of Executive Order 13201 of February 17, 2001, so that such provisions will be binding upon each subcontractor or vendor. The contractor will take such action with respect to any such subcontract or purchase order as may be directed by the Secretary of Labor as a means of enforcing such provisions, including the imposition of sanctions for non compliance: Provided, however, that if the contractor becomes involved in litigation with a subcontractor or vendor, or is threatened with such involvement, as a result of such direction, the contractor may request the United States to enter into such litigation to protect the interests of the United States."

(b) Whenever, through Acts of Congress or through clarification of existing law by the courts or otherwise, it appears that contractual provisions other than, or in addition to, those set out in subsection (a) of this section are needed to inform employees fully and accurately of their rights with respect to union dues, union-security agreements, or the like, the Secretary shall promptly issue such rules, regulations, or orders as are needed to cause the substitution or addition of appropriate contractual provisions in Government contracts thereafter entered into.

Sec. 3. **(a)** The Secretary may, if the Secretary finds that special circumstances require an exemption in order to serve the national interest, exempt a contracting department or agency from the requirements of any or all of the provisions of section 2 of this order with respect to a particular contract, subcontract, or purchase order.

(b) The Secretary may, by rule, regulation, or order, exempt from the provisions of section 2 of this order certain classes of contracts to the extent that they involve (i) work outside the United States and do not involve the recruitment or employment of workers within the United States; (ii) work in jurisdictions where State law forbids enforcement of union-security agreements; (iii) work at sites where the notice to employees described in section 2(a) of this order would be unnecessary because the employees are not represented by a union; (iv) numbers of workers below appropriate thresholds set by the Secretary; or (v) subcontracts below an appropriate tier set by the Secretary.

(c) The Secretary may provide, by rule, regulation, or order, for the exemption of facilities of a contractor, subcontractor, or vendor that are in all respects separate and distinct from activities related to the performance of the contract: Provided, that such exemption will not interfere with or impede the effectuation of the purposes of this order: And provided further, that in the absence of such an exemption all facilities shall be covered by the provisions of this order.

Sec. 4. **(a)** The Secretary may investigate any Government contractor, subcontractor, or vendor to determine whether the contractual provisions required by section 2 of this order have been violated. Such investigations shall be conducted in accordance with procedures established by the Secretary.

(b) The Secretary shall receive and investigate complaints by employees of a Government contractor, subcontractor, or vendor where such complaints allege a failure to perform or a violation of the contractual provisions required by section 2 of this order.

Sec. 5. **(a)** The Secretary, or any agency or officer in the executive branch of the Government designated by rule, regulation, or order of the Secretary, may hold such hearings, public or private, regarding compliance with this order as the Secretary may deem advisable.

(b) The Secretary may hold hearings, or cause hearings to be held, in accordance with subsection (a) of this section prior to imposing, ordering, or recommending the imposition of sanctions under this order. Neither an order for debarment of any contractor from further Government contracts under section 6(b) of this order nor the inclusion of a contractor on a published list of noncomplying contractors under section 6(c) of this order shall be carried out without affording the contractor an opportunity for a hearing.

Sec. 6. In accordance with such rules, regulations, or orders as the Secretary may issue or adopt, the Secretary may:

(a) after consulting with the contracting department or agency, direct that department or agency to cancel, terminate, suspend, or cause to be cancelled, terminated, or suspended, any contract, or any portion or portions thereof, for failure of the contractor to comply with the contractual provisions required by section 2 of this order; contracts may be cancelled, terminated, or suspended absolutely, or continuance of contracts may be conditioned upon future compliance: Provided, that before issuing a directive under this subsection, the Secretary shall provide the head of the contracting department or agency an opportunity to offer written objections to the issuance of such a directive, which objections shall include a complete statement of reasons for the objections, among which reasons shall be a finding that completion of the contract is essential to the agency's mission: And provided further, that no directive shall be issued by the Secretary under this subsection so long as the head of the contracting department or agency continues personally to object to the issuance of such directive;

(b) after consulting with each affected contracting department or agency, provide that one or more contracting departments or agencies shall refrain from entering into further contracts, or extensions or other modifications of existing contracts, with any noncomplying contractor, until such contractor has satisfied the Secretary that such con tractor has complied with and will carry out the provisions of this order: Provided, that before issuing a directive under this subsection, the Secretary shall provide the head of each contracting department or agency an opportunity to offer written objections to the issuance of such a directive, which objections shall include a complete statement of reasons for the objections, among which reasons shall be a finding that further contracts or extensions or other modifications of existing contracts with the noncomplying contractor are essential to the agency's mission: And provided further, that no directive shall be issued by the Secretary under this subsection so long as the head of a contracting department or agency continues personally to object to the issuance of such directive; and

(c) publish, or cause to be published, the names of contractors that have, in the judgment of the Secretary, failed to comply with the provisions of this order or of related rules, regulations, and orders of the Secretary.

Sec. 7. Whenever the Secretary invokes section 6(a) or 6(b) of this order, the contracting department or agency shall report the results of the action it has taken to the Secretary within such time as the Secretary shall specify.

Sec. 8. Each contracting department and agency shall cooperate with the Secretary and provide such information and assistance as the Secretary may require in the performance of the Secretary's functions under this order.

Sec. 9. The Secretary may delegate any function or duty of the Secretary under this order to any officer in the Department of Labor or to any other officer in the executive branch of the Government, with the consent of the head of the department or agency in which that officer serves.

Sec. 10. The Federal Acquisition Regulatory Council (FAR Council) shall take whatever action is required to implement in the Federal Acquisition Regulation (FAR) the provisions of this order and of any related rules, regulations, or orders of the Secretary that were issued to implement this Executive Order. The FAR Council shall amend the FAR to require each solicitation of offers for a contract to include a provision that implements section 2 of this order.

Sec. 11. As it relates to notification of employee rights concerning payment of union dues or fees, Executive Order 12836 of February 1, 1993, which, among other things, revoked Executive Order 12800 of April 13, 1992, is revoked.

Sec. 12. The heads of executive departments and agencies shall revoke expeditiously any orders, rules, regulations, guidelines, or policies implementing or enforcing Executive Order 12836 of February 1, 1993, as it relates to notification of employee rights concerning payment of union dues or fees, to the extent consistent with law.

Sec. 13. This order is intended only to improve the internal management of the executive branch and is not intended to, nor does it, create any right to administrative or judicial review, or any right, whether substantive or procedural, enforceable by any party against the United States, its agencies or instrumentalities, its officers or employees, or any other person.

Sec. 14. The provisions of this order shall apply to contracts resulting from solicitations issued on or after the effective date of this order.

Sec. 15. This order shall become effective 60 days after the date of this order.

GEORGE W. BUSH

CROSS REFERENCES

Alien smuggling and undercover investigation authority and sums appropriated used for leasing space, see 8 USCA § 1363a.
Armed services—
    Examination of contractor's books and records, see 10 USCA § 2313.
    Kinds of contracts, see 10 USCA § 2306.

LIBRARY REFERENCES

American Digest System
    Contracts ☞108(1), 131.
    United States ☞63, 70(18).
    Key Number System Topic Nos. 95, 393.

Research References

ALR Library
    60 ALR, Fed. 263, Requirement Under Defense Procurement and General Procurement Statutes (10 U.S.C.A. § 2306(B); 41 U.S.C.A. § 254(A)) and Regulations Promulgated Thereunder (32 CFR §§ 1-1500 et seq.; 41 CFR §§ 1-1.500 et seq.) That Government Contract for Property and Services Contain Warranty Against Commissions or Contingent Fees.
    148 ALR 768, Validity of Contract to Influence Administrative or Executive Officer or Department.

Encyclopedias
    14 Am. Jur. Trials 437, Representing the Government Contractor.

Treatises and Practice Aids
    Federal Procedure, Lawyers Edition § 39:18, Warranty Against Contingency Fees and the Like.
    Immigration Law Service 2d PSD INA § 294, Undercover Investigation Authority.
    West's Federal Administrative Practice § 610, Laws Applicable--Access to Contractor Records.
    West's Federal Administrative Practice § 613, Laws Applicable--Contract Solicitation.
    West's Federal Administrative Practice § 637, Architect Engineer Acquisitions.
    West's Federal Administrative Practice § 643, Cost or Pricing Data.
    West's Federal Administrative Practice § 648, Cost Contract Problems.

WESTLAW ELECTRONIC RESEARCH

See Westlaw guide following the Explanation pages of this volume.

Notes of Decisions

---

1. Construction with other laws

Section of the Brooks Act providing that a fee not in excess of 6% of the estimated cost is "authorized in contracts for architectural or engineering services related to any public works" was applicable to architectural and engineering (A&E) services rendered by contractor on project, notwithstanding that A&E services were only a minor part of cost-plus-fixed-fee contract; language of statute does not suggest that it applied only to contracts primarily or substantially for A & E services, and Federal Acquisition Regulation (FAR) implementing statute does not limit its applicability to such contracts. Fluor Enterprises, Inc. v. U.S., Fed.Cl.2005, 64 Fed.Cl. 461. United States ☞ 70(18)

2. Purpose

Overall purpose of statute prohibiting private parties from contracting for sales commission from United States government contracts unless agent procuring contract is bona fide established commercial or selling agency maintained by contractor for purpose of securing business, is to prevent improper or undue influence by middlemen from affecting governmental decisions. Furnary v. Merritt, Colo. App.1991, 837 P.2d 192, certiorari denied. Contracts ☞ 131

3. Contingent fee arrangements—Generally

Arrangement by which defendant manufacturer agreed to pay plaintiff, an owner of an engineering consulting and training company, a commission fee and compensation for his services in helping to procure a contract to supply steam turbine blades to the Tennessee Valley Authority was clearly an arrangement for a fee contingent upon defendant's contracting with Authority and, as such, was in violation of federal statutes and regulations and against public policy. Quinn v. Gulf and Western Corp., C.A.2 (Conn.) 1981, 644 F.2d 89. Contracts ☞ 108(2)

Contract between the parties for splitting fees earned by defendant for work done on the renegotiation of a General Services Administration lease was not void as against public policy, since third party, for which the renegotiation services were performed, entered into no contingent fee arrangement with anyone in an attempt to procure the GSA leasing contract, and since the contingent fee arrangement between the parties was thus unrelated to the procurement of a government contract. Vander Zee v. Karabatsos, C.A.D.C.1978, 589 F.2d 723, 191 U.S.App.D.C. 200, certiorari denied 99 S.Ct. 2407, 441 U.S. 962, 60 L.Ed.2d 1066. Contracts ☞ 108(2)

Where prospective purchaser of war surplus real property agreed to pay third person $25,000 if and when prospective purchaser's bid for property was accepted and reason for such agreement was that prospective purchaser was convinced that in no other way could the contract for sale of property to prospective purchaser be secured by the desired date, the agreement was to a pay a "contingent fee" within the contractual prohibition against employing any person to secure the property for a contingent fee. J.D.

Streett & Co., v. U.S., C.A.8 (Mo.) 1958, 256 F.2d 557. Contracts ☞ 131

Contract under which consultant was hired to secure, through renegotiation, new lease with government was contrary to federal policy and, therefore, unenforceable where consultant's commission was contingent upon his negotiating lease acceptable to owner, even though owner as government contractor benefited from illegal contract. Markon v. Unicorp American Corp., D.D.C.1986, 645 F.Supp. 62, affirmed 841 F.2d 428, 268 U.S.App.D.C. 306.

Personal services contract, under which Iranian citizen arranged meetings between Delaware corporation and key officials of Iranian government in connection with oil barter transaction, contravened public policy of the United States and, thus, was unenforceable. Kashfi v. Phibro-Salomon, Inc., S.D.N.Y. 1986, 628 F.Supp. 727. Contracts ☞ 108(2)

Federal statute prohibiting private parties from receiving sales commission from government contracts would not be construed against agent who received contingent fee in exchange for procuring United States Government contract for purchase of manufacturers' product; manufacturers were aware, at time they formed contract with agent, of limitations on such contracts, and manufacturers voluntarily entered into contract despite that knowledge. Furnary v. Merritt, Colo.App.1991, 837 P.2d 192, certiorari denied. Contracts ☞ 131

4. —— Employees or selling agents, contingent fee arrangements

Plaintiff, who entered into an agreement to receive a commission fee from defendant manufacturer in compensation for his services in helping to procure a contract to supply steam turbine blades to the Tennessee Valley Authority did not fall within the exemption for employees or selling agents of government contractors, where he and defendant had never before had any commercial dealings, and evidence was insufficient to support an inference that plaintiff's role in sale of turbine blades was the start of an ongoing relationship. Quinn v. Gulf and Western Corp., C.A.2 (Conn.) 1981, 644 F.2d 89. Contracts ☞ 103

Consultant's expectation, based on conversations with owner's former president and his own perception of owner's needs, that consultant's relationship with property owner would be continuing, when contract itself was of short duration and concerned only single transaction, was insufficient to establish that consultant was employee for purposes of bona fide employee relationship exception to proscription against "influence peddling" in government contracts in form of contingent fee. Markon v. Unicorp American Corp., D.D.C.1986, 645 F.Supp. 62, affirmed 841 F.2d 428, 268 U.S.App.D.C. 306. Contracts ⬠ 131

In action by manufacturers' representative for commission for services rendered in procurement of Government contract containing a warranty against payment of contingent fees, evidence disclosed that representative, was not a bona fide commercial or selling agency "maintained" by contractor to secure business, and hence was not within exception of this section generally prohibiting payment of contingent fees for procuring Government contracts. Weitzel v. Brown-Neil Corp., N.D.W.Va.1957, 152 F.Supp. 540, affirmed 251 F.2d 661. Contracts ⬠ 141(3)

5. —— Liability, contingent fee arrangements

Officers and shareholders of corporation were not individually liable for commissions owed under procurement contract arising from assistance provided in procuring government contract for corporation, in that they did not act outside their capacities as officers in connection with procurement contract and there was no basis for piercing corporate veil. Puma Indus. Consulting, Inc. v. Daal Associates, Inc., C.A.2 (N.Y.) 1987, 808 F.2d 982. Corporations ⬠ 1.6(2); Corporations ⬠ 215; Corporations ⬠ 325

6. —— Recovery of commission, contingent fee arrangements

It is clearly against public policy for the courts to lend themselves to a recovery of contingent fees which are agreed to in violation of valid government regulations, necessary to protect the government against improvident contracts, excessive costs, and the possible corruption of public officials. Quinn v. Gulf and Western Corp., C.A.2 (Conn.) 1981, 644 F.2d 89. Contracts ⬠ 108(1)

The covenant against contingent commissions contained in Atomic Energy Commission's contracts with defendant corporation did not permit manufacturer's representative to recover commission from defendant for services in procuring the contract, where representative was not bona fide employee or bona fide established selling agent maintained by defendant for purpose of securing business as permitted by subsec. (a) of this section; however, the covenants would not preclude representative from asserting claim against defendant's corporate stockholder which did most of the work on the contracts, where representative was such bona fide employee or bona fide established selling agency maintained by such stockholder. Weitzel v. Brown-Neil Corp., C.A.4 (W.Va.) 1958, 251 F.2d 661. Contracts ⬠ 131; Contracts ⬠ 138(1)

In view of prohibition of payment of commission on government contracts, courts should not require a contingent commission to be paid to agent in connection with obtaining government contract. E.F. Higgins, Inc. v. R.L. Pohlman Co., Mo.1973, 491 S.W.2d 249. Contracts ⬠ 131

7. Cost-plus-percentage contracts—Generally

General criteria for determining whether contract is cost-plus-a-percentage-of-cost contract, as prohibited by this section, are: payment is on predetermined percentage rate; predetermined percentage rate is applied to actual performance costs; contractor's entitlement is uncertain at time of contracting; and contractor's entitlement increases commensurately with increased performance costs. Urban Data Systems, Inc. v. U.S., C.A.Fed.1983, 699 F.2d 1147. United States ⬠ 68

Government contractor was not entitled to "lost profit" on cost-reimbursement contracts after decision of Court of Federal Claims determined that it was entitled to reimbursement of state income tax payments, on theory that contractor was entitled to a proportionally greater fee or profit since contracts were negotiated based on the estimated reimbursable costs; award of such "lost profit" was barred by express statutory prohibition against cost-plus-percentage-of-cost contracts. Information Systems & Networks Corp. v. U.S., Fed.Cl.2005, 64 Fed.Cl. 599, appeal dismissed 157 Fed.Appx. 264, 2005 WL 3276164. United States ⬠ 74(15)

8. —— **Ceiling prices, cost-plus-percentage contracts**

Ceiling prices designated in subcontracts between Small Business Administration and private company did not remove those agreements from federal statutory injunction against cost-plus-a-percentage-of-cost contracting. Urban Data Systems, Inc. v. U.S., C.A.Fed. 1983, 699 F.2d 1147. United States ⌐ 68

9. —— **Quantum meruit, cost-plus-percentage contracts**

Government which was liable under quantum meruit for benefits received under invalid concessions contract for transportation services within national park would not be deemed to have assented to payment of more than 10% of total cost of concessioner's performance of contract nor to reimbursement of federal income taxes provided for under contract since such assent would be patently illegal. Yosemite Park and Curry Co. v. U.S., Ct.Cl.1978, 582 F.2d 552, 217 Ct.Cl. 360. United States ⌐ 69(7)

Although cost-plus-fixed-fee contract for provision of architectural and engineering (A&E) services was void as a matter of law for failure to comply with section of Brooks Act limiting fees for A&E services to 6% of estimated cost of contract, contractor which fully performed A&E portion of contract was entitled to recovery in quantum meruit under implied-in-fact contract theory. Fluor Enterprises, Inc. v. U.S., Fed.Cl.2005, 64 Fed.Cl. 461. United States ⌐ 69(4)

10. —— **Quantum valebant, cost-plus-percentage contracts**

While price terms of two subcontracts between Small Business Administration and private company were invalid as cost-plus-a-percentage-of-cost provisions in violation of this section, remaining parts of subcontracts were valid, and thus because government bargained for, agreed to pay for, and accepted supplies delivered by company, company was entitled to reimbursement on quantum valebant basis for reasonable value in marketplace of supplies and concomitant services. Urban Data Systems, Inc. v. U.S., C.A.Fed.1983, 699 F.2d 1147. United States ⌐ 68

11. Cost-plus-fixed-fee contracts

Legal and accounting fees incurred by contractor in renegotiation litigation were "incurred in connection with the prosecution of claims against the government" and thus were not allowable as part of its general and administrative expenses allocated to cost-plus-fixed-fee contract, despite contentions that review in the Court of Claims is part of the entire process of renegotiation involving continuous negotiation and bargaining, and not a formal adversary demand by one party against another, and that, if any "claim" is involved, it is a claim by the government against the contractor and not by the contractor against the government. Grumman Aerospace Corp. v. U.S., Ct.Cl. 1978, 579 F.2d 586, 217 Ct.Cl. 285. United States ⌐ 70(18)

Where legal fees incurred by government contractor in defending itself against suit arising out of commercial venture not connected with government cost plus award fee contracts had no relationship whatever to government contracts or their performance, costs could not properly be charged as direct costs or as indirect costs as part of general and administrative expense costs of contractor in its performance of government contracts. Dynalectron Corp. v. U.S., Ct.Cl. 1976, 545 F.2d 736, 212 Ct.Cl. 118. United States ⌐ 70(18)

Sole proprietor of a cost-plus-fixed-fee contractor could have paid himself a salary so that his contention that he could not have done so did not require that he be compensated for administrative services despite the fact that such constructive compensation would represent nothing actually paid or any proprietor obligation charged or incurred. Norman M. Giller and Associates v. U.S., Ct.Cl.1976, 535 F.2d 37, 210 Ct.Cl. 80. United States ⌐ 70(18)

Where, subsequent to decision that plaintiff was entitled to reimbursement from government under cost-plus fixed fee contracts for rental payments made, government had paid to plaintiff amounts such that any additional amounts would exceed estimated cost of respective contracts and plaintiff did not during progress of work under contracts notify contracting officer that plaintiff had reason to believe that costs would exceed total estimated costs and plaintiff indicated that it was no longer demanding any additional payments under five contracts specifically enumerated, plaintiff was not entitled to recover anything further on the contracts. Loral Electronics Corp. v. U.S., Ct.Cl.1969, 409 F.2d 578, 187 Ct.Cl. 499. United States ⟶ 70(36)

That cash disbursement method of pension plan necessarily related, in form, to services performed prior to performance under cost-plus-fixed-fee government contract was not bar to recovery by contractor of such costs. U.S. Steel Corp. v. U.S., Ct.Cl.1966, 367 F.2d 399, 177 Ct.Cl. 26. United States ⟶ 70(18)

Cost plus fixed fee contract between Pennsylvania corporation and Government for manufacture of tanks in corporation's Illinois plant, which contract provided for proportional payment of certain indirect costs, could not be construed as obligating Government to reimburse corporation for payment of Pennsylvania capital stock tax which was roughly based only on that part of market value of corporation's stock which was created by profits made by operation of corporation's plant in Pennsylvania and value of physical assets of its plant in Pennsylvania. Pressed Steel Car Co. v. U.S., Ct.Cl. 1958, 157 F.Supp. 950, 141 Ct.Cl. 318, certiorari denied 78 S.Ct. 1007, 356 U.S. 967, 2 L.Ed.2d 1074. United States ⟶ 70(18)

Under cost plus a fixed fee contract between United States and ammunition manufacturer for operation of "Twin Cities Ordnance Plant," where ordnance plant had no connection with operations of manufacturer's peacetime plant, and manufacturer would not have become liable for special war risk tax under Minnesota employment and security law, Laws Minn.1943, c. 650, except for operation of ordnance plant, payment of tax was an expense incident to carrying out of contract, and under its terms manufacturer was entitled to be reimbursed in full by the United States for amount of such special taxes paid the state. Federal Car-

tridge Corp. v. U.S., Ct.Cl.1948, 77 F.Supp. 380, 111 Ct.Cl. 372. United States ⟶ 70(18)

Government contractor was not entitled to "reimbursement" for state income tax payments incurred under its negotiated fixed-price contracts, because in the normal course there is no such thing as "reimbursement" of any costs in a fixed-price undertaking. Information Systems & Networks Corp. v. U.S., Fed.Cl.2005, 64 Fed.Cl. 599, appeal dismissed 157 Fed.Appx. 264, 2005 WL 3276164. United States ⟶ 70(18)

Portion of cost-plus-fixed-fee contract for project planning and construction management services which involved the provision of architectural and engineering (A&E) services for modernization of weather forecasting offices was void as a matter of law, where contracting officer failed to make a pre-contract estimate of the cost of the project, and thus failed to comply with section of the Brooks Act limiting fee for architectural and engineering (A&E) services in a government contract to 6% of the estimated cost of the contract as determined by the agency at the time of entering into the contract. Fluor Enterprises, Inc. v. U.S., Fed.Cl. 2005, 64 Fed.Cl. 461. United States ⟶ 68

12. Examination of records

Under fixed-price negotiated contracts between private contractor and agencies of the federal government, the Comptroller General had statutory authority to inspect contractor's records of direct costs but not records of indirect costs since they were not "directly pertinent" to the contracts in question within meaning of this section. Bowsher v. Merck & Co., Inc., U.S.Dist.Col.1983, 103 S.Ct. 1587, 460 U.S. 824, 75 L.Ed.2d 580. United States ⟶ 75(1)

---

§ 254a. Cost-type research and development contracts with educational institutions

On and after September 5, 1962, provision may be made in cost-type research and development contracts (including grants) with universities, colleges, or other educational institutions for payment of reimbursable indirect costs on the basis of predetermined fixed-percentage rates applied to the total, or an element thereof, of the reimbursable direct costs incurred.

(Pub.L. 87–638, Sept. 5, 1962, 76 Stat. 437.)

HISTORICAL AND STATUTORY NOTES

Codifications

Section was not enacted as part of Title III of Act June 30, 1949, c. 288, 63 Stat. 393, which comprises this subchapter.

LIBRARY REFERENCES

American Digest System

United States ☞70(21).

Key Number System Topic No. 393.

WESTLAW ELECTRONIC RESEARCH

See Westlaw guide following the Explanation pages of this volume.

§ 254b. Cost or pricing data: truth in negotiations

(a) Required cost or pricing data and certification

(1) The head of an executive agency shall require offerors, contractors, and subcontractors to make cost or pricing data available as follows:

(A) An offeror for a prime contract under this subchapter to be entered into using procedures other than sealed-bid procedures shall be required to submit cost or pricing data before the award of a contract if—

(i) in the case of a prime contract entered into after October 13, 1994, the price of the contract to the United States is expected to exceed $500,000; and

(ii) in the case of a prime contract entered into on or before October 13, 1994, the price of the contract to the United States is expected to exceed $100,000.

(B) The contractor for a prime contract under this subchapter shall be required to submit cost or pricing data before the pricing of a change or modification to the contract if—

(i) in the case of a change or modification made to a prime contract referred to in subparagraph (A)(i), the price adjustment is expected to exceed $500,000;

(ii) in the case of a change or modification made to a prime contract that was entered into on or before October 13, 1994, and that has been modified pursuant to paragraph (6), the price adjustment is expected to exceed $500,000; and

(iii) in the case of a change or modification not covered by clause (i) or (ii), the price adjustment is expected to exceed $100,000.

(C) An offeror for a subcontract (at any tier) of a contract under this subchapter shall be required to submit cost or pricing data before the award of the subcontract if the prime contractor and each higher-tier subcontractor have been required to make available cost or pricing data under this section and—

    (i) in the case of a subcontract under a prime contract referred to in subparagraph (A)(i), the price of the subcontract is expected to exceed $500,000;

    (ii) in the case of a subcontract entered into under a prime contract that was entered into on or before October 13, 1994, and that has been modified pursuant to paragraph (6), the price of the subcontract is expected to exceed $500,000; and

    (iii) in the case of a subcontract not covered by clause (i) or (ii), the price of the subcontract is expected to exceed $100,000.

(D) The subcontractor for a subcontract covered by subparagraph (C) shall be required to submit cost or pricing data before the pricing of a change or modification to the subcontract if—

    (i) in the case of a change or modification to a subcontract referred to in subparagraph (C)(i) or (C)(ii), the price adjustment is expected to exceed $500,000; and

    (ii) in the case of a change or modification to a subcontract referred to in subparagraph (C)(iii), the price adjustment is expected to exceed $100,000.

(2) A person required, as an offeror, contractor, or subcontractor, to submit cost or pricing data under paragraph (1) (or required by the head of the procuring activity concerned to submit such data under subsection (c) of this section) shall be required to certify that, to the best of the person's knowledge and belief, the cost or pricing data submitted are accurate, complete, and current.

(3) Cost or pricing data required to be submitted under paragraph (1) (or under subsection (c) of this section), and a certification required to be submitted under paragraph (2), shall be submitted—

    (A) in the case of a submission by a prime contractor (or an offeror for a prime contract), to the contracting officer for the contract (or to a designated representative of the contracting officer); or

    (B) in the case of a submission by a subcontractor (or an offeror for a subcontract), to the prime contractor.

(4) Except as provided under subsection (b) of this section, this section applies to contracts entered into by the head of an executive agency on behalf of a foreign government.

(5) A waiver of requirements for submission of certified cost or pricing data that is granted under subsection (b)(1)(C) of this section in the case of a contract or subcontract does not waive the requirement under paragraph (1)(C) for submission of cost or pricing data in the case of subcontracts under that contract or subcontract unless the head of the procuring activity granting the waiver determines that the requirement under that paragraph should be waived in the case of such subcontracts and justifies in writing the reasons for the determination.

(6) Upon the request of a contractor that was required to submit cost or pricing data under paragraph (1) in connection with a prime contract entered into on or before October 13, 1994, the head of the executive agency that entered into such contract shall modify the contract to reflect subparagraphs (B)(ii) and (C)(ii) of paragraph (1). All such modifications shall be made without requiring consideration.

(7) Effective on October 1 of each year that is divisible by 5, each amount set forth in paragraph (1) shall be adjusted to the amount that is equal to the fiscal year 1994 constant dollar value of the amount set forth. Any amount, as so adjusted, that is not evenly divisible by $50,000 shall be rounded to the nearest multiple of $50,000. In the case of an amount that is evenly divisible by $25,000 but not evenly divisible by $50,000, the amount shall be rounded to the next higher multiple of $50,000.

(b) Exceptions

(1) In general

Submission of certified cost or pricing data shall not be required under subsection (a) of this section in the case of a contract, a subcontract, or a modification of a contract or subcontract—

(A) for which the price agreed upon is based on—

(i) adequate price competition; or

(ii) prices set by law or regulation;

(B) for the acquisition of a commercial item; or

(C) in an exceptional case when the head of the procuring activity, without delegation, determines that the requirements of this section may be waived and justifies in writing the reasons for such determination.

(2) Modifications of contracts and subcontracts for commercial items

In the case of a modification of a contract or subcontract for a commercial item that is not covered by the exception to the

494

submission of certified cost or pricing data in paragraph (1)(A) or (1)(B), submission of certified cost or pricing data shall not be required under subsection (a) of this section if—

    (A) the contract or subcontract being modified is a contract or subcontract for which submission of certified cost or pricing data may not be required by reason of paragraph (1)(A) or (1)(B); and

    (B) the modification would not change the contract or subcontract, as the case may be, from a contract or subcontract for the acquisition of a commercial item to a contract or subcontract for the acquisition of an item other than a commercial item.

(c) Cost or pricing data on below–threshold contracts

    (1) Authority to require submission

    Subject to paragraph (2), when certified cost or pricing data are not required to be submitted by subsection (a) of this section for a contract, subcontract, or modification of a contract or subcontract, such data may nevertheless be required to be submitted by the head of the procuring activity, but only if the head of the procuring activity determines that such data are necessary for the evaluation by the agency of the reasonableness of the price of the contract, subcontract, or modification of a contract or subcontract. In any case in which the head of the procuring activity requires such data to be submitted under this subsection, the head of the procuring activity shall justify in writing the reason for such requirement.

    (2) Exception

    The head of the procuring activity may not require certified cost or pricing data to be submitted under this paragraph for any contract or subcontract, or modification of a contract or subcontract, covered by the exceptions in subparagraph (A) or (B) of subsection (b)(1) of this section.

    (3) Delegation of authority prohibited

    The head of a procuring activity may not delegate the functions under this paragraph.

(d) Submission of other information

    (1) Authority to require submission

    When certified cost or pricing data are not required to be submitted under this section for a contract, subcontract, or modification of a contract or subcontract, the contracting officer shall require submission of data other than certified cost or pricing data to the extent necessary to determine the reasonableness of the price of the contract, subcontract, or modification of the contract or subcontract. Except in the case of a contract or subcontract covered by the exceptions in subsection (b)(1)(A) of this section, the contracting officer shall require that the data submitted include, at a minimum, appropriate information on the prices at which the same item or similar items have previously been sold that is adequate for evaluating the reasonableness of the price for the procurement.

(2) Limitations on authority

The Federal Acquisition Regulation shall include the following provisions regarding the types of information that contracting officers may require under paragraph (1):

(A) Reasonable limitations on requests for sales data relating to commercial items.

(B) A requirement that a contracting officer limit, to the maximum extent practicable, the scope of any request for information relating to commercial items from an offeror to only that information that is in the form regularly maintained by the offeror in commercial operations.

(C) A statement that any information received relating to commercial items that is exempt from disclosure under section 552(b) of Title 5 shall not be disclosed by the Federal Government.

(e) Price reductions for defective cost or pricing data

(1)(A) A prime contract (or change or modification to a prime contract) under which a certificate under subsection (a)(2) of this section is required shall contain a provision that the price of the contract to the United States, including profit or fee, shall be adjusted to exclude any significant amount by which it may be determined by the head of the executive agency that such price was increased because the contractor (or any subcontractor required to make available such a certificate) submitted defective cost or pricing data.

(B) For the purposes of this section, defective cost or pricing data are cost or pricing data which, as of the date of agreement on the price of the contract (or another date agreed upon between the parties), were inaccurate, incomplete, or noncurrent. If for purposes of the preceding sentence the parties agree upon a date other than the date of agreement on the price of the contract, the date agreed upon by the parties shall be as close to the date of agreement on the price of the contract as is practicable.

(2) In determining for purposes of a contract price adjustment under a contract provision required by paragraph (1) whether, and to what extent, a contract price was increased because the contractor (or a subcontractor) submitted defective cost or pricing data, it shall be a defense that the United States did not rely on the defective data submitted by the contractor or subcontractor.

(3) It is not a defense to an adjustment of the price of a contract under a contract provision required by paragraph (1) that—

(A) the price of the contract would not have been modified even if accurate, complete, and current cost or pricing data had been submitted by the contractor or subcontractor because the contractor or subcontractor—

(i) was the sole source of the property or services procured; or

(ii) otherwise was in a superior bargaining position with respect to the property or services procured;

(B) the contracting officer should have known that the cost or pricing data in issue were defective even though the contractor or subcontractor took no affirmative action to bring the character of the data to the attention of the contracting officer;

(C) the contract was based on an agreement between the contractor and the United States about the total cost of the contract and there was no agreement about the cost of each item procured under such contract; or

(D) the prime contractor or subcontractor did not submit a certification of cost or pricing data relating to the contract as required under subsection (a)(2) of this section.

(4)(A) A contractor shall be allowed to offset an amount against the amount of a contract price adjustment under a contract provision required by paragraph (1) if—

(i) the contractor certifies to the contracting officer (or to a designated representative of the contracting officer) that, to the best of the contractor's knowledge and belief, the contractor is entitled to the offset; and

(ii) the contractor proves that the cost or pricing data were available before the date of agreement on the price of the contract (or price of the modification), or, if applicable consistent with paragraph (1)(B), another date agreed upon between the parties, and that the data were not submitted as specified in subsection (a)(3) of this section before such date.

(B) A contractor shall not be allowed to offset an amount otherwise authorized to be offset under subparagraph (A) if—

(i) the certification under subsection (a)(2) of this section with respect to the cost or pricing data involved was known to be false when signed; or

(ii) the United States proves that, had the cost or pricing data referred to in subparagraph (A)(ii) been submitted to the United States before the date of agreement on the price of the contract (or price of the modification) or, if applicable under paragraph (1)(B), another date agreed upon between the parties, the submission of such cost or pricing data would not have resulted in an increase in that price in the amount to be offset.

(f) Interest and penalties for certain overpayments

(1) If the United States makes an overpayment to a contractor under a contract with an executive agency subject to this section and the overpayment was due to the submission by the contractor of defective cost or pricing data, the contractor shall be liable to the United States—

(A) for interest on the amount of such overpayment, to be computed—

(i) for the period beginning on the date the overpayment was made to the contractor and ending on the date the contractor repays the amount of such overpayment to the United States; and

(ii) at the current rate prescribed by the Secretary of the Treasury under section 6621 of Title 26; and

(B) if the submission of such defective data was a knowing submission, for an additional amount equal to the amount of the overpayment.

(2) Any liability under this subsection of a contractor that submits cost or pricing data but refuses to submit the certification required by subsection (a)(2) of this section with respect to the cost or pricing data shall not be affected by the refusal to submit such certification.

(g) Right of United States to examine contractor records

For the purpose of evaluating the accuracy, completeness, and currency of cost or pricing data required to be submitted by this section, an executive agency shall have the authority provided by section 254d(a)(2) of this title.

(h) Definitions

In this section:

(1) Cost or pricing data

The term "cost or pricing data" means all facts that, as of the date of agreement on the price of a contract (or the price of a contract modification) or, if applicable consistent with subsection (e)(1)(B) of this section, another date agreed upon between the parties, a prudent buyer or seller would reasonably expect to affect price negotiations significantly. Such term does not include information that is judgmental, but does include the factual information from which a judgment was derived.

(2) Subcontract

The term "subcontract" includes a transfer of commercial items between divisions, subsidiaries, or affiliates of a contractor or a subcontractor.

(3) Commercial item

The term "commercial item" has the meaning provided such term by section 403(12) of this title.

(i) Redesignated (h)

(June 30, 1949, c. 288, Title III, § 304A, as added Oct. 13, 1994, Pub.L. 103–355, Title I, § 1251(a)(2), 108 Stat. 3278, and amended Feb. 10, 1996, Pub.L. 104–106, Div. D, Title XLII, § 4201(b), Title XLIII, § 4321(e)(3), (4), 110 Stat. 651, 675; Oct. 17, 1998, Pub.L. 105–261, Div. A, Title VIII, §§ 805(b), 808(b), 112 Stat. 2083, 2085.)

HISTORICAL AND STATUTORY NOTES

Revision Notes and Legislative Reports
 1994 Acts. Senate Report Nos. 103–258 and 103–259, and House Conference Report No. 103–712, see 1994 U.S. Code Cong. and Adm. News, p. 2561.

 1996 Acts. House Conference Report No. 104–450, see 1996 U.S. Code Cong. and Adm. News, p. 238.

 1998 Acts. House Conference Report No. 105–736 and Statement by President, see 1998 U.S. Code Cong. and Adm. News, p. 513.

Amendments
 1998 Amendments. Subsec. (a)(5). Pub.L. 105–261, § 805(b), revised par. (5). Prior to amendment, par. (5) read as follows: "**(5)** For purposes of paragraph (1)(C), a contractor or subcontractor granted a waiver under subsection (b)(1)(B) of this section shall be considered as having been required to make available cost or pricing data under this section."

 Subsec. (d)(1). Pub.L. 105–261, § 808(b), struck out "the data submitted shall" in the second sentence and inserted in lieu thereof the following: "the

contracting officer shall require that the data submitted".

 1996 Amendments. Subsec. (b). Pub.L. 104–106, § 4201(b), added provisions relating to certified cost or pricing data, the acquisition of a commercial item, and references to par. (1)(B), and struck out provisions relating to established catalog or market prices, and FAR standards.

 Subsec. (c). Pub.L. 104–106, § 4201(b), added provisions relating to certified cost or pricing data.

 Subsec. (c)(1). Pub.L. 104–106, § 4321(e)(3), made technical changes which, for purposes of codification, required no further changes in text.

 Subsec. (d). Pub.L. 104–106, § 4201(b), added provisions relating to certified cost or pricing provisions and struck out provisions relating to authority to audit.

 Subsec. (d)(2)(A)(ii). Pub.L. 104–106, § 4321(e)(4), which directed the addition of "to" following "The information referred", could not be executed due to the revision of subsec. (d) by section 4201(b) of Pub.L. 104–106.

Subsecs. (h), (i). Pub.L. 104–106, § 4101(a)(2), redesignated subsec. (i) as subsec. (h), and struck out former subsec. (h), which related to required regulations.

Effective and Applicability Provisions

1996 Acts. Amendment by Pub.L. 104–106 effective Feb. 10, 1996, except as otherwise provided, see section 4401 of Pub.L. 104–106, set out as a note under section 251 of this title.

1994 Acts. Section effective Oct. 13, 1994, except as otherwise provided, see section 10001 of Pub.L. 103–355, set out as a note under section 251 of this title.

Section 1251(b) of Pub.L. 103–355, as amended by Pub.L. 104–106, Div. D, Title XLIII, § 4321(a)(3), Feb. 10, 1996, 110 Stat. 671, provided that: "Subsection (a) of section 304A of the Federal Property and Administrative Services Act of 1949 as added by subsection (a) [subsec. (a) of this section], shall apply according to the provisions thereof on and after the date of the enactment of this Act [Oct. 13, 1994], notwithstanding section 10001(b) [set out as an Effective Date of 1994 Amendments note under section 254 of this title]."

[Amendment by Pub.L. 104–106 effective Oct. 13, 1994, see section 4321(a) of Pub.L. 104–106, set out as a note under section 2306a of Title 10, Armed Forces.]

Eligibility for Contracts and Subcontracts To Be Conditioned On Compliance

Pub.L. 105–261, Div. A, Title VIII, § 808(c), Oct. 17, 1998, 112 Stat. 2085, provided that: "Not later than 180 days after the date of the enactment of this Act [Oct. 17, 1998], the Federal Acquisition Regulation shall be amended to provide that an offeror's compliance with a requirement to submit data for a contract or subcontract in accordance with section 2306a(d)(1) of title 10, United States Code, or section 304A(d)(1) of the Federal Property and Administrative Services Act of 1949 [subsec. (d)(1) of this section] shall be a condition for the offeror to be eligible to enter into the contract or subcontract, subject to such exceptions as the Federal Acquisition Regulatory Council determines appropriate."

Criteria for Certain Determinations Regarding Price Information

Pub.L. 105–261, Div. A, Title VIII, § 808(d), Oct. 17, 1998, 112 Stat. 2085, provided that: "Not later than 180 days after the date of the enactment of this Act [Oct. 17, 1998], the Federal Acquisition Regulation shall be amended to include criteria for contracting officers to apply for determining the specific price information that an offeror should be required to submit under section 2306a(d) of title 10, United States Code, or section 304A(d) of the Federal Property and Administrative Services Act of 1949 (41 U.S.C. 254b(d))."

CROSS REFERENCES

"Cost or pricing data or price analysis" defined as having same meaning as in this section for purposes of metric conversion, see 15 USCA § 205c.

Restrictions on discharging and obtaining contractor bid or proposal information or source selection information, see 41 USCA § 423.

LIBRARY REFERENCES

American Digest System

United States ⚷64.15, 72(1), 75(5).
Key Number System Topic No. 393.

Research References

Treatises and Practice Aids

Federal Procedure, Lawyers Edition § 39:92, Requirement That Cost and Pricing Data Be Submitted.

WESTLAW ELECTRONIC RESEARCH

See Westlaw guide following the Explanation pages of this volume.

§ 254c.   Multiyear contracts

(a) Authority

An executive agency may enter into a multiyear contract for the acquisition of property or services if—

(1) funds are available and obligated for such contract, for the full period of the contract or for the first fiscal year in which the contract is in effect, and for the estimated costs associated with any necessary termination of such contract; and

(2) the executive agency determines that—

(A) the need for the property or services is reasonably firm and continuing over the period of the contract; and

(B) a multiyear contract will serve the best interests of the United States by encouraging full and open competition or promoting economy in administration, performance, and operation of the agency's programs.

(b) Termination clause

A multiyear contract entered into under the authority of this section shall include a clause that provides that the contract shall be terminated if funds are not made available for the continuation of such contract in any fiscal year covered by the contract. Amounts available for paying termination costs shall remain available for such purpose until the costs associated with termination of the contract are paid.

(c) Cancellation ceiling notice

Before any contract described in subsection (a) of this section that contains a clause setting forth a cancellation ceiling in excess of $10,000,000 may be awarded, the executive agency shall give written notification of the proposed contract and of the proposed cancellation ceiling for that contract to the Congress, and such contract may not then be awarded until the end of a period of 30 days beginning on the date of such notification.

(d) Multiyear contract defined

For the purposes of this section, a multiyear contract is a contract for the purchase of property or services for more than one, but not more than five, program years. Such a contract may provide that performance under the contract during the second and subsequent years of the contract is contingent upon the appropriation of funds and (if it does so provide) may provide for a cancellation payment to be made to the contractor if such appropriations are not made.

(e) Rule of construction

Nothing in this section is intended to modify or affect any other provision of law that authorizes multiyear contracts.

(June 30, 1949, c. 288, Title III, § 304B, as added Oct. 13, 1994, Pub.L. 103–355, Title I, § 1072, 108 Stat. 3270.)

HISTORICAL AND STATUTORY NOTES

Revision Notes and Legislative Reports
1994 Acts. Senate Report Nos. 103–258 and 103–259, and House Conference Report No. 103–712, see 1994 U.S. Code Cong. and Adm. News, p. 2561.

Effective and Applicability Provisions
1994 Acts. Section effective Oct. 13, 1994, except as otherwise provided, see section 10001 of Pub.L. 103–355, set out as a note under section 251 of this title.

CROSS REFERENCES

Projects to accelerate closure activities at defense nuclear facilities and multiyear contracts, see 42 USCA § 7274n.

LIBRARY REFERENCES

American Digest System
United States ⊱60.
Key Number System Topic No. 393.

WESTLAW ELECTRONIC RESEARCH

See Westlaw guide following the Explanation pages of this volume.

§ 254d. Examination of records of contractor

(a) Agency authority

(1) The head of an executive agency, acting through an authorized representative, is authorized to inspect the plant and audit the records of—

 (A) a contractor performing a cost-reimbursement, incentive, time-and-materials, labor-hour, or price-redeterminable contract, or any combination of such contracts, made by that executive agency under this subchapter; and

 (B) a subcontractor performing any cost-reimbursement, incentive, time-and-materials, labor-hour, or price-redeterminable subcontract or any combination of such subcontracts under a contract referred to in subparagraph (A).

(2) The head of an executive agency, acting through an authorized representative, is authorized, for the purpose of evaluating the accuracy, completeness, and currency of certified cost or pricing data required to be submitted pursuant to section 254b of this title with respect to a contract or subcontract, to examine all records of the contractor or subcontractor related to—

 (A) the proposal for the contract or subcontract;

   (B) the discussions conducted on the proposal;

   (C) pricing of the contract or subcontract; or

   (D) performance of the contract or subcontract.

(b) Subpoena power

   (1) The Inspector General of an executive agency appointed under section 3 or 8G of the Inspector General Act of 1978 (5 U.S.C.App.) or, upon request of the head of an executive agency, the Director of the Defense Contract Audit Agency (or any successor agency) of the Department of Defense or the Inspector General of the General Services Administration may require by subpoena the production of records of a contractor, access to which is provided for that executive agency by subsection (a) of this section.

   (2) Any such subpoena, in the case of contumacy or refusal to obey, shall be enforceable by order of an appropriate United States district court.

   (3) The authority provided by paragraph (1) may not be delegated.

   (4) In the year following a year in which authority provided in paragraph (1) is exercised for an executive agency, the head of the executive agency shall submit to the Committee on Governmental Affairs of the Senate and the Committee on Government Operations of the House of Representatives a report on the exercise of such authority during such preceding year and the reasons why such authority was exercised in any instance.

(c) Comptroller General authority

   (1) Except as provided in paragraph (2), each contract awarded after using procedures other than sealed bid procedures shall provide that the Comptroller General and his representatives are authorized to examine any records of the contractor, or any of its subcontractors, that directly pertain to, and involve transactions relating to, the contract or subcontract.

   (2) Paragraph (1) does not apply to a contract or subcontract with a foreign contractor or foreign subcontractor if the executive agency concerned determines, with the concurrence of the Comptroller General or his designee, that the application of that paragraph to the contract or subcontract would not be in the public interest. However, the concurrence of the Comptroller General or his designee is not required—

   (A) where the contractor or subcontractor is a foreign government or agency thereof or is precluded by the laws of the country involved from making its records available for examination; and

(B) where the executive agency determines, after taking into account the price and availability of the property and services from United States sources, that the public interest would be best served by not applying paragraph (1).

(3) Paragraph (1) may not be construed to require a contractor or subcontractor to create or maintain any record that the contractor or subcontractor does not maintain in the ordinary course of business or pursuant to another provision of law.

(d) Limitation on audits relating to indirect costs

An executive agency may not perform an audit of indirect costs under a contract, subcontract, or modification before or after entering into the contract, subcontract, or modification in any case in which the contracting officer determines that the objectives of the audit can reasonably be met by accepting the results of an audit that was conducted by any other department or agency of the Federal Government within one year preceding the date of the contracting officer's determination.

(e) Limitation

The authority of an executive agency under subsection (a) of this section, and the authority of the Comptroller General under subsection (c) of this section, with respect to a contract or subcontract shall expire three years after final payment under such contract or subcontract.

(f) Inapplicability to certain contracts

This section does not apply to the following contracts:

(1) Contracts for utility services at rates not exceeding those established to apply uniformly to the public, plus any applicable reasonable connection charge.

(2) A contract or subcontract that is not greater than the simplified acquisition threshold.

(g) Form of original record storage

Nothing in this section shall be construed to preclude a contractor from duplicating or storing original records in electronic form.

(h) Use of images of original records

An executive agency shall not require a contractor or subcontractor to provide original records in an audit carried out pursuant to this section if the contractor or subcontractor provides photographic or electronic images of the original records and meets the following requirements:

(1) The contractor or subcontractor has established procedures to ensure that the imaging process preserves the integrity, reliability, and security of the original records.

(2) The contractor or subcontractor maintains an effective indexing system to permit timely and convenient access to the imaged records.

(3) The contractor or subcontractor retains the original records for a minimum of one year after imaging to permit periodic validation of the imaging systems.

(i) "Records" defined

In this section, the term "records" includes books, documents, accounting procedures and practices, and other data, regardless of type and regardless of whether such items are in written form, in the form of computer data, or in any other form.

(June 30, 1949, c. 288, Title III, § 304C, as added and amended Oct. 13, 1994, Pub.L. 103–355, Title II, § 2251(a), Title IV, § 4103(d), 108 Stat. 3318, 3341; Feb. 10, 1996, Pub.L. 104–106, Div. D, Title XLIII, § 4321(e)(5), 110 Stat. 675; Sept. 23, 1996, Pub.L. 104–201, Div. A, Title VIII, § 808(b), 110 Stat. 2607.)

HISTORICAL AND STATUTORY NOTES

Revision Notes and Legislative Reports

1994 Acts. Senate Report Nos. 103–258 and 103–259, and House Conference Report No. 103–712, see 1994 U.S. Code Cong. and Adm. News, p. 2561.

1996 Acts. House Conference Report No. 104–450, see 1996 U.S. Code Cong. and Adm. News, p. 238.

House Report No. 104–563 and House Conference Report No. 104–724, see 1996 U.S. Code Cong. and Adm. News, p. 2948.

References in Text

Section 3 and 8G of the Inspector General Act of 1978, referred to in subsec. (b)(1), are sections 3 and 8G, respectively, of Pub.L. 95–452, Oct. 12, 1978, 92 Stat. 1101, as amended, which are set out in Appendix 3 to Title 5, Government Organization and Employees.

Amendments

1996 Amendments. Subsec. (a)(2). Pub.L. 104–106, § 4321(e)(5), substituted "section 254b" for "section 254c".

Subsec. (d). Pub.L. 104–201, § 808(b), substituted provisions relating to limitation on audits relating to indirect costs for provisions relating to limitation on preaward audits relating to indirect costs.

1994 Amendments. Subsec. (f)(2). Pub.L. 103–355, § 4103(d), added par. (2).

Effective and Applicability Provisions

1996 Acts. Amendment by Pub.L. 104–106 effective Feb. 10, 1996, except as otherwise provided, see section 4401 of Pub.L. 104–106, set out as a note under section 251 of this title.

1994 Acts. This section, as added by section 2251(a) of Pub.L. 103–355, and amendment of this section by section 4103(d) of Pub.L. 103–355, effective Oct. 13, 1994, except as otherwise provided, see section 10001 of Pub.L. 103–355, set out as a note under section 251 of this title.

Change of Name

Any reference in any provision of law enacted before Jan. 4, 1995, to the Committee on Government Operations of the House of Representatives treated as referring to the Committee on Government Reform and Oversight of the House of Representatives, except that any reference in any provision of law enacted before Jan. 4, 1995, to the Committee on Government Operations of the House of Representatives treated as referring to the Committee on the Budget of the

House of Representatives in the case of a provision of law relating to the establishment, extension, and enforcement of special controls over the Federal budget, see section 1(a)(6) and (c)(2) of Pub.L. 104–14, set out as a note preceding section 21 of Title 2, The Congress.

LIBRARY REFERENCES

American Digest System
  United States ☞75(1).
  Key Number System Topic No. 393.

WESTLAW ELECTRONIC RESEARCH

See Westlaw guide following the Explanation pages of this volume.

§ 255. Contract financing

(a) Payment authority

Any executive agency may—

  (1) make advance, partial, progress or other payments under contracts for property or services made by the agency; and

  (2) insert in solicitations for procurement of property or services a provision limiting to small business concerns advance or progress payments.

(b) Performance-based payments

Whenever practicable, payments under subsection (a) of this section shall be made on any of the following bases:

  (1) Performance measured by objective, quantifiable methods such as delivery of acceptable items, work measurement, or statistical process controls.

  (2) Accomplishment of events defined in the program management plan.

  (3) Other quantifiable measures of results.

(c) Payment amount

Payments made under subsection (a) of this section may not exceed the unpaid contract price.

(d) Security for advance payments

Advance payments under subsection (a) of this section may be made only upon adequate security and a determination by the agency head that to do so would be in the public interest. Such security may be in the form of a lien in favor of the Government on the property contracted for, on the balance in an account in which such payments are deposited, and on such of the property acquired for performance of the contract as the parties may agree. This lien shall be paramount to all other liens and is effective immediately upon the first advancement of funds without filing, notice, or any other action by the United States.

(e) Conditions for progress payments

(1) The executive agency shall ensure that any payment for work in progress (including materials, labor, and other items) under a contract of an executive agency that provides for such payments is commensurate with the work accomplished that meets standards established under the contract. The contractor shall provide such information and evidence as the executive agency determines necessary to permit the executive agency to carry out the preceding sentence.

(2) The executive agency shall ensure that progress payments referred to in paragraph (1) are not made for more than 80 percent of the work accomplished under the contract so long as the executive agency has not made the contractual terms, specifications, and price definite.

(3) This subsection applies to any contract in an amount greater than $25,000.

(f) Conditions for payments for commercial items

(1) Payments under subsection (a) of this section for commercial items may be made under such terms and conditions as the head of the executive agency determines are appropriate or customary in the commercial marketplace and are in the best interests of the United States. The head of the executive agency shall obtain adequate security for such payments. If the security is in the form of a lien in favor of the United States, such lien is paramount to all other liens and is effective immediately upon the first payment, without filing, notice, or other action by the United States.

(2) Advance payments made under subsection (a) of this section for commercial items may include payments, in a total amount of not more than 15 percent of the contract price, in advance of any performance of work under the contract.

(3) The conditions of subsections (d) and (e) of this section need not be applied if they would be inconsistent, as determined by the head of the executive agency, with commercial terms and conditions pursuant to paragraphs (1) and (2).

(g) Action in case of fraud

(1) In any case in which the remedy coordination official of an executive agency finds that there is substantial evidence that the request of a contractor for advance, partial, or progress payment under a contract awarded by that executive agency is based on fraud,

the remedy coordination official shall recommend that the executive agency reduce or suspend further payments to such contractor.

(2) The head of an executive agency receiving a recommendation under paragraph (1) in the case of a contractor's request for payment under a contract shall determine whether there is substantial evidence that the request is based on fraud. Upon making such a determination, the head of the executive agency may reduce or suspend further payments to the contractor under such contract.

(3) The extent of any reduction or suspension of payments by an executive agency under paragraph (2) on the basis of fraud shall be reasonably commensurate with the anticipated loss to the United States resulting from the fraud.

(4) A written justification for each decision of the head of an executive agency whether to reduce or suspend payments under paragraph (2), and for each recommendation received by the executive agency in connection with such decision, shall be prepared and be retained in the files of the executive agency.

(5) The head of each executive agency shall prescribe procedures to ensure that, before the head of the executive agency decides to reduce or suspend payments in the case of a contractor under paragraph (2), the contractor is afforded notice of the proposed reduction or suspension and an opportunity to submit matters to the executive agency in response to such proposed reduction or suspension.

(6) Not later than 180 days after the date on which the head of an executive agency reduces or suspends payments to a contractor under paragraph (2), the remedy coordination official of the executive agency shall—

  (A) review the determination of fraud on which the reduction or suspension is based; and

  (B) transmit a recommendation to the head of such executive agency whether the suspension or reduction should continue.

(7) The head of each executive agency who receives recommendations made by a remedy coordination official of the executive agency to reduce or suspend payments under paragraph (2) during a fiscal year shall prepare for such year a report that contains the recommendations, the actions taken on the recommendations and the reasons for such actions, and an assessment of the effects of such actions on the Federal Government. Any such report shall be available to any Member of Congress upon request.

(8) The head of an executive agency may not delegate responsibilities under this subsection to any person in a position below level IV of the Executive Schedule.

(9) In this subsection, the term "remedy coordination official", with respect to an executive agency, means the person or entity in that executive agency who coordinates within that executive agency the administration of criminal, civil, administrative, and contractual remedies resulting from investigations of fraud or corruption related to procurement activities.

(June 30, 1949, c. 288, Title III, § 305, 63 Stat. 396; July 12, 1952, c. 703, § 1(m), 66 Stat. 594; Aug. 28, 1958, Pub.L. 85–800, § 4, 72 Stat. 966; Oct. 13, 1994, Pub.L. 103–355, Title II, § 2051(a)-(e), 108 Stat. 3303–3306; Feb. 10, 1996, Pub.L. 104–106, Div. D, Title XLIII, § 4321(a)(4), 110 Stat. 671.)

HISTORICAL AND STATUTORY NOTES

Revision Notes and Legislative Reports
1958 Acts. Senate Report No. 2201, see 1958 U.S.Code Cong. and Adm.News, p. 4021.

1994 Acts. Senate Report Nos. 103–258 and 103–259, and House Conference Report No. 103–712, see 1994 U.S. Code Cong. and Adm. News, p. 2561.

1996 Acts. House Conference Report No. 104–450, see 1996 U.S. Code Cong. and Adm. News, p. 238.

Amendments
1996 Amendments. Subsec. (f)(3). Pub.L. 104–106, § 4321(a)(4), as amended by Pub.L. 103–355, § 2051(e), made technical changes which, for purposes of codification, required no further changes in text.

1994 Amendments. Heading. Pub.L. 103–355, § 2051(a)(1), substituted "Contract financing" for "Advance or other payments; restriction; conditions".

Subsec. (a). Pub.L. 103–355, § 2051(a)(2), (c), enacted subsec. (a) heading and substituted in item (2) "solicitations" for "bid solicitations".

Subsec. (b). Pub.L. 103–355, § 2052(b), added subsec. (b). Former subsec. (b) redesignated (c).

Subsec. (c). Pub.L. 103–355, § 2051(a)(3), (5), enacted subsec. (b) heading and redesignated subsec. (b), and amended, as subsec. (c). Former subsec. (c) redesignated (d).

Subsec. (d). Pub.L. 103–355, § 2051(a)(4), (5), (d), enacted subsec. (c) heading, redesignated subsec. (c), as

amended, as subsec. (d), and added to third sentence provision making the lien effective immediately upon the first advancement of funds without filing, notice, or any other action by the United States.

Subsecs. (e) to (g). Pub.L. 103–355, § 2051(e), added subsecs. (e) to (g).

1958 Amendments. Pub.L. 85–800 authorized advance or other payments under contracts for property or services by agency and insertion in bid solicitations of provision limiting advance or progress payments to small business concerns, restricted payments under subsec. (a) to unpaid contract price, and reworded generally conditions for making advance payments.

1952 Amendments. Subsec. (b). Act July 12, 1952, substituted "property" for "supplies" wherever appearing.

Effective and Applicability Provisions
1996 Acts. Amendment by Pub.L. 104–106 effective Oct. 13, 1994, see section 4321(a) of Pub.L. 104–106, set out as a note under section 2306a of Title 10, Armed Forces.

1994 Acts. Amendment by section 2051(a) through (e) of Pub.L. 103–355 effective Oct. 13, 1994, except as otherwise provided, see section 10001 of Pub.L. 103–355, set out as a note under section 251 of this title.

1949 Acts. Act June 30, 1949, § 605, which set July 1, 1949, as the effective date for this section, was repealed by

Pub.L. 107–217, § 6(b), Aug. 21, 2002, 116 Stat. 1313.

Definitions

The definitions in 40 U.S.C.A. § 102 apply to terms appearing in this subchapter.

Exemption of Functions

Functions authorized by Foreign Assistance Act of 1961, as amended, as exempt, see Ex. Ord. No. 11223, May 12, 1965, 30 F.R. 6635, set out as a note under section 2393 of Title 22, Foreign Relations and Intercourse.

Relationship Between 1994 Amendments and Prompt Payment Requirements

Section 2051(f) of Pub.L. 103–355 provided that: "The amendments made by this section [amending this section] are not intended to impair or modify procedures required by the provisions of chapter 39 of title 31, United States Code [section 3901 et seq. of Title 31, Money and Finance], and the regulations issued pursuant to such provisions of law (as such procedures are in effect on the date of the enactment of this Act [Oct. 13, 1994]), except that the Government may accept payment terms offered by a contractor offering a commercial item."

CROSS REFERENCES

Alien smuggling and undercover investigation authority and sums appropriated for leasing space, see 8 USCA § 1363a.

Armed services contracts, advance payments, see 10 USCA § 2307.

LIBRARY REFERENCES

American Digest System

United States ☞70(15), 73(16).

Key Number System Topic No. 393.

Research References

Encyclopedias

Am. Jur. 2d Public Works and Contracts § 143, Advance, Progress, or Installment Payments.

14 Am. Jur. Trials 437, Representing the Government Contractor.

Treatises and Practice Aids

Immigration Law Service 2d PSD INA § 294, Undercover Investigation Authority.

WESTLAW ELECTRONIC RESEARCH

See Westlaw guide following the Explanation pages of this volume.

Notes of Decisions

Discounts 5
Form or currency of payments 4
Overpayments 3
Partial payments 1
Priority of liens 6
Progress payments 2

1. Partial payments

"Partial payments" amendment to prime contract was authorized by law, even though contract was not a "negotiated" one but was one awarded to lowest responsible bidder. Shepard Engineering Co. v. U.S., C.A.8 (Mo.) 1961, 287 F.2d 737, rehearing denied 289 F.2d 681. United States ☞ 72(1.1)

2. Progress payments

Evidence supported determination that supplier to United States Navy voluntarily agreed to increase the progress payments to be made to corporation with which it subcontracted and, thus, supplier would not be entitled to recover anything as a result of increase in progress payment limitation in subcontract from 70% to 90%. CRF - a Joint Venture of Cemco, Inc. v. U.S., Ct.Cl.1980, 624 F.2d 1054, 224 Ct.Cl. 312. United States ☞ 74(11)

In general, a "finding" amounts to a reasonable inference from the evidence presented, and a contracting officer required to make a finding that the contractor was in such unsatisfactory financial condition as to endanger his performance of the contract and therefore to justify the contracting officer in holding up a progress payment, does not have to recite verbatim one of the reasons given in the reduction or suspension provision of the contract, but must merely use language which makes it clear that the substance of the subsection has been met and the provision properly applied. Davis v. U.S., Ct.Cl.1967, 180 Ct.Cl. 20. United States ☞ 73(9)

3. Overpayments

In action by United States to recover overpayment on supply contracts, federal law and not S.H.A. ch. 121½, § 49 applied. Fansteel Metallurgical Corp. v. U.S., Ct.Cl.1959, 172 F.Supp. 268, 145 Ct.Cl. 496. Federal Courts ☞ 413

Where the plaintiffs purchased from the San Antonio office of the War Assets Administration in 1946, 15 pumping stations with R–41 (four cylinder) gasoline engines at a fixed and agreed price of $1,659 each, and where payment in full was made by plaintiffs and likewise the plaintiffs later purchased from the Cincinnati Regional Office 3 pumping stations with similar equipment at a unit price of $1,659 and thereafter the price of this equipment was fixed at $1,253 per unit and the Cincinnati Regional Office allowed plaintiffs' claim for the difference, $1,218, with respect to three units purchased from the Cincinnati office and refunded the amount to the plaintiffs, in the circumstances it cannot be said that in making the refund of $1,218 the officials of the War Assets Administration acted arbitrarily and without authority. Zink v. U.S., Ct.Cl.1952, 123 Ct.Cl. 85. United States ☞ 58(4)

4. Form or currency of payments

Contracting officer did not have authority to agree to provision in Department of Housing and Urban Development (HUD) property maintenance contract that allowed contractor to satisfy its ad-vance payments indebtedness by purchasing equipment for contract performance; such provision converted loan by government in form of advance payments into gift in event of default by contractor. Johnson Management Group CFC, Inc. v. Martinez, C.A.Fed.2002, 308 F.3d 1245. United States ☞ 60

Where contract provided that consideration should be paid in dollars obligation is not met by payment in francs, in conformity to certain rules and regulations of Treasury Department for payment of our military forces abroad. Jackson v. U.S., Ct.Cl.1925, 60 Ct.Cl. 599. United States ☞ 70(15.1)

5. Discounts

Where contractor offered 2.1% discount for payment within ten days, 2% for payment within twenty days, and net percent thirty days and Government's notice to contractor stated that discount limitation under which Government would consider discount in excess of 2% as trade or special discount available to Government as reduction from prices quoted without regard to whether invoices were actually paid within designated period, Government was entitled to reduce price by 2.1 percent but was not entitled to take additional discount for prompt payment even though payment was made within time period permitting discount. Rawleigh, Moses & Co., Inc. v. U.S., Ct.Cl.1973, 475 F.2d 606, 201 Ct.Cl. 295. United States ☞ 70(15.1)

6. Priority of liens

Suppliers to participant in disadvantaged business development program did not have equitable lien against advance payment loan made by Small Business Administration so as to override government's paramount lien on advance payments. ATC Petroleum, Inc. v. Sanders, D.D.C.1987, 661 F.Supp. 182, affirmed in part, reversed in part 860 F.2d 1104, 274 U.S.App.D.C. 12. United States ☞ 53(8)

§ 256. Allowable costs

(a) Indirect cost that violates FAR cost principle

An executive agency shall require that a covered contract provide that if the contractor submits to the executive agency a proposal for settlement of indirect costs incurred by the contractor for any period after such costs have been accrued and if that proposal includes the submission of a cost which is unallowable because the cost violates a cost principle in the Federal Acquisition Regulation (referred to in section 421(c)(1) of this title) or an executive agency supplement to the Federal Acquisition Regulation, the cost shall be disallowed.

(b) Penalty for violation of cost principle

(1) If the executive agency determines that a cost submitted by a contractor in its proposal for settlement is expressly unallowable under a cost principle referred to in subsection (a) of this section that defines the allowability of specific selected costs, the executive agency shall assess a penalty against the contractor in an amount equal to—

    (A) the amount of the disallowed cost allocated to covered contracts for which a proposal for settlement of indirect costs has been submitted; plus

    (B) interest (to be computed based on provisions in the Federal Acquisition Regulation) to compensate the United States for the use of any funds which a contractor has been paid in excess of the amount to which the contractor was entitled.

(2) If the executive agency determines that a proposal for settlement of indirect costs submitted by a contractor includes a cost determined to be unallowable in the case of such contractor before the submission of such proposal, the executive agency shall assess a penalty against the contractor in an amount equal to two times the amount of the disallowed cost allocated to covered contracts for which a proposal for settlement of indirect costs has been submitted.

(c) Waiver of penalty

The Federal Acquisition Regulation shall provide for a penalty under subsection (b) of this section to be waived in the case of a contractor's proposal for settlement of indirect costs when—

    (1) the contractor withdraws the proposal before the formal initiation of an audit of the proposal by the Federal Government and resubmits a revised proposal;

    (2) the amount of unallowable costs subject to the penalty is insignificant; or

    (3) the contractor demonstrates, to the contracting officer's satisfaction, that—

        (A) it has established appropriate policies and personnel training and an internal control and review system that provide assurances that unallowable costs subject to penalties are precluded from being included in the contractor's proposal for settlement of indirect costs; and

(B) the unallowable costs subject to the penalty were inadvertently incorporated into the proposal.

(d) **Applicability of contract disputes procedure to disallowance of cost and assessment of penalty**

An action of an executive agency under subsection (a) or (b) of this section—

(1) shall be considered a final decision for the purposes of section 605 of this title; and

(2) is appealable in the manner provided in section 606 of this title.

(e) **Specific costs not allowable**

(1) The following costs are not allowable under a covered contract:

(A) Costs of entertainment, including amusement, diversion, and social activities, and any costs directly associated with such costs (such as tickets to shows or sports events, meals, lodging, rentals, transportation, and gratuities).

(B) Costs incurred to influence (directly or indirectly) legislative action on any matter pending before Congress, a State legislature, or a legislative body of a political subdivision of a State.

(C) Costs incurred in defense of any civil or criminal fraud proceeding or similar proceeding (including filing of any false certification) brought by the United States where the contractor is found liable or had pleaded nolo contendere to a charge of fraud or similar proceeding (including filing of a false certification).

(D) Payments of fines and penalties resulting from violations of, or failure to comply with, Federal, State, local, or foreign laws and regulations, except when incurred as a result of compliance with specific terms and conditions of the contract or specific written instructions from the contracting officer authorizing in advance such payments in accordance with applicable provisions of the Federal Acquisition Regulation.

(E) Costs of membership in any social, dining, or country club or organization.

(F) Costs of alcoholic beverages.

(G) Contributions or donations, regardless of the recipient.

(H) Costs of advertising designed to promote the contractor or its products.

(I) Costs of promotional items and memorabilia, including models, gifts, and souvenirs.

(J) Costs for travel by commercial aircraft which exceed the amount of the standard commercial fare.

(K) Costs incurred in making any payment (commonly known as a "golden parachute payment") which is—

　　(i) in an amount in excess of the normal severance pay paid by the contractor to an employee upon termination of employment; and

　　(ii) is paid to the employee contingent upon, and following, a change in management control over, or ownership of, the contractor or a substantial portion of the contractor's assets.

(L) Costs of commercial insurance that protects against the costs of the contractor for correction of the contractor's own defects in materials or workmanship.

(M) Costs of severance pay paid by the contractor to foreign nationals employed by the contractor under a service contract performed outside the United States, to the extent that the amount of severance pay paid in any case exceeds the amount paid in the industry involved under the customary or prevailing practice for firms in that industry providing similar services in the United States, as determined under the Federal Acquisition Regulation.

(N) Costs of severance pay paid by the contractor to a foreign national employed by the contractor under a service contract performed in a foreign country if the termination of the employment of the foreign national is the result of the closing of, or the curtailment of activities at, a United States facility in that country at the request of the government of that country.

(O) Costs incurred by a contractor in connection with any criminal, civil, or administrative proceeding commenced by the United States or a State, to the extent provided in subsection (k) of this section.

(P) Costs of compensation of senior executives of contractors for a fiscal year, regardless of the contract funding source, to the extent that such compensation exceeds the benchmark compensation amount determined applicable for the fiscal year by the Administrator for Federal Procurement Policy under section 435 of this title.

(2)(A) Pursuant to the Federal Acquisition Regulation and subject to the availability of appropriations, an executive agency, in awarding a covered contract, may waive the application of the provisions of paragraphs (1)(M) and (1)(N) to that contract if the executive agency determines that—

(i) the application of such provisions to the contract would adversely affect the continuation of a program, project, or activity that provides significant support services for employees of the executive agency posted outside the United States;

(ii) the contractor has taken (or has established plans to take) appropriate actions within the contractor's control to minimize the amount and number of incidents of the payment of severance pay by the contractor to employees under the contract who are foreign nationals; and

(iii) the payment of severance pay is necessary in order to comply with a law that is generally applicable to a significant number of businesses in the country in which the foreign national receiving the payment performed services under the contract or is necessary to comply with a collective bargaining agreement.

(B) An executive agency shall include in the solicitation for a covered contract a statement indicating—

(i) that a waiver has been granted under subparagraph (A) for the contract; or

(ii) whether the executive agency will consider granting such a waiver, and, if the executive agency will consider granting a waiver, the criteria to be used in granting the waiver.

(C) An executive agency shall make the final determination regarding whether to grant a waiver under subparagraph (A) with respect to a covered contract before award of the contract.

(3) The provisions of the Federal Acquisition Regulation implementing this section may establish appropriate definitions, exclusions, limitations, and qualifications. Any submission by a contractor of costs which are incurred by the contractor and which are claimed to be allowable under Department of Energy management and operating contracts shall be considered a "proposal for settlement of indirect costs incurred by the contractor for any period after such costs have been accrued", as used in this section.

(f) Required regulations

(1) The Federal Acquisition Regulation shall contain provisions on the allowability of contractor costs. Such provisions shall define in detail and in specific terms those costs which are unallowable, in whole or in part, under covered contracts. The regulations shall, at a minimum, clarify the cost principles applicable to contractor costs of the following:

(A) Air shows.

(B) Membership in civic, community, and professional organizations.

515

(C) Recruitment.

(D) Employee morale and welfare.

(E) Actions to influence (directly or indirectly) executive branch action on regulatory and contract matters (other than costs incurred in regard to contract proposals pursuant to solicited or unsolicited bids).

(F) Community relations.

(G) Dining facilities.

(H) Professional and consulting services, including legal services.

(I) Compensation.

(J) Selling and marketing.

(K) Travel.

(L) Public relations.

(M) Hotel and meal expenses.

(N) Expense of corporate aircraft.

(O) Company-furnished automobiles.

(P) Advertising.

(Q) Conventions.

(2) The Federal Acquisition Regulation shall require that a contracting officer not resolve any questioned costs until the contracting officer has obtained—

(A) adequate documentation with respect to such costs; and

(B) the opinion of the contract auditor on the allowability of such costs.

(3) The Federal Acquisition Regulation shall provide that, to the maximum extent practicable, a contract auditor be present at any negotiation or meeting with the contractor regarding a determination of the allowability of indirect costs of the contractor.

(4) The Federal Acquisition Regulation shall require that all categories of costs designated in the report of a contract auditor as questioned with respect to a proposal for settlement be resolved in such a manner that the amount of the individual questioned costs that are paid will be reflected in the settlement.

(g) Applicability of regulations to subcontractors

The regulations referred to in subsections (e) and (f)(1) of this section shall require prime contractors of a covered contract, to the maximum extent practicable, to apply the provisions of such regulations to all subcontractors of the covered contract.

516

(h) Contractor certification required

(1) A proposal for settlement of indirect costs applicable to a covered contract shall include a certification by an official of the contractor that, to the best of the certifying official's knowledge and belief, all indirect costs included in the proposal are allowable. Any such certification shall be in a form prescribed in the Federal Acquisition Regulation.

(2) An executive agency may, in an exceptional case, waive the requirement for certification under paragraph (1) in the case of any contract if the agency—

(A) determines in such case that it would be in the interest of the United States to waive such certification; and

(B) states in writing the reasons for that determination and makes such determination available to the public.

(i) Penalties for submission of cost known as not allowable

The submission to an executive agency of a proposal for settlement of costs for any period after such costs have been accrued that includes a cost that is expressly specified by statute or regulation as being unallowable, with the knowledge that such cost is unallowable, shall be subject to the provisions of section 287 of Title 18 and section 3729 of Title 31.

(j) Contractor to have burden of proof

In a proceeding before a board of contract appeals, the United States Court of Federal Claims, or any other Federal court in which the reasonableness of indirect costs for which a contractor seeks reimbursement from the United States is in issue, the burden of proof shall be upon the contractor to establish that those costs are reasonable.

(k) Proceeding costs not allowable

(1) Except as otherwise provided in this subsection, costs incurred by a contractor in connection with any criminal, civil, or administrative proceeding commenced by the United States or a State are not allowable as reimbursable costs under a covered contract if the proceeding (A) relates to a violation of, or failure to comply with, a Federal or State statute or regulation, and (B) results in a disposition described in paragraph (2).

(2) A disposition referred to in paragraph (1)(B) is any of the following:

(A) In the case of a criminal proceeding, a conviction (including a conviction pursuant to a plea of nolo contendere) by reason of the violation or failure referred to in paragraph (1).

(B) In the case of a civil or administrative proceeding involving an allegation of fraud or similar misconduct, a determination of contractor liability on the basis of the violation or failure referred to in paragraph (1).

(C) In the case of any civil or administrative proceeding, the imposition of a monetary penalty by reason of the violation or failure referred to in paragraph (1).

(D) A final decision—

    (i) to debar or suspend the contractor,

    (ii) to rescind or void the contract, or

    (iii) to terminate the contract for default,

by reason of the violation or failure referred to in paragraph (1).

(E) A disposition of the proceeding by consent or compromise if such action could have resulted in a disposition described in subparagraph (A), (B), (C), or (D).

(3) In the case of a proceeding referred to in paragraph (1) that is commenced by the United States and is resolved by consent or compromise pursuant to an agreement entered into by a contractor and the United States, the costs incurred by the contractor in connection with such proceeding that are otherwise not allowable as reimbursable costs under such paragraph may be allowed to the extent specifically provided in such agreement.

(4) In the case of a proceeding referred to in paragraph (1) that is commenced by a State, the executive agency that awarded the covered contract involved in the proceeding may allow the costs incurred by the contractor in connection with such proceeding as reimbursable costs if the executive agency determines, in accordance with the Federal Acquisition Regulation, that the costs were incurred as a result of (A) a specific term or condition of the contract, or (B) specific written instructions of the executive agency.

(5)(A) Except as provided in subparagraph (C), costs incurred by a contractor in connection with a criminal, civil, or administrative proceeding commenced by the United States or a State in connection with a covered contract may be allowed as reimbursable costs under the contract if such costs are not disallowable under paragraph (1), but only to the extent provided in subparagraph (B).

(B)(i) The amount of the costs allowable under subparagraph (A) in any case may not exceed the amount equal to 80 percent of the amount of the costs incurred, to the extent that such costs are determined to be otherwise allowable and allocable under the Federal Acquisition Regulation.

(ii) Regulations issued for the purpose of clause (i) shall provide for appropriate consideration of the complexity of procurement litigation, generally accepted principles governing the award of legal fees in civil actions involving the United States as a party, and such other factors as may be appropriate.

(C) In the case of a proceeding referred to in subparagraph (A), contractor costs otherwise allowable as reimbursable costs under this paragraph are not allowable if (i) such proceeding involves the same contractor misconduct alleged as the basis of another criminal, civil, or administrative proceeding, and (ii) the costs of such other proceeding are not allowable under paragraph (1).

(6) In this subsection:

(A) The term "proceeding" includes an investigation.

(B) The term "costs", with respect to a proceeding—

(i) means all costs incurred by a contractor, whether before or after the commencement of any such proceeding; and

(ii) includes—

(I) administrative and clerical expenses;

(II) the cost of legal services, including legal services performed by an employee of the contractor;

(III) the cost of the services of accountants and consultants retained by the contractor; and

(IV) the pay of directors, officers, and employees of the contractor for time devoted by such directors, officers, and employees to such proceeding.

(C) The term "penalty" does not include restitution, reimbursement, or compensatory damages.

(l) "Covered contract" defined

(1) In this section, the term "covered contract" means a contract for an amount in excess of $500,000 that is entered into by an executive agency, except that such term does not include a fixed-price contract without cost incentives or any firm, fixed price contract for the purchase of commercial items.

(2) Effective on October 1 of each year that is divisible by five, the amount set forth in paragraph (1) shall be adjusted to the equivalent amount in constant fiscal year 1994 dollars. An amount, as so adjusted, that is not evenly divisible by $50,000 shall be rounded to the nearest multiple of $50,000. In the case of an amount that is evenly divisible by $25,000 but is not evenly divisible by $50,000, the amount shall be rounded to the next higher multiple of $50,000.

(m) Other definitions

In this section:

(1) The term "compensation", for a fiscal year, means the total amount of wages, salary, bonuses and deferred compensation for the fiscal year, whether paid, earned, or otherwise accruing, as recorded in an employer's cost accounting records for the fiscal year.

(2) The term "senior executives", with respect to a contractor, means the five most highly compensated employees in management positions at each home office and each segment of the contractor.

(3) The term "fiscal year" means a fiscal year established by a contractor for accounting purposes.

(June 30, 1949, c. 288, Title III, § 306, as added Nov. 19, 1988, Pub.L. 100–700, § 8(a)(1), 102 Stat. 4635, and amended Oct. 13, 1994, Pub.L. 103–355, Title II, § 2151, 108 Stat. 3309; Nov. 18, 1997, Pub.L. 105–85, Div. A, Title VIII, § 808(b), 111 Stat. 1836; Oct. 17, 1998, Pub.L. 105–261, Div. A, Title VIII, § 804(b), 112 Stat. 2083.)

HISTORICAL AND STATUTORY NOTES

Revision Notes and Legislative Reports
 1988 Acts. Senate Report No. 100–503, see 1988 U.S.Code Cong. and Adm.News, p. 5969.

 1994 Acts. Senate Report Nos. 103–258 and 103–259, and House Conference Report No. 103–712, see 1994 U.S. Code Cong. and Adm. News, p. 2561.

 1997 Acts. House Conference Report No. 105–340 and Statement by President, see 1997 U.S. Code Cong. and Adm. News, p. 2251.

 1998 Acts. House Conference Report No. 105–736 and Statement by President, see 1998 U.S. Code Cong. and Adm. News, p. 513.

Amendments
 1998 Amendments. Subsec. (m)(2). Pub.L. 105–261, § 804(b), revised par. (2). Prior to amendment, par. (2) read as follows:

 "**(2)** The term 'senior executive', with respect to a contractor, means—

 "**(A)** the chief executive officer of the contractor or any individual acting in a similar capacity for the contractor;

 "**(B)** the four most highly compensated employees in management positions of the contractor other than the chief executive officer; and

 "**(C)** in the case of a contractor that has components which report directly

to the contractor's headquarters, the five most highly compensated individuals in management positions at each such component."

 1997 Amendments. Subsec. (e)(1)(P). Pub.L. 105–85, § 808(b)(1), added subpar. (P).

 Subsec. (m). Pub.L. 105–85, § 808(b)(2), added subsec. (m).

 1994 Amendments. Subsecs. (a) to (j). Pub.L. 103–355, § 2151, added subsecs. (a) to (j). Former subsecs. (a) to (f), reenacted, with conforming changes, as subsecs. (k)(1) to (6) and (*l*)(1) of this section.

 Subsec. (k). Pub.L. 103–355, § 2151, added subsec. (k), reenacting former subsecs. (a) to (f), with conforming changes.

 Subsec. (*l*). Pub.L. 103–355, § 2151, added par. (1), incorporating in part former subsec. (f)(1), defining the term "covered contract" as a contract for an amount more than $100,000 entered into by an executive agency other than a fixed-price contract without cost incentives, and added par. (2).

Prior Provisions
 A prior section 256, Act June 30, 1949, c. 288, Title III, § 306, 63 Stat. 396, which related to waiver of liquidated damages, and is now covered by section 256a of this title, was repealed by Act

Sept. 5, 1950, c. 849, § 10(b), 64 Stat. 591.

Effective and Applicability Provisions

1998 Acts. Amendment by section 804 of Pub.L. 105–261 to apply with respect to costs of compensation of senior executives incurred after Jan. 1, 1999, under covered contracts (as defined in section 2324(*l*) of Title 10 and section 256(*l*) of this title) entered into before, on, or after Oct. 17, 1998, see section 804(d) of Pub.L. 105–261, set out as a note under section 2324 of Title 10.

1997 Acts. Amendment by section 808 of Pub.L. 105–85 to take effect on the date that is 90 days after Nov. 18, 1997, and apply with respect to costs of compensation incurred after Jan. 1, 1998, under covered contracts entered into before, on, or after Nov. 18, 1997, see section 808(e) of Pub.L. 105–85, set out as a note under section 435 of Title 41, Public Contracts.

1994 Acts. Amendment by Pub.L. 103–355 effective Oct. 13, 1994, except as otherwise provided, see section 10001 of Pub.L. 103–355, set out as a note under section 251 of this title.

1988 Acts. Section effective with respect to contracts awarded after Nov. 19, 1988, see section 8(e) of Pub.L. 100–700, set out as a note under section 2324 of Title 10, Armed Forces.

Implementing Regulations

Implementing regulations for subsec. (e) of this section to be prescribed not later than 120 days after Nov. 19, 1988, and applicable to contracts entered into more than 30 days after date on which such regulations are issued, see section 8(d) of Pub.L. 100–700, set out as a note under section 2324 of Title 10, Armed Forces.

Revision of Cost Principle Relating to Entertainment, Gift, and Recreation Costs for Contractor Employees

Section 2192 of Pub.L. 103–355 provided that:

"**(a) Costs not allowable.—(1)** The costs of gifts or recreation for employees of a contractor or members of their families that are provided by the contractor to improve employee morale or performance or for any other purpose are not allowable under a covered contract unless, within 120 days after the date of the enactment of this Act [Oct. 13, 1994], the Federal Acquisition Regulatory Council prescribes amendments to the Federal Acquisition Regulation specifying circumstances under which such costs are allowable under a covered contract.

"**(2)** Not later than 90 days after the date of the enactment of this Act [Oct. 13, 1994], the Federal Acquisition Regulatory Council shall amend the cost principle in the Federal Acquisition Regulation that is set out in section 31.205–14 of title 48, Code of Federal Regulations, relating to unallowability of entertainment costs—

"**(A)** by inserting in the cost principle a statement that costs made specifically unallowable under that cost principle are not allowable under any other cost principle; and

"**(B)** by striking out '(but see 31.205–1 and 31.205–13)'.

"**(b) Definitions.**—In this section:

"**(1)** The term 'employee' includes officers and directors of a contractor.

"**(2)** The term 'covered contract' has the meaning given such term in section 2324(1) of title 10, United States Code (as amended by section 2101(c) ([section 2324(*l*) of Title 10, Armed Forces], and section 306(1) of the Federal Property and Administrative Services Act of 1949 (as added by section 2151) [subsec. (*l*) of this section].

"**(c) Effective date.**—Any amendments to the Federal Acquisition Regulation made pursuant to subsection (a) shall apply with respect to costs incurred after the date on which the amendments made by section 2101 apply (as provided in section 10001 [Oct. 1, 1995, or earlier, see section 10001 of Pub.L. 103–355, set out as a note under section 251 of this title]) or the date on which the amendments made by section 2151 apply (as provided in section 10001 [Oct. 1, 1995, or earlier, see section 10001 of Pub.L. 103–355, set out as a note under section 251 of this title]), whichever is later."

LIBRARY REFERENCES

American Digest System
United States ☞70(18), 70(21).
Key Number System Topic No. 393.

Research References

Treatises and Practice Aids
West's Federal Administrative Practice § 616, False Claims Act--Qui Tam Actions.

WESTLAW ELECTRONIC RESEARCH

See Westlaw guide following the Explanation pages of this volume.

§ 256a. Waiver of liquidated damages

Whenever any contract made on behalf of the Government by the head of any Federal Agency, or by officers authorized by him so to do, includes a provision for liquidated damages for delay, the Secretary of the Treasury upon recommendation of such head is authorized and empowered to remit the whole or any part of such damages as in his discretion may be just and equitable.

(Sept. 5, 1950, c. 849, § 10(a), 64 Stat. 591; Oct. 19, 1996, Pub.L. 104–316, Title II, § 202(u), 110 Stat. 3845.)

HISTORICAL AND STATUTORY NOTES

Revision Notes and Legislative Reports
1950 Acts. Senate Report No. 2140, see 1950 U.S.Code Cong.Service, p. 3547.

Codifications
Section was not enacted as part of Title III of Act June 30, 1949, c. 288, 63 Stat. 393, which comprises this subchapter.

Amendments
1996 Amendments. Pub.L. 104–316, § 202(u), substituted "Secretary of the Treasury" for "Comptroller General".

Transfer of Functions
Effective June 30, 1996, the functions of the Comptroller General under this section to be transferred to the Director of the Office of Management and Budget, contingent upon the additional transfer to the Office of Management and Budget of such personnel, budget authority, records, and property of the General Accounting Office relating to such functions as the Comptroller General and the Director jointly determine to be necessary, see section 211 of Pub.L. 104–53, set out as a note under section 501 of Title 31, Money and Finance.

CROSS REFERENCES

Armed services contracts, remission of liquidated damages, see 10 USCA § 2312.

LIBRARY REFERENCES

American Digest System
United States ⟐73(21), 73(26), 74(14).
Key Number System Topic No. 393.

Research References

Treatises and Practice Aids
Federal Procedure, Lawyers Edition § 39:775, Request for Remission.
West's Federal Administrative Practice § 526, Remission of Liquidated Damages.

WESTLAW ELECTRONIC RESEARCH

See Westlaw guide following the Explanation pages of this volume.

Notes of Decisions

---

1. Generally

Under former section 269 of Title 40 [now covered by this section] a provision of a Government contract for liquidated damages for each day's delay in completion of the work was not against public policy. Robinson v. U.S., U.S.1923, 43 S.Ct. 420, 261 U.S. 486, 67 L.Ed. 760. Damages ⟲ 76; United States ⟲ 66

The Government can take from a contractor an enforceable agreement to perform his contract within a specified period or receive compensation ratably diminished according to a reasonable scale for late performance, even if no actual damages are or can be proved. Lebanon Woolen Mills v. U.S., Ct.Cl. 1943, 99 Ct.Cl. 318. Contracts ⟲ 244; United States ⟲ 72(1.1)

It is well settled that the parties to a contract may stipulate for and agree in the contract upon liquidated damages in

case of delay in the performance of the contract work. Morris v. U.S., Ct.Cl. 1915, 50 Ct.Cl. 154. Damages ⟲ 74

2. Law governing

In seller's action in federal court against United States, on contract made in District of Columbia for sale of pumps, clause providing for liquidated damages was enforceable under federal principles irrespective of Erie R. Co. v. Tompkins and irrespective of actual damages, notwithstanding law of California, where contract was to be performed, whereby such clauses would not be conclusive. Byron Jackson Co. v. U.S., S.D.Cal.1940, 35 F.Supp. 665. Federal Courts ⟲ 413

3. Contracts within section

In the absence of any indication that the authority for remission of liquidated damages in this section is limited to procurement contracts, it may be regarded as applicable to all types of contracts, including sales contracts. 1960, 40 Comp.Gen. 143.

4. Penalty, payments considered as

Provision of contract for erecting for $1,200,000 two laboratory buildings for Department of Agriculture, that if buildings are not completed in 30 months Government shall be entitled to $200 as liquidated damages, "computed, estimated, and agreed on" for each day's delay, is not to be considered as one for penalty, because making no distinction whether delay be in completion of one or both buildings. Wise v. U.S., U.S.1919, 39 S.Ct. 303, 249 U.S. 361, 63 L.Ed. 647. Damages ⟲ 78(4)

Liquidated damages clause in government contract for calibration, preventive maintenance and repair of test, measuring, and diagnostic equipment at government sites located in foreign country was not invalid as penalty where damages calculation represented reasonable estimation, as of contract date, of any actual damages that might result to government if contractor failed to provide specified performance level. International Electronics Corp. v. U.S., Ct.Cl.1981, 646 F.2d 496, 227 Ct.Cl. 208. Damages ⟲ 80(1)

Liquidated damages clause in $312,712.40 government road construction contract, which authorized a charge of $100 for each day of delay, was not unenforceable as a penalty, where amount stipulated was reasonable for this agreement at time it was made. Young Associates, Inc. v. U.S., Ct.Cl.1973, 471 F.2d 618, 200 Ct.Cl. 438. Damages ☞ 80(2)

Under contract for road construction containing provision for liquidated damages of $100 per day for each day of unjustified delay beyond completion date, liquidated damages of $9,300 were not improperly assessed, as against contention that they amounted to a penalty because of their size in proportion to the total contract price, which as reduced by Government's change order amounted to $47,882.52. Dineen v. U.S., Ct.Cl.1947, 71 F.Supp. 742, 109 Ct.Cl. 18, certiorari denied 68 S.Ct. 658, 333 U.S. 842, 92 L.Ed. 1125, rehearing denied 68 S.Ct. 1070, 334 U.S. 816, 92 L.Ed. 1746. Damages ☞ 80(2)

Provision in a contract that the proper officer may waive the damages, and that where none have resulted from the delay none will be exacted, indicates that penalty was really intended by the parties. Pacific Hardware & Steel Co. v. U.S., Ct.Cl.1913, 48 Ct.Cl. 399. Damages ☞ 78(4)

A deduction for delay was liquidated damages and not penalty. Crane Co. v. U.S., Ct.Cl.1911, 46 Ct.Cl. 343.

A per diem forfeiture was according to intention of the parties, ascertained from a view of a contract, a penalty, the object of which was to secure the Government against actual loss or damage arising from delay in the completion of the work, the use of the words "liquidated damages" not being, in itself, conclusive of such intention. 1877, 15 Op.Atty.Gen. 418.

5. Absence of provision

Where there is no liquidated-damage clause in a contract and no provision for a penalty, except a provision authorizing the Government to take the contract away from the contractor in case of default, under which no action was taken, the only claim for damages on account of delay is that provided by the common law. Camden Iron Works v. U.S., Ct.Cl. 1915, 50 Ct.Cl. 191. Damages ☞ 122

6. Errors or omissions in clause

Where it was clear what was intended by parties, Government and contractor,

in entering into contract, erroneous reference in liquidated damages clause to armed services procurement regulation did not invalidate the clause. Simmonds Precision Products, Inc. v. U.S., Ct.Cl. 1976, 546 F.2d 886, 212 Ct.Cl. 305. United States ☞ 74(12.1)

7. Breach of contract by government

Failure to make particular progress payments to surety completing contract for construction of auditorium for United States did not constitute a breach of contract which would prevent assessment of liquidated damages for delay in completion of contract, in view of complications arising from death of contractor and fact that delay in payments did not handicap progress of work. U.S. Cas. Co. v. U.S., Ct.Cl.1946, 67 F.Supp. 950, 107 Ct.Cl. 46. Damages ☞ 85

A contractor was not entitled to compensation for disproportionate time devoted by its executives in attempting to resume construction of post office delayed by Government's unjustified stop order, where amount of such excess time was not proved with measurable definiteness. Brand Inv. Co. v. U.S., Ct.Cl.1944, 58 F.Supp. 749, 102 Ct.Cl. 40, certiorari denied 65 S.Ct. 684, 324 U.S. 850, 89 L.Ed. 1410. Postal Service ☞ 6; United States ☞ 73(20)

8. Termination of contract

Under contract providing that "if the government does not terminate the right of contractor to proceed" the contractor should continue and pay as liquidated damages a fixed amount for each day's delay, the right to liquidated damages is conditioned upon the Government not terminating contractor's right to proceed, and where there is such termination, even though it be subsequent to the stipulated completion date, the right to liquidated damages disappears. The Anaconda v. American Sugar Refining Co., U.S.Fla.1944, 64 S.Ct. 863, 322 U.S. 42, 88 L.Ed. 1117.

Under terms of Government contract, which provided for liquidated damages in case contractor failed or refused to deliver, accruing until Government might reasonably procure similar material elsewhere, liquidated damages could be charged on terminated portion of contract. Wyoming Nat. Bank of Wilkes-Barre, Pa. v. U.S., Ct.Cl.1961, 292 F.2d 511, 154 Ct.Cl. 590. Damages ☞ 85

Where the Government, before the time was up, terminated the contractor's right to proceed and engaged another party to complete the contract, the Government was not entitled to collect from surety completing the contract liquidated damages for the delay, and plaintiff is entitled to recover an amount so withheld. Fireman's Fund Indemnity Co. v. U.S., Ct.Cl. 1941, 93 Ct.Cl. 138. Contracts ⟨⟩ 303(4); United States ⟨⟩ 75

9. Delay in performance—Generally

Where contract to furnish dried eggs to Federal Surplus Commodity Corporation provided that May 18, 1942, should be first day of a 10-day period within which Corporation would accept delivery, particular day being at Corporation's option, and that failure to have specified quantities of dried egg products inspected and ready for delivery by date specified in offer would be cause for payment of liquidated damages, but inspection was not completed and certificates issued until May 22 and Corporation gave first notice for shipment of eggs on May 26, the Government was not entitled to liquidated damages. Priebe & Sons v. U.S., U.S. 1947, 68 S.Ct. 123, 332 U.S. 407, 92 L.Ed. 32. Damages ⟨⟩ 85

Where the original "Invitation, Bid and Acceptance," signed by representatives of contractor and the United States, contained no specific reference to a date for completion of work to be performed or a date for expiration of contract, unsigned copies thereof furnished to contractor and containing typewritten notation that contract was to expire on a certain date could not be regarded as a part of the contract. Northwestern Engineering Co. v. U. S., C.C.A.8 (S.D.) 1946, 154 F.2d 793. United States ⟨⟩ 70(4)

Provision for liquidated damages for delay in completion of contract for construction of a post office building will be enforced if the intention of the parties is clear. Consolidated Engineering Co. v. U.S., W.D.Wash.1940, 35 F.Supp. 980, appeal dismissed 123 F.2d 1015. Damages ⟨⟩ 85

Where work not provided for in the contract was ordered by the Government engineer after the date fixed for the completion of the contract, the Government had no right to deduct liquidated damages for delay covering the period between the date fixed for completion and the date when the work was actually

completed. Snare & Triest Co. v. U.S., Ct.Cl.1920, 55 Ct.Cl. 386. Damages ⟨⟩ 78(4)

10. —— Party causing delay, delay in performance

Under Government contract providing that the contractor should be allowed one day additional for each day of delay caused by the Government, that no claim for damages should be made for delay so caused, and that the contractor should pay $420 for each day's delay not caused by the Government, the fact that part of the delay was caused by the Government did not relieve the contractor of liability for the stipulated damages for the part of the delay not so caused. Robinson v. U.S., U.S.1923, 43 S.Ct. 420, 261 U.S. 486, 67 L.Ed. 760. United States ⟨⟩ 73(26)

Delay in completion of post office building, as result of arbitrary refusal to surrender building to Government until complete clearance had been given as to certain details which were being questioned, justified imposition of liquidated damages under provision therefor in contract, in absence of evidence that any delays were caused by demands on part of Government without right, or of evidence that controversies allegedly causing delay resulted in complete stoppage of work. Consolidated Engineering Co. v. U.S., W.D.Wash.1940, 35 F.Supp. 980, appeal dismissed 123 F.2d 1015. Damages ⟨⟩ 85

Apportionment of liquidated damages assessed against government construction contractor was proper with respect to period of 22 days of sequential delay attributable to contracting agency. Sunshine Const. & Engineering, Inc. v. U.S., 2005, 64 Fed.Cl. 346. United States ⟨⟩ 75(5)

Government was not entitled to liquidated damages from contractor for delay in substantial completion of Phases II and III of naval training center renovation project, where both contractor and Navy were responsible for critical path delays, and such delays could not be apportioned. George Sollitt Const. Co. v. U.S., 2005, 64 Fed.Cl. 229. United States ⟨⟩ 73(26)

Where delays have been caused by both parties to a contract, and the period for completing the work has been thereby extended beyond the time fixed for the completion of the contract, the obligation to pay liquidated damages is annulled and cannot be revived, and any recovery for delays must be based on the actual loss sustained. New York Continental Jewell Filtration Co. v. U.S., Ct.Cl.1920, 55 Ct.Cl. 288. Damages ⊂⇛ 78(4)

Where the contractor's delay in completing the work was caused by the other party to the contract, he cannot be charged with liquidated damages during the period of delay so occasioned. Morris v. U.S., Ct.Cl.1915, 50 Ct.Cl. 154. United States ⊂⇛ 75

11. —— Extensions, delay in performance

Government contractor was not entitled to be relieved from payment of liquidated damages for delay despite requested extension, unsupported by any reasons, on ground that contractor had lost "several months of our best working time" on account of delay in commencement of the work. Broome Const., Inc. v. U.S., Ct.Cl.1974, 492 F.2d 829, 203 Ct.Cl. 521. Damages ⊂⇛ 85

Where contractor entered into unit price contract with Government, during work various stop orders were issued by Government but none of the stop orders was actually released until contractor had resumed work in substantially normal manner and extension of one week was granted when contractor objected to release of a stop order, contractor was not entitled to remission of liquidated damages, assessed for inexcusable delay in completing work, because he was allegedly not given credit for time spent in getting ready to assume work after stop orders were lifted. Palumbo v. U.S., Ct. Cl.1953, 113 F.Supp. 450, 125 Ct.Cl. 678. United States ⊂⇛ 73(26)

Where a contract provides for liquidated damages in the event of delay in the completion of the contract, and any extension of the contract is left to the decision of a designated tribunal, whose action is made conclusive upon the parties, the courts have no jurisdiction to review its decision. Warren, Moore & Co. v. U.S., Ct.Cl.1922, 57 Ct.Cl. 576. Contracts ⊂⇛ 284(4)

12. —— Excusal of delay, delay in performance

Proof that plaintiffs' delay in completing their contract for construction of temporary barracks was caused by diffi-

culties which their subcontractor had in obtaining heating equipment and sheet metal workers necessary to install it did not establish that delay was excusable within meaning of the contract, so as to preclude Government from deducting liquidated damages for late completion of the contract. Walsh Bros. v. U.S., Ct.Cl. 1947, 69 F.Supp. 125, 107 Ct.Cl. 627. Contracts ⊂⇛ 300(1); United States ⊂⇛ 73(26)

13. Measure of liquidated damages—Generally

Former section 269 of Title 40 [now covered by this section] did not purport to require liquidated damages to be paid in amounts or under circumstances beyond those stipulated by the parties. U.S. v. American Surety Co., U.S.Mont.1944, 64 S.Ct. 866, 322 U.S. 96, 88 L.Ed. 1158. Damages ⊂⇛ 85

Amount of liquidated damages which prime contract required be paid to government did not govern amount of damages which prime contractor was entitled to recover from subcontractor for the latter's failure to timely perform its obligations in absence of provision in subcontract adopting such amount as measure of damages. U.S. for Use and Benefit of Federal Roofing & Painting, Inc. v. Foster Const. (Panama) S.A., C.A.5 (Canal Zone) 1972, 456 F.2d 250. Damages ⊂⇛ 85

In case of penalty, measure of damages is ordinarily the actual loss; but in the case of liquidated damages the whole amount is recoverable, if consistent with the policy of the law. Illinois Surety Co. v. U.S., C.C.A.2 (N.Y.) 1916, 229 F. 527, 143 C.C.A. 595. See, also, Illinois Surety Co. v. U.S., N.Y.1916, 229 F. 533, 143 C.C.A. 601. Damages ⊂⇛ 85

14. —— Excess cost to government, measure of liquidated damages

The fact that contract price of garments to be delivered to United States for troops was $53,000 and that agreed liquidated damages for delay in delivery or failure to deliver amounted to about $20,000, and that only excess cost to which Government was put in procuring on open market the garments not furnished by contractor was $3.56, could not be considered on contention that liquidated damages were excessive. In re Lion Overall Co., S.D.N.Y.1943, 55

F.Supp. 789, affirmed 144 F.2d 75. Damages ☞ 80(3)

15. —— Items compensable, measure of liquidated damages

Provision of a building contract, that, in case of failure to complete in specified time, contractor shall pay in addition to $100 a day as liquidated damages, all expenses for inspection and superintendence, was valid. J.E. Hathaway & Co. v. U.S., U.S.1919, 39 S.Ct. 346, 249 U.S. 460, 63 L.Ed. 707. Damages ☞ 85

Where plaintiff contracted to deliver specified number of trousers to United States, and delivery schedule was expressed in percentages of total number every 30 days, and contract provided for assessment of liquidated damages at specified percentage of contract price for each day's delay in delivery of each item, and when there was delay United States terminated plaintiff's right to deliver a specified number of trousers pursuant to contract provision so authorizing, and contract contained no provision that delivery schedule would be recomputed in accordance with percentages set forth in delivery schedule on basis of reduced quantity if portion of contract quantity was terminated, in computing liquidated damages percentages were properly applied to total of number of trousers contracted for and were properly not based upon reduced contract quantity. MacLaren Sportswear Co. v. U.S., Ct.Cl.1952, 101 F.Supp. 885, 121 Ct.Cl. 396. Damages ☞ 85

Where contract of partnership to manufacture canvas leggings for Government provided that in case of delay in delivery, Government had right to terminate contract with respect to all or any portion of undelivered leggings and purchase similar leggings in the open market and charge partnership with any excess costs and liquidated damages, and when there was a delay in delivery of leggings Government cancelled contract and purchased no more leggings from partnership or any other contractor, Government was not entitled to liquidated damages with respect to undelivered leggings. Manart Textile Co. v. U.S., Ct.Cl.1948, 77 F.Supp. 924, 111 Ct.Cl. 540. Damages ☞ 76

Where a contract clearly provided for liquidated damages and had another clause which would apparently authorize a further deduction of the cost of inspec-

tion, and the Government deducted both sums from the amount due the contractor, in view of the action on the parties, the liquidated damage as fixed by the contract was the measure of the damages and the contractor could recover the amount withheld by the Government as the cost of inspection. Sorensen v. U.S., Ct.Cl.1916, 51 Ct.Cl. 69. Damages ☞ 85

16. —— Per diem rates, measure of liquidated damages

In a provision for liquidated damages in which the aggregate of damages is to be determined with a per diem rate as the basis of computation, a definite date from which the liquidated damage clause is to operate must be determined from the contract, and the court cannot assume or otherwise fix a date from which the liquidated clause is to operate. Camden Iron Works v. U.S., Ct.Cl.1915, 51 Ct.Cl. 9. Damages ☞ 85

17. Actual damages

Liquidated damage clause of supply contracts executed under Department of Agriculture commodity support and domestic food consumption program could not be deemed unenforceable on ground that actual damages were easily ascertainable in that Department could have obtained substitute performance where damages could consist of more than just higher market price difference and could include administrative expenses which would be difficult to measure with precision. Jennie-O Foods, Inc. v. U.S., Ct.Cl. 1978, 580 F.2d 400, 217 Ct.Cl. 314. Damages ☞ 79(5)

Fact that Government was not in position to invoke stipulation in construction contract for liquidated damages for delay did not strip Government of its right to recover such actual damages for the delay as it might be able to prove. American Surety Co. v. U.S., C.C.A.9 (Mont.) 1943, 136 F.2d 437, certiorari granted 64 S.Ct. 190, 320 U.S. 729, 88 L.Ed. 430, affirmed 64 S.Ct. 866, 322 U.S. 96, 88 L.Ed. 1158. United States ☞ 75(2)

18. Reduction

Liquidated damages were not subject to being reduced because government caused much of delay, notwithstanding that Armed Services Board of Contract Appeals and Comptroller General reduced original amount of liquidated damages assessed against contractor, where reduced damages represented amount as-

sessed for period of time line was discon-
nected by reprocurement contractor. Olson Plumbing & Heating Co. v. U.S., Ct.
Cl.1979, 602 F.2d 950, 221 Ct.Cl. 197.
United States ⊕ 74(4)

19. Notice of delay

Damages by delay are not recoverable
from the United States by a contractor
for public work failing to notify Secretary
of the Interior when delay occurred, as
required by the contract. Plumley v.
U.S., U.S.1913, 33 S.Ct. 139, 226 U.S.
545, 57 L.Ed. 342. United States ⊕
73(20)

Where contractor, at time bid was
made for paving work on existing airport,
had knowledge of the conditions under
which the work would have to be performed, contractor must be deemed to
have entered into contract with notice of
the possibility of delay as a result of those
conditions. Northwestern Engineering
Co. v. U.S., C.C.A.8 (S.D.) 1946, 154 F.2d
793. United States ⊕ 73(20)

The provision in a construction contract entered into by the United States,
requiring contractor within ten days from
beginning of any delay to notify contracting officer in writing of causes of delay,
was a "condition precedent" required to
be complied with, and hence contractor's
receiver could not recover from the United States damages allegedly caused by
failure of the United States to supply on
time preliminary information called for
under contract where contractor did not
give required written notice of delay but
did give oral notice shortly after contract
was awarded. U.S. v. Cunningham, App.
D.C.1941, 125 F.2d 28, 75 U.S.App.D.C.
95. United States ⊕ 73(26)

20. Election of remedy

Where construction contract provided
that if Government did not terminate contractor's right to proceed with contract,
contractor should pay certain amount as
liquidated damages for each calendar day
of delay until work was completed, provision could not be construed as entitling
Government to "liquidated damages"
where Government elected to allow contractor to continue after date specified for
completion, but contractor failed to finish
work even at later date, and Government
then elected to terminate contractor's
right to proceed with contract. American Surety Co. v. U.S., C.C.A.9 (Mont.)
1943, 136 F.2d 437, certiorari granted 64

S.Ct. 190, 320 U.S. 729, 88 L.Ed. 430,
affirmed 64 S.Ct. 866, 322 U.S. 96, 88
L.Ed. 1158. Damages ⊕ 85

Under construction contract requiring
contractor to prosecute work to completion within specified time and giving the
United States, upon failure to do so, the
right to take over work and complete it
and hold contractor for any excess cost or
to permit contractor to continue work
subject to right to retain out of contract
price liquidated damages for each calendar day of delay until completion, those
rights of the United States were alternative, and the United States, having chosen
to take over and complete work and collect excess costs, could not also claim the
other alternative of liquidated damages.
U.S. v. Cunningham, App.D.C.1941, 125
F.2d 28, 75 U.S.App.D.C. 95. Damages
⊕ 85

Where the Government, in accordance
with the terms of a construction contract,
because of delay and default on the part
of the contractor terminated said contract
after the time provided for the completion thereof, and took over and completed
the work, the Government may not collect both liquidated damages for the period that elapsed after the time provided
for completion and before the Government exercised its option to terminate
said contract and the excess costs which
were incurred by the Government in
completing the work. Maryland Casualty
Co. v. U.S., Ct.Cl.1941, 93 Ct.Cl. 247.
Contracts ⊕ 234; Contracts ⊕ 303(4);
United States ⊕ 70(35); United States
⊕ 75

21. Waiver

Purported waivers of damages for delays, in government contract modifications, were ineffective for lack of consideration where waiver clauses were
inserted gratuitously and price adjustments in modifications covered only
cost of actual changes. Paccon, Inc. v.
U.S., Ct.Cl.1968, 399 F.2d 162, 185 Ct.
Cl. 24. United States ⊕ 73(3)

In statutory action by contractor's receiver to recover from the United States
damages allegedly caused by the Government's failure to supply on time preliminary information called for under construction contract, the Government did
not "waive" defense of contractor's failure to give written notice of delay in
supplying information as required by
contract by failure to plead that failure,

where entire correspondence between the parties was without objection received in evidence, counsel for receiver admitted that no written notice had been given counsel, for the Government then moved for a directed finding with respect to issue of damages for delay, and the question was fully argued. U.S. v. Cunningham, App.D.C.1941, 125 F.2d 28, 75 U.S.App.D.C. 95. United States ⇨ 74(8)

The Government may not escape responsibility by merely waiving the right to collect liquidated damages, regardless of additional costs to the contractor by delay caused by the Government. Rogers v. U.S., Ct.Cl.1943, 99 Ct.Cl. 393. Navigable Waters ⇨ 22(2)

The defendant having unreasonably delayed plaintiff, the liquidated damage clauses of the contracts in suit were waived. Hirsch v. U.S., Ct.Cl.1941, 94 Ct.Cl. 602. Contracts ⇨ 300(3); United States ⇨ 73(20)

The Government, having exercised its right to terminate a construction contract and to proceed with its completion, thereby waived its claim to liquidated damages. Maryland Casualty Co. v. U.S., Ct. Cl.1941, 93 Ct.Cl. 247. Contracts ⇨ 303(4); United States ⇨ 75

Where the Secretary of the Treasury, acting according to the contract and former section 269 of Title 40 [now covered by this section], waived liquidated damages, and charged the contractor on final settlement with the cost of maintaining the Government's forces during the delay, it was too late for contractor to question such settlement after its acceptance without protests. McIntyre v. U.S., Ct.Cl. 1917, 52 Ct.Cl. 503. United States ⇨ 118

While it was not expected or believed by any of the parties to a contract that it could be performed within the time prescribed by its terms, the same was given life from its date with all of its conditions and obligations, including the payment of liquidated damages for the nonperformance within the time limit, and no waiver of the liquidated damage clause was thereby contemplated. Stannard v. U.S., Ct.Cl.1916, 51 Ct.Cl. 251. Damages ⇨ 85

Where work has been completed, and no damage has been sustained by the delay, the conditions necessary to warrant the exaction of a penalty do not exist, and the Department is accordingly at liberty to relieve the contractor therefrom. 1877, 15 Op.Atty.Gen. 418. See, also, 1894, 21 Op.Atty.Gen. 27.

§ 257. Administrative determinations

(a) Conclusiveness; delegation of powers

Determinations and decisions provided in this Act to be made by the Administrator or other agency head shall be final. Such determinations or decisions may be made with respect to individual purchases or contracts or, except for determinations or decisions under sections 253, 253a, and 253b of this title, with respect to classes of purchases or contracts. Except as provided in section 253(d)(2) of this title, and except as provided in section 121(d)(1) and (2) of Title 40 with respect to the Administrator, the agency head is authorized to delegate his powers provided by this Act, including the making of such determinations and decisions, in his discretion and subject to his direction, to any other officer or officers or officials of the agency.

(b) Basis of determinations; finding conclusive; preservation of findings; copy

Each determination or decision required by section 254 or by section 255(d) of this title shall be based upon written findings made by the official making such determination, which findings shall be final and shall be available within the agency for a period of at least six years following the date of the determination.

(June 30, 1949, c. 288, Title III, § 307, 63 Stat. 396; Aug. 28, 1958, Pub.L. 85–800, § 5, 72 Stat. 967; Nov. 8, 1965, Pub.L. 89–343, §§ 3, 4, 79 Stat. 1303; July 18, 1984, Pub.L. 98–369, Div. B, Title VII, § 2714(a)(4), 98 Stat. 1184; Feb. 10, 1996, Pub.L. 104–106, Div. D, Title XLIII, § 4321(e)(6), 110 Stat. 675; Oct. 19, 1996, Pub.L. 104–316, Title I, § 121(c), 110 Stat. 3836.)

HISTORICAL AND STATUTORY NOTES

Revision Notes and Legislative Reports
1958 Acts. Senate Report No. 2201, see 1958 U.S. Code Cong. and Adm. News, p. 4021.

1965 Acts. House Report No. 1166, see 1965 U.S. Code Cong. and Adm. News, p. 4217.

1984 Acts. House Report No. 98–432(Part II), Senate Report Nos. 98–50 and 98–297, and House Conference Report No. 98–861, see 1984 U.S. Code Cong. and Adm. News, p. 697.

1996 Acts. House Conference Report No. 104–450, see 1996 U.S. Code Cong. and Adm. News, p. 238.

References in Text
This Act, referred to in subsec. (a), means the Federal Property and Administrative Services Act of 1949, the short title for Act June 30, 1949, c. 288, 63 Stat. 377, as amended, which is currently classified to subchapter IV of chapter 4 of Title 41, 41 U.S.C.A. § 251 et seq., and was formerly classified to chapter 10 of former Title 40, 40 U.S.C.A. § 471 et seq., prior to being repealed by Pub.L. 107–217, § 6(b), Aug. 21, 2002, 116 Stat. 1313; see now generally chapter 1 of Title 40, 40 U.S.C.A. § 101 et seq. Included in the repeal was § 1(a) of the Act, which contained the short title provision.

Codifications
In subsec. (a), "section 121(d)(1) and (2) of Title 40" substituted for "section 486(d) of Title 40", which originally read "section 205(d)", meaning section 205(d) of the Federal Property and Administrative Services Act of 1949, on authority of Pub.L. 107–217, § 5(c), Aug. 21, 2002, 116 Stat. 1301, which is set out as a note preceding 40 U.S.C.A. § 101. Pub.L. 107–217, § 1, enacted Title 40 into positive law. Section 205(d) of the Federal Property and Administrative Services Act of 1949 was classified to section 486(d) of Title 40 prior to being repealed by Pub.L.

107–217, § 6(b), Aug. 21, 2002, 116 Stat. 1313, and its substance reenacted as 40 U.S.C.A. § 121(d)(1), (2). See also References in Text note below.

Amendments
1996 Amendments. Subsec. (b). Pub.L. 104–316, § 121(c), struck out provisions requiring copies of findings to be submitted with the contract to the General Accounting Office.

Subsec. (b). Pub.L. 104–106, § 4321(e)(6), substituted "section 255(d)" for "section 255(c)".

1984 Amendments. Subsec. (a). Pub.L. 98–369, § 2714(a)(4), substituted provision that determinations and decisions provided in this Act to be made by the Administrator or other agency head shall be final for provision that such determinations and decisions provided in this subchapter to be made by such official would be final, and added exception for determinations or decisions under sections 253, 253a, and 253b of this title, substituted "Except as provided in section 253(d)(2) of this title" for "Except as provided in subsection (b) of this section", and directed the substitution of "this Act" for "this chapter" after "powers provided by", which substitution was not capable of literal execution because the original text read "this title". Consequently, the amendment was executed by substituting "this Act" for "this title" as the probable intent of Congress.

Subsec. (b). Pub.L. 98–369, § 2714(a)(4)(D)–(F), redesignated former subsec. (c) as (b) and, in subsec. (b) as so redesignated, struck out "by paragraphs (11), (12), (13), or (14) of section 252(c)," following "Each determination or decision by". Former subsec. (b), which related to nondelegable powers and powers delegable to certain persons, was struck out.

Subsec. (c). Pub.L. 98–369, § 2714(a)(4)(F), redesignated former subsec. (c) as (b).

Subsec. (d). Pub.L. 98–369, § 2714(a)(4)(G), struck out subsec. (d), which related to preservation of data relating to contracts negotiated pursuant to the former provisions of section 252(c) of this title.

1965 Amendments. Subsec. (a). Pub.L. 89–343, § 3, inserted "and except as provided in section 486(d) of Title 40 with respect to the Administrator".

Subsec. (b). Pub.L. 89–343, § 4, deleted provisions which made the power of the Administrator to make the delegations and determinations specified in section 252(a) of this title delegable only to the Deputy Administrator or to the chief official of any principal organizational unit of the General Services Administration.

1958 Amendments. Subsec. (b). Pub.L. 85–800, § 5(a), (b), substituted "(12)" for "(11)", "(13)" for "(12)", and "(11)" for "(10)" and eliminated "and in section 255(a) of this title" preceding "shall not be delegable" in first sentence.

Subsec. (c). Pub.L. 85–800, § 5(a), (c), substituted "(11), (12), (13), or (14)" for

"(10), (11), (12), or (13)", and "255(c)" for "255(a)".

Effective and Applicability Provisions
1996 Acts. Amendment by Pub.L. 104–316 effective Oct. 19, 1996, see section 101(e) of Pub.L. 104–316, set out as a note under section 130c of Title 2, The Congress.

Amendment by Pub.L. 104–106 effective Feb. 10, 1996, except as otherwise provided, see section 4401 of Pub.L. 104–106, set out as a note under section 251 of this title.

1984 Acts. Amendment by Pub.L. 98–369 applicable with respect to any solicitation for bids or proposals issued after Mar. 31, 1985, see section 2751(a) of Pub.L. 98–369, set out as a note under section 251 of this title.

1949 Acts. Act June 30, 1949, § 605, which set July 1, 1949, as the effective date for this section, was repealed by Pub.L. 107–217, § 6(b), Aug. 21, 2002, 116 Stat. 1313.

Definitions
The definitions in 40 U.S.C.A. § 102 apply to terms appearing in this subchapter.

CROSS REFERENCES

Determinations and decisions on armed services contracts, see 10 USCA § 2310.

LIBRARY REFERENCES

American Digest System
United States ☞73(14).
Key Number System Topic No. 393.

WESTLAW ELECTRONIC RESEARCH

See Westlaw guide following the Explanation pages of this volume.

§ 258. Repealed. Pub.L. 103–355, Title VII, § 7205, Oct. 13, 1994, 108 Stat. 3382

HISTORICAL AND STATUTORY NOTES

Section, Act June 30, 1949, c. 288, Title III, § 308, 63 Stat. 397; July 18, 1984, Pub.L. 98–369, Div. B, Title VII, § 2714(a)(5), 98 Stat. 1185, provided that no purchase or contract was to be exempt from sections 35 to 45 of this title or from sections 276a to 276a–6 of former Title 40 solely by reason of having been made or awarded after using procedures other

than sealed-bid procedures, and that such sections and sections 324 and 325a of former Title 40, if otherwise applicable, were to apply to such purchases and contracts.

Effective Date of Repeal
Repeal of section effective Oct. 13, 1994, and to apply on and after such

date, see section 10001 of Pub.L.
103–355, set out as a note under section
251 of this title.

§ 259. Definitions

As used in this subchapter—

(a) The term "agency head" shall mean the head or any assistant head of any executive agency, and may at the option of the Administrator include the chief official of any principal organizational unit of the General Services Administration.

(b) The term "competitive procedures" means procedures under which an executive agency enters into a contract pursuant to full and open competition. Such term also includes—

    (1) procurement of architectural or engineering services conducted in accordance with title XI of this Act;

    (2) the competitive selection of basic research proposals resulting from a general solicitation and the peer review or scientific review (as appropriate) of such proposals;

    (3) the procedures established by the Administrator for the multiple awards schedule program of the General Services Administration if—

        (A) participation in the program has been open to all responsible sources; and

        (B) orders and contracts under such procedures result in the lowest overall cost alternative to meet the needs of the Government;

    (4) procurements conducted in furtherance of section 644 of Title 15 as long as all responsible business concerns that are entitled to submit offers for such procurements are permitted to compete; and

    (5) a competitive selection of research proposals resulting from a general solicitation and peer review or scientific review (as appropriate) solicited pursuant to section 638 of Title 15.

(c) The following terms have the meanings provided such terms in section 403 of this title:

    (1) The term "procurement".

    (2) The term "procurement system".

    (3) The term "standards".

    (4) The term "full and open competition".

    (5) The term "responsible source".

    (6) The term "technical data".

(7) The term "major system".

(8) The term "item".

(9) The term "item of supply".

(10) The term "supplies".

(11) The term "commercial item".

(12) The term "nondevelopmental item".

(13) The term "commercial component".

(14) The term "component".

(d)(1) The term "simplified acquisition threshold" has the meaning provided that term in section 403 of this title, except that, in the case of any contract to be awarded and performed, or purchase to be made, outside the United States in support of a contingency operation or a humanitarian or peacekeeping operation, the term means an amount equal to two times the amount specified for that term in section 403 of this title.

(2) In paragraph (1):

(A) The term "contingency operation" has the meaning given such term in section 101(a) of Title 10.

(B) The term "humanitarian or peacekeeping operation" means a military operation in support of the provision of humanitarian or foreign disaster assistance or in support of a peacekeeping operation under chapter VI or VII of the Charter of the United Nations. The term does not include routine training, force rotation, or stationing.

(e) The term "Federal Acquisition Regulation" means the Federal Acquisition Regulation issued pursuant to section 421(c)(1) of this title.

(June 30, 1949, c. 288, Title III, § 309, 63 Stat. 397; July 12, 1952, c. 703, § 1(h), 66 Stat. 593; July 18, 1984, Pub.L. 98–369, Div. B, Title VII, § 2711(a)(3), 98 Stat. 1180; Oct. 30, 1984, Pub.L. 98–577, Title IV, § 504(a)(3), (4), 98 Stat. 3086; Oct. 13, 1994, Pub.L. 103–355, Title I, § 1551, 108 Stat. 3298; Sept. 23, 1996, Pub.L. 104–201, Div. A, Title VIII, § 807(b), 110 Stat. 2606; Nov. 18, 1997, Pub.L. 105–85, Div. A, Title X, § 1073(g)(1), 111 Stat. 1906.)

HISTORICAL AND STATUTORY NOTES

Revision Notes and Legislative Reports

1984 Acts. Senate Report No. 98–523, see 1984 U.S.Code Cong. and Adm.News, p. 5347.

House Report No. 98–432, Pt. II, Senate Report Nos. 98–50 and 98–297, and House Conference Report No. 98–861, see 1984 U.S.Code Cong. and Adm.News, p. 697.

1994 Acts. Senate Report Nos. 103–258 and 103–259, and House Conference Report No. 103–712, see 1994 U.S. Code Cong. and Adm. News, p. 2561.

1996 Acts. House Report No. 104–563 and House Conference Report No. 104–724, see 1996 U.S. Code Cong. and Adm. News, p. 2948.

1997 Acts. House Conference Report No. 105–340 and Statement by President, see 1997 U.S. Code Cong. and Adm. News, p. 2251.

References in Text
This Act, referred to in subsec. (b)(1), is the Federal Property and Administrative Services Act of 1949, Act June 30, 1949, c. 288, 63 Stat. 377, as amended. Title IX of this Act, which was classified generally to subchapter VI of chapter 10 of former Title 40 U.S.C.A. § 541 et seq., was reenacted by Pub.L. 107–217, §§ 1, 6(b), Aug. 21, 2002, 116 Stat. 1062, 1304, as chapter 11 of Title 40, 40 U.S.C.A. § 1101 et seq. For disposition of sections of former Title 40 to revised Title 40, see Table preceding 40 U.S.C.A. § 101. For complete classification, see Tables.

Codifications
In subsec. (b)(1), "chapter 11 of Title 40" substituted for "Title IX of this Act", on authority of Pub.L. 107–217, § 5(c), Aug. 21, 2002, 116 Stat. 1301, which is set out as a note preceding 40 U.S.C.A. § 101. Pub.L. 107–217, § 1, enacted Title 40 into positive law. Title IX of this Act means Title IX of the Federal Property and Administrative Services Act of 1949, known as the Brooks Architect–Engineers Act, Act June 30, 1949, c. 288, Title IX, §§ 901 to 904, as added Oct. 27, 1972, Pub.L. 92–582, 86 Stat. 1278, as amended, which was classified generally to subchapter VI of chapter 10 of former Title 40, 40 U.S.C.A. § 541 et seq., prior to being repealed by Pub.L. 107–217, § 6(b), Aug. 21, 2002, 116 Stat. 1319, and its substance reenacted as chapter 11 of Title 40, 40 U.S.C.A. § 1101 et seq.

Amendments
1997 Amendments. Subsec. (b)(2). Pub.L. 105–85, § 1073(g)(1), struck out "and" following "such proposals;".

1996 Amendments. Subsec. (d)(1). Pub.L. 104–201, § 807(b)(1), added "(1)" following "(d)".

Pub.L. 104–201, § 807(b)(2), added "or a humanitarian or peacekeeping operation" following "contingency operation".

Subsec. (d)(2). Pub.L. 104–201, § 807(b)(3), added par. (2).

1994 Amendments. Subsec. (c). Pub.L. 103–355, § 1551, enacted references to the terms set out in cls. (1) to (3)

and (11) to (14) and designated references to existing terms as cls. (4) to (10).

Subsecs. (d), (e). Pub.L. 103–355, § 1551, added subsecs. (d) and (e).

1984 Amendments. Subsec. (b). Pub.L. 98–577, § 504(a)(3), added pars. (4) and (5).

Pub.L. 98–369 added subsec. (b).

Subsec. (c). Pub.L. 98–577, § 504(a)(4), substituted ", 'responsible source', 'technical data', 'major system', 'item', 'item of supply', and 'supplies' have" for "and 'responsible source' have" before "the meaning".

Pub.L. 98–369 added subsec. (c).

1952 Amendments. Subsec. (b). Act July 12, 1952, repealed subsec. (b), which defined "supplies".

Effective and Applicability Provisions
1994 Acts. Amendment by section 1551 of Pub.L. 103–355 effective Oct. 13, 1994, except as otherwise provided, see section 10001 of Pub.L. 103–355, set out as a note under section 251 of this title.

1984 Acts. Amendment by Pub.L. 98–369 applicable with respect to any solicitation for bids or proposals issued after Mar. 31, 1985, see section 2751(a) of Pub.L. 98–369, set out as a note under section 251 of this title.

1949 Acts. Act June 30, 1949, § 605, which set July 1, 1949, as the effective date for this section, was repealed by Pub.L. 107–217, § 6(b), Aug. 21, 2002, 116 Stat. 1313.

Coordination with Other Amendments
Amendments by section 1073 of Pub.L. 105–85 to be treated as having been enacted immediately before the other provisions of Pub.L. 105–85, see section 1073(i) of Pub.L. 105–85, set out as a note under section 5315 of Title 5, Government Organization and Employees.

Definitions
The definitions in 40 U.S.C.A. § 102 apply to terms appearing in this subchapter.

Small Business Act
Amendment to this section by Pub.L. 98–369 not to affect or supersede the provisions of section 637(a) of Title 15, Commerce and Trade, see section 2711(c) of Pub.L. 98–369, set out as a note under section 253 of this title.

Research References

Treatises and Practice Aids
West's Federal Administrative Practice § 630, Contracting by Negotiation--Federal Supply Schedule.

WESTLAW ELECTRONIC RESEARCH

See Westlaw guide following the Explanation pages of this volume.

Notes of Decisions

Procurements 1

1. Procurements
Arrangement whereby private hospital agreed to pay one half of the cost of acquisition by Veterans Affairs Medical Center of a piece of medical equipment, with the equipment to be placed in the private hospital and used by both the VA and the hospital, was not a "procurement" for purposes of the Competition in Contracting Act (CICA). Rapides Regional Medical Center v. Secretary, Dept. of Veterans' Affairs, C.A.5 (La.) 1992, 974 F.2d 565, rehearing denied 979 F.2d 211, certiorari denied 113 S.Ct. 2413, 508 U.S. 939, 124 L.Ed.2d 636. United States ⊱ 64.10

§ 260. Laws not applicable to contracts

Sections 5, 8, and 13 of this title shall not apply to the procurement of property or services made by an executive agency pursuant to this subchapter. Any provision of law which authorizes an executive agency (other than an executive agency which is exempted from the provisions of this subchapter by section 252(a) of this title), to procure any property or services without advertising or without regard to said section 5 of this title shall be construed to authorize the procurement of such property or services pursuant to the provisions of this subchapter relating to procedures other than sealed-bid procedures.

(June 30, 1949, c. 288, Title III, § 310, 63 Stat. 397; July 12, 1952, c. 703, § 1(m), (n), 66 Stat. 594; Aug. 28, 1958, Pub.L. 85–800, § 6, 72 Stat. 967; Nov. 8, 1965, Pub.L. 89–343, § 5, 79 Stat. 1303; July 18, 1984, Pub.L. 98–369, Div. B, Title VII, § 2714(a)(6), 98 Stat. 1185.)

HISTORICAL AND STATUTORY NOTES

Revision Notes and Legislative Reports
1958 Acts. Senate Report No. 2201, see 1958 U.S.Code Cong. and Adm.News, p. 4021.

1965 Acts. House Report No. 1166, see 1965 U.S.Code Cong. and Adm.News, p. 4217.

1984 Acts. House Report No. 98–432, Pt. II, Senate Report Nos. 98–50 and 98–297, and House Conference Report No. 98–861, see 1984 U.S.Code Cong. and Adm.News, p. 697.

Amendments
1984 Amendments. Pub.L. 98–369, § 2714(a)(6), substituted "the provisions of this chapter relating to procedures other than sealed-bid procedures" for "section 252(c)(15) of this title without regard to the advertising requirements of sections 252(c) and 253 of this title".

1965 Amendments. Pub.L. 89–343 substituted provisions making sections 5, 8, and 13 of this title inapplicable to the procurement of property or services made by an executive agency pursuant to this subchapter, and requiring any provision of law which authorizes an executive agency (other than an executive agency which is exempted from the provisions of this subchapter by section 252(a) of this title) to procure any property or services without advertising or without regard to said section 5 of this title to be construed to authorize the procurement of such property or services pursuant to section 252(c)(15) of this title without regard to the advertising requirements of sections 252(c) and 253 of this title, for provisions which made sections 5, 6, 6a, and 13 of this title inapplicable to the procurement of property or services by the General Services Administration, or within the scope of authority delegated by the Administrator to any other executive agency, and which required reference in any Act to the applicability of section 5 of this title to the procurement of property or services by the General Services Administration or any constituent organization thereof or any other executive agency delegated authority pursuant to section

252(a)(2) of this title to be deemed a reference to section 252(c) of this title.

1958　Amendments. Subsec.　(b). Pub.L. 85–800 inserted "or any other executive agency delegated authority pursuant to section 252(a)(2) of this title,".

1952 Amendments. Act July 12, 1952, designated existing provisions as subsec. (a) and, in subsec. (a) as so designated, substituted "property" for "supplies", and added subsec. (b).

Effective and Applicability Provisions
1984　Acts. Amendment by Pub.L. 98–369 applicable with respect to any solicitation for bids or proposals issued after Mar. 31, 1985, see section 2751(a) of Pub.L. 98–369, set out as a note under section 251 of this title.

1949 Acts. Act June 30, 1949, § 605, which set July 1, 1949, as the effective date for this section, was repealed by Pub.L. 107–217, § 6(b), Aug. 21, 2002, 116 Stat. 1313.

CROSS REFERENCES

Laws inapplicable to armed services contracts, see 10 USCA § 2314.

Research References

ALR Library
　　30 ALR, Fed. 355, Recovery from United States of Costs Incurred by Unsuccessful Bidder in Preparing and Submitting Contract Bid in Response to Government Solicitation.
　　23 ALR, Fed. 301, Standing of Unsuccessful Bidder for Federal Procurement Contract to Seek Judicial Review of Award.
Encyclopedias
　　14 Am. Jur. Trials 437, Representing the Government Contractor.

WESTLAW ELECTRONIC RESEARCH

See Westlaw guide following the Explanation pages of this volume.

§ 261. Assignment and delegation of procurement functions and responsibilities

(a) In general

Except to the extent expressly prohibited by another provision of law, the head of an executive agency may delegate to any other officer or official of that agency, any power under this subchapter.

(b) Procurements for or with other agencies

Subject to subsection (a) of this section, to facilitate the procurement of property and services covered by this subchapter by each executive agency for any other executive agency, and to facilitate joint procurement by those executive agencies—

(1) the head of an executive agency may delegate functions and assign responsibilities relating to procurement to any officer or employee within such agency;

(2) the heads of two or more executive agencies may by agreement delegate procurement functions and assign procurement responsibilities, consistent with section 1535 of Title 31 and regulations issued under section 1074 of the Federal Acquisition Streamlining Act of 1994, from one executive agency to another of those executive agencies or to an officer or civilian employee of another of those executive agencies; and

(3) the heads of two or more executive agencies may establish joint or combined offices to exercise procurement functions and responsibilities.

(June 30, 1949, c. 288, Title III, § 311, as added Oct. 13, 1994, Pub.L. 103–355, Title I, § 1552, 108 Stat. 3299.)

HISTORICAL AND STATUTORY NOTES

Revision Notes and Legislative Reports
1994   Acts. Senate   Report   Nos. 103–258 and 103–259, and House Conference Report No. 103–712, see 1994 U.S. Code Cong. and Adm. News, p. 2561.

References in Text
Section 1074 of the Federal Acquisition Streamlining Act of 1994, referred to in subsec. (b)(2), is section 1074 of Pub.L. 103–355, Title I, Oct. 13, 1994, 108 Stat. 3271, which is set out as a note under section 1535 of Title 31, Money and Finance.

Effective and Applicability Provisions
1994 Acts. Section effective Oct. 13, 1994, except as otherwise provided, see

section 10001 of Pub.L. 103–355, set out as a note under section 251 of this title.

Prior Provisions
A prior section 261, Pub.L. 101–509, Title V, § 532, Nov. 5, 1990, 104 Stat. 1470; Pub.L. 102–393, Title V, § 529, Oct. 6, 1992, 106 Stat. 1761, relating to Internal Revenue Service procurement of expert services, was repealed by Pub.L. 103–355, Title I, § 1055(c), Oct. 13, 1994, 108 Stat. 3266, effective Oct. 13, 1994, except as otherwise provided, pursuant to section 10001 of Pub.L. 103–355, set out as a note under section 251 of this title.

LIBRARY REFERENCES

American Digest System
United States ⚖➞60.
Key Number System Topic No. 393.

WESTLAW ELECTRONIC RESEARCH

See Westlaw guide following the Explanation pages of this volume.

§ 262. Determinations and decisions

(a) Individual or class determinations and decisions authorized

Determinations and decisions required to be made under this subchapter by the head of an executive agency may be made for an individual purchase or contract or, except to the extent expressly prohibited by another provision of law, for a class of purchases or contracts. Such determinations and decisions are final.

(b) Written findings required

(1) Each determination under section 255(d) of this title or section 254d(c)(2)(B) of this title shall be based on a written finding by the person making the determination or decision. The finding shall set out facts and circumstances that support the determination or decision.

(2) Each finding referred to in paragraph (1) is final.

(3) The head of an executive agency shall maintain for a period of not less than 6 years a copy of each finding referred to in paragraph (1) that is made by a person in that executive agency. The period begins on the date of the determination or decision to which the finding relates.

(June 30, 1949, c. 288, Title III, § 312, as added Oct. 13, 1994, Pub.L. 103–355, Title I, § 1553, 108 Stat. 3300.)

HISTORICAL AND STATUTORY NOTES

Revision Notes and Legislative Reports
  1994 Acts. Senate Report Nos. 103–258 and 103–259, and House Conference Report No. 103–712, see 1994 U.S. Code Cong. and Adm. News, p. 2561.

Effective and Applicability Provisions
  1994 Acts. Section effective Oct. 13, 1994, except as otherwise provided, see section 10001 of Pub.L. 103–355, set out as a note under section 251 of this title.

LIBRARY REFERENCES

American Digest System
  United States ⟚73(8).
  Key Number System Topic No. 393.

WESTLAW ELECTRONIC RESEARCH

See Westlaw guide following the Explanation pages of this volume.

§ 263. Performance based management: acquisition programs

(a) Congressional policy

It is the policy of Congress that the head of each executive agency should achieve, on average, 90 percent of the cost, performance, and schedule goals established for major acquisition programs of the agency.

(b) Establishment of goals

(1) The head of each executive agency shall approve or define the cost, performance, and schedule goals for major acquisition programs of the agency.

(2) The chief financial officer of an executive agency shall evaluate the cost goals proposed for each major acquisition program of the agency.

(c) Identification of noncompliant programs

Whenever it is necessary to do so in order to implement the policy set out in subsection (a) of this section, the head of an executive agency shall—

(1) determine whether there is a continuing need for programs that are significantly behind schedule, over budget, or not in compliance with performance or capability requirements; and

(2) identify suitable actions to be taken, including termination, with respect to such programs.

(June 30, 1949, c. 288, Title III, § 313, as added Oct. 13, 1994, Pub.L. 103–355, Title V, § 5051(a), 108 Stat. 3351; Nov. 18, 1997, Pub.L. 105–85, Div. A, Title VIII, § 851(a), 111 Stat. 1851.)

HISTORICAL AND STATUTORY NOTES

Revision Notes and Legislative Reports
1994   Acts. Senate Report Nos. 103–258 and 103–259, and House Conference Report No. 103–712, see 1994 U.S. Code Cong. and Adm. News, p. 2561.
1997 Acts. House Conference Report No. 105–340 and Statement by President, see 1997 U.S. Code Cong. and Adm. News, p. 2251.

Amendments
1997   Amendments. Subsec.   (a). Pub.L. 105–85, § 851(a), substituted "It is the policy of Congress that the head of each executive agency should achieve, on average, 90 percent of the cost, performance, and schedule goals established for major acquisition programs of the agency" for "It is the policy of Congress that the head of each executive agency should achieve, on average, 90 percent of the cost and schedule goals established for major and nonmajor acquisition programs of the agency without reducing the performance or capabilities of the items being acquired."

Effective and Applicability Provisions
1994 Acts. Section effective Oct. 13, 1994, and applicable on and after such date, see section 10001 of Pub.L. 103–355, set out as a note under section 251 of this title.

Enhanced System of Performance Incentives
Section 5051(c) of Pub.L. 103–355 provided that: "Within one year after the date of the enactment of this Act [Oct. 13, 1994], the Deputy Director for Management of the Office of Management and Budget, in consultation with appropriate officials in other departments and agencies of the Federal Government, shall, to the maximum extent consistent with applicable law—

"**(1)** establish policies and procedures for the heads of such departments and agencies to designate acquisition positions and manage employees (including the accession, education, training and career development of employees) in the designated acquisition positions; and

"**(2)** review the incentives and personnel actions available to the heads of departments and agencies of the Federal Government for encouraging excellence in the acquisition workforce of the Federal Government and provide an enhanced system of incentives for the encouragement of excellence in such workforce which—

"**(A)** relates pay to performance (including the extent to which the performance of personnel in such workforce contributes to achieving the cost goals, schedule goals, and performance goals established for acquisition programs pursuant to section 313(b) of the Federal Property and Administrative Services Act of 1949, as added by subsection (a) [subsec. (b) of this section]); and

"(B) provides for consideration, in personnel evaluations and promotion decisions, of the extent to which the performance of personnel in such workforce contributes to achieving such cost goals, schedule goals, and performance goals."

[Section 5051(c) of Pub.L. 103–355 effective Oct. 13, 1994, and applicable on and after such date, see section 10001 of Pub.L. 103–355, set out as a note under section 251 of this title.]

Recommended Legislation

Section 5051(d) of Pub.L. 103–355 provided that: "Not later than one year after the date of the enactment of this Act [Oct. 13, 1994], the Administrator for Federal Procurement Policy shall submit to Congress any recommended legislation that the Secretary considers necessary to carry out section 313 of the Federal Property and Administrative Services Act of 1949, as added by subsection (a) [this section], and otherwise to facilitate and enhance management of Federal Government acquisition programs and the acquisition workforce of the Federal Government on the basis of performance."

[Section 5051(d) of Pub.L. 103–355 effective Oct. 13, 1994, and applicable on and after such date, see section 10001 of Pub.L. 103–355, set out as a note under section 251 of this title.]

LIBRARY REFERENCES

American Digest System
United States ⏀60.
Key Number System Topic No. 393.

WESTLAW ELECTRONIC RESEARCH

See Westlaw guide following the Explanation pages of this volume.

§ 264. Relationship of commercial item provisions to other provisions of law

(a) Applicability of subchapter

Unless otherwise specifically provided, nothing in this section, section 264a of this title, or section 264b of this title shall be construed as providing that any other provision of this subchapter relating to procurement is inapplicable to the procurement of commercial items.

(b) List of laws inapplicable to contracts for acquisition of commercial items

No contract for the procurement of a commercial item entered into by the head of an executive agency shall be subject to any law properly listed in the Federal Acquisition Regulation (pursuant to section 430 of this title).

(June 30, 1949, c. 288, Title III, § 314, as added Oct. 13, 1994, Pub.L. 103–355, Title VIII, § 8201, 108 Stat. 3394.)

HISTORICAL AND STATUTORY NOTES

Revision Notes and Legislative Reports
  1994 Acts. Senate Report Nos. 103–258 and 103–259, and House Conference Report No. 103–712, see 1994 U.S. Code Cong. and Adm. News, p. 2561.

Effective and Applicability Provisions
  1994 Acts. Section effective Oct. 13, 1994, except as otherwise provided, see

section 10001 of Pub.L. 103–355, set out as a note under section 251 of this title.

Provisions Not Affected by Title VIII of Pub.L. 103–355
Section 8304 of Pub.L. 103–355 provided that: "Nothing in this title [Pub.L. 103–355, Title VIII, § 8001 et seq., Oct. 13, 1994, 108 Stat. 3384 et seq., which enacted this section and sections 264a, 264b, and 430 of this title, sections 2375 through 2377 of Title 10, Armed Forces, and section 334 of former Title 40, Public Buildings, Property, and Works, amended sections 57, 58, 253g, 254, 403, 416, 418, 422, 423, and 701 of this title, sections 2306, 2320, 2321, 2384, 2393, 2397, 2397b, 2397c, 2402, 2408, and 2410b of Title 10, section 1368 of Title 33, Navigation and Navigable Waters, and section 40118 of Title 49, Transportation, repealed section 424 of this title and section 2325 of Title 10, enacted provisions set out as notes under this section and sections 264b and 430 of this title, section 2327 of Title 10, and section 7606 of Title 42, The Public Health and Welfare, and amended provisions set out as a note under section 2301 of Title 10; for complete classification of this title to the Code, see Tables] shall be construed as modifying or superseding, or as intended to impair or restrict, authorities or responsibilities under—

"(1) section 2323 of title 10, United States Code [section 2323 of Title 10], or section 7102 of the Federal Acquisition Streamlining Act of 1994 [section 7102 of Pub.L. 103–355, set out as a note under section 644 of Title 15, Commerce and Trade];

"(2) the Brooks Automatic Data Processing Act (section 111 of the Federal Property and Administrative Services Act of 1949 (40 U.S.C. 759)) [repealed by Pub.L. 104–106, Div. E, Title LI, § 5101, Feb. 10, 1996, 110 Stat. 680] section 759 of Title 40];

"(3) Brooks Architect-Engineers Act (title IX of the Federal Property and Administrative Services Act of 1949 (40 U.S.C. 541 et seq.)) [see now 40 U.S.C.A. § 1101 et seq.];

"(4) subsections (a) and (d) of section 8 of the Small Business Act (15 U.S.C. 637(a) and (d)) [section 637(a) and (d) of Title 15]; or

"(5) the Javits-Wagner-O'Day Act (41 U.S.C. 46–48c) [sections 46 through 48c of this title]."

[Section 8304 of Pub.L. 103–355 effective Oct. 13, 1994, except as otherwise provided, see section 10001 of Pub.L. 103–355, set out as a note under section 251 of this title.]

Regulations on Acquisition of Commercial Items
Section 8002 of Pub.L. 103–355, as amended, Pub.L. 108–136, Div. A, Title XIV, § 1432, Nov. 24, 2003, 117 Stat. 1672, provided that:

"(a) In general.—The Federal Acquisition Regulation shall provide regulations to implement paragraphs (12) through (15) of section 4 of the Office of Federal Procurement Policy Act [section 403(12) through (15) of this title], chapter 140 of title 10, United States Code [section 2375 et seq. of Title 10, Armed Forces], and sections 314 through 314B of the Federal Property and Administrative Services Act of 1949 [this section and sections 264a and 264b of this title].

"(b) Contract clauses.—(1) The regulations prescribed under subsection (a) shall contain a list of contract clauses to be included in contracts for the acquisition of commercial end items. Such list shall, to the maximum extent practicable, include only those contract clauses—

"(A) that are required to implement provisions of law or executive orders applicable to acquisitions of commercial items or commercial components, as the case may be; or

"(B) that are determined to be consistent with standard commercial practice.

"(2) Such regulations shall provide that a prime contractor shall not be required by the Federal Government to apply to any of its divisions, subsidiaries, affiliates, subcontractors, or suppliers that are furnishing commercial items any contract clause except those—

"(A) that are required to implement provisions of law or executive orders applicable to subcontractors furnishing commercial items or commercial components, as the case may be; or

"(B) that are determined to be consistent with standard commercial practice.

"**(3)** To the maximum extent practicable, only the contract clauses listed pursuant to paragraph (1) may be used in a contract, and only the contract clauses referred to in paragraph (2) may be required to be used in a subcontract, for the acquisition of commercial items or commercial components by or for an executive agency.

"**(4)** The Federal Acquisition Regulation shall provide standards and procedures for waiving the use of contract clauses required pursuant to paragraph (1), other than those required by law, including standards for determining the cases in which a waiver is appropriate.

"**(5)** For purposes of this subsection, the term 'subcontract' includes a transfer of commercial items between divisions, subsidiaries, or affiliates of a contractor or subcontractor.

"**(c) Market acceptance.**—(1) The Federal Acquisition Regulation shall provide that under appropriate conditions the head of an executive agency may require offerors to demonstrate that the items offered—

"**(A)** have either—

"**(i)** achieved commercial market acceptance; or

"**(ii)** been satisfactorily supplied to an executive agency under current or recent contracts for the same or similar requirements; and

"**(B)** otherwise meet the item description, specifications, or other criteria prescribed in the public notice and solicitation relating to the contract.

"**(2)** The Federal Acquisition Regulation shall provide guidance to ensure that the criteria for determining commercial market acceptance include the consideration of—

"**(A)** the minimum needs of the executive agency concerned; and

"**(B)** the entire relevant commercial market, including small businesses.

"**(d) Provisions relating to types of contracts for commercial items.**—(1) The Federal Acquisition Regulation shall include, for acquisitions of commercial items—

"**(A)** a requirement that firm, fixed price contracts or fixed price with economic price adjustment contracts be used to the maximum extent practicable;

"**(B)** a prohibition on use of cost type contracts; and

"**(C)** subject to paragraph (2), authority for use of a time-and-materials contract or a labor-hour contract for the procurement of commercial services that are commonly sold to the general public through such contracts and are purchased by the procuring agency on a competitive basis.

"**(2)** A time-and-materials contract or a labor-hour contract may be used pursuant to the authority referred to in paragraph (1)(c)—

"**(A)** Only for a procurement of commercial services in a category of commercial services described in paragraph (3); and—

"**(B)** Only if the contracting officer for such procurement—

"**(i)** executes a determination and findings that no other contract type is suitable;

"**(ii)** includes in the contract a ceiling price that the contractor exceeds at its own risk; and

"**(iii)** authorizes any subsequent change in the ceiling price only upon a determination, documented in the contract file, that it is in the best interest of the procuring agency to change such ceiling price.

"**(3)** The categories of commercial services referred to in paragraph (2) are as follows:

"**(A)** Commercial services procured for support of a commercial item, as described in section 4(12)(E) of the Office of Federal Procurement Policy Act (41 U.S.C. 403(12)(E)).

"**(B)** Any other category of commercial services that is designated by the administrator for Federal procurement policy in the Federal acquisition regulation for the purposes of this paragraph on the basis that—

"**(i)** the commercial services in such category are of a type of commercial services that are commonly sold to the general public through use of time-and-materials or labor-hour contracts; and

"**(ii)** it would be in the best interests of the Federal Government to authorize use of time-and-materials or labor-hour contracts for purchases of the commercial services in such category.

"(e) Contract quality requirements.— The regulations prescribed under subsection (a) shall include provisions that—

"(1) permit, to the maximum extent practicable, a contractor under a commercial items acquisition to use the existing quality assurance system of the contractor as a substitute for compliance with an otherwise applicable requirement for the Government to inspect or test the commercial items before the contractor's tender of those items for acceptance by the Government;

"(2) require that, to the maximum extent practicable, the executive agency take advantage of warranties (including extended warranties) offered by offerors of commercial items and use such warranties for the repair and replacement of commercial items; and

"(3) set forth guidance regarding the use of past performance of commercial items and sources as a factor in contract award decisions.

"(f) Defense contract clauses.—(1) Section 824(b) of the National Defense Authorization Act for Fiscal Years 1990 and 1991 (Public Law 101–189; 10 U.S.C. 2325 note) [section 824(b) of Pub.L 101–189, set out as a note under section 2325 of Title 10] shall cease to be effective on the date on which the regulations implementing this section become effective.

"(2) Notwithstanding subsection (b), a contract of the Department of Defense entered into before the date on which section 824(b) [section 824(b) of Pub.L. 101–189, set out as a note under section 2325 of Title of 10] ceases to be effective under paragraph (1), and a subcontract entered into before such date under such a contract, may include clauses developed pursuant to paragraphs (2) and (3) of section 824(b) of the National Defense Authorization Act for Fiscal Years 1990 and 1991 (Public Law 101–189; 10 U.S.C. 2325 note) [section 824(b)(2) and (3) of Pub.L. 101–189, set out as a note under section 2325 of Title 10]."

[Section 8002 of Pub.L. 103–355 effective Oct. 13, 1994, except as otherwise provided, see section 10001 of Pub.L. 103–355, set out as a note under section 251 of this title.]

WESTLAW ELECTRONIC RESEARCH

See Westlaw guide following the Explanation pages of this volume.

§ 264a. Definitions relating to procurement of commercial items

As used in this subchapter, the terms "commercial item", "nondevelopmental item", "component", and "commercial component" have the meanings provided in section 403 of this title.

(June 30, 1949, c. 288, Title III, § 314A, as added Oct. 13, 1994, Pub.L. 103–355, Title VIII, § 8202, 108 Stat. 3394, and amended Feb. 10, 1996, Pub.L. 104–106, Div. D, Title XLIII, § 4321(e)(7), 110 Stat. 675.)

HISTORICAL AND STATUTORY NOTES

Revision Notes and Legislative Reports

1994 Acts. Senate Report Nos. 103–258 and 103–259, and House Conference Report No. 103–712, see 1994 U.S. Code Cong. and Adm. News, p. 2561.

1996 Acts. House Conference Report No. 104–450, see 1996 U.S. Code Cong. and Adm. News, p. 238.

Amendments

1996 Amendments. Catchline. Pub.L. 104–106, § 4321(e)(7), added "relating to procurement of commercial items" following "Definitions".

Effective and Applicability Provisions

1996 Acts. Amendment by Pub.L. 104–106 effective Feb. 10, 1996, except as otherwise provided, see section 4401 of Pub.L. 104–106, set out as a note under section 251 of this title.

1994 Acts. Section effective Oct. 13, 1994, except as otherwise provided, see

section 10001 of Pub.L. 103–355, set out
as a note under section 251 of this title.

WESTLAW ELECTRONIC RESEARCH

See Westlaw guide following the Explanation pages of this volume.

§ 264b.　Preference for acquisition of commercial items

(a) Preference

The head of each executive agency shall ensure that, to the maximum extent practicable—

    (1) requirements of the executive agency with respect to a procurement of supplies or services are stated in terms of—

        (A) functions to be performed;

        (B) performance required; or

        (C) essential physical characteristics;

    (2) such requirements are defined so that commercial items or, to the extent that commercial items suitable to meet the executive agency's needs are not available, nondevelopmental items other than commercial items, may be procured to fulfill such requirements; and

    (3) offerors of commercial items and nondevelopmental items other than commercial items are provided an opportunity to compete in any procurement to fill such requirements.

(b) Implementation

The head of each executive agency shall ensure that procurement officials in that executive agency, to the maximum extent practicable—

    (1) acquire commercial items or nondevelopmental items other than commercial items to meet the needs of the executive agency;

    (2) require prime contractors and subcontractors at all levels under the executive agency contracts to incorporate commercial items or nondevelopmental items other than commercial items as components of items supplied to the executive agency;

    (3) modify requirements in appropriate cases to ensure that the requirements can be met by commercial items or, to the extent that commercial items suitable to meet the executive agency's needs are not available, nondevelopmental items other than commercial items;

    (4) state specifications in terms that enable and encourage bidders and offerors to supply commercial items or, to the extent that commercial items suitable to meet the executive agency's needs are not available, nondevelopmental items other than commercial items in response to the executive agency solicitations;

(5) revise the executive agency's procurement policies, practices, and procedures not required by law to reduce any impediments in those policies, practices, and procedures to the acquisition of commercial items; and

(6) require training of appropriate personnel in the acquisition of commercial items.

(c) Preliminary market research

(1) The head of an executive agency shall conduct market research appropriate to the circumstances—

(A) before developing new specifications for a procurement by that executive agency; and

(B) before soliciting bids or proposals for a contract in excess of the simplified acquisition threshold.

(2) The head of an executive agency shall use the results of market research to determine whether there are commercial items or, to the extent that commercial items suitable to meet the executive agency's needs are not available, nondevelopmental items other than commercial items available that—

(A) meet the executive agency's requirements;

(B) could be modified to meet the executive agency's requirements; or

(C) could meet the executive agency's requirements if those requirements were modified to a reasonable extent.

(3) In conducting market research, the head of an executive agency should not require potential sources to submit more than the minimum information that is necessary to make the determinations required in paragraph (2).

(June 30, 1949, c. 288, Title III, § 314B, as added Oct. 13, 1994, Pub.L. 103–355, Title VIII, § 8203, 108 Stat. 3394.)

HISTORICAL AND STATUTORY NOTES

Revision Notes and Legislative Reports
1994 Acts. Senate Report Nos. 103–258 and 103–259, and House Conference Report No. 103–712, see 1994 U.S. Code Cong. and Adm. News, p. 2561.

Effective and Applicability Provisions
1994 Acts. Section effective Oct. 13, 1994, except as otherwise provided, see section 10001 of Pub.L. 103–355, set out as a note under section 251 of this title.

Comptroller General Review of Federal Government Use of Market Research Section 8305 of Pub.L. 103–355 provided that:

"(a) **Report required.**—Not later than 2 years after the date of the enactment of this Act [Oct. 13, 1994], the Comptroller General of the United States shall submit to the Congress a report on the use of market research by the Federal Government in support of the procurement of commercial items and nondevelopmental items.

"(b) Content of report.—The report shall include the following:

"(1) A review of existing Federal Government market research efforts to gather data concerning commercial and other nondevelopmental items.

"(2) A review of the feasibility of creating a Government-wide data base for storing, retrieving, and analyzing market data, including use of existing Federal Government resources.

"(3) Any recommendations for changes in law or regulations that the Comptroller General considers appropriate."

CROSS REFERENCES

Metric conversion implementation in acquisition of construction services and materials for Federal facilities, see 15 USCA § 205*l*.

LIBRARY REFERENCES

American Digest System
  United States ☞64.15.
  Key Number System Topic No. 393.

WESTLAW ELECTRONIC RESEARCH

See Westlaw guide following the Explanation pages of this volume.

§ 265. Contractor employees: protection from reprisal for disclosure of certain information

(a) Prohibition of reprisals

An employee of a contractor may not be discharged, demoted, or otherwise discriminated against as a reprisal for disclosing to a Member of Congress or an authorized official of an executive agency or the Department of Justice information relating to a substantial violation of law related to a contract (including the competition for or negotiation of a contract).

(b) Investigation of complaints

A person who believes that the person has been subjected to a reprisal prohibited by subsection (a) of this section may submit a complaint to the Inspector General of the executive agency. Unless the Inspector General determines that the complaint is frivolous, the Inspector General shall investigate the complaint and, upon completion of such investigation, submit a report of the findings of the investigation to the person, the contractor concerned, and the head of the agency. In the case of an executive agency that does not have an Inspector General, the duties of the Inspector General under this section shall be performed by an official designated by the head of the executive agency.

(c) Remedy and enforcement authority

(1) If the head of an executive agency determines that a contractor has subjected a person to a reprisal prohibited by subsection (a) of

this section, the head of the executive agency may take one or more of the following actions:

(A) Order the contractor to take affirmative action to abate the reprisal.

(B) Order the contractor to reinstate the person to the position that the person held before the reprisal, together with the compensation (including back pay), employment benefits, and other terms and conditions of employment that would apply to the person in that position if the reprisal had not been taken.

(C) Order the contractor to pay the complainant an amount equal to the aggregate amount of all costs and expenses (including attorneys' fees and expert witnesses' fees) that were reasonably incurred by the complainant for, or in connection with, bringing the complaint regarding the reprisal, as determined by the head of the executive agency.

(2) Whenever a person fails to comply with an order issued under paragraph (1), the head of the executive agency shall file an action for enforcement of such order in the United States district court for a district in which the reprisal was found to have occurred. In any action brought under this paragraph, the court may grant appropriate relief, including injunctive relief and compensatory and exemplary damages.

(3) Any person adversely affected or aggrieved by an order issued under paragraph (1) may obtain review of the order's conformance with this subsection, and any regulations issued to carry out this section, in the United States court of appeals for a circuit in which the reprisal is alleged in the order to have occurred. No petition seeking such review may be filed more than 60 days after issuance of the order by the head of the agency. Review shall conform to chapter 7 of Title 5.

(d) Construction

Nothing in this section may be construed to authorize the discharge of, demotion of, or discrimination against an employee for a disclosure other than a disclosure protected by subsection (a) of this section or to modify or derogate from a right or remedy otherwise available to the employee.

(e) Definitions

In this section:

(1) The term "contract" means a contract awarded by the head of an executive agency.

(2) The term "contractor" means a person awarded a contract with an executive agency.

(3) The term "Inspector General" means an Inspector General appointed under the Inspector General Act of 1978.

(June 30, 1949, c. 288, Title III, § 315, as added Oct. 13, 1994, Pub.L. 103–355, Title VI, § 6006, 108 Stat. 3365, and amended Feb. 10, 1996, Pub.L. 104–106, Div. D, Title XLIII, § 4321(e)(8), 110 Stat. 675.)

HISTORICAL AND STATUTORY NOTES

Revision Notes and Legislative Reports
1994 Acts. Senate Report Nos. 103–258 and 103–259, and House Conference Report No. 103–712, see 1994 U.S. Code Cong. and Adm. News, p. 2561.

1996 Acts. House Conference Report No. 104–450, see 1996 U.S. Code Cong. and Adm. News, p. 238.

References in Text
The Inspector General Act of 1978, referred to in subsec. (e)(3), is Pub.L. 95–452, Oct. 12, 1978, 92 Stat. 1101, as amended, which is classified to 5 U.S.C.A. App. 3 § 1 et seq.

Amendments
1996 Amendments. Subsec. (b). Pub.L. 104–106, § 4321(e)(8), substituted "Inspector General" for "inspector general" following "does not have an" and "the duties of the", respectively.

Effective and Applicability Provisions
1996 Acts. Amendment by Pub.L. 104–106 effective Feb. 10, 1996, except as otherwise provided, see section 4401 of Pub.L. 104–106, set out as a note under section 251 of this title.

1994 Acts. Section effective Oct. 13, 1994, except as otherwise provided, see section 10001 of Pub.L. 103–355, set out as a note under section 251 of this title.

LIBRARY REFERENCES

American Digest System
Labor and Employment ⊜776.
Key Number System Topic No. 231H.

Corpus Juris Secundum
CJS Employer-Employee Relationship § 82, Whistleblowing--Federal Statutes.

Research References

Encyclopedias
Am. Jur. 2d Wrongful Discharge § 118, Federal Statutes.

Forms
Federal Procedural Forms § 34:530, Whistleblower Protection.
Federal Procedural Forms § 34:531, Whistleblower Protection--Notice of Complaint; Investigation.
Federal Procedural Forms § 34:532, Whistleblower Protection--Order Providing Relief.
Federal Procedural Forms § 34:533, Judicial Review of Order.
Federal Procedural Forms § 34:534, Judicial Review of Order--Enforcement Action.

Treatises and Practice Aids
Federal Procedure, Lawyers Edition § 39:1384, Complaint.
Federal Procedure, Lawyers Edition § 39:1385, Investigation; Findings and Response Thereto.
Federal Procedure, Lawyers Edition § 39:1386, Order Providing Relief.
Federal Procedure, Lawyers Edition § 39:1387, Order Providing Relief--Judicial Review.
Federal Procedure, Lawyers Edition § 39:1388, Order Providing Relief--Enforcement Action.

WESTLAW ELECTRONIC RESEARCH

See Westlaw guide following the Explanation pages of this volume.

§ 266.   Merit-based award of grants for research and development

(a) Policy

It is the policy of Congress that an executive agency should not be required by legislation to award a new grant for research, development, test, or evaluation to a non-Federal Government entity. It is further the policy of Congress that any program, project, or technology identified in legislation be awarded through merit-based selection procedures.

(b) Rule of construction

A provision of law may not be construed as requiring a new grant to be awarded to a specified non-Federal Government entity unless that provision of law—

(1) specifically refers to this subsection;

(2) specifically identifies the particular non-Federal Government entity involved; and

(3) specifically states that the award to that entity is required by such provision of law in contravention of the policy set forth in subsection (a) of this section.

(c) New grant defined

For purposes of this section, a grant is a new grant unless the work provided for in the grant is a continuation of the work performed by the specified entity under a preceding grant.

(d) Inapplicability to certain grants

This section shall not apply with respect to any grant that calls upon the National Academy of Sciences to investigate, examine, or experiment upon any subject of science or art of significance to an executive agency and to report on such matters to Congress or any agency of the Federal Government.

(June 30, 1949, c. 288, Title III, § 316, as added Oct. 13, 1994, Pub.L. 103–355, Title VII, § 7203(b)(2), 108 Stat. 3381, and amended Feb. 10, 1996, Pub.L. 104–106, Div. D, Title XLIII, § 4321(e)(9), 110 Stat. 675.)

HISTORICAL AND STATUTORY NOTES

Revision Notes and Legislative Reports
1994   Acts. Senate   Report   Nos. 103–258 and 103–259 and House Conference Report No. 103–712, see 1994 U.S. Code Cong. and Adm. News, p. 2561.

1996 Acts. House Conference Report No. 104–450, see 1996 U.S. Code Cong. and Adm. News, p. 238.

Amendments
1996 Amendments. Catchline. Pub.L.
104–106, § 4321(e)(9), made technical
changes which, for purposes of codification, required further no changes in text.

Effective and Applicability Provisions
1996 Acts. Amendment by Pub.L.
104–106 effective Feb. 10, 1996, except as

otherwise provided, see section 4401 of
Pub.L. 104–106, set out as a note under
section 251 of this title.

1994 Acts. Section effective Oct. 13,
1994, except as otherwise provided, see
section 10001 of Pub.L. 103–355, set out
as a note under section 251 of this title.

LIBRARY REFERENCES

American Digest System
　United States ⬤⟲60.
　Key Number System Topic No. 393.

WESTLAW ELECTRONIC RESEARCH

See Westlaw guide following the Explanation pages of this volume.

§ 266a. Share-in-savings contracts

(a) Authority to enter into share-in-savings contracts

(1) The head of an executive agency may enter into a share-in-savings contract for information technology (as defined in section 11101(6) of Title 40) in which the Government awards a contract to improve mission-related or administrative processes or to accelerate the achievement of its mission and share with the contractor in savings achieved through contract performance.

(2)(A) Except as provided in subparagraph (B), a share-in-savings contract shall be awarded for a period of not more than five years.

(B) A share-in-savings contract may be awarded for a period greater than five years, but not more than 10 years, if the head of the agency determines in writing prior to award of the contract that—

(i) the level of risk to be assumed and the investment to be undertaken by the contractor is likely to inhibit the government from obtaining the needed information technology competitively at a fair and reasonable price if the contract is limited in duration to a period of five years or less; and

(ii) usage of the information technology to be acquired is likely to continue for a period of time sufficient to generate reasonable benefit for the government.

(3) Contracts awarded pursuant to the authority of this section shall, to the maximum extent practicable, be performance-based contracts that identify objective outcomes and contain performance standards that will be used to measure achievement and milestones that must be met before payment is made.

(4) Contracts awarded pursuant to the authority of this section shall include a provision containing a quantifiable baseline that is to

be the basis upon which a savings share ratio is established that governs the amount of payment a contractor is to receive under the contract. Before commencement of performance of such a contract, the senior procurement executive of the agency shall determine in writing that the terms of the provision are quantifiable and will likely yield value to the Government.

(5)(A) The head of the agency may retain savings realized through the use of a share-in-savings contract under this section that are in excess of the total amount of savings paid to the contractor under the contract, but may not retain any portion of such savings that is attributable to a decrease in the number of civilian employees of the Federal Government performing the function. Except as provided in subparagraph (B), savings shall be credited to the appropriation or fund against which charges were made to carry out the contract and shall be used for information technology.

(B) Amounts retained by the agency under this subsection shall—

(i) without further appropriation, remain available until expended; and

(ii) be applied first to fund any contingent liabilities associated with share-in-savings procurements that are not fully funded.

(b) Cancellation and termination

(1) If funds are not made available for the continuation of a share-in-savings contract entered into under this section in a subsequent fiscal year, the contract shall be canceled or terminated. The costs of cancellation or termination may be paid out of—

(A) appropriations available for the performance of the contract;

(B) appropriations available for acquisition of the information technology procured under the contract, and not otherwise obligated; or

(C) funds subsequently appropriated for payments of costs of cancellation or termination, subject to the limitations in paragraph (3).

(2) The amount payable in the event of cancellation or termination of a share-in-savings contract shall be negotiated with the contractor at the time the contract is entered into.

(3)(A) Subject to subparagraph (B), the head of an executive agency may enter into share-in-savings contracts under this section in any given fiscal year even if funds are not made specifically available for the full costs of cancellation or termination of the contract if funds are available and sufficient to make payments with respect to the first fiscal year of the contract and the following

551

conditions are met regarding the funding of cancellation and termination liability:

(i) The amount of unfunded contingent liability for the contract does not exceed the lesser of—

(I) 25 percent of the estimated costs of a cancellation or termination; or

(II) $5,000,000.

(ii) Unfunded contingent liability in excess of $1,000,000 has been approved by the Director of the Office of Management and Budget or the Director's designee.

(B) The aggregate number of share-in-savings contracts that may be entered into under subparagraph (A) by all executive agencies to which this subchapter applies in a fiscal year may not exceed 5 in each of fiscal years 2003, 2004, and 2005.

(c) Definitions

In this section:

(1) The term "contractor" means a private entity that enters into a contract with an agency.

(2) The term "savings" means—

(A) monetary savings to an agency; or

(B) savings in time or other benefits realized by the agency, including enhanced revenues (other than enhanced revenues from the collection of fees, taxes, debts, claims, or other amounts owed the Federal Government).

(3) The term "share-in-savings contract" means a contract under which—

(A) a contractor provides solutions for—

(i) improving the agency's mission-related or administrative processes; or

(ii) accelerating the achievement of agency missions; and

(B) the head of the agency pays the contractor an amount equal to a portion of the savings derived by the agency from—

(i) any improvements in mission-related or administrative processes that result from implementation of the solution; or

(ii) acceleration of achievement of agency missions.

(June 30, 1949, c. 288, Title III, § 317, as added Dec. 17, 2002, Pub.L. 107–347, Title II, § 210(b), 116 Stat. 2934.)

HISTORICAL AND STATUTORY NOTES

Revision Notes and Legislative Reports
2002   Acts. House   Report   No.
107–787(Part I) and Statement by President, see 2002 U.S. Code Cong. and Adm. News, p. 1880.

References in Text
This subchapter, referred to in subsec. (b)(3)(B), was in the original "this chapter" and has been translated as if it read "this title" in the original, meaning Title

III of Act June 30, 1949, c. 288, to reflect the probable intent of Congress.

Effective and Applicability Provisions
2002 Acts. Except as otherwise provided by section 402(a)(2) of Pub.L. 107–347, amendments made by Pub.L. 107–347, Titles I and II, §§ 101 to 216, effective 120 days after December 17, 2002, see section 402(a) of Pub.L. 107–347, set out as a note under 44 U.S.C.A. § 3601.

LIBRARY REFERENCES

American Digest System
United States ⊛60.
Key Number System Topic No. 393.

Research References

Forms
Federal Procedural Forms § 34:1, Introduction to the FAR.
Federal Procedural Forms § 34:4, Procedures to Promote Competition--Contracting Without Open Competition.

Treatises and Practice Aids
Federal Procedure, Lawyers Edition § 39:1, Introduction to the Federal Acquisition Regulations System.

WESTLAW ELECTRONIC RESEARCH

See Westlaw guide following the Explanation pages of this volume.

SUBCHAPTER V—FOREIGN EXCESS PROPERTY

§§ 271 to 274. Transferred

HISTORICAL AND STATUTORY NOTES

Codifications
Section 271, Act June 30, 1949, c. 288, Title IV, § 401, 63 Stat. 397, which related to disposal of foreign excess property, was transferred to former 40 U.S.C.A. § 511 prior to being repealed by Pub.L. 107–217, § 6(b), Aug. 21, 2002, 116 Stat. 1313 and its substance reenacted as 40 U.S.C.A. § 701.

Section 272, Act June 30, 1949, c. 288, Title IV, § 402, 63 Stat. 398, which related to methods and terms of disposal, was transferred to former 40 U.S.C.A. § 512 prior to being repealed by Pub.L. 107–217, § 6(b), Aug. 21, 2002, 116 Stat. 1313 and its substance reenacted as 40 U.S.C.A. §§ 702 to 703.

Section 273, Act June 30, 1949, c. 288, Title IV, § 403, 63 Stat. 398, which related to proceeds from disposals, was transferred to former 40 U.S.C.A. § 513 prior to being repealed by Pub.L. 107–217, § 6(b), Aug. 21, 2002, 116 Stat. 1313 and its substance reenacted as 40 U.S.C.A. § 705.

Section 274, Act June 30, 1949, c. 288, Title IV, § 404, 63 Stat. 398, which related to general provisions, was transferred to former 40 U.S.C.A. § 514 prior to being repealed by Pub.L. 107–217, § 6(b), Aug. 21, 2002, 116 Stat. 1313 and its substance reenacted as 40 U.S.C.A. § 701.

SUBCHAPTER VI—FEDERAL RECORD MANAGEMENT

§§ 281 to 291.   Transferred

HISTORICAL AND STATUTORY NOTES

Codifications

Section 281, Acts June 30, 1949, c. 288, Title V, § 502; Sept. 5, 1950, c. 849, § 6(d), 64 Stat. 583, which related to custody and control of property, was transferred to section 392 of former Title 44, Public Printing and Documents.

Section 282, Acts June 30, 1949, c. 288, Title V, § 503; Sept. 5, 1950, c. 849, § 6(d), 64 Stat. 583, which related to National Historical Publications Commission, was transferred to section 393 of former Title 44.

Section 283, Acts June 30, 1949, c. 288, Title V, § 504; Sept. 5, 1950, c. 849, § 6(d), 64 Stat. 583, which related to the establishment of the Federal Records Council, was transferred to section 394 of former Title 44.

Section 284, Acts June 30, 1949, c. 288, Title V, § 505; Sept. 5, 1950, c. 849, § 6(d), 64 Stat. 583, which related to records management by Administrator, was transferred to section 395 of former Title 44.

Section 285, Acts June 30, 1949, c. 288, Title V, § 506; Sept. 5, 1950, c. 849, § 6(d), 64 Stat. 583, which related to records management by agency heads, was transferred to section 396 of former Title 44.

Section 286, Acts June 30, 1949, c. 288, Title V, § 507; Sept. 5, 1950, c. 849, § 6(d), 64 Stat. 583, which related to Archival administration, was transferred to section 397 of former Title 44.

Section 287, Acts June 30, 1949, c. 288, Title V, § 508; Sept. 5, 1950, c. 849, § 6(d), 64 Stat. 583, which related to reports, was transferred to section 398 of former Title 44.

Section 288, Acts June 30, 1949, c. 288, Title V, § 509; Sept. 5, 1950, c. 849, § 6(d), 64 Stat. 583, which related to legal status of reproductions; official seal; fees for copies and reproductions, was transferred to section 399 of former Title 44.

Section 289, Acts June 30, 1949, c. 288, Title V, § 510; Sept. 5, 1950, c. 849, § 6(d), 64 Stat. 583, which related to limitation on liability, was transferred to section 400 of former Title 44.

Section 290, June 30, 1949, c. 288, Title V, § 511; Sept. 5, 1950, c. 849, § 6(d), 64 Stat. 583, which related to definitions, was transferred to section 401 of former Title 44.

Section 291, Act Aug. 2, 1946, c. 753, Title I, § 140, 60 Stat. 833, which related to transfer of records of Congress, was transferred to section 402 of former Title 44.

Sections 392 to 402 of former Title 44 are covered by chapter 21 (section 2101 et seq.), chapter 25 (section 2501 et seq.), chapter 27 (section 2701 et seq.), chapter 29 (section 2901 et seq.), and chapter 31 (section 3101 et seq.) of Title 44, Public Printing and Documents.

CHAPTER 5—JUDICIAL REVIEW OF ADMINISTRATIVE DECISIONS

Sec.
321. Limitation on pleading contract provisions relating to finality; standards of review.
322. Contract provisions making decisions final on questions of law.

WESTLAW COMPUTER ASSISTED LEGAL RESEARCH

Westlaw supplements your legal research in many ways. Westlaw allows you to

- update your research with the most current information
- expand your library with additional resources
- retrieve current, comprehensive history citing references to a case with KeyCite

For more information on using Westlaw to supplement your research, see the Westlaw Electronic Research Guide, which follows the Explanation.

---

§ 321. Limitation on pleading contract provisions relating to finality; standards of review

No provision of any contract entered into by the United States, relating to the finality or conclusiveness of any decision of the head of any department or agency or his duly authorized representative or board in a dispute involving a question arising under such contract, shall be pleaded in any suit now filed or to be filed as limiting judicial review of any such decision to cases where fraud by such official or his said representative or board is alleged: *Provided, however,* That any such decision shall be final and conclusive unless the same is fradulent[1] or capricious or arbitrary or so grossly erroneous as necessarily to imply bad faith, or is not supported by substantial evidence.

(May 11, 1954, c. 199, § 1, 68 Stat. 81.)

[1] So in original. Probably should be "fraudulent".

HISTORICAL AND STATUTORY NOTES

Revision Notes and Legislative Reports
  1954 Acts. The purpose of the proposed legislation, as amended, is to overcome the effect of the Supreme Court decision in the case of United States v. Wunderlich, 342 U.S. 98, 72 S.Ct. 154, rendered on November 26, 1951, under which the decisions of Government officers rendered pursuant to the standard disputes clauses in Government contracts are held to be final absent fraud on the part of such Government officers.

  The Supreme Court there defined fraud to mean "conscious wrongdoing, an intention to cheat or be dishonest." The proposed legislation also prescribes fair and uniform standards for the judicial review of such administrative decisions in the light of the reasonable requirements of the various Government departments and agencies, of the General Accounting Office and of Government contractors. It will also prohibit the insertion in Government contracts hereafter executed of provisions making the decisions of Government officers final on questions of law arising under such contracts....

After extensive hearings it has been concluded that it is neither to the interests of the Government nor to the interests of any of the industry groups that are engaged in the performance of Government contracts to repose in Government officials such unbridled power of finally determining either disputed questions of law or disputed questions of fact arising under Government contracts, nor is the situation presently created by the Wunderlich decision consonant with tradition that everyone should have his day in court and that contracts should be mutually enforceable. A continuation of this situation will render the performance of Government work less attractive to the responsible industries upon whom the Government must rely for the performance of such work, and will adversely affect the free and competitive nature of such work. It will discourage the more responsible element of every industry from engaging in Government work and will attract more speculative elements whose bids will contain contingent allowances intended to protect them from unconscionable decisions of Government officials rendered during the performance of their contracts.

A principal change which the amendment effects in S. 24 is to restore the standards of review based on arbitrariness and capriciousness. These have long been recognized as constituting a sufficient basis for judicial review of administrative decisions, a reference to capricious action on the part of a Government contracting official vested with discretionary power of decision being found as early as 1911 in the decision

of the Supreme Court in Ripley v. United States, 223 U.S. 695, 32 S.Ct. 352. The standards of arbitrariness and capriciousness in relation to the review of administrative action were also prescribed in the Administrative Procedures Act (act of June 11, 1946, ch. 324, sec. 10, 60 Stat. 243; 5 U.S.C. 1009). There is a wealth of judicial precedent behind these standards of review and it is the committee's belief that they should not be abandoned.

"The proposed amendment also adopts the additional standard that the administrative decision must be supported by substantial evidence. The requirement that administrative action be supported by substantial evidence is found in the Administrative Procedures Act, supra. As understood by the committee and as interpreted by the Supreme Court in Consolidated Edison Company of New York v. National Labor Relations Board, 305 U.S. 197, 229, 59 S.Ct. 206, "substantial evidence" means "such relevant evidence as a reasonable mind might accept as adequate to support a conclusion."

The inclusion of the standard "not supported by substantial evidence" should also correct another condition arising out of the lack of uniformity between the various departments and agencies concerned in the appellate hearing procedures under the disputes clause. It has been brought to light in public hearings that it is the exception rather than the rule that contractors in the presentation of their disputes are afforded an opportunity to become acquainted with the evidence in support of the Government's position. It is believed that if the standard of substantial evidence is adopted this condition will be corrected and that the records of hearing officers will hereafter contain all of the testimony and evidence upon which they have relied in making their decisions. It would not be possible to justify the retention of the finality causes in Government contracts unless the hearing procedures were conducted in such a way as to require each party to present openly its side of the controversy and afford an opportunity of rebuttal. House Report No. 1380.

CROSS REFERENCES

Judicial review of agency actions generally, see 5 USCA § 701 et seq.

LIBRARY REFERENCES

American Digest System

United States ☞73(14), 73(15).

Key Number System Topic No. 393.

Research References

ALR Library

13 ALR, Fed. 2nd Series 261, Construction and Application of Patent Ambiguity Doctrine to Federal Government Contracts.

200 ALR, Fed. 475, "Total Cost Method (or Approach)" and "Modified Total Cost Method (or Approach)" to Proving Damages in Federal Contract Cases.

59 ALR, Fed. 905, Application of 28 U.S.C.A. § 2516(A) to Government Contractor's Claim for Interest Expense or for Loss of Use of Its Capital Caused by Delay Attributable to Government.

24 ALR, Fed. 317, Construction and Application of Truth in Negotiations Act (10 U.S.C.A. § 2306(F)), Requiring Prime Contractors and Subcontractors to Submit Cost or Pricing Data, Certified to Be Accurate, Complete, and Current, Respecting Certain Government Contracts.

19 ALR, Fed. 645, Reformation by United States Court of Claims of Government Contract.

2 ALR, Fed. 691, Judicial Review Under Wunderlich Act (41 U.S.C.A. §§ 321, 322), of Federal Administrative Decisions Made Under Standard "Disputes" Clauses in Government Contracts.

86 ALR 3rd 182, Public Contracts: Duty of Public Authority to Disclose to Contractor Information, Allegedly in Its Possession, Affecting Cost or Feasibility of Project.

85 ALR 3rd 1085, Construction Contract Provision Excusing Delay Caused by "Severe Weather".

163 ALR 1300, Validity, Construction, and Effect of Statutory or Contractual Provision in Government Construction Contract Referring to Secretary of Labor Questions Respecting Wage Rates or Classification of Employees of Contractor.

126 ALR 837, Constitutionality, Construction, and Application of Statute Providing for Correction or Relief from Consequences of Error or Mistake in Bids for Public Contract.

115 ALR 65, Right of Building or Construction Contractor to Recover Damages Resulting from Delay Caused by Default of Contractee.

92 ALR 663, Stipulation of Parties as to the Law.

88 ALR 1223, Power to Allow Additional Compensation to Public Contractor Over Amount Called for by His Contract.

Encyclopedias

Am. Jur. 2d Federal Tort Claims Act § 32, Other Legislation.

Am. Jur. 2d Public Works and Contracts § 117, Construction of Contract by Architect or Engineer--Administrative Decisions Under the Wunderlich Act.

14 Am. Jur. Trials 437, Representing the Government Contractor.

Forms

Am. Jur. Pl. & Pr. Forms Public Works & Contracts § 98, Complaint in Federal Court--By Contractor--For Recovery of Reasonable Costs of Extra Work--Adjustment Sought Under Changes Clause.

Federal Procedural Forms § 34:313, Petition in Court of Appeals--For Review of Decision of Board of Contract Appeals--Equitable Adjustment Pursuant to Changes Clause; Issuance of Constructive Change Order Alleged [28 U.S.C.A. § 1295(a)(10); 41 U.S.C.A. § 607(g)(1); Fed. R. App. P. Rule 15(a)].

Treatises and Practice Aids

Federal Procedure, Lawyers Edition § 42:1954, Remedial Actions--Notice and Opportunity for Hearing.

557

Federal Procedure, Lawyers Edition § 53:182, Administrative Disallowance--Effect of Contractual Disputes Clause.

WESTLAW ELECTRONIC RESEARCH

See Westlaw guide following the Explanation pages of this volume.

Notes of Decisions

I. GENERALLY

Subdivision Index

1. Construction

By this section making decisions of Government officers rendered pursuant to standard dispute clause in Government contracts final and conclusive unless such decision is fraudulent, capricious, arbitrary, or so grossly erroneous as necessarily to imply bad faith, or is not supported by substantial evidence, Congress intended to establish a general policy for review of decisions made by Government officers, and such policy should not be interpreted in a niggardly manner. U.S. for Use of Bangor Roofing & Sheet Metal Co. v. T.W. Cunningham, Inc., D.C.Me. 1956, 141 F.Supp. 205. United States ☞ 73(14)

2. Purpose

This chapter evidences congressional purpose to insure adequate judicial review of administrative decisions on claims arising under government contracts. Crown Coat Front Co. v. U.S., U.S.N.Y.1967, 87 S.Ct. 1177, 386 U.S. 503, 18 L.Ed.2d 256. United States ☞ 73(15)

One of major reasons for passage of this chapter regarding review of administrative ruling is to assure to General Accounting Office a limited right of scrutiny comparable to that given in the courts. C.J. Langenfelder & Son, Inc. v. U.S., Ct.Cl.1965, 341 F.2d 600, 169 Ct.Cl. 465. United States ☞ 73(15)

3. Retroactive effect

This section providing in effect that administrative decisions on questions of fact arising out of Government contracts are final and conclusive unless shown to be fraudulent or capricious or arbitrary or so grossly erroneous as necessarily to imply bad faith, or unless not supported by substantial evidence, was made applicable to contracts in force at the time of its enactment by provision therein that this chapter was applicable to any suit now filed or to be filed. Hoffmann v. U.S., C.A.10 (Kan.) 1960, 276 F.2d 199. United States ☞ 73(14)

Where claims against United States arising out of construction contract had been dismissed pursuant to provision in such contract that all disputed questions of fact arising under contract should be decided upon by contracting officer, subject to written appeal within 30 days to head of department, whose decision would be final and conclusive, subsequent enactment of this section and section 322 of this title prohibiting pleading of such contract provision would not serve to reopen previously adjudicated claims. United Foundation Corp. v. U.S., Ct.Cl.1955, 127 F.Supp. 798, 130 Ct.Cl. 666. United States ☞ 73(14)

4. District of Columbia as party

Principles of this chapter applied to contract dispute to which District of Columbia was party and that contractor was not entitled to trial de novo in district court. Gunnell Const. Co., Inc. v. District of Columbia, C.A.D.C.1977, 551 F.2d 425, 179 U.S.App.D.C. 239. District Of Columbia ☞ 9

5. Implied contracts

Action by unsuccessful bidder on a government contract, alleging that the government, through its agents, illegally communicated with another bidder while the solicitation was still outstanding, thus resulting unfairly in award of the contract to that bidder, could not be characterized as a request for review of the General Accounting Office's denial of his protest, since this section does not apply to implied contracts between the government and bidders, under a contract solicitation. Rogers v. U.S., Cl.Ct.1984, 6 Cl. Ct. 829. United States ⬙ 64.60(1)

II. ADMINISTRATIVE REVIEW

Subdivision Index

---

31. Power of contracting parties, administrative review

Contracting parties have power to provide for administrative determination of disputes arising incident to contract performance and by appropriate provision to convert breach of contract claims to claims cognizable under contract. Monroe Garment Co., Inc. v. U.S., Ct.Cl.1973, 488 F.2d 989, 203 Ct.Cl. 324. United States ⬙ 73(9)

32. Time of final decisions of contracting officer, administrative review

Where contractor did not claim breach of government's implied covenant to render a timely and appropriate decision on its claim and purchaser was laggard in failing to push contracting officer to award final decision and failure to render final decision was formal, rather than substantial, government did not forfeit its contractual right to an initial administrative determination of claim despite its undue delay in rendering timely and appropriate decision on claim. Zidell Explorations, Inc. v. U.S., Ct.Cl.1970, 427 F.2d 735, 192 Ct.Cl. 331. United States ⬙ 74(8)

33. Notice of appeal, administrative review

A government contractor's letter expressing hardships which the termination would cause and stating "We respectfully ask that you again consider the 'development' nature of our effort and advise if further reconsideration can be granted for a termination other than for default, or advise if we have any recourse for further review" did not constitute a sufficient notice of appeal from a final decision of termination of contract which was required to be made within 30 days from date of termination. Richardson Camera Co., Inc. v. U.S., Ct.Cl.1972, 467 F.2d 491, 199 Ct.Cl. 657. United States ⟾ 73(15)

Where contracting officer prior to adoption of regulation requiring contracting officer to give contractor notice of his final decision and to alert contractor to appeal rights had made decision but continued to negotiate with contractor and subcontractor and finally sent notice affirming his prior decision, first notice was not a final determination, and appeal by contractor after expiration of 30 days after second notice which did not comply with requirements of regulation should not be deemed untimely and Board should decide dispute on merits. Roscoe-Ajax Const. Co. v. U.S., Ct.Cl.1972, 458 F.2d 55, 198 Ct.Cl. 133. United States ⟾ 73(15)

34. Time of appeal, administrative review

Armed services board of contract appeals did not abuse discretion in denying contractor's request for waiver of contractor's six-day delay in mailing its appeal from adverse decision of contracting officer in connection with contractor's claim for additional costs where, under facts presented to board, decision to waive or not to waive six-day delay of contractor could reasonably have gone either way. J.R. Youngdale Const. Co., Inc. v. U.S., Ct.Cl.1976, 536 F.2d 369, 210 Ct.Cl. 459. United States ⟾ 73(15)

Strict compliance with time limit prescribed in the standard type of "disputes" provision for the taking of appeals is not jurisdictional, and Boards of Contract Appeals have the power, in proper circumstances, to extend or waive compliance with such time limit. J.R. Youngdale Const. Co., Inc. v. U.S., Ct.Cl.1974, 504 F.2d 1124, 205 Ct.Cl. 578. United States ⟾ 73(15)

Decision of contracting officer under dispute clause in government contract is final on any factual matter unless appealed by a contractor within 30 days to the head of the department administering the contract or his authorized representative. American Export Isbrandtsen Lines, Inc. v. U.S., Ct.Cl.1974, 499 F.2d 552, 204 Ct.Cl. 424. United States ⟾ 73(14)

Burden rests on contractor who fails to comply with requirement that appeal to

Board of Contract Appeals be filed within 30-day period to persuade and convince Board that under the circumstances of his case a waiver of the time limit should be granted and prejudice to the government is a factor to be considered, but lack of such prejudice does not automatically entitle the plaintiff to a waiver. Maney Aircraft Parts, Inc. v. U.S., Ct.Cl.1973, 479 F.2d 1350, 202 Ct.Cl. 54. United States ⟾ 73(15)

The Court of Claims would not suspend its action for 90 days while plaintiff, which had failed to file an appeal to appeal board within 30 days after termination of contract, was permitted to seek a discretionary waiver from the board, where while contractor might have jumped to conclusion, by government's original requests for settlement costs, that a termination for convenience was contemplated, it was apparent that delay was, in vital part, a product of contractor's own neglect and that, since all the pertinent facts appeared to have been raised at initial board hearing, a suspension to permit an appeal for discretionary waiver would serve little purpose. Richardson Camera Co., Inc. v. U.S., Ct.Cl. 1972, 467 F.2d 491, 199 Ct.Cl. 657. United States ⟾ 73(15)

Government contractor, whose appeal from termination of contract for default was not timely since it was filed one day after running of the 30-day appeal period set forth in contract and in notice of termination, should be permitted to apply to Armed Services Board of Contract Appeals for consideration of a discretionary waiver of the 30-day appeal period, where it did not appear certain that accountant of contractor, who receipted for termination telegram on Saturday when contractor's plant was officially closed, was at the plant on company business, that accountant knew or appreciated the importance of the notice, or that he opened it to find out its contents. Maney Aircraft Parts, Inc. v. U.S., Ct.Cl.1972, 453 F.2d 1260, 197 Ct.Cl. 159, supplemented 479 F.2d 1350, 202 Ct.Cl. 54. United States ⟾ 73(15)

Refusal to toll 30-day period set forth in disputes clause for appealing from administrative denial of claims against government on ground that claimant's attorney and claimant's wife had died was not an abuse of the Armed Services Board of Contract Appeals' discretion where claimant showed by his response to a decision on third claim that he knew how to compose and file the brief notice of appeal required and where that notice did not refer in any way to the two earlier decisions which had been received less than three weeks earlier. Schlesinger v. U.S., Ct.Cl.1967, 383 F.2d 1004, 181 Ct. Cl. 21. United States ☞ 73(15)

Government contractor who failed to appeal within 30 days from contracting officer's decision, made final in absence of appeal within 30 days, that it was not entitled to damages for injuries to its leased truck was foreclosed from any possibility of recovery as it had agreed to disposition of claims based on disputed questions of fact by contract. U.S. v. Peter Kiewit Sons' Co., C.A.8 (Neb.) 1965, 345 F.2d 879. United States ☞ 73(14)

Where the Navy Board of Contract Appeals dismissed the plaintiff's appeal with respect to Contract NObs–206 because the appeal had not been made within the period of 30 days, as required by instructions to his subordinates issued by the Secretary after all of plaintiff's contracts had been made, although the Board recognized that the dispute involved a "question of law" not covered by the disputes provision of the contract and since the plaintiff was not bound by the administrative determination of the question of law, plaintiff lost nothing by its failure to appeal within 30 days. Cramp Shipbuilding Co. v. U.S., Ct.Cl.1952, 122 Ct. Cl. 72. United States ☞ 73(15)

Where the plaintiff appealed in writing to the Chief of Engineers from the decision of the contracting officer with respect to changed conditions encountered, and where the Chief of Engineers refused to pass on the merits of the claim because the appeal had not been filed within the time limit prescribed by the contract, plaintiff was not entitled to recover. Stiers Bros. Const. Co. v. U.S., Ct.Cl.1947, 109 Ct.Cl. 353. Contracts ☞ 285(1); United States ☞ 73(13)

Where the work was begun but after the contract had been signed, the contractor took exception to the contracting officer's ruling as to the amount of concrete to be used, but did not appeal from the decision until after the work had been concluded, the time to appeal was when the ruling was made. Union Paving Co.

v. U.S., Ct.Cl.1946, 107 Ct.Cl. 405. Contracts ☞ 285(1); United States ☞ 73(15)

35. Issues reviewable, administrative review

Veterans' Administration Contract Appeals Board had jurisdiction over successful bidder's claim under this chapter for an equitable adjustment recovery with regard to award of certain contracts on ground that Government had allegedly provided defective drawing upon which it had the right to rely in making its bids. Johnson Controls, Inc. v. U.S., Ct.Cl. 1982, 671 F.2d 1312, 229 Ct.Cl. 445. United States ☞ 73(15)

Government's counsel at proceeding before Armed Services Board of Contract Appeals could agree to modification whereby Board would hear licensing controversy, and did so implicitly agree, vesting Board with all necessary authority to hear and decide licensing dispute with all formality of this chapter, by going forward without objecting to propriety of the forum. General Dynamics Corp. v. U.S., Ct.Cl.1977, 558 F.2d 985, 214 Ct.Cl. 607, 198 U.S.P.Q. 215. United States ☞ 73(9)

Under general provisions of government contract which limited jurisdiction of board of contract appeals to a dispute concerning a question of fact arising under the contract, breach of contract claims were excluded whether for the purpose of granting relief or of making binding findings of fact. Broome Const., Inc. v. U.S., Ct.Cl.1974, 492 F.2d 829, 203 Ct.Cl. 521. United States ☞ 73(14)

Where government delivered armor plate to defense contractor to be used in manufacture of gun carriage parts under the contract, and where contract had no provision for storage charges by contractor with respect to armor plate remaining at completion of contract, contractor was not required to appeal to Armed Services Board of Contract Appeals with respect to his claim for storage charges and Board would not have had jurisdiction thereof, and thus Court of Claims had jurisdiction of the storage claim, notwithstanding contention that contractor had not exhausted administrative remedies. Algonac Mfg. Co. v. U.S., Ct.Cl.1970, 428 F.2d 1241, 192 Ct.Cl. 649, supplemented 458 F.2d 1373, 198 Ct.Cl. 258. United States ☞ 74(11)

Where only clause in government contract which was or could have been invoked in support of administrative relief was not applicable, claim of breach of duty of Federal Maritime Board to supply working plans to contractor was pure breach of contract claim over which administrative authorities had no jurisdiction. National Steel & Shipbuilding Co. v. U.S., Ct.Cl.1969, 419 F.2d 863, 190 Ct.Cl. 247. United States ☞ 73(9)

Contractor was entitled to hearing before Armed Services Board of Contract Appeals as to extent, if any, of damage to underground utilities directly attributable to change in grading on housing project at Air Force base required by contracting officer. Electronic & Missile Facilities, Inc. v. U.S., Ct.Cl.1969, 416 F.2d 1345, 189 Ct.Cl. 237. United States ☞ 73(9)

Veterans Administration Contract Appeals Board had duty to consider issue as to whether government had been prejudiced by delay of government contractor in presenting its claim, even though contracting officer did not mention prejudice in his decision letter or in his findings, inasmuch as issue was inherent in question as to whether there had been abuse of discretion by contracting officer and his refusal to consider contractor's claim on the merits for lack of timely notice. Eggers & Higgins & Edwin A. Keeble Associates, Inc. v. U.S., Ct.Cl.1968, 403 F.2d 225, 185 Ct.Cl. 765. United States ☞ 73(9)

Contractor's asserted breach of contract claims against government arising out of government's claiming a five per cent cost reduction under price discount provision of contract were matters for administrative determination and were not considered independently as breach of contract actions. Schlesinger v. U.S., Ct.Cl.1967, 383 F.2d 1004, 181 Ct.Cl. 21. United States ☞ 73(9)

All of contractor's claims against government, including claims for alleged breaches of contract, were within jurisdiction of board of contract appeals, where relief to contractor on claims for failure to award equitable adjustments would be complete relief under breach of contract claims. Conn v. U.S., Ct.Cl. 1966, 366 F.2d 1019, 177 Ct.Cl. 319. United States ☞ 73(9)

Question as to whether Government was justified in terminating supply contract with defendant did not involve construction of contract which Armed Services Board of Contract Appeals lacked

authority to make. Silverman Bros., Inc. v. U.S., C.A.1 (R.I.) 1963, 324 F.2d 287. United States ☞ 73(9)

36. Questions of law or fact, administrative review

Armed services board of contract appeals may consider questions of law as well as questions of fact. R.E.D.M. Corp. v. Lo Secco, S.D.N.Y.1968, 291 F.Supp. 53, affirmed 412 F.2d 303. United States ☞ 73(15)

Where contractor claimed damages for breach of contract whereunder he was to remove old poles, erect new ones, install antenna and build a culvert with old poles, and United States contracting officer admitted delay in United States' performance and granted recovery for resultant extra antenna work but denied, as in nature of damages, recovery for idle time of rented road machinery, officer's decision was one of law, and contractor was not required to appeal decision through administrative channels before seeking judicial relief. Allied Contractors v. U.S., Ct.Cl.1954, 124 F.Supp. 366, 129 Ct.Cl. 400. United States ☞ 74(8)

37. Standard of review, administrative review

With regard to questions of fact, findings by contracting officer are not necessarily binding upon Armed Services Board of Contract Appeals, since proceedings before Board are de novo, and Board may base its decision on a preponderance of evidence in its entire record. Monroe Garment Co., Inc. v. U.S., Ct.Cl. 1973, 488 F.2d 989, 203 Ct.Cl. 324. United States ☞ 73(15)

Board of contract appeals was entitled to examine matter de novo on appeal from contracting officer. Blount Bros. Corp. v. U.S., Ct.Cl.1970, 424 F.2d 1074, 191 Ct.Cl. 784. United States ☞ 73(15)

On appeal to chief of engineers, or board representing him, decision of contracting officer, which enjoyed no presumption of validity under disputes article of government contract, was vacated, and board owed contractor a de novo hearing and a de novo decision based on applicable law, contract terms, and a preponderance of evidence; board could not abdicate that responsibility by applying tests provided by this section to contracting officer's decision—such tests were reserved for court engaged in subsequent judicial review of Board decision. Southwest Welding & Mfg. Co. v. U.S., Ct.Cl. 1969, 413 F.2d 1167, 188 Ct.Cl. 925. United States ☞ 73(15)

In reviewing the decision of the contracting officer in a factual dispute arising under the contract, a board of contract appeals may examine the dispute de novo and resolve it on appeal on the basis of a preponderance of the evidence before it and without regard to what evidence was before the contracting officer and it is only in the course of judicial review of the board's decision that the court will apply the usual substantial evidence test using only the administrative record on which the board's decision was based. Davis v. U.S., Ct.Cl.1967, 180 Ct. Cl. 20.   United States ☞ 73(15)

38. Default judgment, administrative review

The Corps of Engineers Board of Contract Appeals did not have authority to enter default judgment for the failure of the Government to timely file its answer in proceeding on contractor's claim against the Government. Carl M. Halvorson, Inc. v. U.S., Ct.Cl.1972, 461 F.2d 1337, 198 Ct.Cl. 882.   United States ☞ 73(15)

39. Defenses, administrative review

Previous action of contracting officer in considering contractor's claim for increase in price on its merits did not constitute a waiver on behalf of Government of any defense based upon lack of notice of subsurface conditions differing from those described in contract documents inasmuch as subsequent proceedings before Armed Services Board of Contract Appeals were wholly de novo. Schnip Bldg. Co. v. U.S., Ct.Cl.1981, 645 F.2d 950, 227 Ct.Cl. 148.   United States ☞ 70(36)

40. Dismissal, administrative review

Where claim had been remanded to the Armed Services Board of Contract Appeals to permit the contractor to cross-examine the contracting officer on whether his decision to terminate the contractor's supply contract was reached in good faith and where contractor had failed to comply with ASBCA order directing it to file a statement setting forth its proposed schedule for completion of discovery and the date on when it expected to be ready for a hearing if one was desired, Board was justified in dismissing the claim. Fairfield Scientific Corp. v. U.S., Ct.Cl.

1981, 655 F.2d 1062, 228 Ct.Cl. 264. United States ☞ 73(9)

Board of Contract Appeals should not have dismissed, as untimely, general contractor's appeal from contracting officer's decision without considering whether appeal period specified in prime contract should have been waived in view of fact that general contractor left almost all of the dealings with the government with respect to construction to subcontractor and the government considered subcontractor's request for compensation for alleged "extras" on the merits and did not send copy of contracting officer's decision to subcontractor but only to general contractor, who was on vacation at the time and who received decision late because his secretary had misfiled it. Monroe M. Tapper and Associates v. U.S., Ct.Cl.1972, 458 F.2d 66, 198 Ct.Cl. 72. United States ☞ 73(15)

Claim of government contractor based on damage resulting from delay attributable to government's inaction following notice of changed conditions was not readjustable under the standard, mandatory "changes" clause but would be redressable under a "pay-for-delay" or suspension of work type of contract clause and, in absence of such clause being present in contract, claim was properly dismissed by Board of Contract Appeals for want of jurisdiction. Cosmo Const. Co. v. U.S., Ct.Cl.1971, 439 F.2d 160, 194 Ct.Cl. 559. United States ☞ 70(22.1); United States ☞ 73(9); United States ☞ 73(20)

Electrical equipment subcontractor's cause of action against general contractors on government contract for failure to supply "station piping" was properly dismissed, where ambiguity existed as to meaning of "station piping" which was expressly excluded from specifications of subcontract defining obligations of electrical equipment supplier, extrinsic evidence of meaning of term was received, and determination of officer in charge of construction was conclusive as to questions of fact and mixed questions of fact, under the subcontract and the applicable statutes.   Construction Management Corp. v. Brown & Root, Inc., N.Y.A.D. 1 Dept.1966, 270 N.Y.S.2d 95, 25 A.D.2d 843.   Contracts ☞ 284(4)

41. Burden of proof, administrative review

Plaintiff contractor had burden of proof before Interior Board of Contract Appeals

567

where contractor sought additional payment under terms of its contracts with government on ground that it was entitled to have all materials excavated from certain areas of construction work treated as rock excavation rather than 35% of such materials as allowed by contracting officer. L.B. Samford, Inc. v. U.S., Ct.Cl. 1969, 410 F.2d 782, 187 Ct.Cl. 714. United States ⊱ 74(10)

42. Discovery, administrative review

Contractor was not denied due process and board of contract appeals did not abuse discretion in denying contractor's motion for production of documents in part on ground that there was no showing that documents existed or were relevant and in part on uncontroverted claim that laboratory tests sought were confidential property of nongovernmental agency. Blount Bros. Corp. v. U.S., Ct. Cl.1970, 424 F.2d 1074, 191 Ct.Cl. 784. Constitutional Law ⊱ 4256; United States ⊱ 73(15)

43. Admissibility of evidence, administrative review

Administrative tribunal is not required to exclude hearsay evidence in form of document if its authenticity is sufficiently convincing to a reasonable mind and if it carried sufficient assurance as to truthfulness. Fairfield Scientific Corp. v. U.S., Ct.Cl.1979, 611 F.2d 854, 222 Ct.Cl. 167. Administrative Law And Procedure ⊱ 461

Matter before board of contract appeals is a de novo proceeding and whether certain materials were before contracting officer or not is immaterial to determination of substantiality of board's determination. Arundel Corp. v. U.S., Ct.Cl. 1975, 515 F.2d 1116, 207 Ct.Cl. 84. United States ⊱ 73(14)

Where witness testifying as to how estimate was compiled stated that although he was author of final document figures on which it was based came from information gathered by two other individuals and he assumed figures had been checked, hearing examiner's refusal to admit document into evidence was proper. Nager Elec. Co. v. U.S., Ct.Cl.1971, 442 F.2d 936, 194 Ct.Cl. 835. Evidence ⊱ 355(5)

Armed Services Board of Contract Appeals was not required to accept contractor's affidavit if deemed to be nonpersuasive, merely because it was un-

contradicted, where affidavit, relating to costs in performance of government contract, consisted of brief general statement not accompanied by underlying figures, as the subject matter would be more appropriately proven by books and records rather than by conclusory assertions. Rice v. U.S., Ct.Cl.1970, 428 F.2d 1311, 192 Ct.Cl. 903. United States ⊱ 73(9)

Common-law exclusionary rules of evidence are not applicable in proceedings before Contract Disputes Board. U.S. v. Hamden Co-op. Creamery Co., E.D.N.Y. 1960, 185 F.Supp. 541, affirmed 297 F.2d 130. United States ⊱ 73(9)

Where, in a claim arising under the disputes article of a Government contract, plaintiff has offered in evidence parts of the administrative record and defendant has refused to introduce any part thereof despite commissioner's repeated statements that he would accept and consider any part or parts of the record defendant wished to offer, the commissioner was entitled to decide the issue of liability on the basis of those parts of the record offered in evidence by plaintiff. H.R. Henderson & Co., Inc. v. U.S., Ct.Cl.1965, 169 Ct.Cl. 228. Federal Courts ⊱ 1117

When a contractor appeals from the adverse decision of a contracting officer to the head of the department or the Board designated as his representative under the disputes article of the contract, the evidence presented to the contracting officer is properly a part of the record on appeal to the department head and does not need to be formally proffered at the hearing on appeal. Twombly Tree Experts v. U.S., Ct.Cl.1964, 168 Ct.Cl. 921. United States ⊱ 73(15)

44. Weight and sufficiency of evidence, administrative review

Board of contract appeals could properly give more attention to testimony of geologist which was more detailed than that of other geologists. Arundel Corp. v. U.S., Ct.Cl.1975, 515 F.2d 1116, 207 Ct. Cl. 84. United States ⊱ 73(9)

Answers to leading questions asked by government counsel in hearing before armed services board of contract appeals were not probative of government's claim that contractor voluntarily assumed acceleration clauses. Tombigbee Constructors v. U.S., Ct.Cl.1970, 420 F.2d 1037, 190 Ct.Cl. 615.   United States ⬱ 74(11)

General Services Administration Board of Contract Appeals, as trier of facts in proceeding on claim of general contractor for equitable price adjustment or for damages, was vested with discretion to accept testimony of government's witnesses and to reject that of contractor's witnesses. Ambrose-Augusterfer Corp. v. U.S., Ct.Cl.1968, 394 F.2d 536, 184 Ct.Cl. 18.   United States ⬱ 73(9)

Under a Government contract which provides that disputes concerning questions of fact shall be decided by a written decision of the contracting officer which decision shall be final unless appealed to the head of the contracting agency, and that the decision of such agency head (or that of his duly authorized representative) shall likewise be final unless overturned by a court of competent jurisdiction on the grounds specified in this chapter, the decision on appeal must be one to which the agency head or his representative has directed his individual attention after personal consideration of the evidence or record relative to the dispute but department head's decision based upon the recommendation of a subordinate who had neither heard nor weighed the evidence and who had no record before him except a memorandum from the Board Panel member who conducted an ex parte "hearing" on the appeal, does not comply with the minimum standards for an administrative decision under the contract disputes provision. Johnson v. U.S., Ct. Cl.1965, 173 Ct.Cl. 561.   United States ⬱ 73(9)

45.   Calling or production of witnesses, administrative review

Government contractor was not denied due process by failure of board of contract appeals (which does not have subpoena power) to call contracting officer, where no prejudice or an independent effort to secure his appearance was shown. Blount Bros. Corp. v. U.S., Ct.Cl. 1970, 424 F.2d 1074, 191 Ct.Cl. 784. Constitutional Law ⬱ 4256

46.   Cross-examination, administrative review

Hearing before Veterans Administration Construction Contract Appeals Board at which none of the Government's evidence was testimonial or subject to cross-examination, while part of contrac-

tor's evidence was oral and subject to inquiry and at which both presentations were primarily ex parte was not a clear violation of due process or wholly invalid. J.D. Hedin Const. Co. v. U.S., Ct.Cl.1969, 408 F.2d 424, 187 Ct.Cl. 45.   Administrative Law And Procedure ⬱ 472; Constitutional Law ⬱ 4256; United States ⬱ 73(9)

47.   Theory of recovery, administrative review

Although neither party to claim against government by contractor had presented or advanced theory of changed conditions on level of the contracting officer or to Interior Board of Contract Appeals in presentation of the administrative claim, Board was not precluded from deciding claim on that theory. L.B. Samford, Inc. v. U.S., Ct.Cl.1969, 410 F.2d 782, 187 Ct.Cl. 714.   United States ⬱ 73(12)

A Government board of contract appeals is not precluded from deciding a claim on a theory not advanced by the parties, nor is it obligated to accept an agreement by the parties concerning a particular theory if it concludes the theory is legally improper. Law v. U.S., Ct. Cl.1971, 195 Ct.Cl. 370.   United States ⬱ 73(9)

48.   Findings of fact, administrative review

Where contractors failed to demand findings of fact from Armed Services Board of Contract Appeals in regard to excuses for delay in completion of government contract, and evidence proffered by contractors concerned issue of validity of release from claims signed by them and did not go to merits of their excuses, it was not improper for Board to fail to make specific findings on merits of contractors' excuses. Johnson, Drake & Piper, Inc. v. U.S., Ct.Cl.1976, 531 F.2d 1037, 209 Ct.Cl. 313.   United States ⬱ 73(13)

Fact findings by Armed Services Board of Contract Appeals were not invalid because presiding member did not write the decision and was not a party thereto. Sundstrand Turbo v. U.S., Ct.Cl.1968, 389 F.2d 406, 182 Ct.Cl. 31.   United States ⬱ 73(9)

Lack of findings by contracting officer did not render his decision denying builder an upward adjustment of aircraft carrier construction contract price unconstitutional as contrary to due process.

Newport News Shipbuilding & Dry Dock Co. v. U.S., Ct.Cl.1967, 374 F.2d 516, 179 Ct.Cl. 97. Constitutional Law ⮑ 4256

So long as the officer charged with the duty of deciding considers the evidence, opinion written by a member of an Armed Services Board of Contract Appeals, other than the one who presided at the hearing, does not result in a failure of due process. Peterson-Sharpe Engineering Corp. v. U.S., Cl.Ct.1984, 6 Cl.Ct. 288. Constitutional Law ⮑ 4246

49. Reopening of decisions, administrative review

Boards of contract appeals considering disputes appealed to them from decisions of the contracting officer have authority to reopen decisions made by them and consider new evidence and they also have discretion to refuse to reopen their decisions. Tankersley v. U.S., Ct.Cl.1967, 179 Ct.Cl. 294. United States ⮑ 73(9)

50. General Accounting Office review, administrative review

General Accounting Office review of contract appeals board decisions in favor of the Government is not a necessary corollary of such Office's power to disallow board decisions against the Government in the course of such Office's audit and account settlement authority; in the latter case, but not in the former, such Office's disallowance can lead to judicial review of the board decision. 1969, 42 Op.Atty.Gen., January 16.

51. Election of remedies, administrative review

Where a contractor has proceeded administratively to obtain an equitable adjustment under the changed conditions clause of its contract, claiming that the failure of the off-site drainage contractor to complete its work resulted in plaintiff's encountering a changed condition, and where the administrative Board of Contract Appeals decides this issue adversely to plaintiff, the plaintiff is in no position to assert a claim for breach of contract seeking the same relief on the same set of facts. Fort Sill Associates v. U.S., Ct.Cl. 1968, 183 Ct.Cl. 301. United States ⮑ 73(14)

52. Exclusiveness of remedy, administrative review

Where contractor elected to submit appeal from contracting officer's denial of redress for Government's claimed breach

of government contract to Army Adjustment Board, contractor irrevocably extinguished its rights to sue on contract. Hicks Corp. v. U.S., Ct.Cl.1973, 487 F.2d 520, 203 Ct.Cl. 65. United States ⮑ 74(7)

Exclusive administrative remedy as provided in government contracts for termination substitutes for "breach" claim which would otherwise exist for improper default-termination, and such remedy becomes contractor's sole form of relief, and is an adequate replacement for common-law cause of action. William Green Const. Co., Inc. v. U.S., Ct.Cl.1973, 477 F.2d 930, 201 Ct.Cl. 616, certiorari denied 94 S.Ct. 2606, 417 U.S. 909, 41 L.Ed.2d 213. United States ⮑ 74(7)

Federal contractor's claims for changes, extra costs and extensions of time based on improper rejections and double inspection under contract providing for single inspection only are administratively redressable by armed services board of contract appeals by an award of an equitable adjustment; accordingly, the claims may not by redescription be converted into breach of contract claims to be tried by court. Marley v. U.S., Ct.Cl. 1970, 423 F.2d 324, 191 Ct.Cl. 205. United States ⮑ 74(7)

Where third-party plaintiff and third-party defendants had entered into ship construction contract that contained clause that any dispute arising thereunder should be decided by maritime administration, third-party plaintiff did not waive its rights to administrative determination by filing third-party complaints for indemnity. Farrell Marine Devices, Inc. v. Lykes Bros. S.S. Co., E.D.La.1969, 299 F.Supp. 1270. Alternative Dispute Resolution ⮑ 182(2)

There can be a contractually binding representation of proper timely delivery of Government-furnished property without any administrative relief being available under the contract if the representation is unfulfilled and the breach of such representation is actionable outside the contract if the Government–Furnished Property clause does not provide an exclusive administrative remedy or does not expressly exculpate the Government from breach of contract liability. Koppers/Clough, v. U.S., Ct.Cl.1973, 201 Ct. Cl. 344. United States ⮑ 74(3)

53. Exhaustion of administrative remedies, administrative review—Generally

Under changes clause of typical government contract, contractor must present his claim to contracting officer whose decision is final unless appealed for final action by department head or his representatives and, until such department head or representative has acted, contractor's claim is not subject to adjudication in courts. Crown Coat Front Co. v. U.S., U.S.N.Y.1967, 87 S.Ct. 1177, 386 U.S. 503, 18 L.Ed.2d 256. United States ☞ 73(9); United States ☞ 73(14)

Government contractor, who did not pursue administrative remedy under contract with disputes clause, was not deprived of due process through being prevented from asserting disputes claims as defense to government's action for liquidated damages. U.S. v. Ulvedal, C.A.8 (N.D.) 1967, 372 F.2d 31. Constitutional Law ☞ 4412

Action of Board of Contract Appeals on claim under government contract requiring submission of disputes to Board is integral to converting claim, and there can be no judicially cognizable injury, no violation of contract, and no claim for court relief until Board has acted or had a chance to act. Nager Elec. Co. v. U.S., Ct.Cl.1966, 368 F.2d 847, 177 Ct.Cl. 234. United States ☞ 74(8)

Ordinarily, procedure contained in standard disputes clause in government contract providing for determinations of controversy by contracting officers and Armed Services Board of Contract Appeals must be exhausted before contractor may appeal to courts. Northern Metal Co. v. U.S., C.A.3 (Pa.) 1965, 350 F.2d 833. United States ☞ 74(8)

This chapter forbids use of court as means of automatically enforcing administrative decision in favor of government contractor. ACME Process Equipment Co. v. U.S., Ct.Cl.1965, 347 F.2d 538, 171 Ct.Cl. 251, motion denied 351 F.2d 656, 171 Ct.Cl. 251. United States ☞ 73(15)

Provision in contract between United States and dredging company that all disputes concerning questions of fact arising under contract should be decided by contracting officer subject to written appeal by contractor within thirty days to head of department required, under ordinary circumstances, that such an appeal be made before bringing of action in Court of Claims [now United States Court of Federal Claims]. Guion v. U.S., Ct.Cl. 1947, 69 F.Supp. 341, 108 Ct.Cl. 186. Navigable Waters ☞ 6; United States ☞ 74(8)

Where plaintiff failed to appeal the adverse decisions of the contracting officer to the head of the department, as provided by the contract, there could be no recovery. B-W Const. Co. v. U.S., Ct.Cl. 1945, 104 Ct.Cl. 608, certiorari denied 66 S.Ct. 704, 327 U.S. 785, 90 L.Ed. 1012. Contracts ☞ 285(1)

54. —— Claims subject to exhaustion requirement, exhaustion of administrative remedies, administrative review

Disputes clause of construction contract with Atomic Energy Commission did not cover all disputes relating to contract, and did not render contractor's claim for breach of contract causing unreasonable delay one subject to administrative determination, or make administrative findings on claim conclusive so as to preclude de novo determination in Court of Claims. U.S. v. Utah Const. & Min. Co., U.S.Ct.Cl.1966, 86 S.Ct. 1545, 384 U.S. 394, 16 L.Ed.2d 642. United States ☞ 73(9); United States ☞ 73(14)

Where disputes clause in government contract provided that "Any dispute arising out of or connected in any way with any obligation of the parties arising out of the performance or nonperformance of the contract, whether arising before or after completion of performance, including disputes as to any alleged violation or breach thereof, shall be decided by the Contracting Officer," by its own terms it conferred breach of contract jurisdiction to defendant's general manager subject to review under this chapter and contractor's suit was barred for failure to exhaust contractually established disputes procedure with regard to claim that government's projected failure to supply adequate work constituted an anticipatory breach. Patton Wrecking & Demolition Co. v. Tennessee Val. Authority, C.A.5 (Miss.) 1972, 465 F.2d 1073. United States ☞ 73(9); United States ☞ 74(8)

Where government contract specifically provided that, if the contractor was not in default, the rights and obligations of the parties would be the same as if notice of termination had been issued pursuant to the convenience-termination clause, allegedly improper default termination was not a "breach", but fell "under the contract", and contractor was required to first appeal to the Armed Services Board of Contract Appeals before suing in the Court of Claims. Maney Aircraft Parts, Inc. v. U.S., Ct.Cl.1972, 453 F.2d 1260, 197 Ct.Cl. 159, supplemented 479 F.2d 1350, 202 Ct.Cl. 54. United States ☞ 74(8)

Government claimant does not avoid limitations on judicial review of administrative action by bringing suit for breach of contract. Northbridge Electronics, Inc. v. U.S., Ct.Cl.1971, 444 F.2d 1124, 195 Ct.Cl. 453. United States ☞ 73(15)

No basis existed upon which contractor, which filed suit against government to recover either in quantum meruit the reasonable value of goods and services delivered to and accepted by Navy Department or for breach of contract because defendant failed to definitize letter contract, was obliged to proceed to Armed Services Board of Contract Appeals and exhaust its administrative remedies, where there was no finding or decision of a contracting officer on a question of fact from which the contractor could appeal to the Board, nor any dispute regarding a question of fact arising under the letter contract. Sanders Associates, Inc. v. U.S., Ct.Cl.1970, 423 F.2d 291, 191 Ct.Cl. 157. United States ☞ 74(8)

Determination of equitable adjustment, if any, due plaintiff government contractor for changes ordered by government could not be made in first instances by court of claims but must be made by Armed Services Board of Contract Appeals. Emerson-Sack-Warner Corp. v. U.S., Ct.Cl.1969, 416 F.2d 1335, 189 Ct. Cl. 264. United States ☞ 73(15)

Where suit in which recovery was sought against government by corporate government contractor, its insurer and its major stockholder for loss of certain equipment was based on theories of negligence and unseaworthiness of vessel and there was no "specific contract adjustment provision" with regard to claims of such nature, fact that contract contained a "dispute clause" providing administrative procedure for disposition of disputes did not require that court proceedings be stayed until procedure set forth in contract was exhausted. Aetna Ins. Co. v. U.S., E.D.La.1971, 327 F.Supp. 865. United States ☞ 127(1)

Standard disputes clause of government construction contract does not apply to factual issues involved after completion or termination of the contract; the clause requires exhaustion of administrative remedies only when the factual question arises during performance of contract. Compudyne Corp. v. Maxon Const. Co., E.D.Pa.1965, 248 F.Supp. 83. United States ☞ 73(9)

55. —— Jurisdiction of administrative body or officer, exhaustion of administrative remedies, administrative review

Where plaintiff manufacturer had entered into a contract with the Navy Department for the construction of certain units of ships, but contract was amended and modified and manufacturer operated under a new cost basis instead of original fixed fee basis, the fact that the Government did not appeal from the contracting officer's findings of fact was not relevant to manufacturer's right to have that part of high initial cost incurred before modification date allocated to production after that date, since the question of allocation of normal high initial costs was not for the contracting officer to decide. Merrill-Stevens Dry Dock & Repair Co. v. U.S., Ct.Cl.1951, 96 F.Supp. 464, 119 Ct.Cl. 310. United States ☞ 73(14)

A contractor's claim for unliquidated damages against the United States is a claim over which the contracting officer has no jurisdiction and the contractor need not pursue the "Disputes" clause remedy of appeal to the head of the department from an adverse decision by the contracting officer. Commercial Cable Co. v. U.S., Ct.Cl.1965, 170 Ct.Cl. 813. United States ☞ 73(9); United States ☞ 74(8)

56. —— De novo adjudication, exhaustion of administrative remedies, administrative review

Government contractor, which had not received a final "de novo" adjudication pursuant to disputes clause of its contract, had not exhausted its intra-agency remedies before the Armed Services Board of Contract Appeals to which it had appealed contracting officer's adverse decision and was not entitled to maintain mandamus action by which it sought to receive findings additional to those filed by contracting officer when he denied claim for equitable upward adjust-

ment in contract price. R.E.D.M. Corp.
v. Lo Secco, C.A.2 (N.Y.) 1969, 412 F.2d
303. Mandamus ⚮ 4(5)

57.   —— Ignorance of regulations, exhaustion of administrative remedies, administrative review

Although, generally, a party cannot assign an error in Court of Claims that he has not given administrative tribunal a chance to correct, an exception must be made in the interest of fairness when the error consists of a mutual ignoring of a whole body of applicable agency regulations, considering that agency officials have the means and the duty to be aware of their own regulations to a greater extent than outsiders and that it is not fair to throw the consequences of such a mutual mistake wholly on the party least responsible for causing it. Bethlehem Steel Corp. v. U.S., Ct.Cl.1970, 423 F.2d 300, 191 Ct.Cl. 141. United States ⚮ 73(15)

58.   —— Inadequacy or futility, exhaustion of administrative remedies, administrative review

Parties to government contract will not be required to exhaust administrative procedure if it is shown by clear evidence that such procedure is inadequate or unavailable, but these circumstances are exceptions and inadequacy or unavailability of administrative relief must clearly appear before party may circumvent his own contractual agreement. U.S. v. Anthony Grace & Sons, Inc., U.S.Ct.Cl. 1966, 86 S.Ct. 1539, 384 U.S. 424, 16 L.Ed.2d 662. United States ⚮ 74(8)

Government contractor's administrative remedy of appeal to contracting officer and Postal Service Board of Contract Appeals was not inadequate and unavailable, notwithstanding delay of some seven years during which Board of Contract Appeals first dismissed contractor's appeal on ground that it could not waive contractual time limit and, following remand by Court of Claims, arbitrarily refused to waive time limit. Monroe M. Tapper and Associates v. U.S., Ct.Cl.1975, 514 F.2d 1003, 206 Ct.Cl. 446. United States ⚮ 73(15)

Where Government contracting officer, by refusing to make a record, makes it impossible for contractor to prepare a memorandum asserting issues to be considered on appeal from contractor's decision, the appellate procedure is inade-

quate and failure to pursue appellate procedure under contract does not prevent contractor from seeking judicial relief. U.S. v. Lennox Metal Mfg. Co., E.D.N.Y.1954, 131 F.Supp. 717, affirmed 225 F.2d 302. United States ⚮ 74(8)

Contractor's failure to act under clause of Government hauling contract requiring disputes concerning questions of fact arising under the contract to be decided by contracting officer did not preclude recovery on contract, where contracting officer had specifically announced a construction adverse to contractor, so that it would have been a vain thing to have him act as arbitrator and had threatened contractor with penalties. Lundstrom v. U.S., D.C.Or.1941, 53 F.Supp. 709, affirmed 139 F.2d 792. United States ⚮ 74(1)

Where deductions from contract price for shelving installed in federal office building were approved by department head before they were made, contractor would not be deprived of any rights by failure to take written appeal to departmental head, and its action to recover amount of deductions would be decided as though departmental appeal had been timely taken and disallowed. General Steel Products Corporation v. U.S., E.D.N.Y.1941, 36 F.Supp. 498. United States ⚮ 127(1)

Where the relief sought in the court is relief which could not have been given the contractor administratively under the provisions of the contract, the claim being for damages for defendant's failure to accept delivery under the contract, the issue of damages may be initially determined by the Court of Claims and the case need not be referred to the contracting agency for a computation of such damages as the recent Supreme Court decision in U.S. v. Anthony Grace & Sons, Inc., 86 S.Ct. 1539, 384 U.S. 424, 16 L.Ed.2d 662 (1966), reversing Anthony Grace & Sons, Inc. v. U.S., 170 Ct.Cl. 688, 345 F.2d 808 (1965), requires referral back for the computation of damages only those cases where the relief requested could have been granted under some provision of the contract. Mauricio Hochschild, S.A. M.I. v. U.S., Ct.Cl.1966, 176 Ct.Cl. 808. United States ⚮ 73(15)

59.   —— Refusal to take action, exhaustion of administrative remedies, administrative review

Where contracting officer of agency had refused to take action on claim filed by contractor on basis of final determination by agency administrator in contractor's favor contractor had, in substance, exhausted his administrative remedies and properly brought suit in federal court to recover from agency. C.J. Langenfelder & Son, Inc. v. U.S., Ct.Cl.1965, 341 F.2d 600, 169 Ct.Cl. 465. Administrative Law And Procedure ☞ 229

Where the head of the contracting agency has failed to act upon an appeal by rendering a valid decision, the court has jurisdiction to consider and determine the contractor's right to an equitable adjustment and the amount of such adjustment. Johnson v. U.S., Ct.Cl.1965, 173 Ct.Cl. 561. United States ☞ 73(13)

60.   —— Delay, exhaustion of administrative remedies, administrative review

Contracting officer's letter to government contractor, which had submitted claim for equitable adjustment, that the total cost method was totally unacceptable for pricing equitable adjustment and inviting contractor to submit further proof did not constitute, in effect, an adverse decision which would render failure of Navy to issue a technical final decision a formal rather than substantial defect for purpose of determining whether contractor was entitled to file suit without exhausting administrative remedies because of undue delay. Manpower, Inc. of Tidewater v. U.S., Ct.Cl.1975, 513 F.2d 1396, 206 Ct.Cl. 726. United States ☞ 73(13)

Delay by Maritime Administration in considering ship builder's demand for an increase in price under "changes" mechanism in ship building contract was not so unreasonable as to have caused Government to breach its covenant to render a timely decision, and contractor did not become immediately entitled to a court adjudication, where contractor had in large measure occasioned postponement of evaluation of its cost estimate until Maritime Subsidy Board had made a decision on another of contractor's claims, and where, under circumstances, it was reasonable for Maritime Administration to wait for action of Maritime Subsidy Board. Sun Shipbuilding & Dry Dock Co. v. U.S., Ct.Cl.1972, 461 F.2d 1352, 198 Ct.Cl. 693, certiorari denied 93 S.Ct. 465, 409 U.S. 1023, 34 L.Ed.2d 315. United States ☞ 73(9)

61.   —— Strength of support for claim, exhaustion of administrative remedies, administrative review

Plaintiff contractors who presented to hearing officer claim based on government's termination of contract after allegedly justifiable default and who were ready to present witnesses if hearing officer decided he had authority to grant relief adequately pursued administrative remedy; strength of support of claim was irrelevant for purpose of deciding issue of exhaustion. Nager Elec. Co. v. U.S., Ct. Cl.1968, 396 F.2d 977, 184 Ct.Cl. 390. United States ☞ 74(8)

62.   —— Miscellaneous cases administrative remedies exhausted, exhaustion of administrative remedies, administrative review

Where government contract contained standard suspension of work clause, contractor's claim against government for extra costs incurred during a delay in completing contract was redressable at administrative level, but where contractor had exhausted his administrative remedies, except for amount of his damages, case was properly before Court of Claims for review. Urban Plumbing & Heating Co. v. U.S., Ct.Cl.1969, 408 F.2d 382, 187 Ct.Cl. 15, certiorari denied 90 S.Ct. 2164, 398 U.S. 958, 26 L.Ed.2d 542. United States ☞ 73(15)

Failure of contractor which brought claims against government for breach of contract to initially seek administrative relief did not warrant dismissal of claims in light of fact that administrative proceedings were held. Schlesinger v. U.S., Ct.Cl.1967, 383 F.2d 1004, 181 Ct.Cl. 21. United States ☞ 74(8)

Contracting officer did not transgress limits of his authority when he entered into agreement with plaintiff contractor delineating the actual dispute between the parties by stipulating the underlying facts spawning the controversy, thereby sparing the prosecution of a perfunctory appeal from decision of contracting officer to its obvious administrative conclusion and plaintiff's timely appeal, the stipulation and final board decision, on appeal of another claim presenting same basic facts, discharged plaintiff's obligation to exhaust its administrative remedies and plaintiff was entitled to bring court action. Arthur Venneri Co. v. U.S., Ct.Cl.1967, 381 F.2d 748, 180 Ct.Cl. 920.

United States ☞ 73(9); United States ☞ 74(8)

Where the contracting officer's decisions on plaintiff's claims appealed to the Board of Contract Appeals are decided adversely to the contractor on the matter of liability, with the minor exceptions of one or two claims remanded to the contracting officer to make an adjustment on a theory challenged by the contractor, the contractor is free to elect to test in court its major claims which were rejected as well as the minor claims where the relief from the contracting officer on remand would be unsatisfactory under the Board's challenged theory of relief and no facts would be found which would bear on issues before the court on the major claims of the contractor and in such a case the contractor is deemed to have properly exhausted his administrative remedies of appeal under the contract. N. Fiorito Co. v. U.S., Ct.Cl.1967, 180 Ct.Cl. 1285. United States ☞ 73(15)

63. —— Miscellaneous cases administrative remedies not exhausted, exhaustion of administrative remedies, administrative review

Contractor's contention that it should not be disadvantaged by its failure to comply with contractual provisions concerning request for clarification of conflicts between drawings and specifications of federal contract on ground that its failure was attributable to failure of the United States to abide by provisions of section 253 of this title would not be considered by trial division of Court of Claims where contractor failed to exhaust its administrative remedy with respect to that contention. William F. Klingensmith, Inc. v. U.S., Ct.Cl.1974, 505 F.2d 1257, 205 Ct.Cl. 651. United States ☞ 73(15)

Where Government contract provided that all disputes concerning question of fact arising out of contract which were not disposed of by agreement should be decided by contracting officer and contractor would have 30 days from receipt of decision to appeal, and dispute arose over amount contractor was entitled to recover for services in filling a borrow pit, measure of which was necessarily fixed by contract but amount which was an ultimate question of fact, and contractor did not appeal from adverse decision of contracting officer, he failed to exhaust his administrative remedies and contract-

ing officer's decision became final and conclusive. Happel v. U.S., C.A.8 (Mo.) 1960, 279 F.2d 88. United States ☞ 73(14); United States ☞ 74(8)

Where Government contract provided that all disputes as to questions of fact arising under contract not disposed of by agreement should be decided by contracting officer whose decision was final and conclusive if no appeal were taken therefrom within 30 days, since contractor agreed to settlement of disputes by this procedure when contract was entered into and he failed to exhaust administrative remedies under contract, court was precluded from hearing any issue of fact, and contracting officer's decision that goods did not conform to specifications stood. B.H. Deacon Co. v. U.S., E.D.Pa. 1960, 189 F.Supp. 146. United States ☞ 73(14)

Where Government contract provided that disputes thereunder would be settled by contracting officer who should reduce decision to writing and within 30 days thereafter contractor might appeal to chief of engineers whose decision would be conclusive unless contractor then appealed in writing to the Secretary, and it appeared that contractor failed to appeal the Corps of Engineers Claims and Appeals Board decision to Secretary, contractor having failed to exhaust his administrative remedies, could not bring action in Court of Claims [now United States Court of Federal Claims] seeking increased cost due to alleged change of conditions on theory that decision of Claims and Appeals Board was not supported by substantial evidence. Henry E. Wile Co. v. U.S., Ct.Cl.1959, 169 F.Supp. 249, 144 Ct.Cl. 394. United States ☞ 73(15)

In action to recover for additional work performed under a Government construction contract, where contract provided that a dispute not disposed of by agreement should be decided by the contracting officer, and that his decision should be final unless appealed from, and plaintiff failed to exhaust his administrative remedy by appeal to the Secretary within 30 days, plaintiff was not entitled to maintain the action. Pyle v. U.S., Ct.Cl. 1958, 163 F.Supp. 853, 143 Ct.Cl. 339. United States ☞ 74(8)

Where following an adverse decision of the contracting officer on his claim, plaintiff elected to present the claim to the Comptroller General rather than to assert his right under the "disputes clause" of the contract by an appeal in writing to the head of the department, such failure to follow the remedy provided by the contract precluded plaintiff from presenting the claim to the Court of Claims [now United States Court of Federal Claims] for decision on the merits. Olsen v. U.S., Ct.Cl.1952, 122 Ct.Cl. 106. United States ☞ 74(8)

Where, after amended instructions were given with reference to the inspector's requirement that the plastered partitions be exactly plumb and true, plaintiff made no further written protest against the requirements of the inspectors and also failed to take any appeal to the head of the department from the adverse ruling of the contracting officer on its claim, plaintiff was not entitled to recover on this item. Cauldwell-Wingate Co. v. U.S., Ct.Cl.1947, 109 Ct.Cl. 193. Contracts ☞ 284(4); United States ☞ 70(36)

64. Waiver, administrative review

Objections of a party based on a nonjurisdictional ground will be deemed waived if not asserted in a timely manner, and, because the Wunderlich Act, this chapter, is not a condition imposed upon suit against the sovereign since it is applicable to suits by as well as against the United States, if defendant or plaintiff wishes to impose the limitations on the right to a trial de novo in the Court of Claims in cases coming within the purview of the Wunderlich Act, such limitations must be asserted prior to trial in this court and if not raised until proof is closed, the right to insist on an administrative determination of the claim will be deemed to have been waived. WRB Corp. v. U.S., Ct.Cl.1966, 177 Ct.Cl. 909. Federal Courts ☞ 1114.1; United States ☞ 74(8)

III. JUDICIAL REVIEW GENERALLY

Subdivision Index

---

91. Construction with other laws, judicial review generally

This section, providing that no provision of any contract entered into by the United States, relating to conclusiveness of decision of head of any department in dispute arising under contract shall be pleaded as limiting judicial review of such decision to cases where fraud by such official and his representative or board is alleged, has no application to pleading defense afforded by another statute. Peerless Cas. Co. v. U.S., for Use and Benefit of Bangor Roofing & Sheet Metal Co., C.A.1 (Me.) 1957, 241 F.2d 811. United States ☞ 73(14)

This section, providing for judicial review of administrative decisions pursuant to disputes clauses in contracts, was not intended to alter limitation statutes otherwise applicable. Atlantic Carriers, Inc. v. U.S., S.D.N.Y.1955, 131 F.Supp. 1. Limitation Of Actions ☞ 3(2)

92. Jurisdiction, judicial review generally

Contract clause, requiring all disputes concerning questions of fact to be decided by contracting officer, subject to appeal to Secretary of War, whose decision was to be final and conclusive, deprived court of jurisdiction over fact dispute pending completion of administrative process. U.S. v. Smith, E.D.Pa.1957, 152 F.Supp. 322. United States ☞ 73(15)

After completion of administrative process under disputes clause in contract, court has jurisdiction of claim covered thereby only if complaint in court action alleges that administrative decision is fraudulent, capricious, arbitrary, so grossly erroneous as necessarily to imply bad faith, or not supported by substantial evidence. Atlantic Carriers, Inc. v. U.S., S.D.N.Y.1955, 131 F.Supp. 1. Administrative Law And Procedure ⬅➡ 763; Administrative Law And Procedure ⬅➡ 791

Wunderlich Act did not provide jurisdiction over contractor's suit in the Court of Federal Claims, where contractor contracted with an agency within the executive branch, and contract was entered into well after the effective date of the Contract Disputes Act (CDA). Parker v. U.S., Fed.Cl.2007, 2007 WL 1893172. United States ⬅➡ 73(15)

Fraud is a tort, and Claims Court does not have jurisdiction to consider claims sounding in tort in review proceeding under this section. Degenaars Co. v. U.S., Cl.Ct.1983, 2 Cl.Ct. 482. United States ⬅➡ 73(15)

93. Persons entitled to maintain action, judicial review generally

This chapter does not confer upon the Department of Justice the right to appeal from a decision of an administrative agency. S & E Contractors, Inc. v. U.S., U.S.Ct.Cl.1972, 92 S.Ct. 1411, 406 U.S. 1, 31 L.Ed.2d 658. Attorney General ⬅➡ 6

Government claimant may challenge administrative board's decision as based upon errors of law and as lacking supporting substantial evidence, entailing judicial review of administrative decision on record before board. Northbridge Electronics, Inc. v. U.S., Ct.Cl.1971, 444 F.2d 1124, 195 Ct.Cl. 453. United States ⬅➡ 113

Any reference in caption of claim against government to subcontractors, which were not in privity with government, was considered solely as descriptive of prime contractor's complaint and suit was viewed as one by prime contractor for use and benefit of the subcontractors so that prime contractor had right to appeal on behalf of subcontractors, the real parties in interest, and case would be considered on merits. Owens-Corning Fiberglas Corp. v. U.S., Ct.Cl.1969, 419 F.2d 439, 190 Ct.Cl. 211. United States ⬅➡ 73(15)

This chapter regarding review of administrative decisions applied to administrative decisions favoring contractor as well as those which are adverse. C.J. Langenfelder & Son, Inc. v. U.S., Ct.Cl. 1965, 341 F.2d 600, 169 Ct.Cl. 465. United States ⬅➡ 73(15)

A contracting agency, acting through the Department of Justice, is able on its own initiative to obtain, and has the responsibility in appropriate cases to seek, judicial review of contract appeals board decisions adverse to the Government. 1969, 42 Op.Atty.Gen., January 16.

94. Complaint, judicial review generally—Generally

Pleadings and moving papers, which, for most part, merely adumbrated statutory factors and ultimate circumstances for which this chapter would deny finality to decision of Armed Services Board of Contract Appeals, were insufficient to bring merits of such decision into issue. Hicks Corp. v. U.S., Ct.Cl.1973, 487 F.2d 520, 203 Ct.Cl. 65. United States ⬅➡ 74(9)

Contractor's petition to review Board of Contract Appeals' denial of increased compensation was not defective in substance for failure to allege that decision was not supported by substantial evidence, where it did assert that decision was arbitrary and capricious and disputes article involved was approved for use before enactment of this chapter and did not contain "substantial evidence" phraseology thereafter incorporated into law and most dispute provisions. Hoffman v. U.S., Ct.Cl.1964, 340 F.2d 645, 166 Ct.Cl. 39. United States ⬅➡ 73(15)

In suit to recover for additional work performed under a Government construction contract where there was no allegation whether the adverse decision of the contracting officer or the Claims and Appeals Board or any other action of the Government or its agents was arbitrary, capricious or done in bad faith, there was a fatal defect. Pyle v. U.S., Ct.Cl.1958, 163 F.Supp. 853, 143 Ct.Cl. 339. United States ⬅➡ 74(9)

Petition of contractor for breach of Government contract lodging in Government's contracting officer power to decide disputes concerning questions of fact and giving contractor right to appeal to department head whose decision should be final must do more than repeat language of this section and must allege facts which, if proved, will show that departmental decision was intolerable and hence was deprived of finality. Volentine & Littleton v. U.S., Ct.Cl.1956, 145 F.Supp. 952, 136 Ct.Cl. 638. United States ⬅➡ 74(9)

95. —— **Amendment, complaint, judicial review generally**

Where plaintiff contractor improperly asserted as claim for breach of contract a wrong that, if established, would be redressable under changed conditions or changes clause of contract and it was almost five years after original petition was filed in court of claims, almost two years after plaintiff first sought leave to file count as a breach claim and over six years after plaintiff's correspondence with contracting officer, it was too late to permit plaintiff to amend again to show claim under the contract. Briscoe v. U.S., Ct.Cl.1971, 442 F.2d 953, 194 Ct.Cl. 866. United States ☞ 74(9)

96. —— **Specificity, complaint, judicial review generally**

Where government contractor, in its brief to the Court of Claims, simply cited its motion for reconsideration without specifying the alleged factual errors that were complained of, contractor did not supply the substantive particularity, supported by appropriate record references, necessary to overcome the finality that otherwise attaches to findings made by a board whose decision is subject to review under this section and section 322 of this title. Robert L. Guyler Co. v. U.S., Ct.Cl. 1979, 593 F.2d 406, 219 Ct.Cl. 403, certiorari denied 100 S.Ct. 85, 444 U.S. 843, 62 L.Ed.2d 55, rehearing denied 100 S.Ct. 438, 444 U.S. 957, 62 L.Ed.2d 330. United States ☞ 73(14)

When government contractor seeking recovery for miscellaneous delay claims failed to comply with Court of Claims order requiring it to file assignment of errors specifying factual errors which administrative board made and citing those portions of administrative record on which it relied to demonstrate that board decision was erroneous, but, instead, merely alleged generally right to recover, court studied parties' submissions and parts of record cited by government and concluded that contractor had not shown that board's decision allowing only portions of contractor's claims lacked substantial support. United Contractors v. U.S., Ct.Cl.1966, 368 F.2d 585, 177 Ct.Cl. 151. United States ☞ 73(14)

In actions where decision of Armed Services Board of Contract Appeals is contested, plaintiffs must do more than repeat derogatory language of this section to effect that decision was capricious or arbitrary or so grossly erroneous as necessarily to imply bad faith or was not supported by substantial evidence, and facts must be alleged which if proved will show that under language of this section the Board's decision cannot stand. PLS Coat & Suit Corp. v. U.S., Ct.Cl.1960, 180 F.Supp. 400, 148 Ct.Cl. 296. United States ☞ 74(9)

With exception of contractor's allegations regarding bad faith in the so-called "on-board review" of its submissions, contractor had not alleged error by the Armed Services Board of Contract Appeals with sufficient specificity, where contractor merely referenced the Board's findings, and did not allege or establish specific error, and thus contractor had failed to meet its burden to maintain a Wunderlich Act review suit. Quality Environment Systems, Inc. v. U.S., Cl.Ct. 1985, 7 Cl.Ct. 428. United States ☞ 73(15)

97. Counterclaims, judicial review generally

Though Armed Services Board of Contract Appeals, while upholding default termination of contract, did not rule on demand of the Government for repayment of unliquidated progress payments, counterclaim for repayment would properly be allowed in Court of Claims without remand to the Board for purely formalistic administrative findings respecting facts which were conceded. Piasecki Aircraft Corp. v. U.S., Ct.Cl.1981, 667 F.2d 50, 229 Ct.Cl. 208. Federal Courts ☞ 1118

Where government contractor seeking review under this chapter did not attack any of the contract appeal board's actual determinations, either as to entitlement or quantum, and sole ground of challenge by contractor was with respect to ultimate method of computation under determination of amount due for individual changes by which an overpayment was found, Government was precluded from attacking by counterclaim administrative finding with respect to particular modification, the overhead allowed to subcontractor and cost of other individual changes. Roscoe-Ajax Const. Co., Inc. v. U.S., Ct.Cl.1974, 499 F.2d 639, 204 Ct.Cl. 726. United States ☞ 73(15)

98.   Stay of judicial proceedings, judicial review generally

This chapter was intended to require utilization of administrative procedures contractually bargained for, and in case administrative record is defective or inadequate or reveals commission of prejudicial error, judicial proceedings should be stayed pending further action before agency, or judgment granted for complaining contractor in proper case. U.S. v. Anthony Grace & Sons, Inc., U.S.Ct.Cl. 1966, 86 S.Ct. 1539, 384 U.S. 424, 16 L.Ed.2d 662.   Action ☞ 69(7); United States ☞ 73(9); United States ☞ 74(7)

Under this chapter, where administrative record was highly confused on matter of force-account determinations and contractor contended that Court of Claims should disregard all Board's rulings on force-account phase of case because of insufficient evidence on subject before Board, question of accounting having been reserved, Court of Claims would not entertain piecemeal review of administrative decisions with respect to force-account determinations but would await final determination administratively of all issues relating to such subject matter. Pacific Alaska Contractors, Inc. v. U.S., Ct.Cl.1971, 436 F.2d 461, 193 Ct.Cl. 850. United States ☞ 73(15)

Where decision by Armed Forces Board of Contract Appeals was imminent, board had not been dilatory and claimants had advanced no reason for failure to act within period when administrative process could reasonably have been considered to be dormant, claimant's motion to vacate order which stayed proceedings in action on claim against United States and which required claimants to exhaust their administrative remedy would be denied. Moran Towing & Transp. Co. v. U.S., S.D.N.Y.1966, 263 F.Supp. 787. United States ☞ 74(8)

Where relief is available to a contractor under some clause of his contract by appeal to the head of the contracting agency and the decision on appeal is adequately supported by substantial evidence, and where the board properly refused to change its decision on the basis of new evidence offered at a second trial on a second appeal regarding the same dispute, the Court of Claims will not suspend for a further administrative hearing or permit a trial de novo in the Court of

Claims.   Tankersley v. U.S., Ct.Cl.1967, 179 Ct.Cl. 294.   United States ☞ 73(15)

99.   Limitations, judicial review generally

If claim filed by government contractor was a claim arising under contract and therefore subject to administrative determination under disputes clause of contract, contractor's right to bring civil action would have first accrued when Armed Services Board of Contract Appeals finally ruled adversely on his claim and his suit brought within six years after that ruling would be timely. Crown Coat Front Co. v. U.S., U.S.N.Y.1967, 87 S.Ct. 1177, 386 U.S. 503, 18 L.Ed.2d 256. Limitation Of Actions ☞ 65(3)

Claim against United States does not accrue for purpose of beginning period of limitations until damages are ascertainable. Johnson, Drake & Piper, Inc. v. U.S., Ct.Cl.1976, 531 F.2d 1037, 209 Ct. Cl. 313.   United States ☞ 113

Limitation on filing of claim in Court of Claims does not run during pendency of administrative proceedings pursuant to government contract requiring submission of disputes to administrative board so that "claim under contract" and "breach claim" which spawn "disputes-type" items in litigation may be submitted to court of law after administrative determination. Nager Elec. Co. v. U.S., Ct.Cl. 1966, 368 F.2d 847, 177 Ct.Cl. 234.   Federal Courts ☞ 1108

Although there was inordinately long time between contractor's appeal in March 1946 under disputes clause of government contract and decision of Board of Contract Appeals in October 1958, inasmuch as government had allowed proceedings to remain dormant for over ten years, no detriment to government from delay appeared, interest was not allowable on any recovery and there was no claim that evidence or records had been lost, destroyed or grown stale, action brought in 1962 was not time barred. U.S. Steel Corp. v. U.S., Ct.Cl.1966, 367 F.2d 399, 177 Ct.Cl. 26.   Federal Courts ☞ 1108

Statute of limitations for institution of suit on contract claims, which are within jurisdiction of board of contract appeals, cannot commence to run until final board action.   Conn v. U.S., Ct.Cl.1966, 366 F.2d 1019, 177 Ct.Cl. 319.   Federal Courts ☞ 1108

Fact that during a three-year period a contractor, because of a judicial decision, could not have pursued a cause of action grounded on capricious action of Army Board of Contract Appeals, afforded the contractor no relief from running of limitations, where contractor's cause of action accrued more than three years prior to the decision. Cosmopolitan Mfg. Co. v. U.S., Ct.Cl.1962, 297 F.2d 546, 156 Ct.Cl. 142, certiorari denied 83 S.Ct. 36, 371 U.S. 818, 9 L.Ed.2d 60. Limitation Of Actions ⟶ 104.5

Statute of limitations was tolled on government contractor's claims for extra work required by changes that government had ordered in its original contract when contractor sought review of government's decision in Corps of Engineers Board of Contract Appeals. General Ry. Signal Co. v. Washington Metropolitan Area Transit Authority, D.C.D.C.1979, 527 F.Supp. 359, affirmed 664 F.2d 296, 214 U.S.App.D.C. 170, certiorari denied 101 S.Ct. 3049, 452 U.S. 915, 69 L.Ed.2d 418. Limitation Of Actions ⟶ 105(1)

In Government's action for breach of aerial photography contract, Government was not bound by state statute of limitations. U.S. v. Smith, E.D.Pa.1957, 152 F.Supp. 322. Limitation Of Actions ⟶ 11(1)

100. Estoppel, judicial review generally

Where contractor received, in 1972, refund of state corporation franchise tax paid for 1968 as result of carry-back to 1968 of substantial net operating loss realized by contractor in 1971, government was not estopped from allocating credit to 1968, even assuming that estoppel issue was properly before court. Grumman Aerospace Corp. v. U.S., Ct.Cl.1978, 587 F.2d 498, 218 Ct.Cl. 441, certiorari denied 99 S.Ct. 2837, 442 U.S. 917, 61 L.Ed.2d 283. Estoppel ⟶ 62.2(4)

Where contentions had been placed before the Armed Services Board of Contract Appeals by contractor under the disputes clause of the contract as changed conditions which entitled contractor to an equitable adjustment, and where the Board considered the claim and awarded contractor an equitable adjustment, contractor in case under this chapter could not relitigate the same claim and the same issues in Court of Claims under a reformation theory. Dale Ingram, Inc. v. U.S., Ct.Cl.1973, 475 F.2d 1177, 201 Ct. Cl. 56. United States ⟶ 73(15)

Where findings of Armed Services Board of Contract Appeals were not gratuitous but were properly made in resolution of disputes under pier construction contract, United States was estopped from contesting findings in contractor's breach of contract proceeding. Hardeman-Monier-Hutcherson v. U.S., Ct.Cl. 1972, 458 F.2d 1364, 198 Ct.Cl. 472. Estoppel ⟶ 62.2(4)

Under doctrine of collateral estoppel, United States may not contend that, in absence of relevant new facts or circumstances, holding between parties on same issue previously determined by court should be rejected. Lockheed Aircraft Corp. v. U.S., Ct.Cl.1970, 426 F.2d 322, 192 Ct.Cl. 36. Judgment ⟶ 739; Judgment ⟶ 720

Government contractor was foreclosed from defending on the merits the government's action to enforce final decisions of contracting officer assessing damages against contractor, where contract provided exclusive procedure by which, in event of dispute, parties would present issue to contracting officer and where contractor's appeal from decisions of the contracting officer to the Armed Services Board of Contract Appeals were dismissed for failure to prosecute. U.S. v. Mystic Fuel, Inc., D.C.Md.1985, 622 F.Supp. 601. United States ⟶ 73(15)

General contractor, which had entered into construction contract with the United States General Services Administration and which claimed payment from subcontractor's surety for expenses purportedly incurred due to subcontractor's delays, was, under both federal and Illinois law, collaterally estopped to relitigate factual issues decided by the General Services Board of Contract Appeals even though surety was not party to Administration proceeding. Blackhawk Heating & Plumbing Co., Inc. v. Seaboard Sur. Co., N.D.Ill.1982, 534 F.Supp. 309. United States ⟶ 73(14)

Where a Government contractor has appealed from a decision of the contracting officer under the "Disputes" clause of the contract and there have been lengthy hearings by appeals boards, the contractor is estopped from denying in the Court of Claims that the factual determinations made by the administrative agency were within the scope of the "Disputes" provision of the contract and the related provision of this chapter. H.R. Henderson &

Co., Inc. v. U.S., Ct.Cl.1965, 169 Ct.Cl. 228.   United States ☞ 73(14)

101.   Waiver, judicial review generally
Right to procedural review limited to administrative record is procedural right, and is not jurisdictional, and thus may be waived.   Bennett v. U.S., Ct.Cl.1967, 371 F.2d 859, 178 Ct.Cl. 61.   United States ☞ 73(15)

102.   Judicial notice, judicial review generally
District court in suit against warehouseman by United States seeking recovery for loss of household goods of military personnel may take notice of evidence from outside administrative record where there is no objection by parties.   U.S. v. Morrison, E.D.Va.1974, 370 F.Supp. 193.   United States ☞ 75(4)

103.   Presumptions, judicial review generally
Presumption that prime contractor would benefit by saving involved in contractual change was overcome by evidence showing that prime contractor did not benefit from reduction in costs to subcontractor of performing subcontract.   Varo, Inc. v. U.S., Ct.Cl.1977, 548 F.2d 953, 212 Ct.Cl. 432.   United States ☞ 74(10)

In reviewing equitable adjustment awarded contractor under contract for operation of food service facilities at air force base because number of meals actually served was below 70% of estimated requirements, it would be assumed that contracting officer who made the equitable adjustment did his best to follow requirements of law.   Pacific Architects & Engineers, Inc. v. U.S., Ct.Cl.1974, 491 F.2d 734, 203 Ct.Cl. 499.   United States ☞ 73(15)

Contractor complaining of finding of nonconformities in product furnished under government contract had burden to rebut presumption that tests were properly conducted.   Astro Science Corp. v. U.S., Ct.Cl.1973, 471 F.2d 624, 200 Ct.Cl. 354.   United States ☞ 74(10)

United States failed to rebut presumption arising from findings of government contracting officer as to extent of government's liability for breach of its implied warranty that satisfactory performance would result if government specifications were complied with.   J.D. Hedin Const.

Co. v. U.S., Ct.Cl.1965, 347 F.2d 235, 171 Ct.Cl. 70.   United States ☞ 74(10)

104.   Inferences, judicial review generally
Inference from Government's failure to introduce evidence is more proper for board of contract appeals rather than for court.   Arundel Corp. v. U.S., Ct.Cl.1975, 515 F.2d 1116, 207 Ct.Cl. 84.   United States ☞ 73(15)

Where two equally reasonable but contrary inferences might be drawn from record on appeal from Armed Services Board of Contract Appeals in disputes over government contracts, and each could be sustained as supported by substantial evidence, inference adopted by Board should be sustained.   Koppers Co. v. U.S., Ct.Cl.1968, 405 F.2d 554, 186 Ct.Cl. 142.   United States ☞ 73(15)

105.   Burden of proof, judicial review generally
The challenger of the factual findings of the Armed Services Board of Contract Appeals has the burden of persuading the Court of Claims that each challenged finding is not entitled to finality because it is fraudulent, or capricious, or arbitrary, or so grossly erroneous as necessarily to imply bad faith, or because it is not supported by substantial evidence.   Schnip Bldg. Co. v. U.S., Ct.Cl.1981, 645 F.2d 950, 227 Ct.Cl. 148.   United States ☞ 73(15)

In contractor's action against the government alleging breach of contract for sale and removal of smokeless gunpowder, contractor failed to meet his burden of showing that government's failure to disclose information concerning access and outloading capacity interfered with his efforts to remove the powder during extension period of the contract.   Petrofsky v. U.S., Ct.Cl.1980, 616 F.2d 494, 222 Ct.Cl. 450, certiorari denied 101 S.Ct. 1488, 450 U.S. 968, 67 L.Ed.2d 618.   United States ☞ 74(11)

The burden is on the party appealing from a decision of the Armed Services Board of Contract Appeals, otherwise the findings of the Board must be deemed to be final pursuant to the standards of review under this chapter.   B.D. Click Co., Inc. v. U.S., Ct.Cl.1980, 614 F.2d 748, 222 Ct.Cl. 290.   United States ☞ 73(15)

Judicial review of administrative factual determinations under standards of this section is narrow and limited; the findings of fact of the Corps of Engineers Board of Contract Appeals are presumptively correct and plaintiff carries heavy burden in seeking to set aside factual determinations made by the Board, questions of law decided by the Board, on the other hand, are not binding on the court nor entitled to finality. Dravo Corp. v. U.S., Ct.Cl.1979, 594 F.2d 842, 219 Ct.Cl. 416. United States ☞ 73(15)

Plaintiff who seeks to set aside factual determinations of board of contract appeals carries heavy burden. Arundel Corp. v. U.S., Ct.Cl.1975, 515 F.2d 1116, 207 Ct.Cl. 84. United States ☞ 73(14)

In action against United States to recover additional moneys due subcontractor for estimate quantity items used in overrun on contract for modification of existing flood control structures on Mississippi River, Corps of Engineers Board of Contract Appeals erred when it agreed with contracting officer that it was up to contractor to affirmatively justify amount that it sought rather than being government's burden to prove why amount paid should be less than that called for by contract's unit prices. Victory Const. Co., Inc. v. U.S., Ct.Cl.1975, 510 F.2d 1379, 206 Ct.Cl. 274. United States ☞ 74.2

In seeking to overturn decisions of fact made by Army Corps of Engineers Board of Contract Appeals, a plaintiff assumes a heavy burden of showing that there is no evidence of substance to support the Board's findings and that the evidence of substance compellingly supports a contrary finding. Donald M. Drake Co. v. U.S., Ct.Cl.1971, 439 F.2d 169, 194 Ct.Cl. 549. United States ☞ 73(15)

Government failed to sustain burden of proving that plaintiff contractor which was responsible for design, manufacture, testing and supervision of erection of hydraulic turbines for power plant units at dam project, and which was one of four prime contractors, was responsible for misfunctioning of turbines. Baldwin-Lima-Hamilton Corp. v. U.S., Ct.Cl.1970, 434 F.2d 1371, 193 Ct.Cl. 556. United States ☞ 74(11)

To upset decision of Armed Services Board of Contract Appeals with respect to right of government to adjustment under contract for cleaning Navy mess facilities, contractor was obliged to demonstrate that the evidence was such as

compellingly required findings in his favor. Rice v. U.S., Ct.Cl.1970, 428 F.2d 1311, 192 Ct.Cl. 903. United States ☞ 73(15)

Where on review of decision of armed services board of contract appeals the claim is that evidence did not support findings and supported a contrary finding, Court of Claims does not reweigh evidence to determine whether it is in agreement with findings of board, but inquiry is directed to whether on disputed facts board had substantial evidence to support its determinations; and plaintiff has burden of showing that no such evidence is in record, or that evidence contrary to the board's findings is either overwhelming in itself or so detracts from evidence in support of board's findings as to render it less than substantial on record as a whole. Marley v. U.S., Ct.Cl. 1970, 423 F.2d 324, 191 Ct.Cl. 205. United States ☞ 73(15)

Contractor suing United States has burden of showing specifically why findings of fact of the Armed Services Board of Contract Appeals are arbitrary, capricious or not supported by substantial evidence. Electronic & Missile Facilities, Inc. v. U.S., Ct.Cl.1969, 416 F.2d 1345, 189 Ct.Cl. 237. See, also, J. A. Jones Const. Co. v. U.S., 1968, 395 F.2d 783, 184 Ct.Cl. 1. United States ☞ 73(15)

Burden was on contractor, seeking to avoid liquidated damages for overrun on government contract, to demonstrate to Court of Claims that in rejecting contractor's request for extension of time, board of contract appeals arbitrarily rejected contractor's evidence or that facts affirmatively found by board were based on insubstantial evidence. Dean Const. Co. v. U.S., Ct.Cl.1969, 411 F.2d 1238, 188 Ct.Cl. 62. Federal Courts ☞ 1113

Inasmuch as trustee in bankruptcy for corporate government contractor solicited a "jury verdict" on self-contradictory and otherwise noncompelling testimony, trustee was under heavy burden to upset that verdict in proceeding on its claim against government for delays and changes. Sternberger v. U.S., Ct.Cl. 1968, 401 F.2d 1012, 185 Ct.Cl. 528. United States ☞ 73(14)

Government contractor has burden of establishing that record does not support finding by Armed Services Board of Contract Appeals, and it is not court's function to supply deficiency in such proof by independent excursion along the administrative trail. Sundstrand Turbo v. U.S., Ct.Cl.1968, 389 F.2d 406, 182 Ct.Cl. 31. United States ⟶ 74(11)

Claimant who seeks recovery in Court of Claims of additional compensation for work performed under government contract in cases involving alleged changes or government caused delays must single out facts or evidence showing that administrative decision denying recovery cannot stand under standards of this chapter. United Contractors v. U.S., Ct.Cl.1966, 368 F.2d 585, 177 Ct.Cl. 151. United States ⟶ 73(14)

Government contractor challenging sufficiency of evidence to support findings of Board of Contract Appeals had burden of showing facts and circumstances contained in board's record making board's decision lacking in substantial evidence. Jefferson Const. Co. v. U.S., Ct.Cl.1966, 368 F.2d 247, 177 Ct.Cl. 581. Federal Courts ⟶ 1113

In proceeding in which factual issues were presented that had been determined by Armed Services Board of Contract Appeals with respect to contract, Government had burden to show that Board's finding of fact was not binding upon trial court. Lowell O. West Lumber Sales v. U.S., C.A.9 (Cal.) 1959, 270 F.2d 12. United States ⟶ 74(10)

Where United States contract with supplier vested a broad discretion in contracting officer with respect to terminating such contract and reletting same and holding original contracting party liable for damages because of excess costs, burden was upon original contracting party to show an abuse of discretion by contracting officer. U.S. v. Elliott Truck Parts, Inc., E.D.Mich.1957, 149 F.Supp. 52, affirmed 261 F.2d 835. United States ⟶ 75(4)

106. Summary judgment, judicial review generally

Concession by contractor that it was not suing under an alleged oral order for sandbags by an employee of the Army Corps of Engineers nor for an alleged misrepresentation by an officer of the Corps with respect to authority of the employee to place the oral order meant that the contractor was no longer challenging the correctness of the decision of the Corps of Engineers Board of Contract Appeals that order was not a valid contract and that the officer of the Corps did not misrepresent the true facts and meant, therefore, that the United States was entitled to summary judgment on issue of validity of alleged contract arising out of order. Northwestern Bag Corp. v. U.S., Ct.Cl.1980, 619 F.2d 896, 223 Ct.Cl. 333. United States ⟶ 66

Whether or not the Armed Services Board of Contract Appeals record was comprehensive, in supplier's breach of contract action against the United States, where the board did not engage in fact-finding specifically with regard to whether sale of government machinery constituted a cardinal change, as this issue was not raised by either party at the Armed Services Board of Contract Appeals level, drawing of conclusions of ultimate facts was still a fact-finding function, and case was not ripe for summary judgment. Allied Materials & Equipment Co., Inc. v. U.S., Ct.Cl.1978, 569 F.2d 562, 215 Ct.Cl. 406. Federal Civil Procedure ⟶ 2492

Where four specific allegations of bad faith by Government were made in briefs or at oral argument as to claim against United States, so they were decided by order stating that court did not agree that facts shown in record would enable it to determine that Government was guilty of bad faith and, following court's request that parties submit supplemental brief to determine whether defendant had evinced bad faith or clear abuse of discretion in its actions, there were no new claims of bad faith and no evidence beyond plaintiff's vague offer to produce testimony by cognizant personnel of plaintiff, court could justifiably deny plaintiff's motion for summary judgment. Kalvar Corp., Inc. v. U.S., Ct.Cl.1976, 543 F.2d 1298, 211 Ct.Cl. 192, certiorari denied 98 S.Ct. 112, 434 U.S. 830, 54 L.Ed.2d 89. Federal Courts ⟶ 1120

In proceeding on petition wherein contractor challenged correctness of Armed Services Board of Contract Appeals' decisions upholding default termination of four contracts for supply of missile components to Army and Navy, genuine issues of material fact precluded summary judgment from Government on its counterclaims for recovery of unliquidated progress payments assertedly advanced during two of such contracts and for recovery of progress payments due under contracts extrinsic to suit. Hicks Corp. v.

U.S., Ct.Cl.1973, 487 F.2d 520, 203 Ct.Cl. 65. Federal Courts ⟨= 1120

In review under this section government could not have summary judgment in specific monetary amount on contention totally unexplored administratively. Martin Lane Co. v. U.S., Ct.Cl.1970, 432 F.2d 1013, 193 Ct.Cl. 203. Federal Courts ⟨= 1120

Where armed services board of contract appeals denied government's claim for excess costs against contractor whose contract was terminated for default, contracting officer was not authorized to reassess excess costs, and government's motion for summary judgment for excess costs was denied insofar as it was grounded upon failure to appeal from board decision. Marley v. U.S., Ct.Cl. 1970, 423 F.2d 324, 191 Ct.Cl. 205. Federal Courts ⟨= 1120; United States ⟨= 73(1)

Affidavits of government contractor, seeking damages for government's alleged breach of contract by delaying contractor's completion of work, and government's opposing affidavits raised question of material fact as to correctness of unappealed findings of contracting officer, precluding summary judgment. Dean Const. Co. v. U.S., Ct.Cl.1969, 411 F.2d 1238, 188 Ct.Cl. 62. Federal Courts ⟨= 1120

Where there has been formal and final decision of contracting officer as to factual issue in accordance with disputes clause in Government contract and failure to appeal that decision, United States may be granted summary judgment on issue of liability, as failure to pursue administrative appeal deprives court of jurisdiction of issue. U.S. v. Hammer Contracting Corp., E.D.N.Y.1963, 216 F.Supp. 948, affirmed 331 F.2d 173. Federal Civil Procedure ⟨= 2557

Summary judgment is particularly appropriate in reviewing an administrative order where the plaintiff has no right to trial de novo and where therefore the question of whether or not the evidence meets the statutory standard is purely a matter of law. General Ship Contracting Corp. v. U.S., D.C.N.J.1962, 205 F.Supp. 658. Federal Civil Procedure ⟨= 2464

Each case involving review of decision of Armed Services Board of Contract Appeals as to claim for adjustment of contract price with Government must, with respect to motions for summary judgment be viewed on basis of its own facts and circumstances and in each case it must be decided whether there is any reasonable prospect that a trial would eventuate in a decision contrary to the summary judgment sought. PLS Coat & Suit Corp. v. U.S., Ct.Cl.1960, 180 F.Supp. 400, 148 Ct.Cl. 296. Federal Civil Procedure ⟨= 2492

107. Moot questions, judicial review generally

Where Court of Claims found against contractor on substantive issues, procedural issues with respect to other claims, which presented same substantive issues, were moot. Timber Access Industries Co., Inc. v. U.S., Ct.Cl.1977, 553 F.2d 1250, 213 Ct.Cl. 648. Federal Courts ⟨= 13

Entry of final administrative decision on contract bidder's petition for review mooted agency's motion to dismiss bidder's action for failure to exhaust administrative remedies. Neeb-Kearney & Co. v. U.S. Dept. of Labor, E.D.La.1991, 779 F.Supp. 841. Federal Courts ⟨= 13

108. Remedies or relief, judicial review generally

Where munitions manufacturer based its judgment that production changes were needed on a set of erroneous assumptions, manufacturer was not entitled to recover under this section for additional costs incurred in making the changes in production. Manufacturers Hanover Trust Co. v. U.S., Ct.Cl.1978, 590 F.2d 893, 218 Ct.Cl. 563. United States ⟨= 70(31)

Recovery by government from government contractor of sum of $8,050, alleged to be amount by which contract for total of $548,100 was "overpriced" by contractor, was not prevented by this section and contract clause which required that "significant sums" by which contract is overpriced due to defective cost data disclosure are to be refunded to government; government could recover amount of overpricing despite fact that it might incur litigation expenses in excess of such amount. Conrac Corp. v. U.S., Ct.Cl. 1977, 558 F.2d 994, 214 Ct.Cl. 561. United States ⟨= 75(5)

If administrative decision falls before criteria of this chapter, court could recognize changes or changed conditions or a suspension for convenience of the government and grant equitable adjustments therefor or allow damages for breach of contract, if proved. Banks Const. Co. v. U.S., Ct.Cl.1966, 364 F.2d 357, 176 Ct.Cl. 1302. United States ⊂⇒ 70(25.1); United States ⊂⇒ 74(3)

Where contractor's recovery against United States was not required to be determined administratively and case came to Court of Claims without prior proceeding before agency tribunals, amount of recovery would be determined under rule and trial commissioner would take necessary evidence and make initial determination following as nearly as possible the criteria of termination article of contract, though contract had not been terminated under that article. Brown & Son Elec. Co. v. U.S., Ct.Cl.1963, 325 F.2d 446, 163 Ct.Cl. 465. Federal Courts ⊂⇒ 1116.1

109. Remand, judicial review generally

In proceeding involving contract calling for delivery to Navy Department of 500,000 impulse cartridges, remand to Armed Services Board of Contract Appeals was required in order to determine whether contracting officer was improperly influenced by competitor in arriving at decision to terminate contractor's contract. Fairfield Scientific Corp. v. U.S., Ct.Cl.1979, 611 F.2d 854, 222 Ct.Cl. 167. United States ⊂⇒ 75(3)

Where, after having heard oral argument, court on appeal from decision of Armed Services Board of Contract Appeals remains unsure of exact findings made and legal standard used by Board and evidence is not so overwhelming as to justify court in making its own findings, case should be remanded to Board for clarification. Ordnance Research, Inc. v. U.S., Ct.Cl.1979, 609 F.2d 462, 221 Ct.Cl. 641. United States ⊂⇒ 73(15)

Court hearing action challenging Government's default termination of contract would remand Government's counterclaims to recover amounts paid contractor under alleged fraudulent payment vouchers, amounts contractor was allegedly overpaid as result of excise tax exemption effective after tax inclusion date established by contract and amounts Government incurred due to contractor's failure to meet warranty obligations for administrative processing, where administrative remedies as to counterclaims had not been pursued because of pendency of contractor's action challenging default termination. Universal Fiber-

glass Corp. v. U.S., Ct.Cl.1976, 537 F.2d 393, 210 Ct.Cl. 206. United States ⊂⇒ 73(15)

Where contractor alleged that some items of documentary evidence in 12 exhibits introduced during hearings before District of Columbia Contract Appeals Board were not before the district court when it rendered its decision on basis of "whole administrative record," in the interests of justice, the case would be remanded so that district court, if it had not already done so, might consider all pertinent parts of administrative record, and file amended and supplemental finding reflecting either that it had considered all documentary evidence and exhibits in reaching its conclusion or had, since remand, considered same and amended or affirmed, as it deemed appropriate, its judgment order. Jonal Corp. v. District of Columbia, C.A.D.C.1976, 533 F.2d 1192, 175 U.S.App.D.C. 57, certiorari denied 97 S.Ct. 80, 429 U.S. 825, 50 L.Ed.2d 88. Federal Courts ⊂⇒ 941

If circumstances justify such leniency, Court of Claims can send a case back to determine whether there should be an administrative determination, despite absence of a timely appeal to Armed Services Board of Contract Appeals by contractor. Airco, Inc. v. U.S., Ct.Cl.1974, 504 F.2d 1133, 205 Ct.Cl. 493. United States ⊂⇒ 74(8)

Actions in which carriers sought to recover from government for increase in the price of fuel would be remanded to the Armed Services Board of Contract Appeals for determination of whether the increase in cost had been foreseen by each individual carrier when it entered into contract with the government or was reasonably foreseeable at the time of contracting as likely to arise during the contract period. Gulf & South Am. S.S. Co., Inc. v. U.S., Ct.Cl.1974, 500 F.2d 549, 205 Ct.Cl. 135. United States ⊂⇒ 74(7)

Court of Claims on proceeding to review Board's denial of equitable adjustment pursuant to changed condition clause would not determine whether changed condition had in fact occurred but would remand case to Board for such determination. Roscoe-Ajax Const. Co. v. U.S., Ct.Cl.1972, 458 F.2d 55, 198 Ct.Cl. 133. United States ⊂⇒ 73(15)

Where, after having heard oral argument, court on appeal from decision of Armed Services Board of Contract Appeals remains unsure of exact findings made and legal standard used by Board, and evidence is not so overwhelming as to justify court in making its own finding, case should be remanded to Board for clarification. Koppers Co. v. U.S., Ct.Cl. 1968, 405 F.2d 554, 186 Ct.Cl. 142. United States ⌖ 73(15)

This section and section 322 of this title are not contravened by trying damages issues in Court of Claims where agency has not reached or passed upon them; and it was appropriate for Court of Claims, which concluded that Government had breached contract, to return case to trial commissioner for determination of amount of recovery where neither contracting officer nor Board of Contract Appeals had reached issue of compensation or recovery. Stein Bros. Mfg. Co. v. U.S., Ct.Cl.1963, 337 F.2d 861, 162 Ct.Cl. 802. Federal Courts ⌖ 1115; United States ⌖ 73(14)

Where there were pleadings in suit by United States as assignee of contractor's claims against subcontractor for overpayment to support issues of finality and conclusiveness of disputes award and as to alleged defense under state Statute of Frauds, though summary judgment for subcontractor, reversed on appeal on ground that subcontractor's withdrawal from disputes procedure did not invalidate disputes determination, was not based upon them, reviewing court would remand on such issues alone. U.S. v. Taylor, C.A.5 (Miss.) 1964, 336 F.2d 149. Federal Courts ⌖ 944

In proceeding to determine whether contract between Government and lumber mill was an at-call agreement not binding upon Government or was a requirements contract and therefore binding upon Government, wherein it appeared that Armed Services Board of Contract Appeals had determined that contract was binding, in view of fact that record of proceeding before Board was not brought before reviewing court, matter would be returned to district court for determination of whether Board's determination was fraudulent or capricious or arbitrary or so grossly erroneous as necessarily to imply bad faith or was not supported by substantial evidence. Lowell O. West Lumber Sales v. U.S., C.A.9 (Cal.) 1959, 270 F.2d 12. Federal Courts ⌖ 942

Claims Court would remand contractor's claim to the Department of Agriculture Board of Contract Appeals for further evidentiary proceedings instead of assuming jurisdiction of case for de novo trial on Wunderlich Act appeal, although claim had been before AGBCA for more than ten years before AGBCA required contractor to submit proof of costs; there had been no showing of bias and no assertion of reason for Claims Court to doubt fairness of proceedings before AGBCA, and mere delay was not itself indication of bias. Griffin & Dickson v. U.S., Cl.Ct.1989, 16 Cl.Ct. 347. Federal Courts ⌖ 1118

IV. FINALITY OF ADMINISTRATIVE DECISIONS

Subdivision Index

---

131.   Finality of administrative decisions generally

Should government contractor be dissatisfied with administrative decision and bring suit under section 1346(a) of Title 26 for breach of contract in Court of Claims or district court, finality accorded administrative fact-finding by disputes clause of contract is limited by this chapter. U.S. v. Utah Const. & Min. Co., U.S.Ct.Cl.1966, 86 S.Ct. 1545, 384 U.S. 394, 16 L.Ed.2d 642.   United States ⊕ 73(14)

Attaching finality to the decision of no waiver and no estoppel by the Corps of Engineers Board of Contract Appeals meant that the holding of the Board that the termination of the sandbag contract was due to the default of the contractor was correct as a matter of law and was, therefore, final and conclusive. Northwestern Bag Corp. v. U.S., Ct.Cl.1980, 619 F.2d 896, 223 Ct.Cl. 333.   United States ⊕ 73(14)

In determining whether a letter sent by government contracting officer to contractor terminating contract was a final decision, no magic formula exists for determining what constitutes "finality" absent a specific statutory requirement; the precise word "final" is not required if a sufficient equivalent is used. Richardson Camera Co., Inc. v. U.S., Ct.Cl.1972, 467 F.2d 491, 199 Ct.Cl. 657.   United States ⊕ 73(15)

Decision of head of a department is final and conclusive unless it is fraudulent, arbitrary, or capricious, is so grossly erroneous as to imply bad faith, or is not supported by substantial evidence. Wagner Whirler & Derrick Corp. v. U.S., Ct.

Cl.1954, 121 F.Supp. 664, 128 Ct.Cl. 382. Administrative Law And Procedure ☞ 763; Administrative Law And Procedure ☞ 791

Except in rare cases, such as a suit by the contractor for damages, or in case of fraud or mistake, the defendant is and should be bound by the decision of the person the Government selected to make final decisions. Fred R. Comb Co. v. U.S., Ct.Cl.1943, 100 Ct.Cl. 259. Contracts ☞ 285(1); United States ☞ 73(14)

132. Claims subject to finality requirement, finality of administrative decisions

Disputes clause of construction contract with Atomic Energy Commission excluded breach of contract claims from its coverage, whether for purpose of granting relief or for purpose of making binding findings of fact that would be reviewable under standards contained in this chapter rather than de novo. U.S. v. Utah Const. & Min. Co., U.S.Ct.Cl.1966, 86 S.Ct. 1545, 384 U.S. 394, 16 L.Ed.2d 642. United States ☞ 73(14)

The rule expressed by the Supreme Court in U.S. v. Carlo Bianchi & Co., 83 S.Ct. 1409, 373 U.S. 709, 10 L.Ed.2d 652 (1963), regarding the scope of judicial review by the Court of Claims in contract disputes involving questions of fact, is expressly limited to matters reviewed by the court which have been administratively decided by the contracting agency under some contract provision in which the parties have agreed that the administrative decision shall be final, and the rule does not apply in litigation by a claimant seeking to recover civilian Government pay lost through an alleged improper separation from his Government position following an administrative hearing and adverse decision by the employing agency. Morelli v. U.S., Ct.Cl.1966, 177 Ct.Cl. 848. United States ☞ 39(13); United States ☞ 73(15)

133. Majority opinion of agency, finality of administrative decisions

Where general services administration board of contract appeals divided evenly on question of claimant's liability so that decision of contracting officer was affirmed, there were no findings of fact which could be accorded finality as would otherwise be required by this section since there was no majority decision. L. Rosenman Corp. v. U.S., Ct.Cl.1968, 390 F.2d 711, 182 Ct.Cl. 586. United States ☞ 73(14)

134. Contractual finality provisions, finality of administrative decisions

Where contractor's contract with Atomic Energy Commission for construction of a testing facility contained disputes clause stating that decision of Commission shall be "final and conclusive," Commission decision sustaining examiner's determination that amounts due contractor could not be retained to offset claims allegedly owed by contractor to other contractors and other agencies of government was final in absence of fraud or bad faith and neither the contract nor this chapter permitted further administrative review by the general accounting office. S & E Contractors, Inc. v. U.S., U.S.Ct.Cl.1972, 92 S.Ct. 1411, 406 U.S. 1, 31 L.Ed.2d 658. United States ☞ 73(14); United States ☞ 73(15)

Exception in contractor's agreement settling claims against government to effect that instrument would not be binding if the decision of board is subsequently found to be in violation of standard set forth in provision of this chapter did not bar contractor's suit to review decisions against his claims against government arising out of contract since suit was one in which it might be found that board decision was in violation of standard set forth in this chapter relating to finality and nonreviewability of administrative decisions. Vann v. U.S., Ct.Cl.1970, 420 F.2d 968, 190 Ct.Cl. 546. United States ☞ 74(6)

When government contractor believes government is wrongfully withholding his funds, courts afford remedy only if contractor shows his entitlement thereto under standards of review set forth in this chapter, and aside from true settlements or compromises, the parties cannot bypass this chapter by endowing administrative decisions with absolute finality in advance. ACME Process Equipment Co. v. U.S., Ct.Cl.1965, 347 F.2d 538, 171 Ct.Cl. 251, motion denied 351 F.2d 656, 171 Ct.Cl. 251. United States ☞ 73(14); United States ☞ 73(15)

Where contracts of sale between dried milk producer and Commodity Credit Corporation provided for submission of disputes to contracting officer of Commodity Credit Corporation and for appeals to Contract Disputes Board of the Commodity Credit Corporation, resulting decisions were binding unless fraudulent, capricious, arbitrary, or so grossly erroneous as necessarily implying bad faith or unless not supported by substantial evidence. Land O'Lakes Creameries, Inc. v. Commodity Credit Corp., D.C.Minn.1960, 185 F.Supp. 412, affirmed 308 F.2d 604. United States ⬿ 53(7)

135. Failure to object, finality of administrative decisions

Government contractor petitioning for review of administrative agency determination on contract dispute should not be barred from adopting trial judge's holding on the administrative finality question though neither party addressed itself to such issue at first. Roscoe-Ajax Const. Co., Inc. v. U.S., Ct.Cl.1974, 499 F.2d 639, 204 Ct.Cl. 726. United States ⬿ 73(15)

Where government contractor assigned no error with respect to decision of Corps of Engineers Board of Contract Appeals that government had incurred excess costs as result of contractor's default, such decision was required to be accorded finality by Court of Claims. Stoeckert v. U.S., Ct.Cl.1968, 391 F.2d 639, 183 Ct.Cl. 152. United States ⬿ 73(14)

136. Lack of jurisdiction, finality of administrative decisions

Claim for redress for cardinal changes in government contract, if valid, is a breach claim, and it takes case outside jurisdiction of Armed Services Board of Contract Appeals, rendering its findings gratuitous; however, absent a cardinal change, Board findings enjoy finality. General Dynamics Corp. v. U.S., Ct.Cl. 1978, 585 F.2d 457, 218 Ct.Cl. 40. United States ⬿ 73(9); United States ⬿ 73(14)

Where findings of Armed Services Board of Contract Appeals are made in case within its jurisdiction they must be applied in any collateral proceeding where same facts are in issue, and so applied without challenge on government's part, but where Board conducts proceeding beyond its jurisdiction its findings of fact therein are advisory only. General Dynamics Corp. v. U.S., Ct.Cl. 1977, 558 F.2d 985, 214 Ct.Cl. 607, 198 U.S.P.Q. 215. United States ⬿ 73(14)

Where plaintiff and defendant in changed conditions and disputes provisions of contract for construction of earthen dam across creek jointly con-

ferred on Board of Contract Appeals jurisdiction to determine whether plaintiff encountered changed conditions and, to determine amount of equitable adjustment and plaintiff did not seek review by court of portion of Commissioner's order overruling his request for trial de novo, Board was acting within scope of its jurisdiction when it considered plaintiff's claim and decided that plaintiff had encountered changed condition which entitled him to equitable adjustment upward in contract price and factual determinations contained in Board's decisions were entitled to finality if they met standards prescribed in this section. Briscoe v. U.S., Ct.Cl.1971, 442 F.2d 953, 194 Ct.Cl. 866. United States ⬿ 73(9); United States ⬿ 73(15)

Government contractor's claim that specifications for aircraft maintenance hangar at naval air station were defective in failing to specify that tie rods had to be installed before arches were released on buttresses, that structure collapsed due to this defect, that plaintiff was ordered to reconstruct the hangar and that this resulted in increased costs of almost double the contract price was not encompassed by the changes clause and was not redressable under the contract, and the armed services board of contract appeals was without jurisdiction to consider the claim, and Board's findings of fact on that claim were gratuitous and did not preclude or eliminate trial de novo on the merits of claim for breach of contract in the Court of Claims. Edward R. Marden Corp. v. U.S., Ct.Cl.1971, 442 F.2d 364, 194 Ct.Cl. 799. United States ⬿ 73(9); United States ⬿ 73(15)

Findings of fact by armed services board of contract appeals that federal contractor defaulted, without excuse, and that contract was properly terminated for his default were entitled to final and binding weight in litigation by government against contractor for breach of contract; a matter beyond the board's jurisdiction. Marley v. U.S., Ct.Cl.1970, 423 F.2d 324, 191 Ct.Cl. 205. United States ⬿ 73(14)

Where neither government contractor's claim for administrative relief under contract nor its breach of contract claim was within hearing board's jurisdiction, any findings made by board on either branch of case had no finality. National Steel & Shipbuilding Co. v. U.S., Ct.Cl.1969, 419

F.2d 863, 190 Ct.Cl. 247. United States
☞ 73(14)

Where Department of Commerce
Board of Appeals was without authority
to grant relief to road contractor on his
claim against United States for breach of
implied obligation under contract not to
interfere unreasonably with contractor in
performance of the work, board's findings of fact with respect to claim were
not necessarily entitled to finality even
though supported by substantial evidence. Clack v. U.S., Ct.Cl.1968, 395
F.2d 773, 184 Ct.Cl. 40. Highways ☞
113(4)

Action of Interior Board of Contract
Appeals in making findings of fact on
claim for delay damage due to winter
shutdown was gratuitous, inasmuch as
Board had no jurisdiction of claim and
findings did not preclude or limit trial de
novo on merits of the claim with respect
to government contract. Morrison-Knudsen Co. v. U.S., Ct.Cl.1965, 345 F.2d 833,
170 Ct.Cl. 757. United States ☞ 73(14)

**137. Reconsideration of agency deter-
mination, finality of administrative
decisions**
Ungranted request by a successor contracting officer to Army Board of Contract Appeals, for reconsideration of a
decision of the Secretary of the Army, did
not deprive the decision of finality, for
purposes of determining whether limitations ran on a claim grounded on arbitrariness of such decision, and limitations
was not tolled during period request was
not acted upon. Cosmopolitan Mfg. Co.
v. U.S., Ct.Cl.1962, 297 F.2d 546, 156
Ct.Cl. 142, certiorari denied 83 S.Ct. 36,
371 U.S. 818, 9 L.Ed.2d 60. Limitation
Of Actions ☞ 105(2)

**138. Questions of fact, finality of ad-
ministrative decisions—Generally**
Ordinarily, when questions of fact arise
in suits against the United States founded
upon an express or implied contract with
the United States, function of the Court of
Claims is to receive evidence and to make
appropriate findings as to the facts in
dispute, but the function of the Court of
Claims is limited in cases governed by
this section and section 322 of this title.
U.S. v. Carlo Bianchi & Co., U.S.Ct.Cl.
1963, 83 S.Ct. 1409, 373 U.S. 709, 10
L.Ed.2d 652. Federal Courts ☞ 1114.1;
United States ☞ 73(15)

Any factual determination made by the
Armed Services Board of Contract Appeals must be accepted by the Court of
Claims as final and conclusive for the
purposes of the litigation unless such determination is shown to be fraudulent, or
capricious, or arbitrary, or so grossly erroneous as necessarily to imply bad faith,
or unsupported by substantial evidence.
Schnip Bldg. Co. v. U.S., Ct.Cl.1981, 645
F.2d 950, 227 Ct.Cl. 148. See, also, Philadelphia Regent Builders v. U.S.,Ct.Cl.
1980, 634 F.2d 569, 225 Ct.Cl. 234; Sea-
Land Service, Inc. v. U.S., 1974, 493 F.2d
1357, 204 Ct.Cl. 57, certiorari denied 95
S.Ct. 69, 419 U.S. 840, 42 L.Ed.2d 67;
Northwestern Indus; Piping, Inc. v. U.S.,
1972, 467 F.2d 1308, 199 Ct.Cl. 540; T.
F. Scholes, Inc. v. U.S., 1966, 357 F.2d
963, 174 Ct.Cl. 1215; Lowell O. West
Lumber Sales v. U.S., C.A.Cal.1959, 270
F.2d 12; Meinberg v. U.S., D.C.Mo.1969,
310 F.Supp. 86. United States ☞ 73(15)

In the process of reaching its own conclusions concerning the meaning of a
contract, the Court of Claims must accord finality to administrative factual
findings where there is no showing that
such findings are in any way arbitrary,
capricious or unsupported by substantial
evidence. Robert L. Guyler Co. v. U.S.,
Ct.Cl.1979, 593 F.2d 406, 219 Ct.Cl. 403,
certiorari denied 100 S.Ct. 85, 444 U.S.
843, 62 L.Ed.2d 55, rehearing denied 100
S.Ct. 438, 444 U.S. 957, 62 L.Ed.2d 330.
See, also, Tri–Cor, Inc. v. U.S., 1972, 458
F.2d 112, 198 Ct.Cl. 187; Beryllium
Corp. v. U.S., 1971, 449 F.2d 362, 196
Ct.Cl. 12; National Movers Co. v. U.S.,
1967, 386 F.2d 999, 181 Ct.Cl. 419.
United States ☞ 73(14)

Under this chapter, findings of fact by
Armed Services Board of Contract Appeals are final if supported by substantial
evidence and Board's decisions of questions of law are open to independent judicial consideration. La Crosse Garment
Mfg. Co. v. U.S., Ct.Cl.1970, 432 F.2d
1377, 193 Ct.Cl. 168. United States ☞
73(15)

Clause of standard governmentwide
construction contract requiring "all disputes concerning questions of fact arising
under this contract" to be submitted to
government contracting officer, and providing that officer's decision, subject to
departmental appeal, "shall be final and
conclusive upon the parties thereto" extends only to controversies redressable by

specific provisions in contract, i.e., fact dispute is one "arising under this contract" only when disputed fact is capable of complete resolution by procedures specified in contract. Bethlehem Steel Corp. v. Grace Line, Inc., C.A.D.C.1969, 416 F.2d 1096, 135 U.S.App.D.C. 81. United States ⊂⇛ 73(9)

Factual determinations in actions redressable under government contract provisions are initially the exclusive prerogative of contracting agencies. Capobianco v. U.S., Ct.Cl.1968, 394 F.2d 515, 184 Ct.Cl. 160. United States ⊂⇛ 73(14)

Finality of relevant findings of fact, supported by sufficient evidence, made by administrative board in disposing of claim over which it has power to grant relief, cannot be denuded by trial de novo in Court of Claims on breach claim which is dependent upon same underlying facts that have been previously determined by board. Jefferson Const. Co. v. U.S., Ct. Cl.1968, 392 F.2d 1006, 183 Ct.Cl. 720, certiorari denied 89 S.Ct. 122, 393 U.S. 842, 21 L.Ed.2d 113. Federal Courts ⊂⇛ 1115

An administrative decision as to factual questions is final unless fraudulent, capricious, arbitrary, or so grossly erroneous as necessarily to imply bad faith or unless not supported by substantial evidence. Dittmore-Freimuth Corp. v. U.S., Ct.Cl. 1968, 390 F.2d 664, 182 Ct.Cl. 507. United States ⊂⇛ 73(14)

Where both contractor and government in their requested findings of fact ignored Armed Services Board of Contract Appeals' findings and instead asked for factual findings from court based on evidence, there was no occasion for court to determine whether board findings of fact were or were not entitled to finality under disputes provisions of contracts. Specialty Assembling & Packing Co. v. U.S., Ct. Cl.1966, 355 F.2d 554, 174 Ct.Cl. 153. Federal Courts ⊂⇛ 1118

Where issue is one of fact, administrative appeals board's decision is binding upon district court, unless it comes within reach of exclusions of this section, limiting Government contract provisions as to the finality of administrative decisions with reference to contract. U.S. Nat. Bank of Portland v. U.S., D.C.Or. 1959, 178 F.Supp. 910. United States ⊂⇛ 73(14)

Findings of fact of a Government contracting officer, affirmed on appeal, are conclusive, unless he acted arbitrarily or capriciously or his decisions were so grossly erroneous as to show bad faith. Penner Installation Corp. v. U.S., Ct.Cl. 1950, 89 F.Supp. 545, 116 Ct.Cl. 550, certiorari granted 71 S.Ct. 55, 340 U.S. 808, 95 L.Ed. 594, affirmed 71 S.Ct. 278, 340 U.S. 898, 95 L.Ed. 651, rehearing denied 71 S.Ct. 356, 340 U.S. 923, 95 L.Ed. 666. United States ⊂⇛ 73(14)

A contract "disputes" decision by the Corps of Engineers Board of Contract Appeals is final if the decision relates to a question of fact unless the decision is fraudulent, arbitrary, grossly erroneous, or not supported by substantial evidence. Richards & Associates v. U.S., Ct.Cl.1966, 177 Ct.Cl. 1037. United States ⊂⇛ 73(14)

Disputes concerning questions of fact appealed to the head of the contracting agency under the contract Disputes clause are matters for final decision by such department head and the decision is binding on the parties and the court unless arbitrary or not supported by substantial evidence. Allied Contractors, Inc. v. U.S., Ct.Cl.1966, 176 Ct.Cl. 1095. United States ⊂⇛ 73(14); United States ⊂⇛ 73(15)

The decision by the head of the contracting agency or department in a contract dispute concerning a question of fact will not be deprived of the finality prescribed in this section by reason of minor errors which may have been committed by the Armed Services Board of Contract Appeals in the course of deciding the dispute, where the decision is, on the whole, not arbitrary, grossly erroneous or unsupported by substantial evidence. Heers v. U.S., Ct.Cl.1964, 165 Ct.Cl. 294. United States ⊂⇛ 73(14)

Under the provisions of this section and section 322 of this title, decisions of a contracting officer, affirmed by the head of the contracting agency, on disputes concerning questions of fact are final and binding unless arbitrary, capricious, so grossly erroneous as necessarily to imply bad faith, or are unsupported by substantial evidence. United Foundation Corp. v. U.S., Ct.Cl.1962, 158 Ct.Cl. 41. United States ⊂⇛ 73(14)

139. —— **Amount of equitable adjustment, questions of fact, finality of administrative decisions**

Generally, administrative determination of amount of equitable adjustment of contract costs is pure question of fact. Teledyne McCormick-Selph v. U.S., Ct.Cl. 1978, 588 F.2d 808, 218 Ct.Cl. 513. United States ☞ 74(12.1)

Equitable adjustment due contractor for additional fill on housing project at Air Force base was question of fact for Armed Services Board of Contract Appeals. Electronic & Missile Facilities, Inc. v. U.S., Ct.Cl.1969, 416 F.2d 1345, 189 Ct.Cl. 237. United States ☞ 73(15)

Amount of an equitable adjustment due a contractor on contract price when a suspension of work order is issued is a question of fact to be determined, in first instance, by Armed Services Board of Contract Appeals. Urban Plumbing & Heating Co. v. U.S., Ct.Cl.1969, 408 F.2d 382, 187 Ct.Cl. 15, certiorari denied 90 S.Ct. 2164, 398 U.S. 958, 26 L.Ed.2d 542. United States ☞ 73(15)

Determination of amount of equitable adjustment to which government contractor is entitled as result of changed condition is pure question of fact. Phillips Const. Co. v. U.S., Ct.Cl.1968, 394 F.2d 834, 184 Ct.Cl. 249. United States ☞ 74(12.1)

The amount due for extra concrete work computed at unit prices set out in construction contract was a question of fact, and finding of contracting officer on that question was final, since there was no appeal to head of the department. Gerhardt F. Meyne Co. v. U.S., Ct.Cl. 1948, 76 F.Supp. 811, 110 Ct.Cl. 527. United States ☞ 73(14)

140. —— **Changed conditions, questions of fact, finality of administrative decisions**

Government, which was not in position of having to resort to administrative remedy to protect itself against risk of losing all remedies under changes article of contract for smoke generator was bound, in proceeding to determine whether changes in contract constituted cardinal change, by armed forces board of contract appeals factual findings, in prior administrative hearing on issue of equitable adjustment under changes clause of the contract, as to scope and nature of changes as far as those factual findings

go. Air-A-Plane Corp. v. U.S., Ct.Cl. 1969, 408 F.2d 1030, 187 Ct.Cl. 269. United States ☞ 73(14)

Whether or not a condition encountered by the contractor in connection with the performance of his Government contract amounts to a "Changed Condition" within the meaning of the standard form Government contract, is a question of fact upon which the decision of the head of the contracting agency is final unless fraudulent, arbitrary, grossly erroneous, or not supported by substantial evidence. National Concrete & Foundation Co. v. U.S., Ct.Cl.1965, 170 Ct.Cl. 470. United States ☞ 73(14)

141. —— **Date of contract settlement, questions of fact, finality of administrative decisions**

In action for use of subcontractor to recover on payment bond furnished by Government contractor, this section making decisions of Government officers rendered pursuant to standard dispute clause in Government contracts final and conclusive, unless such decision is fraudulent, capricious, arbitrary, or so grossly erroneous as necessarily to imply bad faith, or is not supported by substantial evidence, was applicable and controlling on question of date of final settlement of contract. U.S. for Use of Bangor Roofing & Sheet Metal Co. v. T.W. Cunningham, Inc., D.C.Me.1956, 141 F.Supp. 205. United States ☞ 67(17)

142. —— **Delay in performance, questions of fact, finality of administrative decisions**

Specific findings of the Court of Claims as to how much of the delay in performance of a Government contract was attributable to the fault of each party are conclusive. Robinson v. U.S., U.S.1923, 43 S.Ct. 420, 261 U.S. 486, 67 L.Ed. 760. Federal Courts ☞ 492

Where contract appeals board in declining jurisdiction on breach of contract claim made finding as to cause and extent of delay experienced by plaintiff contractor in performance and completion of piling work while determining contractor's claims relating to additional work for restoring foundation and with respect to time extensions, such findings, which also were acknowledged by government as factually correct, were conclusive with respect to determination of breach of contract claim for delay damages resulting from foundation failure. J.L. Simmons Co. v. U.S., Ct.Cl.1969, 412 F.2d 1360, 188 Ct.Cl. 684. United States ☞ 73(14)

143. ──── Employee status or position, questions of fact, finality of administrative decisions

Under Government construction subcontract whereby parties agreed upon procedure as to how a dispute concerning question of fact should be decided, determination of whether subcontractor's employee was "project manager" whose salary was reimbursable item of cost of project was a "question of fact". Evans Elec. Const. Co. v. Wm. S. Lozier, Inc., W.D.Mo.1946, 68 F.Supp. 256, appeal dismissed 162 F.2d 717. Contracts ☞ 285(2)

144. ──── Excusability of default, questions of fact, finality of administrative decisions

Whether default of federal contractor is excusable is most often a question of fact. Marley v. U.S., Ct.Cl.1970, 423 F.2d 324, 191 Ct.Cl. 205. United States ☞ 74(7)

Whether or not a default is excusable is a question of fact and a decision thereon by the head of the contracting agency under the disputes article of the contract is conclusive on the parties in the absence of a showing that the decision was fraudulent, capricious, arbitrary or not supported by substantial evidence. H & H Mfg. Co. Inc. v. U.S., Ct.Cl.1964, 168 Ct.Cl. 873. See, also, Dale Const. Co. v. U.S., 1964, 168 Ct.Cl. 692. United States ☞ 73(14)

145. ──── Impossibility of performance, questions of fact, finality of administrative decisions

Question whether government contract has become impossible of performance is proper subject for factual finding by Armed Services Board of Contract Appeals, but ultimate question is legal one. International Electronics Corp. v. U.S., Ct.Cl.1981, 646 F.2d 496, 227 Ct.Cl. 208. United States ☞ 73(15)

Whether specifications for landing mats set forth in government contract were factually impossible or commercially impracticable to perform was a question of fact for Armed Services Board of Contract Appeals, and would not be disturbed on appeal when supported by substantial evidence, but ultimate issue,

namely whether manufacturer's default was excusable because performance was impossible, was one of law, which was not subject to substantial evidence rule. Koppers Co. v. U.S., Ct.Cl.1968, 405 F.2d 554, 186 Ct.Cl. 142. United States ☞ 73(15)

146. ──── Interference with contract, questions of fact, finality of administrative decisions

Issues bearing on government's termination of contract, including alleged interference with plaintiff contractor's performance and reasonableness of excess costs claimed by government, were questions of fact subject to decision by hearing officer under disputes article of contract. Nager Elec. Co. v. U.S., Ct.Cl. 1968, 396 F.2d 977, 184 Ct.Cl. 390. United States ☞ 73(9)

147. ──── Notice to negotiate, questions of fact, finality of administrative decisions

If findings by Armed Services Board of Contract Appeals that supplier waived right to insist on notice to negotiate and could not participate in negotiations until it discovered likelihood of unfavorable outcome and then decline to continue were fact findings, they were supported by evidence, if questions of law, they were correct; in either event, supplier was precluded from insisting on notice to negotiate. Copco Steel & Engineering Co. v. U.S., Ct.Cl.1965, 341 F.2d 590, 169 Ct.Cl. 601. United States ☞ 70(18); United States ☞ 74(11)

148. ──── Profit level determination, questions of fact, finality of administrative decisions

The determination of a reasonable profit level for a government contractor is a factual issue which must be left by the Court of Claims for determination by the Armed Services Board of Contract Appeals, despite previous errors, unless the Board procedure is inadequate and unavailable. Bethlehem Steel Corp. v. U.S., Ct.Cl.1975, 511 F.2d 529, 206 Ct.Cl. 122, certiorari denied 96 S.Ct. 71, 423 U.S. 840, 46 L.Ed.2d 60. United States ☞ 73(15)

149. ──── Standard of workmanship, questions of fact, finality of administrative decisions

Question whether Government applied too high a standard of workmanship in inspecting work done by subcontractor on whose behalf contractor sought equitable adjustment was a question of fact. Chris Berg, Inc. v. U.S., Ct.Cl.1972, 455 F.2d 1037, 197 Ct.Cl. 503. United States ⟷ 74(7)

150. —— Miscellaneous findings final, questions of fact, finality of administrative decisions

In view of identity of controlling factual issues, Court of Claims was bound by factual findings of Armed Services Board of Contract Appeals, which demonstrated that contract was not breached. ITT Gilfillan, Inc. v. U.S., Ct.Cl.1973, 471 F.2d 1382, 200 Ct.Cl. 367. United States ⟷ 73(15)

Government contractor's claim, which had been subject of decision by Army Corps of Engineers' contracting officer and the board of contract appeal, was, to the extent it was a decision on question of fact, subject to review by Court of Claims against record compiled by agency. Merritt-Chapman & Scott Corp. v. U.S., Ct. Cl.1970, 429 F.2d 431, 192 Ct.Cl. 848. United States ⟷ 73(15)

As finding of Board of Contract Appeals that negative master mold failed to meet contract specifications was supported by substantial record evidence, the finding, under this section had to be accepted by court as final and conclusive without an independent weighing of pertinent evidence, since question of whether material furnished under the contract complied with the specifications was one of fact. Panoramic Studios, Inc. v. U.S., Ct.Cl.1969, 413 F.2d 1156, 188 Ct.Cl. 1092. United States ⟷ 73(15)

Mathematical computations of Armed Services Board of Contract Appeals concerning question of fact are final and binding on Court of Claims if supported by substantial evidence. J. A. Jones Const. Co. v. U.S., Ct.Cl.1968, 395 F.2d 783, 184 Ct.Cl. 1. United States ⟷ 73(14)

Exercise of judgment by Armed Services Board of Contract Appeals as to how to apply a guideline established by regulation to particular established facts is decision of fact not reviewable under this chapter. Newport News Shipbuilding & Dry Dock Co. v. U.S., Ct.Cl.1967, 374 F.2d 516, 179 Ct.Cl. 97. United States ⟷ 73(15)

In determining whether owner of vessel was entitled to recover from United States for loss of anchor and part of anchor chain while vessel was operating under time charter to Military Sea Transportation Service of Department of Navy, federal district court was bound by facts found by Board of Contract Appeals as provided in time charter agreement, but had power to review any questions of law. American President Lines, Limited v. U.S., N.D.Cal.1961, 208 F.Supp. 573. Shipping ⟷ 55

151. —— Miscellaneous findings not final, questions of fact, finality of administrative decisions

In action by contractor against United States for sums allegedly due contractor under contract to manufacture and erect two 20-ton jib cranes at Philadelphia Navy Yard, contracting officer's decision involving construction of specification was not binding upon the Court of Claims because it was not a finding of fact, and the disputes clause, which accorded finality to contracting officer's findings, was limited to findings of fact. Wagner Whirler & Derrick Corp. v. U.S., Ct.Cl.1954, 121 F.Supp. 664, 128 Ct.Cl. 382. United States ⟷ 73(14)

152. Questions of law, finality of administrative decisions—Generally

Provision of government contract barring action against government based on contracting officer's refusal to approve substitution of subcontractors was an attempt to accord finality to administrative decision whether or not based on errors of law would be contrary to this section unless the exceptions under this section are read into it. Hoel-Steffen Const. Co. v. U.S., Ct.Cl.1982, 684 F.2d 843, 231 Ct.Cl. 128. United States ⟷ 70(35)

In a case under this chapter, Court of Claims' review is limited; however, when questions for review are those of law, court has duty independently to review decision of administrative board which first passed on the issues. Monroe M. Tapper & Associates v. U.S., Ct.Cl.1979, 602 F.2d 311, 221 Ct.Cl. 27. United States ⟷ 73(15)

Prior administrative decision with respect to questions of law was not binding on Court of Claims trial judge. American Elec. Contracting Corp. v. U.S., Ct.Cl. 1978, 579 F.2d 602, 217 Ct.Cl. 338. See, also, Nager Elec. Co. v. U.S., 1971, 442

F.2d 936, 194 Ct.Cl. 835. United States
☞ 73(14)

Under this chapter, board's decisions
on questions of law are not entitled to
finality. Northwestern Indus. Piping,
Inc. v. U.S., Ct.Cl.1972, 467 F.2d 1308,
199 Ct.Cl. 540.

Administrative decision that government contractor had no breach of contract claim was not final, and was reviewable by court of claims, not only because
administrative board had had no jurisdiction to render such decision but also because it was decision of question of law,
where decision rested not only on simple
facts but was in essence judgment of law
on nature of government's duty to employ
all reasonable effort and reasonable diligence to supply working plans to contractor as required by contract. National
Steel & Shipbuilding Co. v. U.S., Ct.Cl.
1969, 419 F.2d 863, 190 Ct.Cl. 247.
United States ☞ 73(15)

Under this chapter, all legal questions
are to be resolved independently by court
with respect to Government contract and
subordinate factual findings are wholly
subsumed in larger legal problem of contract interpretation. WPC Enterprises,
Inc. v. U.S., Ct.Cl.1963, 323 F.2d 874,
163 Ct.Cl. 1. United States ☞ 74(7)

Where a dispute arising under a contract involves a question of law, the court
is at liberty to make an independent determination. N. Fiorito Co., Inc. v. U.S.,
Ct.Cl.1967, 180 Ct.Cl. 281. United States
☞ 73(15)

A decision made by the head of a contracting agency on a dispute concerning a
question of law is not final and binding
on the parties or the court. Johnson v.
U.S., Ct.Cl.1965, 173 Ct.Cl. 561. See,
also, Bishop Engineering Co. v. U.S.,
1967, 180 Ct.Cl. 411. United States ☞
73(8)

**153. —— Interpretation of contracts
generally, questions of law, finality
of administrative decisions**

The interpretation of a government
contract is a question of law to be decided by the Court of Claims, which is not
bound by the interpretation of the Armed
Services Board of Contract Appeals.
B.D. Click Co., Inc. v. U.S., Ct.Cl.1980,
614 F.2d 748, 222 Ct.Cl. 290. See, also,
H. N. Bailey and Associates v. U.S., 1971,
449 F.2d 387, 196 Ct.Cl. 156; Sea-Land
Service, Inc. v. U.S., 1977, 553 F.2d 651,

213 Ct.Cl. 555, certiorari denied 98 S.Ct.
724, 434 U.S. 1012, 54 L.Ed.2d 755; N.
Fiorito Co. v. U.S., 1969, 416 F.2d 1284,
189 Ct.Cl. 215; Bailey Specialized Bldgs.,
Inc. v. U.S., 1968, 404 F.2d 355, 186
Ct.Cl. 71. United States ☞ 73(15)

In cases the Court of Claims decides
questions of contract interpretation de
novo. Coley Properties Corp. v. U.S.,
Ct.Cl.1979, 593 F.2d 380, 219 Ct.Cl. 227.
See, also, LTV Aerospace Corp. v. U.S.,
1970, 425 F.2d 1237, 192 Ct.Cl. 191;
Electronic & Missile Facilities, Inc. v.
U.S., 1969, 416 F.2d 1345, 189 Ct.Cl.
237; Tecon Corp. v. U.S., 1969, 411 F.2d
1262, 188 Ct.Cl. 15. United States ☞
73(15)

The interpretation of a contract by the
General Services Administration Board of
Contract Appeals will be given careful
consideration and accorded great respect
by court. George Hyman Const. Co. v.
U.S., Ct.Cl.1977, 564 F.2d 939, 215 Ct.Cl.
70. United States ☞ 73(15)

Court of Claims is free to decide question of contract interpretation for itself
regardless of decision of Board of Contract Appeals. C.H. Leavell & Co. v.
U.S., Ct.Cl.1976, 530 F.2d 878, 208 Ct.Cl.
776. See, also, John McShain, Inc. v.
U.S., 1972, 462 F.2d 489, 199 Ct.Cl. 364;
Morrison–Knudsen Co. v. U.S., 1968, 397
F.2d 826, 184 Ct.Cl. 661. United States
☞ 73(14)

Interpretation of contract documents is
judicial function to be performed independently of any decision by board of
contract appeals. Arundel Corp. v. U.S.,
Ct.Cl.1975, 515 F.2d 1116, 207 Ct.Cl. 84.
United States ☞ 73(14)

Interpretation of provisions of government contract is basically a question of
law on which the court, on review under
the Wunderlich Act, may reach its own
conclusion independent of that reached
by administrative appeal board. Petrofsky v. U.S., Ct.Cl.1973, 488 F.2d 1394,
203 Ct.Cl. 347. United States ☞ 73(15)

While interpretation of the meanings of
the provisions of a contract is a question
of law for the court, decision of Armed
Services Board of Contract Appeals in a
case under this section is entitled to great
weight if it is based on the Board's expertise and is not unreasonable. Dale Ingram, Inc. v. U.S., Ct.Cl.1973, 475 F.2d
1177, 201 Ct.Cl. 56. United States ☞
73(15)

Interpretation of contract between United States and Government contractor involves question of law. Dana Corp. v. U.S., Ct.Cl.1972, 470 F.2d 1032, 200 Ct. Cl. 200. See, also, Gelco Builders & Burjay Const. Corp. v. U.S., 1966, 369 F.2d 992, 177 Ct.Cl. 1025; Crowder v. U.S., D.C.Cal.1964, 255 F.Supp. 873, affirmed 362 F.2d 1011. United States ⊂⇒ 74(7)

Decision of Board of Contract Appeals in interpretation of Government contract is not entitled to finality and Court of Claims is free to reexamine contract language and independently reach its own conclusion. Dana Corp. v. U.S., Ct.Cl. 1972, 470 F.2d 1032, 200 Ct.Cl. 200. United States ⊂⇒ 73(14); United States ⊂⇒ 73(15)

Under standards of this chapter, issue as to meaning of language in contract of General Services Administration is for the Court of Claims to decide independently as no finality is attached to a conclusion of law reached by the General Services Board of Contract Appeals. Allied Paint Mfg. Co., Inc. v. U.S., Ct.Cl. 1972, 470 F.2d 556, 200 Ct.Cl. 313. See, also, J.B. Williams Co. v. U.S., 1971, 450 F.2d 1379, 196 Ct.Cl. 491. United States ⊂⇒ 73(15)

Board of contract appeals' decision which rested on interpretation of contract was on question of law and not binding on court. Corbetta Const. Co. v. U.S., Ct.Cl.1972, 461 F.2d 1330, 198 Ct.Cl. 712. United States ⊂⇒ 73(15)

Administrative determination based on contract interpretation is one of law and not binding on court. Nager Elec. Co. v. U.S., Ct.Cl.1971, 442 F.2d 936, 194 Ct.Cl. 835. See, also, Mountain Home Contractors v. U.S., 1970, 425 F.2d 1260, 192 Ct.Cl. 16. United States ⊂⇒ 73(15)

Question of matter of interpretation of specifications in government contract is a question of law and, consequently, neither the court nor government contractor is bound by determination of general services contract board of appeals. Jamsar, Inc. v. U.S., Ct.Cl.1971, 442 F.2d 930, 194 Ct.Cl. 819. United States ⊂⇒ 73(14); United States ⊂⇒ 73(15)

Where each claim of government contractor hinged upon a proper interpretation of the contract terms, and therefore each essentially involved an administrative decision on question of law, the administrative decisions were not final and were subject to plenary consideration by Court of Claims. Paschen Contractors, Inc. v. U.S., Ct.Cl.1969, 418 F.2d 1360, 190 Ct.Cl. 177. See, also, Hol–Gar Mfg. Corp. v. U.S., 1965, 351 F.2d 972, 169 Ct.Cl. 384; Blanchard v. U.S., 1965, 347 F.2d 268, 171 Ct.Cl. 559. United States ⊂⇒ 73(15)

Armed Services Board of Contract Appeals had authority to make interpretation where problem arose under contract and was covered by disputes clause, but court was not bound to accept it as final, since interpretation is a question of law. Sundstrand Turbo v. U.S., Ct.Cl.1968, 389 F.2d 406, 182 Ct.Cl. 31. United States ⊂⇒ 73(12); United States ⊂⇒ 73(15)

Where basic and ultimate issue in contract dispute between contractor and United States involved interpretation of contract specifications which was a question of law, decision of Armed Services Board of Contract Appeals was not entitled to finality under this chapter. Maxwell Dynamometer Co. V . U.S., Ct.Cl. 1967, 386 F.2d 855, 181 Ct.Cl. 607. See, also, Kings Electronics Co. v. U.S., 1965, 341 F.2d 632, 169 Ct.Cl. 433. United States ⊂⇒ 73(14); United States ⊂⇒ 73(15)

Where basic and ultimate issue in contract dispute between contractor and United States involved interpretation of contract specifications which was a question of law, Court of Claims was not bound by determination of Armed Services Board of Contract Appeals and Court of Claims was not bound by determination of Board, and therefore Court of Claims was free to re-examine question and reach its own conclusion as to what contract required. Maxwell Dynamometer Co. v. U.S., Ct.Cl.1967, 386 F.2d 855, 181 Ct.Cl. 607. United States ⊂⇒ 73(14); United States ⊂⇒ 73(15)

Limitations on judicial review of administratively determined factual matters had no application where issue was limited to attack on interpretation of contract provision by board of contract appeals. George Hyman Const. Co. v. U.S., Ct.Cl. 1966, 366 F.2d 1015, 177 Ct.Cl. 313. United States ⊂⇒ 73(15)

Legal interpretations by Board of Contract Appeals are considered helpful, even if not compelling, and such interpretations are given great weight by Claims Court, especially if reasonable and based on particular board's expertise. Flexible

Metal Hose Mfg. Co. v. U.S., Cl.Ct.1984, 4 Cl.Ct. 522, affirmed 765 F.2d 156. United States ☞ 73(15)

Interpretation of public contract is question of law that, under standard of this section, is for court to decide; administrative interpretation is not binding, but is entitled to careful consideration, and accorded due respect, if not unreasonable. Shuey Aircraft, Inc. v. U.S., Cl. Ct.1983, 3 Cl.Ct. 243. United States ☞ 73(15)

The interpretation of contract specifications involves the meaning of the contract and is a proper subject for judicial determination. Bishop Engineering Co., Inc. v. U.S., Ct.Cl.1967, 180 Ct.Cl. 411. Contracts ☞ 176(9)

The parties' contemporaneous construction of their contract is entitled to considerable weight by the Court of Claims in undertaking to interpret the contract. Merritt-Chapman & Scott Corp. v. U.S., Ct.Cl.1967, 178 Ct.Cl. 883, certiorari denied 88 S.Ct. 48, 389 U.S. 851, 19 L.Ed.2d 120. United States ☞ 70(3); United States ☞ 70(14)

154. —— Additional compensation, questions of law, finality of administrative decisions

To extent that government contractor's claim for additional compensation dealt with questions of law, court was required to examine de novo decision of agency administrator in contractor's favor, even though all the factual findings were undisputed or indisputable. C.J. Langenfelder & Son, Inc. v. U.S., Ct.Cl.1965, 341 F.2d 600, 169 Ct.Cl. 465. United States ☞ 73(15)

Where dispute arose between contractor and United States respecting charge for work done which allegedly was not within the terms of contract, and such dispute called for an interpretation of contract, issue constituted a question of law and hence trial court had original jurisdiction. Kayfield Construction Corp. v. United States, C.A.2 (N.Y.) 1960, 278 F.2d 217. United States ☞ 73(14)

155. —— Allocation of taxes, questions of law, finality of administrative decisions

Issue as to whether manufacturer could allocate to fixed-price, incentive type contracts with government a portion of personal property taxes which had been assessed with respect to commercial productive material and work-in-process inventories was question of law where contracts set out accounting rules (albeit vague) and, therefore, decision of Armed Services Board of Contract Appeals was not entitled to finality. Lockheed Aircraft Corp. v. U.S., Ct.Cl.1967, 375 F.2d 786, 179 Ct.Cl. 545. United States ☞ 73(14)

156. —— Changed conditions, questions of law, finality of administrative decisions

Issue of changed conditions, with respect to designated quarry from which contrary to contract indication, contractor was unable to obtain armor rock meeting specifications, was primarily one of law for purposes of this section. Stock & Grove, Inc. v. U.S., Ct.Cl.1974, 493 F.2d 629, 204 Ct.Cl. 103. United States ☞ 73(15)

In dispute as to alleged changed conditions and changes under standard government construction contract, decision on claimed contract indications was matter of analysis and interpretation of contract documents and presented question of law to be decided by Court of Claims independently of decision of appeals board. Foster Const. C.A. & Williams Bros. Co. v. U.S., Ct.Cl.1970, 435 F.2d 873, 193 Ct.Cl. 587. United States ☞ 73(15)

Since decision of Corps of Engineers Claims and Appeals Board with respect to fact that an overrun of 150% of estimated quantities was not a condition materially differing from those indicated involved proper legal standards to be applied under the changed conditions article of government contract, a question of law was presented so that Court of Claims was free to answer independently of Board's decision. Perini Corp. v. U.S., Ct.Cl.1967, 381 F.2d 403, 180 Ct. Cl. 768. United States ☞ 73(15)

When administrative decision concerning allowability of equitable adjustment under "changed conditions" provision of government contract turns on proper interpretation of contract, in order to determine whether subsurface or latent physical conditions at work site differed materially from those indicated in contract, agency is deciding question of law, and its decision is not necessarily final and conclusive. T.F. Scholes, Inc. v. U.S., Ct.Cl.1966, 357 F.2d 963, 174 Ct.Cl. 1215. United States ☞ 73(14)

Claim by government contractor for equitable adjustment under changes clause or damages for breach of contract arising out of deletion of certain pay item from contract involved questions of law relating to interpretation of the contract and decision of Interior Board of Contract Appeals on suit questions were not final. Morrison-Knudsen Co. v. U.S., Ct.Cl. 1965, 345 F.2d 833, 170 Ct.Cl. 757. United States ☞ 73(14)

When an ultimate determination regarding contract turns on question of law, such as whether changes ordered were cardinal and thus in breach of contract, a court is not bound by government officer's or board's decision. S.J. Groves & Sons Co. v. U.S., D.C.Colo.1980, 495 F.Supp. 201. United States ☞ 73(15)

Whether a subsurface or latent physical condition exists within the meaning of the Changed Conditions article of a contract, as indicated by the terms of a compaction specification, is a question of law, and the court is not bound by the board's decision thereon, nor by its rationale. Ray D. Bolander Co., Inc. v. U.S., Ct.Cl.1968, 186 Ct.Cl. 398. United States ☞ 73(15)

Where a contractor submits a claim under the "disputes" provision of a Government contract, the claim requesting an equitable adjustment under the "changes" and "changed conditions" articles for the additional work and expenses required to restore the project to its condition prior to hurricane damage, the decision by the Board of Contract Appeals dismissing the contractor's appeal on the ground that the complaint failed to state a case upon which relief could be granted and without making any factual determination, involves a legal conclusion, and is not entitled to finality. Richards & Associates v. U.S., Ct.Cl.1966, 177 Ct.Cl. 1037. United States ☞ 73(14)

157. —— Drawing or diagram interpretation, questions of law, finality of administrative decisions

Decision of Armed Services Board of Contract Appeals interpreting specification drawings of government is one of law open to independent review in Court of Claims. La Crosse Garment Mfg. Co. v. U.S., Ct.Cl.1970, 432 F.2d 1377, 193 Ct.Cl. 168. United States ☞ 73(15)

Whether government contract drawing reasonably indicated the bottom to be of rock, as contended by contractor in claim

against government, was a question of interpretation of contract documents and presented a question of law on which Court of Claims ruled without regard to a board conclusion. Vann v. U.S., Ct.Cl. 1970, 420 F.2d 968, 190 Ct.Cl. 546. United States ☞ 73(15)

Whether placement on drawings of symbol "A.P.S.", meaning "Construction Required for Assigned Peace Time Strength", by manholes in front of buildings and failure to cross-hatch laterals leading to building in accordance with legend indicating that work to be performed by contractor was cross-hatched led contractor to reasonably believe that such work was outside scope of his contract was a question of contract interpretation and, therefore, of law for decision by Court of Claims on appeal by contractor from adverse determination by administrative agency. United Contractors v. U.S., Ct.Cl.1966, 368 F.2d 585, 177 Ct.Cl. 151. United States ☞ 73(14)

Conclusion of Armed Services Board of Contract Appeals regarding reasonableness of fabricator's interpretation of government contract drawing involved a construction of the terms of the contract and was a decision on a question of law that was not final against fabricator or binding on Court of Claims. Kraus v. U.S., Ct.Cl.1966, 366 F.2d 975, 177 Ct.Cl. 108. United States ☞ 73(14)

158. —— Duress or coercion, questions of law, finality of administrative decisions

Decision of Armed Services Board of Contract Appeals that release executed by buyer of used airplanes and parts was not executed under circumstances of economic duress was a decision upon a question of law and was not entitled to finality. Aircraft Associates & Mfg. Co. v. U.S., Ct.Cl.1966, 357 F.2d 373, 174 Ct.Cl. 886. United States ☞ 73(14)

159. —— Equitable adjustment computation, questions of law, finality of administrative decisions

Dispute between contractor which had contracted to operate food service facilities at air force base and the United States as to proper amount of equitable adjustment due contractor under provision for equitable adjustment in contract price if less than 70% of estimated meals was actually served related to proper construction and application of contract clause; thus, dispute presented question of law and decision of board with respect thereto was not final. Pacific Architects & Engineers, Inc. v. U.S., Ct.Cl.1974, 491 F.2d 734, 203 Ct.Cl. 499. United States ⟶ 73(14)

In deciding that an equitable adjustment for serving of any number of meals less than 70% of estimated requirements by government contractor could not exceed the amount payable had 70% of estimated requirements been served, the contracting officer was actually interpreting the language and specifications of the contract, which interpretation involved a question of law and was therefore subject to independent resolution by the courts. U.S. v. Pickett's Food Service, C.A.5 (La.) 1966, 360 F.2d 338. United States ⟶ 73(14)

In determining whether a dispute involves a question of fact or law, it is necessary to determine whether the fact or the law ingredient is central and crucial to the decision, and where an administrative contract decision concerns the allowability of an equitable adjustment under the changed conditions article of the contract turning on the proper interpretation of certain contract provisions as indications of conditions to be encountered, a question of law is involved. Ray D. Bolander Co., Inc. v. U.S., Ct.Cl.1968, 186 Ct.Cl. 398. United States ⟶ 73(9)

160. —— Intended use of goods, questions of law, finality of administrative decisions

Since the question whether the making of prints from microfilm which government agreed to furnish to contractor manufacturing radio transmitters was an "intended use" for which the government furnished the microfilm was an issue of interpretation which might be decided on basis of undisputed facts in record before Armed Services Board of Contract Appeals, the Court of Claims could independently resolve such issue under this chapter. Thompson Ramo Wooldridge Inc. v. U.S., Ct.Cl.1966, 361 F.2d 222, 175 Ct.Cl. 527. United States ⟶ 73(14)

161. —— Negligence or fault, questions of law, finality of administrative decisions

District court in suit against warehouseman by United States seeking recovery for loss of household goods of military personnel may consider de novo the legal question of warehouseman's negligence or fault. U.S. v. Morrison, E.D.Va.1974, 370 F.Supp. 193. United States ⟶ 75(3)

Question of whether government contractor's failure to perform contract arose out of causes beyond its control and without its fault or negligence is in certain instances question of law. Meinberg v. U.S., W.D.Mo.1969, 310 F.Supp. 86. United States ⟶ 74(7)

A United States contracting officer's finding that contractor's failure to perform was not beyond contractor's control or without its fault or negligence, which finding was affirmed by Armed Services Board of Contract Appeals, was final and conclusive on the parties absent showing that the decision was arbitrary, capricious, fraudulent or not based on substantial evidence, and finding was not a matter of law beyond administrative competence. Whitlock Corp. v. U.S., Ct.Cl. 1958, 159 F.Supp. 602, 141 Ct.Cl. 758, certiorari denied 79 S.Ct. 23, 358 U.S. 815, 3 L.Ed.2d 58. United States ⟶ 73(14)

162. —— Pension funding, questions of law, finality of administrative decisions

Whether general reference to pension cost in government publication "Explanation of Principles for Determination of Costs under Government Contract, War Department—Navy Department", called the "Green Book" and used in large portion of military cost-plus-fixed-fee contracts during World War II, covered government contractor's funding of its past service liability for pensions was an issue of law for independent determination by court under this chapter. U.S. Steel Corp. v. U.S., Ct.Cl.1966, 367 F.2d 399, 177 Ct.Cl. 26. United States ⟶ 73(15)

163. —— Reformation of contract, questions of law, finality of administrative decisions

Question whether Government contract should be reformed was one for court, rather than General Services Administration Board of Review, and Board's finding that renegotiation provision had been inadvertently omitted from formal contract was not binding on court. Blake Const. Co. v. U.S., C.A.D.C.1961, 296 F.2d 393, 111 U.S.App.D.C. 271. United States ⟶ 73(14)

164. —— Reimbursement of costs, questions of law, finality of administrative decisions

On question of law concerned with meaning of pertinent provisions of contract and incorporated regulations permitting reimbursement for reasonable costs of settlement, prior administrative determinations are not binding. ACME Process Equipment Co. v. U.S., Ct.Cl. 1965, 347 F.2d 538, 171 Ct.Cl. 251, motion denied 351 F.2d 656, 171 Ct.Cl. 251. United States ☞ 73(14)

165. —— Schedule enforcement, questions of law, finality of administrative decisions

Contract appeals board's conclusion that government's agreement to set up priorities for respective contractors' work did not imply promise to do what government reasonably could to enforce schedule was not finding of fact as to parties' intent but legal conclusion as to scope of contractual agreement, and as such not binding on Court of Claims. Paccon, Inc. v. U.S., Ct.Cl.1968, 399 F.2d 162, 185 Ct.Cl. 24. United States ☞ 73(15)

166. —— Specifications, questions of law, finality of administrative decisions

In action governed by this chapter, board's decision as to whether contract required certain work was not binding on court since interpretation of contract specifications was question of law. Northwestern Indus. Piping, Inc. v. U.S., Ct.Cl.1972, 467 F.2d 1308, 199 Ct.Cl. 540. United States ☞ 73(15)

167. —— Standard of quality, questions of law, finality of administrative decisions

Whether the "or equal" or "standard of quality" clause contained in government contract was applicable regarding component furnished in performance of contract was a question of law so that the prior administrative decision on the question was not binding on the court. Sherwin v. U.S., Ct.Cl.1971, 436 F.2d 992, 193 Ct.Cl. 962. United States ☞ 73(15)

168. —— Testing of product, questions of law, finality of administrative decisions

A decision by an administrative appeals board that defendant's requirement that plaintiff-contractor test 16-foot rather than 8-foot sections of pipe did not ex- ceed the contract specifications because the specifications did not mention the length of pipe to be tested, is a decision on a question involving interpretation of the contract, i.e., a question of law, as to which the board's decision is not final. River Const. Corp. v. U.S., Ct.Cl.1962, 159 Ct.Cl. 254. United States ☞ 73(14)

169. —— Time of completion of contract, questions of law, finality of administrative decisions

Issue, under undisputed facts, as to when completion of government supply contract took place was question of contract interpretation and accordingly was question of law concerning which decision by Armed Services Board of Contract Appeals had no binding effect. Copco Steel & Engineering Co. v. U.S., Ct.Cl. 1965, 341 F.2d 590, 169 Ct.Cl. 601. United States ☞ 73(14)

170. —— Timeliness of appeal, questions of law, finality of administrative decisions

The issue of timeliness of an appeal from a decision of contracting officer terminating government contract is a question of law for court to decide. Richardson Camera Co., Inc. v. U.S., Ct.Cl.1972, 467 F.2d 491, 199 Ct.Cl. 657. United States ☞ 73(15)

Although Armed Services Board of Contract Appeals, despite Government's assertion of untimeliness of claim with respect to Government contract, rendered decision against contractor on merits of claim, question as to whether claim was timely and in conformity with contract provisions was one of law which might be decided by Court of Claims. PLS Coat & Suit Corp. v. U.S., Ct.Cl. 1960, 180 F.Supp. 400, 148 Ct.Cl. 296. United States ☞ 73(14)

171. —— Miscellaneous questions of law, finality of administrative decisions

The Court of Claims is not bound by the views of the comptroller general nor do they operate as a legal or judicial determination of the rights of the parties. Burroughs Corp. v. U.S., Ct.Cl.1980, 617 F.2d 590, 223 Ct.Cl. 53. United States ☞ 70(1)

No finality is attached by the Court of Claims to a conclusion of law that was reached by the General Services Administration Board of Contract Appeals. Blake

Const. Co., Inc. v. U.S., Ct.Cl.1979, 597 F.2d 1357, 220 Ct.Cl. 56. United States ⊕ 73(14)

Determination of the Armed Services Board of Contract Appeals on a question of law is entitled to no degree of finality. Dairy Sales Corp. v. U.S., Ct.Cl.1979, 593 F.2d 1002, 219 Ct.Cl. 431. See, also, Gorn Corp. v. U.S., 1970, 424 F.2d 588, 191 Ct.Cl. 560. United States ⊕ 73(14)

Court of Claims, as reviewing court, was free to draw its own legal conclusions from facts found below and affirmance of contract appeals board's result did not demand endorsement of all board had to say. Alfred A. Altimont, Inc. v. U.S., Ct.Cl.1978, 579 F.2d 622, 217 Ct.Cl. 628. Federal Courts ⊕ 1118

Department of Commerce Appeals Board decision is not final on issue of contract interpretation. H & M Moving, Inc. v. U.S., Ct.Cl.1974, 499 F.2d 660, 204 Ct.Cl. 696, 204 Ct.Cl. 938. United States ⊕ 73(12)

The Court of Claims is not constrained by the Maritime Administrator's determinations with respect to matters of law, and is free to reach its own conclusions. Sea-Land Service, Inc. v. U.S., Ct.Cl. 1974, 493 F.2d 1357, 204 Ct.Cl. 57, certiorari denied 95 S.Ct. 69, 419 U.S. 840, 42 L.Ed.2d 67. United States ⊕ 73(15)

No finality is attached to board of contract appeals decision of question of law under standards for judicial review prescribed by this chapter. John McShain, Inc. v. U.S., Ct.Cl.1972, 462 F.2d 489, 199 Ct.Cl. 364. United States ⊕ 73(15)

Board of contract appeals had authority to construe agreement, in course of adjudicating claim, but Court of Claims was not bound to accept its interpretation as final but could determine question of law de novo. LTV Aerospace Corp. v. U.S., Ct.Cl.1970, 425 F.2d 1237, 192 Ct. Cl. 191. United States ⊕ 73(12); United States ⊕ 73(15)

On a contention of law Court of Claims is not bound by decision of armed services board of contract appeals. Marley v. U.S., Ct.Cl.1970, 423 F.2d 324, 191 Ct.Cl. 205. See, also, Urban Plumbing & Heating Co. v. U.S., 1969, 408 F.2d 382, 187 Ct.Cl. 15, certiorari denied 90 S.Ct. 2164, 398 U.S. 958, 26 L.Ed.2d 542. United States ⊕ 73(15)

Conclusion of law of Atomic Energy Commission concerning claim of prime contractor carried with it no characteristics of finality on review in suit in Court of Claims. Owens-Corning Fiberglas Corp. v. U.S., Ct.Cl.1969, 419 F.2d 439, 190 Ct.Cl. 211. United States ⊕ 73(15)

Where rejection by Armed Services Board of Contract Appeals of contractor's claim against United States rested on question of legal duty rather than of disputed fact, no finality attached to rejection under this chapter. Aerodex, Inc. v. U.S., Ct.Cl.1969, 417 F.2d 1361, 189 Ct. Cl. 344. United States ⊕ 73(14)

Under this chapter, Court of Claims accords no finality to rulings of law by Veterans Administration Contract Board of Appeals and makes its own independent judgment thereon. Eggers & Higgins & Edwin A. Keeble Associates, Inc. v. U.S., Ct.Cl.1968, 403 F.2d 225, 185 Ct.Cl. 765. United States ⊕ 73(15)

Where factual determination in dispute involving government contract for application of insulation to air-conditioning ducts was dependent upon proper construction of contract specifications a question of law was ultimately involved and administrative determination thereof was not conclusive even though it could not be said that decision was fraudulent, capricious, arbitrary or so grossly erroneous as necessarily to imply bad faith. W.G. Cornell Co. of Washington D.C., Inc. v. U.S., Ct.Cl.1967, 376 F.2d 299, 179 Ct.Cl. 651. United States ⊕ 73(14)

The Armed Services Board of Contract Appeals is not delegated uncontrolled discretion, and its failure to apply guidelines prescribed by regulation is an error of law reviewable under this chapter. Newport News Shipbuilding & Dry Dock Co. v. U.S., Ct.Cl.1967, 374 F.2d 516, 179 Ct.Cl. 97. United States ⊕ 73(9); United States ⊕ 73(15)

Where ultimate issue of suit against United States under contract for air conditioning of post office was one of contract interpretation and thus a question of law, decision by the Government Service Administration Board of Contract Appeals was not conclusive and not beyond review by court. Gelco Builders & Burjay Const. Corp. v. U.S., Ct.Cl.1966, 369 F.2d 992, 177 Ct.Cl. 1025. United States ⊕ 73(15)

Where Armed Services Board of Contract Appeals concluded that, read as a whole, specifications were unambiguous in requiring painting of existing interior plaster surfaces, and that such interpretation gave meaning to all provisions of the specifications and avoided conflict, the contest of such conclusions by contractor raised questions of law to be decided by court without according finality to Board's decision thereof. Southern Const. Co. v. U.S., Ct.Cl.1966, 364 F.2d 439, 176 Ct.Cl. 1339. United States ⟜ 73(14)

Where dispute between contractor and United States was a legal one, turning on meaning and application of contract terms, neither the contractor nor the Court of Claims was bound by adverse administrative rulings within Public Housing Administration. Beacon Const. Co. of Mass. v. U.S., Ct.Cl.1963, 314 F.2d 501, 161 Ct.Cl. 1. United States ⟜ 73(14)

Where facts presented to Armed Services Board of Appeals were not in conflict, and based upon that record, Board reached conclusion that contract was properly terminated by Government for default on part of contractor and for anticipatory breach, and bankruptcy referee, on same record, reached the opposite conclusion and held that termination was for convenience of Government, and district court approved decision of referee, the problem of court of appeals was to determine whether conclusion of district court was contrary to law as applied to undisputed facts, and no limitation was placed upon court of appeals by either statute or federal rule in respect to passing upon questions of law. U.S. v. Chichester, C.A.9 (Cal.) 1963, 312 F.2d 275. Bankruptcy ⟜ 3787

Where paint contractor brought action against United States for alleged breach of contract after decision of Armed Services Board of Contract Appeals adverse to contractor, federal district court was right, at least initially, in considering interpretation of contract provisions question of law for independent decision of district court under this chapter. Allied Paint & Color Works, Inc. v. U.S., C.A.2 (N.Y.) 1962, 309 F.2d 133, certiorari denied 84 S.Ct. 41, 375 U.S. 813, 11 L.Ed.2d 48. United States ⟜ 73(14)

Legal error gives reviewing court cause to reverse decision of Armed Services Board of Contract Appeals. Meinberg v. U.S., W.D.Mo.1969, 310 F.Supp. 86. United States ⟜ 73(15)

Regardless of determinations made by armed services board of contract appeals to which contractor appealed from decision of contracting officer favorable to United States from which contractor sought recovery of contract price for work and materials allegedly expended and placed in and upon building located at air force base, district court was free to make its own determination of all questions of law. Crowder v. U.S., N.D.Cal. 1964, 255 F.Supp. 873, affirmed 362 F.2d 1011. United States ⟜ 73(14)

If Contract Disputes Board's decisions on the facts are not fraudulent or capricious or arbitrary or so grossly erroneous as necessarily to imply bad faith, and are supported by substantial evidence, decisions are final and conclusive but such finality does not attach to decisions of law made by the board. U.S. v. Hamden Co-op. Creamery Co., E.D.N.Y.1960, 185 F.Supp. 541, affirmed 297 F.2d 130. United States ⟜ 73(14)

The question of whether or not the contracting agency has rendered the contractor all the assistance required by the contract is a question of contract interpretation and therefore a question of law. Commercial Cable Co. v. U.S., Ct.Cl. 1965, 170 Ct.Cl. 813. United States ⟜ 73(14)

172. Mixed questions of law and fact, finality of administrative decisions

Whether or not the quality assurance representative made a statement in agreement with government contractor's interpretation of specifications as not requiring automatic detergent dispenser with dishwashing machines was a question of fact which properly could be the subject of a stipulation, but the correctness or legal effect of the quality assurance representative's interpretation was an issue of law not binding on court. Gresham & Co., Inc. v. U.S., Ct.Cl.1972, 470 F.2d 542, 200 Ct.Cl. 97. Stipulations ⟜ 3; Stipulations ⟜ 17(3)

Since interpretation of a contract is an issue of law, decision of an administrative board interpreting a contract specification is not entitled to finality and is not binding on Court of Claims, but even if ultimate interpretation is a question of law, underlying factual determinations of administrative board are entitled to finality if substantially supported. Tri-Cor, Inc. v. U.S., Ct.Cl.1972, 458 F.2d 112, 198 Ct.Cl. 187. See, also, D & L Const.

Co. and Associates v. U.S., 1968, 402 F.2d 990, 187 Ct.Cl. 736. United States ☞ 73(15)

Even when decisive issue is interpretation of contract itself, underlying factual determinations by contract appeals board are entitled to finality if supported by substantial evidence. Liles Const. Co. v. U.S., Ct.Cl.1972, 455 F.2d 527, 197 Ct.Cl. 164. United States ☞ 73(14)

Even where predominant issue of claim against United States is one of law, such as interpretation of contract provisions, findings of a contract appeals board as to facts directly related to legal issue are accorded finality as long as the claim is one upon which the board could grant relief under the contract. Clack v. U.S., Ct.Cl.1968, 395 F.2d 773, 184 Ct.Cl. 40. United States ☞ 73(14)

From standpoint of finality of administrative decision, if contract ambiguity is susceptible to interpretation within four corners of instrument, it is purely question of law, but if there be need to resort to extraneous evidence, for construction rather than interpretation, it is mixed question, the ultimate law question depending on preliminary determination of the fact question. Construction Management Corp. v. Brown & Root, Inc., N.Y.Sup.1964, 246 N.Y.S.2d 465, 41 Misc.2d 864, modified 270 N.Y.S.2d 95, 25 A.D.2d 843. Administrative Law And Procedure ☞ 784.1; Administrative Law And Procedure ☞ 796

173. Persons decisions final against, finality of administrative decisions

Administrative findings made within overriding requirements of this chapter on factual issues relevant to questions arising under contract are final and conclusive on parties for all purposes. Monroe Garment Co., Inc. v. U.S., Ct.Cl.1973, 488 F.2d 989, 203 Ct.Cl. 324. United States ☞ 73(14)

Decision of contracting officer and of Contract Board of Appeals requiring prime contractor to parge all of basement walls was not final or binding on masonry subcontractor in its suit under sections 270a–270d of Title 40 for balance claimed due on subcontract, wherein defendant prime contractor counterclaimed for cost of parging. U.S. for Use of White Masonry, Inc. v. F.D. Rich Co., C.A.9 (Alaska) 1970, 434 F.2d 855. United States ☞ 73(14)

174. Miscellaneous decisions final, finality of administrative decisions

Where Armed Services Board of Contract Appeals' decision that United States properly terminated contract to produce electronic testers for default was not based on any conclusion of law, the finding was entitled to finality. Bromion, Inc. v. U.S., Ct.Cl.1969, 411 F.2d 1020, 188 Ct.Cl. 31. United States ☞ 73(14)

Where, upon rejection by Armed Services Board of Contract Appeals of demand for all "past service" pension costs in connection with cost-plus-fixed-fee contracts, plaintiff contractor elected to test that claim in court, contractor would not be entitled to bring new suit to review any administrative determination thereafter made on the "current service" question arising under the same contracts. U.S. Steel Corp. v. U.S., Ct.Cl.1966, 367 F.2d 399, 177 Ct.Cl. 26. United States ☞ 74(7)

Where, under the provisions of the contract, plaintiffs agreed that if the work was delayed by nondelivery of allocated materials, they would accept extensions of time within which to complete the work without further liability on the part of the Government and plaintiffs accepted the extension of time granted by the Area Engineer for multiple causes of delay, reserving the right of appeal and no appeal was taken, the Area Engineer's determination was final. Dunnigan Const. Co. v. U.S., Ct.Cl.1952, 122 Ct.Cl. 262. United States ☞ 73(14)

175. Miscellaneous decisions not final, finality of administrative decisions

Administrative decision that contract required insulating of flexible connectors which connected air conditioning duct work on low pressure side of system with ceiling slot diffusers was not entitled to finality under this chapter. Leavell-Morrison-Knudsen-Hardeman v. U.S., Ct.Cl. 1971, 436 F.2d 451, 193 Ct.Cl. 949. United States ☞ 73(15)

Government contracting officer's written findings determining amount due government under changes clause were not final, conclusive and binding in absence of proof of delivery to contractor. Beaconwear Clothing Co. v. U.S., Ct.Cl. 1966, 355 F.2d 583, 174 Ct.Cl. 40. United States ☞ 73(14)

V. STANDARDS OF REVIEW GENERALLY

201. Standards of review generally

Authority of the Court of Claims to review a decision of a Board of Contract Appeals under this section is limited to a determination of whether the Board's findings are fraudulent, arbitrary or ca-

pricious or so erroneous as to imply bad faith, or are not supported by substantial evidence, and whether the Board's decision is erroneous as a matter of law. National Civil Service League v. U.S., Ct. Cl.1981, 643 F.2d 768, 226 Ct.Cl. 478. See, also, B.D. Click Co., Inc. v. U.S., Ct.Cl.1980, 614 F.2d 748, 222 Ct.Cl. 290. United States ☞ 73(15)

Where question presented is one of simple fact arising under changed conditions article, decision of board of contract appeals thereon, unless fraudulent, capricious, arbitrary, or so grossly erroneous as to imply bad faith, or not supported by "substantial evidence" (meaning such relevant evidence as reasonable mind might accept as adequate to support conclusion after considering record as whole) is entitled to finality but where ultimate determination turns on proper legal standard to be applied, question of law is presented which Court of Claims is free to answer independently of board's decision. Blount Bros. Corp. v. U.S., Ct.Cl.1970, 424 F.2d 1074, 191 Ct.Cl. 784. United States ☞ 73(14); United States ☞ 73(15)

Where Armed Services Board of Contract Appeals had jurisdiction of claims, conducted full trial, received evidence and briefs, made findings and conclusions and disposed of all claims involved, scope of review by Court of Claims was narrow and limited but court would determine what finality should be given to the findings, conclusions and decision. Sundstrand Turbo v. U.S., Ct.Cl.1968, 389 F.2d 406, 182 Ct.Cl. 31. United States ☞ 73(14)

Under this chapter the factual finding by Armed Services Board of Contract Appeals may be overturned only if found to be arbitrary, capricious, so grossly erroneous as to imply bad faith, or unsupported by substantial evidence. Thompson Ramo Wooldridge Inc. v. U.S., Ct.Cl. 1966, 361 F.2d 222, 175 Ct.Cl. 527. United States ☞ 73(15)

In negotiated procurement, contracting officer has broad discretion, and review is limited to determination of whether his acts were arbitrary, capricious, an abuse of discretion or otherwise not in accordance with law, or were in excess of his authority. Shuey Aircraft, Inc. v. U.S., Cl.Ct.1983, 3 Cl.Ct. 243. United States ☞ 64.60(3.1)

Under the provisions of this section, the scope of review of the Court of Claims is the same as that exercised by the federal courts of appeals under the standards defined by the Supreme Court in its decision in Universal Camera Corp. v. NLRB, 71 S.Ct. 456, 340 U.S. 474, 95 L.Ed. 456, the record as a whole must be considered in making the determination, including the evidence introduced by the party against whom the decision was rendered and the fact that the reviewing court might have decided, as an original matter, with the other party on balance, is not sufficient reason for not upholding the decision of the administrative body. Carlo Bianchi & Co. v. U.S., Ct.Cl.1964, 167 Ct.Cl. 364. See, also, Woodcrest Const. Co. v. U.S., 1969, 408 F.2d 406, 187 Ct.Cl. 249, certiorari denied 90 S.Ct. 2164, 398 U.S. 958, 26 L.Ed.2d 542.

202. Cases subject to standard of review, standards of review generally

Standard of review under this section applied where case came before court following determination by Department of Agriculture Board of Forest Appeals. Timber Access Industries Co., Inc. v. U.S., Ct.Cl.1977, 553 F.2d 1250, 213 Ct. Cl. 648.   United States ⚖ 73(15)

203. Issues reviewable, standards of review generally—Generally

It is vital to proper functioning of government contract system that a contractor not be forced to risk what he has gained before agency, regardless of lack of or minimal connection between favorable and adverse components of its determination, whenever he seeks review under this chapter of an unfavorable portion of an administrative decision. Roscoe-Ajax Const. Co., Inc. v. U.S., Ct.Cl.1974, 499 F.2d 639, 204 Ct.Cl. 726. United States ⚖ 73(15)

Review under this chapter is necessarily tied to particular contracts. Loral Electronics Corp. v. U.S., Ct.Cl.1969, 409 F.2d 578, 187 Ct.Cl. 499. United States ⚖ 73(15)

Contractor, which claimed that government's changes in fixed price contract were so numerous that contract took on aspects of design or development contract and were so frequent and of such nature that production was disrupted, had right to trial in Court of Claims on claim that government imposed cardinal change on it. Air-A-Plane Corp. v. U.S., Ct.Cl.1969, 408 F.2d 1030, 187 Ct.Cl. 269.   United States ⚖ 74(7)

Claim of government contractor for amounts allegedly due for breach of contract was properly in the Court of Claims where it could not be resolved administratively under the contract provisions for adjustment of disputes. L.L. Hall Const. Co. v. U.S., Ct.Cl.1966, 379 F.2d 559, 177 Ct.Cl. 870.   Federal Courts ⚖ 1076

This section slightly extended judicial review to cases other than fraud involving government contracts. Northern Metal Co. v. U.S., C.A.3 (Pa.) 1965, 350 F.2d 833.   United States ⚖ 74(4)

Final selection of contractor by Government contracting officer involves discretion and is not subject to review by judicial branch of Government. Friend v. Lee, C.A.D.C.1955, 221 F.2d 96, 95 U.S.App.D.C. 224.   United States ⚖ 64.60(1)

204. —— Questions or issues not raised below, issues reviewable, standards of review generally

Where only five Navy cost-plus contracts were specifically referred to in previous petition in Court of Claims which decided that plaintiff was entitled to reimbursement from government and only those five contracts were before Armed Services Board of Contract Appeals, petition would not support any judgment relating to a contract other than those five. Loral Electronics Corp. v. U.S., Ct.Cl. 1969, 409 F.2d 578, 187 Ct.Cl. 499.   Federal Courts ⚖ 1111

Issue not raised before Corps of Engineers Board of Contract Appeals could not be raised for first time before Court of Claims. Ace Const. Co. v. U.S., Ct.Cl. 1968, 401 F.2d 816, 185 Ct.Cl. 487. United States ⚖ 73(15)

This section and section 322 of this title are not contravened by trying damages issues in Court of Claims where agency has not reached or passed upon them. Stein Bros. Mfg. Co. v. U.S., Ct.Cl.1963, 337 F.2d 861, 162 Ct.Cl. 802.

District court in ruling that award of damages by Contract Disputes Board of Commodity Credit Corporation to Commodity Credit Corporation for sale by dried milk producer of insect-infested dried milk to Commodity Credit Corporation was supported as recovery of minimum damages for breach of warranty without regard to legal doctrine of rescission did not intrude on domain of Contract Disputes Board and render

judgment on ground not considered by
Contract Disputes Board or disclosed by
record made before it, where district
court properly found that Commodity
Credit Corporation was entitled to rescind contract. Land O'Lakes Creameries, Inc. v. Commodity Credit Corp.,
C.A.8 (Minn.) 1962, 308 F.2d 604. United States ⮫ 53(18)

Contractor's failure to raise issue before Armed Services Board of Contract
Appeals precludes considering that issue
in a review under this section. Degenaars Co. v. U.S., Cl.Ct.1983, 2 Cl.Ct. 482.
United States ⮫ 73(15)

**205. Arbitrary or capricious standard,
standards of review generally—
Generally**

In suit by government contractor
against United States, court performs
principally a reviewing function and only
if it is alleged and proved that administrative determination adverse to contractor was arbitrary, capricious, or not supported by substantial evidence may court
refuse to honor it. Crown Coat Front Co.
v. U.S., U.S.N.Y.1967, 87 S.Ct. 1177, 386
U.S. 503, 18 L.Ed.2d 256. United States
⮫ 73(15)

In reviewing determination of the Department of Interior Board of Contract
Appeals, the court of appeals must decide
whether, with respect to facts, the
Board's decision is fraudulent, or arbitrary, or capricious, or so grossly erroneous as necessarily to imply bad faith, or is
not supported by substantial evidence;
the legal conclusions of the Board are
freely reviewable by court of appeals.
Systems Technology Associates, Inc. v.
U.S., C.A.Fed.1983, 699 F.2d 1383. United States ⮫ 73(15)

Standard to be used in reviewing decisions made by government contracting
officers is whether the government's conduct was arbitrary and capricious toward
the bidder claimant. Old Dominion
Dairy Products, Inc. v. Secretary of Defense, C.A.D.C.1980, 631 F.2d 953, 203
U.S.App.D.C. 371. United States ⮫
64.60(4)

Court of Claims standard in reviewing
armed services board of contract appeals'
decision on whether or not to waive appealing contractor's six-day delay in mailing its appeal from contracting officer's
decision in connection with contractor's
claim for additional costs is not whether

court itself, upon consideration of pertinent facts, believes that waiver of six-day
delay would be justified, but rather
whether board abused its discretionary
power by exercising such power in arbitrary manner. J.R. Youngdale Const.
Co., Inc. v. U.S., Ct.Cl.1976, 536 F.2d
369, 210 Ct.Cl. 459. United States ⮫
73(15)

Where relief from decision of armed
services board of contract appeals is
sought, only issue before court, unless it
is alleged that decision was fraudulent, is
whether decision was arbitrary, capricious, so grossly erroneous as necessarily
to imply bad faith, or not supported by
substantial evidence. H.N. Bailey and
Associates v. U.S., Ct.Cl.1971, 449 F.2d
376, 196 Ct.Cl. 166. United States ⮫
73(15)

Determination of Armed Services
Board of Contract Appeals as to acceptability of rope delivered under Government contract was final under this
section unless fraudulent, capricious,
arbitrary or so grossly erroneous as to
imply bad faith, and court could not
reverse decision of Board merely because it might prefer another course.
U.S. v. Seaboard Sur. Co., C.A.2 (N.Y.)
1964, 339 F.2d 1. United States ⮫
73(14)

In suit brought against the Tennessee
Valley Authority by a former coal supplier, challenging Authority's final administrative decision which found plaintiff in
violation of contracts that contained reclamation provisions, the scope of district
court's review was governed by the "Disputes" clause in the contracts between
the parties; under this clause, the court
was required to confine its examination
to questions of law presented and to
whether the final decision of Authority's
hearing officer was capricious, arbitrary,
grossly erroneous or not supported by
substantial evidence. Crass v. Tennessee
Valley Authority, E.D.Tenn.1978, 460
F.Supp. 941, affirmed 627 F.2d 1089.
Mines And Minerals ⮫ 83

Review by district court of decision
of Armed Services Board of Contract
Appeals is on the record and decision
of Board is conclusive unless it is
fraudulent, arbitrary, grossly erroneous
to indicate bad faith of Board or is not
supported by substantial evidence.
Meinberg v. U.S., W.D.Mo.1969, 310
F.Supp. 86. United States ⮫ 73(15)

When reviewing actions by Armed Services Board of Contract Appeals under Wunderlich Act, Claims Court performs appellate function; Court may determine whether Board's legal determinations are erroneous and, with respect to Board's factual findings, may determine whether Board's actions are fraudulent, arbitrary, capricious, or unsupported by substantial evidence. Maitland Bros. Co. v. U.S., Cl.Ct.1990, 20 Cl.Ct. 53. United States ☞ 73(15)

Absent deficiency, such as finding that National Aeronautics and Space Administration Board of Contract Appeals' factual findings were arbitrary, capricious, grossly erroneous, or not supported by substantial evidence, Claims Court is bound by Board's factual findings, even though administrative record might support different or contrary findings. Flexible Metal Hose Mfg. Co. v. U.S., Cl.Ct. 1984, 4 Cl.Ct. 522, affirmed 765 F.2d 156. United States ☞ 73(15)

In order to show that an adverse administrative decision in a contract dispute was arbitrary and capricious, the plaintiff must do more than repeat the derogatory language of the statute; the plaintiff must allege and prove specific facts which will show that the decision was arbitrary and capricious. River Const. Corp. v. U.S., Ct.Cl.1962, 159 Ct. Cl. 254. United States ☞ 74(9)

206. —— Miscellaneous decisions arbitrary or capricious, standards of review generally

Corps of Engineers' decision to reject nonconforming waterstop installed in dam project without consideration of requisite performance standards for project and without providing rational basis for rejecting contractor's proposed repairs was arbitrary and capricious; government's only criterion in directing removal and replacement of waterstop was strict compliance with specifications, in contravention of contract which gave government discretion to accept nonconforming waterstop if deemed adequate and required government to consider public interest when deciding whether to replace nonconforming waterstop. Granite Const. Co. v. U.S., C.A.Fed.1992, 962 F.2d 998, rehearing denied, certiorari denied 113 S.Ct. 965, 506 U.S. 1048, 122 L.Ed.2d 121. United States ☞ 73(9)

To extent contracting officer denied general contractor's request for substitu-

tion of subcontractors, after determining that general contractor's predicament fell within purview of unusual situation, solely because subcontractor's quotations were made by telephone, such determination was arbitrary and capricious. Hoel-Steffen Const. Co. v. U.S., Ct.Cl.1982, 684 F.2d 843, 231 Ct.Cl. 128. United States ☞ 72(3)

Armed Services Board of Contract Appeals' failure to award any recovery for rework costs incurred by government contractor in replacing rotary switches which were incorporated into military aircraft radio receiving set because of defective design specification furnished by the government was arbitrary, capricious, and unsupported by substantial evidence where board was convinced that contractor had suffered damages due to government's fault, notwithstanding that contractor failed to establish exact damages with mathematical precision as there was sufficient evidence to enable Board to make a fair and reasonable proximation and, under evidence, contracting officer's award was a fair and reasonable proximation of damages. S.W. Electronics & Mfg. Corp. v. U.S., Ct.Cl.1981, 655 F.2d 1078, 228 Ct.Cl. 333. United States ☞ 74(12.1)

In government contractor's proceeding against United States to recover for increased costs incurred as consequence of explosions allegedly caused by defective government contract specifications for production of igniters used in fire bombs, finding of Armed Services Board of Contract Appeals that wet-blending process set forth in specifications resulted in more "aged" atomized magnesium and safer pelletizing operation than "dry blend" process used by contractor was arbitrary, capricious and unsupported by substantial evidence and record established that blending method employed was unrelated to safety. Ordnance Research, Inc. v. U.S., Ct.Cl.1979, 609 F.2d 462, 221 Ct.Cl. 641. United States ☞ 70(29)

Postal Service Board of Contract Appeals' finding that government's course of dealing with subcontractor as real party in interest did not induce subcontractor to believe that he would promptly receive copy of contracting officer's final decision on claim and thus enable him to make timely appeal was arbitrary and capricious, and thus, Board should have waived appeal period specified in contract. Monroe M. Tapper and Associates v. U.S., Ct.Cl.1975, 514 F.2d 1003, 206 Ct.Cl. 446. United States 73(15)

Decision of armed services board of contract appeals that contractor, contesting default termination and assessment of excess cost, had failed to meet deadline for furnishing airborne terrain clearance radar systems notwithstanding government's delay in furnishing essential drawings, which contractor was entitled to as a matter of right under agreement, was arbitrary, unsupported by substantial evidence, legally erroneous, and not entitled to finality. Whittaker Corp. v. U.S., Ct. Cl.1971, 443 F.2d 1373, 195 Ct.Cl. 161. United States 72.1(2); United States 73(14)

207. —— Miscellaneous decisions not arbitrary or capricious, standards of review generally

Interpretation which the Armed Services Board of Contract Appeals gave to contract calling for contractor to construct a storage paint and dope building at an air force base and which was to effect that specifications, which were to supply any omission or deficiency in drawings, called for installation of a complete sprinkler system so as to preclude contractor from obtaining an equitable adjustment for its installation of system was neither arbitrary, capricious, unsupported by substantial evidence, or so grossly erroneous as to imply bad faith. B.D. Click Co., Inc. v. U.S., Ct.Cl.1980, 614 F.2d 748, 222 Ct.Cl. 290. United States 70(29)

Decision of Armed Services Board of Contract Appeals which denied government contractor's claim for equitable adjustment in contract price pursuant to changes clause in contract because the claim was not properly asserted prior to final payment was neither arbitrary, capricious, unsupported by substantial evidence, nor legally erroneous. Jo-Bar Mfg. Corp. v. U.S., Ct.Cl.1976, 535 F.2d 62, 210 Ct.Cl. 149. United States 70(36)

Fact that Department of Agriculture Board of Contract Appeals failed to ascertain cause of explosion of boiler installed by contractor in government building did not render Board's decision that cause of explosion was of uncertain origin arbitrary or capricious. John C. Kohler Co.

v. U.S., Ct.Cl.1974, 498 F.2d 1360, 204 Ct.Cl. 777. United States 73(14)

Architect of the Capitol, who awarded bid to plaintiff's competitor, was not arbitrary and capricious in concluding that errors in competitor's bid, which involved an addendum, and a wrong job number on bid bond, constituted waivable minor informalities. Excavation Const., Inc. v. U.S., Ct.Cl.1974, 494 F.2d 1289, 204 Ct.Cl. 299. United States 64.30

Armed Services Board of Contract Appeals decision based on its acceptance of testimony of one apparently qualified expert witness over another as to reasonable fees to be paid for services rendered by government contractor's accountants was not arbitrary, capricious, and unsupported by substantial evidence, and contractor's recovery for post-termination accounting expenses should be limited to amount awarded by Board. ACME Process Equipment Co. v. U.S., Ct.Cl.1965, 347 F.2d 538, 171 Ct.Cl. 251, motion denied 351 F.2d 656, 171 Ct.Cl. 251. United States 73(14)

Forest Service did not act arbitrarily or capriciously when, relying on circumstantial evidence that logging company had placed counterfeit marks on trees standing in tract affected by timber sale contract, it found logging company in breach of such contract and terminated it. Roberts Logging Co., Inc. v. Yurich, E.D.Wis.1980, 482 F.Supp. 1231. Public Lands 9.1

Where proper administrative consideration was granted to contractor who had claims against United States arising under contract for conversion of Veterans Administration Building, substantial evidence supported administrative findings and conclusions, and its findings being neither arbitrary nor capricious, ruling of administrative body would be affirmed. Wells & Wells, Inc. v. U.S., E.D.Mo.1958, 164 F.Supp. 26, affirmed 269 F.2d 412. United States 73(15)

An administrative decision holding that where the contract specifications required that lighting fixtures must be "substantially mounted to ceiling supports," the installation by the contractor of the fixtures by use of toggle bolts attaching the fixtures to the metal lath of suspended ceilings was improper because the metal lath was a part of the ceiling itself and not a ceiling support, is not arbitrary or capricious, particularly where qualified experts in the electrical construction field testified that the lath was a part of the ceiling. J.D. Steele, Inc. v. U.S., Ct.Cl.1967, 180 Ct.Cl. 1213. United States ⊛ 73(12)

The allowance by the Board of Contract Appeals of 5 percent of plaintiff's unit cost of production for officers' salaries was not arbitrary or capricious. Kalis Clothing Mfg. Co. v. U.S., Ct.Cl.1957, 137 Ct.Cl. 718. United States ⊛ 70(19)

208. Bad faith, standards of review generally

That GSA relied solely upon representation of plaintiff's competitor that competitor's film was beyond plaintiff's primary source contract for film and did not test film independently did not establish bad faith of GSA, where it had always relied upon manufacturers' representations regarding specifications of film, because it had no testing equipment of its own, and, even if GSA's reliance upon information furnished by competitor was misguided or if the information was erroneous, that would not be sufficient to show bad faith for purpose of avoiding limitations of termination for convenience clause. Kalvar Corp., Inc. v. U.S., Ct.Cl.1976, 543 F.2d 1298, 211 Ct.Cl. 192, certiorari denied 98 S.Ct. 112, 434 U.S. 830, 54 L.Ed.2d 89. United States ⊛ 70(35)

Within provision of this section that decision of head of department or agency or his representative or board in dispute involving contract with United States shall be final and conclusive unless it is so grossly erroneous as necessarily to imply bad faith, the grossly erroneous standard should be equated with the constitutional due process standard. Jonal Corp. v. District of Columbia, C.A.D.C.1976, 533 F.2d 1192, 175 U.S.App.D.C. 57, certiorari denied 97 S.Ct. 80, 429 U.S. 825, 50 L.Ed.2d 88. United States ⊛ 73(14)

209. Bias, standards of review generally

Government contractor was entitled to relief from judgment upholding decision of Armed Services Board of Contract Appeals upon revelation of ex parte communications to Government counsel from, and initiated by, same administrative law judge who determined contractor's case regarding another case involving different claim by same contractor, based on copending status of two actions and ap-

pearance of potential bias and prejudice. Gulf & Western Industries, Inc. v. U.S., Ct.Cl.1981, 655 F.2d 1106, on remand 6 Cl.Ct. 742. United States ⊛ 73(15)

Where the record in a contract dispute appeal decided adversely to plaintiff by the Armed Services Board of Contract Appeals indicates a possibility of some harsh comment by the presiding board member to plaintiff at the administrative hearing on the appeal, that plaintiff made no protest and that there was no partiality or unfairness in rulings made by the presiding board member, and where the ultimate findings and conclusions are amply supported by the record, there is no evidence for the court to conclude that any unfairness or bias existed in connection with the proceedings. Remler Co. v. U.S., Ct.Cl.1967, 179 Ct.Cl. 459, certiorari denied 88 S.Ct. 66, 389 U.S. 840, 19 L.Ed.2d 102.

210. Convincing evidence standard, standards of review generally

Opinion of Board of Appeals for Department of Commerce was not rendered erroneous as a matter of law because the term "convincing evidence" was used in the discussion in the manner in which the Board evaluated the available evidence under this chapter, where the factual matters decided by the Board had already been made and Court of Claims found that substantial evidence supported the Board's decision. Wm. A. Smith Contracting Co. v. U.S., Ct.Cl.1969, 412 F.2d 1325, 188 Ct.Cl. 1062. United States ⊛ 73(9)

211. Correctness of decision, standards of review generally

Factual determination by government board of contract appeals can be overturned by court only if it is not supported by substantial evidence or otherwise fails to satisfy the standards set forth by this chapter; the court's inquiry does not go to the absolute correctness of the appeals board decision. Kaminer Const. Corp. v. U.S., Ct.Cl.1973, 488 F.2d 980, 203 Ct.Cl. 182. United States ⊛ 73(15)

212. Fraud, standards of review generally

Even where contractor has obtained a judgment and the time for review of it has expired, fraud on an administrative agency or on the court enforcing the agency action is ground for setting aside the judgment. S & E Contractors, Inc. v.

U.S., U.S.Ct.Cl.1972, 92 S.Ct. 1411, 406 U.S. 1, 31 L.Ed.2d 658. Federal Civil Procedure ⟷ 2654

Where factual determination of Armed Services Board of Contract Appeals to the effect that contractor should have expected perma-frost in certain excavating sites was not shown to be fraudulent, arbitrary, capricious or so grossly erroneous as to necessarily imply bad faith, and such factual determination was supported by substantial evidence, with respect to contractor's claim for an equitable adjustment the factual finding was final and conclusive under disputes provision of contract and this section. Morrison-Knudsen Co. v. U.S., Ct.Cl.1965, 345 F.2d 535, 170 Ct.Cl. 712. United States ⟷ 73(14)

Where it was not alleged that a contract officer acted fraudulently, capriciously, or in bad faith, in canceling a contract the Government had entered into with a contractor for procurement of certain goods, factual determination of the Armed Services Board of Contract Appeals that contractor's default was due to failure of contractor to purchase available goods because he was required to pay a higher price than he had anticipated, was binding on contractor, unless such determination was shown not to be supported by substantial evidence. Hoffmann v. U.S., C.A.10 (Kan.) 1960, 276 F.2d 199. United States ⟷ 73(14)

In action by Government as sole stockholder of Commodity Credit Corporation for damages for breach of implied warranty in connection with six contracts for purchase by corporation of powdered milk, findings of Contract Disputes Board that milk had been infested at time of delivery of powder to Government but infestation could not have been discovered by visual inspection thereof and that after delivery infestation developed to stage where it became readily apparent by visual inspection were not based upon fraud, bad faith or capricious or arbitrary conduct and were supported by substantial evidence. U.S. v. Hamden Co-op. Creamery Co., E.D.N.Y.1960, 185 F.Supp. 541, affirmed 297 F.2d 130. United States ⟷ 53(17)

Where action of Government contracting officer made it impossible for contractor to assert before Board of Contract Appeals its defenses to United States' claims, and United States itself brought action to recover under contract, contractor could be granted relief, notwithstanding findings of fact made by contracting officer, without alleging and proving fraud. U.S. v. Lennox Metal Mfg. Co., E.D.N.Y.1954, 131 F.Supp. 717, affirmed 225 F.2d 302. United States ⟷ 75(2)

Court of Claims was not at liberty to narrow, in order to alleviate its harshness, construction of contract provision relieving Government for all liability for delays caused by it in absence of fraudulent or malicious or arbitrary conduct of its agents causing the delays complained of. George J. Grant Const. Co. v. U.S., Ct.Cl.1953, 109 F.Supp. 245, 124 Ct.Cl. 202. United States ⟷ 73(20)

A decision by the Armed Services Board of Contract Appeals to allow a contractor a claim that may be partially tainted with possible fraud may not be regarded as imposing any obligation on the United States in view of the fact that it is judicially recognized that administrative accounting and auditing officers have a duty to refuse and to prevent payment of public moneys when they have a reasonable basis for suspecting fraud, and to reserve such matters for scrutiny of the courts. 1964, 44 Comp.Gen. 110.

213. Grossly erroneous standard, standards of review generally

Where the head of the contracting department acting through a board of contract appeals finds that the contractor was not required to perform any work not required by the contract specifications, and the record before the board and additional evidence before the Court of Claims reveals that the manner in which the contractor was required to perform the work was clearly more than the specifications reasonably required, the decision of the board is grossly erroneous and not supported by credible and probative evidence and therefore is not final and binding on the contractor. Fox Valley Engineering, Inc. v. U.S., Ct.Cl.1960, 151 Ct.Cl. 228. United States ⟷ 73(14)

214. Preponderance of evidence standard, standards of review generally

Under circumstances of action by general contractor seeking remission of liquidated damages, decision of contracting officer was not entitled to finality and a resolution of factual issues was to be made on basis of preponderance of evidence before court. Wertheimer Const.

Corp. v. U.S., Ct.Cl.1969, 406 F.2d 1071, 186 Ct.Cl. 836.   United States ⟢ 73(15)

215. Rational basis standard, standards of review generally

In reviewing contracting officer's decision denying substitution of subcontractors, court's role is not to determine proper administration and application of procurement regulations but must restrict its inquiry to determination of whether procurement agency's decision had reasonable basis.   Hoel-Steffen Const. Co. v. U.S., Ct.Cl.1982, 684 F.2d 843, 231 Ct.Cl. 128.   United States ⟢ 72(3)

Judicial review of purchasing decision of Army Corps of Engineers, including its interpretation of procurement regulations, was quite limited, and it was for court to determine whether procurement decision was rational one, in which event decision was to be upheld.   Allis-Chalmers Corp., Hydro-Turbine Division v. Friedkin, C.A.3 (Pa.) 1980, 635 F.2d 248.   United States ⟢ 64.60(3.1)

On review of decision of Department of Agriculture Board of Contract Appeals, test to be applied is whether, on the basis of the evidence before it, the action taken by the Board was a reasonable one.   John C. Kohler Co. v. U.S., Ct.Cl.1974, 498 F.2d 1360, 204 Ct.Cl. 777.   United States ⟢ 73(14)

In reviewing decision of Corps of Engineers Board of Contract Appeals, consideration must be given to all evidence and if there was such evidence as might convince reasonable men to reach conclusion made by the board, board must be sustained even though reviewing court might have decided otherwise.   Tecon Corp. v. U.S., Ct.Cl.1969, 411 F.2d 1271, 188 Ct. Cl. 436.   United States ⟢ 73(15)

Allegation that finding of General Services Administration Board of Contract Appeals that fixtures, for the removing and rehanging of which contractor sought compensation, were affixed to ducts and provided with essential wire connections was wholly unreasonable was insufficient to overturn Board's factual determination.   Ambrose-Augusterfer Corp. v. U.S., Ct.Cl.1968, 394 F.2d 536, 184 Ct.Cl. 18.   United States ⟢ 73(15)

Court should not overturn a federal procurement determination unless the aggrieved debtor demonstrates that there was no rational basis for the decision.

Fairplain Development Co. v. Freeman, N.D.Ill.1981, 512 F.Supp. 201.   United States ⟢ 55

Courts should not overrule any government contract procurement determination unless aggrieved bidder demonstrates that there was no rational basis for agency's decision and, even if such determination is made, there is room for sound judicial discretion, in presence of overriding public interest considerations, to refuse to entertain declaratory or injunctive actions in preprocurement context.   General Elec. Co. v. Kreps, D.C.D.C.1978, 456 F.Supp. 468.   United States ⟢ 64.60(4)

216. Substitution of judgment, standards of review generally

Where record of hearing before Department of Agriculture Board of Contract Appeals disclosed substantial evidence in support of two proffered theories explaining explosion of boiler installed by contractor in government building, Court of Claims could not substitute its view of the facts for that of the Board which found cause of explosion was of uncertain origin.   John C. Kohler Co. v. U.S., Ct.Cl. 1974, 498 F.2d 1360, 204 Ct.Cl. 777.   United States ⟢ 73(14)

If upon review of the entire record a reasonable man could have reached the conclusion arrived at by administrative tribunal, Court of Claims is precluded from substituting its judgment for that of agency involved on factual matters.   Dittmore-Freimuth Corp. v. U.S., Ct.Cl.1968, 390 F.2d 664, 182 Ct.Cl. 507.   United States ⟢ 73(15)

Court cannot substitute its own judgment for that of the Construction Contract Appeals Board of the Veterans Administration.   Wells & Wells, Inc. v. U.S., E.D.Mo.1958, 164 F.Supp. 26, affirmed 269 F.2d 412.   United States ⟢ 73(14)

217. Trial de novo—Generally, standards of review generally

When board of contract appeals has made findings relevant to dispute properly before it and which parties have agreed shall be final and conclusive, these findings cannot be disregarded and factual issues tried de novo in Court of Claims when contractor sues for relief which board was not empowered to give.   U.S. v. Utah Const. & Min. Co., U.S.Ct.Cl. 1966, 86 S.Ct. 1545, 384 U.S. 394, 16 L.Ed.2d 642.   United States ⟢ 73(14)

Where MA–4 jobs contract was partially terminated by government for government's convenience, contractor's remedy was exclusively administrative and it was not entitled to de novo trial to recover damages allegedly resulting from breach of such contract. Kisco Co., Inc. v. U.S., Ct.Cl.1979, 610 F.2d 742, 221 Ct.Cl. 806. United States ⚏ 74(5)

Contractor's delay-damage claim, i.e., that Government improperly invoked supply warranty clause or exercised options available thereunder after an unreasonable delay, was not cognizable in a trial de novo before court of claims, even though claim was not encompassed by any contract provision and was not redressable under contract, where factors underlying claim were resolved by findings of Armed Services Board of Contract Appeals, and determinations made under supply warranty clause were subject to disputes article. Monroe Garment Co., Inc. v. U.S., Ct.Cl.1973, 488 F.2d 989, 203 Ct.Cl. 324. United States ⚏ 73(15)

When complete administrative relief is available to a contractor under government contract, contractor is not entitled to a trial de novo on factual questions decided administratively. W.G. Cornell Co. of Washington D.C., Inc. v. U.S., Ct.Cl.1967, 376 F.2d 299, 179 Ct.Cl. 651. See, also, Newport News Shipbuilding & Dry Dock Co. v. U.S., 1967, 374 F.2d 516, 179 Ct.Cl. 97. United States ⚏ 73(15)

Contractors, whose claims against Government for additional compensation were denied by contracting officer, Board of Contract Appeals, and commanding general, were not entitled to trial de novo or to submit additional testimony in support of claims, and court must determine issues upon transcripts in evidence, and additional evidence, as to whether administrative findings were fraudulent, arbitrary, grossly erroneous or not supported by substantial evidence. Union Painting Co. v. U.S., D.C.Alaska 1961, 194 F.Supp. 803, supplemented 198 F.Supp. 282. United States ⚏ 73(14); United States ⚏ 74(7)

Courts do not have authority to try de novo claims against United States that have been determined by Construction Contract Appeals Board of Veterans Administration, but courts are vested with power to review administrative rulings and findings and conclusions of the administrative body and such rulings are

only to be altered by courts in those instances where there is no substantial evidence to support the ruling. Wells & Wells, Inc. v. U.S., E.D.Mo.1958, 164 F.Supp. 26, affirmed 269 F.2d 412. United States ⚏ 73(15)

218. ——— Waiver by contractor, trial de novo, standards of review generally

By contractor's lack of objection to government's motion to limit proceedings to administrative record and by contractor's uncontested acceptance of commissioner's pretrial order for assignment of errors limited to that record, contractor effectively waived any right it might have had to a de novo trial and was estopped to claim one. Banks Const. Co. v. U.S., Ct.Cl.1966, 364 F.2d 357, 176 Ct.Cl. 1302. Federal Courts ⚏ 1115

219. ——— Waiver by government, trial de novo, standards of review generally

Government, by failing to object to de novo proceedings in Court of Claims until after close of proof, waived right to assert inappropriateness of de novo proceeding. Bennett v. U.S., Ct.Cl.1967, 371 F.2d 859, 178 Ct.Cl. 61. United States ⚏ 73(15)

United States waived objection to use of de novo evidence on review of decision of Armed Services Board of Contract Appeals where it made no objection to introduction of such evidence at trial before Court of Claims commissioner. Kings Electronics Co. v. U.S., Ct.Cl.1965, 341 F.2d 632, 169 Ct.Cl. 433. Federal Courts ⚏ 1115

The limitations on a trial de novo are not entirely nonwaivable by virtue of this chapter, and a motion to suspend and require the plaintiff to seek an administrative determination of his claim must be made before a complete trial on the merits has been held in court and such a motion or objection by defendant stands on the same footing as an affirmative defense and should be made when the answer, the amended or supplemental answer, is filed and not after close of proof by both parties. WRB Corp. v. U.S., Ct.Cl.1966, 177 Ct.Cl. 909.

220. Record of administrative proceeding, standards of review generally—Generally

Under standard disputes clause in government contract, even when contractual

612

scheme for relief has run its course and government contractor is free to file his suit against United States in court, he is not entitled to demand de novo determination of his claim for equitable adjustment, evidence in support of his case must have been presented administratively and record there made will be record before the reviewing court. Crown Coat Front Co. v. U.S., U.S.N.Y.1967, 87 S.Ct. 1177, 386 U.S. 503, 18 L.Ed.2d 256. United States ⊛ 73(15)

That administrative record is defective or inadequate or reveals prejudicial error does not permit Court of Claims, in an action to review decision of a federal department under a disputes clause in a Government contract, to hold an evidentiary hearing in order for the court to proceed to judgment, as the court may either grant judgment on basis of existing record or stay its own proceedings pending some further action before the agency involved. U.S. v. Carlo Bianchi & Co., U.S.Ct.Cl.1963, 83 S.Ct. 1409, 373 U.S. 709, 10 L.Ed.2d 652. United States ⊛ 73(15)

Operating methods and procedures of the house board which was to review challenges to architect's decisions on government contract for construction of underground garages and related structures were so defective that its decision was not entitled to usual finality accorded board's decision under this section; however, remedy was not a trial de novo but, rather, a de novo decision based on record before the board, by a different trial judge. Baltimore Contractors, Inc. v. U.S., Ct.Cl.1981, 643 F.2d 729, 226 Ct.Cl. 394. United States ⊛ 73(15)

It was immaterial that the release signed by the contractor was not introduced into evidence before the Armed Services Board of Contract Appeals where it was before the court of appeals as a part of the record on the appeal. B.D. Click Co., Inc. v. U.S., Ct.Cl.1980, 614 F.2d 748, 222 Ct.Cl. 290. United States ⊛ 73(15)

Court of Claims' review of decision of Armed Services Board of Contract Appeals takes place on the record before the Board. Rice v. U.S., Ct.Cl.1970, 428 F.2d 1311, 192 Ct.Cl. 903. United States ⊛ 73(15)

Statement made by government contractor in course of pretrial proceedings in court of claims that proceedings herein should be by way of review of the administrative record pursuant to the standards prescribed by this chapter was consent that issues be decided on a written administrative record by standards of this chapter as applicable and not by trial de novo, and was not waiver of claim of breach of contract over which administrative board had had no jurisdiction. National Steel & Shipbuilding Co. v. U.S., Ct.Cl.1969, 419 F.2d 863, 190 Ct.Cl. 247. Federal Courts ⊛ 1115

Court when considering factual questions within scope of disputes clause of standard government construction contracts is restricted to review of administrative record under standards of this section which immunizes from judicial correction the ultimate administrative determination of such factual dispute unless the decision therein is fraudulent, capricious or arbitrary or so grossly erroneous as necessarily to imply bad faith, or is not supported by substantial evidence. W.G. Cornell Co. of Washington D.C., Inc. v. U.S., Ct.Cl.1967, 376 F.2d 299, 179 Ct.Cl. 651. United States ⊛ 73(15)

Review in Court of Claims on facts pertaining to government contractor's claim for breach of contract to remodel dormitories at Air Force Base was limited to review of administrative record in accordance with standards prescribed by Wunderlich Act. Jefferson Const. Co. v. U.S., Ct.Cl.1966, 368 F.2d 247, 177 Ct.Cl. 581. United States ⊛ 73(15)

Before a hearing record compiled by designee of the head of a contract agency can be properly reviewed by a court for testing against statutory standards, its metes and bounds must be identifiable and available to reviewing tribunal. Roberts v. U.S., Ct.Cl.1966, 357 F.2d 938, 174 Ct.Cl. 940. United States ⊛ 73(15)

Scope of review of trial in Court of Claims on facts pertaining to government contractor's claim for increased costs of furnishing subgrade in connection with highway project was limited to review of administrative record under standards prescribed by this section and section 322 of this title. Morrison-Knudsen Co. v. U.S., Ct.Cl.1965, 345 F.2d 833, 170 Ct.Cl. 757. Federal Courts ⊛ 1118

Record of proceeding in Court of Claims to review Board of Contract Appeals' denial of contractor's claim for increased compensation established that trial commissioner had made correct conclusion on basis of administrative record alone and had not considered evidentiary record as though produced at actual trial de novo before him. Hoffman v. U.S., Ct.Cl.1964, 340 F.2d 645, 166 Ct.Cl. 39. Federal Courts ☞ 1117

Federal district court properly limited its review to record made before Armed Services Board of Contract Appeals when paint contractor brought action against United States for alleged breach of contract, where parties had proceeded through full hearing before Board. Allied Paint & Color Works, Inc. v. U.S., C.A.2 (N.Y.) 1962, 309 F.2d 133, certiorari denied 84 S.Ct. 41, 375 U.S. 813, 11 L.Ed.2d 48. United States ☞ 73(15)

In determining legal question of fault or negligence and liability of warehouseman under contract covering storage of household goods of military personnel, court would normally be limited to administrative record. U.S. v. Morrison, E.D.Va.1974, 370 F.Supp. 193. United States ☞ 73(15)

Where determination by chief of office of ship construction that contractor was in default was upheld by maritime administrator, without notice to government contractor, on same date chief's determination was made and administrator attempted to rectify his premature action by holding hearings on subsequent date with notice to contractor, the purported review did not comport with procedural requirements of contract providing that contractor be given chance to be heard and to produce evidence, so that this chapter restricting subsequent judicial review to administrative hearing record was inapplicable. U.S. v. Marietta Mfg. Co., S.D.W.Va.1967, 268 F.Supp. 176. United States ☞ 73(15)

In Government contractor's action in federal district court for review of denial of compensation following Government's termination of painting contract, contractor was not entitled to a trial de novo and United States properly was permitted to rely instead upon the administrative record of proceedings before Navy Contract Appeals Panel of the Armed Services Board of Contract Appeals, before which contractor had received a quasi-judicial due process hearing. General Ship Contracting Corp. v. U.S., D.C.N.J.1962, 205 F.Supp. 658. United States ☞ 73(14)

Court was confined to record made before Armed Services Board of Contract Appeals, and would decide questions of law based upon evidence adduced before the Board, in an action arising out of a purchase of surplus Government property, and court would not try the case de novo, where the findings of the Board were supported by substantial evidence. M. Berger Co. v. U.S., W.D.Pa.1961, 199 F.Supp. 22. United States ☞ 73(15)

In action under Tucker Act, section 1346(a)(2) of Title 28, in nature of appeal from Corps of Engineer's Claims and Appeals Board decision refusing plaintiff's claim, for additional excavation work and return of liquidated damages, under contract for channel clearing and other work on river, wherein plaintiff did not claim that Board had been guilty of fraud or caprice but merely asserted that its decision was erroneous and not supported by substantial evidence, determination as to whether Board's decision was supported by substantial evidence would have to be made by viewing administrative appeal record, reading it as a whole, and not by taking further testimony or having a trial de novo. U.S. Nat. Bank of Portland v. U.S., D.C.Or.1959, 178 F.Supp. 910. United States ☞ 74(7)

In view of this section and section 322 of this title regulating actions against United States on disputes growing out of Government contracts, Government contractor, in suit which it brought against United States, on contract, after its claims had been administratively denied, was not entitled to trial de novo but hearing was to be confined to review of administrative record. Mann Chemical Laboratories, Inc. v. U.S., D.C.Mass. 1958, 174 F.Supp. 563. United States ☞ 74(7)

This chapter does not require the reviewing court to consider evidence in the administrative record which the administrative tribunal had a right to and did disregard in arriving at its decision concerning a dispute appealed to it by the contractor. Tankersley v. U.S., Ct.Cl. 1967, 179 Ct.Cl. 294. United States ☞ 73(15)

Where a plaintiff alleges that the contracting officer and the Contract Appeals Board for the contracting agency acted arbitrarily and capriciously in denying plaintiff's claim under its contract, the plaintiff is entitled to a full hearing on its case in the Court of Claims and is not limited to the administrative record made

at the contracting agency level. Lester
Bros., Inc. v. U.S., Ct.Cl.1960, 151 Ct.Cl.
536. United States ☞ 74(7)

221. —— Independent search of record, record of administrative proceeding, standards of review generally

It is not incumbent upon the Court of
Claims to make an independent search of
the entire record to determine whether
the factual findings of the Armed Services
Board of Contract Appeals meet the statutory finality standards; the parties have
the responsibility of calling the attention
of the Court of Claims specifically to the
portions of the administrative record that
are relevant to the challenged factual
findings. Schnip Bldg. Co. v. U.S., Ct.Cl.
1981, 645 F.2d 950, 227 Ct.Cl. 148.
United States ☞ 73(15)

It is not function of Court of Claims to
undertake independent and/or de novo
review of record to supply deficiency in
plaintiff's petition lacking substantive
particularity necessary to overcome finality that otherwise attaches to findings
made by board whose decision is subject
to review under this chapter. Wickham
Contracting Co., Inc. v. U.S., Ct.Cl.1976,
546 F.2d 395, 212 Ct.Cl. 318. United
States ☞ 73(15)

It is not function of Court of Claims to
conduct an independent excursion to find
factual or legal error in decision of Board
of Contract Appeals. Jet Const. Co., Inc.
v. U.S., Ct.Cl.1976, 531 F.2d 538, 209
Ct.Cl. 200. United States ☞ 73(15)

On appeal from Army Board of Contract Appeals decision, it is for complaining parties and their attorneys, and not
for court, to search the record for errors,
and if they do not do so, court is justified
in assuming that no errors have been
made. Algonac Mfg. Co. v. U.S., Ct.Cl.
1970, 428 F.2d 1241, 192 Ct.Cl. 649, supplemented 458 F.2d 1373, 198 Ct.Cl. 258.
Administrative Law And Procedure ☞
749

Where claimant who seeks recovery
against government has been directed by
Court of Claims to file an assignment of
errors specifying factual errors which administrative board made and citing those
portions of administrative record on
which it relies to demonstrate that board
decision was erroneous but fails to do so
and merely alleges generally a right to
recover, court is not required to search

record for itself. United Contractors v.
U.S., Ct.Cl.1966, 368 F.2d 585, 177 Ct.Cl.
151. United States ☞ 73(15)

When plaintiff who seeks Wunderlich
Act review fails to meet its burden of
specifying facts and circumstances contained in record of Armed Services Board
of Contract Appeals, which make the
Board's decision lacking in substantial
evidence, it is not function of Claims
Court to supply deficiency by an independent excursion along the administrative
trail. Roflan Co. v. U.S., Cl.Ct.1985, 7
Cl.Ct. 242. United States ☞ 73(15)

222. New evidence, reception of, standards of review generally

Apart from questions of fraud, determination of the finality to be attached to a
departmental decision on a question arising under a disputes clause in a contract
with the Government must rest solely on
consideration of the record before the
department, and new evidence may not
be received thereon. U.S. v. Carlo Bianchi & Co., U.S.Ct.Cl.1963, 83 S.Ct. 1409,
373 U.S. 709, 10 L.Ed.2d 652. United
States ☞ 73(14); United States ☞ 73(15)

In proceeding for review of an agency
appeals board decision, which review can
be made only on the basis of board record, court cannot receive or consider new
evidence on an issue that was never presented to or considered by the board.
McKee v. U.S., Ct.Cl.1974, 500 F.2d 525,
205 Ct.Cl. 303. United States ☞ 73(15)

In reviewing a decision of the Armed
Services Board of Contract Appeals,
court of claims may only consider evidence presented to agency and contained
in administrative record. Monroe Garment Co., Inc. v. U.S., Ct.Cl.1973, 488
F.2d 989, 203 Ct.Cl. 324. United States
☞ 73(15)

On review under this chapter, court
may not consider evidence other than
that presented to agency and contained in
administrative record. Northbridge Electronics, Inc. v. U.S., Ct.Cl.1971, 444 F.2d
1124, 195 Ct.Cl. 453. United States ☞
73(15)

In reviewing trial commissioner's opinion passing upon factual determination of
Board of Contract Appeals or similar contractual agency, Court of Claims will not,
except in exceptional circumstances, consider points and record references which
should have been presented to trial commissioner but were not. Jefferson Const.

Co. v. U.S., Ct.Cl.1966, 368 F.2d 247, 177 Ct.Cl. 581. Federal Courts ⚬⟹ 1117

Government contractor's request to present de novo evidence would be denied since decision of Board of Contract Appeals on related facts must necessarily be accorded finality and could not be judicially supplemented by a new trial. Jefferson Const. Co. of Fla. v. U.S., Ct.Cl. 1966, 364 F.2d 420, 176 Ct.Cl. 1363, certiorari denied 87 S.Ct. 865, 386 U.S. 914, 17 L.Ed.2d 786. United States ⚬⟹ 73(15)

Under circumstances including showing that Secretary of Smithsonian Institution had merely asked for advice of Board of Review of a claim of contractor for construction of concrete roadway for National Air Museum Storage Area, leaving himself free to make the final decision, and that contracting officer's decision which was affirmed by the head of the department did not show what the secretary considered in making his determination, the trial commissioner properly admitted de novo evidence in trial of the action on contractor's claim. Roberts v. U.S., Ct.Cl.1966, 357 F.2d 938, 174 Ct.Cl. 940. United States ⚬⟹ 74(10)

Ultimate issue, relating to meaning of contract specifications, being one of law, it might have been that Court of Claims was not precluded from considering any evidence bearing on legal issues, no matter what Board of Contract Appeals had determined or what was in record before it; but, in any event, new evidence could be considered where Government made no objection to admission or consideration thereof at trial in Court of Claims until after argument. Stein Bros. Mfg. Co. v. U.S., Ct.Cl.1963, 337 F.2d 861, 162 Ct.Cl. 802. Federal Courts ⚬⟹ 1115

In its consideration of matters within scope of standard disputes clause in Government contract, district court is confined to review of administrative record under standards in this chapter, and it may not receive new evidence on such issues. Silverman Bros., Inc. v. U.S., C.A.1 (R.I.) 1963, 324 F.2d 287. United States ⚬⟹ 73(15)

Government which made no objection to receipt of evidence additional to that presented by both sides in hearing before Board of Contract Appeals concerning Government contract and which did not seek to raise objection until oral argument waived objection and Court of Claims was free to take account of such evidence. WPC Enterprises, Inc. v. U.S., Ct.Cl.1963, 323 F.2d 874, 163 Ct.Cl. 1. Federal Courts ⚬⟹ 1115

Government contractor's newly discovered evidence that other powdered milk in Government warehouses had been found to be infested was insufficient to shake Contract Disputes Board's determination that milk sold by contractor had been infested at time of delivery to Government. U.S. v. Hamden Co-op. Creamery Co., C.A.2 (N.Y.) 1961, 297 F.2d 130. United States ⚬⟹ 73(15)

In reviewing administrative decision in Government contract case, court was required to make independent determination of meaning of contract based on evidence adduced before administrative tribunal, and it would make determination of legal question of whether paint furnished by contractor and accepted by Government inspector became Government-furnished property under one contract on record made before Board of Contract Appeals and would preclude further taking of testimony. Allied Paint & Color Works, Inc. v. U.S., S.D.N.Y. 1960, 199 F.Supp. 285. United States ⚬⟹ 73(15)

Additional evidence presented in court in support of contention that findings of Government contracting officer and Board of Contract Appeals were not supported by substantial evidence must be limited to proof that findings were not based on evidence presented. Union Painting Co. v. U.S., D.C.Alaska 1961, 194 F.Supp. 803, supplemented 198 F.Supp. 282. United States ⚬⟹ 74(10)

In action by Government for breach of implied warranty in connection with contracts for sale of powdered milk, court had no authority to consider seller's belated evidence which it could have discovered before or at hearing before Contract Disputes Board and which tended to show that powder from two other manufacturers stored in Government warehouse was suspect contrary to finding of Board that no other shipments of powder in Government warehouses were infested. U.S. v. Hamden Co-op. Creamery Co., E.D.N.Y.1960, 185 F.Supp. 541, affirmed 297 F.2d 130. United States ⚬⟹ 73(14)

There may be some instances, under this section limiting effect of contract provisions as to finality of administrative decisions, where court may be required to take additional testimony, as, for example, where it is alleged that administrative appeals board acted fraudulently, and in that case party charging fraud should not be limited to record before board but should be permitted to introduce evidence to prove such fraud. U.S. Nat. Bank of Portland v. U.S., D.C.Or. 1959, 178 F.Supp. 910. United States ⚭ 73(14)

In review cases under this chapter the parties, as a general rule, cannot supplement the record with additional fact-oriented materials not placed before the administrative board initially, and this is so in cases where the dispositive issue is deemed to be one of law. Truong Xuan Truc v. U.S., Ct.Cl.1976, 212 Ct.Cl. 51. United States ⚭ 73(15)

The introduction and admission in evidence of parts of the administrative record compiled in a contract dispute appealed to the head of the contracting agency and decided adversely to the plaintiff who then seeks relief in the Court of Claims, is not a trial de novo in the Court of Claims and is not the receipt of evidence de novo and this is so even where the defendant refuses to introduce all or any part of the administrative record and permits the commissioner to decide the issue of liability solely on the basis of the parts of the administrative record offered in evidence by the plaintiff and the parties have an obligation to help the commissioner in his consideration of the administrative record and they cannot dictate his procedure so long as their rights are not prejudiced by his method of trying the case. H.R. Henderson & Co., Inc. v. U.S., Ct.Cl.1965, 169 Ct.Cl. 228. Federal Courts ⚭ 1115; Federal Courts ⚭ 1117

223. Credibility of witnesses, standards of review generally

Credibility of witnesses and probative value of their testimony are matters for determination of the Corps of Engineers Board of Contract Appeals as trier of the facts and the Board's determination is not to be overruled unless it is found that testimony by the witnesses is discredited by undisputed evidence or by fact. Seger v. U.S., Ct.Cl.1972, 469 F.2d 292, 199 Ct.Cl. 766. United States ⚭ 73(15)

Acceptance by board of contract appeals of testimony of government's expert could not be disturbed by court. D & L Const. Co. and Associates v. U.S., Ct.Cl.

1968, 402 F.2d 990, 185 Ct.Cl. 736. United States ⚭ 73(15)

Court of Claims normally defers to judgment of Armed Services Board of Contract Appeals and credibility of witnesses who have testified before Board, at least in absence of contradictory uncontrovertible documentary evidence or physical fact, or studied arbitrary design. Sternberger v. U.S., Ct.Cl.1968, 401 F.2d 1012, 185 Ct.Cl. 528. United States ⚭ 73(15)

Claims Court must accept evaluation by Armed Services Board of Contract Appeals of conflicting conclusions of expert witnesses, unless testimony is inherently improbable or discredited by uncontrovertible evidence. Maitland Bros. Co. v. U.S., Cl.Ct.1990, 20 Cl.Ct. 53. United States ⚭ 73(15)

Credibility of witnesses is a function of Postal Service Board of Contract Appeals, and that function is not to be disregarded by Claims Court merely because the testimony was heard by only one member of the three-member Board panel whose decision is under review. Iconco v. U.S., Cl.Ct.1984, 6 Cl.Ct. 149, affirmed 770 F.2d 179. United States ⚭ 73(15)

224. Weight and sufficiency of evidence, standards of review generally

That author of decision of Armed Services Board of Contract Appeals had been assigned to Board following closing of administrative record and thus had not participated in hearing before the Board did not give Court of Claims greater liberty to make its own assessment of weight and inferences to be drawn from the evidence than it would have had in other circumstances and did not alter the applicable standards of review. Ordnance Research, Inc. v. U.S., Ct.Cl.1979, 609 F.2d 462, 221 Ct.Cl. 641. United States ⚭ 73(15)

Where Armed Services Board of Contract Appeals elected to accept one party's evidence as more persuasive than the others', its determination of such factual issue cannot be upset by court which cannot weigh evidence independently to determine where preponderance lies. Switlik Parachute Co., Inc. v. U.S., Ct.Cl. 1978, 573 F.2d 1228, 216 Ct.Cl. 362. United States ⚭ 73(15)

Where hearing before Veterans Administration Construction Contract Appeals Board involved primarily ex parte presentations of evidence which included conclusory written statements and remote hearsay, Board findings were not entitled to weight which they would have been given in true adversary process. J.D. Hedin Const. Co. v. U.S., Ct.Cl.1969, 408 F.2d 424, 187 Ct.Cl. 45. Administrative Law And Procedure ☞ 484.1; United States ☞ 73(14)

Weight to be given to affidavits of persons who did not appear before Veterans Administration Contract Appeals Board was within peculiar province of that body, especially in absence of any showing of arbitrariness or caprice in choice of Board to accept affidavits of defendant government's representatives rather than that of government contractor's affiant. Eggers & Higgins & Edwin A. Keeble Associates, Inc. v. U.S., Ct.Cl.1968, 403 F.2d 225, 185 Ct.Cl. 765. United States ☞ 73(15)

Where explanation by the Armed Services Board of Contract Appeals of its reasoning was so summary and sketchy that on review of the board's decision the Court of Claims could not tell the basis of the decision, the court was not required to accord such great weight to the board's determination as it would if the board had given detailed findings to support its conclusion. Loral Electronics Corp. v. U.S., Ct.Cl.1967, 387 F.2d 975, 181 Ct.Cl. 822. United States ☞ 73(15)

Court of Claims in contractor's suit on government contract, wherein evidence adduced at trial de novo was same as evidence presented to Board of Contract Appeals, would not search every subsidiary finding to ascertain whether it was supported or could be supported solely on evidence presented to the Board. Amino Bros. Co. v. U.S., Ct.Cl.1967, 372 F.2d 485, 178 Ct.Cl. 515, certiorari denied 88 S.Ct. 98, 389 U.S. 846, 19 L.Ed.2d 112. Federal Courts ☞ 1115

225. Findings of fact, standards of review generally

Claims Court trial judge, in reviewing decision of the Armed Services Board of Contract Appeals relating to contract for design and manufacture of radio transceivers, did not improperly make de novo fact findings. Teledyne Lewisburg v. U.S., C.A.Fed.1983, 699 F.2d 1336. Federal Courts ☞ 1115

Where board fails to make a finding of fact on evidence that is undisputed, the

Court of Claims can make the finding even if the evidence is disputed but is of such a nature that as a matter of law the board could only make one finding of fact or decide the fact in only one way. B.D. Click Co., Inc. v. U.S., Ct.Cl.1980, 614 F.2d 748, 222 Ct.Cl. 290. United States ☞ 73(15)

If Armed Services Board of Contract Appeals has failed to make a relevant finding of fact, and evidence relating to fact question is undisputed, court on appeal may make a supplemental finding without returning case to Board, but where evidence is disputed and its overwhelming weight strongly points to one conclusion of fact, court may make a necessary contrary finding without returning case to Board. Ordnance Research, Inc. v. U.S., Ct.Cl.1979, 609 F.2d 462, 221 Ct.Cl. 641. United States ☞ 73(15)

Without specifically supported demonstration of factual error on part of Armed Services Board of Contract Appeals, Board's statement of facts would be accepted on petition for review to Court of Claims. ITT Arctic Services, Inc. v. U.S., Ct.Cl.1975, 524 F.2d 680, 207 Ct.Cl. 743. United States ☞ 73(15)

Supplementation of facts as recited by board of contract appeals for purpose of explanation, clarity of presentation, or proper perspective, is permissible in review proceeding under this section as long as supplementary facts are undisputed or uncontroverted. Arundel Corp. v. U.S., Ct.Cl.1975, 515 F.2d 1116, 207 Ct. Cl. 84. United States ☞ 73(15)

Where contract appeal board fails to make findings of fact fully supported and required by record, court may make such findings in order to avoid remanding. Liles Const. Co. v. U.S., Ct.Cl.1972, 455 F.2d 527, 197 Ct.Cl. 164. See, also, Sherwin v. U.S., 1971, 436 F.2d 992, 193 Ct.Cl. 962; Max Drill, Inc. v. U.S., 1970, 427 F.2d 1233, 192 Ct.Cl. 608; Dittmore–Freimuth Corp. v. U.S., 1968, 390 F.2d 664, 182 Ct.Cl. 507; S. S. Mullen, Inc. v. U.S., 1968, 389 F.2d 390, 182 Ct.Cl. 1. Federal Courts ☞ 1118

Finding of Armed Services Board of Contract Appeals, namely that contracting officer offered 69 days' time extension to contractor because of delay in approvals and that it was not as much as was due for excusable cause, would be regarded as a finding by Board that government did delay contractor 69 days, but even if Board did not so find, evidence on matter was such that as a matter of law the Board could have made only one finding of fact with respect to it, so that Court of Claims, on appeal from Board's finding, was authorized to make finding on question. Urban Plumbing & Heating Co. v. U.S., Ct.Cl.1969, 408 F.2d 382, 187 Ct.Cl. 15, certiorari denied 90 S.Ct. 2164, 398 U.S. 958, 26 L.Ed.2d 542. United States ⟶ 73(15)

If Armed Services Board of Contract Appeals has failed to make a relevant finding of fact, and evidence relating to fact question is undisputed, court on appeal may make a supplementary finding without returning case to Board, but where evidence is disputed and its overwhelming weight strongly points to one conclusion of fact, court may make a necessary contrary finding without returning case to Board. Koppers Co. v. U.S., Ct.Cl.1968, 405 F.2d 554, 186 Ct.Cl. 142. United States ⟶ 73(15)

Where evidence is disputed in dispute involving contract between contractor and United States, but evidence is of such nature that, as matter of law, administrative board could have made only one finding of fact, Court of Claims can make that finding without sending the matter back to the board for determination of factual issues. S.S. Mullen, Inc. v. U.S., Ct.Cl.1968, 389 F.2d 390, 182 Ct.Cl. 1. Federal Courts ⟶ 1118

Where United States contracting officer, upon default of contract to supply quartermaster depot with brass buckles, did not make findings on facts relating to a repurchase contract, and Armed Services Board of Contract Appeals found that the award of the repurchase contract to the second lowest bidder was proper, to the extent Board went beyond facts found by contracting officer, Court of Claims was not bound to accept Board's verdict as final. Whitlock Corp. v. U.S., Ct.Cl.1958, 159 F.Supp. 602, 141 Ct.Cl. 758, certiorari denied 79 S.Ct. 23, 358 U.S. 815, 3 L.Ed.2d 58. United States ⟶ 73(14)

Where the administrative decision on a contract dispute fails to include subsidiary findings fully supported by the board record and required by that record, the court may make such findings in articulating its decision. Ray D. Bolander Co.,

Inc. v. U.S., Ct.Cl.1968, 186 Ct.Cl. 398. United States ⟶ 73(15)

VI. SUBSTANTIAL EVIDENCE FOR DECISION

Subdivision Index

251. Substantial evidence for decision generally

It is duty of Court of Claims to determine whether findings of fact and conclusions of law of the Corps of Engineers Board of Contract Appeals are supported by substantial evidence and are correct as a matter of law. Dravo Corp. v. U.S., Ct.Cl.1979, 594 F.2d 842, 219 Ct.Cl. 416. United States ⟶ 73(15)

Factual determinations of Armed Services Board of Contract Appeals are conclusive when supported by substantial evidence. Pelliccia v. U.S., Ct.Cl.1975, 525 F.2d 1035, 208 Ct.Cl. 278. See, also, Phillips Const. Co. v. U.S., 1968, 394 F.2d 834, 184 Ct.Cl. 249. United States ⟐ 73(14)

Findings by Armed Services Board of Contract Appeals on question of manufacturer's rights against Government for cancellation of contracts were binding in Court of Claims action for breach of contract unless Government could show that the findings were not supported by substantial evidence. National Factors, Inc. v. U.S., Ct.Cl.1974, 492 F.2d 1383, 204 Ct.Cl. 98. United States ⟐ 73(15)

Decision of board of contract appeals was binding on the court and the parties under disputes clause of contract and this section, where it was in no way arbitrary or capricious, was supported by substantial evidence, and was not erroneous as a matter of law. Broome Const., Inc. v. U.S., Ct.Cl.1974, 492 F.2d 829, 203 Ct.Cl. 521. United States ⟐ 73(15)

Whether or not factual findings and conclusions of Armed Services Board of Contract Appeals are supported by substantial evidence goes to reasonableness of what Board did on basis of evidence before it. Hardeman-Monier-Hutcherson v. U.S., Ct.Cl.1972, 458 F.2d 1364, 198 Ct.Cl. 472. United States ⟐ 73(15)

Under this chapter, the findings of fact of the Army Corps of Engineers Board of Contract Appeals are final if supported by substantial evidence, and its decisions of questions of law are open to independent judicial consideration. Donald M. Drake Co. v. U.S., Ct.Cl.1971, 439 F.2d 169, 194 Ct.Cl. 549. United States ⟐ 73(15)

Findings of Armed Services Board of Contract Appeals are binding upon Court of Claims if supported by substantial evidence. Preuss v. U.S., Ct.Cl.1969, 412 F.2d 1293, 188 Ct.Cl. 469. See, also, Chris Berg, Inc. v. U.S., 1968, 389 F.2d 401, 182 Ct.Cl. 23. United States ⟐ 73(15)

Fact that there is evidence, considered of and by itself, to support decision of Armed Services Board of Contract Appeals is not sufficient where there is opposing evidence so substantial in character as to detract from its weight and render it less than substantial on record

as a whole, but where opposing evidence is not overwhelmingly in favor of opposing view, view of facts adopted by Board, if otherwise proper, will be sustained when supported by evidence. Koppers Co. v. U.S., Ct.Cl.1968, 405 F.2d 554, 186 Ct.Cl. 142. United States ⟐ 73(15)

Factual conclusions of General Services Administration Board of Contract Appeals when supported by substantial evidence are immunized from attack in Court of Claims. Ambrose-Augusterfer Corp. v. U.S., Ct.Cl.1968, 394 F.2d 536, 184 Ct.Cl. 18. United States ⟐ 73(15)

The Court of Claims in contractor's suit on government contract is bound by findings of Corps of Engineers Board of Contract Appeals if they are supported by substantial evidence. Amino Bros. Co. v. U.S., Ct.Cl.1967, 372 F.2d 485, 178 Ct.Cl. 515, certiorari denied 88 S.Ct. 98, 389 U.S. 846, 19 L.Ed.2d 112. United States ⟐ 73(14)

Where government contractor challenging sufficiency of evidence to support finding of Board of Contract Appeals failed to allege or specify in what respects finding was not supported by substantial evidence, finding was final. Jefferson Const. Co. v. U.S., Ct.Cl.1966, 368 F.2d 247, 177 Ct.Cl. 581. United States ⟐ 73(14)

In this section providing that any decision by the head of any department or agency of United States or his duly authorized representative in dispute involving question arising under public contract is conclusive unless it is not "supported by substantial evidence", the quoted words are a term of art implying review on the record only. Mann Chemical Laboratories, Inc. v. U.S., D.C.Mass.1958, 174 F.Supp. 563. United States ⟐ 73(14)

In a dispute concerning a question of fact arising under a Government contract, the findings of the department head or a contract appeal board are binding unless not supported by substantial evidence in the record before such administrative officer on appeal; Court of Claims does not determine where the preponderance of the evidence lies, nor weigh the evidence independently, but examines it to see if in the entire record there is substantial evidence to sustain the administrative findings and decision; where the evidence before the administrative officer or board consists of conflicting testimony, the court will not substitute its judgment on matters of credibility for the board's unless there is uncontrovertible evidence or physical fact contradicting the board's inferences; and if the decision is reasonable and is supported by substantial evidence, Court of Claims will not disturb it. Phillips Const. Co., Inc. v. U.S., Ct.Cl. 1967, 179 Ct.Cl. 883. United States ⊂⇒ 73(14); United States ⊂⇒ 73(15)

Where the decision of the Corps of Engineers Claims and Appeals Board adverse to the contractor is based on substantial evidence contained in the record before that Board, and where nothing presented to the Court of Claims in plaintiff-contractor's suit tends to detract from the substantiality of the evidence supporting the adverse board decision, that decision must prevail. River Const. Corp. v. U.S., Ct.Cl.1962, 159 Ct.Cl. 254. United States ⊂⇒ 73(14)

The decision of the contracting officer affirmed by the Armed Services Board of Contract Appeals on a dispute concerning a question of fact is final where the court is persuaded, on consideration of all the evidence, that the decision is supported by substantial evidence. Rheem Mfg. Co. v. U.S., Ct.Cl.1961, 153 Ct.Cl. 465. United States ⊂⇒ 73(14)

252. Adequate to support conclusion, substantial evidence for decision

"Substantial evidence" is such relevant evidence as a reasonable mind might accept as adequate to support a conclusion. U.S. v. Hamden Co-op. Creamery Co., E.D.N.Y.1960, 185 F.Supp. 541, affirmed 297 F.2d 130. Evidence ⊂⇒ 597

In this section providing that reviewing board's decision on contract entered into by United States is final unless not supported by substantial evidence, "substantial evidence" means more than a mere scintilla and means such relevant evidence as reasonable mind might accept as adequate to support a conclusion. Langoma Lumber Corp. v. U.S., E.D.Pa. 1955, 140 F.Supp. 460, affirmed 232 F.2d 886. United States ⊂⇒ 73(14)

Where administrative record showed fully such relevant evidence as reasonable mind might accept as adequate to support conclusion, findings and conclusions were sustained by substantial evidence. Construction Management Corp. v. Brown & Root, Inc., N.Y.Sup.1964, 246

N.Y.S.2d 465, 41 Misc.2d 864, modified 270 N.Y.S.2d 95, 25 A.D.2d 843. Administrative Law And Procedure ⊂⇒ 791

253. Failure to present evidence or witnesses, substantial evidence for decision

That government presented no witnesses did not make plaintiff's evidence in proceeding on claim against United States compelling or substantial. Sternberger v. U.S., Ct.Cl.1968, 401 F.2d 1012, 185 Ct.Cl. 528. Evidence ⊂⇒ 589

Finding of Board of Contract Appeals that contractor could have ascertained borrow pit widths by mathematical analysis data in the contract document would be accepted as unchallenged where neither party pointed out the precise mechanics of the mathematical computation, so that it could not be determined whether such finding of the Board was supported by substantial evidence. Jefferson Const. Co. of Fla. v. U.S., Ct.Cl. 1966, 364 F.2d 420, 176 Ct.Cl. 1363, certiorari denied 87 S.Ct. 865, 386 U.S. 914, 17 L.Ed.2d 786. United States ⊂⇒ 73(14)

254. Evidence considered, substantial evidence for decision

To decide whether substantial evidence supports findings of Board of Appeals in contract case, evidence presented by both parties, including testimony elicited by cross-examination as well as direct examination, must be considered. Wm. A. Smith Contracting Co. v. U.S., Ct.Cl. 1969, 412 F.2d 1325, 188 Ct.Cl. 1062. United States ⊂⇒ 73(15)

In reviewing administrative decision in a contract case, the Court of Claims applies the substantial evidence test to the administrative record on which the board of contract appeals' decision is based, rather than to findings of the contracting officer. Dean Const. Co. v. U.S., Ct.Cl. 1969, 411 F.2d 1238, 188 Ct.Cl. 62. Federal Courts ⊂⇒ 1114.1

Rule providing that substantial evidence must exist to support findings of Armed Services Board of Contract Appeals requires a consideration of the evidence on both sides in order to determine whether it appears that evidence in support of decision can fairly be said to be substantial in face of opposing evidence. Koppers Co. v. U.S., Ct.Cl.1968, 405 F.2d 554, 186 Ct.Cl. 142. United States ⊂⇒ 73(15)

Standard for determining whether Corps of Engineers Claims and Appeals Board finding is supported by record is whether finding is supported by substantial evidence in record as a whole. Farnsworth & Chambers Co. v. U.S., Ct. Cl.1965, 346 F.2d 577, 171 Ct.Cl. 30. United States ⊕ 73(15)

In determining whether decision of Comptroller General as to date of final settlement of Government contract was supported by substantial evidence, the record as a whole must be reviewed, and not merely the evidence on which official based his decision. U.S. for Use of Bangor Roofing & Sheet Metal Co. v. T.W. Cunningham, Inc., D.C.Me.1956, 141 F.Supp. 205. United States ⊕ 67(20)

255. Conflicting evidence, substantial evidence for decision

The factual conclusions of the comptroller general would be accepted by the Court of Claims on cross motions for summary judgment where the parties did not dispute the factual conclusions. Burroughs Corp. v. U.S., Ct.Cl.1980, 617 F.2d 590, 223 Ct.Cl. 53. Federal Courts ⊕ 1120

Despite absence of decision by Armed Service Board of Contract Appeals, Court of Claims could properly decide issues as to constructive acceleration without returning case to Board where, even though evidence might be disputed, it was of such nature that as matter of law Board could have made only one finding of fact and where it was clear from facts actually found by the Board on another issue that plaintiff could not establish valid claim of constructive acceleration. Simmonds Precision Products, Inc. v. U.S., Ct.Cl.1976, 546 F.2d 886, 212 Ct.Cl. 305. Federal Courts ⊕ 1118

Conclusion of Armed Services Board of Contract Appeals is binding upon the Court of Claims if the court finds a reasonable conclusion based on the evidence even though there may be other evidence which refutes conclusion. Sylvania Elec. Products, Inc. v. U.S., Ct.Cl.1973, 479 F.2d 1342, 202 Ct.Cl. 16. United States ⊕ 73(15)

In proceeding to review decision of Post Office Department Board of Contract Appeals denying claim for additional compensation for packaging charges on shipments of items sold to Post Office Department by plaintiff, where plaintiff's

employee and Government's employee gave conflicting accounts of telephone conversations between them and both accounts were credible, Board's finding as to what took place would be adopted. Dana Corp. v. U.S., Ct.Cl.1972, 470 F.2d 1032, 200 Ct.Cl. 200. United States ⊕ 73(15)

Administrative finding may not be disturbed where contrary inferences may be drawn, each is supported by evidence, and evidence contrary to administrative conclusion is neither overwhelming in itself nor so detracts from evidence in support of finding as to render it less than substantial on record as a whole. Vann v. U.S., Ct.Cl.1970, 420 F.2d 968, 190 Ct.Cl. 546. Administrative Law And Procedure ⊕ 788; Administrative Law And Procedure ⊕ 789; Administrative Law And Procedure ⊕ 791

Evaluation of conflicting conclusions of expert witnesses by Corps of Engineers Board of Contract Appeals should be accepted unless testimony is inherently improbable or discredited by uncontrovertible evidence or physical fact. Tecon Corp. v. U.S., Ct.Cl.1969, 411 F.2d 1271, 188 Ct.Cl. 436. United States ⊕ 73(15)

Where conflicting testimony is in record on appeal from Armed Services Board of Contract Appeals in disputes over government contracts, Board's preference will, generally, not be disturbed unless court can conclude that findings are not supported by some evidence which qualitatively and in appropriate circumstances, quantitatively, can be deemed substantial evidence when record is viewed as a whole. Koppers Co. v. U.S., Ct.Cl.1968, 405 F.2d 554, 186 Ct.Cl. 142. United States ⊕ 73(15)

Court may not displace Armed Services Board of Contract Appeals choice between two fairly conflicting views, even though court might justifiably have made different choice had matter been before it de novo. Phillips Const. Co. v. U.S., Ct. Cl.1968, 394 F.2d 834, 184 Ct.Cl. 249. United States ⊕ 73(15)

Where there was a sharp dispute as to accuracy of time records kept by truck drivers and as to government's determination of portion of compensation allocable for truck rental, and contracting officer's report, disputed by general contractor, was accepted as factual basis for decision by Department of Labor, the findings of fact could not be accepted as correct, and were not entitled to limited scope of review provided by this chapter. H.B. Zachry Co. v. U.S., Ct.Cl.1965, 344 F.2d 352, 170 Ct.Cl. 115. United States ⮞ 73(14)

Where there were varying degrees of conflict in the testimony of the plaintiff's and defendant's witnesses at the hearing on appeal before the contracting agency's Board of Contract Appeals, but a fair reading of the entire record indicates that the findings of the Board are supported by substantial evidence, the Court of Claims will be bound by the administrative decision. Fort Sill Associates v. U.S., Ct.Cl.1968, 183 Ct.Cl. 301. United States ⮞ 73(15)

Where the court is reviewing a record made in an appeal of a contract dispute to the head of the contracting agency under the disputes clause of the contract and the provisions of this section, the conclusion of the department head must stand where there is a conflict in testimony by witnesses shown to have had enough knowledge of the subject matter of the dispute to make them competent to express conclusions, i.e., where there is substantial evidence to support varying decisions. Carlo Bianchi & Co. v. U.S., Ct.Cl.1964, 167 Ct.Cl. 364. United States ⮞ 73(15)

256. Abandonment of claim, substantial evidence for decision

Record supported finding that tramway contractor had abandoned his claim against the United States for increased expenses in construction of tramway for air force because of United States' failure to extend completion date of contract to reflect delays caused by strike of ironworkers. S.S. Mullen, Inc. v. U.S., Ct.Cl. 1968, 389 F.2d 390, 182 Ct.Cl. 1. United States ⮞ 73(3)

257. Acquiescence in interpretation, substantial evidence for decision

Evidence did not sustain finding of Board of Contract Appeals that contractor had acquiesced in Government's interpretation of contract, after bids were made but before award. WPC Enterprises, Inc. v. U.S., Ct.Cl.1963, 323 F.2d 874, 163 Ct.Cl. 1. United States ⮞ 74(11)

258. Acts of God, substantial evidence for decision

Evidence supported finding that prolonged flooding during construction of highway by contractor was caused by an act of God, in action by contractor's assignee against government for breach of contract wherein plaintiff contended that construction of dam by government caused the prolonged and abnormal inundation. Security Nat. Bank of Kansas City, Kansas City, Kan. v. U.S., Ct.Cl. 1968, 397 F.2d 984, 184 Ct.Cl. 741. Highways ⮞ 113(4)

259. Changed conditions, substantial evidence for decision

Determination by board of contract appeals that levee construction contractor had not encountered changed conditions during contract performance, in that quantity of rock encountered in borrow area did not greatly exceed that which it anticipated from examination of contract documents and other available information, was reasonable and supported by substantial evidence. Arundel Corp. v. U.S., Ct.Cl.1975, 515 F.2d 1116, 207 Ct. Cl. 84. United States ⮞ 73(14)

Evidence in highway repair contractor's proceeding for equitable adjustment on account of changed conditions in that designated quarry did not produce armor stone meeting specifications did not support contract appeal board's findings that contractor's inability to quarry armor stone was caused by its failure properly to evaluate site conditions, failure to plan and execute proper quarry production methods, and failure to utilize all of the indicated source. Stock & Grove, Inc. v. U.S., Ct.Cl.1974, 493 F.2d 629, 204 Ct.Cl. 103. Highways ⮞ 113(4)

Evidence supported finding of commerce department's board of contract appeals that road construction contractors' claimed additional costs, in performing unclassified excavation, due to hardness and abrasiveness of rock, and its effect on drilling costs were not, for purposes of recovery of equitable adjustment for changed conditions, causally related to discovery of unknown and unusual physical conditions differing materially from those ordinarily encountered and generally recognized as adhering in work of character provided for in contract. Charles T. Parker Const. Co. v. U.S., Ct. Cl.1970, 433 F.2d 771, 193 Ct.Cl. 320. Highways ⮞ 113(4)

Evidence in government contractor's action on claim under changed conditions provisions of construction contract support finding that, although pile driving proved difficult, soil conditions were not shown to be different than those disclosed by contract documents. Blount Bros. Corp. v. U.S., Ct.Cl.1970, 424 F.2d 1074, 191 Ct.Cl. 784. United States ☞ 74(11)

Finding by Armed Services Board of Contract Appeals that additional and excess cleaning costs in housing project at Air Force base were not result of conditions caused by change in grading was supported by substantial evidence. Electronic & Missile Facilities, Inc. v. U.S., Ct.Cl.1969, 416 F.2d 1345, 189 Ct.Cl. 237. United States ☞ 74(11)

In proceeding on claim against United States by contractor constructing for the Navy a dry dock at Brooklyn Naval Shipyard, record established that parties intended by change order and accompanying letter agreement to settle any and all claims for additional costs, including delay costs arising out of changed conditions. Corbetta Const. Co. v. U.S., Ct.Cl. 1969, 408 F.2d 450, 187 Ct.Cl. 409. United States ☞ 74(10)

Evidence, in action by road builder to recover additional compensation under changes and changed conditions clauses of contract for construction of road, supported findings that after deletion of surface course the roadway which was constructed was substantially identical to roadway provided for by specifications and drawings, that under specifications a reasonable variation of tolerances was allowable, and that flexible tolerances were required by the road commission which were not unreasonable. Morrison-Knudsen Co. v. U.S., Ct.Cl.1968, 397 F.2d 826, 184 Ct.Cl. 661. Highways ☞ 113(4)

Evidence in proceeding by excavation contractor to recover from the United States added costs allegedly incurred because of changed condition was sufficient to support determination of board of contract appeals of Department of Interior that contractor did not encounter, within purview of "changed conditions" clause, either (1) "subsurface and/or latent conditions at the site materially differing from those shown on the drawings or indicated in the specifications" or (2) "unknown conditions of an unusual nature differing materially from those ordinarily encountered and generally recognized as inhering in work of the character provided for in the plans and specifications." J.A. Terteling & Sons,

Inc. v. U.S., Ct.Cl.1968, 390 F.2d 926, 182 Ct.Cl. 691. United States ☞ 74(11)

Record in contractor's claim for extra work required under construction contract because of unforeseen changed condition established that 57¼ days of delay in completion of contract was caused by changed condition. Farnsworth & Chambers Co. v. U.S., Ct.Cl.1967, 383 F.2d 407, 180 Ct.Cl. 992. United States ☞ 74(12.1)

Corps of Engineers Claims and Appeals Board finding that there was no large channel or opening in river bed permitting water to flow into cofferdam area from which it was being pumped by government contractor who claimed changed condition because of asserted backflow was unsupported by substantial evidence and record as a whole. Farnsworth & Chambers Co. v. U.S., Ct.Cl.1965, 346 F.2d 577, 171 Ct.Cl. 30. United States ☞ 74(11)

Finding by Board of Contract Appeals, in proceeding on bridge contractor's claim for additional compensation for increased costs on account of changed conditions, that upstream contractor's cofferdam, which diverted water onto bridge contractor's worksite, was not a changed condition since it was foreseeable, was not supported by substantial evidence. Hoffman v. U.S., Ct.Cl.1964, 340 F.2d 645, 166 Ct.Cl. 39. United States ☞ 74(11)

In action by contractor against United States for sums allegedly due contractor under contract to manufacture and erect two 20-ton jib cranes at Philadelphia Navy Yard, evidence established that contracting officer's decision upon some items, which made up amount by which contract price was to be reduced as result of changes in contract, was incorrect. Wagner Whirler & Derrick Corp. v. U.S., Ct.Cl.1954, 121 F.Supp. 664, 128 Ct.Cl. 382. United States ☞ 74(11)

260. Custom or trade, substantial evidence for decision

Evidence supported finding of Armed Services Board of Contract Appeals that it was not custom of trade in locality that equipment removed and replaced be retained by contractor unless contract specifically provides that salvaged material be retained by owner. Eder Elec. Co. v. U.S., E.D.Pa.1962, 205 F.Supp. 305. United States ☞ 74(11)

261.   Damages, substantial evidence for decision—Generally

Finding that government contractor had not suffered loss due to decrease in labor efficiency was supported by substantial evidence, despite claim that testimony of claimant's witnesses rendered opposing evidence insubstantial. Northbridge Electronics, Inc. v. U.S., Ct.Cl. 1971, 444 F.2d 1124, 195 Ct.Cl. 453. United States ☜ 74(11)

Evidence sustained finding of Armed Services Board of Contract Appeals that stop shipment order of velour between October 4 and November 12 for Air Force overcoats did not damage contractor in manufacture of overcoats. Leopold Morse Tailoring Co. v. U.S., Ct.Cl.1969, 408 F.2d 739, 187 Ct.Cl. 304. United States ☜ 74(11)

262.   —— Amount, damages, substantial evidence for decision

In action to recover for government's breach of contract to produce and supply helium, evidence established that producer was entitled to award of $33,457,400. Northern Helex Co. v. U.S., Ct.Cl.1980, 634 F.2d 557, 225 Ct.Cl. 194. United States ☜ 74(13)

On termination of contract for convenience of government, evidence supported action of board of contract appeals in allowing contractor $275,275 for profit. Nolan Bros., Inc. v. U.S., Ct.Cl.1971, 437 F.2d 1371, 194 Ct.Cl. 1. United States ☜ 74(15)

In proceeding culminating in administrative decision adverse to contractor's claim, for additional excavation work and return of liquidated damages paid under contract for channel clearing and other work on river, evidence supported Board's findings that contractor had not used either reasonable precautions or sound engineering and construction practices, as required by contract, and that liquidated damages for not completing contract in time had been properly assessed. U.S. Nat. Bank of Portland v. U.S., D.C.Or.1959, 178 F.Supp. 910. United States ☜ 74(11)

263.   Date of delivery, substantial evidence for decision

Finding of Armed Services Board of Contract Appeals that contracting officer offered contractor an extension delivery date for electronic equipment to October 29, 1966 and that contractor accepted

that date was supported by substantial evidence in contractor's appeal from default termination. Bromion, Inc. v. U.S., Ct.Cl.1969, 411 F.2d 1020, 188 Ct.Cl. 31. United States ☜ 74(11)

264.   Delays, substantial evidence for decision

Evidence supported finding of Armed Services Board of Contract Appeals that failure of supplier to United States Navy to obtain a reduction of subcontract price was due to supplier's own avoidable delay with respect to negotiating a price reduction with corporation with which supplier subcontracted and, finding supported conclusion that government was not liable on theory that actions by Navy Department personnel prevented supplier from obtaining a deductive pricing change from corporation in connection with a net reduction in scope of work under subcontract resulting from a modification to the prime contract. CRF - a Joint Venture of Cemco, Inc. v. U.S., Ct. Cl.1980, 624 F.2d 1054, 224 Ct.Cl. 312. United States ☜ 74(11)

Findings of Corps of Engineers Board of Contract Appeals that, except for specified instances in which the government directed contractor to perform corrective work, flood damage and cleanup in and around certain portions of street relocation project were not the cause of delays and interruptions which increased the costs of contract performance were supported by substantial evidence. Carl M. Halvorson, Inc. v. U.S., Ct.Cl.1972, 461 F.2d 1337, 198 Ct.Cl. 882. United States ☜ 74(11)

Evidence supported finding of Department of the Interior board of contract appeals that there was no suspension, delay or interruption in construction of gateway arch of the Jefferson National Expansion Memorial which resulted from act of the contracting officer or any of his representatives during April, May or June 1966 which caused substantial delay of ductwork which would permit contractor to recover price adjustment for the period prior to July 1, 1966. Hoel-Steffen Const. Co. v. U.S., Ct.Cl.1972, 456 F.2d 760, 197 Ct.Cl. 561. United States ☜ 74(11)

Evidence sustained Armed Services Board of Contract Appeals finding that contractor on housing project under Capehart Housing Act suffered only 75 days of delay which was attributable to changed conditions for which government was liable. Phillips Const. Co. v. U.S., Ct.Cl.1971, 440 F.2d 429, 194 Ct.Cl. 695. United States ⟾ 74(11)

Evidence, in proceeding on claim by contractor against government to recover adjustment under special work provision of contract for construction of air traffic control center, supported Federal Aviation Agency Contract Appeals Panel's determination that unreasonable portion of delay caused by issuance of stop order in connection with lath and plaster work was only 55 days. Chaney & James Const. Co. v. U.S., Ct.Cl.1970, 421 F.2d 728, 190 Ct.Cl. 699. United States ⟾ 74(11)

There was substantial evidence to support conclusion of board that delay in performance of contract for repair of light for Coast Guard due to change in conditions was not caused by contractor but was chargeable to government which was responsible for more of the indecision than contractor. Vann v. U.S., Ct. Cl.1970, 420 F.2d 968, 190 Ct.Cl. 546. United States ⟾ 74(11)

Findings of Veterans Administration Construction Contract Appeals Board that much of the delay in construction was due to contractor's unsatisfactory relations with its concrete supplier, to contractor's failure to reorganize project so as to minimize disruption of planned sequence of operations, to lack of adequate equipment and labor, to performance of defective concrete work, and to failure to coordinate work of the various trades were not supported by substantial evidence. J. D. Hedin Const. Co. v. U.S., Ct.Cl.1969, 408 F.2d 424, 187 Ct.Cl. 45. United States ⟾ 73(14)

Evidence supported findings of Board of Contract Appeals that government contractor's work in remodeling dormitories at Air Force Base was not unreasonably delayed, except for one day, by government's failure to evacuate buildings on schedule, to clarify in timely manner errors and ambiguities in contract drawings and specifications, to promptly approve samples of material submitted by contractor, or to promptly accept buildings on completion. Jefferson Const. Co. v. U.S., Ct.Cl.1966, 368 F.2d 247, 177 Ct.Cl. 581. United States ⟾ 74(11)

Determination by Board of Contract Appeals that delay in start of replacement of built up roofing and insulation project,

which contractor agreed to perform under contract providing for liquidated damages of $40 for each day of delay beyond 100 days from date of receipt of notice to proceed unless delay arose from unforeseeable causes beyond control and without fault of contractor, due to late approval of contractor's material list and certificates was fault of contractor and not Government was supported by substantial evidence. Missouri Roofing Co., Inc. v. U.S., E.D.Mo.1973, 357 F.Supp. 918. United States ⟾ 74(11)

265. Duress, substantial evidence for decision

Settlement agreement between contractor and federal government was not secured by coercion or duress on part of government and would not be set aside, in that delay for which government was responsible was not sufficient to establish duress in light of circumstances surrounding negotiation of settlement agreement, record did not support contractor's claim that government was aware of, had caused, and had used contractor's precarious financial condition to coerce a settlement, contractor was not coerced by use of total cost basis methodology, and bad faith was not established. Systems Technology Associates, Inc. v. U.S., C.A.Fed. 1983, 699 F.2d 1383. United States ⟾ 74(6)

Evidence failed to establish that contractor was subjected by Government to duress in negotiations concerning extended delivery dates and liquidated damages clauses. Simmonds Precision Products, Inc. v. U.S., Ct.Cl.1976, 546 F.2d 886, 212 Ct.Cl. 305. United States ⟾ 74(11)

266. Equitable adjustment, substantial evidence for decision

Record with respect to contract for aerial banner tow targets failed to support contention that, despite default termination, contractor was entitled to equitable adjustment for constructive changes. Piasecki Aircraft Corp. v. U.S., Ct.Cl. 1981, 667 F.2d 50, 229 Ct.Cl. 208. United States ⟾ 72.1(6)

In proceeding on claim of government contractor to be reimbursed for its cost of correcting government-furnished drawings, the cost of which it contended was at least $527,579.06, evidence supported equitable adjustment by Armed Services Board of Contract Appeals of $46,058 for drawing changes. Teitelbaum v. U.S., Ct.

Cl.1972, 458 F.2d 72, 198 Ct.Cl. 150. United States ⊂⇒ 74(12.1)

Evidence established that government was entitled to credit of $10,258.02 for deleted work performed by substituted contractor. Nager Elec. Co. v. U.S., Ct. Cl.1971, 442 F.2d 936, 194 Ct.Cl. 835. United States ⊂⇒ 75(4)

Evidence established that specification drafter did not regard flexible connectors which connected air conditioning duct work on low pressure side of system with ceiling slot diffusers as ducts which were required to be insulated according to contract and directive requiring such insulation was constructive change order entitling contractor to apply for adjustment in contract price. Leavell-Morrison-Knudsen-Hardeman v. U.S., Ct.Cl.1971, 436 F.2d 451, 193 Ct.Cl. 949. United States ⊂⇒ 74(11)

Evidence that trade practice where work was performed on United States Air Force contract was to pay haul rate of 16¢ per cubic yard per mile and to consider any fraction of one-half mile as one-half mile failed to sustain conclusion of Armed Services Board of Contract Appeals that practice was not established, and equitable adjustment to embrace any fraction of one-half mile as one-half mile was required. N. Fiorito Co. v. U.S., Ct.Cl.1969, 416 F.2d 1284, 189 Ct.Cl. 215. Customs And Usages ⊂⇒ 19(3)

Armed Services Board of Contract Appeals' findings that contractor's failure to proceed with production of radio transmitting set was direct result of its inadequate financial situation and that United States' refusal to grant an equitable adjustment for defective microfilm did not cause such financial difficulties were supported by substantial evidence. Preuss v. U.S., Ct.Cl.1969, 412 F.2d 1293, 188 Ct. Cl. 469. United States ⊂⇒ 74(11)

Evidence failed to support finding of Armed Services Board of Contract Appeals that difficulties encountered by contractor in process of manufacturing flying jackets for Navy because of defects in specification requirements were the normal, minor, and relatively insignificant specification requirements which often necessitate slight adjustment in mass production and for which additional compensation is neither sought nor expected. L.W. Foster Sportswear Co. v. U.S., Ct.Cl. 1969, 405 F.2d 1285, 186 Ct.Cl. 499. United States ⊂⇒ 74(11)

Findings of armed services board of contract appeals that contractor's rocket launcher adapters were not subjected by government to tests more severe than those required by the adapter manufacturing contracts was supported by substantial evidence and thus was binding upon Court of Claims, in proceeding on contractor's claim for equitable adjustment for additional costs incurred in performance of the contracts. Dittmore-Freimuth Corp. v. U.S., Ct.Cl.1968, 390 F.2d 664, 182 Ct.Cl. 507. United States ⊂⇒ 73(15); United States ⊂⇒ 74(11)

Determination of armed services board of contract appeals that $48,512.84 was amount of equitable adjustment due prime contractor for change from "walls and roofs first" construction plan to "floors first" construction plan was supported by substantial evidence. Turnbull, Inc. v. U.S., Ct.Cl.1967, 389 F.2d 1007, 180 Ct.Cl. 1010. United States ⊂⇒ 74(12.1)

Findings of Armed Services Board of Contract Appeals that tramway at air force radar site contained defects which existed and could have been found before contract to construct new tramway was awarded to contractor were supported by substantial evidence in contractor's action to obtain equitable adjustment of contract price. Chris Berg, Inc. v. U.S., Ct.Cl.1968, 389 F.2d 401, 182 Ct.Cl. 23. United States ⊂⇒ 74(11)

Findings of Armed Forces Board of Contract Appeals that if tramway contractor had made adequate site investigation it would have discovered that its plan to use existing tramway to assemble new towers was not safe and feasible were not supported by substantial evidence in tramway contractor's action for equitable adjustment of contract price for additional construction costs due to inability to use existing tramway. S.S. Mullen, Inc. v. U.S., Ct.Cl.1968, 389 F.2d 390, 182 Ct.Cl. 1. United States ⊂⇒ 74(11)

Finding that contractor performing work under contract with government encountered a large amount of subsurface water was supported by evidence, so as to bring contractor within provision of contract allowing equitable adjustment in price if contractor encounters subsurface and/or latent physical conditions materially differing from those in specifications or unknown physical conditions of an unusual nature. United Contractors v. U.S.,

Ct.Cl.1966, 368 F.2d 585, 177 Ct.Cl. 151. Federal Courts ☞ 1113

Evidence sustained finding of Armed Services Board of Contract Appeals that successful bidder on certain surplus Government property, in failing to inspect all boxes of bandages on which it bid, assumed the risk in regard to color of the bandages in the uninspected boxes, and was therefore not entitled to an adjustment of price on basis that some of the bandages were brown, and that bandages were described in the sales invitation as white. M. Berger Co. v. U.S., W.D.Pa. 1961, 199 F.Supp. 22. United States ☞ 74(11)

Corps of Engineers' willingness to permit beach restoration contractor to use dredging method that proved to be inefficient did not amount to differing site condition or failure to disclose superior knowledge that entitled contractor to equitable adjustment; contractor was given wide discretion to choose appropriate dredging method and its choice of dredging method was a business decision and business risk. Hydromar Corp. of Delaware and Eastern Seaboard Pile Driving, Inc. v. U.S., Cl.Ct.1992, 25 Cl.Ct. 555, affirmed 980 F.2d 744. United States ☞ 70(22.1); United States ☞ 70(30)

267. Existence of agreement, substantial evidence for decision

Under evidence, there was agreement reached between contractor and government pursuant to which contractor agreed to provide variable pairing of buffer processors as consideration for government's willingness to accept reduction of L–119s from eight to four in data processing subsystem, and, in view of such compromise, there was no extracontractual requirement unilaterally imposed by government for which contractor could recover. Singer Co. Librascope Div. v. U.S., Ct.Cl.1977, 568 F.2d 695, 215 Ct.Cl. 281. United States ☞ 70(25.1)

Where the Armed Services Board of Contract Appeals determined that the testimony of the contractor's witnesses in a contract dispute appeal failed to establish a binding agreement to eliminate certain production procedures and that the discussions concerning their elimination were between two Government representatives without any participation by the contractor or his representatives, and where the record before the Board contained undisputed testimony that the dis-

cussions relative to the elimination of the procedure were between authorized Government personnel and authorized representatives of the contractor, the Board's determination is not supported by substantial evidence and is not binding on the court or the parties. Northbridge Electronics, Inc. v. U.S., Ct.Cl.1966, 175 Ct.Cl. 426. United States ☞ 73(14)

268. Fees and expenses, substantial evidence for decision

In determining general and administrative expenses incurred by government contractor during period prior to termination of contract for convenience of government, evidence warranted action of board of contract appeals in allowing depreciation on office equipment and automobiles at home office. Nolan Bros., Inc. v. U.S., Ct.Cl.1971, 437 F.2d 1371, 194 Ct.Cl. 1. United States ☞ 74(12.1)

269. Financial inability to perform, substantial evidence for decision

Evidence would not support finding of Armed Services Board of Contract Appeals that contractor was financially unable to perform his contract or that excess cost assessment would be justified in light of evidence that contractor by virtue of commitment made by bank was fully able to pay for successive deliveries by manufacturer and that payment was guaranteed by bank and that manufacturer had accepted the credit arrangements. Meinberg v. U.S., W.D.Mo.1969, 310 F.Supp. 86. United States ☞ 74(11)

270. Good faith, substantial evidence for decision

Substantial evidence sustained finding that United States had acted in good faith in work assignments under an indefinite delivery requirements type contract, notwithstanding claim of contractor that government had failed to provide sufficient projects under contract. Franklin Co. v. U.S., Ct.Cl.1967, 381 F.2d 416, 180 Ct.Cl. 666. United States ☞ 74(11)

271. Impossibility of performance, substantial evidence for decision

Finding by Department of Agriculture Board of Contract Appeals that contractor which knew of cholera difficulties being experienced by its supplier at time it entered supply contracts under commodity support and domestic food consumption program had sufficient supplies to fulfill contracts was supported by substantial evidence and would not be disturbed by court on contractor's appeal from Board's assessment of liquidated damages against contractor due to its failure to make timely deliveries of processed turkeys. Jennie-O Foods, Inc. v. U.S., Ct.Cl.1978, 580 F.2d 400, 217 Ct.Cl. 314. United States ☞ 73(15)

Record established that contractor did not recognize sole impossibility of specifications for jamming antennas until it had completed testing every alternative method of performance at which point it so informed the Air Force. Dynalectron Corp. (Pacific Division) v. U.S., Ct.Cl. 1975, 518 F.2d 594, 207 Ct.Cl. 349. United States ☞ 70(30)

Evidence supported finding of armed services board of contract appeals that achievement of degree of compaction required by construction contract was practical impossibility, as claimed by contractor in seeking recovery of expenses incurred in attaining required compaction. Tombigbee Constructors v. U.S., Ct.Cl.1970, 420 F.2d 1037, 190 Ct. Cl. 615. United States ☞ 74(11)

Evidence supported findings of Corps of Engineers Board of Contract Appeals that government contract for installation of tile floor in powerhouse of federal dam required bond between setting bed and slab, that conditions existing at site did not render such requirement impossible of performance, and that government inspectors did not interfere with contractor's work to such a degree as to indicate bad faith and deliberate effort to ruin contractor. Stoeckert v. U.S., Ct.Cl.1968, 391 F.2d 639, 183 Ct.Cl. 152. United States ☞ 74(11)

In suit by the Government against a procurement contractor for damages due to his default on a procurement contract, evidence sustained finding of Armed Services Board of Contract Appeals that it was possible for contractor to secure component parts, but that contractor failed to purchase them because he was required to pay a higher price than he had anticipated, thus cutting his margin of profit, and in any event, trial court's judgment sustaining the Board's finding was not clearly erroneous. Hoffmann v. U.S., C.A.10 (Kan.) 1960, 276 F.2d 199. United States ☞ 75(4)

272. Increased costs, substantial evidence for decision

Substantial evidence sustained finding of Armed Services Board of Contract Appeals that government incurred $46,964.60 in excess cost for reprocurement of impulse cartridges following contractor's failure to perform contract. Fairfield Scientific Corp. v. U.S., Ct.Cl. 1979, 611 F.2d 854, 222 Ct.Cl. 167. United States ☞ 75(5)

Substantial evidence supported determinations of armed services board of contract appeals in proceeding to review assessment and collection by government of excess reprocurement costs that government did not withhold superior knowledge which would have expedited production of pole hooks and loop hooks used to recover scientific instruments returning from space, that government did not waive contract delivery schedule, that contractor was not misled by request for proposals, and that reprocured articles were essentially the same as those which contractor had agreed to furnish. H.N. Bailey and Associates v. U.S., Ct.Cl.1971, 449 F.2d 376, 196 Ct.Cl. 166. United States ☞ 74(11)

Where conclusion of board with respect to whether government contractor, claiming additional funds from government, had worked on Sundays when weather permitted was nicely balanced, board's conclusion that contractor did not work on Sundays when weather permitted lay within zone of reasonableness provided by record and met the substantial evidence standard of this chapter. Vann v. U.S., Ct.Cl.1970, 420 F.2d 968, 190 Ct.Cl. 546. United States ☞ 74(11)

Findings of the Armed Services Board of Contract Appeals in regard to whether a contractor incurred additional costs in fulfilling a government contract, as a result of faulty specifications or design by the government, were binding on appeal from decision of the Board where such findings were supported by substantial evidence. Bell v. U.S., Ct.Cl.1968, 404 F.2d 975, 186 Ct.Cl. 189. United States ☞ 73(15)

Evidence failed to support decision of government appeals board upholding contracting officer's determination that contractor was not entitled to be reimbursed for increased costs incurred as result of change in government specifications for pilings for veterans administration hospital facility. J.D. Hedin Const. Co. v. U.S., Ct.Cl.1965, 347 F.2d 235, 171 Ct.Cl. 70. United States ⚖ 74(11)

In action against Government by contractor who had converted Veterans Administration building for compensation for additional work resulting from error in plans furnished by Government and for recovery of liquidated damages assessed against it by Government because work was not completed within time provided for in contract as extended, evidence sustained finding of Construction Contract Appeals Board of Veterans Administration adverse to contractor. Wells & Wells, Inc. v. U.S., C.A.8 (Mo.) 1959, 269 F.2d 412. United States ⚖ 74(11)

Evidence sustained decision of Veterans Administration's Construction Contract Appeals Board adverse to contractor claiming additional compensation after contracting officer ordered subcontractor to paint underside of steel deck roofing. Malan Const. Corp. v. U.S., S.D.N.Y. 1962, 217 F.Supp. 955, affirmed 318 F.2d 709. United States ⚖ 74(11)

Evidence, in suit by Government against contractor and his bonding company to recover excess cost to Government of completing a contract, including secondary records made in the regular course of business, sustained finding of Advisory Board of Contract Appeals that Government had a valid claim against contractor for $5,192.04. U.S. v. Dykes, E.D.Tenn.1960, 194 F.Supp. 478. United States ⚖ 75(4)

In action against Government for extra compensation for mistakes in Government plans with respect to conversion of Veterans Administration Building, and for form work and reinforcing steel and concrete walls, extra time, and for liquidated damages, evidence sustained findings of Construction Contract Appeals Board of Veterans Administration allowing certain extra time and compensation and decisions were not arbitrary or capricious. Wells & Wells, Inc. v. U.S., E.D.Mo.1958, 164 F.Supp. 26, affirmed 269 F.2d 412. United States ⚖ 74(11)

In suit by contractor to recover increased cost of performance on Government contract claimed to have resulted from delays caused by Government's failure to give proper notice to proceed as required by contract, evidence sustained findings as to actual loss suffered by contractor because of delay which caused

performance during bad weather and at time when contractor was obligated to pay increased wage rates. Abbett Elec. Corp.v. U.S., Ct.Cl.1958, 162 F.Supp. 772, 142 Ct.Cl. 609. United States ⚖ 74(11)

In action to recover excess costs incurred by plaintiff in manufacture of Women's Army Corps exercise suits, wherein plaintiff claimed that pattern to which suits were required to conform had not been made available until after bids had been submitted and that its bid was made on basis of sample garment which was shorter in length than pattern, and wherein defendant claimed that plaintiff had no authority to bid on any article not in accordance with contract and that plaintiff had assumed risk of any loss suffered by mistake of judgment in estimating amount of material that would be required by pattern, evidence sustained Board's denial of relief. L.W. Foster Sportswear Co. v. U.S., E.D.Pa.1956, 145 F.Supp. 148. United States ⚖ 74(11)

In an action by plaintiff under its contract to construct maintenance hangars at an Air Force Base, to recover the cost of extra work of installing remedial piers, on the ground that the remedial work was occasioned by the Government's faulty concrete mix designs, the decision by the Armed Services Board of Contract Appeals adverse to plaintiff and holding that the defective concrete had resulted from insufficient or improper mixing by plaintiff's subcontractor, was a determination under the disputes clause of the contract on a question of fact, and because the record before Court of Claims contained substantial evidence to support such determination, the decision of the Board was final and binding on the plaintiff. T.C. Bateson Const. Co. v. U.S., Ct. Cl.1960, 149 Ct.Cl. 514. United States ⚖ 73(14)

273. Indemnity for nonperformance, substantial evidence for decision

Substantial evidence sustained determination of board of contract appeals that mail carrier had by letter accepted specified amount as indemnity for nonperformance of services on two days when mail service was curtailed. Lough v. Klassen, D.C.Mont.1972, 348 F.Supp. 754. Postal Service ⚖ 21(1)

274. Inspections, substantial evidence for decision

Evidence, in dispute over contract for manufacture and delivery of artillery shell components to the United States, supported decision of the Armed Services Board of Contract Appeals that while Government was not entitled to threaten discontinuation of inspection, that event had no bearing upon contractor's halt in production. A.B.G. Instrument & Engineering, Inc. v. U.S., Ct.Cl.1979, 593 F.2d 394, 219 Ct.Cl. 381. United States ☞ 74(11)

Findings of Armed Services Board of Contract Appeals that producer of pork roasts for military had in fact agreed to an inspection plan and that it could not complain that morning production was already frozen by time of inspection, thus preventing reworking and/or reinspection, were supported by substantial evidence. Max Bauer Meat Packer, Inc. v. U.S., Ct.Cl.1972, 458 F.2d 88, 198 Ct.Cl. 97. United States ☞ 74(11)

Evidence in support of contractor's claim for equitable adjustment would not support contractor's charge that Government made overly critical or meticulous inspections of paint job by subcontractor or that Government's inspection procedure resulted in the expenditure of excessive material and labor. Chris Berg, Inc. v. U.S., Ct.Cl.1972, 455 F.2d 1037, 197 Ct.Cl. 503. United States ☞ 74(11)

275. Interest, substantial evidence for decision

Administrative determination of Washington Metropolitan Area Transit Authority that contracting officer did not take unreasonable amount of time in processing contractor's two claims for extra work required by changes that Authority had ordered in its original contract, and that contractor was thus not entitled to interest, was not supported by substantial evidence. General Ry. Signal Co. v. Washington Metropolitan Area Transit Authority, D.C.D.C.1979, 527 F.Supp. 359, affirmed 664 F.2d 296, 214 U.S.App. D.C. 170, certiorari denied 101 S.Ct. 3049, 452 U.S. 915, 69 L.Ed.2d 418. District Of Columbia ☞ 14

276. Interference with performance, substantial evidence for decision

Evidence failed to show that certain work which government contractor had completed was damaged through fault of

members of the Air Force. Banks Const. Co. v. U. S., Ct.Cl.1966, 364 F.2d 357, 176 Ct.Cl. 1302. United States ☞ 74(11)

277. Knowledge or notice, substantial evidence for decision

Claims Court properly found that finding of the Armed Services Board of Contract Appeals that contractor knew a prior contractor had received Government waivers was not supported by substantial evidence. Teledyne Lewisburg v. U.S., C.A.Fed.1983, 699 F.2d 1336. United States ☞ 74(11)

In proceeding on claim by electronics manufacturer under contract for multi-year procurement of aircraft carrier radar systems, evidence supported determination of Armed Services Board of Contract Appeals that funds for contract were not available to contracting officer and that manufacturer therefore never became entitled to receive notice that they were available. Applied Devices Corp. v. U.S., Ct.Cl.1979, 591 F.2d 635, 219 Ct.Cl. 109. United States ☞ 74(11)

Evidence supported finding that contractor knew what it was expected to do under contract to study and report on lineal survey methods for air force test track, and that level of satisfactory performance under contract was not imprecise. J.A. Maurer, Inc. v. U.S., Ct.Cl. 1973, 485 F.2d 588, 202 Ct.Cl. 813. United States ☞ 74(11)

Evidence supported finding of Board of Contract Appeals that shirt manufacturer was fully aware or should have been that, in ascertaining whether cloth for military shirts was good approximation of the standard sample, United States would compare sample swatches with its own shade range. Doyle Shirt Mfg. Corp. v. U.S., Ct.Cl.1972, 462 F.2d 1150, 199 Ct. Cl. 150. United States ☞ 74(11)

Substantial evidence failed to support determination of Corps of Engineers Board of Contract Appeals that government contractor knew or should have known of the existence of a high groundwater table at project site, and that contractor thus was not misled by erroneous failure of the United States to show the ground-water table on core boring logs. Woodcrest Const. Co. v. U.S., Ct. Cl.1969, 408 F.2d 406, 187 Ct.Cl. 249, certiorari denied 90 S.Ct. 2164, 398 U.S. 958, 26 L.Ed.2d 542. United States ☞ 73(14)

Evidence in action by contractor on federal construction project against United States for premium wages which were paid by contractor and its subcontractors as result of local labor shortage caused by high priority federal construction program in area and as to which contractor, in making bid, was misled by nondisclosure sustained finding that contractor was not aware of program. J.A. Jones Const. Co. v. U.S., Ct.Cl.1968, 390 F.2d 886, 182 Ct.Cl. 615. United States ⬉ 74(11)

Substantial evidence supported Contract Disputes Board's determinations that milk powder sold to Government had been infested at time of delivery, that infestation was not discoverable until later, and that Government, which discovered infestation in September and gave notice to contractor on October 17, had given timely and adequate notice. U.S. v. Hamden Co-op. Creamery Co., C.A.2 (N.Y.) 1961, 297 F.2d 130. United States ⬉ 73(15)

278. Payment, adequacy of, substantial evidence for decision

Evidence failed to sustain board's finding that payment to contractor adequately compensated contractor for title to storage tanks in place. Norcoast Constructors, Inc. v. U.S., Ct.Cl.1971, 448 F.2d 1400, 196 Ct.Cl. 1. United States ⬉ 74(11)

279. Price warranties, substantial evidence for decision

Armed Services Board of Contract Appeals' decision that plaintiff contractor breached the price warranty provision of two consecutive requirements contracts for lift truck replacement parts, under which provision plaintiff warranted that the prices to be paid by the Government were as low as those charged to any commercial or nongovernmental customer, was supported by substantial evidence, notwithstanding plaintiff's claim that its franchise dealers, who were charged a lower price, were not "customers" within the meaning of the price warranty clause because, under normal trade parlance and usage, a customer is an end-user and not, like a dealer, one who is obliged to perform service functions in relation to products that he buys for eventual resale to an end-user. Eaton Corp., Indus. Truck Div. v. U.S., Ct.Cl.1979, 591

F.2d 682, 219 Ct.Cl. 217. United States ⬉ 70(19)

280. Rejection of goods or performance, substantial evidence for decision

Evidence sustained findings of Armed Services Board of Contract Appeals that 60% of roofing and siding sheets for hangars at air force base were properly rejected on ground that they lacked zinc coating requirements contained in specifications and that half of remaining 40% of such sheets and half of galvanized sheets for hangar doors were properly rejected on ground that they were corroded. J.A. Jones Const. Co. v. U.S., Ct.Cl. 1968, 395 F.2d 783, 184 Ct.Cl. 1. United States ⬉ 74(11)

281. Representations, substantial evidence for decision

In action under this section by contractors for production of steel track shoes for armored personnel carriers, record supported determination that plaintiffs were not misled to their detriment by government representative's statement at bidders' conference that steel required by specifications and steel previously used could be expected to machine substantially the same, in light of evidence that the representation proved to be essentially correct once contractors adjusted their heat treatment procedures so as to achieve comparability of hardness. Firestone Tire & Rubber Co. v. U.S., Ct.Cl. 1977, 558 F.2d 577, 214 Ct.Cl. 457. United States ⬉ 74(11)

Testimony by contractor's officer that contractor wanted to get contract and thought supplying steel welded tanks for storage of diesel fuel would please engineers was not substantial evidence that any such undertaking was conveyed to Government in time to be inducement for award of contract. Norcoast Constructors, Inc. v. U.S., Ct.Cl.1971, 448 F.2d 1400, 196 Ct.Cl. 1. United States ⬉ 74(11)

Evidence as to what defendant's representative told plaintiff's representative during visit to jobsite for construction of earthen dam across creek supported finding of Board of Contract Appeals that defendant did not represent to plaintiff's representative that contractor would have right to use water in natural basin for construction purposes. Briscoe v. U.S., Ct.Cl.1971, 442 F.2d 953, 194 Ct.Cl. 866. United States ⬉ 74(11)

282. Severance payments, substantial evidence for decision

Record supported decision of National Aeronautics and Space Administration Board of Contract Appeals denying reimbursement of severance pay costs incurred by subcontractor under contract to furnish security guards and fire protection services at Kennedy Space Center, and supported finding that severance payments were not required by law, by established policy constituting implied agreement, or by circumstances of particular employment. Trans World Airlines, Inc. for and on Behalf of Wackenhut Corp. v. U.S., Ct.Cl.1978, 587 F.2d 44, 218 Ct.Cl. 376. United States ☞ 70(18)

283. Specifications, substantial evidence for decision

Evidence supported finding of Board of Contract Appeals that air-conditioning units which contractor proposed to use for renovation of Government's building did not meet the contract specifications. Jet Const. Co., Inc. v. U.S., Ct.Cl.1976, 531 F.2d 538, 209 Ct.Cl. 200. United States ☞ 74(11)

Substantial evidence supported findings of Armed Services Board of Contract Appeals that contract specification, which required contractor to tear up (or "break out") and remove six narrow strips of concrete or "laterals" from existing apron of airfield by jackhammers or percussion drills and hydraulic or mechanical expanders without cracking or damaging adjacent concrete or subgrade, did not explicitly permit use of heavy wheel-mounted pavement breakers known in industry as "stompers," and that damage which occurred to adjacent concrete and subgrade not only resulted from use of stompers but was excessive and would not have occurred had breakout been achieved by use of portable jackhammers, percussion drills and pavement expanders. Tri-Cor, Inc. v. U.S., Ct.Cl.1972, 458 F.2d 112, 198 Ct.Cl. 187. United States ☞ 74(11)

Evidence, in action by contractor against the United States to recover damages in its own behalf and in behalf of several of its subcontractors for alleged breach of warranty by the United States in connection with a construction contract, authorized finding that original drawings and addenda were in fact defective and inadequate. John McShain, Inc.

v. U.S., Ct.Cl.1969, 412 F.2d 1281, 188 Ct.Cl. 830. United States ☞ 74(11)

Substantial evidence supported finding of Corps of Engineers Board of Contract Appeals that contractor seeking damages resulting from necessary reworking of steel girders for dam had not proved that specifications were followed in initial fabrication of girders, that subcontractor deviated from specifications causing results which were a possible cause of cracking of welds, and that contractor failed to prove practical impossibility of performance pursuant to specifications. Tecon Corp. v. U.S., Ct.Cl.1969, 411 F.2d 1271, 188 Ct.Cl. 436. United States ☞ 74(11)

Finding that failure of certain lot of raincoats produced under government specifications was not due to surplus material but due to poor workmanship on part of contractor's employees was not supported by substantial evidence on the whole record. Centre Mfg. Co. v. U.S., Ct.Cl.1968, 392 F.2d 229, 183 Ct.Cl. 115. United States ☞ 74(11)

Finding by Armed Services Board of Contract Appeals that certain specification did not apply to contract was not based upon substantial evidence. Kings Electronics Co. v. U.S., Ct.Cl.1965, 341 F.2d 632, 169 Ct.Cl. 433. United States ☞ 74(11)

Evidence supported finding that no change in specifications under government contract for manufacture of photographic processing tray sets was authorized by any person having authority to make such a change, and finding was thus final and conclusive under this chapter. Bar Ray Products, Inc. v. U.S., Ct. Cl.1964, 340 F.2d 343, 167 Ct.Cl. 839. United States ☞ 73(14); United States ☞ 74(11)

Evidence supported finding of Armed Services Board of Contract Appeals that military supply contractor had submitted cable sample which complied with specifications of contract. Klein v. U.S., Ct.Cl. 1961, 285 F.2d 778, 152 Ct.Cl. 8. United States ☞ 74(11)

284. Suitability for use, substantial evidence for decision

Evidence supported finding of Armed Services Board of Contract Appeals that the microfilm furnished to contractor of radio transmitters was not suitable for making prints, on issue of government's liability for breach of warranty of the microfilm. Thompson Ramo Wooldridge Inc. v. U.S., Ct.Cl.1966, 361 F.2d 222, 175 Ct.Cl. 527. United States ⊶ 74(11)

285. Termination of contract, substantial evidence for decision

Findings of Department of Agriculture Board of Contract Appeals in respect to termination of contract to construct a campground in a national forest, when supported by substantial evidence in record and in harmony with relevant contract law, would be affirmed. Discount Co., Inc. v. U.S., Ct.Cl.1977, 554 F.2d 435, 213 Ct.Cl. 567, certiorari denied 98 S.Ct. 428, 434 U.S. 938, 54 L.Ed.2d 298. United States ⊶ 73(15)

Evidence in action challenging partial termination of contract for ignition cartridges for default of plaintiff's supply contract showed that plaintiff failed to sustain burden of showing that rejection of one lot of cartridges because of excess glue in flashtube, was improper because data package or specifications did not specify such defect as a critical defect or specify that as a point of inspection since method of applying glue was left to manufacturer and it was readily apparent that excessive glue could interfere with transmission of flash employed to ignite Cartridge. Penguin Industries, Inc. v. U.S., Ct.Cl.1976, 530 F.2d 934, 209 Ct.Cl. 121. United States ⊶ 74(11)

Evidence supported finding that there were substantial nonconformities in sample shelter furnished under government contract, not attributable to improper testing or defective specifications, justifying default termination. Astro Science Corp. v. U.S., Ct.Cl.1973, 471 F.2d 624, 200 Ct.Cl. 354. United States ⊶ 74(11)

Substantial evidence supported determination by General Services Board of Contract Appeals that failure of government contractor, which had entered into an indefinite quantity term contract with General Services Administration for manufacture and delivery of paint, to undertake production or to offer for delivery items to be procured under terminated purchase orders justified a default termination notwithstanding fact that acts by General Services Administration in administration of other contracts admittedly adversely affected contractor's ability to perform under all contracts. Allied Paint Mfg. Co., Inc. v. U.S., Ct.Cl.1972, 470

F.2d 556, 200 Ct.Cl. 313. United States ⊶ 74(11)

There was substantial evidence to support finding of armed services board of contract appeals that the government's termination of contract calling for production and delivery of 131 pressure ratio transducers of which four were preproduction samples for default because of inability of plaintiff contractor to produce acceptable preproduction samples meeting specifications as amended was a proper action by government and in exercise of the right reserved to it by contract, despite contractor's claim of impossibility of performance. Astronautics Corp. of America v. U.S., Ct.Cl.1971, 436 F.2d 430, 193 Ct.Cl. 910. United States ⊶ 74(11)

Decision of Armed Services Board of Contract Appeals with respect to amount payable under contracts terminated "for the convenience of the government" was supported by substantial evidence. Algonac Mfg. Co. v. U.S., Ct.Cl.1970, 428 F.2d 1241, 192 Ct.Cl. 649, supplemented 458 F.2d 1373, 198 Ct.Cl. 258. United States ⊶ 74(11)

In action by contractor against United States to recover either in quantum meruit the reasonable value of goods and services delivered to and accepted by Navy Department or for breach of contract because defendant failed to definitize letter contract, evidence established that the letter contract was never terminated, directly or constructively; in fact, evidence showed that the defendant, if anything, encouraged contractor to continue performance subsequent to emergence of dispute regarding contractor's fee. Sanders Associates, Inc. v. U.S., Ct.Cl.1970, 423 F.2d 291, 191 Ct.Cl. 157. United States ⊶ 74(11)

Finding of Armed Services Board of Contract Appeals in contractor's appeal from default termination that contracting officer was not mistaken in calculation of modified delivery date was supported by substantial evidence. Bromion, Inc. v. U.S., Ct.Cl.1969, 411 F.2d 1020, 188 Ct. Cl. 31. United States ⊶ 74(11)

286. Waiver, substantial evidence for decision

Evidence in government contract dispute in which contractor sought to have default termination by Government converted into a termination for convenience of Government supported finding of Armed Services Board of Contract Appeals that Government, whose offer to extend delivery schedule for a specified reduction in contract price was not accepted by contractor which did request clarification of specification while it halted production, did not waive a delivery schedule specified in contract. Switlik Parachute Co., Inc. v. U.S., Ct.Cl.1978, 573 F.2d 1228, 216 Ct.Cl. 362. United States ☞ 74(11)

287. Miscellaneous issues, substantial evidence for decision

Record supported finding of Board of Contract Appeals that contract specifications for air-conditioning units to be installed in government building were not restricted to a single manufacturer's unit. Jet Const. Co., Inc. v. U.S., Ct.Cl.1976, 531 F.2d 538, 209 Ct.Cl. 200. United States ☞ 74(11)

Presumption indulged in by Board of Contract Appeals in contract dispute that trail which contractor was to use to reach work area was entirely on government land, and that contractor's trespass onto Indian land was therefore due to his negligence in straying off the trail while improving it, was not supported by any substantial evidence. McKee v. U.S., Ct.Cl. 1974, 500 F.2d 525, 205 Ct.Cl. 303. United States ☞ 73(9)

Record did not establish that contract for construction of drydock required that cofferdam also serve as permanent water cut-off wall. Corbetta Const. Co. v. U.S., Ct.Cl.1972, 461 F.2d 1330, 198 Ct.Cl. 712. United States ☞ 70(8)

Finding by Armed Services Board of Contract Appeals that contractor's outside utility subcontractor's delays were not result of grading change made by the government was supported by evidence and entitled to finality. Electronic & Missile Facilities, Inc. v. U.S., Ct.Cl.1969, 416 F.2d 1345, 189 Ct.Cl. 237. United States ☞ 73(15); United States ☞ 74(11)

Finding of Corps of Engineers Board of Contract Appeals that contractor did not safely and economically operate two cranes at same time on then constructed portion of trestle in dam construction was supported by substantial evidence in contracts dispute proceeding. Paul Hardeman, Inc. v. U.S., Ct.Cl.1969, 406 F.2d 1357, 186 Ct.Cl. 743. United States ☞ 74(11)

Substantial evidence supported finding of Department of Commerce Appeals Board that road construction contractor's task of removing from roadway and disposing of uprooted trees, brush and other vegetation that had been deposited by landslides constituted "clearing and grubbing" work and that work involved in removing fallen timber from slide was no greater than work that would have been necessary if clearing and grubbing had been performed in advance of the slides. Clack v. U.S., Ct.Cl.1968, 395 F.2d 773, 184 Ct.Cl. 40. Highways ☞ 113(4)

Where contract imposed liability on warehouseman for loss of goods only if loss resulted from warehouseman's negligence or fault, and evidence disclosed that warehouse complied with fire safety regulations and fire was of unknown origin, and contracting officer's report recited no facts to support conclusion of negligence or fault on part of warehouseman, warehouseman could not be held liable for loss. U.S. v. Morrison, E.D.Va.1974, 370 F.Supp. 193. United States ☞ 75(2)

In action by dried milk producer against Commodity Credit Corporation for unpaid balance of price of dried milk sold, wherein Commodity Credit Corporation counterclaimed for same amount on ground that part of sale had been properly rescinded because some of dried milk had been infested with insects, evidence was sufficient to establish existence of insect infestation at Government warehouses. Land O'Lakes Creameries, Inc. v. Commodity Credit Corp., D.C.Minn. 1960, 185 F.Supp. 412, affirmed 308 F.2d 604. United States ☞ 53(17)

§ 322. Contract provisions making decisions final on questions of law

No Government contract shall contain a provision making final on a question of law the decision of any administrative official, representative, or board.

(May 11, 1954, c. 199, § 2, 68 Stat. 81.)

LIBRARY REFERENCES

American Digest System
United States ☞73(14), 73(15).
Key Number System Topic No. 393.

Research References

ALR Library

13 ALR, Fed. 2nd Series 261, Construction and Application of Patent Ambiguity Doctrine to Federal Government Contracts.

59 ALR, Fed. 905, Application of 28 U.S.C.A. § 2516(A) to Government Contractor's Claim for Interest Expense or for Loss of Use of Its Capital Caused by Delay Attributable to Government.

24 ALR, Fed. 317, Construction and Application of Truth in Negotiations Act (10 U.S.C.A. § 2306(F)), Requiring Prime Contractors and Subcontractors to Submit Cost or Pricing Data, Certified to Be Accurate, Complete, and Current, Respecting Certain Government Contracts.

19 ALR, Fed. 645, Reformation by United States Court of Claims of Government Contract.

2 ALR, Fed. 691, Judicial Review Under Wunderlich Act (41 U.S.C.A. §§ 321, 322), of Federal Administrative Decisions Made Under Standard "Disputes" Clauses in Government Contracts.

86 ALR 3rd 182, Public Contracts: Duty of Public Authority to Disclose to Contractor Information, Allegedly in Its Possession, Affecting Cost or Feasibility of Project.

85 ALR 3rd 1085, Construction Contract Provision Excusing Delay Caused by "Severe Weather".

163 ALR 1300, Validity, Construction, and Effect of Statutory or Contractual Provision in Government Construction Contract Referring to Secretary of Labor Questions Respecting Wage Rates or Classification of Employees of Contractor.

126 ALR 837, Constitutionality, Construction, and Application of Statute Providing for Correction or Relief from Consequences of Error or Mistake in Bids for Public Contract.

115 ALR 65, Right of Building or Construction Contractor to Recover Damages Resulting from Delay Caused by Default of Contractee.

88 ALR 1223, Power to Allow Additional Compensation to Public Contractor Over Amount Called for by His Contract.

Encyclopedias

Am. Jur. 2d Federal Tort Claims Act § 32, Other Legislation.

Am. Jur. 2d Public Works and Contracts § 117, Construction of Contract by Architect or Engineer--Administrative Decisions Under the Wunderlich Act.

14 Am. Jur. Trials 437, Representing the Government Contractor.

Forms

Am. Jur. Pl. & Pr. Forms Public Works & Contracts § 86, Petition--In Court of Federal Claims--For Review of Decision of Board of Contract Appeals--Under Contract Disputes Act of 1978--Improper Denial of Claims for Financing Costs.

Am. Jur. Pl. & Pr. Forms Public Works & Contracts § 98, Complaint in Federal Court--By Contractor--For Recovery of Reasonable Costs of Extra Work--Adjustment Sought Under Changes Clause.

Am. Jur. Pl. & Pr. Forms Public Works & Contracts § 103, Petition--In United States Court of Federal Claims--For Remission of Liquidated Damages Wrongfully Assessed Against Contractor.

Federal Procedural Forms § 34:313, Petition in Court of Appeals--For Review of Decision of Board of Contract Appeals--Equitable Adjustment Pursuant to Changes Clause; Issuance of Constructive Change Order Alleged [28 U.S.C.A. § 1295(a)(10); 41 U.S.C.A. § 607(g)(1); Fed. R. App. P. Rule 15(a)].

Federal Procedural Forms § 34:346, Petition--For Review of Decision of Board of Contract Appeals--Under Contract Disputes Act of 1978--Improper Denial of Claims for Financing Costs.

Treatises and Practice Aids
Federal Procedure, Lawyers Edition § 42:1954, Remedial Actions--Notice and Opportunity for Hearing.

WESTLAW ELECTRONIC RESEARCH

See Westlaw guide following the Explanation pages of this volume.

Notes of Decisions

Contract interpretation, questions of law
  5
Questions of fact   3
Questions of law   4, 5
  Generally   4
  Contract interpretation   5
Right to judicial review   2
Rulemaking   1
Waiver   6

_____

1. Rulemaking

This section did not afford affected parties basis on which to challenge rulemaking procedures by which Bureau of Reclamation effected rate increase for electrical power. Northern California Power Agency v. Morton, D.C.D.C.1975, 396 F.Supp. 1187, affirmed 539 F.2d 243, 176 U.S.App.D.C. 241. Electricity ☞ 11.3(7)

2. Right to judicial review

Eligibility of ship operators who had 20-year contracts with the United States providing for operating-differential subsidies to reimburse operators for part of a fair and reasonable cost of wages of officers and crews was governed by principles of contract law and not by the auguries of agency discretion and were subject, under this section, to the guarantee of at least a minimal measure of judicial review of administrative determination under any contract entered into by the United States. American Export Isbrandtsen Lines, Inc. v. U.S., Ct.Cl. 1974, 499 F.2d 552, 204 Ct.Cl. 424. Shipping ☞ 3; United States ☞ 73(15)

3. Questions of fact

Government and contractor may enter agreement which, by its terms, makes final a contracting officer's decision in dispute involving question of fact arising out of contract. U.S. v. Ulvedal, C.A.8 (N.D.) 1967, 372 F.2d 31. United States ☞ 73(14)

Standard disputes clause in Government contract includes any dispute concerning question of fact arising under contract, whether it arises during performance of contract or after completion. Silverman Bros., Inc. v. U.S., C.A.1 (R.I.) 1963, 324 F.2d 287. United States ☞ 73(9)

Amount of work performed by a contractor, and quantity of borrow pit fill used by a contractor in performing a Government contract for construction of riverside berm revetment and repair borrow pits, was a "question of fact" within provision of contract that any dispute concerning a question of fact arising under the contract shall be decided by the contracting officer. Happel v. U.S., E.D.Mo.1959, 176 F.Supp. 787, affirmed 279 F.2d 88. United States ☞ 73(9)

Where contract for sale of potatoes to Army provided that any dispute concerning a question of fact arising out of contract was to be decided by contracting officer, and only dispute arising between seller and Government was whether or not seller had been guilty of fraud in performance of its contract on facts arising wholly outside contract itself, contracting officer had neither authority nor duty to render decision with respect to controversy between seller and Government, and his failure in this regard could not affect accrual of seller's claim or right to prosecute claim in court. International Potato Corp. v. U.S., Ct.Cl.1958, 161 F.Supp. 602, 142 Ct.Cl. 604. United States ☞ 73(9)

Where suit against United States for breach of contract for purchase of rock and gravel involved construction of contract and presented no real dispute as to any facts, contract provision that decision of Secretary of Navy or his duly authorized representative was final and conclusive on any disputes concerning questions of fact was inapplicable, and fact that Board of Contract Appeals of Department of Navy had affirmed contracting officer's decision that plaintiff had no claim under contract was not controlling on question involved. Ready-Mix Concrete Co. v. U.S., Ct.Cl.1958, 158 F.Supp. 571, 141 Ct.Cl. 168. United States ☞ 73(14)

Under contract providing that all disputes concerning questions of fact arising under contract shall be decided by contracting officer of the United States subject to written appeal by contractor within 30 days to head of department, whose decision shall be final and conclusive, upon parties thereto decisions of fact of head of department were final and conclusive, in action by contractor against the United States. Palumbo v. U.S., Ct. Cl.1953, 113 F.Supp. 450, 125 Ct.Cl. 678. United States ☞ 73(14)

Whether unforeseeable and unusually severe weather existed, excusing performance of contract with Government for delivery of canned blackberries, was a question of fact, within provision of contract making the contracting officer's findings of fact conclusive on the parties. Mitchell Canneries v. U.S., Ct.Cl.1948, 77 F.Supp. 498, 111 Ct.Cl. 228. United States ☞ 73(14)

Where Government construction subcontract provided that dispute concerning question of fact should be decided by contracting officer and that his decision was appealable to chief of army engineers, whose decision should be conclusive upon the parties, and disputed question of fact had been submitted by parties to contracting officer and finally determined in favor of subcontractor by such officer and chief of engineers, decision of such officers was conclusive upon court in absence of fraud on part of officers. Evans Elec. Const. Co. v. Wm. S. Lozier, Inc., W.D.Mo.1946, 68 F.Supp. 256, appeal dismissed 162 F.2d 717. Contracts ☞ 285(1)

Interpretation of hauling contract was not a "question of fact" within provision that all disputes concerning questions of fact arising under contract should be decided by contracting officer, etc. Lundstrom v. U.S., D.C.Or.1941, 53 F.Supp. 709, affirmed 139 F.2d 792. United States ☞ 73(12)

When plaintiff was denied the right to retain its cash discounts up to one percent plaintiff appealed to the Secretary of the Navy who referred the question to the Navy Department Board of Contract Appeals for its report and recommendations and the Board reported the facts and recommended that the plaintiff's appeal be sustained as to one contract, designated as Contract NObs–100 and the Secretary adopted the Board's finding of facts but refused to make the decision on the merits which the Board had recommended, and dismissed the appeal and under the provisions of the contract the determination of the Secretary on appeal was final as to all matters of fact involved in the contract, the question of the retention of discounts was not a "matter of fact" within the meaning of the language of Government contracts, but was a question of the interpretation of a written document, commonly called a "question of law". McWilliams Dredging Co. v. U.S., Ct.Cl.1950, 118 Ct.Cl. 1. See, also, Cramp Shipbuilding Co. v. U.S., 1952, 122 Ct.Cl. 72.

Under the provisions of the contract entered into by the plaintiff with the Government to supply a quantity of rust compound the question of whether the rust compound met the required specifications was a question of fact to be decided by the contracting officer, whose decision was final under the contract, and plaintiff was not entitled to recover. Crystal Soap & Chemical Co. v. U.S., Ct.Cl.1945, 103 Ct.Cl. 166. Sales ☞ 168(1); United States ☞ 73(14)

4. Questions of law—Generally

Contractors cannot bargain away their right to full scale judicial review of administrative decisions on questions of law. Lockheed Aircraft Corp. v. U.S., Ct.Cl.1967, 375 F.2d 786, 179 Ct.Cl. 545. United States ☞ 73(15)

Question whether modification of contract is a "change" or a "termination" is question of law, and not within Government contract provision that questions of fact should be decided by contracting officer. J. W. Bateson Co. v. U.S., C.A.5 (Tex.) 1962, 308 F.2d 510. United States ☞ 73(9)

Claim of Government contractor for additional compensation for extra track lifting in performance of Government railroad rehabilitation contract arose out of dispute as to meaning of contract bid item, and was question of law on which administrative decision was not made final by contract, and contractor was entitled to review of claim. Wm. A. Smith Contracting Co. v. U.S., Ct.Cl.1961, 292 F.2d 854, 155 Ct.Cl. 44. United States ⏣ 73(14)

Where only questions of law were involved which were (1) whether retained 10% by District of Columbia was limited to insuring only that actual work of street and sewer construction be completed, or whether it also covered restoration of damaged property, and (2) whether interest should be allowed on sum retained in excess of 10%, decision of District Contract Appeals Board was not final and binding on the parties on such questions notwithstanding provision of contract that decision of such board should be final in view of this section providing that no Government contract should contain a provision making final on question of law, decision of any administrative official or board, and hence contractor could maintain action to recover the money withheld. Kenny Const. Co. v. District of Columbia, C.A.D.C.1959, 262 F.2d 926, 105 U.S.App.D.C. 8. District Of Columbia ⏣ 14

Provision of contract with housing authority for removal of prefabricated houses that decision of head of department should be final in case of disputes concerning questions of fact was not applicable to legal question whether contractor could recover for replacements and repairs necessitated by hurricane. Blair v. U.S., C.C.A.5 (Ala.) 1947, 164 F.2d 115, certiorari denied 68 S.Ct. 910, 333 U.S. 880, 92 L.Ed. 1155, rehearing denied 68 S.Ct. 1336, 334 U.S. 830, 92 L.Ed. 1758. United States ⏣ 73(14)

Authority of a Government contracting officer to render decision under contract providing that any dispute concerning questions of fact arising under contract which is not disposed of by agreement shall be decided by contracting officer, is limited strictly to factual questions arising from contract itself and does not extend to questions of law. International Potato Corp. v. U.S., Ct.Cl.1958, 161 F.Supp. 602, 142 Ct.Cl. 604. United States ⏣ 73(9)

Whether or not the contract required plaintiff to pay the increased wages to common laborers was not a question of fact but of law, and the contract did not require plaintiff to appeal to the contracting officer a ruling of the project engineer on the legal interpretation of the contract.

A.J. Paretta Contracting Co. v. U.S., Ct. Cl.1947, 109 Ct.Cl. 324. Contracts ⏣ 285(1); United States ⏣ 73(12)

5. ⸺ Contract interpretation, questions of law

In a suit under this section, it is for the Court of Claims to decide independently any issue as to the meaning of language in a contract. Blake Const. Co., Inc. v. U.S., Ct.Cl.1979, 597 F.2d 1357, 220 Ct. Cl. 56. United States ⏣ 73(14)

Armed Services Board of Contract Appeals' conclusion as to contract interpretation is not final and binding on court in action under this section and section 321 of this title since such is a question of law. Merando, Inc. v. U.S., Ct.Cl.1973, 475 F.2d 601, 201 Ct.Cl. 23. United States ⏣ 73(15)

In actions under this section and section 321 of this title, court is not bound by Armed Services Board of Contract Appeals interpretation of contract provisions since such is a matter of law which the court is free to answer independently. Merando, Inc. v. U.S., Ct.Cl.1973, 475 F.2d 598, 201 Ct.Cl. 19. United States ⏣ 73(15)

As the decisions of the Corps of Engineers Board of Contract Appeals on "changes" claims involved (with one exception) the interpretation of contract drawings or specifications, the administrative decisions related to questions of law, and the Board's decision were not binding on the Court of Claims, which was authorized by this section to consider those legal questions de novo. Woodcrest Const. Co. v. U.S., Ct.Cl.1969, 408 F.2d 406, 187 Ct.Cl. 249, certiorari denied 90 S.Ct. 2164, 398 U.S. 958, 26 L.Ed.2d 542. United States ⏣ 73(14)

Question whether United States violated contractual duty was one of law, and decision thereon by Agency for International Development Board of Contract Appeals was not entitled to finality, and rejection by Court of Claims of view of AID Board of Contract Appeals was not inconsistent with requirements of this section. Scherr & McDermott, Inc. v. U.S., Ct.Cl.1966, 360 F.2d 966, 175 Ct.Cl. 440. United States ⏣ 73(14)

Issue requiring interpretation of language of contract involved question of law, not question of fact as to which decision of Armed Services Board of Contract Appeals was made final by the contract. Guyler v. U.S., Ct.Cl.1963, 314 F.2d 506, 161 Ct.Cl. 159. United States ☞ 73(14)

Under this chapter providing that decision of Government board on Government contract is final unless fraudulent, capricious or arbitrary or not supported by substantial evidence, but providing that Government contracts may not contain provisions making final such decision on question of law, interpretation of contract remains question of law and board's decision thereon is subject to judicial review. John A. Johnson Contracting Corp. v. U.S., Ct.Cl.1955, 132 F.Supp. 698, 132 Ct.Cl. 645. United States ☞ 73(15)

In Wunderlich Act case, General Services Administration Board of Contract Appeals correctly interpreted terms of office space lease agreement using ordinary meaning, rather than adding gloss or attempting to glean subjective intentions of particular party; Board's statement that escalation clause was "poorly written" did not mean that Board was unable to find clear and controlling language on issues to be resolved, and thus parties' prior conduct, even if inconsistent with lease terms, was irrelevant. Town Center Management Corp. v. U.S., Fed.Cl.1994, 31 Fed.Cl. 763. United States ☞ 70(18)

The decision of a department head concerning a contract dispute involving a question of contract interpretation, i.e., a question of law, is not binding on the parties under this section. Commercial Metals Co. v. U.S., Ct.Cl.1966, 176 Ct.Cl. 343. United States ☞ 73(14)

Questions of interpretation of contract terms and specifications are not disputes as to questions of fact, and determination by U.S. Army contracting officer, under contract making his decisions of questions of fact binding on parties, was not binding on plaintiff where such determination involved interpretation of written specifications. Forest Box & Lumber Co. v. Fraser Brace Overseas Corp., N.Y.Sup. 1959, 184 N.Y.S.2d 66, 17 Misc.2d 619. Alternative Dispute Resolution ☞ 350

6. Waiver

Use of disputes mechanism in public contract can be waived as can bar to judicial trial of issues arising under the contract. Nager Elec. Co. v. U.S., Ct.Cl. 1968, 396 F.2d 977, 184 Ct.Cl. 390. United States ☞ 73(9)

A waiver by government agency of right to have issue resolved pursuant to disputes claim may be explicit or implied by agency's conduct; government agency's selection of a judicial forum constitutes a waiver of the right to invoke disputes clause. Tennessee Valley Authority v. Westinghouse Elec. Corp., E.D.Va. 1977, 429 F.Supp. 940. United States ☞ 73(9)

CHAPTER 6—SERVICE CONTRACT LABOR STANDARDS

CROSS REFERENCES

Fair labor standards, see 29 USCA § 201 et seq.
Indian Self–Determination Act contracts, see 25 USCA § 450j.
Occupational safety and health, see 29 USCA § 651 et seq.

LAW REVIEW AND JOURNAL COMMENTARIES

Representing the federal government contractor. James S. Ganther, 70 Fla.B.J. 58 (April 1996).

WESTLAW COMPUTER ASSISTED LEGAL RESEARCH

Westlaw supplements your legal research in many ways. Westlaw allows you to

● update your research with the most current information

● expand your library with additional resources

● retrieve current, comprehensive history citing references to a case with KeyCite

For more information on using Westlaw to supplement your research, see the Westlaw Electronic Research Guide, which follows the Explanation.

§ 351. Required contract provisions; minimum wages

(a) Every contract (and any bid specification therefor) entered into by the United States or the District of Columbia in excess of $2,500, except as provided in section 356 of this title, whether negotiated or advertised, the principal purpose of which is to furnish services in the United States through the use of service employees, shall contain the following:

(1) A provision specifying the minimum monetary wages to be paid the various classes of service employees in the performance of the contract or any subcontract thereunder, as determined by

641

the Secretary, or his authorized representative, in accordance with prevailing rates for such employees in the locality, or, where a collective-bargaining agreement covers any such service employees, in accordance with the rates for such employees provided for in such agreement, including prospective wage increases provided for in such agreement as a result of arm's length negotiations. In no case shall such wages be lower than the minimum specified in subsection (b) of this section.

(2) A provision specifying the fringe benefits to be furnished in the various classes of service employees, engaged in the performance of the contract or any subcontract thereunder, as determined by the Secretary or his authorized representative to be prevailing for such employees in the locality, or, where a collective-bargaining agreement covers any such service employees, to be provided for in such agreement, including prospective fringe benefits increases provided for in such agreement as a result of arm's-length negotiations. Such fringe benefits shall include medical or hospital care, pensions on retirement or death, compensation for injuries or illness resulting from occupational activity, or insurance to provide any of the foregoing, unemployment benefits, life insurance, disability and sickness insurance, accident insurance, vacation and holiday pay, costs of apprenticeship or other similar programs and other bona fide fringe benefits not otherwise required by Federal, State, or local law to be provided by the contractor or subcontractor. The obligation under this subparagraph may be discharged by furnishing any equivalent combinations of fringe benefits or by making equivalent or differential payments in cash under rules and regulations established by the Secretary.

(3) A provision that no part of the services covered by this chapter will be performed in buildings or surroundings or under working conditions, provided by or under the control or supervision of the contractor or any subcontractor, which are unsanitary or hazardous or dangerous to the health or safety of service employees engaged to furnish the services.

(4) A provision that on the date a service employee commences work on a contract to which this chapter applies, the contractor or subcontractor will deliver to the employee a notice of the compensation required under paragraphs (1) and (2) of this subsection, on a form prepared by the Federal agency, or will post a notice of the required compensation in a prominent place at the worksite.

(5) A statement of the rates that would be paid by the Federal agency to the various classes of service employees if section 5341 or section 5332 of Title 5 were applicable to them. The Secre-

tary shall give due consideration to such rates in making the wage and fringe benefit determinations specified in this section.

(b)(1) No contractor who enters into any contract with the Federal Government the principal purpose of which is to furnish services through the use of service employees and no subcontractor thereunder shall pay any of his employees engaged in performing work on such contracts less than the minimum wage specified under section 206(a)(1) of Title 29.

(2) The provisions of sections 352 to 354 of this title shall be applicable to violations of this subsection.

(Pub.L. 89–286, § 2, Oct. 22, 1965, 79 Stat. 1034; Pub.L. 92–473, §§ 1, 2, Oct. 9, 1972, 86 Stat. 789; Pub.L. 94–489, §§ 1, 2, Oct. 13, 1976, 90 Stat. 2358.)

HISTORICAL AND STATUTORY NOTES

Revision Notes and Legislative Reports

1965 Acts. The purpose of this bill is to provide labor standards for the protection of employees of contractors and subcontractors furnishing services to or performing maintenance service for Federal agencies. The service contract is the only remaining category of Federal contracts to which no labor standards protection applies. Federal construction contracts require compliance with labor standards under the Davis–Bacon Act and related statutes. Federal supply contracts also provide labor standards under the Walsh–Healey Public Contracts Act.

The bill is applicable to advertised or negotiated contracts in excess of $2,500, the principal purpose of which is to furnish services through the use of service employees. Service employees are defined in the bill as guards, watchmen, and any person in a recognized trade or craft, or other skilled mechanical craft, or in unskilled, semiskilled, or skilled manual labor occupations. Typical services furnished would also include laundry and drycleaning, custodial, janitorial, cafeteria, food, and miscellaneous housekeeping.

Persons covered by the bill must be paid no less than the prevailing rate in the locality as determined by the Secretary, including fringe benefits as an element of the wages. No less than the applicable minimum wage provided in the Fair Labor Standards Act, as amended, can be paid. In determining the prevailing rate in the locality, the Secretary will consider the compensation paid persons engaged in such service-type work and work of a similar type in the locality. The Secretary in determining the locality for such purpose would take a realistic view of the type of service contract intended to be covered by the determination.

In addition, the bill requires that work shall not be performed under unsafe or unsanitary working conditions.

Enforcement procedures are provided in the bill including the withholding of payments due the contractor under the contract and payments to the employees of amounts due them; suit by the United States against the contractor or surety to recover the amount of underpayment; cancellation of the contract for any violation with the contractor liable for any resulting cost to the United States; authority for the Secretary to list and withhold awarding further contracts to contractors violating this bill for up to 3 years; and authority to issue regulation under sections 4 and 5 of the Walsh–Healey Public Contracts Act to enforce this bill. The authority to list contractors violating this act specified in the bill and to recommend no further contracts of the United States be awarded such violators is subject to the provision of sections 4 and 5 of the Walsh–Healey Public Contracts Act. Contractors would therefore be entitled to the notice, hearing, and other procedures provided for in said act.

There are certain specific exemptions from coverage listed in section 7 including contracts covered by the Davis–Bacon

Act, the Walsh–Healey Public Contracts Act, the Interstate Commerce Commission, the Communication Acts of 1934; also, contracts for public utility services, direct employment by individuals, and for postal contract stations. Senate Report No. 89–748.

1972 Acts. Senate Report No. 92–1131, see 1972 U.S.Code Cong. and Adm.News, p. 3534.

1976 Acts. House Report No. 94–1571, see 1976 U.S.Code Cong. and Adm.News, p. 5211.

Amendments

1976   Amendments. Subsec. (a). Pub.L. 94–489, § 1(a), struck out "as defined herein" following "use of service employees".

Subsec. (a)(5). Pub.L. 94–489, § 2, added "or section 5332" following "section 5341".

Subsec. (b)(1). Pub.L. 94–489, § 1(b), struck out "as defined herein" following "use of service employees".

1972   Amendments. Subsec. (a)(1). Pub.L. 92–473, § 1(a), provided for minimum monetary wages to be paid service employees where collective-bargaining agreement covers any such service employees in accordance with the rates for such employees provided for in such agreement, including prospective wage increases provided for in such agreement as a result of arm's-length negotiations.

Subsec. (a)(2). Pub.L. 92–473, § 1(b), provided for fringe benefits to be furnished service employees where collective-bargaining agreement covers any such service employees, to be provided for in such agreement, including prospective fringe increases provided for in such agreement as a result of arm's-length negotiations.

Subsec. (a)(5). Pub.L. 92–473, § 2, added par. (5).

Effective and Applicability Provisions
1965 Acts. Section 9 of Pub.L. 89–286 provided that: "This Act [enacting this chapter] shall apply to all contracts entered into pursuant to negotiations concluded or invitations for bids issued on or after ninety days from the date of enactment of this Act [Oct. 22, 1965]."

Short Title
1965 Acts. Section 1 of Pub.L. 89–286 provided that: "This Act [enacting this chapter] may be cited as the 'Service Contract Act of 1965'."

CROSS REFERENCES

Determinations of minimum wage and fringe benefits to be made as soon as administratively feasible, see 41 USCA § 358.

CODE OF FEDERAL REGULATIONS

Federal Acquisition Regulations System, see 48 CFR § 1.000 et seq.
Labor standards, federal service contracts, see 29 CFR § 4.1 et seq.
Occupational safety and health standards, see 29 CFR § 1910.1 et seq.
Procedural rules for modification, etc., of occupational safety or health standards, see 29 CFR § 1911.1 et seq.
Safety and health standards in general, see 29 CFR § 1925.1 et seq.

LAW REVIEW AND JOURNAL COMMENTARIES

Comparable worth—The theory, its legal foundation, and the feasibility of implementation. Carin Ann Clauss, 20 U.Mich.J.L.Ref. 7 (1986).
Employer obligations under the Service Contract Act: Just another minimum wage law? James C. Fontana, 25 Public Contract L.J. 483 (1996).
The Department of Labor's regulations for the determination of minimum wages and benefits under this provision are at 29 C.F.R. pt. 4 (1994).

LIBRARY REFERENCES

American Digest System
Labor and Employment ⊙2243, 2304, 2350, 2563, 2838.
Key Number System Topic No. 231H.

Corpus Juris Secundum
CJS Labor Relations § 1103, Public Employees; Employees on Public Works.

CJS Labor Relations § 1293, Federal Service Contract Labor Standards Act.
CJS Labor Relations § 1302, Under Federal Law.

Research References

ALR Library

8 ALR, Fed. 2nd Series 611, Application of Local District Court Summary Judgment Rules to Nonmoving Party in Federal Courts--Statements of Facts.

152 ALR, Fed. 605, Construction and Application of Federal Tort Claims Act Provision (28 U.S.C.A. § 2680(H)) Excepting from Coverage Claims Arising Out of False Imprisonment, False Arrest, Malicious Prosecution, or Abuse of Process.

96 ALR, Fed. 411, What Constitutes Adequate Notice of Proposed Federal Agency Rule Against Objection That Rule Adopted Differed in Substance from That Published as Proposed in Notice.

63 ALR, Fed. 794, Obligations of Successor Contractor Under § 4(C) of Service Contract Act of 1965 (41 U.S.C.A. § 353(C)).

53 ALR, Fed. 272, Legal Issues Relating to Wage Rate Determinations by Secretary of Labor Under § 1 of Davis-Bacon Act (40 U.S.C.A. § 276a).

31 ALR, Fed. 348, What Limitation Periods Apply Under 28 U.S.C.A. § 2415 to Government Suits.

27 ALR, Fed. 702, Modern Status of Applicability of Doctrine of Estoppel Against Federal Government and Its Agencies.

2 ALR, Fed. 637, What Contracts Are Subject to Wage and Hour Requirements of Walsh-Healey Act (41 U.S.C.A. § 35).

161 ALR 1161, Relief from Stipulations.

153 ALR 1188, Comment Note.--Retroactive Operation of Regulation of Administrative Authority Amending a Previous Regulation.

150 ALR 700, What Constitutes a "Service Establishment" Within Exemption Provision of Fair Labor Standards Act.

134 ALR 1149, Civil Service Laws, Rules, or Regulations as Applicable to Persons Employed by One Under Contract with Municipal Corporation or Other Governmental Body to Do Certain Work for It or Its Residents.

126 ALR 837, Constitutionality, Construction, and Application of Statute Providing for Correction or Relief from Consequences of Error or Mistake in Bids for Public Contract.

118 ALR 715, Jurisdictional Amount Involved in Suit Arising Out of Labor Disputes.

65 ALR 835, Bidder's Variation from Specifications on Bid for Public Work.

Encyclopedias

Am. Jur. 2d Aliens and Citizens § 711, Calculation and Determination of Prevailing Wage--Occupation Subject to Wage Determination Under.

Am. Jur. 2d Bankruptcy § 1787, Property Held in Trust.

Am. Jur. 2d Bankruptcy § 1834, Labor and Employment.

Am. Jur. 2d Public Works and Contracts § 217, The Federal Service Contract Labor Standards Act.

Am. Jur. 2d Public Works and Contracts § 226, Service Contract Labor Standards Act.

Forms

Federal Procedural Forms § 37:96, Preemption--Federal Laws.

24A West's Legal Forms § 4.7, Prevailing Wage Laws.

28 West's Legal Forms § 21.18, Labor Standards Clauses -- Federal Service Contracts Exceeding $2,500.

Treatises and Practice Aids

Bankruptcy Service Lawyers Edition § 19:116, Service Contract Act.

Bankruptcy Service Lawyers Edition § 19:617, Service Contract Act.

Bankruptcy Service Lawyers Edition § 21:322, Nature of Court Order Needed-- Illustrative Particular Orders.

Bankruptcy Service Lawyers Edition § 21:336, Other Determinations.
Bankruptcy Service Lawyers Edition § 29:353, Contract Rights, Generally.
Federal Procedure, Lawyers Edition § 39:452, Labor Law Violations.
Federal Procedure, Lawyers Edition § 39:468, Protest Based Upon Apparent
    Solicitation Defect.
Federal Procedure, Lawyers Edition § 42:2298, Laws Which OSHA Supersedes.
Federal Procedure, Lawyers Edition § 42:2310, Government Contracting.
Federal Procedure, Lawyers Edition § 45:620, Calculation of Prevailing Wage--
    Davis-Bacon Act and Service Contract Act Occupations.
Immigration Law Service 2d § 4:249, Wages.
Immigration Law Service 2d § 4:253, Establishing Prevailing Wage: SWA Wage
    Determination--Service Contract Act (SCA) Wages.
Immigration Law Service 2d § 4:259, Documentation Supporting Wage State-
    ment--Prevailing Wage.
Immigration Law Service 2d § 8:114, Pre-Recruitment Considerations--Prevailing
    Wage Determination.
Immigration Law Service 2d BALCA DB CH 18, Prevailing Wage.
Labor Certification Handbook § 8:1, PERM Regulations.
West's Federal Administrative Practice § 320, Department of Labor--Office of
    Administrative Appeals.
West's Federal Administrative Practice § 615, Laws Applicable--Labor Conditions.

WESTLAW ELECTRONIC RESEARCH

See Westlaw guide following the Explanation pages of this volume.

Notes of Decisions

Unemployment   compensation,   fringe
  benefits   27
Vacation benefits, fringe benefits   28

1. Construction

This chapter is remedial labor legislation which must be liberally construed.
Midwest Maintenance & Const. Co., Inc.
v. Vela, C.A.10 (Okla.) 1980, 621 F.2d
1046.   Labor And Employment ☞ 2304

2. Construction with other laws

Qui tam False Claims Act (FCA) action
brought against federal contractor by former employee, for allegedly making
fraudulent reports to the United States
that it was in compliance with the Service Contract Act (SCA), was not equivalent of suit for SCA damages, which
would be foreclosed by SCA's bar on private actions; FCA claim was based on
contractor's reports to the United States
rather than its nonpayment of prevailing
wages, and amounts recoverable included
civil penalties plus three times damage to
the United States rather than lost wages.
U.S. ex rel. Sutton v. Double Day Office
Services, Inc., C.A.9 (Cal.) 1997, 121 F.3d
531.   United States ☞ 122

Firefighters and engineers who alleged
that government contractor did not properly compensate them stated claim under
Fair Labor Standards Act (FLSA), and
there was no conflict with Service Contract Act (SCA). Lee v. Flightsafety Services Corp., C.A.11 (Ga.) 1994, 20 F.3d
428.   Labor And Employment ☞ 2243;
Labor And Employment ☞ 2380(1)

Contract Work Hours Standards Act,
section 327 et seq. of Title 40, and this
chapter where applicable are both mutually supplemental to the Fair Labor Standards Act of 1938, section 201 et seq. of
Title 29; laborer is ordinarily entitled to
be paid in accordance with provisions
requiring greatest pay, but this does not
mean no other provisions may affect him.
Masters v. Maryland Management Co.,
C.A.4 (Md.) 1974, 493 F.2d 1329. Labor
And Employment ☞ 2220(1); Statutes
☞ 223.2(19)

Service Contract Act (SCA), which provides only administrative remedy to enforce wage protections it affords to employees of federal service contractors, did
not impliedly repeal FLSA's private enforcement provisions, and therefore employee of federal service contractor could
maintain suit against contractor for viola-

tion of FLSA despite fact that SCA also
governed employee's employment.   Ko-
ren v. Martin Marietta Services, Inc.,
D.Puerto Rico 1998, 997 F.Supp. 196.
Labor And Employment ☞ 2361; Labor
And Employment ☞ 2218(11)

Close intertwining of this section setting forth scope of coverage of this chapter with section 5102 of Title 5 setting
forth certain exclusions from section
5101 et seq. of Title 5 demonstrated that
Congress intended that this chapter
should cover no greater field than the
traditional blue collar definition applied
to section 5101 et seq. of Title 5. Federal
Elec. Corp. v. Dunlop, M.D.Fla.1976, 419
F.Supp. 221.   United States ☞ 66

3. Purpose

In passing the Service Contract Act,
Congress clearly intended to close a gap
in the otherwise comprehensive net of
federal contract legislation.   Menlo Service Corp. v. U.S., C.A.9 (Cal.) 1985, 765
F.2d 805.   Labor And Employment ☞
2243

Principal purpose of this chapter was
to establish minimum wage and fringe
benefit standards to be provided by successor employers.   Trinity Services, Inc.
v. Marshall, C.A.D.C.1978, 593 F.2d
1250, 193 U.S.App.D.C. 96.   Labor And
Employment ☞ 2217(1)

This chapter was passed to provide labor standards for protection of employees
of contractors who perform maintenance
service for federal agencies.   Masters v.
Maryland Management Co., C.A.4 (Md.)
1974, 493 F.2d 1329.   Labor And Employment ☞ 2217(1)

Primary purpose of Service Contract
Act is to provide wage and benefit protec-
tion to employees of federal contractors.
Halifax Technical Services, Inc. v. U.S.,
D.D.C.1994, 848 F.Supp. 240.   Labor
And Employment ☞ 2217(1)

Purpose of this chapter is to require
contractors to pay their employees working on a federal service contract in accordance with the prevailing rates and benefits for such employees in the locality.
Berry v. Andrews, M.D.Ala.1982, 535
F.Supp. 1317.

4. Contracts within section—Generally

Secretary of Labor was within his authority in adopting regulation providing
that Service Contract Act applied only to
contracts principally for provision of ser-

vices, even though Act once applied to separate line items for provision of services in contract not principally for services as a whole. American Federation of Labor and Congress of Indus. Organizations v. Donovan, C.A.D.C.1985, 757 F.2d 330, 244 U.S.App.D.C. 255. Labor And Employment ⬅ 2338

5. —— Principal purpose of contract, contracts within section

If principal purpose of contract was not clearing of land but was, rather, sale of salvaged materials, then, under principal-purpose test, contract would not be within scope of Service Contract Act. American Federation of Labor and Congress of Indus. Organizations v. Donovan, C.A.D.C.1985, 757 F.2d 330, 244 U.S.App.D.C. 255. Labor And Employment ⬅ 2243

6. —— Demolition contracts, contracts within section

Regulations with respect to timber sales, demolition/salvage, and engine rebuilding rested on common premise that Service Contract Act applied only to contracts principally for services and not to bid specifications for services in contracts not in whole principally for service, and that premise was properly reviewable as an interpretive rule, enjoying high protection of agency discretion under traditional "arbitrary and capricious" standard. American Federation of Labor and Congress of Indus. Organizations v. Donovan, C.A.D.C.1985, 757 F.2d 330, 244 U.S.App.D.C. 255. Labor And Employment ⬅ 2357

7. —— Mail haul contracts, contracts within section

Mail haul contracts between private employer and United States Postal Service were "service contracts" governed by this chapter. Nichols v. Mower's News Service, Inc., D.C.Vt.1980, 492 F.Supp. 258. Labor And Employment ⬅ 2243

8. —— Maintenance and operation of vessels, contracts within section

Secretary of Labor's determination that Service Contract Act applied to Department of the Navy's procurement for operation and maintenance of 12 oceanographic vessels had a rational basis and was consistent with statute and regulation. Marine Transport Lines, Inc. v.

Lehman, D.C.D.C.1985, 623 F.Supp. 330. Labor And Employment ⬅ 2350(2)

9. —— Maintenance and repair of equipment, contracts within section

Regulation granting exemption from requirements of Service Contract Act for contracts for maintenance and repair of certain automated data processing, scientific and medical, and office and business equipment, was not arbitrary or capricious, and was in accordance with law. American Federation of Labor and Congress of Indus. Organizations v. Donovan, C.A.D.C.1985, 757 F.2d 330, 244 U.S.App.D.C. 255. Labor And Employment ⬅ 2338

10. —— Reserve bank contracts, contracts within section

In light of previous judicial precedents finding Federal Reserve banks to be federal agencies or instrumentalities, in light of opinion of Attorney General concluding that reserve banks were covered by this chapter, and in light of general remedial nature and purposes of that provision, this chapter applied to service contracts of the Federal Reserve bank of Richmond, Virginia, with armored car companies, and declaratory and injunctive relief would be granted to bring those contracts into compliance with this chapter. Brink's, Inc. v. Board of Governors of Federal Reserve System, D.C.D.C. 1979, 466 F.Supp. 116. Labor And Employment ⬅ 2243

11. —— Timber sale contracts, contracts within section

If principal purpose of contract is sale of timber by government, any individual contract provision for services would not be within scope of Service Contract Act, which applies only when principal purpose of contract is for services. American Federation of Labor and Congress of Indus. Organizations v. Donovan, C.A.D.C.1985, 757 F.2d 330, 244 U.S.App.D.C. 255. Labor And Employment ⬅ 2243

Contract for sale of timber on Indian reservation was not principally for "services," within meaning of Service Contract Act, and thus that Act's requirement that contractor provide its employees with occupational compensation insurance and accident insurance was not applicable. Bear Medicine v. U.S., D.Mont. 1999, 47 F.Supp.2d 1172, reversed 241

F.3d 1208, on remand 192 F.Supp.2d
1053. Labor And Employment ⚬ 185

12. —— Travel management contracts, contracts within section

Secretary of Labor did not act arbitrarily and capriciously in determining that principal purpose of government travel management contracts was to furnish services, as opposed to selling concession rights to travel agencies, and that travel agencies entering into such contracts thus were covered by wage and benefit requirements of Service Contract Act; government did not enter into such contracts until after deregulation of airlines made services provided by travel agents particularly important. Ober United Travel Agency, Inc. v. U.S. Dept. of Labor, C.A.D.C.1998, 135 F.3d 822, 328 U.S.App.D.C. 410. Labor And Employment ⚬ 2295

13. —— Miscellaneous contracts, contracts within section

Recital in purchase orders concerning referral of employees to research facility operated by state university on behalf of United States that contract under which purchase orders issued was subject to Service Contract Act did not determine whether agreement was subject to the Act and, thus, Government's attempt to characterize service corporation's noncompliance with the Act as a breach of a voluntary contractual commitment was unpersuasive. Menlo Service Corp. v. U.S., C.A.9 (Cal.) 1985, 765 F.2d 805. Labor And Employment ⚬ 2243

Space shuttle processing contract, which eliminated all still photography positions and numerous film processor positions which had been performed by union members, was covered by Service Contract Act. Locals 666 and 780 of Intern. Alliance of Theatrical Stage Employees and Moving Picture Mach. Operators of United States and Canada, AFL-CIO v. U.S. Dept. of Labor, C.A.7 (Ill.) 1985, 760 F.2d 141, certiorari denied 106 S.Ct. 227, 474 U.S. 901, 88 L.Ed.2d 227. Labor And Employment ⚬ 2243

14. Illegibility of contract

Ambiguity because of illegible number in wage determination in government contract could not be construed in favor of government contractor under contra proferentem rule where contract would violate this chapter if it was so interpreted. Saavedra v. Donovan, C.A.9 (Cal.)

1983, 700 F.2d 496, certiorari denied 104 S.Ct. 236, 464 U.S. 892, 78 L.Ed.2d 227. Labor And Employment ⚬ 2350(3)

15. Classification of employees

The Navy, as contracting agency, did not owe contractor legal duty to clarify Department of Labor employee classifications for purposes of minimum wages to be paid on government contract, and did not possess authority to do so; it was the Department of Labor which possessed authority to resolve ambiguities. Collins Intern. Service Co. v. U.S., C.A.Fed.1984, 744 F.2d 812. United States ⚬ 70(23)

Price-based reformation of government contract based on improper classification of services under Service Contract Act did not require application of percentage increase in wages to other items of cost and profit in earlier contracts. Richlin Sec. Service Co. v. Ridge, C.A.Fed.2004, 99 Fed.Appx. 906, 2004 WL 1153349, Unreported. Reformation Of Instruments ⚬ 47

16. Expenses

Agency was not required to reimburse government contractor for administrative expenses it incurred in locating former employees and providing escrow services after it was determined that wages to lower level employees fell below level required by Service Contract Act (SCA). Richlin Sec. Service Co. v. Ridge, C.A.Fed.2004, 99 Fed.Appx. 906, 2004 WL 1153349, Unreported. United States ⚬ 70(18)

17. Locality of prevailing wage—Generally

Regulation promulgated by Secretary of Labor interpreting term "the locality," used in Service Contract Act as the location of each individual potential contractor constituted interpretive ruling that carried some weight and attracted some deference, but did not enjoy highest degree of deference available under "arbitrary and capricious" review. American Federation of Labor and Congress of Indus. Organizations v. Donovan, C.A.D.C. 1985, 757 F.2d 330, 244 U.S.App.D.C. 255. Labor And Employment ⚬ 2357

"Locality" as used in Walsh-Healey Act, sections 35 to 45 of this title is not synonymous with "locality" as used in this chapter. Southern Packaging and Storage Co., Inc. v. U.S., C.A.4 (S.C.)

1980, 618 F.2d 1088. Labor And Employment 🗝 2304

The "prevailing" wage rates under this section must be determined with reference to an objective standard of predominance or currency in a given locality, and it would therefore be permissible to define the prevailing wage in terms of the lowest rate only where that rate in fact reflects the wage which occurs most frequently; where no single wage is predominant, it is permissible to use an average. 1981 (Counsel-Inf. Op.) 5 Op. O.L.C. 174.

18. ——— Nature of contract, locality of prevailing wage

In enacting this chapter, Congress required wage levels based on prevailing wage rates in locality and further required Secretary, in determining "locality," to take a realistic view of type of contract intended to be covered by determination. Southern Packaging and Storage Co. v. U.S., D.C.S.C.1978, 458 F.Supp. 726, affirmed 618 F.2d 1088. Labor And Employment 🗝 2304

19. ——— Nationwide determinations, locality of prevailing wage

Regulation establishing two-step process for determining "locally prevailing wage" when locality of performance was unknown at time of bidding, in which potential bidders and their localities were identified, followed by wage determination for each locality, was in accordance with Service Contract Act, despite contention that wage determinations should have been nationwide. American Federation of Labor and Congress of Indus. Organizations v. Donovan, C.A.D.C.1985, 757 F.2d 330, 244 U.S.App.D.C. 255. Labor And Employment 🗝 2338

Appropriate "locality" for determining prevailing minimum wage under this chapter was standard metropolitan statistical area in which contractor was located, not entire nation. Southern Packaging and Storage Co., Inc. v. U.S., C.A.4 (S.C.) 1980, 618 F.2d 1088. Labor And Employment 🗝 2304

Neither this chapter nor Labor Department's manual of policies and procedures for administration of Service Contract Act required delegate of Secretary to limit "locality" covered by wage determination to isolated federal installation, and delegate's policy of avoiding making of enclave determinations under most circumstances did not violate any legal requirement. Kentron Hawaii, Ltd. v. Warner, C.A.D.C.1973, 480 F.2d 1166, 156 U.S.App.D.C. 274. Labor And Employment 🗝 2350(2)

20. ——— Place of contracting facility, locality of prevailing wage

Government contractor did not relinquish its claim that prevailing wage should be determined by county of performance, rather than county of contracting facility, by failing to protest wage determinations prior to making of award, since contractor had right, but not obligation, to seek clarification of bid invitation and contract, contractor did not intend to forsake, abandon or renounce its position, contractor kept adequate and accurate records and was prepared to cooperate with department in defense of its position and there was no showing that it obtained any advantage over competing bidders. Midwest Maintenance & Const. Co., Inc. v. Vela, C.A.10 (Okla.) 1980, 621 F.2d 1046. Labor And Employment 🗝 2345

Even if this chapter applied to keypunch operators, applicable wage determination with respect to bidder on government keypunching contract would be those prevailing for keypunch operators in Wilmington, Delaware area, the locality of bidder's principal place of business, and not the Washington, D.C. area, the locality of government installation. Descomp, Inc. v. Sampson, D.C.Del.1974, 377 F.Supp. 254. Labor And Employment 🗝 2304

21. ——— Place of performance, locality of prevailing wage

When government contract is of type where area of performance cannot be determined prior to bid solicitation, a realistic view dictates that each bidder should base his bid on prevailing wage rate, as determined by Department of Labor, in his own specific locality. Southern Packaging and Storage Co. v. U.S., D.C.S.C. 1978, 458 F.Supp. 726, affirmed 618 F.2d 1088. Labor And Employment 🗝 2243

Term "locality," in this section, refers to area where services are actually performed, rather than locality of government installation. Descomp, Inc. v. Sampson, D.C.Del.1974, 377 F.Supp. 254. United States 🗝 66

22. Retention of wage records

Government service contractor is required, under its contract, to keep complete wage data on hand and available to government for three years following completion of contract. Kentron Hawaii, Ltd. v. Warner, C.A.D.C.1973, 480 F.2d 1166, 156 U.S.App.D.C. 274. United States ⮞ 70(12.1)

23. Fringe benefits—Generally

Aircraft maintenance service contractor was not required to satisfy its fringe-benefit obligations under collective bargaining agreement (CBA) by making equivalent payments directly to its employees, rather than seeking price adjustment under Service Contract Act (SCA) price adjustment clause for increased costs of providing employees with defined-benefit health; if contractor paid its employees the "equivalent" of the fringe benefit, then applicable regulations would require it to pay them an amount equal to its own costs of providing the benefit and the extent of contractor's CBA-based obligations would remain unchanged. Lear Siegler Services, Inc. v. Rumsfeld, C.A.Fed.2006, 457 F.3d 1262. Labor And Employment ⮞ 1313; United States ⮞ 70(23)

Government contractor's method of cross-crediting fringe benefits for its employees, by which benefits were capped at 40 hours per week regardless of number of contracts, or hours per contract, employee actually worked, rather than awarded up to 40 hours per week per contract, did not violate McNamara–O'Hara Service Contract Act, as Act's intent was to base fringe benefits on typical nonovertime work week. Dantran, Inc. v. U.S. Dept. of Labor, C.A.1 (Me.) 1999, 171 F.3d 58. Labor And Employment ⮞ 2185

For purpose of this chapter, a bona fide "fringe benefit" is one which involves the present cost or the present risk of a future cost to the employer of the workers and is a benefit of the type of which its value to the recipient is capable of being ascertained in a different amount. Trinity Services, Inc. v. Marshall, C.A.D.C. 1978, 593 F.2d 1250, 193 U.S.App.D.C. 96. Labor And Employment ⮞ 2304

24. —— Nondirect benefits, fringe benefits

While variance hearing procedure authorized under this chapter might eventu-

ally detect a non-arm's length collective bargaining agreement provision, inclusion of statutory language on arm's length negotiation means that only bona fide wages and fringe benefits are within scope of this chapter; hence, where a nondirect wage benefit is determined not to be a bona fide fringe benefit no hearing is required to determine whether such benefit is substantially at variance with those prevailing for services of a character similar in the locality. Trinity Services, Inc. v. Marshall, C.A.D.C.1978, 593 F.2d 1250, 193 U.S.App.D.C. 96. Labor And Employment ⮞ 2348

25. —— Pension programs, fringe benefits

Findings of Secretary that janitorial service company's self-insurance health and welfare and pension program were fatally defective and did not satisfy requirements of this chapter were not supported by substantial evidence. White Glove Bldg. Maintenance, Inc. v. Hodgson, C.A.9 (Cal.) 1972, 459 F.2d 175. Labor And Employment ⮞ 256(1)

26. —— Severance payments, fringe benefits

Provision of incumbent contractor's bargaining agreement requiring a successor employer to make severance payment to incumbent's employees if successor did not hire the employees was not a bona fide "fringe benefit" within meaning of this chapter. Trinity Services, Inc. v. Marshall, C.A.D.C.1978, 593 F.2d 1250, 193 U.S.App.D.C. 96. Labor And Employment ⮞ 2300

27. —— Unemployment compensation, fringe benefits

Contractor's mistake in calculating a fixed hourly rate which undercompensated it for federal and state unemployment taxes was a mistake of judgment for which there was no remedy of contract reformation, as contractor was clearly on notice that its 2008–hour cost calculation was not consistent with the base period of the contract, and it could conceivably have adjusted its profit margin or other more flexible cost elements accordingly. United Intern. Investigative Services, Inc. v. U.S., Fed.Cl.2003, 56 Fed.Cl. 619. Reformation Of Instruments ⮞ 17(1)

Workers' compensation and unemployment insurance are "fringe benefits" within meaning of the Services Contract Act (SCA) which requires every government contract to contain provision specifying fringe benefits to be furnished employees. Aleman Food Services, Inc. v. U.S., Cl.Ct.1992, 25 Cl.Ct. 201, reversed 994 F.2d 819. Labor And Employment ☞ 2299

This section providing that federal government contract shall contain provision specifying the fringe benefits which contractor was required to furnish employees engaged in performance of contract as determined by the Secretary of Labor or his authorized representative to be prevailing for such employees in locality did not require unemployment compensation coverage for state political subdivision which did not elect coverage under Employment Security Act, section 1101 et seq. of Title 42, and did not make contributions to employment security fund; thus, where Secretary never made any determination as to fringe benefits, employee who was employed by political subdivision in performance of federal government contract was not entitled to unemployment compensation. Baldisserotto v. State Employment Sec. Dept., Wash.App.1973, 507 P.2d 891, 8 Wash. App. 531, review denied. Unemployment Compensation ☞ 26

28. —— Vacation benefits, fringe benefits

Under the Service Contract Act, contracting agency had no discretion to authorize successor contractor to pay vacation benefits which accrued under

predecessor contractors or to warrant reimbursement after the fact; to the extent government had other, ongoing contracts with the predecessor contractors, it could only, upon findings of fact after notice and hearings, withhold payment under those other contracts in order to make compensation "directly to the underpaid employees," not to successor contractor. United Intern. Investigative Services, Inc. v. U.S., Fed.Cl. 2003, 56 Fed.Cl. 619. Labor And Employment ☞ 2337

29. Injunctions

Unsuccessful bidder on Marine Corps contract for maintenance of military equipment and supplies loaded aboard prepositioning ships was not entitled to preliminary injunction preventing award of contract to successful bidder, as its likelihood of success on merits of claim that costs realism analysis was flawed and that bid would cause successful bidder to violate Service Contract Act was negligible, and both Marine Corps and successful bidder would suffer substantial harm if performance of contract was stayed. Halifax Technical Services, Inc. v. U.S., D.D.C.1994, 848 F.Supp. 240. Injunction ☞ 138.63

30. Private right of action

No private right of action exists under Service Contract Act (SCA). Lee v. Flightsafety Services Corp., C.A.11 (Ga.) 1994, 20 F.3d 428. Action ☞ 3

§ 352. Violations

(a) Liability of responsible party; withholding payments due on contract; payment of underpaid employees from withheld payments

Any violation of any of the contract stipulations required by section 351(a)(1) or (2) or of section 351(b) of this title shall render the party responsible therefor liable for a sum equal to the amount of any deductions, rebates, refunds, or underpayment of compensation due to any employee engaged in the performance of such contract. So much of the accrued payment due on the contract or any other contract between the same contractor and the Federal Government may be withheld as is necessary to pay such employees. Such withheld sums shall be held in a deposit fund. On order of the Secretary, any compensation which the head of the Federal agency or the Secretary has found to be due pursuant to this chapter shall be paid directly to the underpaid employees from any accrued payments withheld under this chapter.

(b) Enforcement of section

In accordance with regulations prescribed pursuant to section 353 of this title, the Federal agency head or the Secretary is hereby authorized to carry out the provisions of this section.

(c) Cancellation of contract; contracts for completion of original contract; liability of original contractor for additional cost

In addition, when a violation is found of any contract stipulation, the contract is subject upon written notice to cancellation by the contracting agency. Whereupon, the United States may enter into other contracts or arrangements for the completion of the original contract, charging any additional cost to the original contractor.

(Pub.L. 89–286, § 3, Oct. 22, 1965, 79 Stat. 1035.)

HISTORICAL AND STATUTORY NOTES

Revision Notes and Legislative Reports
1965 Acts. Senate Report No. 89–748, see 1965 U.S.Code Cong. and Adm.News, p. 3737.

LIBRARY REFERENCES

American Digest System
Labor and Employment ⟐2337.
United States ⟐75(1).
Key Number System Topic Nos. 231H, 393.

Research References

Encyclopedias
Am. Jur. 2d Public Works and Contracts § 217, The Federal Service Contract Labor Standards Act.
Am. Jur. 2d Public Works and Contracts § 226, Service Contract Labor Standards Act.

Treatises and Practice Aids
Bankruptcy Service Lawyers Edition § 29:353, Contract Rights, Generally.

WESTLAW ELECTRONIC RESEARCH

See Westlaw guide following the Explanation pages of this volume.

Notes of Decisions

Amount of repayments   5
Authority of Secretary   1
Garnishment, withholding of payments   4
Persons bound by administrative determinations   2
Persons entitled to maintain action   6
Persons liable   7
Withholding of payments   3, 4
Generally   3
Garnishment   4

1. Authority of Secretary
Secretary of Labor had not failed to discharge statutory duty to enforce mini-

mum wage provisions of Service Contract Act, by declining to pursue more than two years of arrearage on affected employees' back pay entitlement, so as to permit affected employee to maintain mandamus action against Secretary; policy helped to conserve scarce resources and enable more cases to be investigated. Barron v. Reich, C.A.9 (Cal.) 1994, 13 F.3d 1370. Mandamus ⚖ 73(1)

In order to insure that no employee of government contractor suffers underpayment of compensation in form of fringe benefits, Secretary may properly order the government contractor to make cash payments. White Glove Bldg. Maintenance, Inc. v. Hodgson, C.A.9 (Cal.) 1972, 459 F.2d 175. Labor And Employment ⚖ 2184

2. Persons bound by administrative determinations

Findings, conclusions and decision of hearing examiner as to amounts of underpayments by defendant to its employees in violation of this chapter and government contracts were binding on defendant employer's surety, even though surety was not a party to the administrative hearing and had no actual notice thereof. U.S. v. Powers Bldg. Maintenance Co., W.D.Okla.1972, 336 F.Supp. 819. Labor And Employment ⚖ 2357

3. Withholding of payments—Generally

Equities did not justify bankruptcy court's revocation of its approval of stipulation whereby funds were withheld by government from payments due debtor to cure debtor's arrears in benefit payments to union fund under Service Contract Act under debtor's contract to provide mess attendant services at two Army bases, where government did not pursue other available remedies for debtor's default and debtor's employees continued to work under the contract, which remained in force by reason of the court's first order, and bankruptcy estate would have been depleted without their labor. In re Harris Management Co., Inc., C.A.9 (Cal.) 1986, 791 F.2d 1412. Stipulations ⚖ 13

Under the Service Contract Act, contracting agency had no discretion to authorize successor contractor to pay vacation benefits which accrued under predecessor contractors or to warrant reimbursement after the fact; to the extent government had other, ongoing contracts with the predecessor contrac-

tors, it could only, upon findings of fact after notice and hearings, withhold payment under those other contracts in order to make compensation "directly to the underpaid employees," not to successor contractor. United Intern. Investigative Services, Inc. v. U.S., Fed.Cl. 2003, 56 Fed.Cl. 619. Labor And Employment ⚖ 2337

Withholding procedures accomplished by Department of Labor under Services Contract Act, which allows federal government to withhold payment due contractor in amount equal to compensation found to be due workers under the Act, did not extinguish all of debtor's rights and interests in accounts receivable withheld, where no definitive amount was found to be due debtor's employees under Act, payment withheld was not deposited into deposit fund as statutorily required, and no order to pay amount withheld to underpaid employees was ever issued by Secretary of Labor. In re Professional Technical Services, Inc., Bkrtcy.E.D.Mo. 1987, 71 B.R. 946, reversed. Bankruptcy ⚖ 2531

Even if withholding of payments on mail hauling contract with Chapter 11 debtor's principal at direction of Department of Labor were to enforce employee claims, debtor's principal was personally liable as "party responsible" for violation, so that withholding was against principal personally and not levy against debtor in violation of automatic stay, where record showed no transfers or assignments of mail hauling contracts from principal to debtor and principal directed and controlled employment practices and management policy both before and after incorporation of debtor. In re Frank Mossa Trucking, Inc., Bkrtcy.D.Mass. 1985, 65 B.R. 715. Bankruptcy ⚖ 2394.1

4. —— Garnishment, withholding of payments

Funds withheld at Department of Labor's request pursuant to Service Contract Act [Service Contract Act of 1965, §§ 2 et seq., 41 U.S.C.A. §§ 351 et seq.] to compensate underpaid employees of judgment debtor were not subject to garnishment prior to commencement of administrative proceeding to reduce Department's claim to judgment. Amoco Oil Co. v. Southeastern Mail Transport, Inc., M.D.Fla.1985, 628 F.Supp. 37. Garnishment ⚖ 58

5. Amount of repayments

Where janitorial service company, which performed services at air force base, obtained windfall by reason of inefficient distribution of notice of the company's self-insurance health and welfare and pension plans, the company would be required to pay 20 cents an hour for each hour worked by employees who worked between August 7, 1967, and date on which union implemented its health, welfare and pension plans and who had received no benefits or filed no claim, or until the employee's name appeared on January 10, 1968, or March 10, 1969, payroll lists, or until company could prove that the particular employee had actual notice of the self-insurance plan, whichever was sooner. Amoco Oil Co. v. Southeastern Mail Transport, Inc., M.D.Fla.1985, 628 F.Supp. 37.

6. Persons entitled to maintain action

Incumbent contractor waived its objection to terms of government solicitation for contract to provide concession services at national historic landmark site based upon solicitation's failure to require compliance with Service Contract Act when, despite having opportunity to do so, incumbent contractor failed to raise issue prior to closing of bidding process. Blue & Gold Fleet, L.P. v. U.S., C.A.Fed.2007, 2007 WL 1815678. United States ☞ 64.60(3.1)

Unions representing members employed by unsuccessful bidders for public contract lacked standing to challenge any violations of Service Contract Act in awarding of contract; members' injury, due to loss of jobs, was neither fairly traceable to allegedly illegal omission of wage determination from contract nor fairly redressable by resolicitation of contract remedies sought by unions. National Maritime Union of America v. Commander, Military Sealift Command, C.A.D.C.1987, 824 F.2d 1228, 263

U.S.App.D.C. 248. Labor And Employment ☞ 1982

Bid protestor's contention that United States Park Service violated the Service Contract Act in solicitation for ferry services by not requiring bidders to submit wages computed in accordance with the Act constituted a challenge to term of solicitation, and protestor's failure to contest term before submission of proposals precluded its subsequent protest of term in bid protest before the Court of Federal Claims. Blue & Gold Fleet, LP v. U.S., Fed.Cl.2006, 70 Fed.Cl. 487. United States ☞ 64.55(2)

7. Persons liable

Service Contract Act does not hold a successor contractor liable if the predecessor contractor does not pay accrued benefits; provisions of implementing regulation merely confirm that, if a contractor succeeds to a contract, he must maintain the level of wages and benefits already in place, not that he then takes on legal responsibility for obligations over which the predecessor contractor has defaulted. United Intern. Investigative Services, Inc. v. U.S., Fed.Cl.2003, 56 Fed.Cl. 619. Labor And Employment ☞ 2227

Conclusion that president of company that provided security-guard services at Navy base was the party responsible for company's violations of the McNamara–O'Hara Service Contract Act (SCA), as well as the factual findings underlying conclusion, were supported by evidence, including testimony of operations manager for company's security contract, even if there was conflicting evidence suggesting that manager's supervisor had been responsible for the day-to-day operations of the company. Johnson v. U.S. Dept. of Labor, C.A.6 (Ohio) 2006, 205 Fed.Appx. 312, 2006 WL 2373390, Unreported. Labor And Employment ☞ 2347

§ 353. Law governing authority of Secretary

(a) Enforcement of chapter

Sections 38 and 39 of this title shall govern the Secretary's authority to enforce this chapter, make rules, regulations, issue orders, hold hearings, and make decisions based upon findings of fact, and take other appropriate action hereunder.

(b) Limitations and regulations allowing variations, tolerances, and exemptions

The Secretary may provide such reasonable limitations and may make such rules and regulations allowing reasonable variation, tolerances, and exemptions to and from any or all provisions of this chapter (other than section 358 of this title), but only in special circumstances where he determines that such limitation, variation, tolerance, or exemption is necessary and proper in the public interest or to avoid the serious impairment of government business, and is in accord with the remedial purpose of this chapter to protect prevailing labor standards.

(c) Predecessor contracts; employees' wages and fringe benefits

No contractor or subcontractor under a contract, which succeeds a contract subject to this chapter and under which substantially the same services are furnished, shall pay any service employee under such contract less than the wages and fringe benefits, including accrued wages and fringe benefits, and any prospective increases in wages and fringe benefits provided for in a collective-bargaining agreement as a result of arm's-length negotiations, to which such service employees would have been entitled if they were employed under the predecessor contract: *Provided,* That in any of the foregoing circumstances such obligations shall not apply if the Secretary finds after a hearing in accordance with regulations adopted by the Secretary that such wages and fringe benefits are substantially at variance with those which prevail for services of a character similar in the locality.

(d) Duration of contract

Subject to limitations in annual appropriation Acts but notwithstanding any other provision of law, contracts to which this chapter applies may, if authorized by the Secretary, be for any term of years not exceeding five, if each such contract provides for the periodic adjustment of wages and fringe benefits pursuant to future determinations, issued in the manner prescribed in section 351 of this title no less often than once every two years during the term of the contract, covering the various classes of service employees.

(Pub.L. 89–286, § 4, Oct. 22, 1965, 79 Stat. 1035; Pub.L. 92–473, § 3, Oct. 9, 1972, 86 Stat. 789.)

HISTORICAL AND STATUTORY NOTES

Revision Notes and Legislative Reports
1965 Acts. Senate Report No. 89–748, see 1965 U.S.Code Cong. and Adm.News, p. 3737.

1972 Acts. Senate Report No. 92–1131, see 1972 U.S.Code Cong. and Adm.News, p. 3534.

Amendments

1972   Amendments. Subsec. (b). Pub.L. 92–473, § 3(a), excluded section 358 of this title from being subject to Secretary's authority to provide limitations and to make regulations respecting application of provisions of this chapter, substituted "but only in special circumstances where he determines that such limitation, variation, tolerance, or exemption is necessary and proper" for "as he may find necessary and proper", and authorized administrative action in accord with the remedial purpose of this chapter to protect prevailing labor standards.

Subsecs. (c), (d). Pub.L. 92–473, § 3(b), added subsecs. (c) and (d).

CODE OF FEDERAL REGULATIONS

Rules of practice, see 29 CFR § 6.1 et seq., 41 CFR § 50–203.1 et seq.

Rules of procedure, promulgating occupational safety or health standards, see 29 CFR § 1911.1 et seq.

LIBRARY REFERENCES

American Digest System

Labor and Employment ☞2336 to 2351.

Key Number System Topic No. 231H.

Corpus Juris Secundum

CJS Labor Relations § 1293, Federal Service Contract Labor Standards Act.

Research References

ALR Library

63 ALR, Fed. 794, Obligations of Successor Contractor Under § 4(C) of Service Contract Act of 1965 (41 U.S.C.A. § 353(C)).

149 ALR 276, Claims Based on Provisions of Statutes Relating Specifically to Rights, Duties, and Obligations Between Employer and Employee as Subject to Arbitration Provisions of Contracts or Statutes.

Treatises and Practice Aids

Federal Procedure, Lawyers Edition § 39:306, How to Request Exemption or Variance.

Federal Procedure, Lawyers Edition § 39:315, Introduction.

West's Federal Administrative Practice § 615, Laws Applicable--Labor Conditions.

WESTLAW ELECTRONIC RESEARCH

See Westlaw guide following the Explanation pages of this volume.

Notes of Decisions

Administrative review 14-17
    Generally 14
    Burden of proof 15
    Exclusiveness of enforcement proce-
        dure 16
    Interim appellate authority 17
Attorney fees 29
Bid preparation costs 30
Burden of proof 28
Burden of proof, administrative review
    15
Complaint 25
Displaced employees, persons entitled to
    maintain action 21
Exclusiveness of enforcement procedure,
    administrative review 16

Failure of Secretary to issue, wage deter-
    mination 8
Good-faith bargaining, predecessor con-
    tracts 2
Hearing, wage determination 12
Injunction 31
Interim appellate authority, administra-
    tive review 17
Jurisdiction 19
Labor Department review, wage determi-
    nation 13
Number of employees, wage determina-
    tion 9
Persons entitled to maintain action
    20-24
    Generally 20
    Displaced employees 21

---

1. Predecessor contracts—Generally

Aircraft maintenance service contractor was subject to Service Contract Act's (SCA) successor contractor rule; contractor succeeded another contractor on original contract and succeeded itself during its first option year. Lear Siegler Services, Inc. v. Rumsfeld, C.A.Fed.2006, 457 F.3d 1262. Labor And Employment ☞ 1291

Successor contractor asserting that collective bargaining agreement to which his predecessor was party was not result of arm's length negotiations, such that successor would not be bound by agreement's wage rate under McNamara-O'Hara Service Contract Act, had to ap-

ply to Secretary of Labor for determination; it was not open to successor contractor to take it on its own to decide that predecessor's agreement was not properly negotiated and leave all in suspense until there was administrative complaint and trial. Vigilantes, Inc. v. Administrator of Wage and Hour Div., U.S. Dept. of Labor, C.A.1 (Puerto Rico) 1992, 968 F.2d 1412. Labor And Employment ☞ 2345

Regulations, under which successor contract provisions of Service Contract Act would apply only when successor contractor would provide substantially same services in same locality, were in accordance with law. American Federation of Labor and Congress of Indus. Organizations v. Donovan, C.A.D.C.1985, 757 F.2d 330, 244 U.S.App.D.C. 255. Labor And Employment ☞ 2338

Any wage determination issued under this chapter must contain the wage and fringe benefit provisions of any collective bargaining agreement between the incumbent employer and any union representing the service employees to the extent that this chapter requires their inclusion and the successor contractor must pay the wages and provide the benefits unless it is found that such wages and fringe benefits are substantially at variance with those which prevail for services of a character similar in the locality. Trinity Services, Inc. v. Marshall, C.A.D.C.1978, 593 F.2d 1250, 193 U.S.App.D.C. 96. Labor And Employment ☞ 1225

Where relationship between predecessor and successor employers is one of replacement in the periodic rebidding context, so that demonstration of continuity in the identity of the enterprise depends completely upon the continuity of the employee complement, the continuity in the identity of the work force must be more substantially established to oblige successor to arbitrate under its predecessor's union contract than would be required where the relationship between the predecessor and successor employers is one of merger, or purchase and sale. Boeing Co. v. International Ass'n of Machinists and Aerospace Workers, AFL-CIO, C.A.5 (Fla.) 1974, 504 F.2d 307, certiorari denied 95 S.Ct. 1570, 421 U.S. 913, 43 L.Ed.2d 779. Labor And Employment ☞ 1547

When operation-maintenance contract was awarded on 21st May 1971, requirement that successor employer honor collective agreement to which predecessor and its union were parties did not apply to government contractors. Kentron Hawaii, Ltd. v. Warner, C.A.D.C.1973, 480 F.2d 1166, 156 U.S.App.D.C. 274. Labor And Employment ⬤➡ 1291

2. ——— Good-faith bargaining, predecessor contracts

Where new collective bargaining agreement between government contractor and its employees' union was not result of arms-length negotiations, it did not provide basis for price adjustment during contract renewal periods. Guardian Moving and Storage Company, Inc. v. Hayden, C.A.Fed.2005, 421 F.3d 1268, rehearing denied. United States ⬤➡ 70(21)

Even if government contracting officer in awarding service contract should have anticipated application of "successor employer" doctrine which was not, under existing law, applicable when contract was awarded, and even if there was an accompanying requirement of good-faith bargaining, there was no inherent illegality in nonunion contractor's proposal where, though proposal did envision some efforts to avoid unionization, it did not appear that a refusal to bargain in good faith would necessarily occur if legal duty were to arise. Kentron Hawaii, Ltd. v. Warner, C.A.D.C.1973, 480 F.2d 1166, 156 U.S.App.D.C. 274. Labor And Employment ⬤➡ 1265

3. ——— Remittance of union dues, predecessor contracts

Even though labor contract of predecessor National Aeronautics and Space Administration contractor was not applicable to successor, inasmuch as successor had labor contract with union, successor's remittance to union of union dues which successor had checked off and escrowed would not violate Labor Management Relations Act, 1947, section 141 et seq. of Title 29. Boeing Co. v. International Ass'n of Machinists and Aerospace Workers, AFL–CIO, C.A.5 (Fla.) 1974, 504 F.2d 307, certiorari denied 95 S.Ct. 1570, 421 U.S. 913, 43 L.Ed.2d 779. Labor And Employment ⬤➡ 1291

4. ——— Retention of benefit levels, predecessor contracts

Changes in costs arising from collective bargaining agreement (CBA), that required aircraft maintenance service contractor to pay whatever was necessary for it to meet its obligations to its employees, in light of changes in costs of providing employees with an agreed-upon level of health care benefit, triggered Service Contract Act's (SCA) price adjustment clause, even though there were no increases in the benefits themselves. Lear Siegler Services, Inc. v. Rumsfeld, C.A.Fed.2006, 457 F.3d 1262. United States ⬤➡ 70(23)

5. ——— Retention of employees, predecessor contracts

Successor government building cleaning contractor was not required under this chapter, imposing upon successor employer to pay wages and fringe benefits agreed to in predecessor's collective bargaining agreement, to retain the predecessor's employees who were members of local union which had collective bargaining contract with predecessor and to arbitrate disputes under such contract. Service Emp. Intern. Union, Local Union No. 36 v. General Services Administration, E.D.Pa.1977, 443 F.Supp. 575. Labor And Employment ⬤➡ 1291; Labor And Employment ⬤➡ 1547

6. ——— Seniority rights, predecessor contracts

Under this chapter, which requires that successor contractor grant employees the same wages and fringe benefits as were provided under predecessor's collective bargaining agreement, successor contractor was not required to recognize successorship and seniority rights acquired by predecessor contractor's employees under collective bargaining agreement with predecessor. Clark v. Unified Services, Inc., C.A.5 (Fla.) 1981, 659 F.2d 49. Labor And Employment ⬤➡ 2304

In considering seniority requirements in a wage determination under this chapter, requires no more than that the successor employer must give an employee it hires credit for similar work performed at the federal facility and that the successor provide workers with an equal amount of seniority the same wage and fringe benefits they would have received under the predecessor's contract; as regarded seniority, this chapter requires no more than the above. Trinity Services, Inc. v. Marshall, C.A.D.C.1978, 593 F.2d 1250, 193 U.S.App.D.C. 96. Labor And Employment ☞ 1225

7. Wage determination—Generally

While 1972 amendment to this chapter may have further restricted Secretary of Labor's discretion not to issue wage determination, such amendments did not create new remedies against contractors. International Ass'n of Machinists and Aerospace Workers, AFL-CIO v. Hodgson, C.A.D.C.1975, 515 F.2d 373, 169 U.S.App.D.C. 142. Labor And Employment ☞ 2362

Exemption standards as provided by this chapter gave Labor Department discretion to allocate its own scarce resources in determining whether, in particular case, to issue complete area wage determination, partial wage determination, enclave wage determination, or no determination at all. Kentron Hawaii, Ltd. v. Warner, C.A.D.C.1973, 480 F.2d 1166, 156 U.S.App.D.C. 274. Labor And Employment ☞ 2350(1)

8. —— Failure of Secretary to issue, wage determination

Service contract between National Aeronautics and Space Administration and government contractor was valid despite failure of Secretary of Labor to make pervasive wage determination pursuant to this chapter. International Ass'n of Machinists and Aerospace Workers, AFL-CIO v. Hodgson, C.A.D.C.1975, 515 F.2d 373, 169 U.S.App.D.C. 142. United States ☞ 66

Labor Department does not have unlimited discretion in deciding whether to issue wage determination under this chapter, but Labor Department does have authority to withhold wage determination in some cases, including instances in which refusal to issue determination is justified as necessary and proper in public interest or to avoid serious impairment of government business. Kentron Hawaii, Ltd. v. Warner, C.A.D.C.1973, 480 F.2d 1166, 156 U.S.App.D.C. 274. Labor And Employment ☞ 2350(1)

9. —— Number of employees, wage determination

Under evidence, including evidence showing that government service contract involved relatively few employees, great diversity of job classifications and wide

geographical distribution of employment sites, deputy assistant administrator of wage and hour division, employment standards administration, acted within his discretion under this chapter in declining to issue complete area wage determination, partial wage determination or enclave wage determination. Kentron Hawaii, Ltd. v. Warner, C.A.D.C.1973, 480 F.2d 1166, 156 U.S.App.D.C. 274. Labor And Employment ☞ 2347

10. —— Regular rate, wage determination

For purposes of Fair Labor Standards Act of 1938, section 201 et seq. of Title 29, Contract Work Hours Standards Act, section 327 et seq. of Title 40, and this section, "regular rate" was properly computed by dividing wage by hours worked, and where employment contract was for weekly wage with variable or fluctuating hours, same method of computation produced "regular rate" for each week though week by week the regular rate varied with number of hours worked. Masters v. Maryland Management Co., C.A.4 (Md.) 1974, 493 F.2d 1329. Labor And Employment ☞ 2307

11. —— Withholding of wage data, wage determination

To extent that critical wage data was readily available to Navy, Navy's failure to forward same to Labor Department with standard form 98 or later under this chapter was clear violation of this chapter and armed services procurement regulations. Kentron Hawaii, Ltd. v. Warner, C.A.D.C.1973, 480 F.2d 1166, 156 U.S.App.D.C. 274. United States ☞ 64.20

12. —— Hearing, wage determination

Proviso in Service Contract Act, that obligation of successful bidder on service contract to pay at or above predecessor contract rate shall not apply if Secretary of Department of Labor finds after hearing that such wages and fringe benefits are substantially at variance with those which prevail for services of character similar in locality, does not permit Secretary to hold hearing whenever wage rates are substantially at variance with those in locality, but only permits Secretary to suspend wage and fringe benefits floor of predecessor contract when wages and benefits are already higher than local rates for similar services, as proviso only pertains to earlier provision of statute providing wage and fringe benefits floor by requiring wages in successor arms-length agreement to be no less than wages and fringe benefits to which such service employees would have been entitled if they were employed under predecessor contract. Gracey v. International Broth. of Elec. Workers, Local Union No. 1340, AFL-CIO, C.A.4 (Va.) 1989, 868 F.2d 671, rehearing denied. Labor And Employment ⏎ 2185

Purpose of hearing required under this chapter to determine if wage and fringe benefits in a collective bargaining agreement between an incumbent employer and labor union are at variance with those which prevail for services of a character similar in the locality is to determine the factual question of whether a particular fringe benefit or wage is at variance with those prevailing in the locality, and before variance hearing is required it must first be determined that the particular benefit or wage in question is a monetary wage required to be paid by a contractor. Trinity Services, Inc. v. Marshall, C.A.D.C.1978, 593 F.2d 1250, 193 U.S.App.D.C. 96. Labor And Employment ⏎ 2348

13. —— Labor Department review, wage determination

Labor Department wage and hour administrator was entitled to waive the deadline for filing objections to administrative law judge's findings in the interests of justice in a proceeding alleging minimum wage and benefits violations pursuant to the Service Contract Act. Amcor, Inc. v. Brock, C.A.11 (Fla.) 1986, 780 F.2d 897. Labor And Employment ⏎ 2351

Statute relied upon by Department of Labor (DOL) as legal basis for initiating investigations regarding violations of Service Contract Act (SCA), which referenced statute granting DOL authority to conduct investigations in matters covered by Walsh–Healey Act, granted DOL same enforcement authority for employee service contracts covered by SCA as it had under Walsh–Healey Act, and therefore DOL did not act in excess of its jurisdiction when it initiated investigation into wages and benefits paid by government contractor to its employees. Bannum, Inc. v. Sawyer, D.D.C.2003, 251 F.Supp.2d 7. Labor And Employment ⏎ 2339

General Accounting Office does not review wage rate determinations established by Labor Secretary pursuant to this section; Labor Department is appropriate forum in which to complain regarding determination. 1984, 63 Op. Comp.Gen. 208.

14. Administrative review—Generally

Employee's sole remedy under this chapter for underpaid wages and lost fringe benefits is the administrative channel created by Congress. Berry v. Andrews, M.D.Ala.1982, 535 F.Supp. 1317. Labor And Employment ⏎ 2361

15. —— Burden of proof, administrative review

Evidence, including testimony of former employees, as supported by compliance officer, and documentary evidence sufficiently established a pattern of violations of this chapter, by government contractor, charged with failing to pay required minimum wage and fringe benefits, thereby causing burden to shift to the contractor in the administrative proceeding. American Waste Removal Co. v. Donovan, C.A.10 (N.M.) 1984, 748 F.2d 1406. Labor And Employment ⏎ 2347

16. —— Exclusiveness of enforcement procedure, administrative review

Exclusive remedy of employees of Navy aircraft maintenance contractors for contractors' alleged failure to pay prevailing wages was statutory scheme for administrative relief set forth in Service Contract Act, which barred any private civil action, even couched in terms of Racketeer Influenced and Corrupt Organizations Act (RICO). Danielsen v. Burnside-Ott Aviation Training Center, Inc., C.A.D.C.1991, 941 F.2d 1220, 291 U.S.App.D.C. 303. Labor And Employment ⏎ 2362

Employees of defense contractors were precluded from bringing a RICO claim premised on alleged violations of Service Contract Act; RICO claims were inextricably intertwined with wage determinations under Act and Congress intended to confine claims to administrative process. Danielsen v. Burnside-Ott Aviation Training Center, Inc., D.D.C.1990, 746 F.Supp. 170, affirmed 941 F.2d 1220, 291 U.S.App.D.C. 303. Racketeer Influenced And Corrupt Organizations ⏎ 12

17. —— Interim appellate authority, administrative review

Delay by the Secretary of Labor in implementing regulation calling for establishment of Board of Service Contract Appeals to hear appeals from administrative law judge (ALJ) determinations under the Service Contract Act did not divest interim appellate authority appointed by Secretary to hear appeals until Board could be established of its jurisdiction to hear such appeals. Nationwide Bldg. Maintenance, Inc. v. Reich, C.A.6 (Ohio) 1994, 14 F.3d 1102. United States ☞ 73(15)

18. Scope of judicial review

It was duty of district court in reviewing action of United States and its agents with respect to bidding on ration assembly contracts to determine whether Secretary had applied bidding requirements of this chapter in accordance with law. Southern Packaging and Storage Co. v. U.S., D.C.S.C.1978, 458 F.Supp. 726, affirmed 618 F.2d 1088. Labor And Employment ☞ 2354

Where bidder on government keypunching contract contended that Secretary of Labor, in making Washington, D.C. wage level applicable to the contract, disregarded clear intent of Congress as to certain terms of this chapter as well as the, department's own regulations, the Secretary could not preclude judicial review by claiming that matters in question had been committed to agency discretion, and federal district court could review the Secretary's decision at least to extent of determining whether it was in violation of this chapter or the department's regulations promulgated pursuant to this chapter. Descomp, Inc. v. Sampson, D.C.Del.1974, 377 F.Supp. 254. Labor And Employment ☞ 2354

19. Jurisdiction

Federal district court had no subject matter jurisdiction to hear employees' complaint that employer reduced their wages and benefits in violation of the Service Contract Act (SCA) and furnish them with some type of relief because SCA neither explicitly nor implicitly authorizes private cause of action and Secretary of Labor, and not private parties, has exclusive jurisdiction to enforce SCA. Gautier Rodriguez v. Mason Technologies, Inc., D.Puerto Rico 1996, 931

F.Supp. 114. Labor And Employment ☞ 2367

Federal Reserve bank located in Richmond, Virginia, whose Federal Reserve district encompassed District of Columbia, and which provided regular currency, coin, and check collection services for its member commercial banks located in District of Columbia, was within jurisdiction of United States District Court for the District of Columbia as a federal agency located within District of Columbia for purposes of action brought under this chapter. Brink's, Inc. v. Board of Governors of Federal Reserve System, D.C.D.C.1979, 466 F.Supp. 116. Federal Courts ☞ 71

Assertion that successful bidder was incapable of ably performing Air Force procurement contract for overhaul, repair and rebuilding of jet engines was a matter peculiarly within jurisdiction of Secretary of Labor to resolve in determining whether contract was subject to this chapter relating to payment of prevailing wage and fringe benefits. Curtiss-Wright Corp. v. McLucas, D.C.N.J.1974, 381 F.Supp. 657. Labor And Employment ☞ 2354

20. Persons entitled to maintain action—Generally

Fair Labor Standards Act of 1938, section 201 et seq. of Title 29, and this chapter are mutually supplemental and person whose contract was subject to provisions of this chapter could bring a private action, under the terms of the Fair Labor Standards Act for his alleged retaliatory discharge. Berry v. Andrews, M.D.Ala.1982, 535 F.Supp. 1317. Labor And Employment ☞ 851

This chapter does not create private right of action by service employees against their employers. Foster v. Parker Transfer Co., W.D.Pa.1981, 528 F.Supp. 906. Labor And Employment ☞ 2362

21. —— Displaced employees, persons entitled to maintain action

Former civil service custodial workers at Air Force base, who had been separated from Air Force via reduction in force after Air Force contracted out custodial services as economy measure, and whose interests were antithetical to those of private employees who replaced them, had no standing to challenge as inordinately low wage-rate determination required by this chapter, which requires that every contract in excess of $2,500 contain provisions specifying minimum wage to be paid contract employees. American Federation of Government Emp., AFL-CIO v. Stetson, C.A.5 (Tex.) 1981, 640 F.2d 642. Labor And Employment ☞ 2372

This chapter, requiring determination of minimum wage to be paid contract employees in connection with government contracts, was passed for the benefit and protection of employees of contractors and subcontractors performing services for the government, and thus, for purposes of standing, civil service employees who were displaced when outside contractor was retained to provide services which civil service employees had previously provided were not within the zone of interests to be protected by this chapter. American Federation of Government Employees, Local 1668 v. Dunn, C.A.9 (Alaska) 1977, 561 F.2d 1310. Labor And Employment ☞ 2372

22. —— Successor employees, persons entitled to maintain action

Employees of successor to air force contract for the operation of missile-tracking station did not have standing under this chapter, as amended, to institute a private action alleging that such successor contractor violated this chapter by refusing to recognize certain seniority rights held by them by virtue of their employment with a previous contractor, thereby altering their entitlement to pension benefits; redress of the employees' grievances lay with the Secretary of Labor. Miscellaneous Service Workers, Drivers & Helpers, Teamsters Local No. 427 v. Philco-Ford Corp., WDL Division, C.A.9 (Hawai'i) 1981, 661 F.2d 776. Labor And Employment ☞ 2372

23. —— Unions, persons entitled to maintain action

Union and its members, who previously performed still photography and film processing tasks which were eliminated in space shuttle processing contract, did not have standing to bring claim that employer violated Service Contract Act, where members were not "predecessors" of engineers, technicians, and inspectors who fulfilled limited photography services needed under replacement contract. Locals 666 and 780 of Intern. Alliance of Theatrical Stage Employees and Moving Picture Mach. Operators of United States and Canada, AFL–CIO v. U.S. Dept. of Labor, C.A.7 (Ill.) 1985, 760 F.2d 141, certiorari denied 106 S.Ct. 227, 474 U.S. 901, 88 L.Ed.2d 227. Federal Civil Procedure ☞ 103.4

Union could not under this chapter maintain private right of action against employer who entered into agreement with National Aeronautics and Space Administration for operation and maintenance of visitors information center at space center, to recover directly for differences between wages and fringe benefits actually paid and those that would have been paid had wage determinations been issued for concession agreement entered into in connection with expansion of employer's duties. District Lodge No. 166, Intern. Ass'n of Machinists and Aerospace Workers, AFL–CIO v. TWA Services, Inc., C.A.11 (Fla.) 1984, 731 F.2d 711, certiorari denied 105 S.Ct. 1175, 469 U.S. 1209, 84 L.Ed.2d 324. Action ☞ 3

Union had standing to bring action challenging decision of Secretary of Labor not to issue pervasive wage determination pursuant to this chapter where, in addition to complaining that contractor paid lower wages than those paid to same employees by preceding contractor, union contended that wage rates were less than those prevailing in locality. International Ass'n of Machinists and Aerospace Workers, AFL-CIO v. Hodgson, C.A.D.C.1975, 515 F.2d 373, 169 U.S.App.D.C. 142. Labor And Employment ☞ 2429

Union had standing to challenge General Services Administration (GSA) regulation, providing that contractors must retroactively reimburse GSA for any wage or fringe benefit increases paid by GSA which are later determined by Secretary of Labor to be at substantial variance with prevailing wage and fringe benefits in the area or which have not been arrived at in arms-length negotiations; regulation would have negative impact on wages and fringe benefits of union members and fact that causality could depend to some extent on actions of third party, the service contractors, was not bar to standing. Service Employees Intern. Union, AFL-CIO v. General Services Admin., D.D.C.1993, 830 F.Supp. 5. Labor And Employment ☞ 2372

Unions representing seamen on government-owned oceanographic vessels lacked standing to enforce provisions of agency circular governing contracting-out determinations because those provisions did not protect any interest that unions could claim, and even if unions have standing, circular granted them no substantive rights they could enforce. National Maritime Union of America, AFL-CIO v. Commander, Military Sealift Command, D.D.C.1986, 632 F.Supp. 409, affirmed 824 F.2d 1228, 263 U.S.App. D.C. 248. Labor And Employment ⬅ 2372

Union local, representing employees of former government contractor under collective bargaining agreement, lacked standing to sue under this chapter after new contractor took over cleaning services contract for government building, since enforcement of this chapter is a function granted only to Secretary. Service Emp. Intern. Union, Local Union No. 36 v. General Services Administration, E.D.Pa.1977, 443 F.Supp. 575. Labor And Employment ⬅ 2372

24. ⸺ United States, persons entitled to maintain action

The Service Contract Act, this chapter, incorporates only those sections of the Walsh–Healey Act, which govern administrative enforcement of that Act, and does not incorporate section of the Walsh–Healey Act which authorizes suits thereunder to be brought in the name of the United States to recover amounts due under the provisions thereof. U.S. v. Deluxe Cleaners & Laundry, Inc., C.A.4 (S.C.) 1975, 511 F.2d 926. United States ⬅ 75(1)

25. Complaint

Local union, representing employees of predecessor government cleaning contractor and suing to compel successor contractor to retain predecessor's employees and submit disputes to arbitration under predecessor's collective bargaining agreement, was not entitled to amend complaint to add Secretary as a defendant in order to compel Secretary to enforce this chapter against successor contractor, since this chapter did not provide for damages and injunctive, relief as sought by union and union lacked standing since it did not represent successor's employees. Service Emp. Intern. Union, Local Union No. 36 v. General Services Administration, E.D.Pa.1977, 443 F.Supp. 575. Federal Civil Procedure ⬅ 286

26. Standard of judicial review

Preponderance of the evidence standard for reviewing administrative fact findings in proceedings under McNamara–O'Hara Service Contract Act is not equivalent of substantial evidence standard, but is equivalent of clear erroneous standard of review. Dantran, Inc. v. U.S. Dept. of Labor, C.A.1 (Me.) 1999, 171 F.3d 58. Labor And Employment ⬅ 2355

Decisions of government contracting officer on cost realism and feasibility are squarely within area of his expertise, and Court of Appeals cannot second-guess such determination unless it is not supported by any reasonable basis. Kentron Hawaii, Ltd. v. Warner, C.A.D.C.1973, 480 F.2d 1166, 156 U.S.App.D.C. 274. United States ⬅ 73(15)

Secretary of Labor's interpretation of Service Contract Act is of controlling weight unless plainly erroneous or inconsistent with regulation. Marine Transport Lines, Inc. v. Lehman, D.C.D.C. 1985, 623 F.Supp. 330. Labor And Employment ⬅ 2357

Appropriate standard for review by district court of action by United States and its agents with respect to bidding on ration assembly contracts was somewhat expanded where primary issue was one of statutory interpretation. Southern Packaging and Storage Co. v. U.S., D.C.S.C. 1978, 458 F.Supp. 726, affirmed 618 F.2d 1088. United States ⬅ 64.60(3.1)

Determination of Secretary as to the applicability of this chapter to specific classifications must be upheld by the court if it has warrant in the record and a reasonable basis in law. Federal Elec. Corp. v. Dunlop, M.D.Fla.1976, 419 F.Supp. 221. United States ⬅ 66

Secretary of Labor's determination of applicability of this chapter would be reviewed under rational basis standard, but his determination that Washington, D.C. area wage levels should apply would be reviewed under substitution of judgment standard. Descomp, Inc. v. Sampson, D.C.Del.1974, 377 F.Supp. 254. United States ⬅ 66

Findings of fact made by hearing examiner in administrative proceedings conducted pursuant to this chapter are conclusive in any court of the United States, if supported by preponderance of evidence, and, in government's suit to recover amount found due, defendants were not entitled to trial de novo on appeal. U.S. v. Powers Bldg. Maintenance Co., W.D.Okla.1972, 336 F.Supp. 819. Labor And Employment ⏝ 2357

27. Weight and conclusiveness of administrative determinations

Department of Labor's wage determination in effect at beginning of contract renewal period was controlling, for purpose of determining whether government contractor was entitled to price adjustment for renewal period, even though determination was withdrawn during renewal period on ground it had been issued in error. Guardian Moving and Storage Company, Inc. v. Hayden, C.A.Fed.2005, 421 F.3d 1268, rehearing denied. United States ⏝ 70(23)

Administrative law judge's (ALJ) decision in Department of Labor's (DOL) action under McNamara-O'Hara Service Contract Act became final when 40-day appeals period expired and unless district court held that ALJ's findings were not supported by preponderance of the evidence, there was no legal basis that could have sustained district court's order to remand matter for another round of administrative proceedings; rather, responsibility fell on district court either to grant DOL's action to recover an underpayment or to make a formal determination that ALJ's findings were not supported by a preponderance of the evidence. U.S. v. Todd, C.A.6 (Mich.) 1994, 38 F.3d 277. Labor And Employment ⏝ 2358

Where hearing examiner determined, in proceeding under this chapter that contractor had underpaid employees, such decision was affirmed by the Administrator, and no appeal or application for relief was sought, findings of fact and decision of the hearing examiner became final and conclusive on all agencies of the United States and, if supported by a preponderance of the evidence, conclusive in any court of the United States. U.S. v. Deluxe Cleaners & Laundry, Inc., C.A.4 (S.C.) 1975, 511 F.2d 926. United States ⏝ 73(14)

Secretary of Labor's interpretation of Service Contract Act has controlling weight unless plainly erroneous or inconsistent with Act. Service Employees Intern. Union, AFL-CIO v. General Services Admin., D.D.C.1993, 830 F.Supp. 5. Statutes ⏝ 219(8)

Findings by Secretary of Labor pursuant to this chapter regarding claims that employer had not paid its service employees prevailing labor rates were conclusive and binding on all parties, unless timely appeal was taken. Foster v. Parker Transfer Co., W.D.Pa.1981, 528 F.Supp. 906. Labor And Employment ⏝ 2350(3)

Although court must accord due deference to expertise of Secretary in determining applicability of this chapter, court must hold, when necessary, that Secretary's determination has exceeded the boundaries set by Congress. Federal Elec. Corp. v. Dunlop, M.D.Fla.1976, 419 F.Supp. 221. United States ⏝ 66

Decision of Secretary of Labor as to applicability of this chapter to particular contract in question was final and binding. Curtiss-Wright Corp. v. McLucas, D.C.N.J.1974, 381 F.Supp. 657. United States ⏝ 66

28. Burden of proof

In action pursuant to this section providing for enforcement of provisions of this chapter by United States bringing action against contractor or any sureties, burden is on defendants to show that findings of hearing examiner were not supported by preponderance of the evidence. U.S. v. Powers Bldg. Maintenance Co., W.D.Okla.1972, 336 F.Supp. 819. Labor And Employment ⏝ 2355

29. Attorney fees

Absent any statute or court-made exception authorizing award of protest costs and attorney fees, bidder on government keypunching contract, who was incorrectly required by General Services Administration to agree to pay its keypunchers at wage level prevailing in Washington, D.C. area, in order to bid on the contract, would not be awarded such damages. Descomp, Inc. v. Sampson, D.C.Del.1974, 377 F.Supp. 254. United States ⏝ 64.60(5.1)

30. Bid preparation costs

Department of Labor did not act arbitrarily in ruling that both contract and commercial time could be counted to establish eligibility for benefits under wage determination made under this chapter, with benefit prorated to reflect percentage of time spent on contract work. Saavedra v. Donovan, C.A.9 (Cal.) 1983, 700 F.2d 496, certiorari denied 104 S.Ct.

236, 464 U.S. 892, 78 L.Ed.2d 227. Labor And Employment ⟨⟩ 2350(2)

Bidder on government keypunching contract, who was incorrectly required by General Services Administration to agree to pay its keypunchers at wage levels prevailing in Washington, D.C., area in order to bid on the contract, would not be awarded its bid preparation costs, absent showing that the expenditure of bid preparation costs was related to the arbitrary wage condition placed in the solicitation for bids. Descomp, Inc. v. Sampson, D.C.Del.1974, 377 F.Supp. 254. United States ⟨⟩ 64.60(6)

31. Injunction

Unsuccessful bidder on contract for operation and maintenance services at two Air Force bases was not entitled to preliminary injunction restraining the Air Force from permitting the performance to begin on two contracts awarded to the lowest bidder where unsuccessful bidder did not make showing of probability of success on the merits on contention that the award lacked rational basis. ServAir, Inc. v. Seamans, C.A.D.C.1972, 473 F.2d 158, 154 U.S.App.D.C. 28. Injunction ⟨⟩ 147

In view of fact that, if this chapter was applicable as plaintiffs claimed, such applicability would militate against plaintiffs' being permitted to continue performance under their concurrent nonconforming contract, they failed to show likelihood of success on merits, for purposes of temporary injunctive relief. Brink's, Inc. v. Board of Governors of Federal Reserve System, D.C.D.C.1979, 466 F.Supp. 112. Injunction ⟨⟩ 138.63

§ 354. List of violators; prohibition of contract award to firms appearing on list; actions to recover underpayments; payment of sums recovered

(a) The Comptroller General is directed to distribute a list to all agencies of the Government giving the names of persons or firms that the Federal agencies or the Secretary have found to have violated this chapter. Unless the Secretary otherwise recommends because of unusual circumstances, no contract of the United States shall be awarded to the persons or firms appearing on this list or to any firm, corporation, partnership, or association in which such persons or firms have a substantial interest until three years have elapsed from the date of publication of the list containing the name of such persons or firms. Where the Secretary does not otherwise recommend because of unusual circumstances, he shall, not later than ninety days after a hearing examiner has made a finding of a violation of this chapter, forward to the Comptroller General the name of the individual or firm found to have violated the provisions of this chapter.

(b) If the accrued payments withheld under the terms of the contract are insufficient to reimburse all service employees with respect to whom there has been a failure to pay the compensation required pursuant to this chapter, the United States may bring action against the contractor, subcontractor, or any sureties in any court of competent jurisdiction to recover the remaining amount of underpayments. Any sums thus recovered by the United States shall be held in the deposit fund and shall be paid, on order of the Secretary, directly to the underpaid employee or employees. Any sum not paid

to an employee because of inability to do so within three years shall
be covered into the Treasury of the United States as miscellaneous
receipts.

(Pub.L. 89–286, § 5, Oct. 22, 1965, 79 Stat. 1035; Pub.L. 92–473, § 4, Oct. 9,
1972, 86 Stat. 790.)

HISTORICAL AND STATUTORY NOTES

Revision Notes and Legislative Reports
1965 Acts. Senate Report No. 89–748,
see 1965 U.S.Code Cong. and Adm.News,
p. 3737.

1972 Acts. Senate Report No. 92–1131,
see 1972 U.S.Code Cong. and Adm.News,
p. 3534.

Amendments
1972   Amendments. Subsec. (a).
Pub.L. 92–473 authorized award of con-

tracts to violators because of unusual circumstances and required the Secretary to
forward names of violators to Comptroller General within ninety days of hearing
examiner's finding of a violation where
the Secretary does not recommend
awards because of unusual circumstances.

CODE OF FEDERAL REGULATIONS

Rules of practice, enforcing standards in construction and federal service con-
tracts, see 29 CFR § 6.1 et seq.
Rules of procedure, promulgating occupational safety or health standards, see 29
CFR § 1911.1 et seq.

LIBRARY REFERENCES

American Digest System
Labor and Employment ☞2302.
United States ☞64.20, 75(1).
Key Number System Topic Nos. 231H, 393.

Research References

ALR Library
31 ALR, Fed. 348, What Limitation Periods Apply Under 28 U.S.C.A. § 2415 to
Government Suits.
Encyclopedias
Am. Jur. 2d Public Works and Contracts § 217, The Federal Service Contract
Labor Standards Act.
Am. Jur. 2d Public Works and Contracts § 226, Service Contract Labor Standards
Act.

Treatises and Practice Aids
Federal Procedure, Lawyers Edition § 39:360, Action by United States.
West's Federal Administrative Practice § 659, Debarment and Suspension.

WESTLAW ELECTRONIC RESEARCH

See Westlaw guide following the Explanation pages of this volume.

Notes of Decisions

Debarment 2-6	List of violators 2-6
Injunction 11	Generally 2
Interest, recovery of underpayments 9	Period of debarment 5
Jurisdiction 10	Persons barred from contracting 6
Law governing 1	

---

1. Law governing

Action by the United States against government contractor for failure to pay its employees minimum wage as required under the terms of its contract and by this chapter was governed by general six-year period of limitations under section 2415 of Title 28, and not by two-year period of limitations of the Portal-to-Portal Act, section 255 of Title 29, despite contention, inter alia, that it was illogical to assume that Congress intended to discriminate between employers covered by this chapter and those covered by other acts. U.S. v. Deluxe Cleaners & Laundry, Inc., C.A.4 (S.C.) 1975, 511 F.2d 926. United States ☞ 133

Right to interest on amounts recovered as underpayments of wages by United States in action under this chapter was a question of federal law. U.S. v. Powers Bldg. Maintenance Co., W.D.Okla.1972, 336 F.Supp. 819. Federal Courts ☞ 415

2. List of violators—Generally

In reviewing debarments under this section's provision that violators of Act are ineligible for award of government contracts for three-year period unless Secretary of Labor recommends otherwise because of unusual circumstances, Secretary has broad discretion, but when findings are made, they must respect guidelines by which Secretary exercised his discretion. Federal Food Service, Inc. v. Donovan, C.A.D.C.1981, 658 F.2d 830, 212 U.S.App.D.C. 82. Labor And Employment ☞ 2351; Labor And Employment ☞ 2349

3. ―― Unusual circumstances, list of violators

Continuing pursuit of debarment based on government contractor's use of longer-than-semimonthly pay periods in violation of government regulations was not substantially justified under Equal Access to Justice Act (EAJA) after ALJ determined that unusual circumstances justified excusing contractor, and thus contractor was entitled to fee award under EAJA, where, by time of ALJ's decision, Secretary's enforcement actions had imposed severe punishment by triggering loss of contractor's business due to freezing of funds owed under contract, contractor had fully complied with its remedial obligations, and contractor had made repeated offers to settle, which included acquiescence to government's legal stance in exchange for relief from debarment. Dantran, Inc. v. U.S. Dept. of Labor, C.A.1 (Me.) 2001, 246 F.3d 36. United States ☞ 147(12)

Department of Labor (DOL) should not have refused to extend unusual circumstances exception to Service Contract Act violations based upon findings that violations resulted from culpable conduct, as what constituted culpability could not be discerned from administrative law judge's (ALJ's) opinion. Elaine's Cleaning Service, Inc. v. U.S. Dept. of Labor, C.A.6 (Ohio) 1997, 106 F.3d 726. United States ☞ 64.20

As to provision of this section that underpayment of government contractor's employees makes contractor ineligible for award of government contracts for three-year period, unless Secretary of Labor recommends otherwise because of unusual circumstances, if administrative law judge finds improper management solely on basis of virtually de minimis underpayments, Secretary must consider particular circumstances of business under review, and, if previous violation is relied on to support disbarment, standard of reasonable management must be applied to them as well, but if administrative law judge has made such findings on record, Secretary need not make independent investigation. Federal Food Service, Inc. v. Donovan, C.A.D.C.1981, 658 F.2d 830, 212 U.S.App.D.C. 82. Labor And Employment ☞ 2351

There were no "unusual circumstances" such as to preclude debarment of minority contractor under McNamara-O'Hara Service Contract Act for failing to meet its responsibilities as successor contractor and repeated violations of numerous regulations. Vigilantes, Inc. v. Administrator, Wage and Hour Div., U.S. Dept. of Labor, D.Puerto Rico 1991, 769 F.Supp. 57, affirmed 968 F.2d 1412. Labor And Employment ☞ 2243

Administrator of Wage and Hour Division of Department of Labor acted arbitrarily and capriciously in rejecting administrative law judge's determination that contractor had demonstrated that unusual circumstances militating against debarment for violations of this chapter were present. Mastercraft Flooring, Inc. v. Donovan, D.C.D.C.1984, 589 F.Supp. 258. Labor And Employment ☞ 2357

President of company that provided security-guard services at Navy base failed to demonstrate unusual circumstances that would entitle him to relief from the ordinary remedy of debarment from bidding on government contracts for a period of three years for violations of the McNamara–O'Hara Service Contract Act (SCA), after receiving guidance as to wage payments. Johnson v. U.S. Dept. of Labor, C.A.6 (Ohio) 2006, 205 Fed.Appx. 312, 2006 WL 2373390, Unreported. Labor And Employment ☞ 2302

4. —— Removal from list, list of violators

Secretary of Labor's decision that there were no "unusual circumstances" to justify removal of government contractors' names from list of those ineligible to bid on government contracts, after contractors had underpaid certain employees, was an abuse of discretion, where there were several factors favorable to contractors and no evidentiary support for administrative law judge's finding of negligence in use of improper management technique. Federal Food Service, Inc. v. Donovan, C.A.D.C.1981, 658 F.2d 830, 212 U.S.App.D.C. 82. Labor And Employment ☞ 2347

Recommendation of administrator that Secretary take affirmative action to remove name of janitorial service company from the list of persons or firms that had violated this chapter was supported by the evidence. White Glove Bldg. Maintenance, Inc. v. Hodgson, C.A.9 (Cal.) 1972, 459 F.2d 175. Labor And Employment ☞ 2347

5. —— Period of debarment, list of violators

The 90–day period for forwarding the name of a wage and fringe benefit violator to the Comptroller General for place-

ment on list of debarred contractors ran from date order of administrative law judge became final, after expiration of time for appeal, not from date of initial order and, in any event, period of debarment ran from date of publication of violator's name on debarment list, not from date on which name was forwarded to the Comptroller. Cimpi v. Dole, D.D.C. 1990, 739 F.Supp. 25. United States ☞ 64.20

6. —— Persons barred from contracting, list of violators

Debarment of minority contractor for three years was warranted for its violations of labor standards of McNamara-O'Hara Service Contract Act, considering contract's numerous deficiencies under several contracts amounting to more than $70,000, contractor's failure to make prompt payment of monies due, and absence of "unusual circumstances" bearing on good faith. Vigilantes, Inc. v. Administrator of Wage and Hour Div., U.S. Dept. of Labor, C.A.1 (Puerto Rico) 1992, 968 F.2d 1412. Labor And Employment ☞ 2302

Evidence was sufficient to support administrative law judge's finding that government contractor was guilty of "repeated violations" of Service Contract Act, barring it from contracting with United States for period of three years; contractor failed to pay individual uniform allowances due as required by contract, and failed to pay health, welfare and pension benefits when due. A to Z Maintenance Corp. v. Dole, D.D.C.1989, 710 F.Supp. 853. United States ☞ 64.20

In view of the contractor's past history which reflected violations of this chapter during several years, in view of the fact that violations continued to occur, that proper management would have precluded continuing occurrences of widespread underpayments, and that there had been culpable violations, decision of the Secretary to debar contractor was not arbitrary, capricious, or an abuse of discretion despite claim of unusual circumstances by the contractor. Federal Food Service, Inc. v. Marshall, D.C.D.C. 1979, 481 F.Supp. 816. Labor And Employment ☞ 2357

7. Recovery of underpayments—Generally

Award against government contractor for back wages and benefits for unnamed, unlocated employees was not a penalty or fine unauthorized by this chapter but was a proper means of effectuating purposes of this chapter, with award to be paid to the treasury if the employees could not be located. American Waste Removal Co. v. Donovan, C.A.10 (N.M.) 1984, 748 F.2d 1406. Labor And Employment ☞ 2389

8. —— Notice of payment, recovery of underpayments

Under mandate of Court of Appeals that employer pay 20 cent an hour for each hour worked by employees who worked between August 7, 1967, and day on which union implemented its health, welfare and pension plans and who had received no benefits or filed no claim, or until employee's name appeared on certain payroll lists or until company could prove that "the particular employee had actual notice" of the self-insurance plan, whichever was sooner, written take-home notice was not required, and testimony concerning notice, including written notice on bulletin board which was called to attention of all and explained to those that could not read, was sufficient to establish strong prima facie in absence of contradiction or impeachment. White Glove Bldg. Maintenance, Inc. v. Brennan, C.A.9 (Cal.) 1975, 518 F.2d 1271. Labor And Employment ☞ 2358

9. —— Interest, recovery of underpayments

The United States was entitled to prejudgment interest at rate of 6% on amounts recovered as underpayments of wages, from date wages were due to date paid, in government's action for amounts which defendant failed to pay as minimum wages required by this chapter. U.S. v. Powers Bldg. Maintenance Co., W.D.Okla.1972, 336 F.Supp. 819. Interest ☞ 39(2.40)

10. Jurisdiction

District court had jurisdiction to consider Secretary's ruling that government contractor was ineligible to bid on government contract for three years because of violation of this chapter. Midwest Maintenance & Const. Co., Inc. v. Vela, C.A.10 (Okla.) 1980, 621 F.2d 1046. Labor And Employment ☞ 2354

11. Injunction

For purposes of determining whether government contractor was entitled to preliminary injunction against debarment, the harm to other interested parties and the public interest weighed against the contractor as this chapter was designed to provide fair wage standards for employees performing work on federal service contracts and any decision setting aside actions which are consistent with this chapter could cause substantial injury to enforcement of this chapter. Federal Food Service, Inc. v. Marshall, D.C.D.C.1979, 481 F.Supp. 816. Injunction ☞ 138.63

§ 355. Exclusion of fringe benefit payments in determining overtime pay

In determining any overtime pay to which such service employees are entitled under any Federal law, the regular or basic hourly rate of pay of such an employee shall not include any fringe benefit payments computed hereunder which are excluded from the regular rate under the Fair Labor Standards Act [29 U.S.C.A. § 201 et seq.] by provisions of section 7(d) thereof [29 U.S.C.A. § 207(d)].

(Pub.L. 89–286, § 6, Oct. 22, 1965, 79 Stat. 1035.)

HISTORICAL AND STATUTORY NOTES

Revision Notes and Legislative Reports

1965 Acts. Senate Report No. 89–748, see 1965 U.S.Code Cong. and Adm.News, p. 3737.

References in Text

The Fair Labor Standards Act, referred to in text, is Act June 25, 1938, c. 676, 52 Stat. 1060, which is classified principally to chapter 8 (section 201 et seq.) of Title 29, Labor. For complete classification of

this Act to the Code, see section 201 of
Title 29 and Tables.

LIBRARY REFERENCES

American Digest System
Labor and Employment ⟐2243.
Key Number System Topic No. 231H.

WESTLAW ELECTRONIC RESEARCH

See Westlaw guide following the Explanation pages of this volume.

§ 356. Exemptions

This chapter shall not apply to—

(1) any contract of the United States or District of Columbia for construction, alteration and/or repair, including painting and decorating of public buildings or public works;

(2) any work required to be done in accordance with the provisions of the Walsh–Healey Public Contracts Act [41 U.S.C.A. § 35 et seq.];

(3) any contract for the carriage of freight or personnel by vessel, airplane, bus, truck, express, railway line or oil or gas pipeline where published tariff rates are in effect;

(4) any contract for the furnishing of services by radio, telephone, telegraph, or cable companies, subject to the Communications Act of 1934 [47 U.S.C.A. § 151 et seq.];

(5) any contract for public utility services, including electric light and power, water, steam, and gas;

(6) any employment contract providing for direct services to a Federal agency by an individual or individuals; and

(7) any contract with the United States Postal Service, the principal purpose of which is the operation of postal contract stations.

(Pub.L.89–286, § 7, Oct. 22, 1965, 79 Stat. 1035; Pub.L. 91–375, §§ 4(a), 6(o), Aug. 12, 1970, 84 Stat. 773, 783.)

HISTORICAL AND STATUTORY NOTES

Revision Notes and Legislative Reports
1965 Acts. Senate Report No. 89–748, see 1965 U.S.Code Cong. and Adm.News, p. 3737.

References in Text
The Walsh–Healey Public Contracts Act, referred to in in par. (2), probably means Act June 30, 1936, c. 881, 49 Stat. 2036, commonly known as the Walsh–Healey Act, which is classified generally to sections 35 to 45 of this title. For complete classification of this Act to the Code, see Short Title note under section 35 of this title and Tables. See, also, section 262 of Title 29, Labor.

The Communication Act of 1934, as amended, referred to in par. (4), is Act June 19, 1934, c. 652, 48 Stat. 1064, which is classified principally to chapter 5 (section 151 et seq.) of Title 47, Telegraphs, Telephones, and Radiotelegraphs. For complete classification of this Act to the Code, see Tables.

Change of Name

In par. (7), "United States Postal Service" was substituted for "Post Office Department" pursuant to Pub.L. 91–375, §§ 4(a), 6(o), Aug. 12, 1970, 84 Stat. 773, 783, which are set out as notes preceding

section 101 of Title 39, Postal Service, and under section 201 of Title 39, respectively, which abolished the Post Office Department, transferred its functions to the United States Postal Service, and provided that references in other laws to the Post Office Department shall be considered a reference to the United States Postal Service.

LIBRARY REFERENCES

American Digest System

Labor and Employment ⟐2292(3).
Key Number System Topic No. 231H.

Corpus Juris Secundum

CJS Steam § 9, Contracts.

Research References

Encyclopedias

Am. Jur. 2d Public Works and Contracts § 226, Service Contract Labor Standards Act.

WESTLAW ELECTRONIC RESEARCH

See Westlaw guide following the Explanation pages of this volume.

Notes of Decisions

Carriage of freight contracts   2
Construction   1
Direct service contracts   3
Walsh-Healey Public Contracts Act employees   4

———

1. Construction

Remedial labor statutes like the Service Contract Act are to be liberally construed; however, exemptions in such statutes should be read narrowly. Menlo Service Corp. v. U.S., C.A.9 (Cal.) 1985, 765 F.2d 805. Labor And Employment ⟐ 2220(2); Labor And Employment ⟐ 2251

Exemptions from remedial legislation, should be narrowly construed against party asserting the applicability of the exemption. Williams v. U.S. Dept. of Labor, C.A.8 (Mo.) 1983, 697 F.2d 842. Labor And Employment ⟐ 2251

2. Carriage of freight contracts

In proceeding wherein contractor, who entered into contracts with Air Force for preparation of personal property of military personnel for movement and storage and for related services, was found to have violated this chapter by underpaying

his employees, Department of Labor's administrative law judge's determination to effect that the contracts were not primarily for the carriage of freight, within meaning of this section under which the requirement that government contractor's employees not be paid less than the prevailing rates in the locality was not to apply to contracts for carriage of freight by truck if published tariffs were in effect, was supported by preponderance of the evidence. Williams v. U.S. Dept. of Labor, C.A.8 (Mo.) 1983, 697 F.2d 842. Labor And Employment ⟐ 2350(2)

3. Direct service contracts

Exemption from Service Contract Act for any employment contract providing for direct services did not apply to employees of service corporation which referred workers to federally owned research facility operated by state university, on ground that referrals provided services to the laboratory; regulation construed exemption to apply only when the contractor as an individual provides direct services to the government and no service employees are used. Menlo Service Corp. v. U.S.,

C.A.9 (Cal.) 1985, 765 F.2d 805. Labor And Employment ⬚ 2292(3)

4. Walsh-Healey Public Contracts Act employees

Regulation exempting from Service Contract Act the type of engine and equipment overhaul and modification which was so extensive as to constitute remanufacturing was not arbitrary or capricious and was in accordance with law. American Federation of Labor and Congress of Indus. Organizations v. Donovan,

C.A.D.C.1985, 757 F.2d 330, 244 U.S.App.D.C. 255. Labor And Employment ⬚ 2338

Company which assembled the component parts of "Meal Combat Individual" field rations was not a "manufacturer" for purposes of Walsh–Healey Act, sections 35 to 45 of this title, and thus came within coverage of this chapter. Southern Packaging and Storage Co., Inc. v. U.S., C.A.4 (S.C.) 1980, 618 F.2d 1088. Labor And Employment ⬚ 2243

§ 357. Definitions

For the purposes of this chapter—

(a) "Secretary" means Secretary of Labor.

(b) The term "service employee" means any person engaged in the performance of a contract entered into by the United States and not exempted under section 356 of this title, whether negotiated or advertised, the principal purpose of which is to furnish services in the United States (other than any person employed in a bona fide executive, administrative, or professional capacity, as those terms are defined in part 541 of Title 29, Code of Federal Regulations, as of July 30, 1976, and any subsequent revision of those regulations); and shall include all such persons regardless of any contractual relationship that may be alleged to exist between a contractor or subcontractor and such persons.

(c) The term "compensation" means any of the payments or fringe benefits described in section 351 of this title.

(d) The term "United States" when used in a geographical sense shall include any State of the United States, the District of Columbia, Puerto Rico, the Virgin Islands, Outer Continental Shelf lands as defined in the Outer Continental Shelf Lands Act, American Samoa, Guam, Wake Island, Eniwetok Atoll, Kwajalein Atoll, Johnston Island, and Canton Island, but shall not include any other territory under the jurisdiction of the United States or any United States base or possession within a foreign country.

(Pub.L. 89–286, § 8, Oct. 22, 1965, 79 Stat. 1036; Pub.L. 93–57, § 1, July 6, 1973, 87 Stat. 140; Pub.L. 94–489, § 3, Oct. 13, 1976, 90 Stat. 2358.)

HISTORICAL AND STATUTORY NOTES

Revision Notes and Legislative Reports
1965 Acts. Senate Report No. 89–748, see 1965 U.S.Code Cong. and Adm.News, p. 3737.

1976 Acts. House Report No. 94–1571, see 1976 U.S. Code Cong. and Adm. News, p. 5211.

References in Text

The Outer Continental Shelf Lands Act, referred to in subsec. (d), is Act Aug. 7, 1953, c. 345, 67 Stat. 462, which is classified generally to subchapter III (section 1331 et seq.) of chapter 29 of Title 43, Public Lands. For complete classification of this Act to the Code, see Short Title note set out under section 1331 of Title 43 and Tables.

Amendments

1976 Amendments. Subsec. (b). Pub.L. 94–489 substituted provision defining service employees to include all employees, but excluding bona fide executive, administrative, and professional employees, for provision defining service employees as guards, watchmen, any person engaged in a recognized trade or craft, or in unskilled, semiskilled, or skilled manual labor occupations; and any other employee including a foreman or supervisor in a position having trade, craft, or laboring experience as the paramount requirement.

1973 Amendments. Subsec. (d). Pub.L. 93–57 defined term "United States" to include Canton Island.

Effective and Applicability Provisions

1973 Acts. Section 2 of Pub.L. 93–57 provided that: "The amendment [to subsec. (d) of this section] made hereby shall be effective with respect to all contracts entered into at any time after the date of enactment [July 6, 1973]."

CODE OF FEDERAL REGULATIONS

Definitions, interpretations, etc., see 29 CFR § 541.0 et seq.

Research References

Encyclopedias

Am. Jur. 2d Bankruptcy § 1787, Property Held in Trust.

Am. Jur. 2d Public Works and Contracts § 217, The Federal Service Contract Labor Standards Act.

Am. Jur. 2d Public Works and Contracts § 226, Service Contract Labor Standards Act.

Treatises and Practice Aids

Immigration Law Service 2d § 4:253, Establishing Prevailing Wage: SWA Wage Determination--Service Contract Act (SCA) Wages.

WESTLAW ELECTRONIC RESEARCH

See Westlaw guide following the Explanation pages of this volume.

Notes of Decisions

1. Service employees—Generally

Terms "any" and "all" as used in provision of this section setting forth persons who are covered by this section operate simply to include within the term "service employee" the totality of those persons who fit within the job categories set out in the remainder of this section, the words have no talismanic or independent effect and are not indicative, one way or the other, of the legislative intent as to the scope of the term "service employee." Federal Elec. Corp. v. Dunlop, M.D.Fla. 1976, 419 F.Supp. 221. United States ⟐ 66

Criterion to be applied in determining whether a given worker is a "service employee" within this chapter is to see how his or her counterpart in federal service would be classified. Descomp, Inc. v. Sampson, D.C.Del.1974, 377 F.Supp. 254. United States ⟐ 66

2. —— Keypunch operators, service employees

Department of Labor regulation adopted under this chapter and providing in effect that the coverage of this chapter extended to classes of employees described in Civil Service Commission's Handbook of Blue Collar Occupational Families and Series militated against a wider interpretation of this chapter and deprived the Secretary's subsequent determination that non "blue collar" key punch operators, technical clerks and computer operators were covered by this chapter of the rational basis necessary to uphold that determination. Federal Elec. Corp. v. Dunlop, M.D.Fla.1976, 419 F.Supp. 221. United States ⮑ 66

Keypunch operators were not "service employees" within this chapter and Secretary of Labor's determination to contrary had no reasonable basis in law and would be set aside. Descomp, Inc. v. Sampson, D.C.Del.1974, 377 F.Supp. 254. United States ⮑ 66

3. —— Supervisory employees, service employees

Finding of Secretary that none of janitorial service company's employees at air force base was within the supervisory employee exemption from the fringe benefit payment requirements of this chapter was supported by evidence. White Glove Bldg. Maintenance, Inc. v. Hodgson, C.A.9 (Cal.) 1972, 459 F.2d 175. Labor And Employment ⮑ 2347

4. —— Truck drivers, service employees

Truck driver who delivered mail under mail haul contract between his employer and United States Postal Service was a "service employee" within meaning of this chapter; thus his wage grievances must be brought under such chapter which vests in Secretary the sole authority for enforcing the chapter and district court lacked subject-matter jurisdiction to hear truck driver's claims that he had not been paid for some straight-time labor and had not been paid one and one-half his regular rate for hours of overtime work. Nichols v. Mower's News Service, Inc., D.C.Vt.1980, 492 F.Supp. 258. Labor And Employment ⮑ 2233; Labor And Employment ⮑ 2367

5. —— Miscellaneous employees, service employees

Purchase agreement whereby service corporation located and referred desired personnel to federally owned laboratory operated by state university fell within scope of Service Contract Act where service corporation contractually agreed not only to administer payroll but to set rates of compensation for its referrals and was required to provide almost immediate replacements should any of its referrals prove unfit and service corporation was paid for each hour of service rendered by a referral, notwithstanding that service corporation had no control over work of the referrals, each of whom served along side regular employees of the laboratory, performed similar tasks and were subject to the same supervision; Act's coverage was not limited to those office employees of the corporation who arranged the referrals and prepared the payrolls. Menlo Service Corp. v. U.S., C.A.9 (Cal.) 1985, 765 F.2d 805. Labor And Employment ⮑ 2243

§ 358. Wage and fringe benefit determinations of Secretary

It is the intent of the Congress that determinations of minimum monetary wages and fringe benefits for the various classes of service employees under the provisions of paragraphs (1) and (2) of section 351 [1] of this title should be made with respect to all contracts subject to this chapter, as soon as it is administratively feasible to do so. In any event, the Secretary shall make such determinations with respect to at least the following contracts subject to this chapter which are entered into during the applicable fiscal year:

(1) For the fiscal year ending June 30, 1973, all contracts under which more than twenty-five service employees are to be employed.

(2) For the fiscal year ending June 30, 1974, all contracts, under which more than twenty service employees are to be employed.

(3) For the fiscal year ending June 30, 1975, all contracts under which more than fifteen service employees are to be employed.

(4) For the fiscal year ending June 30, 1976, all contracts under which more than ten service employees are to be employed.

(5) On or after July 1, 1976, all contracts under which more than five service employees are to be employed.

(Pub.L. 89–286, § 10, as added Pub.L. 92–473, § 5, Oct. 9, 1972, 86 Stat. 790, and amended Pub.L. 94–273, § 29, Apr. 21, 1976, 90 Stat. 380.)

¹ So in original.   Probably should be "section 351 (a)".

HISTORICAL AND STATUTORY NOTES

Revision Notes and Legislative Reports
1965 Acts. Senate Report No. 89–748, see 1965 U.S.Code Cong. and Adm.News, p. 3737.

1972 Acts. Senate Report No. 92–1131, see 1972 U.S.Code Cong. and Adm.News, p. 3534.

1976 Acts. House Report No. 94–1571, see 1976 U.S.Code Cong. and Adm.News, p. 5211.

Amendments
1976   Amendments. Par. (5).   Pub.L. 94–273 substituted "On or after July 1, 1976" for "For the fiscal year ending June 30, 1977, and for each fiscal year thereafter".

LIBRARY REFERENCES

American Digest System
Labor and Employment ⟾2336 to 2351.
Key Number System Topic No. 231H.

Corpus Juris Secundum
CJS Labor Relations § 1103, Public Employees; Employees on Public Works.
CJS Labor Relations § 1293, Federal Service Contract Labor Standards Act.
CJS Labor Relations § 1302, Under Federal Law.

Research References

ALR Library
8 ALR, Fed. 2nd Series 611, Application of Local District Court Summary Judgment Rules to Nonmoving Party in Federal Courts--Statements of Facts.
96 ALR, Fed. 411, What Constitutes Adequate Notice of Proposed Federal Agency Rule Against Objection That Rule Adopted Differed in Substance from That Published as Proposed in Notice.

Forms
24A West's Legal Forms § 4.7, Prevailing Wage Laws.

Treatises and Practice Aids
Bankruptcy Service Lawyers Edition § 19:617, Service Contract Act.
Federal Procedure, Lawyers Edition § 39:452, Labor Law Violations.
Federal Procedure, Lawyers Edition § 39:468, Protest Based Upon Apparent Solicitation Defect.

West's Federal Administrative Practice § 615, Laws Applicable--Labor Conditions.

WESTLAW ELECTRONIC RESEARCH

See Westlaw guide following the Explanation pages of this volume.

CHAPTER 7—OFFICE OF FEDERAL PROCUREMENT POLICY

Sec.
435.   Levels of compensation of certain contractor personnel not allowable as costs under certain contracts.
436.   Protection of constitutional rights of contractors.
437.   Incentives for efficient performance of services contracts.
438.   Civilian Board of Contract Appeals.

CROSS REFERENCES

Indian Self–Determination Act contracts and construction, see 25 USCA § 450j.
Tribal self-governance funding agreements and construction projects, see 25 USCA § 458cc.

WESTLAW COMPUTER ASSISTED LEGAL RESEARCH

Westlaw supplements your legal research in many ways. Westlaw allows you to

● update your research with the most current information

● expand your library with additional resources

● retrieve current, comprehensive history citing references to a case with KeyCite

For more information on using Westlaw to supplement your research, see the Westlaw Electronic Research Guide, which follows the Explanation.

---

§§ 401, 402. Repealed. Pub.L. 104–106, Div. D, Title XLIII, § 4305(a)(2), Feb. 10, 1996, 110 Stat. 665

HISTORICAL AND STATUTORY NOTES

Section 401, Pub.L. 93–400, § 2, Aug. 30, 1974, 88 Stat. 796; Pub.L. 96–83, § 2, Oct. 10, 1979, 93 Stat. 648; Pub.L. 98–191, § 3, Dec. 1, 1983, 97 Stat. 1325; as amended Pub.L. 100–679, § 2(a), Nov. 17, 1988, 102 Stat. 4055; Pub.L. 103–355, Title I, § 1091(a), Oct. 13, 1994, 108 Stat. 3272, stated policy of U.S. government relating to procurement of property and services.

Section 402, Pub.L. 93–400, § 3, Aug. 30, 1974, 88 Stat. 796, as amended Pub.L. 100–679, § 2(b), Nov. 17, 1988, 102 Stat. 4055, related to Congressional findings and purpose.

Effective Date of Repeal

Repeal of sections by Pub.L. 104–106 effective Feb. 10, 1996, except as otherwise provided, see section 4401 of Pub.L.

104–106, set out as a note under section 251 of this title.

Short Title

2003 Amendments. Pub.L. 108–136, § 1401, provided that: "This title [enacting 41 U.S.C.A. §§414b, 428a, and 437, amending 10 U.S.C.A. § 2855, 31 U.S.C.A. § 1115, and 41 U.S.C.A. §§ 403, 414, 433, and 436, enacting provisions set out as notes under 31 U.S.C.A. § 501, 40 U.S.C.A. § 1103, and 41 U.S.C.A. §§ 253, 253a, 405, 428a, and 433, amending provisions set out as notes under 10 U.S.C.A. § 2304 and 41 U.S.C.A. § 264, and repealing provisions set out as a note under 10 U.S.C.A. § 2302] may be cited as the 'Services Acquisition Reform Act of 2003'."

§ 403. Definitions

As used in this chapter:

(1) The term "executive agency" means—

(A) an executive department specified in section 101 of Title 5;

(B) a military department specified in section 102 of such Title;

(C) an independent establishment as defined in section 104(1) of such Title; and

(D) a wholly owned Government corporation fully subject to the provisions of chapter 91 of Title 31.

(2) The term "procurement" includes all stages of the process of acquiring property or services, beginning with the process for determining a need for property or services and ending with contract completion and closeout.

(3) The term "procurement system" means the integration of the procurement process, the professional development of procurement personnel, and the management structure for carrying out the procurement function.

(4) The term "standards" means the criteria for determining the effectiveness of the procurement system by measuring the performance of the various elements of such system.

(5) The term "competitive procedures" means procedures under which an agency enters into a contract pursuant to full and open competition.

(6) The term "full and open competition", when used with respect to a procurement, means that all responsible sources are permitted to submit sealed bids or competitive proposals on the procurement.

(7) The term "responsible source" means a prospective contractor who—

(A) has adequate financial resources to perform the contract or the ability to obtain such resources;

(B) is able to comply with the required or proposed delivery or performance schedule, taking into consideration all existing commercial and Government business commitments;

(C) has a satisfactory performance record;

(D) has a satisfactory record of integrity and business ethics;

(E) has the necessary organization, experience, accounting and operational controls, and technical skills, or the ability to obtain such organization, experience, controls, and skills;

(F) has the necessary production, construction, and technical equipment and facilities, or the ability to obtain such equipment and facilities; and

(G) is otherwise qualified and eligible to receive an award under applicable laws and regulations.

(8) The term "technical data" means recorded information (regardless of the form or method of the recording) of a scientific or technical nature (including computer software documentation) relating to supplies procured by an agency. Such term does not include computer software or financial, administrative, cost or pricing, or management data or other information incidental to contract administration.

(9)(A) The term "major system" means a combination of elements that will function together to produce the capabilities required to fulfill a mission need, which elements may include hardware, equipment, software or any combination thereof, but excludes construction or other improvements to real property; and

(B) a system shall be considered a major system if (i) the Department of Defense is responsible for the system and the total expenditures for research, development, test and evaluation for the system are estimated to be more than $75,000,000 (based on fiscal year 1980 constant dollars) or the eventual total expenditure for procurement of more than $300,000,000 (based on fiscal year 1980 constant dollars); (ii) a civilian agency is responsible for the system and total expenditures for the system are estimated to exceed $750,000 (based on fiscal year 1980 constant dollars) or the dollar threshold for a "major system" established by the agency pursuant to Office of Management and Budget (OMB) Circular A–109, entitled "Major Systems Acquisitions", whichever is greater; or (iii) the system is designated a "major system" by the head of the agency responsible for the system.

(10) The term "item", "item of supply", or "supplies" means any individual part, component, subassembly, assembly, or subsystem integral to a major system, and other property which may be replaced during the service life of the system, and includes spare parts and replenishment spare parts, but does not include packaging or labeling associated with shipment or identification of an "item".

(11) The term "simplified acquisition threshold" means $100,000.

(12) The term "commercial item" means any of the following:

(A) Any item, other than real property, that is of a type customarily used by the general public or by nongovernmental entities for purposes other than governmental purposes, and that—

(i) has been sold, leased, or licensed to the general public; or

(ii) has been offered for sale, lease, or license to the general public.

(B) Any item that evolved from an item described in subparagraph (A) through advances in technology or performance and that is not yet available in the commercial marketplace, but will be available in the commercial marketplace in time to satisfy the delivery requirements under a Federal Government solicitation.

(C) Any item that, but for—

(i) modifications of a type customarily available in the commercial marketplace, or

(ii) minor modifications made to meet Federal Government requirements,

would satisfy the criteria in subparagraph (A) or (B).

(D) Any combination of items meeting the requirements of subparagraph (A), (B), (C), or (E) that are of a type customarily combined and sold in combination to the general public.

(E) Installation services, maintenance services, repair services, training services, and other services if—

(i) the services are procured for support of an item referred to in subparagraph (A), (B), (C), or (D), regardless of whether such services are provided by the same source or at the same time as the item; and

(ii) the source of the services provides similar services contemporaneously to the general public under terms and conditions similar to those offered to the Federal Government.

(F) Services offered and sold competitively, in substantial quantities, in the commercial marketplace based on established catalog or market prices for specific tasks performed or specific outcomes to be achieved and under standard commercial terms and conditions.

(G) Any item, combination of items, or service referred to in subparagraphs (A) through (F) notwithstanding the fact that the item, combination of items, or service is transferred between or among separate divisions, subsidiaries, or affiliates of a contractor.

(H) A nondevelopmental item, if the procuring agency determines, in accordance with conditions set forth in the Federal Acquisition Regulation, that the item was developed exclusively at private expense and has been sold in substantial quantities, on a competitive basis, to multiple State and local governments.

(13) The term "nondevelopmental item" means any of the following:

(A) Any commercial item.

(B) Any previously developed item of supply that is in use by a department or agency of the United States, a State or local government, or a foreign government with which the United States has a mutual defense cooperation agreement.

(C) Any item of supply described in subparagraph (A) or (B) that requires only minor modification or modification of the type customarily available in the commercial marketplace in order to meet the requirements of the procuring department or agency.

(D) Any item of supply currently being produced that does not meet the requirements of subparagraph (A), (B), or (C) solely because the item is not yet in use.

(14) The term "component" means any item supplied to the Federal Government as part of an end item or of another component.

(15) The term "commercial component" means any component that is a commercial item.

(16) The term "acquisition"—

(A) means the process of acquiring, with appropriated funds, by contract for purchase or lease, property or services (including construction) that support the missions and goals of an executive agency, from the point at which the requirements of the executive agency are established in consultation with the chief acquisition officer of the executive agency; and

(B) includes—

(i) the process of acquiring property or services that are already in existence, or that must be created, developed, demonstrated, and evaluated;

683

(ii) the description of requirements to satisfy agency needs;

(iii) solicitation and selection of sources;

(iv) award of contracts;

(v) contract performance;

(vi) contract financing;

(vii) management and measurement of contract performance through final delivery and payment; and

(viii) technical and management functions directly related to the process of fulfilling agency requirements by contract.

(17) The term "Federal Acquisition Regulatory Council" means the Federal Acquisition Regulatory Council established under section 421 of this title.

(Pub.L. 93–400, § 4, Aug. 30, 1974, 88 Stat. 797; Pub.L. 96–83, § 3, Oct. 10, 1979, 93 Stat. 649; Pub.L. 98–191, § 4, Dec. 1, 1983, 97 Stat. 1326; Pub.L. 98–369, Div. B, Title VII, § 2731, July 18, 1984, 98 Stat. 1195; Pub.L. 98–577, Title I, § 102, Oct. 30, 1984, 98 Stat. 3067; Pub.L. 100–679, § 3(c), Nov. 17, 1988, 102 Stat. 4056; Pub.L. 101–510, § 806(a)(1), Nov. 5, 1990, 104 Stat. 1592; Pub.L. 103–355, Title IV, § 4001, Title VIII, § 8001, Oct. 13, 1994, 108 Stat. 3338, 3384; Pub.L. 104–106, Div. D, Title XLII, § 4204, Feb. 10, 1996, 110 Stat. 655; Pub.L. 106–65, Div. A, Title VIII, § 805, Oct. 5, 1999, 113 Stat. 705; Pub.L. 108–136, Div. A, Title XIV, §§ 1411, 1433, Nov. 24, 2003, 117 Stat. 1663, 1673; Pub.L. 108–375, Div. A, Title VIII, § 807(b), Oct. 28, 2004, 118 Stat. 2011.)

HISTORICAL AND STATUTORY NOTES

Revision Notes and Legislative Reports

1974 Acts. Senate Report No. 93–692, see 1974 U.S.Code Cong. and Adm.News, p. 4589.

1979 Acts. House Report No. 96–178, see 1979 U.S.Code Cong. and Adm.News, p. 1492.

1983 Acts. Senate Report No. 98–214, see 1983 U.S.Code Cong. and Adm.News, p. 2027.

1984 Acts. Senate Report No. 98–523, see 1984 U.S.Code Cong. and Adm.News, p. 5347.

1988 Acts. Senate Report No. 100–424, see 1988 U.S.Code Cong. and Adm.News. p. 5687.

1990 Acts. House Report No. 101–665 and House Conference Report No. 101–923, see 1990 Act U.S.Code Cong. and Adm.News, p. 2931.

1994 Acts. Senate Report Nos. 103–258 and 103–259, and House Confer-

ence Report No. 103–712, see 1994 U.S. Code Cong. and Adm. News, p. 2561.

1996 Acts. House Conference Report No. 104–450, see 1996 U.S. Code Cong. and Adm. News, p. 238.

1999 Acts. House Conference Report No. 106–301 and Statement by President, see 1999 U.S. Code Cong. and Adm. News, p. 94.

2003 Acts. House Conference Report No. 108–354 and Statement by President, see 2003 U.S. Code Cong. and Adm. News, p. 1407.

2004 Acts. House Conference Report No. 108–767, see 2004 U.S. Code Cong. and Adm. News, p. 1961.

Statement by President, see 2004 U.S. Code Cong. and Adm. News, p. S37.

References in Text

This chapter, referred to in text, was in the original "this Act", meaning Pub.L. 93–400, which is classified principally to this chapter. For complete classification of this Act to the Code, see Short Title note set out under 41 U.S.C.A. § 401 and Tables.

Codifications

Section 2731 of Pub.L. 98–369 directed in part that this section be redesignated as section 4 of Pub.L. 93–400 to correct an inconsistency in the language of the amendment by Pub.L. 98–191, which amended this section generally but referred to it as "Sec. 3". Since this section was enacted as section 4 of Pub.L. 93–400 no change was required.

Amendments

2004 Amendments. Par. (17). Pub.L. 108–375, § 807(b), added par. (17).

2003 Amendments. Par. (12)(F). Pub.L. 108–136, § 1433, inserted "or specific outcomes to be achieved" after "performed".

Par. (16). Pub.L. 108–136, § 1411, added par. (16).

1999 Amendments. Par. (12)(E). Pub.L. 106–65, § 805, rewrote subpar. (E), which formerly read:

"**(E)** Installation services, maintenance services, repair services, training services, and other services if such services are procured for support of an item referred to in subparagraph (A), (B), (C), or (D) and if the source of such services—

"**(i)** offers such services to the general public and the Federal Government contemporaneously and under similar terms and conditions; and

"**(ii)** offers to use the same work force for providing the Federal Government with such services as the source uses for providing such services to the general public."

1996 Amendments. Par. (12)(F). Pub.L. 104–106, § 4204, added "or market" following "catalog".

1994 Amendments. Pub.L. 103–355, § 8001(b)(1), substituted "this chapter:" for "this chapter—".

Pars. (1) to (3). Pub.L. 103–355, § 8001(b)(2), (3), capitalized the introductory word to read "The" and substituted for the semicolon a period.

Par. (4). Pub.L. 103–355, § 8001(b)(2)(4), capitalized the introductory word to read "The" and substituted for "; and" a period.

Pars. (5) to (9). Pub.L. 103–355, § 8001(b)(2), (3), capitalized the introductory word to read "The" and substituted for the semicolon a period.

Par. (10). Pub.L. 103–355, § 8001(b)(2), (4), capitalized the introductory word to read "The" and substituted for "; and" a period.

Par. (11). Pub.L. 103–355, § 4001, substituted the definition of the term "simplified acquisition threshold" as meaning $100,000 for the definition of the term "small purchase threshold" as meaning $25,000, adjusted on October 1 of each year divisible by 5 to the amount equal to $25,000 in constant fiscal year 1990 dollars (rounded to the nearest $1,000).

Pub.L. 103–355, §§ 4001, 8001(b)(2), enacted identical amendments, capitalizing the introductory word to read "The".

Pars. (12) to (15). Pub.L. 103–355, § 8001(a), added pars. (12) to (15).

1990 Amendments. Subsec. (a)(11). Pub.L. 101–510, § 806(a)(1), added par. (11).

1988 Amendments. Par. (4). Pub.L. 100–679 redesignated former par. (5) as (4) and struck out former par. (4), which defined the term "single system of Government-wide procurement regulations" for purposes of this chapter.

Pars. (5) to (10). Pub.L. 100–679 redesignated former pars. (6) to (11) as (5) to (10), respectively.

Par. (11). Pub.L. 100–679 redesignated former par. (11) as (10).

1984 Amendments. Pars. (6) to (8). Pub.L. 98–369 added pars. (6) to (8).

Pars. (9) to (11). Pub.L. 98–577 added pars. (9) to (11).

1983 Amendments. Pub.L. 98–191 redesignated former subsecs. (a) and (b) as pars. (1) and (2), respectively, and, in pars. (1) and (2) as so redesignated, restated definitions of "executive agency" and "procurement", and added pars. (3) to (5).

1979 Amendments. Pub.L. 96–83 designated existing provisions as subsec. (a), and added subsec. (b).

Effective and Applicability Provisions

1996 Acts. Amendment by Pub.L. 104–106 effective Feb. 10, 1996, except as otherwise provided, see section 4401 of

Pub.L. 104–106, set out as a note under section 251 of this title.

1994 Acts. Amendment by sections 4001 and 8001 of Pub.L. 103–355 effective Oct. 13, 1994, except as otherwise provided, see section 10001 of Pub.L. 103–355, set out as a note under section 251 of this title.

1984 Acts. Amendment by Pub.L. 98–369 applicable with respect to any solicitation for bids or proposals issued after Mar. 31, 1985, see section 2751(a) of Pub.L. 98–369, set out as a note under section 251 of this title.

1979 Acts. Amendment by Pub.L. 96–83 effective Oct. 1, 1979, see section 12 of Pub.L. 96–83, set out as a note under section 401 of this title.

Partnership and Cooperation Agreements and References to Agreements
Any reference in a law, regulation, document, or other paper of the United States to a "cooperation agreement" or "project cooperation agreement" deemed to be a reference to a "partnership agreement" or a "project partnership agree-

ment", respectively, see Pub.L. 110–114, Title II, § 2003(f), Nov. 8, 2007, 121 Stat. 1070, set out as a note under 42 U.S.C.A. § 1962d–5b.

First Adjustment of Small Purchase Threshold
Section 806(a)(2) of Pub.L. 101–510 provided that: "The first adjustment under section 4(11) of such Act [par. (11) of this section], as amended by paragraph (1), shall be made on October 1, 1995."

Modification of Federal Acquisition Regulations
Section 2752 of Pub.L. 98–369 provided that: "Not later than March 31, 1985, the single Government-wide procurement regulation referred to in section 4(4)(A) of the Office of Federal Procurement Policy Act (41 U.S.C. 403(4)(A)) [par. (4)(A) of this section] shall be modified to conform to the requirements of this title [Title VII of Pub.L. 98–369, §§ 2701 to 2753, July 18, 1984, 98 Stat. 1175 to 1203] and the amendments made by this title [see Short Title of 1984 Amendment note set out under section 251 of this title]".

CROSS REFERENCES

Armed services acquisitions—
    Applicability of limitation on exception of appropriations to contracts at or below simplified acquisition threshold, see 10 USCA § 2207.
    Applicability of prohibition of contractors limiting subcontractors sales directly to the United States, see 10 USCA § 2402.
    Applicability of prohibition on persons convicted of defense-contract related felonies, see 10 USCA § 2408.
    Supplies and marking with name of contractor, see 10 USCA § 2384.
"Commercial item", "non-developmental item", "component", and "commercial component" defined as having the same meaning as under this section for purposes of—
    Armed services acquisitions, see 10 USCA § 2376.
    Civilian agency acquisitions, see 41 USCA § 264a.
"Commercial item" defined as having same meaning as under this section for purposes of—
    Applicability of prohibition on limitation of subcontractor direct sales, see 10 USCA § 2402.
    Federal procurement, see 33 USCA § 1368.
    Government-financed air transportation fly American requirement, see 49 USCA § 40118.
Contractor inventory accounting system standards, see 10 USCA § 2410b.
Inspection authority and exception, see 41 USCA § 58.
"Procurement, procurement system, standards, etc." defined as having same meaning as under this section for purposes of—
    Armed services acquisition, see 10 USCA § 2302.
    Civilian agency acquisitions, see 41 USCA § 259.
Prohibition against doing business with certain officers or contractors, see 10 USCA § 2393.
Simplified acquisition threshold—
    Defined as having same meaning as under this section for purposes of armed services acquisition and certification, see 10 USCA § 2410.

Simplified acquisition threshold——Cont'd
Executive agencies, see 41 USCA § 252a.
Federal acquisition regulation, see 10 USCA § 2302a.

LAW REVIEW AND JOURNAL COMMENTARIES

Enforcing competition through government contract claims. Michael K. Love, 20 U.Rich.L.Rev. 525 (1986).

Research References

ALR Library
21 ALR 180, False Pretense: Presentation of and Attempt to Establish Fraudulent Claim Against Governmental Agency.
Encyclopedias
Am. Jur. 2d Job Discrimination § 410, Obligations of Employers.

Forms
Federal Procedural Forms § 34:11, Small Purchase and Other Simplified Procedures.

Treatises and Practice Aids
Emp. Discrim. Coord. Analysis of Federal Law § 20:92, Which Employers Must Maintain a Drug-Free Workplace.
West's Federal Administrative Practice § 627, Contracting by Negotiation--Commercial Item Contracting.
West's Federal Administrative Practice § 2157, Historically Underutilized Business Zone Program ("Hubzone").

WESTLAW ELECTRONIC RESEARCH

See Westlaw guide following the Explanation pages of this volume.

Notes of Decisions

Construction with other laws 1

---

1. Construction with other laws
Office of Federal Procurement Policy Act Amendments of 1979 (OFPPAA) could not serve as "a relevant statute" under which civilian employees of military base could establish prudential standing to challenge decision to outsource base support services contract pursuant to Administrative Procedure Act (APA), inasmuch as employees' cognizable interests in maintaining their employment at base were not within zone of interests protected by OFPPAA; rather, underlying procurement policy reflected desire to outsource government work whenever doing so would result in increased cost efficiency, and nothing in OFPPAA or its legisla-

tive history supported conclusion that Congress intended to protect employment of federal workers. Courtney v. Smith, C.A.6 (Ohio) 2002, 297 F.3d 455, certiorari denied 124 S.Ct. 64, 540 U.S. 814, 157 L.Ed.2d 28. United States ☞ 64.60(2)

Definition of "procurement" in the Federal Procurement Policy Act which establishes the Office of Federal Procurement Policy within the Office of Management and Budget does not apply to the Competition in Contracting Act (CICA). Rapides Regional Medical Center v. Secretary, Dept. of Veterans' Affairs, C.A.5 (La.) 1992, 974 F.2d 565, rehearing denied 979 F.2d 211, certiorari denied 113 S.Ct. 2413, 508 U.S. 939, 124 L.Ed.2d 636. United States ☞ 64.10

§ 404. Establishment of Office of Federal Procurement Policy; appointment of Administrator

(a) There is in the Office of Management and Budget an Office of Federal Procurement Policy (hereinafter referred to as the "Office") to provide overall direction of Government-wide procurement policies, regulations, procedures, and forms for executive agencies and to promote economy, efficiency, and effectiveness in the procurement of property and services by the executive branch of the Federal Government.

(b) There shall be at the head of the Office an Administrator for Federal Procurement Policy (hereinafter referred to as the "Administrator"), who shall be appointed by the President, by and with the advice and consent of the Senate.

(Pub.L. 93–400, § 5, Aug. 30, 1974, 88 Stat. 797; Pub.L. 104–106, Div. D, Title XLIII, § 4305(a)(1), Feb. 10, 1996, 110 Stat. 665.)

HISTORICAL AND STATUTORY NOTES

Revision Notes and Legislative Reports
1974 Acts. Section 5 establishes the Office of Federal Procurement Policy in the Executive Office of the President. It is to be headed by an Administrator. There shall also be a Deputy Administrator in the OFPP, who shall serve as Acting Administrator during the absence or disability of the Administrator until the President designates a person to fill the vacancy. Both the Administrator and Deputy Administrator are to be appointed by the President with the advice and consent of the Senate. The Office is to function subject to the policies and directives of the President. Senate Report No. 93–692.

1996 Acts. House Conference Report No. 104–450, see 1996 U.S. Code Cong. and Adm. News, p. 238.

Amendments
1996 Amendments. Subsec. (a). Pub.L. 104–106, § 4305(a)(1), added provisions relating to purpose of Office of Federal Procurement Policy.

Effective and Applicability Provisions
1996 Acts. Amendment by Pub.L. 104–106 effective Feb. 10, 1996, except as otherwise provided, see section 4401 of Pub.L. 104–106, set out as a note under section 251 of this title.

LIBRARY REFERENCES

American Digest System
   United States ☞33.
   Key Number System Topic No. 393.

WESTLAW ELECTRONIC RESEARCH

See Westlaw guide following the Explanation pages of this volume.

§ 405. Authority and functions of the Administrator

(a) Development of procurement policy; leadership

The Administrator shall provide overall direction of procurement policy and leadership in the development of procurement systems of the executive agencies. To the extent that the Administrator considers appropriate, in carrying out the policies and functions set forth in this chapter, and with due regard for applicable laws and the program activities of the executive agencies, the Administrator may prescribe Government-wide procurement policies. These policies shall be implemented in a single Government-wide procurement regulation called the Federal Acquisition Regulation and shall be followed by executive agencies in the procurement of—

(1) property other than real property in being;

(2) services, including research and development; and

(3) construction, alteration, repair, or maintenance of real property.

(b) Government–wide procurement regulations

In any instance in which the Administrator determines that the Department of Defense, the National Aeronautics and Space Administration, and the General Services Administration are unable to agree on or fail to issue Government-wide regulations, procedures and forms in a timely manner, including any such regulations, procedures, and forms as are necessary to implement prescribed policy initiated by the Administrator under subsection (a) of this section, the Administrator shall, with due regard for applicable laws and the program activities of the executive agencies and consistent with the policies and functions set forth in this chapter, prescribe Government-wide regulations, procedures and forms which shall be followed by executive agencies in the procurement of—

(1) property other than real property in being;

(2) services, including research and development; and

(3) construction, alteration, repair, or maintenance of real property.

(c) Noninterference with executive agencies

The authority of the Administrator under this chapter shall not be construed to—

(1) impair or interfere with the determination by executive agencies of their need for, or their use of, specific property, services, or construction, including particular specifications therefor; or

(2) interfere with the determination by executive agencies of specific actions in the award or administration of procurement contracts.

(d) Enumeration of included functions

The functions of the Administrator shall include—

(1) providing leadership and ensuring action by the executive agencies in the establishment, development and maintenance of the single system of simplified Government-wide procurement regulations and resolving differences among the executive agencies in the development of simplified Government-wide procurement regulations, procedures and forms;

(2) coordinating the development of Government-wide procurement system standards that shall be implemented by the executive agencies in their procurement systems;

(3) providing leadership and coordination in the formulation of the executive branch position on legislation relating to procurement;

(4)(A) providing for and directing the activities of the computer-based Federal Procurement Data System (including recommending to the Administrator of General Services a sufficient budget for such activities), which shall be located in the General Services Administration, in order to adequately collect, develop, and disseminate procurement data; and

(B) ensuring executive agency compliance with the record requirements of section 417 of this title;

(5) providing for and directing the activities of the Federal Acquisition Institute (including recommending to the Administrator of General Services a sufficient budget for such activities), which shall be located in the General Services Administration, in order to—

(A) foster and promote the development of a professional acquisition workforce Government-wide;

(B) promote and coordinate Government-wide research and studies to improve the procurement process and the laws, policies, methods, regulations, procedures, and forms relating to acquisition by the executive agencies;

(C) collect data and analyze acquisition workforce data from the Office of Personnel Management, the heads of executive agencies, and, through periodic surveys, from individual employees;

(D) periodically analyze acquisition career fields to identify critical competencies, duties, tasks, and related academic prerequisites, skills, and knowledge;

(E) coordinate and assist agencies in identifying and recruiting highly qualified candidates for acquisition fields;

(F) develop instructional materials for acquisition personnel in coordination with private and public acquisition colleges and training facilities;

(G) evaluate the effectiveness of training and career development programs for acquisition personnel;

(H) promote the establishment and utilization of academic programs by colleges and universities in acquisition fields;

(I) facilitate, to the extent requested by agencies, interagency intern and training programs; and

(J) perform other career management or research functions as directed by the Administrator;

(6) administering the provisions of section 433 of this title;

(7) establishing criteria and procedures to ensure the effective and timely solicitation of the viewpoints of interested parties in the development of procurement policies, regulations, procedures, and forms;

(8) developing standard contract forms and contract language in order to reduce the Government's cost of procuring property and services and the private sector's cost of doing business with the Government;

(9) providing for a Government-wide award to recognize and promote vendor excellence;

(10) providing for a Government-wide award to recognize and promote excellence in officers and employees of the Federal Government serving in procurement-related positions;

(11) developing policies, in consultation with the Administrator of the Small Business Administration, that ensure that small businesses, qualified HUBZone small business concerns (as defined in section 632(p) of Title 15), small businesses owned and controlled by socially and economically disadvantaged individuals, and small businesses owned and controlled by women are provided with the maximum practicable opportunities to participate in procurements that are conducted for amounts below the simplified acquisition threshold;

(12) developing policies that will promote achievement of goals for participation by small businesses, qualified HUBZone small business concerns (as defined in section 632(p) of Title 15), small businesses owned and controlled by socially and economically disadvantaged individuals, and small businesses owned and controlled by women; and

(13) completing action, as appropriate, on the recommendations of the Commission on Government Procurement.

(e) Consultation; assistance of existing executive agencies; advisory committees and interagency groups

In carrying out the functions set forth in subsection (d) of this section, the Administrator—

(1) shall consult with the affected executive agencies, including the Small Business Administration;

(2) may, with the concurrence of the heads of affected executive agencies, designate an executive agency or executive agencies to assist in the performance of such functions; and

(3) may establish advisory committees or other interagency groups to assist in providing for the establishment, development, and maintenance of a single system of simplified Government-wide procurement regulations and to assist in the performance of any of the other functions which the Administrator considers appropriate.

(f) Oversight of regulations promulgated by other agencies relating to procurement

The Administrator, with the concurrence of the Director of the Office of Management and Budget, and with consultation with the head of the agency or agencies concerned, may deny the promulgation of or rescind any Government–wide regulation or final rule or regulation of any executive agency relating to procurement if the Administrator determines that such rule or regulation is inconsistent with any policies, regulations, or procedures issued pursuant to subsection (a) of this section.

(g) Assignment, delegation, or transfer of functions prohibited

Except as otherwise provided by law, no duties, functions, or responsibilities, other than those expressly assigned by this chapter, shall be assigned, delegated, or transferred to the Administrator.

(h) Automatic data processing and telecommunications equipment; real property procurement; Office of Management and Budget

Nothing in this chapter shall be construed to—

(1) impair or affect the authorities or responsibilities conferred by the Federal Property and Administrative Services Act of 1949 [41 U.S.C.A. § 251 et seq.] with respect to the procurement of real property; or

(2) limit the current authorities and responsibilities of the Director of the Office of Management and Budget.

(i) Recipients of Federal grants or assistance

(1) With due regard to applicable laws and the program activities of the executive agencies administering Federal programs of grants or assistance, the Administrator may prescribe Government-wide policies, regulations, procedures, and forms which the Administrator considers appropriate and which shall be followed by such executive agencies in providing for the procurement, to the extent required under such programs, of property or services referred to in clauses (1), (2), and (3) of subsection (a) of this section by recipients of Federal grants or assistance under such programs.

(2) Nothing in paragraph (1) shall be construed to—

(A) permit the Administrator to authorize procurement or supply support, either directly or indirectly, to recipients of Federal grants or assistance; or

(B) authorize any action by such recipients contrary to State and local laws, in the case of programs to provide Federal grants or assistance to States and political subdivisions.

(j) Policy regarding consideration of contractor past performance

(1) The Administrator shall prescribe for executive agencies guidance regarding consideration of the past contract performance of offerors in awarding contracts. The guidance shall include—

(A) standards for evaluating past performance with respect to cost (when appropriate), schedule, compliance with technical or functional specifications, and other relevant performance factors that facilitate consistent and fair evaluation by all executive agencies;

(B) policies for the collection and maintenance of information on past contract performance that, to the maximum extent practicable, facilitate automated collection, maintenance, and dissemination of information and provide for ease of collection, maintenance, and dissemination of information by other methods, as necessary;

(C) policies for ensuring that—

(i) offerors are afforded an opportunity to submit relevant information on past contract performance, including performance under contracts entered into by the executive agency concerned, contracts entered into by other departments and agencies of the Federal Government, contracts entered into by agencies of State and local governments, and contracts entered into by commercial customers; and

(ii) such information submitted by offerors is considered; and

(D) the period for which information on past performance of offerors may be maintained and considered.

(2) In the case of an offeror with respect to which there is no information on past contract performance or with respect to which information on past contract performance is not available, the offeror may not be evaluated favorably or unfavorably on the factor of past contract performance.

(k) Annual reporting requirement

The Administrator shall submit to Congress, on an annual basis, an assessment of the progress made in executive agencies in implementing the policy regarding major acquisitions that is stated in section 263(a) of this title. The Administrator shall use data from existing management systems in making the assessment.

(Pub.L. 93–400, § 6, Aug. 30, 1974, 88 Stat. 797; Pub.L. 96–83, § 4, Oct. 10, 1979, 93 Stat. 649; Pub.L. 98–191, § 5, Dec. 1, 1983, 97 Stat. 1326; Pub.L. 98–369, Div. B, Title VII, § 2732(b)(1), July 18, 1984, 98 Stat. 1199; Pub.L. 100–679, § 3(a), Nov. 17, 1988, 102 Stat. 4055; Pub.L. 103–355, Title I, § 1091(b)(2), Title V, §§ 5051(b), 5091, Title VII, § 7108(a), (b), Oct. 13, 1994, 108 Stat. 3272, 3351, 3361, 3378; Pub.L. 104–106, Div. D, Title XLIII, §§ 4307(b), 4321(h)(1), (2), 4322(a)(1), Div. E, Title LVI, § 5607(d), Feb. 10, 1996, 110 Stat. 668, 675, 677, 702; Pub.L. 104–201, Div. A, Title X, § 1074(f)(1), Sept. 23, 1996, 110 Stat. 2661; Pub.L. 105–85, Div. A, Title VIII, § 851(b), Title X, § 1073(g)(2)(B), Nov. 18, 1997, 111 Stat. 1851, 1906; Pub.L. 105–135, Title VI, § 604(f)(1), Dec. 2, 1997, 111 Stat. 2634.)

HISTORICAL AND STATUTORY NOTES

Revision Notes and Legislative Reports

1974 Acts. Senate Report No. 93–692, see 1974 U.S.Code Cong. and Adm.News, p. 4589.

1979 Acts. House Report No. 96–178, see 1979 U.S.Code Cong. and Adm.News, p. 1492.

1983 Acts. Senate Report No. 98–214, see 1983 U.S.Code Cong. and Adm.News, p. 2027.

1984 Acts. House Report No. 98–432, Pt. II, Senate Report Nos. 98–50 and 98–297, and House Conference Report No. 98–861, see 1984 U.S.Code Cong. and Adm.News, p. 697.

1988 Acts. Senate Report No. 100–424, see 1988 U.S.Code Cong. and Adm.News, p. 5687.

1994 Acts. Senate Report Nos. 103–258 and 103–259, and House Conference Report No. 103–712, see 1994 U.S. Code Cong. and Adm. News, p. 2561.

1996 Acts. House Conference Report No. 104–450, see 1996 U.S. Code Cong. and Adm. News, p. 238.

House Report No. 104–563 and House Conference Report No. 104–724, see 1996 U.S. Code Cong. and Adm. News, p. 2948.

1997 Acts. House Conference Report No. 105–340 and Statement by President, see 1997 U.S. Code Cong. and Adm. News, p. 2251.

Senate Report No. 105–62, see 1997 U.S. Code Cong. and Adm. News, p. 3077.

References in Text

The Federal Property and Administrative Services Act of 1949, referred to in subsec. (h)(1), is Act June 30, 1949, c. 288, 63 Stat. 377, as amended, Title III of which is currently classified to subchapter IV of chapter 4 of Title 41, 41 U.S.C.A. § 251 et seq., and the remainder of which was formerly classified to chapter 10 of former Title 40, 40 U.S.C.A. § 471 et seq., prior to being repealed by Pub.L. 107–217, § 6(b), Aug. 21, 2002, 116 Stat. 1313; see now generally chapter 1 of Title 40, 40 U.S.C.A. § 101 et seq.

Codifications

Amendment by Pub.L. 104–106, § 4321(h)(1) was executed to subsec. (d)(13) of this section, in view of redesignation of pars. (6) through (12) as pars. (7) through (13) in section 4307(b)(1). Amendment by § 4321(h)(2) was executed to subsec. (d)(12) of this section, in view of such redesignation and notwithstanding directory language indicating only par. (11), as the probable intent of Congress.

Amendments

1997 Amendments. Subsec. (d)(5)(J). Pub.L. 105–85, § 1073(g)(2)(B)(i), substituted a semicolon for a period following "by the Administrator".

Subsec. (d)(6). Pub.L. 105–85, § 1073(g)(2)(B)(ii), repositioned par. (6).

Subsec. (d)(11). Pub.L. 105–135, § 604(f)(1)(A), inserted "qualified HUBZone small business concerns (as defined in section 632(p) of Title 15),".

Subsec. (d)(12). Pub.L. 105–85, § 1073(g)(2)(B)(iii), which directed that "small businesses" be substituted for "small business" was incapable of execution, as this change had already been made by Pub.L. 104–106, § 4321(h)(2). See 1996 Amendment notes and Codification note set out under this section.

Subsec. (d)(12). Pub.L. 105–135, § 604(f)(1)(B), inserted "qualified HUBZone small business concerns (as defined in section 632(p) of Title 15),".

Subsec. (k). Pub.L. 105–85, § 851(b), inserted "regarding major acquisitions that is" following "implementing the policy".

1996 Amendments. Subsec. (b). Pub.L. 104–106, § 4322(a)(1), struck out the second comma following "subsection (a) of this section".

Subsec. (d)(5)(A). Pub.L. 104–106, § 4307(b)(2)(A), substituted "the development of a professional acquisition workforce Government-wide" for "Government-wide career management programs for a professional procurement work force".

Subsec. (d)(5)(B). Pub.L. 104–106, § 4307(b)(2)(B)(i), substituted "acquisition by the" for "procurement by the".

Subsec. (d)(5)(C). Pub.L. 104–106, § 4307(b)(2)(B)(iii), substituted provisions relating to collecting data and analyzing acquisition workforce data for provisions relating to policies and procedures for establishment and implementation of education and training programs.

Subsec. (d)(5)(D) to (J). Pub.L. 104–106, § 4307(b)(2)(B)(iii), added subpars. (D) through (J).

Subsec. (d)(6). Pub.L. 104–106, § 4307(b)(1), redesignated par. (6) as par. (7).

Pub.L. 104–106, § 4307(b)(3), added par. (6).

Subsec. (d)(7) to (11). Pub.L. 104–106, § 4307(b)(1), redesignated pars. (7) through (11) as pars. (8) through (12).

Subsec. (d)(12). Pub.L. 104–106, § 4307(b)(1), redesignated par. (12) as par. (13).

Pub.L. 104–106, § 4321(h)(2), substituted "small businesses" for "small business". See Codification note set out under this section.

Subsec. (d)(13). Pub.L. 104–106, § 4307(b)(1), redesignated par. (12) as par. (13).

Pub.L. 104–106, § 4321(h)(1), transferred par. (13) to end of subsection, which amendment had already been executed, thereby requiring no further change in text. See Codification note set out under this section.

Subsec. (f). Pub.L. 104–201, § 1074(f)(1), struck out reference to inconsistency with policies of section 401 of this title.

Subsec. (h)(1). Pub.L. 104–106, § 5607(d), struck out "of automatic data processing and telecommunications equipment and services or" following "procurement".

1994 Amendments. Subsec. (d)(5). Pub.L. 103–355, § 7108(b)(1)-(3), struck "and" at the end of subpar. (A), substituted "; and" for the period at the end of subpar. (B), and added subpar. (C).

Subsec. (d)(7). Pub.L. 103–355, § 5091(1), struck "and" at the end of par. (7).

Subsec. (d)(8). Pub.L. 103–355, § 5091(3), added par. (8). Former par. (8) redesignated (12).

Subsec. (d)(9). Pub.L. 103–355, § 5091(3), added par. (9).

Subsec. (d)(10), (11). Pub.L. 103–355, § 7108(a), added pars. (10) and (11).

Subsec. (d)(12). Pub.L. 103–355, § 5091(2), redesignated par. (8) as (12).

Subsec. (j). Pub.L. 103–355, § 1091(b)(2), added subsec. (j).

Subsec. (k). Pub.L. 103–355, § 5051(b), added subsec. (k).

1988 Amendments. Subsec. (a). Pub.L. 100–679, § 3(a)(1), inserted a period after "policies" and substituted "These policies shall be implemented in a single Government-wide procurement regulation called the Federal Acquisition Regulation and shall be" for "which shall be implemented in a single system of Government-wide procurement regulations and shall be".

Subsec. (b). Pub.L. 100–679, § 3(a)(2), inserted ", including any such regulations, procedures, and forms as are necessary to implement prescribed policy initiated by the Administrator under subsection (a) of this section," after "timely manner" and substituted "shall" for "may".

Subsec. (d)(4). Pub.L. 100–679, § 3(a)(3), included within the functions of the Administrator directing the activities of the computer-based Federal Procurement Data System, including recommending to the Administrator of General Services a sufficient budget for such activities, and ensuring executive agency compliance with the record requirements of section 417 of this title.

Subsec. (d)(5). Pub.L. 100–679, § 3(a)(3), included within the functions of the administrator directing the activities of the Federal Acquisition Institute, including recommending to the Administrator of general Services a sufficient budget for such activities.

Subsec. (f). Pub.L. 100–679, § 3(a)(4), substituted "The Administrator, with the concurrence of the Director of the Office of Management and Budget, and with consultation with the head of the agency or agencies concerned," for "The Director of the Office Management and Budget".

1984 Amendments. Subsec. (e). Pub.L. 98–369 substituted "subsection (d)" for "subsection (c)".

1983 Amendments. Pub.L. 98–191 generally strengthened and expanded the authority and functions of the Administrator for Federal Procurement Policy by revising and restating as subsecs. (a), (c), (d), (e), (g), (h), and (i) provisions of former subsecs. (a), (f), (d), (e), (g), (j), and (b), respectively, and by adding provisions set out in new subsecs. (b) and (f).

1979 Amendments. Subsec. (a). Pub.L. 96–83, § 4(a), substituted provisions setting forth the responsibilities of the Administrator with respect to the development and implementation of procurement policies, the coordination of programs to improve the quality and performance of personnel, and the development of a uniform procurement system, for provisions setting forth overall directive responsibility of the Administrator, and functions with respect to issuance of policy directions, regulations, procedures, and forms.

Subsec. (c). Pub.L. 96–83, § 4(b), substituted provisions relating to development and proposal of a central management system, for provisions setting forth limitation of authority to procurement

from appropriated funds and provisions relating to a study and report of procurement from nonappropriated funds.

Subsec. (d). Pub.L. 96–83, § 4(c), substituted provisions setting forth the review, development, etc., functions of the Administrator with respect to procurement policies, regulations, procedures, and forms, procurement data, procurement personnel, and procurement contracts, for provisions setting forth the establishment, monitoring, etc., functions of the Administrator with respect to uniform procurement regulations, procurement policies, regulations, procedures, and forms, procurement data, and procurement personnel.

Subsec. (e). Pub.L. 96–83, § 4(d), substituted provisions relating to consultative functions of the Administrator with respect to the development and implementation of the uniform procurement system, for provisions relating to the consultative functions of the Administrator with respect to the development of policies, regulations, procedures and forms to be authorized or prescribed by such Administrator.

Subsecs. (h) to (j). Pub.L. 96–83, § 4(e), added subsecs. (h) to (j).

Effective and Applicability Provisions

1997 Acts. Pub.L. 105–135 and the amendments made by Pub.L. 105–135 effective on October 1, 1997, see section 3 of Pub.L. 105–135, set out as a note under section 631 of Title 15, Commerce and Trade.

1996 Acts. Amendment by sections 4307(b), 4321(h)(1), (2), and 4322(a)(1) of Pub.L. 104–106 effective Feb. 10, 1996, except as otherwise provided, see section 4401 of Pub.L. 104–106, set out as a note under section 251 of this title.

Pub.L. 104–106, Div. E, Title LVII, § 5701, Feb. 10, 1996, 110 Stat. 702, which provided that amendment by section 5607(d) of Pub.L. 104–106 was to be effective 180 days after Feb. 10, 1996, was repealed by Pub.L. 107–217, § 6(b), Aug. 21, 2002, 116 Stat. 1325.

1994 Acts. Amendment by sections 1091(b)(2) and 7108 of Pub.L. 103–355 effective Oct. 13, 1994, except as otherwise provided, see section 10001 of Pub.L. 103–355, set out as a note under section 251 of this title.

Amendment by sections 5051(b) and 5091 of Pub.L. 103–355 effective Oct. 13, 1994, and applicable on and after such date, see section 10001 of Pub.L. 103–355, set out as a note under section 251 of this title.

1984 Acts. Amendment by Pub.L. 98–369 applicable with respect to any solicitation for bids or proposals issued after Mar. 31, 1985, see section 2751(a) of Pub.L. 98–369, set out as a note under section 251 of this title.

1979 Acts. Amendment by Pub.L. 96–83 effective Oct. 1, 1979, see section 12 of Pub.L. 96–83, set out as a note under section 401 of this title.

Pilot Program for Development and Implementation of an Inventory to Track the Cost and Size of Service Contracts
Pub.L. 110–161, Div. D, Title VII, § 748, Dec. 26, 2007, 121 Stat. 2035, provided that: "No later than 180 days after enactment of this Act [Dec. 26, 2007], the Office of Management and Budget shall establish a pilot program to develop and implement an inventory to track the cost and size (in contractor manpower equivalents) of service contracts, particularly with respect to contracts that have been performed poorly by a contractor because of excessive costs or inferior quality, as determined by a contracting officer within the last five years, involve inherently governmental functions, or were undertaken without competition. The pilot program shall be established in at least three Cabinet-level departments, based on varying levels of annual contracting for services, as reported by the Federal Procurement Data System's Federal Procurement Report for fiscal year 2005, including at least one Cabinet-level department that contracts out annually for $10,000,000,000 or more in services, at least one Cabinet-level department that contracts out annually for between $5,000,000,000 and $9,000,000,000 in services, and at least one Cabinet-level department that contracts out annually for under $5,000,000,000 in services."

Federal Support for Enhancement of State and Local Anti-Terrorism Response Capabilities
Pub.L. 108–136, Div. A, Title VIII, § 803, Nov. 24, 2003, 117 Stat. 1541, provided that:

"**(a) Procurements of anti-terrorism technologies and services by State and local Governments.**—The Administrator for Federal Procurement Policy shall establish a program under which States and units of local government may procure through contracts entered into by the Department of Defense or the Department of Homeland Security anti-terrorism technologies or anti-terrorism services for the purpose of preventing, detecting, identifying, deterring, or recovering from acts of terrorism.

"**(b) Authorities.**—Under the program, the Secretary of Defense and the Secretary of Homeland Security may, but shall not be required to, award contracts using the procedures established by the Administrator of General Services for the multiple awards schedule program of the General Services Administration.

"**(c) Definition.**—In this section, the term 'State or local government' has the meaning provided in section 502(c)(3) of title 40, United States Code."

Statutory and Regulatory Review
Pub.L. 108–136, Div. A, Title XIV, § 1423, Nov. 24, 2003, 117 Stat. 1669, as amended Pub.L. 109–163, Div. A, Title VIII, § 843, Jan. 6, 2006, 119 Stat. 3389, provided that:

"**(a) Establishment.**—Not later than 90 days after the date of the enactment of this Act [Nov. 24, 2003], the Administrator for Federal Procurement Policy shall establish an advisory panel to review laws and regulations regarding the use of commercial practices, performance-based contracting, the performance of acquisition functions across agency lines of responsibility, and the use of Government-wide contracts.

"**(b) Membership.**—The panel shall be composed of at least nine individuals who are recognized experts in acquisition law and Government acquisition policy. In making appointments to the panel, the Administrator shall—

"**(1)** consult with the Secretary of Defense, the Administrator of General Services, the Committees on Armed Services and Government Reform of the House of Representatives, and the Committees on Armed Services and Governmental Affairs of the Senate; and

"**(2)** ensure that the members of the panel reflect the diverse experiences in both the public and private sectors, including academia.

"(c) Duties.—The panel shall—

"(1) review all Federal acquisition laws and regulations, and, to the extent practicable, government-wide acquisition policies, with a view toward ensuring effective and appropriate use of commercial practices and performance-based contracting; and

"(2) Make any recommendations for the modification of such laws, regulations, or policies that are considered necessary as a result of such review—

"(A) to protect the best interests of the Federal Government;

"(B) to ensure the continuing financial and ethical integrity of acquisitions by the Federal Government; and

"(C) to amend or eliminate any provisions in such laws, regulations, or policies that are unnecessary for the effective, efficient, and fair award and administration of contracts for the acquisition by the Federal Government of goods and services.

"(d) Report.—Not later than 18 months after the establishment of the panel, the panel shall submit to the Administrator and to the Committees on Armed Services and Government Reform of the House of Representatives and the Committees on Armed Services and Governmental Affairs of the Senate a report containing a detailed statement of the findings, conclusions, and recommendations of the panel."

Center of Excellence in Service Contracting
Pub.L. 108–136, Div. A, Title XIV, § 1431(b), Nov. 24, 2003, 117 Stat. 1671, provided that: "Not later than 180 days after the date of the enactment of this Act [Nov. 24, 2003], the Administrator for Federal Procurement Policy shall establish a center of excellence in contracting for services. The center of excellence shall assist the acquisition community by identifying, and serving as a clearinghouse for, best practices in contracting for services in the public and private sectors."

Congressional Findings and Policy Regarding Consideration of Contractor Past Performance
Section 1091(b)(1) of Pub.L. 103–355 provided that:

"(1) Congress makes the following findings:

"(A) Past contract performance of an offeror is one of the relevant factors that a contracting official of an executive agency should consider in awarding a contract.

"(B) It is appropriate for a contracting official to consider past contract performance of an offeror as an indicator of the likelihood that the offeror will successfully perform a contract to be awarded by that official."

Coordination with Other Amendments
Amendments by section 1073 of Pub.L. 105–85 to be treated as having been enacted immediately before the other provisions of Pub.L. 105–85, see section 1073(i) of Pub.L. 105–85, set out as a note under section 5315 of Title 5, Government Organization and Employees.

Data Collection Through the Federal Procurement Data System
Section 10004 of Pub.L. 103–355 provided that:

"(a) Data collection required.—The Federal Procurement Data System described in section 6(d)(4)(A) of the Office of Federal Procurement Policy Act (41 U.S.C. 405(d)(4)(A)) [subsec.(d)(4)(A) of this section] shall be modified to collect from contracts in excess of the simplified acquisition threshold data identifying the following matters:

"(1) Contract awards made pursuant to competitions conducted pursuant to section 2323 of title 10, United States Code [section 2323 of Title 10, Armed Forces], or section 7102 of the Federal Acquisition Streamlining Act of 1994 [section 7102 of Pub.L. 103–355, set out as a note under section 644 of Title 15, Commerce and Trade].

"(2) Awards to business concerns owned and controlled by women.

"(3) Number of offers received in response to a solicitation.

"(4) Task order contracts.

"(5) Contracts for the acquisition of commercial items.

"(b) Definition.—In this section, the term 'simplified acquisition threshold' has the meaning given such term in section 4(11) of the Office of Federal Procurement Policy Act (41 U.S.C. 403(11)) [section 403(11) of this title]."

Development of Definitions Regarding Certain Small Business Concerns

Section 7107 of Pub.L. 103–355 provided that:

"(a) **Review required.**—(1) The Administrator for Federal Procurement Policy shall conduct a comprehensive review of Federal laws, as in effect on November 1, 1994, to identify and catalogue all of the provisions in such laws that define (or describe for definitional purposes) the small business concerns set forth in paragraph (2) for purposes of authorizing the participation of such small business concerns as prime contractors or subcontractors in—

"(A) contracts awarded directly by the Federal Government or subcontracts awarded under such contracts; or

"(B) contracts and subcontracts funded, in whole or in part, by Federal financial assistance under grants, cooperative agreements, or other forms of Federal assistance.

"(2) The small business concerns referred to in paragraph (1) are as follows:

"(A) Small business concerns owned and controlled by socially and economically disadvantaged individuals.

"(B) Minority-owned small business concerns.

"(C) Small business concerns owned and controlled by women.

"(D) Woman-owned small business concerns.

"(b) **Matters to be developed.**—On the basis of the results of the review carried out under subsection (a), the Administrator for Federal Procurement Policy shall develop—

"(1) uniform definitions for the small business concerns referred to in subsection (a)(2);

"(2) uniform agency certification standards and procedures for—

"(A) determinations of whether a small business concern qualifies as a small business concern referred to in subsection (a)(2) under an applicable standard for purposes of contracts and subcontracts referred to in subsection (a)(1); and

"(B) reciprocal recognition by an agency of a decision of another agency regarding whether a small business concern qualifies as a small business concern referred to in subsection (a)(2) for such purposes; and

"(3) such other related recommendations as the Administrator determines appropriate consistent with the review results.

"(c) **Procedures and schedule.**—(1) The Administrator for Federal Procurement Policy shall provide for the participation in the review and activities under subsections (a) and (b) by representatives of—

"(A) the Small Business Administration (including the Office of the Chief Counsel for Advocacy);

"(B) the Minority Business Development Agency of the Department of Commerce;

"(C) the Department of Transportation;

"(D) the Environmental Protection Agency; and

"(E) such other executive departments and agencies as the Administrator considers appropriate.

"(2) In carrying out subsections (a) and (b), the Administrator shall consult with representatives of organizations representing—

"(A) minority-owned business enterprises;

"(B) women-owned business enterprises; and

"(C) other organizations that the Administrator considers appropriate.

"(3) Not later than 60 days after the date of the enactment of this Act [Oct. 13, 1994], the Administrator shall publish in the Federal Register a notice which—

"(A) lists the provisions of law identified in the review carried out under subsection (a);

"(B) describes the matters to be developed on the basis of the results of the review pursuant to subsection (b);

"(C) solicits public comment regarding the matters described in the notice pursuant to subparagraphs (A) and (B) for a period of not less than 60 days; and

"(D) addresses such other matters as the Administrator considers appropriate to ensure the comprehensiveness of the review and activities under subsections (a) and (b).

"(d) Report.—Not later than May 1, 1996, the Administrator for Federal Procurement Policy shall submit to the Committees on Small Business of the Senate and the House of Representatives a report on the results of the review carried out under subsection (a) and the actions taken under subsection (b). The report shall include a discussion of the results of the review, a description of the consultations conducted and public comments received, and the Administrator's recommendations with regard to the matters identified under subsection (b)."

Profit Methodology Study
Section 7 of Pub.L. 100–679 provided that:

"(a) In general.—The Administrator shall conduct a study to develop a consistent methodology which executive agencies should use for measuring the profits earned by government contractors on procurements, other than procurements where the price is based on adequate price competition or on established catalog or market prices of commercial items sold in substantial quantities to the general public.

"(b) Contractors' financial data.—The methodology developed under subsection (a) shall include adequate procedures for verifying and maintaining the confidentiality of contractors' financial data."

Reporting of bundled contract opportunities
Section 414 of Pub.L. 105–135 provided that:

"(a) Data collection required
"The Federal Procurement Data System described in section 6(d)(4)(A) of the Office of Federal Procurement Policy Act (41 U.S.C. 405(d)(4)(A)) shall be modified to collect data regarding bundling of contract requirements when the contracting

officer anticipates that the resulting contract price, including all options, is expected to exceed $5,000,000. The data shall reflect a determination made by the contracting officer regarding whether a particular solicitation constitutes a contract bundling.

"(b) Definitions
"In this section, the term 'bundling of contract requirements' has the meaning given that term in section 3(*o*) of the Small Business Act (15 U.S.C. 632(*o*)) (as added by section 412 of this subtitle [Pub.L. 105–135, Title IV, § 412, Dec. 2, 1997, 111 Stat. 2617])."

[Pub.L. 105–135 effective Oct. 1, 1997, see section 3 of Pub.L. 105–135, set out as a note under section 631 of this title.]

Results-Oriented Acquisition Process
Section 5052 of Pub.L. 103–355 provided that:

"(a) Development of process required.—The Administrator for Federal Procurement Policy, in consultation with the heads of appropriate Federal agencies, shall develop results-oriented acquisition process guidelines for implementation by agencies in acquisitions of property and services by the Federal agencies. The process guidelines shall include the identification of quantitative measures and standards for determining the extent to which an acquisition of items other than commercial items by a Federal agency satisfies the needs for which the items are being acquired.

"(b) Inapplicability of process to Department of Defense.—The process guidelines developed pursuant to subsection (a) may not be applied to the Department of Defense."

[Section 5052 of Pub.L. 103–355 effective Oct. 13, 1994, and applicable on and after such date, see section 10001 of Pub.L. 103–355, set out as a note under section 251 of this title.]

LIBRARY REFERENCES

American Digest System
United States ⊚➡40.
Key Number System Topic No. 393.

WESTLAW ELECTRONIC RESEARCH

See Westlaw guide following the Explanation pages of this volume.

Notes of Decisions

Attorney fees 3
Rules and regulations   1, 2
  Generally 1
  Telecommunications   procurements
  2
Telecommunications procurements, rules
  and regulations   2

---

1. Rules and regulations—Generally

The authority of the Administrator of the Office of Federal Procurement Policy includes the authority to promulgate regulations governing the procurement aspects of the Service Contract Act, section 351 et seq. of this title, the Walsh–Healey Act, section 35 et seq. of this title, and the Davis–Bacon Act, section 276a et seq. of Title 40, Public Buildings, Property, and Works, but that authority does not include the authority to decide whether or not a specific procurement contract is

subject to one or more of those Acts. 1979, 43 Op.Atty.Gen., Mar. 9.

2. —— Telecommunications procurements

Federal information resources management regulation did not apply to telecommunications procurements involving the army. New York Telephone Co. v. Secretary of Army, D.D.C.1986, 657 F.Supp. 18. United States ☞ 64.5

3. Attorney fees

In enacting the Federal Acquisition Regulation (FAR) governing the recovery of legal fees incurred by a government contractor in defense of criminal proceedings, Congress intended to confer broad authority on the agencies to adopt cost disallowance principles. Brownlee v. DynCorp., C.A.Fed.2003, 349 F.3d 1343, rehearing and rehearing en banc denied, on remand 2006 WL 225580. United States ☞ 70(18)

§ 405a. Uniform Federal procurement regulations and procedures

The Administrator of the Office of Federal Procurement Policy is authorized and directed, pursuant to the authority conferred by Public Law 93–400 [41 U.S.C.A. § 401 et seq.] and subject to the procedures set forth in such Public Law, to promulgate a single, simplified, uniform Federal procurement regulation and to establish procedures for insuring compliance with such provisions by all Federal agencies. In formulating such regulations and procedures the Administrator of the Office of Federal Procurement Policy shall, in consultation with the Small Business Administration, conduct analyses of the impact on small business concerns resulting from revised procurement regulations, and incorporate into revised procurement regulations simplified bidding, contract performance, and contract administration procedures for small business concerns.

(Pub.L. 95–507, Title II, § 222, Oct. 24, 1978, 92 Stat. 1771.)

HISTORICAL AND STATUTORY NOTES

Revision Notes and Legislative Reports

1978 Acts. This section amends section 8(d) of the Small Business Act, stating that it is the policy of the Federal Government to afford the maximum practicable opportunity for participation in the performance of Federal contract to small business. This policy shall be stated as a clause in all Federal contracts specified in this section. For specified Federal contracts let pursuant to the negotiated method of procurement, or by formal advertising, a final subcontracting plan must be negotiated between the offering business concern and the procuring department or agency. The approved subcontracting plan shall be included in and made a material part of the contract.

The Small Business Administration is authorized to review subcontracting plans, evaluate compliance with these plans, and submit an annual report to the House and Senate Small Business Committees on those plans failing to comply with stated Federal policy. Senate Report No. 95–1070.

References in Text
Public Law 93–400, referred to in text, is Pub.L. 93–400, Aug. 30, 1974, 88 Stat. 796, as amended, known as the Office of Federal Procurement Policy Act, which classified principally to this chapter. For complete classification, see Short Title note set out under 41 U.S.C.A. § 401 and Tables.

Codifications
Section was not enacted as part of the Office of Federal Procurement Policy Act which comprises this chapter.

Definitions
The definitions in section 637c of Title 15, Commerce and Trade, apply to terms appearing in this section.

Supersedure of Inconsistent Statutory Provisions
Pub.L. 96–83, § 11, Oct. 10, 1979, 93 Stat. 652, provided that: "The provisions of the Act as amended by this Act [see Short Title and Short Title of 1979 Amendment notes set out under section 401 of this title] shall supersede the provisions of section 222 of the Act of October 24, 1978, entitled 'An Act to amend the Small Business Act and the Small Business Investment Act of 1958' (41 U.S.C. 405a) [this section] to the extent they are inconsistent therewith."

LIBRARY REFERENCES

American Digest System
United States ⚭41.
Key Number System Topic No. 393.

WESTLAW ELECTRONIC RESEARCH

See Westlaw guide following the Explanation pages of this volume.

§ 405b. Conflict of interest standards for individuals providing consulting services

(a) Issuance of policy and regulations

Not later than 90 days after October 1, 1988, the Administrator of the Office of Federal Procurement Policy shall issue a policy, and not later than 180 days thereafter Government–wide regulations shall be issued under the Office of Federal Procurement Policy Act [41 U.S.C.A. § 401 et seq.] which set forth—

(1) conflict of interest standards for persons who provide consulting services described in subsection (b) of this section; and

(2) procedures, including such registration, certification, and enforcement requirements as may be appropriate, to promote compliance with such standards.

(b) Services subject to regulations

The regulations required by subsection (a) of this section shall apply to the following types of consulting services:

(1) advisory and assistance services provided to the Government to the extent necessary to identify and evaluate the poten-

tial for conflicts of interest that could be prejudicial to the interests of the United States;

(2) services related to support of the preparation or submission of bids and proposals for Federal contracts to the extent that inclusion of such services in such regulations is necessary to identify and evaluate the potential for conflicts of interest that could be prejudicial to the interests of the United States; and

(3) such other services related to Federal contracts as may be specified in the regulations prescribed under subsection (a) of this section to the extent necessary to identify and evaluate the potential for conflicts of interest that could be prejudicial to the interests of the United States.

(c) Report to Congress by Comptroller General on effectiveness of regulations

The Comptroller General shall report to Congress not later than one year after October 1, 1988, his assessment of the effectiveness of the regulations prescribed under this section.

(d) Intelligence activities exemption; annual report by Director of Central Intelligence

Intelligence activities as defined in section 3.4(e) of Executive order 12333 or a comparable definitional section in any successor order may be exempt from the regulations required by subsection (a) of this section: *Provided,* That the Director of Central Intelligence shall report to the Intelligence and Appropriations Committees of the Congress no later than January 1, 1990, and annually thereafter delineating those activities and organizations which have been exempted from the regulations required by subsection (a) of this section in accordance with the provisions of this subsection.

(e) Adverse effect determination by President prior to issuance of regulations; report to Congressional committees; voiding of regulations requirement

The President shall, before issuance of the regulations required by subsection (a) of this section, determine if the promulgation of such regulations would have a significantly adverse effect on the accomplishment of the mission of the Department of Defense or other Federal Government agencies: *Provided,* That if the President determines that the regulations required by subsection (a) of this section would have such an adverse effect, the President shall so report to the appropriate committees of the Senate and the House of Representatives, stating in full the reasons for such a determination: *Provided further,* That in the event of submission of a report to the committees containing an adverse effect determination, the requirement for the regulations prescribed by subsection (a) of this section shall be null and void.

(Pub.L. 100–463, Title VIII, § 8141, Oct. 1, 1988, 102 Stat. 2270–47.)

HISTORICAL AND STATUTORY NOTES

References in Text

The Office of Federal Procurement Policy Act, referred to in subsec. (a), is Pub.L. 93–400, Aug. 30, 1974, 88 Stat. 796, as amended, which is classified principally to this chapter. For complete classification of this Act to the Code, see Short Title note set out under section 401 of this title and Tables.

Executive Order 12333, referred to in subsec. (d), is Ex. Ord. No. 12333, Dec. 4, 1981, 46 F.R. 59941, which is set out as a note under section 401 of Title 50, War and National Defense.

Codifications

Section was enacted as part of the Department of Defense Appropriations Act, 1989, and not as part of the Office of Federal Procurement Policy Act, which comprises this chapter.

Termination of Reporting Requirements

For termination of reporting provisions of subsec. (d) of this section, effective May 15, 2000, see Pub.L. 104–66, § 3003, as amended, set out as a note under 31 U.S.C.A. § 1113, and the 9th item on page 156 of House Document No. 103–7.

Change of Name

Reference to the Director of Central Intelligence or the Director of the Central Intelligence Agency in the Director's capacity as the head of the intelligence community deemed to be a reference to the Director of National Intelligence. Reference to the Director of Central Intelligence or the Director of the Central Intelligence Agency in the Director's capacity as the head of the Central Intelligence Agency deemed to be a reference to the Director of the Central Intelligence Agency. See section 1081(a), (b) of Pub.L. 108–458, set out as a note under 50 U.S.C.A. § 401.

LIBRARY REFERENCES

American Digest System

United States ☞41, 64.5.
Key Number System Topic No. 393.

WESTLAW ELECTRONIC RESEARCH

See Westlaw guide following the Explanation pages of this volume.

§ 406. Administrative powers

Upon the request of the Administrator, each executive agency is directed to—

(1) make its services, personnel, and facilities available to the Office to the greatest practicable extent for the performance of functions under this chapter; and

(2) except when prohibited by law, furnish to the Administrator and give him access to all information and records in its possession which the Administrator may determine to be necessary for the performance of the functions of the Office.

(Pub.L. 93–400, § 7, Aug. 30, 1974, 88 Stat. 798.)

HISTORICAL AND STATUTORY NOTES

Revision Notes and Legislative Reports
1974 Acts. Senate Report No. 93–692,
see 1974 U.S.Code Cong. and Adm.News,
p. 4589.

LIBRARY REFERENCES

American Digest System
United States ⚖41.
Key Number System Topic No. 393.

WESTLAW ELECTRONIC RESEARCH

See Westlaw guide following the Explanation pages of this volume.

§ 407. Repealed. Pub.L. 104–106, Div. D, Title XLIII, § 4305(b), Feb. 10, 1996, 110 Stat. 665

HISTORICAL AND STATUTORY NOTES

Section, Pub.L. 93–400, § 8, Aug. 30, 1974, 88 Stat. 798; Pub.L. 96–83, § 5, Oct. 10, 1979, 93 Stat. 651; Pub.L. 98–191, § 8(a), Dec. 1, 1983, 97 Stat. 1331, related to responsiveness to Congress.

Effective Date of Repeal
Repeal by Pub.L. 104–106 effective Feb. 10, 1996, except as otherwise provided, see section 4401 of Pub.L. 104–106, set out as a note under section 251 of this title.

Plan for Alternatives to Increase Opportunities to Achieve Full and Open Competition; Study to Congress, Criteria, Etc.
Pub.L. 98–369, Div. B, Title VII, § 2753, July 18, 1984, 98 Stat. 1203, provided that:

"**(a)** Not later than January 31, 1985, the Administrator of the Office of Federal Procurement Policy, in consultation with the Secretary of Defense, the Administrator of General Services and the Administrator of the National Aeronautics and Space Administration, shall complete a study of alternatives and recommend to the Committee on Governmental Affairs of the Senate and the Committee on Government Operations of the House of Representatives a plan to

increase the opportunities to achieve full and open competition on the basis of technical qualifications, quality, and other factors in the procurement of professional, technical, and managerial services.

"**(b)** Such plan shall provide for testing the recommended alternative and be developed in accordance with section 15 of the Office of Federal Procurement Policy Act (41 U.S.C. 413) and be consistent with the policies set forth in section 2 of such Act (41 U.S.C. 401)."

[Any reference in any provision of law enacted before Jan. 4, 1995, to the Committee on Government Operations of the House of Representatives treated as referring to the Committee on Government Reform and Oversight of the House of Representatives, except that any reference in any provision of law enacted before Jan. 4, 1995, to the Committee on Government Operations of the House of Representatives treated as referring to the Committee on the Budget of the House of Representatives in the case of a provision of law relating to the establishment, extension, and enforcement of special controls over the Federal budget, see section 1(a)(6) and (c)(2) of Pub.L. 104–14, set out as a note preceding section 21 of Title 2, The Congress.]

§ 408. Applicability of existing laws

The authority of an executive agency under any other law to prescribe policies, regulations, procedures, and forms for procurement is subject to the authority conferred in section 405 of this title.

(Pub.L. 93–400, § 9, Aug. 30, 1974, 88 Stat. 799.)

HISTORICAL AND STATUTORY NOTES

Revision Notes and Legislative Reports
1974 Acts. Section 9 is basic to the intent to make the OFPP the controlling force for the government-wide integration and issuance of procurement policy. It provides that any other agency authority to prescribe policy is subject to that of the OFPP. This provision relates only to the authority of an agency to prescribe policy. Neither it nor the following section gives the Office authority to contravene an existing statute. Outmoded, inconsistent or duplicative statutes having an adverse impact on procurement will be reported to Congress, with recommendations for amendment or repeal of existing laws or adoption of new laws. Senate Report No. 93–692.

WESTLAW ELECTRONIC RESEARCH

See Westlaw guide following the Explanation pages of this volume.

Notes of Decisions

Power of Secretary of Labor   1
―――――

1. Power of Secretary of Labor
The question of whether a particular class of contracts is covered by the Walsh–Healey Act, section 35 et seq. of this title, or the Service Contract Act, section 351 et seq. of this title, is one for the decision of the Secretary of Labor, not one to be decided by the Administrator of the Office of Federal Procurement Policy under authority granted the Administrator by this chapter. 1979, 43 Op. Atty.Gen., Mar. 9.

§ 409. Repealed. Pub.L. 104–106, Div. D, Title XLIII, § 4305(c)(1), Feb. 10, 1996, 110 Stat. 665

HISTORICAL AND STATUTORY NOTES

Section, Pub.L. 93–400, § 10, Aug. 30, 1974, 88 Stat. 799; Pub.L. 96–83, § 6, Oct. 10, 1979, 93 Stat. 651; Pub.L. 98–191, § 8(b), Dec. 1, 1983, 97 Stat. 1331, related to effect on existing regulations.

Effective Date of Repeal
Repeal by Pub.L. 104–106 effective Feb. 10, 1996, except as otherwise provided, see section 4401 of Pub.L. 104–106, set out as a note under section 251 of this title.

§ 410. Authorization of appropriations.

There is authorized to be appropriated for the Office of Federal Procurement Policy each fiscal year such sums as may be necessary for carrying out the responsibilities of that office for such fiscal year.

(Pub.L. 93–400, § 11, Aug. 30, 1974, 88 Stat. 799; Pub.L. 96–83, § 7, Oct. 10, 1979, 93 Stat. 651; Pub.L. 98–191, § 6, Dec. 1, 1983, 97 Stat. 1329; Pub.L. 100–679, § 3(b), Nov. 17, 1988, 102 Stat. 4056; Pub.L. 104–106, Div. D, Title XLIII, § 4305(c)(2), Feb. 10, 1996, 110 Stat. 665.)

HISTORICAL AND STATUTORY NOTES

Revision Notes and Legislative Reports

1974 Acts. Section 11 places a limitation on the appropriations to support the Office during the first year after enactment of this legislation; establishes a sublimitation on funds used for research during that year; and provides that funds for operations of the Office are authorized to be appropriated for only five years. Subsequent proposals for authorization of funds to be appropriated are to be referred to the Government Operations Committee and will be contingent on a conclusion by the Government Operations Committee that the Office has and will continue to promote the economy, efficiency, and effectiveness of Government procurement. Fiscal year funding for the Office will be a concern of both the Government Operations and the Appropriation Committees. Senate Report No. 93–692.

1979 Acts. House Report No. 96–178, see 1979 U.S.Code Cong. and Adm.News, p. 1492.

1983 Acts. Senate Report No. 98–214, see 1983 U.S.Code Cong. and Adm.News, p. 2027.

1988 Acts. Senate Report No. 100–424, see 1988 U.S.Code Cong. and Adm.News, p. 5687.

1996 Acts. House Conference Report No. 104–450, see 1996 U.S. Code Cong. and Adm. News, p. 238.

Amendments

1996 Amendments. Pub.L. 104–106 amended section generally. Prior to amendment, section read as follows: "There are authorized to be appropriated to carry out the provisions of this chapter, and for no other purpose, $4,500,000 for the fiscal year ending September 30, 1984, and such sums as may be necessary for each succeeding fiscal year."

1988 Amendments. Pub.L. 100–679 substituted "such sums as may be necessary for each succeeding fiscal year" for "for each of the three succeeding fiscal years".

1983 Amendments. Pub.L. 98–191 substituted provisions authorizing appropriations of $4,500,000 for the fiscal year ending Sept. 30, 1984, and for each of the three succeeding fiscal years for former provisions which had authorized appropriations of $4,000,000 for the fiscal year ending Sept. 30, 1980, and for each of the three succeeding fiscal years and had required that future authorization of appropriations to carry out the purposes of this chapter be referred to the Senate Committee on Governmental Affairs.

1979 Amendments. Pub.L. 96–83 substituted provisions authorizing appropriations of $4,000,000 for the fiscal year ending Sept. 30, 1980, and for each of the three succeeding fiscal years, such funds not to be used for any other purpose, with one-third of the appropriations to be made available to the Federal Acquisition Institute, for provisions authorizing appropriations of not to exceed $2,000,000 for the fiscal year ending June 30, 1975, of which not to exceed $150,000 was to be available for the purposes of former section 405(d)(4) of this title, and such other sums as necessary for each of the four fiscal years thereafter, and substituted "Governmental Affairs" for "Government Operations".

Effective and Applicability Provisions

1996 Acts. Amendment by Pub.L. 104–106 effective Feb. 10, 1996, except as otherwise provided, see section 4401 of Pub.L. 104–106, set out as a note under section 251 of this title.

1979 Acts. Amendment by Pub.L. 96–83 effective Oct. 1, 1979, see section 12 of Pub.L. 96–83, set out as a note under section 401 of this title.

LIBRARY REFERENCES

American Digest System

United States ⟊22.
Key Number System Topic No. 393.

WESTLAW ELECTRONIC RESEARCH

See Westlaw guide following the Explanation pages of this volume.

§ 411. Delegation of authority by Administrator

(a) The Administrator may delegate, and authorize successive redelegations of, any authority, function, or power of the Administrator under this chapter (other than the authority to provide overall direction of Federal procurement policy and to prescribe policies and regulations to carry out such policy), to any other executive agency with the consent of the head of such executive agency or at the direction of the President.

(b) The Administrator may make and authorize such delegations within the Office as he determines to be necessary to carry out the provisions of this chapter.

(Pub.L. 93–400, § 12, Aug. 30, 1974, 88 Stat. 799; Pub.L. 96–83, § 8, Oct. 10, 1979, 93 Stat. 652; Pub.L. 98–191, § 8(c), Dec. 1, 1983, 97 Stat. 1331.)

HISTORICAL AND STATUTORY NOTES

Revision Notes and Legislative Reports

1974 Acts. Section 12 authorizes the Administrator to delegate his functions to personnel in his office or to executive agencies with their consent or with the approval of the President, provided he does not delegate the final policy-making decision to other agencies. The Administrator is expected and encouraged to use the executive agencies to develop policies and regulations, but the final approval authority cannot be delegated. Subject to this restriction, delegation to other agencies of technical and detailed aspects of policy development is considered a necessary option if the Office is to operate with the small staff envisioned by the Commission. Senate Report No. 93–692.

1979 Acts. House Report No. 96–178, see 1979 U.S.Code Cong. and Adm.News, p. 1492.

1983 Acts. Senate Report No. 98–214, see 1983 U.S.Code Cong. and Adm.News, p. 2027.

Amendments

1983 Amendments. Subsec. (a). Pub.L. 98–191 substituted "The Administrator may delegate, and authorize successive redelegations of, any authority, function, or power of the Administrator under this chapter (other than the authority to provide overall direction of Federal procurement policy and to prescribe policies and regulations to carry out such policy), to any other executive agency with the consent of the head of such executive agency or at the direction of the President" for "The Administrator may delegate, and authorize successive redelegations of, any authority, function, or power under this chapter, other than his basic authority to provide overall leadership in the development of Federal procurement policy, to any other executive agency with the consent of such agency or at the direction of the President".

1979 Amendments. Subsec. (a). Pub.L. 96–83 substituted provisions respecting delegation of the leadership role in the development of policy, for provisions respecting delegation of the direction of policy and the authority to prescribe rules and regulations to effectuate that policy.

Effective and Applicability Provisions

1979 Acts. Amendment by Pub.L. 96–83 effective Oct. 1, 1979, see section 12 of Pub.L. 96–83, set out as a note under section 401 of this title.

LIBRARY REFERENCES

American Digest System

United States ⟐40, 41.
Key Number System Topic No. 393.

WESTLAW ELECTRONIC RESEARCH

See Westlaw guide following the Explanation pages of this volume.

§ 412. Comptroller General's access to information from Administrator; rule making procedure

(a) The Administrator and personnel in his Office shall furnish such information as the Comptroller General may require for the discharge of his responsibilities. For this purpose, the Comptroller General or his representatives shall have access to all books, documents, papers, and records of the Office.

(b) The Administrator shall, by regulation, require that formal meetings of the Office, as designated by him, for the purpose of developing procurement policies and regulations shall be open to the public, and that public notice of each such meeting shall be given not less than ten days prior thereto.

(Pub.L. 93–400, § 14, Aug. 30, 1974, 88 Stat. 800; Pub.L. 96–83, § 9, Oct. 10, 1979, 93 Stat. 652.)

HISTORICAL AND STATUTORY NOTES

Revision Notes and Legislative Reports
1974 Acts. Section 14(a) provides for the General Accounting Office to obtain information from the OFPP and have access to its records.

Section 14(b) requires the Administrator to open to the public formal, scheduled meetings to promulgate procurement policies and regulations, specifies that a ten-day notice will be given of such meetings, and gives him the authority to determine those policies and regulations to which this requirement is applicable. These meetings will give the public an additional opportunity to express their views on highly sensitive or significant issuances of the OFPP. This subsection complements the provisions of the bill calling for the timely, effective solicitation of the viewpoints of interested parties.

In general, it is intended that the affairs of the Office will be conducted so as to give maximum practical public visibility to its rule-making activities. Senate Report No. 93–692.

1979 Acts. House Report No. 96–178, see 1979 U.S.Code Cong. and Adm.News, p. 1492.

Amendments
1979 **Amendments.** Subsec. (b). Pub.L. 96–83 substituted "developing" for "establishing".

Effective and Applicability Provisions
1979 Acts. Amendment by Pub.L. 96–83 effective Oct. 1, 1979, see section 12 of Pub.L. 96–83, set out as a note under section 401 of this title.

LIBRARY REFERENCES

American Digest System
United States ⚜40, 41.
Key Number System Topic No. 393.

WESTLAW ELECTRONIC RESEARCH

See Westlaw guide following the Explanation pages of this volume.

§ 413. Tests of innovative procurement methods and procedures

(a) The Administrator may develop innovative procurement methods and procedures to be tested by selected executive agencies. In developing any program to test innovative procurement methods and procedures under this subsection, the Administrator shall consult with the heads of executive agencies to—

(1) ascertain the need for and specify the objectives of such program;

(2) develop the guidelines and procedures for carrying out such program and the criteria to be used in measuring the success of such program;

(3) evaluate the potential costs and benefits which may be derived from the innovative procurement methods and procedures tested under such program;

(4) select the appropriate executive agencies or components of executive agencies to carry out such program;

(5) specify the categories and types of products or services to be procured under such program; and

(6) develop the methods to be used to analyze the results of such program.

A program to test innovative procurement methods and procedures may not be carried out unless approved by the heads of the executive agencies selected to carry out such program.

(b) If the Administrator determines that it is necessary to waive the application of any provision of law in order to carry out a proposed program to test innovative procurement methods and procedures under subsection (a) of this section, the Administrator shall transmit notice of the proposed program to the Committee on Government Operations of the House of Representatives and the Committee on Governmental Affairs of the Senate and request that such committees take such action as may be necessary to provide that such provision of law does not apply with respect to the proposed program. The notification to Congress shall include a description of the proposed program (including the scope and purpose of the proposed program), the procedures to be followed in carrying out the proposed program, the provisions of law affected and any provision of law the application of which must be waived in order to carry out the proposed program, and the executive agencies involved in carrying out the proposed program.

(Pub.L. 93–400, § 15, as added Pub.L. 98–191, § 7, Dec. 1, 1983, 97 Stat. 1329, and amended Pub.L. 104–201, Title X, § 1074(f)(2), Sept. 23, 1996, 110 Stat. 2661.)

HISTORICAL AND STATUTORY NOTES

Revision Notes and Legislative Reports
1983 Acts. Section 7 amends the OFPP Act by adding a new section 15 which authorizes the Administrator to develop innovative procurement methods and procedures to be tested by selected agencies. Such methods and procedures are required to be consistent with the policies set forth in section 2.

This section requires the Administrator, in developing a test program, to consult with the agency heads to (1) ascertain the need for and specify the functions of such programs, (2) develop guidelines for carrying out such program and criteria to be used in measuring its success, (3) evaluate the costs and benefits, (4) select the appropriate agencies to carry out such program, (5) specify the products or services to be procured, and (6) develop the methods for analyzing the results.

This section prohibits any testing unless the program has been approved by the head of the executive agencies selected to carry out such program.

If the Administrator determines that it is necessary to waive existing laws in order to implement a proposed test program, this section requires the Administrator to notify the House Committee on Government Operations and the Senate Committee on Governmental Affairs and request that both committees take the necessary action to waive such laws. The notice shall include a description of the proposed test program, the procedures to be followed in carrying out such program, the laws affected and those which must be waived in order to implement such program, and the agencies involved. Senate Report No. 98–214.

1996 Acts. House Report No. 104–563 and House Conference Report No. 104–724, see 1996 U.S. Code Cong. and Adm. News, p. 2949.

Codifications
Another section 15 of Pub.L. 93–400, Aug. 30, 1974, 88 Stat. 800, which amended sections 474, 481, and 487 of former Title 40, was repealed by Pub.L. 107–217, § 6(b), Aug. 21, 2002, 116 Stat. 1319.

Amendments
1996 Amendments. Subsec. (a). Pub.L. 104–201, § 1074(f)(2), struck out

reference to consistency with policies of section 401 of this title.

Change of Name
Any reference in any provision of law enacted before Jan. 4, 1995, to the Committee on Government Operations of the House of Representatives treated as referring to the Committee on Government Reform and Oversight of the House of Representatives, except that any reference in any provision of law enacted before Jan. 4, 1995, to the Committee on Government Operations of the House of Representatives treated as referring to the Committee on the Budget of the House of Representatives in the case of a provision of law relating to the establishment, extension, and enforcement of special controls over the Federal budget, see section 1(a)(6) and (c)(2) of Pub.L. 104–14, set out as a note preceding section 21 of Title 2, The Congress.

Test Program for Executive Agencies
Pub.L. 103–355, Title V, § 5061, Oct. 13, 1994, 108 Stat. 3352, as amended Pub.L. 104–106, Div. D, Title XLIII, § 4302(a), Feb. 10, 1996, 110 Stat. 658, as amended Pub.L. 105–85, Div. A, Title VIII, § 850(f)(1), Nov. 18, 1997, 111 Stat. 1849, provided that:

"**(a) In general.**—The Administrator for Federal Procurement Policy (in this section referred to as the 'Administrator') may conduct a program of tests of alternative and innovative procurement procedures. To the extent consistent with this section, such program shall be conducted consistent with section 15 of the Office of Federal Procurement Policy Act (41 U.S.C. 413) [this section]. No more than 6 such tests shall be conducted under the authority of this subsection, and not more than 1 such test shall be conducted under such authority in an agency.

"**(b) Designation of agencies.**—Each test conducted pursuant to subsection (a) shall be carried out in not more than 2 specific procuring activities in an agency designated by the Administrator. Each agency so designated shall select the procuring activities participating in the test with the approval of the Administrator and shall designate a procurement testing official who shall be responsible for the conduct and evaluation of tests within that agency.

"**(c) Test requirements and limitations.**—(1) Each test conducted under subsection (a)—

"**(A)** shall be developed and structured by the Administrator or by the agency senior procurement executive designated pursuant to section 16(3) of the Office of Federal Procurement Policy Act (41 U.S.C. 414(3)) [section 414(3) of this title in close coordination with the Administrator; and

"**(B)** shall be limited to specific programs of agencies or specific acquisitions.

"**(2)** The total estimated life-cycle cost to the Federal Government for each test conducted under subsection (a) may not exceed $100,000,000.

"**(3)(A)** Except as provided in subparagraph (B), each contract awarded in conducting the tests under subsection (a) (including the cost of options if all options were to be exercised) may not exceed $5,000,000.

"**(B)** For one of the tests conducted under subsection (a), the amount of each contract awarded in conducting the test (including options) may exceed $5,000,000.

"**(4)** The program of tests conducted under subsection (a) shall include, either as a test or as part of a test, the use of the electronic commerce capability required by section 30 of the Office of Federal Procurement Policy Act [section 426 of this title] for procurement actions in amounts greater than the simplified acquisition threshold.

"**(d) Limitation on total value of contracts under program.**—(1) The Administrator shall ensure that the total amount obligated under contracts awarded pursuant to the program under this section does not exceed $600,000,000. In calculating such amount, the Administrator shall not include any contract awarded for the test conducted by the National Aeronautics and Space Administration pursuant to section 5062 of this Act [section 5062 of Pub.L. 103–335, which is set out as a note under section 2473 of Title 42, The Public Health and Welfare].

"**(2)** The Administrator shall monitor the value of contracts awarded pursuant to the program under this section.

"**(3)** No contract may be awarded under the program under this section if the award of the contract would result in an obligation of more than $600,000,000 under contracts awarded pursuant to the program under this section.

"**(e) Procedures authorized.**—Tests conducted under this section may include any of the following procedures:

"**(1)** Publication of agency needs before drafting of a solicitation.

"**(2)** Issuance of draft solicitations for comment.

"**(3)** Streamlined solicitations that specify as the evaluation factors the minimum factors necessary, require sources to submit the minimum information necessary, provide abbreviated periods for submission of offers, and specify page limitations for offers.

"**(4)** Limitation of source selection factors to—

"**(A)** cost to the Federal Government;

"**(B)** past experience and performance; and

"**(C)** quality of the content of the offer.

"**(5)** Evaluation of proposals by small teams of highly qualified people over a period not greater than 30 days.

"**(6)** Restriction of competitions to sources determined capable in a precompetition screening process, provided that the screening process affords all interested sources a fair opportunity to be considered.

"**(7)** Restriction of competitions to sources of preevaluated products, provided that the preevaluation process affords all interested sources a fair opportunity to be considered.

"**(8)** Alternative notice and publication requirements.

"**(9)** A process in which—

"**(A)** the competitive process is initiated by publication in the Commerce Business Daily of a notice that—

"**(i)** contains a synopsis of the functional and performance needs of the executive agency conducting the test, and, for purposes of guidance only, other specifications; and

"**(ii)** invites any interested source to submit information or samples showing the suitability of its product for meeting those needs, together with a price quotation, or, if appropriate, showing the source's technical capability, past performance, product supportability, or other qualifications (including, as appropriate, information regarding rates and other cost-related factors);

"**(B)** contracting officials develop a request for proposals (including appropriate specifications and evaluation criteria) after reviewing the submissions of interested sources and, if the officials determine necessary, after consultation with those sources; and

"**(C)** a contract is awarded after a streamlined competition that is limited to all sources that timely provided product information in response to the notice or, if appropriate, to those sources determined most capable based on the qualification-based factors included in an invitation to submit information pursuant to subparagraph (A).

"**(f) Measurable test criteria.**—The Administrator shall require each agency conducting a test pursuant to subsection (a) to establish, to the maximum extent practicable, measurable criteria for evaluation of the effects of the procedure or technique to be tested.

"**(g) Test plan.**—At least 270 days before a test may be conducted under this section, the Administrator shall—

"**(1)** provide a detailed test plan, including lists of any regulations that are to be waived, and any written determination under subsection (h)(1)(B) to the Committee on Government Operations of the House of Representatives and the Committee on Governmental Affairs of the Senate;

"**(2)** provide a copy of the plan to the appropriate authorization and appropriations committees of the House of Representatives and the Senate; and

"**(3)** publish the plan in the Federal Register and provide an opportunity for public comment.

"**(h) Waiver of procurement regulations.**—**(1)** For purposes of a test conducted under subsection (a), the Administrator may waive—

"**(A)** any provision of the Federal Acquisition Regulation that is not required by statute; and

"**(B)** any provision of the Federal Acquisition Regulation that is required by a provision of law described in para-

graph (2), the waiver of which the Administrator determines in writing to be necessary to conduct any test of any of the procedures described in subsection (e).

"**(2)** The provisions of law referred to in paragraph (1) are as follows:

"**(A)** The following provisions of title 10, United States Code:

"**(i)** Section 2304 [section 2304 of Title 10, Armed Forces].

"**(ii)** Section 2305 [section 2305 of Title 10].

"**(iii)** Section 2319 [section 2319 of Title 10].

"**(B)** Subsections (e), (f), and (g) of section 8 of the Small Business Act (15 U.S.C. 637) [section 637 of Title 15, Commerce and Trade].

"**(C)** The following provisions of the Revised Statutes:

"**(i)** Section 3709 (41 U.S.C. 5) [section 5 of this title].

"**(ii)** Section 3710 (41 U.S.C. 8) [section 8 of this title].

"**(iii)** Section 3735 (41 U.S.C. 13) [section 13 of this title].

"**(D)** The following provisions of the Federal Property and Administrative Services Act of 1949 [Act June 30, 1949, c. 288, 63 Stat. 377]:

"**(i)** Section 303 (41 U.S.C. 253) [section 253 of this title].

"**(ii)** Section 303A (41 U.S.C. 253a) [section 253a of this title].

"**(iii)** Section 303B (41 U.S.C. 253b) [section 253b of this title].

"**(iv)** Section 303C (41 U.S.C. 253c) [section 253c of this title].

"**(v)** Section 310 (41 U.S.C. 260) [section 260 of this title].

"**(E)** The following provisions of the Office of Federal Procurement Policy Act [Pub.L. 93–400, Aug. 30, 1974, 88 Stat. 796, as amended]:

"**(i)** Section 4(6) (41 U.S.C. 403(6)) [section 403(6) of this title].

"**(ii)** Section 18 (41 U.S.C. 416) [section 416 of this title].

"**(3)** If the Administrator determines that the conduct of a test requires the waiver of a law not listed in paragraph (2) or requires approval of an estimated dollar amount not permitted under subsection (c)(4), the Administrator may propose legislation to authorize the waiver or

grant the approval. Before proposing
such legislation, the Administrator may
provide and publish a test plan as described in subsection (g).

"(i) Report.—Not later than 6 months
after completion of a test conducted under subsection (a), the Comptroller General shall submit to Congress a report for
the test setting forth in detail the results
of the test, including such recommendations as the Comptroller General considers appropriate.

**"(j) Commencement and expiration of
authority.**—The authority to conduct a
test under subsection (a) in an agency
and to award contracts under such a test
shall take effect on January 1, 1997, and
shall expire on January 1, 2001. A contract entered into before such authority
expires in an agency pursuant to a test
shall remain in effect, in accordance with
the terms of the contract, the notwithstanding of expiration the authority to
conduct the test under this section.

"(k) Rule of construction.—Nothing in
this section shall be construed as authorizing the appropriation or obligation of
funds for the tests conducted pursuant to
subsection (a)."

[Amendment by section 4302(a) of
Pub.L. 104-106 effective Feb. 10, 1996,
except as otherwise provided, see section

4401 of Pub.L. 104-106, set out as a note
under section 251 of this title.]

[Section 5061 of Pub.L. 103-355 effective Oct. 13, 1994, and applicable on and
after such date, see section 10001 of
Pub.L. 103-355, set out as a note under
section 251 of this title.]

[Any reference in any provision of law
enacted before Jan. 4, 1995, to the Committee on Government Operations of the
House of Representatives treated as referring to the Committee on Government
Reform and Oversight of the House of
Representatives, except that any reference in any provision of law enacted before Jan. 4, 1995, to the Committee on
Government Operations of the House of
Representatives treated as referring to
the Committee on the Budget of the
House of Representatives in the case of a
provision of law relating to the establishment, extension, and enforcement of special controls over the Federal budget, see
section 1(a)(6) and (c)(2) of Pub.L.
104-14, set out as a note preceding section 21 of Title 2, The Congress.]

[Provisions of amendment, to the note
immediately preceding, by section
850(f)(1) of Pub.L. 105-85, to take effect
180 days after Nov. 18, 1997, see section
850(g) of Pub.L. 105-85, set out as an
Effective Date of 1997 Acts note under
section 2302c of Title 10, Armed Forces.]

LIBRARY REFERENCES

American Digest System
   United States ⬚60.
   Key Number System Topic No. 393.

WESTLAW ELECTRONIC RESEARCH

   See Westlaw guide following the Explanation pages of this volume.

§ 414. Chief acquisition officers and senior procurement execu-
tives

(a) Establishment of agency chief acquisition officers

   (1) The head of each executive agency described in section
901(b)(1) (other than the Department of Defense) or section
901(b)(2)(C) of Title 31, with a Chief Financial Officer appointed or
designated under section 901(a) of Title 31 shall appoint or designate
a non-career employee as Chief Acquisition Officer for the agency,
who shall—

   (A) have acquisition management as that official's primary
   duty; and

(B) advise and assist the head of the executive agency and other agency officials to ensure that the mission of the executive agency is achieved through the management of the agency's acquisition activities.

(b) Authority and functions of agency chief acquisition officers

The functions of each Chief Acquisition Officer shall include—

(1) monitoring the performance of acquisition activities and acquisition programs of the executive agency, evaluating the performance of those programs on the basis of applicable performance measurements, and advising the head of the executive agency regarding the appropriate business strategy to achieve the mission of the executive agency;

(2) increasing the use of full and open competition in the acquisition of property and services by the executive agency by establishing policies, procedures, and practices that ensure that the executive agency receives a sufficient number of sealed bids or competitive proposals from responsible sources to fulfill the Government's requirements (including performance and delivery schedules) at the lowest cost or best value considering the nature of the property or service procured;

(3) increasing appropriate use of performance-based contracting and performance specifications;

(4) making acquisition decisions consistent with all applicable laws and establishing clear lines of authority, accountability, and responsibility for acquisition decisionmaking within the executive agency;

(5) managing the direction of acquisition policy for the executive agency, including implementation of the unique acquisition policies, regulations, and standards of the executive agency;

(6) developing and maintaining an acquisition career management program in the executive agency to ensure that there is an adequate professional workforce; and

(7) as part of the strategic planning and performance evaluation process required under section 306 of Title 5, and sections 1105(a)(28), 1115, 1116, and 9703 of Title 31—

    (A) assessing the requirements established for agency personnel regarding knowledge and skill in acquisition resources management and the adequacy of such requirements for facilitating the achievement of the performance goals established for acquisition management;

    (B) in order to rectify any deficiency in meeting such requirements, developing strategies and specific plans for hiring, training, and professional development; and

(C) reporting to the head of the executive agency on the progress made in improving acquisition management capability.

(c) Senior procurement executive

(1) The head of each executive agency shall designate a senior procurement executive who shall be responsible for management direction of the procurement system of the executive agency, including implementation of the unique procurement policies, regulations, and standards of the executive agency.

(2) In the case of an executive agency for which a chief acquisition officer has been appointed or designated under subsection (a) of this section, the head of such executive agency shall either

(A) designate the Chief Acquisition Officer as the senior procurement executive for the executive agency; or

(B) ensure that the senior procurement executive designated for the executive agency under paragraph (1) reports directly to the Chief Acquisition Officer without intervening authority.

(Pub.L. 93–400, § 16, as added Pub.L. 98–191, § 7, Dec. 1, 1983, 97 Stat. 1330, and amended Pub.L. 98–369, Div. B, Title VII, § 2732(b)(2), July 18, 1984, 98 Stat. 1199; Pub.L. 108–136, Div. A, Title XIV, § 1421(a)(1), Nov. 24, 2003, 117 Stat. 1666.)

HISTORICAL AND STATUTORY NOTES

Revision Notes and Legislative Reports
1983 Acts. Section 7 also amends the OFPP Act by adding a section 16 on Executive Agency Responsibilities. This section incorporates management directives prescribed by Executive order 12352, which require the head of each executive agency to (1) increase the use of effective competition, (2) establish clear lines of authority, accountability and responsibility for procurement decisionmaking, (3) designate a procurement executive who will be responsible for managing the agency's procurement system, and (4) develop and maintain a procurement career management program. In addition, agencies are required to participate, to the extent practicable, in interagency groups established by the Administrator. Senate Report No. 98–214.

1984 Acts. House Report No. 98–432(Part II), Senate Report Nos. 98–50 and 98–297, and House Conference Report No. 98–861, see 1984 U.S. Code Cong. and Adm. News, p. 697.

2003 Acts. House Conference Report No. 108–354 and Statement by President,

see 2003 U.S. Code Cong. and Adm. News, p. 1407.

Amendments
2003 Amendments. Pub.L. 108–136, § 1421(a)(1), rewrote this section, which formerly read:

"**§ 414. Executive agency responsibilities**

"To further achieve effective, efficient, and economic administration of the Federal procurement system, the head of each executive agency shall, in accordance with applicable laws, Government-wide policies and regulations, and good business practices—

"(1) increase the use of full and open competition in the procurement of property or services by the executive agency by establishing policies, procedures, and practices that assure that the executive agency receives a sufficient number of sealed bids or competitive proposals from responsible sources to fulfill the Government's requirements (including performance and delivery schedules) at the lowest reasonable cost considering the nature of the property or service procured;

"(2) establish clear lines of authority, accountability, and responsibility for procurement decisionmaking within the executive agency, including placing the procurement function at a sufficiently high level in the executive agency to provide—

"(A) direct access to the head of the major organizational element of the executive agency served; and

"(B) comparative equality with organizational counterparts;

"(3) designate a senior procurement executive who shall be responsible for management direction of the procurement system of the executive agency, including implementation of the unique procurement policies, regulations, and standards of the executive agency; and

"(4) develop and maintain a procurement career management program in the executive agency to assure an adequate professional work force."

1984 Amendments. Par. (1).   Pub.L. 98–369 substituted provision directing an increase in the use of full and open competition in procurement by establishing policies, procedures, and practices that assure the receipt of a sufficient number of sealed bids or competitive proposals to fulfill the Government's requirements at the lowest possible cost for provision directing an increase in the use of effective competition in procurement by the executive agency.

Effective and Applicability Provisions
1984 Acts. Amendment by Pub.L. 98–369 applicable with respect to any solicitation for bids or proposals issued after Mar. 31, 1985, see section 2751(a) of Pub.L. 98–369, set out as a note under section 251 of this title.

CROSS REFERENCES

Aviation programs general procurement authority and duties and powers of senior procurement executive, see 49 USCA § 40110.

LIBRARY REFERENCES

American Digest System
United States ⊂⇒60, 64.5.
Key Number System Topic No. 393.

WESTLAW ELECTRONIC RESEARCH

See Westlaw guide following the Explanation pages of this volume.

§ 414a. Personnel evaluation

The head of each executive agency that is subject to the provisions of Title III of the Federal Property and Administrative Services Act of 1949 [41 U.S.C.A. § 251 et seq.] shall ensure, with respect to the employees of that agency whose primary duties and responsibilities pertain to the award of contracts subject to the provisions of this Act, that the performance appraisal system applicable to such employees affords appropriate recognition to, among other factors, efforts—

(1) to increase competition and achieve cost savings through the elimination of procedures that unnecessarily inhibit full and open competition;

(2) to further the purposes of the Small Business and Federal Procurement Competition Enhancement Act of 1984 and the Defense Procurement Reform Act of 1984; and

(3) to further such other objectives and purposes of the Federal acquisition system as may be authorized by law.

(Pub.L. 98–577, Title V, § 502, Oct. 30, 1984, 98 Stat. 3085.)

HISTORICAL AND STATUTORY NOTES

Revision Notes and Legislative Reports
1984 Acts. Senate Report No. 98–523, see 1984 U.S. Code Cong. and Adm. News, p. 5347.

References in Text
The Federal Property and Administrative Services Act of 1949, referred to in text, is Act June 30, 1949, c. 288, 63 Stat. 377, as amended, Title III of which is currently classified to subchapter IV of chapter 4 of Title 41, 41 U.S.C.A. § 251 et seq., and the remainder of which was formerly classified to chapter 10 of former Title 40, 40 U.S.C.A. § 471 et seq., prior to being repealed by Pub.L. 107–217, § 6(b), Aug. 21, 2002, 116 Stat. 1313; see now generally chapter 1 of Title 40, 40 U.S.C.A. § 101 et seq.

This Act and the Small Business and Federal Procurement Competition Enhancement Act of 1984, referred to in provision preceding par. (1) and par. (2), is Pub.L. 98–577, Oct. 30, 1984, 98 Stat. 3066. For complete classification of this Act to the Code see Short Title note set out under section 251 of this title and Tables.

The Defense Procurement Reform Act of 1984, referred to in par. (2), is Pub.L. 98–525, Title XII, Oct. 19, 1984, 98 Stat. 2588. For complete classification of this Act to the Code see Short Title note set out under section 2301 of Title 10, Armed Forces and Tables.

Codifications
Section was enacted as part of the Small Business and Federal Procurement Competition Enhancement Act of 1984, and not as part of the Office of Federal Procurement Policy Act, which comprises this chapter.

LIBRARY REFERENCES

American Digest System
United States ⊚64.5.
Key Number System Topic No. 393.

WESTLAW ELECTRONIC RESEARCH

See Westlaw guide following the Explanation pages of this volume.

§ 414b. Chief acquisition officers council

(a) Establishment

There is established in the executive branch a Chief Acquisition Officers Council.

(b) Membership

The members of the Council shall be as follows:

(1) The Deputy Director for Management of the Office of Management and Budget, who shall act as Chairman of the Council.

(2) The Administrator for Federal Procurement Policy.

(3) The Under Secretary of Defense for Acquisition, Technology, and Logistics.

(4) The chief acquisition officer of each executive agency that is required to have a chief acquisition officer under section 414 of this title and the senior procurement executive of each military department.

(5) Any other senior agency officer of each executive agency, appointed by the head of the agency in consultation with the Chairman, who can effectively assist the Council in performing the functions set forth in subsection (e) of this section and supporting the associated range of acquisition activities.

(c) Leadership; support

(1) The Administrator for Federal Procurement Policy shall lead the activities of the Council on behalf of the Deputy Director for Management.

(2)(A) The Vice Chairman of the Council shall be selected by the Council from among its members.

(B) The Vice Chairman shall serve a 1–year term, and may serve multiple terms.

(3) The Administrator of General Services shall provide administrative and other support for the Council.

(d) Principal forum

The Council is designated the principal interagency forum for monitoring and improving the Federal acquisition system.

(e) Functions

The Council shall perform functions that include the following:

(1) Develop recommendations for the Director of the Office of Management and Budget on Federal acquisition policies and requirements.

(2) Share experiences, ideas, best practices, and innovative approaches related to Federal acquisition.

(3) Assist the Administrator in the identification, development, and coordination of multiagency projects and other innovative initiatives to improve Federal acquisition.

(4) Promote effective business practices that ensure the timely delivery of best value products to the Federal Government and achieve appropriate public policy objectives.

(5) Further integrity, fairness, competition, openness, and efficiency in the Federal acquisition system.

(6) Work with the Office of Personnel Management to assess and address the hiring, training, and professional development needs of the Federal Government related to acquisition.

(7) Work with the Administrator and the Federal Acquisition Regulatory Council to promote the business practices referred to in paragraph (4) and other results of the functions carried out under this subsection.

(Pub.L. 93–400, § 16A, as added Pub.L. 108–136, Div. A, Title XIV, § 1422(a), Nov. 24, 2003, 117 Stat. 1668.)

HISTORICAL AND STATUTORY NOTES

Revision Notes and Legislative Reports
2003 Acts. House Conference Report No. 108–354 and Statement by President, see 2003 U.S. Code Cong. and Adm. News, p. 1407.

LIBRARY REFERENCES

American Digest System
United States ⊕33.
Key Number System Topic No. 393.

WESTLAW ELECTRONIC RESEARCH

See Westlaw guide following the Explanation pages of this volume.

§ 415. Repealed. Pub.L. 103–355, Title VI, § 6003, Oct. 13, 1994, 108 Stat. 3364

HISTORICAL AND STATUTORY NOTES

Section, Pub.L. 93–400, § 17, as added Pub.L. 98–191, § 7, Dec. 1, 1983, 97 Stat. 1330, required Administrator to conduct studies and issue report to Congressional committees on extent of competition in award of subcontracts by Federal prime contractors, and related to contents of report and deadline for its submission.

Effective Date of Repeal
Repeal of section effective Oct. 13, 1994, except as otherwise provided, see section 10001 of Pub.L. 103–355, set out as a note under section 251 of this title.

§ 416. Procurement notice

(a) Covered executive agency activities; publication of notice; time limitations

(1) Except as provided in subsection (c) of this section—

(A) an executive agency intending to—

(i) solicit bids or proposals for a contract for property or services for a price expected to exceed $25,000; or

(ii) place an order, expected to exceed $25,000, under a basic agreement, basic ordering agreement, or similar arrangement,

shall publish a notice of solicitation described in subsection (b) of this section;

(B) an executive agency intending to solicit bids or proposals for a contract for property or services for a price expected to exceed $10,000, but not to exceed $25,000, shall post, for a period of not less than ten days, in a public place at the contracting office issuing the solicitation a notice of solicitation described in subsection (b) of this section; and

(C) an executive agency awarding a contract for property or services for a price exceeding $25,000, or placing an order referred to in clause (A)(ii) exceeding $25,000, shall furnish for publication by the Secretary of Commerce a notice announcing the award or order if there is likely to be any subcontract under such contract or order.

(2)(A) A notice of solicitation required to be published under paragraph (1) may be published

(i) by electronic means that meets the requirements for accessibility under paragraph (7); or

(ii) by the Secretary of Commerce in the Commerce Business Daily.

(B) The Secretary of Commerce shall promptly publish in the Commerce Business Daily each notice or announcement received under this subsection for publication by that means.

(3) Whenever an executive agency is required by paragraph (1)(A) to publish a notice of solicitation, such executive agency may not—

(A) issue the solicitation earlier than 15 days after the date on which the notice is published; or

(B) in the case of a contract or order expected to be greater than the simplified acquisition threshold, establish a deadline for the submission of all bids or proposals in response to the notice required by paragraph (1)(A) that—

(i) in the case of an order under a basic agreement, basic ordering agreement, or similar arrangement, is earlier than the date 30 days after the date the notice required by paragraph (1)(A)(ii) is published;

(ii) in the case of a solicitation for research and development, is earlier than the date 45 days after the date the notice required by paragraph (1)(A)(i) is published; or

(iii) in any other case, is earlier than the date 30 days after the date the solicitation is issued.

(4) An executive agency intending to solicit offers for a contract for which a notice of solicitation is required to be posted under paragraph (1)(B) shall ensure that contracting officers consider each responsive offer timely received from an offeror.

(5) An executive agency shall establish a deadline for the submission of all bids or proposals in response to a solicitation with respect to which no such deadline is provided by statute. Each deadline for the submission of offers shall afford potential offerors a reasonable opportunity to respond.

(6) The Administrator shall prescribe regulations defining limited circumstances in which flexible deadlines can be used under paragraph (3) for the issuance of solicitations and the submission of bids or proposals for the procurement of commercial items.

(7) A publication of a notice of solicitation by electronic means meets the requirements for accessibility under this paragraph if the notice is electronically accessible in a form that allows convenient and universal user access through the single Government-wide point of entry designated in the Federal Acquisition Regulation.

(b) Contents of notice

Each notice of solicitation required by subparagraph (A) or (B) of subsection (a)(1) shall include—

　(1) an accurate description of the property or services to be contracted for, which description (A) shall not be unnecessarily restrictive of competition, and (B) shall include, as appropriate, the agency nomenclature, National Stock Number or other part number, and a brief description of the item's form, fit, or function, physical dimensions, predominant material of manufacture, or similar information that will assist a prospective contractor to make an informed business judgment as to whether a copy of the solicitation should be requested;

　(2) provisions that—

　　(A) state whether the technical data required to respond to the solicitation will not be furnished as part of such solicitation, and identify the source in the Government, if any, from which the technical data may be obtained; and

　　(B) state whether an offeror, its product, or service must meet a qualification requirement in order to be eligible for award, and, if so, identify the office from which the qualification requirement may be obtained;

　(3) the name, business address, and telephone number of the contracting officer;

　(4) a statement that all responsible sources may submit a bid, proposal, or quotation (as appropriate) which shall be considered by the agency;

　(5) in the case of a procurement using procedures other than competitive procedures, a statement of the reason justifying the use of such procedures and the identity of the intended source; and

(6) in the case of a contract in an amount estimated to be greater than $25,000 but not greater than the simplified acquisition threshold, or a contract for the procurement of commercial items using special simplified procedures—

(A) a description of the procedures to be used in awarding the contract; and

(B) a statement specifying the periods for prospective offerors and the contracting officer to take the necessary preaward and award actions.

(c) Exempted, etc., activities of executive agency

(1) A notice is not required under subsection (a)(1) of this section if—

(A) the proposed procurement is for an amount not greater than the simplified acquisition threshold and is to be conducted by—

(i) using widespread electronic public notice of the solicitation in a form that allows convenient and universal user access through a single, Government-wide point of entry; and

(ii) permitting the public to respond to the solicitation electronically;

(B) the notice would disclose the executive agency's needs and the disclosure of such needs would compromise the national security;

(C) the proposed procurement would result from acceptance of—

(i) any unsolicited proposal that demonstrates a unique and innovative research concept and the publication of any notice of such unsolicited research proposal would disclose the originality of thought or innovativeness of the proposal or would disclose proprietary information associated with the proposal; or

(ii) a proposal submitted under section 638 of Title 15;

(D) the procurement is made against an order placed under a requirements contract, a task order contract, or a delivery order contract;

(E) the procurement is made for perishable subsistence supplies;

(F) the procurement is for utility services, other than telecommunication services, and only one source is available;

723

(G) the procurement is for the services of an expert for use in any litigation or dispute (including any reasonably foreseeable litigation or dispute) involving the Federal Government in any trial, hearing, or proceeding before any court, administrative tribunal, or agency, or in any part of an alternative dispute resolution process, whether or not the expert is expected to testify; or

(H) the procurement is by the Secretary of Homeland Security pursuant to the special procedures provided in section 393(c) of Title 6.

(2) The requirements of subsection (a)(1)(A) of this section do not apply to any procurement under conditions described in paragraph (2), (3), (4), (5), or (7) of section 253(c) of this title or paragraph (2), (3), (4), (5), or (7) of section 2304(c) of Title 10.

(3) The requirements of subsection (a)(1)(A) of this section shall not apply in the case of any procurement for which the head of the executive agency makes a determination in writing, after consultation with the Administrator for Federal Procurement Policy and the Administrator of the Small Business Administration, that it is not appropriate or reasonable to publish a notice before issuing a solicitation.

(d) Availability of complete solicitation package; payment of fee

An executive agency shall make available to any business concern, or the authorized representative of such concern, the complete solicitation package for any on-going procurement announced pursuant to a notice of solicitation under subsection (a) of this section. An executive agency may require the payment of a fee, not exceeding the actual cost of duplication, for a copy of such package.

(Pub.L. 93–400, § 18, as added Pub.L. 98–369, Div. B, Title VII, § 2732(a), July 18, 1984, 98 Stat. 1195, and amended Pub.L. 98–577, Title III, § 303(a), Oct. 30, 1984, 98 Stat. 3077; Pub.L. 99–500, Title I, § 101(c) [Title X, § 922(b), (d)(2)], Oct. 18, 1986, 100 Stat. 1783–151, 1783–152; Pub.L. 99–591, Title I, § 101(c) [Title X, § 922(b), (d)(2)], Oct. 30, 1986, 100 Stat. 3341–151, 3341–152; Pub.L. 99–661, Div. A, Title IX, formerly Title IV, § 922(b), (d)(2), Nov. 14, 1986, 100 Stat. 3931, 3932, renumbered Pub.L. 100–26, § 3(5), Apr. 21, 1987, 101 Stat. 273; Pub.L. 101–510, Div. A, Title VIII, § 806(d), Nov. 5, 1990, 104 Stat. 1592; Pub.L. 103–355, Title I, § 1055(b)(1), Title IV, §§ 4201(b), (c), 4202(a) to (c), Title VIII, § 8302, Title IX, § 9001(b), Oct. 13, 1994, 108 Stat. 3265, 3344, 3398, 3402; Pub.L. 104–106, Div. D, Title XLI, § 4101(c), Title XLII, § 4202(d)(1), Title XLIII, §§ 4310, 4321(h)(3), Feb. 10, 1996, 110 Stat. 642, 654, 670, 675; Pub.L. 105–85, Div. A, Title VIII, § 850(e)(2), Nov. 18, 1997, 111 Stat. 1849; Pub.L. 105–261, Div. A, Title X, § 1069(d)(1), Oct. 17, 1998, 112 Stat. 2136; Pub.L. 106–398, § 1 [Div. A, Title VIII, § 810(a), (b)], Oct. 30, 2000, 114 Stat. 1654, 1654A–209; Pub.L. 107–296, Title VIII, § 833(c)(2), Nov. 25, 2002, 116 Stat. 2226.)

HISTORICAL AND STATUTORY NOTES

Revision Notes and Legislative Reports
1984 Acts. Senate Report No. 98–523, see 1984 U.S.Code Cong. and Adm.News, p. 5347.

House Report No. 98–432, Pt. II, Senate Report Nos. 98–50 and 98–297, and House Conference Report No. 98–861, see 1984 U.S.Code Cong. and Adm.News, p. 697.

1986 Acts. Senate Report No. 99–331, House Conference Report No. 99–1001, and Statement by President, see 1986 U.S.Code Cong. and Adm.News, p. 6413.

Statement by President, see 1986 U.S.Code Cong. and Adm.News, p. 5627.

1990 Acts. House Report No. 101–665 and House Conference Report No. 101–923, see 1990 Act U.S.Code Cong. and Adm.News, p. 2931.

1994 Acts. Senate Report Nos. 103–258 and 103–259, and House Conference Report No. 103–712, see 1994 U.S. Code Cong. and Adm. News, p. 2561.

1996 Acts. House Conference Report No. 104–450, see 1996 U.S. Code Cong. and Adm. News, p. 238.

1997 Acts. House Conference Report No. 105–340 and Statement by President, see 1997 U.S. Code Cong. and Adm. News, p. 2251.

1998 Acts. House Conference Report No. 105–736 and Statement by President, see 1998 U.S. Code Cong. and Adm. News, p. 513.

2000 Acts. House Conference Report No. 106–945 and Statement by President, see 2000 U.S. Code Cong. and Adm. News, p. 1516.

2002 Acts. House Report No. 107–609(Part I) and Statement by President, see 2002 U.S. Code Cong. and Adm. News, p. 1352.

Codifications
Pub.L. 99–591, cited in the credit for this section, is a corrected version of Pub.L. 99–500, also cited in the credit for this section.

Amendments
2002 Amendments. Subsec. (c)(1)(F). Pub.L. 107–296, § 833(c)(2)(A), struck out "or" at the end.

Subsec. (c)(1)(G). Pub.L. 107–296, § 833(c)(2)(B), struck out the period at the end and inserted "; or".

Subsec. (c)(1)(H). Pub.L. 107–296, § 833(c)(2)(C), added subpar. (H).

2000 Amendments. Subsec. (a)(1)(A). Pub.L. 106–398, [Div. A, Title VIII, § 810(a)(1)], in subpar. (A), struck out "furnish for publication by the Secretary of Commerce" and inserted "publish".

Subsec. (a)(2). Pub.L. 106–398, [Div. A, Title VIII, § 809(a)(2)], rewrote par. (2), which formerly read: "(2) The Secretary of Commerce shall publish promptly in the Commerce Business Daily each notice required by paragraph (1).".

Subsec. (a)(3). Pub.L. 106–398, [Div. A, Title VIII, § 809(b)(1)], struck out "furnish a notice to the Secretary of Commerce" and inserted "publish a notice of solicitation".

Subsec. (a)(3)(A). Pub.L. 106–398, [Div. A, Title VIII, § 809(b)(2)], in subpar. (A), struck out "by the Secretary of Commerce" following "published".

Subsec. (a)(7). Pub.L. 106–398, [Div. A, Title VIII, § 809(a)(3)], added par. (7).

1998 Amendments. Subsec. (c)(1). Pub.L. 105–261, § 1069(d)(1), struck out the period at the end of subpar. (A) and inserted in lieu thereof a semicolon.

1997 Amendments. Subsec. (c)(1)(A) to (H). Pub.L. 105–85, § 850(g)(2), redesignated subpars. (C) through (H) as (B) through (G), respectively, added subpar. (A), and struck out former subpars. (A) and (B), which read as follows:

"(A) the proposed procurement is for an amount not greater than the simplified acquisition threshold and is to be made through a system with interim FACNET capability certified pursuant to section 426a(a)(1) of this title or with full FACNET capability certified pursuant to section 426a(a)(2) of this title;

"(B)(i) the proposed procurement is for an amount not greater than $250,000 and is to be made through a system with full FACNET capability certified pursuant to section 426a(a)(1) of this title; and

"(ii) a certification has been made pursuant to section 426a(b) of this title that Government-wide FACNET capability has been implemented;".

1996 Amendments. Subsec. (a)(1)(B). Pub.L. 104–106, § 4101(c), added "for a price expected to exceed $10,000, but not to exceed $25,000," following "property or services", substituted "subsection (b) of this section; and" for "subsection (f)—", and struck out provisions relating to the Department of Defense and other executive agencies.

Subsec. (a)(6). Pub.L. 104–106, § 4202(d)(1)(A), added "issuance of solicitations and the" following "paragraph (3) for the".

Subsec. (b)(5). Pub.L. 104–106, § 4321(h)(3), added "and" following "source;".

Subsec. (b)(6). Pub.L. 104–106, § 4202(d)(1)(B), substituted "threshold, or a contract for the procurement of commercial items using special simplified procedures—" for "threshold—".

Subsec. (c)(1)(E). Pub.L. 104–106, § 4310, added ", a task order contract, or a delivery order contract" following "requirements contract".

1994 Amendments. Subsec. (a)(1). Pub.L. 103–355, § 4202(a)(1), substituted "$25,000" for "the small purchase threshold" wherever appearing in subpars. (A)(i), (ii), (B)(i), (ii) and (C).

Subsec. (a)(1)(A). Pub.L. 103–355, § 9001(b)(1), substituted "notice of solicitation " for "notice".

Subsec. (a)(3)(B). Pub.L. 103–355, § 4202(a)(2), inserted the introductory phrase "in the case of a contract or order estimated to be greater than the simplified acquisition threshold,".

Subsec. (a)(4), (5). Pub.L. 103–355, § 4201(b), (c), added pars. (4) and (5), respectively.

Subsec. (a)(6). Pub.L. 103–355, § 8302, added par. (6).

Subsec. (b). Pub.L. 103–355, § 4202(b)(1)-(3), struck out "and" at the end of par. (4), substituted a semicolon for the period at the end of par. (5), and added par. (6).

Subsec. (c)(1)(A). Pub.L. 103–355, § 4202(c)(2), added subpar. (A). Former subpar. (A) redesignated (C).

Subsec. (c)(1)(B). Pub.L. 103–355, § 4202(c)(2), added subpar. (B). Former subpar. (B) redesignated (D).

Subsec. (c)(1)(C). Pub.L. 103–355, § 4202(c)(1), redesignated subpar. (A) as

(C). Former subpar. (C) redesignated (E).

Subsec. (c)(1)(D). Pub.L. 103–355, § 4202(c)(1), redesignated subpar. (B) as (D). Former subpar. (D) redesignated (F).

Subsec. (c)(1)(E). Pub.L. 103–355, § 4202(c)(1), redesignated subpar. (C) as (E). Former subpar. (E) redesignated (G).

Subsec. (c)(1)(F). Pub.L. 103–355, §§ 1055(b)(1)(A), 4202(c)(1), struck out "or" at the end of subpar. (D) and redesignated subpar. (D), as amended, as subpar. (F). Former subpar. (F) redesignated (H).

Subsec. (c)(1)(G). Pub.L. 103–355, §§ 1055(b)(1)(B), 4202(c)(1), substituted "; or" for the period at the end of subpar. (E), and redesignated subpar. (E), and amended, as subpar. (G).

Subsec. (c)(1)(H). Pub.L. 103–355, §§ 1055(b)(1)(C), 4202(c)(1), added subpar. (F) and redesignated subpar. (F), as added, as subpar. (H).

Subsec. (d). Pub.L. 103–355, § 9001(b)(2), substituted "notice of solicitation under subsection (a)" for "notice under subsection (e)".

1990 Amendments. Subsec. (a)(1)(A)(i). Pub.L. 101–510, § 806(d)(1), substituted "the small purchase threshold" for "$25,000".

Subsec. (a)(1)(A)(ii). Pub.L. 101–510, § 806(d)(1), substituted "the small purchase threshold" for "$25,000".

Subsec. (a)(1)(A)(iii). Pub.L. 101–510, § 806(d)(2), struck out cl. (iii), which made the notice requirement applicable to agencies intending to solicit bids or proposals for a contract for property or services for a price expected to exceed $10,000 if there is no reasonable expectation of at least two offers from responsive and responsible offerors.

Subsec. (a)(1)(B)(i). Pub.L. 101–510, § 806(d)(1), substituted "the small purchase threshold" for "$25,000".

Subsec. (a)(1)(B)(ii). Pub.L. 101–510, § 806(d)(1), substituted "the small purchase threshold" for "$25,000".

Subsec. (a)(1)(C). Pub.L. 101–510, § 806(d)(1), substituted "the small purchase threshold" for "$25,000" wherever appearing.

1986   Amendments. Subsec. (a)(1). Pub.L. 99–500, Title I, § 101(c) [Title X, § 922(b)], in subpar. (A) substituted "$25,000" for "$10,000" in cls. (i) and (ii), added cl. (iii), added subpar. (B), and redesignated former subpar. (B) as (C).

Pub.L. 99–591, Title I, § 101(c) [Title X, § 922(b)] and Pub.L. 99–661, § 922(b), made an amendment identical to Pub.L. 99–500, Title I, § 101(c) [Title X, § 922(c)].

Subsec. (b). Pub.L. 99–500, Title I, § 101(c) [Title X, § 922(d)(2)], substituted "subparagraph (A) or (B) of subsection (a)(1) of this section" for "subsection (a)(1)(A) of this section".

Pub.L. 99–591, Title I, § 101(c) [Title X, § 922(d)(2)] and Pub.L. 99–661, § 922(d)(2), made an amendment identical to Pub.L. 99–500, Title I, § 101(c) [Title X, § 922(d)(2)].

1984   Amendments. Subsec. (a)(1)(A). Pub. L. 98–577 designated existing provisions as cl. (i) and added cl. (ii).

Subsec. (a)(1)(B). Pub.L. 98–577 added ",or placing an order referred to in clause (A)(ii) exceeding $25,000," before "shall furnish".

Subsec. (a)(3)(B). Pub. L. 98–577 designated existing provisions as cl. (i), and in cl. (i) as so designated substituted provisions relating to an order under a basic agreement for provisions which related to all bids, and added cls. (ii) and (iii).

Subsec. (b)(1). Pub. L. 98–577 designated existing provisions as subpar. (A) and added subpar. (B).

Subsec. (b)(2). Pub. L. 98–577 added par. (2). Former par (2), which related to information about the officer or employee of the executive agency who may be contacted for purposes of obtaining a copy of the solicitation, was struck out.

Subsec. (c)(1)(B). Pub. L. 98–577 designated existing provisions as cl. (i) and added cl. (ii).

Subsec. (c)(1)(E). Pub. L. 98–577 added subpar. (E).

Subsec. (d). Pub. L. 98–577 added subsec. (d).

Effective and Applicability Provisions

2002 Acts. Amendments to this section by Pub.L. 107–296 effective 60 days after Nov. 25, 2002, see Pub.L. 107–296, § 4, set out as a note under 6 U.S.C.A. § 101.

2000   Acts. Amendment by Pub.L. 106–398, § 1 [Div. A, Title VIII, § 810(a), (b)], effective October 1, 2000, see Pub.L. 106–398, § 1 [Div. A, Title VIII, § 810(e)], set out as a note under section 637 of Title 15.

1997 Acts. Amendment by section 850 of Pub.L. 105–85 to take effect 180 days after Nov. 18, 1997, see section 850(g) of Pub.L. 105–85, set out as a note under section 2302c of Title 10, Armed Forces.

1996   Acts. Amendment by Pub.L. 104–106 effective Feb. 10, 1996, except as otherwise provided, see section 4401 of Pub.L. 104–106, set out as a note under section 251 of this title.

1994   Acts. Amendment by Pub.L. 103–355 effective Oct. 13, 1994, except as otherwise provided, see section 10001 of Pub.L. 103–355, set out as a note under section 251 of this title.

1984 Acts. Section 303(b) of Pub. L. 98–577 provided that: "The amendment made by subsection (a) [amending this section] shall take effect with respect to any solicitation issued after March 31, 1985."

Section applicable to any solicitation for bids or proposals issued after Mar. 31, 1985, see section 2751(a) of Pub.L. 98–369, set out as a note under section 251 of this title.

Coordination of Amendments by Pub.L. 105–261

For provisions stating that for purposes of applying amendments made by provisions of Pub.L. 105–261, Oct. 17, 1998, 112 Stat. 1920 [see Tables for classification], other than provisions of section 1069 of Pub.L. 105–261, Oct. 17, 1998, 112 Stat. 1920 [see Tables for classification], section 1069 of Pub.L. 105–261 shall be treated as having been enacted immediately before the other provisions of Pub.L. 105–261, see Pub.L. 105–261, Div. A, Title X, § 1069(e), Oct. 17, 1998, 112 Stat. 2137, set out as a note under section 101 of Title 10.

Implementation of Amendments by Section 850(e) of Pub.L. 105–85

Amendment by section 850(e)(2) of Pub.L. 105–85 to be implemented in a manner consistent with any applicable international agreements, see section 850(e)(3) of Pub.L. 105–85, set out as a note under section 637 of Title 15, Commerce and Trade.

[Provisions of the note immediately preceding, i.e., section 850(e)(3) of Pub.L. 105–85, to take effect 180 days after Nov. 18, 1997, see section 850(g) of Pub.L. 105–85, set out as an Effective Date of 1997 Acts note under section 2302c of Title 10, Armed Forces.]

Applicability to Tennessee Valley Authority

Section 303(c) of Pub. L. 98–577 provided that: "The provisions of the amendments made by subsection (a) of this section [amending this section] shall apply to the Tennessee Valley Authority only with respect to procurements to be paid from appropriated funds."

Rule of Construction for Duplicate Authorization and Appropriation Provisions of Public Laws 99–500, 99–591, and 99–661

For rule of construction for certain duplicate provisions of Public Laws 99–500, 99–591, and 99–661, see Pub.L. 100–26, § 6, Apr. 21, 1987, 101 Stat. 274, set out as a note under section 2302 of Title 10.

CROSS REFERENCES

Armed services acquisitions—
 Task and delivery order contracts and issuance of orders, see 10 USCA § 2304c.
 Task order contracts and advisory and assistant services, see 10 USCA § 2304b.
Civilian agency acquisitions—
 Task and delivery order contracts, see 41 USCA § 253j.
 Task order contracts and advisory and assistant services and content of notice, see 41 USCA § 253i.

LIBRARY REFERENCES

American Digest System
United States ☞64.25.
Key Number System Topic No. 393.

Research References

Treatises and Practice Aids
West's Federal Administrative Practice § 623, Sealed Bidding.
West's Federal Administrative Practice § 639, Simplified Purchases.

WESTLAW ELECTRONIC RESEARCH

See Westlaw guide following the Explanation pages of this volume.

§ 417. Record requirements

(a) Establishment and maintenance of computer file by executive agency; time period coverage

Each executive agency shall establish and maintain for a period of five years a computer file, by fiscal year, containing unclassified records of all procurements greater than the simplified acquisition threshold in such fiscal year.

(b) Contents

The record established under subsection (a) of this section shall include—

 (1) with respect to each procurement carried out using competitive procedures—

(A) the date of contract award;

(B) information identifying the source to whom the contract was awarded;

(C) the property or services obtained by the Government under the procurement; and

(D) the total cost of the procurement;

(2) with respect to each procurement carried out using procedures other than competitive procedures—

(A) the information described in clauses (1)(A), (1)(B), (1)(C), and (1)(D);

(B) the reason under section 253(c) of this title or section 2304(c) of Title 10, as the case may be, for the use of such procedures; and

(C) the identity of the organization or activity which conducted the procurement.

(c) Record categories

The information that is included in such record pursuant to subsection (b)(1) of this section and relates to procurements resulting in the submission of a bid or proposal by only one responsible source shall be separately categorized from the information relating to other procurements included in such record. The record of such information shall be designated "noncompetitive procurements using competitive procedures".

(d) Transmission and data system entry of information

The information included in the record established and maintained under subsection (a) of this section shall be transmitted to the General Services Administration and shall be entered in the Federal Procurement Data System referred to in section 405(d)(4) of this title.

(Pub.L. 93–400, § 19, as added Pub.L. 98–369, Title VII, § 2732(a), July 18, 1984, 98 Stat. 1197, and amended Pub.L. 103–355, Title IV, § 4403, Oct. 13, 1994, 108 Stat. 3349.)

HISTORICAL AND STATUTORY NOTES

Revision Notes and Legislative Reports
  1984 Acts. House Report No. 98–432, Pt. II, Senate Report Nos. 98–50 and 98–297, and House Conference Report No. 98–861, see 1984 U.S.Code Cong. and Adm.News, p. 697.

  1994 Acts. Senate Report Nos. 103–258 and 103–259, and House Conference Report No. 103–712, see 1994 U.S. Code Cong. and Adm. News, p. 2561.

Amendments
  1994 Amendments. Subsec. (a). Pub.L. 103–355, § 4403, substituted "procurements greater than the simplified acquisition threshold" for "procurements, other than small purchases".

Effective and Applicability Provisions
  1994 Acts. Amendment by section 4403 of Pub.L. 103–355 effective Oct. 13, 1994, except as otherwise provided, see section 10001 of Pub.L. 103–355, set out as a note under section 251 of this title.

1984 Acts. Section applicable to any solicitation for bids or proposals issued after Mar. 31, 1985, see section 2751(a)

of Pub.L. 98–369, set out as a note under section 251 of this title.

LIBRARY REFERENCES

American Digest System
United States ☞41.
Key Number System Topic No. 393.

WESTLAW ELECTRONIC RESEARCH

See Westlaw guide following the Explanation pages of this volume.

§ 417a. Procurement data

(a) Reporting

Each Federal agency shall report to the Office of Federal Procurement Policy the number of qualified HUBZone small business concerns, the number of small businesses owned and controlled by women, and the number of small business concerns owned and controlled by socially and economically disadvantaged businesses, by gender, that are first time recipients of contracts from such agency. The Office of Federal Procurement Policy shall take such actions as may be appropriate to ascertain for each fiscal year the number of such small businesses that have newly entered the Federal market.

(b) Definitions

For purposes of this section the terms "small business concern owned and controlled by women" and "small business concerns owned and controlled by socially and economically disadvantaged individuals" shall be given the same meaning as those terms are given under section 637(d) of Title 15 and section 204 of this Act, and the term "qualified HUBZone small business concern" has the meaning given that term in section 632(p) of Title 15..[1]

(Pub.L. 100–533, Title V, § 502, Oct. 25, 1988, 102 Stat. 2697; Pub.L. 105–135, Title VI, § 604(f)(2), Dec. 2, 1997, 111 Stat. 2634.)

[1] So in original. The second period probably should not appear.

HISTORICAL AND STATUTORY NOTES

Revision Notes and Legislative Reports
1988 Acts. House Report No. 100–955, see 1988 U.S. Code Cong. and Adm. News, p. 3530.
1997 Acts. Senate Report No. 105–62, see 1997 U.S. Code Cong. and Adm. News, p. 3077.

References in Text
Section 204 of this Act, referred to in subsec. (b), is section 204 of Pub.L.

100–533, Title II, Oct. 25, 1988, 102 Stat. 2692, which is set out as a note under section 637 of Title 15, Commerce and Trade.

Codifications
Section was enacted as part of the Women's Business Ownership Act of 1988, and not as part of the Office of Federal Procurement Policy Act, which comprises this chapter.

Amendments

1997   Amendments. Subsec.   (a).
Pub.L. 105–135, § 604(f)(2)(A)(i), (ii), inserted "the   number   of   qualified
HUBZone small business concerns,", and
inserted a comma following "women".

Subsec.   (b).   Pub.L.   105–135,
§ 604(f)(2)(B), inserted ", and the term
'qualified HUBZone small business con-

cern' has the meaning given that term in
section 632(p) of Title 15".

Effective and Applicability Provisions
Acts 1997. Pub.L. 105–135 and the
amendments made by Pub.L. 105–135 effective on October 1, 1997, see section 3
of Pub.L. 105–135, set out as a note under section 631 of Title 15, Commerce
and Trade.

LIBRARY REFERENCES

American Digest System
United States ☞41.
Key Number System Topic No. 393.

WESTLAW ELECTRONIC RESEARCH

See Westlaw guide following the Explanation pages of this volume.

§ 418. Advocates for competition

(a) Establishment, designation, etc., in executive agency

(1) There is established in each executive agency an advocate for
competition.

(2) The head of each executive agency shall—

(A) designate for the executive agency and for each procuring
activity of the executive agency one officer or employee serving
in a position authorized for such executive agency on July 18,
1984, (other than the senior procurement executive designated
pursuant to section 414(3) of this title) to serve as the advocate
for competition;

(B) not assign such officers or employees any duties or responsibilities that are inconsistent with the duties and responsibilities of the advocates for competition; and

(C) provide such officers or employees with such staff or
assistance as may be necessary to carry out the duties and
responsibilities of the advocate for competition, such as persons
who are specialists in engineering, technical operations, contract
administration, financial management, supply management, and
utilization of small and disadvantaged business concerns.

(b) Duties and functions

The advocate for competition of an executive agency shall—

(1) be responsible for challenging barriers to and promoting
full and open competition in the procurement of property and
services by the executive agency;

(2) review the procurement activities of the executive agency;

(3) identify and report to the senior procurement executive of the executive agency designated pursuant to section 414(3) of this title—

   (A) opportunities and actions taken to achieve full and open competition in the procurement activities of the executive agency; and

   (B) any condition or action which has the effect of unnecessarily restricting competition in the procurement actions of the executive agency; and [1]

(4) prepare and transmit to such senior procurement executive an annual report describing—

   (A) such advocate's activities under this section;

   (B) new initiatives required to increase competition; and

   (C) barriers to full and open competition that remain;

(5) recommend to the senior procurement executive of the executive agency goals and the plans for increasing competition on a fiscal year basis;

(6) recommend to the senior procurement executive of the executive agency a system of personal and organizational accountability for competition, which may include the use of recognition and awards to motivate program managers, contracting officers, and others in authority to promote competition in procurement programs; and

(7) describe other ways in which the executive agency has emphasized competition in programs for procurement training and research.

(c) Responsibilities

The advocate for competition for each procuring activity shall be responsible for promoting full and open competition, promoting the acquisition of commercial items, and challenging barriers to such acquisition, including such barriers as unnecessarily restrictive statements of need, unnecessarily detailed specifications, and unnecessarily burdensome contract clauses.

(Pub.L. 93–400, § 20, as added Pub.L. 98–369, Div. B, Title VII, § 2732(a), July 18, 1984, 98 Stat. 1197, and amended Pub.L. 103–355, Title VIII, § 8303(a), Oct. 13, 1994, 108 Stat. 3398.)

[1] So in original. The word "and" probably should not appear.

HISTORICAL AND STATUTORY NOTES

Revision Notes and Legislative Reports
1984 Acts. House Report No. 98–432, Pt. II, Senate Report Nos. 98–50 and 98–297, and House Conference Report

No. 98–861, see 1984 U.S.Code Cong. and Adm.News, p. 697.

1994   Acts. Senate   Report   Nos. 103–258 and 103–259, and House Conference Report No. 103–712, see 1994 U.S. Code Cong. and Adm. News, p. 2561.

Amendments
1994 Amendments. Subsec. (c). Pub.L. 103–355, § 8303(a), substituted "responsible for promoting full and open competition promoting the acquisition of commercial items, and challenging barriers to such acquisition, including such barriers as unnecessarily restrictive statements of need, unnecessarily detailed specifications, and unnecessarily burdensome contract clauses" for "responsible for challenging barriers to and promoting full and open competition in the procuring activity, including unnecessarily de-

tailed specifications and unnecessarily restrictive statements of need".

Effective and Applicability Provisions
1994 Acts. Amendment by section 8303(a) of Pub.L. 103–355 effective Oct. 13, 1994, except as otherwise provided, see section 10001 of Pub.L. 103–355, set out as a note under section 251 of this title.

1984 Acts. Section applicable to any solicitation for bids or proposals issued after Mar. 31, 1985, see section 2751(a) of Pub.L. 98–369, set out as a note under section 251 of this title.

CROSS REFERENCES

Defense Logistics Agency, advocate for competition, designation by Secretary of Defense, see 10 USCA § 2318.

LIBRARY REFERENCES

American Digest System
United States ☞41.
Key Number System Topic No. 393.

WESTLAW ELECTRONIC RESEARCH

See Westlaw guide following the Explanation pages of this volume.

§ 418a. Rights in technical data

(a) Regulations; legitimate proprietary interest of United States

The legitimate proprietary interest of the United States and of a contractor in technical or other data shall be defined in regulations prescribed as part of the single system of Government-wide procurement regulations as defined in section 403(4) of this title. Such regulations may not impair any right of the United States or of any contractor with respect to patents or copyrights or any other right in technical data otherwise established by law. Such regulations shall provide, with respect to executive agencies that are subject to the provisions of Title III of the Federal Property and Administrative Services Act of 1949 [41 U.S.C.A. § 251 et seq.], that the United States may not require persons who have developed products or processes offered or to be offered for sale to the public as a condition for the procurement of such products or processes by the United States, to provide to the United States technical data relating to the design, development, or manufacture of such products or processes (except for such data as may be necessary for the United States to operate and maintain the product or use the process if obtained by the United States as an element of performance under the contract).

733

(b) Unlimited rights; technical data; developed with Federal funds; unrestricted, royalty-free right to use; rights under law

(1) Except as otherwise expressly provided by Federal statute, the regulations prescribed pursuant to subsection (a) of this section shall provide, with respect to executive agencies that are subject to the provisions of Title III of the Federal Property and Administrative Services Act of 1949 [41 U.S.C.A. § 251 et seq.], that the United States shall have unlimited rights in technical data developed exclusively with Federal funds if delivery of such data—

(A) was required as an element of performance under a contract; and

(B) is needed to ensure the competitive acquisition of supplies or services that will be required in substantial quantities in the future.

(2) Except as otherwise expressly provided by Federal statute, the regulations prescribed pursuant to subsection (a) of this section shall provide, with respect to executive agencies that are subject to the provisions of Title III of the Federal Property and Administrative Services Act of 1949 [41 U.S.C.A. § 251 et seq.], that the United States (and each agency thereof) shall have an unrestricted, royalty-free right to use, or to have its contractors use, for governmental purposes (excluding publication outside the Government) technical data developed exclusively with Federal funds.

(3) The requirements of paragraphs (1) and (2) shall be in addition to and not in lieu of any other rights that the United States may have pursuant to law.

(c) Factors; regulations

The following factors shall be considered in prescribing regulations pursuant to subsection (a) of this section:

(1) Whether the item or process to which the technical data pertains was developed—

(A) exclusively with Federal funds;

(B) exclusively at private expense; or

(C) in part with Federal funds and in part at private expense.

(2) The statement of congressional policy and objectives in section 200 of Title 35, the statement of purposes in section 2(b) of the Small Business Innovation Development Act of 1982 (Public Law 97–219; 15 U.S.C.638 note), and the declaration of policy in section 631 of Title 15.

(3) The interest of the United States in increasing competition and lowering costs by developing and locating alternative sources of supply and manufacture.

(d) Provisions; contracts; regulations

Regulations prescribed under subsection (a) of this section shall require that a contract for property or services entered into by an executive agency contain appropriate provisions relating to technical data, including provisions—

(1) defining the respective rights of the United States and the contractor or subcontractor (at any tier) regarding any technical data to be delivered under the contract;

(2) specifying the technical data, if any, to be delivered under the contract and delivery schedules for such delivery;

(3) establishing or referencing procedures for determining the acceptability of technical data to be delivered under the contract;

(4) establishing separate contract line items for the technical data, if any, to be delivered under the contract;

(5) to the maximum practicable extent, identifying, in advance of delivery, technical data which is to be delivered with restrictions on the right of the United States to use such data;

(6) requiring the contractor to revise any technical data delivered under the contract to reflect engineering design changes made during the performance of the contract and affecting the form, fit, and function of the items specified in the contract and to deliver such revised technical data to an agency within a time specified in the contract;

(7) requiring the contractor to furnish written assurance at the time the technical data is delivered or is made available that the technical data is complete and accurate and satisfies the requirements of the contract concerning technical data;

(8) establishing remedies to be available to the United States when technical data required to be delivered or made available under the contract is found to be incomplete or inadequate or to not satisfy the requirements of the contract concerning technical data; and

(9) authorizing the head of the agency to withhold payments under the contract (or exercise such other remedies as the head of the agency considers appropriate) during any period if the contractor does not meet the requirements of the contract pertaining to the delivery of technical data.

(Pub.L. 93–400, § 21, as added Pub.L. 98–577, Title III, § 301(a), Oct. 30, 1984, 98 Stat. 3074, and amended Pub.L. 99–145, Title IX, § 961(d)(2), Nov. 8, 1985, 99 Stat. 704.)

HISTORICAL AND STATUTORY NOTES

Revision Notes and Legislative Reports

1984 Acts. Paragraph (4) of new section 15(o) requires the inclusion of a contract provision defining the respective rights of the Government and a contractor or subcontractor regarding any technical data to be delivered under the contract. It requires that the contract provision include a definition of the phrase "developed at private expense."

However, technical data is not always delivered to the Government without restriction on its subsequent use by the Government. Technical data delivered by the contractor may include "trade secrets" in which the contractor claims a proprietary interest, that is, a property right. If such trade secrets are kept out of the public domain, that is are kept "secret" and unpublished, they are protected under common law, and enforceable through state court action. Trade secrets are not presently regulated through Federal statute.

Current procurement regulations, and the contract clauses through which they are implemented, recognize a contractor's right to deliver the technical data to the Government with limitations on its subsequent use by the Government in a manner that would not violate their character as trade secrets. Specifically, such "limited rights technical data", or "proprietary" technical data cannot be published by the Government, as would be the case if it were included in a technical data package for a competitive procurement.

If the proprietary data is essential to define what it is the Government wants to purchase, or is essential to enable another contractor to fulfill the Government's requirement, competition is foreclosed. At that point, the Government is forced to procure the item on a "sole source" basis from the contractor that owns the proprietary data. ....

Paragraph (5) of new section 15(o) requires the inclusion of a contract provision that will require the contractor to identify to the Government technical data which the contractor intends to deliver with limitations on the Government's right to use the data. This provision closely parallels the requirements of DAR 7–2003.61 (Predetermination of Rights in Technical Data and Computer Software).

Having early access to information regarding whether competition for a particular component will be restricted due to a contractor's assertion of a limitation on the Government's rights on the technical data will better enable the executive agency to take remedial action: mount a challenge, if the limited rights assertion is suspected of being unwarranted, or exercise an option to purchase or license the restricted technical data, if the contractor extended such an offer to the government. The AFMAG suggested that such a predetermination clause should be mandatory in all contract solicitations issued by the Air Force for major systems. II AFMAG Report at 42–43. Senate Report No. 98–523.

1985 Acts. House Report No. 99–81 and House Conference Report No. 99–235, see 1985 U.S.Code Cong. and Adm.News, p. 472.

References in Text

The Federal Property and Administrative Services Act of 1949, referred to in subsecs. (a) and (b), is Act June 30, 1949, c. 288, 63 Stat. 377, as amended, Title III of which is currently classified to subchapter IV of chapter 4 of Title 41, 41 U.S.C.A. § 251 et seq., and the remainder of which was formerly classified to chapter 10 of former Title 40, 40 U.S.C.A. § 471 et seq., prior to being repealed by Pub.L. 107–217, § 6(b), Aug. 21, 2002, 116 Stat. 1313; see now generally chapter 1 of Title 40, 40 U.S.C.A. § 101 et seq.

Section 2(b) of the Small Business Innovation Development Act of 1982, referred to in subsec. (c)(2) of this section, is section 2(b) of Pub.L. 97–219, July 22, 1982, 96 Stat. 217, which is set out as a note under section 638 of Title 15, Commerce and Trade.

Amendments

1985 Amendments. Subsec. (c)(1). Pub.L. 99–145, § 961(d)(2), substituted "the item or process to which the technical data pertains" for "the technical data".

Effective and Applicability Provisions

1984 Acts. Section 301(c) of Pub.L. 98–577, as amended Pub.L. 99–145, Title IX, § 961(d)(3), Nov. 8, 1985, 99 Stat. 704, provided that: "The amendment made by subsection (a) [enacting this section] shall take effect on the date of enactment of this Act [Oct. 30, 1984]. The regulations required by such amendment shall be issued not later than October 19, 1985."

Prior Provisions

A prior section 21 of Pub.L. 93–400, as added Pub.L. 98–369, Div. B, Title VII,

§ 2732(a), July 18, 1984, 98 Stat. 1198, was renumbered as section 23 of Pub.L. 93–400 by Pub.L. 98–577, Title III, § 301(a), Oct. 30, 1984, 98 Stat. 3074. See section 419 of this title.

LIBRARY REFERENCES

American Digest System
Labor and Employment ⚍312.
Key Number System Topic No. 231H.

WESTLAW ELECTRONIC RESEARCH

See Westlaw guide following the Explanation pages of this volume.

§ 418b.   Publication of proposed regulations

(a) Effective date; procurement policy, regulations, procedure or form; publication in Federal Register

Except as provided in subsection (d) of this section, no procurement policy, regulation, procedure, or form (including amendments or modifications thereto) relating to the expenditure of appropriated funds that has (1) a significant effect beyond the internal operating procedures of the agency issuing the procurement policy, regulation, procedure or form, or (2) a significant cost or administrative impact on contractors or offerors, may take effect until 60 days after the procurement policy, regulation, procedure, or form is published for public comment in the Federal Register pursuant to subsection (b) of this section. Notwithstanding the preceding sentence, such a policy, regulation, procedure, or form may take effect earlier than 60 days after the publication date when there are compelling circumstances for the earlier effective date, but in no event may that effective date be less than 30 days after the publication date.

(b) Publication in Federal Register

Subject to subsection (c) of this section, the head of the agency shall cause to be published in the Federal Register a notice of the proposed procurement policy, regulation, procedure, or form and provide for a public comment period for receiving and considering the views of all interested parties on such proposal. The length of such comment period may not be less than 30 days.

(c) Notice; proposed policy; contents

Any notice of a proposed procurement policy, regulation, procedure, or form prepared for publication in the Federal Register shall include—

(1) the text of the proposal or, if it is impracticable to publish the full text of the proposal, a summary of the proposal and a statement specifying the name, address, and telephone number of the officer or employee of the executive agency from whom the full text may be obtained; and

(2) a request for interested parties to submit comments on the proposal and shall include the name and address of the officer or employee of the Government designated to receive such comments.

(d) Waiver

(1) The requirements of subsections (a) and (b) of this section may be waived by the officer authorized to issue a procurement policy, regulation, procedure, or form if urgent and compelling circumstances make compliance with such requirements impracticable.

(2) A procurement policy, regulation, procedure, or form with respect to which the requirements of subsections (a) and (b) of this section are waived under paragraph (1) shall be effective on a temporary basis if—

(A) a notice of such procurement policy, regulation, procedure, or form is published in the Federal Register and includes a statement that the procurement policy, regulation, procedure, or form is temporary; and

(B) provision is made for a public comment period of 30 days beginning on the date on which the notice is published.

(3) After considering the comments received, the head of the agency waiving the requirements of subsections (a) and (b) of this section under paragraph (1) may issue the final procurement policy, regulation, procedure, or form.

(Pub.L. 93–400, § 22, as added Pub.L. 98–577, Title III, § 302(a), Oct. 30, 1984, 98 Stat. 3076, and amended Pub.L. 103–355, Title V, § 5092, Oct. 13, 1994, 108 Stat. 3362; Pub.L. 104–106, Div. D, Title XLIII, § 4321(a)(9), Feb. 10, 1996, 110 Stat. 671.)

HISTORICAL AND STATUTORY NOTES

Revision Notes and Legislative Reports
1984 Acts. Senate Report No. 98–523, see 1984 U.S. Code Cong. and Adm. News, p. 5347.

1994 Acts. Senate Report Nos. 103–258 and 103–259, and House Conference Report No. 103–712, see 1994 U.S. Code Cong. and Adm. News, p. 2561.

1996 Acts. House Conference Report No. 104–450, see 1996 U.S. Code Cong. and Adm. News, p. 238.

Codifications
Amendment to subsec. (d) by section 5092(b) of Pub.L. 103–355, purporting to require the designation of the second sentence of subsec. (d) as par. (3), has been executed by designating the second sentence of subsec. (d)(2), which had previously been undesignated, as (d)(3), as the probable intent of Congress.

Amendments
1996 Amendments. Subsec. (d)(3). Pub.L. 104–106, § 4321(a)(9), as amend-

ing Pub.L. 103–355, § 5092(b), made technical changes to directory language, adding "of paragraph (2)" following "second sentence" which, for purposes of codification, required no changes in text.

1994 Amendments. Subsec. (a). Pub.L. 103–355, § 5092(a)(1), (2), substituted "60 days" for "30 days" and authorized an earlier effective date when there are compelling circumstances but in no event earlier than 30 days after the publication date.

Effective and Applicability Provisions
1996 Acts. Amendment by Pub.L. 104–106 effective Oct. 13, 1994, see section 4321(a) of Pub.L. 104–106, set out as a note under section 2306a of Title 10, Armed Forces.

1994 Acts. Amendment by section 5092 of Pub.L. 103–355 effective Oct. 13, 1994,

and applicable on and after such date, see section 10001 of Pub.L. 103–355, set out as a note under section 251 of this title.

1984 Acts. Section 302(b) of Pub.L. 98–577 provided that: "The procedures required by the amendment made by subsection (a) [enacting this section] shall apply with respect to procurement policies, regulations, procedures, or forms that an agency issues in final form on or after the date which is 30 days after the date of enactment of this Act [Oct. 30, 1984]."

Prior Provisions
A prior section 21 of Pub.L. 93–400, as added Pub.L. 98–369, Div. B, Title VII, § 2732(a), July 18, 1984, 98 Stat. 1198, was renumbered section 23 by Pub.L. 98–577 and is classified to 41 U.S.C.A. § 419.

CROSS REFERENCES

Authority to secure health-care resources and publication of procedures in accordance with this section, see 38 USCA § 8153.

LIBRARY REFERENCES

American Digest System
United States ⚷64.5.
Key Number System Topic No. 393.

Research References

ALR Library
15 ALR, Fed. 2nd Series 273, Validity, Construction, and Effect of Economic Price Adjustment (EPA) Clauses in Federal Contracts.

WESTLAW ELECTRONIC RESEARCH

See Westlaw guide following the Explanation pages of this volume.

Notes of Decisions

Constructive notice   1
Failure to provide notice   2
———

1. Constructive notice
Statute imposing notice and comment requirements in connection with procurement policies was not satisfied by constructive notice and opportunity to comment allegedly enjoyed by carrier groups challenging Military Traffic Management Command (MTMC) notice requiring carriers seeking government's general traffic (GT) and voluntary tender business to agree to accept Foreign Military Sales (FMS) work at same rate; there was no

evidence that all of carriers received notice, and statute required publication "for public comment," whereas it appeared that MTMC would abide by terms of notice in spite of any comments received, and no explicit comment period was set forth in notice. Munitions Carriers Conference, Inc. v. U.S., D.D.C.1996, 932 F.Supp. 334, reversed 147 F.3d 1027, 331 U.S.App.D.C. 213. United States ⚷ 64.5

2. Failure to provide notice
Class deviation from the Federal Acquisition Regulation (FAR) for economic price adjustment (EPA) clause employing price indexes in military jet fuel supply

contracts was not valid, where contracting agency did not comply with publication requirements in the Defense Logistics Acquisition Regulation (DLAR), and the Office of Federal Procurement Policy (OFPP) Act; agency did not publish notice of the proposed class deviation and its published notice of proposed permanent revision of FAR section governing EPA clauses did not provide notice of the class deviation. Navajo Refining Co., L.P. v. U.S., Fed.Cl.2003, 58 Fed.Cl. 200. United States ⊕ 70(18)

Class deviation from the Federal Acquisition Regulation (FAR) for economic price adjustment clause based on price index was not authorized and was not valid for 1997, 1998, and 1999 contracts for the procurement of military jet and diesel fuel, where the government obtained the class deviation in contravention of the publication requirements established by section of the Defense Logistics Acquisition Regulation, and section of the Office of Federal Procurement Policy (OFPP) Act; government did not publish notice of the proposed class deviation and published notice of a proposed permanent revision did not provide notice of the class deviation. La Gloria Oil and Gas Co. v. U.S., Fed.Cl.2003, 56 Fed.Cl. 211. United States ⊕ 70(18)

§ 419. Contracting functions performed by Federal personnel

(a) Limitation on payment for advisory and assistance services

(1) No person who is not a person described in subsection (b) of this section may be paid by an executive agency for services to conduct evaluations or analyses of any aspect of a proposal submitted for an acquisition unless personnel described in subsection (b) of this section with adequate training and capabilities to perform such evaluations and analyses are not readily available within the agency or another Federal agency, as determined in accordance with standards and procedures prescribed in the Federal Acquisition Regulation.

(2) In the administration of this subsection, the head of each executive agency shall determine in accordance with the standards and procedures set forth in the Federal Acquisition Regulation whether—

(A) a sufficient number of personnel described in subsection (b) of this section within the agency or another Federal agency are readily available to perform a particular evaluation or analysis for the head of the executive agency making the determination; and

(B) the readily available personnel have the training and capabilities necessary to perform the evaluation or analysis.

(b) Covered personnel

For purposes of subsection (a) of this section, the personnel described in this subsection are as follows:

(1) An employee, as defined in section 2105 of Title 5.

(2) A member of the Armed Forces of the United States.

(3) A person assigned to a Federal agency pursuant to subchapter VI of chapter 33 of Title 5.

(c) Rule of construction

Nothing in this section is intended to affect the relationship between the Federal Government and a federally funded research and development center.

(Pub.L. 93–400, § 23, as added Oct. 13, 1994, Pub.L. 103–355, Title VI, § 6002(a), 108 Stat. 3363.)

HISTORICAL AND STATUTORY NOTES

Revision Notes and Legislative Reports
1994 Acts. Senate Report Nos. 103–258 and 103–259, and House Conference Report No. 103–712, see 1994 U.S. Code Cong. and Adm. News, p. 2561.

Effective and Applicability Provisions
1994 Acts. Section effective Oct. 13, 1994, except as otherwise provided, see section 10001 of Pub.L. 103–355, set out as a note under section 251 of this title.

Prior Provisions
A prior section 419, Pub.L. 93–400, § 23, formerly § 21, as added Pub.L. 98–369, Div. B, Title VII, § 2732(a), July 18, 1984, 98 Stat. 1198, and renumbered Pub.L. 98–577, Title III, § 301(a), Oct. 30, 1984, 98 Stat. 3074, which related to annual report to be submitted to Congress by agency heads concerning actions taken to increase competition for contracts and reduce number and dollar value of noncompetitive contracts, was repealed, effective Oct. 13, 1994, and applicable on and after such date, by Pub.L. 103–355, Title I, § 1092, Title X, § 10001, Oct. 13, 1994, 108 Stat. 3273, 3404.

Requirement for Guidance and Regulations
Section 6002(b) of Pub.L. 103–355 provided that:

"The Federal Acquisition Regulatory Council established by section 25(a) of the Office of Federal Procurement Policy Act (41 U.S.C. 421(a)) [section 421(a) of this title] shall—

"**(1)** review part 37 of title 48 of the Code of Federal Regulations as it relates to the use of advisory and assistance services; and

"**(2)** provide guidance and promulgate regulations regarding—

"**(A)** what actions Federal agencies are required to take to determine whether expertise is readily available within the Federal Government before contracting for advisory and technical services to conduct acquisitions; and

"**(B)** the manner in which personnel with expertise may be shared with agencies needing expertise for such acquisitions."

WESTLAW ELECTRONIC RESEARCH

See Westlaw guide following the Explanation pages of this volume.

§ 420. Repealed. Pub.L. 103–355, Title II, § 2191, Oct. 13, 1994, 108 Stat. 3315

HISTORICAL AND STATUTORY NOTES

Section, Pub.L. 93–400, § 24, as added Pub.L. 99–234, Title II, § 201, Jan. 2, 1986, 99 Stat. 1759, and amended Pub.L. 100–679, § 12, Nov. 17, 1988, 102 Stat. 4070, related to limits on allowable costs

for travel expenses of government contractors.

Effective Date of Repeal
Repeal of section effective Oct. 13, 1994, and applicable on and after such

date, see section 10001 of Pub.L.
103–355, set out as a note under section
251 of this title.

§ 421. Federal Acquisition Regulatory Council

(a) Establishment

There is established a Federal Acquisition Regulatory Council (hereinafter in this section referred to as the "Council") to assist in the direction and coordination of Government-wide procurement policy and Government-wide procurement regulatory activities in the Federal Government.

(b) Membership

(1) The Council shall consist of the Administrator for Federal Procurement Policy and—

   (A) the Secretary of Defense,

   (B) the Administrator of National Aeronautics and Space; and

   (C) the Administrator of General Services.

(2) Notwithstanding section 121(d)(1) and (2) of Title 40 [40 U.S.C. 486(d)], the officials specified in subparagraphs (A), (B), and (C) of paragraph (1) may designate to serve on and attend meetings of the Council in place of that official (A) the official assigned by statute with the responsibility for acquisition policy in each of their respective agencies or, in the case of the Secretary of Defense, an official at an organizational level not lower than an Assistant Secretary of Defense within the Office of the Under Secretary of Defense for Acquisition, Technology, and Logistics; or (B) if no official of such agency is assigned by statute with the responsibility for acquisition policy for that agency, the official designated pursuant to section 414(3) of this title. No other official or employee may be designated to serve on the Council.

(c) Functions

(1) Subject to the provisions of section 405 of this title, the General Services Administration, the Department of Defense, and the National Aeronautics and Space Administration, pursuant to their respective authorities under title III of the Federal Property and Administrative Services Act of 1949 (41 U.S.C. 251, et seq.), chapters 4 and 137 of Title 10, and the National Aeronautics and Space Act of 1958 (42 U.S.C. 2451, et seq.), shall jointly issue and maintain in accordance with subsection (f) of this section a single Government-wide procurement regulation, to be known as the "Federal Acquisition Regulation".

(2) Any other regulations relating to procurement issued by an executive agency shall be limited to (A) regulations essential to implement Government-wide policies and procedures within the agency, and (B) additional policies and procedures required to satisfy the specific and unique needs of the agency.

(3) The Administrator, in consultation with the Council, shall ensure that procurement regulations promulgated by executive agencies are consistent with the Federal Acquisition Regulation and in accordance with any policies issued pursuant to section 405(a) of this title.

(4)(A) Under procedures established by the Administrator, a person may request the Administrator to review any regulation relating to procurement on the basis that such regulation is inconsistent with the Federal Acquisition Regulation.

(B) Unless the request is frivolous or does not, on its face, state a valid basis for such review, the Administrator shall complete such a review not later than 60 days after receiving the request. The time for completion of the review may be extended if the Administrator determines that an additional period of review is required. The Administrator shall advise the requester of the reasons for the extension and the date by which the review will be completed.

(5) If the Administrator determines that a regulation relating to procurement is inconsistent with the Federal Acquisition Regulation or that the regulation should otherwise be revised to remove an inconsistency with any policies issued under section 405(a) of this title, the Administrator shall rescind or deny the promulgation of the regulation or take such other action authorized under section 405 of this title as may be necessary to remove the inconsistency. If the Administrator determines that such a regulation, although not inconsistent with the Federal Acquisition Regulation or such policies, should be revised to improve compliance with such Regulation or policies, the Administrator shall take such action authorized under section 405 of this title as may be necessary and appropriate.

(6) The decisions of the Administrator shall be in writing and made publicly available. The Administrator shall provide a listing of such decisions in the annual report to Congress required by section 407 of this title.

(d) Additional responsibilities of membership

Subject to the authority, direction, and control of the head of the agency concerned, each official who represents an agency on the Council pursuant to subsection (b) of this section shall—

(1) approve or disapprove all regulations that are, after 60 days after November 17, 1988, proposed for public comment, promulgated in final form, or otherwise made effective by such agency relating to procurement before such regulation may be promulgated in final form, or otherwise made effective, except that such official may grant an interim approval, without review, for not more than 60 days for a procurement regulation in urgent and compelling circumstances;

(2) carry out the responsibilities of such agency set forth in chapter 35 of Title 44 for each information collection request (as that term is defined in section 3502(11) of Title 44) that relates to procurement rules or regulations; and

(3) eliminate or reduce (A) any redundant or unnecessary levels of review and approval, in the procurement system of such agency, and (B) redundant or unnecessary procurement regulations which are unique to that agency.

The authority to review and approve or disapprove regulations under paragraph (1) of this subsection may not be delegated to any person outside the office of the official who represents the agency on the Council pursuant to subsection (b) of this section.

(e) Governing policies

All actions of the Council and of members of the Council shall be in accordance with and furtherance of the policies prescribed under section 405(a) of this title.

(f) General authority with respect to FAR

Subject to section 405(b) of this title, the Council shall manage, coordinate, control, and monitor the maintenance of, and issuance of and changes in, the Federal Acquisition Regulation.

(Pub.L. 93–400, § 25, as added Pub.L. 100–679, § 4, Nov. 17, 1988, 102 Stat. 4056, and amended Pub.L. 101–510, Div. A, Title VIII, § 807, Nov. 5, 1990, 104 Stat. 1593; Pub.L. 103–160, Div. A, Title IX, § 904(f), Nov. 30, 1993, 107 Stat. 1729; Pub.L. 104–106, Div. D, Title XLIII, § 4322(a)(2), Feb. 10, 1996, 110 Stat. 677; Pub.L. 104–201, Div. A, Title VIII, § 822, Title X, § 1074(f)(3), Sept. 23, 1996, 110 Stat. 2609, 2661; Pub.L. 105–85, Div. A, Title VIII, § 841(d), Nov. 18, 1997, 111 Stat. 1843; Pub.L. 106–65, Div. A, Title IX, § 911(a)(1), Oct. 5, 1999, 113 Stat. 717.)

HISTORICAL AND STATUTORY NOTES

Revision Notes and Legislative Reports
1988 Acts. Senate Report No. 100–424, see 1988 U.S. Code Cong. and Adm. News, p. 5687.
1993 Acts. House Report No. 103–200 and House Conference Report No.

103–357, see 1993 U.S. Code Cong. and Adm. News, p. 2013.

1996 Acts. House Conference Report No. 104–450, see 1996 U.S. Code Cong. and Adm. News, p. 238.

House Report No. 104–563 and House Conference Report No. 104–724, see 1996 U.S. Code Cong. and Adm. News, p. 2948.

1997 Acts. House Conference Report No. 105–340 and Statement by President, see 1997 U.S. Code Cong. and Adm. News, p. 2251.

1999 Acts. House Conference Report No. 106–301 and Statement by President, see 1999 U.S. Code Cong. and Adm. News, p. 94.

References in Text

The Federal Property and Administrative Services Act of 1949, referred to in subsec. (c)(1), is Act June 30, 1949, c. 288, 63 Stat. 377, as amended, which is currently classified to subchapter IV of chapter 4 of Title 41, 41 U.S.C.A. § 251 et seq., and was formerly classified to chapter 10 of former Title 40, 40 U.S.C.A. § 471 et seq., prior to being repealed by Pub.L. 107–217, § 6(b), Aug. 21, 2002, 116 Stat. 1313; see now generally chapter 1 of Title 40, 40 U.S.C.A. § 101 et seq.

The National Aeronautics and Space Act of 1958, referred to in subsec. (c)(1), is classified generally to chapter 26 of Title 42 (42 U.S.C.A. § 2451 et seq.). For complete classification, see Short Title note set out under section 2451 of Title 42 and Tables.

Section 407 of this title, referred to in subsec. (c)(6), was repealed by Pub.L. 104–106, Div. D, Title XLIII, § 4305(b), Feb. 10, 1996, 110 Stat. 665.

Section 3502 of Title 44, referred to in subsec. (d)(2), which in par. (11) defined the term "information collection request", was omitted in the general amendment of chapter 35 of Title 44 by Pub.L. 104–913, § 2, May 22, 1995, 109 Stat. 163. Pub.L. 104 –13 enacted a new 44 U.S.C.A. § 3502 which does not define that term.

Codifications

In subsec. (b)(2), "section 121(d)(1) and (2) of Title 40" substituted for "section 205(d) of the Federal Property and Administrative Services Act of 1949", on authority of Pub.L. 107–217, § 5(c), Aug. 21, 2002, 116 Stat. 1301, which is set out as a note preceding 40 U.S.C.A. § 101. Pub.L. 107–217, § 1, enacted Title 40 into positive law. Section 205(d) of the Federal Property and Administrative Services Act of 1949 was classified to section

486(d) of Title 40 prior to being repealed by Pub.L. 107–217, § 6(b), Aug. 21, 2002, 116 Stat. 1313, and its substance reenacted as 40 U.S.C.A. § 121(d)(1), (2). See also References in Text note below.

Amendments

1999 Amendments. Subsec. (b)(2). Pub.L. 106–65, § 911(a)(1), struck out "Under Secretary of Defense for Acquisition and Technology" and inserted "Under Secretary of Defense for Acquisition, Technology, and Logistics".

1997 Amendments. Subsec. (g). Pub.L. 105–85, § 841(d), struck out subsec. (g). Prior to repeal, subsec. (g) read as follows:

"(g) Reports

"The Administrator for Federal Procurement Policy shall—

"(1) publish a report every 12 months relating to the development of procurement regulations to be issued in accordance with subsection (c) of this section;

"(2) include in each report published under paragraph (1)—

"(A) the status of each such regulation;

"(B) a description of those regulations which are required by statute;

"(C) a description of the methods by which public comment was sought with regard to each proposed regulation in accordance with section 418b of this title, and to the extent appropriate, sections 3504(h) and 3507 of Title 44;

"(D) regulatory activities completed and initiated since the last report;

"(E) regulations, policies, procedures, practices, and forms that are under consideration or review by the Office of Federal Procurement Policy;

"(F) whether the regulations have paperwork requirements;

"(G) the progress made in promulgating and implementing the Federal Acquisition Regulation; and

"(H) such other matters as the Administrator determines would be useful."

1996 Amendments. Subsec. (b)(2). Pub.L. 104–106, § 4322(a)(2), substituted "Under Secretary of Defense for Acquisition and Technology" for "Under Secretary of Defense for Acquisition", which amendment had already been executed, thereby requiring no further change in text.

Subsec. (c)(3). Pub.L. 104–201, § 1074(f)(3)(A)(i), struck out reference to accord with policies of section 401 of this title.

Subsec. (c)(5). Pub.L. 104–201, § 1074(f)(3)(A)(ii), struck out reference to consistency with policies of section 401 of this title.

Subsec. (e). Pub.L. 104–201, § 1074(f)(3)(B), struck out reference to furthering policies of section 401 of this title.

Subsec. (g)(1). Pub.L. 104–201, § 822(1)(A), substituted "every 12 months" for "within 6 months after November 17, 1988, and every 6 months thereafter".

Pub.L. 104–201, § 822(1)(B), made technical corrections.

Subsec. (g)(2)(H). Pub.L. 104–201, § 822(2), made technical corrections.

Subsec. (g)(3). Pub.L 104–201, § 822(3), struck out par. (3) which related to the mandatory report to Congress regarding the extent of the paperwork burden and the extent to which the Federal procurement system can be streamlined.

1993 Amendments. Subsec. (b)(2). Pub.L. 103–160, § 904(f), substituted "Under Secretary of Defense for Acquisi-

tion and Technology" for "Under Secretary of Defense for Acquisition".

1990 Amendments. Subsec. (b)(2)(A). Pub.L. 101–510, § 807, authorized an official at an organizational level not lower than an Assistant Secretary of Defense within the Office of the Under Secretary of Defense for Acquisition, to serve on and attend meetings of the Council in place of the Secretary of Defense.

Effective and Applicability Provisions
1996 Acts. Amendment by Pub.L. 104–106 effective Feb. 10, 1996, except as otherwise provided, see section 4401 of Pub.L. 104–106, set out as a note under section 251 of this title.

Status of the Director of Defense Procurement
Pub.L. 102–190, Div. A, Title VIII, § 809, Dec. 5, 1991, 105 Stat. 1423, as amended Pub.L. 103–160, Div. A, Title IX, § 904(f), Nov. 30, 1993, 107 Stat. 1729; Pub.L. 106–65, Div. A, Title IX, § 911(a)(1), Oct. 5, 1999, 113 Stat. 717, provided that: "For the purposes of the amendment made by section 807 of the National Defense Authorization Act for Fiscal Year 1991 (Public Law 101–510; 104 Stat. 1593) to section 25(b)(2) of the Office of Federal Procurement Policy Act (41 U.S.C. 421(b)(2)) [subsec. (b)(2) of this section], the Director of Defense Procurement of the Department of Defense shall be considered to be an official at an organizational level of an Assistant Secretary of Defense within the Office of the Under Secretary of Defense for Acquisition, Technology, and Logistics."

CROSS REFERENCES

Civilian agency acquisition allowable contract costs and indirect costs that violates FAR costs principle, see 41 USCA § 256.

"Federal Acquisition Regulation" defined as in this section for purposes of civilian agency acquisitions, see 41 USCA § 259.

LIBRARY REFERENCES

American Digest System
United States ⚮33.
Key Number System Topic No. 393.

WESTLAW ELECTRONIC RESEARCH

See Westlaw guide following the Explanation pages of this volume.

§ 422. Cost Accounting Standards Board

(a) Establishment; membership; terms

(1) There is established within the Office of Federal Procurement Policy an independent board to be known as the "Cost Accounting Standards Board" (hereinafter referred to as the "Board"). The Board shall consist of 5 members, including the Administrator, who shall serve as Chairman, and 4 members, all of whom shall have experience in Government contract cost accounting, and who shall be appointed as follows:

(A) two representatives of the Federal Government—

(i) one of whom shall be a representative of the Department of Defense and be appointed by the Secretary of Defense; and

(ii) one of whom shall be an officer or employee of the General Services Administration appointed by the Administrator of General Services; and

(B) two individuals from the private sector, each of whom shall be appointed by the Administrator and—

(i) one of whom shall be a representative of industry; and

(ii) one of whom shall be particularly knowledgeable about cost accounting problems and systems.

(2)(A) The term of office of each of the members of the Board, other than the Administrator for Federal Procurement Policy, shall be 4 years, except that—

(i) of the initial members, two shall be appointed for terms of two years, one shall be appointed for a term of three years, and one shall be appointed for a term of four years;

(ii) any member appointed to fill a vacancy in the Board shall serve for the remainder of the term for which his predecessor was appointed; and

(iii) no individual who is appointed under paragraph (1)(A) of this subsection shall continue to serve after ceasing to be an officer or employee of the agency from which he or she was appointed.

(B) A vacancy on the Board shall be filled in the same manner in which the original appointment was made.

(C) The initial members of the Board shall be appointed within 120 days after November 17, 1988.

(b) Senior staff

The Administrator, after consultation with the Board, may appoint an executive secretary and two additional staff members without regard to the provisions of Title 5 governing appointments in the competitive service, and may pay such employees without regard to the provisions of chapter 51 and subchapter III of chapter 53 of such title relating to classification and General Schedule pay rates, except that no individual so appointed may receive pay in excess of the annual rate of basic pay payable for GS–18 of the General Schedule.

(c) Other staff

The Administrator may appoint, fix the compensation, and remove additional employees of the Board under the applicable provisions of Title 5.

(d) Detailed and temporary personnel

(1) The Board may use, without reimbursement, any personnel of a Federal agency (with the consent of the head of the agency concerned) to serve on advisory committees and task forces to assist the Board in carrying out the functions and responsibilities of the Board under this section.

(2) The Administrator, after consultation with the Board, may procure temporary and intermittent services under section 3109(b) of Title 5 of personnel for the purpose of serving on advisory committees and task forces to assist the Board in carrying out the functions and responsibilities of the Board under this section.

(e) Compensation

Except as otherwise provided in subsection (a) of this section, the members of the Board who are officers or employees of the Federal Government, and officers and employees of other agencies of the Federal Government who are used under subsection (d)(1) of this section, shall receive no additional compensation for services, but shall continue to be compensated by the employing Department or agency of such officer or employee. Each member of the Board appointed from private life shall receive compensation at a rate not to exceed the daily equivalent of the rate prescribed for level IV of the Executive Schedule for each day (including travel time) in which the member is engaged in the actual performance of duties vested in the Board. Individuals hired under subsection (d)(2) of this section may receive compensation at rates fixed by the Administrator, but not to exceed the daily equivalent of the rate prescribed for level V of the Federal Executive Salary Schedule under section 5316 of Title 5 for each day (including travel time) in which such appointees are properly engaged in the actual performance of duties under this section. While serving away from homes or the regular place of business, Board members and other appointees serving on an intermittent basis under this section shall be allowed travel expenses in accordance with section 5703 of Title 5.

(f) Cost accounting standards authority

(1) The Board shall have the exclusive authority to make, promulgate, amend, and rescind cost accounting standards and interpretations thereof designed to achieve uniformity and consistency in the cost accounting standards governing measurement, assignment, and allocation of costs to contracts with the United States.

(2)(A) Cost accounting standards promulgated under this section shall be mandatory for use by all executive agencies and by contractors and subcontractors in estimating, accumulating, and reporting costs in connection with pricing and administration of, and settlement of disputes concerning, all negotiated prime contract and subcontract procurements with the United States in excess of the amount set forth in section 2306a(a)(1)(A)(i) of title 10, United States Code, as such amount is adjusted in accordance with applicable requirements of law.

(B) Subparagraph (A) does not apply to the following contracts or subcontracts:

(i) Contracts or subcontracts for the acquisition of commercial items.

(ii) Contracts or subcontracts where the price negotiated is based on prices set by law or regulation.

(iii) Firm, fixed-price contracts or subcontracts awarded on the basis of adequate price competition without submission of certified cost or pricing data.

(iv) A contract or subcontract with a value of less than $7,500,000 if, at the time the contract or subcontract is entered into, the segment of the contractor or subcontractor that will perform the work has not been awarded at least one contract or subcontract with a value of more than $7,500,000 that is covered by the cost accounting standards.

(C) In this paragraph, the term "subcontract" includes a transfer of commercial items between divisions, subsidiaries, or affiliates of a contractor or subcontractor.

(3) The Administrator, after consultation with the Board, shall prescribe rules and procedures governing actions of the Board under this section. Such rules and procedures shall require that any cost accounting standard promulgated, amended, or rescinded (and interpretations thereof) shall be adopted by majority vote of the Board members.

(4) The Board is authorized—

(A) to exempt classes or categories of contractors and subcontractors from the requirements of this section; and

(B) to establish procedures for the waiver of the requirements of this section with respect to individual contracts and subcontracts.

(5)(A) The head of an executive agency may waive the applicability of the cost accounting standards for a contract or subcontract with a value less than $15,000,000 if that official determines in writing that the segment of the contractor or subcontractor that will perform the work—

(i) is primarily engaged in the sale of commercial items; and

(ii) would not otherwise be subject to the cost accounting standards under this section, as in effect on or after the effective date of this paragraph.

(B) The head of an executive agency may also waive the applicability of the cost accounting standards for a contract or subcontract under exceptional circumstances when necessary to meet the needs of the agency. A determination to waive the applicability of the cost accounting standards under this subparagraph shall be set forth in writing and shall include a statement of the circumstances justifying the waiver.

(C) The head of an executive agency may not delegate the authority under subparagraph (A) or (B) to any official in the executive agency below the senior policymaking level in the executive agency.

(D) The Federal Acquisition Regulation shall include the following:

(i) Criteria for selecting an official to be delegated authority to grant waivers under subparagraph (A) or (B).

(ii) The specific circumstances under which such a waiver may be granted.

(E) The head of each executive agency shall report the waivers granted under subparagraphs (A) and (B) for that agency to the Board on an annual basis.

(g) Requirements for standards

(1) Prior to the promulgation under this section of cost accounting standards and interpretations thereof, the Board shall—

(A) take into account, after consultation and discussions with the Comptroller General and professional accounting organizations, contractors, and other interested parties—

(i) the probable costs of implementation, including inflationary effects, if any, compared to the probable benefits;

(ii) the advantages, disadvantages, and improvements anticipated in the pricing and administration of, and settlement of disputes concerning, contracts; and

(iii) the scope of, and alternatives available to, the action proposed to be taken;

(B) prepare and publish a report in the Federal Register on the issues reviewed under paragraph (1)(A);

(C)(i) publish an advanced notice of proposed rulemaking in the Federal Register in order to solicit comments on the report prepared pursuant to subparagraph (B);

(ii) provide all parties affected a period of not less than 60 days after such publication to submit their views and comments; and

(iii) during this 60-day period, consult with the Comptroller General and consider any recommendation the Comptroller General may make; and

(D) publish a notice of such proposed rulemaking in the Federal Register and provide all parties affected a period of not less than 60 days after such publication to submit their views and comments.

(2) Rules, regulations, cost accounting standards, and modifications thereof promulgated or amended under this section shall have the full force and effect of law, and shall become effective within 120 days after publication in the Federal Register in final form, unless the Board determines a longer period is necessary. Implementation dates for contractors and subcontractors shall be determined by the Board, but in no event shall such dates be later than the beginning of the second fiscal year of the contractor or subcontractor after the standard becomes effective. Rules, regulations, cost accounting standards, and modifications thereof promulgated or amended under this section shall be accompanied by prefatory comments and by illustrations, if necessary.

(3) The functions exercised under this section are excluded from the operation of sections 551, 553 through 559, and 701 through 706 of Title 5.

(h) Implementing regulations

(1) The Board shall promulgate rules and regulations for the implementation of cost accounting standards promulgated or interpreted under subsection (f) of this section. Such regulations shall be incorporated into the Federal Acquisition Regulation and shall re-

quire contractors and subcontractors as a condition of contracting with the United States to—

(A) disclose in writing their cost accounting practices, including methods of distinguishing direct costs from indirect costs and the basis used for allocating indirect costs; and

(B) agree to a contract price adjustment, with interest, for any increased costs paid to such contractor or subcontractor by the United States by reason of a change in the contractor's or subcontractor's cost accounting practices or by reason of a failure by the contractor or subcontractor to comply with applicable cost accounting standards.

(2) If the United States and a contractor or subcontractor fail to agree on a contract price adjustment, including whether the contractor or subcontractor has complied with the applicable cost accounting standards, the disagreement will constitute a dispute under the Contract Disputes Act [41 U.S.C.A. § 601 et seq.].

(3) Any contract price adjustment undertaken pursuant to paragraph (1)(B) shall be made, where applicable, on relevant contracts between the United States and the contractor that are subject to the cost accounting standards so as to protect the United States from payment, in the aggregate, of increased costs (as defined by the Board). In no case shall the Government recover costs greater than the increased cost (as defined by the Board) to the Government, in the aggregate, on the relevant contracts subject to the price adjustment, unless the contractor made a change in its cost accounting practices of which it was aware or should have been aware at the time of the price negotiation and which it failed to disclose to the Government.

(4) The interest rate applicable to any contract price adjustment shall be the annual rate of interest established under section 6621 of Title 26 for such period. Such interest shall accrue from the time payments of the increased costs were made to the contractor or subcontractor to the time the United States receives full compensation for the price adjustment.

(i) Omitted

(j) Effect on other standards and regulations

(1) All cost accounting standards, waivers, exemptions, interpretations, modifications, rules, and regulations promulgated by the Cost Accounting Standards Board under section 2168 of this Title 50, Appendix shall remain in effect unless and until amended, superseded, or rescinded by the Board pursuant to this section.

(2) Existing cost accounting standards referred to in paragraph (1) shall be subject to the provisions of this Act in the same manner as if promulgated by the Board under this chapter.

(3) The Administrator, under the authority set forth in section 405 of this title, shall ensure that no regulation or proposed regulation of an executive agency is inconsistent with a cost accounting standard promulgated or amended under this section by rescinding or denying the promulgation of any such inconsistent regulation or proposed regulation and taking such other action authorized under section 405 of this title as may be appropriate.

(4) Costs which are the subject of cost accounting standards promulgated under this section shall not be subject to regulations that are established by another executive agency that differ from such standards with respect to the measurement, assignment, and allocation of such costs.

(k) Examinations

For the purpose of determining whether a contractor or subcontractor has complied with cost accounting standards promulgated under this section and has followed consistently the contractor's or subcontractor's disclosed cost accounting practices, any authorized representative of the head of the agency concerned, of the offices of inspector general established pursuant to the Inspector General Act of 1978, or of the Comptroller General of the United States shall have the right to examine and make copies of any documents, papers, or records of such contractor or subcontractor relating to compliance with such cost accounting standards.

(*l*) Authorization of appropriations

There are authorized to be appropriated such sums as may be necessary to carry out the provisions of this section.

(Pub.L. 93–400, § 26, as added Pub.L. 100–679, § 5(a), Nov. 17, 1988, 102 Stat. 4056, and amended Pub.L. 103–355, Title II, § 2453, Title VIII, § 8301(d), Oct. 13, 1994, 108 Stat. 3326, 3397; Pub.L. 104–106, Div. D, Title XLII, § 4205, Title XLIII, § 4321(h)(4), Feb. 10, 1996, 110 Stat. 656, 675; Pub.L. 106–65, Title VIII, § 802(a), (b), Oct. 5, 1999, 113 Stat. 701; Pub.L. 109–163, Div. A, Title VIII, § 822, Jan. 6, 2006, 119 Stat. 3386.)

HISTORICAL AND STATUTORY NOTES

Revision Notes and Legislative Reports

1988 Acts. Senate Report No. 100–424, see 1988 U.S.Code Cong. and Adm.News, p. 5687.

1994   Acts. Senate   Report   Nos. 103–258 and 103–259, and House Conference Report No. 103–712, see 1994 U.S. Code Cong. and Adm. News, p. 2561.

1996 Acts. House Conference Report No. 104–450, see 1996 U.S. Code Cong. and Adm. News, p. 238.

1999 Acts. House Conference Report No. 106–301 and Statement by President, see 1999 U.S. Code Cong. and Adm. News, p. 94.

2006 Acts. House Conference Report No. 109–360, see 2005 U.S. Code Cong. and Adm. News, p. 1678.

Statement by President, see 2005 U.S. Code Cong. and Adm. News, p. S54.

References in Text

The provisions of Title 5 governing appointments in the competitive service, referred to in subsec. (b), are classified generally to 5 U.S.C.A. § 3301 et seq.

The General Schedule, referred to in subsec. (b), is set out under 5 U.S.C.A. § 5332.

Level IV of the Executive Schedule, referred to in subsec. (e), is set out in 5 U.S.C.A. § 5315.

For the effective date of this paragraph, referred to in subsec. (f)(5)(A)(ii), as 180 days after Oct. 5, 1999, see section 802(i) of Pub.L. 106–65, set out as an Effective and Applicability Provisions note below.

The Contract Disputes Act, referred to in subsec. (h)(2), is Pub.L. 95–563, Nov. 1, 1978, 92 Stat. 2383, which is classified generally to chapter 9 (section 601 et seq.) of this title. For complete classification of that Act to the Code, see Short Title note set out under section 601 of this title and Tables.

Section 2168 of Title 50, Appendix, referred to in subsec. (j)(1), was repealed by Pub.L. 100–679, § 5(b), Nov. 17, 1988, 102 Stat. 4063.

The Inspector General Act of 1978, referred to in subsec. (k), is Pub.L. 95–452, Oct. 12, 1978, 92 Stat. 1101, as amended, which is classified generally to section 1 et seq. of Appendix 3 of Title 5, Government Organization and Employees. For complete classification of that Act to the Code, see section 1 of Appendix 3 to Title 5, and Tables.

Codifications

Subsec. (i) of this section, which required the Board to submit an annual report to Congress on the activities and operations of the Board under this section, terminated effective May 15, 2000, pursuant to section 3003 of Pub.L. 104–66, as amended, which is set out as a note under 31 U.S.C.A. § 1113. See, also, page 158 of House Document No. 103–7.

Amendments

2006 Amendments. Subsec. (f)(2)(A). Pub.L. 109–163, § 822, struck out

"$500,000" following "in excess of" and inserted "the amount set forth in section 2306a(a)(1)(A)(i) of title 10, United States Code, as such amount is adjusted in accordance with applicable requirements of law".

1999   Amendments. Subsec. (f)(2)(B)(iii),   (iv).   Pub.L.   106–65, § 802(a), added clauses (iii) and (iv).

Subsec.   (f)(5).   Pub.L.   106–65, § 802(b), added par. (5).

1996 Amendments. Subsec. (f)(2)(B)(i). Pub.L. 104–106, § 4205(1), substituted provisions relating to acquisition of commercial items for provisions relating to catalog or market prices of commercial items.

Subsec. (f)(2)(B)(iii). Pub.L. 104–106, § 4205(2), struck out cl. (iii) relating to firm fixed-price contract or subcontract (without cost incentives) for commercial items.

Subsec.   (f)(3).   Pub.L.   104–106, § 4321(h)(4), substituted "The Administrator" for "Not later than 180 days after November 17, 1988, the Administrator", which amendment had already been executed, thereby requiring no further change in text.

1994   Amendments. Subsec.   (f)(2). Pub.L. 103–355, § 8301(d)(1)-(3), designated existing provision as subpar. (A), struck therefrom provision for nonapplication to contracts or subcontracts where the price is based on (A) established catalog or market prices of commercial items sold in substantial quantities to the general public, or (B) prices set by law or regulation (now incorporated in subpar. (B)(i) and (ii)), and added subpars. (B) and (C).

Subsec.   (f)(3).   Pub.L.   103–355, § 2453, substituted "The Administrator" for "Not later than 180 days after November 17, 1988, the Administrator".

Effective and Applicability Provisions

1999 Acts. Pub.L. 106–65, Div. A, Title VIII, § 802(i), Oct. 5, 1999, 113 Stat. 702, provided that:

"The amendments made by subsections (a) and (b) [amending this section] shall take effect 180 days after the date of enactment of this Act [Oct. 5, 1999], and shall apply with respect to—

"(1) contracts that are entered into on or after such effective date; and

"**(2)** determinations made on or after such effective date regarding whether a segment of a contractor or subcontractor is subject to the cost accounting standards under section 26(f) of the Office of Federal Procurement Policy Act (41 U.S.C. 422(f)), regardless of whether the contracts on which such determinations are made were entered into before, on, or after such date."

1996 Acts. Amendment by Pub.L. 104–106 effective Feb. 10, 1996, except as otherwise provided, see section 4401 of Pub.L. 104–106, set out as a note under section 251 of this title.

1994 Acts. Amendment by sections 2453 and 8301(d) of Pub.L. 103–355 effective Oct. 13, 1994, except as otherwise provided, see section 10001 of Pub.L. 103–355, set out as a note under section 251 of this title.

Inapplicability of Standards to Certain Contracts; Construction Regarding Certain Not-for-Profit Entities
Pub.L. 106–65, Div. A, Title VIII, § 802(g), (h), Oct. 5, 1999, 113 Stat. 702, provided that:

"**(g) Inapplicability of standards to certain contracts.**—The cost accounting standards issued pursuant to section 26(f) of the Office of Federal Procurement Policy Act (41 U.S.C. 422(f)) [subsec. (f) of this section], as amended by this section, shall not apply during fiscal year 2000 with respect to a contract entered into under the authority provided in chapter 89 of title 5, United States Code [5 U.S.C.A. § 8901 et seq.] (relating to health benefits for Federal employees).

"**(h) Construction regarding certain not-for-profit entities.**—The amendments made by subsections (a) and (b) [amending this section] shall not be construed as modifying or superseding, nor as intended to impair or restrict, the applicability of the cost accounting standards described in section 26(f) of the Office of Federal Procurement Policy Act (41 U.S.C. 422(f)) [subsec. (f) of this section] to—

"**(1)** any educational institution or federally funded research and development center that is associated with an educational institution in accordance with Office of Management and Budget Circular A–21, as in effect on January 1, 1999; or

"**(2)** any contract with a nonprofit entity that provides research and development and related products or services to the Department of Defense."

Regulations; Implementation
Pub.L. 106–65, Div. A, Title VIII, § 802(c) to (e), Oct. 5, 1999, 113 Stat. 701, provided that:

"**(c) Regulation on types of CAS coverage.**—(1) The Administrator for Federal Procurement Policy shall revise the rules and procedures prescribed pursuant to section 26(f) of the Office of Federal Procurement Policy Act (41 U.S.C. 422(f)) to the extent necessary to increase the thresholds established in section 9903.201–2 of title 48 of the Code of Federal Regulations from $25,000,000 to $50,000,000.

"**(2)** Paragraph (1) requires only a change of the statement of a threshold condition in the regulation referred to by section number in that paragraph, and shall not be construed as—

"**(A)** a ratification or expression of approval of—

"**(i)** any aspect of the regulation; or

"**(ii)** the manner in which section 26 of the Office of Federal Procurement Policy Act [this section] is administered through the regulation; or

"**(B)** a requirement to apply the regulation.

"**(d) Implementation.**—The Administrator for Federal Procurement Policy shall ensure that this section and the amendments made by this section [amending this section] are implemented in a manner that ensures that the Federal Government can recover costs, as appropriate, in a case in which noncompliance with cost accounting standards, or a change in the cost accounting system of a contractor segment or subcontractor segment that is not determined to be desirable by the Federal Government, results in a shift of costs from contracts that are not covered by the cost accounting standards to contracts that are covered by the cost accounting standards.

"**(e) Implementation of requirements for revision of regulations.**—(1) Final regulations required by subsection (c) shall be issued not later than 180 days after the date of the enactment of this Act [Oct. 5, 1999].

"(2) Subsection (c) shall cease to be effective one year after the date on which final regulations issued in accordance with that subsection take effect."

References in Other Laws to GS–16, 17, or 18 Pay Rates

References in laws to the rates of pay for GS–16, 17, or 18, or to maximum rates of pay under the General Schedule, to be considered references to rates payable under specified sections of Title 5, see section 529 [Title I, § 101(c)(1)] of Pub.L. 101–509, set out in a note under 5 U.S.C.A. § 5376.

LIBRARY REFERENCES

American Digest System
United States ☞33, 70(18).
Key Number System Topic No. 393.

Research References

Treatises and Practice Aids
West's Federal Administrative Practice § 642, Cost Principles and Pricing.

WESTLAW ELECTRONIC RESEARCH

See Westlaw guide following the Explanation pages of this volume.

Notes of Decisions

Costs and attorneys fees　2
Price adjustments　3
Standards　1

_____

1. Standards

Legal expenses incurred by government contractor in shareholder derivative action were allocable to specific contracts under Cost Accounting Standards (CAS). Boeing North American, Inc. v. Roche, C.A.Fed.2002, 298 F.3d 1274. United States ☞ 70(18)

Cost Accounting Standards Board (CASB) complied with procedural requirements of the Office of Federal Procurement Policy Act (OFPPA) when it issued amended Cost Accounting Standard (CAS) making government contractor liable for pension surplus attributable to firm-fixed-price contracts in a segment closing adjustment; CASB gave adequate notice of the inclusion of firm-fixed-price contracts in the new segment closing adjustment provision in proposed illustrations, and received comments that addressed issue. Teledyne, Inc. v. U.S., Fed.Cl.2001, 50 Fed.Cl. 155, appeal granted 20 Fed.Appx. 849, 2001 WL 1173207, affirmed 316 F.3d 1366, rehearing and rehearing en banc denied, certiorari denied 124 S.Ct. 804, 540 U.S. 1068,

157 L.Ed.2d 732. United States ☞ 70(18)

Multistate contractor did not satisfy its obligations under contractually mandatory cost accounting standards when it charged state income taxes to government-owned contractor-operated (GOCO) facilities under one scheme of allocation and relied on different scheme of allocation for non-GOCO contracts for purposes of cost reimbursement; government was entitled to charges determined under single allocation scheme. Hercules, Inc. v. U.S., Cl.Ct.1992, 26 Cl.Ct. 662. United States ☞ 70(18)

2. Costs and attorneys fees

Legal expenses incurred by government contractor in subsequently settled shareholder derivative action based on contractor's alleged failure to maintain adequate controls to prevent wrongdoing against the government were allowable if contractor could show that the allegations in that action had very little likelihood of success on the merits; costs could not be disallowed because they would not have been incurred "but for" misconduct by contractor's employees. Boeing North American, Inc. v. Roche, C.A.Fed.2002, 298 F.3d 1274. United States ☞ 70(18)

3. Price adjustments
Government contractor may offset or eliminate cost increases associated with a change in cost accounting practices in cost-reimbursement contracts with cost decreases triggered in fixed-priced contracts by the same accounting change. Lockheed Martin Corp. v. U.S., Fed.Cl. 2006, 70 Fed.Cl. 745. United States ⊶ 70(18)

§ 423. Restrictions on disclosing and obtaining contractor bid or proposal information or source selection information

(a) Prohibition on disclosing procurement information

(1) A person described in paragraph (2) shall not, other than as provided by law, knowingly disclose contractor bid or proposal information or source selection information before the award of a Federal agency procurement contract to which the information relates. In the case of an employee of a private sector organization assigned to an agency under chapter 37 of Title 5, in addition to the restriction in the preceding sentence, such employee shall not, other than as provided by law, knowingly disclose contractor bid or proposal information or source selection information during the three-year period after the end of the assignment of such employee.

(2) Paragraph (1) applies to any person who—

(A) is a present or former official of the United States, or a person who is acting or has acted for or on behalf of, or who is advising or has advised the United States with respect to, a Federal agency procurement; and

(B) by virtue of that office, employment, or relationship has or had access to contractor bid or proposal information or source selection information.

(b) Prohibition on obtaining procurement information

A person shall not, other than as provided by law, knowingly obtain contractor bid or proposal information or source selection information before the award of a Federal agency procurement contract to which the information relates.

(c) Actions required of procurement officers when contacted by offerors regarding non–Federal employment

(1) If an agency official who is participating personally and substantially in a Federal agency procurement for a contract in excess of the simplified acquisition threshold contacts or is contacted by a person who is a bidder or offeror in that Federal agency procurement regarding possible non–Federal employment for that official, the official shall—

(A) promptly report the contact in writing to the official's supervisor and to the designated agency ethics official (or designee) of the agency in which the official is employed; and

(B)(i) reject the possibility of non–Federal employment; or

(ii) disqualify himself or herself from further personal and substantial participation in that Federal agency procurement until such time as the agency has authorized the official to resume participation in such procurement, in accordance with the requirements of section 208 of Title 18 and applicable agency regulations on the grounds that—

> **(I)** the person is no longer a bidder or offeror in that Federal agency procurement; or

> **(II)** all discussions with the bidder or offeror regarding possible non–Federal employment have terminated without an agreement or arrangement for employment.

(2) Each report required by this subsection shall be retained by the agency for not less than two years following the submission of the report. All such reports shall be made available to the public upon request, except that any part of a report that is exempt from the disclosure requirements of section 552 of Title 5 under subsection (b)(1) of such section may be withheld from disclosure to the public.

(3) An official who knowingly fails to comply with the requirements of this subsection shall be subject to the penalties and administrative actions set forth in subsection (e) of this section.

(4) A bidder or offeror who engages in employment discussions with an official who is subject to the restrictions of this subsection, knowing that the official has not complied with subparagraph (A) or (B) of paragraph (1), shall be subject to the penalties and administrative actions set forth in subsection (e) of this section.

(d) Prohibition on former official's acceptance of compensation from contractor

(1) A former official of a Federal agency may not accept compensation from a contractor as an employee, officer, director, or consultant of the contractor within a period of one year after such former official—

> **(A)** served, at the time of selection of the contractor or the award of a contract to that contractor, as the procuring contracting officer, the source selection authority, a member of the source selection evaluation board, or the chief of a financial or technical evaluation team in a procurement in which that contractor was selected for award of a contract in excess of $10,000,000;

> **(B)** served as the program manager, deputy program manager, or administrative contracting officer for a contract in excess of $10,000,000 awarded to that contractor; or

(C) personally made for the Federal agency—

(i) a decision to award a contract, subcontract, modification of a contract or subcontract, or a task order or delivery order in excess of $10,000,000 to that contractor;

(ii) a decision to establish overhead or other rates applicable to a contract or contracts for that contractor that are valued in excess of $10,000,000;

(iii) a decision to approve issuance of a contract payment or payments in excess of $10,000,000 to that contractor; or

(iv) a decision to pay or settle a claim in excess of $10,000,000 with that contractor.

(2) Nothing in paragraph (1) may be construed to prohibit a former official of a Federal agency from accepting compensation from any division or affiliate of a contractor that does not produce the same or similar products or services as the entity of the contractor that is responsible for the contract referred to in subparagraph (A), (B), or (C) of such paragraph.

(3) A former official who knowingly accepts compensation in violation of this subsection shall be subject to penalties and administrative actions as set forth in subsection (e) of this section.

(4) A contractor who provides compensation to a former official knowing that such compensation is accepted by the former official in violation of this subsection shall be subject to penalties and administrative actions as set forth in subsection (e) of this section.

(5) Regulations implementing this subsection shall include procedures for an official or former official of a Federal agency to request advice from the appropriate designated agency ethics official regarding whether the official or former official is or would be precluded by this subsection from accepting compensation from a particular contractor.

(e) Penalties and administrative actions

(1) Criminal penalties

Whoever engages in conduct constituting a violation of subsection (a) or (b) of this section for the purpose of either—

(A) exchanging the information covered by such subsection for anything of value, or

(B) obtaining or giving anyone a competitive advantage in the award of a Federal agency procurement contract,

shall be imprisoned for not more than 5 years or fined as provided under Title 18, or both.

(2) Civil penalties

The Attorney General may bring a civil action in an appropriate United States district court against any person who engages in conduct constituting a violation of subsection (a), (b), (c), or (d) of this section. Upon proof of such conduct by a preponderance of the evidence, the person is subject to a civil penalty. An individual who engages in such conduct is subject to a civil penalty of not more than $50,000 for each violation plus twice the amount of compensation which the individual received or offered for the prohibited conduct. An organization that engages in such conduct is subject to a civil penalty of not more than $500,000 for each violation plus twice the amount of compensation which the organization received or offered for the prohibited conduct.

(3) Administrative actions

(A) If a Federal agency receives information that a contractor or a person has engaged in conduct constituting a violation of subsection (a), (b), (c), or (d) of this section, the Federal agency shall consider taking one or more of the following actions, as appropriate:

 (i) Cancellation of the Federal agency procurement, if a contract has not yet been awarded.

 (ii) Rescission of a contract with respect to which—

  (I) the contractor or someone acting for the contractor has been convicted for an offense punishable under paragraph (1), or

  (II) the head of the agency that awarded the contract has determined, based upon a preponderance of the evidence, that the contractor or someone acting for the contractor has engaged in conduct constituting such an offense.

 (iii) Initiation of suspension or debarment proceedings for the protection of the Government in accordance with procedures in the Federal Acquisition Regulation.

 (iv) Initiation of adverse personnel action, pursuant to the procedures in chapter 75 of Title 5 or other applicable law or regulation.

(B) If a Federal agency rescinds a contract pursuant to subparagraph (A)(ii), the United States is entitled to recover, in addition to any penalty prescribed by law, the amount expended under the contract.

(C) For purposes of any suspension or debarment proceedings initiated pursuant to subparagraph (A)(iii), engaging in conduct constituting an offense under subsection (a), (b), (c), or (d) of this section affects the present responsibility of a Government contractor or subcontractor.

(f) Definitions

As used in this section:

(1) The term "contractor bid or proposal information" means any of the following information submitted to a Federal agency as part of or in connection with a bid or proposal to enter into a Federal agency procurement contract, if that information has not been previously made available to the public or disclosed publicly:

(A) Cost or pricing data (as defined by section 2306a(h) of Title 10, with respect to procurements subject to that section, and section 254b(h) of this title, with respect to procurements subject to that section).

(B) Indirect costs and direct labor rates.

(C) Proprietary information about manufacturing processes, operations, or techniques marked by the contractor in accordance with applicable law or regulation.

(D) Information marked by the contractor as "contractor bid or proposal information", in accordance with applicable law or regulation.

(2) The term "source selection information" means any of the following information prepared for use by a Federal agency for the purpose of evaluating a bid or proposal to enter into a Federal agency procurement contract, if that information has not been previously made available to the public or disclosed publicly:

(A) Bid prices submitted in response to a Federal agency solicitation for sealed bids, or lists of those bid prices before public bid opening.

(B) Proposed costs or prices submitted in response to a Federal agency solicitation, or lists of those proposed costs or prices.

(C) Source selection plans.

(D) Technical evaluation plans.

(E) Technical evaluations of proposals.

(F) Cost or price evaluations of proposals.

(G) Competitive range determinations that identify proposals that have a reasonable chance of being selected for award of a contract.

(H) Rankings of bids, proposals, or competitors.

(I) The reports and evaluations of source selection panels, boards, or advisory councils.

(J) Other information marked as "source selection information" based on a case-by-case determination by the head of the agency, his designee, or the contracting officer that its disclosure would jeopardize the integrity or successful completion of the Federal agency procurement to which the information relates.

(3) The term "Federal agency" has the meaning provided such term in section 102 of Title 40.

(4) The term "Federal agency procurement" means the acquisition (by using competitive procedures and awarding a contract) of goods or services (including construction) from non–Federal sources by a Federal agency using appropriated funds.

(5) The term "contracting officer" means a person who, by appointment in accordance with applicable regulations, has the authority to enter into a Federal agency procurement contract on behalf of the Government and to make determinations and findings with respect to such a contract.

(6) The term "protest" means a written objection by an interested party to the award or proposed award of a Federal agency procurement contract, pursuant to subchapter V of chapter 35 of Title 31.

(7) The term "official" means the following:

(A) An officer, as defined in section 2104 of Title 5.

(B) An employee, as defined in section 2105 of Title 5.

(C) A member of the uniformed services, as defined in section 2101(3) of Title 5.

(g) Limitation on protests

No person may file a protest against the award or proposed award of a Federal agency procurement contract alleging a violation of subsection (a), (b), (c), or (d) of this section, nor may the Comptroller General of the United States consider such an allegation in deciding a protest, unless that person reported to the Federal agency responsible for the procurement, no later than 14 days after the person first discovered the possible violation, the information that the person believed constitutes evidence of the offense.

(h) Savings provisions

This section does not—

(1) restrict the disclosure of information to, or its receipt by, any person or class of persons authorized, in accordance with

applicable agency regulations or procedures, to receive that information;

(2) restrict a contractor from disclosing its own bid or proposal information or the recipient from receiving that information;

(3) restrict the disclosure or receipt of information relating to a Federal agency procurement after it has been canceled by the Federal agency before contract award unless the Federal agency plans to resume the procurement;

(4) prohibit individual meetings between a Federal agency official and an offeror or potential offeror for, or a recipient of, a contract or subcontract under a Federal agency procurement, provided that unauthorized disclosure or receipt of contractor bid or proposal information or source selection information does not occur;

(5) authorize the withholding of information from, nor restrict its receipt by, Congress, a committee or subcommittee of Congress, the Comptroller General, a Federal agency, or an inspector general of a Federal agency;

(6) authorize the withholding of information from, nor restrict its receipt by, the Comptroller General of the United States in the course of a protest against the award or proposed award of a Federal agency procurement contract; or

(7) limit the applicability of any requirements, sanctions, contract penalties, and remedies established under any other law or regulation.

(Pub.L. 93–400, § 27, as added Pub.L. 100–679, § 6(a), Nov. 17, 1988, 102 Stat. 4063, and amended Pub.L. 101–189, Div. A, Title VIII, § 814(a) to (d)(1), Nov. 29, 1989, 103 Stat. 1495–1498; Pub.L. 101–510, Title XIV, § 1484(*l*)(6), Nov. 5, 1990, 104 Stat. 1720; Pub.L. 102–25, Title VII, § 705(i), Apr. 6, 1991, 105 Stat. 121; Pub.L. 103–355, Title VIII, § 8301(e), Oct. 13, 1994, 108 Stat. 3397; Pub.L. 104–106, Div. D, Title XLIII, § 4304(a), Feb. 10, 1996, 110 Stat. 659; Pub.L. 107–347, Title II, § 209(d)(4), Dec. 17, 2002, 116 Stat. 2930.)

HISTORICAL AND STATUTORY NOTES

Revision Notes and Legislative Reports
1988 Acts. Senate Report No. 100–424, see 1988 U.S.Code Cong. and Adm.News, p. 5687.

1989 Acts. House Report No. 101–121, House Conference Report No. 331 and Statement by President, see 1989 U.S. Code Cong. and Adm. News, p. 838.

1990 Acts. House Report No. 101–665 and House Conference Report No. 101–923, see 1990 U.S. Code Cong. and Adm. News, p. 2931.

1991 Acts. House Report No. 102–16, see 1991 U.S. Code Cong. and Adm. News, p. 36.

1994 Acts. Senate Report Nos. 103–258 and 103–259, and House Conference Report No. 103–712, see 1994 U.S. Code Cong. and Adm. News, p. 2561.

1996 Acts. House Conference Report No. 104–450, see 1996 U.S. Code Cong. and Adm. News, p. 238.

2002 Acts. House Report No. 107–787(Part I) and Statement by President, see 2002 U.S. Code Cong. and Adm. News, p. 1880.

References in Text
Chapter 37 of Title 5, referred to in subsec. (a)(1), is 5 U.S.C.A. § 3701 et seq.

Codifications
In subsec. (f)(3), "section 102 of Title 40" substituted for "section 472 of Title 40", which originally read "section 3 of the Federal Property and Administrative Services Act of 1949 (40 U.S.C. 472)", on authority of Pub.L. 107–217, § 5(c), Aug. 21, 2002, 116 Stat. 1301, which is set out as a note preceding 40 U.S.C.A. § 101. Pub.L. 107–217, § 1, enacted Title 40 into positive law. Section 3 of the Federal Property and Administrative Services Act of 1949, Act June 30, 1949, c. 288, § 3, 63 Stat. 378, as amended, was classified to former 40 U.S.C.A. § 472, prior to being repealed by Pub.L. 107–217, § 6(b), Aug. 21, 2002, 116 Stat. 1313, and its substance reenacted as 40 U.S.C.A. § 102. The term "Federal agency" is currently defined by 40 U.S.C.A. § 102(5).

Amendments
2002 Amendments. Subsec. (a)(1). Pub.L. 107–347, § 209(d)(4), in par. (1), added "In the case of an employee of a private sector organization assigned to an agency under chapter 37 of Title 5, in addition to the restriction in the preceding sentence, such employee shall not, other than as provided by law, knowingly disclose contractor bid or proposal information or source selection information during the three-year period after the end of the assignment of such employee." at the end.

1996 Amendments. Pub.L. 104–106, § 4304(a), amended section generally by enacting provisions as subsecs. (a) to (h) relating to prohibition on disclosing procurement information, prohibition on obtaining procurement information, actions required of procurement officers when contacted by offerors regarding non–Federal employment, prohibition on former official's acceptance of compensation from contractor, penalties and administrative actions, definitions, limitation on protests, and savings provisions, respectively, for provisions previously set out as subsecs. (a) to (p) relating to prohibited conduct by competing contractors, prohibited conduct by procurement officials, recusal, disclosure to unauthorized persons, certification and enforcement mat-

ters, restrictions resulting from procurement activities of procurement officials, contractual penalties, administrative actions, civil penalties, criminal penalties, ethics advice, training, remedies not exclusive, no authority to withhold information, implementing regulations and guidelines, and definitions, respectively.

1994 Amendments. Subsec. (e)(1)(B). Pub.L. 103–355, § 8301(e), inserted after "certifies in writing to such contracting officer" the phrase ", except in the case of a contract for the procurement of commercial items,".

1991 Amendments. Subsec. (p)(8). Pub.L. 102–25 substituted "has the meaning given such term by section 109(3) of the Ethics in Government Act of 1978 (5 U.S.C.App.)" for "has the same meaning as the term 'designated agency official' in section 209(10) of the Ethics in Government Act of 1978 (92 Stat. 1850; 5 U.S.C.App.)".

1990 Amendments. Subsec. (f)(3)(F). Pub.L. 101–510 redesignated as subpar. (F) former last subpar. designated (D) and defining term "civil service".

1989 Amendments. Subsec. (a)(1). Pub.L. 101–189, § 814(a)(1)(A), inserted ", except as provided in subsection (c)" before the semicolon.

Subsec. (b)(1). Pub.L. 101–189, § 814(a)(1)(A), inserted ", except as provided in subsection (c)" before the semicolon.

Subsec. (c). Pub.L. 101–189, § 814(a)(1)(C), added subsec. (c). Former subsec. (c) redesignated (d).

Subsec. (d). Pub.L. 101–189, § 814(a)(1)(B)(ii), redesignated former subsec. (c) as (d). Former subsec. (d) redesignated (e).

Subsec. (e). Pub.L. 101–189, § 814(a)(1)(B)(ii), redesignated former subsec. (d) as (e). Former subsec. (e) redesignated (f).

Subsec. (e)(1)(A)(i). Pub.L. 101–189, § 814(c)(1)(A), substituted "(d), or (f)" for "(c), or (e)".

Subsec. (e)(1)(B)(ii). Pub.L. 101–189, § 814(c)(1)(B), substituted "(d), or (f)" for "(c), or (e)".

Subsec. (e)(2)(A). Pub.L. 101–189, § 814(c)(1)(C), substituted "(d), or (f)" for "(c), or (e)".

Subsec. (e)(3)(A). Pub.L. 101–189, § 814(c)(1)(D), substituted "(d), or (f)" for "(c), or (e)".

Subsec. (e)(7)(B)(ii). Pub.L. 101–189, § 814(c)(1)(E), substituted "subsection (o)" for "subsection (m)".

Subsec. (f). Pub.L. 101–189, § 814(a)(1)(B)(ii), redesignated former subsec. (e) as (f). Former subsec. (f) redesignated (g).

Pub.L. 101–189, § 814(a)(2)(B), in subsec. (f), as so redesignated, substituted "Restrictions resulting from procurement activities of procurement officials" for "Restrictions on government officials and employees" as the subsection catchline.

Subsec. (f)(1). Pub.L. 101–189, § 814(a)(2)(A), (B), in subsec. (f), as so redesignated, designated existing provisions as par. (1), in par. (1), as so designated, in provisions preceding subpar. (A), substituted "No individual who, while serving as an officer or employee of the Government or member of the Armed Forces, was a procurement official with respect to a particular procurement may knowingly—" for "No Government official or employee, civilian, or military, who has participated personally and substantially in the conduct of any Federal agency procurement or who has personally reviewed and approved the award, modification, or extension of any contract for such procurement shall—" and redesignated former pars. (1) and (2) as subpars. (A) and (B), respectively.

Subsec. (f)(2). Pub.L. 101–189, § 814(a)(2)(C), added par. (2).

Subsec. (f)(3). Pub.L. 101–189, § 814(d)(1), added par. (3).

Subsec. (g). Pub.L. 101–189, § 814(a)(1)(B)(ii), redesignated former subsec. (f) as (g). Former subsec. (g) redesignated (h).

Subsec. (g)(1). Pub.L. 101–189, § 814(c)(2), in par. (1) of subsec. (g), as so redesignated, substituted "subsection (o)" for "subsection (m)".

Subsec. (h). Pub.L. 101–189, § 814(a)(1)(B)(ii), redesignated former subsec. (g) as (h). Former subsec. (h) redesignated (i).

Subsec. (h)(1). Pub.L. 101–189, § 814(c)(3)(A), in par. (1) of subsec. (h), as so redesignated, substituted "subsection (e)" for "subsection (d)".

Subsec. (h)(2). Pub.L. 101–189, § 814(c)(3)(B), substituted "(b) or (d)" for "(b) or (c)".

Subsec. (h)(3). Pub.L. 101–189, § 814(c)(3)(C), substituted "(i) and (j)" for "(h) and (i)".

Subsec. (i). Pub.L. 101–189, § 814(a)(1)(B)(ii), redesignated former subsec. (h) as (i). Former subsec. (i) redesignated (j).

Pub.L. 101–189, § 814(c)(4), in subsec. (i), as so redesignated, substituted "(d), or (f)" for "(c), or (e).

Subsec. (j). Pub.L. 101–189, § 814(a)(1)(B)(ii), redesignated former subsec. (i) as (j). Former subsec. (j) redesignated (l).

Subsec. (j)(1). Pub.L. 101–189, § 814(c)(5), in par. (1) of subsec. (j), as so redesignated, substituted "subsection (p)" for "subsection (n)" and "subsection (o)" for "subsection (m)", respectively.

Subsec. (k). Pub.L. 101–189, § 814(a)(3), added subsec. (k). Former subsec. (k) redesignated (m).

Subsec. (l). Pub.L. 101–189, § 814(a)(1)(B)(i), redesignated former subsec. (j) as (l). Former subsec. (l) redesignated (n).

Subsec. (l)(1). Pub.L. 101–189, § 814(c)(6)(A), in par. (1) of subsec. (l), as so redesignated, substituted "subsections (b), (c), and (e)" for "subsection (b)".

Subsec. (l)(2). Pub.L. 101–189, § 814(c)(6)(B), substituted "subsections (b), (c), and (e)" for "subsection (b)" and "(d), or (f)" for "(c), or (e)", respectively.

Subsec. (m). Pub.L. 101–189, § 814(a)(1)(B)(i), redesignated former subsec. (k) as (m). Former subsec. (m) redesignated (o).

Subsec. (n). Pub.L. 101–189, § 814(a)(1)(B)(i), redesignated former subsec. (l) as (n). Former subsec. (n) redesignated (p).

Subsec. (o). Pub.L. 101–189, § 814(a)(1)(B)(i), redesignated former subsec. (m) as (o).

Pub.L. 101–189, § 814(a)(4), in subsec. (o), as so redesignated, designated existing provisions as par. (1), in par. (1), as so redesignated, substituted "appropriate to carry out this section shall be included in the Federal Acquisition Regulation" for "deemed appropriate to carry out this section shall be issued in the Federal Acquisition Regulation within 180 days after November 17, 1988'', and added pars. (2) and (3).

Subsec. (p). Pub.L. 101–189, § 814(a)(1)(B)(i), redesignated former subsec. (n) as (p).

Subsec. (p)(1). Pub.L. 101–189, § 814(b)(1), in par. (1) of subsec. (p), as so redesignated, substituted "on the earliest specific date, as determined under implementing regulations, on which an authorized official orders or requests an action described in clauses (i)—(viii) of paragraph (3)(A)," for "with the development, preparation, and issuance of a procurement solicitation,".

Subsec. (p)(3)(A). Pub.L. 101–189, § 814(b)(2), substituted provisions defining the term procurement official as meaning, with respect to any procurement (including the modification or extension of a contract), any civilian or military official or employee of an agency who has participated personally and substantially in any of the activities enumerated in cls. (i) to (viii) for provision which defined such term as meaning any civilian or military official or employee of an agency who participated personally and substantially in the conduct of the agency procurement concerned, including all officials and employees who were responsible for reviewing or approving the procurement, as further defined by applicable implementing regulations.

Subsec. (p)(8). Pub.L. 101–189, § 814(b)(3), added par. (8).

Effective and Applicability Provisions

2002 Acts. Except as otherwise provided by section 402(a)(2) of Pub.L. 107–347, amendments made by Pub.L. 107–347, Titles I and II, §§ 101 to 216, effective 120 days after December 17, 2002, see section 402(a) of Pub.L. 107–347, set out as a note under 44 U.S.C.A. § 3601.

1996 Acts. Amendment by Pub.L. 104–106 effective Feb. 10, 1996, except as otherwise provided, see section 4401 of Pub.L. 104–106, set out as a note under section 251 of this title.

1994 Acts. Amendment by section 8301(e) of Pub.L. 103–355 effective Oct. 13, 1994, except as otherwise provided, see section 10001 of Pub.L. 103–355, set out as a note under section 251 of this title.

1988 Acts. Section 6(b) of Pub.L. 100–679, as amended Pub.L. 101–28, May 15, 1989, 103 Stat. 57, provided that: "The amendment made by subsection (a) [enacting this section] shall take effect July 16, 1989."

Clarification of Frequency of Certification by Employees and Contractors

Pub.L. 101–510, Div. A, Title VIII, § 815(b), Nov. 5, 1990, 104 Stat. 1597, provided that: "Not later than 30 days after the date of the enactment of this Act [Nov. 5, 1990], the regulations implementing section 27(e)(1)(B) of the Office of Federal Procurement Policy Act (41 U.S.C. 423(e)(1)(B)) [subsec. (e)(1)(B) of this section] shall be revised to ensure that a contractor is required to obtain from each officer, employee, agent, representative, and consultant of the contractor only one certification (as described in clauses (i) and (ii) of that section) during the person's employment or association with the contractor and that such certification shall be made at the earliest possible date after the person begins his or her employment or association with the contractor."

Promulgation of Regulations

Section 814(e) of Pub.L. 101–189 provided that: "Not later than 90 days after the date of the enactment of this section [Nov. 29, 1989], regulations implementing the amendments made by this section to the provisions of section 27 of the Office of Federal Procurement Policy Act (41 U.S.C. 423) [this section] shall be issued in accordance with sections 6 and 25 of such Act (41 U.S.C. 405, 421) [sections 405 and 421 of this title], after coordination with the Director of the Office of Government Ethics."

Suspension of Effect of Section

This section had no force or effect during the period beginning Dec. 1, 1989 and ending one year following such date, pursuant to Pub.L. 101–194, Title V, § 507, Nov. 30, 1989, 103 Stat. 1759.

Suspension of Effect of Subsec. (f)

Pub.L. 101–510, Div. A, Title VIII, § 815(a)(1), Nov. 5, 1990, 104 Stat. 1597, provided that subsec. (f) of this section have no force or effect during the period beginning on Dec. 1, 1990, and ending on May 31, 1991.

LAW REVIEW AND JOURNAL COMMENTARIES

Byrd shot: Congress takes a broad aim at government contract lobbyists. Thomas M. Susman and Clayton S. Marsh, 37 Fed.B.News & J. 387 (1990).

The potential for criminal liability in government contracting: A closer look at The Procurement Integrity Act. Note, 34 Pub. Cont. L.J. 521 (2005).

LIBRARY REFERENCES

American Digest System

Records ☞31, 55.

United States ☞61, 75(1).

Key Number System Topic Nos. 326, 393.

Research References

Forms

Nichols Cyclopedia of Legal Forms Annotated § 7:2530, United States Lessee--General Clauses.

Treatises and Practice Aids

Federal Procedure, Lawyers Edition § 38:101, Other Agencies.

Federal Procedure, Lawyers Edition § 39:20, Protection of Contractor Bid or Proposal Information and Source Selection Information.

Federal Procedure, Lawyers Edition § 39:21, Voiding or Rescinding Contract Upon Conviction of Crime.

Federal Procedure, Lawyers Edition § 39:103, Exchanges with Offerors After Receipt of Proposals.

Federal Procedure, Lawyers Edition § 39:527, Regulatory Criteria for For Dismissal of Protest.

West's Federal Administrative Practice § 525, Bid Protests.

West's Federal Administrative Practice § 608, Procurement Integrity.

West's Federal Administrative Practice § 611, Laws Applicable--Access to Government Procurement Records.

West's Federal Administrative Practice § 613, Laws Applicable--Contract Solicitation.

West's Federal Administrative Practice § 625, Contracting by Negotiation.

West's Federal Administrative Practice § 666, Federal Acquisition Reform Act of 1996 (Clinger Cohen Act of 1996).

West's Federal Administrative Practice § 2157, Historically Underutilized Business Zone Program ("HUBZone").

West's Federal Administrative Practice § 2158, Government Contract Procurement for Businesses of Service-Disabled Veterans.

WESTLAW ELECTRONIC RESEARCH

See Westlaw guide following the Explanation pages of this volume.

Notes of Decisions

Certification   1
Conflict of interest   2
Disclosure   3

———

1. Certification

Regulation of the General Services Administration (GSA) requiring that certificate of procurement integrity (CPI) be submitted with the bid was not arbitrary and capricious, even though governing statute did not require the CPI to be submitted before the contract was awarded. S.J. Amoroso Const. Co. v. U.S., C.A.9 (Cal.) 1992, 981 F.2d 1073. United States ☞ 64.30

2. Conflict of interest

Whether or not conduct of Postal Service evaluator comported with Procurement Policy Act was irrelevant on challenge to Postal Service contract, where evaluator had conflict of interest due to fact that he had not immediately rejected

offer for future employment from poten-
tial bidder. Express One Intern., Inc. v.
U.S. Postal Service, D.D.C.1992, 814
F.Supp. 93. United States ☞ 64.40(2)

Incumbent contractor who lost out in
competition for successor aircraft maintenance contract failed to establish bias on
part of source selection evaluation board
(SSEB) based on e-mail of member of
board critical of contractor's policy of
farming out certain work to subcontractors, where contracting agency, in an
abundance of caution, removed member
who sent e-mail and member who received e-mail from the SSEB, and destroyed hard copy evaluations to ensure
that the opinions of former members and
their work product did not find their way
to reconstructed SSEB. Avtel Services,
Inc. v. U.S., Fed.Cl.2006, 70 Fed.Cl. 173.
United States ☞ 64.40(2)

3. Disclosure

Contracting officer's decision not to
disqualify offeror under the Procurement
Integrity Act for obtaining information
concerning incumbent contractor's working conditions, pay, and other deployment details had a reasonable basis, in
that such deployment information was in
the public domain and incumbent contractor did not demonstrate competitive
harm from release of the information.
Avtel Services, Inc. v. U.S., Fed.Cl.2006,
70 Fed.Cl. 173. United States ☞
64.45(2)

Procurement Integrity Act, prohibiting
disclosure of procurement-related information "other than as provided by law,"
does not restrict information to which bid
protester is ordinarily entitled by means
of discovery for litigation purposes, or
otherwise circumscribe Court of Federal
Claims' authority to administer pretrial
proceedings in bid protest actions; Act is
directed at situations in which a present
or former government procurement officer secretly leaks information concerning
a pending solicitation to an offeror participating therein, in hopes of securing post-
government employment or other compensation. Pikes Peak Family Housing,
LLC v. U.S., Fed.Cl.1998, 40 Fed.Cl. 673.
Federal Courts ☞ 1072; Federal Courts
☞ 1112

§ 424. Repealed. Pub.L. 103–355, Title VIII, § 8303(b), Oct. 13, 1994, 108 Stat. 3398

HISTORICAL AND STATUTORY NOTES

Section, Pub.L. 93–400, § 28, as added
Pub.L. 100–679, § 9, Nov. 17, 1988, 102
Stat. 4069, related to establishment and
duties of position of Advocate for the Acquisition of Commercial Products.

Effective Date of Repeal

Repeal of section effective Oct. 13,
1994, except as otherwise provided, see
section 10001 of Pub.L. 103–355, set out
as a note under section 251 of this title.

§ 425. Contract clauses and certifications

(a) Nonstandard contract clauses

The Federal Acquisition Regulatory Council shall promulgate regulations to discourage the use of a nonstandard contract clause on a
repetitive basis. The regulations shall include provisions that—

(1) clearly define what types of contract clauses are to be
treated as nonstandard clauses; and

(2) require prior approval for the use of a nonstandard clause
on a repetitive basis by an official at a level of responsibility
above the contracting officer.

(b) Construction of certification requirements

A provision of law may not be construed as requiring a certification by a contractor or offeror in a procurement made or to be made

by the Federal Government unless that provision of law specifically provides that such a certification shall be required.

(c) Prohibition on certification requirements

(1) A requirement for a certification by a contractor or offeror may not be included in the Federal Acquisition Regulation unless—

(A) the certification requirement is specifically imposed by statute; or

(B) written justification for such certification requirement is provided to the Administrator for Federal Procurement Policy by the Federal Acquisition Regulatory Council, and the Administrator approves in writing the inclusion of such certification requirement.

(2)(A) A requirement for a certification by a contractor or offeror may not be included in a procurement regulation of an executive agency unless—

(i) the certification requirement is specifically imposed by statute; or

(ii) written justification for such certification requirement is provided to the head of the executive agency by the senior procurement executive of the agency, and the head of the executive agency approves in writing the inclusion of such certification requirement.

(B) For purposes of subparagraph (A), the term "head of the executive agency" with respect to a military department means the Secretary of Defense.

(Pub.L. 93–400, § 29, as added Oct. 13, 1994, Pub.L. 103–355, Title I, § 1093, 108 Stat. 3273, and amended Pub.L. 104–106, Div. D, Title XLIII, § 4301(b)(2)(A), (c), Feb. 10, 1996, 110 Stat. 657, 658.)

HISTORICAL AND STATUTORY NOTES

Revision Notes and Legislative Reports
1994 Acts. Senate Report Nos. 103–258 and 103–259, and House Conference Report No. 103–712, see 1994 U.S. Code Cong. and Adm. News, p. 2561.

1996 Acts. House Conference Report No. 104–450, see 1996 U.S. Code Cong. and Adm. News, p. 238.

Amendments
1996 Amendments. Catchline. Pub.L. 104–106, § 4301(b)(2)(A)(i), substituted "Contract clauses and certifications" for "Nonstandard contract clauses" in section catchline.

Subsec. (a). Pub.L. 104–106, § 4301(b)(2)(A)(ii), added heading "(a)

Nonstandard contract clauses" preceding "The Federal Acquisition" and redesignated existing provisions as subsec. (a).

Subsec. (b). Pub.L. 104–106, § 4301(c), added subsec. (b).

Subsec. (c). Pub.L. 104–106, § 4301(b)(2)(A)(iii), added subsec. (c).

Effective and Applicability Provisions
1996 Acts. Amendment by Pub.L. 104–106 effective Feb. 10, 1996, except as otherwise provided, see section 4401 of Pub.L. 104–106, set out as a note under section 251 of this title.

1994 Acts. Section effective Oct. 13, 1994, except as otherwise provided, see section 10001 of Pub.L. 103–355, set out as a note under section 251 of this title.

Current Certification Requirements
Section 4301(b)(1) of Pub.L. 104–106, provided that:

"**(A)** Not later than 210 days after the date of the enactment of this Act [Feb. 10, 1996], the Administrator for Federal Procurement Policy shall issue for public comment a proposal to amend the Federal Acquisition Regulation to remove from the Federal Acquisition Regulation certification requirements for contractors and offerors that are not specifically imposed by statute. The Administrator may omit such a certification requirement from the proposal only if—

"**(i)** the Federal Acquisition Regulatory Council provides the Administrator with a written justification for the requirement and a determination that there is no less burdensome means for administering and enforcing the particular regulation that contains the certification requirement; and

"**(ii)** the Administrator approves in writing the retention of the certification requirement.

"**(B)(i)** Not later than 210 days after the date of the enactment of this Act [Feb. 10, 1996], the head of each executive agency that has agency procurement regulations containing one or more certification requirements for contractors and offerors that are not specifically imposed by statute shall issue for public comment a proposal to amend the regulations to remove the certification requirements. The head of the executive agency may omit such a certification requirement from the proposal only if—

"**(I)** the senior procurement executive for the executive agency provides the head of the executive agency with a written justification for the requirement and a determination that there is no less burdensome means for administering and enforcing the particular regulation that contains the certification requirement; and

"**(II)** the head of the executive agency approves in writing the retention of such certification requirement.

"**(ii)** For purposes of clause (i), the term 'head of the executive agency' with respect to a military department means the Secretary of Defense."

LIBRARY REFERENCES

American Digest System
United States ☞73(9).
Key Number System Topic No. 393.

WESTLAW ELECTRONIC RESEARCH
See Westlaw guide following the Explanation pages of this volume.

§ 426.　Use of electronic commerce in Federal procurement

(a) In general

The head of each executive agency, after consulting with the Administrator, shall establish, maintain, and use, to the maximum extent that is practicable and cost-effective, procedures and processes that employ electronic commerce in the conduct and administration of its procurement system.

(b) Applicable standards

In conducting electronic commerce, the head of an agency shall apply nationally and internationally recognized standards that broaden interoperability and ease the electronic interchange of information.

(c) Agency procedures

The head of each executive agency shall ensure that systems, technologies, procedures, and processes established pursuant to this section—

(1) are implemented with uniformity throughout the agency, to the extent practicable;

(2) are implemented only after granting due consideration to the use or partial use, as appropriate, of existing electronic commerce and electronic data interchange systems and infrastructures such [1] the Federal acquisition computer network architecture known as FACNET;

(3) facilitate access to Federal Government procurement opportunities, including opportunities for small business concerns, socially and economically disadvantaged small business concerns, and business concerns owned predominantly by women; and

(4) ensure that any notice of agency requirements or agency solicitation for contract opportunities is provided in a form that allows convenient and universal user access through a single, Government-wide point of entry.

(d) Implementation

The Administrator shall, in carrying out the requirements of this section—

(1) issue policies to promote, to the maximum extent practicable, uniform implementation of this section by executive agencies, with due regard for differences in program requirements among agencies that may require departures from uniform procedures and processes in appropriate cases, when warranted because of the agency mission;

(2) ensure that the head of each executive agency complies with the requirements of subsection (c) of this section with respect to the agency systems, technologies, procedures, and processes established pursuant to this section; and

(3) consult with the heads of appropriate Federal agencies with applicable technical and functional expertise, including the Office of Information and Regulatory Affairs, the National Institute of Standards and Technology, the General Services Administration, and the Department of Defense.

(e) Report

Not later than March 1 of each even-numbered year through 2004, the Administrator shall submit to Congress a report setting forth in detail the progress made in implementing the requirements of this section. The report shall include the following:

(1) A strategic plan for the implementation of a Government-wide electronic commerce capability.

(2) An agency-by-agency summary of implementation of the requirements of subsection (c) of this section, including timetables, as appropriate, addressing when individual agencies will come into full compliance.

(3) A specific assessment of compliance with the requirement in subsection (c) of this section to provide universal public access through a single, Government-wide point of entry.

(4) An agency-by-agency summary of the volume and dollar value of transactions that were conducted using electronic commerce methods during the previous two fiscal years.

(5) A discussion of possible incremental changes to the electronic commerce capability referred to in subsection (c)(4) of this section to increase the level of government contract information available to the private sector, including an assessment of the advisability of including contract award information in the electronic commerce functional standard.

(f) "Electronic commerce" defined

For the purposes of this section, the term "electronic commerce" means electronic techniques for accomplishing business transactions, including electronic mail or messaging, World Wide Web technology, electronic bulletin boards, purchase cards, electronic funds transfers, and electronic data interchange.

(Pub.L. 93–400, § 30, as added Pub.L. 103–355, Title IX, § 9001(a), Oct. 13, 1994, 108 Stat. 3399, and amended Pub.L. 105–85, Div. A, Title VIII, § 850(a), Nov. 18, 1997, 111 Stat. 1847; Pub.L. 106–398, § 1 [Div. A, Title VIII, § 810(d)], Oct. 30, 2000, 114 Stat. 1654, 1654A–210.)

[1] So in original. Probably should be "such as".

HISTORICAL AND STATUTORY NOTES

Revision Notes and Legislative Reports

1994 Acts. Senate Report Nos. 103–258, 103–259 and House Conference Report No. 103–712, see 1994 U.S. Code Cong. and Adm. News, p. 2561.

1997 Acts. House Conference Report No. 105–340 and Statement by President, see 1997 U.S. Code Cong. and Adm. News, p. 2251.

2000 Acts. House Conference Report No. 106–945 and Statement by President, see 2000 U.S. Code Cong. and Adm. News, p. 1516.

Amendments

2000 Amendments. Subsec. (e). Pub.L. 106–398, [Div. A, Title VIII, § 810(d)(1)], substituted "Not later than March 1 of each even-numbered year through 2004" for "Not later than March 1, 1998, and every year afterward through 2003".

Subsec. (e)(4). Pub.L. 106–398, [Div. A, Title VIII, § 810(d)(2)], in par. (4), substituted "An" for "Beginning with the report submitted on March 1, 1999, an" and "two fiscal years" for "calendar year", respectively.

1997 Amendments. Pub.L. 105–85, § 850(a), substituted provisions relating to use of electronic commerce in Federal procurement for provisions relating to Federal acquisition computer network (FACNET) architecture. Prior to revision, section read as follows:

"**§ 426. Federal acquisition computer network (FACNET) architecture**

"**(a) In general**

"**(1)** The Administrator shall establish a program for the development and implementation of a Federal acquisition computer network architecture (hereinafter in this section referred to as "FACNET") that will be Government-wide and provide interoperability among users. The Administrator shall assign a program manager for FACNET and shall provide for overall direction of policy and leadership in the development, coordination, installation, operation, and completion of implementation of FACNET by executive agencies.

"**(2)** In carrying out paragraph (1), the Administrator shall consult with the heads of appropriate Federal agencies with applicable technical and functional expertise, including the Office of Information and Regulatory Affairs, the National Institute of Standards and Technology, the General Services Administration, and the Department of Defense.

"**(3)** Government-wide FACNET capability (as defined in section 426a(b) of this title) shall be implemented not later than January 1, 2000.

"**(b) Functions of FACNET**

"The FACNET architecture shall provide for the following functions:

"**(1) Government functions**

"Allow executive agencies to do the following electronically:

"**(A)** Provide widespread public notice of solicitations for contract opportunities issued by an executive agency.

"**(B)** Receive responses to solicitations and associated requests for information through such system.

"**(C)** Provide public notice of contract awards (including price) through such system.

"**(D)** In cases in which it is practicable, receive questions regarding solicitations through such system.

"**(E)** In cases in which it is practicable, issue orders to be made through such system.

"**(F)** In cases in which it is practicable, make payments to contractors by bank card, electronic funds transfer, or other automated methods.

"**(G)** Archive data relating to each procurement action made using such system.

"**(2) Private sector user functions**

"Allow private sector users to do the following electronically:

"**(A)** Access notice of solicitations for contract opportunities issued by an executive agency.

"**(B)** Access and review solicitations issued by an executive agency.

"**(C)** Respond to solicitations issued by the executive agency.

"**(D)** In cases in which it is practicable, receive orders from the executive agency.

"**(E)** Access information on contract awards (including price) made by the executive agency.

"**(F)** In cases in which it is practicable, receive payment by bank card, electronic funds transfer, or other automated means.

"**(3) General functions**

"**(A)** Allow the electronic interchange of procurement information between the private sector and the Federal Government and among Federal agencies.

"**(B)** Employ nationally and internationally recognized data formats that serve to broaden and ease the electronic interchange of data.

"**(C)** Allow convenient and universal user access through any point of entry.

"**(c) Notice and solicitation regulations**

"In connection with implementation of the architecture referred to in subsection (a) of this section, the Federal Acquisition Regulatory Council shall ensure that the Federal Acquisition Regulation contains appropriate notice and solicitation provisions applicable to acquisitions conducted through a FACNET capability. The provisions shall specify the required form and content of notices of acquisitions and the minimum periods for notifications of solicitations and for deadlines for the submission of offers under solicitations. Each minimum period specified for a notification of solicitation and each deadline for the submission of offers under a solicitation shall afford potential offerors a reasonable opportunity to respond.

"(d) 'Architecture' defined

"For purposes of this section, the term 'architecture' means the conceptual framework that—

"**(1)** uses a combination of commercial hardware and commercial software to enable contractors to conduct business with the Federal Government by electronic means; and

"**(2)** includes a description of the functions to be performed to achieve the mission of streamlining procurement through electronic commerce, the system elements and interfaces needed to perform the functions, and the designation of performance levels of those system elements."

Effective and Applicability Provisions

2000 Acts. Amendment by Pub.L. 106–398, § 1 [Div. A, Title VIII, § 810(d)], effective Oct. 1, 2000, see Pub.L. 106–398, § 1 [Div. A, Title VIII, § 810(e)], set out as a note under 15 U.S.C.A. § 637.

1997 Acts. Amendment by section 850 of Pub.L. 105–85 to take effect 180 days after Nov. 18, 1997, see section 850(g) of Pub.L. 105–85, set out as a note under section 2302c of Title 10, Armed Forces.

1994 Acts. Section effective Oct. 13, 1994, except as otherwise provided, see section 10001 of Pub.L. 103–355, set out as a note under section 251 of this title.

CROSS REFERENCES

Executive agency heads to implement FACNET capability, see 41 USCA § 252c.

LIBRARY REFERENCES

American Digest System
> United States ⊶64.5.
> Key Number System Topic No. 393.

WESTLAW ELECTRONIC RESEARCH

See Westlaw guide following the Explanation pages of this volume.

§ 426a. Repealed. Pub.L. 105–85, Div. A, Title VIII, § 850(b), Nov. 18, 1997, 111 Stat. 1848

HISTORICAL AND STATUTORY NOTES

Section, Pub.L. 93–400, § 30A, as added Pub.L. 103–355, Title IX, § 9001(a), Oct. 13, 1994, 108 Stat. 3400, related to the implementation of the federal acquisition computer network.

Effective Date of Repeal

Repeal by section 850 of Pub.L. 105–85 to take effect 180 days after Nov. 18, 1997, see section 850(g) of Pub.L. 105–85, set out as a note under section 2302c of Title 10, Armed Forces.

GAO Determination of Eligible Agency Contracts

Section 9004 of Pub.L. 103–355, which required reports to the Administrator for Federal Procurement Policy and certain enumerated Congressional committees on contracts not suitable for acquisition through full FACNET capability, together with appropriate FAR Council determinations applicable for purposes of determining eligibility of contracts under subsec. (e) of this section, such determinations also to be submitted to such Committees, was repealed by Pub.L. 105–85, Div. A, Title VIII, § 850(c), Nov. 18, 1997, 111 Stat. 1848.

§ 427. Simplified acquisition procedures

(a) Requirement

In order to promote efficiency and economy in contracting and to avoid unnecessary burdens for agencies and contractors, the Federal Acquisition Regulation shall provide for—

(1) special simplified procedures for purchases of property and services for amounts not greater than the simplified acquisition threshold; and

(2) special simplified procedures for purchases of property and services for amounts greater than the simplified acquisition threshold but not greater than $5,000,000 with respect to which the contracting officer reasonably expects, based on the nature of the property or services sought and on market research, that offers will include only commercial items.

(b) Prohibition on dividing purchases

A proposed purchase or contract for an amount above the simplified acquisition threshold may not be divided into several purchases or contracts for lesser amounts in order to use the simplified acquisition procedures required by subsection (a) of this section.

(c) Promotion of competition required

In using simplified acquisition procedures, the head of an executive agency shall promote competition to the maximum extent practicable.

(d) Consideration of offers timely received

The simplified acquisition procedures contained in the Federal Acquisition Regulation shall include a requirement that a contracting officer consider each responsive offer timely received from an eligible offeror.

(e) Interim reporting rule

Until October 1, 2004, procuring activities shall continue to report under section 417(d) of this title procurement awards with a dollar value of at least $25,000, but less than $100,000, in conformity with the procedures for the reporting of a contract award greater than $25,000 that were in effect on October 1, 1992.

(f) Special rules for commercial items

The Federal Acquisition Regulation shall provide that, in the case of a purchase of commercial items using special simplified procedures, an executive agency—

(1) shall publish a notice in accordance with section 416 of this title and, as provided in subsection (b)(4) of such section, permit all responsible sources to submit a bid, proposal, or quotation (as appropriate) which shall be considered by the agency;

(2) may not conduct the purchase on a sole source basis unless the need to do so is justified in writing and approved in accordance with section 2304 of Title 10 or section 253 of this title, as applicable; and

(3) shall include in the contract file a written description of the procedures used in awarding the contract and the number of offers received.

(g) Redesignated as (f)

(Pub.L. 93–400, § 31, as added Pub.L. 103–355, Title IV, § 4201(a), Oct. 13, 1994, 108 Stat. 3342, and amended Pub.L. 104–106, Div. D, Title XLII, §§ 4202(c), 4302(b), Feb. 10, 1996, 110 Stat. 653, 658; Pub.L. 104–201, Div. A, Title X, § 1074(b)(6), Sept. 23, 1996, 110 Stat. 2660; Pub.L. 105–85, Div. A, Title VIII, § 850(d), Nov. 18, 1997, 111 Stat. 1848; Pub.L. 106–65, Div. A, Title VIII, § 818, Oct. 5, 1999, 113 Stat. 712.)

HISTORICAL AND STATUTORY NOTES

Revision Notes and Legislative Reports
1994 Acts. Senate Report Nos. 103–258 and 103–259, and House Conference Report No. 103–712, see 1994 U.S. Code Cong. and Adm. News, p. 2561.

1996 Acts. House Conference Report No. 104–450, see 1996 U.S. Code Cong. and Adm. News, p. 238.

House Report No. 104–563 and House Conference Report No. 104–724, see 1996 U.S. Code Cong. and Adm. News, p. 2948.

1997 Acts. House Conference Report No. 105–340 and Statement by President, see 1997 U.S. Code Cong. and Adm. News, p. 2251.

1999 Acts. House Conference Report No. 106–301 and Statement by President, see 1999 U.S. Code Cong. and Adm. News, p. 94.

Amendments
1999 Amendments. Subsec. (e). Pub.L. 106–65, § 818, struck out "October 1, 1999" and inserted "October 1, 2004".

1997 Amendments. Subsecs. (e) to (g). Pub.L. 105–85, § 850(d), redesignated subsecs. (f) and (g) as (e) and (f), respectively, and struck out former subsec. (e), which read as follows:

"(e) Special rules for use of simplified acquisition procedures

"The simplified acquisition procedures provided in the Federal Acquisition Regulation pursuant to section 2304(g)(1)(A) of Title 10, section 253(g)(1)(A) of this title, and subsection (a)(1) of this section may not be used by an agency after December 31, 1999, for contracts in amounts greater than $50,000 and not greater than the simplified acquisition threshold until a certification has been made pursuant to section 426a(a)(2) of this title that the agency has implemented a full FACNET capability."

1996 Amendments. Subsec. (a). Pub.L. 104–201, § 1074(b)(6), amended Pub.L. 104–106, § 4202(c)(1), by substituting "contracts for" for "purchases of", which no required no change in the text.

Pub.L. 104–106, § 4202(c)(1), restructured existing provisions into par. (1) and added par. (2).

Subsec. (e). Pub.L. 104–106, § 4302(b)(1), redesignated par. (2)(B) as subsec. (e), and struck out former par. (1), relating to effect of interim FACNET capability and former par. (2)(A), relating to effect of full FACNET capability.

Pub.L. 104–106, § 4302(b)(2), substituted "pursuant to section 2304(g)(1)(A) of Title 10, section 253(g)(1)(A) of this title, and subsection (a)(1) of this section" for "pursuant to this section".

Subsec. (g). Pub.L. 104–106, § 4202(c)(2), added subsec. (g).

Effective and Applicability Provisions
1997 Acts. Amendment by section 850 of Pub.L. 105–85 to take effect 180 days after Nov. 18, 1997, see section 850(g) of Pub.L. 105–85, set out as a note under section 2302c of Title 10, Armed Forces.

1996 Acts. Section 1074(b)(6) of Pub.L. 104–201 provided in part that Pub.L. 104–106, § 4202(c)(1), is amended, effective Feb. 10, 1996.

Amendment by Pub.L. 104–106 effective Feb. 10, 1996, except as otherwise

provided, see section 4401 of Pub.L. 104–106, set out as a note under section 251 of this title.

1994 Acts. Section effective Oct. 13, 1994, except as otherwise provided, see section 10001 of Pub.L. 103–355, set out as a note under section 251 of this title.

Termination of Authority to Issue Solicitations for Purchases of Commercial Items in Excess of Simplified Acquisition Threshold
Authority to issue solicitations for purchases of commercial items in excess of simplified acquisition threshold pursuant to special simplified procedures authorized by subsec. (a) of this section expires Jan. 1, 2002, see section 4202(e) of Pub.L. 104–106, set out as a note under section 2304 of Title 10.

CROSS REFERENCES

Implementation of simplified acquisition procedures, see 10 USCA § 2302b and 41 USCA § 252b.

LIBRARY REFERENCES

American Digest System
United States ☜64.5.
Key Number System Topic No. 393.

Research References

Forms
Federal Procedural Forms § 34:11, Small Purchase and Other Simplified Procedures.

WESTLAW ELECTRONIC RESEARCH

See Westlaw guide following the Explanation pages of this volume.

§ 428. Procedures applicable to purchases below micro-purchase threshold

(a) Requirements

(1) The head of each executive agency shall ensure that procuring activities of that agency, in awarding a contract with a price exceeding the micro-purchase threshold, comply with the requirements of section 637(a) of Title 15, section 2323 of Title 10, and section 7102 of the Federal Acquisition Streamlining Act of 1994.

(2) The authority under part 13.106(a)(1) of the Federal Acquisition Regulation (48 C.F.R. 13.106(a)(1)), as in effect on November 18, 1993, to make purchases without securing competitive quotations

does not apply to any purchases with a price exceeding the micro-purchase threshold.

(b) Exclusion for micro-purchases

A purchase by an executive agency with an anticipated value of the micro-purchase threshold or less is not subject to section 644(j) of Title 15 and the Buy American Act (41 U.S.C. 10a–10c).

(c) Purchases without competitive quotations

A purchase not greater than $2,500 may be made without obtaining competitive quotations if an employee of an executive agency or a member of the Armed Forces of the United States authorized to do so determines that the price for the purchase is reasonable.

(d) Equitable distribution

Purchases not greater than $2,500 shall be distributed equitably among qualified suppliers.

(e) Implementation through FAR

This section shall be implemented through the Federal Acquisition Regulation.

(f) Micro-purchase threshold defined

For purposes of this section, the micro-purchase threshold is the amount of $2,500.

(g) Redesignated (f)

(Pub.L. 93–400, § 32, as added Pub.L. 103–355, Title IV, § 4301(a), Oct. 13, 1994, 108 Stat. 3346, and amended Pub.L. 104–106, Div. D, Title XLIII, §§ 4304(b)(4), (c)(3), 4311, Feb. 10, 1996, 110 Stat. 664, 671.)

HISTORICAL AND STATUTORY NOTES

Revision Notes and Legislative Reports

1994 Acts. Senate Report Nos. 103–258 and 103–259, and House Conference Report No. 103–712, see 1994 U.S. Code Cong. and Adm. News, p. 2561.

1996 Acts. House Conference Report No. 104–450, see 1996 U.S. Code Cong. and Adm. News, p. 238.

References in Text

Section 7102 of the Federal Acquisition Streamlining Act of 1994, referred to in subsec. (a)(1), is section 7102 of Pub.L. 103–355, Title VII, Oct. 13, 1994, 108 Stat. 3367, which is set out as a note under section 644 of Title 15, Commerce and Trade.

The Buy American Act, referred to in subsec. (b), is Act Mar. 3, 1933, c. 212,

Title III, 47 Stat. 1520, as amended, which is classified to sections 10a, 10b, 10b–1, and 10c of this title. For complete classification of this Act to the Code, see Short Title note set out under section 10a of this title and Tables.

Amendments

1996 Amendments. Subsec. (c). Pub.L. 104–106, § 4304(b)(4), struck out subsec. (c) relating to applicability of certain provisions.

Pub.L. 104–106, § 4304(c)(3), redesignated former subsec. (d) as subsec. (c).

Pub.L. 104–106, § 4311, substituted "an employee of an executive agency or a member of the Armed Forces of the United States authorized to do so" for "the contracting officer".

Subsecs. (d) to (g). Pub.L. 104–106, § 4304(c)(3), redesignated former subsecs. (e) to (g) as subsecs. (d) to (f), respectively.

Effective and Applicability Provisions

1996 Acts. Amendment by Pub.L. 104–106 effective Feb. 10, 1996, except as

otherwise provided, see section 4401 of Pub.L. 104–106, set out as a note under section 251 of this title.

1994 Acts. Section effective on Oct. 13, 1994, and shall be implemented in the Federal Acquisition Regulation not later than 60 days after Oct. 13, 1994, see section 4301(c) of Pub.L. 103–355, set out as a note under section 10a of this title.

CROSS REFERENCES

Exception to buy American Act for micro-purchases, see 41 USCA § 10a.

LIBRARY REFERENCES

American Digest System
United States ☞64.5.
Key Number System Topic No. 393.

Research References

ALR Library
185 ALR, Fed. 253, Validity, Construction, and Operation of Buy American Act (41 U.S.C.A. § 10a–10d).

WESTLAW ELECTRONIC RESEARCH

See Westlaw guide following the Explanation pages of this volume.

§ 428a. Special emergency procurement authority

(a) Applicability

The authorities provided in this section apply with respect to any procurement of property or services by or for an executive agency that, as determined by the head of such executive agency, are to be used—

    (1) in support of a contingency operation; or

    (2) to facilitate the defense against or recovery from nuclear, biological, chemical, or radiological attack against the United States.

(b) Increased thresholds

For a procurement to which this section applies under subsection (a) of this section—

    (1) the amount specified in subsections (c), (d), and (f) of section 428 of this title shall be deemed to be—

        (A) $15,000 in the case of any contract to be awarded and performed, or purchase to be made, inside the United States; and

(B) $25,000 in the case of any contract to be awarded and performed, or purchase to be made, outside the United States; and

(2) the term "simplified acquisition threshold" means—

(A) $250,000 in the case of any contract to be awarded and performed, or purchase to be made, inside the United States; and

(B) $1,000,000 in the case of any contract to be awarded and performed, or purchase to be made, outside the United States.

(c) Increased limitation on use of simplified acquisition procedures

For a procurement to which this section applies under subsection (a) of this section, the $5,000,000 limitation in the following provisions of law shall be deemed to be $10,000,000:

(1) Section 427(a)(2) of this title.

(2) Section 2304(g)(1)(B) of Title 10.

(3) Section 253(g)(1)(B) of this title.

(d) Commercial items authority

(1) The head of an executive agency carrying out a procurement of property or a service to which this section applies under subsection (a)(2) of this section may treat such property or service as a commercial item for the purpose of carrying out such procurement.

(2) A contract in an amount greater than $15,000,000 that is awarded on a sole source basis for an item or service treated as a commercial item under paragraph (1) shall not be exempt from—

(A) cost accounting standards promulgated pursuant to section 422 of this title; or

(B) cost or pricing data requirements (commonly referred to as truth in negotiating) under section 2306a of Title 10 and section 254b of this title.

(e) Contingency operation defined

In this section, the term "contingency operation" has the meaning given such term in section 101(a) (13) of Title 10.

(Pub.L. 93–400, § 32A, as added Pub.L. 108–136, Div. A, Title XIV, § 1443(a)(1), Nov. 24, 2003, 117 Stat. 1675, and amended Pub.L. 108–375, Div. A, Title VIII, § 822, Oct. 28, 2004, 118 Stat. 2016.)

HISTORICAL AND STATUTORY NOTES

Revision Notes and Legislative Reports
2003 Acts. House Conference Report No. 108–354 and Statement by President, see 2003 U.S. Code Cong. and Adm. News, p. 1407.

2004 Acts. House Conference Report No. 108–767, see 2004 U.S. Code Cong. and Adm. News, p. 1961.

Statement by President, see 2004 U.S. Code Cong. and Adm. News, p. S37.

Amendments

2004 Amendments. Subsec. (b)(1). Pub.L. 108–375, § 822(1), rewrote par. (1), which formerly read: "**(1)** the amount specified in subsections (c), (d), and (f) of section 428 of this title shall be deemed to be $15,000; and".

Subsec. (b)(2)(B). Pub.L. 108–375, § 822(2), in subpar. (B), substituted "$1,000,000" for "$500,000".

Authority to Enter into Certain Transactions for Defense Against or Recovery from Terrorism or Nuclear, Biological, Chemical, or Radiological Attack
Pub.L. 108–136, Div. A, Title XIV, § 1441, Nov. 24, 2003, 117 Stat. 1673, provided that:

"**(a) Authority.—**

"**(1) In general.**—The head of an executive agency who engages in basic research, applied research, advanced research, and development projects that—

"**(A)** are necessary to the responsibilities of such official's executive agency in the field of research and development, and

"**(B)** have the potential to facilitate defense against or recovery from terrorism or nuclear, biological, chemical, or radiological attack,

may exercise the same authority (subject to the same restrictions and conditions) with respect to such research and projects as the Secretary of Defense may exercise under section 2371 of title 10, United States Code, except for subsections (b) and (f) of such section 2371.

"**(2) Prototype projects.**—The head of an executive agency may, under the authority of paragraph (1), carry out prototype projects that meet the requirements of subparagraphs (A) and (B) of paragraph (1) in accordance with the requirements and conditions provided for carrying out prototype projects under section 845 of the National Defense Authorization Act for Fiscal Year 1994 (Public Law 103–160; 10 U.S.C. 2371 note), including that, to the maximum extent practicable, com-

petitive procedures shall be used when entering into agreements to carry out projects under subsection (a) of that section and that the period of authority to carry out projects under such subsection (a) terminates as provided in subsection (g) of that section.

"**(3) Application of requirements and conditions.**—In applying the requirements and conditions of section 845 of the National Defense Authorization Act for Fiscal Year 1994 [10 U.S.C.A. § 2371 note] under this subsection—

"**(A)** subsection (c) of that section [10 U.S.C.A. § 2371 note] shall apply with respect to prototype projects carried out under this paragraph; and

"**(B)** the Director of the Office of Management and Budget shall perform the functions of the Secretary of Defense under subsection (d) of that section [10 U.S.C.A. § 2371 note] .

"**(4) Applicability to selected executive agencies.—**

"**(A) OMB authorization required.**—The head of an executive agency may exercise authority under this subsection [this note] for a project only if authorized by the Director of the Office of Management and Budget to use the authority for such project.

"**(B) Relationship to authority of department of homeland security.**—The authority under this subsection [this note] shall not apply to the Secretary of Homeland Security while section 831 of the Homeland Security Act of 2002 (Public Law 107–296; 116 Stat. 2224) [6 U.S.C.A. § 391] is in effect.

"**(b) Annual report.**—The annual report of the head of an executive agency that is required under subsection (h) of section 2371 of title 10, United States Code, as applied to the head of the executive agency by subsection (a) [of this note], shall be submitted to the Committee on Governmental Affairs of the Senate and the Committee on Government Reform of the House of Representatives.

"**(c) Regulations.**—The Director of the Office of Management and Budget shall prescribe regulations to carry out this section [this note]. No transaction may be conducted under the authority of this section [this note] before the date on which such regulations take effect.

"(d) Termination of authority.—The authority to carry out transactions under subsection (a) [of this note] shall terminate on September 30, 2008."

LIBRARY REFERENCES

American Digest System
United States ⬤60.
Key Number System Topic No. 393.

WESTLAW ELECTRONIC RESEARCH

See Westlaw guide following the Explanation pages of this volume.

§ 429. List of laws inapplicable to contracts not greater than simplified acquisition threshold in Federal Acquisition Regulation

(a) List of inapplicable provisions of law

(1) The Federal Acquisition Regulation shall include a list of provisions of law that are inapplicable to contracts or subcontracts in amounts not greater than the simplified acquisition threshold. A provision of law that is properly included on the list pursuant to paragraph (2) may not be construed as applicable to such contracts or subcontracts (as the case may be) by an executive agency. Nothing in this section shall be construed to render inapplicable to contracts and subcontracts in amounts not greater than the simplified acquisition threshold any provision of law that is not included on such list.

(2) A provision of law described in subsection (b) of this section that is enacted after October 13, 1994, shall be included on the list of inapplicable provisions of law required by paragraph (1), unless the Federal Acquisition Regulatory Council makes a written determination that it would not be in the best interest of the Federal Government to exempt contracts or subcontracts in amounts not greater than the simplified acquisition threshold from the applicability of the provision.

(b) Covered law

A provision of law referred to in subsection (a)(2) of this section is any provision of law that, as determined by the Federal Acquisition Regulatory Council, sets forth policies, procedures, requirements, or restrictions for the procurement of property or services by the Federal Government, except for a provision of law that—

(1) provides for criminal or civil penalties; or

(2) specifically refers to this section and provides that, notwithstanding this section, it shall be applicable to contracts or

subcontracts in amounts not greater than the simplified acquisition threshold.

(c) Petition

In the event that a provision of law described in subsection (b) of this section is not included on the list of inapplicable provisions of law as required by subsection (a) of this section, and no written determination has been made by the Federal Acquisition Regulatory Council pursuant to subsection (a)(2) of this section, a person may petition the Administrator for Federal Procurement Policy to take appropriate action. The Administrator shall revise the Federal Acquisition Regulation to include the provision on the list of inapplicable provisions of law unless the Federal Acquisition Regulatory Council makes a determination pursuant to subsection (a)(2) of this section within 60 days after the date on which the petition is received.

(Pub.L. 93–400, § 33, as added Pub.L. 103–355, Title IV, § 4101, Oct. 13, 1994, 108 Stat. 3339.)

HISTORICAL AND STATUTORY NOTES

Revision Notes and Legislative Reports
1994 Acts. Senate Report Nos. 103–258 and 103–259, and House Conference Report No. 103–712, see 1994 U.S. Code Cong. and Adm. News, p. 2561.

Effective and Applicability Provisions
1994 Acts. Section effective Oct. 13, 1994, except as otherwise provided, see section 10001 of Pub.L. 103–355, set out as a note under section 251 of this title.

CROSS REFERENCES

Addition of certain items to domestic source limitations and applicability to contracts for ball bearings and roller bearings, see 10 USCA § 2534.
Armed services acquisition and simplified acquisition threshold, see 10 USCA § 2302a.
Civilian agency acquisitions and simplified acquisition threshold, see 41 USCA § 252a.

WESTLAW ELECTRONIC RESEARCH

See Westlaw guide following the Explanation pages of this volume.

§ 430. List of laws inapplicable to procurements of commercial items in Federal Acquisition Regulation

(a) List of inapplicable provisions of law

(1) The Federal Acquisition Regulation shall include a list of provisions of law that are inapplicable to contracts for the procurement of commercial items. A provision of law that is properly included on the list pursuant to paragraph (2) may not be construed as applicable to purchases of commercial items by an executive agency. Nothing in this section shall be construed to render inapplicable to contracts

for the procurement of commercial items any provision of law that is not included on such list.

(2) A provision of law described in subsection (c) of this section that is enacted after October 13, 1994, shall be included on the list of inapplicable provisions of law required by paragraph (1), unless the Federal Acquisition Regulatory Council makes a written determination that it would not be in the best interest of the Federal Government to exempt contracts for the procurement of commercial items from the applicability of the provision.

(b) Subcontracts

(1) The Federal Acquisition Regulation shall include a list of provisions of law that are inapplicable to subcontracts under either a contract for the procurement of commercial items or a subcontract for the procurement of commercial items. A provision of law that is properly included on the list pursuant to paragraph (2) may not be construed as applicable to such subcontracts. Nothing in this section shall be construed to render inapplicable to subcontracts under a contract for the procurement of commercial items any provision of law that is not included on such list.

(2) A provision of law described in subsection (c) of this section shall be included on the list of inapplicable provisions of law required by paragraph (1) unless the Federal Acquisition Regulatory Council makes a written determination that it would not be in the best interest of the Federal Government to exempt subcontracts under a contract for the procurement of commercial items from the applicability of the provision.

(3) Nothing in this subsection shall be construed to authorize the waiver of the applicability of any provision of law with respect to any subcontract under a contract with a prime contractor reselling or distributing commercial items of another contractor without adding value.

(4) In this subsection, the term "subcontract" includes a transfer of commercial items between divisions, subsidiaries, or affiliates of a contractor or subcontractor.

(c) Covered law

A provision of law referred to in subsections (a)(2) and (b) of this section is any provision of law that, as determined by the Federal Acquisition Regulatory Council, sets forth policies, procedures, requirements, or restrictions for the procurement of property or services by the Federal Government, except for a provision of law that—

(1) provides for criminal or civil penalties; or

(2) specifically refers to this section and provides that, notwithstanding this section, it shall be applicable to contracts for the procurement of commercial items.

(d) Petition

In the event that a provision of law described in subsection (c) of this section is not included on the list of inapplicable provisions of law as required by subsection (a) or (b) of this section, and no written determination has been made by the Federal Acquisition Regulatory Council pursuant to subsection (a)(2) or (b)(2) of this section, a person may petition the Administrator for Federal Procurement Policy to take appropriate action. The Administrator shall revise the Federal Acquisition Regulation to include the provision on the list of inapplicable provisions of law unless the Federal Acquisition Regulatory Council makes a determination pursuant to subsection (a)(2) or (b)(2) of this section within 60 days after the date on which the petition is received.

(Pub.L. 93–400, § 34, as added Pub.L. 103–355, Title VIII, § 8003(a), Oct. 13, 1994, 108 Stat. 3388.)

HISTORICAL AND STATUTORY NOTES

Revision Notes and Legislative Reports
   1994   Acts. Senate   Report   Nos. 103–258 and 103–259, and House Conference Report No. 103–712, see 1994 U.S. Code Cong. and Adm. News, p. 2561.

Effective and Applicability Provisions
   1994 Acts. Section 8003(b) of Pub.L. 103–355 provided that: "No petition may be filed under section 34(d) of the Office of Federal Procurement Policy Act, as added by subsection (a) [subsec. (d) of this section], until after the date occurring 6 months after the date of the enactment of this Act [Oct. 13, 1994]."

   Section effective Oct. 13, 1994, except as otherwise provided, see section 10001 of Pub.L. 103–355, set out as a note under section 251 of this title.

WESTLAW ELECTRONIC RESEARCH

See Westlaw guide following the Explanation pages of this volume.

§ 431. Commercially available off-the-shelf item acquisitions: lists of inapplicable laws in Federal Acquisition Regulation

(a) Lists of inapplicable provisions of law

(1) The Federal Acquisition Regulation shall include a list of provisions of law that are inapplicable to contracts for the procurement of commercially available off-the-shelf items.

(2) A provision of law that, pursuant to paragraph (3), is properly included on a list referred to in paragraph (1) may not be construed as being applicable to contracts referred to in paragraph (1). Nothing in this section shall be construed to render inapplicable to such contracts any provision of law that is not included on such list.

(3) A provision of law described in subsection (b) of this section shall be included on the list of inapplicable provisions of law required by paragraph (1) unless the Administrator for Federal Procurement Policy makes a written determination that it would not be in the best interest of the United States to exempt such contracts from the applicability of that provision of law. Nothing in this section shall be construed as modifying or superseding, or as being intended to impair or restrict authorities or responsibilities under—

　(A) section 644 of Title 15; or

　(B) bid protest procedures developed under the authority of subchapter V of chapter 35 of Title 31; subsections (e) and (f) of section 2305 of Title 10; or subsections (h) and (i) of section 253b of this title.

(b) Covered law

Except as provided in subsection (a)(3) of this section, the list referred to in subsection (a)(1) of this section shall include each provision of law that, as determined by the Administrator, imposes on persons who have been awarded contracts by the Federal Government for the procurement of commercially available off-the-shelf items Government-unique policies, procedures, requirements, or restrictions for the procurement of property or services, except the following:

　(1) A provision of law that provides for criminal or civil penalties.

　(2) A provision of law that specifically refers to this section and provides that, notwithstanding this section, such provision of law shall be applicable to contracts for the procurement of commercially available off-the-shelf items.

(c) "Commercially available off-the-shelf item" defined

　(1) As used in this section, the term "commercially available off-the-shelf item" means, except as provided in paragraph (2), an item that—

　　(A) is a commercial item (as described in section 403(12)(A) of this title);

　　(B) is sold in substantial quantities in the commercial marketplace; and

　　(C) is offered to the Government, without modification, in the same form in which it is sold in the commercial marketplace.

　(2) The term "commercially available off-the-shelf item" does not include bulk cargo, as defined in section 40102 of Title 46, such as agricultural products and petroleum products.

(Pub.L. 93–400, § 35, as added Pub.L. 104–106, Div. D, Title XLII, § 4203(a), Feb. 10, 1996, 110 Stat. 654, and amended Pub.L. 105–85, Div. A, Title X, § 1073(g)(2)(C), Nov. 18, 1997, 111 Stat. 1906.)

HISTORICAL AND STATUTORY NOTES

Revision Notes and Legislative Reports
   1996 Acts. House Conference Report No. 104–450, see 1996 U.S. Code Cong. and Adm. News, p. 238.

   1997 Acts. House Conference Report No. 105–340 and Statement by President, see 1997 U.S. Code Cong. and Adm. News, p. 2251.

Codifications
   "Section 40102 of Title 46" substituted in subsec. (c)(2) for "section 1702 of Title 46, Appendix" on authority of Pub. L. 109–304, § 18(c), Oct. 6, 2006, 120 Stat. 1709, which completed the codification of T. 46, Shipping, as positive law.

   Another section 35 of the Office of Federal Procurement Policy Act, Pub.L. 93–400, Aug. 30, 1974, 88 Stat. 796, as amended, was added by section 5202(a)

of Pub.L. 104–106 and is set out as section 434 of this title.

Amendments
   1997 Amendments. Subsec. (b)(2). Pub.L. 105–85, § 1073(g)(2)(C), substituted "commercially available" for "commercial".

Effective and Applicability Provisions
   1996 Acts. Section effective Feb. 10, 1996, except as otherwise provided, see section 4401 of Pub.L. 104–106, set out as a note under section 251 of this title.

Coordination with Other Amendments
   Amendments by section 1073 of Pub.L. 105–85 to be treated as having been enacted immediately before the other provisions of Pub.L. 105–85, see section 1073(i) of Pub.L. 105–85, set out as a note under section 5315 of Title 5, Government Organization and Employees.

WESTLAW ELECTRONIC RESEARCH

See Westlaw guide following the Explanation pages of this volume.

§ 431a. Inflation adjustment of acquisition-related dollar thresholds

(a) Requirement for periodic adjustment

   (1) On October 1 of each year that is evenly divisible by five, the Federal Acquisition Regulatory Council shall adjust each acquisition-related dollar threshold provided by law, as described in subsection (c) of this section, to the baseline constant dollar value of that threshold.

   (2) For the purposes of paragraph (1), the baseline constant dollar value—

   (A) for a dollar threshold in effect on October 1, 2000, that was first specified in a law that took effect on or before such date shall be the October 1, 2000, constant dollar value of that dollar threshold; and

   (B) for a dollar threshold specified in a law that takes effect after October 1, 2000, shall be the constant dollar value of that threshold as of the effective date of that dollar threshold pursuant to such law.

(b) Adjustments effective upon publication

   The Federal Acquisition Regulatory Council shall publish a notice of the adjusted dollar thresholds under this section in the Federal

Register. The adjusted dollar thresholds shall take effect on the date of publication.

(c) Acquisition-related dollar thresholds

Except as provided in subsection (d) of this section, the requirement for adjustment under subsection (a) of this section applies to a dollar threshold that is specified in law as a factor in defining the scope of the applicability of a policy, procedure, requirement, or restriction provided in that law to the procurement of property or services by an executive agency, as determined by the Federal Acquisition Regulatory Council.

(d) Excluded thresholds

Subsection (a) of this section does not apply to—

    (1) dollar thresholds in sections 3141 through 3144, 3146, and 3147 of Title 40;

    (2) dollar thresholds in the Service Contract Act of 1965 (41 U.S.C. 351 et seq.); or

    (3) dollar thresholds established by the United States Trade Representative pursuant to title III of the Trade Agreements Act of 1979 (19 U.S.C. 2511 et seq.).

(e) Calculation of adjustments

An adjustment under this section shall—

    (1) be calculated on the basis of changes in the Consumer Price Index for all-urban consumers published monthly by the Department of Labor; and

    (2) be rounded—

        (A) in the case of a dollar threshold that (as in effect on the day before the adjustment) is less than $10,000, to the nearest $500;

        (B) in the case of a dollar threshold that (as in effect on the day before the adjustment) is not less than $10,000, but is less than $100,000, to the nearest $5,000;

        (C) in the case of a dollar threshold that (as in effect on the day before the adjustment) is not less than $100,000, but is less than $1,000,000, to the nearest $50,000; and

        (D) in the case of a dollar threshold that (as in effect on the day before the adjustment) is $1,000,000 or more, to the nearest $500,000.

(f) Petition for inclusion of omitted threshold

    (1) If a dollar threshold adjustable under this section is not included in a notice of adjustment published under subsection (b) of this section, any person may request adjustment of that dollar threshold by submitting a petition for adjustment to the Administrator for Federal Procurement Policy.

(2) Upon receipt of a petition for adjustment of a dollar threshold under paragraph (1), the Administrator shall—

(A) determine, in writing, whether that dollar threshold is required to be adjusted under this section; and

(B) if so, shall publish in the Federal Register a revised notice of the adjusted dollar thresholds under this section that includes the adjustment of the dollar threshold covered by the petition.

(3) The adjustment of a dollar threshold pursuant to a petition under this subsection shall take effect on the date of the publication of the revised notice adding the adjustment of that dollar threshold under paragraph (2)(B).

(Pub.L. 93–400, § 35A, as added Pub.L. 108–375, Div. A, Title VIII, § 807(a), Oct. 28, 2004, 118 Stat. 2010.)

HISTORICAL AND STATUTORY NOTES

Revision Notes and Legislative Reports
2004 Acts. House Conference Report No. 108–767, see 2004 U.S. Code Cong. and Adm. News, p. 1961.

Statement by President, see 2004 U.S. Code Cong. and Adm. News, p. S37.

References in Text
The Service Contract Act of 1965, referred to in subsec. (d)(2), is Pub.L. 89–286, Oct. 22, 1965, 79 Stat. 1034, as amended, which enacted chapter 6 of this title, 41 U.S.C.A. § 351 et seq.

Title III of the Trade Agreements Act of 1979, referred to in subsec. (d)(3), is Pub.L. 96–39, Title III, § 301 et seq., July 26, 1979, 93 Stat. 236, as amended, which is classified to subchapter I of chapter 13 of Title 19, 19 U.S.C.A. § 2511 et seq.

Relationship to Other Inflation Adjustment Authorities
Pub.L. 108–375, Div. A, Title VIII, § 807(c), Oct. 28, 2004. 118 Stat. 2011, provided that:

"**(1)** Section 35A of the Office of Federal Procurement Policy Act, as added by subsection (a) [Pub.L. 108–375, Div. A, Title VIII, § 807(a), which enacted this section], supersedes the applicability of any other provision of law that provides for the adjustment of a dollar threshold that is adjustable under such section.

"**(2)** After the date of the enactment of this Act [Oct. 28, 2004], a dollar threshold adjustable under section 35A of the Office of Federal Procurement Policy Act, as added by subsection (a) [this section], shall be adjusted only as provided under that section."

LIBRARY REFERENCES

American Digest System
United States ⊙64.5.
Key Number System Topic No. 393.

WESTLAW ELECTRONIC RESEARCH

See Westlaw guide following the Explanation pages of this volume.

§ 432. Value engineering

(a) In general

Each executive agency shall establish and maintain cost-effective value engineering procedures and processes.

(b) "Value engineering" defined

As used in this section, the term "value engineering" means an analysis of the functions of a program, project, system, product, item of equipment, building, facility, service, or supply of an executive agency, performed by qualified agency or contractor personnel, directed at improving performance, reliability, quality, safety, and life cycle costs.

(Pub.L. 93–400, § 36, as added Pub.L. 104–106, Div. D, Title XLIII, § 4306(a), Feb. 10, 1996, 110 Stat. 665.)

HISTORICAL AND STATUTORY NOTES

Revision Notes and Legislative Reports
  1996 Acts. House Conference Report No. 104–450, see 1996 U.S. Code Cong. and Adm. News, p. 238.

Effective and Applicability Provisions
  1996 Acts. Section effective Feb. 10, 1996, except as otherwise provided, see section 4401 of Pub.L. 104–106, set out as a note under section 251 of this title.

LIBRARY REFERENCES

American Digest System
  United States ⌾64.45.
  Key Number System Topic No. 393.

WESTLAW ELECTRONIC RESEARCH

See Westlaw guide following the Explanation pages of this volume.

§ 433 Acquisition workforce

(a) Applicability

Except as provided in subsection (h)(3) of this section, this section does not apply to an executive agency that is subject to chapter 87 of Title 10.

(b) Management policies

(1) Policies and procedures

The head of each executive agency, after consultation with the Administrator for Federal Procurement Policy, shall establish policies and procedures for the effective management (including accession, education, training, career development, and performance incentives) of the acquisition workforce of the agency. The development of acquisition workforce policies under this section shall be carried out consistent with the merit system principles set forth in section 2301(b) of Title 5.

(2) Uniform implementation

The head of each executive agency shall ensure that, to the maximum extent practicable, acquisition workforce policies and procedures established are uniform in their implementation throughout the agency.

(3) Government-wide policies and evaluation

The Administrator shall issue policies to promote uniform implementation of this section by executive agencies, with due regard for differences in program requirements among agencies that may be appropriate and warranted in view of the agency mission. The Administrator shall coordinate with the Deputy Director for Management of the Office of Management and Budget to ensure that such policies are consistent with the policies and procedures established and enhanced system of incentives provided pursuant to section 5051(c) of the Federal Acquisition Streamlining Act of 1994 (41 U.S.C. 263 note). The Administrator shall evaluate the implementation of the provisions of this section by executive agencies.

(c) Senior procurement executive authorities and responsibilities

Subject to the authority, direction, and control of the head of an executive agency, the senior procurement executive of the agency shall carry out all powers, functions, and duties of the head of the agency with respect to implementation of this section. The senior procurement executive shall ensure that the policies of the head of the executive agency established in accordance with this section are implemented throughout the agency.

(d) Management information systems

The Administrator shall ensure that the heads of executive agencies collect and maintain standardized information on the acquisition workforce related to implementation of this section. To the maximum extent practicable, such data requirements shall conform to standards established by the Office of Personnel Management for the Central Personnel Data File.

(e) Applicability to acquisition workforce

The programs established by this section shall apply to the acquisition workforce of each executive agency. For purposes of this section, the acquisition workforce of an agency consists of all employees serving in acquisition positions listed in subsection (g)(1)(A) of this section.

(f) Career development

(1) Career paths

The head of each executive agency shall ensure that appropriate career paths for personnel who desire to pursue careers in acquisition are identified in terms of the education, training, experience, and assignments necessary for career progression to the most senior acquisition positions. The head of each executive agency shall make information available on such career paths.

(2) Critical duties and tasks

For each career path, the head of each executive agency shall identify the critical acquisition-related duties and tasks in which, at minimum, employees of the agency in the career path shall be competent to perform at full performance grade levels. For this purpose, the head of the executive agency shall provide appropriate coverage of the critical duties and tasks identified by the Director of the Federal Acquisition Institute.

(3) Mandatory training and education

For each career path, the head of each executive agency shall establish requirements for the completion of course work and related on-the-job training in the critical acquisition-related duties and tasks of the career path. The head of each executive agency shall also encourage employees to maintain the currency of their acquisition knowledge and generally enhance their knowledge of related acquisition management disciplines through academic programs and other self-developmental activities.

(4) Performance incentives

The head of each executive agency shall provide for an enhanced system of incentives for the encouragement of excellence in the acquisition workforce which rewards performance of employees that contribute to achieving the agency's performance goals. The system of incentives shall include provisions that—

(A) relate pay to performance (including the extent to which the performance of personnel in such workforce contributes to achieving the cost goals, schedule goals, and performance goals established for acquisition programs pursuant to section 263(b) of this title); and

(B) provide for consideration, in personnel evaluations and promotion decisions, of the extent to which the performance of personnel in such workforce contributes to achieving such cost goals, schedule goals, and performance goals.

(g) Qualification requirements

(1) In general

(A) Subject to paragraph (2), the Administrator shall establish qualification requirements, including education requirements, for the following positions:

(i) Entry-level positions in the General Schedule Contracting series(GS–1102).

(ii) Senior positions in the General Schedule Contracting series (GS–1102).

(iii) All positions in the General Schedule Purchasing series (GS–1105).

(iv) Positions in other General Schedule series in which significant acquisition-related functions are performed.

(B) Subject to paragraph (2), the Administrator shall prescribe the manner and extent to which such qualification requirements shall apply to any person serving in a position described in subparagraph (A) at the time such requirements are established.

(2) Relationship to requirements applicable to defense acquisition workforce

The Administrator shall establish qualification requirements and make prescriptions under paragraph (1) that are comparable to those established for the same or equivalent positions pursuant to chapter 87 of Title 10 with appropriate modifications.

(3) Approval of requirements

The Administrator shall submit any requirement established or prescription made under paragraph (1) to the Director of the Office of Personnel Management for approval. If the Director does not disapprove a requirement or prescription within 30 days after the date on which the Director receives it, the requirement or prescription is deemed to be approved by the Director.

(h) Education and training

(1) Funding levels

(A) The head of an executive agency shall set forth separately the funding levels requested for education and training of the acquisition workforce in the budget justification documents submitted in support of the President's budget submitted to Congress under section 1105 of Title 31.

(B) Funds appropriated for education and training under this section may not be obligated for any other purpose.

(2) Tuition assistance

The head of an executive agency may provide tuition reimbursement in education (including a full-time course of study leading to a degree) in accordance with section 4107 of Title 5 for personnel serving in acquisition positions in the agency.

(3) Acquisition workforce training fund

(A) The Administrator of General Services shall establish an acquisition workforce training fund. The Administrator shall manage the fund through the Federal Acquisition Institute to support the training of the acquisition workforce of the executive agencies, except as provided in subparagraph (D). The Administrator shall consult with the Administrator for Federal Procurement Policy in managing the fund.

(B) There shall be credited to the acquisition workforce training fund 5 percent of the fees collected by executive agencies (other than the Department of Defense) under the following contracts:

(i) Governmentwide task and delivery-order contracts entered into under sections 253h and 253i of this title.

(ii) Governmentwide contracts for the acquisition of information technology as defined in section 11101 of Title 40, and multiagency acquisition contracts for such technology authorized by section 11314 of Title 40.

(iii) Multiple–award schedule contracts entered into by the Administrator of General Services.

(C) The head of an executive agency that administers a contract described in subparagraph (B) shall remit to the General Services Administration the amount required to be credited to the fund with respect to such contract at the end of each quarter of the fiscal year.

(D) The Administrator of General Services shall transfer to the Secretary of Defense fees collected from the Department of Defense pursuant to subparagraph (B), to be used by the Defense Acquisition University for purposes of acquisition workforce training.

(E) The Administrator of General Services, through the Office of Federal Acquisition Policy, shall ensure that funds collected for training under this section are not used for any purpose other than the purpose specified in subparagraph (A).

(F) Amounts credited to the fund shall be in addition to funds requested and appropriated for education and training referred to in paragraph (1).

(G) Amounts credited to the fund shall remain available to be expended only in the fiscal year for which credited and the two succeeding fiscal years.

(H) This paragraph shall cease to be effective five years after November 24, 2003.

(i) Provisions relating to reemployment

(1) Policies and procedures

The head of each executive agency, after consultation with the Administrator and the Director of the Office of Personnel Management, shall establish policies and procedures under which the agency head may reemploy in an acquisition-related position (as described in subsection (g)(1)(A) of this section) an individual receiving an annuity from the Civil Service Retirement and Disability Fund, on the basis of such individual's service, without discontinuing such annuity. The head of each executive agency shall keep the Administrator informed of the agency's use of this authority.

(2) Service not subject to CSRs or FERs

An individual so reemployed shall not be considered an employee for the purposes of chapter 83 or 84 of title 5, United States Code.

(3) Criteria for exercise of authority

Polices and procedures established pursuant to this subsection shall authorize the head of the executive agency, on a case-by-case basis, to continue an annuity if—

(A) the unusually high or unique qualifications of an individual receiving an annuity from the Civil Service Retirement and Disability Fund on the basis of such individual's service,

(B) the exceptional difficulty in recruiting or retaining a qualified employee, or

(C) a temporary emergency hiring need, makes the reemployment of an individual essential.

(4) Reporting requirement

The Administrator shall submit annually to the Committee on Government Reform of the House of Representatives and the Committee on Homeland Security and Governmental Affairs of the Senate a report on the use of the authority under this subsection, including the number of employees reemployed under authority of this subsection.

(5) Sunset provision

The authority under this subsection shall expire on December 31, 2011.

(Pub.L. 93–400, § 37, as added Pub.L. 104–106, Div. D, Title XLIII, § 4307(a)(1), Feb. 10, 1996, 110 Stat. 666, and amended Pub.L. 108–136, Div. A, Title XIV, § 1412(b), Nov. 24, 2003, 117 Stat. 1664; Pub.L. 109–163, Div. A, Title VIII, § 821(a), (b)(1), Jan. 6, 2006, 119 Stat. 3386; Pub.L. 109–313, § 4, Oct. 6, 2006, 120 Stat. 1737.)

Termination of Subsec. (h)(3)

Subsec. (h)(3) to cease to be effective five years after Nov. 24, 2003, see subsec. (h)(3)(H).

HISTORICAL AND STATUTORY NOTES

Revision Notes and Legislative Reports
  1996 Acts. House Conference Report No. 104–450, see 1996 U.S. Code Cong. and Adm. News, p. 238.

  2003 Acts. House Conference Report No. 108–354 and Statement by President, see 2003 U.S. Code Cong. and Adm. News, p. 1407.

  2006 Acts. House Conference Report No. 109–360, see 2005 U.S. Code Cong. and Adm. News, p. 1678.

  Statement by President, see 2005 U.S. Code Cong. and Adm. News, p. S54.

  House Report No. 109–91, see 2006 U.S. Code Cong. and Adm. News, p. 1098.

References in Text
  Section 5051(c) of the Federal Acquisition Streamlining Act of 1994, referred to in subsec. (b)(3), is section 5051(c) of Pub.L. 103–355, Title V, Oct. 13, 1994, 108 Stat. 3351, which is set out as a note under section 263 of this title.

  The General Schedule, referred to in subsec. (g)(1)(A), is set out under 5 U.S.C.A. § 5332.

  Chapter 83 or 84 of title 5, referred to in subsec. (i)(2), are Retirement, 5 U.S.C.A. § 8301 et seq., and Federal Employees' Retirement System, 5 U.S.C.A. § 8401 et seq.

Amendments
  2006 Amendments. Subsec. (a). Pub.L. 109–163, § 821(b)(1), substituted "Except as provided in subsection (h)(3) of this section, this section" for "This section".

  Subsec. (h)(3)(A). Pub.L. 109–163, § 821(a)(1), struck out "other than the Department of Defense" following "executive agencies" and inserted ", except as provided in subparagraph (D)".

  Subsec. (h)(3)(D). Pub.L. 109–163, § 821(a)(2), added subpar. (D) and redesignated former subpar. (D) as (E).

  Subsec. (h)(3)(E). Pub.L. 109–163, § 821(a)(2), redesignated former subpar. (D) as (E). Former subpar. (E) was redesignated as (F).

  Subsec. (h)(3)(F). Pub.L. 109–163, § 821(a)(2), redesignated former subpar. (E) as (F). Former subpar. (F) was redesignated as (G).

  Subsec. (h)(3)(G). Pub.L. 109–163, § 821(a)(2), redesignated former subpar. (F) as (G). Former subpar. (G) was redesignated as (H).

  Subsec. (h)(3)(H). Pub.L. 109–163, § 821(a)(2), redesignated former subpar. (G) as subpar. (H).

  Subsec. (i). Pub.L. 109–313, § 4, added subsec. (i).

  2003 Amendments. Subsec. (h)(3). Pub.L. 108–136, § 1412(a), added par. (3).

Effective and Applicability Provisions
  2006 Acts. Amendments by Pub.L. 109–313 effective 60 days after Oct. 6, 2006, see Pub.L. 109–313, § 6, set out as a note under 5 U.S.C.A. § 5316.

Pub.L. 109–163, Div. A, Title VIII, § 821(d), Jan. 6, 2006, 119 Stat. 3386, provided that: "The amendments made by this section [amending subsecs. (a) and (h)(3) of this section, enacting provisions set out as a note under this section, and repealing provisions set out as a note under this section] shall apply with respect to fees collected under contracts described in section 37(h)(3)(B) of the Office of Federal Procurement Policy Act (41 U.S.C. 433(h)(3)(B) [subsec. (h)(3)(B) of this section]) after the date of the enactment of this Act [Jan. 6, 2006]."

1996 Acts. Section effective Feb. 10, 1996, except as otherwise provided, see section 4401 of Pub.L. 104–106, set out as a note under section 251 of this title.

Defense Acquisition University Funding
Pub.L. 109–163, Div. A, Title VIII, § 821(c), Jan. 6, 2006, 119 Stat. 3386, provided that: "Amounts transferred under section 37(h)(3)(D) of the Office of Federal Procurement Policy Act as amended by subsection (a) [Pub.L. 109–163, Div. A, Title VIII, § 821(a), Jan. 6, 2006, 119 Stat. 3386, which amended subsec. (h)(3) of this section] for use by the Defense Acquisition University shall be in addition to other amounts authorized for the University."

Acquisition Workforce Training Fund
Pub.L. 108–136, Div. A, Title XIV, § 1412(a), Nov. 24, 2003, 117 Stat. 1664, provided that:

"**(a) Purposes.**—The purposes of this section [this note] are to ensure that the Federal acquisition workforce—

"**(1)** adapts to fundamental changes in the nature of Federal Government acquisition of property and services associated with the changing roles of the Federal Government; and

"**(2)** acquires new skills and a new perspective to enable it to contribute effectively in the changing environment of the 21st century."

Department of Defense Acquisition Workforce—Exception
Pub.L. 108–136, Div. A, Title XIV, § 1412(c), Nov. 24, 2003, 117 Stat. 1665, which provided an exception for the acquisition workforce of the Department of Defense and provided for a reduction of fees charged to the Department of Defense, was repealed by Pub.L. 109–163, Div. A, Title VIII, § 821(b)(2), Jan. 6, 2006, 119 Stat. 3386.

Acquisition Workforce Recruitment Program
Pub.L. 108–136, Div. A, Title XVI, § 1413, Nov. 24, 2003, 117 Stat. 1665, provided that:

"**(a) Determination of shortage category positions.**—For purposes of sections 3304, 5333, and 5753 of title 5, United States Code, the head of a department or agency of the United States (other than the Secretary of Defense) may determine, under regulations prescribed by the Office of Personnel Management, that certain Federal acquisition positions (as described in section 37(g)(1)(A) of the Office of Federal Procurement Policy Act (41 U.S.C. 433(g)(1)(A)) [subsec. (g)(1)(A) of this section] are shortage category positions in order to use the authorities in those sections to recruit and appoint highly qualified persons directly to such positions in the department or agency.

"**(b) Termination of authority.**—The head of a department or agency may not appoint a person to a position of employment under this section after September 30, 2007.

"**(c) Report.**—Not later than March 31, 2007, the Director of the Office of Personnel Management, in consultation with the Administrator for Federal Procurement Policy, shall submit to Congress a report on the implementation of this section [this note]. The report shall include—

"**(1)** a list of the departments and agencies that exercised the authority provided in this section [this note], and whether the exercise of the authority was carried out in accordance with the regulations prescribed by the Office of Personnel Management;

"**(2)** the Director's assessment of the efficacy of the exercise of the authority provided in this section [this note] in attracting employees with unusually high qualifications to the acquisition workforce; and

"**(3)** any recommendations considered appropriate by the Director on whether the authority to carry out the program should be extended."

Architectural and Engineering Acquisition Workforce
Pub.L. 108–136, Div. A, Title XIV, § 1414, Nov. 24, 2003, 117 Stat. 1666, provided that:

"The Administrator for Federal Procurement Policy, in consultation with the

Secretary of Defense, the Administrator of General Services, and the Director of the Office of Personnel Management, shall develop and implement a plan to ensure that the Federal Government maintains the necessary capability with respect to the acquisition of architectural and engineering services to—

"(1) ensure that Federal Government employees have the expertise to determine agency requirements for such services;

"(2) establish priorities and programs (including acquisition plans);

"(3) establish professional standards;

"(4) develop scopes of work; and

"(5) award and administer contracts for such services."

LIBRARY REFERENCES

American Digest System
United States ☞41.
Key Number System Topic No. 393.

WESTLAW ELECTRONIC RESEARCH

See Westlaw guide following the Explanation pages of this volume.

§ 434. Modular contracting for information technology

(a) In general

The head of an executive agency should, to the maximum extent practicable, use modular contracting for an acquisition of a major system of information technology.

(b) Modular contracting described

Under modular contracting, an executive agency's need for a system is satisfied in successive acquisitions of interoperable increments. Each increment complies with common or commercially accepted standards applicable to information technology so that the increments are compatible with other increments of information technology comprising the system.

(c) Implementation

The Federal Acquisition Regulation shall provide that—

(1) under the modular contracting process, an acquisition of a major system of information technology may be divided into several smaller acquisition increments that—

(A) are easier to manage individually than would be one comprehensive acquisition;

(B) address complex information technology objectives incrementally in order to enhance the likelihood of achieving workable solutions for attainment of those objectives;

(C) provide for delivery, implementation, and testing of workable systems or solutions in discrete increments each of which comprises a system or solution that is not dependent on any subsequent increment in order to perform its principal functions; and

    (D) provide an opportunity for subsequent increments of the acquisition to take advantage of any evolution in technology or needs that occur during conduct of the earlier increments;

    (2) a contract for an increment of an information technology acquisition should, to the maximum extent practicable, be awarded within 180 days after the date on which the solicitation is issued and, if the contract for that increment cannot be awarded within such period, the increment should be considered for cancellation; and

    (3) the information technology provided for in a contract for acquisition of information technology should be delivered within 18 months after the date on which the solicitation resulting in award of the contract was issued.

(Pub.L. 93–400, § 38, formerly § 35, as added Pub.L. 104–106, Div. E, Title LII, § 5202(a), Feb. 10, 1996, 110 Stat. 690; renumbered § 38, Pub.L. 104–201, Div. A, Title X, § 1074(d)(1), Sept. 23, 1996, 110 Stat. 2660.)

HISTORICAL AND STATUTORY NOTES

Revision Notes and Legislative Reports
1996 Acts. House Conference Report No. 104–450, see 1996 U.S. Code Cong. and Adm. News, p. 238.

House Report No. 104–563 and House Conference Report No. 104–724, see 1996 U.S. Code Cong. and Adm. News, p. 2948.

Codifications
Another section 35 of the Office of Federal Procurement Policy Act, Pub.L.

93–400, Aug. 30, 1974, 88 Stat. 796, as amended, was added by section 4203(a) of Pub.L. 104–106 and is set out as section 431 of this title.

Effective and Applicability Provisions
1996 Acts. Pub.L. 104–106, Div. E, Title LVII, § 5701, Feb. 10, 1996, 110 Stat. 702, which provided that this section was effective 180 days after Feb. 10, 1996, was repealed by Pub.L. 107–217, § 6(b), Aug. 21, 2002, 116 Stat. 1325.

LIBRARY REFERENCES

American Digest System
United States ⚮64.5.
Key Number System Topic No. 393.

WESTLAW ELECTRONIC RESEARCH

See Westlaw guide following the Explanation pages of this volume.

§ 435. Levels of compensation of certain contractor personnel not allowable as costs under certain contracts

(a) Determination required

For purposes of section 2324(e)(1)(P) of Title 10 and section 256(e)(1)(P) of this title, the Administrator shall review commercially available surveys of executive compensation and, on the basis of the results of the review, determine a benchmark compensation amount to apply for each fiscal year. In making determinations under this subsection the Administrator shall consult with the Director of the Defense Contract Audit Agency and such other officials of executive agencies as the Administrator considers appropriate.

(b) Benchmark compensation amount

The benchmark compensation amount applicable for a fiscal year is the median amount of the compensation provided for all senior executives of all benchmark corporations for the most recent year for which data is available at the time the determination under subsection (a) of this section is made.

(c) Definitions

In this section:

(1) The term "compensation", for a fiscal year, means the total amount of wages, salary, bonuses and deferred compensation for the fiscal year, whether paid, earned, or otherwise accruing, as recorded in an employer's cost accounting records for the fiscal year.

(2) The term "senior executives", with respect to a contractor, means the five most highly compensated employees in management positions at each home office and each segment of the contractor.

(3) The term "benchmark corporation", with respect to a fiscal year, means a publicly-owned United States corporation that has annual sales in excess of $50,000,000 for the fiscal year.

(4) The term "publicly-owned United States corporation" means a corporation organized under the laws of a State of the United States, the District of Columbia, the Commonwealth of Puerto Rico, or a possession of the United States the voting stock of which is publicly traded.

(5) The term "fiscal year" means a fiscal year established by a contractor for accounting purposes.

(Pub.L. 93–400, § 39, as added Pub.L. 105–85, Div. A, Title VIII, § 808(c)(1), Nov. 18, 1997, 111 Stat. 1837, and amended Pub.L. 105–261, Div. A, Title VIII, § 804(c)(1), Oct. 17, 1998, 112 Stat. 2083.)

HISTORICAL AND STATUTORY NOTES

Revision Notes and Legislative Reports
1997 Acts. House Conference Report No. 105–340 and Statement by President, see 1997 U.S. Code Cong. and Adm. News, p. 2251.

1998 Acts. House Conference Report No. 105–736 and Statement by President, see 1998 U.S. Code Cong. and Adm. News, p. 513.

Codifications

Another section 39 of the Office of Federal Procurement Policy Act, Pub.L. 93–400, was added by Pub.L. 105–277, Div. I, Title III, § 308, Oct. 21, 1998, 112 Stat. 2681–879, and is classified to section 436 of this title.

Amendments

1998 Amendments. Subsec. (c)(2). Pub.L. 105–261, § 804(c)(1), revised par. (2). Prior to amendment, par. (2) read as follows:

"**(2)** The term 'senior executive', with respect to a corporation, means—

"**(A)** the chief executive officer of the corporation or any individual acting in a similar capacity for the corporation;

"**(B)** the four most highly compensated employees in management positions of the corporation other than the chief executive officer; and

"**(C)** in the case of a corporation that has components which report directly to the corporate headquarters, the five most highly compensated individuals in management positions at each such component."

Effective Date of 1998 Amendments

Amendment by section 804 of Pub.L. 105–261, which, among other changes, amended this section and provisions set out as notes under this section, to apply with respect to costs of compensation of senior executives incurred after Jan. 1, 1999, under covered contracts (as defined in section 2324(*l*) of Title 10 and section 256(*l*) of this title) entered into before, on, or after Oct. 17, 1998, see section 804(d) of Pub.L. 105–261, set out as a note under section 2324 of Title 10.

Effective Date of 1997 Amendments

Section 808(e) of Pub.L. 105–85 provided that: "The amendments made by this section [enacting this section, amending section 256 of this title and section 2324 of Title 10, and enacting provisions set out as notes under this section] shall—

"**(1)** take effect on the date that is 90 days after the date of the enactment of this Act [Nov. 18, 1997]; and

"**(2)** apply with respect to costs of compensation incurred after January 1, 1998, under covered contracts entered into before, on, or after the date of the enactment of this Act [Nov. 18, 1997]."

Definition of Certain Terms for Purposes of Section 808 of Pub.L. 105–85

Section 808(g) of Pub.L. 105–85, as amended Pub.L. 105–261, Div. A, Title VIII, § 804(c)(2), Oct. 17, 1998, 112 Stat. 2083, provided that: "In this section:

"**(1)** The term 'covered contract' has the meaning given such term in section 2324(*l*) of title 10, United States Code [section 2324(*l*) of Title 10], and section 306(*l*) of the Federal Property and Administrative Services Act of 1949 (41 U.S.C. 256(*l*)).

"**(2)** The terms 'compensation' and 'senior executives' have the meanings given such terms in section 2324(*l*) of title 10, United States Code [section 2324(*l*) of Title 10], and section 306(m) of the Federal Property and Administrative Services Act of 1949 [section 256 of this title]."

Exclusive Applicability of Provisions Limiting Allowability of Compensation for Certain Contractor Personnel

Section 808(f) of Pub.L. 105–85 provided that: "Notwithstanding any other provision of law, no other limitation in law on the allowability of costs of compensation of senior executives under covered contracts shall apply to such costs of compensation incurred after January 1, 1998."

Promulgation of Regulations

Section 808(d) of Pub.L. 105–85 provided that: "Regulations implementing the amendments made by this section [enacting this section, amending section 256 of this title and section 2324 of Title 10, and enacting provisions set out as notes under this section] shall be published in the Federal Register not later than the effective date of the amendments under subsection (e) [set out as a note under this section]."

LIBRARY REFERENCES

American Digest System

United States ⬤⇒70(18).

Key Number System Topic No. 393.

WESTLAW ELECTRONIC RESEARCH
See Westlaw guide following the Explanation pages of this volume.

§ 436. Protection of constitutional rights of contractors

(a) Prohibition

A contractor may not be required, as a condition for entering into a contract with the Federal Government, to waive any right under the Constitution for any purpose related to Chemical Weapons Convention Implementation Act of 1997 [22 U.S.C.A. § 6701 et seq.] or the Chemical Weapons Convention (as defined in section 3 of such Act [22 U.S.C.A. § 6701]).

(b) Construction

Nothing in subsection (a) of this section shall be construed to prohibit an executive agency from including in a contract a clause that requires the contractor to permit inspections for the purpose of ensuring that the contractor is performing the contract in accordance with the provisions of the contract.

(Pub.L. 93–400, § 40, formerly § 39, as added Pub.L. 105–277, Div. I, Title III, § 308, Oct. 21, 1998, 112 Stat. 2681–879; renumbered § 40, Pub.L. 108–136, Div. A, Title IV, § 1431(d)(2), Nov. 24, 2003, 117 Stat. 1672.)

HISTORICAL AND STATUTORY NOTES

Revision Notes and Legislative Reports
1998 Acts. Statement by President, see 1998 U.S. Code Cong. and Adm. News, p. 582.

2003 Acts. House Conference Report No. 108–354 and Statement by President, see 2003 U.S. Code Cong. and Adm. News, p. 1407.

References in Text
The Chemical Weapons Convention Implementation Act of 1997, referred to in subsec. (a) of the text, probably means the Chemical Weapons Convention Implementation Act of 1998, which is Pub.L. 105–277, Div. I, Oct. 21, 1998, 112 Stat. 2681–879, which enacted this section. For complete classification, see Tables.

LIBRARY REFERENCES

American Digest System
United States ⬾64.5.
Key Number System Topic No. 393.

WESTLAW ELECTRONIC RESEARCH
See Westlaw guide following the Explanation pages of this volume.

§ 437. Incentives for efficient performance of services contracts

(a) Incentive for use of performance-based services contracts

A performance-based contract for the procurement of services entered into by an executive agency or a performance-based task order for services issued by an executive agency may be treated as a contract for the procurement of commercial items if—

(1) the value of the contract or task order is estimated not to exceed $25,000,000;

(2) the contract or task order sets forth specifically each task to be performed and, for each task—

(A) defines the task in measurable, mission-related terms;

(B) identifies the specific end products or output to be achieved; and

(C) contains firm, fixed prices for specific tasks to be performed or outcomes to be achieved; and

(3) the source of the services provides similar services to the general public under terms and conditions similar to those offered to the Federal Government.

(b) Regulations

The regulations implementing this section shall require agencies to collect and maintain reliable data sufficient to identify the contracts or task orders treated as contracts for commercial items using the authority of this section. The data may be collected using the Federal Procurement Data System or other reporting mechanism.

(c) Report

Not later than two years after November 24, 2003, the Director of the Office of Management and Budget shall prepare and submit to the Committees on Governmental Affairs and on Armed Services of the Senate and the Committees on Government Reform and on Armed Services of the House of Representatives a report on the contracts or task orders treated as contracts for commercial items using the authority of this section. The report shall include data on the use of such authority both government-wide and for each department and agency.

(d) Expiration

The authority under this section shall expire 10 years after November 24, 2003.

(Pub.L. 93–400, § 41, as added Pub.L. 108–136, Div. A, Title XIV, § 1431(a), Nov. 24, 2003, 117 Stat. 1671.)

Expiration of Section

Authority under this section expires 10 years after Nov. 24, 2003, see subsec. (d).

HISTORICAL AND STATUTORY NOTES

Revision Notes and Legislative Reports   see 2003 U.S. Code Cong. and Adm.
2003 Acts. House Conference Report   News, p. 1407.
No. 108–354 and Statement by President,

LIBRARY REFERENCES

American Digest System
   United States ⚮70(6.1), 73.
   Key Number System Topic No. 393.

WESTLAW ELECTRONIC RESEARCH

See Westlaw guide following the Explanation pages of this volume.

§ 438. Civilian Board of Contract Appeals

(a) Board established

There is established in the General Services Administration a board of contract appeals to be known as the Civilian Board of Contract Appeals (in this section referred to as the "Civilian Board").

(b) Membership

(1) Appointment

(A) The Civilian Board shall consist of members appointed by the Administrator of General Services (in consultation with the Administrator for Federal Procurement Policy) from a register of applicants maintained by the Administrator of General Services, in accordance with rules issued by the Administrator of General Services (in consultation with the Administrator for Federal Procurement Policy) for establishing and maintaining a register of eligible applicants and selecting Civilian Board members. The Administrator of General Services shall appoint a member without regard to political affiliation and solely on the basis of the professional qualifications required to perform the duties and responsibilities of a Civilian Board member.

(B) The members of the Civilian Board shall be selected and appointed to serve in the same manner as administrative law judges appointed pursuant to section 3105 of Title 5, with an additional requirement that such members shall have had not fewer than five years of experience in public contract law.

(C) Notwithstanding subparagraph (B) and subject to paragraph (2), the following persons shall serve as Civilian Board members: any full-time member of any agency board of contract appeals other than the Armed Services Board of Contract Appeals, the Postal Service Board of Contract Appeals, and the board of contract appeals of the Tennessee Valley Authority serving as such on the day before the effective date of this section.

(2) Removal

Members of the Civilian Board shall be subject to removal in the same manner as administrative law judges, as provided in section 7521 of Title 5.

(3) Compensation

Compensation for members of the Civilian Board shall be determined under section 5372a of Title 5.

(c) Functions

(1) In general

The Civilian Board shall have jurisdiction as provided by section 607(d) of this title.

(2) Additional jurisdiction

The Civilian Board may, with the concurrence of the Federal agency or agencies affected—

(A) assume jurisdiction over any additional category of laws or disputes over which an agency board of contract appeals established pursuant to section 607 of this title exercised jurisdiction before the effective date of this section; and

(B) assume any other functions performed by such a board before such effective date on behalf of such agencies.

(Pub.L. 93–400, § 42, as added Pub.L. 109–163, Div. A, Title VIII, § 847(a), Jan. 6, 2006, 119 Stat. 3391.)

HISTORICAL AND STATUTORY NOTES

Revision Notes and Legislative Reports
2006 Acts. House Conference Report No. 109–360, see 2005 U.S. Code Cong. and Adm. News, p. 1678.

Statement by President, see 2005 U.S. Code Cong. and Adm. News, p. S54.

References in Text
The effective date of this section, referred to in subsecs. (b)(1)(C), (c)(2), is

one year after Jan. 6, 2006, see Pub.L. 109–163, § 847(g), set out as a note under 5 U.S.C.A. § 5372a.

Effective and Applicability Provisions
2006 Acts. Enactment of section by Pub.L. 109–163, § 847, effective 1 year after Jan. 6, 2006, see Pub.L. 109–163, § 847(g), set out as a note under 5 U.S.C.A. § 5372a.

LIBRARY REFERENCES

American Digest System
United States ☞73(15).
Key Number System Topic No. 393.

WESTLAW ELECTRONIC RESEARCH

See Westlaw guide following the Explanation pages of this volume.

CHAPTER 8—FEDERAL GRANTS AND COOPERATIVE AGREEMENTS

§§ 501 to 509. Repealed. Pub.L. 97–258, § 5(b), Sept. 13, 1982, 96 Stat. 1083

HISTORICAL AND STATUTORY NOTES

Section 501, Pub.L. 95–224, § 2, Feb. 3, 1978, 92 Stat. 3, set out the Congressional findings and statement of purposes in enacting the Federal Grant and Cooperative Agreement Act of 1977 [this chapter]. Sections 1 and 10(b) of Pub.L. 95–224, setting out the short title provisions and savings provisions respectively of that Act, were set out as notes under this section, and were repealed by Pub.L. 97–258, § 5(b), Sept. 13, 1982, 96 Stat. 1083. See section 6301 of Title 31, Money and Finance. Section 10(d) of Pub.L. 95–224, as amended by Pub.L. 97–162, Apr. 1, 1982, 96 Stat. 23, setting out the excepted transactions provisions of that Act was set out as a note under this section, and was repealed by Pub.L. 97–258, § 5(b), Sept. 13, 1982, 96 Stat. 1083. See section 6307(2) of Title 31.

Section 502, Pub.L. 95–224, § 3, Feb. 3, 1978, 92 Stat. 4, defined the terms "State government", "local government", "other recipient", "executive agency", and "grant or cooperative agreement". See section 6302 of Title 31, Money and Finance.

Section 503, Pub.L. 95–224, § 4, Feb. 3, 1978, 92 Stat. 4, provided for the use of procurement contracts by executive agencies. See section 6303 of Title 31, Money and Finance.

Section 504, Pub.L. 95–224, § 5, Feb. 3, 1978, 92 Stat. 4, provided for the use of grant agreements by executive agencies. See section 6304 of Title 31, Money and Finance.

Section 505, Pub.L. 95–224, § 6, Feb. 3, 1978, 92 Stat. 5, provided for the use of cooperative agreements by executive agencies. See section 6305 of Title 31, Money and Finance.

Section 506, Pub.L. 95–224, § 7, Feb. 3, 1978, 92 Stat. 5, pertained to required and discretionary authorities. See section 6306 of Title 31, Money and Finance.

Section 507, Pub.L. 95–224, § 8, Feb. 3, 1978, 92 Stat. 5, directed the Director of the Office of Management and Budget to undertake a study to develop a better understanding of alternate means of implementing Federal assistance programs.

Section 508, Pub.L. 95–224, § 9, Feb. 3, 1978, 92 Stat. 6, authorized the Director of the Office of Management and Budget to issue supplemental interpretive guidelines to promote consistent and efficient use of contracts, grant agreements, and cooperative agreements. See section 6307 of Title 31, Money and Finance.

Section 509, Pub.L. 95–224, § 10(c), Feb. 3, 1978, 92 Stat. 6, related to the use of multiple relationships for different components of jointly funded projects. See section 6308 of Title 31, Money and Finance.

CHAPTER 9—CONTRACT DISPUTES

CROSS REFERENCES

Claim pertaining to validity of proprietary data restrictions considered claim within meaning of this chapter, see 41 USCA § 253d.
Indian Self–Determination Act contracts regulations promulgated by Secretary of Health and Human Services, see 25 USCA § 450k.

LAW REVIEW AND JOURNAL COMMENTARIES

Representing the federal government contractor. James S. Ganther, 70 Fla.B.J. 58 (April 1996).

WESTLAW COMPUTER ASSISTED LEGAL RESEARCH

Westlaw supplements your legal research in many ways. Westlaw allows you to

• update your research with the most current information
• expand your library with additional resources
• retrieve current, comprehensive history citing references to a case with KeyCite

For more information on using Westlaw to supplement your research, see the Westlaw Electronic Research Guide, which follows the Explanation.

§ 601. Definitions

As used in this chapter—

(1) the term "agency head" means the head and any assistant head of an executive agency, and may "upon the designation by" the head of an executive agency include the chief official of any principal division of the agency;

(2) the term "executive agency" means an executive department as defined in section 101 of Title 5, an independent establishment as defined by section 104 of Title 5 (except that it shall not include the Government Accountability Office), a military department as defined by section 102 of Title 5, and a wholly owned Government corporation as defined by section 9101(3) of Title 31;

(3) the term "contracting officer" means any person who, by appointment in accordance with applicable regulations, has the authority to enter into and administer contracts and make determinations and findings with respect thereto. The term also includes the authorized representative of the contracting officer, acting within the limits of his authority;

(4) the term "contractor" means a party to a Government contract other than the Government;

(5) the term "Administrator" means the Administrator for Federal Procurement Policy appointed pursuant to the Office of Federal Procurement Policy Act [41 U.S.C.A. § 401 et seq.];

(6) the terms "agency board" or "agency board of contract appeals" mean—

    (A) the Armed Services Board of Contract Appeals established under section 607(a)(1) of this title;

    (B) the Civilian Board of Contract Appeals established under section 438 of this title;

    (C) the board of contract appeals of the Tennessee Valley Authority; or

    (D) the Postal Service Board of Contract Appeals established under 607(c) of this title;

(7) the term "Armed Services Board" means the Armed Services Board of Contract Appeals established under section 607(a)(1) of this title;

(8) the term "Civilian Board" means the Civilian Board of Contract Appeals established under section 438 of this title; and

(9) the term "misrepresentation of fact" means a false statement of substantive fact, or any conduct which leads to a belief of a substantive fact material to proper understanding of the matter in hand, made with intent to deceive or mislead.

(Pub.L. 95–563, § 2, Nov. 1, 1978, 92 Stat. 2383; Pub.L. 104–106, Div. D, Title XLIII, § 4322(b)(5), Feb. 10, 1996, 110 Stat. 677; Pub.L. 108–271, § 8(b), July 7, 2004, 118 Stat. 814; Pub.L. 109–163, Div. A, Title VIII, § 847(d)(1), Jan. 6, 2006, 119 Stat. 3393.)

HISTORICAL AND STATUTORY NOTES

Revision Notes and Legislative Reports
1978 Acts. The Contract Disputes Act of 1978 provides a fair, balanced, and comprehensive statutory system of legal and administrative remedies in resolving Government contract claims. The act's provisions help to induce resolution of more contract disputes by negotiation prior to litigation; equalize the bargaining power of the parties when a dispute exists; provide alternate forums suitable to handle the different types of disputes; and insure fair and equitable treatment to contractors and Government agencies....

Section 2 defines "agency head," "executive agency," "contracting officer," "contractor," "Administrator," "agency board," and "misrepresentation."

The term "executive agency" includes the executive departments, independent establishments, military departments, the U.S. Postal Service, and wholly owned Government corporations.

The judicial and legislative branches, including the General Accounting Office, are not subject to the provisions of this legislation. Acquisition activity by these agencies is relatively small, and subjecting them to regulations promulgated by the executive branch agencies could raise constitutional questions under "the separation of powers" doctrine.

The U.S. Postal Service is covered, since it continues to receive a significant portion of its operating expenses from appropriated funds.

The term "contractor" means a party to a Government contract other than the Government.

The recommendations of the Procurement Commission specifically exclude bringing subcontractors under the provisions of S. 3178. It is expected that the present sponsorship rules would remain in effect. There are a number of advantages in the present sponsorship approach. From the Government's point of view, the sponsorship approach is the best method of administering complex procurements. By administering its procurement through a single point of contact, the Government's job is made both simpler and cheaper. The single point of contact approach also helps suppress frivolous claims. If direct access were allowed to all Government subcontrac-tors, contracting officers might, without appropriate safeguards, be presented with numerous frivolous claims that the prime contractor would not have sponsored. By forcing the prime contractor to administer its subcontractor network, the Government permits prime contractors and subcontractors at all tiers to use to some extent their familiar commercial procedures in contract award and administration. This advantage should not be underestimated, since the considerable variation between Government and commercial contract administration often requires extensive revisions in the administrative procedures of Government prime contractors and considerable reeducation of contract personnel. Finally, by denying the subcontractors direct access to administrative remedies, the Government is forcing the prime contractor and the subcontractor to negotiate their disputes. Allowing direct access would eliminate some incentive to negotiate a settlement. This might result in additional time-consuming and expensive litigation. The forced negotiation under the present system can create a psychological familiarity between the prime contractor and subcontractor, resulting in a greater likelihood of successful negotiation in future dealings.

On balance, although some inequities presently exist with respect to the treatment of subcontractor claims, these inequities are best handled by improved subcontract administration by the prime contractor with appropriate supervision by the Government. The additional problems of contract administration and program management that would arise if subcontractors were given direct access to the Government in disputes and claims outweigh the benefit to be gained. However, Government contracting agencies must remain alert to problems associated with subcontractor claims and assure that those resulting from Government actions are decided fairly.

The term "misrepresentation" means a false statement of substantive fact, or any conduct which leads to a belief of a substantive fact material to proper understanding of the matter in hand, made with intent to deceive or mislead.

In the context of this act, the term "misrepresentation" is used in section 4(b). For additional comments on the context in which the term is applied, refer to the analysis of section 4(b).

The key section of the definition lies in the reference to "made with intent to deceive or mislead." It is not the intent of the committees to punish contractors who may through ignorance or lack of understanding misrepresent some portion of the facts on a claim. It is the specific desire of the committees to punish those who knowingly misrepresent the facts of their claims in order to benefit from the misrepresentation, thus the definition of "misrepresentation" specifies that there must be intent to deceive or mislead before a contractor can be liable for misrepresentation. Senate Report No. 95–1118.

1996 Acts. House Conference Report No. 104–450, see 1996 U.S. Code Cong. and Adm. News, p. 238.

2006 Acts. House Conference Report No. 109–360, see 2005 U.S. Code Cong. and Adm. News, p. 1678.

Statement by President, see 2005 U.S. Code Cong. and Adm. News, p. S54.

References in Text

"This chapter", referred to in text preceding par. (1), was in the original, "this Act", meaning Pub.L. 95–563, which, in addition to enacting this chapter, amended section 5108 of Title 5, Government Organization and Employees, sections 1346, 1491, 2401, 2414, 2510, and 2517 of Title 28, Judiciary and Judicial Procedure, and section 724a of Title 31, Money and Finance, and enacted provisions set out as notes under this section. For complete classification of this Act to the Code, see Short Title note below and Tables.

The Office of Federal Procurement Policy Act, referred to in par. (5), is Pub.L. 93–400, Aug. 30, 1974, 88 Stat. 796, as amended, which is classified principally to chapter 7 (section 401 et seq.) of this title. For complete classification of this Act to the Code, see Short Title note set out under section 401 of this title and Tables.

Codifications

In par. (2), "section 9101(3) of Title 31" was substituted for "section 846 of Title 31, United States Code" on authority of Pub.L. 97–258, § 4(b), Sept. 13, 1982, 96 Stat. 1067, the first section of which enacted Title 31, Money and Finance.

Amendments

2006 Amendments. Par. (2). Pub.L. 109–163, § 847(d)(1)(A), struck out ", the United States Postal Service, and the Postal Rate Commission" following "section 9101(3) of Title 31".

Par. (6). Pub.L. 109–163, § 847(d)(1)(C), rewrote par. (6), which formerly read: "the term 'agency board' means an agency board of contract appeals established under section 607 of this title; and".

Par. (7). Pub.L. 109–163, § 847(d)(1)(B), (D), added par. (7) and redesignated former par. (7) as (9).

Par. (8). Pub.L. 109–163, § 847(d)(1)(D), added par. (8).

Par. (9). Pub.L. 109–163, § 847(d)(1)(B), redesignated former par. (7) as (9).

1996 Amendments. Pars. (3), (5) to (7). Pub.L. 104–106, § 4322(b)(5), substituted "the" for "The".

Effective and Applicability Provisions

2006 Acts. Amendments by Pub.L. 109–163, § 847, effective 1 year after Jan. 6, 2006, see Pub.L. 109–163, § 847(g), set out as a note under 5 U.S.C.A. § 5372a.

1996 Acts. Amendment by Pub.L. 104–106 effective Feb. 10, 1996, except as otherwise provided, see section 4401 of Pub.L. 104–106, set out as a note under section 251 of this title.

1978 Acts. Section 16 of Pub.L. 95–563 provided that: "This Act [enacting this chapter and amending section 5108 of Title 5, Government Organization and Employees, sections 1346, 1491, 2401, 2414, 2510, and 2517 of Title 28, Judiciary and Judicial Procedure, and section 724a of Title 31, Money and Finance] shall apply to contracts entered into one hundred twenty days after the date of enactment [Nov. 1, 1978]. Notwithstanding any provision in a contract made before the effective date of this Act, the contractor may elect to proceed under this Act with respect to any claim pending then before the contracting officer or initiated thereafter."

Change of Name

"Government Accountability Office" substituted for "General Accounting Office" in par. (2) on authority of Pub.L. 108–271, § 8(b), cited in the credit to this section and set out as a note under 31 U.S.C.A. § 702, which provided that any reference to the General Accounting Office in any law, rule, regulation, certificate, directive, instruction, or other official paper in force on July 17, 2004, to refer and apply to the Government Accountability Office.

Short Title

1978 Acts. Section 1 of Pub.L. 95–563 provided: "That this Act [enacting this

chapter, amending section 5108 of Title 5, Government Organization and Employees, sections 1346, 1491, 2401, 2414, 2510, and 2517 of Title 28, Judiciary and Judicial Procedure, and section 724a of Title 31, Money and Finance, and enacting provisions set out as notes under this section] may be cited as the 'Contract Disputes Act of 1978'."

CODE OF FEDERAL REGULATIONS

Appeals, procedures, etc.—
    Office of Secretary of Interior, see 43 CFR § 4.1 et seq.

LAW REVIEW AND JOURNAL COMMENTARIES

Contractor claims for relief under illegal contracts with the government. Michael T. Janik and Margaret C. Rhodes, 45 Am.U.L.Rev. 1949 (1996).

Determining the adequacy of a claim: *Blake Construction* reconciles the conflict between *Gauntt* and *Westclox*. M. Lee Kristeller, 18 Pub.Cont.L.J. 494 (1989).

Doing business with the government. Peter C. Mieres (February 1982) 4 L.A.Law. 34.

When a termination for convenience settlement proposal constitutes a claim under the Contract Disputes Act. Eric R. Fish, 26 Public Contract L.J. 423 (1997).

Research References

ALR Library

13 ALR, Fed. 2nd Series 261, Construction and Application of Patent Ambiguity Doctrine to Federal Government Contracts.

190 ALR, Fed. 249, Validity, Construction, and Application of Indian Self-Determination and Education Assistance Act.

106 ALR, Fed. 191, What Constitutes "Special Circumstances" Precluding Award of Attorneys' Fees Under Equal Access to Justice Act (28 U.S.C.A. § 2412(D)).

97 ALR, Fed. 694, Jurisdiction of United States Court of Appeals for Federal Circuit Under 28 U.S.C.A. §§ 1292 and 1295.

96 ALR, Fed. 336, What Constitutes "Adversary Adjudication" by Administrative Agency Entitling Prevailing Party to Award of Attorneys' Fees Under Equal Access to Justice Act (5 U.S.C.A. § 504).

59 ALR, Fed. 905, Application of 28 U.S.C.A. § 2516(A) to Government Contractor's Claim for Interest Expense or for Loss of Use of Its Capital Caused by Delay Attributable to Government.

44 ALR, Fed. 775, Modern Status and Application of Rule That Only Voluntary Transfer or Assignment of Claim Against United States Is Within Assignment of Claims Act (31 U.S.C.A. § 203, 41 U.S.C.A. § 15).

27 ALR, Fed. 702, Modern Status of Applicability of Doctrine of Estoppel Against Federal Government and Its Agencies.

2 ALR, Fed. 691, Judicial Review Under Wunderlich Act (41 U.S.C.A. §§ 321, 322), of Federal Administrative Decisions Made Under Standard "Disputes" Clauses in Government Contracts.

24 ALR 2nd 928, Recovery of Interest on Claim Against a Governmental Unit in Absence of Provision in Contract or Express Statutory Provision.

140 ALR 1518, Validity and Construction of War Enactments in United States Suspending Operation of Statute of Limitations.

92 ALR 663, Stipulation of Parties as to the Law.

77 ALR 1044, Estoppel Against Defense of Limitation in Tort Actions.

Encyclopedias

Am. Jur. 2d Admiralty § 45, United States.

Am. Jur. 2d United States § 39, Generally; Priority of Government Claims.
70 Am. Jur. Proof of Facts 3d 97, Proof That a Government Agency Was Liable for Improperly Granting a Bid Award to a Bid Applicant.
14 Am. Jur. Trials 437, Representing the Government Contractor.
100 Am. Jur. Trials 45, Construction Dispute Resolution Arbitration and Beyond.

Forms

Am. Jur. Pl. & Pr. Forms Public Works & Contracts § 85, Petition--In Court of Federal Claims--For Review of Decision of Board of Contract Appeals-- Under Contract Disputes Act of 1978--Breach of Contract--Building Maintenance Services.

Am. Jur. Pl. & Pr. Forms Public Works & Contracts § 87, Petition--In Court of Federal Claims--For Review of Decision of Board of Contract Appeals-- Under Contract Disputes Act of 1978--Denial of Claim for Value of Extra Work Done Under Contract.

Am. Jur. Pl. & Pr. Forms Public Works & Contracts § 88, Petition--For Increased Costs of Performance--Government's Failure to Give Timely Notice to Proceed as Constituting Breach of Contract.

Am. Jur. Pl. & Pr. Forms Space Law § 21, Introductory Comments.

Am. Jur. Pl. & Pr. Forms Space Law § 28, Petition--In U.S. Court of Federal Claims--For Review of Denial of Award of Contract--And for Recovery of Bid Preparation Costs.

Am. Jur. Pl. & Pr. Forms Space Law § 29, Petition--In U.S. Court of Federal Claims--For Review of Denial of Award of Contract--And to Declare Contract Awarded to Another Void.

Am. Jur. Pl. & Pr. Forms Space Law § 30, Petition--In U.S. Court of Federal Claims--By Contractor--For Funds Wrongfully Withheld as Offset--Government's Breach of Contract.

Am. Jur. Pl. & Pr. Forms Space Law § 31, Petition--In U.S. Court of Federal Claims--By Contractor--For Damages--Cancellation of Award of Contract as Breach.

Am. Jur. Pl. & Pr. Forms Space Law § 32, Petition--In U.S. Court of Federal Claims--By Contractor--For Increased Costs of Performance--Failure to Give Timely Notice to Proceed as Breach.

Federal Procedural Forms § 34:74, Petition--By Unsuccessful Bidder--For Recovery of Bid-Preparation Costs--Denial of Award of Contract Arbitrary and Capricious [28 U.S.C.A. § 1491; 41 U.S.C.A. § 607; United States Claims Court Rule 8].

Federal Procedural Forms § 34:75, Petition--By Unsuccessful Bidder--To Have Contract Arbitrarily Awarded to Another Declared Void [28 U.S.C.A. § 1491; 41 U.S.C.A. § 609; United States Claims Court Rule 8].

Federal Procedural Forms § 34:78, Introduction to CDA.

Federal Procedural Forms § 34:79, Disputes Subject to CDA's Resolution Procedures.

Federal Procedural Forms § 34:80, Disputes Excluded from CDA's Resolution Procedures.

Federal Procedural Forms § 34:89, Alternative Dispute Resolution.

Federal Procedural Forms § 34:102, Introduction to Boards of Contract Appeals.

Federal Procedural Forms § 34:121, Contractor Versus Government Agency.

Federal Procedural Forms § 34:255, Notice of Appeal--To General Services Administration--Alternative Form, with Statement of Dispute [48 C.F.R. § 6101, GSBCA Rule 101].

Federal Procedural Forms § 34:306, Exhaustion of Administrative Remedies.

Federal Procedural Forms § 34:339, Petition--For an Accounting and Damages-- For Government's Breach of Contract [41 U.S.C.A. § 609(A)(3); United States Court of Federal Claims Rule 8].

Federal Procedural Forms § 34:341, Petition--By Contractor--For Recovery of Funds Wrongfully Withheld as Offset Against Alleged Prior Indebtedness [28 U.S.C.A. § 1491; 41 U.S.C.A. § 609; United States Court of Federal Claims Rule 8].

Federal Procedural Forms § 34:342, Petition--By Contractor for Damages--Cancellation of Award of Contract, Pursuant to Opinion of Comptroller General, as Constituting Breach of Contract [28 U.S.C.A. § 1491; 41 U.S.C.A. § 609; United States Court of Federal Claims Rule 8].

Federal Procedural Forms § 34:343, Petition--For Increased Costs of Performance--Government's Failure to Give Timely Notice to Proceed as Constituting Breach of Contract [28 U.S.C.A. § 1491; 41 U.S.C.A. § 609; United States Court of Federal Claims Rule 8].

Federal Procedural Forms § 34:344, Petition--For Recovery of Forfeited Bid Deposits--Mistake in Bid [28 U.S.C.A. § 1491; 41 U.S.C.A. § 609; United States Court of Federal Claims Rule 8].

Federal Procedural Forms § 34:345, Petition--For Review of Decision of Board of Contract Appeals--Under Contract Disputes Act of 1978--Breach of Contract--Building Maintenance Services.

Federal Procedural Forms § 55:107, Sale of Personal Property Through Competitive Bidding.

Nichols Cyclopedia of Legal Forms Annotated § 7:2518, Supply Contract with United States--General Provisions.

Nichols Cyclopedia of Legal Forms Annotated § 7:2530, United States Lessee--General Clauses.

Nichols Cyclopedia of Legal Forms Annotated § 7:2536, Construction Contract with United States--General Provisions.

8 West's Federal Forms § 13102, Formal Brief of Appellant--Appeal from Board of Contract Appeals.

8 West's Federal Forms § 13126, Tucker Act--Contract Claims.

8 West's Federal Forms § 13129, Contract Disputes Act.

12A West's Legal Forms § 38.4 Form 4, Emergency Equipment Rental Agreement.

Treatises and Practice Aids

Americans with Disab. Pract. & Compliance Manual § 9:41, Judicial Enforcement--Private Right of Action.

Eckstrom's Licensing in Foreign & Domestic Ops. App. 11A, Patent Rights in Inventions Made with Federal Assistance (35 U.S.C.A. §§ 200 to 212).

Federal Procedure, Lawyers Edition § 19:65, Suits Under Contract Disputes Act.

Federal Procedure, Lawyers Edition § 19:179, Motions for Notice or Summons to Third Parties.

Federal Procedure, Lawyers Edition § 39:370, Jurisdiction of Boards of Contract Appeals.

Federal Procedure, Lawyers Edition § 39:425, Nonconsideration or Dismissal of Protests.

Federal Procedure, Lawyers Edition § 39:438, Administration of Contracts.

Federal Procedure, Lawyers Edition § 39:635, Sufficiency of Claim.

Federal Procedure, Lawyers Edition § 39:671, Inadequacy of Other Legal Authority for Relief.

Federal Procedure, Lawyers Edition § 39:696, Review of Decision to Terminate.

Federal Procedure, Lawyers Edition § 39:786, Introduction to CDA.

Federal Procedure, Lawyers Edition § 39:793, Sufficiency of Supporting Information.

Federal Procedure, Lawyers Edition § 39:849, Introduction.

Federal Procedure, Lawyers Edition § 39:897, Contractor as Appellant.

Federal Procedure, Lawyers Edition § 39:1409, Introduction.

Federal Procedure, Lawyers Edition § 46:435, Necessity of Filing Claim.

Federal Procedure, Lawyers Edition § 46:436, Claim Defined.

Federal Procedure, Lawyers Edition § 46:443, Finality of Decision by Awarding Official.

Federal Procedure, Lawyers Edition § 53:167, Scope of Jurisdiction--Suits in Admiralty Act.

Federal Procedure, Lawyers Edition § 57:412, Filing and Content of Notice of Appeal.

Federal Procedure, Lawyers Edition § 60:862, Factual Review of Decision to Request Conveyance of Title.

Federal Procedure, Lawyers Edition § 63:2, Statutory Bases for Jurisdiction.

West's Federal Administrative Practice § 4, The Judicial Branch.

West's Federal Administrative Practice § 379, Department of Transportation-- Board of Contract Appeals.

West's Federal Administrative Practice § 446, Department of Veterans Affairs-- Board of Contract Appeals.

West's Federal Administrative Practice § 511, GAO Decisions: Nature and Effect.

West's Federal Administrative Practice § 516, Claims Against the United States.

West's Federal Administrative Practice § 519, Demand and Setoff.

West's Federal Administrative Practice § 521, Government Claims and Statutes of Limitation.

West's Federal Administrative Practice § 524, Contract Jurisdiction--Limitations.

West's Federal Administrative Practice § 603, Differences from Private Contracts.

West's Federal Administrative Practice § 605, Common Contractor Mistakes and Contract Pitfalls.

West's Federal Administrative Practice § 615, Laws Applicable--Labor Conditions.

West's Federal Administrative Practice § 633, Contract Quality and Warranties.

West's Federal Administrative Practice § 634, Value Engineering.

West's Federal Administrative Practice § 650, Changes and Equitable Adjustments.

West's Federal Administrative Practice § 653, Extraordinary Contractual Actions.

West's Federal Administrative Practice § 660, Financing.

West's Federal Administrative Practice § 664, Protests and Appeals.

West's Federal Administrative Practice § 671, Contract Forms and Clauses.

West's Federal Administrative Practice § 672, Contract Disputes Litigation--Overview.

West's Federal Administrative Practice § 817, Interest on Claims and Judgments; Payment and Conclusiveness of Judgments.

West's Federal Administrative Practice § 822, Subject Matter Jurisdiction--Contract Claim: Jurisdiction, Limitations, Appeals and Interest.

West's Federal Administrative Practice § 5321, Office of the Secretary--Organization--Board of Contract Appeals.

West's Federal Administrative Practice § 5457, Authority of Administrator--Special Procurement Authority.

West's Federal Administrative Practice § 8006, Courts of Special Jurisdiction-- Claims Court.

13 Wright & Miller: Federal Prac. & Proc. § 3527, Exclusive Federal Court Jurisdiction.

14 Wright & Miller: Federal Prac. & Proc. § 3657, Statutory Exceptions to Sovereign Immunity--Actions Under the Tucker Act.

17 Wright & Miller: Federal Prac. & Proc. § 4101, The Claims Court.

33 Wright & Miller: Federal Prac. & Proc. § 8293, Courts of Special Jurisdiction.

WESTLAW ELECTRONIC RESEARCH

See Westlaw guide following the Explanation pages of this volume.

Notes of Decisions

1. Construction

Contract Disputes Act is waiver of sovereign immunity and must, therefore, be strictly construed. Sigmon Fuel Co. v. Tennessee Valley Authority, C.A.6 (Tenn.) 1985, 754 F.2d 162. United States ☞ 73(9)

2. Construction with other laws

The Debt Collection Act (DCA) which affords notice and other procedural protections when the government undertakes to collect a debt by administrative offset does not supplant or restrict established procedures for contractual offsets accommodated by the Contracts Disputes Act (CDA). Cecile Industries, Inc. v. Cheney, C.A.Fed.1993, 995 F.2d 1052, rehearing denied. United States ⚖ 130(3)

Proviso in statute granting district courts jurisdiction over any civil action or claim against United States not exceeding $10,000, that is founded upon contract with United States, that district courts shall not have jurisdiction over any civil action or claim against United States founded on contract subject to Contract Disputes Act restricts only jurisdiction that is granted in that statute. North Side Lumber Co. v. Block, C.A.9 (Or.) 1985, 753 F.2d 1482, certiorari denied 106 S.Ct. 248, 474 U.S. 919, 88 L.Ed.2d 256, certiorari denied 106 S.Ct. 265, 474 U.S. 931, 88 L.Ed.2d 271. Federal Courts ⚖ 976

Contract Disputes Act (CDA) precluded District Court from exercising subject matter jurisdiction under Postal Reorganization Act's (PRA) "sue and be sued" clause in subcontractor's action against Postal Service. Tradesmen Intern., Inc. v. U.S. Postal Service, D.Kan.2002, 234 F.Supp.2d 1191. United States ⚖ 74.2

Contract Disputes Act (CDA), which applies to any express or implied contract entered into by an executive agency for the procurement of services, and under which contract disputes with the United States Postal Service (USPS) are to be heard before a contracting officer and are appealable to the USPS's Board of Contract Appeals (BCA) and the Federal Claims Court (FCC), trumps the Postal Reorganization Act (PRA), which gave the USPS the general power to sue and be sued in its official name and gave the United States district courts original but not exclusive jurisdiction over all actions brought by or against the USPS. B & B Industries, Inc. v. U.S. Postal Service, E.D.Mich.2002, 185 F.Supp.2d 760, reversed in part 363 F.3d 404, rehearing en banc granted, opinion superseded on rehearing 406 F.3d 766. Federal Courts ⚖ 1141; Postal Service ⚖ 3.1; United States ⚖ 73(9); United States ⚖ 73(15)

Congress did not contemplate or intend application of Contract Disputes Act [41 U.S.C.A. § 601 et seq.] to include Miller Act [40 U.S.C.A. §§ 270a–270d] and suits between sureties and government. U.S. v. Seaboard Surety Co., E.D.N.Y.1985, 622 F.Supp. 882.

The Contract Disputes Act preempted whatever jurisdiction federal district courts previously had under the Postal Reorganization Act, in the case of contract suits against the Postal Service, and conferred exclusive jurisdiction of contract claims against the Postal Service in the United States Claims Court. Prefab Products, Inc. v. U.S. Postal Service, S.D.Fla.1984, 600 F.Supp. 89. Federal Courts ⚖ 1139

3. Purpose

Generally, purpose of Contract Disputes Act was to divest district courts and regional circuits of all jurisdiction over government contract disputes and to concentrate that authority in contracting officer, Armed Services Board of Contract Appeals, or claims court, at contractor's option, and eventually in Court of Appeals for Federal Circuit. McDonnell Douglas Corp. v. U.S., C.A.Fed.1985, 754 F.2d 365. United States ⚖ 73(9)

Purpose of enacting Contract Disputes Act (CDA) was to create comprehensive statutory scheme of administrative and legal remedies so that contract claims against government could be uniformly resolved. Richland-Lexington Airport Dist. v. Atlas Properties, Inc., D.S.C.1994, 854 F.Supp. 400. United States ⚖ 73(9)

Legislative history indicates that this chapter was intended to induce resolution of contract disputes with government by negotiation rather than litigation, and provide alternative forums for dispute resolution. Great Lakes Educational Consultants v. Federal Emergency Management Agency, a Div. of Federal Government, W.D.Mich.1984, 582 F.Supp. 193. United States ⚖ 73(9)

4. Effective date

This chapter was inapplicable to claim which was not pending before contracting officer on effective date of this chapter but was pending before Armed Services Board of Contract Appeals. North American Corp. v. U.S., C.A.Fed.1983, 706 F.2d 1212. United States ⚖ 73(9)

Where contractor's claim was not pending before contracting officer on effective date of this chapter, direct access to the Court of Claims was not available, and, therefore, contractor was required to exhaust its administrative remedies. S.J. Groves & Sons Co. v. U.S., Ct.Cl. 1981, 661 F.2d 170, 228 Ct.Cl. 598. United States ☞ 73(15)

Word "then", within section 16 of Pub.L. 95–563, set out as a note under this section, authorizing an award of interest on "any claim pending then before the contracting officer", refers to effective date of Pub.L. 95–563 rather than to date of enactment. Monroe M. Tapper & Associates v. U.S., Ct.Cl.1979, 611 F.2d 354, 222 Ct.Cl. 34. United States ☞ 110

Where contractor's claim was "pending" on, or "initiated" after, March 1, 1979, contractor, which took no action to appeal decision of contracting officer, either to agency or to Claims Court, could elect to proceed under this chapter. Z.A.N. Co. v. U.S., Cl.Ct.1984, 6 Cl.Ct. 298. United States ☞ 73(9)

Government contractor's claim for amount due it in consequence of convenience termination of contract was within jurisdiction of Claims Court, as a "direct access" claim authorized by this section, notwithstanding contention that contractor's claim had its origins prior to effective date thereof, since dispute on amount due in consequence of convenience termination did not arise until long after such effective date. Semco, Inc. v. U.S., Cl.Ct. 1984, 6 Cl.Ct. 81. Federal Courts ☞ 1076

Where contracting officer had entered final determination adverse to contractor on claim for unanticipated subsurface timber pilings, determination was filed with contract appeals board prior to effective date of this chapter, and, upon being reversed on appeal, was then returned to contracting officer for negotiation of amount, fact that pricing dispute emerged upon remand would not alter status of underlying claim which remained pending before board; thus, contractor was not entitled to proceed under this chapter, with respect to quantum determination on its pile claim, since claim neither was pending before contracting officer on effective date of this chapter, nor was it initiated thereafter. P.J. Maffei Bldg. Wrecking Corp. v. U.S., Cl.Ct.

1983, 3 Cl.Ct. 482, affirmed 732 F.2d 913. United States ☞ 73(9)

5. Executive agency

Since the Government Printing Office was not an "executive agency" within the meaning of this chapter, Federal Circuit was without jurisdiction to decide an appeal from a decision of the Government Printing Office Board of Contract Appeals and transferred the appeal to the claims court, assuming, without deciding, that the Claims Court has jurisdiction under section 1346 of Title 29. Tatelbaum v. U.S., C.A.Fed.1984, 749 F.2d 729, transferred to 10 Cl.Ct. 207. Federal Courts ☞ 1139; Federal Courts ☞ 1158

This section defines "executive agency" as wholly owned government corporation as defined by section 9101(3) of Title 31, and such definition expressly lists Federal Savings and Loan Insurance Corporation as wholly owned government corporation; therefore, Federal Savings and Loan Insurance Corporation is "executive agency" within meaning of this section. APA, Inc. v. Federal Sav. and Loan Ins. Corp., W.D.La.1983, 562 F.Supp. 884. Building And Loan Associations ☞ 48

6. Contractor—Generally

Contract Disputes Act's waiver of sovereign immunity with respect to "contractor" includes those who are in privity of contract with government, even though they are not properly parties to government contract. Hodgdon v. U.S., D.Me. 1996, 919 F.Supp. 37. United States ☞ 125(16)

Government contractor's president had no standing to bring a claim on contractor's behalf under the Contract Disputes Act (CDA) and no privity of contract to bring a CDA claim in his own name. Schickler v. U.S., Fed.Cl.2002, 54 Fed.Cl. 264, appeal dismissed 70 Fed.Appx. 584, 2003 WL 21774141. Federal Courts ☞ 1110

United States Claims Court lacked subject matter jurisdiction, pursuant to Contract Disputes Act, over completion contractor's complaint seeking recovery of alleged omission of home office overhead under contract completed pursuant to surety takeover agreement since completion contractor was not party to government contract and was not party to surety takeover agreement executed by United States Army Corps of Engineers. George

W. Kane, Inc. v. U.S., Cl.Ct.1992, 26 Cl. Ct. 655. United States ☞ 74(1)

Disappointed bidder was not a "contractor" under Contract Disputes Act since it was not a party to a Forest Service contract and therefore could not base its claim that Forest Service breached duty to fairly consider its bid under the solicitation upon Contract Disputes Act. Monchamp Corp. v. U.S., Cl.Ct. 1990, 19 Cl.Ct. 797. United States ☞ 64.60(1)

Neither corporate parent of dissolved subsidiary which had contract with Government were "contractors" as defined by the Contract Disputes Act, and thus, were not liable under subsidiary's contract; there was no express contract between parents and Government, there was no implied in fact contract given lack of evidence that parents received benefit as result of their dealing with Government, and parents were not third-party beneficiaries. BLH Inc. v. U.S., Cl.Ct. 1987, 13 Cl.Ct. 265. Corporations ☞ 254

7. —— Subcontractor

Subcontractor was not entitled to interest on portion of award obtained by government contractor from Interior Board of Contract Appeals (IBCA) that related to subcontractor's work on canal project, as subcontractor was not "contractor" under Contract Disputes Act, and terms of subcontract did not authorize such award. MRT Const. Inc. v. Hardrives, Inc., C.A.9 (Ariz.) 1998, 158 F.3d 478. United States ☞ 110

All claims by food service supplier against Government stemmed from its failure to be awarded subcontract for Air Force base, and thus, supplier was "subcontractor" and claims court did not have jurisdiction to hear claims under Contract Disputes Act, which is limited to claims by contractors. Clean Giant, Inc. v. U.S., Cl.Ct.1990, 19 Cl.Ct. 390. Federal Courts ☞ 1076

Subcontractor's failure to fulfill jurisdictional prerequisites of the Contract Disputes Act mandated dismissal of its complaint alleging that the Government breached two contracts in connection with a NASA construction project; if subcontractor had any contract with the Government, as opposed to prime contractor, it would be in privity and thus was within purview of the CDA, which

defines "contractor" as "a party to a government contract other than the government." Acousti Engineering Co. of Florida v. U.S., Cl.Ct.1988, 15 Cl.Ct. 698.

8. —— Surety, contractor

Armed Services Board of Contract Appeals lacked jurisdiction over claims for equitable adjustment asserted by surety that completed performance of defaulting contractor, pursuant to surety's takeover agreement with government, to the extent that claims related to and depended upon events which occurred before takeover agreement was executed, such that surety was not "contractor" under Contract Disputes Act when claims arose. United Pacific Ins. Co. v. Roche, C.A.Fed.2004, 380 F.3d 1352, rehearing denied. United States ☞ 73(15)

Surety was not a contractor under Contract Disputes Act, and, consequently, Board of Contract Appeals did not have subject matter jurisdiction to address surety's claim against federal government relating to pre-takeover activities, even though surety claimed it should be considered a contractor under equitable subrogation doctrine; surety was not party to any contract with government prior to takeover agreement it had with government, and its pre-takeover claims did not arise under such contract. Fireman's Fund Ins. Co. v. England, C.A.Fed.2002, 313 F.3d 1344. United States ☞ 73(15)

Performance and payment bond surety was not "contractor" and, therefore, could not appeal alone to Armed Services Board of Contract Appeals following decision by contracting officer; surety did not enter takeover agreement to complete the project and was not in privity with the Navy. Admiralty Const., Inc. by Nat. American Ins. Co. v. Dalton, C.A.Fed. 1998, 156 F.3d 1217. United States ☞ 73(15)

Performance bond surety that has not made payment pursuant to its obligation, or entered separate takeover agreement with government, is not party to government contract and hence is not "contractor" within meaning of Contract Disputes Act for purpose of allowing it to assert claims under Act. Fidelity & Deposit Co. of Maryland v. U.S., Fed.Cl.1994, 31 Fed. Cl. 540. United States ☞ 74.1

Prime contractor's surety was not "contractor" entitled to maintain contract claim under Contract Disputes Act of 1978 after surety was required to make payments to prime contractor's subcontractors, prime contractor abandoned project and Government terminated for default; Act required that contract sued upon be government contract and did not apply to bond issued by surety. Westech Corp. v. U.S., Cl.Ct.1990, 20 Cl.Ct. 745. United States ⌖ 74.1

Surety, which was appointed to act on behalf of parties that executed performance bond and payment bond with original contractor and which executed takeover agreement to complete performance under original construction contract upon original contractor's default, became prime party in privity with Government and was therefore a "contractor" within meaning of Contract Disputes Act and had standing to maintain action with reference to alleged breaches of takeover agreement and construction contract to the extent that construction contract terms were incorporated by reference into takeover agreement. Travelers Indem. Co. v. U.S., Cl.Ct.1988, 16 Cl.Ct. 142. United States ⌖ 74.1

Government contractor's surety, which sought to set aside default termination as to contractor so as to preclude necessity of surety's performance on performance and payment bonds, was not "contractor" within meaning of Contract Disputes Act so as to have standing to bring action directly against Government. Fidelity & Deposit Co. of Maryland v. U.S., Cl.Ct. 1988, 14 Cl.Ct. 421. United States ⌖ 74.1

Surety of construction company which entered into contract with Government was not a party to the construction contract and therefore not a "contractor" under the Contract Disputes Act for the purpose of allowing it to assert claims under Act. Universal Sur. Co. v. U.S.,

Cl.Ct.1986, 10 Cl.Ct. 794. United States ⌖ 73(9)

9. Third party beneficiaries

Lender, as holder of debtor's note, could have required Small Business Administration (SBA), as loan's guarantor, to provide written consent to foreclose on loan, pursuant to guaranty agreement between lender and SBA, but waived that right when it acted upon SBA's oral consent, and therefore debtor, as third-party beneficiary of guaranty agreement, could not rely upon such right in suing SBA for breach of contract. Audio Odyssey, Ltd. v. U.S., S.D.Iowa 2003, 243 F.Supp.2d 951, affirmed 373 F.3d 870, rehearing and rehearing en banc denied. United States ⌖ 53(8)

For purposes of Contract Disputes Act's waiver of sovereign immunity with respect to "contractor," contractor's employee was not third-party beneficiary of contractor's contract with government to manage and operate vessel; contract reflected no intent of parties to benefit third parties such as employee who suffered injury by contractor's negligence or unseaworthiness of vessel, and contained no provision demonstrating intent to provide employee with direct right to compensation or to enforce that right against United States. Hodgdon v. U.S., D.Me.1996, 919 F.Supp. 37. United States ⌖ 125(12)

Subcontractor, as third-party beneficiary of government contract, was not a "contractor" within meaning of the Contract Disputes Act (CDA), as it was not a party to the contract, and thus could not assert a claim for prejudgment interest under the CDA. JGB Enterprises, Inc. v. U.S., Fed.Cl.2004, 63 Fed.Cl. 319, motion for relief from judgment denied 71 Fed. Cl. 468, appeal dismissed 192 Fed.Appx. 962, 2006 WL 2382737. United States ⌖ 73(9)

§ 602. Applicability of law

(a) Executive agency contracts

Unless otherwise specifically provided herein, this chapter applies to any express or implied contract (including those of the nonappropriated fund activities described in sections 1346 and 1491 of Title 28) entered into by an executive agency for—

(1) the procurement of property, other than real property in being;

(2) the procurement of services;

(3) the procurement of construction, alteration, repair or maintenance of real property; or,

(4) the disposal of personal property.

(b) Tennessee Valley Authority contracts

With respect to contracts of the Tennessee Valley Authority, the provisions of this chapter shall apply only to those contracts which contain a disputes clause requiring that a contract dispute be resolved through an agency administrative process. Notwithstanding any other provision of this chapter, contracts of the Tennessee Valley Authority for the sale of fertilizer or electric power or related to the conduct or operation of the electric power system shall be excluded from the chapter.

(c) Foreign government or international organization contracts

This chapter does not apply to a contract with a foreign government, or agency thereof, or international organization, or subsidiary body thereof, if the head of the agency determines that the application of the chapter to the contract would not be in the public interest.

(Pub.L. 95–563, § 3, Nov. 1, 1978, 92 Stat. 2383.)

HISTORICAL AND STATUTORY NOTES

Revision Notes and Legislative Reports

1978 Acts. Section 3 would make the provisions of the bill applicable to all express or implied contracts entered into by an executive agency of the United States (including those nonappropriated fund activities described in sections 1346 and 1491 of title 28 of the United States Code) for the procurement of property (other than real property in being), services, for construction, alteration, repair, or maintenance of real property, for disposal of personal property and applicable to any other contract or agreement with the United States which by its terms is expressly made subject to its provisions.

The bill would have broad application in order to unify the diverse and often inconsistent procedures presently existing among the many procuring agencies, a goal defined in the Report of the Commission on Government Procurement, volume I, pages 1, 2.

The bill applies to contracts entered into by the executive departments, an independent establishment (except that it shall not include the General Accounting Office), wholly owned Government corporations, the military departments, the U.S. Postal Service, and the Postal Rate Commission (see "definitions," sec. 2(2)).

The bill expressly states its applicability to those nonappropriated fund activities over which the courts presently have jurisdiction under 28 U.S.C. 1346 and 1491. Consideration was given to including all nonappropriated fund activities. However, since the court's present jurisdiction over nonappropriated fund contracts is limited to certain post exchanges, and as there appears to be no problem with remedies relating to other nonappropriated fund activities, it was deemed unnecessary to include all or any additional nonappropriated fund activities within the scope of the bill.

Consideration was also given to having the bill apply to maritime contracts for the employment, use, restoration, repair, or salvage of vessels and aids to navigation. Jurisdiction over these contracts arise in Admiralty and presently reside wholly within the Federal district courts. This jurisdiction is not shared by the Court of Claims. See: *Matson Navigation Co. v. United States*, 284 U.S. 352

(1932); *Amell v. United States*, 384 U.S. 158 (1966). A variety of factors militated against the inclusion of such contracts within the bill.

Jurisdiction over matters arising in admiralty including maritime contracts has vested exclusively with the Federal district courts since 1920 (See: Suits in Admiralty Act, 46 U.S.C. 741–752; *Matson Navigation Co. v. United States*, supra). As a result, the district courts have developed an expertise in admiralty matters, which has resulted in a common body of procedural and substantive law, applicable to private litigants and the United States alike. Inclusion of maritime contracts within the bill would have created an exception to the district courts' otherwise exclusive admiralty jurisdiction and divided maritime contract disputes between the Court of Claims and district courts depending upon whether the United States was a party plaintiff or defendant. Admiralty matters sounding in contract involve issues and procedural questions considered sufficiently unique so as to warrant the continued maintenance of these actions within the exclusive jurisdiction of the district courts.

Contracts for the disposal of personal property are included within the coverage of the bill even though they are for the sale rather than the procurement of property. These contracts are generally referred to as "surplus sales" contracts. The General Services Administration has cognizance over all such sales. Under its personal property management regulations Federal agencies currently include the standard disputes clause in contracts for the disposal of personal property. (Standard form 114C, Sale of Government Property—General Sale Terms and Conditions (January 1970 edi-

tion), prescribed by GSA regulations, 41 C.F.R. 101–45.304–8(c)(4), for all sales of personal property, includes the standard disputes clause.)

The inclusion of the disputes procedure in disposal contracts has worked well for many years and justifies its incorporation into the bill. Moreover, the omission of contracts for the disposal of personal property from section 3 of the bill might be construed to imply a congressional intention to exclude personal property disposal contracts from the blanket coverage of the bill notwithstanding current agency requirements to treat such disputes in the same manner as procurement disputes. Since no such exclusion is intended, contracts for the disposal of personal property were made expressly covered by the bill. Senate Report No. 95–1118.

References in Text

"This chapter", referred to in text, was, in the original, "this Act", meaning Pub.L. 95–563, which, in addition to enacting this chapter, amended section 5108 of Title 5, Government Organization and Employees, sections 1346, 1491, 2401, 2414, 2510, and 2517 of Title 28, Judiciary and Judicial Procedure, and section 724a of Title 31, Money and Finance, and enacted provisions set out as notes under section 2201 of this title.

Effective and Applicability Provisions

1978 Acts. Section effective with respect to contracts entered into 120 days after Nov. 1, 1978 and, at the election of the contractor, with respect to any claim pending at such time before the contracting officer or initiated thereafter, see section 16 of Pub.L. 95–563, set out as a note under section 601 of this title.

LAW REVIEW AND JOURNAL COMMENTARIES

Government contract cases in the United States Court of Appeals for the Federal Circuit: 1995 in review. Thomas F. Williamson, Stacey L. Valerio and Stephanie P. Gilson, 45 Am.U.L.Rev. 1657 (1996).

LIBRARY REFERENCES

American Digest System
United States ☞53(6), 73(8).
Key Number System Topic No. 393.

Research References

Forms

Federal Procedural Forms § 34:79, Disputes Subject to CDA's Resolution Procedures.

Federal Procedural Forms § 34:80, Disputes Excluded from CDA's Resolution Procedures.

8 West's Federal Forms § 13129, Contract Disputes Act.

Treatises and Practice Aids

Federal Procedure, Lawyers Edition § 39:786, Introduction to CDA.

Federal Procedure, Lawyers Edition § 39:790, Disputes Excluded from CDA's Resolution Procedures.

Patent Law Fundamentals § 18:18, Government Access to Privately Owned Inventions--Adjudication of Claims Against the United States for Intellectual Property Infringement.

West's Federal Administrative Practice § 822, Subject Matter Jurisdiction--Contract Claim: Jurisdiction, Limitations, Appeals and Interest.

WESTLAW ELECTRONIC RESEARCH

See Westlaw guide following the Explanation pages of this volume.

Notes of Decisions

Generally 1
Broker's fee contracts 13
Common carrier contracts 14
Confidentiality and disclosure 15
Construction, alteration, repair or maintenance, real property contracts 9
Disposal of personal property 12
Executive agency 3
Financing and subsidy, real property contracts 8
Government provision of services, services procured 11
Guaranties 16
Implied contracts 2
Leases, real property contracts 7
Miscellaneous claims CDA applicable 21
Miscellaneous claims CDA not applicable 22
Nonappropriated fund activities 4
Postal Services contracts 17
Procurement contracts generally 5
Real property contracts 6-9
    Generally 6
    Construction, alteration, repair or maintenance 9
    Financing and subsidy 8
    Leases 7
Research contracts 18
Services procured 10, 11
    Generally 10
    Government provision of services 11
Subcontracts 19

Sureties 20

___

1. Generally

When the Contract Disputes Act (CDA) applies, it provides the exclusive mechanism for dispute resolution; CDA was not designed to serve as an alternative administrative remedy, available at the contractor's option. Texas Health Choice, L.C. v. Office of Personnel Management, C.A.Fed.2005, 400 F.3d 895, rehearing and rehearing en banc denied. United States ☞ 73(9)

Unless Tucker Act and Contract Disputes Act specify otherwise, these statutes apply only to agencies that operate using appropriated funds, and as a result do not waive federal sovereign immunity from contract actions for all agencies. Research Triangle Institute v. Board of Governors of the Federal Reserve System, C.A.4 (N.C.) 1997, 132 F.3d 985, certiorari denied 119 S.Ct. 44, 525 U.S. 811, 142 L.Ed.2d 34. United States ☞ 125(16)

Once Contract Disputes Act is applicable, it controls all avenues of appeal available to the contractor. Mark Smith Const. Co., Inc. v. U.S., Cl.Ct.1986, 10 Cl.Ct. 540. United States ☞ 73(15)

2. Implied contracts

Implied contract to treat a bidder on a government contract honestly and fairly is not a contract for the "procurement of goods or services" for purpose of this section and, hence, this section did not give Department of Energy Board of Contract Appeals jurisdiction of claim for bid preparation costs incurred in connection with government's solicitation for petroleum storage proposals which was cancelled before any contract was awarded. Coastal Corp. v. U.S., C.A.Fed.1983, 713 F.2d 728. United States ☞ 64.60(6)

Any implied contract arising when informant responded to offer of reward by United States Postal Inspection Service (USPIS) for information about assailant who attacked postal worker was one for "procurement of services," and thus within exclusive jurisdiction of Court of Federal Claims under Contract Disputes Act over implied contracts with executive agencies. Goodin v. U.S. Postal Inspection Service, D.Minn.2005, 393 F.Supp.2d 869, affirmed 444 F.3d 998, certiorari denied 127 S.Ct. 930, 166 L.Ed.2d 702. Federal Courts ☞ 1141

Bidder's claim against the United States for breach of an implied contract arising out of government bid for the sale of recyclable aluminum scrap was in effect a bid protest which was not cognizable under the Contract Disputes Act (CDA). Resource Recycling Corp., Inc. v. U.S., Fed.Cl.2003, 56 Fed.Cl. 612. United States ☞ 64.60(1)

Agreement between corporation and government contractor under which corporation would act as subcontractor for work to be perform for Air Force did not create implied contract with government which would support award of quantum meruit relief; corporation was not joint venturer with government contractor but rather was subcontractor. Eastern Trans-Waste of Maryland, Inc. v. U.S., Fed.Cl.1992, 27 Fed.Cl. 146. United States ☞ 69(2); United States ☞ 74.2

Contract Disputes Act was applicable to implied-in-fact contract under which Government was liable for emergency medical care rendered to illegal aliens. City of El Centro v. U.S., Cl.Ct.1989, 17 Cl.Ct. 794. United States ☞ 73(1)

Contract Disputes Act did not embrace implied contract of fair dealing that arose from lowest bidder's submission of bid on contract to provide meals and lodging for armed forces applicants so as to permit bidder to recover for lost profits based on rooms it allegedly set aside in order to be able to meet government's contemplated needs. La Strada Inn, Inc. v. U.S., Cl.Ct.

1987, 12 Cl.Ct. 110. United States ☞ 64.55(1)

3. Executive agency

Contract Disputes Act (CDA) vests exclusive jurisdiction with either Agency Board of Contract Appeals or United States Court of Federal Claims over claims regarding procurement contracts entered into by executive agency, such as United States Postal Service (USPS). Four Star Aviation, Inc. v. U.S. Postal Service, D.Virgin Islands 2000, 120 F.Supp.2d 523. Federal Courts ☞ 1141; United States ☞ 73(15)

Government Printing Office is not "executive agency," and, thus, contract with Office is not subject to Contract Disputes Act. Fry Communications, Inc. v. U.S., Cl.Ct.1991, 22 Cl.Ct. 497, on remand. United States ☞ 33

4. Nonappropriated fund activities

Vendor's contract with morale, welfare, and recreation activity, a local, base level nonappropriated fund instrumentality (NAFI) located at overseas Marine Corps air station, to provide fast food services at the Marine Corps air station for a ten-year period, was with a local morale, welfare, and recreation entity with supervision and contracting structures separate and distinct from a military exchange, and therefore was not closely affiliated with a post exchange, and thus, the morale, welfare, and recreation activity was not a covered entity under the Contract Disputes Act, and vendor's contract was not subject to the Contract Disputes Act (CDA). Pacrim Pizza Co. v. Pirie, C.A.Fed.2002, 304 F.3d 1291. United States ☞ 73(9)

Contract between Nonappropriated Fund Risk Management Program (RIMP) and child care provider in Army child care program, by which government agreed to insure provider under certain circumstances, was not subject to Contract Disputes Act. Lee by Lee v. U.S., C.A.Fed.1997, 129 F.3d 1482. United States ☞ 73(9)

5. Procurement contracts generally

Army's purchase orders for prototypes of hydration systems constituted "procurement contracts," and thus Armed Services Board of Contract Appeals had subject matter jurisdiction under Contract Disputes Act (CDA) over manufacturer's claim that United States improperly disclosed proprietary data in purchase orders to non-governmental third parties to extent that orders incorporated confidentiality provisions of Defense Acquisition Regulation (DAR) legend on manufacturer's unsolicited proposals, even though Army had not awarded manufacturer final contract, and manufacturer did not sign purchase orders, where purchase orders specified parties involved, delivery instructions, price, payment terms, and transportation instructions. Wesleyan Co., Inc. v. Harvey, C.A.Fed.2006, 454 F.3d 1375, rehearing denied. United States ☞ 73(15)

Agreement between mushroom grower and the National Resource Conservation Service (NRCS) in Department of Agriculture, pursuant to which grower would construct and operate spent mushroom substrate (SMS) transfer facility according to NRCS specifications in return for cost-share payments, was a "cooperative agreement" rather than a "procurement contract," and thus it was not subject to the Contract Disputes Act (CDA). Rick's Mushroom Service, Inc. v. U.S., Fed.Cl. 2007, 2007 WL 1095555. United States ☞ 73(9)

Alleged bailment contract between professional artist and the government regarding storage of artist's artwork in an American cultural center in Belgium did not fall within scope of the Contract Disputes Act (CDA) or the Overseas Procurement Handbook, as bailment contract is not a contract for procurement of goods and services. Leonardo v. U.S., Fed.Cl. 2004, 60 Fed.Cl. 126. United States ☞ 64.5; United States ☞ 73(9)

Although competing in contest for war memorial design and winning same may have served to create contract, contract did not constitute procurement covered by Contract Disputes Act. Lucas v. U.S., Cl.Ct.1992, 25 Cl.Ct. 298. United States ☞ 63

Contracts between the Bureau of Indian Affairs and Indian school board relating to funds for repair of high school were not "procurement" oriented contracts, but, rather, basically grant or sociological type contracts designed to accomplish government social policy provision, placing contracts outside scope of the Contract Disputes Act of 1978, § 3, 41 U.S.C.A. § 602; therefore, claims for breach of such contracts

were not covered by the Act. Busby School of Northern Cheyenne Tribe v. U.S., Cl.Ct.1985, 8 Cl.Ct. 596. United States ☞ 73(9)

Since post-award mistake in bid claim is matter relating to government procurement contract, error must be resolved according to prescribed procedures. 1984, 63 Op.Comp.Gen. 166.

6.   Real property contracts—Generally

Contract by which government purchased office building and received fee simple title to property involved conveyance of preexisting real property interest to government and not creation of new property interest so that contract was one for "procurement" of real property, as well as for repair and alteration of building, for purposes of determining jurisdiction over contract dispute. Bonneville Associates v. U.S., C.A.Fed.1994, 43 F.3d 649. United States ☞ 73(15)

Agreement by which contractor was assigned Government's options to purchase land in exchange for promise to build office building thereon for lease to Government was within scope of Contract Disputes Act, even though agreement dealt with real property. Sterling-Kates v. U.S., Cl.Ct.1987, 12 Cl.Ct. 290. United States ☞ 73(15)

Alleged contract, implied in fact, on which owner of parking lot relied, based upon irregular use by government employees, of parking spaces on the parking lot, for temporary storage of their privately owned automobiles, was not a contract for the "procurement of * * * realty in being," and therefore was not excluded from applicability of this section; thus, lack of a proper certification deprived Claims Court of jurisdiction to consider parking lot owner's claim for over $62,000, allegedly due under implied contract with United States. Parking Co. of America, Inc. v. U.S., Cl.Ct.1984, 5 Cl.Ct. 139. United States ☞ 70(9)

7.   —— Leases, real property contracts

By entering into lease government does not acquire preexisting interest in land, it establishes new one; thus, language in both Office of Federal Procurement Policy Act [41 U.S.C.A. § 405(a)(1)] and Contract Disputes Act [41 U.S.C.A. § 602(a)(1)] excluding contracts to procure "real property in being" did not apply to newly-created lease agreement, and agreement fell within purview of statutes. Forman v. U.S., C.A.Fed.1985, 767 F.2d 875. United States ⟲ 55

The Contract Disputes Act (CDA) applies to leases of real property. 1-10 Industry Associates, Inc. v. U.S. Postal Service, E.D.N.Y.2001, 133 F.Supp.2d 194. United States ⟲ 73(7)

Government leases of real property are governed by Contract Disputes Act (CDA), as they are considered the procurement of property, "other than real property in being," within CDA provisions; lease contract entered into by executive agency creates new interest in land, rather than resulting in acquisition of preexisting interest in land. Spodek v. U.S., E.D.Pa. 1998, 26 F.Supp.2d 750. United States ⟲ 73(9)

The Contract Disputes Act applies to leases of real property, including those by the Postal Service. U.S. v. Black Hawk Masonic Temple Ass'n, Inc., D.Colo.1992, 798 F.Supp. 646. United States ⟲ 55

Concession lease allowing contractor to operate a marina business at government reservoir was not governed by the Contract Disputes Act (CDA), as it was not a contract for the procurement of property, services, or construction, and thus failure of lessees to file a CDA claim did not defeat jurisdiction of the Court of Federal Claims over their breach of lease claim. Frazier v. U.S., Fed.Cl.2005, 67 Fed.Cl. 56, appeal filed, affirmed 186 Fed.Appx. 990, 2006 WL 1737429. United States ⟲ 73(9)

Lease which was acquired by the Postal Service incident to its purchase of the underlying fee interest from a foreclosing lender was "real property in being" with meaning of provision of the Contract Disputes Act (CDA) excluding the procurement of "real property in being" from its purview. Coconut Grove Entertainment, Inc. v. U.S., Fed.Cl.2000, 46 Fed.Cl. 249, reconsideration denied. United States ⟲ 55

Lease of Saudi Arabian property to United States fell within purview of CDA; although "real property in being" was excluded from scope of statute, execution of a lease established a new interest. Hamza v. U.S., Fed.Cl.1994, 31 Fed.Cl. 315. United States ⟲ 55

8. —— Financing and subsidy, real property contracts

Turnkey contract between contractor and housing authority was not contract for "the procurement of construction * * * of real property" by executive agency within meaning of Contract Disputes Act; contract was merely for financing of procurement of construction by nonfederal agency, the housing authority. New Era Const. v. U.S., C.A.Fed.1989, 890 F.2d 1152, rehearing denied. United States ⟲ 74(7)

Construction-differential subsidy contracts are not the type of conventional contracts for direct procurement by government of tangible property or services which Congress contemplated including within scope of the Contract Disputes Act. Newport News Shipbuilding and Dry Dock Co. v. U.S., Cl.Ct.1985, 7 Cl.Ct. 549. United States ⟲ 73(9)

9. —— Construction, alteration, repair or maintenance, real property contracts

Contract by which irrigation district was to operate and maintain particular unit of dam project which was constructed and owned by government was contract involving "procurement of construction, alteration, repair or maintenance of real property," thus, dispute arising under contract was subject to CDA. Oroville-Tonasket Irr. Dist. v. U.S., Fed.Cl. 1995, 33 Fed.Cl. 14. United States ⟲ 73(9)

10. Services procured—Generally

Forensic toxicology expert's claim against the United States Air Force for sums owed to him for expert services rendered was subject to Contract Disputes Act of 1978, and, therefore, federal district court lacked jurisdiction over dispute. Vasiliades v. U.S., D.Neb.1997, 991 F.Supp. 1136. Federal Courts ⟲ 976; United States ⟲ 73(9)

Contracts Dispute Act (CDA) was applicable to written contracts of employment entered into by Native Americans with the Bureau of Indian Affairs (BIA) to fill "educator" positions at tribal school, as the contracts were express contracts with an executive agency for the "procurement of services" within meaning of the CDA. Flying Horse v. U.S., Fed.Cl.2001, 49 Fed.Cl. 419. United States ⟲ 73(9)

Contract Disputes Act is not applicable to service contract involving judiciary. Erwin v. U.S., Cl.Ct.1989, 19 Cl.Ct. 47. United States ⟲ 73(1)

Fact that Farmers Home Administration subordinated loan agreements to certain private financial institutions did not transform the contracts into ones for which the government was procuring services and therefore Contract Disputes Act of 1978, § 3(a) [41 U.S.C.A. § 602(a)] was not implicated. Hester v. Farmers Home Admin., E.D.Mo.1985, 49 B.R. 593. United States ⊕ 53(7); United States ⊕ 73(9)

Services abroad agreement under which employee of Central Intelligence Agency (CIA) agreed to reimburse government for relocation expenses if she terminated her assignment abroad prematurely was not contract for procurement of services and thus was not governed by Contract Disputes Act (CDA). Roberta B. v. Tenet, C.A.Fed.2003, 71 Fed.Appx. 45, 2003 WL 21675123, Unreported. United States ⊕ 73(9)

11.   —— Government provision of services, services procured

Contract Disputes Act (CDA) did not apply to consolidated arrangements contract (CAC) because it was a contract for the provision of services by the government; nevertheless, jurisdiction over claim arising out of the CAC was proper in the Court of Federal Claims under the Tucker Act. North Star Steel Co. v. U.S., C.A.Fed.2007, 477 F.3d 1324. Federal Courts ⊕ 1076; United States ⊕ 73(9)

Park Service regulation providing that National Park concession contracts were not contracts within coverage of Contract Dispute Act, which provides alternative forum to judicial relief in Court of Federal Claims, was in conformity with Contract Disputes act as concession contracts did not involve procurement of property or services for government but rather provision of services to third party National Park visitors. Amfac Resorts, L.L.C. v. U.S. Dept. of the Interior, C.A.D.C.2002, 282 F.3d 818, 350 U.S.App.D.C. 191, rehearing and rehearing en banc denied, certiorari granted 123 S.Ct. 549, 537 U.S. 1018, 154 L.Ed.2d 424, vacated in part 123 S.Ct. 2026, 538 U.S. 803, 155 L.Ed.2d 1017, on remand 2003 WL 22327068. United States ⊕ 73(9)

Contract Disputes Act (CDA) did not apply to uranium enrichment contracts pursuant to which the Department of Energy (DOE) was to provide uranium enrichment services to electric utilities,

since they did not involve the "procurement of property" or the "disposal of personal property" by the government. Florida Power & Light Co. v. U.S., Fed. Cl.2001, 49 Fed.Cl. 656, vacated 307 F.3d 1364, on remand 56 Fed.Cl. 555.

12.   Disposal of personal property

Government contractor's claim against Forest Service contracting officer for breach of timber sales contracts was subject to provisions of Contract Disputes Act and within jurisdiction of Claims Court; although contractor contended claim was constitutional rather than contractual in nature, claim was founded upon express contract with United States, and timber sale contract was a contract for disposal of personal property within meaning of the Act. Mendenhall v. Kusicko, C.A.9 (Idaho) 1988, 857 F.2d 1378. Federal Courts ⊕ 1076

Lease of government real property was not contract for "disposal of personal property," even though lease included various items of equipment, and, thus, Government's ejectment action against lessee following expiration of lease was not governed by Contract Disputes Act. U.S. v. Triple A Mach. Shop, Inc., C.A.9 (Cal.) 1988, 857 F.2d 579. United States ⊕ 57

13.   Broker's fee contracts

This chapter was applicable to real estate agent's action against Federal Savings and Loan Insurance Corporation to recover brokerage fee; thus, district court lacked jurisdiction to hear matter. APA, Inc. v. Federal Sav. and Loan Ins. Corp., W.D.La.1983, 562 F.Supp. 884. Building And Loan Associations ⊕ 48

14.   Common carrier contracts

When common carrier provides transportation services to government agency under the Transportation Act and government bill of lading serves as contract between parties, claims arising in connection with that contract are not subject to Contract Disputes Act. Dalton v. Sherwood Van Lines, Inc., C.A.Fed.1995, 50 F.3d 1014. United States ⊕ 73(9)

15.   Confidentiality and disclosure

Conceptual information disclosed by manufacturer of hydration system to Army prior to submission of its first unsolicited proposal was not protected by confidentiality provisions, and thus Armed Services Board of Contract Appeals did not have subject matter jurisdiction over manufacturer's claim against Army for improper disclosure of its proprietary data to non-governmental third parties, where proposal did not contain Defense Acquisition Regulation (DAR) legend discussing government use of unsolicited information, and there was no contract between parties at time of disclosure. Wesleyan Co., Inc. v. Harvey, C.A.Fed.2006, 454 F.3d 1375, rehearing denied. United States ⊂⇒ 73(15)

16. Guaranties

United States' guarantees for payment of transportation charges, should contractor fail to comply with obligations imposed by contract between contractor and motor common carrier, were not "contracts" for purposes of the Contract Disputes Act, so as to deprive federal district court of jurisdiction over carrier's claim and contractor's cross claim that were both based upon the guarantees. Jones Motor Co., Inc. v. Teledyne, Inc., D.Del.1988, 690 F.Supp. 310. Federal Courts ⊂⇒ 976

Contract Disputes Act did not confer jurisdiction upon Claims Court of bank's action against the United States, based on allegedly wrongful retention of funds paid to the Department of State, Office of Foreign Buildings Operations, pursuant to bond obligation, given determination that bank was acting as guarantor in regard to public contract rather than as surety. Egyptian American Bank, S.A.E. v. U.S., Cl.Ct.1987, 13 Cl.Ct. 337, affirmed 861 F.2d 728. Federal Courts ⊂⇒ 1076

17. Postal Services contracts

United States Postal Service's solicitation of suggestions under employee suggestion program constituted "procurement of services" under Contract Disputes Act; thus, former postal employee's suit alleging failure to be compensated for suggestion he had made under that program had to be pursued in Court of Claims, not federal district court. Hayes v. U.S. Postal Service, C.A.5 (La.) 1988, 859 F.2d 354. Federal Courts ⊂⇒ 1079

Claim of mail transporters who had contract with the United States Postal Service (USPS) to transport mail by truck, that USPS's implementation of requirement that the transporters purchase fuel from designated suppliers violated their Fifth Amendment rights, in

that it denied them of their freedom to contract by arbitrarily incorporating the requirement into all renewal and new mail contracts, and in that the requirement constituted a taking of property, was "essentially contractual," and thus, pursuant to the Contract Disputes Act (CDA), the district court lacked subject matter jurisdiction over the claim. B & B Industries, Inc. v. U.S. Postal Service, E.D.Mich.2002, 185 F.Supp.2d 760, reversed in part 363 F.3d 404, rehearing en banc granted, opinion superseded on rehearing 406 F.3d 766. Federal Courts ⊂⇒ 1141

Contract Disputes Act's (CDA) procedures for appeal to Court of Federal Claims provided exclusive method of adjudication of landlord's dispute over rent payments allegedly owed by United States Postal Service (USPS). 1-10 Industry Associates, Inc. v. U.S. Postal Service, E.D.N.Y.2001, 133 F.Supp.2d 194. Federal Courts ⊂⇒ 1141

Even with general jurisdiction grant to the district courts, the Claims Court retained jurisdiction over contract claims involving the United States Postal Service. Prefab Products, Inc. v. U.S. Postal Service, S.D.Fla.1984, 600 F.Supp. 89. Federal Courts ⊂⇒ 1141

Postal Service employee's receipt of certificate in return for submitting suggestion according to Postal Service's employee suggestion program was not a "procurement of services" under the Contract Disputes Act necessary to invoke contractual jurisdiction of the Claims Court. Hayes v. U.S., Cl.Ct.1990, 20 Cl. Ct. 150, affirmed 928 F.2d 411. Federal Courts ⊂⇒ 1076

Alleged contract between Postal Service customer and Postal Service for delivery of third-class political mail within 48 hours was not a contract cognizable under Contract Disputes Act, since alleged contract was one for a governmental entity to provide services, rather than to procure services, as Contract Disputes Act envisioned. Rider v. U.S., Cl.Ct. 1985, 7 Cl.Ct. 770, affirmed 790 F.2d 91. United States ⊂⇒ 73(15)

18. Research contracts

Contract Disputes Act was not applicable to pleaded contracts, primary function of which was facilitation of transfer of AIDS-related research materials among scientists engaged in collaborative research effort, not procurement of property or services; thus, Claims Court did not lack jurisdiction on ground that there had been no prior presentation of claim, over $50,000, to agency contracting officer and decision or failure to decide by that officer. Institut Pasteur v. U.S., C.A.Fed.1987, 814 F.2d 624, 2 U.S.P.Q.2d 1048. Federal Courts ⟜ 1102

19. Subcontracts

Supply subcontractor which was "teamed" with prime contractor for purposes of federal agency's procurement program lacked standing to assert claim that agency, after terminating prior contract with subcontractor, blacklisted subcontractor from competing for new contract, where procurement program permitted only prime contractors to submit bids and where prime contractor and subcontractor rather than government had made decision that they would work together. Information Systems & Networks Corp. v. U.S. Dept. of Health and Human Services, D.D.C. 1997, 970 F.Supp. 1. United States ⟜ 74.2

Subcontract with prime government contractor was governed by Contract Disputes Act's alternative dispute resolution mechanism; prime contract, which was governed by Act, was incorporated into subcontract by reference, and, although work was commenced under oral agreement and prime contract was voluminous, subcontractor had been in business for many years, had rendered services under government contracts before, and had ample opportunity to become acquainted with prime contract. COSMCO, Inc. v. Head, Inc., Ohio App. 10 Dist. 1990, 591 N.E.2d 803, 70 Ohio App.3d 544. Alternative Dispute Resolution ⟜ 100

20. Sureties

A suit for breach of surety agreement is not Contract Disputes Act (CDA) claim, and therefore such a claim does not have to be litigated according to procedures established by the CDA. U.S. v. American States Ins. Co., C.A.11 (Fla.) 2001, 252 F.3d 1268. United States ⟜ 73(15)

Contract Disputes Act, which requires that "contract" sued upon be government contract, did not apply to performance bond issued by surety to contractor, so as to negate district court subject matter jurisdiction, in action by United States

against Miller Act sureties, on theory sureties were contractors under the CDA. U.S. v. Seaboard Sur. Co., C.A.2 (N.Y.) 1987, 817 F.2d 956, certiorari denied 108 S.Ct. 161, 484 U.S. 855, 98 L.Ed.2d 115. Federal Courts ⟜ 233

21. Miscellaneous claims CDA applicable

Telecommunications company's claims against United States for unconstitutional taking and inverse condemnation and claims under Federal Tort Claims Act, which were all based upon claims of ownership of telecommunications equipment and facilities installed and maintained pursuant to contract with Department of Energy and of drawings and plats of telecommunications system, were "essentially contractual in nature," and, thus, had to be resolved under Contract Disputes Act and Tucker Act, with sole proper forum for judicial consideration being Court of Federal Claims. BellSouth Telecommunications, Inc. v. U.S., E.D.Tenn.1996, 991 F.Supp. 920. Federal Courts ⟜ 1139; United States ⟜ 73(9)

Sculptor's claim against the General Services Administration, arising from GSA's decision to move outdoor sculpture, arose from the contract between sculptor and the agency, and was therefore subject to the Contract Disputes Act, and district court lacked jurisdiction to hear claim. Serra v. U.S. General Services Admin., S.D.N.Y.1987, 667 F.Supp. 1042, affirmed 847 F.2d 1045. Federal Courts ⟜ 976

Farmer's claim against Commodity Credit Corporation based on allegation that CCC agents had wrongfully altered farmer's bid under payment in kind program, thereby violating farmer's agreement to transfer grain to CCC in exchange for government's discharge of farm loan, was subject to Contract Disputes Act [Contract Disputes Act of 1978, § 2 et seq., 41 U.S.C.A. § 601 et seq.] with exclusive jurisdiction in the Claims Court. Coffey v. U.S. on Behalf of Commodity Credit Corp., D.Kan.1986, 626 F.Supp. 1246. Federal Courts ⟜ 1139

22. Miscellaneous claims CDA not applicable

Contract Disputes Act did not apply to "host country contracts" between Syria and contractor to improve water supply in Damascus, even though contracts were adopted by administrator of Agency for International Development, since contract was not for direct procurement of goods or services by executive agency of United States Government and, thus, Federal Circuit lacked jurisdiction to hear appeal from decision from Armed Services Board of Contract Appeals denying contractor's claims. G.E. Boggs & Associates, Inc. v. Roskens, C.A.Fed.1992, 969 F.2d 1023. United States ☞ 73(15)

Contract Disputes Act (CDA) did not apply to crop insurer's action against Federal Crop Insurance Corporation (FCIC) seeking damages for agency's alleged violation of standard reinsurance agreement (SRA), and thus did not preclude federal district court's exercise of jurisdiction over action; insurer did not have to bring claim in United States Court of Federal Claims. American Growers Ins. Co. v. Federal Crop Ins. Corp., S.D.Iowa 2002, 210 F.Supp.2d 1088. Federal Courts ☞ 1141; United States ☞ 73(9)

Contract Disputes Act (CDA) was not applicable to lodge owner's claim for compensation pursuant to termination provision of term special use permit issued for operation of resort in the Sho-

shone National Forest, as permit was not issued for the procurement of services for the federal government, which did not own the improvements of the resort site. The Sweetwater, A Wilderness Lodge LLC v. U.S., Fed.Cl.2006, 72 Fed.Cl. 208, modified on reconsideration. United States ☞ 73(9)

Court of Federal Claims lacked subject matter jurisdiction under the Contract Disputes Act (CDA) over claim of federal prisoner that the government breached his guilty plea agreement, as the statute applies only to contracts with executive agencies for the procurement of goods or services. Houston v. U.S., Fed.Cl.2004, 60 Fed.Cl. 507. Federal Courts ☞ 1076

Court of Federal Claims lacked jurisdiction under the Contract Disputes Act (CDA) over claim of contractor's president that wrongful debarment unfairly excluded him from the possibility of entering into future government contracts, resulting in lost profits and other business damages, as claim was not based upon a breach of a contract within the scope of the CDA. Schickler v. U.S., Fed.Cl.2002, 54 Fed.Cl. 264, appeal dismissed 70 Fed.Appx. 584, 2003 WL 21774141. Federal Courts ☞ 1076

§ 603. Maritime contracts

Appeals under paragraph (g) of section 607 of this title and suits under section 609 of this title, arising out of maritime contracts, shall be governed by chapter 20 or 22 of Title 46, Appendix, as applicable, to the extent that those chapters are not inconsistent with this chapter.

(Pub.L. 95–563, § 4, Nov. 1, 1978, 92 Stat. 2384.)

HISTORICAL AND STATUTORY NOTES

Revision Notes and Legislative Reports
1978 Acts. Senate Report No. 95–1118, see 1978 U.S.Code Cong. and Adm.News, p. 5235.

References in Text
Chapter 20 of Title 46, Appendix, referred to in text, was in the original a reference to the Act of Mar. 9, 1920 (41 Stat. 525, as amended), known as the Suits in Admiralty Act, which was classified generally to chapter 20 (section 741 et seq.) of Title 46, Shipping, prior to repeal by Pub.L. 109–304, § 19, Oct. 6, 2006, 120 Stat. 1710. See now chapter

309 of Title 46, 46 U.S.C.A. § 30901 et seq.

Chapter 22 of Title 46, Appendix, referred to in text, was in the original a reference to the Act of Mar. 3, 1925 (43 Stat. 1112, as amended), known as the Public Vessels Act, which was classified principally to chapter 22 of the Appendix to Title 46, 46 App. U.S.C.A. § 781 et seq., prior to repeal by Pub.L. 109–304, § 19, Oct. 6, 2006, 120 Stat. 1710. See, now, chapter 311 of Title 46, 46 U.S.C.A. § 31101 et seq.

"This chapter", referred to in text, was, in the original, "this Act", meaning Pub.L. 95–563, which, in addition to enacting this chapter, amended section 5108 of Title 5, Government Organization and Employees, sections 1346, 1491, 2401, 2414, 2510, and 2517 of Title 28, Judiciary and Judiciary Procedure, and section 724a of Title 31, Money and Finance, and enacted provisions set out as notes under section 601 of this title.

Effective and Applicability Provisions

1978 Acts. Section effective with respect to contracts entered into 120 days after Nov. 1, 1978 and, at the election of the contractor, with respect to any claim pending at such time before the contracting officer or initiated thereafter, see section 16 of Pub.L. 95–563, set out as a note under section 601 of this title.

LIBRARY REFERENCES

American Digest System

Federal Courts ☞1136.
United States ☞73(8).
Key Number System Topic Nos. 170B, 393.

Research References

ALR Library

59 ALR, Fed. 905, Application of 28 U.S.C.A. § 2516(A) to Government Contractor's Claim for Interest Expense or for Loss of Use of Its Capital Caused by Delay Attributable to Government.

29 ALR, Fed. 325, Comment Note.--Admiralty Jurisdiction in Matters of Contract.

Forms

Federal Procedural Forms § 34:79, Disputes Subject to CDA's Resolution Procedures.

Federal Procedural Forms § 34:92, Form.

Federal Procedural Forms § 34:305, Appeals Involving Maritime Contracts.

Federal Procedural Forms § 34:324, Actions Involving Maritime Contracts.

Federal Procedural Forms § 34:348, Complaint--For Equitable Adjustment [41 U.S.C.A. § 603].

8 West's Federal Forms § 13023, Appeals from the Boards of Contract Appeals Under the Contract Disputes Act.

Treatises and Practice Aids

Federal Procedure, Lawyers Edition § 39:801, Time for Submission.

Federal Procedure, Lawyers Edition § 39:1027, Dismissal Without Prejudice--Particular Circumstances as Justifying.

Federal Procedure, Lawyers Edition § 39:1124, Appeals Involving Maritime Contracts.

Federal Procedure, Lawyers Edition § 39:1130, Questions of Law.

Federal Procedure, Lawyers Edition § 39:1135, Remand for Further Action.

Federal Procedure, Lawyers Edition § 39:1140, Parties.

Federal Procedure, Lawyers Edition § 39:1146, Submission of Claim to Contracting Officer.

Federal Procedure, Lawyers Edition § 39:1160, Actions Involving Maritime Contracts.

West's Federal Administrative Practice § 822, Subject Matter Jurisdiction--Contract Claim: Jurisdiction, Limitations, Appeals and Interest.

13 Wright & Miller: Federal Prac. & Proc. § 3526, Congressional Control of Lower Federal Court Jurisdiction.

13 Wright & Miller: Federal Prac. & Proc. § 3527, Exclusive Federal Court Jurisdiction.

14 Wright & Miller: Federal Prac. & Proc. § 3657, Statutory Exceptions to Sovereign Immunity--Actions Under the Tucker Act.

WESTLAW ELECTRONIC RESEARCH

See Westlaw guide following the Explanation pages of this volume.

Notes of Decisions

Generally 1
Construction with other laws 2
Purpose 3
Transfer to district court 4

___

1. Generally

While Contract Disputes Act authorizes Court of Appeals for the Federal Circuit to review decisions of the boards of contract appeals, appeals arising out of maritime contracts must be brought in the federal district courts. Marine Logistics, Inc. v. England, C.A.Fed.2001, 265 F.3d 1322. Federal Courts ☞ 1136; Federal Courts ☞ 1141

Reference in Contract Disputes Act to disputes "arising out of maritime contracts" incorporates the law regarding scope of admiralty jurisdiction, which provides that admiralty extends only to contracts that are "wholly maritime" in nature, but that general rule is subject to two exceptions, such that admiralty court will retain jurisdiction over contract that is not wholly maritime in nature if (1) the non-maritime feature of the contract is merely incidental, or (2) the non-maritime feature of the contract is separable from the maritime elements, so that it may be severed and litigated independently without prejudice to any party. Sea-Land Service, Inc. v. Danzig, C.A.Fed.2000, 211 F.3d 1373. Federal Courts ☞ 1136

Appeals from government contracting board determinations generally lie in the Court of Appeals for the Federal Circuit; however, direct appeals from contracting officer's decisions and appeals from board of contracting appeal are treated differently when they arise from maritime contracts. Southwest Marine, Inc. v. U.S., N.D.Cal.1988, 680 F.Supp. 1400, reconsideration denied 680 F.Supp. 327. Administrative Law And Procedure ☞ 663; United States ☞ 73(15)

2. Construction with other laws

The Federal Courts Improvement Act did not create an exception to the district courts' exclusive jurisdiction over maritime contracts for government contracts relating to the repair of ships. Southwest Marine of San Francisco, Inc. v. U.S., C.A.Fed.1990, 896 F.2d 532. United States ☞ 73(15)

3. Purpose

Intent of Congress was to retain maritime contract claims within the exclusive jurisdiction of district courts. Whitey's Welding and Fabrication, Inc. v. U.S., Cl.Ct.1984, 5 Cl.Ct. 284.

4. Transfer to district court

Transfer of suit against the United States challenging default termination of maritime contract to district court was appropriate, considering that Court of Federal Claims lacked jurisdiction under the Contract Disputes Act (CDA), that district court would have jurisdiction, and that transfer was in the interest of justice given risk that twelve-month limitation period set forth in the CDA would render action stale if refiled. Thrustmaster of Texas, Inc. v. U.S., Fed.Cl.2004, 59 Fed. Cl. 672. Federal Courts ☞ 1155

§ 604. Fraudulent claims

If a contractor is unable to support any part of his claim and it is determined that such inability is attributable to misrepresentation of fact or fraud on the part of the contractor, he shall be liable to the Government for an amount equal to such unsupported part of the claim in addition to all costs to the Government attributable to the cost of reviewing said part of his claim. Liability under this subsection [1] shall be determined within six years of the commission of such misrepresentation of fact or fraud.

(Pub.L. 95–563, § 5, Nov. 1, 1978, 92 Stat. 2384.)

[1] So in original. Probably should be "section".

HISTORICAL AND STATUTORY NOTES

Revision Notes and Legislative Reports

1978 Acts. Section 4(b) states that if a contractor is unable to support any part of his claim and it is determined that such inability is attributable to misrepresentation of fact made with intent to deceive or mislead or fraud on the part of the contractor, he shall be liable to the Government for an amount equal to such unsupported part of the claim in addition to all costs to the Government attributable to the cost of reviewing said part of his claim.

This subsection is included out of concern that the submission of baseless claims contribute to the so-called horsetrading theory where an amount beyond that which can be legitimately claimed is submitted merely as a negotiating tactic. Hence, payment of such a claim by the Government would constitute a windfall to the contractor. It is the committee's view that to the extent that this practice is utilized, it should be eliminated so that disputes encompass only the amount which is truly contested.

Consistent with the limitations expressed in section 4(a) excluding issues of fraud against the United States from the authority of contracting agencies to consider or resolve, actions to enforce the Government's rights under section 4(b) would be solely the responsibility of the Department of Justice and would be instituted by the United States in a court of competent jurisdiction. The procedures now utilized by procurement agencies for reporting suspected fraudulent activity to the Department of Justice would be equally applicable to section 4(b) matters. See, for example, ASPR 1–111.

If such cases do arise and are thus handled in the courts, other parts of the claim not associated with possible fraud or misrepresentation of fact will continue on in the agency board or in the Court of Claims where the claim originated.

However, any claim to be paid to a contractor will be subject to a setoff where a false claim dispute is resolved against the contractor prior to such payment. The court in its discretion may enjoin any payment to a contractor who is the subject of an action under section 4(b).

This provision is intended to be separate and distinct from the rights now possessed by the Government in legislation such as the False Claims Act, 31 U.S.C. 231 et seq., or the Forfeiture Statute, 28 U.S.C. 2514. That is, section 4(b) is not intended in any way to diminish the rights now afforded to the Government under current legislation. To the extent that contractors set forth claim items and costs on which they can submit a legitimate argument for recovery, this provision would not apply. However, to the extent a contractor increases the claim submission by the fraudulent addition of items or costs or by misrepresenting its claim items or costs, this provision would apply. Under present law, if such fraud or misrepresentation is discovered prior to any payments by the Government, the claim can, in certain circumstances, be forfeited under 28 U.S.C. 2514. Any affirmative recovery by the Government in such a circumstance (where no Government payment has been made) is, however, limited to a $2,000 penalty under the provisions of the False Claims Act, 31 U.S.C. et seq. Section 4(b) will afford the Government a separate and additional remedy of recovering an amount equal to the fraudulent or misrepresented amount. The present $2,000 penalty bears no relation to the extent of the fraud attempted by a person who submits such a claim. This small sum lacks sufficient deterrent impact. Providing for a recovery equal to any proven attempted fraud means that the larger the fraud attempted, the greater is the liability to the Government.

It is not contemplated that the administration of section 4(b) would delay legitimate payments to contractors in any way, but to the extent any delay should occur in payments eventually found to be owing to a contractor, section 12 of the act requires that the contractor be compensated by the payment of interest. Senate Report No. 95–1118.

Effective and Applicability Provisions

1978 Acts. Section effective with respect to contracts entered into 120 days after Nov. 1, 1978 and, at the election of the contractor, with respect to any claim pending at such time before the contracting officer or initiated thereafter, see section 16 of Pub.L. 95–563, set out as a note under section 601 of this title.

LIBRARY REFERENCES

American Digest System
United States ☞75(5), 122.
Key Number System Topic No. 393.

Research References

Treatises and Practice Aids
Federal Procedure, Lawyers Edition § 39:793, Sufficiency of Supporting Information.

WESTLAW ELECTRONIC RESEARCH

See Westlaw guide following the Explanation pages of this volume.

Notes of Decisions

Contractors liable 2
Timeliness of claims 1

---

1. Timeliness of claims

Award of damages under anti-fraud provision of the Contract Disputes Act (CDA) was not time barred on ground that more than six years had passed since contractor's claim for equitable adjustment was determined to be fraudulent by contracting officer, where contractor's commission of fraud was repeated and ongoing in subsequent submissions to federal bankruptcy court, in multiple complaints filed in the Court of Federal Claims, and in filings submitted to the Court during trial and post-trial. UMC Elec. Co. v. U.S., Fed.Cl.1999, 45 Fed.Cl. 507. Federal Courts ☞ 1105

Six-year limitation period for government to bring claim under Contract Disputes Act (CDA) arises no earlier than submission of contractor's certified claim under CDA, regardless of when conduct rendering contractor's claim false allegedly occurred. Jana, Inc. v. U.S., Fed.Cl. 1995, 34 Fed.Cl. 447. Federal Courts ☞ 1107

Earliest that Government could have been aware of alleged fraud in contractor's supply of rifle barrels was when rifle barrel malfunctioned, and claims based on that fraud filed within six years of that

date were timely. SGW, Inc. v. U.S., Cl.Ct.1990, 20 Cl.Ct. 174. Limitation Of Actions ☞ 100(12)

2. Contractors liable

Government proved that certified claim of contractor for $64 million was fraudulent to the extent of $50 million, rendering contractor liable for that amount under fraud provision of the Contract Disputes Act (CDA); evidence revealed that contractor did not believe that the government owed it $64 million as a matter of right, but that it submitted claim as a negotiating ploy. Daewoo Engineering and Const. Co., Ltd. v. U.S., Fed.Cl.2006, 73 Fed.Cl. 547. United States ☞ 122

Contractor was liable to United States for amount equal to unsupported part of its claim for equitable adjustment of contract with government for replacement of underground water lines in addition to all costs to government attributable to cost of reviewing portion of its claim under anti-fraud provision of Contract Disputes Act (CDA), since contractor's conduct was devoid of any reasonable attempt to verify its claim or other conduct showing that it did not intend to defraud the government. Larry D. Barnes, Inc. v. U.S., C.A.Fed.2002, 45 Fed.Appx. 907, 2002 WL 1890798, Unreported. United States ☞ 75(5)

§ 605. Decision by contracting officer

(a) Contractor claims

All claims by a contractor against the government relating to a contract shall be in writing and shall be submitted to the contracting officer for a decision. All claims by the government against a contractor relating to a contract shall be the subject of a decision by the contracting officer. Each claim by a contractor against the government relating to a contract and each claim by the government against a contractor relating to a contract shall be submitted within 6 years after the accrual of the claim. The preceding sentence does not apply to a claim by the government against a contractor that is based on a claim by the contractor involving fraud. The contracting officer shall issue his decisions in writing, and shall mail or otherwise furnish a copy of the decision to the contractor. The decision shall state the reasons for the decision reached, and shall inform the contractor of his rights as provided in this chapter. Specific findings of fact are not required, but, if made, shall not be binding in any subsequent proceeding. The authority of this subsection shall not extend to a claim or dispute for penalties or forfeitures prescribed by statute or regulation which another Federal agency is specifically authorized to administer, settle, or determine. This section shall not authorize any agency head to settle, compromise, pay, or otherwise adjust any claim involving fraud.

(b) Review; performance of contract pending appeal

The contracting officer's decision on the claim shall be final and conclusive and not subject to review by any forum, tribunal, or Government agency, unless an appeal or suit is timely commenced as authorized by this chapter. Nothing in this chapter shall prohibit executive agencies from including a clause in government contracts requiring that pending final decision of an appeal, action, or final settlement, a contractor shall proceed diligently with performance of the contract in accordance with the contracting officer's decision.

(c) Amount of claim; certification; notification; time of issuance; presumption

(1) A contracting officer shall issue a decision on any submitted claim of $100,000 or less within sixty days from his receipt of a written request from the contractor that a decision be rendered within that period. For claims of more than $100,000, the contractor shall certify that the claim is made in good faith, that the supporting data are accurate and complete to the best of his knowledge and belief, that the amount requested accurately reflects the contract adjustment for which the contractor believes the government is liable, and that the certifier is duly authorized to certify the claim on behalf of the contractor.

(2) A contracting officer shall, within sixty days of receipt of a submitted certified claim over $100,000—

　　(A) issue a decision; or

(B) notify the contractor of the time within which a decision will be issued.

(3) The decision of a contracting officer on submitted claims shall be issued within a reasonable time, in accordance with regulations promulgated by the agency, taking into account such factors as the size and complexity of the claim and the adequacy of the information in support of the claim provided by the contractor.

(4) A contractor may request the tribunal concerned to direct a contracting officer to issue a decision in a specified period of time, as determined by the tribunal concerned, in the event of undue delay on the part of the contracting officer.

(5) Any failure by the contracting officer to issue a decision on a contract claim within the period required will be deemed to be a decision by the contracting officer denying the claim and will authorize the commencement of the appeal or suit on the claim as otherwise provided in this chapter. However, in the event an appeal or suit is so commenced in the absence of a prior decision by the contracting officer, the tribunal concerned may, at its option, stay the proceedings to obtain a decision on the claim by the contracting officer.

(6) The contracting officer shall have no obligation to render a final decision on any claim of more than $100,000 that is not certified in accordance with paragraph (1) if, within 60 days after receipt of the claim, the contracting officer notifies the contractor in writing of the reasons why any attempted certification was found to be defective. A defect in the certification of a claim shall not deprive a court or an agency board of contract appeals of jurisdiction over that claim. Prior to the entry of a final judgment by a court or a decision by an agency board of contract appeals, the court or agency board shall require a defective certification to be corrected.

(7) The certification required by paragraph (1) may be executed by any person duly authorized to bind the contractor with respect to the claim.

(d) Alternative means of dispute resolution

Notwithstanding any other provision of this chapter, a contractor and a contracting officer may use any alternative means of dispute resolution under subchapter IV of chapter 5 of Title 5, or other mutually agreeable procedures, for resolving claims. The contractor shall certify the claim when required to do so as provided under subsection (c)(1) of this section or as otherwise required by law. All provisions of subchapter IV of chapter 5 of Title 5 shall apply to such alternative means of dispute resolution.

(e) Termination of authority to engage in alternative means of dispute resolution; savings provision

In any case in which the contracting officer rejects a contractor's request for alternative dispute resolution proceedings, the contracting officer shall provide the contractor with a written explanation, citing one or more of the conditions in section 572(b) of Title 5 or such other specific reasons that alternative dispute resolution procedures are inappropriate for the resolution of the dispute. In any case in which a contractor rejects a request of an agency for alternative dispute resolution proceedings, the contractor shall inform the agency in writing of the contractor's specific reasons for rejecting the request.

(Pub.L. 95–563, § 6, Nov. 1, 1978, 92 Stat. 2384; Pub.L. 101–552, § 6(a), Nov. 15, 1990, 104 Stat. 2745; Pub.L. 102–572, Title IX, § 907(a)(1), Oct. 29, 1992, 106 Stat. 4518; Pub.L. 103–355, Title II, §§ 2351(a)(1), (b), (e), 2352, Oct. 13, 1994, 108 Stat. 3322; Pub.L. 104–106, Div. D, Title XLIII, §§ 4321(a)(6), (7), 4322(b)(6), Feb. 10, 1996, 110 Stat. 671, 677; Pub.L. 104–320, § 6, Oct. 19, 1996, 110 Stat. 3871; Pub.L. 105–85, Div. A, Title X, § 1073(g)(3), Nov. 18, 1997, 111 Stat. 1906.)

HISTORICAL AND STATUTORY NOTES

Revision Notes and Legislative Reports

1978 Acts. Section 5(a) states that all claims are to be submitted in writing and that it is the responsibility of the contracting officer to issue a decision on the claim in writing to the contractor and to inform the contractor of his rights as provided in the Contract Disputes Act. The written decision is to state the reasons for the decision. Specific findings of fact are not required, but, if made will not be binding in any subsequent appeal.

Section 5(b) states that the contracting officer's decision on the claim is final and conclusive unless an appeal or suit is instituted.

Section 5(c) states that upon written request from the contractor that a decision be made on the claim, the contracting officer will make that decision within a 60-day period from receipt of the request. This period may be extended by written agreement between both parties. The establishment of this 60-day period is to insure that a contracting officer will act promptly on all claims and if he should arbitrarily delay, the contractor has recourse to obtaining a decision. Should the contracting officer continued to deny issuing a written decision within the period required, that failure will be construed as his denying the claim and

will authorize the commencement of the appeals process. Should the appeals process start without the decision of the contracting officer, the tribunal concerned may, at its option, stay the proceedings to obtain a decision on the claim by the contracting officer.

Section 5 describes explicitly the decisionmaking role of the contracting officer. Equally important is a thorough knowledge by the contractor of the role and authority that the contracting officer plays in the decisionmaking process of the agency he represents. This importance is highlighted as recommendation No. 1 in the Procurement Commission's report. While the objective may be to make the contracting officer the focal point for decisions, practicability dictates that the extent to which the contracting officer relies on his own judgment or abides by the advice or determination of others is dependent on a variety of factors, including the officer's personal knowledge, capability, and executive qualities, as well as the nature of the particular procurement. With so many variables, it is impossible to generalize as to what the contracting officer's role should be in all situations. In addition, it is unrealistic to suggest that the various levels of management responsible for the projects and programs to which a contract relates and that bear the responsibility for the propriety and wisdom of the agency's action should at all times remain aloof from the manner in which contracts are administered and contractual actions are taken.

Thus, in the disputes and remedies area, the procuring agencies should have flexibility in deciding what role the contracting officer will have. Most importantly, the agencies, whatever role they decide to give the contracting officer, must make clear that role to the contractor. Thus, if for one reason or another, the contracting officer is not the primary decisionmaker on a contract matter, the Government must tell the contractor this, and tell the contractor who is making the decision. From this course of action the contractor will at all times know with whom he is dealing in matters under dispute.

It is expected that procedures will be established by the agencies to carry out this recommendation and course of action. Senate Report No. 95–1118.

1990 Acts. Senate Report No. 101–543, see 1990 U.S.Cong. and Adm.News, p. 3931.

1992 Acts. House Report No. 102–1006, see 1992 U.S. Code Cong. and Adm. News, p. 3921.

1994 Acts. Senate Report Nos. 103–258 and 103–259, and House Conference Report No. 103–712, see 1994 U.S. Code Cong. and Adm. News, p. 2561.

1996 Acts. House Conference Report No. 104–450, see 1996 U.S. Code Cong. and Adm. News, p. 238.

1997 Acts. House Conference Report No. 105–340 and Statement by President, see 1997 U.S. Code Cong. and Adm. News, p. 2251.

References in Text

"This chapter", referred to in subsecs. (a), (b), (c)(5), was, in the original, "this Act", meaning Pub.L. 95–563, which, in addition to enacting this chapter, amended section 5108 of Title 5, Government Organization and Employees, sections 1346, 1491, 2401, 2414, 2510, and 2517 of Title 28, Judiciary and Judicial Procedure, and section 724a of Title 31, Money and Finance, and enacted provisions set out as notes under section 601 of this title.

Codifications

Pub.L. 101–552, § 6(a) directed that section 6 of the Contract Disputes Act of 1978 (41 U.S.C. 606) be amended by adding new subsecs. (d) and (e). The amendment was executed to this section as the probable intent of Congress.

Amendments

1997 Amendments. Subsecs. (d), (e). Pub.L. 105–85, § 1073(g)(3), struck out "as in effect on September 30, 1995)" following "of Title 5" wherever appearing.

1996 Amendments. Subsec. (a). Pub.L. 104–106, § 4321(a)(6), amended Pub.L. 103–355, § 2351(a), making technical changes which, for the purposes of codification, required no changes in text.

Subsec. (d). Pub.L. 104–320, § 6(1), substituted provisions requiring a contractor to certify the claim when required to do so as provided under subsection (c)(1) of this section or as otherwise required by law for provisions requiring a contractor to certify the claim is in good faith, the supporting data is accurate, and amount requested accurately reflects the contract adjustment.

Pub.L. 104–106, § 4322(b)(6), inserted "(as in effect on September 30, 1995)" following "chapter 5 of Title 5", wherever appearing.

Subsec. (e). Pub.L. 104–320, § 6(2), struck out provisions relating to authority of agencies to engage in alternative means of dispute resolution proceedings under subsection (d) of this section until October 1, 1999, except with respect to then pending dispute resolution proceedings, until such proceedings terminate.

Pub.L. 104–106, § 4322(b)(6), inserted "(as in effect on September 30, 1995)" following "section 572(b) of Title 5".

Pub.L. 104–106, § 4321(a)(7), amended Pub.L. 103–355, § 2352(b), making technical changes which, for purposes of codification, required no changes in text.

1994 Amendments. Subsec. (a). Pub.L. 103–355, § 2351(a)[(1)], inserted after the second sentence "Each claim by a contractor against the government relating to a contract shall be submitted within 6 years after the accrual of the claim. The preceding sentence does not apply to a claim by the government against a contractor that is based on a claim by the contractor involving fraud.".

Subsec. (c). Pub.L. 103–355, § 2351(b), (e)(1), (2), substituted: in pars. (1), (2), and (6), "$100,000" for "$50,000" wherever appearing; and in par. (4), "tribunal concerned" for "agency board of contract appeals" and "determined by the tribunal concerned" for "determined by the board", respectively.

Subsec. (e). Pub.L. 103–355, § 2352(a), (b), extended, the date for the exercise of alternative dispute resolution authority to Oct. 1, 1999, from Oct. 1, 1995, and imposed reciprocal requirements on the contracting officer and the contractor to provide written explanations for rejection of alternative dispute resolution proceedings.

1992 Amendments. Subsec. (c)(1). Pub.L. 102–572, § 907(a)(1)(A), struck out "and" after "belief" and inserted provision relating to authorization of certifier to certify claim on behalf of contractor.

Subsec. (c)(6), (7). Pub.L. 102–572, § 907(a)(1)(B), added pars. (6) and (7).

1990 Amendments. Subsecs. (d), (e). Pub.L. 101–552 temporarily added subsecs. (d) and (e). See Effective and Termination Date of 1990 Acts note set out under this section.

Effective and Applicability Provisions
1996 Acts. Amendment by section 4321 of Pub.L. 104–106 effective as of Oct. 13, 1994, and as if included in Pub.L. 103–355, see section 4321(a) of Pub.L. 104–106, set out as a note under section 2306a of Title 10.

For effective date and applicability of amendment by section 4322(b)(6) of Pub.L. 104–106, see section 4401 of Pub.L. 104–106, set out as a note under section 251 of this title.

1994 Acts. Amendment by Pub.L. 103–355 effective Oct. 13, 1994, except as otherwise provided, see section 10001 of Pub.L. 103–355, set out as a note under section 251 of this title.

1992 Acts. Section 907(a)(2) of Pub.L. 102–572 provided that: "The amendment made by paragraph (1)(B) [enacting subsec. (c)(6) and (7) of this section] shall be effective with respect to all claims filed before, on, or after the date of the enactment of this Act [Oct. 29, 1992], except for those claims which, before such date of enactment, have been the subject of an appeal to an agency board of contract appeals or a suit in the United States Claims Court."

Section 907(a)(4) of Pub.L. 102–572 provided that: "The amendments made by paragraph (1)(A) [amending subsec. (c)(1) of this section] shall be effective with respect to certifications executed more than 60 days after the effective date of amendments to the Federal Acquisition Regulations implementing the amendments made by paragraph (1)(A) with respect to the certification of claims." [Regulation amended Oct. 25, 1993. See 58 F.R. 57243–01.]

1990 Acts. The termination of amendments by Pub.L. 101–552 and authority to use dispute resolution proceedings on Oct. 1, 1995, provided by section 11 of Pub.L. 101–552, set out as a note under section 571 of Title 5, Government Organization and Employees, was repealed by section 9 of Pub.L. 104–320.

1978 Acts. Section effective with respect to contracts entered into 120 days after Nov. 1, 1978 and, at the election of the contractor, with respect to any claim pending at such time before the contracting officer or initiated thereafter, see section 16 of Pub.L. 95–563, set out as a note under section 601 of this title.

Coordination with Other Amendments
Amendments by section 1073 of Pub.L. 105–85 to be treated as having been enacted immediately before the other provisions of Pub.L. 105–85, see section 1073(i) of Pub.L. 105–85, set out as a note under section 5315 of Title 5, Government Organization and Employees.

Definitions
Definitions of terms "agency", "administrative program" and "alternative means of dispute resolution" set forth in section 581 applicable to this section, see section 10 of Pub.L. 101–552, set out as a note under section 581 of Title 5, Government Organization and Employees.

Limitations Period for Submissions of Claims Against Government Less Than 6 Years for Certain Contracts in Existence on October 13, 1994
Section 2351(a)(2) of Pub.L. 103–355 provided that: "Notwithstanding the third sentence of section 6(a) of the Contract Disputes Act of 1978, as added by paragraph (1) [the third sentence of subsec. (a) of this section], if a contract in existence on the date of the enactment of

this Act [Oct. 13, 1994] requires that a claim referred to in that sentence be submitted earlier than 6 years after the accrual of the claim, then the claim shall be submitted within the period required by the contract. The preceding sentence does not apply to a claim by the Federal Government against a contractor that is based on a claim by the contractor involving fraud."

CROSS REFERENCES

Civilian agency acquisition allowable contract costs and applicability of contract disputes procedures to disallowance of costs and assessment of penalty, see 41 USCA § 256.

Costs and fees of parties, see 5 USCA § 504.

Defense contracts, allowable costs, see 10 USCA § 2324.

LAW REVIEW AND JOURNAL COMMENTARIES

Arbitration: A permissible or desirable method for resolving disputes involving federal acquisition and assistance contracts? Kirby Behre, 16 Pub.Cont.L.J. 66 (1986).

Determining the adequacy of a claim: *Blake Construction* reconciles the conflict between *Gauntt* and *Westclox*. M. Lee Kristeller, 18 Pub.Cont.L.J. 494 (1989).

Doing business with the government. Peter C. Mieres (February 1982) 4 L.A.Law. 34.

Government contract cases in the United States Court of Appeals for the Federal Circuit: 1995 in review. Thomas F. Williamson, Stacey L. Valerio and Stephanie P. Gilson, 45 Am.U.L.Rev. 1657 (1996).

Recovering look-back interest penalties under construction contracts after Illinois Contractors. William M. Simmons, 23 Pub.Cont.L.J. 305 (1994).

LIBRARY REFERENCES

American Digest System
United States ☞73(8), 75(2).
Key Number System Topic No. 393.

Research References

ALR Library
8 ALR, Fed. 2nd Series 1, Validity, Construction, and Application of Federal Employees Health Benefits Act (FEHBA), 5 U.S.C.A. §§ 8901 to 8914.
96 ALR, Fed. 336, What Constitutes "Adversary Adjudication" by Administrative Agency Entitling Prevailing Party to Award of Attorneys' Fees Under Equal Access to Justice Act (5 U.S.C.A. § 504).
27 ALR, Fed. 702, Modern Status of Applicability of Doctrine of Estoppel Against Federal Government and Its Agencies.
115 ALR 65, Right of Building or Construction Contractor to Recover Damages Resulting from Delay Caused by Default of Contractee.
21 ALR 180, False Pretense: Presentation of and Attempt to Establish Fraudulent Claim Against Governmental Agency.

Encyclopedias
Am. Jur. 2d Federal Courts § 2011, Suits Under Contract Disputes Act.
Am. Jur. 2d Public Works and Contracts § 207, Jurisdiction of Contracting Officer.
Am. Jur. 2d Public Works and Contracts § 210, Certification Requirement.
Am. Jur. 2d Public Works and Contracts § 211, Finality of Decisions of Contracting Officer.
Am. Jur. 2d Public Works and Contracts § 212, Appeal to an Agency Board of Contract Appeals.
67 Am. Jur. Proof of Facts 3d 339, Liability of Owner and Contractor for Delay in Completion of Building or Construction Project.

Forms

Federal Procedural Forms § 18:36, Contract Disputes Act.

Federal Procedural Forms § 34:78, Introduction to CDA.

Federal Procedural Forms § 34:80, Disputes Excluded from CDA's Resolution Procedures.

Federal Procedural Forms § 34:81, Form of Claim.

Federal Procedural Forms § 34:82, Time for Submitting Claim.

Federal Procedural Forms § 34:83, Certification of Claim--Affidavit.

Federal Procedural Forms § 34:85, Certification of Claim--Necessity of Stating Good Faith.

Federal Procedural Forms § 34:86, Certification of Claim--Who May Certify.

Federal Procedural Forms § 34:87, Claim Must Be Submitted to Contracting Officer.

Federal Procedural Forms § 34:89, Alternative Dispute Resolution.

Federal Procedural Forms § 34:91, Deadline for Issuing Decision; Contractor's Request for Decision.

Federal Procedural Forms § 34:92, Form.

Federal Procedural Forms § 34:93, Service.

Federal Procedural Forms § 34:94, Decision as Final Absent Appeal.

Federal Procedural Forms § 34:98, Election of Forum for Appeal of Contracting Officer's Decision.

Federal Procedural Forms § 34:116, Relief Available.

Federal Procedural Forms § 34:120, Requirement That Claim Be Certified.

Federal Procedural Forms § 34:130, Time for Filing--Effect of Contracting Officer's Failure to Issue Decision.

Federal Procedural Forms § 34:131, Effect of Failure to File or Untimely Filing.

Federal Procedural Forms § 34:133, Form and Content of Notice.

Federal Procedural Forms § 34:277, Motion in Limine to Establish Order of Proof and Limit Proof--Before Armed Services Board of Contract Appeals [48 C.F.R. Ch. 2, Appx. A, ASBCA Rule 5(B)].

Federal Procedural Forms § 34:302, Appeals by Contractors.

Federal Procedural Forms § 34:329, Necessity of Obtaining Contracting Officer's Decision.

Federal Procedural Forms § 34:330, Necessity of Obtaining Contracting Officer's Decision--Certification.

Federal Procedural Forms § 34:347, Complaint--For Damages--For Government's Breach of Contract [28 U.S.C.A. § 1491; 41 U.S.C.A. § 609; United States Court of Federal Claims Rule 8].

8 West's Federal Forms § 13023, Appeals from the Boards of Contract Appeals Under the Contract Disputes Act.

8 West's Federal Forms § 13112, History.

8 West's Federal Forms § 13223, Government Contract Claims--Claims Under the Contract Disputes Act.

26 West's Legal Forms § 1.3, Statutes Mandating or Encouraging Alternative Dispute Resolution.

Treatises and Practice Aids

Bankruptcy Service Lawyers Edition § 45:470, Relationship to Other Federal Laws or Regulations.

Bankruptcy Service Lawyers Edition § 45:490, Miscellaneous.

Federal Procedure, Lawyers Edition § 2:253, Adversary Adjudication Defined.

Federal Procedure, Lawyers Edition § 7:902, Introduction; Covered Proceedings and Applicants.

Federal Procedure, Lawyers Edition § 19:65, Suits Under Contract Disputes Act.

Federal Procedure, Lawyers Edition § 34:126, Types of Proceedings Covered.

Federal Procedure, Lawyers Edition § 34:134, Further Proceedings.

Federal Procedure, Lawyers Edition § 34:136, Administrative and Judicial Review.

Federal Procedure, Lawyers Edition § 39:790, Disputes Excluded from CDA's Resolution Procedures.

Federal Procedure, Lawyers Edition § 39:800, Submission to Contracting Officer.

WESTLAW ELECTRONIC RESEARCH

See Westlaw guide following the Explanation pages of this volume.

Notes of Decisions

1. Generally

Contract Dispute Act (CDA) establishes comprehensive scheme of legal and administrative remedies for resolution of government contract disputes; this scheme is designed to foster administrative resolution of government contract disputes and to this end it excludes those disputes from federal district court. U.S. v. Unified Industries, Inc., E.D.Va.1996, 929 F.Supp. 947. United States ⛒ 73(9)

2. Construction with other laws

That claim was submitted in conformity with the Contract Disputes Act did not preclude it from satisfying notice requirements of the Federal Tort Claims Act (FTCA). FGS Constructors, Inc. v. Carlow, D.S.D.1993, 823 F.Supp. 1508. United States ⛒ 127(2)

3. Mandatory nature of section

Unless requirements of this section are satisfied, there is no claim upon which a contracting officer can render a valid decision. Halec Const. Co., Inc. v. U.S., Cl.Ct.1984, 6 Cl.Ct. 439. United States ⛒ 73(9)

4. Claims within section—Generally

Procuring agencies have authority under this chapter to reform contracts and award proper monetary relief to mitigate effect of a unilateral bid mistake and a reformation claim for such purpose is cognizable before contracting officer. Paragon Energy Corp. v. U.S., Ct.Cl. 1981, 645 F.2d 966, 227 Ct.Cl. 176, affirmed 230 Ct.Cl. 884. United States ⛒ 73(9)

There is no requirement in the Contract Disputes Act (CDA) that a contractor's "claim" be submitted in any particular form or use any particular wording; all that is required is that the contractor submit in writing to the contracting officer (CO) a clear and unequivocal statement that gives the CO adequate notice of the basis and amount of the claim. Sarang Corp. v. U.S., Fed.Cl.2007, 76 Fed.Cl. 560. United States ⛒ 73(9)

Demand for monetary relief can be "claim" under Contract Disputes Act even absent antecedent dispute that specifically took into consideration amount of demand.   American Tel. & Tel. Co. v. U.S., Fed.Cl.1995, 32 Fed.Cl. 672, amended 33 Fed.Cl. 540, appeal granted 66 F.3d 344, affirmed in part, reversed in part 124 F.3d 1471, rehearing granted, vacated 136 F.3d 793, on rehearing 177 F.3d 1368, on remand 48 Fed.Cl. 156. United States ⬱ 73(9)

Even if contractor had claimed that Navy's nonrenewal breached contract awarded to contractor pursuant to solicitation, Court of Federal Claims would not have had jurisdiction, as claim would have been postaward dispute, which could not be brought to Court of Federal Claims, as contractor had not submitted claim to contracting officer that had been denied or deemed denied, and Court of Federal Claims had no equitable powers over postaward disputes.   Control Data Systems, Inc. v. U.S., Fed.Cl.1994, 32 Fed.Cl. 520.   United States ⬱ 73(15)

Routine request for payment, such as submission of as yet undisputed voucher, is not considered to be "claim" within subsec. (c) of this section.   Z.A.N. Co. v. U.S., Cl.Ct.1984, 6 Cl.Ct. 298.   United States ⬱ 73(9)

5. —— Counterclaims, claims within section

Where Government contractor elected to proceed under Contract Disputes Act with respect to contract which was initiated prior to effective date of Act, Government was required to raise its counterclaims before a contracting officer before Government could assert them in claims court.   Joseph Morton Co., Inc. v. U.S., C.A.Fed.1985, 757 F.2d 1273. United States ⬱ 73(15)

In action by shipowner to recover on its claim against government for balance of unpaid charter hire for use of ship, government's counterclaim that shipowner breached implied warranty of seaworthiness by failing to furnish properly trained crew members was improperly dismissed in view of fact that this section which would preclude such counterclaim does not apply to government.   Woods Hole Oceanographic Inst. v. U.S., C.A.1 (Mass.) 1982, 677 F.2d 149.   United States ⬱ 75(2)

6. —— Penalties or forfeitures, claims within section

Court of Federal Claims had jurisdiction under the Contract Disputes Act (CDA) over contractor's claim to the contract balance following default termination, notwithstanding that contractor did not submit a certified claim to contracting officer (CO) for the contract balance, where government submitted liquidated damages claim to the CO, who issued final decision setting off the damages against the contract balance, and thus contractor's request for the contract balance was an appeal of CO's final decision regarding liquidated damages award and the contract balance. Roxco, Ltd. v. U.S., Fed.Cl.2007, 77 Fed.Cl. 138.   United States ⬱ 73(9)

Dispute over liquidated damages could not be jurisdictional basis for Court of Federal Claims to consider complaint seeking money allegedly due for contract performance.   Kalamazoo Contractors, Inc. v. U.S., Fed.Cl.1997, 37 Fed.Cl. 362. United States ⬱ 74(1)

Claims court lacked jurisdiction over contractor's claim for liquidated damages and over contractor's challenge to Government's claim for such damages; contractor did not refer to liquidated damages in either its claim letter or complaint and neither its claim nor that of Government was made subject of decision in writing by contracting officer.   Wilner v. U.S., Cl.Ct.1991, 23 Cl.Ct. 241.   United States ⬱ 74(14)

Contractor's claim that contracting officer erred in withholding and assessing monies for its subcontractor's wage deficiencies against it instead of the subcontractor did not fall within the "penalty or forfeiture" exception to Contract Disputes Act's requirement that claim be presented to contracting officer in order to be redressable in Claims Court pursuant to direct access provision.   Mark Smith Const. Co., Inc. v. U.S., Cl.Ct.1986, 10 Cl.Ct. 540.   United States ⬱ 73(9)

Where public contractor seeks to contest assessment of liquidated damages by claiming entitlement to time extensions or other relief, court is presented with claim by contractor against government which, under Contract Disputes Act, must first be presented to the contracting officer.   Elgin Builders, Inc. v. U.S., Cl.Ct. 1986, 10 Cl.Ct. 40.   United States ⬱ 73(9)

Requirement of subsec. (c) of this section, that claims of more than $50,000 be certified to contracting officer beforehand, applied to contractor's claim for liquidated damages retained by United States as result of delays in completion of contract attributed to contractor; facts showed that request for time extensions from which final decision was rendered was made as result of meeting at which parties addressed question concerning retention of liquidated damages of more than $50,000, and communications between parties subsequent to meeting made clear that parties treated request for time extensions as single, unitary claim. Warchol Const. Co., Inc. v. U.S., Cl.Ct.1983, 2 Cl.Ct. 384. United States ☞ 73(15)

7. —— Subcontractor claims, claims within section

Subcontractor's claims against prime contractor on Air Force project were arbitrable under parties' contract, and did not have to be submitted to contracting officer under Contract Disputes Act; while parties' contract required that decision of contracting officer about prime contract would be binding on parties in disputes about subcontract, it also provided that any dispute not settled by agreement of parties would be submitted to arbitration; subcontractor's claims related to increased costs incurred as result of testing standards that were imposed by contractor and that were allegedly higher than Air Force's standards, and thus could not be considered to be claims against government. NavCom Defense Electronics, Inc. v. Ball Corp., C.A.9 (Cal.) 1996, 92 F.3d 877. United States ☞ 73(9)

Subcontractor's status as a subcontractor did not defeat CDA preemption of its claims against prime management contractor, where subcontractor had had a direct contractual relationship with government for over 25 years before prime contractor entered the scene, subcontract contained express disputes clause which expressly authorized and directed subcontractor to bring its claims before Department of Energy (DOE) contracting officer with a direct right of appeal to Energy Board of Contract Appeals (EBCA), there was no disclaimer of privity with DOE in subcontract, and prime contractor was not required to obtain Miller Act payment bond for subcontract.

RMI Titanium Co. v. Westinghouse Elec. Corp., C.A.6 (Ohio) 1996, 78 F.3d 1125. United States ☞ 73(9)

"Claims" provision in the "Construction Management Special General Provisions" of the prime contract between government and prime contractor did not contemplate that subcontractors should have the right to proceed directly against the government; by its terms, the provision did not expressly authorize a direct subcontractor appeal. U.S. v. Johnson Controls, Inc., C.A.Fed.1983, 713 F.2d 1541. United States ☞ 74.2

Contract Disputes Act (CDA) preempted entire field of government contract remedies, such that subcontractor was prevented from obtaining jurisdiction in federal district court in action against United States Postal Service (USPS), although CDA expressly applied only to claims by contractors; it was unlikely that Congress intended to create comprehensive system for streamlining resolution of claims by contractors while at same time allowing subcontractors to continue to bring claims in federal district court, and other avenues of relief were available. Eagle Fence Co., Inc. v. V.S. Elec., Inc., E.D.Pa.2004, 324 F.Supp.2d 621. United States ☞ 74.2

Contract Disputes Act did not govern dispute between subcontractor and prime contractor performing work at federally owned installation which was operated by a private entity and thus, section of private contract which required submission of disputes to appropriate contracting officer was insufficient to deprive district court of jurisdiction over dispute. Riley Elec. Co. v. American Dist. Telegraph Co., W.D.Ky.1989, 715 F.Supp. 813. Federal Courts ☞ 1102

Letter of subcontractor and cover letter of general contractor submitted to contracting officer (CO) together constituted a valid non-monetary claim under the Contract Disputes Act (CDA), and subsequent response by CO was a final decision, triggering time limit for appeal, where letters clearly and unequivocally stated contractor's disagreement with government's interpretation of contract modification, and sought interpretation of the modification as a matter of right. Clearwater Constructors, Inc. v. U.S., Fed.Cl.2003, 56 Fed.Cl. 303. United States ☞ 73(9); United States ☞ 73(15)

Government contractor's unqualified certification of subcontractor's claim that complied with Contract Disputes Act (CDA) was sufficient to support exercise of jurisdiction over claim by Court of Federal Claims, even if contractor did not believe claim was based on good grounds. Dillingham Const., N.A., Inc. v. U.S., Fed.Cl.1995, 33 Fed.Cl. 495, affirmed 91 F.3d 167. United States ⏛ 73(9)

Prime Government contractor's submission of claim on behalf of subcontractor to officer in charge of construction satisfied requirement of Contract Disputes Act that claims be submitted to contracting officer, where submission of claim to officer in charge of construction did not preclude full hearing on that claim. Blake Const. Co., Inc. v. U.S., Cl.Ct.1992, 25 Cl.Ct. 177, reversed 987 F.2d 743, rehearing denied, in banc suggestion declined, certiorari denied 114 S.Ct. 438, 510 U.S. 963, 126 L.Ed.2d 372. United States ⏛ 73(9)

Subcontractor had standing under Contract Disputes Act and Tucker Act to advance claim for retainage against Government where Government had undertaken obligation to pay subcontractor directly for all work performed under general contract. Wallace O'Connor Intern., Ltd. v. U.S., Cl.Ct.1991, 23 Cl.Ct. 754. United States ⏛ 74.2

Contracting officer lacks authority to settle claims of subcontractors who are not parties to prime contract, even when subcontractors agree to accept pro rata settlement from available contract funds; subcontractor claims should not be paid until court, or trustee in bankruptcy, settles other accounts. 1983, 62 Op.Comp. Gen. 633.

8. —— Miscellaneous requests considered claims, claims within section

Letters sent to contracting officer requesting equitable adjustments and time extension, explaining the circumstances warranting the increased performance cost and time, and requesting a sum were valid Contract Disputes Act (CDA) claims and Armed Services Board of Contract Appeals had jurisdiction over them, even in the absence of cost breakdown. H.L. Smith, Inc. v. Dalton, C.A.Fed.1995, 49 F.3d 1563, rehearing denied, in banc suggestion declined. United States ⏛ 73(9)

Contractor's letter submitting to contracting officer subcontractor's request for equitable adjustment qualified as "claim" under Contract Disputes Act, even though letter did not explicitly request final decision; letter requested payment of sum certain and gave adequate notice of basis and amount of claim, and contracting officer was on notice that subcontractor wanted final decision on claim. Transamerica Ins. Corp., Inc. for and on Behalf of Stroup Sheet Metal Works v. U.S., C.A.Fed.1992, 973 F.2d 1572, on remand 28 Fed.Cl. 418. United States ⏛ 73(9)

Letters submitted by public contractor requesting payment for contract amount constituted "claims" under Contract Disputes Act. Contract Cleaning Maintenance, Inc. v. U.S., C.A.Fed.1987, 811 F.2d 586. United States ⏛ 73(9)

Contractor stated "claim" under the Contract Disputes Act (CDA) when he sent e-mail to contracting agency's program manager requesting determination from contracting officer (CO) that agency's cautionary statement in official correspondence regarding the disclosure of communications related to contract be removed from agency's correspondence with him, as e-mail stated in attachments the factual and legal grounds for contractor's contention that contract could not unilaterally be changed by terms of cautionary notice. Parker v. U.S., Fed.Cl. 2007, 2007 WL 1893172. United States ⏛ 73(9)

Contractor properly presented equitable adjustment claim to contracting officer as required by the Contract Disputes Act (CDA) when it submitted its claim in writing for equitable adjustment arising from quantity shortfall in the amount of radiologically contaminated soil that it excavated from storage site and transported to a third-party facility, asserted its request for an equitable adjustment as a matter of right under changes clause of contract, and sought damages in a sum certain amount. Engineered Demolition, Inc. v. U.S., Fed.Cl.2006, 70 Fed.Cl. 580. United States ⏛ 73(9)

Letter from timber purchaser to contracting officer (CO) asserting that timber sale contract was modified pursuant to prior letters from CO proposing modification and its acceptance by down payment, and requesting CO to respond within ten days, constituted a "claim" within meaning of the Contract Disputes Act (CDA). Mills v. U.S., Fed.Cl.2006, 69 Fed.Cl. 358. United States ☞ 73(9)

Contractor's letters to contracting officer (CO) in which it asked CO to "confirm" its interpretation of exclusivity provision of contract constituted a valid "claim" within meaning of the Contract Disputes Act (CDA), since they sought "interpretation of contract terms" by the CO, in light of impending solicitation which contractor believed violated exclusivity provision. CW Government Travel, Inc. v. U.S., Fed.Cl.2004, 63 Fed.Cl. 369. United States ☞ 73(9)

Forest Service's demand for damages for purchaser's default on timber sale contracts constituted a "claim" under the Contract Disputes Act (CDA), notwithstanding that amount of breach damages was not "in dispute" when contracting officers issued final decisions assessing default damages on the contracts, and thus Court of Federal Claims had jurisdiction over government's counterclaim seeking default damages in purchaser's suit for breach. Precision Pine & Timber, Inc. v. U.S., Fed.Cl.2004, 62 Fed.Cl. 635. Federal Courts ☞ 1076; United States ☞ 73(9)

Contractor's letter to contracting officer (CO) constituted a "claim" under the Contract Disputes Act (CDA), where letter demanded a sum certain and conveyed contractor's position that the government "should pay" that amount, and CO was explicit in his treatment of the letter as a claim. Kanag'Iq Const. Co. v. U.S., Fed. Cl.2001, 51 Fed.Cl. 38. United States ☞ 73(9)

Under the Contract Disputes Act (CDA), government contractor filed valid termination for convenience claim with contracting officer (CO) when it submitted second filing to the CO, which was specifically labeled a "claim," updating with increased costs the claims asserted in termination settlement proposal (TSP), and explicitly requesting a final decision from the CO. Advanced Materials, Inc. v. U.S., Fed.Cl.2000, 46 Fed.Cl. 697. United States ☞ 73(9)

Claim letter that contractor sent agency was sufficient to invoke the jurisdiction of the Court of Federal Claims under the Contract Disputes Act (CDA); although contractor altered basis of claim from an express agreement entered into on certain date to an implied-in-fact contract

that evolved over several years and was authorized by ratification, claimed breach in failing to transfer title to aircraft to contractor remained the same. Hawkins and Powers Aviation, Inc. v. U.S., Fed.Cl. 2000, 46 Fed.Cl. 238. United States ☞ 73(15)

Government contractor's letter to contracting officer, asserting a cardinal change and a breach of contract by the government, satisfied requirements for a "claim" under the Contract Disputes Act (CDA); contractor submitted written document demanding the payment of $9,150,596.00, the letter asserted that the submission was certified, and requested contracting officer's final decision pursuant to the CDA. Kentucky Bridge & Dam, Inc. v. U.S., Fed.Cl.1998, 42 Fed. Cl. 501. United States ☞ 73(9)

Government contractor's claim for rental expenses which accrued during different period from that for which claim was submitted to contracting officer was a new "claim" for purposes of determining whether court of federal claims had subject matter jurisdiction. Cupey Bajo Nursing Home, Inc. v. U.S., Fed.Cl.1996, 36 Fed.Cl. 122. Federal Courts ☞ 1107

Because data processing service contractor's complaint alleged breach of an implied contract between the parties and contractor's letter to contracting officer constituted claim within meaning of Contract Disputes Act (CDA) and was, in fact, acted upon as a claim, Court of Federal Claims had jurisdiction over claim for breach of implied contract. OCR, Inc. v. U.S., Fed.Cl.1994, 31 Fed.Cl. 716, appeal dismissed 79 F.3d 1164. United States ☞ 73(9)

Even though government contractor's letter presented to contracting officer lacked request that contracting officer render final decision on the "claim," letter was sufficient to establish jurisdiction under Contract Disputes Act (CDA), where letter, other writings and conversations with contracting officer and officer's representatives impliedly expressed contractor's desire for final decision of contracting officer on claims; moreover, contracting officer in his correspondence with contractor specifically referred to the submission as a claim. Mega Const. Co., Inc. v. U.S., Fed.Cl.1993, 29 Fed.Cl. 396. United States ☞ 73(9)

Claim existed under Contract Disputes Act as to whether rigid electrical conduit instead of PVC conduit was specified in contract for construction at naval regional medical center, thereby entitling contractor to equitable adjustment to contract price where general contractor intended for government to treat electrical subcontractor's claim as its own and series of letters from general contractor requested contracting officer's final decision for sum certain established general contractor's certification of claim. Blake Const. Co., Inc. v. U.S., Fed.Cl. 1993, 28 Fed.Cl. 672, affirmed 29 F.3d 645. United States ☞ 73(9)

Contracting officer and government contractor for flame retardant denim trousers were in dispute within meaning of Contract Disputes Act (CDA); contractor's submittal enumerating effects of alleged delay and disruption in contractor's production process was not prepared at government's request, nothing indicated that contractor and government were in negotiating posture concerning possibility of upward equitable adjustment for alleged defective government testing at time of submittal or at any time thereafter, and contracting officer's treatment of contractor's submittal was consistent with recognizing that it contained disputed claims within contemplation of CDA. Coastal Industries, Inc. v. U.S., Fed.Cl. 1993, 27 Fed.Cl. 713. United States ☞ 73(9)

Contractor's certified request for equitable adjustment and its letter requesting a final decision of contracting officer constituted a valid claim within meaning of Contract Disputes Act; fact that letter also suggested the possibility, or hope, for a negotiated solution to the dispute did not detract from its validity of perfecting the contractor's claim under the Act. Isles Engineering & Const., Inc. v. U.S., Cl.Ct.1992, 26 Cl.Ct. 240. United States ☞ 73(9)

Contractor "submitted" claim to contracting officer within meaning of Contract Disputes Act even though claim was embodied in letter addressed to office in charge of construction rather than contracting officer; letter set forth basis in amount of claim and unequivocally requested final decision by contracting officer; moreover, office ultimately sent letter directly to contracting officer. Tri-Ad

Constructors v. U.S., Cl.Ct.1990, 21 Cl.Ct. 789. United States ☞ 73(9)

Contractor's action in sending written claim to resident officer in charge of construction requesting final decision from contracting officer and resident officer's forwarding claim to contracting officer satisfied terms of direct access provision of Contract Disputes Act that claim be in writing and be submitted to contracting officer for decision. American Pacific Roofing Co. v. U.S., Cl.Ct.1990, 21 Cl.Ct. 265. United States ☞ 73(9)

Contractor's request for equitable adjustment submitted under contract's changes clause was "affirmative claim" under Contract Disputes Act, where had Government regarded request as routine request for payment it would logically have promptly paid amount claimed as undisputed "contract payable" without further negotiation or argument, but, rather than doing so, continued its vigorous denial of any liability. Cubic Corp. v. U.S., Cl.Ct.1990, 20 Cl.Ct. 610. United States ☞ 73(9)

9. —— Miscellaneous requests not considered claims, claims within section

Letter sent by contractor to Navy, which identified contractor's cost proposal regarding building of facility as a claim and attached certification, did not meet requirements of a claim under Contract Disputes Act; there was no dispute between parties at time letter was sent, because representatives of Navy did not deny contractor's right to compensation for any part of amount set forth in proposal. Santa Fe Engineers, Inc. v. Garrett, C.A.Fed.1993, 991 F.2d 1579. United States ☞ 73(9)

Submissions of contractor to contracting agency were not "claims" within meaning of the Contract Disputes Act (CDA) where amounts asserted were not in dispute at time submissions were made; each of the submissions suggested in one way or another that contractor and government were still negotiating, and none of the submissions requested a final decision, explicitly or implicitly. Heyl & Patterson, Inc. v. O'Keefe, C.A.Fed.1993, 986 F.2d 480, on remand 1996 WL 202566. United States ☞ 73(9)

Unilateral cost proposals or correspondence suggesting disagreement during negotiations do not, for purposes of appeal provision of Contract Disputes Act, satisfy clear requirement of contract containing standard defense acquisition dispute clause that request be in dispute to qualify as "claim"; contractor and contracting agency must already be in dispute over amount requested. Dawco Const., Inc. v. U.S., C.A.Fed.1991, 930 F.2d 872. United States ☞ 73(9)

Contractor's contract reformation claim, which sought modification of contract to mitigate effect of a unilateral bid mistake, constituted a valid, cognizable "claim" within meaning of this chapter but contractor's request for reconsideration of denial of its unilateral bid mistake under public law providing for extra contractual relief to contractors did not. Paragon Energy Corp. v. U.S., Ct.Cl. 1981, 645 F.2d 966, 227 Ct.Cl. 176, affirmed 230 Ct.Cl. 884. United States ☞ 73(9)

Three letters sent by government contractor to contracting officer (CO) which attempted to convince CO that contractor was an "authorized manufacturer" capable of fulfilling contracts for supply of circuit card did not constitute a valid claim under the Contract Disputes Act (CDA) challenging agency's cancellation of contracts, as the letters were submitted to CO prior to cancellation and thus could not have challenged that event or claimed attendant monetary losses. Ulysses, Inc. v. U.S., Fed.Cl.2005, 66 Fed.Cl. 161. United States ☞ 73(9)

Reservation of general right to file future claim is not itself submission of claim, for purpose of invoking right to resolution under either Contract Disputes Act or contract dispute process. New Valley Corp. v. U.S., Fed.Cl.1996, 34 Fed. Cl. 703, reversed 119 F.3d 1576, rehearing denied, in banc suggestion declined, subsequent mandamus proceeding 155 F.3d 569. United States ☞ 73(9)

Claim submitted to Navy contracting officer was insufficient to notify officer of basis and amount of claim, and therefore was insufficient to confer jurisdiction over action under Contract Disputes Act (CDA), where written claim consisted of allegation that contract at issue did not require contractor to provide any insulation for structure it had contracted to build and complaint filed in Court of Federal Claims referred to dispute as to type of insulation required. Orbas & Associates v. U.S., Fed.Cl.1995, 34 Fed.Cl. 68. United States ☞ 73(9)

Public contractor's letter was not valid claim for CDA purposes, as it failed to request sum certain or final decision; figures in letter allegedly representing Government's debts to contractor were merely speculative, and letter contained no explicit or implicit request for final decision. Pevar Co. v. U.S., Fed.Cl.1995, 32 Fed.Cl. 822. United States ☞ 73(9)

Contractor's letter to contracting officer requesting increase in price on purchase orders did not qualify as claim under Contract Disputes Act (CDA), so that contractor had not requested final decision from contracting officer over which Claims Court would have jurisdiction; letters did not include request for rescission of cancellation of orders which contractor sought in his Claims Court action against government and fact that there was no underlying dispute over amounts contractor requested rendered price increase a unilateral cost proposal to which government had yet to respond. Krueger v. U.S., Cl.Ct.1992, 26 Cl.Ct. 841. United States ☞ 73(9)

Federal contractor's letters to Army contracting officer were requests for payment, rather than "claims" under Contract Disputes Act, even though letters repeatedly invoked Act and requested written decisions, where Government did not attempt to challenge its liability, and exchange of letters served only to clarify United State's payment history; thus, Claims Court lacked jurisdiction. CPT Corp. v. U.S., Cl.Ct.1992, 25 Cl.Ct. 451. United States ☞ 73(9)

Letter of contractor to contracting officer did not constitute a "claim" triggering one-year limitation period of the Contract Disputes Act (CDA); although letter asserted specific rights to payment of additional overhead costs and extension of time, and contractor requested specific relief in form of a sum certain, contractor did not expressly request a final decision, nor was there any implication that contractor desired a final decision; moreover, letter contained request to meet and discuss disagreement, indicating that negotiations were not clearly abandoned. Sun Eagle Corp. v. U.S., Cl.Ct.1991, 23 Cl.Ct. 465. United States ☞ 73(9)

Contractor's letters relating to change orders did not constitute "claims," within meaning of Contract Disputes Act, and therefore contractor was not entitled to award of interest from date of letters, even though contractor's assertion of rights was not tentative, contractor invoked Act, there was no question that change order had taken place, and contractor reserved claim for delay or interest, where it was not clear at that time that there would be dispute as to amount of compensation.   Essex Electro Engineers, Inc. v. U.S., Cl.Ct.1991, 22 Cl.Ct. 757, affirmed 960 F.2d 1576, certiorari denied 113 S.Ct. 408, 506 U.S. 953, 121 L.Ed.2d 333.   United States ☞ 73(9)

Contracting officer's indirect receipt of contractor's letters sent to contract manager and passed to officer by assistant United States attorney did not satisfy requirements for making claim under Contract Disputes Act.   Robert Irsay Co. v. U.S. Postal Service, Cl.Ct.1990, 21 Cl.Ct. 502.   United States ☞ 73(9)

10.   Relating to a contract

Government contractor's claim for reformation of existing contract with United States Army related to contract within meaning of Contract Disputes Act (CDA) and, thus Armed Services Board of Contract Appeals had jurisdiction over claim; claim asserted violation of regulation prohibiting auction techniques during bidding, rather than merely protesting bid solely on basis of alleged violation of implied contract of fair dealing.   LaBarge Products, Inc. v. West, C.A.Fed.1995, 46 F.3d 1547.   United States ☞ 73(9)

Government's claims against contractors for unjust enrichment and payment by mistake were "claims relating to a contract" within meaning of Contract Disputes Act (CDA) and, thus, like government's breach of contract claim, were governed exclusively by CDA.   U.S. v. Marovic, N.D.Cal.1999, 69 F.Supp.2d 1190.   United States ☞ 73(9)

Fact that surety which issued payment and performance bonds in connection with contracts for construction of school and commissary executed takeover agreement when contractor defaulted on school contract did not render CDA applicable to surety's equitable subrogation claim; surety's right to equitable subrogation was not claim "arising under" takeover agreement and was not claim "relating to" takeover agreement for purpose of provision in CDA requiring submission of certified equitable subrogation claim to contracting officer as jurisdictional prerequisite.   Transamerica Ins. Co. v. U.S., Fed.Cl.1994, 31 Fed.Cl. 602.

United States ☞ 74.1; United States ☞ 127(2)

11.   Exhaustion of remedies

Exhaustion of administrative remedies under Contract Disputes Act (CDA) could not be avoided by Indian tribe seeking additional amounts allegedly due under contract with Indian Health Service (IHS) by framing its claim as "statutory" as opposed to contractual claim under ISHA.   Pueblo of Zuni v. U.S., D.N.M. 2006, 467 F.Supp.2d 1114.   United States ☞ 73(9)

Contract Disputes Act's (CDA) administrative exhaustion provision required that government contractor prior to asserting breach of contract claim against government submit requests for amounts in dispute to contracting officer for his decision; mere submission of invoices, without showing that invoices were in dispute at time of submission, was insufficient.   U.S. v. Intrados/International Management Group, D.D.C.2003, 277 F.Supp.2d 55.   United States ☞ 73(9)

Failure of educators terminated by the Bureau of Indian Affairs (BIA) to exhaust the administrative remedies provided under the Bureau of Indian Affairs Manual (BIAM) before bringing breach of employment contract suit under the Contract Disputes Act (CDA) did not divest the Court of Federal Claims of jurisdiction over their CDA claims, as the CDA does not mandate exhaustion of such remedies.   Flying Horse v. U.S., Fed.Cl. 2001, 49 Fed.Cl. 419.   United States ☞ 73(15)

12.   Settlement proposals

Finding that government contractor's termination settlement proposal was not "claim," within meaning of Contract Disputes Act, was sufficiently supported by evidence that no dispute existed between Government and contractor as to amount of settlement; where final settlement agreement gave contractor only $25,213.88 less than it had requested in its final settlement proposal of $463,559.88, parties could be characterized as being in "predispute, negotiation posture."   Mayfair Const. Co. v. U.S., C.A.Fed.1988, 841 F.2d 1576, certiorari denied 109 S.Ct. 528, 488 U.S. 980, 102 L.Ed.2d 560.   United States ☞ 74(11)

Letter from contractor to resident officer in charge of construction concerning claimed impact and delay costs resulting from change order was a settlement proposal, rather than a claim, for purposes of Contract Disputes Act's certification requirements; although letter used word "claim" and discussed specific cost items for which contractor was seeking reimbursement, letter did not request decision by contracting officer, and contractor failed to challenge Government's comment that it would be treating letter as request for change order and not claim. Lakeview Const. Co. v. U.S., Cl.Ct.1990, 21 Cl.Ct. 269. United States ⬥ 73(9)

Claim by real estate broker for damages arising from Federal Communications Commission's failure to enter into lease for office space located by broker may be settled by contracting officer under this section. 1982, 61 Comp.Gen. 568.

13. Persons entitled to maintain claim

Government contractor whose value engineering change proposal for replacement of air dampers in government building was rejected by Government did not acquire proprietary rights in proposal that would allow him priority over subsequent proposals based upon same idea; thus, contractor could not maintain action on claim pursuant to Contract Disputes Act. John J. Kirlin, Inc. v. U.S., C.A.Fed.1987, 827 F.2d 1538. United States ⬥ 74(1)

Letter to the Secretary of Defense from chairman of nonprofit organization asking that American-made products be made available for purchase at military exchange stores as a matter of policy, was not a "claim" as contemplated by the Contract Disputes Act (CDA), as it was not made by one of the contracting parties, and did not request a sum certain arising from a contract or a final decision. Made in the USA Foundation v. U.S., Fed.Cl.2001, 51 Fed.Cl. 252. United States ⬥ 73(9)

Letter to contracting officer from counsel representing two individuals associated with contractor, which requested new progress payment after contractor had absconded with prior payment, did not constitute a "claim" under the Contract Disputes Act (CDA), as the CDA requires that the claim be "by a contractor," and letter did not purport to constitute a claim from contractor. Construction Equipment Lease Co. v. U.S., Cl.Ct.1992, 26 Cl.Ct. 341. United States ⬥ 73(9)

Assignee of contractor's rights under public contract was not a "contractor" and thus could not maintain breach of contract action under Contract Disputes Act. Thomas Funding Corp. v. U.S., Cl. Ct.1988, 15 Cl.Ct. 495. United States ⬥ 111(12)

14. Time of presentment of claim to contracting officer

Genuine issues of material fact as to when government contractor's equitable adjustment claims relating to air gun developed to test batteries accrued precluded summary judgment on issue of whether claims were barred by statute of limitations of the Contract Disputes Act (CDA). Axion Corp. v. U.S., Fed.Cl. 2005, 68 Fed.Cl. 468. Federal Courts ⬥ 1120

Government contractor's claim for equitable adjustment was not barred by laches, despite government's contention that three-year period between execution of first contract modification giving rise to claim and filing of claim was an undue delay; contractor filed its claim within the six-year limitation period specified in the Contract Disputes Act (CDA), and government did not carry its burden of showing that it was sufficiently prejudiced by any delay. Cygnus Corp. v. U.S., Fed.Cl.2004, 63 Fed.Cl. 150, affirmed 177 Fed.Appx. 86, 2006 WL 1049326. Federal Courts ⬥ 1104

Contractor's failure to respond to contracting officer's show cause letter on default termination which had 48-hour deadline did not waive contractor's claims for equitable adjustment for which the Contract Disputes Act (CDA) sets a six-year statute of limitation. Roxco, Ltd. v. U.S., Fed.Cl.2004, 60 Fed.Cl. 39. United States ⬥ 74(5)

Contractor's claim of mutual mistake, which had been brought before Court of Federal Claims, and contractor's subsequent duress claim were "related" within meaning of Contract Disputes Act and, thus, contracting officer lacked authority to act on duress claim so as to commence running of 60–day deemed denial period and contractor could not bring duress claim before Court of Federal Claims under deemed denial provisions of Act; both claims sought same relief, namely, rescission of contract modification. Peterson Builders, Inc. v. U.S., Fed.Cl.1993, 27 Fed.Cl. 443. United States ⬥ 73(9)

Plaintiffs' failure to comply with contractual time limitation provisions for submission of claims under timber sales contract barred claims; contract language was not ambiguous, and plaintiffs were free to waive their rights to statute of limitations provided in Contract Disputes Act. Stone Forest Industries, Inc. v. U.S., Cl.Ct.1992, 26 Cl.Ct. 410. United States ☞ 58(8)

University's presentment of claim under Contract Disputes Act to contracting officer was not untimely, though general six-year statute of limitations for bringing claim in Claims Court had already expired, in that Contract Disputes Act provides no limitations period for presentment of claims and Claims Court had no jurisdiction over claim until decision had been issued by contracting officer, following proper presentment of claim to him. Board of Governors of University of North Carolina v. U.S., Cl.Ct.1986, 10 Cl.Ct. 27. United States ☞ 73(9)

Contractor's retroactive filing of claim with contracting officer some 11 months after filing complaint in Claims Court was ineffective under Contract Disputes Act and did not cure failure to certify the claim at proper time. Prefab Products, Inc. v. U.S., Cl.Ct.1986, 9 Cl.Ct. 786. United States ☞ 73(15)

15. Government claims

Contract Disputes Act did not require United States to file its own administrative claim in order to recover overpayment that ensued from decision by Armed Services Board of Contract Appeals that United States owed less than contracting officer awarded; contractor was required to submit a claim to contracting officer, but when government sought recovery it was enough that issue was subject of decision by contracting officer. U.S. v. T & W Edmier Corp., C.A.7 (Ill.) 2006, 465 F.3d 764. United States ☞ 73(9); United States ☞ 75(2)

Under government contract making permissive a conversion of request for payment to a "claim," where it was the United States which made request for payment that was not paid, it was the United States and not contractor that would have option to convert the request to a claim, and where the United States did not do so, it did not activate the contract dispute resolution mechanism of the Contract Disputes Act, and contractor was not entitled to appeal to Board of

Contract Appeals or Claims Court after contracting officer failed to make a decision within a reasonable time. A.E. Finley & Associates, Inc. v. U.S., C.A.6 (Tenn.) 1990, 898 F.2d 1165. United States ☞ 73(9)

Failure of contractor to first submit claim for money to contracting officer did not deprive Armed Services Board of Contract Appeals of jurisdiction to determine propriety of termination for default; default termination was "government claim," and Contract Disputes Act states that contractor may appeal Government claim to appropriate board of contract appeals without having to submit monetary claim of its own to contracting officer. Malone v. U.S., C.A.Fed.1988, 849 F.2d 1441, modified 857 F.2d 787. United States ☞ 73(15)

United States' claim for setoff for paint deficiencies in renovation and restoration contract with general contractor did not qualify as valid CDA claim and, therefore, Court of Federal Claims lacked jurisdiction over this government setoff where contracting officer did not determine both basis and amount of liability. Volmar Const., Inc. v. U.S., Fed.Cl.1995, 32 Fed.Cl. 746. United States ☞ 73(9)

16. Sum certain requests

Even if there are circumstances in which separate communications from contracting officer can be considered together in determining whether Court of Federal Claims has subject matter jurisdiction under Contract Disputes Act, such combination was not appropriate with respect to contracting officer's default termination letter and letter requesting repayment of unliquidated progress payments; default termination letter made no reference to any money entitlement, and amount specified in subsequent letter was merely proposed by contracting officer and had not been rejected by contractor. Sharman Co., Inc. v. U.S., C.A.Fed.1993, 2 F.3d 1564, on remand 30 Fed.Cl. 231. United States ☞ 73(9)

Contractor's submissions were not Contract Disputes Act "claims," as was necessary for contractor to be entitled to recover interest, because submissions did not seek sum certain as matter of right, as required by federal acquisition regulation that implemented Act. Essex Electro Engineers, Inc. v. U.S., C.A.Fed.1992, 960 F.2d 1576, certiorari denied 113

S.Ct. 408, 506 U.S. 953, 121 L.Ed.2d 333. United States ⊕ 110

Letter in which lessor of building notified the government, as a holdover tenant performing final condition of lease requiring cleanup of hazardous materials, that "the Government is a holdover tenant with rent accruing at the pro rata rate of $793,509 per year until clean up is complete" satisfied the "sum certain" requirement for a "claim" under the Contract Disputes Act (CDA); letter could be read as requesting a final decision from contracting officer on claim for one month's holdover rent on the property, which was stated to be "rent accruing at the pro rata rate of $793,509 per year," or $66,125.75. Modeer v. U.S., Fed.Cl. 2005, 68 Fed.Cl. 131, affirmed 183 Fed. Appx. 975, 2006 WL 1582178. United States ⊕ 73(9)

Contractor's submissions to contracting officer (CO) concerning additional work outside scope of contract failed to satisfy certain sum of money requirement for a valid claim under the Contract Disputes Act (CDA), where submissions contained no dollar figure or documentation that could be used to calculate a dollar figure. CPS Mechanical Contractors, Inc. v. U.S., Fed.Cl.2004, 59 Fed.Cl. 760. United States ⊕ 73(9)

Contractors' claims letter to contracting officer (CO) satisfied requirement of the Contract Disputes Act (CDA) that claim specify a sum certain, where letter made reference to enclosed contracts, and each contract specified the exact amount of monetary compensation each contractor was to receive. Flying Horse v. U.S., Fed.Cl.2001, 49 Fed.Cl. 419. United States ⊕ 73(9)

Letter demanding return of property but containing no specific allegations of resulting losses from breach of lease agreement and no claim for any specific amount of money was insufficient to constitute valid claim under Contract Disputes Act (CDA). Colon v. U.S., Fed.Cl. 1996, 35 Fed.Cl. 337. United States ⊕ 73(9)

Communications of contractor did not constitute valid "claim" as jurisdictional prerequisite to filing suit under Contract Disputes Act (CDA); communications failed to make requisite request for "sum certain," in that they did not request same monetary damages and they did not contain requisite language of finality to

put contracting officer on notice as to which communication was intended to be final claim. Sam Gray Enterprises, Inc. v. U.S., Fed.Cl.1995, 32 Fed.Cl. 526. United States ⊕ 73(9)

Bidder's letter "protesting" breach of alleged oral promise to award government contract did not constitute "claim" required before Court of Federal Claims could exercise jurisdiction over dispute; letter did not request payment of money in sum certain. Domagala v. U.S., Fed. Cl.1993, 30 Fed.Cl. 149, affirmed 39 F.3d 1196. United States ⊕ 73(9)

Government contractor failed to submit valid "claim" to contracting officer, and thus Court of Federal Claims lacked jurisdiction over dispute, where contractor never included sum-certain in any of his written correspondence; agency's statement that it would not compensate contractor in any manner did not excuse compliance with sum-certain requirement. Executive Court Reporters, Inc. v. U.S., Fed.Cl.1993, 29 Fed.Cl. 769, appeal dismissed 22 F.3d 1106. United States ⊕ 73(9)

Government contractor's request for "aggregate net payment" to which contractor was entitled under claim of $140,203,709, pursuant to partially terminated contract, was not "sum certain" then due it, and thus was not "claim" subject to jurisdiction of the Claims Court under the Contract Disputes Act; several portions of contract remain to be performed, contractor indicated that no contract price currently existed, and contractor would be unable to price value of completed and uncompleted, but nonterminated work until it either reached agreement with government or performed rest of work. Boeing Co. v. U.S., Cl.Ct.1992, 26 Cl.Ct. 872. United States ⊕ 73(9)

Psychiatric and medical care provider first filed Contract Disputes Act "claim" for services provided to veterans on date when it actually asserted per diem rate, number of days of inpatient care provided to veterans, and total amount of additional payment that provider claimed it was entitled to, for purposes of motion by Veterans Administration (VA) to dismiss claim by provider for lack of jurisdiction, even though provider had previously provided contracting officer with statement outlining statistical data, where only second submission clearly sought payment of additional monies for services purportedly supplied under contract and VA eventually disputed contents of second submission. Cupey Bajo Nursing Home, Inc. v. U.S., Cl.Ct.1991, 23 Cl.Ct. 406. United States ☞ 73(9)

Government contractor's letter claiming additional costs was valid claim under Contract Disputes Act, even though it did not indicate specific amount being sought; previous letter, referred to in claim, had specified amount sought. Kvaas Const. Co. v. U.S., Cl.Ct.1991, 22 Cl.Ct. 740. United States ☞ 73(9)

Claims Court did not lack jurisdiction over contractor's claims under timber sale contracts on ground that contractor did not state in any of its letters its monetary claims in an amount certain, where dispute between the parties concerned rates and conversion factors that should be employed in determining payment for timber and, if contractor's contentions were correct, the United States could arithmetically calculate the amount of overpayment claimed for each contract. Little River Lumber Co. v. U.S., Cl.Ct.1990, 21 Cl.Ct. 527. United States ☞ 73(9)

Contractor adequately certified its claim to contracting officer, and thus could maintain action under the Contract Disputes Act, by initially requesting damages in the amount of $34 per month per unit for each of the 14 months remaining on the contract after it was terminated for the convenience of the Government and then submitting a claim for $600,000 in damages, where information necessary to determine the number of units involved was in the possession of the Government. Embrey v. U.S., Cl.Ct.1989, 17 Cl.Ct. 617. United States ☞ 73(9)

Contractor's demands upon contracting officer for extended home office overhead costs in "an amount exceeding $91,000" and for third-party indemnification fees "exceeding $7,500" allegedly incurred in performance of Army contract were not sum-certain claims cognizable under the Contract Disputes Act, which would allow contractor's resort to judicial remedies; moreover, exhibits to the letter were voluminous and consisted of many different letters and forms, nearly all of which contained some dollar amounts; it would not have been a matter of simple arithmetic for contracting officer to determine the sum-certain amounts of the claims from such items. Metric Const.

Co., Inc. v. U.S., Cl.Ct.1988, 14 Cl.Ct. 177, review denied. United States ☞ 73(9)

17. Certification of claim—Generally

Absent appropriate certification, contracting officer has no claim on which to issue decision under Contract Disputes Act (CDA). Newport News Shipbuilding and Dry Dock Co. v. Garrett, C.A.Fed. 1993, 6 F.3d 1547, rehearing denied, in banc suggestion declined. United States ☞ 73(9)

Exact recitation of statutory language is not required for contractor to certify claim as accurate and complete to best of knowledge and belief. Fischbach and Moore Intern. Corp. v. Christopher, C.A.Fed.1993, 987 F.2d 759. United States ☞ 73(9)

Under provisions of Contract Disputes Act, in order for contractor to collect debt of $50,000 or more, or interest thereon, or both, from Government, he must submit claim in writing to contracting officer, which describes the debt, or the interest, or both, with specificity, and which is dated, signed and certified by contractor in accordance with Contract Disputes Act, and which demands decision by contracting officer. J.M.T. Mach. Co., Inc. v. U.S., C.A.Fed.1987, 826 F.2d 1042. United States ☞ 73(9)

Mandate that all claims over $50,000 must be certified is one of most significant provisions of this chapter; thus, certification is not mere technicality to be disregarded at whim of contractor, but is unequivocal prerequisite to claim being considered under this section, and unless certification requirement is met, there is simply no claim on which contracting officer could issue decision. Fidelity Const. Co. v. U.S., C.A.Fed.1983, 700 F.2d 1379, certiorari denied 104 S.Ct. 97, 464 U.S. 826, 78 L.Ed.2d 103. United States ☞ 73(9)

To satisfy the administrative claim requirement of the Contract Disputes Act (CDA) a contractor must make a written, non-routine demand to a contracting officer, request a final decision, and seek the payment of money in a sum certain, the adjustment or interpretation of contract terms, or other relief arising from or relating to the contract. Ace Constructors, Inc. v. U.S., Fed.Cl.2006, 70 Fed.Cl. 253. United States ☞ 73(9)

Because contract at issue set forth the requirements for certified claim under Contracts Disputes Act, failure to comply with the requirements could not be excused on grounds that "very few American lawyers are familiar with the governmental claim process" and that few attorneys have Claims Court experience. American Nat. Bank and Trust Co. of Chicago v. U.S., Cl.Ct.1990, 20 Cl.Ct. 530. United States ⚮ 73(9)

18. ——— Amount of claim generally, certification of claim

In determining whether contractor's claim was for more than $50,000, so as to require contractor to certify claim, claims court should have focused on original claim of $31,500 made by contractor to contracting officer, rather than on $66,570.32 contractor prayed for in complaint to claims court, an amount resulting from denial of contractor's initial claim in contracting officer's liability decision and additional setoffs determined in quantum decision, and complaint thus should not have been dismissed for lack of jurisdiction on ground contractor had failed to certify claim as required. Glenn v. U.S., C.A.Fed.1988, 858 F.2d 1577. United States ⚮ 73(9)

Certification of contractor's administrative tort claim did not meet certification requirements of contractor's breach of contract claim under Contract Disputes Act (CDA); amount requested in tort claim could not accurately reflect amount of damages based solely on contract. Colon v. U.S., Fed.Cl.1996, 35 Fed.Cl. 337. United States ⚮ 73(9)

Eight separate claims submitted to the Court of Federal Claims in connection with contract to install laboratory equipment for Department of Agriculture (USDA) arose from two sets of closely related facts and, thus, comprised two claims for less than $50,000 each, as opposed to one claim for more than $50,000, for purposes of determining whether certification was required under Contract Disputes Act. Reliance Ins. Co. v. U.S., Fed.Cl.1993, 27 Fed.Cl. 815. United States ⚮ 73(9)

The Contract Disputes Act does not bar plaintiff from seeking an amount of damages that exceeds the quantum in the claim to the contracting officer; however, the excess quantum must spring from the same certified claim; plaintiff may not seek damages for a new claim which has

not yet been submitted to and decided by the contracting officer. SMS Data Products Group, Inc. v. U.S., Cl.Ct.1990, 19 Cl.Ct. 612. United States ⚮ 73(9)

Submission of post office lessor's claim to contracting officer without certification addressed to the quantum deprived Claims Court of jurisdiction over lessor's suit for cost of heating and air conditioning; lessor stated only belief that amount of claim would exceed $50,000, but did not include any costs it had incurred or any basis upon which contracting officer could compute amount involved and, thus, contracting officer's decision was invalid. 25 New Chardon Street Ltd. Partnership v. U.S., Cl.Ct.1990, 19 Cl.Ct. 208. United States ⚮ 73(9)

Contractor was not required to submit signed certificate to contracting officer as called for in contract for claims over $50,000 where the claim was for less than $50,000, but the inapplicability of the certification provision did not excuse the contractor from satisfying other requirements for presenting a claim to the contracting officer. RSH Constructors, Inc. v. U.S., Cl.Ct.1988, 14 Cl.Ct. 655. United States ⚮ 73(9)

Government contractor's submission of a single, unitary claim for over $50,000, based on a common nucleus of operative facts, was outside the jurisdiction of the Claims Court, for failure to certify claim, even though contractor contended that its demand exceeded $50,000 boundary only because of government's refusal to pay; once contractor realized that the amount in question might have risen above $50,000, contractor was under a duty to certify its demand to a contracting officer. Black Star Sec., Inc. v. U.S., Cl.Ct. 1984, 5 Cl.Ct. 110. United States ⚮ 73(9)

For purposes of subsec. (c)(1) of this section, contractor's claim for payment allegedly due for work completed before contract terminated was a request for contract adjustment, and was to be included in determining contractor's obligation to certify; furthermore, where contractor's claim, including the pretermination item, amounted to $128,373, contractor was required to certify that the claim was made in good faith, that supporting data was accurate and complete, and that amount requested accurately reflected the contract adjustment for which contractor believed government was liable. Palmer & Sicard, Inc. v. U.S., Cl.Ct. 1984, 4 Cl.Ct. 420.

19. —— Good faith, certification of claim

Prime contractor acted in "good faith," for purposes of Contract Disputes Act (CDA), in certifying claim of subcontractor to Navy in face of bankruptcy court order in subcontractor's Chapter 11 case directing prime contractor to certify and sponsor subcontractor's claim in specified amount and to submit it to Navy with prime contractor's own claim; it was clear from record that prime contractor had no intention either to defraud or deceive Navy and took every measure that could reasonably have been expected of prime contractor to obtain subcontractor's support and justification for its claim in amount which prime contractor felt it could conscientiously certify and there was possibility that if prime contractor had disobeyed order of bankruptcy court, prime contractor would have been cited by that court for civil contempt. Arnold M. Diamond, Inc. v. Dalton, C.A.Fed.1994, 25 F.3d 1006, rehearing denied. United States ⮌ 73(9)

Contractor's certification as to validity of subcontractor's claim for equitable adjustment was at least in substantial compliance with statutory requirement to certify good-faith basis of claim and accuracy and completeness of data, even though contractor stated in cover letter that it did not have access to subcontractor's books and records and could not make statement with respect to amount of claim; certification submitted contractor to liability for fraud. Transamerica Ins. Corp., Inc. for and on Behalf of Stroup Sheet Metal Works v. U.S., C.A.Fed.1992, 973 F.2d 1572, on remand 28 Fed.Cl. 418. United States ⮌ 73(9)

Prime contractor's certification of subcontractor's claim for equitable adjustment, encompassing all statutory requirements, was effective to confer jurisdiction on Armed Services Board of Contract Appeals to hear merits of subcontractor's claim; prime contractor was not required to believe that subcontractor's claim was certain, only that it believed there was good ground for the claim. U.S. v. Turner Const. Co., C.A.Fed.1987, 827 F.2d 1554. United States ⮌ 73(9)

20. —— Accurate and complete supporting data, certification of claim

Purpose of statutory requirement that contractor must certify claim as accurate and complete to best of knowledge and belief is to trigger contractor's potential liability for fraudulent claim. Fischbach and Moore Intern. Corp. v. Christopher, C.A.Fed.1993, 987 F.2d 759. United States ⮌ 73(9)

Government contractor's claim was properly certified despite its failure to attach specifically referenced prior claim letter; contractor had only one claim pending before contracting officer and it was reasonable to infer from context in which it was submitted that certification's reference to "supporting data" included prior letter. Kirkham Constructors, Inc. v. U.S., Fed.Cl.1993, 30 Fed.Cl. 90. United States ⮌ 73(9)

Contractor did not provide certification of data sufficient to vest claims court with jurisdiction over delay claim; contractor did not state that data was accurate to best of contractor's knowledge and belief, up to date of certification. Ingersoll-Rand Co. v. U.S., Cl.Ct.1991, 24 Cl.Ct. 692. United States ⮌ 73(9)

Contractor did not comply with certification requirement of Contract Disputes Act so as to confer jurisdiction upon Claims Court over $2,000,000 claim against Government; certification relied on supporting document prepared by Government to fulfill requirement that contractor certify that supporting data was accurate and complete. Aeronetics Div., AAR Brooks & Perkins Corp. v. U.S., Cl.Ct.1987, 12 Cl.Ct. 132. United States ⮌ 73(15)

21. —— Knowledge and belief, certification of claim

Contractor's certification of claim to best of "understanding and belief" substantially complied with statutory requirement to certify claim to best of "knowledge and belief" and, therefore, was acceptable. Fischbach and Moore Intern. Corp. v. Christopher, C.A.Fed. 1993, 987 F.2d 759. United States ⮌ 73(9)

Contractor's claim neither fully nor substantially complied with statutory certification requirement; certification that claims were true and correct to best of certifier's knowledge, information and belief was not sufficient to certify that supporting data were accurate and complete to the best of the certifier's knowledge and belief, and accompanying documents setting forth "costs" were insufficient to certify that amount requested accurately reflected contract adjustment for which contractor believed government was liable. Sipco Services & Marine Inc. v. U.S., Fed.Cl. 1994, 30 Fed.Cl. 478. United States ⊂⇨ 73(9)

Government contractor's certification of claim over $50,000 substantially complied with Contract Disputes Act, even though it omitted words "and belief" after stating that "supporting data is accurate and complete to the best of my knowledge * * *." Young Enterprises, Inc. v. U.S., Cl.Ct.1992, 26 Cl.Ct. 858. United States ⊂⇨ 73(9)

Government contractor's certification of claim which stated that "The following claim report is made . . . with accurate supporting data and to the best of our knowledge is complete." substantially complied with Contract Disputes Act and was not invalid, although Act required that properly certified claim indicate that supporting data are accurate and complete to the best of contractor's knowledge "and belief"; omission of words "and belief" in no way undermined purpose and rationale of Act. Alcan Elec. & Engineering Co., Inc. v. U.S., Cl.Ct.1992, 24 Cl.Ct. 704. United States ⊂⇨ 73(9)

22. —— Amendment of claim, certification of claim

Claim seeking over $50,000 submitted after effective date of Contract Disputes Act did not convert that claim into one which superseded earlier claim, which was for less than $50,000 and which was submitted before effective date of Contract Disputes Act, for purposes of determining whether claim had to be certified under Act to be appealed to Claims Court. Contract Cleaning Maintenance, Inc. v. U.S., C.A.Fed.1987, 811 F.2d 586. United States ⊂⇨ 73(9)

Government contractor's monetary claim which was properly considered by contracting officer without certification, in that claim was less than $50,000 and covered only one year, was not required to be certified when very same claim came before board of contract appeals or court of appeals, notwithstanding that claim at postcontracting officer level had been amended to amount greater than

$50,000 due to intervening extension of contract. Tecom, Inc. v. U.S., C.A.Fed. 1984, 732 F.2d 935. United States ⊂⇨ 73(9)

Contractor which brought suit on "test" contract to recover independent research and development (IR&D) costs and production costs incurred to upgrade launch motor for commercial market as indirect costs of government contracts would be permitted to amend complaint to seek relief for contacting officer's disallowance of such costs with respect to all affected contracts, and not just "test" contract, considering absence of prior requests to amend, government received timely notice through certified claim that contractor claimed entitlement to entirety of the disallowance, and complaint which sought relief for that portion of disallowance attributable to "test" contract alleged that entire disallowance was improper. ATK Thiokol, Inc. v. U.S., Fed. Cl.2006, 72 Fed.Cl. 306. Federal Courts ⊂⇨ 1111

Jurisdictional requirement of the Contract Disputes Act (CDA) that claims for more than $100,000 must be certified did not apply to government contractor's original claim for the sum certain of $66,125.75, representing one month's holdover rent, notwithstanding that claim amount increased to $330,628.75 to cover entire holdover period of five months; moreover, even if certification was required, contractor's claim letter concluded with a technically defective certification statement which could be corrected before entry of final judgment. Modeer v. U.S., Fed.Cl.2005, 68 Fed.Cl. 131, affirmed 183 Fed.Appx. 975, 2006 WL 1582178. United States ⊂⇨ 73(9)

Contractor's motion to amend its claim against government to add claim for unpaid contract earnings did not relate back to differing site conditions claims pleaded in its original complaint for purposes of subject matter jurisdiction; new claim was not presented to a contracting officer, claims were not legally and factually intertwined such that demand for relief under one would necessarily be demand for relief under the other, and entitlement to additional contract earnings did not depend on successful prosecution of claim for additional compensation due to alleged differing site conditions. Renda Marine, Inc. v. U.S., Fed.Cl.2005, 65 Fed. Cl. 152, reconsideration denied 71 Fed.

Cl. 782, appeal dismissed 208 Fed.Appx. 880, 2006 WL 3497269, order recalled and vacated 2006 WL 3922781. Federal Courts ⊜ 1106

With regard to section of the Contract Disputes Act (CDA) providing that "[a] defect in the certification of a claim shall not deprive a court or an agency board of contract appeals of jurisdiction over that claim," and that court or board "shall require a defective certification to be corrected," terms "defect in the certification" and "defective certification" include missing certifications when two or more claims not requiring certification are deemed by the court or board to be a larger claim requiring certification. Engineered Demolition, Inc. v. U.S., Fed.Cl. 2004, 60 Fed.Cl. 822. United States ⊜ 73(9)

Lessor's lack of certification of claim under CDA was not subject to correction, where lessor made no attempt to certify his claim; he produced no certification, defective or otherwise. Hamza v. U.S., Fed.Cl.1994, 31 Fed.Cl. 315. United States ⊜ 73(9)

After it was determined that contractor had failed to establish jurisdiction over its preliminary complaint against government, contractor could not cure lack of certification defect by bringing certification demand before termination contracting officer who no longer had authority to act upon demand, waiting requisite 60 days, then amending its complaint. Boeing Co. v. U.S., Cl.Ct.1992, 25 Cl.Ct. 441, reversed 991 F.2d 811, rehearing denied, on remand 31 Fed.Cl. 289. United States ⊜ 73(9)

Where claim submitted to contracting officer and contained in the original complaint, as well as claim in the first amended complaint, were both based on the contention that the Government had accepted the contractor's value engineering change proposals (VECP), the amended claim was submitted to the contracting officer and Claims Court had jurisdiction over it. AAI Corp. v. U.S., Cl.Ct.1991, 22 Cl.Ct. 541. United States ⊜ 73(9)

Following determination that contractor's failure to properly certify its claim to the contracting officer deprived the Claims Court of subject matter jurisdiction, contractor could not circumvent certification requirement by amending its complaint to delete the claim for money damages, where contractor's monetary

damage claim was inseparable from the claim that contracting officer improperly terminated contract for default. Halec Const. Co., Inc. v. U.S., Cl.Ct.1984, 6 Cl.Ct. 439. United States ⊜ 73(15)

23.   —— Separate or joint claims, certification of claim

For purposes of Contract Disputes Act's certification requirement and determination of whether two or more separate claims rather than only fragmented single claim exists, court must assess whether claims are based on common or related set of operative facts; if court will have to review same or related evidence to make its decision, then only one claim exists for which certification is required if it seeks more than $50,000; if, however, claims as presented to contracting officer will necessitate focus on different or unrelated set of operative facts as to each claim, then separate claims exist that avoid the certification requirement, provided that none of them exceed $50,000. Placeway Const. Corp. v. U.S., C.A.Fed.1990, 920 F.2d 903. United States ⊜ 73(9)

The critical test for determining whether the operative facts are the same in later claims, such that federal court will have jurisdiction over later claims in addition to those presented to contracting officer under Contract Disputes Act (CDA), is whether claim circumvents statutory role of the contracting officer to receive and pass judgment on the contractor's entire claim. Pueblo of Zuni v. U.S., D.N.M.2006, 467 F.Supp.2d 1099, reconsideration denied 467 F.Supp.2d 1114. United States ⊜ 73(9)

Court of Federal Claims lacked jurisdiction over contractor's claim that government constructively changed contract in its response to request for information (RFI) by requiring controlled compaction in top 1.5 meters in roadway areas, as claim was never presented to contracting officer (CO); claim arose from different set of operative facts than claim presented to CO which sought reimbursement for increased cost of crushing stone to 3 inches as opposed to 6 inches, and for increased cost of spreading 6–inch material in layers with a thickness of 30 cm as compared to spreading 3–inch material in layers with a thickness of 20 cm. AAB Joint Venture v. U.S., Fed.Cl.2007, 75 Fed.Cl. 414. United States ⊜ 73(9)

Contractor's claim requesting compensation on behalf of subcontractor for increased costs caused by delays in subcontractor's earthworks operations due to differing site condition did not arise from same set of operative facts as certified claim that contractor presented to contracting officer on its own behalf, and thus failure to separately certify subcontractor's claim precluded jurisdiction in the Court of Federal Claims; factual evidence and proof required for subcontractor's claim for delay costs was entirely different from that required for contractor's certified claim for increased costs for disposal of excess material. AAB Joint Venture v. U.S., Fed.Cl.2005, 74 Fed.Cl. 367. United States ☞ 73(9)

Under the Contract Disputes Act (CDA), government contractor which brought suit challenging determination of contracting officer (CO) that it was liable for increased costs due to its violation of cost accounting standard governing allocation of supercomputer costs could not raise by way of offset alleged losses which it incurred on disposition of the supercomputers without a formal claim having been filed and denied by CO, as contractor's offset claim did not arise from same set of operative facts as those considered by CO in rendering his decision. Lockheed Martin Corp. v. U.S., Fed.Cl.2006, 70 Fed.Cl. 745. United States ☞ 73(9)

Court of Federal Claims lacked jurisdiction under the Contract Disputes Act (CDA) over contractor's claims that government breached contract by providing defective specifications and by abusing its discretion, where sole claim that contractor submitted to contracting officer (CO) was a request for reconsideration of the default termination; breach of contract claims were new claims not within scope of claim presented to CO, as they presented different factual and legal issues. Armour of America v. U.S., Fed.Cl.2006, 69 Fed.Cl. 587. United States ☞ 73(15)

Contractor's claim for $69,047 in under-absorbed overhead associated with shortfall in quantity of contaminated soil removed, and subcontractor's claim for $38,940 relating to excess numbers of railcars ordered to transport the soil, were separate and independent claims for purposes of certification requirement of the Contract Disputes Act (CDA), and since each was less than $100,000 no CDA certification was required; claims arose out of factual predicates that were separate and apart from each other, and

proof of contractor's claim would not be sufficient to prove subcontractor's claim. Engineered Demolition, Inc. v. U.S., Fed. Cl.2004, 60 Fed.Cl. 822. United States ☞ 73(9)

Under the Contract Disputes Act (CDA), a single government contract may give rise to more than one claim and a contractor may pursue its rights by filing "two or more suits" in either one or more fora; the only limitation is that a single, unified claim based on a common and related set of facts cannot be fragmented for the purpose of eluding the CDA's certification requirement. Kanag'Iq Const. Co. v. U.S., Fed.Cl.2001, 51 Fed.Cl. 38. United States ☞ 73(9); United States ☞ 73(15)

Corporations which were working jointly to complete government job filed certifications which substantially complied with Contract Disputes Act requirement although they filed their certifications separately, as no provision of Act or its implementing regulations required that dual prime contractors submit joint certification. McDonnell Douglas Corp. v. U.S., Cl.Ct.1992, 25 Cl.Ct. 342. United States ☞ 73(9)

City's 14 claims for reimbursement of emergency medical care rendered to 14 illegal aliens did not constitute "unitary claim" over $50,000, as would have triggered certification requirement of Contract Disputes Act; city did not treat its claims as unitary at agency level or in its complaint, and viewing city's separately submitted claims as separate would neither confuse nor mislead. City of El Centro v. U.S., Cl.Ct.1989, 17 Cl.Ct. 794. United States ☞ 73(9)

Government contractor's separate claims against Government arose out of unrelated conduct and did not involve closely connected facts so as to warrant consideration of claims as unitary claims requiring certification by contracting officer, and thus four claims ruled on by contracting officer, which involved amounts under $50,000, did not require certification so that contracting officer's decision on claims had vitality and finality absent other considerations. H.H.O. Co. v. U.S., Cl.Ct.1987, 12 Cl.Ct. 147. United States ☞ 73(9)

In determining, for purposes of subsec. (c) of this section, whether separately stated claims are unitary, neither language employed by contractor, nor how they are organized, governs; vital, however, is whether demands arose out of essentially interrelated conduct or services, and same or closely connected facts. Walsky Const. Co. v. U.S., Cl.Ct. 1983, 3 Cl.Ct. 615. United States ⊙ 73(9)

Requirement of subsec. (c) of this section, that claims of more than $50,000 be certified to contracting officer beforehand, applied to claims by contractor, which submitted its differing site claim in three separate installments, each seeking amount less than $50,000, but with aggregate amount exceeding $50,000, notwithstanding fact that contractor had received final decision on request for under $50,000 from original complaint, and had filed suit in Claims Court seeking relief thereon. Warchol Const. Co., Inc. v. U.S., Cl.Ct.1983, 2 Cl.Ct. 384. United States ⊙ 73(15)

Submissions to contracting officer for additional sum due on dredging contract constituted unitary claim in excess of certification requirement threshold for action to be brought under this section, and submissions could not be fragmented into multiple claims, each below certification threshold, based on delay in notice to proceed, survey errors, rejection of conforming work, defective specifications, and costs associated with extra work, as there was but a single demand, and fragmentation was for no apparent purpose other than to escape certification requirement; absent proper certification, the Claims Court was without jurisdiction. Fidelity and Deposit Co. of Maryland v. U.S., Cl.Ct.1983, 2 Cl.Ct. 137. Federal Courts ⊙ 1102

24. —— Waiver, certification of claim

Government may not be estopped, by any asserted "waiver" by the contracting officer of the claim certification prerequisite to a direct challenge in the Court of Claims of contracting officer's decision, to claim that proper certification is lacking. W.H. Moseley Co., Inc. v. U.S., Ct. Cl.1982, 677 F.2d 850, 230 Ct.Cl. 405, certiorari denied 103 S.Ct. 81, 459 U.S. 836, 74 L.Ed.2d 77. Estoppel ⊙ 62.2(4)

Contracting officer, who rejected contractor's claim against United States after fully considering the claim, had not had authority to waive certification requirement of this section which provided that, for claims of more than $50,000, contractor was to certify that claim was

made in good faith, that supporting data was accurate and complete to best of his knowledge and belief and that amount requested accurately reflected contract adjustment for which contractor believed government was liable and that, within 60 days of receipt of a submitted certified claim, contracting officer was to issue a decision or notify contractor when decision would be issued. Paul E. Lehman, Inc. v. U.S., Ct.Cl.1982, 673 F.2d 352, 230 Ct.Cl. 11. United States ⊙ 73(9)

Energy Board of Contract Appeals can not waive certification requirement of Contract Disputes Act, nor can it manipulate election requirement of Act. Beacon Oil Co. v. U.S., Cl.Ct.1985, 8 Cl.Ct. 695. United States ⊙ 73(9)

Fact that a government contracting officer has rendered a final decision on merits of an uncertified claim under the Contract Disputes Act is of no consequence, as officer has no authority to waive a requirement that Congress imposed. Rider v. U.S., Cl.Ct.1985, 7 Cl.Ct. 770, affirmed 790 F.2d 91. United States ⊙ 73(9)

Contracting officer cannot waive certification requirement of subsec. (c) of this section. Warchol Const. Co., Inc. v. U.S., Cl.Ct.1983, 2 Cl.Ct. 384. United States ⊙ 73(15)

25. —— Adequacy of claim certification, certification of claim

Government contractor's letter to contracting officer was claim submission, under Contract Disputes Act (CDA), even though letter was not accompanied by contemporaneous certification, where letter referred to valid certification included with previous letter to resident engineer, and claim was not altered since certification; thus, contracting officer's final decision on claim was valid, and contractor's failure to timely appeal from decision deprived Corps of Engineers Board of Contract Appeals of jurisdiction to review claim. D.L. Braughler Co., Inc. v. West, C.A.Fed.1997, 127 F.3d 1476. United States ⊙ 73(9)

Letter sent by contractor to Navy, which requested issuance of written final decision from contracting officer regarding claim concerning contractor's cost proposal for facility, did not meet requirements of a claim under Contract Disputes Act; contractor did not execute certification to letter and, although letter referred to contractor's previous certification, that certification was not effective at time it was submitted because it did not relate to existing dispute. Santa Fe Engineers, Inc. v. Garrett, C.A.Fed.1993, 991 F.2d 1579. United States ☞ 73(9)

Finding of the Agricultural Board of Contract Appeals that claims by buyer of timber from Forest Service were not certified as required pursuant to contract and the Contract Disputes Act was unsupported by substantial evidence, in light of evidence that contracting officer who considered claims on merits expressed no doubt about proper certification. Cedar Lumber, Inc. v. U.S., C.A.Fed.1986, 799 F.2d 743. United States ☞ 73(9)

Act of contractor in sending certified copy of his Claims Court complaint to contracting office did not satisfy statutory requirement [41 U.S.C.A. § 605] that contractor submit certified claim to contracting officer in first instance. Thoen v. U.S., C.A.Fed.1985, 765 F.2d 1110. United States ☞ 73(9)

Public contractor's claim for payment of overceiling costs which listed contracts for which costs were sought, enclosed statement of prior overceiling costs allocable to subject contracts, requested final decision from contracting officer regarding claim, specified nature of costs, and certified that claim was made in good faith was in substantial compliance with this chapter, and thus, Armed Services Board of Contract Appeals had jurisdiction to consider claim; contractor was not further required to swear to belief in legal theory of recovery. U.S. v. General Elec. Corp., C.A.Fed.1984, 727 F.2d 1567. United States ☞ 73(9)

This section does not leave the determination of the adequacy of the claim's certification to the contracting officer's discretion. W.H. Moseley Co., Inc. v. U.S., Ct.Cl.1982, 677 F.2d 850, 230 Ct.Cl. 405, certiorari denied 103 S.Ct. 81, 459 U.S. 836, 74 L.Ed.2d 77. United States ☞ 73(15)

Court of Federal Claims had subject matter jurisdiction under the Contract Disputes Act (CDA) over contractor's economic waste claim that government failed to mitigate damages by unreasonably rejecting the delivered aggregate material and ordering contractor to replace the material; contractor's certified claim to contracting officer (CO) clearly and unequivocally alleged that the aggregate

substantially complied with specifications, that it was otherwise adequate for its intended purpose, and that its replacement was economically wasteful. M.A. DeAtley Const., Inc. v. U.S., Fed.Cl.2007, 75 Fed.Cl. 575. United States ☞ 73(15)

Claim certifications filed by contractor under the Contract Disputes Act (CDA) were technically deficient, where they failed to include the required representations that the claim was made in good faith and that the certifier was duly authorized to certify the claim. Trafalgar House Constr., Inc. v. U.S., Fed.Cl.2006, 73 Fed.Cl. 675. United States ☞ 73(9)

Contractor's certified claim submitted to contracting officer (CO) which sought final decision on "test" contract with respect to indirect cost disallowance was a "claim" within meaning of the Contract Disputes Act (CDA) for entire disallowance for all affected contracts, and not just "test" contract, where CO's final decision indicated that dispute was not limited to "test" contract, and that decision encompassed entire disallowance for all affected contracts. ATK Thiokol, Inc. v. U.S., Fed.Cl.2006, 72 Fed.Cl. 306. United States ☞ 73(9)

Contractor's certified Type I differing site conditions claim submitted to contracting officer (CO) pursuant to the Contract Disputes Act (CDA) did not give CO adequate notice of a defective design specifications claim, precluding jurisdiction over that claim in the Court of Federal Claims, despite contractor's contention that both claims arose from the same set of operative facts; moreover, letter informing CO that contractor intended to pursue multiple claims under various entitlement theories, including defective design, was too vague for adequate notice. Kiewit Constr. Co. v. U.S., Fed.Cl.2003, 56 Fed.Cl. 414. Federal Courts ☞ 1076; United States ☞ 73(9)

A technically deficient claim certification under the Contract Disputes Act (CDA) neither prevents a contractor from stating a claim nor precludes the Court of Federal Claims from exercising jurisdiction over the matter. Medina Const., Ltd. v. U.S., Fed.Cl.1999, 43 Fed.Cl. 537. United States ☞ 73(9)

Qualification in contractor's final proposal that claim was presented "subject to review" of subcontractor's proposal rendered certification defective for not being in substantial compliance with

Contract Disputes Act. Alvarado Const., Inc. v. U.S., Fed.Cl.1994, 32 Fed.Cl. 184. United States ☞ 73(9)

Documents submitted to government contracting officer by contractor, taken together, were valid "claim" for purposes of Contract Disputes Act; certified list of expenses and letter stating that list was monetary claim presented for payment adequately notified officer that contractor sought final decision and that amount claimed was in dispute, and complaint filed in district court and prelitigation correspondence in suit that was later dismissed provided officer with basis of claim. Al Munford, Inc. v. U.S., Fed.Cl. 1993, 30 Fed.Cl. 185. United States ☞ 73(9)

Two letters submitted by contractor to contracting officer, which were each insufficient individually to constitute certified claim for extended overhead, could not be combined to satisfy Contract Dispute Act's (CDA's) certification requirements. Foley Co. v. U.S., Cl.Ct.1992, 26 Cl.Ct. 936, affirmed 11 F.3d 1032. United States ☞ 73(9)

Contractor's letter to Department of Energy (DOE) failed to satisfy Contract Disputes Act's requirement that certified claim be filed with contracting officer; there was no indication that dispute existed between contractor and DOE at time letter was written, letter did not request final decision, and letter was not received by contracting officer. Facilities Systems Engineering Corp. v. U.S., Cl.Ct.1992, 25 Cl.Ct. 761. United States ☞ 73(9)

Landlord's facsimile sent to Postal Service stating that, pursuant to the surrender of the lease, the Postal Service's continued failure to vacate would be charged at the rate of $1,000 per day in addition to other remedies available against it and second facsimile stating that the continuing obligation of maintenance and security would continue until the premises were surrendered were not sufficient to meet the Contract Disputes Act requirements of certification of claim and presentation of the claim to the contracting officer where landlord asserted two sets of claims, one to recover for failure to repair and maintain the premises, and one for damages incident to breach of alleged agreement for termination of the lease. Nussinow v. U.S., Cl.Ct.1991, 23 Cl.Ct. 556. United States ☞ 73(9)

Fact that joint venture, which was named in claim letter as contractor and referred to in body of certification as contractor, was not identified by name in certification was not fatal to certification of claim of more than $50,000. KDH Corp. v. U.S., Cl.Ct.1991, 23 Cl.Ct. 34. United States ☞ 73(9)

Even if contractor's cover letter and settlement proposal sent to Government which terminated contract for convenience was sufficient "claim" under Contract Disputes Act, Claims Court would not have jurisdiction over dispute; contractor failed to properly certify that claim, which was in excess of $50,000, was made in good faith, that data was accurate and complete, and that claim accurately reflected contract adjustment for which contractor believed Government was liable. Gardner Machinery Corp. v. U.S., Cl.Ct.1988, 14 Cl.Ct. 286. United States ☞ 73(9)

Contractor's statements in letter to contracting officer, that contractor again certified claim set forth on government form was made in good faith, that supporting data and documentation were accurate and complete to best of contractor's knowledge and belief, and that amount requested therein accurately reflected contract adjustment for which contractor believed Government was liable, were not effective to retroactively certify alleged claim after contract was terminated for default, for purposes of the Contract Disputes Act, where the claim had not been properly certified, and accordingly, the letter was not sufficient certification of the previously made claim to permit the contractor to file direct access suit in Claims Court. Technassociates, Inc. v. U.S., Cl.Ct.1988, 14 Cl.Ct. 200. United States ☞ 73(9)

United States Claims Court did not have jurisdiction over contracting party's direct access contract action under Contract Disputes Act, where letter to contracting officer upon which contracting party relied for certification merely stated that supporting data were accurate and where contracting party failed to certify both his good faith and accuracy of claim amount requested. Fredenburg v. U.S., Cl.Ct.1986, 10 Cl.Ct. 216. Federal Courts ☞ 1076; United States ☞ 73(15)

26. Persons authorized to certify—Generally

Because contractor who is not natural person cannot act except through persons or entities with authority to bind it, Contract Disputes Act clearly requires that person or entity acting on behalf of contractor have authority as to claim; however, such authority, standing alone, is not enough, and person certifying claim under federal acquisition regulations implementing Contract Disputes Act must also have general authority over affairs of contractor. Kiewit/Tulsa-Houston v. U.S., C.A.Fed.1992, 981 F.2d 531. United States ⊕ 73(9)

Senior corporate officer's signature on government contractor's claim for equitable adjustment was insufficient to give Armed Services Board of Contract Appeals jurisdiction over claim, absent evidence that officer participated in performance of contract, was present at contract site, prosecuted claim, or had general corporate authority. Universal Canvas, Inc. v. Stone, C.A.Fed.1992, 975 F.2d 847. United States ⊕ 73(9)

In addition to status requirements of the Federal Acquisition Regulation dealing with certification of claims under the Contracts Disputes Act where contractor is not individual, certifier must also have authority to bind contractor. Kiewit/Tulsa-Houston v. U.S., Cl.Ct.1992, 25 Cl.Ct. 110, affirmed 981 F.2d 531. United States ⊕ 73(9)

Only senior company official or officer or general partner of corporate contractor would have been able to properly certify claim under the Contract Disputes Act. Donald M. Drake Co. v. U.S., Cl.Ct. 1987, 12 Cl.Ct. 518. United States ⊕ 73(9)

27. —— Attorneys, persons authorized to certify

Under the Contracts Dispute Act (CDA), attorney for contractors was a proper person who could file their claims letter with contracting officer (CO), in light of CDA provision that "certification may be executed by any person duly authorized to bind the contractor with respect to the claim," and fact that the CDA does not specify who must submit claim to the CO. Flying Horse v. U.S., Fed.Cl.2001, 49 Fed.Cl. 419. United States ⊕ 73(9)

Contractor was required personally to certify written claim for damages under

Contract Disputes Act, and, thus, certification of claim by attorney, who was neither senior official nor individual having supervisory responsibility for contractor's affairs, was insufficient to confer jurisdiction upon claims court. Romala Corp. v. U.S., Cl.Ct.1987, 12 Cl.Ct. 411. Federal Courts ⊕ 1076

28. —— Joint ventures, persons authorized to certify

Joint venture which successfully bid on contract to build military housing properly certified claim to Navy's contracting officer in accordance with Contract Disputes Act, where claim was signed by only one of two voting members of joint venture's management committee; member who signed claim was also joint venture's sole signatory to contract, and Navy never questioned his authority to bind joint venture. Sadelmi Joint Venture v. Dalton, C.A.Fed.1993, 5 F.3d 510. United States ⊕ 73(9)

Contract claims against United States were not properly certified, where claim certifications were submitted on letterhead of dissolved joint venture and were signed by vice president of joint venturer, and where use of joint venturer's name was not inadvertent. Price/CIRI Const., J.V. v. U.S., Fed.Cl.1993, 27 Fed.Cl. 695. United States ⊕ 73(9)

President of one of coventurers did not have requisite status to properly certify claim of joint venture contractor under the Contract Disputes Act; joint venture agreement did not designate a representative in the capacity of "senior company official" with respect to joint venture, he was not in charge at location involved with regard to contract performance, and coventurer could not meet overall responsibility prong of certification regulations, as joint venture agreement did not designate any officers or general partners of joint venture. Universal Coatings/Won Ill Co., Ltd. (Joint Venture) v. U.S., Cl.Ct. 1991, 24 Cl.Ct. 241. United States ⊕ 73(9)

Joint venture seeking equitable adjustment of its contract substantially complied with claim certification requirement, even though only one member of venture signed certification and did so without indicating that certification was submitted on behalf of joint venture; record showed that member had overall responsibility for conduct of venture's affairs and documents attached to claim referred to joint venture and member's position. Cox Const. Co. v. U.S., Cl.Ct. 1990, 21 Cl.Ct. 98. United States ☞ 73(9)

29. ── Miscellaneous persons, persons authorized to certify

Contractor's controller lacked authority to certify claim to contracting officer, even though contractor's vice president of finance stated that controller had unrestricted authority to certify and submit claim, even if claim involved accounting issue, and even though contracting officer was elected corporate officer; controller lacked primary responsibility for contract performance, had no physical presence at primary location for contract performance, and lacked overall responsibility for conduct of contractor's affairs. Newport News Shipbuilding and Dry Dock Co. v. Garrett, C.A.Fed.1993, 6 F.3d 1547, rehearing denied, in banc suggestion declined. United States ☞ 73(9)

Contractor's executive vice president had overall responsibility for contractor's affairs and, therefore, was qualified to certify claim. Fischbach and Moore Intern. Corp. v. Christopher, C.A.Fed.1993, 987 F.2d 759. United States ☞ 73(9)

Corporate secretary and general counsel for public contractor had overall responsibility for conduct of contractor's affairs and, thus, was qualified to certify contractor's equitable adjustment claim, even though he reported to vice president who was general manager of corporation where secretary had overall responsibility for 95% of contractor's business. Johnson Controls World Services, Inc. v. Garrett, C.A.Fed.1993, 987 F.2d 738. United States ☞ 73(9)

Corporation's executive vice president was qualified to certify claim after defense contract audit agency suspended payments under public contracts with corporation, where contractor specifically asserted that executive vice president had unlimited authority to bind company and it had overall responsibility for conduct of its affairs. U.S. v. Newport News Shipbuilding and Dry Dock Co., C.A.Fed. 1991, 933 F.2d 996. United States ☞ 73(9)

Contractor failed to show that its Senior Vice President and Treasurer was proper person to certify that claim for disallowed contract costs was made in good faith; officer in question was not

"in charge," as there was no indication that he was responsible for anything more than simply deciding and reporting on whether particular dividend-like costs were employee compensation chargeable to series of government contracts, and evidence that his functions included overall responsibility for contractor's financial affairs was insufficient. U.S. v. Grumman Aerospace Corp., C.A.Fed. 1991, 927 F.2d 575, certiorari denied 112 S.Ct. 330, 502 U.S. 919, 116 L.Ed.2d 270. United States ☞ 73(9)

Chief cost engineer for corporate public contractor was not person authorized under Federal Acquisitions Regulations to certify contractor's claims for additional compensation under Contract Disputes Act. Ball, Ball & Brosamer, Inc. v. U.S., C.A.Fed.1989, 878 F.2d 1426. United States ☞ 73(9)

Corporate contractor's regional vice president was appropriate official to certify contractor's claim in the amount of $325,114, for repairs to fuel line of aircraft fueling system, both because he qualified as official having overall authority for conduct of contractor's affairs and because he had responsibility for contract at issue. M.A. Mortenson Co. v. U.S., Fed.Cl.1993, 29 Fed.Cl. 82. United States ☞ 73(9)

Senior official of government contractor was qualified to submit certified claim to contracting officer under Contract Disputes Act (CDA), where official had primary responsibility for execution of contract and visited contract site 40 to 50 times for two to three hours each visit over two-year period, although he was not located at contract site on permanent basis. T.L. Roof & Associates Const. Co. v. U.S., Fed.Cl.1993, 28 Fed.Cl. 572. United States ☞ 73(15)

Vice president and secretary of small closely held construction company was, at time he certified company's claim, officer of company having overall responsibility for conduct of its affairs within meaning of Federal Acquisition Regulations and could properly certify claims for company; although day-to-day management of construction project was responsibility of company's president, president and vice president/secretary shared overall responsibility for conduct of company's affairs. Valcon II, Inc. v. U.S., Cl.Ct.1991, 24 Cl.Ct. 479. United States ☞ 73(9)

General manager of contractor lacked authority to certify contract claims to contacting officer under the Contract Disputes Act (CDA), considering that manager's employment contract did not give him the right to make any contracts or commitments for or on behalf of contractor without first obtaining written consent of contractor, and that only president of contractor had authority to sign a contract and any amendments to a contract. Choggiung Ltd. v. U.S., Cl.Ct. 1991, 24 Cl.Ct. 320. United States ☞ 73(9)

Contractor's chief estimator was not appropriate person to certify contractor's claim for damages sustained as result of contracting officer's refusal to reform government contract, as the chief estimator did not qualify as senior company official in charge at contractor's plant or location involved or as officer or general partner of contractor having overall responsibility for conduct of contractor's affairs. Shirley Const. Corp. v. U.S., Cl.Ct.1991, 23 Cl.Ct. 686. United States ☞ 73(9)

Assistant vice president of bond claims in regional office and bond claims manager for region was not qualified to certify surety's claim for equitable adjustment to government construction contract brought under Contract Disputes Act, even though he was corporate officer, since officer was not senior company official in charge of plant or location involved and officer did not have overall responsibility for contractor's affairs. Reliance Ins. Co. v. U.S., Cl.Ct.1991, 23 Cl.Ct. 108. United States ☞ 73(9)

Contractor's employee who supervised 20 different projects and exercised general supervisory powers and responsibilities, including the negotiation of all contract changes and the preparation and filing of all contract claims without any dollar limitation, who had authority to run his projects as he thought necessary and full contract authority to bind the company, and who was specifically in charge of the work at issue was the proper person to certify contractor's claim under the Contract Disputes Act. Manning Elec. & Repair Co., Inc. v. U.S., Cl.Ct.1991, 22 Cl.Ct. 240. United States ☞ 73(9)

Vice-president and chief financial officer of general partner of limited partnership, which was contractor, was a person qualified to certify claim under Contract Disputes Act; since under Texas law limited partnership acts only through its general partner, general partner was appropriate entity to act for limited partnership in submission of claim under public contract and vice-president and chief financial officer was official responsible for completion of contract. Sun Cal, Inc. v. U.S., Cl.Ct.1990, 21 Cl.Ct. 31. United States ☞ 73(9)

Claim of defaulting contractor that went out of business could not be properly certified by on-site project manager where work force was demobilized at time of certification and manager was no longer employee of contractor, notwithstanding assertion that no one had more authority than manager at time of certification; mere assertion that former manager acted as agent of contractor, and thus was authorized to certify claim, was unavailing. Westech Corp. v. U.S., Cl.Ct. 1990, 20 Cl.Ct. 745. United States ☞ 73(9)

Contractor's project manager validly certified equitable adjustment claim under Contracts Disputes Act, as he was "senior company official in charge" at construction site. Western Empire Constructors, Inc. v. U.S., Cl.Ct.1990, 20 Cl. Ct. 668. United States ☞ 73(9)

Certification of equitable adjustment claim made to contracting officer by officer of parent corporation of surety on construction project did not satisfy requirement that claim be certified by officer of contractor. National Sur. Corp. v. U.S., Cl.Ct.1990, 20 Cl.Ct. 407. United States ☞ 73(9)

Project manager was not a senior company official in charge of the contractor's location and thus could not properly certify claim under Contract Disputes Act where his authority to deal with change orders was limited to those of $50,000 or less and where he was not otherwise shown to be a senior company official. Al Johnson Const. Co. v. U.S., Cl.Ct.1990, 19 Cl.Ct. 732. United States ☞ 73(9)

Contractor's general manager's signature of photocopy of claim for equitable adjustment of contract was valid certification, even if unauthorized party also signed claim, and general manager did not date signature; general manager had full authority to represent and bind contractor, and cover letter provided date on which certification was executed. Todd

Bldg. Co. v. U.S., Cl.Ct.1987, 13 Cl.Ct. 587. United States ⋘ 73(9)

30. Jurisdictional prerequisite of certification

Armed Services Board of Contract Appeals did not have jurisdiction under Contract Disputes Act (CDA) over contractor's appeal from contracting officer's award of termination settlement costs following termination of its contract with Navy to provide guard services at shipyard, where contractor did not submit either a claim or termination settlement proposal that could have ripened into a claim prior to the contracting officer's settlement proposal. England v. The Swanson Group, Inc., C.A.Fed.2004, 353 F.3d 1375. United States ⋘ 73(15)

Certification is a jurisdictional prerequisite to consideration of public contractor's claim for equitable adjustment. Johnson Controls World Services, Inc. v. Garrett, C.A.Fed.1993, 987 F.2d 738. United States ⋘ 73(9)

District court had no admiralty jurisdiction over contractor's action to recover monies owed under government contract for ship repairs, where contractor did not file proper administrative claim against government seeking recovery for such repairs. Bethlehem Steel Corp. v. Avondale Shipyards, Inc., C.A.5 (La.) 1992, 951 F.2d 92. United States ⋘ 73(9)

Energy Department Board of Contract Appeals had no jurisdiction over claim in excess of $50,000 by buyer of crude oil from naval petroleum reserve which had made binding election to proceed under Contract Disputes Act, even though claim was originally uncertified. Beacon Oil Co. v. U.S., C.A.Fed.1987, 832 F.2d 593, on remand. United States ⋘ 73(15)

If public contract claim of more than $50,000 has not been certified, as required by the Contract Disputes Act, Claims Court lacks jurisdiction over appeal from decision of contracting officer denying claim. Contract Cleaning Maintenance, Inc. v. U.S., C.A.Fed.1987, 811 F.2d 586. Federal Courts ⋘ 1076

Lack of required certification of government contractor's claims deprives contracting officer, board of contract appeals, and court of appeals of jurisdiction to proceed on claim. Tecom, Inc. v. U.S., C.A.Fed.1984, 732 F.2d 935. United States ⋘ 73(9)

Court of Federal Claims lacked jurisdiction over federal government's breach of contract and Contract Disputes Act counterclaims, with respect to action initiated by contractor seeking payment for construction of government facilities, since such claims had not been first submitted to Contracting Officer. Morse Diesel Intern., Inc. v. U.S., Fed.Cl.2007, 74 Fed.Cl. 601. United States ⋘ 73(9)

Court of Federal Claims lacked jurisdiction to adjudicate contracting officer's denial of contractor's request for equitable adjustment in an amount in excess of $100,000, where request was never certified, and thus government's denial did not comply with jurisdictional requirement of the Contract Disputes Act (CDA). Information Intern. Associates, Inc. v. U.S., Fed.Cl.2006, 74 Fed.Cl. 192. United States ⋘ 73(9)

Court of Federal Claims lacked jurisdiction over aspect of contractor's claim seeking to convert default termination to termination for convenience which sought convenience damages, where only letter from contractor to contracting officer (CO) merely requested reconsideration of default termination, and there was no evidence of record to show that contractor requested monetary damages of a sum certain, and there was no final decision by CO on a claim for convenience termination monetary damages. Armour of America v. U.S., Fed.Cl.2006, 69 Fed. Cl. 587. United States ⋘ 73(15)

Court of Federal Claims lacked jurisdiction over contractor's claim seeking to recover increased costs on part of subcontractor, where claim was not certified and presented contracting officer (CO) for final decision as required by the Contract Disputes Act (CDA) for claims exceeding $100,000, notwithstanding contractor's contention that claim was not a new claim but merely an increase in amount of properly certified claim presented to CO on behalf of another subcontractor, as the two subcontractor claims were based on a different set of operative facts. AAB Joint Venture v. U.S., Fed.Cl.2005, 68 Fed.Cl. 363. United States ⋘ 73(15)

Pursuant to Contract Disputes Act (CDA), government contractor failed to invoke jurisdiction of Court of Federal Claims with respect to its claim for $109,040.91 allegedly due on copy machines purportedly covered under lease-to-own plan when contractor did not make written demand upon contracting officer for such amount, and did not certify that claim was made in good faith, that supporting data was accurate and complete to the best of contractor's knowledge and belief, and that amount accurately reflected contract adjustment for which contractor believed government was liable. Danka de Puerto Rico, Inc. v. U.S., Fed.Cl.2004, 63 Fed.Cl. 20. Federal Courts ⚖ 1076

Court of Federal Claims lacked jurisdiction under the Contract Disputes Act (CDA) over claims by electric utilities that they were improperly charged by the government for imputed interest and for the production of High Assay Uranium price for uranium enrichment services, where the claims were not presented to the contracting officer (CO), despite their contention that such claims were encompassed in original claim based on the inclusion of remedial action and depleted uranium costs in the price. Florida Power & Light Co. v. U.S., Fed.Cl.2001, 49 Fed.Cl. 656, vacated 307 F.3d 1364, on remand 56 Fed.Cl. 555. Federal Courts ⚖ 1076

Court of Federal Claims lacked jurisdiction under the Contract Disputes Act (CDA) over contractor's breach of contract claim, where claim was not presented to the contracting officer (CO). Advanced Materials, Inc. v. U.S., Fed.Cl. 2000, 46 Fed.Cl. 697. Federal Courts ⚖ 1076

Prerequisite to access to Court of Federal Claims is that the claim at issue first be certified and submitted in writing to the contracting officer pursuant to statute, and a contractor may change the amount of his claim, but may not raise any new claims not subject to a decision by the contracting officer. ThermoCor, Inc. v. U.S., Fed.Cl.1996, 35 Fed.Cl. 480. Federal Courts ⚖ 1102

Under Contract Disputes Act, alleged implied in fact contract between airlines and Immigration and Naturalization Service (INS) to compensate airline for expenses would have to be certified and submitted to contracting officer for decision before suit could be filed in Court of Federal Claims. Aerolineas Argentinas v. U.S., Fed.Cl.1994, 31 Fed.Cl. 25, vacated 77 F.3d 1564, rehearing denied, in banc suggestion declined. United States ⚖ 73(9)

Claims Court lacked subject matter jurisdiction over breach of contract claim by contractor with Federal Bureau of Investigation (FBI), in light of contractor's failure to satisfy mandatory jurisdictional prerequisite that he submit written claim to contracting officer before filing suit. Cox v. U.S., Cl.Ct.1992, 26 Cl.Ct. 199. Federal Courts ⚖ 1102

Even if letter from contractor was sufficient claim under Contract Disputes Act, Claims Court lacked subject matter jurisdiction over direct access appeal where contractor failed to certify purported claim in accordance with statutory and regulatory mandates. Robin Industries, Inc., Tadcol Government Services Div. v. U.S., Cl.Ct.1991, 22 Cl.Ct. 448. United States ⚖ 73(9)

A government contractor's claim certification substituting the word "subcontractor" for "contractor" when seeking an equitable adjustment on behalf of the subcontractor failed to meet the Contract Disputes Act requirement's jurisdictional requirement that the contractor certify that there was good ground for the amount claimed by the subcontractor, and thus deprived the Claims Court of jurisdiction. Century Const. Co. v. U.S., Cl.Ct.1990, 22 Cl.Ct. 63. United States ⚖ 73(9)

Requirement that claim presented to contracting officer be certified by appropriate officer of contractor is jurisdictional, and complaint must be dismissed if certification is defective. National Sur. Corp. v. U.S., Cl.Ct.1990, 20 Cl.Ct. 407. United States ⚖ 73(9)

Filing of a properly certified claim with a contracting officer is a jurisdictional prerequisite to asserting a claim under the Contract Disputes Act. Al Johnson Const. Co. v. U.S., Cl.Ct.1990, 19 Cl.Ct. 732. United States ⚖ 73(9)

Even if food service supplier were contractor rather than subcontractor, supplier failed to submit properly certified claim for monetary damages to contracting officer, and thus claims court did not have jurisdiction under Contract Disputes Act over supplier's claims. Clean Giant, Inc. v. U.S., Cl.Ct.1990, 19 Cl.Ct. 390. United States ⚖ 73(9)

Claims Court lacked jurisdiction over partnership's claims against the United States for breach of express or implied contract where claim had not been certified and presented for decision to contracting officer. Haberman v. U.S., Cl. Ct.1989, 18 Cl.Ct. 302. Federal Courts ⚖ 1102

Failure of government contractor to comply with jurisdictional requirements of submitting claim to agency contracting officer and receiving opinion from that official prior to seeking monetary relief in Claims Court rendered complaint of a nullity, and contractor's later filing of complaint with contracting officer, and latter's rendering of decision on claim, did not have retroactive effect of curing jurisdictional defect in original complaint. Christian Appalachian Project, Inc. v. U.S., Cl.Ct.1986, 10 Cl.Ct. 595. Federal Courts ⚖ 1102

31. Hearing

Contract Disputes Act does not require that contracting officer hold hearing prior to reaching decision on claims by contractor against government. Girard v. Klopfenstein, C.A.9 (Ariz.) 1991, 930 F.2d 738, certiorari denied 112 S.Ct. 173, 502 U.S. 858, 116 L.Ed.2d 136. United States ⚖ 73(9)

32. Authority to issue final decision

Contractor's CDA claim challenging contracting officer's default termination of contract and government's demand for return of unliquidated progress payments was not "mirror image" of later claim challenging contracting officer's deemed denial of claim for equitable adjustment and lost profits under same contract and thus later claim was not "in litigation," as would have divested contracting officer of authority to issue final decision, and vested exclusive authority in Department of Justice to act in pending litigation. Case, Inc. v. U.S., C.A.Fed.1996, 88 F.3d 1004. United States ⚖ 73(9)

Air Force's contracting officer lacked authority to issue "final decision" on contractor's claim for work completed on prefabricated modular building in light of excusability defense raised by contractor; contractor had Multiple Award Schedule (MAS) contract as part of Federal Supply Schedule (FSS) program with General Services Administration (GSA) to provide prefabricated buildings to federal agencies for five years, Air Force chose to purchase from contractor after solicitation to FSS-MAS contract holders, and contractual default clause and regulation applicable to FSS schedule contracts provided that determination of whether failure was excusable was to be made by GSA's contracting officer. United Partition Systems, Inc. v. U.S., Fed.Cl.2004, 59 Fed.Cl. 627. United States ⚖ 73(9)

General Services Administration's (GSA's) contracting officer would be revested by Court of Federal Claims with authority to issue final decision on claim; Court had jurisdiction over case by deemed denial of claim based on absence of timely decision by authorized contracting officer, Court acted pursuant to statute to issue stay to obtain final decision from contracting officer on excusability aspect of claim, and Court did so after proceedings that involved full participation of claimant and Government. United Partition Systems, Inc. v. U.S., Fed.Cl.2004, 59 Fed.Cl. 627. United States ⚖ 73(9)

33. Failure to issue decision deemed denial of claim

If contracting officer fails to issue final decision on contractor's claim under Contract Disputes Act or to notify contractor of time within which decision will be issued, and at least 60 days have passed since date claim was submitted for decision, claim is deemed denied. Dalton v. Cessna Aircraft Co., C.A.Fed. 1996, 98 F.3d 1298, rehearing denied, in banc suggestion declined. United States ⚖ 73(9)

Terminating contracting officer's failure to issue decision within statutory 60–day time period in regard to Government contractor's claim for termination for convenience costs, satisfied jurisdictional prerequisites for Armed Services Board of Contract Appeals to consider appeal of contractor's claim. Do-Well Mach. Shop, Inc. v. U.S., C.A.Fed.1989, 870 F.2d 637. United States ⚖ 73(13)

Contracting officer's decision to extend the time for reaching a final decision on contractor's claim, issued 7 days before, but not received by contractor until 2 days after the expiration of the 60–day period allowed by the Contract Disputes Act (CDA) for contracting officer to issue a decision on claim or notify contractor that decision will be delayed, extended the 60–day period, thus precluding contractor's reliance on a "deemed denial" to file suit on the claim. Logicvision, Inc. v. U.S., Fed.Cl.2002, 54 Fed.Cl. 549. United States ⚖ 73(13)

Failure of contracting officer to issue or give date certain for decision on claims asserted by party which had contracted to purchase surplus aircraft parts from government within 60 days after receipt of claim constituted deemed denial of claim, allowing commencement of suit on claim under Contract Disputes Act (CDA); however, because decision by contracting officer would be beneficial, proceedings in court of federal claims were stayed until after issuance of such an opinion, which was required to be within 60 days. Sparks v. U.S., Fed.Cl. 1996, 36 Fed.Cl. 488, as modified. Federal Courts ☞ 1101; Federal Courts ☞ 1102; United States ☞ 73(9)

Claims by company which contracted with Bureau of Prisons to provide housing, supervision, and counseling of inmates were in dispute for purposes of CDA: for each claim, company submitted letters requesting payment and identified for each claim the amount, in sum certain, that company requested; company sought "speedy resolution" and expressed disappointment over the "lack of progress"; and company's attempts to resolve its claims spanned a period of several years; company sought final decision with respect to claims and Bureau failed to render decision within the 60 days mandated by statute. Bannum, Inc. v. U.S., Fed.Cl.1995, 33 Fed.Cl. 672. United States ☞ 73(9)

In light of contracting officer's (CO's) failure to timely issue decision on contractor's termination for convenience claim, due to CO's erroneous view that claim had been placed before Court of Federal Claims and that final decision would not be issued while case was pending, claim could be treated as denied and Court of Federal Claims had jurisdiction over claim. Cincinnati Electronics Corp. v. U.S., Fed.Cl.1994, 32 Fed.Cl. 496. United States ☞ 73(9)

Language in contracting officer's letter to contractor that contractor should not expect final decision "prior to" June 30th failed to satisfy Contract Claims Act provision requiring notification of contractor of time within which decision will be issued, and thus, claim was "deemed denied" and action could be brought in claims court. Orbas & Associates v. U.S., Cl.Ct.1992, 26 Cl.Ct. 647. United States ☞ 73(9)

The Claims Court could not assert jurisdiction over government contractor's termination for convenience claim under the Contract Dispute Act, as the 60-day period necessary to create "deemed" denial for exercise of jurisdiction had not run, where contracting officer had certified claims before her which were also subject of pending Claims Court termination for default suit. Boeing Co. v. U.S., Cl.Ct.1992, 26 Cl.Ct. 529, reversed 991 F.2d 811, rehearing denied, on remand 31 Fed.Cl. 289. United States ☞ 73(9); United States ☞ 73(15)

A termination contracting officer's letter to a contractor, which fixed a date by which she would respond or advise contractor when she would respond to its claims, did not obligate officer to make her decision on the contractor's claims by a specific date, so as to trigger a tolling of the period after which the claim would be deemed denied; fixing a date by which some later date would be identified did not afford the contractor, within 60 days of filing the claim, a date for issuance of a final decision as required by real estate Contract Disputes Act. Boeing Co. v. U.S., Cl.Ct.1992, 26 Cl.Ct. 257. United States ☞ 73(9)

Suit commenced pursuant to "deemed denial" provision of Contract Disputes Act is one which is commenced following passage of 60 days after submission of claim to contracting officer without decision, not one that is commenced before claims are submitted to contracting officer. Tecom Industries, Inc. v. U.S., Cl. Ct.1991, 24 Cl.Ct. 611. United States ☞ 73(13)

Where government contractor chooses to deem his claim denied by contracting officer's failure to issue timely decision, and file suit in United States Claims Court, contracting officer is divested of his authority over claim unless Claims Court, in its discretion, concludes to stay action and remand it to contracting officer for determination. Durable Metal Products, Inc. v. U.S., Cl.Ct.1990, 21 Cl. Ct. 41. United States ☞ 73(9)

Controlling statute, specifically referenced in government contract, providing that failure to allow a contractor's claim would be deemed a denial of the claim, and that contractor could, through appeal or suit, contest that denial, entitled Government to contest contractor's claim for damages upon Government cancellation of contract, and Government was not, as claimed by contractor, "in default," based upon failure to respond to his claim within specified period, so as to obligate Government to pay full amount requested. Maki v. U.S., Cl.Ct.1987, 13 Cl.Ct. 779, affirmed 852 F.2d 1293, certiorari denied 109 S.Ct. 368, 488 U.S. 943, 102 L.Ed.2d 358. United States ⟜ 74(5)

Statute declaring failure of contracting officer to issue decision on contract claim within 60 days to be decision by officer denying claim is permissible, not mandatory. W & J Const. Corp. v. U.S., Cl.Ct. 1987, 12 Cl.Ct. 507. United States ⟜ 73(13)

Statute declaring failure of contracting officer to issue decision on contract claim within 60 days to be a decision by the officer denying the claim, Contract Disputes Act of 1978, § 6(c)(5), 41 U.S.C.A. § 605(c)(5), is permissive, thereby giving contractor choice of filing or not filing suit if contracting officer has not reached a final decision within the relevant 60–day time period. Vemo Co. v. U.S., Cl.Ct.1985, 9 Cl.Ct. 217. United States ⟜ 73(13)

34. Final decision—Generally

Six-year limitations period applicable to actions for money damages brought by United States did not apply to government's claim under Contract Disputes Act (CDA), which could not be asserted in federal court before issuance of contracting officer's final decision. Motorola, Inc. v. West, C.A.Fed.1997, 125 F.3d 1470, rehearing denied. United States ⟜ 73(15)

35. —— Jurisdictional prerequisite, final decision

Under Contract Disputes Act, final decision by contracting officer on claim, whether asserted by contractor or government, is jurisdictional prerequisite to further legal action on claim. Sharman Co., Inc. v. U.S., C.A.Fed.1993, 2 F.3d 1564, on remand 30 Fed.Cl. 231. United States ⟜ 73(9)

Claims Court did not have jurisdiction over government contractor's action requesting conversion of termination of contract for default into termination for convenience, where contracting officer had not made final decision; without final decision from contracting officer, contractor's complaint in effect sought

declaratory judgment. Scott Aviation v. U.S., C.A.Fed.1992, 953 F.2d 1377. Federal Courts ⟜ 1078; Federal Courts ⟜ 1102

Absent submission of a contract "claim" in writing to contracting officer, no "decision" by contracting officer is possible and therefore no basis for jurisdiction in Court of Claims under this chapter. Paragon Energy Corp. v. U.S., Ct.Cl.1981, 645 F.2d 966, 227 Ct.Cl. 176, affirmed 230 Ct.Cl. 884. United States ⟜ 73(15)

Plaintiff's failure to submit his claim against General Services Administration (GSA) to GSA contracting officer before he brought suit in federal court precluded his cause of action against GSA under Contract Dispute Act (CDA). Mosseri v. F.D.I.C., S.D.N.Y.1996, 924 F.Supp. 605, affirmed in part, reversed in part 104 F.3d 356. United States ⟜ 73(9)

Company hired by Environmental Protection Agency (EPA) to remove hazardous waste failed to comply with Contract Disputes Act (CDA) and, therefore, could not bring action against EPA in federal court for breach of contract, where record did not reveal that contracting officer ever issued decision with respect to company's claim. Richland-Lexington Airport Dist. v. Atlas Properties, Inc., D.S.C. 1994, 854 F.Supp. 400. United States ⟜ 73(9)

Court of Federal Claims did not have jurisdiction to adjudicate contractor's claim for interest under the Contract Disputes Act (CDA) on $25,000 contract payment, where contractor did not submit a CDA "claim" to and receive a "final decision" from the contracting officer (CO) for the $25,000 amount or interest thereon; contractor's application for payment which included the $25,000 amount had all the characteristics of a routine invoice, and thus did not qualify as a CDA claim. Sarang Corp. v. U.S., Fed.Cl. 2007, 76 Fed.Cl. 560. United States ⟜ 73(9)

Claim by contractor seeking determination of rights under land patent was not within the jurisdiction of the Court of Federal Claims, where claim was never submitted to the contracting officer and there was no final decision or deemed denial by the contracting officer. Alaska Pulp Corp. v. U.S., Fed.Cl.1997, 38 Fed. Cl. 141. Federal Courts ⟜ 1073.1

Where payment to contractor was made under Contract Disputes Act, contracting officer's decision asserting the government's right to recover the erroneous modification payment was a prerequisite to suit in Court of Federal Claims. Crown Laundry and Dry Cleaners, Inc. v. U.S., Fed.Cl.1993, 29 Fed.Cl. 506. United States ☞ 73(9)

Government contractor's claims for demobilization costs, reduction in liquidated damages because of delays in diverting river channel related to low water, and for compensation for dredging performed by subcontractor were affirmative claims for money damages which were required to be presented to contracting officer for final decision before Court of Federal Claims could exercise subject-matter jurisdiction. John Massman Contracting Co. v. U.S., Fed.Cl. 1993, 28 Fed.Cl. 235. United States ☞ 73(9)

Claims Court did not have jurisdiction over indemnity corporation that took over and completed performance of contract upon original contractor's default as its certifying official did not meet requirements of Contract Disputes Act; indemnity corporation was "contractor" for definitional purposes, and the certifying official, its Bond Counsel, was not officer of contractor and had made only one visit to construction site and thus did not satisfy either prong of Federal Acquisition Regulation. Industrial Indem. Co. v. U.S., Cl.Ct.1992, 26 Cl.Ct. 443. United States ☞ 73(9)

Claims Court had no jurisdiction over government contractor's claim for equitable adjustment to contract price, where claim was never subject to contracting officer's final decision. Continental Heller Const. v. U.S., Cl.Ct.1990, 21 Cl.Ct. 471. United States ☞ 73(9)

Jurisdictional prerequisites for suit in Claims Court under Contract Disputes Act are that contractor must have presented written claim to contracting officer, and that there was either an actual contracting officer's decision on claim or contracting officer must have failed to issue decision within statutory time period, in which case Act provides that contracting officer is deemed to have made decision denying claim. Mendenhall v. U.S., Cl.Ct.1990, 20 Cl.Ct. 78. United States ☞ 73(9)

Claims Court lacked jurisdiction to consider government's claim for reimbursement of progress payments in connection with case brought by contractor challenging Army's termination of contract; letter notifying contractor of purported default stated that it was not a final decision, and only final decisions were reviewable by Court. Crippen & Graen Corp. v. U.S., Cl.Ct.1989, 18 Cl.Ct. 237. United States ☞ 73(15)

36. —— Request for final decision

Letter of contractor's representative stating to contracting officer stating that contractor was "very anxious to put this matter to rest and move on to other projects" implicitly requested a final decision of contracting officer under the Contract Disputes Act (CDA); statement suggested a desire for finality, which only a contractor officer's final decision could provide. Scan-Tech Sec., L.P. v. U.S., Fed.Cl.2000, 46 Fed.Cl. 326. United States ☞ 73(9)

Letter sent from salvage company to Assistant United States Attorney was not submission of valid claim under Contract Disputes Act (CDA), as salvage company failed to provide contractual basis that would entitle it to relief, and by failing to send letter to proper procurement agency did not express desire for final decision within meaning of CDA, although letter eventually found its way into hands of appropriate contracting officer. J & E Salvage Co. v. U.S., Fed.Cl.1997, 37 Fed. Cl. 256, affirmed 152 F.3d 945, certiorari denied 119 S.Ct. 76, 525 U.S. 827, 142 L.Ed.2d 59. United States ☞ 73(9)

Contractor's letter to contracting officer constituted "claim" with respect to contracts with Department of Agriculture covering the harvesting of timber in national forest, even though letter did not use legal term "final decision" or mention Contract Disputes Act, where letter clearly requested decision on contractor's request to cancel contracts and refund money he had paid, and letter referred to harvesting areas covered by contract. Mendenhall v. U.S., Cl.Ct.1990, 20 Cl.Ct. 78. United States ☞ 73(9)

Letter with attached settlement proposal that was submitted to contracting officer did not constitute written demand by contractor for final decision by contracting officer, for purposes of Contract Disputes Act requirement that claim be submitted to contracting officer for decision before contractor files direct access suit in claims court; there was no demand for finite amount or request for final decision thereon, and letter and attached settlement proposal could be viewed as further attempt by contractor to get contracting officer to renegotiate terms of contract, although contractor used words "convenience termination claim" and included definite amount of money. Technassociates, Inc. v. U.S., Cl.Ct.1988, 14 Cl.Ct. 200. United States ☞ 73(9)

Purchaser's request to be notified if volume of government crude oil required to be purchased would be altered in response to purchaser's protests qualified as demand for decision by contracting officer for purposes of claim under Contracts Disputes Act. Alliance Oil & Refining Co. v. U.S., Cl.Ct.1987, 13 Cl.Ct. 496, affirmed 856 F.2d 201. United States ☞ 73(9)

Letter from claimant to contracting officer identifying compensation requested and asking that matter be resolved within 60 days satisfied Contract Disputes Act requirement that written claim be submitted requesting final decision. Malissa Co., Inc. v. U.S., Cl.Ct.1986, 11 Cl.Ct. 389. United States ☞ 73(13)

37. —— Miscellaneous decisions, final decision

Letter by contracting officer terminating government contract for default based on failure to timely perform, in accordance with standard Federal Acquisition Regulations (FAR) default clause included in contract, was valid final decision for purposes of establishing jurisdiction under Contract Disputes Act (CDA) over action brought by contractor challenging termination, even though contractor contended that termination was technically defective due to lack of cure notice. Daff v. U.S., C.A.Fed.1996, 78 F.3d 1566, rehearing denied, in banc suggestion declined. United States ☞ 73(9)

Contracting officer rendered final decision on government claim for purposes of Claims Court jurisdiction when he declined to pay contractor balance due on contract on ground that contractor had failed to complete contract in timely manner, delaying issuance of start-work notices to other contractors who might later submit delay claims against Government; contract price was undisputed and was due upon completion of work, and, although officer may have implied that amount of Government's claimed setoff

would be redetermined in future, he effectively granted Government's claim in full amount of contract price balance sought by contractor. Placeway Const. Corp. v. U.S., C.A.Fed.1990, 920 F.2d 903. United States ☞ 73(9)

Court of Federal Claims had jurisdiction under the Contract Disputes Act (CDA) over contractor's claim requesting that termination for default be converted to termination for convenience, where contractor sent letter to contracting officer (CO) requesting reconsideration of default termination, and CO reaffirmed the default termination in a letter to Plaintiff, thereby rendering her final decision regarding the default termination. Armour of America v. U.S., Fed.Cl.2006, 69 Fed.Cl. 587. United States ☞ 73(15)

Decision of contracting officer (CO) regarding monetary claims of contractor was not a valid "final decision" under the Contract Disputes Act (CDA), where decision was rendered after contractor brought suit on the claims, precluding jurisdiction in the Court of Federal Claims. Witherington Const. Corp. v. U.S., Fed.Cl.1999, 45 Fed.Cl. 208. United States ☞ 73(15)

Final decisions of contracting officer denying contractors' claims were invalid and could not serve as a basis for jurisdiction in the Court of Federal Claims under the Contract Disputes Act (CDA), where the claims were incorporated into complaint filed in district court, and claims were not submitted to contracting officer until after suit was filed; district court action extinguished contracting officer's prerogative to issue a decision on the claims. Ervin and Associates, Inc. v. U.S., Fed.Cl.1999, 44 Fed.Cl. 646. Federal Courts ☞ 1076

Letter from contracting officer to contractor, acknowledging receipt of contractor's termination for convenience proposed settlement costs and stating that government did not grant such costs under contracts terminated for default when purchase orders for them were withdrawn or cancelled, was final decision of contracting officer for Contracts Disputes Act purposes even though it did not contain "boilerplate" language indicating it was a final decision. Davies Precision Machining, Inc. v. U.S., Fed.Cl. 1996, 35 Fed.Cl. 651. United States ☞ 73(9)

Military installation contracting officer's letter setting forth his decision concerning violation of Anti-Kickback Act constituted final decision and provided basis for appeal pursuant to Contracts Dispute Act (CDA), where letter was titled "contracting officer's final decision on third government claim" and where letter set forth contracting officer's findings and rationale and informed party of his avenues for appeal. Haustechnik v. U.S., Fed.Cl.1996, 34 Fed.Cl. 740. United States ☞ 73(15)

Contracting officer's letters that adopted district court's ruling respecting nonconformance of contractor's accounting practices and that based immediately effective payment redeterminations on those rulings were "final decisions" for purposes of Contract Disputes Act, even though letters were not so labeled. Litton Systems, Inc., Litton Computer Services Div. v. U.S., Fed.Cl.1992, 27 Fed.Cl. 306, dismissed 36 F.3d 1111. United States ☞ 73(9)

Court of Federal Claims had jurisdiction over contractor's action under Contract Disputes Act, as there was deemed final decision by contracting officer relating to subject claims; contracting officer's notices did not comply with Act as time within which contracting officer would issue final decision was left openended and, alternatively, because contracting officer had not committed to issue a decision by the specified dates. Claude E. Atkins Enterprises, Inc. v. U.S., Fed.Cl.1992, 27 Fed.Cl. 142. United States ☞ 73(9)

Decision by contracting officer not to make payment to government contractor above $55 million cap would constitute "decision" denying contractor's claim under contract's termination for convenience clause and within meaning of Contracts Dispute Act over which Claims Court had jurisdiction—since contractor had already received $55 million. Solar Turbines, Inc. v. U.S., Cl.Ct.1989, 16 Cl. Ct. 304. United States ☞ 73(9)

38. Dismissal of claim

Where contractor did not submit his claims for fair price of his services and fair value of services realized by Government to contracting officer, and sole grounds for dismissing claims was lack of jurisdiction, dismissal without prejudice was proper course. Thoen v. U.S.,

C.A.Fed.1985, 765 F.2d 1110. United States ☞ 73(15)

While sovereign immunity of United States with respect to contract claim arising out of operation of public vessel could have been waived by United States, where contractor failed to provide a certified claim to contracting officer as required by Contract Disputes Act for waiver to occur, contract claim against United States was subject to being dismissed for want of subject matter jurisdiction. River and Offshore Services Co., Inc. v. U.S., E.D.La.1987, 651 F.Supp. 276. United States ☞ 125(12)

Result of a failure to certify a claim for more than $50,000 is dismissal thereof. Palmer & Sicard, Inc. v. U.S., Cl.Ct.1984, 4 Cl.Ct. 420.

Proper course of action for contractor, whose case is dismissed for lack of jurisdiction, is to properly certify claim, resubmit it to contracting officer, and, if there is then adverse decision, appeal either directly to the board of contract appeals, or directly to the Claims Court. Conoc Const. Corp. v. U.S., Cl.Ct.1983, 3 Cl.Ct. 146. United States ☞ 73(15)

39. Reasons for decision

Final decision of contracting officer which stated that the claim was not timely and attached letter in which the basis for the claim of untimeliness was set forth were sufficient to satisfy requirements of the Contract Disputes Act that the contracting officer state the reasons for the decision. Summit Contractors v. U.S., Cl.Ct.1988, 15 Cl.Ct. 806. United States ☞ 73(9)

40. Right of appeal—Generally

This chapter does not contemplate a right of direct appellate review from orders under this section providing that contractor may request agency board of contract appeals to direct contracting officer to issue a decision in a specified period of time. U.S. v. W.H. Moseley Co., C.A.Fed.1984, 730 F.2d 1472. United States ☞ 73(15)

Marine fuel supply contractor which failed to challenge contracting officer's decisions holding contractor liable to Government for demurrage claims could not challenge decisions in Government's enforcement action; contract between contractor and Government provided schedule of demurrage rates for delays in vessel loading designed to approximate and not exceed actual damage costs involved with such delay. U.S. v. Roarda, Inc., D.Md.1987, 671 F.Supp. 1084. United States ☞ 73(14)

41. —— Notice of appeal rights, right of appeal

Construction company surety's termination for default, after surety took over federal postal facility project, would not be converted into termination for convenience of government, even though termination notice failed to advise surety of its appeal rights in violation of Contract Disputes Act, as omission of any reference to appeal rights was harmless; surety had actual notice of appeal rights, and surety challenged postal service's actions by appealing denial of payment request and filing instant suit. State of Fla., Dept. of Ins. v. U.S., C.A.Fed.1996, 81 F.3d 1093. United States ☞ 73(5)

Contract Disputes Act (CDA) requires that government provide contractor sufficient information concerning his rights to make informed choice as to whether, and in what forum, he will pursue appeal; focus of requirement is protection of contractor, and when contractor's determination regarding appeal is unaffected by defect, notice does not fail in its protective purpose, and continues to be effective Contracting Officer's decision under CDA with respect to triggering limitations period for appeal. Decker & Co. v. West, C.A.Fed.1996, 76 F.3d 1573, on remand 1998 WL 195944. United States ☞ 73(15)

Notice given to Postal Service contractor of its appeal rights following denial by the Service of its contract claims was adequate under this section where contractor was notified that it could elect to appeal decision to Postal Service Board of Contract Appeals or, in lieu of appealing decision to Board, could bring action directly on claim in Court of Claims. Santa Fe Engineers, Inc. v. U.S., Ct.Cl. 1982, 677 F.2d 876, 230 Ct.Cl. 512. United States ☞ 73(15)

Letter from contracting officer informing lessor of finality of his decision on lessor's claim with respect to obligations that United States Postal Service (USPS) allegedly incurred in conjunction with its tenancy and informing lessor of 12–month filing deadline mandated by CDA fulfilled USPS's obligation to notify lessor of his appeal rights and because

lessor failed to bring suit within 12–month period, his claim was time barred. Thomas v. U.S., Fed.Cl.1995, 34 Fed.Cl. 619, affirmed 101 F.3d 714. United States ☞ 73(15)

Contracting officer's decision letter considering and denying government contractor's claim was final decision subject to Contract Disputes Act requirement that government contractor be informed of appeal rights, even though letter advised that contractor could pursue matter further by complying with disputes clause of government contract or Contract Disputes Act; nothing in disputes clause of contract required contractor to do more than was done to alert contracting officer of claim or to take further steps to perfect claim. Alliance Oil & Refining Co. v. U.S., Cl.Ct.1987, 13 Cl.Ct. 496, affirmed 856 F.2d 201. United States ☞ 73(9)

42. —— Time of appeal, right of appeal

Incorrect statement by contracting officer in issuing default termination of contract that government contractor could appeal within 12 months to Court of Federal Claims, which at time of notice did not have jurisdiction over pure default terminations, did not in and of itself render termination notice invalid and did not prevent operation of time bar on contractor's claim against government absent evidence that detrimental reliance by contractor on statement caused contractor's failure to appeal to Armed Services Board of Contract Appeals within 90 days. Decker & Co. v. West, C.A.Fed. 1996, 76 F.3d 1573, on remand 1998 WL 195944. United States ☞ 73(15)

Contracting officer's letter denying contractor's monetary claim because contractor had not yet provided requested documentation was final decision denying contractor's claim and thus commenced 12–month period for contractor to bring direct action in Court of Federal Claims; contracting officer classified her decision as a "final decision" and offered contractor only two possible avenues of recourse, an appeal to Board of Contract Appeals or direct action in Court of Federal Claims. L & D Services, Inc. v. U.S., Fed.Cl.1996, 34 Fed.Cl. 673. United States ☞ 73(15)

Contract Disputes Act subjects each claim submitted individually by contractor to statute of limitations by providing that decision of contracting officer with respect to claim shall be final unless timely appealed; thus, contractor who chooses to submit discrete claims may not avoid statutory restriction by amendment. Design and Production, Inc. v. U.S., Cl. Ct.1986, 10 Cl.Ct. 80. Limitation Of Actions ☞ 127(13); United States ☞ 73(15)

Contracting officer's decision based on uncertified claim cannot trigger running of limitations periods under this section, since such decision has no life apart from underlying claim. United Const. Co., Inc. v. U.S., Cl.Ct.1984, 7 Cl.Ct. 47. United States ☞ 73(15)

43. General Accounting office, review by

General Accounting Office generally does not consider mistake in bid claims alleged after award, since claims relate to contract within meaning of this section, which requires such claims to be filed with contracting officer for decision. 1985, 64 Op.Comp.Gen. 330.

Since subsec. (a) of this section provides that all claims by contractor against government should be submitted to contracting officer for decision, General Accounting Office is not proper tribunal for resolving such disputes. 1984, 63 Op. Comp.Gen. 338.

44. Fraud exception

Government's claims against contractors for unjust enrichment, payment by mistake, and breach of contract did not involve fraud and, thus, fraud exception to Contract Disputes Act (CDA) did not apply; although contractor sought payments from government based on subcontractors' false invoices, there was no allegation that contractors engaged in fraud and success of government's claims did not depend on whether subcontractors committed fraud. U.S. v. Marovic, N.D.Cal.1999, 69 F.Supp.2d 1190. United States ☞ 73(9)

Government's breach of contract and unjust enrichment claims against government contractors, alleging that government was overbilled approximately $330,000 for contractor's leases of equipment from its own subsidiaries and for full salary of contractor's employee who spent only 62% of her time on government contracts, were claims "involving fraud," for purposes of Contract Dispute Act (CDA) section that generally precludes government from filing federal court action related to contract dispute, except for claims "involving fraud";

thus, because those claims were intimately bound up with and part of same case or controversy as government's False Claims Act (FCA) claim, government was not required to pursue claim in two separate fora, but could instead pursue all claims in federal district court. U.S. v. Unified Industries, Inc., E.D.Va.1996, 929 F.Supp. 947. United States ☞ 73(9)

Government's claims against defense contractor for breach of contract, payment under mistake of fact and unjust enrichment were claims involving fraud, excluded from Contract Disputes Act; each claim represented another theory of recovery for contractor's alleged fraud. U.S. ex rel. O'Keefe v. McDonnell Douglas Corp., E.D.Mo.1996, 918 F.Supp. 1338. United States ☞ 73(9)

United States' claims that defense contractor violated Federal False Claims Act (FCA) through its conduct in negotiating contract were exempt from coverage under Contract Disputes Act (CDA), so that they were subject to jurisdiction of federal district court, as those claims involved allegations of fraud. U.S. v. Rockwell Intern. Corp., N.D.Ga.1992, 795 F.Supp. 1131. Federal Courts ☞ 976; United States ☞ 120.1

All matters involving fraud are excepted from application of the Contract Disputes Act provision for resolving claims by decision of contracting officer and claims under the False Claims Act need not be submitted to administrative agency for determination. U.S. v. JT Const. Co., Inc., W.D.Tex.1987, 668 F.Supp. 592. United States ☞ 122

Under the Contract Disputes Act (CDA), contractor's claim certifications were substantively defective as to subcontractor's portion of claim, where contractor did not certify subcontractor's portion of claim in disregard of requirement that prime contractor must certify claim of subcontractor, where contractor was advised by outside consultant that subcontractor's claim might be fraudulent. Trafalgar House Constr., Inc. v. U.S., Fed.Cl.2006, 73 Fed.Cl. 675. United States ☞ 73(9)

Last sentence of provision of Contract Disputes Act (CDA) limiting authority of any agency head to settle, compromise, pay, or otherwise adjust any claim involving fraud does not limit contracting officer's right to deny claims, terminate contracts for default, or issue affirmative government claims, at least insofar as latter does not result in settlement of contractor claim. Daff v. U.S., Fed.Cl.1994, 31 Fed.Cl. 682, affirmed 78 F.3d 1566, rehearing denied, in banc suggestion declined. United States ☞ 73(9); United States ☞ 74(6)

United States Claims Court had jurisdiction over counterclaims by United States Army under Contracts Disputes Act in connection with contractor's delivery of self-propelled howitzers, even though no final decision had been issued by contracting officer, since alleged breach of contract involved fraud. BMY-Combat Systems Div. of Harsco Corp. v. U.S., Cl.Ct.1992, 26 Cl.Ct. 846. Federal Courts ☞ 1102

45. Rules and regulations—Generally

Regulation requiring senior company official to certify government contractor's claim to contracting officer is consistent with language and intent of underlying statute, which was intended to deter and redress fraud. Ingalls Shipbuilding, Inc. v. O'Keefe, C.A.Fed.1993, 986 F.2d 486. United States ☞ 73(9)

Office of Federal Procurement Policy was not required to follow Administrative Procedure Act (APA) requirements in promulgating federal acquisition regulation implementing Contract Disputes Act, in view of APA exemption for matters related to public contract. Essex Electro Engineers, Inc. v. U.S., C.A.Fed.1992, 960 F.2d 1576, certiorari denied 113 S.Ct. 408, 506 U.S. 953, 121 L.Ed.2d 333. Administrative Law And Procedure ☞ 392.1; United States ☞ 73(9)

46. —— Federal Acquisition Regulations, rules and regulations

Where parties agreed that they would try to reach mutually agreeable settlement upon government's termination of contract and agreed that, if they were unable to do so, contracting officer would issue a final decision which contractor could appeal to the court, contractor's termination settlement proposal met the Federal Acquisition Regulation (FAR) definition of a claim but, at time of submission it was not a claim because it was not submitted to contracting officer for decision; once negotiations reached an impasse and the proposal, by the terms of the FAR and the contract, was submitted for decision, it became a claim. James M. Ellett Const. Co., Inc. v. U.S., C.A.Fed.

1996, 93 F.3d 1537. United States ☞ 73(9)

Request for equitable adjustment (REA) submitted to contracting officer by contractor qualified as "claim" within meaning of Contract Disputes Act (CDA) and Federal Acquisitions Regulation (FAR), even without preexisting dispute; requirement for a preexisting dispute applied only to "routine" requests for payment, and submitted REA was not "routine." Reflectone, Inc. v. Dalton, C.A.Fed.1995, 60 F.3d 1572, rehearing denied. United States ☞ 73(9)

Federal Acquisition Regulation (FAR) on who may certify claim to contracting officer is not interpretative and, therefore, could not be waived by contracting officer. Newport News Shipbuilding and Dry Dock Co. v. Garrett, C.A.Fed.1993, 6 F.3d 1547, rehearing denied, in banc suggestion declined. United States ☞ 73(9)

Navy's directive to contractor to correct or replace defective engines, constituted "other relief" within federal acquisition regulations' (FAR) third category of "claims," and, thus, was within Contract Disputes Act concept of "claim," and Court of Appeals had jurisdiction over contractor's appeal from directive. Garrett v. General Elec. Co., C.A.Fed.1993, 987 F.2d 747, rehearing denied, in banc suggestion declined. United States ☞ 73(15)

Federal Acquisition Regulation which specifies persons in contractor's organization who may certify that claim for over $50,000 is made in good faith furthers important objective of Congress by triggering contractor's potential liability for fraudulent claim under Contract Disputes Act; thus, regulation is valid. U.S. v. Grumman Aerospace Corp., C.A.Fed. 1991, 927 F.2d 575, certiorari denied 112 S.Ct. 330, 502 U.S. 919, 116 L.Ed.2d 270. United States ☞ 73(9)

Under governing version of federal acquisition regulation, request for equitable adjustment (REA) was not "claim" under Contract Disputes Act (CDA) when submitted by government contractor to contracting officer, inasmuch as regulation excluded from definition of "claim" a written demand or assertion seeking payment of more than $100,000 that had not been certified under CDA, and REA, while certified pursuant to defense acquisition regulations, was not certified in accordance with regulation applicable to contractor claims submitted under CDA. Johnson v. Advanced Engineering & Planning Corp., Inc., E.D.Va.2003, 292 F.Supp.2d 846. United States ⟲ 73(9)

Dispute concerning whether Navy adequately followed steps set out in Department of Defense Federal Acquisition Regulations before beginning arrangements to reverse engineer ram tensioner for which plaintiff had been sole supplier was not founded upon contract between parties, but rather arose as controversy over proprietary rights; thus, matter was properly before district court, and was not required to be brought in Court of Claims. Westech Gear Corp. v. Department of Navy, D.D.C.1989, 733 F.Supp. 390, affirmed 907 F.2d 1225, 285 U.S.App.D.C. 219. Action ⟲ 27(1)

Section of the Federal Acquisition Regulation (FAR) interpreting the Contract Disputes Act (CDA), and providing that "[f]ailure to certify shall not be deemed to be a defective certification" is overbroad and invalid insofar as it would treat as a jurisdictional defect missing certifications when two or more claims not requiring certification are deemed by the court or board to be a larger claim requiring certi-

fication. Engineered Demolition, Inc. v. U.S., Fed.Cl.2004, 60 Fed.Cl. 822. United States ⟲ 73(9)

47. Alternative dispute resolution

Contract agreements which provide for alternate resolution proceedings prior to a final decision by the contracting officer are not inconsistent with the Contract Disputes Act. OSHCO-PAE-SOMC v. U.S., Cl.Ct.1989, 16 Cl.Ct. 614. United States ⟲ 74(7)

Federal Aviation Administration, and hence the United States, remained liable for contract claims which contractor had pending before contracting officer at time of transfer of operating authority over airport from federal Government to independent regional authority under Metropolitan Washington Airports Act; phrase "procedure for disputes resolution" in Act providing that such procedures would continue to govern performance of contract meant all contract disputes procedures and related obligations enumerated in parties' contract and Contract Disputes Act. Jonal Corp. v. U.S., Cl.Ct.1988, 14 Cl.Ct. 337. United States ⟲ 73(9)

§ 606. Contractor's right of appeal to board of contract appeals

Within ninety days from the date of receipt of a contracting officer's decision under section 605 of this title, the contractor may appeal such decision to an agency board of contract appeals, as provided in section 607 of this title.

(Pub.L. 95–563, § 7, Nov. 1, 1978, 92 Stat. 2385.)

HISTORICAL AND STATUTORY NOTES

Revision Notes and Legislative Reports
1978 Acts. Section 7 establishes the time limits available to the contractor to initiate an appeal to an agency board of contract appeals. This time frame (90 days) is considered adequate to insure the contractor the necessary time to review his position and to decide whether to appeal to an agency board. Senate Report No. 95–1118.

Effective and Applicability Provisions
1978 Acts. Section effective with respect to contracts entered into 120 days after Nov. 1, 1978 and, at the election of the contractor, with respect to any claim pending at such time before the contracting officer or initiated thereafter, see section 16 of Pub.L. 95–563, set out as a note under section 601 of this title.

CROSS REFERENCES

Civilian agency acquisition allowable contract costs and applicability of contract disputes procedures to disallowance of costs and assessment of penalty, see 41 USCA § 256.

LIBRARY REFERENCES

American Digest System
United States ⊙73(15).
Key Number System Topic No. 393.

Corpus Juris Secundum
CJS Limitations of Actions § 156, Stay of Proceedings.

Research References

ALR Library
8 ALR, Fed. 2nd Series 1, Validity, Construction, and Application of Federal Employees Health Benefits Act (FEHBA), 5 U.S.C.A. §§ 8901 to 8914.

Encyclopedias
Am. Jur. 2d Public Works and Contracts § 212, Appeal to an Agency Board of Contract Appeals.

Forms
Am. Jur. Pl. & Pr. Forms Public Works & Contracts § 79, Notice of Appeal--To Board of Contract Appeals--Under Contract Disputes Act of 1978.
Am. Jur. Pl. & Pr. Forms Space Law § 25, Notice of Appeal--To Board of Contract Appeals--Under Contract Disputes Act of 1978.
Federal Procedural Forms § 34:96, Payment of Claim Pending Appeal.
Federal Procedural Forms § 34:102, Introduction to Boards of Contract Appeals.
Federal Procedural Forms § 34:121, Contractor Versus Government Agency.
Federal Procedural Forms § 34:129, Time for Filing.
Federal Procedural Forms § 34:132, Effect of Failure to File or Untimely Filing-- Premature Appeal.
Federal Procedural Forms § 34:251, Notice of Appeal--To Board of Contract Appeals--Under Contract Disputes Act of 1978 [41 U.S.C.A. §§ 606, 607(D); 48 C.F.R. §§ 33.201 et seq.].
8 West's Federal Forms § 13023, Appeals from the Boards of Contract Appeals Under the Contract Disputes Act.
8 West's Federal Forms § 13129, Contract Disputes Act.
8 West's Federal Forms § 13223, Government Contract Claims--Claims Under the Contract Disputes Act.

Treatises and Practice Aids
Federal Procedure, Lawyers Edition § 39:849, Introduction.
Federal Procedure, Lawyers Edition § 39:897, Contractor as Appellant.
Federal Procedure, Lawyers Edition § 39:911, Form and Content of Notice.
Federal Procedure, Lawyers Edition § 44:128, Eligible Applicants--Determination of Net Worth and Number of Employees.
West's Federal Administrative Practice § 664, Protests and Appeals.
West's Federal Administrative Practice § 674, Contract Disputes Litigation--Prerequisites for Valid Appeal Before Boards of Contract Appeal.

WESTLAW ELECTRONIC RESEARCH

See Westlaw guide following the Explanation pages of this volume.

Notes of Decisions

Construction   1
Election of forum   2
Time of filing appeal   4

Waiver   3

_____

1. Construction
This section, of which 90-day deadline for appeal from contracting officer's decision was a part and which defined jurisdiction of appeal tribunal, was statute

waiving sovereign immunity and therefore had to be strictly construed. Cosmic Const. Co. v. U.S., C.A.Fed.1982, 697 F.2d 1389. United States ⟐ 73(15)

2. Election of forum

Where contracting officer did not notify contractor that it had any right to elect to appeal under Contract Disputes Act, contractor's appeal under disputes clause of contract could not be considered "knowing election" under Act so as to preclude contractor from changing its avenue of appeal thereafter. S.E.R., Jobs For Progress, Inc. v. U.S., C.A.Fed.1985, 759 F.2d 1. United States ⟐ 73(15)

Where there was no statutory or regulatory provision detailing the way in which election to proceed under this chapter was to be made, the only real requirement was that the election be informed and voluntary. Essex Electro Engineers, Inc. v. U.S., C.A.Fed.1983, 702 F.2d 998. United States ⟐ 73(9)

Contractor made a valid election to come under this chapter at time it filed its timely complaint with the Postal Service Board of Contract Appeals. Nab-Lord Associates v. U.S., Ct.Cl.1982, 682 F.2d 940, 230 Ct.Cl. 694. United States ⟐ 73(9)

When contractor made conscious election to go to board of contract appeals, and actually filed there, contractor was bound by its choice and could not file court action without exhausting its administrative remedies. S.J. Groves & Sons Co. v. U.S., Ct.Cl.1981, 661 F.2d 170, 228 Ct.Cl. 598. Election Of Remedies ⟐ 15

Under Contract Disputes Act of 1978, contractor who contests a contracting officer's decision has a choice between two exclusive remedies: (1) contractor may appeal the decision to an agency board of contract appeals (BCA) within 90 days from date of receipt of the decision, or (2) contractor may bring an action directly on the claim in the United States Court of Federal Claims within 12 months from the date of receipt. Vasiliades v. U.S., D.Neb.1997, 991 F.Supp. 1136. United States ⟐ 74(7)

Federal district court could not exercise jurisdiction over licensor's claims against Government under Trade Secrets Act in view of licensor's earlier election to certify under Contract Dispute Act breach of contract claim for withholding of royalty payments, which was same claim underlying trade secrets claims. Colt Industries, Inc. v. U.S., D.D.C.1989, 716 F.Supp. 660, 12 U.S.P.Q.2d 1926. United States ⟐ 73(9)

Contract Disputes Act [§ 2 et seq., 41 U.S.C.A. § 601 et seq.] provides for review of contract dispute decision by only two methods: appeal of contracting officer's decision to the Board of Contract Appeals; or direct relief from the Court of Claims, and once contractor makes an election to go to the Board, it has chosen a means of review. Sealtite Corp. v. General Services Admin., D.C.Colo.1985, 614 F.Supp. 352. United States ⟐ 73(15)

This chapter provides for review for resolving government contracts disputes by only two methods: appeal of contracting officer's decision to Board of Contract Appeals or action for relief directly in court of claims. Group Health Inc. v. Schweiker, S.D.Fla.1982, 549 F.Supp. 135. United States ⟐ 73(15)

Under the "Election Doctrine," once a government contractor contesting a contracting officer's final decision makes a binding election to appeal to the appropriate board of contract appeals or bring a direct action in the Court of Federal Claims, that decision must stand, and the contractor thereby relinquishes his right to pursue an appeal with the alternative forum; however, an election does not become binding until the selected forum determines that it has jurisdiction over the appeal. Grinnell v. U.S., Fed.Cl. 2006, 71 Fed.Cl. 202. United States ⟐ 73(15)

Where contractor elected to appeal the merits of default termination of contract to agency's board of contract appeals before voluntarily dismissing appeal with limited reservation of its right to challenge assessment of reprocurement costs, it was precluded under the Election Doctrine from seeking damages in connection with its default termination in the Court of Federal Claims; however, *Fulford* Doctrine permitted contractor to challenge assessment of reprocurement costs by asserting any defense it might have had to default termination decision. American Telecom Corp. v. U.S., Fed.Cl.2004, 59 Fed.Cl. 467. United States ⟐ 73(15)

Contractor's president did not make binding election to bring wrongful debarment claim before agency board of contract appeals, where board determined that it did not have the ability to exercise jurisdiction at the time president attempted to bring the wrongful debarment claim before it. Schickler v. U.S., Fed.Cl.2002, 54 Fed.Cl. 264, appeal dismissed 70 Fed. Appx. 584, 2003 WL 21774141. United States ☞ 73(15)

Under the election doctrine of the Contract Disputes Act (CDA), contractor who appealed default terminations to the agency board of contract appeals made a binding election, precluding subsequent suit in the Court of Federal Claims, where contracting officer (CO) advised contractor of his option to appeal to the board or the Court. Mobility Systems and Equipment Company v. U.S., Fed.Cl. 2001, 51 Fed.Cl. 233. United States ☞ 73(9)

Election of lessors to file appeal of contracting officer's final decision denying rent claim with agency board of contract appeals was an informed one, and thus election was binding, where lessors received notice of their alternative option to appeal to the board or the Court of Federal Claims in the contracting officer's final decision. Spodek v. U.S., Fed.Cl. 2001, 51 Fed.Cl. 221, affirmed in part and vacated in part 52 Fed.Appx. 497, 2002 WL 31724959. United States ☞ 73(9)

Breach of contract claim involving dual-purpose agreement for both repair and sale of office building was covered by Contract Disputes Act, in that dispute involved only contractor's obligations under repair clauses of contract; thus contractor was bound by its initial decision to appeal final decision of contracting officer to General Services Administration Board of Contract Appeals (GSBCA) and could not file claim in Court of Federal Claims. Bonneville Associates v. U.S., Fed.Cl.1993, 30 Fed.Cl. 85, affirmed 43 F.3d 649. United States ☞ 73(15)

Navy contractor's petition to Armed Services Board of Contract Appeals requesting that contracting officer be required to render decision on claim under contract's termination for convenience clause within specified time did not constitute binding election which prevented contractor from subsequently relying on 60–day or "reasonable time" provision of Contract Disputes Act to invoke jurisdiction of Claims Court. Solar Turbines, Inc. v. U.S., Cl.Ct.1989, 16 Cl.Ct. 304. United States ☞ 73(9)

Under this section which applies to all claims initiated after its enactment, a contractor can either appeal an adverse final decision of contracting officer to appropriate board of contract appeals, or seek relief from contracting officer's decision in Claims Court, but cannot do both. Diamond Mfg. Co. v. U.S., Cl.Ct.1983, 3 Cl.Ct. 424. United States ☞ 74(7)

After government contractor elected to file a claim with the Board of Contract Appeals (Board) on the issue of increased rent for postal facility, Court of Federal Claims properly dismissed government contractor's subsequent increased rent claim for lack of subject matter jurisdiction, where all of the facts at issue arose from an unexecuted lease for the postal facility, and the two suits would have formed a convenient trial unit because both involved substantially the same incidents evincing the same relationships between government contractor and postal service as landlord and holdover tenant, respectively, and involved generally the same witnesses and evidence. Spodek v. U.S., C.A.Fed.2002, 52 Fed.Appx. 497, 2002 WL 31724959, Unreported. Federal Courts ☞ 1076

3. Waiver

Armed Services Board of Contract Appeals lacked jurisdiction to waive 90-day period provided by this section for appeal from contracting officer's decision. Cosmic Const. Co. v. U.S., C.A.Fed.1982, 697 F.2d 1389. United States ☞ 73(15)

4. Time of filing appeal

District court's stay order in False Claims Act (FCA) qui tam action against air tanker contractor with the Forest Service not only enjoined government from bringing future administrative proceedings against contractor, it also tolled running of limitations period in which contractor had to file Contract Dispute Act (CDA) suit challenging decision of contracting officer (CO) with respect to contractor's agreement with government. International Air Response v. U.S., C.A.Fed.2002, 302 F.3d 1363, rehearing denied 324 F.3d 1376, rehearing and rehearing in banc denied 324 F.3d 1380. Limitation Of Actions ☞ 107

Contractor seeking to appeal decision of contracting officer to General Services Administration's Board of Contract Appeals was not entitled to equitable tolling of Contract Disputes Act's 90–day limitations period for bringing such appeal, during time that contractor unsuccessfully pursued relief in Court of Federal Claims, where contractor took no action to preserve appeal during pendency of court action, and any error was comparable only to garden variety claim of excusable neglect. Bonneville Associates, Ltd. Partnership v. Barram, C.A.Fed.1999, 165 F.3d 1360, certiorari denied 120 S.Ct. 40, 528 U.S. 809, 145 L.Ed.2d 37. United States ☞ 73(15)

District court could transfer maritime contract claim against United States to Armed Services Board of Contract Appeals, even though action would have been untimely had it been brought before Board of Contract Appeals originally; requirement that actions before agency board be filed within 90 days applies only to direct appeals of contracting officer's decisions, not to suits transferred from district court to agency board. Southwest Marine, Inc., on Behalf of Universal

Painting & Sandblasting Corp. v. U.S., N.D.Cal.1988, 680 F.Supp. 327. Federal Courts ☞ 1154

Contractor, who brought untimely appeal of contracting officer's decision to board of contract appeals, was not precluded from bringing direct suit in Claims Court to recover on its claims. Cosmic Const. Co. v. U.S., Cl.Ct.1984, 5 Cl.Ct. 237. United States ☞ 73(15)

Where contractor has option to appeal contracting officer's decision to agency board of contract appeals, within finite time frame, but fails to do so within prescribed period, option ceases to exist; compliance with time requirements is prerequisite to board's jurisdiction, and failure to satisfy such requirements is bar to administrative consideration of contracting officer's adverse decision. Olsberg Excavating Co. v. U.S., Cl.Ct.1983, 3 Cl.Ct. 249. United States ☞ 73(15)

§ 607. Agency boards of contract appeals

(a) Establishment; consultation; Tennessee Valley Authority

(1) An Armed Services Board of Contract Appeals may be established within the Department of Defense when the Secretary of Defense, after consultation with the Administrator, determines from a workload study that the volume of contract claims justifies the establishment of a full-time agency board of at least three members who shall have no other inconsistent duties. Workload studies will be updated at least once every three years and submitted to the Administrator.

(2) The Board of Directors of the Tennessee Valley Authority may establish a board of contract appeals for the Authority of an indeterminate number of members.

(b) Appointment of members; chairman; compensation

(1) The members of the Armed Services Board of Contract Appeals shall be selected and appointed to serve in the same manner as administrative law judges appointed pursuant to section 3105 of Title 5 with an additional requirement that such members shall have had not fewer than five years' experience in public contract law. Full-time members of such Board serving as such on the effective date of this chapter shall be considered qualified. The chairman and vice chairman of such Board shall be designated by the Secretary of Defense from members so appointed. Compensation for the chair-

man, the vice chairman, and all other members of such Board shall be determined under section 5372a of Title 5.

(2) The Board of Directors of the Tennessee Valley Authority shall establish criteria for the appointment of members to its agency board of contract appeals established in subsection (a)(2) of this section, and shall designate a chairman of such board. The chairman and all other members of such board shall receive compensation, at the daily equivalent of the rates determined under section 5372a of Title 5 for each day they are engaged in the actual performance of their duties as members of the board.

(c) Appeals; inter-agency arrangements

There is established an agency board of contract appeals to be known as the "Postal Service Board of Contract Appeals". Such board shall have jurisdiction to decide any appeal from a decision of a contracting officer of the United States Postal Service or the Postal Regulatory Commission relative to a contract made by either agency. Such board shall consist of judges appointed by the Postmaster General who shall meet the qualifications of and serve in the same manner as members of the Civilian Board of Contract Appeals. This chapter shall apply to contract disputes before the Postal Service Board of Contract Appeals in the same manner as they apply to contract disputes before the Civilian Board.

(d) Jurisdiction

The Armed Services Board shall have jurisdiction to decide any appeal from a decision of a contracting officer of the Department of Defense, the Department of the Army, the Department of the Navy, the Department of the Air Force, or the National Aeronautics and Space Administration relative to a contract made by that department or agency. The Civilian Board shall have jurisdiction to decide any appeal from a decision of a contracting officer of any executive agency (other than the Department of Defense, the Department of the Army, the Department of the Navy, the Department of the Air Force, the National Aeronautics and Space Administration, the United States Postal Service, the Postal Regulatory Commission, or the Tennessee Valley Authority) relative to a contract made by that agency. Each other agency board shall have jurisdiction to decide any appeal from a decision of a contracting officer relative to a contract made by its agency. In exercising this jurisdiction, the agency board is authorized to grant any relief that would be available to a litigant asserting a contract claim in the United States Court of Federal Claims.

(e) Decisions

An agency board shall provide to the fullest extent practicable, informal, expeditious, and inexpensive resolution of disputes, and shall issue a decision in writing or take other appropriate action on each appeal submitted, and shall mail or otherwise furnish a copy of the decision to the contractor and the contracting officer.

(f) Accelerated appeal disposition

The rules of each agency board shall include a procedure for the accelerated disposition of any appeal from a decision of a contracting officer where the amount in dispute is $100,000 or less. The accelerated procedure shall be applicable at the sole election of only the contractor. Appeals under the accelerated procedure shall be resolved, whenever possible, within one hundred and eighty days from the date the contractor elects to utilize such procedure.

(g) Review

(1) The decision of an agency board of contract appeals shall be final, except that—

(A) a contractor may appeal such a decision to the United States Court of Appeals for the Federal Circuit within one hundred twenty days after the date of receipt of a copy of such decision, or

(B) the agency head, if he determines that an appeal should be taken, and with the prior approval of the Attorney General, transmits the decision of the board of contract appeals to the Court of Appeals for the Federal Circuit for judicial review under section 1295 of Title 28, within one hundred and twenty days from the date of the agency's receipt of a copy of the board's decision.

(2) Notwithstanding the provisions of paragraph (1), the decision of the board of contract appeals of the Tennessee Valley Authority shall be final, except that—

(A) a contractor may appeal such a decision to a United States district court pursuant to the provisions of section 1337 of Title 28, within one hundred twenty days after the date of receipt of a copy of such decision, or

(B) The Tennessee Valley Authority may appeal the decision to a United States district court pursuant to the provisions of section 1337 of Title 28, within one hundred twenty days after the date of the decision in any case.

(3) An award by an arbitrator under this chapter shall be reviewed pursuant to sections 9 through 13 of Title 9, except that the court

may set aside or limit any award that is found to violate limitations imposed by Federal statute.

(h), (i) Repealed.   Pub.L. 109–163, Div. A, Title VIII, § 847(d)(4), Jan. 6, 2006, 119 Stat. 3394

(Pub.L. 95–563, § 8, Nov. 1, 1978, 92 Stat. 2385; Pub.L. 97–164, Title I, §§ 156, 160(a)(15), Apr. 2, 1982, 96 Stat. 47, 48; Pub.L. 101–509, Title V, § 529 [Title I, § 104(d)(4)], Nov. 5, 1990, 104 Stat. 1447; Pub.L. 101–552, § 6(b), Nov. 15, 1990, 104 Stat. 2746; Pub.L. 102–572, Title IX, § 902(b)(1), Oct. 29, 1992, 106 Stat. 4516; Pub.L. 103–355, Title II, § 2351(c), Oct. 13, 1994, 108 Stat. 3322; Pub.L. 109–163, Div. A, Title VIII, § 847(d)(2) to (4), Jan. 6, 2006, 119 Stat. 3393, 3394; Pub.L. 109–435, Title VI, § 604(f), Dec. 20, 2006, 120 Stat. 3242.)

HISTORICAL AND STATUTORY NOTES

Revision Notes and Legislative Reports

1978 Acts. Section 8(a)(1) provides that the boards will be full time with at least five members who will have no other inconsistent duties. It will be the responsibility of each agency head who wishes to have an agency board of contract appeals within his agency to develop a workload study of cases of contract appeals based on guidelines established by the Administrator.

Upon completion of the workload study, the agency head must consult with the Administrator on the advisability of setting up a board based on the results of that workload study. It is intended that the agency head have the ultimate responsibility for justifying a board of contract appeals within his agency, but the committees also feel that the knowledge and expertise centered in the Office of Federal Procurement Policy should be utilized through the consultation process. As part of the Administrator's administrative responsibilities under the Act, he is responsible for developing the basic workload study format. His office is to be a central clearing point for the workload studies of all agencies with boards of contract appeals. The committees' intent is that the Office of Federal Procurement Policy be directly involved in an advisory role in the process for justifying the setting up, and should the case be, closing down of agency boards.

Only those duties that are complementary to the hearing and deciding of appeals shall be added to the responsibilities of board members. The Administrator of Federal Procurement Policy is responsible for identifying those duties which are consistent. Where the Administrator finds that the execution of those noninconsistent duties is getting in the way of the primary duty of the boards—the expeditious, less formal, less expensive resolution of Government contract claims—the Administrator shall eliminate those duties he identifies as nonbeneficial.

The establishment of agency boards on a full-time basis with minimum size standards brings the advantages of board consolidation: uniformity, consistency, economy, and efficiency. The boards that meet the minimum standards will be familiar with the procurement mission and operating procedures of those agencies to which they are assigned. Such familiarity does assist the boards in performing their functions and does not make the operation of the boards any less fair to contractors. Conversely, the expertise in agency peculiarities attributed to agency boards does not outweigh the advantages of some consolidation; contract disputes do not vary so widely from agency to agency that each agency needs to have its own board. Thus those agencies that cannot justify their own fulltime board can or may have their cases reviewed by other agency boards.

The rationale for retaining the boards of contract appeals within the agencies is closely tied to section 10(a) which allows contractors direct access to the courts. These administrative boards, with their quasi-judicial nature and powers, will offer a true alternative to a court proceeding. Complete consolidation of the boards, however, would only result in the creation of a completely judicialized and formalized new "court," regardless of its title.

Section 8(a)(2) allows the Board of Directors of the Tennessee Valley Authority (TVA) to establish a board of contract appeals for the TVA of indeterminate number of members. No authority outside the Tennessee Valley Authority has the power to terminate the TVA board.

Section 8(b)(1) details the selection process and grade levels for agency board members (excluding TVA) and the Chairman and Vice Chairman. Where an agency board has more than one Vice Chairman, each shall be in grade 17. The principal purpose of having agency board members selected and appointed to serve in the same manner as hearing examiners appointed pursuant to section 3105 of title 5 is to insure the independence of contract appeals board members as quasi-judicial officers. In other words, the method of appointment prescribed by section 8(b)(1) is intended to guarantee that contract appeals board members, like hearing examiners (administrative law judges), be appointed strictly on the basis of merit, and that in conducting proceedings and deciding cases they would not be subject to direction or control by procuring agency management authorities. The hearing examiners system is perceived as a model for assuring this requisite independence. The intent of S. 3178 is to establish a corps of contract appeals board members comparable to that system.

It is not intended that current agency board members will be deemed qualified to assume the responsibilities of administrative law judges and thus be eligible for appointment to the National Labor Relations Board, Securities and Exchange Commission, or other regulatory agencies. While the current responsibilities and duties of agency board members directly parallel those of hearing examiners, it will be necessary to complete the necessary examinations requisite to becoming a hearing examiner before current agency board members can be deemed qualified.

Section 8(b)(2) gives the Board of Directors of the Tennessee Valley Authority the power to set the criteria for appointment of its agency board members. Since the TVA is not subject to the Civil Service Act, and its board may only be part time, pay levels for the members of the TVA board as well as the Chairman will be at rates equal to the daily rate paid under the General Schedule contained in section 5332, United States Code for each day they are performing duties as members of the TVA board. It is the intent to give the TVA as much latitude as is needed to obtain the services required to settle claims on its contracts without burdening it with requirements only applicable to Government agencies located in Washington, D.C. Conversely, it is also intended that TVA be part of the overall system that establishes fair and equitable remedies system.

Section 8(c) states that if the volume of contract claims is not sufficient to justify an agency board or if the agency head considers it otherwise appropriate, the agency head can arrange to have appeals from decisions of contracting officers of his agency to be decided by a board of contract appeals of another agency. If the agency head is unable to make arrangements with another agency, he may submit the case to the Administrator for placement with another agency board.

The provisions of this section are not applicable to the Tennessee Valley Authority board.

Section 8(d) states that each agency board will have jurisdiction to decide an appeal from a decision of a contracting officer under a contract made by its agency or under a contract made by any other agency when that agency or the Administrator has designated that board to decide the appeal.

Section 8(e) stipulates that the agency board shall provide to the fullest extent practicable, informal, expeditious, and inexpensive resolution of disputes. Counteracting these objectives are the provisions in the act that make the boards more quasi-judicial and courtlike. Rules and regulations developed for the boards be more informal and expeditious and less expensive that comparable proceedings in the courts. The contractor should feel that he is able to obtain his "day in court" at the agency boards and at the same time have saved time and money through the agency board process. If this is not so, then contractors would elect to go directly to court and bypass the boards since there would be no advantage in choosing the agency board route for appeals. The process by which agency board proceedings take place should be of sufficient positive value in time and monetary savings that contractors would elect to take their appeals to the agency boards.

Section 8(f) provides procedures for the accelerated disposition of claims up to and including $50,000. Only the contractor can choose this procedure which sets 180 days as its target for resolution of the claim. The average time today for nonaccelerated cases is 13 months.

The term "accelerated" in S. 3178 means to hasten the progress or development of the claim. This is to be differentiated from the small claims procedure in section 9 which would expedite the resolution of claims. The intent of the accelerated procedure is to reduce the time requirements associated with board deliberations—the two parties would still be afforded the due process trappings of the agency board, but would waive some or all of the time-consuming procedures that are part of the process. For example, the parties with cases proceeding under the accelerated procedures rule would be encouraged, to the extent possible consistent with adequate presentation of their factual and legal positions, to waive pleadings, discovery, and briefs. Written decisions by the agency board normally will be short, hopefully within 30 days after the appeal is ready for decision and contain summary findings of fact and conclusion only.

It is expected that all contractors who have claims of $50,000 or less be made aware by the agency board and the executive agency that an accelerated procedure for claims of that magnitude is available. Equally important to making the contractor aware of the accelerated procedure is the follow through by the agency board member(s) hearing the claim to insure that the procedures for accelerating the processing of claims are carried out. Too often, cases that begin as accelerated procedure cases, tend to become less "accelerated" and more "procedural" just because the board member is more familiar with handling full procedure cases.

While it is not the intent of S. 3178 to establish special board members familiar only with accelerated procedures, it is expected that board members would act diligently in not allowing the differences in board proceedings for accelerated claims to diminish or reduce the opportunity to resolve claims in a speedier and more economical fashion.

The Administrator, pursuant to the authority given him in section 8(h), is to review at least every three years the dollar amount identified as within the guidelines for the accelerated procedure, and based on economic indexes selected by the Administrator adjust that level accordingly.

Section 8(g)(1) deals with the appeals process available to the contractor and the Government from an adverse decision of an agency board. The aggrieved party is afforded 120 days from the date of the board's adverse decision to appeal that decision. It is the intent of the committees to insure that the rights given to the contractor and the Government are equal within the remedies system, and the equalizing of the time afforded to make an appeal goes a long way towards realizing that objective. The committees are not persuaded that the limitation to the contractor of 120 days will cause undue hardship.

Section 8(g)(1)(B) grants to the Government the clear right to seek judicial review of adverse agency board decisions. The agency boards of contract appeals as they exist today, and as they would be strengthened by this bill, function as quasi-judicial bodies. Their members serve as administrative judges in an adversary-type proceeding, make findings of fact, and interpret the law. Their decisions set the bulk of legal precedents in Government contract law, and often involve substantial sums of money. In performing this function they do not act as a representative of the agency, since the agency is contesting the contractor's entitlement to relief. In this context, the Government should have an equal right of judicial review, since it would be an anomaly in the American judicial system for such a trial tribunal to have the final authority on decisions that set important precedents in procurement law.

Moreover, section 10(a) gives the contractor an option to go directly from an adverse contracting officer decision to the Court of Claims. If the contractor chooses direct access to court, the Government can appeal to a higher court as a matter of right. If the Government has no right to seek judicial review of a board decision, there is created a situation where contractors may be prone to take controversial issues involving statutes or case law to the boards in order to obtain a tactical advantage over the Government. If the Government has no appeal rights, but the contractor does, the contractor has an unfair advantage since if he loses before the board, he can seek judicial review of the decision.

Section 8(g)(1)(B) specifies that the agency head of the agency receiving an adverse decision, after receiving the approval of the Attorney General, may appeal the decision for the Government. There was considerable discussion in the Procurement Commission on this subject of Government right to appeal and the final vote was 7 to 5 favoring. The dissenting five members of the Commission were concerned over the executive agency's unfettered right to appeal any decisions to the courts and thus prolong the litigation process for the contractor who has already completed the long process of negotiation with the contracting officer and a trial before the agency board or the court. In order to provide that proper restraints be placed on the executive agency, the Commission recommended that the Attorney General must approve all decisions by an agency head to appeal adverse decisions. The committees agree with this course of action.

The Administrator of the Office of Federal Procurement Policy must be consulted directly in the review process by the Attorney General on determining whether to approve a Government appeal. The knowledge and expertise in determining whether procurement precedents are, or are not, being set by a particular agency board decision should be invaluable to the Attorney General in his decisionmaking process. Nothing in this section, however, is intended to restrict or alter the Attorney General's authority to appeal any contract decision on behalf of the Government.

Section 8(g)(2) excludes the Tennessee Valley Authority from the provisions of section 8(g)(1) and specifies that both the contractor and the Tennessee Valley Authority may appeal an adverse decision directly to the U.S. district court pursuant to the provisions of section 1337 of title 28, United States Code. Neither party may appeal an adverse decision to the Court of Claims.

Section 8(h) defines the authority of the Administrator of Federal Procurement

Policy to issue rules and regulations with respect to the establishment, functions, and procedures of the agency boards.

In order to assure uniformity and high-quality decisions and to insure that the agency boards continue to perform the functions for which they are designed, uniform standards need be applied to each board. If section 8(e) is to become reality—agency boards providing to the fullest extent practicable, informal, expeditious, and inexpensive resolution of disputes—there must be a central focal point for establishing the rules and regulations for the functions and procedures of the boards. This focal point is best placed in the Office of Federal Procurement Policy. It is expected that the Administrator will consult directly with the chairmen of the agency boards in the development of these rules and regulations.

The authority of the Administrator in the establishment of agency boards is limited to developing the workload study formats; being the central clearing point for collection of each of the agency's workload studies; and acting in concert with the agency head in the establishment of each board. The Administrator shall not set up rules and regulations that would give him the power to unilaterally set up or terminate a board.

The Administrator is given the authority in this section to set rules and regulations for the operation of all boards of contract appeals, including the Tennessee Valley Authority, but it is not the intent that any rules and regulations that would affect the operation of the TVA board in any way negate the special provisions given in this act to the Tennessee Valley Authority. Senate Report No. 95–1118.

1990 Acts. Senate Report No. 101–543, see 1990 U.S. Code Cong. and Adm. News, p. 3931.

1992 Acts. House Report No. 102–1006, see 1992 U.S. Code Cong. and Adm. News, p. 3921.

1994 Acts. Senate Report Nos. 103–258 and 103–259, and House Conference Report No. 103–712, see 1994 U.S. Code Cong. and Adm. News, p. 2561.

2006 Acts. House Conference Report No. 109–360, see 2005 U.S. Code Cong. and Adm. News, p. 1678.

Statement by President, see 2005 U.S. Code Cong. and Adm. News, p. S54.

Statement by President, see 2006 U.S. Code Cong. and Adm. News, p. S76.

References in Text
For the effective date of this chapter, referred to in subsec. (b)(1), see section 16 of Pub.L. 95–563, set out as a note under 41 U.S.C.A. § 601.

This chapter, referred to in subsecs. (c) and (g), originally read "this Act", meaning the Contract Disputes Act, Pub.L. 95–563, Nov. 1, 1978, 92 Stat. 2383, which is classified principally to this chapter, 41 U.S.C.A. § 601 et. seq. For complete classification, see Short Title note set out under 41 U.S.C.A. § 601 and Tables.

Codifications
In subsec. (b)(1) of this section, "administrative law judges" was substituted for "hearing examiners" on authority of section 3 of Pub.L. 95–251, Mar. 27, 1978, 92 Stat. 184, which is set out as a note under 5 U.S.C.A. § 3105.

Subsec. (i) of this section, which required all agency boards of three or more full time members, except that of the Tennessee Valley Authority, within one hundred and twenty days after Nov. 1, 1978, to develop workload studies for approval by the agency head specified in subsec. (a)(1) of this section, was omitted. Such subsec. (i) was subsequently repealed by Pub.L. 109–163, see 2006 Amendments notes under this section.

Amendments
2006 Amendments. Subsec. (a)(1). Pub.L. 109–163, § 847(d)(3)(A)(i), struck out "Except as provided in paragraph (2) an agency board of contract appeals" preceding "may be established" and inserted "An Armed Services Board of Contract Appeals".

Pub.L. 109–163, § 847(d)(3)(A)(ii), substituted "the Department of Defense when the Secretary of Defense" for "an executive agency when the agency head".

Subsec. (b)(1). Pub.L. 109–163, § 847(d)(3)(B)(i), struck out "Except as provided in paragraph (2), the members of agency boards" preceding "shall be selected" and inserted "The members of the Armed Services Board of Contract Appeals".

Pub.L. 109–163, § 847(d)(3)(B)(ii), in the second sentence, struck out "agency boards" and inserted "such Board".

Pub.L. 109–163, § 847(d)(3)(B)(iii), in the third sentence, struck out "each board" and inserted "such Board" and substituted "the Secretary of Defense" for "the agency head".

Pub.L. 109–163, § 847(d)(3)(B)(iv), in the fourth sentence, struck out "an agency board" and inserted "such Board".

Subsec. (c). Pub.L. 109–435, § 604(f), substituted "Postal Regulatory Commission" for "Postal Rate Commission".

Pub.L. 109–163, § 847(d)(2)(B), rewrote subsec. (c), which formerly read: "If the volume of contract claims is not sufficient to justify an agency board under subsection (a) of this section or if he otherwise considers it appropriate, any agency head shall arrange for appeals from decisions by contracting officers of his agency to be decided by a board of contract appeals of another executive agency. In the event an agency head is unable to make such an arrangement with another agency, he shall submit the case to the Administrator for placement with an agency board. The provisions of this subsection shall not apply to the Tennessee Valley Authority".

Subsec. (d). Pub.L. 109–435, § 604(f), substituted "Postal Regulatory Commission" for "Postal Rate Commission".

Pub.L. 109–163, § 847(d)(2)(A)(i), struck out "Each agency board shall have jurisdiction to decide any appeal from a decision of a contracting officer (1) relative to a contract made by its agency, and (2) relative to a contract made by any other agency when such agency or the Administrator has designated the agency board to decide the appeal." and inserted "The Armed Services Board shall have jurisdiction to decide any appeal from a decision of a contracting officer of the Department of Defense, the Department of the Army, the Department of the Navy, the Department of the Air Force, or the National Aeronautics and Space Administration relative to a contract made by that department or agency. The Civilian Board shall have jurisdiction to decide any appeal from a decision of a contracting officer of any executive agency (other than the Department of Defense, the Department of the Army, the Department of the Navy, the Department of the Air Force, the National Aeronautics and Space Administration, the United States Postal Service, the Postal Rate Commission, or the Tennessee Valley Authority) relative to a contract made by that agency. Each other agency board shall have jurisdiction to decide any appeal from a decision of a contracting officer relative to a contract made by its agency."

Pub.L. 109–163, § 847(d)(2)(A)(ii), in the fourth sentence, substituted "Court of Federal Claims" for "Claims Court".

Subsec. (h). Pub.L. 109–163, § 847(d)(4), struck out subsec. (h), which formerly read:

"(h) Procedural guidelines

"Pursuant to the authority conferred under the Office of Federal Procurement Policy Act [41 U.S.C.A. § 401 et seq.], the Administrator is authorized and directed, as may be necessary or desirable to carry out the provisions of this chapter, to issue guidelines with respect to criteria for the establishment, functions, and procedures of the agency boards (except for a board established by the Tennessee Valley Authority).".

Subsec. (i). Pub.L. 109–163, § 847(d)(4), struck out subsec. (i), which had been omitted. See Codifications note set out under this section.

1994 Amendments. Subsec. (f). Pub.L. 103–355, § 2351(c), substituted "$100,000" for "$50,000".

1990 Amendments. Subsec. (b)(1). Pub.L. 101–509, § 104(d)(4)(A), substituted provisions directing that compensation for chairman, vice chairman, and other board members be determined under Title 5, § 5372a, for provisions directing that chairman, vice chairman, and other board members receive compensation at GS–18, GS–17, and GS–16 rates, respectively.

Subsec. (b)(2). Pub.L. 101–509, § 104(d)(4)(B), substituted provisions directing that chairman and other members receive compensation at rates determined under Title 5, § 5372a, for provisions directing that chairman receive compensation at GS–18 rate and other members be paid at GS–16 rates.

Subsec. (g)(3). Pub.L. 101–552 temporarily added par. (3). See Effective and Termination Date of 1990 Acts note set out under this section.

1982 Amendments. Subsec. (d). Pub.L. 97–164, § 160(a)(15), substituted "United States Claims Court" for "Court of Claims".

Subsec. (g)(1)(A). Pub.L. 97–164, § 156(1), substituted "United States Court of Appeals for the Federal Circuit" for "Court of Claims".

Subsec. (g)(1)(B). Pub.L. 97–164, § 156(2), substituted "Court of Appeals for the Federal Circuit for judicial review under section 1295 of Title 28" for "United States Court of Claims for judicial review, under section 2510 of Title 28".

Effective and Applicability Provisions
2006 Acts. Amendments by Pub.L. 109–163, § 847, effective 1 year after Jan. 6, 2006, see Pub.L. 109–163, § 847(g), set out as a note under 5 U.S.C.A. § 5372a.

1994 Acts. Amendment by section 2351(c) of Pub.L. 103–355 effective Oct. 13, 1994, except as otherwise provided, see section 10001 of Pub.L. 103–355, set out as a note under section 251 of this title.

1992 Acts. Amendment by section 902(b)(1) of Pub.L. 102–572 effective Oct. 29, 1992, see section 911 of Pub.L. 102–572, set out as a note under 28 U.S.C.A. § 171.

1990 Acts. The termination of amendments by Pub.L. 101–552 and authority to use dispute resolution proceedings on Oct. 1, 1995, provided by section 11 of Pub.L. 101–552, set out as a note under 5 U.S.C.A. § 571, was repealed by section 9 of Pub.L. 104–320.

Amendment to this section (together with any notes enacted or amended hereunder) by the Federal Employees Pay Comparability Act of 1990, as incorporated in section 529 of Pub.L. 101–509, to take effect on May 4, 1991, except that the Office of Personnel Management may establish an earlier effective date, but not earlier than Feb. 3, 1991, for any such provisions with respect to which the Office determines an earlier effective date to be appropriate, see Ex. Ord. No. 12748, Feb. 1, 1991, 56 F.R. 4521, set out as a note under 5 U.S.C.A. § 5304.

Amendment by Pub.L. 101–509 effective on such date as the President shall determine, but not earlier than 90 days, and not later than 180 days, after Nov. 5, 1990, see section 529 [Title III, § 305] of Pub.L. 101–509, set out as a note under 5 U.S.C.A. § 5301.

1982 Acts. Amendment by Pub. L. 97–164 effective Oct. 1, 1982, see section

402 of Pub. L. 97–164, set out as a note under 28 U.S.C.A. § 171.

1978 Acts. Section effective with respect to contracts entered into 120 days after Nov. 1, 1978 and, at the election of the contractor, with respect to any claim pending at such time before the contracting officer or initiated thereafter, see section 16 of Pub.L. 95–563, set out as a note under section 601 of this title.

Change of Name
References to United States Claims Court deemed to refer to United States Court of Federal Claims and references to Claims Court deemed to refer to Court of Federal Claims, see section 902(b) of Pub.L. 102–572, set out as a note under 28 U.S.C.A. § 171.

Boards of Contract Appeals; Transfers; Termination; References
Pub.L. 109–163, Div. A, Title VIII, § 847(b), (c), (e), Jan. 6, 2006, 119 Stat. 3392, 3394, provided that:

"**(b) Transfers.**—The personnel employed in connection with, and the assets, liabilities, contracts, property, records, and unexpended balance of appropriations, authorizations, allocations, and other funds employed, held, used, arising from, available to, or to be made available in connection with the functions vested by law in the agency boards of contract appeals established pursuant to section 8 of the Contract Disputes Act of 1978 (41 U.S.C. 607) (as in effect on the day before the effective date described in subsection (g)) [Pub.L. 109–163, Div. A, Title VIII, § 847(g), Jan. 6, 2006, 119 Stat. 3395, set out as a note under 5 U.S.C.A. § 5372a, which provides for an effective date of 1 year after Jan. 6, 2006], other than the Armed Services Board of Contract Appeals, the board of contract appeals of the Tennessee Valley Authority, and the Postal Service Board of Contract Appeals shall be transferred to the Civilian Board of Contract Appeals for appropriate allocation by the Chairman of that Board.

"**(c) Termination of boards of contract appeals.**—

"**(1) Termination.**—Effective on the effective date described in subsection (g) [Pub.L. 109–163, Div. A, Title VIII,

§ 847(g), Jan. 6, 2006, 119 Stat. 3395, set out as a note under 5 U.S.C.A. § 5372a, which provides for an effective date of 1 year after Jan. 6, 2006], the agency boards of contract appeals established pursuant to section 8 of the Contract Disputes Act of 1978 (41 U.S.C. 607) (as in effect on the day before such effective date), other than the Armed Services Board of Contract Appeals, the board of contract appeals of the Tennessee Valley Authority, and the Postal Service Board of Contract Appeals, shall terminate.

"**(2) Savings provision.**—(A) This section and the amendments made by this section [enacting 41 U.S.C.A. § 438, amending 5 U.S.C.A. § 5372a, 41 U.S.C.A. §§ 601, and 607, and enacting provisions set out as notes under this section and 5 U.S.C.A. § 5372a] shall not affect any proceedings pending on the effective date described in subsection (g) [1 year after Jan. 6, 2006] before any agency board of contract appeals terminated by paragraph (1).

"**(B)** In the case of any such proceedings pending before an agency board of contract appeals other than the Armed Services Board of Contract Appeals or the board of contract appeals of the Tennessee Valley Authority, the proceedings shall be continued by the Civilian Board of Contract Appeals, and orders which were issued in any such proceeding by the agency board shall continue in effect until modified, terminated, superseded, or revoked by the Civilian Board of Contract Appeals, by a court of competent jurisdiction, or by operation of law."

"**(e) References.**—Any reference to an agency board of contract appeals other than the Armed Services Board of Contract Appeals, the board of contract appeals of the Tennessee Valley Authority, or the Postal Service Board of Contract Appeals in any provision of law or in any rule, regulation, or other paper of the United States shall be treated as referring to the Civilian Board of Contract Appeals established under section 42 of the Office of Federal Procurement Policy Act [41 U.S.C.A. § 438]."

CODE OF FEDERAL REGULATIONS

Housing and Urban Development Department, see 24 CFR § 20.1 et seq.

LAW REVIEW AND JOURNAL COMMENTARIES

Arbitration: A permissible or desirable method for resolving disputes involving federal acquisition and assistance contracts? Kirby Behre, 16 Pub.Cont.L.J. 66 (1986)

Doing business with the government. Peter C. Mieres (February 1982) 4 L.A.Law. 34.

LIBRARY REFERENCES

American Digest System
United States ⊘33, 73(15).
Key Number System Topic No. 393.

Research References

ALR Library

185 ALR, Fed. 419, Construction and Application of Federal Crop Insurance Act, 7 U.S.C.A. §§ 1501 et seq.

97 ALR, Fed. 694, Jurisdiction of United States Court of Appeals for Federal Circuit Under 28 U.S.C.A. §§ 1292 and 1295.

96 ALR, Fed. 336, What Constitutes "Adversary Adjudication" by Administrative Agency Entitling Prevailing Party to Award of Attorneys' Fees Under Equal Access to Justice Act (5 U.S.C.A. § 504).

93 ALR, Fed. 886, Federal Government Liability for Loss of, or Damage to, Vessels or Vehicles Seized in Course of Drug Enforcement Activity.

2 ALR, Fed. 691, Judicial Review Under Wunderlich Act (41 U.S.C.A. §§ 321, 322), of Federal Administrative Decisions Made Under Standard "Disputes" Clauses in Government Contracts.

Encyclopedias

Am. Jur. 2d Federal Courts § 2011, Suits Under Contract Disputes Act.

Am. Jur. 2d Public Works and Contracts § 212, Appeal to an Agency Board of Contract Appeals.

Am. Jur. 2d Public Works and Contracts § 213, Appeal to an Agency Board of Contract Appeals--Appeals; Finality of Decisions of Agency Board of Contract Appeals; Questions of Law and Fact.

14 Am. Jur. Trials 437, Representing the Government Contractor.

Forms

Am. Jur. Pl. & Pr. Forms Aviation § 98, Petition in Federal Court--Inverse Condemnation--Invasion of Airspace--Flights of Military Aircraft at Low Level Over Land Adjoining Military Airfield.

Am. Jur. Pl. & Pr. Forms Public Works & Contracts § 79, Notice of Appeal--To Board of Contract Appeals--Under Contract Disputes Act of 1978.

Am. Jur. Pl. & Pr. Forms Public Works & Contracts § 83, Petition--In Court of Federal Claims--For Review of Decision of Board of Contract Appeals--Under Contract Disputes Act of 1978.

Am. Jur. Pl. & Pr. Forms Space Law § 25, Notice of Appeal--To Board of Contract Appeals--Under Contract Disputes Act of 1978.

Federal Procedural Forms § 34:102, Introduction to Boards of Contract Appeals.

Federal Procedural Forms § 34:116, Relief Available.

Federal Procedural Forms § 34:217, Decision--Form.

Federal Procedural Forms § 34:220, Finality of Decision.

Federal Procedural Forms § 34:251, Notice of Appeal--To Board of Contract Appeals--Under Contract Disputes Act of 1978 [41 U.S.C.A. §§ 606, 607(D); 48 C.F.R. §§ 33.201 et seq.].

Federal Procedural Forms § 34:277, Motion in Limine to Establish Order of Proof and Limit Proof--Before Armed Services Board of Contract Appeals [48 C.F.R. Ch. 2, Appx. A, ASBCA Rule 5(B)].

Federal Procedural Forms § 34:302, Appeals by Contractors.

Federal Procedural Forms § 34:303, Appeals by the Government.

Federal Procedural Forms § 34:304, Appeals from Decisions of TVA BCA.

Federal Procedural Forms § 34:311, Petition in Court of Appeals--For Review of Decision of Board of Contract Appeals--Liquidated Damages Wrongfully Assessed Against Contractor [28 U.S.C.A. § 1295(A)(10); 41 U.S.C.A. § 607(G)(1); Fed. R. App. P. Rule 15(a)].

Federal Procedural Forms § 34:516, Introduction.

8 West's Federal Forms § 13011, Overview.

8 West's Federal Forms § 13023, Appeals from the Boards of Contract Appeals Under the Contract Disputes Act.

8 West's Federal Forms § 13102, Formal Brief of Appellant--Appeal from Board of Contract Appeals.

8 West's Federal Forms § 13223, Government Contract Claims--Claims Under the Contract Disputes Act.

Treatises and Practice Aids

Federal Procedure, Lawyers Edition § 2:253, Adversary Adjudication Defined.

Federal Procedure, Lawyers Edition § 7:902, Introduction; Covered Proceedings and Applicants.

Federal Procedure, Lawyers Edition § 19:65, Suits Under Contract Disputes Act.

Federal Procedure, Lawyers Edition § 34:126, Types of Proceedings Covered.

Federal Procedure, Lawyers Edition § 34:134, Further Proceedings.

Federal Procedure, Lawyers Edition § 34:136, Administrative and Judicial Review.

Federal Procedure, Lawyers Edition § 39:824, Judicial Review of Arbitration Award.

Federal Procedure, Lawyers Edition § 39:849, Introduction.

Federal Procedure, Lawyers Edition § 39:850, Composition of Boards of Contract Appeals.

Federal Procedure, Lawyers Edition § 39:911, Form and Content of Notice.

Federal Procedure, Lawyers Edition § 39:1081, Form of Decision.

Federal Procedure, Lawyers Edition § 39:1082, Transmission to Parties.

Federal Procedure, Lawyers Edition § 39:1083, Finality of Decision.

Federal Procedure, Lawyers Edition § 39:1121, Appeals by Contractors, Generally.

Federal Procedure, Lawyers Edition § 39:1122, Appeals by Government, Generally.

Federal Procedure, Lawyers Edition § 39:1123, Appeals from Decisions of Tennessee Valley Authority BCA.

Federal Procedure, Lawyers Edition § 39:1390, Applicability to NASA Adjudications.

Federal Procedure, Lawyers Edition § 44:126, Proceedings to Which EAJA and Implementing Rules Apply.

Federal Procedure, Lawyers Edition § 76:6, Department of Transportation Proceedings Covered by the Equal Access to Justice Act.

Immigration Law Service 2d PSD 1991 GEN COUNSEL OP, General Counsel's Opinions.

Patent Law Fundamentals App. 20(A), 28 U.S.C.A. § 1295--Jurisdiction of U.S. Court of Appeals for the Federal Circuit.

West's Federal Administrative Practice § 446, Department of Veterans Affairs--Board of Contract Appeals.

West's Federal Administrative Practice § 673, Contract Disputes Litigation--Boards of Contract Appeals.

West's Federal Administrative Practice § 675, Types of Proceedings.

West's Federal Administrative Practice § 676, Remedies and Appeals.

West's Federal Administrative Practice § 810, Time in Which to File; Statutes of Limitations; Laches; Equitable Estoppel.

West's Federal Administrative Practice § 819, Jurisdiction Concurrent with United States District Courts; Transfer of Jurisdiction.

West's Federal Administrative Practice § 8005, Courts of Special Jurisdiction--Federal Circuit.

33A Wright & Miller: Federal Prac. & Proc. App E.A.J.A., Equal Access to Justice Act.

WESTLAW ELECTRONIC RESEARCH

See Westlaw guide following the Explanation pages of this volume.

Notes of Decisions

1. Compensation of agency board members

While subsec. (b)(1) of this section does provide that members of agency boards are to be compensated at supergrade rates, the subsection also contemplates antecedent appointment to allocated supergrade positions. 1982, 61 Comp.Gen. 336.

2. Power and authority of agency boards—Generally

Armed Services Board of Contract Appeals had authority to reduce or nullify awards made by contracting officer to contractor which sought equitable adjustment of Air Force fixed-price contract. Assurance Co. v. U.S., C.A.Fed.1987, 813 F.2d 1202. United States ☞ 73(15)

Although agency boards of contract appeals and the Claims Court are powerless to grant injunctive relief, specific performance or a writ of mandamus in post award cases, they can determine the contract interpretation issues underlying the parties' dispute. U.S. v. Black Hawk Masonic Temple Ass'n, Inc., D.Colo.1992, 798 F.Supp. 646. United States ☞ 64.55(2); United States ☞ 64.60(1)

3. —— Delegation, power and authority of agency boards

Where heads of procuring agencies had expressly delegated their full disputes clause authority to the respective boards of contract appeals without reserving power to review, reconsider, or reject the rulings of the boards, the procuring agency heads could not refuse to accept the determination of the boards of contract appeals favorable to contractors and thus compel contractors to litigate merits of their claims in the Court of Claims, and contractors were entitled to recover on basis of the favorable decisions of the boards of contract appeals. Fischbach and Moore Intern. Corp. v. U.S., Ct.Cl. 1980, 617 F.2d 223, 223 Ct.Cl. 119. United States ☞ 73(14)

4. —— Technical advisers, power and authority of agency boards

The Board of Contract appeals may employ technical advisers to analyze and make recommendations on the technical aspects of evidence, and their reports and recommendations need not be disclosed to the parties unless such advice adds new facts to the record or constitutes evidence in itself. 1981 (Counsel-Inf. Op.) 5 Op. O.L.C. 69.

5. Jurisdiction of agency boards—Generally

Department of Labor, rather than Armed Services Board of Contract Appeals, had jurisdiction over roofing contractor's challenge to prevailing wage determinations and their application to contractor's employees who worked on contracts for reroofing Army housing areas; essence of contractor's complaint related to wage rate paid to all workers doing roofing work, despite contractor's attempt to style its complaint as one relating to defective specification or misrepresentation. Emerald Maintenance, Inc. v. U.S., C.A.Fed.1991, 925 F.2d 1425. Labor And Employment ⊙= 2351; United States ⊙= 73(15)

This section, providing that on appeal from decision of contracting officer the agency board is authorized to grant any relief that would be available to a litigant asserting a contract claim in the claims court does not expand the jurisdiction otherwise specifically granted contracting agencies under this chapter and did not grant Department of Energy Board of Contract Appeals jurisdiction over claim to recover bid preparation costs in connection with solicitation that was cancelled before contract was awarded. Coastal Corp. v. U.S., C.A.Fed.1983, 713 F.2d 728. United States ⊙= 64.60(6); United States ⊙= 73(15)

General Services Board of Contract Appeals operates with narrower jurisdiction than Court of Federal Claims, and for the Board to have jurisdiction, a decision must be issued by a contracting officer from a specific agency, rather than by any contracting authority, as is the case for the Court. United Partition Systems, Inc. v. U.S., Fed.Cl.2004, 59 Fed.Cl. 627. United States ⊙= 73(15)

6. —— Armed Services Board of Contract Appeals, jurisdiction of agency boards

Provision in takeover agreement between government and surety for defaulting contractor by which surety expressly reserved all prior rights, including those respecting alleged overpayments made to contractor, did not give Armed Services Board of Contract Appeals jurisdiction over surety's claim for equitable adjustment based on alleged overpayments, over which Board never had jurisdiction. United Pacific Ins. Co. v. Roche, C.A.Fed. 2004, 380 F.3d 1352, rehearing denied. United States ⊙= 73(15)

Armed Services Board of Contract Appeals lacked jurisdiction to consider government contractor's request that government's termination of contract for default be converted into a termination for the convenience of the government, where contractor failed to adequately raise such issue before the contracting officer. J.C.

Equipment Corp. v. England, C.A.Fed. 2004, 360 F.3d 1311. United States ⊙= 73(15)

Armed Services Board of Contract Appeals had jurisdiction to hear and decide cost reimbursement contractor's claim for reimbursement of legal costs incurred in defending a wrongful discharge lawsuit of terminated employees who claimed they had been discharged for refusing to participate in fraud against the government, in case in which the parties did not dispute that contractor actually incurred the legal fees claimed and the Army made no allegations that contractor could not adequately support its filed claims with appropriate bills and receipts; whether the Board had jurisdiction to make factual determinations concerning contractor's alleged fraudulent behavior leading to the discharge of the employees was a separate question. Caldera v. Northrop Worldwide Aircraft Services, Inc., C.A.Fed.1999, 192 F.3d 962, rehearing denied, in banc suggestion declined. United States ⊙= 73(15)

Contractor's claim for additional compensation for work performed during three-year option period arose under Contract Disputes Act (CDA) and was within jurisdiction of Armed Services Board of Contract Appeals, although contractor argued that Navy violated Antideficiency Act and attendant regulations and sought compensation from Navy based upon theory of implied-in-fact contract for services rendered during option years. Cessna Aircraft Co. v. Dalton, C.A.Fed.1997, 126 F.3d 1442, rehearing denied, in banc suggestion declined, certiorari denied 119 S.Ct. 57, 525 U.S. 818, 142 L.Ed.2d 44. United States ⊙= 73(9)

Contract provision which purportedly divested jurisdiction of Armed Services Board of Contract Appeals to hear dispute concerning calculation of award fee under cost–plus–award–fee (CPAF) contract between Navy and contractor was void; provision otherwise depriving board of jurisdiction was not a matter of statute primacy, and thus parties could not on their own alter board's review under Contract Disputes Act (CDA). Burnside-Ott Aviation Training Center v. Dalton, C.A.Fed.1997, 107 F.3d 854, rehearing denied. United States ⊙= 68

Federal Acquisition Regulation (FAR) on who may certify a claim does not limit statutorily defined jurisdiction of Armed

Services Board of Contract Appeals (ASBCA); it merely fills gap left by statutory silence. Newport News Shipbuilding and Dry Dock Co. v. Garrett, C.A.Fed. 1993, 6 F.3d 1547, rehearing denied, in banc suggestion declined. United States ⬯ 73(9)

Armed Services Board of Contract Appeals erred in assuming jurisdiction over a direct appeal by subcontractor, as the subcontractor was not a "contractor" as that term is defined in this chapter; not only was there no privity of contract between the government and the subcontractor arising either from the contract language or from the doctrine of agency, but no direct appeal by the subcontractor was authorized under either the prime contract or subcontract. U.S. v. Johnson Controls, Inc., C.A.Fed.1983, 713 F.2d 1541. United States ⬯ 73(15); United States ⬯ 74.2

Under this chapter Armed Services Board of Contract Appeals had jurisdiction to entertain contractor's claim for reformation based on Government's failure to notify contractor properly of mistake in bid where certification requirements of this chapter were met. U.S. v. Hamilton Enterprises, Inc., C.A.Fed. 1983, 711 F.2d 1038. United States ⬯ 74(4)

Third-party indemnity claim asserted by defense contractor and its surety against United States was within exclusive jurisdiction of Armed Services Board and Claims Court under Tucker Act and Contract Disputes Act. U.S., for Use and Benefit of Ferguson Door Co., Inc. v. Safeco Ins., S.D.Cal.1989, 707 F.Supp. 1205. Federal Courts ⬯ 1139

In prosecution for conspiracy to defraud the Government based on alleged improprieties with regard to expenditures under defense contract, questions regarding interpretation of the contract, which was ambiguous as to whether it was a firm fixed-price contract or a best efforts contract, would be referred, under doctrine of primary jurisdiction, to Armed Services Board of Contract Appeals. U.S. v. General Dynamics Corp., C.D.Cal. 1986, 644 F.Supp. 1497, reversed 828 F.2d 1356. Administrative Law And Procedure ⬯ 228.1

7. Court of appeals review—Generally

Court of Appeals did not have jurisdiction to hear surety's appeal of Armed

Services Board of Contract Appeals' dismissal in part of surety's complaint that disputed contracting officer's decision denying in part equitable adjustment of contract of which surety completed performance for contractor under takeover agreement; Board's decision was not final since it did not reach full extent of contracting officer's decision which included determination of allowable quantum of surety's claims. United Pacific Ins. Co. v. Roche, C.A.Fed.2002, 294 F.3d 1367. United States ⬯ 73(15)

Government contractor could only appeal decision of Armed Services Board of Contract Appeals to United States Court of Appeals for the Federal Circuit, and suit in Claims Court on contract claim was prohibited. AAAA Enterprises, Inc. v. U.S., Cl.Ct.1986, 10 Cl.Ct. 191. Federal Courts ⬯ 1139

If contractor took an appeal, to the Department of Labor's Board of Contract Appeals, from contracting officer's decision on Department's counterclaim against contractor, and the Board's decision was adverse, review would be by the Court of Appeals for the Federal Circuit, and not by the Claims Court. Opalack v. U.S., Cl.Ct.1984, 5 Cl.Ct. 349. Federal Courts ⬯ 1139

8. —— Issues reviewable, court of appeals review

Court of Appeals lacked jurisdiction under Contract Disputes Act over surety's claims to extent that claims related to and depended upon events that occurred before takeover agreement with government was executed. United Pacific Ins. Co. v. Roche, C.A.Fed.2005, 401 F.3d 1362. United States ⬯ 73(15)

Government contractor was not required to appeal directly from decision of Armed Services Board of Contract Appeals rejecting some of contractor's equitable adjustment claims, but could challenge rejection of those claims in its appeal from Board's subsequent order establishing amount of recovery on claims on which contractor prevailed; fact that Board's earlier entitlement decision may have had sufficient finality to make it immediately appealable did not mean that contractor's failure to take such appeal precluded it from challenging that ruling in its appeal from Board's second decision, which was Board's "final" action in the case. J.C. Equipment Corp. v. England, C.A.Fed.

2004, 360 F.3d 1311.   United States ⊕ 73(15)

Court of Appeals did not have jurisdiction to hear surety's appeal of Armed Services Board of Contract Appeals' dismissal in part of surety's complaint that disputed contracting officer's decision denying in part equitable adjustment of contract of which surety completed performance for contractor under takeover agreement; Board's decision was not final since it did not reach full extent of contracting officer's decision which included determination of allowable quantum of surety's claims.   United Pacific Ins. Co. v. Roche, C.A.Fed.2002, 294 F.3d 1367.   United States ⊕ 73(15)

Decision of Armed Services Board of Contract Appeals, denying contractor's motion for summary judgment on contractor's claim that contracting officer exceeded his authority in unilaterally reducing prime contract price and withholding claimed amount following determination that cost and pricing information furnished by contractor was incomplete, inaccurate, and noncurrent, was not appealable, either under Contract Disputes Act of 1978 or under *Cohen* doctrine, where Board had not yet considered merits of contracting officer's defective pricing determination, and claim that officer had exceeded his authority was not completely separate from issue as to whether contractor's pricing information was defective.   Fairchild Republic Co. v. U.S., C.A.Fed.1987, 810 F.2d 1123.   Administrative Law And Procedure ⊕ 701; United States ⊕ 73(15)

Contractor could raise before court of appeals issue that General Services Administration Board of Contract Appeals' denial of contractor's claim for contract time extension plus impact costs had to be set aside because it failed to address contractor's claim that Government's order to install ten additional caissons in construction of parking ramp was cause of delay in completion of project, despite Government's contention that issue was not properly raised before the Board, where contractor's claim clearly stated that scope of work covered was "over-depth drilling of caissons and additional caissons drilled due to changed conditions," and contractor's answers to interrogatories, posthearing brief, and witnesses' testimony also contained similar allegations that change from footings to caissons was cause of delay.   William F. Klingensmith, Inc. v. U.S., C.A.Fed.1984, 731 F.2d 805.   United States ⊕ 73(15)

Provision of Contract Disputes Act (CDA) authorizing Court of Appeals to review "such a decision" by agency board of contract appeals referred only to board's jurisdiction over appeals from decisions of contracting officer relative to a contract, and did not separately grant Court of Appeals jurisdiction over appeals from all final board decisions; rather, Court of Appeals was vested only with jurisdiction over appeals from board decisions rendered pursuant to CDA.   Roberta B. v. Tenet, C.A.Fed.2003, 71 Fed. Appx. 45, 2003 WL 21675123, Unreported.   United States ⊕ 73(15)

9. ——— Findings of fact, court of appeals review

On appeal, if Armed Services Board of Contract Appeals has failed to make relevant finding of fact which is established by undisputed evidence, court may make supplemental finding.   U.S. v. Hamilton Enterprises, Inc., C.A.Fed.1983, 711 F.2d 1038.   United States ⊕ 73(15)

10. ——— Persons entitled to appeal, court of appeals review

In future government contract cases in the Court of Appeals for the Federal Circuit, only prime contractor may be the appellant, absent special contract or regulatory provisions which might confer standing on subcontractors or persons who normally would be deemed only subcontractors.   Erickson Air Crane Co. of Washington, Inc. v. U.S., C.A.Fed.1984, 731 F.2d 810.   United States ⊕ 74.2

11. ——— Time to appeal, court of appeals review

Armed Services Board of Contract Appeals' decision that disputed settlement proposal was not "claim" under Contract Disputes Act, and thus Board lacked jurisdiction over proposal, was not result of inadvertent error or mistake of law, correctly relied upon precedent then binding, and was not appealed, and thus became final 120 days after it was entered, and could not thereafter be appealed.   Essex Electro Engineers, Inc. v. Widnall, C.A.Fed.1997, 116 F.3d 461, certiorari denied 118 S.Ct. 303, 522 U.S. 916, 139 L.Ed.2d 233.   United States ⊕ 73(15)

To be timely, appeal from decision of Armed Services Board of Contract Appeals had to be received by clerk of court within 120-day period mandated by this section. Placeway Const. Corp. v. U.S., C.A.Fed.1983, 713 F.2d 726. United States ⟷ 73(15)

Principle that motion for reconsideration results in tolling of underlying appeal period applies to decisions of boards of contract appeal and to 120–day period allowed by Contract Disputes Act for appeal of such decisions. K & S Const. v. U.S., Fed.Cl.1996, 35 Fed.Cl. 270, affirmed 121 F.3d 727. United States ⟷ 73(15)

Contractor did not carry his burden of showing that he received copy of decision of Armed Services Board of Contract Ap-

peals, denying his claim against Department of Air Force, two weeks later than when Air Force received its copy of decision, on allegation of that circumstance, particularly where contractor did not respond to Board's request in decision to advise it of "the date, time and the circumstances when [he] first received a copy of the decision," and, consequently, Court of Appeals did not have jurisdiction over appeal which relied upon date of receipt alleged by contractor in order to be timely. Blackman v. Roche, C.A.Fed. 2005, 133 Fed.Appx. 743, 2005 WL 1331137, Unreported, rehearing denied. United States ⟷ 73(15)

§ 608. Small claims

(a) Accelerated disposition of appeals

The rules of each agency board shall include a procedure for the expedited disposition of any appeal from a decision of a contracting officer where the amount in dispute is $50,000 or less or, in the case of a small business concern (as defined in the Small Business Act and regulations under that Act), $150,000 or less. The small claims procedure shall be applicable at the sole election of the contractor.

(b) Simplified rules of procedure

The small claims procedure shall provide for simplified rules of procedure to facilitate the decision of any appeal thereunder. Such appeals may be decided by a single member of the agency board with such concurrences as may be provided by rule or regulation.

(c) Time of decision

Appeals under the small claims procedure shall be resolved, whenever possible, within one hundred twenty days from the date on which the contractor elects to utilize such procedure.

(d) Finality of decision

A decision against the Government or the contractor reached under the small claims procedure shall be final and conclusive and shall not be set aside except in cases of fraud.

(e) Effect of decision

Administrative determinations and final decisions under this section shall have no value as precedent for future cases under this chapter.

(f) Review of requisite amount in controversy

The Administrator is authorized to review at least every three years, beginning with the third year after November 1, 1978, the dollar amount defined in subsection (a) of this section as a small claim, and based upon economic indexes selected by the Administrator adjust that level accordingly.

(Pub.L. 95–563, § 9, Nov. 1, 1978, 92 Stat. 2387; Pub.L. 103–355, Title II, § 2351(d), Oct. 13, 1994, 108 Stat. 3322; Pub.L. 109–364, Div. A, Title VIII, § 857, Oct. 17, 2006, 120 Stat. 2349.)

HISTORICAL AND STATUTORY NOTES

Revision Notes and Legislative Reports
1978 Acts. Section 9 deals with recommendation No. 4 of the Procurement Commission's report and establishes procedures for the expedited disposition of appeals from decisions of contracting officers for claims of $10,000 or less that will be reviewed before agency boards. As discussed in section 8, the aim of any remedial system is to give the parties what is due them as determined by a thorough, impartial, speedy, and economical adjudication. However, it is difficult to be economical, yet thorough; thorough, yet speedy. The key is to provide a flexible system that provides alternatives for resolution of particular kinds of disputes. The claimant should be able to choose a forum according to the needs of his particular case; that is, one where the degree of due process can be balanced by the time and expense considered appropriate for that case.

Section 9(a) deals with a specific class of claims—defined as small claims of $10,000 or less—at the sole election of the contractor. Thus a claim of $10,000 or less could be appealed through the regular procedures of the agency board (Section 8) or, at the election of the contractor, through the simplified and expedited procedures as established for small claims.

Section 9(b) specifies that the small claims procedure shall provide for simplified rules of procedure in order to facilitate the decisionmaking process.

The purpose of the expedited small claims procedure with its lack of due process safeguards is to provide simplicity, speed, and economy. This means that lengthy briefs, formal motions, and burdensome evidentiary rules would be eliminated or cut to a minimum. The proceeding would resemble informal arbitration. Each side would present its case, and witnesses would be interviewed. The board member would issue a written order sustaining or denying the appeal and stating the amount awarded, hopefully that day or the day after a hearing if one is held. No written opinion would be made. While the proceeding is informal, there is no reason why it cannot be fair to both parties.

Section 9(c) establishes a limit, 120 days, whenever possible, for small claims to be resolved. It will be the responsibility of the Administrator under section 8(g) to insure that rules and regulations are established and carried out that will meet this expectation.

Section 9(d) specifies that decisions against both the Government and the contractor reached under the expedited small claims procedure will be final and conclusive except in cases of fraud.

A decision against the Government should be final and binding, since decisions under the small claims procedure will establish no precedents. Therefore the Government has no reason to go to court to avoid an unfavorable precedent.

The expedited procedure for claims of $10,000 or less is intended to satisfy the needs of those contractors who have small money claims and are interested only in getting a quick and simple decision from the agency board. In these circumstances the contractor most often does not wish to employ a lawyer to represent him. The key determining factor to the contractor is to have a procedure whereby if the decision is favorable, he will have something tangible for his victory. If the remedies process costs more than the contractor can make even if he wins the decision, then the process isn't meeting the contractor's needs. Given this background, the contractor, on choosing the expedited small claims procedure, has no further recourse in the remedies process and cannot appeal the decision. If he does not wish to have this finality, then he can process his claim through the regular board procedures or use the accelerated procedures.

The history of the existing agency boards has been one of increasing judicialization even under small claims and this will continue as long as a record is required for judicial review. Creeping judicialization could be the greatest threat to effective, economical handling of small claims. By not allowing appeals by either the contractor or the Government under the small claims procedure, the need to build a record for review is alleviated and one of the major obstacles to speed and economy is done away with.

Section 9(e) states that administrative determinations and final decisions under this section shall not set precedents for future cases under the act. Because of the lack of due process in the expedited procedures, it is important that decisions made under the small claims procedure for $10,000 or less not set precedents for cases that might be worth considerably more but have the same principles.

Section 9(f) is intended to keep the dollar level identified as a small claim up to date by authorizing the Administrator to review at least every 3 years the dollar amount and to adjust the level if he feels the economic indexes justify such a move. Senate Report No. 95–1118.

1994 Acts. Senate Report Nos. 103–258 and 103–259, and House Conference Report No. 103–712, see 1994 U.S. Code Cong. and Adm. News, p. 2561.

2006 Acts. House Conference Report No. 109–702, see 2006 U.S. Code Cong. and Adm. News, p. 1298.

Statement by President, see 2006 U.S. Code Cong. and Adm. News, p. S59.

References in Text

The Small Business Act, referred to in subsec. (a), is Pub.L. 85–536, July 18, 1958, 72 Stat. 384, as amended, which is classified generally to chapter 14A of Title 15, 15 U.S.C.A. § 631 et seq. For complete classification, see Short Title note set out under 15 U.S.C.A. § 631 and Tables.

Regulations under the Small Business Act, referred to in subsec. (a), are principally classified to chapter I of Title 13, C.F.R., 13 C.F.R. § 101.100 et seq.

This chapter, referred to in subsec. (e), was in the original, "this Act", meaning Pub.L. 95–563, which, in addition to enacting this chapter, amended section 5108 of Title 5, Government Organization and Employees, sections 1346, 1491, 2401, 2414, 2510, and 2517 of Title 28, Judiciary and Judicial Procedure, and section 724a of Title 31, Money and Finance, and enacted provisions set out as notes under section 601 of this title.

Codifications

Amendment by Pub.L. 109–364 to "Section 9(a) of the Contract Disputes Act of 1978 (41 U.S.C. 608)" was executed to subsection (a) of this section as the probable intent of Congress. Section 9(a) of the Act is classified to subsec. (a) of this section.

Amendments

2006 Amendments. Subsec. (a). Pub.L. 109–364, § 857, struck out the period following "$50,000 or less" and inserted the following: "or, in the case of a small business concern (as defined in the Small Business Act and regulations under that Act), $150,000 or less.".

1994 Amendments. Subsec. (a). Pub.L. 103–355, § 2351(d), substituted "$50,000" for "$10,000".

Effective and Applicability Provisions

1994 Acts. Amendment by section 2351(d) of Pub.L. 103–355 effective Oct. 13, 1994, except as otherwise provided, see section 10001 of Pub.L. 103–355, set out as a note under section 251 of this title.

1978 Acts. Section effective with respect to contracts entered into 120 days after Nov. 1, 1978 and, at the election of the contractor, with respect to any claim pending at such time before the contracting officer or initiated thereafter, see section 16 of Pub.L. 95–563, set out as a note under section 601 of this title.

LAW REVIEW AND JOURNAL COMMENTARIES

Arbitration: A permissible or desirable method for resolving disputes involving federal acquisition and assistance contracts? Kirby Behre, 16 Pub.Cont.L.J. 66 (1986)

LIBRARY REFERENCES

American Digest System
    United States ☞73(15).
    Key Number System Topic No. 393.

Research References

Forms
    Federal Procedural Forms § 34:239, Decision.
    Federal Procedural Forms § 34:241, Effect of Decision.
    8 West's Federal Forms § 13023, Appeals from the Boards of Contract Appeals
        Under the Contract Disputes Act.
    8 West's Federal Forms § 13223, Government Contract Claims--Claims Under the
        Contract Disputes Act.

Treatises and Practice Aids
    Federal Procedure, Lawyers Edition § 39:1112, Decision.
    Federal Procedure, Lawyers Edition § 39:1114, Finality and Effect of Decision.
    West's Federal Administrative Practice § 675, Types of Proceedings.

WESTLAW ELECTRONIC RESEARCH

See Westlaw guide following the Explanation pages of this volume.

§ 609. Judicial review of board decisions

(a) Actions in United States Court of Federal Claims; district court actions; time for filing

(1) Except as provided in paragraph (2), and in lieu of appealing the decision of the contracting officer under section 605 of this title to an agency board, a contractor may bring an action directly on the claim in the United States Court of Federal Claims, notwithstanding any contract provision, regulation, or rule of law to the contrary.

(2) In the case of an action against the Tennessee Valley Authority, the contractor may only bring an action directly on the claim in a United States district court pursuant to section 1337 of title 28, notwithstanding any contract provision, regulation, or rule of law to the contrary.

(3) Any action under paragraph (1) or (2) shall be filed within twelve months from the date of the receipt by the contractor of the decision of the contracting officer concerning the claim, and shall proceed de novo in accordance with the rules of the appropriate court.

(b) Finality of board decision

In the event of an appeal by a contractor or the Government from a decision of any agency board pursuant to section 607 of this title, notwithstanding any contract provision, regulation, or rules of law to the contrary, the decision of the agency board on any question of law shall not be final or conclusive, but the decision on any question of fact shall be final and conclusive and shall not be set aside unless the decision is fraudulent, or arbitrary, or capricious, or so grossly erroneous as to necessarily imply bad faith, or if such decision is not supported by substantial evidence.

(c) Remand or retention of case

In any appeal by a contractor or the Government from a decision of an agency board pursuant to section 607 of this title, the court may render an opinion and judgment and remand the case for further action by the agency board or by the executive agency as appropriate, with such direction as the court considers just and proper.

(d) Consolidation

If two or more suits arising from one contract are filed in the United States Court of Federal Claims and one or more agency boards, for the convenience of parties or witnesses or in the interest of justice, the United States Court of Federal Claims may order the consolidation of such suits in that court or transfer any suits to or among the agency boards involved.

(e) Judgments as to fewer than all claims

In any suit filed pursuant to this chapter involving two or more claims, counterclaims, cross-claims, or third-party claims, and where a portion of one such claim can be divided for purposes of decision or judgment, and in any such suit where multiple parties are involved, the court, whenever such action is appropriate, may enter a judgment as to one or more but fewer than all of the claims, portions thereof, or parties.

(f) Advisory opinions

(1) Whenever an action involving an issue described in paragraph (2) is pending in a district court of the United States, the district court may request a board of contract appeals to provide the court with an advisory opinion on the matters of contract interpretation at issue.

(2) An issue referred to in paragraph (1) is any issue that could be the proper subject of a final decision of a contracting officer appealable under this chapter.

(3) A district court shall direct any request under paragraph (1) to the board of contract appeals having jurisdiction under this chapter to adjudicate appeals of contract claims under the contract or contracts being interpreted by the court.

(4) After receiving a request for an advisory opinion under paragraph (1), a board of contract appeals shall provide the advisory opinion in a timely manner to the district court making the request.

(Pub.L. 95–563, § 10, Nov. 1, 1978, 92 Stat. 2388; Pub.L. 97–164, Title I, §§ 157, 160(a)(15), 161(10), Apr. 2, 1982, 96 Stat. 47 to 49; Pub.L. 102–572, Title IX, § 902(b)(1), Oct. 29, 1992, 106 Stat. 4516; Pub.L. 103–355, Title II, § 2354, Oct. 13, 1994, 108 Stat. 3323.)

HISTORICAL AND STATUTORY NOTES

Revision Notes and Legislative Reports

1978 Acts. Section 10(a) allows contractors, at their option, to bypass administrative disputes-resolving forums and seek review of adverse contracting officer decisions directly in the Court of Claims. This section responds to the Procurement Commission's recommendation No. 6 and would restore the contractor its right to a day in court—a fully judicialized totally independent forum—which historically has been the forum within which contract rights and duties have been adjudicated.

Suits against the Tennessee Valley Authority are not subject to the dollar limitations of the Tucker Act when brought directly to U.S. district court pursuant to section 1337 of Title 28, United States Code. Such suits only have jurisdiction in the district courts. The Tennessee Valley Authority cannot be sued in the Court of Claims.

Any actions pursuant to this section must be filed within 12 months from the date of the contracting officer's decision. It is the committee's belief that the 12-month period is sufficient for a contractor to make his decision.

Section 10(b) sets the same standard of judicial review on appeal of agency board decisions for both the contractor and the Government: The decision of the agency board on any question of law shall not be final or conclusive, but the decision on any question of fact shall be final and conclusive and shall not be set aside unless the decision is fraudulent or arbitrary, or capricious, or clearly erroneous. It is the intent of S. 3178 to relax the rigid standard established by the Wunderlich Act, a recommendation of the Procurement Commission, and to establish the standard used for appellate reviews of bench decisions—clearly erroneous—as the standard of review for appeals of agency board decision. Although there

may be evidence to support it, the decision of the agency board may be reversed when the appellate judge, upon review on the entire record, is left with the definite and firm conviction that a mistake has been committed. The "substantial evidence" standard of review will no longer be used for review of agency board decisions * * *

Section 10(e) sets in motion a process whereby the Court of Claims, for the convenience of parties and witnesses, may order the consolidation of suits arising from one contract in the Court of Claims or transfer from the court to or among agency boards that may be involved. It is the intent of the committees that splitting of the causes of action, or suits, under one contract be kept to a minimum both within the Court of Claims and within the boards. For example, a $40,000 suit cannot and should not be able to be split into four $10,000 suits that could be handled through the expedited small claims procedure. The boards should have the authority to consolidate these suits when they clearly arise from the same cause of action. Conversely, it is intended that the Court of Claims have the same ultimate authority to consolidate suits that are split between the court and the agency boards, but the committees specifically recommend that the Court of Claims be sensitive to the reasons why the suits have been split, and should not consolidate only for the sake of consolidation. For example, a contractor may have a large and complex claim and wish to take it directly to the Court of Claims. While the case is pending before the court, a smaller claim under the same contract, and possibly the same suit, arises and the contractor wishes to expedite the resolution of that claim through the agency board under the small claims procedure or possibly the accelerated procedure, which would both be considerably shorter than direct action in court. Under these circumstances, the court should allow for the splitting of the claim between the two jurisdictions (the court and the board).

The Court of Claims, when reviewing the decision to consolidate, should not arbitrarily take away the contractor's right to his day in court by consolidating two suits in the agency boards, and thus forcing one suit out of the court. It is the intent of the section to make available the opportunity to consolidate like suits in one jurisdiction, but this action should weigh the positions of the parties involved.

Section 10(f) permits partial judgments where various claims, counterclaims, and cross-claims can be segmented, so that parties do not have to await the final disposition of all of the litigation before receiving judgment. It is the intent of S. 3178 to expedite decisions on claims or portions thereof at the earliest time possible in the appeals process and not to allow unresolved issues on nonrelated claims to hold up the payment on claims that have been decided. Senate Report No. 95-1118.

1994 Acts. Senate Report Nos. 103-258 and 103-259, and House Conference Report No. 103-712, see 1994 U.S. Code Cong. and Adm. News, p. 2561.

1992 Acts. House Report No. 102-1006, see 1992 U.S. Code Cong. and Adm. News, p. 3921.

References in Text
This chapter, referred to in subsec. (e), was in the original, "this Act", meaning Pub.L. 95-563, which, in addition to enacting this chapter, amended section 5108 of Title 5, Government Organization and Employees, sections 1346, 1491, 2401, 2414, 2510, and 2517 of Title 28, Judiciary and Judicial Procedure, and section 724a of Title 31, Money and Finance, and enacted provisions set out as notes under section 601 of this title.

Amendments
1994 Amendments. Subsec. (f). Pub.L. 103-355, § 2354, added subsec. (f).

1982 Amendments. Subsec. (a)(1). Pub.L. 97-164, § 161(10), substituted "Claims Court" for "Court of Claims".

Subsec. (c). Pub.L. 97-164, § 157, struck out ", or, in its discretion and in lieu of remand it may retain the case and take such additional evidence or action as may be necessary for final disposition of the case" following "with such direction as the court considers just and proper".

Subsec. (d). Pub.L. 97-164, § 160(a)(15), substituted "United States Claims Court" for "Court of Claims" in two places.

Effective and Applicability Provisions
1994 Acts. Amendment by section 2354 of Pub.L. 103-355 effective Oct. 13, 1994, except as otherwise provided, see section 10001 of Pub.L. 103-355, set out as a note under section 251 of this title.

1992 Acts. Amendment by section 902(b)(1) of Pub.L. 102-572 effective Oct. 29, 1992, see section 911 of Pub.L. 102-572, set out as a note under section 171 of Title 28, Judiciary and Judicial Procedure.

1982 Acts. Amendment by Pub.L. 97-164 effective Oct. 1, 1982, see section 402 of Pub.L. 97-164, set out as a note under section 171 of Title 28, Judiciary and Judicial Procedure.

1978 Acts. Section effective with respect to contracts entered into 120 days after Nov. 1, 1978 and, at the election of the contractor, with respect to any claim pending at such time before the contracting officer or initiated thereafter, see section 16 of Pub.L. 95-563, set out as a note under 41 U.S.C.A. § 601.

Change of Name
References to United States Claims Court deemed to refer to United States Court of Federal Claims and references to Claims Court deemed to refer to Court of Federal Claims, see section 902(b) of Pub.L. 102-572, set out as a note under section 171 of Title 28, Judiciary and Judicial Procedure.

CROSS REFERENCES

Concurrent jurisdiction of district courts and United States Claims Court, see 28 USCA § 1346.

LAW REVIEW AND JOURNAL COMMENTARIES

Contractor claims for relief under illegal contracts with the government. Michael T. Janik and Margaret C. Rhodes, 45 Am.U.L.Rev. 1949 (1996).

Doing business with the government. Peter C. Mieres (February 1982) 4 L.A.Law. 34.

Government contract cases in the United States Court of Appeals for the Federal Circuit: 1995 in review. Thomas F. Williamson, Stacey L. Valerio and Stephanie P. Gilson, 45 Am.U.L.Rev. 1657 (1996).

Standard of review applied by the United States Court of Appeals for the Federal Circuit in international trade and customs cases. Herbert C. Shelley, Alice A. Kipel, Anne Talbot and Keith R. Marino, 45 Am.U.L.Rev. 1749 (1996).

LIBRARY REFERENCES

American Digest System

Federal Courts ☞1076, 1101, 1110.

United States ☞73(15).

Key Number System Topic Nos. 170B, 393.

Corpus Juris Secundum

CJS Limitations of Actions § 156, Stay of Proceedings.

Research References

ALR Library

8 ALR, Fed. 2nd Series 1, Validity, Construction, and Application of Federal Employees Health Benefits Act (FEHBA), 5 U.S.C.A. §§ 8901 to 8914.

150 ALR, Fed. 543, What Constitutes "Adjudicative Facts" Within Meaning of Rule 201 of Federal Rules of Evidence Concerning Judicial Notice of Adjudicative Facts.

97 ALR, Fed. 694, Jurisdiction of United States Court of Appeals for Federal Circuit Under 28 U.S.C.A. §§ 1292 and 1295.

93 ALR, Fed. 886, Federal Government Liability for Loss of, or Damage to, Vessels or Vehicles Seized in Course of Drug Enforcement Activity.

77 ALR 1044, Estoppel Against Defense of Limitation in Tort Actions.

Encyclopedias

Am. Jur. 2d Federal Courts § 2011, Suits Under Contract Disputes Act.

Am. Jur. 2d Public Works and Contracts § 213, Appeal to an Agency Board of Contract Appeals--Appeals; Finality of Decisions of Agency Board of Contract Appeals; Questions of Law and Fact.

Am. Jur. 2d Public Works and Contracts § 214, Appeal to United States Court of Federal Claims.

Forms

Am. Jur. Pl. & Pr. Forms Aviation § 98, Petition in Federal Court--Inverse Condemnation--Invasion of Airspace--Flights of Military Aircraft at Low Level Over Land Adjoining Military Airfield.

Am. Jur. Pl. & Pr. Forms Public Works & Contracts § 83, Petition--In Court of Federal Claims--For Review of Decision of Board of Contract Appeals--Under Contract Disputes Act of 1978.

Am. Jur. Pl. & Pr. Forms Public Works & Contracts § 84, Complaint, Petition, or Declaration--In Court of Federal Claims--For Review of Decision of Contracting Officer--Under Contract Disputes Act of 1978.

Federal Procedural Forms § 18:36, Contract Disputes Act.

Federal Procedural Forms § 34:98, Election of Forum for Appeal of Contracting Officer's Decision.

Federal Procedural Forms § 34:307, Scope.

Federal Procedural Forms § 34:308, Decision; Consideration of Matters Outside Record.

Federal Procedural Forms § 34:322, Actions in Court of Federal Claims.

Federal Procedural Forms § 34:323, Actions Involving the Tennessee Valley Authority.

Federal Procedural Forms § 34:325, Time for Bringing Action.

Federal Procedural Forms § 34:327, Parties.

Federal Procedural Forms § 34:332, Consolidation of Suits; Transfer to Board of Contract Appeals.

Federal Procedural Forms § 34:335, Decision; Payment of Judgment and Interest.

Federal Procedural Forms § 34:340, Petition--For Additional Compensation and Attorney's Fees--For Additional Work Under Contract [41 U.S.C.A. § 609; United States Court of Federal Claims Rule 8].

Federal Procedural Forms § 34:347, Complaint--For Damages--For Government's Breach of Contract [28 U.S.C.A. § 1491; 41 U.S.C.A. § 609; United States Court of Federal Claims Rule 8].

Federal Procedural Forms § 61:1, Statutes of Limitation, and Other Time Limits, Within United States Code.

8 West's Federal Forms § 13011, Overview.

8 West's Federal Forms § 13023, Appeals from the Boards of Contract Appeals Under the Contract Disputes Act.

8 West's Federal Forms § 13129, Contract Disputes Act.

8 West's Federal Forms § 13156, Time for Filings--Complaint.

8 West's Federal Forms § 13223, Government Contract Claims--Claims Under the Contract Disputes Act.

8 West's Federal Forms § 13249, Appeal of Contracting Officer's Final Decision--Complaint.

Treatises and Practice Aids

Federal Procedure, Lawyers Edition § 19:65, Suits Under Contract Disputes Act.

Federal Procedure, Lawyers Edition § 39:1130, Questions of Law.

Federal Procedure, Lawyers Edition § 39:1135, Remand for Further Action.

Federal Procedure, Lawyers Edition § 39:1137, Time for Bringing Action.

Federal Procedure, Lawyers Edition § 39:1140, Parties.

Federal Procedure, Lawyers Edition § 39:1142, Consolidation of Suits; Transfer to Board of Contract Appeals.

Federal Procedure, Lawyers Edition § 39:1151, Partial Decision.

Federal Procedure, Lawyers Edition § 39:1159, Actions Involving the Tennessee Valley Authority.

Federal Procedure, Lawyers Edition § 39:1174, Claims Governed by Contract Disputes Act; Related Claims--Advisory Opinion of Board of Contract Appeals.

Norton Bankruptcy Law and Practice 2d 28 USC § 1334, Bankruptcy Cases and Proceedings.

Patent Law Fundamentals App. 20(A), 28 U.S.C.A. § 1295--Jurisdiction of U.S. Court of Appeals for the Federal Circuit.

West's Federal Administrative Practice § 664, Protests and Appeals.

West's Federal Administrative Practice § 676, Remedies and Appeals.

West's Federal Administrative Practice § 677, United States Court of Federal Claims.

West's Federal Administrative Practice § 810, Time in Which to File; Statutes of Limitations; Laches; Equitable Estoppel.

West's Federal Administrative Practice § 819, Jurisdiction Concurrent with United States District Courts; Transfer of Jurisdiction.

West's Federal Administrative Practice § 822, Subject Matter Jurisdiction--Contract Claim: Jurisdiction, Limitations, Appeals and Interest.

14 Wright & Miller: Federal Prac. & Proc. § 3657, Statutory Exceptions to Sovereign Immunity--Actions Under the Tucker Act.

WESTLAW ELECTRONIC RESEARCH

See Westlaw guide following the Explanation pages of this volume.

Notes of Decisions

Amendment of complaint, time for filing   Burden of proof 40
16
Bankruptcy court jurisdiction 48

1. Construction

Any jurisdiction granted to the Claims Court, by the Contract Disputes Act, must be strictly construed. Williams Intern. Corp. v. U.S., Cl.Ct.1985, 7 Cl.Ct. 726. Federal Courts ☞ 1076

2. Purpose

Intent behind Contract Disputes Act scheme for review of government contracting officer's decision on government contract claim is to confine these government contract disputes to expert tribunals created expressly for that purpose. U.S. v. Suntip Co., C.A.9 (Or.) 1996, 82 F.3d 1468, certiorari denied 117 S.Ct. 942, 519 U.S. 1108, 136 L.Ed.2d 832, on remand 971 F.Supp. 1354. United States ☞ 73(9)

3. Law governing

Government contractor's claim that government violated federal Debt Collection Act and Administrative Procedures Act (APA) in connection with credit offsets was governed by Contract Disputes Act and federal Tucker Act, and was insufficient to invoke jurisdiction of district court. Thomas Creek Lumber and Log Co. v. Madigan, D.Or.1993, 815 F.Supp. 355. Federal Courts ☞ 974.1

In appeal by paint manufacturer from decision of Tennessee Valley Authority Board of Contract Appeals seeking equitable adjustment under contract with Authority, federal law governed contract rights and obligations of Authority. Tennessee Valley Authority v. Imperial Professional Coatings, E.D.Tenn.1984, 599 F.Supp. 436. Federal Courts ☞ 413

4. Preemption

Contract Disputes Act does not preempt subcontractor actions against the United States Postal Service in light of fact that waiver of immunity under Postal Reorganization Act (PRA) is to be liberally construed and that PRA's "sue and be sued" provision is virtually identical to Small Business Act's provision which has been found not to be preempted by Contract Disputes Act. Wright v. U.S. Postal Service, C.A.9 (Cal.) 1994, 29 F.3d 1426. Postal Service ☞ 3.1

District court's jurisdiction was preempted by a grant of exclusive jurisdiction to the administrative dispute-resolution process and the Court of Federal Claims under the Contract Disputes Act (CDA) in an action brought by contractor against the Defense Contract Audit Agency (DCAA), seeking declaratory and injunctive relief under the Administrative Procedure Act (APA) to prevent the DCAA from rescinding the contractor's direct billing authority or from causing payments due to the contractor under contracts with the Department of Defense to be withheld; action was fundamentally about specific government contracts and how they were administered, and the requested relief was intimately related to the contractor's contractual rights.

Lockheed Martin Corp. v. Defense Contract Audit Agency, D.Md.2005, 397 F.Supp.2d 659. Federal Courts ☞ 1141

Contract Disputes Act (CDA) preempted whatever jurisdiction might previously have existed in federal district courts under Postal Reorganization Act with respect to contract actions involving Postal Service. Four Star Aviation, Inc. v. U.S. Postal Service, D.Virgin Islands 2000, 120 F.Supp.2d 523. Federal Courts ☞ 1141

Subsubcontractor's claim against United States Postal Service (USPS), which sought to obtain payment for labor and materials supplied for post office building project by foreclosing on subsubcontractor's mechanic's lien on contract retainage sums allegedly held by USPS, was preempted by the Contract Disputes Act (CDA). U.S. ex rel. S & G Excavating, Inc. v. Seaboard Sur. Co., S.D.Ind.2000, 93 F.Supp.2d 968, reversed 236 F.3d 883, certiorari dismissed 121 S.Ct. 2022, 532 U.S. 1049, 149 L.Ed.2d 1021. United States ☞ 74.2

Contract Disputes Act preempted subcontractor's suit against United States Postal Service for Service's failure to obtain security bond for post office repair project. Biebel Bros., Inc. v. U.S. Postal Service, E.D.Mo.1991, 772 F.Supp. 1117. States ☞ 18.15; United States ☞ 67(1)

Contract Disputes Act preempted district court suits against United States Post Office by subcontractors as well as contractors. Carroll v. U.S. Postal Service, E.D.Mo.1991, 764 F.Supp. 143. United States ☞ 74.2

The Contract Disputes Act's preemption of district court jurisdiction over a contractor's suit against the United States Postal Service extends to actions brought against the Postal Service by subcontractors, whose only connection to the Postal Service is the subcontract with the general contractor which, in turn, contracted with the Postal Service. Eastern, Inc. v. Shelly's of Delaware, Inc., D.N.J.1989, 721 F.Supp. 649. United States ☞ 74.2

This chapter preempted whatever jurisdiction might previously have existed in the federal district courts under the Postal Reorganization Act, sec. 101 et seq. of Title 39, with respect to contract actions involving the Postal Service; thus, contractor bringing breach of contract action against Postal Service was limited to seeking relief in Court of Claims, even though Court of Claims would probably be without authority to award specific performance, which contractor claimed was its only adequate remedy. Consumers Solar Electric Power Corp. v. U.S. Postal Service, C.D.Cal.1982, 530 F.Supp. 702. Federal Courts ⊂⇒ 1141

5. Election of forum

Postal Service contractor who elected to appeal contract dispute to Postal Service Board of Contract Appeals instead of directly to Court of Claims was foreclosed from bringing dispute to Court of Claims. Santa Fe Engineers, Inc. v. U.S., Ct.Cl. 1982, 677 F.2d 876, 230 Ct.Cl. 512. United States ⊂⇒ 73(15)

Government contractor was precluded from bringing dispute under pre-March 1, 1979 contract with government under this chapter by electing to choose to appeal contracting officer's adverse decision to the Armed Services Board of Contract Appeals where contractor made no response to contracting officer's request that office be advised if contractor elected to have dispute subject to this chapter and contractor notified contracting officer that it desired to take appeal to Armed Services Board of Contract Appeals within the 30-day time period. Tuttle/White Constructors, Inc. v. U.S., Ct.Cl.1981, 656 F.2d 644, 228 Ct.Cl. 354. United States ⊂⇒ 73(9)

A contractor may proceed under this chapter and file suit directly in the Court of Claims with respect to a claim pending before the contracting officer on the effective date of this chapter, but a claim which is before an agency board, that is, one which has been the subject of a contracting officer's final decision, may not be switched to the Court of Claims under provisions of this chapter. Monroe M. Tapper & Associates v. U.S., Ct.Cl.1979, 611 F.2d 354, 222 Ct.Cl. 34. United States ⊂⇒ 73(14)

Government contractor could not circumvent the Contract Disputes Act by characterizing dispute as an action in replevin, or for return of property, where contracting officer had already ruled in favor of the General Services Administration that the supplies on job site where contractor had ceased performance had been paid for and could not be recovered by contractor, and appeal of this decision was pending before the General Services Board of Contract Appeals. Sealtite

Corp. v. General Services Admin., D.C.Colo.1985, 614 F.Supp. 352. United States ⊂⇒ 73(15)

A contractor who contests a contracting officer's decision has a choice between two exclusive remedies under the Contract Disputes Act (CDA): it may appeal the decision to an agency board of contract appeals within ninety days from the date of receipt of the decision; or it may bring an action directly on the claim in the United States Court of Federal Claims "within twelve months from the date of the receipt by the contractor of the decision of the contracting officer concerning the claim." Renda Marine, Inc. v. U.S., Fed.Cl.2006, 71 Fed.Cl. 782. United States ⊂⇒ 73(15)

Under the election of forum doctrine of the Contract Disputes Act (CDA), Court of Federal Claims lacked jurisdiction to enforce awards of Value Engineering Change Proposal (VECP) royalty payments made to contractor by the Armed Services Board of Contract Appeals (ASBCA) but paid to bank as contractor's assignee; since contractor elected to pursue his VECP claims before the ASBCA instead of the Court of Federal Claims, any disagreement concerning payment of the royalties to bank should have been brought to the ASBCA or to the Court of Appeals for the Federal Circuit. Bianchi v. U.S., Fed.Cl.2005, 68 Fed.Cl. 442, affirmed in part, reversed in part and remanded 475 F.3d 1268. United States ⊂⇒ 73(15)

Although the Contract Disputes Act (CDA) affords a contractor with a choice of forums in which to challenge an adverse decision by the contracting officer (CO), the plain language of the statute indicates that the contractor may not pursue dual avenues of appeal but must make an election. American Telecom Corp. v. U.S., Fed.Cl.2004, 59 Fed.Cl. 467. United States ⊂⇒ 73(15)

Monetary claim could not be tried before Court of Federal Claims where it was included within merits of case to be presented before Interior Board of Contract Appeals (IBCA). Marshall Associated Contractors, Inc. v. U.S., Fed.Cl.1994, 31 Fed.Cl. 809. Election Of Remedies ⊂⇒ 15

Contractor with Department of Agriculture did not make binding election to pursue its remedies with Agriculture Board of Contract Appeals, with respect to contracting officer's denial of claim for equitable adjustment, by filing untimely notice of appeal with Board which dismissed appeal for lack of jurisdiction; thus, contractor was not precluded from pursuing timely suit in Claims Court. Information Systems & Networks Corp. v. U.S., Cl.Ct.1989, 17 Cl.Ct. 527. United States ⊙ 73(9)

Government contractor's filing of complaint with Armed Services Board of Contract Appeals, without filing notice of appeal as required by Board's rules, failed to invoke jurisdiction of Board, and thus did not make binding election of forum such as would preclude contractor from filing subsequent complaint in United States Claims Court. Jo-Mar Corp. v. U.S., Cl.Ct.1988, 15 Cl.Ct. 602. United States ⊙ 73(9)

Mere mailing of notice of appeal from contracting officer's denial of additional compensation to contractor, to Armed Services Board of Contract Appeals, which was neither filed nor docketed, and which was retrieved by contractor, did not constitute binding election to proceed before Board so as to deprive Claims Court of jurisdiction over dispute between contractor and Navy; Board's rule which permitted mailing date to serve as filing date was applicable in situations where appeal was timely mailed, but would have been untimely if date of filing was determinative. Blake Const. Co., Inc. v. U.S., Cl.Ct.1987, 13 Cl.Ct. 250. United States ⊙ 73(9)

Claims Court did not have jurisdiction to hear postal contractor's appeals from decisions of contracting officer that had been appealed to Postal Service Board of Contract Appeals, in light of contract appeal procedures under Contract Disputes Act; contractor's election precluded proper filing of cases in Claims Court. Aviation & Transp. Properties, Inc. v. U.S., Cl.Ct.1986, 11 Cl.Ct. 87. United States ⊙ 73(15)

Public contractor, which was awarded contract before effective date of Contract Disputes Act, but which initiated reformation claim after effective date of Act and after effective date of Act elected to take its appeal of contracting officer's adverse decision to the Department of Transportation Contract Appeals Board, lost right to proceed de novo thereafter in the Claims Court under direct access provision of the Act. Bromley Contracting

Co., Inc. v. U.S., Cl.Ct.1986, 10 Cl.Ct. 668. United States ⊙ 73(15)

Contractor's previous filings of identical claims with contract appeals board, notwithstanding their dismissal without prejudice, constituted a binding election within meaning of Contract Disputes Act so as to deprive Claims Court of direct access jurisdiction over those same claims. Mark Smith Const. Co., Inc. v. U.S., Cl.Ct.1986, 10 Cl.Ct. 540. United States ⊙ 73(15)

Public contractor made effective election to proceed under the Contract Disputes Act with respect to claims regarding contract with Postal Service, even though contractor initiated suit in district court rather than in Claims Court as specifically provided in Act; contractor's briefs before district court indicated that contractor intended to pursue its Contract Disputes Act remedies and that it had merely erred in selecting forum, and contractor had successfully requested transfer of action to Claims Court. Elgin Builders, Inc. v. U.S., Cl.Ct.1986, 10 Cl. Ct. 40. United States ⊙ 73(9)

Where, at time contractor purported to "appeal," some nine months after its receipt of contracting officer's final decision on claims, there was no right of election to proceed administratively, no valid means of invoking jurisdiction of Board of Contract Appeals, and no real choice of forums, but rather, only choice was between direct access suit and abandonment of its claims, no valid election of forums took place, and no review process began; therefore, contractor had right under this section to bring action in Claims Court within prescribed time limit. Olsberg Excavating Co. v. U.S., Cl.Ct. 1983, 3 Cl.Ct. 249. United States ⊙ 73(15)

6. Jurisdiction of Court of Federal Claims—Generally

Contract Disputes Act (CDA) vests exclusive jurisdiction over claims brought by contractors regarding procurement contracts entered into by the United States Postal Service (USPS) with either the Agency Board of Contract Appeals or the United States Court of Federal Claims. Eagle Fence Co., Inc. v. V.S. Elec., Inc., E.D.Pa.2004, 324 F.Supp.2d 621. Federal Courts ⊙ 1141; United States ⊙ 73(15)

To proceed under the Contract Disputes Act (CDA), aggrieved contractor must first present its claim to agency contracting officer; if contracting officer denies claim, contractor has two options: it can either appeal to agency board of contract appeals (ABCA), or file suit in Federal Court of Claims. Southwest Marine, Inc. v. U.S., N.D.Cal.1995, 926 F.Supp. 142. United States ⇒ 73(9); United States ⇒ 73(15)

Statute permitting government contractor to bring action on claim directly in Claims Court "notwithstanding any contract provision, regulation, or rule of law to the contrary" only overrides contract provisions, regulations, and court decisions requiring application to agency Boards of Contract Appeals as prerequisite to court action, and does not provide Claims Court with unlimited jurisdiction. United Intern. Investigative Services v. U.S., Cl.Ct.1992, 26 Cl.Ct. 892. Federal Courts ⇒ 1076

7. —— Concurrent jurisdiction, jurisdiction of Court of Federal Claims

Decision of Armed Services Board of Contract Appeals to assert jurisdiction over Navy's claim directing contractor to replace defective parts in engines at no additional cost preserved jurisdictional parity between Court of Federal Claims and the Board. Garrett v. General Elec. Co., C.A.Fed.1993, 987 F.2d 747, rehearing denied, in banc suggestion declined. United States ⇒ 73(15)

New scheme envisioned essentially concurrent jurisdiction by both agency boards and by court, as part of which contracting officer would become focal point for all contract disputes, and, from his decision, appeal would lie in either board or the court, and scope of "claims" was to be read against such background, so that, consonant with purposes of this section, term would be given broad definition encompassing all claims and disputes, whether arising under or related to the contract. Z.A.N. Co. v. U.S., Cl.Ct. 1984, 6 Cl.Ct. 298. United States ⇒ 73(9)

8. —— Submission of claim, jurisdiction of Court of Federal Claims

Contractor's letter to contracting officer (CO) provided sufficient jurisdictional basis under the Contract Disputes Act (CDA) for contractor to assert claims in the Court of Federal Claims for bad faith default termination and equitable adjustment for unissued change orders; letter informed CO of factual basis of each claim and identified a sum certain associated with the claim. C.D. Hayes, Inc. v. U.S., Fed.Cl.2006, 74 Fed.Cl. 699. United States ⇒ 73(9)

Court of Federal Claims had jurisdiction under the Contract Disputes Act (CDA) over contractor's claim to the contract balance following default termination, notwithstanding that contractor did not submit a certified claim to contracting officer (CO) for the contract balance, where government submitted liquidated damages claim to the CO, who issued final decision setting off the damages against the contract balance, and thus contractor's request for the contract balance was an appeal of CO's final decision regarding liquidated damages award and the contract balance. Roxco, Ltd. v. U.S., Fed.Cl.2007, 77 Fed.Cl. 138. United States ⇒ 73(9)

Even if government contractor's claim for amounts allegedly due on copy machines purportedly covered under lease-to-own plan qualified as non-routine request for compensation, such that there did not have to be pre-existing dispute between parties, lack of written demand to contracting officer for payment of sum certain required under Contract Disputes Act (CDA) precluded contractor's invocation of jurisdiction of Court of Federal Claims. Danka de Puerto Rico, Inc. v. U.S., Fed.Cl.2004, 63 Fed.Cl. 20. Federal Courts ⇒ 1076

Under the Contract Disputes Act (CDA), contractor's failure to submit a claim requesting money damages to contracting officer (CO) precluded the Court of Federal Claims from exercising jurisdiction over contractor's request for damages arising from termination of lease for default; moreover, CO's final decision on the lease termination was not an adequate jurisdictional substitute for a CDA claim and final decision on money damages. Deponte Investments, Inc. v. U.S., Fed.Cl.2002, 54 Fed.Cl. 112. Federal Courts ⇒ 1076

Court of Federal Claims lacked jurisdiction under the Contract Disputes Act (CDA) over contractor's claim seeking $1 million in damages for an alleged breach of contract, where contractor never presented its claim to the contracting officer (CO) for a final decision. Atlanta Appraisal Services, Inc. v. U.S., Fed.Cl. 2002, 54 Fed.Cl. 51. Federal Courts ⟜ 1076

Prerequisite under the Contracts Dispute Act (CDA) to the litigation of government contract claims in the Court of Federal Claims is that a prior written claim must be submitted to a contracting officer for decision; when filing a complaint in the Court, contractors may increase the amount of their claim; however, contractors may not raise any new claims that have not been previously presented and certified to the contracting officer. Laidlaw Environmental Services (GS), Inc. v. U.S., Fed.Cl.1999, 43 Fed.Cl. 44. Federal Courts ⟜ 1076

Dispute concerning contractor's value engineering change proposal (VECP), which was submitted under VECP clause of contract, had to follow procedures outlined in the Contract Disputes Act (CDA), and in absence of submission of claim to the contracting officer (CO) and CO's final decision on claim, Court of Federal Claims lacked jurisdiction. Rig Masters, Inc. v. U.S., Fed.Cl.1998, 42 Fed.Cl. 369. United States ⟜ 73(9)

Court of Federal Claims did not have subject matter jurisdiction over reimbursement claim which was not submitted by government contractor to contracting officer. Cupey Bajo Nursing Home, Inc. v. U.S., Fed.Cl.1996, 36 Fed.Cl. 122. Federal Courts ⟜ 1102; United States ⟜ 73(15)

If entitlement to recover funds derives from public contract subject to provisions of Contract Disputes Act, adjudication of entitlement is conditioned on exhaustion of administrative requirements; absent submission of claim to contracting officer for decision, court cannot hear claim. Sharman Co., Inc. v. U.S., Cl.Ct.1991, 24 Cl.Ct. 763. Federal Courts ⟜ 1102

Failure of stenographic reporting firm to submit to contracting officer issue of whether Government breached its contract by having its own reporter report hearings called in cases where there was less than two hour notice rather than having firm report meetings took claim outside jurisdiction of Claims Court. International Verbatim Reporters, Inc. v. U.S., Cl.Ct.1986, 9 Cl.Ct. 710. Federal Courts ⟜ 1102

Claims Court did not have jurisdiction over claim brought by government contractor under contract for salvage sale and logging of timber for costs resulting from logging of mismarked timber where that claim had not been presented to contracting officer as claim upon which final decision could be entered from which appeal directly to Claims Court would lie. LDG Timber Enterprises, Inc. v. U.S., Cl.Ct.1985, 8 Cl.Ct. 445. United States ⟜ 127(2)

Postal Service customer's failure to properly submit written claim for a postal refund and consequential damages for untimely delivery of third-class political mail to a contracting officer within meaning of Contract Disputes Act precluded assumption of subject-matter jurisdiction by Claims Court over claim. Rider v. U.S., Cl.Ct.1985, 7 Cl.Ct. 770, affirmed 790 F.2d 91. United States ⟜ 73(15)

9. ―― Certification of claim, jurisdiction of Court of Federal Claims

Where government contractor, which had option to appeal contracting officer's denial of claim either under the contract's dispute clause or this chapter, chose to proceed under this chapter it was required to abide by this chapter's procedural requirements and where it failed to certify its claim before the contracting officer, the claims court and the Court of Appeals for the Federal Circuit were without jurisdiction of appeal from decision of Board notwithstanding attempted retroactive certification of claim before the Board. W.M. Schlosser Co., Inc. v. U.S., C.A.Fed.1983, 705 F.2d 1336. United States ⟜ 73(15)

Since plaintiff failed to certify its claim as required by section 605, the Court of Claims was without jurisdiction to consider plaintiff's direct appeal. W.H. Moseley Co., Inc. v. U.S., Ct.Cl.1982, 677 F.2d 850, 230 Ct.Cl. 405, certiorari denied 103 S.Ct. 81, 459 U.S. 836, 74 L.Ed.2d 77. United States ⟜ 73(15)

Absent presentment of contractor's claim for money in amount of excess of $50,000 and, if appropriate, certification, claim is not one on which contracting officer could issue, or be deemed to have issued, final decision and, therefore, Claims Court has no jurisdiction to entertain any appeal with respect thereto. LDG Timber Enterprises, Inc. v. U.S., Cl.Ct.1985, 8 Cl.Ct. 445. United States ⟜ 127(2)

10. —— Decision of contracting officer, jurisdiction of Court of Federal Claims

Contracting officer's decision not to accept contractor's value engineering change was not subject to review on merits by Court of Appeals for the Federal Circuit, unless officer acted contrary to law or abused her discretion. NI Industries, Inc. v. U.S., C.A.Fed.1988, 841 F.2d 1104. Administrative Law And Procedure ☞ 756; United States ☞ 73(15)

Linchpin for appealing claims under this chapter is contracting officer's "decision." Paragon Energy Corp. v. U.S., Ct.Cl.1981, 645 F.2d 966, 227 Ct.Cl. 176, affirmed 230 Ct.Cl. 884. United States ☞ 73(15)

Absent an appealable decision by contracting officer on the claim, direct access provision found in Contract Disputes Act is not applicable by its own terms. Mark Smith Const. Co., Inc. v. U.S., Cl. Ct.1986, 10 Cl.Ct. 540. United States ☞ 73(9)

While a contractor can dispute a Government's termination for default by merely filing written claim with contracting officer, seeking to convert the default into a termination for convenience and to recover the contractually authorized damages for such termination for convenience, a contractor's claim, challenging termination for default, is ripe for appeal to the Claims Court under 41 U.S.C.A. § 609(a) only after contractor submits written claim, certified if necessary, to the contracting officer and after contracting officer issues final decision on that claim; accordingly, if contractor has failed to comply with the statutory prerequisites, he cannot invoke direct access jurisdiction of Claims Court, based upon contractor's claim, to challenge validity of termination for default. Gunn-Williams v. U.S., Cl.Ct.1985, 8 Cl.Ct. 531. United States ☞ 73(15)

Where decision of contracting officer asserted government's right to reprocure, because contract was in default, but relief sought as result of reprocurement could not then be completely or specifically stated, statement of government's claim as to reprocurement was not complete until decision determined specific amount of relief sought in assessment of excess reprocurement costs, and contractor's action in Claims Court asserted timely appeal from the latter decision,

which was thus subject to review, and contractor could contest propriety of reprocurement and mitigation, and could defend against assessment on grounds of excusability, though contractor could not appeal from decision that government had right to terminate contract. Z.A.N. Co. v. U.S., Cl.Ct.1984, 6 Cl.Ct. 298. United States ☞ 73(15)

Jurisdictional requirements of filing by contractor with contracting officer of requests for relief in the form of time extensions, and a final decision by contracting officer denying such requests and assessing liquidated damages for delay, having been met, the Claims Court had jurisdiction to consider merits of claim asserted in complaint with respect to that matter. Palmer & Sicard, Inc. v. U.S., Cl.Ct.1984, 6 Cl.Ct. 232. United States ☞ 74(8)

11. Time for filing—Generally

New contracting officer's letter to lessor notifying lessor that United States Postal Service (USPS) was terminating its lease did not serve to initiate a new 12–month period for lessor to bring a CDA action after lessor had already received a final decision letter on his claims. Thomas v. U.S., Fed.Cl.1995, 34 Fed.Cl. 619, affirmed 101 F.3d 714. United States ☞ 73(15)

Jurisdictional defect under Contract Disputes Act of prematurely filing suit less than 60 days after public contractor has made claim to contracting officer cannot be cured by the passage of time after filing of action. Mendenhall v. U.S., Cl.Ct.1990, 20 Cl.Ct. 78. United States ☞ 73(9)

Under Contract Disputes Act, government contractor who submitted claims to contracting officer involving amounts less than $50,000 was required to appeal decision on claims within 12 months of receipt thereof, and failure to do so required Claims Court to dismiss claims. H.H.O. Co. v. U.S., Cl.Ct.1987, 12 Cl.Ct. 147. United States ☞ 73(15)

After issuance of final decision on contractor's claim challenging termination for default, failure of contractor to appeal within statutory time limits, 41 U.S.C.A. § 607 or 41 U.S.C.A. § 609(a), divests Claims Court of jurisdiction. Gunn-Williams v. U.S., Cl.Ct.1985, 8 Cl.Ct. 531. United States ☞ 73(15)

Subsec. (a)(3) of this section does not bar a contractor from contesting propriety of a default determination in a suit appealing a contracting officer's final decision assessing excess reprocurement costs, if such a suit is filed within 12 months of that decision; however, failure to seek judicial review of a default determination within 12 months after decision thereon bars a contractor from judicially challenging such determination, unless excess costs are assessed. D. Moody & Co., Inc. v. U.S., Cl.Ct.1984, 5 Cl.Ct. 70.

Under subsec. (a)(3) of this section, any "direct access" action must be filed within 12 months after contractor receives contracting officer's decision on claim and, absent such timely filed action, contracting officer's decision is final, conclusive and not subject to review by any forum. Hawkins v. U.S., Cl.Ct.1983, 1 Cl.Ct. 221. United States ☞ 73(14); United States ☞ 73(15)

12. ―― Law governing, time for filing

Once contractor elects to proceed under Contract Disputes Act, six-year statute of limitations applicable to claims over which Claims Court has jurisdiction is not applicable. Pathman Const. Co., Inc. v. U.S., C.A.Fed.1987, 817 F.2d 1573. Federal Courts ☞ 1105

Contract Disputes Act limitations period, relating specifically to suits in Claims Court contesting contracting officer's decisions under Contract Disputes Act, governed action by university against Government for reimbursement of expenses under contract, to exclusion of more general statute of limitations for claims over which Claims Court had jurisdiction. Board of Governors of University of North Carolina v. U.S., Cl.Ct.1986, 10 Cl.Ct. 27. Federal Courts ☞ 1105

Limitations period of 12 months contained in Contract Disputes Act [41 U.S.C.A. § 609(a)(3)] displaced general six-year statute of limitations for contractual claims [28 U.S.C.A. § 2501] with respect to claims seeking costs allegedly incurred in performing additional work under contract for construction of space transportation system. Kasler/Continental Heller/Fruin Colnon v. U.S., Cl.Ct. 1985, 9 Cl.Ct. 187. United States ☞ 73(15)

13. ―― Decision of contracting officer, time for filing

Under Contract Disputes Act, 12–month period within which public contractor must file, in Claims Court, suit

challenging decision of contracting officer does not begin to run when claim submitted to contracting officer is "deemed denied" since officer has not decided claim within period specified by Act; rather, limitations period does not begin to run until contracting officer renders actual written decision on claim. Pathman Const. Co., Inc. v. U.S., C.A.Fed.1987, 817 F.2d 1573. Federal Courts ☞ 1107

Alleged "gross mistake" of contracting officer (CO) in issuing a final decision does not provide an exception to the twelve–month statutory time limit provided in the Contract Disputes Act (CDA) for bringing an action in the Court of Federal Claims based on a contracting officer's final decision. Renda Marine, Inc. v. U.S., Fed.Cl.2006, 71 Fed.Cl. 782. United States ☞ 73(15)

A default termination notice labeled as a final decision by contracting officer fulfills the statutory requirements of the Contracts Dispute Act and triggers the 12–month period in which a contractor may directly appeal the termination decision to the Court of Federal Claims, irrespective of whether the contractor has submitted a certified claim to the contracting officer. Educators Associates, Inc. v. U.S., Fed.Cl.1998, 41 Fed.Cl. 811. Federal Courts ☞ 1106

Contracting officer's decision announcing termination of government contract due to contractor's alleged default was "claim" within meaning of statute that allows contractor period of 12 months, measured from date of receipt of contracting officer's final decision on claim, in which to bring action on claim in Court of Federal Claims. K & S Const. v. U.S., Fed.Cl.1996, 35 Fed.Cl. 270, affirmed 121 F.3d 727. United States ☞ 73(15)

Reconsideration of decision by contracting officer suspended the finality of the action pending disposition upon reconsideration and only upon the decision on reconsideration did the action become final; contracting officer's decision upon reconsideration constituted the "final decision" for purposes of the appeal time under the Contract Disputes Act. Summit Contractors v. U.S., Cl.Ct.1988, 15 Cl.Ct. 806. Federal Courts ☞ 1106

Twelve-month statute of limitations contained in Contract Disputes Act, for bringing suit in Claims Court did not begin to run until contracting officer issued his decision on contractor's claim, so that in absence of decision by contracting officer within required time frame, contractor could commence suit in Claims Court more than one year after contractor had submitted certified claim to contracting officer. Dawco Const., Inc. v. U.S., Cl.Ct.1987, 12 Cl.Ct. 445. Federal Courts ⇒ 1107

Government contractor's claims against Government, seeking total recovery of $178,695, required certification by contracting officer, so that contracting officer's denial of claims was of no consequence and did not activate statute of limitations in Contract Disputes Act. H.H.O. Co. v. U.S., Cl.Ct.1987, 12 Cl.Ct. 147. Limitation Of Actions ⇒ 66(6); United States ⇒ 73(9)

One year limitations period applicable to contractor's claim against government commenced to run when contracting officer issued written decision denying claim, rather than 60 days after claim was first submitted to contracting officer, during which no decision was reached. Vemo Co. v. U.S., Cl.Ct.1985, 9 Cl.Ct. 217. United States ⇒ 73(15)

14. ⸺ **Deemed denials, time for filing**
A deemed denial of a contractor's claim under the Contract Disputes Act (CDA) is not subject to the same twelve-month limitations period for seeking judicial relief as a contracting officer's written final decision. United Partition Systems, Inc. v. U.S., Fed.Cl.2004, 59 Fed.Cl. 627. United States ⇒ 73(13)

Where contracting officer (CO) did not render a written decision on contractor's wrongful debarment claim, and instead there was a deemed denial, the 12–month statute of limitations of the Contract Disputes Act (CDA) for suits in the Court of Federal Claims did not begin to run. Schickler v. U.S., Fed.Cl.2002, 54 Fed.Cl. 264, appeal dismissed 70 Fed.Appx. 584, 2003 WL 21774141. Federal Courts ⇒ 1107

Failure of contracting officer to issue decision within 60 days of submission of written claim would not trigger 12–month statute of limitations; disagreeing with *Pathman Construction Co. v. United States*, 10 Cl.Ct. 142. Malissa Co., Inc. v. U.S., Cl.Ct.1986, 11 Cl.Ct. 389. Federal Courts ⇒ 1107

Contractor's suit under Contract Disputes Act was not barred because he did not file within 12 months of date claim was deemed denied; such denial does not start running of Act's 12–month limitations period. LaCoste v. U.S., Cl.Ct.1986, 9 Cl.Ct. 313. Federal Courts ⇒ 1105

Twelve-month limitations provision of the Contract Disputes Act of 1978, § 10(a)(3), 41 U.S.C.A. § 609(a)(3), did not apply to a "deemed" decision which would authorize a direct access suit under § 6(c)(5) of the Act, 41 U.S.C.A. § 605(c)(5), but, rather, would apply to an actual decision issued by a contracting officer. Turner Const. Co. v. U.S., Cl.Ct. 1985, 9 Cl.Ct. 214. United States ⇒ 73(13)

15. ⸺ **Receipt by contractor, time for filing**
Government did not provide sufficient objective proof under Contract Disputes Act (CDA) that contractor received final decision of contracting officer, in order to begin period for filing action on claim in Court of Federal Claims, on evidence that decision was sent by certified mail to post office box for contractor's attorney, since Post Office was not agent for law firm or contractor, Post Office did not complete any portion of certified mail receipt, and letter was never released from custody of postal employees, and, instead, Post Office returned entire letter to contracting officer marked as undeliverable, unaccepted, and unsigned. Riley & Ephriam Const. Co., Inc. v. U.S., C.A.Fed.2005, 408 F.3d 1369. United States ⇒ 73(9)

Contract Disputes Act provision authorizing Claims Court to entertain claims filed within 12 months from date of receipt of decision by contractor means actual physical receipt of decision by contractor; Act defines timely claims in terms of that receipt date, not date of actual notice of contractor's decision. Borough of Alpine v. U.S., C.A.Fed.1991, 923 F.2d 170. Federal Courts ⇒ 1107

Contractor's receipt of final decision of contracting officer (CO) occurred for purposes of twelve-month statute of limitations for suit under Contract Disputes Act (CDA) when CO's certified letter arrived at post office where contractor had its post office (PO) box, and forms notifying contractor of its receipt were placed the box, notwithstanding contractor's objection that the post office was not an agent that could accept mail on its behalf; contractor's officers implicitly consented to allow post office employees to handle and accept mail on behalf of contractor when they rented the box. Riley & Ephriam Const. Co. Inc. v. U.S., Fed.Cl.2004, 61 Fed.Cl. 405, reversed and remanded 408 F.3d 1369. United States ☞ 73(15)

The actual physical receipt by the contractor of the contracting officer's decision is the critical event that starts the running of the limitations period of the Contract Disputes Act (CDA) for filing suit in the Court of Federal Claims. Policy Analysis Co., Inc. v. U.S., Fed.Cl.2001, 50 Fed.Cl. 626, appeal dismissed 49 Fed. Appx. 918, 2002 WL 31439818, order recalled and vacated 54 Fed.Appx. 496, 2002 WL 31939129, affirmed 61 Fed. Appx. 705, 2003 WL 1875580, rehearing denied. Federal Courts ☞ 1107

Facts indicated that attorney was contractor's representative and thus possessed authority to accept on contractor's behalf contracting officer's final decision on claim, so that statute of limitations began to run when attorney received that decision, where attorney initially represented contractor in various correspondence with the United States concerning claim and later submitted contractor's claim to contracting officer. Hamza v. U.S., Fed.Cl.1996, 36 Fed.Cl. 10. Attorney And Client ☞ 64; Federal Courts ☞ 1107

A final decision letter addressed to a borough's mayor, rather than the borough itself as the proper contracting party, nonetheless began the running of the limitations period for a case brought under the Contract Disputes Act. Borough of Alpine v. U.S., Cl.Ct.1990, 19 Cl.Ct. 802, affirmed 923 F.2d 170. Federal Courts ☞ 1107

The 12–month period in which public contractor was required to file direct access complaint in Claims Court began to run when contractor's attorney received contracting officer's decision, and not when contractor received decision from its attorney. Structural Finishing, Inc. v. U.S., Cl.Ct.1988, 14 Cl.Ct. 447. Federal Courts ☞ 1107

16. ——— Amendment of complaint, time for filing

Contractor which brought suit on "test" contract to recover independent research and development (IR&D) costs and production costs incurred to upgrade launch motor for commercial market as indirect costs of government contracts would be permitted to amend complaint to seek relief for contacting officer's disallowance of such costs with respect to all affected contracts, and not just "test" contract, considering absence of prior requests to amend, government received timely notice through certified claim that contractor claimed entitlement to entirety of the disallowance, and complaint which sought relief for that portion of disallowance attributable to "test" contract alleged that entire disallowance was improper. ATK Thiokol, Inc. v. U.S., Fed. Cl.2006, 72 Fed.Cl. 306. Federal Courts ☞ 1111

Court had jurisdiction to adjudicate amended complaint, filed after government contractor submitted claim to agency contracting officer and received opinion from that official, though compliance with these jurisdictional requirements did not cure defect of original complaint, because court could treat amended complaint as new, original complaint. Christian Appalachian Project, Inc. v. U.S., Cl.Ct.1986, 10 Cl.Ct. 595. Federal Courts ☞ 1111

Contractor's attempted amendment of his complaint was not barred by 12–month statute of limitations of Contract Disputes Act, where contractor only sought to specify present action included all elements of certified claim denied by contracting officer, and it was obvious by his complaint that contractor sought redress from adverse decision in its entirety. Design and Production, Inc. v. U.S., Cl.Ct.1986, 10 Cl.Ct. 80. Limitation Of Actions ☞ 127(4)

17. ——— Relation back doctrine, time for filing

Where a Contract Disputes Act claim asserted in an amendment to a complaint arose out of a transaction or occurrence set forth in the original complaint, the amendment was given retroactive effect to the date of the original complaint, such that claim that otherwise might be time barred could be considered timely where "relation back" was applicable. Case, Inc. v. U.S., Cl.Ct.1992, 25 Cl.Ct. 379. Federal Courts ☞ 1106

Government contractor's motion to join real party in interest as plaintiff in its direct action suit against Government, though filed after statute of limitations had passed, nevertheless related back to original, timely filed complaint; failure to include party originally was understandable mistake, and Government failed to demonstrate such extenuating circumstances as would warrant denial of motion to amend. Construction Equipment Lease Co. v. U.S., Cl.Ct.1989, 17 Cl.Ct. 628. Federal Courts ☞ 1106

Under Contract Disputes Act, relation back doctrine has no automatic application to all contractor's claims arising under single contract; in fact, if they are presented separately to contracting officer and are subject of discrete final decisions, Act requires just the opposite. AAAA Enterprises, Inc. v. U.S., Cl.Ct. 1986, 10 Cl.Ct. 191. Federal Courts ☞ 1105

18.   —— Tolling of period, time for filing

District court's stay order in False Claims Act (FCA) qui tam action against air tanker contractor with the Forest Service not only enjoined government from bringing future administrative proceedings against contractor, it also tolled running of limitations period in which contractor had to file Contract Dispute Act (CDA) suit challenging decision of contracting officer (CO) with respect to contractor's agreement with government. International Air Response v. U.S., C.A.Fed.2002, 302 F.3d 1363, rehearing denied 324 F.3d 1376, rehearing and rehearing in banc denied 324 F.3d 1380. Limitation Of Actions ☞ 107

Evidence supported conclusion that contracting officer (CO) recognized and reviewed lessor's request for reconsideration of CO's decision to terminate lease for default, thus suspending finality of CO's decision, and tolling twelve-month period for appeal under the Contract Disputes Act (CDA); in letter to lessor, CO acknowledged that she wanted to resolve rent claim, and her acknowledgement demonstrated that she was willing to review lessor's request and, in fact, was in the process of reviewing request. Arono, Inc. v. U.S., Fed.Cl.2001, 49 Fed.Cl. 544. Federal Courts ☞ 1106

Deadline for filing appeal under the Contract Disputes Act (CDA) of decision of contracting officer was not tolled by district court order in related false claims case "staying the enforcement of the action by the contracting officer and staying any deadlines pertinent to that order for appeal or review," as there is no tolling

provision in the CDA, and district court did not possess the requisite jurisdiction. International Air Response v. U.S., Fed. Cl.2001, 49 Fed.Cl. 509, reversed 302 F.3d 1363, rehearing denied 324 F.3d 1376, rehearing and rehearing in banc denied 324 F.3d 1380. Federal Courts ☞ 1106

Filing contract action in district court did not equitably toll 12–month statute of limitations on a direct contract action against United States based on contracting officer's unilateral decision to exclude area where northern spotted owl nest was discovered from contract for removal of timber given that logging company ignored unequivocal instructions in contracting officer's final decision concerning which court to file action in and, in any event, logging company failed to file complaint in correct court until seven months after district court's dismissal was affirmed on appeal. Janicki Logging Co., Inc. v. U.S., Fed.Cl.1996, 36 Fed.Cl. 338, affirmed 124 F.3d 226. Limitation Of Actions ☞ 104.5

Contracting officer's agreement to reconsider final decision would suspend finality of decision for purposes of time for filing complaint under the Contract Disputes Act if request for reconsideration were made in a timely manner, regardless of whether contracting officer ultimately reconsidered decision. Vepco of Sarasota, Inc. v. U.S., Cl.Ct.1992, 26 Cl. Ct. 639, affirmed 6 F.3d 786. Federal Courts ☞ 1106

Armed Services Board of Contract Appeals' decision in no way tolled 12–month statute of limitations set out in Contract Disputes Act for bringing action in Claims Court; Claims Court is under no statutory obligation to wait for Board to render decision before hearing case. Structural Finishing, Inc. v. U.S., Cl.Ct. 1988, 14 Cl.Ct. 447. Federal Courts ☞ 1106

Misdating of final damage determination by contracting officer with respect to persistent leak in building constructed in accordance with drawings provided and approved by contractor did not provide a basis for applying doctrine of equitable estoppel to toll statute of limitations, even if contractor did in fact rely on date of letter, where reliance was unreasonable because language of statute was clear that key date commencing running of 12–month period was receipt of final decision and, contractor was not only shown to have signed for final decision, but was shown to have actually received decision which stated plainly therein that contractor had 12 months in which to file claim. Shaver Partnership v. U.S., Cl.Ct. 1987, 11 Cl.Ct. 594. Limitation Of Actions ☞ 13

19. —— Miscellaneous filings timely, time for filing

Federal government's appeal from a decision of the Armed Services Board of Contract Appeals awarding, as allowable costs, part of government contractor's legal fees, was not time-barred, even though, instead of appealing from the Board's earlier decision as to contractor's entitlement, the government waited to appeal from the Board's decision resolving the question of quantum; although the earlier entitlement decision was, pursuant to the flexible concept of finality applicable in this context, a "final" decision, allowing the government, as aggrieved party, to wait for a truly final judgment before appealing furthered the purposes of both the Contract Disputes Act (CDA) and the doctrine of finality. Brownlee v. DynCorp., C.A.Fed.2003, 349 F.3d 1343, rehearing and rehearing en banc denied, on remand 2006 WL 225580. United States ☞ 73(15)

Although statutory period for bringing action pursuant to Contract Disputes Act ended on a Saturday, contractor's action filed in Court of Federal Claims on the following Monday was timely pursuant to rule of Court of Federal Claims permitting filing on the next business day after a weekend or holiday. Wood-Ivey Systems Corp. v. U.S., C.A.Fed.1993, 4 F.3d 961. Time ☞ 10(4)

Because 12–month statute of limitations of the Contract Disputes Act would have applied if claimant had ever filed a legal claim with contracting officer, so that general 6–year statute of limitations did not apply, but no claim had been filed, so that the Contract Disputes Act statute of limitations was not available, no statute of limitations barred claimant's equitable claims being considered on Congressional reference. Spalding and Son, Inc. v. U.S., Cl.Ct.1991, 24 Cl.Ct. 112, report and recommendation rejected 28 Fed.Cl. 242. Federal Courts ☞ 1105

Public contractor's complaint seeking recovery of increased costs as a result of changes in original contract performance

ordered by contracting officer during progress of work was timely filed where complaint was filed within 12 months of date contractor received contracting officer's decision on claim for increased costs. Kunz Const. Co. v. U.S., Cl.Ct. 1987, 12 Cl.Ct. 74. Federal Courts ☞ 1105

Contractor's breach of contract claim filed with Claims Court in 1984 for breach which allegedly occurred in 1976 was not barred by 12–month limitations period of Contract Disputes Act where government contracting officer did not render decision on contractor's claim submitted in 1978 at any time before contractor filed complaint with Claims Court. G & H Machinery Co. v. U.S., Cl.Ct.1985, 7 Cl.Ct. 199. Federal Courts ☞ 1105

20. —— Miscellaneous filings not timely, time for filing

Contractor's failure to claim applicability of Contract Disputes Act [41 U.S.C.A. §§ 601–613] in timely fashion foreclosed claim under the Act, where contractor's complaint against Tennessee Valley Authority was not filed until 40 months after its receipt of contracting officer's decision, TVA representative had issued final decision more than one year after Contract Disputes Act became law, and Act clearly provided that action be brought within 12 months from date of receipt by contractor of decision of contracting officer. Massman Const. Co. v. Tennessee Valley Authority, C.A.6 (Tenn.) 1985, 769 F.2d 1114, certiorari denied 106 S.Ct. 1947, 476 U.S. 1104, 90 L.Ed.2d 357.

Contract Disputes Act (CDA) barred judicial review of final decision of contracting officer (CO) in favor of government on its counterclaims against contractor, notwithstanding that decision might have been invalid because counterclaims were the "mirror image" of contractor's claims before the Court of Federal Claims, where contractor failed to challenge decision in the Court within twelve months after receipt of decision. Renda Marine, Inc. v. U.S., Fed.Cl.2006, 71 Fed.Cl. 782. United States ☞ 73(15)

Government contractor whose complaint arrived at Court of Federal Claims one day after expiration of the 12–month limitations period of Contract Disputes Act was not entitled to corrective order showing its complaint as having been filed on the last day of the period, even though contractor presented evidence that complaint should have arrived on that date; court could not create exceptions to or otherwise waive or expand limitations period established by statute, and judicially created rebuttable presumption of actual receipt by date complaint should have arrived in the ordinary course of mail could not be applied to override terms of statute limiting sovereign's waiver of immunity to sue. White Buffalo Const., Inc. v. U.S., Cl.Ct.1992, 28 Fed.Cl. 145. Federal Courts ⟜ 1106

Contract Disputes Act requirement that contractor's action in Claims Court against government be filed within 12 months from date of receipt of decision of contracting officer barred contractor's claim where contractor received final decision in November 1989 and did not file complaint in Claims Court until December 1990, even though November 1989 decision was not marked "duplicate original" and decision marked "duplicate original" was received in February 1990. Krueger v. U.S., Cl.Ct.1992, 26 Cl.Ct. 841. Federal Courts ⟜ 1105

Even if contractor's letter to contracting officer constituted "claim," within meaning of Contract Disputes Act, Claims Court lacked jurisdiction over contractor's "claim," where contractor filed action against United States before expiration of the 60–day period within which contracting officer had to respond to "claim." Mendenhall v. U.S., Cl.Ct.1990, 20 Cl.Ct. 78. United States ⟜ 73(9)

Judicial admission contained in related pleadings in state court, in which executrix of estate of government contractor admitted that earlier claim filed with Government by her son had been made on behalf of estate, constituted, at minimum, ratification by estate of son's actions in making claim and rendered untimely executrix' subsequent action under Contract Disputes Act in Claims Court commenced more than one year after son's claim was denied. Handel v. U.S., Cl.Ct.1988, 16 Cl.Ct. 70. Federal Courts ⟜ 1105

21. Finality of decision

In view of contract provisions, contracting officer's decision, where not timely appealed, was entitled to finality with respect to government's claim against contractor concerning determination that contractor was in default, conferring on government right to terminate the contract, and regarding determination, implicit in the termination, government was relieved of its obligation to pay contract price, and, contractor not having appealed such decision, the determination of default became final and not subject to review in the Claims Court. Z.A.N. Co. v. U.S., Cl.Ct.1984, 6 Cl.Ct. 298. United States ⟜ 73(15)

Original decision by Department of Transportation Board of Contract Appeals, regarding corrections center service company's claim for interest on unpaid wages, fringe benefits, and associated taxes under Contract Dispute Act (CDA), was not final, since quantum issues were still outstanding, and thus board was free to reexamine claim in light of intervening case law. Schleicher Community Corrections Center, Inc. v. Gonzales, C.A.Fed.2007, 2007 WL 43260, Unreported. United States ⟜ 73(15)

22. Review of board decisions—Generally

Under Contract Disputes Act (CDA), court reviews legal conclusions of Armed Services Board of Contract Appeals (ASBCA) without deference, and must accept the ASBCA's findings of fact unless they are: (1) fraudulent; (2) arbitrary or capricious; (3) so grossly erroneous as to necessarily imply bad faith; or (4) not supported by substantial evidence. Ryste & Ricas, Inc. v. Harvey, C.A.Fed.2007, 477 F.3d 1337. United States ⟜ 73(15)

Under scope of review applicable to decision of a board of contract appeals, the board's conclusions of law are freely reviewable by the Court of Appeals, while review of the board's findings of fact is limited to a determination of whether those findings are arbitrary, capricious, based on less than substantial evidence, or rendered in bad faith. Gardiner, Kamya & Associates, P.C. v. Jackson, C.A.Fed.2004, 369 F.3d 1318, on remand 2005 WL 2651155. United States ⟜ 73(15)

Under Contract Disputes Act (CDA), Court of Appeals for the Federal Circuit reviews factual determinations of Armed Services Board of Contract Appeals under substantial evidence standard and legal questions under de novo standard. Perry v. Martin Marietta Corp., C.A.Fed. 1995, 47 F.3d 1134. Administrative Law And Procedure ⟜ 791; Administrative

Law And Procedure ☞ 796; United States ☞ 73(15)

Armed Services Board of Contract Appeal's conclusions of law are not final and are thus freely reviewable by Court of Appeals, while the Board's findings of fact are final and review is limited to a determination of whether those findings are arbitrary, capricious, based on less than substantial evidence, or rendered in bad faith. U.S. v. Boeing Co., C.A.Fed. 1986, 802 F.2d 1390. United States ☞ 73(15)

23. —— Deference, review of board decisions

Agency board of contract appeals has considerable experience and expertise in interpreting government contracts, and its interpretation is given careful consideration and great respect on judicial review pursuant to Contract Disputes Act (CDA). HPI/GSA 3C, LLC v. Perry, C.A.Fed.2004, 364 F.3d 1327. United States ☞ 73(15)

Determinations of Armed Services Board of Contract Appeals on issues of contract interpretation are reviewed de novo, although Court of Appeals' review is mindful of the Board's specialist expertise. Lockheed Martin Corp. v. Walker, C.A.Fed.1998, 149 F.3d 1377, on remand 1999 WL 166193. United States ☞ 73(15)

Since contract interpretation is question of law, Board of Contract Appeals' interpretation is not binding upon Court of Appeals; however, because of Board's expertise on questions of government contracts, court gives some weight to Board's interpretation of particular contractual language. R.B. Wright Const. Co. Through Rembrant, Inc. v. U.S., C.A.Fed.1990, 919 F.2d 1569, affirmed. Administrative Law And Procedure ☞ 792; United States ☞ 73(15)

Under Contract Disputes Act, appellate court will not alter findings of fact by Armed Services Board of Contract Appeals if they are supported by substantial evidence even though record may contain evidence supporting contrary position; however, Board's decision as to question of law is not final or conclusive, and its interpretation of contract is not binding, although entitled to careful consideration and great respect since legal interpretations by tribunals having expertise are helpful even if not compelling. Fruin-

Colnon Corp. v. U.S., C.A.Fed.1990, 912 F.2d 1426. United States ☞ 73(15)

Interpretation of contract by Postal Service Board of Contract Appeals is question of law, and thus not final, although it is afforded careful consideration and great respect. Alvin Ltd. v. U.S. Postal Service, C.A.Fed.1987, 816 F.2d 1562. See, also, S.S. Silberblatt Inc. v. U.S., C.A.Fed.1989, 888 F.2d 829. Postal Service ☞ 3.1

24. —— Questions of law, review of board decisions

Under the Contract Disputes Act (CDA), the Court of Appeals reviews conclusions of law by the Department of Energy Board of Contract Appeals without deference. Cities of Burbank, Glendale and Pasadena, Cal. v. Bodman, C.A.Fed.2006, 464 F.3d 1280. United States ☞ 73(15)

Determining proper method of review by General Services Administration Board of Contract Appeals when examining best value agency procurement decision is question of law, reviewed de novo. Widnall v. B3H Corp., C.A.Fed.1996, 75 F.3d 1577, on remand 1996 WL 233753. United States ☞ 73(15)

Because question of jurisdiction is one of law, Court of Appeals for the Federal Circuit reviews de novo dismissals by the General Services Administration Board of Contract Appeals for lack of jurisdiction. PRC Inc. v. Widnall, C.A.Fed.1995, 64 F.3d 644. United States ☞ 64.60(3.1)

Armed Services Board of Contract Appeals' interpretation of government contract, including whether it incorporates certain Federal Acquisition Regulation (FAR) provisions, is matter of law for de novo review. Aydin Corp. v. Widnall, C.A.Fed.1995, 61 F.3d 1571, rehearing denied, on remand 1995 WL 744609. Administrative Law And Procedure ☞ 796; United States ☞ 73(15)

In reviewing decision of agency board on any question of law under Contract Disputes Act, Court of Appeals is not bound by board's conclusions. Caldwell & Santmyer, Inc. v. Glickman, C.A.Fed. 1995, 55 F.3d 1578. United States ☞ 73(15)

Whether claim exists under Federal Acquisition Regulations is question of law reviewed de novo. Bill Strong Enterprises, Inc. v. Shannon, C.A.Fed.1995, 49 F.3d 1541, on remand 1996 WL 405814.

Administrative Law And Procedure ☞ 796; United States ☞ 73(15)

To extent that determinations of Armed Services Board of Contract Appeals (ASBCA) regarding allocation and allowability of costs of Air Force contract turned on ASBCA's interpretation of defense acquisition regulation (DAR) and cost accounting standard (CAS), they presented questions of law subject to independent review. Rice v. Martin Marietta Corp., C.A.Fed.1993, 13 F.3d 1563. United States ☞ 73(15)

Whether Armed Services Board of Contract Appeals has jurisdiction is question of law. Fischbach and Moore Intern. Corp. v. Christopher, C.A.Fed.1993, 987 F.2d 759. United States ☞ 73(15)

On appeal, legal conclusion of Armed Services Board of Contract Appeals on jurisdiction is not final or conclusive. Garrett v. General Elec. Co., C.A.Fed. 1993, 987 F.2d 747, rehearing denied, in banc suggestion declined. United States ☞ 73(15)

Whether Armed Services Board of Contract Appeals has jurisdiction over public contractor's claim for equitable adjustment is a question of law. Johnson Controls World Services, Inc. v. Garrett, C.A.Fed.1993, 987 F.2d 738. United States ☞ 73(15)

Court of Appeals review of decision of Armed Services Board of Contract Appeals is limited; factual findings are final and conclusive and shall not be set aside unless decision is fraudulent, arbitrary, capricious, so grossly erroneous as to necessarily imply bad faith, or if such decision is not supported by substantial evidence but legal conclusions are freely reviewable. ICSD Corp. v. U.S., C.A.Fed. 1991, 934 F.2d 313. Administrative Law And Procedure ☞ 763; Administrative Law And Procedure ☞ 791; Administrative Law And Procedure ☞ 796; United States ☞ 73(15)

While review by Court of Appeals of decision of General Services Administration Board of Contract Appeals does not permit reconsideration of facts de novo, Board's conclusions of law are not binding on Court of Appeals. Afro-Lecon, Inc. v. U.S., C.A.Fed.1987, 820 F.2d 1198. Administrative Law And Procedure ☞ 796; United States ☞ 73(15)

Court of Appeals is not required to grant finality to legal interpretation by Armed Services Board of Contract Appeals with respect to cost accounting standards and interpretations, as interpretation of regulations incorporated into government contracts is question of law which court is free to resolve. U.S. v. Lockheed Corp., C.A.Fed.1987, 817 F.2d 1565. Administrative Law And Procedure ☞ 413; United States ☞ 73(15)

25. —— Clearly erroneous standard, review of board decisions

The Court of Appeals will not set aside findings of fact by agency board of contract appeals unless fraudulent, arbitrary, or capricious, or so grossly erroneous as to necessarily imply bad faith, or if such decision is not supported by substantial evidence. Cities of Burbank, Glendale and Pasadena, Cal. v. Bodman, C.A.Fed. 2006, 464 F.3d 1280. United States ☞ 73(15)

Court of appeals reviews conclusions of law of Armed Services Board of Contract Appeals anew, and may set aside Board's findings of fact only when they are fraudulent, arbitrary, or capricious, or so grossly erroneous as to necessarily imply bad faith, or if they are not supported by substantial evidence. Decker & Co. v. West, C.A.Fed.1996, 76 F.3d 1573, on remand 1998 WL 195944. United States ☞ 73(15)

The "clearly erroneous" standard was applicable with respect to findings of fact by the United States Claims Court in de novo proceeding on contract claim. Milmark Services, Inc. v. U.S., C.A.Fed.1984, 731 F.2d 855. United States ☞ 73(15)

26. —— Substantial evidence standard, review of board decisions

Substantial evidence standard applicable to bid protest reviewed in the absence of a hearing applies to the trial court's review of agency findings, not the Court of Federal Claims' initial fact-finding. Bannum, Inc. v. U.S., C.A.Fed.2005, 404 F.3d 1346. United States ☞ 64.60(3.1)

Substantial evidence did not support finding by Armed Services Board of Contract Appeals that maintenance contractor was not misled by defective specification in calculating its bid with respect to required policing work, such that contractor was not eligible for equitable adjustment, when although it used mowing acreage to estimate appropriate workweek, contractor otherwise relied on government's understated yearly policing acreage when calculating its policing bid. E.L. Hamm & Associates, Inc. v. England, C.A.Fed.2004, 379 F.3d 1334. United States ⊂⊃ 73(15)

"Substantial evidence," of kind required to support factual findings of the General Services Administration Board of Contract Appeals (GSBCA) in connection with protest decision, means such relevant evidence as reasonable mind might accept as adequate to support conclusion. Statistica, Inc. v. Christopher, C.A.Fed. 1996, 102 F.3d 1577. Administrative Law And Procedure ⊂⊃ 791; United States ⊂⊃ 64.60(3.1)

On appeal from protest decision of the General Services Administration Board of Contract Appeals (GSBCA), Court of Appeals reviews GSBCA's factual findings to determine whether they are fraudulent, arbitrary, or capricious, so grossly erroneous as to necessarily imply bad faith, or not supported by substantial evidence. Statistica, Inc. v. Christopher, C.A.Fed. 1996, 102 F.3d 1577. Administrative Law And Procedure ⊂⊃ 763; Administrative Law And Procedure ⊂⊃ 791; United States ⊂⊃ 64.60(3.1); United States ⊂⊃ 64.60(4)

Court of Appeals must uphold Board of Contract Appeals' decision on any question of fact unless the decision is fraudulent, arbitrary or capricious, so grossly erroneous as to necessarily imply bad faith, or not supported by substantial evidence; "substantial evidence" is such relevant evidence as a reasonable mind might accept as adequate to support a conclusion. Grumman Data Systems Corp. v. Dalton, C.A.Fed.1996, 88 F.3d 990. Administrative Law And Procedure ⊂⊃ 763; Administrative Law And Procedure ⊂⊃ 791; United States ⊂⊃ 64.60(4)

Court of Appeals will not disturb findings of Department of Agriculture Board of Contract Appeals (AGBCA) if they are supported by substantial evidence, despite existence of support for alternative findings in the record. Roseburg Lumber Co. v. Madigan, C.A.Fed.1992, 978 F.2d 660, rehearing denied. United States ⊂⊃ 73(15)

The Board of Contract Appeals' conclusions of law are reviewed de novo, but the reviewing court defers to its findings of fact unless unsupported by substantial evidence. Andersen Consulting v. U.S., C.A.Fed.1992, 959 F.2d 929. United

States ⊂⊃ 64.60(3.1); United States ⊂⊃ 73(15)

Substantial evidence supported finding of the General Services Administration Board of Contract Appeals, which denied contractor's claim for contract time extension plus impact costs, that contractor's actions delayed caisson installation and that contractor had not met its heavy burden of establishing that evidence required a finding in its favor. William F. Klingensmith, Inc. v. U.S., C.A.Fed.1984, 731 F.2d 805. United States ⊂⊃ 74(11)

Decision of Armed Services Board of Contract Appeals which awarded public contractor right to adjustment in price of aircraft engines delivered for foreign military sales, on basis of savings clause in contracts which permitted recovery of overceiling research and development and bid and proposal costs, was supported by substantial evidence. U.S. v. General Elec. Corp., C.A.Fed.1984, 727 F.2d 1567. United States ⊂⊃ 74(11)

In government contractor's proceeding against United States to recover for increased costs incurred as consequence of explosions allegedly caused by defective government contract specifications for production of igniters used in fire bombs, Armed Services Board of Contract Appeals' conclusion that specifications designating igniter as minimum hazard in its invitation of bids, under heading "transportation data," and within section captioned "preservation, packaging and packing," could not reasonably be construed as representing that no explosion would occur during production of igniters, was not arbitrary, capricious, unsupported by substantial evidence, or erroneous as matter of law. Ordnance Research, Inc. v. U.S., Ct.Cl.1979, 609 F.2d 462, 221 Ct.Cl. 641. United States ⊂⊃ 70(29)

Substantial evidence supported finding by Armed Services Board of Contract Appeals that objective purpose of Navy contractor's preparation and submission of request for equitable adjustment (REA) was to seek comprehensive resolution of entire job order, sustaining Board's determination that costs incurred in preparing REA, which did not qualify as claim under Contract Disputes Act (CDA), were contract administration costs, rather than costs incurred in connection with prosecution of CDA claim against government, and thus recoverable by contractor.

Johnson v. Advanced Engineering & Planning Corp., Inc., E.D.Va.2003, 292 F.Supp.2d 846. United States ☞ 73(15)

Decision of Postal Service Board of Contract Appeals that lessor of building leased by the United States Postal Service (USPS) was responsible for the cost of repairing and replacing the roof of the building was supported by substantial evidence; pursuant to lease agreement, lessor was required to maintain building in good repair except in case of damage arising from negligence of USPS employees, there was no evidence that roof repair was necessitated by negligence of USPS employees, USPS gave lessor written notice that roof was leaking and needing repair, and government's roofing expert testified that roof repair was necessary. Spodek v. Potter, C.A.Fed.2003, 57 Fed.Appx. 867, 2003 WL 839423, Unreported. United States ☞ 73(15)

27. Claims or issues reviewable—Generally

Where a contractor has not presented its claims to the contracting officer (CO) in the exact terms of its complaint in the Court of Federal Claims, the contractor has sufficiently established subject matter jurisdiction under the Contract Disputes Act (CDA) when its claims in the complaint arise from the same operative facts, seek essentially the same relief, and merely assert differing legal theories for that recovery when compared with its claim presented to the CO. M.A. DeAtley Const., Inc. v. U.S., Fed.Cl.2007, 75 Fed. Cl. 575. United States ☞ 73(9)

Under the *"Fulford* doctrine," when a contractor timely appeals an assessment of excess reprocurement costs following default termination, the propriety of the government's default termination can be challenged even though the default termination decision was not appealed. Roxco, Ltd. v. U.S., Fed.Cl.2004, 60 Fed.Cl. 39. United States ☞ 74(5)

Court of Federal Claims reviews claims under Contract Disputes Act de novo and, thus, alternative arguments may be raised even though not presented to contracting officer below. Farmers Grain Co. of Esmond v. U.S., Fed.Cl.1995, 33 Fed.Cl. 298. Federal Courts ☞ 1115

Finality of Government's default termination did not allow contractor to bring all possible claims under the contract before the Claims Court, as the Court had jurisdiction only over those claims of the contractor which had been certified by the contractor and presented to the contracting officer for determination. SGW, Inc. v. U.S., Cl.Ct.1990, 20 Cl.Ct. 174. United States ☞ 73(9)

Claims Court's scope of de novo review under Contract Disputes Act permits introduction of new facts and/or legal theories in support of original claim, without affecting Court's jurisdiction. Cerberonics, Inc. v. U.S., Cl.Ct.1987, 13 Cl.Ct. 415. Federal Courts ☞ 1115

Claim for amount of money which has not been presented to contracting officer can subsequently be presented to Claims Court if amount was determined or determinable after presentment to contracting officer as result of newly discovered or newly developed evidence. LDG Timber Enterprises, Inc. v. U.S., Cl.Ct.1985, 8 Cl.Ct. 445. United States ☞ 127(2)

28. ―― Interpretation or construction of contracts, claims or issues reviewable

Government contractor's claims against Office of Personnel Management (OPM) implicated contract by which contractor provided health care services to federal employees and retirees in Texas, pursuant to Federal Employees Health Benefits Act (FEHBA), even though complaint, read literally, sought only to invalidate OPM regulation governing calculation of subscription rates for final year of contract, rather than recovery of reconciliation amount allegedly due under contract, and therefore Court of Federal Claims had exclusive jurisdiction over contractor's action pursuant to Contract Disputes Act (CDA). Texas Health Choice, L.C. v. Office of Personnel Management, C.A.Fed.2005, 400 F.3d 895, rehearing and rehearing en banc denied. Federal Courts ☞ 1139

United States' action against container buyer to recover helicopter transmissions hidden in containers was essentially contract action, and, thus, Contract Disputes Act (CDA) prohibited court from exercising jurisdiction, even though government attempted to present action as tort case alleging conversion and seeking replevin; case involved question of contract interpretation, i.e., did bill of sale and Defense Reutilization and Marketing Officer (DRMO) sales pamphlet allow transfer of ownership of hidden transmissions, it was impossible to ignore terms of contract documents, question could be phrased as whether sale was void for unilateral or mutual mistake of fact, and district court rejected claim for punitive damages. U.S. v. J & E Salvage Co., C.A.4 (N.C.) 1995, 55 F.3d 985. Action ⚖ 27(1); Federal Courts ⚖ 973

Challenge to nonrenewal of medicare provider's contract for provision of services was question of contract interpretation and, pursuant to contract article providing that agreement at issue was subject to this chapter, would more appropriately be before Court of Claims than before federal district court. Group Health Inc. v. Schweiker, S.D.Fla.1982, 549 F.Supp. 135. Federal Courts ⚖ 1141

29. —— Liquidated damages, claims or issues reviewable

Contractor's amended claim against government for unpaid contract earnings was a new claim that had not been the subject of contractor's certified claim, and thus was outside Court of Federal Claims' subject matter jurisdiction under Contract Disputes Act (CDA), although contractor's original complaint sought liquidated damages; request for liquidated damages could not possibly foreshadow contractor's request for unpaid contract earnings. Renda Marine, Inc. v. U.S., Fed.Cl.2005, 65 Fed.Cl. 152, reconsideration denied 71 Fed.Cl. 782, appeal dismissed 208 Fed.Appx. 880, 2006 WL 3497269, order recalled and vacated 2006 WL 3922781. United States ⚖ 73(15)

In suit by public contractor involving dispute over contracting officer's assessment of liquidated damages of $54,000 against contractor, Claims Court did not lack jurisdiction with respect to those claims exceeding $50,000, on grounds that public contractor had not certified claims before contracting officer as required under Contract Disputes Act; contractor could contest before Claims Court the assessment of liquidated damages based on contracting officer's decision that there was delay in completion of contract; however, if contractor intended, in connection with its contest of assessment, to raise any issue of relief to which it might be entitled, such as claim of entitlement to time extensions, such claim would first have to be presented to contracting officer for his decision before claim would be considered by Claims

Court. Elgin Builders, Inc. v. U.S., Cl.Ct. 1986, 10 Cl.Ct. 40. United States ⚖ 73(15)

30. —— Same operative facts, claims or issues reviewable

Federal district court had supplemental jurisdiction over United States' common-law claims of unjust enrichment, payment under mistake of fact, and breach of contract against defense contractor as court had jurisdiction over Federal False Claims Act (FCA) claims under fraud exception to Contract Dispute Act's (CDA) coverage; common-law claims were based upon general allegations of fraud, and both common-law claims and FCA claims arose from single set of operative facts. U.S. v. Rockwell Intern. Corp., N.D.Ga.1992, 795 F.Supp. 1131. Federal Courts ⚖ 15

Court of Federal Claims had subject matter jurisdiction under the Contract Disputes Act (CDA) over contractor's claim for breach of contract based on government's failure to test source of aggregate specified in specifications for road construction contract, as claim arose from same operative facts as those presented to contracting officer (CO); contractor clearly and unequivocally put CO on notice that claim, at least in part, was that it suffered damages because government breached a duty to conduct source testing pursuant to the contract's "Special Contract Requirements." M.A. DeAtley Const., Inc. v. U.S., Fed.Cl.2007, 75 Fed.Cl. 575. United States ⚖ 73(15)

Court of Federal Claims had jurisdiction under the Contract Disputes Act (CDA) to award monetary relief for breach of contract claims asserted in contractor's proposed second amended complaint, where proposed claims contained the very same factual and legal bases as the certified claim previously submitted to the contracting officer. ATK Thiokol, Inc. v. U.S., Fed.Cl.2007, 76 Fed.Cl. 654. United States ⚖ 73(9)

Under the Contract Disputes Act (CDA), a contractor may not present a claim to the Court of Federal Claims that was not first presented to the contracting officer for a final decision; however, a claim presented to the Court is not a new claim if it arises from the same operative facts and seeks the same categories of relief as the original claims. P.R. Contractors, Inc. v. U.S., Fed.Cl.2007, 76 Fed.Cl. 621. United States ⚖ 73(9)

Construction contractor's claim for additional costs it allegedly incurred for replacement of subgrade material under structures as a result of differing site conditions was a new claim which was never certified and presented to contracting officer (CO), and thus Court of Federal Claims lacked jurisdiction over claim under the Contract Disputes Act (CDA); subgrade claim did not arise from same set of operative facts as certified pile length claims, and subgrade replacement claim was not merely a request for additional damages on pile length claims. AAB Joint Venture v. U.S., Fed.Cl.2007, 75 Fed.Cl. 123. United States ⟸ 73(9)

Court of Federal Claims lacked jurisdiction under the Contract Disputes Act (CDA) over claim of lessors that Federal Aviation Administration (FAA) breached the lease by constructing and using air traffic control equipment on property not included in the lease, as claim was a new claim which was not submitted to contracting officer (CO); claim that was submitted to the CO demanded an increase in rent pursuant to "renewal" section of lease agreement, and new claim did not arise from the same set of operative facts. Peterson v. U.S., Fed.Cl.2005, 68 Fed.Cl. 773. United States ⟸ 73(15)

Court of Federal Claims had jurisdiction under the Contract Disputes Act (CDA) over contractor's claim for rent for entire period of government's holdover tenancy, even though contractor's claim submitted to contracting officer (CO) was only for first month of holdover period, as claim for entire period was not a new claim for jurisdictional purposes; holdover rent claim for entire holdover period arose from the same operative facts and the same category of relief as the claim for the first month of the holdover period, and length of holdover tenancy could not have been known by contractor at time he presented claim to CO. Modeer v. U.S., Fed.Cl.2005, 68 Fed.Cl. 131, affirmed 183 Fed.Appx. 975, 2006 WL 1582178. United States ⟸ 73(15)

Claims Court lacked jurisdiction under the Contract Disputes Act over lost profits claim which was not presented to contracting officer, notwithstanding plaintiff's contention that request for lost profits merely constituted an additional quantum of damages that arose from same set of operative facts as compensatory claim; however, claims involved different theories of liability; compensatory damages claim involved proof of circumstances beyond agency's control which rendered contract obsolete or impracticable; lost profits claim involved proof that agency willfully obstructed performance. SMS Data Products Group, Inc. v. U.S., Cl.Ct.1990, 19 Cl.Ct. 612. United States ⟸ 73(9)

Fact that government contractor's claim, under differing site condition clause in contract, as presented to Claims Court in direct access suit, was greater than that presented and certified to contracting officer for decision did not present jurisdictional bar to consideration of the increased claim, inasmuch as contractor did not thereby present new claim, but, rather, factual basis of claim before Court was identical to claim certified to contracting officer, with contractor having merely presented additional evidence pertaining to damages springing from same factual claim. J.F. Shea Co., Inc. v. U.S., Cl.Ct.1983, 4 Cl.Ct. 46. United States ⟸ 73(15)

31. —— Tort claims, claims or issues reviewable

Disguised contract actions may not escape the Contract Disputes Act (CDA); neither contractors nor the government may bring a contract action in federal district court simply by recasting claims in tort language or as some statutory or regulatory violation. Lockheed Martin Corp. v. Defense Contract Audit Agency, D.Md.2005, 397 F.Supp.2d 659. United States ⟸ 73(9)

Two counts of prime contractor's complaint alleging that the United States breached contract by failing to preserve condition of salvage generator while it was stored awaiting shipment and that in derogation of duty to contractor, the United States was negligent in allowing salvage equipment to be pirated and robbed of salvage value by employees were contract claims, and thus, not barred in action brought under this section of Contract Disputes Act of 1978 as being tort claims. Pan Arctic Corp. v. U.S., Cl.Ct.1985, 8 Cl.Ct. 546. Federal Courts ⟸ 1076

32. —— Miscellaneous claims or issues reviewable

Court of Federal Claims had jurisdiction over Contract Disputes Act (CDA) claim of timber contractor that Forest

Service wrongfully suspended timber sales contracts; although contractor may have posed slightly different legal theories for the breach, the contractor gave contracting officer (CO) clear notice of a purported breach of contract based on the prolonged and allegedly unauthorized suspensions, and sought from the CO the same remedy sought from the trial court, namely consequential damages for the alleged breach. Scott Timber Co. v. U.S., C.A.Fed.2003, 333 F.3d 1358, rehearing denied, on remand 64 Fed.Cl. 130. Federal Courts ⊕ 1076

Government contractor's claim for equitable adjustment, which was in essence a request for determination of effect that Department of Labor's (DOL) classification of contractor's employees had on its contract rights, did not arise exclusively out of labor standards provision of contract and, thus, Court of Federal Claims had jurisdiction. Burnside-Ott Aviation Training Center, Inc. v. U.S., C.A.Fed. 1993, 985 F.2d 1574. Federal Courts ⊕ 1076

Winning bidder's postaward substitution of personnel to perform computer facility operation contract was properly reviewable in bid protest action; allegations that winning bidder had misrepresented personnel to be used on contract raised issue of whether full and open competition in bidding and award of contract had been achieved. Planning Research Corp. v. U.S., C.A.Fed.1992, 971 F.2d 736. United States ⊕ 64.60(3.1)

Court of Federal Claims had jurisdiction under the Contract Disputes Act (CDA) over timber purchaser's claim that government's suspension of timber purchase contract for environmental reasons constituted a material breach because such suspension was barred by the Rescissions Act, despite fact that purchaser did not put contracting officer (CO) on notice that the Rescissions Act applied to contract, as actual basis for claim that the suspension was invalid was presented to the CO. Swanson Group, Inc. v. U.S., Fed.Cl.2007, 2007 WL 1031715. United States ⊕ 73(15)

Failure of contractor to plead with specificity a description of the contract or contracts upon which its claim was founded did not preclude jurisdiction in the Court of Federal Claims over its action brought under the Contract Disputes Act (CDA) challenging final decision of

contracting officer, because claim was not based on contract, but instead on agency action that related to its contracts. Information Systems & Networks Corp. v. U.S., Fed.Cl.2005, 64 Fed.Cl. 599, appeal dismissed 157 Fed.Appx. 264, 2005 WL 3276164. Federal Courts ⊕ 1111

Court of Federal Claims had jurisdiction under the Contract Disputes Act (CDA) to consider whether termination for default was justified by contractor's alleged violations of the Davis-Bacon and Buy American Acts, notwithstanding that the violations were not discovered until after termination, and were not considered in the contracting officer's final decision. Glazer Const. Co., Inc. v. U.S., Fed.Cl.2002, 52 Fed.Cl. 513. United States ⊕ 73(15)

Rather than remanding proceedings to contracting officer for final decision, Court of Federal Claims would exercise its discretion to assume role of contracting officer and consider claim for termination-for-convenience costs that public contractors had filed with contracting officer after first filing complaint requesting conversion of termination for default to termination for convenience, where that was most efficient and fair result, in that parties were familiar with claims and issues related to damages, some issues had already been litigated, and parties had stipulated damages. McDonnell Douglas Corp. v. U.S., Fed.Cl.1997, 37 Fed.Cl. 285, reconsideration denied 1997 WL 842408. Federal Courts ⊕ 1118

Contractor's claims for certain sums alleged to have been improperly withheld from contractor by government under federal road construction contract were validly before the Claims Court, where claims had been denied by operation of law in that government official, who purported to deny contractor's request for time extension and to comply with fact-finding and other requirements of default clause, was not then the "contracting officer." Timberland Paving & Const. Co. v. U.S., Cl.Ct.1985, 8 Cl.Ct. 653. Highways ⊕ 113(1)

Court of Federal Claims had jurisdiction to review government contracting officer's decision to deny plumbing repairs, real estate taxes, and anticipated restoration costs of postal facility, even though government contractor had already elected to pursue rent increase claim with Board of Contract Appeals (Board), where government contractor's claim for plumbing repairs, real estate taxes, and anticipated restoration costs had not been before the Board during prior appeal. Spodek v. U.S., C.A.Fed.2002, 52 Fed. Appx. 497, 2002 WL 31724959, Unreported. Federal Courts ⟳ 1076

33. —— Miscellaneous claims or issues not reviewable

Court of Federal Claims did not have jurisdiction under Contract Disputes Act (CDA) over contractual claim by electric utilities that government overcharged electric utilities for enriched uranium; even though transaction between utilities and government arguably had characteristics of sale of product, relationship between parties was that government provided service of enriching uranium for utilities. Florida Power & Light Co. v. U.S., C.A.Fed.2002, 307 F.3d 1364, on remand 56 Fed.Cl. 555. Federal Courts ⟳ 1076

Claims Court lacks jurisdiction over suit challenging termination of contract for default, without any associated claim for money damages. Overall Roofing & Const. Inc. v. U.S., C.A.Fed.1991, 929 F.2d 687. Federal Courts ⟳ 1076

Court of Appeals would not consider contractor's argument that no certification that claim was made in good faith was required for claim of less than $50,000, as that was argument not raised during Armed Services Board of Contract Appeals hearings or to Court of Appeals in either its brief or at oral argument. U.S. v. Grumman Aerospace Corp., C.A.Fed.1991, 927 F.2d 575, certiorari denied 112 S.Ct. 330, 502 U.S. 919, 116 L.Ed.2d 270. United States ⟳ 73(15)

Court of Federal Claims lacked subject matter jurisdiction under the Contract Disputes Act (CDA) over contractor's claim that specifications of road construction contract were defective due to government's failure to permit gradation tolerances; there was no indication that contractor's claim presented to contracting officer (CO) asserted that the specifications were deficient because they did not allow for gradation tolerances, as contractor merely alleged that the source for the aggregate proved to be defective. M.A. DeAtley Const., Inc. v. U.S., Fed.Cl. 2007, 75 Fed.Cl. 575. United States ⟳ 73(9)

Court of Federal Claims lacked jurisdiction under the Contract Disputes Act (CDA) over appeal of purchase order vendor (POV) from decision of contracting officer (CO) denying her claim challenging termination of blanket purchase agreement (BPA), as BPA was not a contract; moreover, there was no implied-in-fact contract obligating government to continuing issuing purchase orders to vendor. Zhengxing v. U.S., Fed.Cl.2006, 71 Fed.Cl. 732, affirmed 204 Fed.Appx. 885, 2006 WL 3228605, rehearing denied. United States ⟳ 73(15)

Bid protest jurisdiction of the Court of Federal Claims under the Contract Disputes Act (CDA) does not extend to bid protests of individual task orders issued under a multiple award indefinite delivery-indefinite quantity (IDIQ) contract. A & D Fire Protection, Inc. v. U.S., Fed. Cl.2006, 72 Fed.Cl. 126. United States ⟳ 64.60(1)

Court of Federal Claims lacked jurisdiction under the Contract Disputes Act (CDA) to consider dredging contractor's claim that government breached its implied duty to cooperate by not affording guidance to contractor concerning realignment of levee, where claim was not based on the same set of operative facts as levee realignment claim presented to contracting officer (CO) which was based on differing site condition, and claim was not based on the same legal theory as claim before CO which sought equitable adjustment for the differing site condition. Renda Marine, Inc. v. U.S., Fed.Cl. 2006, 71 Fed.Cl. 378. United States ⟳ 73(15)

Marine dredging contractor was jurisdictionally barred under the Contract Disputes Act (CDA) from asserting claim for increased costs caused by disruption of its disposal operations due to electric utility's construction of new transmission tower in the vicinity of site used by contractor for disposal of dredged material, based on theory that the government had superior knowledge that a transmission tower would be constructed at the site, where contractor did not present superior knowledge claim to contracting officer in request for equitable adjustment or in its certified claim. Renda Marine, Inc. v. U.S., Fed.Cl.2005, 66 Fed.Cl. 639. United States ⟳ 73(9)

Certified breach of warranty claim presented to the contracting officer by buyer of eighteen sheep at government auction related only to one ram, and not to the other sheep, and thus Court of Federal Claims lacked subject matter jurisdiction under the Contract Disputes Act (CDA) to consider buyer's claims relating to the other seventeen sheep. Dodson Livestock Co. v. U.S., Fed.Cl.1998, 42 Fed.Cl. 455. United States ⊕ 73(15)

Correction of effects of oligopoly as market concept is not program within scope of contract claims to be litigated under Contract Disputes Act (CDA). Smith v. U.S., Fed.Cl.1995, 34 Fed.Cl. 313, appeal dismissed 91 F.3d 165. United States ⊕ 73(9)

34. Specific contracts

Lease to ownership price of Navy contract was not fixed, and thus contractor was not entitled to compensation on fixed price basis; contract and request for proposal (RFP) made clear that estimated quantities of equipment, upon which lease to ownership (LTO) price was based, were subject to change. England v. Contel Advanced Systems, Inc., C.A.Fed.2004, 384 F.3d 1372. United States ⊕ 70(15.1)

Clause in timber sales contracts providing authority to cancel or modify contracts when required to protect threatened or endangered species did not grant the Forest Service authority to unilaterally suspend operations under the contracts upon the threatened species listing of the marbled murrelet, a tiny bird indigenous to the forest areas covered by the contracts; the clause on its face did not contain the word "suspension" or any reference to suspension authority. Scott Timber Co. v. U.S., C.A.Fed.2003, 333 F.3d 1358, rehearing denied, on remand 64 Fed.Cl. 130. Woods And Forests ⊕ 8

Where Defense Logistics Agency (DLA) was aware several months before award of requirements contract that purchased quantity would be only about 10% of that estimated in request for proposals (RFP), DLA had duty to inform successful bidder of that fact. Rumsfeld v. Applied Companies, Inc., C.A.Fed.2003, 325 F.3d 1328, certiorari denied 124 S.Ct. 462, 540 U.S. 981, 157 L.Ed.2d 370, on remand 2004 WL 1616167. United States ⊕ 70(30)

Government contract with telecommunications provider giving the government discounts in exchange for a service real-location resulting in a potential target revenue share of 76% of government business was not breached by the government's withholding of information about the possible difficulties in transferring the Treasury Department to that provider's network where, inter alia, the provider was partly responsible for failing to achieve a 76% revenue share. AT&T Communications, Inc. v. Perry, C.A.Fed. 2002, 296 F.3d 1307. United States ⊕ 73(22)

Where Court of Federal Claims previously ruled that default termination was proper in dismissing contractor's breach of contract claim, law of the case precluded claims that government acted in bad faith, or arbitrarily and capriciously, in issuing default termination. C.D. Hayes, Inc. v. U.S., Fed.Cl.2006, 74 Fed. Cl. 699. Courts ⊕ 99(3)

Evidence based on computerized enrollment system of health maintenance organization (HMO) established that government breached contracts to provide health insurance benefits under the Federal Employees Health Benefits (FEHB) Program by failing to pay $9,128,180 in premiums due for contract years 1990 through 1996; evidence showed that number of enrollees for whom benefits were provided by the HMO during the period exceeded the number for which HMO received payment during that period. Health Ins. Plan of Greater New York v. U.S., Fed.Cl.2004, 62 Fed.Cl. 33. United States ⊕ 74(11)

Soil boring information provided by Army Corps of Engineers for contract to construct levee on river floodplain was generally adequate to warn reasonably prudent contractor of poor subsurface conditions and possibility of high water tables and soft soils and, thus, did not support contractor's claims under Contract Disputes Act (CDA) for excess costs allegedly incurred due to reliance on misleading borings; although borings data provided by Corps was obviously limited and dated, they suggested presence of soft, wet clays that would provide poor support for contractor's equipment, contract contained notice that contractor was responsible for verification of site conditions, and contractor independently investigated conditions only with visual and manual inspections using hand-held auger and stick. Hardwick Bros. Co., II

v. U.S., Fed.Cl.1996, 36 Fed.Cl. 347. Levees And Flood Control ⬥ 16

Government, which did not permit contractor to take acceptance test called for in the initial contract but instead defaulted contractor for not complying with terms of test which were changed after the contract was entered into, did not offer the contractor the opportunity to perform before terminating the contract for default. SMS Data Products Group, Inc. v. U.S., Cl.Ct.1989, 17 Cl.Ct. 1. United States ⬥ 73(1)

Claims court had jurisdiction to resolve accounting dispute which arose during performance of contract between Army Corps of Engineers and contractor from Saudi Arabia; contract agreement removing contractor's option to choose claims court for resolution of claim finally decided by contracting officer under Contract Disputes Act could not deprive claims court of jurisdiction over timely filed suit. OSHCO-PAE-SOMC v. U.S., Cl.Ct.1989, 16 Cl.Ct. 614. Contracts ⬥ 127(1)

35. Consolidation or transfer

Interests of justice warranted district court's transfer to Armed Services Board of Contract Appeals of contractor's action challenging contractor officer's denial of subcontractor's claim; claims already pending before Board arose out of same contract as those pending in contractor's action, and there would be substantial duplication of effort if claim was subsequently tried in district court. Southwest Marine, Inc. v. U.S., N.D.Cal.1988, 680 F.Supp. 1400, reconsideration denied 680 F.Supp. 327. Federal Courts ⬥ 1154

Convenience of the parties and interest of justice did not support transfer of government contractor's claims concerning reprocurement costs assessed against it to the Armed Services Board of Contract Appeals (ASBCA) where contractor's appeals of default terminations were pending, where the ASBCA had made extensive progress in the appeals, and contractor's ability to obtain an efficient resolution of its challenges to the default terminations could be hampered by transferring its damages claims to the ASBCA. American Renovation and Const. Co. v. U.S., Fed.Cl.2007, 77 Fed. Cl. 97. United States ⬥ 73(15)

Consolidation of military contractor's overhead claim before the Armed Services Board of Contract Appeals (ASBCA)

with contractor's breach of contract suit in the Court of Federal Claims was not appropriate under consolidation provision of the Contract Disputes Act (CDA), where the two claims did not overlap because they were not seeking the same costs, and the issues did not appear to be identical, such that a preclusive effect would stem from first forum to rule. Northrop Grumman Corp. v. U.S., Fed. Cl.2006, 70 Fed.Cl. 230. United States ⬥ 73(15)

Action pending in the Department of Energy (DOE) Board of Contract Appeals in which contractor sought to recover unreimbursed costs of defending qui tam action in which government intervened and government asserted claim to recoup previously paid defense costs would not be transferred to the Court of Federal Claims and consolidated with contractor's action seeking recovery of award fees; although issues of reimbursability of defense costs and proper determination of award fees arose from same contract, they were otherwise unrelated to one another and focused on interpretation of different portions of the contractual language. Rockwell Automation, Inc. v. U.S., Fed.Cl.2006, 70 Fed.Cl. 114. Federal Courts ⬥ 1158

Under section of the Contract Disputes Act (CDA) authorizing the Court of Federal Claims to order transfer of suit filed with agency board of contract appeals to the Court of Federal Claims for consolidation with pending suit "if two or more two or more suits arising from one contract are filed in the United States Claims Court and one or more agency boards," Court had jurisdiction to transfer actions filed by contractor with the General Services Board of Contracting Appeals (GSBCA) concerning Phase I of construction contract and consolidate them with consolidated case pending in the Court which concerned Phase II of construction contract, where the government filed counterclaims regarding Phase I in the Court actions. Morse Diesel Intern., Inc. v. U.S., Fed.Cl. 2006, 69 Fed.Cl. 558. Federal Courts ⬥ 1101

Transfer of contractor's suit in the General Services Administration Board of Contract Appeals (GSBCA) to the Court of Federal Claims where other suits of contractor were pending was appropriate, considering that claims before the GSBCA and the Court were related, contractor first filed its claims in the Court, significant progress in the adjudication of the claims had been made in the Court, concurrent resolution would result in an inefficient allocation of resources, separate forums could reach inconsistent results, and the transfer served the interest of justice. Morse Diesel Intern., Inc. v. U.S., Fed.Cl.2005, 66 Fed.Cl. 801, petition denied 163 Fed.Appx. 878, 2006 WL 171763. Federal Courts ⊂⊃ 1101

Litigation of the same timber purchase contract before the Court of Federal Claims and the Agricultural Board of Contract Appeals (AGBCA) was permissible, and consolidation was not warranted, where each forum was hearing an independent controversy; AGBCA appeal concerned whether purchaser was liable to the government for a default, and court case involved whether suspension of the contract to comply with the Endangered Species Act was wrongful. Precision Pine & Timber, Inc. v. U.S., Fed.Cl. 1999, 45 Fed.Cl. 134. Federal Courts ⊂⊃ 1101

Contractor's complaint challenging contracting officer's rejection of claim for delay damages would be transferred to Armed Services Board of Contract Appeals for the interests of justice and convenience of parties and witnesses where two claims on same contract were pending before Board. Giuliani Contracting Co. Inc. v. U.S., Cl.Ct.1990, 21 Cl.Ct. 81. Federal Courts ⊂⊃ 1158

Dispute between the government and contractor over contract for repair of warehouse roof at air force base would be transferred from Claims Court to Armed Services Board of Contract Appeals, where factual issues raised by the complaint in the Claims Court were substantially the same as those pending before the Board, or involved substantially related issues, contractor had originally elected to bring the issues before the Board, and considerable efforts had already been expended by the Board in furthering resolution of the claims. Multi-Roof Systems Co., Inc. v. U.S., Cl.Ct. 1984, 5 Cl.Ct. 245. Federal Courts ⊂⊃ 1154

In case wherein action before the Claims Court and appeals pending before the Agriculture Board of Contract Appeals involved the same timber sale contracts, the Court action was transferred to the Board, in the interests of justice, and

for the convenience of parties. Guy Roberts Lumber Co. v. U.S., Cl.Ct.1984, 5 Cl.Ct. 42. Federal Courts ⊂⊃ 1154

Claims Court is to weigh positions of both parties, in deciding which forum is appropriate for consolidation of two or more suits arising from contract filed in Claims Court and with one or more agency boards. E.D.S. Federal Corp. v. U.S., Cl.Ct.1983, 2 Cl.Ct. 735. Federal Courts ⊂⊃ 1101

Granting of motion under subsec. (d) of this section to transfer a case is discretionary with Claims Court, and court may properly order case transferred sua sponte. Space Age Engineering, Inc. v. U.S., Cl.Ct.1983, 2 Cl.Ct. 164. United States ⊂⊃ 73(15)

36. Dismissal

Board of contract appeals' dismissal of government contractor's complaint contesting contracting officer's adverse decision as untimely did not preclude contractor's pursuit of claim in the Claims Court under the election doctrine of the Contract Disputes Act as board had not determined whether it had jurisdiction over contractor's appeal and thus proceeding before the Claims Court was not ripe for dismissal. National Neighbors, Inc. v. U.S., C.A.Fed.1988, 839 F.2d 1539. Administrative Law And Procedure ⊂⊃ 663; United States ⊂⊃ 73(15)

Following Court of Federal Claims' dismissal of actions brought by federal timber buyer pursuant to Contract Disputes Act (CDA), decisions of contracting officers holding buyer liable for breach of timber sale contract became final and could be enforced, despite claim that they were vacated by filing of actions in Court of Federal Claims. U.S. v. Hampton Tree Farms, Inc., D.Or.1997, 971 F.Supp. 1354. United States ⊂⊃ 75(2)

Where action was one over which federal district court had no subject-matter jurisdiction and where, in requesting direct transfer of case to the claims court, plaintiff sought to bypass administrative procedures provided by this chapter, defense motion to dismiss would be granted, without prejudice. Great Lakes Educational Consultants v. Federal Emergency Management Agency, a Div. of Federal Government, W.D.Mich.1984, 582 F.Supp. 193. Federal Civil Procedure ⊂⊃ 1723.1; Federal Civil Procedure ⊂⊃ 1742(2)

Contractor would be required to show cause why Claims Court should not dismiss for lack of subject matter jurisdiction its complaint seeking declaratory judgment that government's default terminations of two contracts be declared improper and be converted into terminations for convenience and seeking damages for government's alleged termination for convenience. Corporate Air v. U.S., Cl.Ct.1992, 26 Cl.Ct. 204. Federal Courts ☞ 1078; Federal Courts ☞ 1101

Proper course of action for contractor whose direct access contract action under Contract Disputes Act has been dismissed for lack of jurisdiction is to properly certify claim, resubmit certified claim to contracting officer, and, if there is then an adverse decision by contracting officer, appeal either to board of contract appeals, or directly to Claims Court. Fredenburg v. U.S., Cl.Ct.1986, 10 Cl.Ct. 216. United States ☞ 73(15)

37. Evidence

In determining whether costs incurred by Navy contractor in preparing request for equitable adjustment (REA) which did not qualify as claim under Contract Disputes Act (CDA) were recoverable contract administration costs, rather than costs incurred in connection with prosecution of CDA claim against government, Armed Services Board of Contract Appeals could consider the course of negotiations between the parties to determine the objective purpose behind contractor's submission of REA. Johnson v. Advanced Engineering & Planning Corp., Inc., E.D.Va.2003, 292 F.Supp.2d 846. United States ☞ 74(12.1)

Document setting forth contractor's equitable adjustment claim was admissible in action under the Contract Disputes Act (CDA) to show it was duly submitted to the contracting officer (CO) and acted upon, as required for Court of Federal Claims to have a jurisdiction under the CDA. PR Contractors, Inc. v. U.S., Fed. Cl.2006, 69 Fed.Cl. 468. United States ☞ 74(10)

38. Parties

This section did not change law relative to third-party practice in Court of Claims, which was adopted by Claims Court. Myrtle Beach Pipeline Co. v. U.S., Cl.Ct. 1984, 6 Cl.Ct. 363. Federal Courts ☞ 1110

39. Persons entitled to maintain action

Provision of takeover agreement between government and defaulting contractor's surety that entitled surety to exercise such rights as were afforded by Contract Disputes Act merely recognized that surety retained whatever rights it otherwise had under Act, and did not establish jurisdiction of Armed Services Board of Contract Appeals over claims asserted by surety based on events preceding takeover agreement, as to which, under Act, surety had no right to maintain claim before Board. United Pacific Ins. Co. v. Roche, C.A.Fed.2004, 380 F.3d 1352, rehearing denied. United States ☞ 73(15)

Landlord who assigned all of his right, title, and interest in tenant leases, including lease with General Services Administration (GSA), could not be deemed to have transferred his claim to back rent and, therefore, landlord possessed standing to pursue back rent claim under Contract Disputes Act. Ginsberg v. Austin, C.A.Fed.1992, 968 F.2d 1198, on remand. United States ☞ 71

Sureties of government contractor which had not performed their obligations under their performance bonds could not maintain an action in the Court of Federal Claims under the Contract Disputes Act (CDA) contesting default terminations and contracting officer's award of damages to government, as privity of contract was lacking; moreover, sureties were not equitably subrogated to claims of contractor until they took over performance of the contracts and financed their completion. American Renovation and Const. Co. v. U.S., Fed.Cl.2007, 77 Fed.Cl. 97. Federal Courts ☞ 1110

Bid protestor lacked standing to file bid protest, where its bid was nonresponsive because it submitted no bid bond with its proposal, or, in the alternative, because it faxed a bid bond in contravention of terms of solicitation. A & D Fire Protection, Inc. v. U.S., Fed.Cl.2006, 72 Fed.Cl. 126. United States ☞ 64.60(2)

Surety which issued performance and payment bonds for government contractor lacked standing under the Contract Disputes Act (CDA) to appeal final decision of contracting officer (CO) finding contractor in default, where surety was not a party to the contract and did not execute a takeover agreement with the government. Nova Cas. Co. v. U.S., Fed.

Cl.2006, 69 Fed.Cl. 284. United States ⌐ 73(15)

Only a performance bond surety that enters into a takeover agreement with the government can bring an action in the Court of Federal Claims under the Contract Disputes Act (CDA). Westchester Fire Ins. Co. v. U.S., Fed.Cl.2002, 52 Fed. Cl. 567. United States ⌐ 74.1

Certificate of revivor, which reinstated defense contractor's corporate powers, did not reinstate contractor's capacity to bring action against United States under Contract Disputes Act; contractor's corporate powers were suspended when the contract was entered into, claim against United States was filed, and 12–month statute of limitations under Act expired. Computer Products Intern., Inc. v. U.S., Cl.Ct.1992, 26 Cl.Ct. 518. Corporations ⌐ 630(1)

Claims Court had no jurisdiction if plaintiff was subcontractor of government contract. Ward-Schmid Co., Inc. v. U.S., Cl.Ct.1989, 18 Cl.Ct. 572. Federal Courts ⌐ 1076

Subcontractor was not in privity with government, and thus could not bring direct action against it contesting termination by prime contractor; government was not party to subcontract, its monitoring of contract performance did not evidence intent to waive sovereign immunity, and there was no evidence prime contractor was acting as government's purchasing agent. Lockheed Martin Corp. v. U.S., C.A.Fed.2002, 48 Fed. Appx. 752, 2002 WL 31164088, Unreported. United States ⌐ 74.2

40. Burden of proof

In action for review of contracting officer's decision, contracting officer's findings of fact are not binding upon the parties and are not entitled to any deference; rather, contractor has burden to prove fundamental facts of liability and damages de novo. Wilner v. U.S., C.A.Fed.1994, 24 F.3d 1397. United States ⌐ 73(15)

41. Counterclaims

Claims Court had jurisdiction over Commodity Credit Corporation's (CCC) counterclaims against grain storage company, even if company never received written claim for definite amount corresponding to any of CCC's counterclaims, where contracting officer's final decision gave company notice that CCC would seek compensation for grain deterioration through counterclaims. HNV Cent. River Front Corp. v. U.S., Cl.Ct.1992, 25 Cl.Ct. 606. Federal Courts ⌐ 1102

42. Jury trial

Timber contractors' acceptance of contract which provided for appeal of contracting officer's decision as provided for in Contract Disputes Act, which was changed by Federal Courts Improvement Act (FCIA) to provide jurisdiction over direct access suits in Article I court rather than Article III court, was a knowing and voluntary waiver of right to jury trial, even though FCIA was not in effect at time contracts were entered into. Seaboard Lumber Co. v. U.S., C.A.Fed.1990, 903 F.2d 1560, rehearing denied, certiorari denied 111 S.Ct. 1308, 499 U.S. 919, 113 L.Ed.2d 243. Jury ⌐ 28(5)

Though contractor could maintain suit against Tennessee Valley Authority under Contract Disputes Act, it had no right to jury trial in that action; Congress had unequivocally waived government's sovereign immunity as applied to TVA, but Tennessee Valley Authority Act and Contract Disputes Act were silent as to availability of jury trials. Jones-Hailey v. Corporation of Tennessee Valley Authority, E.D.Tenn.1987, 660 F.Supp. 551. Jury ⌐ 14(1)

Though Congress did not specifically provide for jury trial under this chapter, Congress did not intend to deny plaintiff his traditional right to jury trial in contract cases in district court where defending party is independent governmental agency such as Tennessee Valley Authority and where from time of such agency's creation, Congress has expressly conferred on it power to sue and be sued without any limitation. Algernon Blair Indus. Contractors, Inc. v. Tennessee Valley Authority, M.D.Ala.1982, 552 F.Supp. 972. Jury ⌐ 12(1.2)

43. Declaratory judgment

Government contractor stated claim for declaratory judgment that travel management contracts with the Department of the Army required that it be the exclusive provider of traditional commercial travel services to fifty-four Military Entrance Processing Stations (MEPS) while the contracts were in effect; facts as alleged concerning an Army solicitation for MEPS travel services evidenced a live dispute involving an anticipatory breach of contract by the Army. CW Government Travel, Inc. v. U.S., Fed.Cl.2004, 63 Fed.Cl. 369.   Declaratory Judgment ⊕ 203

Court of Federal Claims had jurisdiction under the Contract Disputes Act (CDA) and the Tucker Act over government contractor's claim for declaratory judgment contesting final decision of contracting officer (CO) to assert an offset claim against contractor based upon alleged savings guarantee in contract, and CO's post-suit action of releasing offset funds did not elide the jurisdiction that was established when complaint was filed, especially when release was accompanied by an express reservation of the government's position regarding interpretation of the contract. Tiger Natural Gas, Inc. v. U.S., Fed.Cl.2004, 61 Fed.Cl. 287. Federal Courts ⊕ 1078

Claims court lacked jurisdiction over claim brought by government contractor, under Contract Disputes Act, seeking only a declaration that it was not obligated under warranty clause of its contract with Government to repaint jet fuel storage tanks at air force base, but seeking no money judgment in view of the fact that claims court did not have jurisdiction to render declaratory relief. Alan J. Haynes Const. Systems, Inc. v. U.S., Cl.Ct.1986, 10 Cl.Ct. 526.   Federal Courts ⊕ 1078

44. Summary judgment

Genuine issues of material fact arising from contract ambiguities precluded summary judgment on government contractor's suit seeking declaratory judgment that travel management contracts with the Department of the Army required that it be the exclusive provider of traditional commercial travel services to fifty-four Military Entrance Processing Stations (MEPS) as long as the contracts were in effect. CW Government Travel, Inc. v. U.S., Fed.Cl.2004, 63 Fed.Cl. 369. Federal Courts ⊕ 1120

45. District court jurisdiction—Generally

Contract Disputes Act deprived a district court of jurisdiction to enforce against a union of government employees a settlement agreement concerning various claims on a contingency reserve fund which the Office of Personnel Management (OPM) was maintaining as part of its oversight of a union-sponsored and

insurer-underwritten health insurance plan, where the effect of enforcing the settlement was to extinguish the union's claim on the fund; and moreover, jurisdiction may also have been lacking over the other claims. Mutual of Omaha Ins. Co. v. National Ass'n of Government Employees, Inc., C.A.D.C.1998, 145 F.3d 389, 330 U.S.App.D.C. 262, rehearing denied.   Federal Courts ⊕ 976

Federal district court had no subject-matter jurisdiction over contractor's claim that Army improperly terminated its contract for convenience.   Mark Dunning Industries, Inc. v. Cheney, C.A.11 (Ala.) 1991, 934 F.2d 266.   United States ⊕ 64.60(1)

District court exceeded its jurisdiction by referring, on primary jurisdiction grounds, questions to Armed Services Board of Contract Appeals relating to interpretation of contract upon which criminal charges against defense contractor and several of its officers hinged and by halting criminal proceedings pending action by the ASBCA; the ASBCA's statutory authority was limited to adjudicating contract disputes, and thus, the doctrine of primary jurisdiction did not apply. U.S. v. General Dynamics Corp., C.A.9 (Cal.) 1987, 828 F.2d 1356.   Administrative Law And Procedure ⊕ 228.1; United States ⊕ 40

Federal district courts do not have jurisdiction to hear government contract claims which are subject to Contract Disputes Act (CDA).   U.S. v. Rockwell Intern. Corp., N.D.Ga.1992, 795 F.Supp. 1131.   Federal Courts ⊕ 976

Where contractor received notice of default and his rights under Contract Disputes Act to seek review of that decision, contractor was required by law to pursue any defenses or challenges to contracting officer's final decision, including his mental capacity during contract period, under appellate procedures contained in Act, and therefore, district court lacked jurisdiction to consider challenges asserted by contractor in defense to Government's action seeking excess procurement costs of $16,380 incurred as result of contractor's default under his contract to construct and lease post office building. U.S. v. Dabbs, S.D.Miss.1985, 608 F.Supp. 507.

District Court lacked subject-matter jurisdiction over contract dispute between developer and manufacturer of computer software and the Department of Housing and Urban Development; rather, the claims court had exclusive jurisdiction under this chapter. Management Science America, Inc. v. Pierce, N.D.Ga. 1984, 598 F.Supp. 223, affirmed 778 F.2d 792. Federal Courts ⟋ 1139

46. —— Injunctive or declaratory relief, district court jurisdiction

District court did not have subject matter jurisdiction over a contractor's complaint challenging Government's decision to terminate a contract to supply air compressors and to resolicit bids for the contract; although complaint sought only declaratory and injunctive relief and did not specifically allege breach of contract, the essential rights at stake were contractual and were within the unique expertise of the claims court. Ingersoll-Rand Co. v. U.S., C.A.D.C.1985, 780 F.2d 74, 250 U.S.App.D.C. 412. Federal Courts ⟋ 1139

Government contractor's petition for preliminary injunction to prevent Navy from requiring performance or declaring default until rescission claim was finally adjudicated was inherently contractual and was outside district court's jurisdiction, even though contractor claimed that action was founded upon statutory and common-law right to bring contract action in claims court unimpaired by Navy's out-of-court efforts to compel performance, and even though claims court was unable to grant equitable relief. Manshul Const. Corp. v. U.S., E.D.N.Y. 1988, 687 F.Supp. 60. Federal Courts ⟋ 976

Injunctive relief was available to party whose contract was arbitrarily and capriciously terminated by the Government, given that damages remedy would compensate party only for small percentage of its anticipated profit and would fail to account for increase in party's knowledge and expertise in state of the art vibration transmission and abatement, had party been allowed to complete the contract, and increase in party's prestige in scientific and business community. Vibra-Tech Engineers, Inc. v. U.S., D.C.Colo.1983, 567 F.Supp. 484. United States ⟋ 74(7)

47. —— Tennessee Valley Authority, district court jurisdiction

District court lacked jurisdiction over contractor's claim for compensation for extended overhead costs associated with

60–day delay resulting from field erection coordination problems, as that claim was not properly certified to contracting officer. Stellar Mfg. Co. v. Tennessee Valley Authority, E.D.Pa.1989, 707 F.Supp. 782, affirmed 891 F.2d 283. United States ⟋ 73(9)

48. Bankruptcy court jurisdiction

In matters dealing with government contract disputes under Contract Disputes Act, bankruptcy court should yield to jurisdiction of the Board of Federal Claims Court unless government seeks bankruptcy court's jurisdiction or waives any right to object to bankruptcy court's jurisdiction. Matter of American Ship Bldg. Co., Inc., Bkrtcy.M.D.Fla.1994, 164 B.R. 358. Bankruptcy ⟋ 2061

Bankruptcy court had jurisdiction over proceeding to determine whether escrow fund, which was established under contract between debtor and the United States Department of Energy (DOE) for the acquisition of unclassified and classified gas centrifuge equipment, was estate property; jurisdiction over the proceeding did not rest solely in the United States Claims Court. In re All Chemical Isotope Enrichment, Inc., Bkrtcy.E.D.Tenn.1991, 127 B.R. 829. Bankruptcy ⟋ 2061

49. Estoppel

Finding in prior False Claims Act (FCA) qui tam action against air tanker contractor with the Forest Service, in which government intervened as plaintiff, that district court had authority under All Writs Act to stay running of limitations period for challenging final decision of contracting officer (CO) that aircraft exchange agreement between contractor and Forest Service was illegal under Contract Dispute Act (CDA) precluded relitigation, under doctrine of collateral estoppel, of issue of district court's authority, in contractor's subsequent action against government challenging CO's decision under CDA; authority issue was actually litigated, and district court's determination was necessary to outcome of prior action. International Air Response v. U.S., C.A.Fed.2003, 324 F.3d 1376. Judgment ⟋ 720; Judgment ⟋ 725(6); Judgment ⟋ 744

Government contractor was not equitably estopped from asserting claims for equitable adjustment after default termination, on ground that agency detrimentally relied on contractor's representation in letter that it was abandoning the contract; agency's reliance was not reasonable, as contractor repeatedly served notice in its correspondence with agency that it reserved its rights under the contract and noted that it might take future action. Roxco, Ltd. v. U.S., Fed.Cl.2004, 60 Fed.Cl. 39. Estoppel ⚖ 87

50. Exhaustion of remedies

Contract Disputes Act's (CDA) administrative exhaustion provision required that government contractor prior to asserting breach of contract claim against government submit requests for amounts in dispute to contracting officer for his decision; mere submission of invoices, without showing that invoices were in dispute at time of submission, was insufficient. U.S. v. Intrados/International Management Group, D.D.C.2003, 277 F.Supp.2d 55. United States ⚖ 73(9)

Claim of health maintenance organization (HMO) which provided health insurance benefits under the Federal Employees Health Benefits (FEHB) Program that the government was required to pay a portion of unpaid premiums into contingency reserve was presented to the contracting officer (CO) when HMO presented claims for unpaid premiums, as required for exhaustion under the Contract Disputes Act (CDA); while there was no specific reference to contingency reserve in the claims, government was on notice that duty to pay into contingency reserve would attach if it were found to have underpaid premiums. Health Ins. Plan of Greater New York v. U.S., Fed.Cl. 2004, 62 Fed.Cl. 33. United States ⚖ 73(15)

Until a final decision has been rendered by contracting officer, there has been no exhaustion of administrative remedies as required by direct access to jurisdictional requirements of Contract Disputes Act. Rider v. U.S., Cl.Ct.1985, 7 Cl.Ct. 770, affirmed 790 F.2d 91. See, also, Newport News Shipbuilding and Dry Dock Co. v. U.S., Ct.Cl.1985, 7 Cl.Ct. 549. United States ⚖ 73(15)

51. Remand

Remand to Armed Services Board of Contract Appeals for hearing to determine amount of any equitable adjustment to which contractor was entitled was warranted when, on appeal, it was determined contrary to Board's findings that contractor was misled by defect in speci-

fication for maintenance contract in calculating its bid for policing work, and that such defect was latent, and thus that contractor was eligible for equitable adjustment. E.L. Hamm & Associates, Inc. v. England, C.A.Fed.2004, 379 F.3d 1334. United States ⚖ 73(15)

Court of Appeals would remand, to General Services Administration Board of Contract Appeals, appeal from Board's refusal to award contractor expert consultant fees and employee salaries incurred in filing and successfully pursuing procurement protest, for determination as to what costs should be recovered, as Congress had delegated discretion to Board as to determination of such cost recovery. Sterling Federal Systems, Inc. v. Goldin, C.A.Fed.1994, 16 F.3d 1177, on remand 1995 WL 113358. United States ⚖ 64.60(5.1)

Findings of fact by Department of Labor Board of Contract Appeals were inadequate to determine extent to which contractor was prejudiced by Government's inexcusable delay in pursuing its contract claim and, therefore, remand was necessary for determination of whether Government's claim was barred by laches. S.E.R., Jobs For Progress, Inc. v. U.S., C.A.Fed.1985, 759 F.2d 1. United States ⚖ 73(15)

Case in which contractor was challenging General Services Administration Board of Contract Appeals' denial of its claim for a contract time extension plus impact costs had to be remanded to Board for determination whether government's actions relating to changing of footings to caissons in construction of parking ramp by contractor was cause of delay in completion of project. William F. Klingensmith, Inc. v. U.S., C.A.Fed. 1984, 731 F.2d 805. United States ⚖ 73(15)

Contracting agency's issuance of conflicting contracting officer (CO) decisions tainted by agency's internal discord and interference of agency supervisor who was not a CO violated requirement of Contract Disputes Act (CDA)that contracting officers act independently when adjudicating disputes, and required remand to agency for issuance of proper final decision on contractor's claims. Lavezzo v. U.S., Fed.Cl.2006, 74 Fed.Cl. 502. United States ⚖ 73(9); United States ⚖ 73(15)

General Services Administration's (GSA's) contracting officer would be re-vested by Court of Federal Claims with authority to issue final decision on claim; Court had jurisdiction over case by deemed denial of claim based on absence of timely decision by authorized contracting officer, Court acted pursuant to statute to issue stay to obtain final decision from contracting officer on excusability aspect of claim, and Court did so after proceedings that involved full participation of claimant and Government. United Partition Systems, Inc. v. U.S.,

Fed.Cl.2004, 59 Fed.Cl. 627. United States ⟐ 73(9)

Where contracting officer (CO) based his decision to withdraw request for proposals (RFP) from the small business set aside program on comparison of independent government estimate (IGE) to remaining bidder's price, but there was no supporting documentation or discussion in the record regarding how the IGE was prepared, the Court of Federal Claims had no choice but to remand the matter to the CO for a new IGE. Nutech Laundry & Textile, Inc. v. U.S., Fed.Cl.2003, 56 Fed.Cl. 588. United States ⟐ 64.50

§ 610.   Subpena, discovery, and deposition

A member of an agency board of contract appeals may administer oaths to witnesses, authorize depositions and discovery proceedings, and require by subpena the attendance of witnesses, and production of books and papers, for the taking of testimony or evidence by deposition or in the hearing of an appeal by the agency board. In case of contumacy or refusal to obey a subpena by a person who resides, is found, or transacts business within the jurisdiction of a United States district court, the court, upon application of the agency board through the Attorney General; or upon application by the board of contract appeals of the Tennessee Valley Authority, shall have jurisdiction to issue the person an order requiring him to appear before the agency board or a member thereof, to produce evidence or to give testimony, or both. Any failure of any such person to obey the order of the court may be punished by the court as a contempt thereof.

(Pub.L. 95–563, § 11, Nov. 1, 1978, 92 Stat. 2388.)

HISTORICAL AND STATUTORY NOTES

Revision Notes and Legislative Reports
    1978 Acts. Section 11 effectuates recommendation No. 3 of the Procurement Commission and gives the boards of contract appeals of the agencies power to administer oaths, authorize depositions, and discovery, and issue subpoenas. It further provides a mechanism for enforcing these orders through the courts. It is the intent of this increased authority to improve upon the quality of the board records, and to insure that the tools are available to make complete and accurate

findings, thus minimizing the need for a court to supplement the board record on review. Senate Report No. 95–1118.

Effective and Applicability Provisions
    1978 Acts. Section effective with respect to contracts entered into 120 days after Nov. 1, 1978 and, at the election of the contractor, with respect to any claim pending at such time before the contracting officer or initiated thereafter, see section 16 of Pub.L. 95–563, set out as a note under section 601 of this title.

LAW REVIEW AND JOURNAL COMMENTARIES

Doing business with the government.   Peter C. Mieres (February 1982) 4 L.A.Law. 34.

LIBRARY REFERENCES

American Digest System
United States ⊶73(15).
Key Number System Topic No. 393.

Research References

Forms
Federal Procedural Forms § 34:170, Depositions.
Federal Procedural Forms § 34:190, Effect of Refusal to Obey.

Treatises and Practice Aids
Federal Procedure, Lawyers Edition § 39:1006, Request for Issuance.
West's Federal Administrative Practice § 675, Types of Proceedings.

WESTLAW ELECTRONIC RESEARCH

See Westlaw guide following the Explanation pages of this volume.

§ 611.   Interest

Interest on amounts found due contractors on claims shall be paid to the contractor from the date the contracting officer receives the claim pursuant to section 605(a) of this title from the contractor until payment thereof. The interest provided for in this section shall be paid at the rate established by the Secretary of the Treasury pursuant to Public Law 92–41 (85 Stat. 97) for the Renegotiation Board.

(Pub.L. 95–563, § 12, Nov. 1, 1978, 92 Stat. 2389.)

HISTORICAL AND STATUTORY NOTES

Revision Notes and Legislative Reports
1978 Acts. Section 12 executes recommendation No. 11 of the Procurement Commission and authorizes the payment of interest on claims awarded by administrative and judicial forums. The rights of Government contractors who prevail on claims against the Government are unique since they have been required by language of the contract, for example, the changes article and the disputes article, to perform the work as directed by the Government without stopping to litigate. Thus, Government contractors must perform and then argue about the amount of the equitable adjustment at some later time. Since the contractor has been compelled to perform the work with its own money—in the total absence of contract payments or progress payments—there can be no equitable adjustment to the contractor until the contractor recovers the entire cost of the additional work. The cost of money to finance this additional work while pursuing the administrative remedy, normally called interest,

is a legitimate cost of performing the additional work.

This section provides interest to the contractor upon a favorable decision on his claim from the point in time the cause of action arises or the additional costs are incurred, whichever is later, to the date of payment following either a final decision of the agency board or a court of competent jurisdiction, or a settlement between the contractor and the Government prior to a decision by the agency boards or the courts.

This section does not allow a contractor unlimited discretion on the amount of time when he must notify a contracting officer of a claim subsequent to the contractor's identifying the cause of action or additional costs. Administrative judges in the agency boards and trial judges at the Court of Claims must be very sensitive when fixing a date from which to start interest charges not to allow undue delay in a contractor's notification of a claim to the contracting officer to be of a benefit to the contractor. The contracting officer should know of the claim in a reasonable amount of time after the contractor's identification of such claim so as to give the contracting officer or the agency he represents the opportunity to act so as to limit the dollar exposure in interest.

It is not the intent of this act to provide interest for the period of time after which a decision is made should the appeal of that decision be unsuccessful. For example, a contractor has sued for $100,000 and an agency board or the Court of Claims has awarded him $50,000, but he wishes to appeal that decision trying to obtain the additional $50,000. If he wins his appeal and obtains more than the original $50,000, he would obtain interest on the original $50,000, and the increase above $50,000 through the period of the final decision of the appellate court review. If the appeal is unsuccessful and he is awarded only the original $50,000, interest would only be paid through the date of the original decision and not carry over to the review period. Senate Report No. 95–1118.

References in Text

Provisions of Public Law 92–41, referred to in text, which authorized the Secretary of the Treasury to fix interest rates for the Renegotiation Board, were contained in section 2(a)(3) of Pub.L. 92–41, which was classified to section 1215(b)(2) of the Appendix to Title 50, War and National Defense, and was omitted from the Code. See note under section 1211 of the Appendix to Title 50.

Effective and Applicability Provisions

1978 Acts. Section effective with respect to contracts entered into 120 days after Nov. 1, 1978 and, at the election of the contractor, with respect to any claim pending at such time before the contracting officer or initiated thereafter, see section 16 of Pub.L. 95–563, set out as a note under section 601 of this title.

Accrual of Interest Where Certification is Defective

Pub.L. 102–572, Title IX, § 907(a)(3), Oct. 29, 1992, 106 Stat. 4518, provided that: "If any interest is due under section 12 of the Contract Disputes Act of 1978 [this section] on a claim for which the certification under section 6(c)(1) [section 605(c)(1) of this title] is, on or after the date of the enactment of this Act [Oct. 29, 1992], found to be defective shall be paid from the later of the date on which the contracting officer initially received the claim or the date of the enactment of this Act."

CROSS REFERENCES

Interest penalties, payment of, see 31 USCA § 3902.

LAW REVIEW AND JOURNAL COMMENTARIES

Doing business with the government. Peter C. Mieres (February 1982) 4 L.A.Law. 34.

Government contract cases in the United States Court of Appeals for the Federal Circuit: 1995 in review. Thomas F. Williamson, Stacey L. Valerio and Stephanie P. Gilson, 45 Am.U.L.Rev. 1657 (1996).

LIBRARY REFERENCES

American Digest System
Interest ⬯31.
United States ⬯110.
Key Number System Topic Nos. 219, 393.

Corpus Juris Secundum
CJS United States § 191, Interest.

Research References

ALR Library
4 ALR 2nd 1388, Interest as Element of Damages Recoverable in Action for Breach of Contract for the Sale of a Commodity.

Forms
Federal Procedural Forms § 34:97, Interest.

Federal Procedural Forms § 34:347, Complaint--For Damages--For Government's
  Breach of Contract [28 U.S.C.A. § 1491; 41 U.S.C.A. § 609; United States
  Court of Federal Claims Rule 8].
Nichols Cyclopedia of Legal Forms Annotated § 7:2530, United States Lessee--
  General Clauses.
8 West's Federal Forms § 13223, Government Contract Claims--Claims Under the
  Contract Disputes Act.

Treatises and Practice Aids

Federal Procedure, Lawyers Edition § 39:844, Defectively Certified Claims.
West's Federal Administrative Practice § 822, Subject Matter Jurisdiction--Con-
  tract Claim: Jurisdiction, Limitations, Appeals and Interest.
14 Wright & Miller: Federal Prac. & Proc. § 3654, Jurisdiction Over Actions
  Against the United States.

WESTLAW ELECTRONIC RESEARCH

See Westlaw guide following the Explanation pages of this volume.

Notes of Decisions

Generally 1
Certification of claims 6
Election of remedies 2
Elements of claim 3
Particular claims not requiring payment
  of interest 11
Particular claims requiring payment of
  interest 10
Pending claims 4
Rate of interest 7
Retroactive effect 4
Settlements 8
Specificity 9
Submission of claims 5

_____

1. Generally

Contract Disputes Act allows for interest to be paid in traditional government
contract cases from date contracting officer receives valid claim from contractor
until payment is made. Blaze Const.,
Inc. v. U.S., Fed.Cl.1993, 27 Fed.Cl. 646.
United States ☞ 110

2. Election of remedies

Government contract assignee's decision to proceed by direct action in district
court rather than to appeal administrative decision concerning its right to proceeds due on invoices constituted election
not to proceed under Contract Disputes
Act and precluded award of prejudgment
interest under Act. Sigmon Fuel Co. v.
Tennessee Valley Authority, C.A.6 (Tenn.)
1985, 754 F.2d 162. Election Of Remedies ☞ 7(1); United States ☞ 110

Claims Court did not have jurisdiction
over contractor's interest dispute with
United States after contractor had previ-

ously made binding election under Con-
tract Disputes Act to appeal its underly-
ing equitable adjustment claim to agency
Board of Contract Appeals. Santa Fe,
Inc. v. U.S., Cl.Ct.1987, 13 Cl.Ct. 464.
United States ☞ 73(9)

3. Elements of claim

In order for a contractor to receive
interest under this chapter there must be
an underlying claim for quantum which
is governed by this chapter. Nab-Lord
Associates v. U.S., Ct.Cl.1982, 682 F.2d
940, 230 Ct.Cl. 694. United States ☞
110

4. Pending claims

On effective date of this chapter contractor did not have any claim pending
before contracting officer and, therefore,
underlying claims, with respect to which
contractor attempted to proceed under
this section, themselves failed to come
under this chapter. Nab-Lord Associates
v. U.S., Ct.Cl.1982, 682 F.2d 940, 230
Ct.Cl. 694. United States ☞ 110

Although this section has beneficial effect in providing additional inducement
for settlement of claims short of litigation, that purpose would not be facilitated
by awards of interest on subsequently allowed claims for periods of time prior to
effective date of this chapter; further, denial of such interest harmonizes with
long-established, deeply-imbedded principle that interest is not allowed on monetary claims against federal government
unless Congress or a contract plainly authorizes such addition. Brookfield Const.
Co., Inc. v. U.S., Ct.Cl.1981, 661 F.2d

159, 228 Ct.Cl. 551. United States ☞ 110

This chapter, authorizing awards of interest, was not applicable retroactively to claim pending before Court of Claims on this chapter's effective date. Everett Plywood Corp. v. U.S., Ct.Cl.1981, 651 F.2d 723, 227 Ct.Cl. 415. Interest ☞ 3

Claim which was rejected by final decision of contracting officer on Dec. 23, 1968 was not pending before contracting officer on effective date of this chapter because a judgment in favor of contractor had not as yet been rendered and, hence, was not a basis for an award of interest from time of final decision to date of judgment. Monroe M. Tapper & Associates v. U.S., Ct.Cl.1979, 611 F.2d 354, 222 Ct.Cl. 34. United States ☞ 110

Surety which had underwritten bonds on federal construction contract, and which had undertaken completion of project, was not entitled to interest on contract proceeds withheld by government pursuant to setoff of contractor's tax deficiency, where contract was entered into prior to effective date of this section, and surety had thus made no election thereunder. Morrison Assur. Co., Inc. v. U.S., Cl.Ct.1983, 3 Cl.Ct. 626. United States ☞ 110

No interest would be awarded on amount of subsidy payments wrongfully withheld by government, under construction-differential subsidy contracts for construction of vessels, for various reasons, including fact that this section, under which interest might otherwise be paid, did not encompass pending contract covering subsidy payments for construction of vessels purchased by private parties for their own use. Delta S.S. Lines, Inc. v. U.S., Cl.Ct.1983, 3 Cl.Ct. 559. United States ☞ 73(20)

Under law in effect at time of making of contract, public contractor could not recover prejudgment interest from Washington Metropolitan Area Transit Authority (WMATA) on claims for equitable adjustments under contract, absent specific contract provision authorizing prejudgment interest against government, despite any implied duty to avoid unreasonable administrative delay; contract was made before passage of Contract Disputes Act, before which judicial and administrative tribunals consistently construed interest claims against contractors. Washington Metropolitan Area Transit Authority v.

Nello L. Teer Co., D.C.1992, 618 A.2d 128, answer to certified question conformed to 995 F.2d 305, 301 U.S.App. D.C. 405. Interest ☞ 39(2.30)

5. Submission of claims

Substantial evidence supported findings of Armed Services Board of Contract Appeals that public contractor effectively abandoned its equitable adjustment claim until it was revived in 1982 so that contractor was entitled to interest only from date upon which contracting officer received claim in 1982. Dewey Electronics Corp. v. U.S., C.A.Fed.1986, 803 F.2d 650. United States ☞ 74(11)

Government contractor was not entitled to interest running from date that liquidated price adjustments necessitated by contract modifications became unreasonably delayed until date of actual payment, where contractor failed to convert the undisputed invoices to "claims," within meaning of this section, by submitting necessary writing before receiving payment, on all but one of the price adjustments, and where final price adjustment payment arrived only nine days after contractor submitted necessary writing. Esprit Corp., Inc. v. U.S., Cl.Ct. 1984, 6 Cl.Ct. 546, affirmed 776 F.2d 1062. United States ☞ 110

Architectural engineering firm, which was entitled to refund of amount paid to government under protest, upon finding that delay in project giving rise to payment was not fully attributable to it, was not entitled to interest on the sum, where underlying claim was presented to contracting officer by government, and not by contractor. Ruhnau-Evans-Ruhnau Associates v. U.S., Cl.Ct.1983, 3 Cl.Ct. 217.

Contractor who was awarded payments for wage increases under contracts with the Bureau of Prisons (BOP) was entitled to interest on the award from date that he submitted claim to the contracting officer and requested a final decision, rather than dates of other claims that did not include explicit or implicit request for a final decision. Bannum, Inc. v. U.S., C.A.Fed.2005, 121 Fed.Appx. 849, 2005 WL 78695, Unreported. United States ☞ 110

6. Certification of claims

Public contractor was not entitled to recover interest on its claim for cost overruns for period of delay in payment prior to date on which contractor's certificate of current cost or pricing data was received by contracting officer where the certificate did not meet the requirements for certifying claims and thus could not support allowance for interest. ReCon Paving, Inc. v. U.S., C.A.Fed.1984, 745 F.2d 34.   Interest ⟐ 46(2)

Contractor was entitled to interest only from the date it certified its claims pursuant to section 605 of this title, where its claims were in excess of $50,000.   Essex Electro Engineers, Inc. v. U.S., C.A.Fed. 1983, 702 F.2d 998.   Interest ⟐ 39(1)

Submission of uncertified claim, for purposes of this chapter, is, in effect, legal nullity; thus no interest can accrue on uncertified claim.   Fidelity Const. Co. v. U.S., C.A.Fed.1983, 700 F.2d 1379, certiorari denied 104 S.Ct. 97, 464 U.S. 826, 78 L.Ed.2d 103.   United States ⟐ 73(9)

No interest accrued under Contract Disputes Act on monies withheld from contractually prescribed payments where the contractor failed to file a "proper" certified claim with the contracting officer with respect to the underlying claim. Youngdale & Sons Const. Co., Inc. v. U.S., Fed.Cl.1993, 27 Fed.Cl. 516.   United States ⟐ 73(9); United States ⟐ 110

Failure to properly certify claim against United States caused contractor to forfeit right to any interest that may have accrued.   KDH Corp. v. U.S., Cl.Ct. 1991, 23 Cl.Ct. 34.   United States ⟐ 73(9)

7. Rate of interest

Interest rate set forth in Contract Disputes Act applied for purposes of determining just compensation to mortgagees on their takings claim against government following civil forfeiture of mortgaged property with respect to time period beyond term of note, where neither party introduced evidence on fair market interest rate for comparable mortgage notes.   Shelden v. U.S., Fed.Cl.1995, 34 Fed.Cl. 355, dismissed 152 F.3d 946.   Interest ⟐ 31

Owner of oil and gas equipment taken by United States along with condemned land owned by third party was entitled to simple interest at rate of 8.5% per annum from date of taking until 1979 and at rate utilized by Contract Disputes Act for period beginning January 1, 1980.   Paul v.

U.S., Cl.Ct.1990, 21 Cl.Ct. 415, affirmed 937 F.2d 623.   Interest ⟐ 31

Public contractor was entitled to collect interest on its differing site condition claim at the statutory rate on any recovery as of date of receipt of relevant claim. Servidone Const. Corp. v. U.S., Cl.Ct. 1990, 19 Cl.Ct. 346, affirmed 931 F.2d 860.   Interest ⟐ 31; Interest ⟐ 46(1)

Interest rates established under method required in this section were appropriate for computation of just compensation, in action pending against government for taking of flowage easements over farmlands, as result of construction and operation of dams in Missouri River Basin Water Control Projects.   Jones v. U.S., Cl.Ct.1983, 3 Cl.Ct. 4.   Eminent Domain ⟐ 148

Federal contract law, rather than state law, governed appropriate rate of prejudgment interest, in adversary proceeding brought by purchaser of Chapter 11 debtor-subcontractor's assets, to which debtor had assigned three of its four environmental remediation subcontracts with environmental management contractor for the United States Department of Energy (DOE), to recover for this environmental management contractor's alleged breach of contract in attempting to reduce sums owing to asset purchaser under these assumed and assigned subcontracts by setting off its rejection damages claim against debtor-subcontractor in connection with the rejected subcontract; debtor and environmental management contractor had agreed in their subcontracts that federal contract law would govern disputes between them, if such law was dispositive.   In re The IT Group, Inc., Bkrtcy.D.Del.2006, 359 B.R. 90. Bankruptcy ⟐ 3079

8. Settlements

Public contractor was not entitled to interest on amount of settlement it received upon termination of government contract in that contractor's termination settlement proposals were not "claims" on which interest could be allowed, within meaning of Contract Disputes Act. Mayfair Const. Co. v. U.S., C.A.Fed.1988, 841 F.2d 1576, certiorari denied 109 S.Ct. 528, 488 U.S. 980, 102 L.Ed.2d 560. United States ⟐ 110

Interest provisions of the Contract Disputes Act (CDA) and the Prompt Payment Act (PPA) were applicable to settlement agreement between contractor and government which resolved contractor's request for equitable adjustment. Sarang Corp. v. U.S., Fed.Cl.2007, 76 Fed.Cl. 560. United States ☞ 73(9)

Contractor was not entitled to assert claim under Contract Disputes Act for interest on quantum amounts claimed and ultimately settled, where there were no underlying "claims," within meaning of Act. Essex Electro Engineers, Inc. v. U.S., Cl.Ct.1991, 22 Cl.Ct. 757, affirmed 960 F.2d 1576, certiorari denied 113 S.Ct. 408, 506 U.S. 953, 121 L.Ed.2d 333. United States ☞ 70(33)

9. Specificity

Certified claim that was undifferentiated claim for $250,000 for costs associated with allegedly improper termination for default did not trigger time from which interest would run on claim by contractor against United States; the claim recited circumstances leading to termination and concluded that contractor suffered general and special damages then thought to exceed $250,000, but there was no particularity of claims or itemization of costs, and that lack of specificity was not cured by subsequent correspondence or discovery after commencement of litigation. Timberland Paving and Const. Co. v. U.S., Cl.Ct.1989, 18 Cl.Ct. 129. United States ☞ 110

10. Particular claims requiring payment of interest

Government contractor who was due money damages for government's failure to properly allocate costs was entitled to interest under the Contract Disputes Act (CDA), since contractor incurred the costs at issue. ATK Thiokol, Inc. v. U.S., Fed.Cl.2007, 76 Fed.Cl. 654. United States ☞ 110

Contractor which leased building to the government was entitled to interest under the Contract Disputes Act (CDA) on award of four months rent for period of government's holdover tenancy. Modeer v. U.S., Fed.Cl.2005, 68 Fed.Cl. 131, affirmed 183 Fed.Appx. 975, 2006 WL 1582178. United States ☞ 110

Government contract for the sale of commissary data to contractor was a contract for "disposal of personal property" within purview of the Contract Disputes Act (CDA), and thus contractor was entitled to interest on its recovery of damages for government's breach of contract.

Marketing and Management Information, Inc. v. U.S., Fed.Cl.2004, 62 Fed.Cl. 126. United States ☞ 110

Award of just compensation for temporary taking of property also entitles owner to simple interest from date of taking to date of compensation. Heydt v. U.S., Fed.Cl.1997, 38 Fed.Cl. 286. Eminent Domain ☞ 148

Stevedoring contractor that was awarded equitable adjustment for work performed during Operation Desert Storm was entitled to interest at rate specified by Contract Disputes Act (CDA) from date on which contractor filed its seventh claim, where total claim period was completely encompassed within contractor's cost claims as of that date, although specific amounts allegedly due in the claims were not finalized. Ryan-Walsh, Inc. v. U.S., Fed.Cl.1997, 37 Fed.Cl. 639. United States ☞ 110

Crude oil buyer under crude oil purchase contract with federal government was entitled to damages in amount of $430,572 plus interest from date contracting officer received claim, for government's breach of its duty of good faith and fair dealing by failing to give buyer accurate, nonevasive assessment of wastewater disposal problems; crude oil taken out of buyer's system to compensate for unexpected production shortfall of 113,000 barrels had to be replaced, there was difference between prices of crude oil at time of shortfall and government's later provision of make-up crude oil at different location, and government provided additional make-up deliveries which had to be taken into account. Celeron Gathering Corp. v. U.S., Fed.Cl. 1996, 34 Fed.Cl. 745. United States ☞ 74(13)

Contract Disputes Act (CDA) interest rates should not be applied uniformly in calculating delay component of just compensation in takings cases and the reason is that CDA interest rates typically are not reasonable measure of property owner's economic loss resulting from delay between government's appropriation of property and its payment of value of the property to property owner. NRG Co. v. U.S., Fed.Cl.1994, 31 Fed.Cl. 659. Eminent Domain ☞ 148

Interest could be awarded on equitable claim against the United States allowed by private legislation, since interest could have been awarded under relevant provisions of the Contract Disputes Act, a provision which was not available to the claimant because of the inequitable conduct of the Government. Spalding and Son, Inc. v. U.S., Cl.Ct.1991, 24 Cl.Ct. 112, report and recommendation rejected 28 Fed.Cl. 242. United States ⚖ 110

Where United States, as lessee under month-to-month tenancy, failed to pay rent after being informed that failure to pay would result in default, and lessor elected to cancel lease, lessee's status was effectively that of tenant-at-sufferance, liable for rent from date of default plus simple interest from date contracting officer received lessor's claim. Kelley v. U.S., Cl.Ct.1989, 19 Cl.Ct. 155. United States ⚖ 55

Property owners were entitled to award of prejudgment interest from date of taking to date of payment of judgment, based on computation set forth in Contract Disputes Act. Whitney Benefits, Inc. v. U.S., Cl.Ct.1989, 18 Cl.Ct. 394, opinion corrected 20 Cl.Ct. 324, affirmed 926 F.2d 1169, rehearing denied, rehearing in banc declined, certiorari denied 112 S.Ct. 406, 502 U.S. 952, 116 L.Ed.2d 354. Eminent Domain ⚖ 247(2)

Contract Disputes Act (CDA), which bankrupt subcontractor and environmental management contractor for the United States Department of Energy (DOE) had agreed in subcontracts would govern disputes between them, provided requisite authority for award of prejudgment interest when purchaser of debtor-subcontractor's assets, to which debtor-subcontractor had assigned three of its four subcontracts, successfully sued to prevent this environmental management contractor from reducing payments to which purchaser was entitled under the assumed and assigned subcontracts by setting off its rejection damages claim against debtor-subcontractor on the unassumed subcontract. In re The LTV Group, Inc., Bkrtcy.D.Del.2006, 359 B.R. 90. Bankruptcy ⚖ 3079; Interest ⚖ 39(2.30)

11. Particular claims not requiring payment of interest

Government contractor was not entitled under Contract Disputes Act (CDA) to recover interest on amounts paid by agency to discharge contractor's back wage liability following reformation of contract, even though contractor was obligated by contract to pay employees

amount required by Service Contract Act, and to pay related tax amounts to appropriate tax authorities, where back wages and associated taxes were paid by government through escrow mechanism, and contractor did not itself advance any payments to employees or tax authorities. Richlin Sec. Service Co. v. Chertoff, C.A.Fed.2006, 437 F.3d 1296, rehearing and rehearing en banc denied, certiorari denied 127 S.Ct. 253, 166 L.Ed.2d 149. United States ⚖ 110

Navy contractor's claim seeking to recover interest it paid on extra money it was forced to borrow as result of Navy's delay in reconciling lease to ownership (LTO) price was essentially claim for interest, barred by no-interest rule. England v. Contel Advanced Systems, Inc., C.A.Fed.2004, 384 F.3d 1372. United States ⚖ 110

Government contractor, which sought price adjustments on military supply contract that was terminated pursuant to contract's termination for convenience clause, was not entitled to interest award on amounts allowed as prospective costs under provision of Contract Disputes Act requiring interest to be awarded on any amounts found due to contractor from date on which contracting officer received claim; costs were never actually incurred by contractor, given contract termination, and Armed Services Board of Contract Appeals had not yet established amount "found due." Raytheon Co. v. White, C.A.Fed.2002, 305 F.3d 1354, rehearing denied, on remand 2003 WL 21905428. United States ⚖ 110

Government was not responsible under Contract Disputes Act for interest on amount of interest due timber company for government's material breach of timber contract for removal of timber from National Forest since payment of interest on interest liability was not authorized, even though government failed to pay interest for over five years. Stone Forest Industries, Inc. v. U.S., C.A.Fed.1992, 973 F.2d 1548, rehearing denied. United States ⚖ 110

Contractor bringing delay damage claim against Government relating to completion of a building was not entitled to interest due to alleged violation of Prompt Payment Act; as the adequacy of contractor's performance under contract had been challenged, interest, if any, on contractor's claim was determinable exclusively under the Contract Disputes Act. Wilner v. U.S., Cl.Ct.1991, 23 Cl.Ct. 241. United States ⇔ 110

Public contractor could not recover interest on borrowed funds as an element of costs recoverable on differing site condition claim. Servidone Const. Corp. v. U.S., Cl.Ct.1990, 19 Cl.Ct. 346, affirmed 931 F.2d 860. United States ⇔ 74(12.1)

Agreement under which Environmental Protection Agency agreed to process pesticide manufacturer's indemnification claim expeditiously after cancellation of pesticide's registration was not procurement contract or contract for disposal of government property and, thus, manufacturer was not entitled to interest on indemnification pursuant to Contract Disputes Act. Cedar Chemical Corp. v. U.S., Cl.Ct.1989, 18 Cl.Ct. 25. United States ⇔ 110

Existence of dispute between contractor and government over proper payments for costs incurred in performing

change orders for construction work on Veterans Administration hospital did not constitute "claim" within meaning of either provision of Contract Disputes Act requiring underlying claim for payment of interest or disputes clause of contract between contractor and Veterans Administration. Hoffman Const. Co. v. U.S., Cl.Ct.1985, 7 Cl.Ct. 518. United States ⇔ 110

Corrections center service company was not entitled to interest on increased wages, fringe benefits, and taxes resulting from belated incorporation and subsequent revision of wage determination from Department of Labor (DOL); company was serving as mere conduit for back wages to be transferred to DOL for distribution to employees. Schleicher Community Corrections Center, Inc. v. Gonzales, C.A.Fed.2007, 212 Fed.Appx. 972, 2007 WL 43260, Unreported. United States ⇔ 70(33)

§ 612. Payment of claims

(a) Judgments

Any judgment against the United States on a claim under this chapter shall be paid promptly in accordance with the procedures provided by section 1304 of Title 31.

(b) Monetary awards

Any monetary award to a contractor by an agency board of contract appeals shall be paid promptly in accordance with the procedures contained in subsection (a) of this section.

(c) Reimbursement

Payments made pursuant to subsections (a) and (b) of this section shall be reimbursed to the fund provided by section 1304 of Title 31 by the agency whose appropriations were used for the contract out of available funds or by obtaining additional appropriations for such purposes.

(d) Tennessee Valley Authority

(1) Notwithstanding the provisions of subsection (a) through (c) of this section, any judgment against the Tennessee Valley Authority on a claim under this chapter shall be paid promptly in accordance with the provisions of section 831h(b) of Title 16.

(2) Notwithstanding the provisions of subsection (a) through (c), any monetary award to a contractor by the board of contract appeals

for the Tennessee Valley Authority shall be paid in accordance with the provisions of section 831h(b) of Title 16.

(Pub.L. 95–563, § 13, Nov. 1, 1978, 92 Stat. 2389; Pub.L. 104–106, Div. D, Title XLIII, § 4322(b)(7), Feb. 10, 1996, 110 Stat. 677.)

HISTORICAL AND STATUTORY NOTES

Revision Notes and Legislative Reports

1978 Acts. Section 13 implements Recommendation No. 12 of the Procurement Commission and sets in motion the payment of all judgments, including those of the agency boards, the courts, or settlements, from agency appropriations. It constitutes a definite departure from the present procedure in the payment of judgments and awards of agency boards. It is intended to assure prompt payment of all such judgments and awards in contrast to present procedure which frequently result in serious delays pending appropriations by Congress.

Section 13(a) makes awards of the agency boards payable under the same procedures as court judgments by amending title 31, United States Code 724a.

Section 13(b) provides that the payments made under section 13(a) be made promptly.

Section 13(c) provides that all such payments will be backcharged to the procuring agency involved.

There may be an incentive in certain cases on the part of the procuring agency to avoid settlements and prolong litigation in order to have the final judgment against the agency occur in court, thus avoiding payment out of agency funds. Second, the practice may tend to hide from Congress the true economic costs of some procurements by not requiring the agencies to seek additional appropriations to pay the judgment.

In order to promote settlements and to assure the total economic cost of procurement is charged to those programs, all judgments awarded on contract claims are to be paid from the defendant agency's appropriations. If the agency does not have the funds to make the payment the agency is to request additional appropriations from Congress.

One of the Commission's primary objectives was to induce more resolution of disputes by negotiation and settlement. Requiring the agencies to shoulder the responsibility for interest and payment of judgments brings to bear on them the only real incentives available to induce more management involvement in contract administration and dispute resolution. Either the agencies must use some part of their program funds to pay the interest and the judgment, or they must seek additional funds from Congress for this purpose. The former course can have an impact on current programs; the latter would necessitate an explanation to a congressional committee. While these are negative incentives, they offer some counterpart to the economic considerations a contractor must evaluate in deciding whether to settle a claim or to litigate. Senate Report No. 95–1118.

1996 Acts. House Conference Report No. 104–450, see 1996 U.S. Code Cong. and Adm. News, p. 238.

References in Text

This chapter, referred to in subsec. (a), (d)(1), was in the original, "this Act", meaning Pub.L. 95–563, which, in addition to enacting this chapter, amended section 5108 of Title 5, Government Organization and Employees, sections 1346, 1491, 2401, 2414, 2510, and 2517 of Title 28, Judiciary and Judicial Procedure, and section 724a of Title 31, Money and Finance, and enacted provisions set out as notes under section 601 of this title.

Amendments

1996 Amendments. Subsec. (a). Pub.L. 104–106, § 4322(b)(7)(A), substituted "section 1304 of Title 31" for "section 1302 of the Act of July 27, 1956, (70 Stat. 694, as amended; 31 U.S.C. 724a)", which, for purposes of codification, required no change in text.

Subsec. (c). Pub.L. 104–106, § 4322(b)(7)(B), substituted "section 1304 of Title 31" for "section 1302 of the Act of July 27, 1956, (70 Stat. 694, as amended; 31 U.S.C. 724a)", which for purposes of codification, required no change in text.

Effective and Applicability Provisions
   1996 Acts. Amendment by Pub.L. 104–106 effective Feb. 10, 1996, except as otherwise provided, see section 4401 of Pub.L. 104–106, set out as a note under section 251 of this title.
   1978 Acts. Section effective with respect to contracts entered into 120 days

after Nov. 1, 1978 and, at the election of the contractor, with respect to any claim pending at such time before the contracting officer or initiated thereafter, see section 16 of Pub.L. 95–563, set out as a note under section 601 of this title.

CROSS REFERENCES

Award of fees and expenses to prevailing party, see 28 USCA § 2412.

LIBRARY REFERENCES

American Digest System
   United States ☞118.
   Key Number System Topic No. 393.

Research References

Forms
   Federal Procedural Forms § 34:225, Implementation of Decision.
   Federal Procedural Forms § 34:323, Actions Involving the Tennessee Valley Authority.
   Federal Procedural Forms § 34:335, Decision; Payment of Judgment and Interest.
   8 West's Federal Forms § 13223, Government Contract Claims--Claims Under the Contract Disputes Act.

Treatises and Practice Aids
   Federal Procedure, Lawyers Edition § 39:1156, Payment of Judgment and Interest.
   Federal Procedure, Lawyers Edition § 39:1159, Actions Involving the Tennessee Valley Authority.

WESTLAW ELECTRONIC RESEARCH

See Westlaw guide following the Explanation pages of this volume.

Notes of Decisions

Reimbursement   1

---

1. Reimbursement

Contract Dispute Act's (CDA) provision for reimbursement of claim payments applies only to agencies whose appropriations were used for the contract and not to non-appropriated fund instrumentalities (NAFI) other than the military exchanges and the National Aeronautics and Space Administration (NASA) exchange councils specifically identified in

the Tucker Act. Core Concepts of Florida, Inc. v. U.S., C.A.Fed.2003, 327 F.3d 1331, rehearing and rehearing en banc denied, certiorari denied 124 S.Ct. 805, 540 U.S. 1046, 157 L.Ed.2d 693. United States ☞ 118

For purposes of reimbursement requirement in subsec. (c) of this section, either court judgment or monetary award by board of contract appeals creates new payment liability. 1984, 63 Op.Comp. Gen. 308.

§ 613. Separability

   If any provision of this chapter, or the application of such provision to any persons or circumstances, is held invalid, the remainder of this chapter, or the application of such provision to persons or circumstances other than those to which it is held invalid, shall not be affected thereby.

(Pub.L. 95–563, § 15, Nov. 1, 1978, 92 Stat. 2391.)

HISTORICAL AND STATUTORY NOTES

Revision Notes and Legislative Reports
1978 Acts. Section 15 provides that if any provision of this act, or the application of it to any person or circumstances is held invalid, such provision is separable from the rest the act, and the remainder of the act shall not be affected, nor shall the application of such provision to other person or circumstances be affected. Senate Report No. 95–1118.

References in Text
This chapter, referred to in text, was in the original, "this Act", meaning Pub.L. 95–563, which, in addition to enacting this chapter, amended section 5108 of Title 5, Government Organization and

Employees, sections 1346, 1491, 2401, 2414, 2510, and 2517 of Title 28, Judiciary and Judicial Procedure, and section 724a of Title 31, Money and Finance, and enacted provisions set out as notes under section 601 of this title.

Effective and Applicability Provisions
1978 Acts. Section effective with respect to contracts entered into 120 days after Nov. 1, 1978 and, at the election of the contractor, with respect to any claim pending at such time before the contracting officer or initiated thereafter, see section 16 of Pub.L. 95–563, set out as a note under section 601 of this title.

Research References

ALR Library

13 ALR, Fed. 2nd Series 261, Construction and Application of Patent Ambiguity Doctrine to Federal Government Contracts.

97 ALR, Fed. 694, Jurisdiction of United States Court of Appeals for Federal Circuit Under 28 U.S.C.A. §§ 1292 and 1295.

96 ALR, Fed. 336, What Constitutes "Adversary Adjudication" by Administrative Agency Entitling Prevailing Party to Award of Attorneys' Fees Under Equal Access to Justice Act (5 U.S.C.A. § 504).

24 ALR 2nd 928, Recovery of Interest on Claim Against a Governmental Unit in Absence of Provision in Contract or Express Statutory Provision.

Encyclopedias

Am. Jur. 2d Admiralty § 45, United States.

Am. Jur. 2d United States § 39, Generally; Priority of Government Claims.

100 Am. Jur. Trials 45, Construction Dispute Resolution Arbitration and Beyond.

Forms

Federal Procedural Forms § 34:78, Introduction to CDA.

Federal Procedural Forms § 34:79, Disputes Subject to CDA's Resolution Procedures.

Federal Procedural Forms § 34:80, Disputes Excluded from CDA's Resolution Procedures.

Federal Procedural Forms § 34:89, Alternative Dispute Resolution.

Federal Procedural Forms § 34:102, Introduction to Boards of Contract Appeals.

Federal Procedural Forms § 34:306, Exhaustion of Administrative Remedies.

Federal Procedural Forms § 34:341, Petition--By Contractor--For Recovery of Funds Wrongfully Withheld as Offset Against Alleged Prior Indebtedness [28 U.S.C.A. § 1491; 41 U.S.C.A. § 609; United States Court of Federal Claims Rule 8].

Federal Procedural Forms § 34:342, Petition--By Contractor for Damages--Cancellation of Award of Contract, Pursuant to Opinion of Comptroller General, as Constituting Breach of Contract [28 U.S.C.A. § 1491; 41 U.S.C.A. § 609; United States Court of Federal Claims Rule 8].

Federal Procedural Forms § 34:343, Petition--For Increased Costs of Performance--Government's Failure to Give Timely Notice to Proceed as Constituting Breach of Contract [28 U.S.C.A. § 1491; 41 U.S.C.A. § 609; United States Court of Federal Claims Rule 8].

Federal Procedural Forms § 34:344, Petition--For Recovery of Forfeited Bid Deposits--Mistake in Bid [28 U.S.C.A. § 1491; 41 U.S.C.A. § 609; United States Court of Federal Claims Rule 8].

Federal Procedural Forms § 55:107, Sale of Personal Property Through Competitive Bidding.

Nichols Cyclopedia of Legal Forms Annotated § 7:2518, Supply Contract with United States--General Provisions.

Nichols Cyclopedia of Legal Forms Annotated § 7:2530, United States Lessee--General Clauses.

Nichols Cyclopedia of Legal Forms Annotated § 7:2536, Construction Contract with United States--General Provisions.

8 West's Federal Forms § 13102, Formal Brief of Appellant--Appeal from Board of Contract Appeals.

8 West's Federal Forms § 13126, Tucker Act--Contract Claims.

8 West's Federal Forms § 13129, Contract Disputes Act.

Treatises and Practice Aids

Federal Procedure, Lawyers Edition § 39:370, Jurisdiction of Boards of Contract Appeals.

Federal Procedure, Lawyers Edition § 39:425, Nonconsideration or Dismissal of Protests.

Federal Procedure, Lawyers Edition § 39:438, Administration of Contracts.

Federal Procedure, Lawyers Edition § 39:635, Sufficiency of Claim.

Federal Procedure, Lawyers Edition § 39:671, Inadequacy of Other Legal Authority for Relief.

Federal Procedure, Lawyers Edition § 39:696, Review of Decision to Terminate.

Federal Procedure, Lawyers Edition § 39:786, Introduction to CDA.

Federal Procedure, Lawyers Edition § 39:849, Introduction.

Federal Procedure, Lawyers Edition § 53:167, Scope of Jurisdiction--Suits in Admiralty Act.

Federal Procedure, Lawyers Edition § 57:412, Filing and Content of Notice of Appeal.

Federal Procedure, Lawyers Edition § 60:862, Factual Review of Decision to Request Conveyance of Title.

Federal Procedure, Lawyers Edition § 63:2, Statutory Bases for Jurisdiction.

Patent Law Fundamentals § 18:18, Government Access to Privately Owned Inventions--Adjudication of Claims Against the United States for Intellectual Property Infringement.

West's Federal Administrative Practice § 605, Common Contractor Mistakes and Contract Pitfalls.

West's Federal Administrative Practice § 634, Value Engineering.

West's Federal Administrative Practice § 8006, Courts of Special Jurisdiction--Claims Court.

33 Wright & Miller: Federal Prac. & Proc. § 8293, Courts of Special Jurisdiction.

WESTLAW ELECTRONIC RESEARCH

See Westlaw guide following the Explanation pages of this volume.

CHAPTER 10—DRUG–FREE WORKPLACE

WESTLAW COMPUTER ASSISTED LEGAL RESEARCH

Westlaw supplements your legal research in many ways. Westlaw allows you to

● update your research with the most current information

● expand your library with additional resources

● retrieve current, comprehensive history citing references to a case with KeyCite

For more information on using Westlaw to supplement your research, see the Westlaw Electronic Research Guide, which follows the Explanation.

---

§ 701. Drug-free workplace requirements for Federal contractors

(a) Drug-free workplace requirement

(1) Requirement for persons other than individuals

No person, other than an individual, shall be considered a responsible source, under the meaning of such term as defined in section 403(8) of this title, for the purposes of being awarded a contract for the procurement of any property or services of a value greater than the simplified acquisition threshold (as defined in section 403(11) of this title) by any Federal agency, other than a contract for the procurement of commercial items (as defined in section 403(12) of this title), unless such person agrees to provide a drug-free workplace by—

(A) publishing a statement notifying employees that the unlawful manufacture, distribution, dispensation, possession, or use of a controlled substance is prohibited in the person's workplace and specifying the actions that will be taken against employees for violations of such prohibition;

(B) establishing a drug-free awareness program to inform employees about—

947

(i) the dangers of drug abuse in the workplace;

(ii) the person's policy of maintaining a drug-free workplace;

(iii) any available drug counseling, rehabilitation, and employee assistance programs; and

(iv) the penalties that may be imposed upon employees for drug abuse violations;

(C) making it a requirement that each employee to be engaged in the performance of such contract be given a copy of the statement required by subparagraph (A);

(D) notifying the employee in the statement required by subparagraph (A), that as a condition of employment on such contract, the employee will—

(i) abide by the terms of the statement; and

(ii) notify the employer of any criminal drug statute conviction for a violation occurring in the workplace no later than 5 days after such conviction;

(E) notifying the contracting agency within 10 days after receiving notice under subparagraph (D)(ii) from an employee or otherwise receiving actual notice of such conviction;

(F) imposing a sanction on, or requiring the satisfactory participation in a drug abuse assistance or rehabilitation program by, any employee who is so convicted, as required by section 703 of this title; and

(G) making a good faith effort to continue to maintain a drug-free workplace through implementation of subparagraphs (A), (B), (C), (D), (E), and (F).

(2) Requirement for individuals

No Federal agency shall enter into a contract with an individual unless such individual agrees that the individual will not engage in the unlawful manufacture, distribution, dispensation, possession, or use of a controlled substance in the performance of the contract.

(b) Suspension, termination, or debarment of the contractor

(1) Grounds for suspension, termination, or debarment

Each contract awarded by a Federal agency shall be subject to suspension of payments under the contract or termination of the contract, or both, and the contractor thereunder or the individual who entered the contract with the Federal agency, as applicable, shall be subject to suspension or debarment in accordance with the requirements of this section if the head of the agency determines that—

(A) the contractor violates the requirements of subparagraph (A), (B), (C), (D), (E), or (F) of subsection (a)(1) of this section; or

(B) such a number of employees of such contractor have been convicted of violations of criminal drug statutes for violations occurring in the workplace as to indicate that the contractor has failed to make a good faith effort to provide a drug-free workplace as required by subsection (a) of this section.

(C) Redesignated (B)

(2) Conduct of suspension, termination, and debarment proceedings

(A) If a contracting officer determines, in writing, that cause for suspension of payments, termination, or suspension or debarment exists, an appropriate action shall be initiated by a contracting officer of the agency, to be conducted by the agency concerned in accordance with the Federal Acquisition Regulation and applicable agency procedures.

(B) The Federal Acquisition Regulation shall be revised to include rules for conducting suspension and debarment proceedings under this subsection, including rules providing notice, opportunity to respond in writing or in person, and such other procedures as may be necessary to provide a full and fair proceeding to a contractor or individual in such proceeding.

(3) Effect of debarment

Upon issuance of any final decision under this subsection requiring debarment of a contractor or individual, such contractor or individual shall be ineligible for award of any contract by any Federal agency, and for participation in any future procurement by any Federal agency, for a period specified in the decision, not to exceed 5 years.

(Pub.L. 100–690, Title V, § 5152, Nov. 18, 1988, 102 Stat. 4304; Pub.L. 103–355, Title IV, § 4104(d), Title VIII, § 8301(f), Oct. 13, 1994, 108 Stat. 3342, 3397; Pub.L. 104–106, Div. D, Title XLIII, §§ 4301(a)(3), 4321(i)(13), Feb. 10, 1996, 110 Stat. 656, 677.)

HISTORICAL AND STATUTORY NOTES

Revision Notes and Legislative Reports
1994   Acts. Senate   Report   Nos. 103–258 and 103–259, and House Conference Report No. 103–712, see 1994 U.S. Code Cong. and Adm. News, p. 2561.
1996 Acts. House Conference Report No. 104–450, see 1996 U.S. Code Cong. and Adm. News, p. 238.

Amendments
1996   Amendments. Subsec.   (a)(1). Pub.L.   104–106, § 4301(a)(3)(A), substituted "agrees to" for "has certified to the contracting agency that it will".

Pub.L. 104–106, § 4321(i)(13), substituted "(as defined in section 403(12) of this title)" for "as defined in section 403 of this title".

Subsec. (a)(2). Pub.L. 104–106, § 4301(a)(3)(B), substituted "individual agrees" for "contract includes a certification by the individual".

Subsec. (b)(1)(A) to (C). Pub.L. 104–106, § 4301(a)(3)(C), redesignated subpars. (B) and (C) as subpars. (A) and (B), respectively, struck out former subpar. (A) relating to false certifications and in subpar. (A) as so redesignated, struck out "such certification by failing to carry out" following "violates".

1994 Amendments. Subsec. (a)(1). Pub.L. 103–355, § 4104(d), substituted "greater than the simplified acquisition threshold (as defined in section 403(11) of the title) by any Federal agency" for "of $25,000 or more from any Federal agency".

Pub.L. 103–355, § 8301(f) provided for inapplicability of a drug-free workplace requirement in awarding contracts for procurement of commercial items as defined in section 403 of this title.

Effective and Applicability Provisions
1996 Acts. Amendment by Pub.L. 104–106 effective Feb. 10, 1996, except as otherwise provided, see section 4401 of

Pub.L. 104–106, set out as a note under section 251 of this title.

1994 Acts. Amendment by sections 4104(d) and 8301(f) of Pub.L. 103–355 effective Oct. 13, 1994, except as otherwise provided, see section 10001 of Pub.L. 103–355, set out as a note under section 251 of this title.

1988 Acts. Section 5160 of Pub.L. 100–690 provided that: "Sections 5152 [this section] and 5153 [section 702 of this title] shall be effective 120 days after the date of the enactment of this subtitle [Nov. 18, 1988]."

Short Title
1988 Acts. Section 5151 of Pub.L. 100–690 provided that: "This subtitle [Subtitle D of Title V, §§ 5151 to 5160, of Pub.L. 100–690, enacting this chapter and enacting a provision set out as a note under this section] may be cited as the 'Drug–Free Workplace Act of 1988'."

Consistency of Regulations With International Obligations of United States; Extraterritorial Application
Pub.L. 100–690, Title IV, § 4804, Nov. 18, 1988, 102 Stat. 4295, which required that regulations promulgated by agency heads be consistent with the international obligations of the United States, was repealed by Pub.L. 103–447, Title I, § 103(b), Nov. 2, 1994, 108 Stat. 4693.

CODE OF FEDERAL REGULATIONS
Drug-free workplace grants, Secretary of Labor, see 29 CFR § 98.600 et seq.
Workplace substance abuse programs, Energy Department, see 10 CFR § 707.1 et seq.

LAW REVIEW AND JOURNAL COMMENTARIES
Debarment and suspension revisited: fewer eggs in the basket? Brian D. Shannon, 44 Cath.U.L.Rev. 363 (1995).
Drug-free workplaces: The new requirements for federal grantees and contractors. James A. Kahl, 63 Fla.B.J. 38 (July/August 1989).
Drug testing: Is preemption the answer? 33 Santa Clara L.Rev. 657 (1993).
Just say maybe: A watershed decision on drug testing by the California Supreme Court sets the stage for continued litigation of privacy rights in the workplace. Victor Schachter and Steven Blackburn, 17 L.A.Law. 26 (Nov. 1994).
Sister sovereign states: Preemption and the Second Twentieth Century Revolution in the law of the American workplace. Henry H. Drummonds, 62 Fordham L.Rev. 469 (1993).

LIBRARY REFERENCES
American Digest System
United States ⟜64.15, 64.20.
Key Number System Topic No. 393.
Corpus Juris Secundum
CJS Civil Rights § 296, Illegal Use of Drugs and Alcohol.

Research References

ALR Library
142 ALR, Fed. 387, Vacating on Public Policy Grounds Arbitration Awards Reinstating Discharged Employees.

Encyclopedias
Am. Jur. 2d Job Discrimination § 407, Employer Substance Abuse and Testing Policies Under Americans with Disabilities Act.
Am. Jur. 2d Job Discrimination § 408, Liability Relating to Private Employer Substance Abuse Policies.
Am. Jur. 2d Job Discrimination § 410, Obligations of Employers.
Am. Jur. 2d Job Discrimination § 412, Enforcement and Waivers.
20 Am. Jur. Proof of Facts 3d 361, Disability Discrimination Under the Americans with Disabilities Act.
28 Am. Jur. Proof of Facts 3d 185, Proof of Violation of Privacy Rights in Employment Drug Testing.
42 Am. Jur. Proof of Facts 3d 1, Employer's Defense Under Americans with Disabilities Act.
47 Am. Jur. Proof of Facts 3d 203, Admissibility and Reliability of Hair Sample Testing to Prove Illegal Drug Use.
49 Am. Jur. Trials 171, Defense of Claim Brought Under the Americans with Disabilities Act.
57 Am. Jur. Trials 255, Alternative Dispute Resolution: Employment Law.

Forms
24A West's Legal Forms § 1:19, Drug Testing.
31 West's Legal Forms § 32:179, Drug-Free/Alcohol-Free Workplace.

Treatises and Practice Aids
Americans with Disab. Pract. & Compliance Manual § 7:141, Compliance with Other Regulations.
Americans with Disab. Pract. & Compliance Manual § 8:233, Drug and Alcohol Policies.
Eckstrom's Licensing in Foreign & Domestic Ops. App. 14D, Model Cooperative Research and Development Agreement for the Department of Agriculture.
Emp. Discrim. Coord. Analysis of Federal Law § 6:37, Perceived Impairments: Contagious Diseases, Drug and Alcohol Abuse.
Emp. Discrim. Coord. Analysis of Federal Law § 20:92, Which Employers Must Maintain a Drug-Free Workplace.
Emp. Discrim. Coord. Analysis of Federal Law § 20:93, Specific Employer Obligations.
Emp. Discrim. Coord. Analysis of Federal Law § 20:95, Enforcement and Waivers.
Emp. Discrim. Coord. Analysis of Federal Law § 49A:3, Rules Prohibiting the Illegal Use of Drugs or the Use of Alcohol.
Emp. Discrim. Coord. Analysis of State Law § 11:56, Regulation of Tobacco, Alcohol, and Drug Use.
Emp. Discrim. Coord. Analysis of State Law § 17:74, Rules of Conduct.
Employment Discrimination Law and Litigation App F, Americans with Disabilities Act.
Employment Practices Manual § 2:14, Drug-Free Workplace Act of 1988.
Employment Practices Manual § 6:10, Drug and Alcohol Testing--Overview.
Employment Practices Manual App E, Americans with Disabilities Act of 1990 (42 U.S.C.A. § 12101 et seq.).
Federal Procedure, Lawyers Edition § 39:1347, Causes for Debarment.
West's Federal Administrative Practice § 609, Laws Applicable--In General.
West's Federal Administrative Practice App. O, Title 42--Americans with Disabilities Act.

WESTLAW ELECTRONIC RESEARCH

See Westlaw guide following the Explanation pages of this volume.

Notes of Decisions

Back pay award   3
Mandatory nature of drug testing   1
Reinstatement of employee   2

1. Mandatory nature of drug testing

Drug-Free Workplace Act did not require public utility to perform drug testing on its employees such that utility could be considered "state actor" for purposes of Fourth and Fifth Amendment claims asserted by former employee who was fired following drug test, notwithstanding "requirements" set forth in Act to enable federal contractors and grant recipients to remain eligible for federal funds and notwithstanding former employee's reference to certain federal regulations purportedly mandating testing; regulations relied by employee were promulgated under different statutes, Act did not mandate drug tests, and employee identified no regulations implementing act that did so. Parker v. Atlanta Gas Light Co., S.D.Ga.1993, 818 F.Supp. 345. Constitutional Law ⟊ 3941; Searches And Seizures ⟊ 78

2. Reinstatement of employee

Arbitration award in favor of refinery's unionized process technician violated public policy against reinstating employee in safety-sensitive position after testing positive for cocaine and breaching employer's drug abuse policy on two occasions—breaking pledge of abstinence and failing to disclose relapse—even though nothing indicated that technician possessed or used cocaine on the premises. Gulf Coast Indus. Workers Union v. Exxon Co., U.S.A., C.A.5 (Tex.) 1993, 991 F.2d 244, certiorari denied 114 S.Ct. 441, 510 U.S. 965, 126 L.Ed.2d 375.   Labor And Employment ⟊ 1609(2)

3. Back pay award

Notwithstanding that employee's discharge violated terms of collective bargaining agreement and arbitrator's award did not require that employee be reinstated, award of back pay to employee who, while working in safety sensitive position, tested positive for cocaine use violated well-established public policy against use of drugs by employees in such positions. Exxon Corp. v. Baton Rouge Oil and Chemical Workers Union, C.A.5 (La.) 1996, 77 F.3d 850. Labor And Employment ⟊ 1609(2)

§ 702. Drug-free workplace requirements for Federal grant recipients

(a) Drug-free workplace requirement

(1) Persons other than individuals

No person, other than an individual, shall receive a grant from any Federal agency unless such person agrees to provide a drug-free workplace by—

   (A) publishing a statement notifying employees that the unlawful manufacture, distribution, dispensation, possession, or use of a controlled substance is prohibited in the grantee's workplace and specifying the actions that will be taken against employees for violations of such prohibition;

   (B) establishing a drug-free awareness program to inform employees about—

      (i) the dangers of drug abuse in the workplace;

      (ii) the grantee's policy of maintaining a drug-free workplace;

      (iii) any available drug counseling, rehabilitation, and employee assistance programs; and

(iv) the penalties that may be imposed upon employees for drug abuse violations;

(C) making it a requirement that each employee to be engaged in the performance of such grant be given a copy of the statement required by subparagraph (A);

(D) notifying the employee in the statement required by subparagraph (A), that as a condition of employment in such grant, the employee will—

(i) abide by the terms of the statement; and

(ii) notify the employer of any criminal drug statute conviction for a violation occurring in the workplace no later than 5 days after such conviction;

(E) notifying the granting agency within 10 days after receiving notice of a conviction under subparagraph (D)(ii) from an employee or otherwise receiving actual notice of such conviction;

(F) imposing a sanction on, or requiring the satisfactory participation in a drug abuse assistance or rehabilitation program by, any employee who is so convicted, as required by section 703 of this title; and

(G) making a good faith effort to continue to maintain a drug-free workplace through implementation of subparagraphs (A), (B), (C), (D), (E), and (F).

(2) Individuals

No Federal agency shall make a grant to any individual unless such individual agrees as a condition of such grant that the individual will not engage in the unlawful manufacture, distribution, dispensation, possession, or use of a controlled substance in conducting any activity with such grant.

(b) Suspension, termination, or debarment of grantee

(1) Grounds for suspension, termination, or debarment

Each grant awarded by a Federal agency shall be subject to suspension of payments under the grant or termination of the grant, or both, and the grantee thereunder shall be subject to suspension or debarment, in accordance with the requirements of this section if the agency head of the granting agency or his official designee determines, in writing, that—

(A) the grantee violates the requirements of subparagraph (A), (B), (C), (D), (E), (F), or (G) of subsection (a)(1) of this section; or

(B) such a number of employees of such grantee have been convicted of violations of criminal drug statutes for violations occurring in the workplace as to indicate that the grantee has failed to make a good faith effort to provide a drug-free workplace as required by subsection (a)(1) of this section.

(2) Conduct of suspension, termination, and debarment proceedings

A suspension of payments, termination, or suspension or debarment proceeding subject to this subsection shall be conducted in accordance with applicable law, including Executive Order 12549 or any superseding Executive order and any regulations promulgated to implement such law or Executive order.

(3) Effect of debarment

Upon issuance of any final decision under this subsection requiring debarment of a grantee, such grantee shall be ineligible for award of any grant from any Federal agency and for participation in any future grant from any Federal agency for a period specified in the decision, not to exceed 5 years.

(Pub.L. 100–690, Title V, § 5153, Nov. 18, 1988, 102 Stat. 4306; Pub.L. 105–85, Div. A, Title VIII, § 809, Nov. 18, 1997, 111 Stat. 1838.)

HISTORICAL AND STATUTORY NOTES

Revision Notes and Legislative Reports
1997 Acts. House Conference Report No. 105–340 and Statement by President, see 1997 U.S. Code Cong. and Adm. News, p. 2251.

References in Text
Executive Order 12549, referred to in subsec. (b)(2), is Ex. Ord. No. 12549, Feb. 19, 1986, 51 F.R. 6370, which is set out as a note under section 6101 of Title 31, Money and Finance.

1997 Amendments
Subsec. (a)(1). Pub.L. 105–85, § 809(1)(A), substituted "agrees to" for "has certified to the granting agency that it will".
Subsec. (a)(2). Pub.L. 105–85, § 809(1)(B), substituted "agrees" for "certifies to the agency".

Subsec. (b)(1)(A) to (C). Pub.L. 105–85, § 809(2), redesignated former subpars. (B) and (C) as (A) and (B), respectively, in subpar. (A), as so redesignated, struck out "such certification by failing to carry out" after "The grantee violates", and struck out former subpar. (A), which read as follows:

"**(A)** the grantee has made a false certification under subsection (a) of this section;"

Effective and Applicability Provisions
Section effective 120 days after Nov. 18, 1988, see section 5160 of Pub.L. 100–690, set out as a note under section 701 of this title.

CODE OF FEDERAL REGULATIONS

Drug-free workplace grants, Secretary of Labor, see 29 CFR § 98.600 et seq.
Workplace substance abuse programs, Energy Department, see 10 CFR § 707.1 et seq.

LAW REVIEW AND JOURNAL COMMENTARIES

Debarment and suspension revisited: Fewer eggs in the basket? Brian D. Shannon, 44 Cath.U.L.Rev. 363 (1995).

LIBRARY REFERENCES

American Digest System
United States ⚖️82(1).
Key Number System Topic No. 393.

Research References

Encyclopedias
Am. Jur. 2d Job Discrimination § 410, Obligations of Employers.
Am. Jur. 2d Job Discrimination § 412, Enforcement and Waivers.
28 Am. Jur. Proof of Facts 3d 185, Proof of Violation of Privacy Rights in Employment Drug Testing.
47 Am. Jur. Proof of Facts 3d 203, Admissibility and Reliability of Hair Sample Testing to Prove Illegal Drug Use.

Treatises and Practice Aids
Emp. Discrim. Coord. Analysis of Federal Law § 20:92, Which Employers Must Maintain a Drug-Free Workplace.
Emp. Discrim. Coord. Analysis of Federal Law § 20:93, Specific Employer Obligations.
Emp. Discrim. Coord. Analysis of Federal Law § 20:95, Enforcement and Waivers.

WESTLAW ELECTRONIC RESEARCH

See Westlaw guide following the Explanation pages of this volume.

Notes of Decisions

Mandatory nature of drug testing   1

1. Mandatory nature of drug testing
Drug-Free Workplace Act did not require public utility to perform drug testing on its employees such that utility could be considered "state actor" for purposes of Fourth and Fifth Amendment claims asserted by former employee who was fired following drug test, notwithstanding "requirements" set forth in Act to enable federal contractors and grant recipients to remain eligible for federal funds and notwithstanding former employee's reference to certain federal regulations purportedly mandating testing; regulations relied by employee were promulgated under different statutes, Act did not mandate drug tests, and employee identified no regulations implementing act that did so. Parker v. Atlanta Gas Light Co., S.D.Ga.1993, 818 F.Supp. 345. Constitutional Law ⚖️ 3941; Searches And Seizures ⚖️ 78

§ 703. Employee sanctions and remedies

A grantee or contractor shall, within 30 days after receiving notice from an employee of a conviction pursuant to section 701(a)(1)(D)(ii) or 702(a)(1)(D)(ii) of this title—

(1) take appropriate personnel action against such employee up to and including termination; or

(2) require such employee to satisfactorily participate in a drug abuse assistance or rehabilitation program approved for such purposes by a Federal, State, or local health, law enforcement, or other appropriate agency.

(Pub.L. 100–690, Title V, § 5154, Nov. 18, 1988, 102 Stat. 4307.)

CODE OF FEDERAL REGULATIONS

Drug-free workplace grants, Secretary of Labor, see 29 CFR § 98.600 et seq.
Workplace substance abuse programs, Energy Department, see 10 CFR § 707.1 et seq.

LIBRARY REFERENCES

American Digest System
Labor and Employment ⚮767.
Key Number System Topic No. 231H.

WESTLAW ELECTRONIC RESEARCH

See Westlaw guide following the Explanation pages of this volume.

§ 704. Waiver

(a) In general

A termination, suspension of payments, or suspension or debarment under this chapter may be waived by the head of an agency with respect to a particular contract or grant if—

(1) in the case of a waiver with respect to a contract, the head of the agency determines under section 701(b)(1) of this title, after the issuance of a final determination under such section, that suspension of payments, or termination of the contract, or suspension or debarment of the contractor, or refusal to permit a person to be treated as a responsible source for a contract, as the case may be, would severely disrupt the operation of such agency to the detriment of the Federal Government or the general public; or

(2) in the case of a waiver with respect to a grant, the head of the agency determines that suspension of payments, termination of the grant, or suspension or debarment of the grantee would not be in the public interest.

(b) Exclusive authority

The authority of the head of an agency under this section to waive a termination, suspension, or debarment shall not be delegated.

(Pub.L. 100–690, Title V, § 5155, Nov. 18, 1988, 102 Stat. 4307.)

CODE OF FEDERAL REGULATIONS

Drug-free workplace grants, Secretary of Labor, see 29 CFR § 98.600 et seq.
Workplace substance abuse programs, Energy Department, see 10 CFR § 707.1 et seq.

LIBRARY REFERENCES

American Digest System
United States ⚮73(3).
Key Number System Topic No. 393.

Research References

Encyclopedias
    Am. Jur. 2d Job Discrimination § 412, Enforcement and Waivers.

Treatises and Practice Aids
    Emp. Discrim. Coord. Analysis of Federal Law § 20:95, Enforcement and Waivers.

WESTLAW ELECTRONIC RESEARCH

    See Westlaw guide following the Explanation pages of this volume.

§ 705. Regulations

Not later than 90 days after November 18, 1988, the government-wide regulations governing actions under this chapter shall be issued pursuant to the Office of Federal Procurement Policy Act [41 U.S.C.A. § 401 et seq.].

(Pub.L. 100–690, Title V, § 5156, Nov. 18, 1988, 102 Stat. 4308.)

HISTORICAL AND STATUTORY NOTES

References in Text
    The Office of Federal Procurement Policy Act, referred to in text, is Pub.L. 93–400, Aug. 30, 1974, 88 Stat. 796, as amended, which is classified principally to chapter 7 (section 401 et seq.) of this title. For complete classification of this Act to the Code, see Short Title note set out under section 401 of this title and Tables.

Research References

Encyclopedias
    Am. Jur. 2d Job Discrimination § 411, Adoption of Rules to Implement Drug-Free Workplace Requirements.

Treatises and Practice Aids
    Emp. Discrim. Coord. Analysis of Federal Law § 20:94, Adoption of Rules to Implement Drug-Free Workplace Requirements.

WESTLAW ELECTRONIC RESEARCH

    See Westlaw guide following the Explanation pages of this volume.

§ 706. Definitions

For purposes of this chapter—

    (1) the term "drug-free workplace" means a site for the performance of work done in connection with a specific grant or contract described in section 701 or 702 of this title of an entity at which employees of such entity are prohibited from engaging in the unlawful manufacture, distribution, dispensation, possession, or use of a controlled substance in accordance with the requirements of this Act;

    (2) the term "employee" means the employee of a grantee or contractor directly engaged in the performance of work pursuant to the provisions of the grant or contract described in section 701 or 702 of this title;

(3) the term "controlled substance" means a controlled substance in schedules I through V of section 812 of Title 21;

(4) the term "conviction" means a finding of guilt (including a plea of nolo contendere) or imposition of sentence, or both, by any judicial body charged with the responsibility to determine violations of the Federal or State criminal drug statutes;

(5) the term "criminal drug statute" means a criminal statute involving manufacture, distribution, dispensation, use, or possession of any controlled substance;

(6) the term "grantee" means the department, division, or other unit of a person responsible for the performance under the grant;

(7) the term "contractor" means the department, division, or other unit of a person responsible for the performance under the contract; and

(8) the term "Federal agency" means an agency as that term is defined in section 552(f) of Title 5.

(Pub.L. 100–690, Title V, § 5157, Nov. 18, 1988, 102 Stat. 4308.)

HISTORICAL AND STATUTORY NOTES

References in Text

This Act, referred to in par. (1), is Pub.L. 100–690, Nov. 18, 1988, 102 Stat. 4181, known as the Anti–Drug Abuse Act of 1988. For complete classification of this Act to the Code, see Short Title note set out under section 1501 of Title 21, Food and Drugs, and Tables.

CODE OF FEDERAL REGULATIONS

Drug-free workplace grants, Secretary of Labor, see 29 CFR § 98.600 et seq.
Workplace substance abuse programs, Energy Department, see 10 CFR § 707.1 et seq.

Research References

Encyclopedias

Am. Jur. 2d Job Discrimination § 410, Obligations of Employers.

Treatises and Practice Aids

Emp. Discrim. Coord. Analysis of Federal Law § 20:93, Specific Employer Obligations.

WESTLAW ELECTRONIC RESEARCH

See Westlaw guide following the Explanation pages of this volume.

§ 707. Construction of chapter

Nothing in this chapter shall be construed to require law enforcement agencies, if the head of the agency determines it would be inappropriate in connection with the agency's undercover operations, to comply with the provisions of this chapter.

(Pub.L. 100–690, Title V, § 5158, Nov. 18, 1988, 102 Stat. 4308.)

Research References

ALR Library
142 ALR, Fed. 387, Vacating on Public Policy Grounds Arbitration Awards Reinstating Discharged Employees.

Encyclopedias
Am. Jur. 2d Job Discrimination § 408, Liability Relating to Private Employer Substance Abuse Policies.
Am. Jur. 2d Job Discrimination § 410, Obligations of Employers.
Am. Jur. 2d Job Discrimination § 412, Enforcement and Waivers.
20 Am. Jur. Proof of Facts 3d 361, Disability Discrimination Under the Americans with Disabilities Act.
28 Am. Jur. Proof of Facts 3d 185, Proof of Violation of Privacy Rights in Employment Drug Testing.
42 Am. Jur. Proof of Facts 3d 1, Employer's Defense Under Americans with Disabilities Act.
49 Am. Jur. Trials 171, Defense of Claim Brought Under the Americans with Disabilities Act.

Forms
24A West's Legal Forms § 1:19, Drug Testing.
31 West's Legal Forms § 32:179, Drug-Free/Alcohol-Free Workplace.

Treatises and Practice Aids
Americans with Disab. Pract. & Compliance Manual § 7:141, Compliance with Other Regulations.
Emp. Discrim. Coord. Analysis of Federal Law § 20:95, Enforcement and Waivers.

WESTLAW ELECTRONIC RESEARCH

See Westlaw guide following the Explanation pages of this volume.

*

INDEX TO
TITLE 41—PUBLIC CONTRACTS

References are to U.S.C.A. Sections.

PUBLIC CONTRACTS

INDEX TO TITLE 41

PUBLIC CONTRACTS

PUBLIC CONTRACTS

PUBLIC CONTRACTS

I–13

PUBLIC CONTRACTS

PUBLIC CONTRACTS

I–19

PUBLIC CONTRACTS

PUBLIC CONTRACTS

I–27

PUBLIC CONTRACTS

I–29

INDEX TO TITLE 41

PUBLIC CONTRACTS

I–31

INDEX TO TITLE 41

PUBLIC CONTRACTS

END OF VOLUME